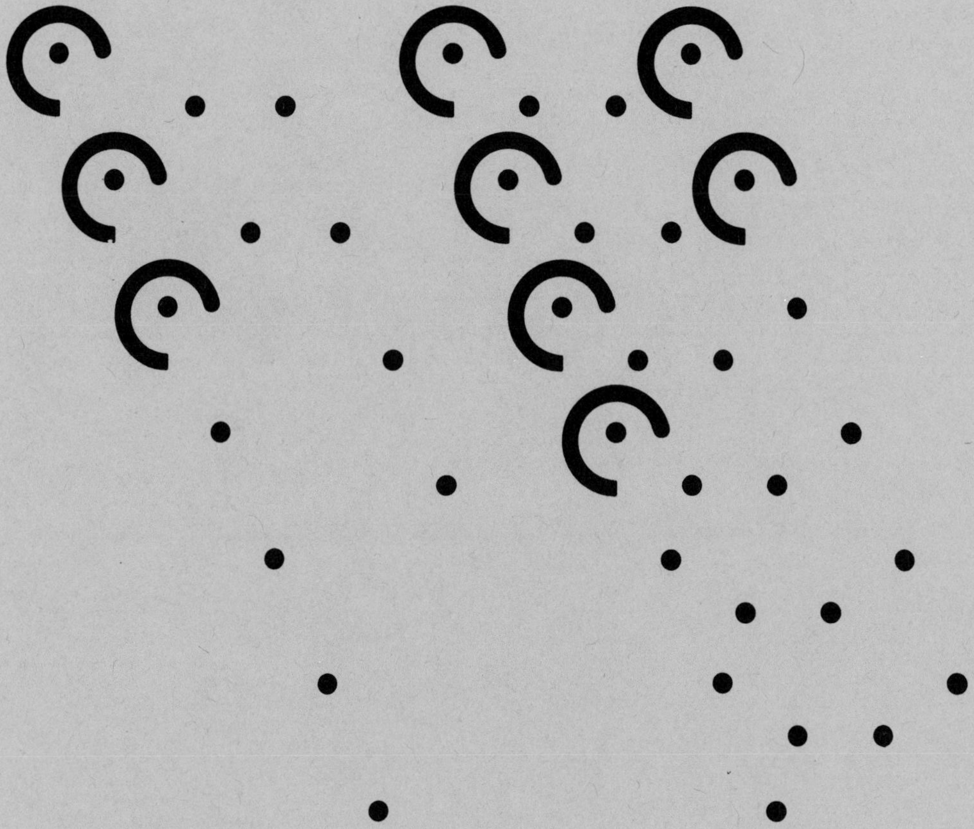

Hermeneia
—A Critical
and Historical
Commentary
on the Bible

Ezekiel 1

A Commentary on the
Book of the Prophet Ezekiel,
Chapters 1–24

by Walther Zimmerli

Translated by
Ronald E. Clements

Edited by
Frank Moore Cross and
Klaus Baltzer with the assistance of
Leonard Jay Greenspoon

**Fortress
Press**   Philadelphia

Translated from the German *Ezechiel 1, I. Teilband* by
Walther Zimmerli. Biblischer Kommentar Altes
Testament, Band XIII/1. © 1969 Neukirchener
Verlag des Erziehungsvereins GmbH, Neukirchen-
Vluyn.

Library of Congress Catalog Card Number 75—21540
ISBN 0—8006—6008—0

Printed in the United States of America
Design by Kenneth Hiebert
Type set by Fyldetype Ltd., the United Kingdom
2634E79   20—6008

Contents
Ezekiel 1

The name *Hermeneia*, Greek ἑρμηνεία, has been chosen as the title of the commentary series to which this volume belongs. The word *Hermeneia* has a rich background in the history of biblical interpretation as a term used in the ancient Greek-speaking world for the detailed, systematic exposition of a scriptural work. It is hoped that the series, like its name, will carry forward this old and venerable tradition. A second entirely practical reason for selecting the name lies in the desire to avoid a long descriptive title and its inevitable acronym, or worse, an unpronounceable abbreviation.

The series is designed to be a critical and historical commentary to the Bible without arbitrary limits in size or scope. It will utilize the full range of philological and historical tools, including textual criticism (often slighted in modern commentaries), the methods of the history of tradition (including genre and prosodic analysis), and the history of religion.

Hermeneia is designed for the serious student of the Bible. It will make full use of ancient Semitic and classical languages; at the same time, English translations of all comparative materials—Greek, Latin, Canaanite, or Akkadian—will be supplied alongside the citation of the source in its original language. Insofar as possible, the aim is to provide the student or scholar with full critical discussion of each problem of interpretation and with the primary data upon which the discussion is based.

Hermeneia is designed to be international and interconfessional in the selection of authors; its editorial boards were formed with this end in view. Occasionally the series will offer translations of distinguished commentaries which originally appeared in languages other than English. Published volumes of the series will be revised continually, and eventually, new commentaries will replace older works in order to preserve the currency of the series. Commentaries are also being assigned for important literary works in the categories of apocryphal and pseudepigraphical works relating to the Old and New Testaments, including some of Essene or Gnostic authorship.

The editors of *Hermeneia* impose no systematic-theological perspective upon the series (directly, or indirectly by selection of authors). It is expected that authors will struggle to lay bare the ancient meaning of a biblical work or pericope. In this way the text's human relevance should become transparent, as is always the case in competent historical discourse. However, the series eschews for itself homiletical translation of the Bible.

The editors are heavily indebted to Fortress Press for its energy and courage in taking up an expensive, long-term project, the rewards of which will accrue chiefly to the field of biblical scholarship.

The translator of this volume is Professor Ronald Clements of Cambridge University. Professor Leonard Jay Greenspoon of Clemson University provided valuable assistance in copy editing the volume, in preparing bibliographic data, and in searching out errors in references and translations.

The editors responsible for this volume are Frank Moore Cross of Harvard University and Klaus Baltzer of the University of Munich.

December, 1977   *Frank Moore Cross*   *Helmut Koester*
                 For the Old Testament   For the New Testament
                 Editorial Board   Editorial Board

The first part of the present commentary was published at the beginning of October, 1955. The last sentences of the excursuses were written in the last days of December in 1968. The author must ask the indulgence of the subscribers of whom he has demanded such patience. The way has been longer than could have been foreseen at the beginning. A visiting professorship in the Divinity School of Yale University in New Haven, Connecticut, which was unexpectedly followed by a year as pro-Rector, two years as Rector, and then a further year as con-Rector of my University in Göttingen, may excuse a part of the delay. For the rest, I must blame the unevenness of the territory through which a way had to be cut and which necessitated proceeding with care. It could not be hastily done. The recollection of Ḥanina ben Hezekiah and the 300 cruses of oil which this scholar of the synagogue used for the exposition of the book of Ezekiel came as a comforting reassurance for the difficult work. However, it would be dishonest of the author if he were silent about the feeling with which he comes to the end—a feeling that he is now ready to begin the work with some understanding. He knows better than any other that for those who follow in the task of expounding this book there is still much new work that remains to be done. Ezekiel, the "theologian" among the prophets with his steep and harsh message behind which any easily grasped humanity lies hidden so deeply, does not make it easy for his commentator. However, even in this harshness and severity he brings us to the depths of the divine reality which needs fear no closer ground.

The long duration of the task of exposition has occasioned that here and there the view of the commentator was slightly changed. The careful reader will notice that the readings of the Greek version at the beginning of the commentary are less sharply examined than at the end. In the excursus on the divine names in the book of Ezekiel something quite different finally emerged than in the exposition of the detailed text. The reader is therefore asked to refer to the excursus for the passages which use the double name of God. Also in the course of the exposition studies were published which could not at first be fully used. Thus, for example, the calculations about chronology of Parker-Dubberstein (1956) are among these. Sperber's edition of the Targum of the text of Ezekiel first came into the author's hand in 1962.

The slow progress of the commentary also allowed many features to reach a fuller development than would have been achieved with a more rapid pace of composition. Many preliminary studies could be dealt with first which ultimately benefited the whole work. No attempt has been made to deal with arguments which appeared in literature after the conclusion of the separate parts of the commentary since this would have increased still further the already all too extensive literature, and to discuss them would have delayed its conclusion still further. The bibliography, which has been continued up to the end of 1968, will in any case point the way to the most recent studies on Ezekiel.

When a road is so long there are many helpers to whom thanks are due. I have to thank my assistants, who in the course of the years shared in the labor of this work and who, I hope, will also share a little in the satisfaction of its completion. Pastor W. Reiser, now in Schaffhausen; Prof. Dr. R. Rendtorff in Heidelberg; Dr. H. U. Boesche, Lecturer for Hebrew in Göttingen; Pastor M. Howald in Basel; and Dr. Chr. Jeremias, who most recently undertook the task of compiling the index and the final verification of the bibliographical references. They deserve my sincere thanks for all their assistance. Among the colleagues to whom I could from time to time turn for advice I would mention as representative of many others Prof. Dr. W. von Soden (Münster), Prof. Dr. R. Borger (Göttingen), and Prof. Dr. B. Hartmann (Leiden). I have mentioned that I am indebted to Prof. Dr. Merkelbach (Cologne) and Prof. Dr. M. Fernandez-Galiano (Madrid). For consultation on Septuagint questions I am indebted to Dr. R. Hanhart, the head of the Göttingen Septuagint Institute. In studying the difficult territory of the divine names in the book of Ezekiel I was able to refer at length by letter to Dr. H. Stegemann and Dr. L. Delekat in Bonn. The preparation of the drawings for Ezek 40–48 was undertaken by U. Nagel of Göttingen University.

A commentary on the book of the prophet Ezekiel, the preacher of God's holy majesty and faithfulness, cannot finally be published without humble thanks to the Lord who has granted both the power to work and the people who have assisted me in the task. Among such people, without whose hidden contribution nothing at all would have been achieved, I should like to mention the name of my wife.

Göttingen
June 1st, 1969.

Walther Zimmerli

1. Sources and Abbreviations

Abbreviations used in this volume for sources and
literature from antiquity are the same as those used
in the *Theological Dictionary of the New Testament*, ed.
Gerhard Kittel, tr. Geoffrey W. Bromiley, vol. 1
(Grand Rapids, Michigan, and London: Eerdmans,
1964), xvi–xl. Some abbreviations are adapted from
that list and can be easily identified.

In addition, the following abbreviations have
been used:

Acts	Acts of the Apostles
AfO	*Archiv für Orientforschung* (Berlin, 1926ff)
AJSL	*American Journal of Semitic Languages and Literatures* (Chicago, 1895–1941)
ALBO	Analecta lovanensia biblica et orientalia
ANEP	*The Ancient Near East in Pictures Relating to the Old Testament*, ed. J. B. Pritchard (Princeton: Princeton Univ. Press, 1954)
ANET[2]	*Ancient Near Eastern Texts Relating to the Old Testament*, ed. J. B. Pritchard (Princeton: Princeton Univ. Press, [2]1955)
AO	Der Alte Orient (Leipzig, 1900ff)
AOBAT	*Altorientalische Bilder zum Alten Testament*, ed. H. Gressmann (Tübingen, [2]1926)
AOT	*Altorientalische Texte zum Alten Testament*, ed. H. Gressmann (Tübingen, [2]1926)
ARW	*Archiv für Religionswissenschaft* (Freiburg, Leipzig, Tübingen, 1898–1941)
ATANT	Abhandlungen zur Theologie des Alten und Neuen Testaments
ATD	Das Alte Testament Deutsch
BA	*The Biblical Archaeologist*
Bar	Baruch
BASOR	*Bulletin of the American Schools of Oriental Research*
BBB	Bonner Biblische Beiträge
BEvTh	Beiträge zur evangelischen Theologie (München)
BFChrTh	Beiträge zur Förderung Christlichen Theologie
BH-	*Biblia Hebraica*, ed. Rudolf Kittel. "Ezechiel" in *BH*[2] (1913) prepared by J. W. Rothstein. "Ezechiel" in *BH*[3] (1937) prepared by Julius A. Bewer
BhEvTh	Beihefte zur evangelischen Theologie (München)
BHTh	Beiträge zur historischen Theologie (Tübingen, 1929ff)
Bibl	*Biblica* (Rome)
BK	Biblischer Kommentar. Altes Testament, eds. Martin Noth, H. W. Wolff, S. Herrmann (Neukirchen)
BRA	Beiträge zur Religionsgeschichte des Altertums
BRL	*Biblisches Reallexikon*, ed. Kurt Galling (Tübingen, 1937)
BSF	Biblische Studien (Freiburg)
BWA(N)T	Beiträge zur Wissenschaft vom Alten (und Neuen) Testament
BZ	*Biblische Zeitschrift*
BZAW	Beihefte zur Zeitschrift fur die alttestamentliche Wissenschaft
BZNW	Beihefte zur Zeitschrift fur die neutestamentliche Wissenschaft
Cent-B	The Century Bible (London)
cf.	Confer, compare with
Chr	Chronicles
cj.	Conjecture
COT	Commentar op het Oude Testament, ed. G. Charles Aalders (Kampen)
CSS	Cursus scripturae (Paris)
CT	*Collectanea theologica*
CultBibl	*Cultura biblica* (Segovia)
DalmanWB	Dalman, Gustaf: *Aramäisch-neuhebräisches Handwörterbuch* ([2]1922)
Dan	Daniel
Dtn	Deuteronomy
Eccl	Ecclesiastes
Echter-B	Die Heilige Schrift in deutscher übersetzung (Würzburg: Echter Verlag)
ed.	Editor; edited by
[Ed.]	Editor of this volume of Hermenia
Est	Esther
ET	*The Expository Times*
EThL	*Ephemerides theologicae lovanienses*
EvTh	*Evangelische Theologie*
Ex	Exodus
Ezek	Ezekiel
Ezr	Ezra
f	Designates one verse or page following the verse or page cited
FRLANT	Forschungen zur Religion und Literatur des Alten und Neuen Testaments (Göttingen)
FuF	*Forschungen und Fortschritte* (Berlin)

Gen	Genesis
H	Holiness Code (Leviticus 17–26)
Hab	Habakkuk
Hag	Haggai
HAT	Handbuch zum Alten Testament, ed. Otto Eissfeldt
HBNT	Handbuch zum Neuen Testament
HKAT	Handkommentar zum Alten Testament, ed. W. Nowack (Göttingen)
HO	*Handbuch der Orientalistik*, ed. B. Spuler (Berlin, 1948ff)
Hos	Hosea
HSAT	Die Heilige Schrift der Alten Testaments, ed. E. Kautzsch (Tübingen)
HTR	*Harvard Theological Review*
HUCA	*Hebrew Union College Annual* (Cincinnati, 1924ff)
IB	*The Interpreter's Bible*
ibid.	In the same place
ICC	The International Critical Commentary of the Holy Scriptures of the Old and New Testament (Edinburgh)
idem	The same (person)
IEJ	*Israel Exploration Journal* (Jerusalem)
Is	Isaiah
JAOS	*Journal of the American Oriental Society* (New Haven, 1843ff)
JBL	*Journal of Biblical Literature*
JBR	*Journal of Bible and Religion*
Jer	Jeremiah
Jn	John
Jon	Jonah
Josh	Joshua
JPOS	*Journal of the Palestine Oriental Society* (Jerusalem, 1920–48)
JPTh	*Jahrbücher für protestantische Theologie* (Leipzig)
JSS	*Journal of Semitic Studies*
JTS	*Journal of Theological Studies*
Ju	Judges
KAT	Kommentar zum Alten Testament, ed. E. Sellin
KeH	Kurzgefasstes exegetisches Handbuch zum Alten Testament (Leipzig)
Kgs	Kings
KHC	Kurzer Hand-Commentar zum Alten Testament, ed. K. Marti
Lam	Lamentations
Lev	Leviticus
LidzEph	Lidzbarski, Mark: *Ephemeris für semitische Epigraphik* (Giessen, 1901—1911)
Lk	Luke
Mal	Malachi
MGWJ	*Monatsschrift für Geschichte und Wissenschaft des Judentums* (Breslau)
Mic	Micah
Mk	Mark
MPL	Migne, J. P.: *Patrologiæ cursus completus. Series latina.*
Mt	Matthew
Museon	*Le Museon*. Revue d'études orientales (Louvain)
MVÄG	Mitteilungen der Vorderasiatisch-Ägyptischen Gesellschaft
Na	Nahum
NC	*La Nouvelle Clio* (Brussels)
Neh	Nehemiah
NKZ	*Neue kirchliche Zeitschrift* (Erlangen)
NTS	*New Testament Studies* (Cambridge)
Nu	Numbers
Ob	Obadiah
OIP	The Oriental Institute Publications (Chicago)
OLZ	*Orientalistische Literaturzeitung*
Or	*Orientalia*. Commentarii periodici Pontificii Instituti Biblici (Rome)
OTS	*Oudtestamentische Studiën* (Leiden)
p.(pp.)	Page(s)
PEQ	*Palestine Exploration Quarterly* (London, 1869ff)
PJ	*Palästinajahrbuch*
Prv	Proverbs
Ps	Psalms
RB	*Revue biblique*
RES	*Revue des études semitiques* (Paris)
RGG	*Die Religion in Geschichte und Gegenwart*
RGL	*Religionsgeschichtliches Lesebuch*, ed. Alfred Bertholet (Tübingen, 1926ff)
RHPhR	*Revue d'histoire et de philosophie religieuses* (Strassbourg)
RLV	*Reallexikon der Vorgeschichte*, ed. Max Ebert (Berlin, 1924–32)
RQ	*Revue de Qumran* (Paris)
Sam	Samuel
SBOT	The Sacred Books of the Old Testament, ed. Paul Haupt
Sir	Jesus Sirach (Ecclesiasticus)
Song	Song of Solomon
StOr	Studia orientalia (Helsinki)
StTh	*Studia theologica*. Cura ordinum theologorum sandinavicorum edita (Lund)
Sumer	*Sumer* (Bagdad)
Syria	*Syria*. Revue d'art oriental et archéologie (Paris)
TeU	Tekst en Uitleg (Den Haag, Groningen)
ThB	Theologische Bücherei (München)
ThGl	*Theologie und Glaube*
ThLZ	*Theologische Literaturzeitung*
ThEx	Theologische Existenz Heute (München)
ThR	*Theologische Rundschau*
ThSt	Theologische Studien
ThStKr	*Theologische Studien und Kritiken*
ThT	*Theologisch Tijdschrift*
TWNT	*Theologisches Wörterbuch Zum Neuen Testament*. Begun by G. Kittel

ThZ	*Theologische Zeitschrift* (Basel)
tr.	Translator, translated by
[Trans.]	Translator of this volume of Hermeneia
[Trans. by Ed.]	Translated by editor of this volume of Hermeneia
UUÅ	Uppsala universitetsårsskrift (Uppsala)
v(v)	Verse(s)
VAB	Vorderasiatische Bibliothek (Leipzig, 1907–1916)
vol(s)	Volume(s)
VT	*Vetus Testamentum*
VT Suppl	Supplements to Vetus Testamentum (Leiden)
WMANT	Wissenschaftliche Monographien zum Alten und Neuen Testament (Neukirchen)
WO	Die Welt des Orients. Wissenschaftliche Beiträge zur Kunde des Morgenlandes (Göttingen)
WuD	*Wort und Dienst.*
WVDOG	Wissenschaftliche Veröffentlichungen der Deutschen Orientgesellschaft
WZ	*Wissenschaftliche Zeitschrift*
WZKM	*Wiener Zeitschrift für die Kunde des Morgenlandes* (Vienna, 1886–1940)
ZAW	*Zeitschrift für die alttestamentliche Wissenschaft*
ZB	*Züricher Bibel*
ZDMG	*Zeitschrift der Deutschen Morgenländischen Gesellschaft*
ZDPV	*Zeitschrift des deutschen Palaestina-Vereins*
Zech	Zechariah
Zeph	Zephaniah
ZKTh	*Zeitschrift für kathologische Theologie*
ZLThK	*Zeitschrift für lutherische Theologie und Kirche*
ZS	*Zeitschrift für Semistik und verwandte Gebiete*
ZThK	*Zeitschrift für Theologie und Kirche*
ZWTh	*Zeitschrift für wissenschaftliche Theologie*

2. Short Titles of Commentaries, Studies, and Articles Often Cited

Commentaries on Ezekiel as well as a few other works are cited by author's name only.

Aalders
Gerhard Charles Aalders, *Ezechiel*, 2 volumes, COT (Kampen: Kok, 1955 and 1957).

Albrecht, "Geschlecht"
Karl Albrecht, "Das Geschlecht der hebräichen Hauptwörter," *ZAW* 16 (1896): 41–121.

Albright, *Archaeology*
W. F. Albright, *Archaeology and the Religion of Israel* (Baltimore: Johns Hopkins University Press, 1956).

Albright, "Seal of Eliakim"
W. F. Albright, "The Seal of Eliakim and the Latest Preëxilic History of Judah, with Some Observations on Ezekiel," *JBL* 51 (1932): 77–106.

Albright, *Stone Age*
W. F. Albright, *From the Stone Age to Christianity* (Baltimore: Johns Hopkins University Press, ²1957).

Alföldi, "Throntabernakels"
A. Alföldi, "Die Geschichte des Throntabernakels," *NC* 1/2 (1949/50): 537–566.

Alt, "Gedanken"
A. Alt, "Gedanken über das Königtum Jahwes" in *Kleine Schriften zur Geschichte des Volkes Israel* 1 (München: Beck, 1953), 345–357.

Alt, "Jerusalems Aufstieg"
A. Alt, "Jerusalems Aufstieg," *ZDMG* NF 4/79 (1925): 1–19; reprinted in *idem, Kleine Schriften zur Geschichte des Volkes Israel* 3 (München: Beck, 1959), 243–257.

Alt, *Kleine Schriften*
A. Alt, *Kleine Schriften zur Geschichte des Volkes Israel*, 3 volumes, (München: Beck, 1953–1959).

Alt, "Origins of Law"
A. Alt, "The Origins of Israelite Law" in *Essays on Old Testament History and Religion*, tr. R. A. Wilson (Garden City, New York: Doubleday, 1967), 101–171.

Auvray
P. Auvray, *Ezéchiel*. Témoins de Dieu (1947).

Bach, *Erwählung*
Robert Bach, *Die Erwählung Israels in der Wüste*, Unpub. Diss. (Bonn, 1951).

Baentsch, "Pathologischer"
B. Baentsch, "Pathologischer Züge in Israels Prophetentum," *ZWTh* 50 (1908): 52–81.

Baer-Delitzsch
S. Baer and F. Delitzsch, *Liber Ezechielis, Textum masoreticum accuratissime expressit, e fontibus Masorae varie illustravit, notis criticis confirmavit* (1884).

Balla, "Ezek 8:1–9:11; 11:24–25"
E. Balla, "Ezechiel 8:1–9:11; 11:24–25" in *Festschrift Rudolf Bultmann zum 65. Geburtstag überreicht* (Stuttgart: Kohlhammer, 1949), 1–11.

Barrois, *Manuel*
A. G. Barrois, *Manuel d'archaéologie biblique* 1 (Paris: Picard, 1939).

Barth, "Zauber"
J. Barth, "Zu dem Zauber des Umnähens der Gelenke," *MGWJ* 57 (1913).

Barton, "Danel"
George A. Barton, "Danel, A Pre-Israelite Hero of Galilee," *JBL* 60 (1941): 213–225.

Bauer, "Hes. xxiv 17"
Johannes Bauer, "Hes. xxiv 17," *VT* 7 (1957): 91–92.

Bauer-Leander
Hans Bauer and Pontus Leander, *Historische Grammatik der hebräischen Sprache des Alten Testaments* 1 (Halle: Niemeyer, 1922).

Baumann, "Hauptvisionen"
Eberhard Baumann, "Die Hauptvisionen Hesekiels in ihrem zeitlichen und sachlichen Zusammenhang untersucht," *ZAW* 67 (1955): 56–67.

Baumann, "Weinranke"
Eberhard Baumann, "Die Weinranke im Walde. Hes. 15, 1–8," *ThLZ* 80 (1955): 119–120.

Baumgärtel, "Formel"
Friedrich Baumgärtel, "Die Formel *neʾum jahwe*," *ZAW* 73 (1961): 277–290.

Baumgartner, *Klagegedichte*
Walter Baumgartner, *Die Klagegedichte des Jeremia*, BZAW 32 (Berlin, 1917).

Beer-Meyer
G. Beer and D. R. Meyer, *Hebräische Grammatik* (Berlin, 1952–55).

Begrich, *Chronologie*
Joachim Begrich, *Die Chronologie der Könige von Israel und Juda und die Quellen des Rahmens der Königsbücher* (Tübingen: Mohr [Siebeck], 1929).

Begrich, *Studien*
Joachim Begrich, *Studien zu Deuterojesaja*, BWANT 4:25 (Stuttgart, 1938).

Begrich, "Tora"
Joachim Begrich, "Die priestliche Tora," in BZAW 66 (Berlin, 1936), 63–88; reprinted in *idem, Gesammelte Studien zum AT*, ThB 21 (München: Kaiser, 1964), 232–260.

Berry, "Exile"
George Ricker Berry, "Was Ezekiel in the Exile?" *JBL* 49 (1930): 83–93.

Berry, "Title"
George Ricker Berry, "The Title of Ezekiel (1:1–3)," *JBL* 51 (1932): 54–57.

Bertholet
Alfred Bertholet, *Das Buch Hesekiel erklärt*, KHC 12 (Freiburg: Mohr, 1897).

Bertholet-Galling
Alfred Bertholet and Kurt Galling, *Hesekiel*, HAT 13 (Tübingen: Mohr [Siebeck], 1936).

Bewer, "Exegese"
Julius A. Bewer, "Beiträge zur Exegese des Buches Ezechiel," *ZAW* 63 (1951): 193–201.

Bewer, "Ezek 7:5–14"
Julius A. Bewer, "On the Text of Ezekiel 7:5–14," *JBL* 45 (1926): 223–231.

Bewer, "Text"
Julius A. Bewer, "The Text of Ezek. 1:1–3," *AJSL* 50 (1934): 96–101.

Bewer, "Textual Notes"
Julius A. Bewer, "Textual and Exegetical Notes on the Book of Ezekiel," *JBL* 72 (1953): 158–168.

Blank, "Profanation"
Sheldon Blank, "Isaiah 52:5 and the Profanation of the Name," *HUCA* 25 (1954): 1–8.

Blau, "Adverbia"
Josia Blau, "Adverbia als psychologische und grammatische Subjekte/Praedikate im Bibel-hebraeisch," *VT* 9 (1959): 130–137.

Blau, "Gebrauch"
Josia Blau, "Zum angeblichen Gebrauch von את vor dem Nominativ," *VT* 4 (1954): 7–22.

Blau, "Hebräisch"
Josia Blau, "Zum Hebräisch der Übersetzer des AT," *VT* 6 (1956): 97–99.

Borger
R. Borger, "Zu שוב שבו/ית," *ZAW* 66 (1954 [1955]): 315–316.

van den Born, *Die historische situatie*
A. van den Born, *Die historische situatie van Ezechiels prophetie*, ALBO 2 (Leuven: Bijbels Seminarie, 1947).

Breuer
Joseph Breuer, *Das Buch Jecheskel übersetzt und erläutert* (Frankfurt: Sänger and Friedberg, 1921).

Brockelmann
C. Brockelmann, *Hebräische Syntax* (Neukirchen-Vluyn: Neukirchen, 1956).

Brooks, "Functionaries"
Beatrice A. Brooks, "Fertility Cult Functionaries in the Old Testament," *JBL* 60 (1941): 227–253.

Broome, "Personality"
Edwin C. Broome, Jr., "Ezekiel's Abnormal Personality," *JBL* 65 (1946): 277–292.

Buber, "Jecheskel 3:12"
Martin Buber, "Zu Jecheskel 3:12," *MGWJ* 78 (1934): 471–473.

C. Budde, "Klagelied"
"Das hebräische Klagelied," *ZAW* 2 (1882): 1–52.

K. Budde, "Eingang"
Karl Budde, "Zum Eingang des Buches Ezechiel," *JBL* 50 (1931): 20–41.

du Mesnil du Buisson, "Tablette"
Le Comte du Mesnil du Buisson, "Une Tablette magique de la région du moyen Euphrate" in *Mélanges syrien offerts à M. René Dussaud 1* (Paris: Geuthner, 1939), 421–434.

Burrows, "Daroma"
Millar Burrows, "Daroma," *JPOS* 12 (1932): 142–148.

Burrows, *Relations*
Millar Burrows, *The Literary Relations of Ezekiel* (Philadelphia: Jewish Publication Society, 1925).

Buzy, "Symboles"
Denis Buzy, "Les symboles prophétiques d'Ezéchiel," *RB* 29 (1920): 203–228; 353–358; 30 (1921): 45–54; 161–194; reprinted in *idem, Les symboles de l'ancien testament* (Paris: LeCoffre, 1923): 157–264.

Černý, *Day of Yahweh*
Ladislav Černý, *The Day of Yahweh and Some Relevant Problems* (Praze: Nákladem Filosofické Fakulty University Karlovy, 1948).

Cheyne, "Image"
T. K. Cheyne, "The Image of Jealousy in Ezekiel," *ZAW* 21 (1901): 201–202.

Cohen, "Studies"
A. Cohen, "Studies in Hebrew Lexicography," *AJSL* 40 (1924): 153–185.

Cooke
G. A. Cooke, *A Critical and Exegetical Commentary on the Book of Ezekiel*, ICC (Edinburgh: Clark, 1936).

Cornill
Carl Heinrich Cornill, *Das Buch des Propheten Ezechiel* (Leipzig, 1886).

Cowley, *Papyri*
Arthur Ernest Cowley, *Aramaic Papyri discovered at Assuan* (London: Moring, 1906).

Dalman, *Arbeit*
Gustaf Dalman, *Arbeit und Sitte in Palästina* 7 volumes (Gütersloh: Bertelsmann, 1928–1942).

Daube, "Umbildung"
D. Daube, Über die Umbildung biblischen Rechtsgutes" in *Symbolae Friburgenses in honorem Ottonis Lenel* (Leipzig: Tauchnitz, 1935), 245–258.

Delitzsch, *Schreibfehler*
Friedrich Delitzsch, *Die Lese- und Schreibfehler im Alten Testament* (Berlin 1920).

Delitzsch, "Schwertlied"
Friedrich Delitzsch, "Assyriologische Notizen zum Alten Testament. IV. Das Schwertlied Ezech. 21, 13–22," *ZK* 2 (1885): 385–398.

Dhorme, *religions*
E. Dhorme, *Les religions de Babylonie et d'Assyrie* (Paris: Presses universitaires de France, ²1949).

Diehl, *Pronomen*
W. Diehl, *Das Pronomen personale suffixum 2. und 3. pers. plur. des hebräischen in der alttestamentlichen Überlieferung*, Unpub. Diss. (Giessen, 1895).

Driver, "Difficult"
G. R. Driver, "Difficult Words in the Hebrew Prophets" in *Studies in Old Testament Prophecy*, ed. H. H. Rowley (Edinburgh: Clark, 1950), 52–72.

Driver, "Ezekiel"
G. R. Driver, "Ezekiel: Linguistic and Textual Problems," *Bibl* 35 (1954): 145–159; 299–312.

Driver, "Hebrew Notes"
  G. R. Driver, "Hebrew Notes," *JBL* 68 (1949):
  57–59.
Driver, "Hebrew Words"
  G. R. Driver, "Some Hebrew Words," *JTS* 29
  (1928): 390–396.
Driver, "Inaugural"
  G. R. Driver, "Ezekiel's Inaugural Vision," *VT* 1
  (1951): 60–62.
Driver, "L'interpretation"
  G. R. Driver, "L'interpretation du texte masoré-
  tique a la lumière de la lexicographie hébraique,"
  EThL 26 (1950): 337–353.
Driver, "Isaiah"
  G. R. Driver, "Linguistic and Textual Problems:
  Isaiah I–XXXIX," *JTS* 38 (1937): 36–50.
Driver, "Linguistic Problems"
  G. R. Driver, "Linguistic and Textual Problems:
  Ezekiel," *Bibl* 19 (1938): 60–69; 175–187.
Driver, "Medical Expressions"
  G. R. Driver, "Some Hebrew Medical Expres-
  sions," *ZAW* 65 (1953): 255–262.
Driver, "Studies. 3"
  G. R. Driver, "Studies in the Vocabulary of the
  Old Testament. 3," *JTS* 32 (1930/31): 361–366.
Driver, "Studies. 8"
  G. R. Driver, "Studies in the Vocabulary of the
  Old Testament. 8," *JTS* 36 (1935): 293–301.
Driver, "Three Notes"
  G. R. Driver, "Three Notes," *VT* 2 (1952): 356–
  357.
Duhm, *Theologie*
  Bernhard Duhm, *Die Theologie der Propheten als
  Grundlage für die innere Entwicklungsgeschichte der
  israelitischen Religion* (Bonn, 1875).
Dupont-Sommer, *Essene*
  A. Dupont-Sommer, *The Essene Writings from
  Qumran*, tr. G. Vermes (Cleveland: World, 1962).
Dürr, *Apokalyptik*
  L. Dürr, *Die Stellung des Propheten Ezechiel in der
  israelitisch-jüdischen Apokalyptik*, AA IX 1 (Mün-
  ster: Aschendorff, 1923).
Dürr, *Ezekiels Vision*
  L. Dürr, *Ezekiels Vision von der Erscheinung Gottes
  (Ez. c. 1 und 10) im Lichte der vorderasiatischen Alter-
  tumskunde* (Würzburg: Richter, 1917).
Dussaud, "L'idole"
  R. Dussaud, "L'idole de la jalousie," *Syria* 21
  (1940): 359–360.
Ehrlich, *Randglossen*
  Arnold B. Ehrlich, *Randglossen zur hebräischen Bibel*
  5 (Leipzig: Hinrichs, 1912).
Eichrodt
  Walther Eichrodt, *Der Prophet Hesekiel*, ATD
  (1970).
Eisler, "gśtj"
  Robert Eisler, "gśtj = κάστυ του γραμματέως =
  קֶסֶת הַסֹּפֵר im Danielkommentar des Hippolytos
  von Rom," *OLZ* 33 (1930): 585–587.

Eissfeldt, *Baal Zaphon*
  Otto Eissfeldt, *Baal Zaphon, Zeus Kasios und der
  Durchzug der Israeliten durchs Meer*, BRA 1 (Halle:
  Niemeyer, 1932).
Eissfeldt, "Ezechiel"
  Otto Eissfeldt, "Ezechiel als Zeuge für Sanheribs
  Eingriff in Palästina," *PJ* 27 (1931): 58–66.
Eissfeldt, "Kap. 16"
  Otto Eissfeldt, "Hesekiel Kap. 16 als Geschichts-
  quelle," *JPOS* 16 (1936): 286–292.
Eissfeldt, *OT Introduction*
  Otto Eissfeldt, *The Old Testament; An Introduction*,
  tr. Peter R. Ackroyd (New York: Harper and
  Row, 1965).
Eissfeldt, "Schwerterschlagene"
  Otto Eissfeldt, "Schwerterschlagene bei Hesekiel"
  in *Studies in Old Testament Prophecy presented to T. H.
  Robinson*, ed. H. H. Rowley (Edinburgh: Clark,
  1950), 73–81.
Eissfeldt, "Zeilenfüllung"
  Otto Eissfeldt, "Zeilenfüllung," *VT* 2 (1952):
  87–92.
Eitan, "Bearing of Ethiopic"
  Israel Eitan, "The Bearing of Ethiopic on Biblical
  Exegesis and Lexicography," *JPOS* 3 (1923):
  136–143.
Elliger, "Chammanim"
  K. Elliger, "Chammanim = Maṣṣeben?" *ZAW*
  57 (1939): 256–265.
Elliger, "Ich bin"
  K. Elliger, "Ich bin der Herr-euer Gott" in *Theo-
  logie als Glaubenswagnis, Festschrift für K. Heim*
  (Hamburg: Furche, 1954), 9–34; reprinted in
  idem, Kleine Schriften zum A.T., ThB 32 (1966),
  211–231.
Elliger, *Leviticus*
  K. Elliger, *Leviticus*, HAT 4 (Tübingen: Mohr
  [Siebeck], 1966).
Erbt, "Fürstensprüche"
  Wilhelm Erbt, "Die Fürstensprüche im Hesekiel-
  buche," *OLZ* 20 (1917): 270–274; 289–296.
Erman, *Religion*
  Adof Erman, *Die Religion der Ägypter* (Berlin: De
  Gruyter, 1934).
Erman-Ranke
  Adolf Erman and Hermann Ranke, *Ägypten und
  aegyptisches Leben im Altertum* (Tübingen: Mohr
  [Siebeck], 1922–23).
Ewald
  Heinrich Ewald, *Die Propheten des Alten Bundes
  erklärt*, volume 2, "Jeremja und Hezeqiel" (Göt-
  tingen, ²1868).
Fahlgren, *Ṣᵉdāḳā*
  Karl Hjalmar Fahlgren, *Ṣᵉdāḳā, nahestehende und
  entgegensetzte Begriffe im Alten Testament* (Uppsala:
  Almquist & Wiksell, 1932).
Falkenstein-von Soden
  A. Falkenstein and W. von Soden, *Sumerische und*

akkadische Hymnen und Gebete (Zürich: Artemis, 1953).

Filson, "Omission"
Floyd V. Filson, "The Omission of Ezek. 12:26–28 and 36:23b–38 in Codex 967," *JBL* 62 (1943): 27–32.

Fink, "Gedanken"
E. Fink, "Gedanken über die כרת-Strafe," *Jeschurun* 4 (1917): 383–393.

Fischer, *Unity*
O. R. Fischer, *The Unity of the Book of Ezekiel*, Unpub. Diss. (Boston, 1939).

Fohrer, *Hauptprobleme*
Georg Fohrer, *Die Hauptprobleme des Buches Ezechiel*, BZAW 72 (Berlin: Töpelmann, 1952).

Fohrer, *symbolischen Handlungen*
Georg Fohrer, *Die symbolischen Handlungen der Propheten*, ATANT 54 (Zürich: Zwingli, ²1968).

Fohrer-Galling
Georg Fohrer and Kurt Galling, *Ezechiel*, HAT 13 (Tübingen: Mohr [Siebeck], ²1955).

Frazer, "Hunting"
James George Frazer, "Hunting for Souls," *ARW* 11 (1908): 197–199.

Friedmann
M. Friedmann, הציון הוא ביאור לנבואת יחזקאל (Vienna, 1888).

Galling, "Beichtspiegel"
Kurt Galling, "Der Beichtspiegel. Eine gattungsgeschichtliche Studie," *ZAW* 47 (1929): 125–130.

Galling, "Ehrenname"
Kurt Galling, "Der Ehrenname Elisas und die Entrückung Elias," *ZThK* 53 (1956): 129–148.

Gaster, "Mysteries"
Theodore Gaster, "Ezekiel and the Mysteries," *JBL* 60 (1941): 289–310.

Gehman, "Relations"
Henry Snyder Gehman, "The Relations between the Hebrew Text of Ezekiel and that of the John H. Scheide Papyri," *JAOS* 58 (1938): 92–102.

Geiger, *Urschrift*
Abraham Geiger, *Urschrift und Uebersetzungen der Bibel in ihrer Abhängigkeit von der innern Entwicklung des Judenthums* (Breslau: Hainauer, 1857).

Gemser, "rîb"
B. Gemser, "The *rîb*—or Controversy—Pattern in Hebrew Mentality" in *Wisdom in Israel and in the Ancient Near East*, ed. Martin Noth, VT Suppl 3 (Leiden: Brill, 1955), 120–137.

Gesenius-Buhl
Walter Gesenius and F. Buhl, *Hebräisches und aramäisches Handwörter zum AT* (Leipzig: ¹⁶1915).

Gesenius-Kautzsch
W. Gesenius, *Hebrew Grammar*, E. Kautzsch (ed.) and A. E. Cowley (tr. and reviser) (Oxford: Clarendon, ²1910).

Goettsberger, "Ez 7:1–16"
J. Goettsberger, "Ez 7:1–16 textkritisch und exegetisch untersucht," *BZ* 22 (1934): 195–223.

Goettsberger, "Ez 9:8, 11:13"
J. Goettsberger, "Zu Ez 9:8 und 11:13," *BZ* 19 (1931): 6–19.

Gordon, *Ugaritic Literature*
Cyrus H. Gordon, *Ugaritic Literature* (Rome: Pontifical Biblical Institute, 1949).

Gordon, *Ugaritic Textbook*
Cyrus H. Gordon, *Ugaritic Textbook*, Analecta Orientalia 38 (Rome: Pontifical Biblical Institute, 1965).

E. I. Gordon, "Princes"
E. I. Gordon, "Of Princes and Foxes: The Neckstock in the newly-discovered Agade Period Stele," *Sumer* 12 (1956): 80–84.

Graetz, "Echtheit"
H. Graetz, "Die Echtheit des Buches des Propheten Ezechiel," *MGWJ* 23 (1874): 433–446; 515–525.

Greenberg, "Ezekiel 17"
Moshe Greenberg, "Ezekiel 17 and the Policy of Psammetichus II," *JBL* 76 (1957): 304–309.

Gressmann, *Messias*
Hugo Gressmann, *Der Messias*, FRLANT 26 (Göttingen, 1929).

Gressmann, *Ursprung*
Hugo Gressmann, *Der Ursprung der israelitisch-jüdischen Eschatologie*, FRLANT 6 (Göttingen, 1905).

Grether, *Name*
Oskar Grether, *Name und Wort Gottes im Alten Testament*, BZAW 64 (Giessen: Töpelmann, 1934).

Grill, "Versionen"
Severin Grill, "Die Alten Versionen und die Partikeln lo', lô, lû, lî," *BZ* NF 1 (1957): 277–281.

Gronkowski, "De natura"
Walter Gronkowski, "De natura Ezechielis 'vinculorum'," *CT* 18 (1937): 374–412.

Gunkel, "Schreiberengel"
Hermann Gunkel, "Der Schreiberengel Nabû im A.T. und im Judentum," *ARW* 1 (1898): 294–300.

Gunkel-Begrich, *Einleitung*
Hermann Gunkel and Joachim Begrich, *Einleitung in die Psalmen* (Göttingen: Vandenhoeck & Ruprecht, ²1966).

Haag, *Untersuchung*
Herbert Haag, *Was lehrt die literarische Untersuchung des Ezechiel-Textes?* (Freiburg in der Schweiz: Paulusdruckerei, 1943).

Haevernick
H. A. C. Haevernick, *Commentar über den Propheten Ezechiel* (1843).

Harford, *Studies*
John Battersby Harford, *Studies in the Book of Ezekiel* (Cambridge: Cambridge University Press, 1935).

Heinisch
Paul Heinisch, *Das Buch Ezechiel übersetzt und er-*

klärt, HSAT 8 (Bonn: Hanstein, 1923).

Heinisch, *Trauergebräuche*
Paul Heinisch, *Die Trauergebräuche bei den Israeliten* (Münster: Aschendorff, 1931).

Hempel, *Literatur*
Johannes Hempel, *Die althebraische Literatur und ihr hellenistisch-juedisches Nachleben* (Wildpark-Potsdam: Akademische Verlagsgesellschaft Athenaion, 1930).

Herntrich, *Ezekielprobleme*
Volkmar Herntrich, *Ezekielprobleme*, BZAW 61 (Giessen: Töpelmann, 1933).

J. Herrmann
J. Herrmann, *Ezechiel, übersetzt und erklärt*, KAT (Leipzig: Deichert, 1924).

J. Herrmann, *Ezechielstudien*
Johannes Herrmann, *Ezechielstudien*, BWAT 2 (Leipzig, 1908).

S. Herrmann, "Königsnovelle"
Siegfried Herrmann, "Die Königsnovelle in Ägypten und in Israel," *WZ* 3 (1953/54): 51–83.

S. Herrmann, *prophetischen Heilserwartungen*
Siegfried Herrmann, *Die prophetischen Heilserwartungen im Alten Testament*, BWANT 85 (Stuttgart: Kohlhammer, 1965).

Hilprecht-Clay, *Expedition*
H. V. Hilprecht and A. T. Clay, *The Babylonian Expedition of the University of Pennsylvania* 9 and 10 (Philadelphia, 1898–1904).

Hines, "Mystic"
Herbert W. Hines, "The Prophet as Mystic," *AJSL* 40 (1923): 37–71.

Hitzig
F. Hitzig, *Der Prophet Ezechiel erklärt*, KeH 8 (Leipzig, 1847).

Höhne, *Thronwagenvision*
Ernst Höhne, *Die Thronwagenvision Hesekiels. Echtheit und Herkunft des Vision Hes. 1: 4–28 und ihrer einzelnen Züge*, Unpub. Diss. (Erlangen, 1953/54).

Hölscher, *Geschichte*
Gustav Hölscher, *Geschichte der israelitischen und jüdischen Religion* (Giessen: Töpelmann, 1922).

Hölscher, *Hesekiel, der Dichter*
Gustav Hölscher, *Hesekiel, der Dichter und das Buch*, BZAW 39 (Giessen: Töpelmann, 1924).

Hölscher, *Profeten*
Gustav Hölscher, *Die Profeten* (Leipzig: Hinrichs, 1914).

Honeyman, "Euphemism"
A. M. Honeyman, "An unnoticed Euphemism in Isaiah ix 19–20," *VT* 1 (1951): 221–223.

Horst, "Eid"
F. Horst, "Der Eid im Alten Testament," *EvTh* 17 (1957): 366–384; reprinted in *idem, Gottes Recht*, ThB 12 (München: Kaiser, 1961), 292–314.

Horst, "Exilsgemeinde"
F. Horst, "Exilsgemeinde und Jerusalem in Ez viii–xi. Eine literarische Untersuchung," *VT* 3 (1953): 337–360.

Horst-Robinson, *kleinen Propheten*
Friedrich Horst and Theodore H. Robinson, *Die zwölf kleinen Propheten*, HAT 14 (Tübingen: Mohr [Siebeck], ³1964).

Howie
Carl Gordon Howie, *The Book of Ezekiel; The Book of Daniel*, The Layman's Bible Commentary 13 (Richmond, Va.: John Knox, 1961).

Howie, *Date*
Carl Gordon Howie, *The Date and Composition of Ezekiel*, Journal of Biblical Literature Monograph Series 4 (Philadelphia: Society of Biblical Literature, 1950).

Hulst, "*Kol baśar*,"
A. R. Hulst, "*Kol baśar* in der priesterlichen Fluterzählung" in *Studies on the Book of Genesis*, OTS 12 (Leiden: Brill, 1958), 28–68.

Humbert, "'hinnenî êlékâ'"
Paul Humbert, "Die Herausforderungsformel 'hinnenî êlékâ'," *ZAW* 51 (1933): 101–108.

Irwin, *Problem*
William A. Irwin, *The Problem of Ezechiel* (Chicago: The University of Chicago Press, 1943).

Jahn, *Buch*
Gustav Jahn, *Das Buch Ezechiel auf Grund der Septuaginta hergestellt, übersetzt und kritisch erklärt* (Leipzig: Pfeiffer, 1905).

Jahnow, *Leichenlied*
Hedwig Jahnow, *Das hebräische Leichenlied im Rahmen der Völkerdichtung*, BZAW 36 (Giessen: Töpelmann, 1923).

Janssen, *Juda*
Enno Janssen, *Juda in der Exilszeit*, FRLANT NF 51 (Göttingen: Vandenhoeck & Ruprecht, 1956).

Jirku, "Ansiedlung"
Anton Jirku, "Eine hethitische Ansiedlung in Jerusalem zur Zeit von El-Amarna," *ZDPV* 43 (1920): 58–61.

Jirku, *Materialen*
Anton Jirku, *Materialen zur Volksreligion Israels* (Leipzig: Deichert, 1914).

Johnson, *Vitality*
Aubrey R. Johnson, *The Vitality of the Individual in the Thought of Ancient Israel* (Cardiff: University of Wales Press, 1949).

Joüon
Paul Joüon, *Grammaire de l'hébreu biblique* (Rome: Pontifical Biblical Institute, ²1947).

Katz, "Septuagina"
Peter Katz, "*Septuaginta id est V.T. graece iuxta LXX*," *ThLZ* 61 (1936): 265–287.

Katz, "Textgestaltung"
Peter Katz, "Zur Textgestaltung der Ezechiel-Septuaginta," *Bibl* 35 (1954): 29–39.

Keil
Karl Friedrich Keil, *Biblical Commentary on the Prophecies of Ezekiel*, 2 volumes, tr. James Martin. Biblical Commentary on the Old Testament

(Grand Rapids, Mich.: Eerdmans, 1950)

Keller, *OTH*

Carl A. Keller, *Das Wort OTH als "Offenbarungs-zeichen Gottes"* (Basel: Hoenen, 1946).

Kelso, "Parable"

J. L. Kelso, "Ezekiel's Parable of the Corroded Copper Cauldron," *JBL* 64 (1945): 391–393.

Kittel, *Geschichte*

Rudolf Kittel, *Geschichte des Volkes Israel* 3 (Stuttgart: Kohlhammer, 1927–29).

Klamroth, *Exulanten*

Erich Klamroth, *Die jüdischen Exulanten in Babylonien*, BWAT 10 (Leipzig: Hinrichs, 1912).

Kliefoth

Th. Kliefoth, *Das Buch Ezechiels übersetzt und erklärt* (Rostock, 1864/65).

Klostermann, "Ezekiel"

A. Klostermann, "Ezekiel. Ein Beitrag zu besserer Würdigung seiner Person und seiner Schrift," *ThStKr* 50 (1877): 391–439.

Klostermann, "Heiligkeitsgesetz"

A. Klostermann, "Beiträge zur Enstehungs-geschichte des Pentateuchs," *ZLThK* 38 (1877): 401–445; reprinted as "Ezechiel und das Heiligkeitsgesetz" in idem, *Der Pentateuch* (Leipzig: Deichert, 1893), 368–418.

Knabenbauer

Joseph Knabenbauer, *Commentarius in Ezechielem prophetam*, CSS (Paris, 1890).

Knudtzon, *Amarna*

Jørgen Alexander Knudtzon, *Die El-Amarna-Tafeln*, 2 volumes (1915 = Aalen: O. Zeller, 1964).

Koch, "Geschichte"

Klaus Koch, "Zur Geschichte der Erwählungs-vorstellung in Israel," *ZAW* 67 (1955 [1956]): 205–226.

Koehler, "Beḏīl"

Ludwig Koehler, "Alttestamentliche Wortforschung. Beḏīl und *beḏīlīm," *ThZ* 3 (1947): 155–156.

Koehler, "Hebräische Vokabeln III"

Ludwig Koehler, "Hebräische Vokabeln III," *ZAW* 58 (1940/41): 228–234.

Koehler, *Lichter*

Ludwig Koehler, *Kleine Lichter: fünfzig Bibelstellen erklärt*, Zwingli-Bücherei 47 (Zürich: Livingli-Verlag, 1945).

Koehler, "Syntatica IV"

Ludwig Koehler, "Syntatica IV," *VT* 3 (1953): 299–305.

Koehler-Baumgartner

Ludwig Koehler and Walter Baumgartner, *Lexicon in Veteris Testamenti libros* (Leiden: Brill, 1953).

Kopf, "Etymologien"

L. Kopf, "Arabische Etymologien und Parallelen zum Bibelwörterbuch," *VT* 8 (1958): 161–215.

Korošec, *Staatsverträge*

V. Korošec, *Hethitische Staatsverträge. Ein Beitrag zu ihrer iuristischen Wertung*, LRSt 60 (Leipzig: Weicher, 1931).

Kraetzschmar

Richard Kraetzschmar, *Das Buch Ezechiel*, HKAT (Göttingen: Vandenhoeck & Ruprecht, 1900).

Kraus, *Klagelieder*

Hans-Joachim Kraus, *Klagelieder (Threni)*, BK 20 (Neukirchen-Vluyn: Neukirchener, 1956).

Kraus, *Königsherrschaft*

Hans-Joachim Kraus, *Die Königsherrschaft Gottes im Alten Testament*, BHTh 13 (Tübingen: Mohr [Siebeck], 1951).

Kuhl, "Schauplatz"

Curt Kuhl, "Der Schauplatz der Wirksamkeit Hesekiel. Ein Lösungsversuch," *ThZ* 8 (1952): 401–418.

Kuhl, " 'Wiederaufnahme' "

Curt Kuhl, "Die 'Wiederaufnahme'—ein literar-kritisches Prinzip?" *ZAW* 64 (1952): 1–11.

Landersdorfer, *Der ΒΑΑΛ*

Simon Landersdorfer, *Der ΒΑΑΛ ΤΕΤΡΑΜΟΡ-ΦΟΣ und die Kerube des Ezechiel*, Studien zur Geschichte und Kultur des Altertums 9, 3 (Paderborn: Schöningh, 1918).

Levy, *Wörterbuch*

Jacob Levy, *Wörterbuch über die Talmudim und Midraschim*, 5 volumes (Berlin: Harz, 1924).

Lewy, "Nāḫ"

J. Lewy, "Nāḫ et Rušpān" in *Mélanges syriens offerts à M. René Dussaud* 1 (Paris: Geuthner, 1939), 273–275.

Loew

Immanuel Loew, *Die Flora der Juden* 1 and 2, Publications of the Alexander Kohut Memorial Foundation 4 (Wien: Löwit, 1928).

Loewe, "Anthropopathism"

Raphael Loewe, "Jerome's Treatment of an Anthropopathism," *VT* 2 (1952): 261–272.

Löwinger, "Tel Abib"

S. Löwinger, "Tel Abib—til Abūbi (Ezek. 3:15)" in *Études orientales à la mémoire de Paul Hirschler* (Budapest, 1950), 62–72.

Malamat, "Jeremiah"

A. Malamat, "Jeremiah and the Last Two Kings of Judah," *PEQ* 83 (1951): 81–87.

Matthews

I. G. Matthews, *Ezekiel. An American Commentary on the Old Testament* (Philadelphia: Judson, 1939).

May

Herbert G. May, "The Book of Ezekiel" in *The Interpreter's Bible* 6 (Nashville: Abingdon, 1956), 41–338.

May, "Departure"

Herbert Gordon May, "The Departure of the Glory of Yahweh," *JBL* 56 (1937): 309–321.

Meissner, *Babylonien*

Bruno Meissner, *Babylonien und Assyrien*, 2 volumes (Heidelberg: Winter, 1920).

Mendenhall, "Covenant Forms"

George E. Mendenhall, "Covenant Forms in Israelite Tradition," *BA* 17 (1954): 50–76.

Merx, "Wert"
A. Merx, "Der Wert der Septuaginta für die Textkritik des Alten Testamentes, am Ezechiel aufgezeigt," *JPTh* 9 (1883): 65–77.

Messel
Nils Messel, *Ezéchielfragen* (Oslo: Dybwad, 1945).

Michaelis, "Zeichen"
Wilhelm Michaelis, "Zeichen, Siegel, Kreuz. Ein Ausschnitt aus der Bedeutungsgeschichte biblischen Begriff," *ThZ* 12 (1956): 505–525.

Michel, "Studien"
Diethelm Michel, "Studien zu den sogenannten Thronbesteigungspsalmen," *VT* 6 (1956): 40–68.

Miller, *Verhältnis*
John Wolf Miller, *Das Verhältnis Jeremias und Hesekiels sprachlich und theologisch untersucht* (Assen: Van Gorcum, 1955).

Montgomery, "Hebraica"
James A. Montgomery, "Hebraica," *JAOS* 58 (1938): 130–139.

Moore, *Judaism*
George Foot Moore, *Judaism in the first centuries of the Christian era, the age of the Tannaim*, 2 volumes (New York: Schocken, 1971).

Moran, "Gen. 49:10"
William L. Moran, "Gen. 49:10 and Its Use in Ez 21:32," *Bibl.* 39 (1958): 405–425.

Morgenstern, "Additional Notes"
Julian Morgenstern, "Additional Notes on 'Beena Marriage (Matriarchat) in Ancient Israel'," *ZAW* 49 (1931): 46–58.

Mowinckel, *Décalogue*
Sigmund Mowinckel, *Le Décalogue* (Paris: Alcan, 1927).

Mowinckel, *Prophecy*
Sigmund Mowinckel, *Prophecy and Tradition* (Oslo: Dybwad, 1946).

Mülinen, "Galgal"
Eberhard von Mülinen, "Galgal. Hesekiel kapitel 10:13," *ZDPV* 46 (1923): 79–107.

Müller, *Ezechiel-studien*
David Heinrich Müller, *Ezechiel-studien* (Berlin: Reuther & Reichard, 1895); reprinted as *idem*, *Biblische Studien* 1 (Wien: Hölder, 1904).

Müller, *Strophenbau*
David Heinrich Müller, *Biblische Studien 4: Strophenbau und Responsion in Ezechiel und den Psalmen* (Wien: Hölder, 1908).

Müller, "Zephanja"
David Heinrich Müller, "Der Prophet Ezechiel entlehnt eine Stelle des Propheten Zephanja und glossiert sie," *WZKM* 19 (1905): 263–270; reprinted in *idem*, *Biblische Studien* 3 (Wien: Hölder, 1907), 30–36.

Néher, "symbolisme"
A. Néher, "Le symbolisme conjugal: expression de l'historie dans l'Ancien Testament," *RHPhR* 34 (1954): 30–49.

Neufeld, *Marriage Laws*
E. Neufeld, *Ancient Hebrew Marriage Laws* (London: Longmans Green, 1944).

Neuss, *Buch*
Wilhelm Neuss, *Das Buch Ezechiel in Theologie und Kunst bis zum Ende des XII. Jahrhunderts*, Beiträge zur Geschichte des Alten Mönchtums und des Benediktinerordens 1–2 (Münster: Aschendorff, 1912).

Noth, "Einnahme"
Martin Noth, "Die Einnahme von Jerusalem im Jahre 597 v. Chr.," *ZDPV* 74 (1958): 133–157.

Noth, *israelitischen Personennamen*
Martin Noth, *Die israelitischen Personennamen im Rahmen der gemeinsemitischen Namengebung*, BWANT 3, 10 (Stuttgart: Kohlhammer, 1928).

Noth, "Jerusalem Catastrophe"
Martin Noth, "The Jerusalem Catastrophe of 587 B.C., and its significance for Israel" in *The Laws in the Pentateuch and Other Studies*, tr. D. R. Ap-Thomas (Philadelphia: Fortress, 1967), 260–280.

Noth, "Noah"
Martin Noth, "Noah, Daniel und Hiob in Ezechiel xiv," *VT* 1 (1951): 251–260.

Noth, *Pentateuchal Traditions*
Martin Noth, *A History of Pentateuchal Traditions*, tr. Bernhard W. Anderson (Englewood Cliffs, N.J.: Prentice Hall, 1972).

Noth, *System*
Martin Noth, *Das System der zwölf Stämme Israels*, BWANT 4, 1 (Stuttgart: Kohlhammer, 1930).

Oort, "Ezechiël"
H. Oort, "Ezechiël 19; 21:18, 19v., 24v.," *ThT* 23 (1889): 504–514.

Oppenheim, *Tell Halaf*
Max Freiherr von Oppenheim, *Der Tell Halaf; eine neue Kultur im aeltesten Mesopotamien* (Leipzig: Brockhaus, 1931).

von Orelli
Conrad von Orelli, *Das Buch Ezechiel und die zwölf kleinen Propheten*, Kurzgefasster Kommentar zu den Schriften des Alten und Neuen Testaments (Nördlingen, ²1896).

Parker-Dubberstein
Richard Anthony Parker and Waldo H. Dubberstein, *Babylonian Chronology 626 B.C.–A.D. 75*, Brown University Studies 19 (Providence: Brown University Press, 1956).

Parrot, *Babylon*
André Parrot, *Babylon and the Old Testament*, tr. B. E. Hooke. Studies in Biblical Archaeology 8 (London: SCM, 1958).

Perles, "Glossen"
F. Perles, "Babylonisch-biblische Glossen," *OLZ* 8 (1905): 125–130; 179–183.

van der Ploeg, "Règle de la Guerre"
J. van der Ploeg, "La Règle de la Guerre, Traduc-

tion et Notes," *VT* 5 (1955): 373–420.

Procksch, "Berufungsvision"
O. Procksch, "Die Berufungsvision Hesekiels" in *K. Budde zum 70. Geburtstag überreicht*, BZAW 34 (Giessen: Töpelmann, 1920), 141–149.

Quell, *Propheten*
Gottfried Quell, *Wahre und falsche Propheten*, BFChrTh 46, 1 (Gütersloh: Bertelsmann, 1952).

von Rabenau, "Rätsels"
Kurt von Rabenau, "Die Form des Rätsels im Buche Hesekiel," *Wiss. Z. Halle* GR 7, 5 (1958): 1055–1058.

von Rabenau, "Zukunftswort"
Kurt von Rabenau, "Das prophetische Zukunftswort im Buch Hesekiel" in *Studien zur Theologie der alttestamentlichen Überlieferungen*, ed. R. Rendtorff and K. Koch (Neukirchen-Vluyn: Neukirchener, 1961), 61–80.

von Rad, "Faith"
Gerhard von Rad, "Faith Reckoned as Righteousness" in *The Problem of the Hexateuch and Other Essays*, tr. E. W. Trueman Dicken (New York: McGraw-Hill, 1966), 125–130.

von Rad, *Krieg*
Gerhard von Rad, *Der heilige Krieg im alten Israel*, ATANT 20 (Göttingen: Vandenhoeck & Ruprecht, ⁵1969).

von Rad, *OT Theology*
Gerhard von Rad, *Old Testament Theology*, 2 volumes, tr. D. M. G. Stalker (New York: Harper and Row, 1962 and 1965).

von Rad, "Promised Land"
Gerhard von Rad, "The Promised Land and Yahweh's Land in the Hexateuch" in *The Problem of the Hexateuch and Other Essays*, tr. E. W. Trueman Dicken (New York: McGraw-Hill, 1966), 79–93.

von Rad, " 'Righteousness' "
Gerhard von Rad, " 'Righteousness' and 'Life' in the Cultic Language of the Psalms" in *The Problem of the Hexateuch and Other Essays*, tr. E. W. Trueman Dicken (New York: McGraw-Hill, 1966), 243–266.

Ratschow, *Werden*
Carl Heinz Ratschow, *Werden und Wirken. Eine Untersuchung des Wortes hajah als Beitrag zur Wirklichkeitserfassung des Alten Testamentes*, BZAW 70 (Berlin: Töpelmann, 1941).

Reider, "Contributions"
Joseph Reider, "Contributions to the Scriptural Text," *HUCA* 24 (1952/3): 85–106.

Reider, "Etymological Studies"
Joseph Reider, "Etymological Studies in Biblical Hebrew," *VT* 2 (1952): 113–130.

Reider, "Studies"
Joseph Reider, "Etymological Studies in Biblical Hebrew," *VT* 4 (1954): 276–295.

Reider, "ידע"
Joseph Reider, "Etymological Studies: ידע or

ירע and רעע," *JBL* 66 (1947): 315–317.

Rendtorff, "Gebrauch"
Rolf Rendtorff, "Zum Gebrauch der Formel nᵉʾum jahwe im Jeremiabuch," *ZAW* 66 (1954): 27–37.

Rendtorff, *Gesetze*
Rolf Rendtorff, *Die Gesetze in der Priesterschrift*, FRLANT NF 44 (Göttingen: Vandenhoeck & Ruprecht, 1954).

Reventlow, "Mazkir"
Henning Graf Reventlow, "Das Amt des Mazkir. Zur Rechtsstruktur des öffentlichen Lebens in Israel," *ThZ* 15 (1959): 161–175.

Reventlow, "Die Völker"
Henning Graf Reventlow, "Die Völker als Jahwes Zeugen bei Ezechiel," *ZAW* 71 (1959): 33–43.

Riessler
Paul Riessler, *Altjüdisches Schrifttum ausserhalb der Bibel, übersetzt und erläutert* (1928 = Heidelberg, 1966).

Rohland, *Erwählungstraditionen*
Edzard Rohland, *Die Bedeutung der Erwählungstraditionen Israels für die Eschatologie der alttestamentlichen Propheten*, Unpub. Diss. (Heidelberg, 1956).

L. Rost, *Israel*
Leonhard Rost, *Israel bei den Propheten*, BWANT 4, 19 (Stuttgart: Kohlhammer, 1937).

L. Rost, *Vorstufen*
Leonhard Rost, *Die Vorstufen von Kirche und Synagoge im Alten Testament*, BWANT 4, 24 (Stuttgart: Kohlhammer, 1938).

P. Rost, "Miscellen"
Paul Rost, "Miscellen I," *OLZ* 7 (1904): 390–393; 479–483.

Rothstein
J. W. Rothstein, *Das Buch Ezechiel*, HSAT (Tübingen, ⁴1922).

Rubinstein, "Finite Verb"
A. Rubinstein, "A Finite Verb continued by an Infinitive Absolute in Biblical Hebrew," *VT* 2 (1952): 362–367.

Rudolph, *Jeremia*
Wilhelm Rudolph, *Jeremia*, HAT 1, 12 (Tübingen: Mohr [Siebeck], ³1968).

Schmidt, "Kerubenthron"
H. Schmidt, "Kerubenthron und Lade" in *Eucharisterion für H. Gunkel*, FRLANT 36, 1 (Göttingen, 1923), 120–144.

Schulthess, "רִיפוֹת"
Friedrich Schulthess, "רִיפוֹת 2 Sam. 17:19, רְפֹת Prov. 27:22," *ZAW* 25 (1905): 357–359.

Schumpp
Meinrad Schumpp, *Das Buch Ezechiel übersetzt und erklärt*, Herders Bibelkommentar (Freiburg: Herder, 1942).

Schwarzenbach, *Terminologie*
Armin Schwarzenbach, *Die geographische Terminologie im hebräischen des Alten Testamentes* (Leiden:

Brill, 1954).

Seeligmann, "Midraschexegese"

I. L. Seeligmann, "Voraussetzungen der Midraschexegese" in *Congress Volume: Copenhagen*, VT Suppl 1 (Leiden, 1953), 150–181.

Selbie, "Ezek 13:18–21"

J. A. Selbie, "Ezekiel 13:18–21," *ET* 15 (1903/1904).

Selle, *De Aramaismis*

Fridericus Philippus Selle, *De Aramaismis libri Ezechielis* (Halis Saxonum: Formis Kaemmererianis, 1890).

Silbermann, *Targum*

Samuel Silbermann, *Das Targum zu Ezechiel nach einer südarabischen Handschrift* (Strassburg, 1902).

Simons, *Jerusalem*

Jan Jozef Simons, *Jerusalem in the Old Testament; researches and theories* (Leiden: E. J. Brill, 1952).

Slotki, "Ezek. 18:10"

Israel W. Slotki, "Ezek. 18:10," *AJSL* 43 (1926): 63–66.

Smend

Rudolf Smend, *Der Prophet Ezechiel*, KeH (Leipzig, ²1880).

J. Smith, *Book*

James Smith, *The Book of the Prophet Ezekiel; a new interpretation* (London: S.P.C.K., 1931).

L. P. Smith, "Eagle(s)"

Louise Pettibone Smith, "The Eagle(s) of Ezekiel 17," *JBL* 58 (1939): 43–50.

Snijders, "Meaning"

L. A. Snijders, "The meaning of זר in the Old Testament. An Exegetical Study," *OTS* 10 (1954): 1–154.

Speier, "Wortforschung"

Salomon Speier, "Alttestamentliche Wortforschung. Ṭārāf, Genesis 8, 11," *ThZ* 2 (1946): 153–154.

Spiegel, "Ezekiel"

Shalom Spiegel, "Ezekiel or Pseudo-Ezekiel?" *HTR* 24 (1931): 245–321.

Spiegel, "Noah"

Shalom Spiegel, "Noah, Daniel and Job, Touching on Canaanite Relics in the Legends of the Jews" in *Louis Ginzberg Jubilee Volume* (N.Y.: Amer. Acad. Jewish Research, 1945), 305–355 (English section).

Sprank, *Studien*

Siegfried Sprank and Kurt Wiese, *Studien zu Ezechiel und dem Buch der Richter*, BWANT 3, 4 (Stuttgart: Kohlhammer, 1926).

Stade, "Aequivalent"

Bernhard Stade, "Das vermeintliche aramäisch-assyrische Aequivalent der מלכת השמים Jer. 7.44," *ZAW* 6 (1886): 289–339.

Steinmann, *Le prophète Ézéchiel*

Jean Steinmann, *Le prophète Ézéchiel et les débuts de l'exil*, Lectio Divina 13 (Paris: Cerf, 1953).

Steuernagel, *Lehrbuch*

Carl Steuernagel, *Lehrbuch der Einleitung in das Alte Testament* (Tübingen: Mohr [Siebeck], 1912).

Stoebe, "Gut"

Hans Joachim Stoebe, "Gut und Böse in der jahwistischen Quelle des Pentateuch," *ZAW* 65 (1953): 188–204.

Strack-Billerbeck

Hermann L. Strack and Paul Billerbeck, *Kommentar zum Neuen Testament aus Talmud und Midrasch*, 6 volumes (München: Beck, ²1956–1961).

Stummer, "אָמְלָה"

F. Stummer, "אָמְלָה (Ez xvi 30 A)," *VT* 4 (1954): 34–40.

Sutcliffe, "Effect as Purpose"

Edmund F. Sutcliffe, "Effect as Purpose: A Study in Hebrew Thought Patterns," *Bibl* 35 (1954): 320–327.

Tallqvist, *Himmelsgegenden*

Knut Tallqvist, *Himmelsgegenden und Winde*, StOr 2 (Helsinki, 1928).

Torrey, *Pseudo-Ezekiel*

C. C. Torrey, *Pseudo-Ezekiel and the Original Prophecy* (New Haven: Yale University Press, 1930 = New York: KTAV Publishing House, 1970).

Tournay, "Review"

R. Tournay, "Review of *Die Hauptprobleme des Buches Ezechiel*," *RB* 60 (1953): 417–419.

Toy

C. H. Toy, *The Book of the Prophet Ezekiel*, SBOT 12 (New York: Dodd, Mead, 1899).

Troelstra

A. Troelstra, *Ezechiel*, 2 vols, TeU (Groningen: Wolters, 1931).

Tsevat, "Vassal Oaths"

Matitiahu Tsevat, "The Neo-Assyrian and Neo-Babylonian Vassal Oaths and the Prophet Ezekiel," *JBL* 78 (1959): 199–204.

Ungnad, *Religion*

A. Ungnad, *Die Religion der Babylonier und Assyrer* (Jena: Diederich, 1921).

Virolleaud, "l'idole"

Charles Virolleaud, "Sur l'idole de la jalousie du temple de Jérusalem," *RES* 1 (1945): 59–63.

Vischer, "Jerusalem"

W. Vischer, "Jerusalem du hast deine Schwestern gerechtfertigt durch alle deine Greuel, die du getan hast. Hesekiel 16" in *Versöhnung zwischen West und Ost*, ThEx NF 56 (München, 1957), 16–38.

Vogt, "Ioiakîn"

E. Vogt, "Ioiakîn collari ligneo vinctus (Ez 19:9)," *Bibl* 37 (1956): 388–389.

Volz, *Geist Gottes*

Paul Volz, *Der Geist Gottes und die verwandten Erscheinungen im Alten Testament und im anschliessenden Judentum* (Tübingen, 1910).

Vriezen, "'Ehje"

Theodorus Christiaan Vriezen, "'Ehje ᵃšer 'ehje"

in *Festschrift A. Bertholet* (Tuebingen: Mohr [Paul Siebeck], 1950), 498–512.

Wagner, *Aramaismen*
Max Wagner, *Die lexikalischen und grammatikalischen Aramaismen im alttestamentlichen Hebräisch*, BZAW 96 (Berlin: Töpelmann, 1966).

Watzinger, *Denkmäler*
Carl Watzinger, *Denkmäler Palästinas*, 2 volumes (Leipzig: Hinrichs, 1933–35).

Wellhausen, *Text*
Julius Wellhausen, *Der Text der Bücher Samuelis* (Göttingen: Vandenhoeck & Ruprecht, 1871).

Wernberg-Møller, "'Pleonastic'"
P. Wernberg-Møller, "'Pleonastic' *Waw* in Classical Hebrew," *JSS* 3 (1958): 321–326.

Wevers
John W. Wevers, *Ezekiel*, Cent-B (London: Nelson, 1969).

Wevers, "Septuaginta-Forschungen"
John W. Wevers, "Septuaginta-Forschungen," *ThR* NF 22 (1954): 85–138.

Wiesner, *Fahren*
J. Wiesner, *Fahren und Reiten in Alteuropa und im Alten Orient*, AO 38, 2–4 (Leipzig: 1939).

Wildberger, "Israel"
Hans Wildberger, "Israel und sein Land," *EvTh* 16 (1956): 404–422.

Wiseman, *Chronicles*
Donald John Wiseman, *Chronicles of Chaldaean Kings (626–556 B.C.) in the British Museum* (London: The British Museum, 1956).

Wolff, "Begründungen"
Hans Walter Wolff, "Die Begründungen der prophetischen Heils- und Unheilssprüche," *ZAW* 52 (1934): 1–22; reprinted in *idem, Gesammelte Studien zum AT*, ThB 22 (München: Kaiser, 1964), 9–35.

Wolff, *Hosea*
Hans Walter Wolff, *Hosea: A Commentary on the Book of the Prophet Hosea*, tr. Gary Stansell. Hermeneia (Philadelphia: Fortress, 1974).

Wolff, *Zitat*
Hans Walter Wolff, *Das Zitat im Prophetenspruch*, BhEvTh 4 (München: Kaiser, 1937); reprinted in *idem, Ges. Stud. zum AT*, ThB 22 (München: Kaiser, 1964), 36–129.

Würthwein, ʿamm
Ernst Würthwein, *Der ʿamm haʾarez im Alten Testament*, BWANT 4, 17 (Stuttgart: Kohlhammer, 1936).

Würthwein, *Text*
Ernst Würthwein, *The Text of the Old Testament; an Introduction to Kittel-Kahle's Biblia Hebraica*, tr. Peter R. Ackroyd (Oxford: Basil Blackwell, 1957).

Ziegler
Joseph Ziegler, *Ezechiel*, Echter-B (Würzburg: Echter, 1948).

Ziegler, *Ezechiel*
Joseph Ziegler, *Ezechiel*, Septuaginta. Vetus Testamentum graecum 16, 1 (Göttingen: Vandenhoeck & Ruprecht, 1952).

Zimmerli, "Eigenart"
Walther Zimmerli, "Die Eigenart der prophetischen Rede des Ezechiel. Ein Beitrag zum Problem an Hand von Ez. 14: 1–11," *ZAW* 66 (1954): 1–26.

Zimmerli, *Erkenntnis*
Walther Zimmerli, *Erkenntnis Gottes nach dem Buche Ezechiel*, ATANT 27 (Zürich: Zwingli, 1954); reprinted in *idem, Gottes Offenbarung*, ThB 19 (München: Kaiser, 1963), 41–119.

Zimmerli, "Jahwe"
Walther Zimmerli, "Ich bin Jahwe" in *Festschrift für A. Alt* (Tübingen: Mohr [Siebeck], 1953): 179–209; reprinted in *idem, Gottes Offenbarung*, ThB 19 (München: Kaiser, 1963), 11–40.

Zimmerli, "'Leben' und 'Tod'"
Walther Zimmerli, "'Leben' und 'Tod' im Buche des Propheten Ezechiel," *ThZ* 13 (1957): 494–508; reprinted in *idem, Gottes Offenbarung*, ThB 19 (München: Kaiser, 1963), 178–191.

Zimmerli, "Planungen"
Walther Zimmerli, "Planungen für den Wiederaufbau nach der Katastrophe von 587," *VT* 18 (1968): 229–255.

Zimmerli, "Wort"
Walther Zimmerli, "Das Wort des göttlichen Selbsterweises" in *Mélanges bibliques rédigés en l'honneur de André Robert*, Travaux de l'Institut Catholique de Paris 4 (Paris, 1957), 154–164; reprinted in *idem, Gottes Offenbarung*, ThB 19 (München: Kaiser, 1963), 120–132.

Zorell
Franciscus Zorell, *Lexicon hebraicum et aramaicum Veteris Testamenti* (Rome: Pontifical Biblical Institute, 1946–1954).

Zunz, "Ezechiel"
L. Zunz, "Bibelkritisches II. Ezechiel," *ZDMG* 27 (1873): 676–681.

1. Commentaries (listed in order of their publication)

Haevernick, H. A. C.
Commentar über den Propheten Ezechiel (1843).

Hitzig, F.
Der Prophet Ezechiel erklärt, KeH 8 (Leipzig, 1847).

Kliefoth, Th.
Das Buch Ezechiels übersetzt und erklärt (Rostock, 1864/65).

Ewald, Heinrich
Die Propheten des Alten Bundes erklärt, volume 2, "Jeremja und Hezeqiel" (Göttingen, ²1868).

Smend, Rudolf
Der Prophet Ezechiel, KeH (Leipzig, ²1880).

Cornill, Carl Heinrich
Das Buch des Propheten Ezechiel (Leipzig, 1886).

Knabenbauer, Joseph
Commentarius in Ezechielem prophetam, CSS (Paris, 1890).

Bertholet, Alfred
Das Buch Hesekiel erklärt, KHC 12 (Freiburg: Mohr, 1897).

Toy, C. H.
The Book of the Prophet Ezekiel, SBOT 12 (New York: Dodd, Mead, 1899).

Kraetzschmar, Richard
Das Buch Ezekiel, HKAT (Göttingen: Vandenhoeck & Ruprecht, 1900).

Breuer, Joseph
Das Buch Jecheskel übersetzt und erläutert (Frankfurt: Sänger and Friedburg, 1921).

Rothstein, J. W.
Das Buch Ezekiel, HSAT (Tübingen: ⁴1922).

Heinisch, Paul
Das Buch Ezechiel übersetzt und erklärt, HSAT 8 (Bonn: Hanstein, 1923).

Herrmann, Johannes
Ezechiel, übersetzt und erklärt, KAT (Leipzig: Deichert, 1924).

Troelstra, A.
Ezechiel, 2 vols, TeU (Groningen: Wolters, 1931).

Bertholet, Alfred and Galling, Kurt
Hesekiel, HAT 13 (Tübingen: Mohr [Siebeck], 1936).

Cooke, G. A.
A Critical and Exegetical Commentary on the Book of Ezekiel, ICC (Edinburgh: Clark, 1936).

Matthews, I. G.
Ezekiel. An American Commentary on the Old Testament (Philadelphia: Judson, 1939).

Schumpp, Meinrad
Das Buch Ezechiel übersetzt und erklärt, Herders Bibelkommentar (Freiburg: Herder, 1942).

Auvray, P.
Ezéchiel, Témoins de Dieu (1947).

Ziegler, Joseph
Ezechiel, Echter-B (Würzburg: Echter, 1948).

Fohrer, Georg and Galling, Kurt
Ezechiel, HAT 13 (Tübingen: Mohr [Siebeck], ²1955).

Aalders, Gerhard Charles
Ezechiel, 2 volumes, COT (Kampen: Kok, 1955 and 1957).

May, Herbert G.
"The Book of Ezekiel" in *The Interpreter's Bible* 6 (Nashville: Abingdon, 1956), 41–338.

Howie, Carl Gordon
The Book of Ezekiel; The Book of Daniel, The Layman's Bible Commentary 13 (Richmond, Va.: John Knox, 1961).

Wevers, John W.
Ezekiel, Cent-B (London: Nelson, 1969).

Eichrodt, Walther
Der Prophet Hesekiel, ATD (1970).

2. Select Books, Monographs, and Articles (alphabetically)

Ackroyd, Peter R.
"The Teraphim," *ET* 62 (1950/51): 378–380.

Albrecht, Karl
"Das Geschlecht der hebräischen Hauptwörter," *ZAW* 16 (1896): 41–121.

Albright, W. F.
Archaeology and the Religion of Israel (Baltimore: Johns Hopkins University Press, 1956).

Idem
From the Stone Age to Christianity (Baltimore: Johns Hopkins University Press, ²1957).

Idem
"The High Place in Ancient Palestine" in *Volume du Congrès, Strasbourg 1956*, VT Suppl 4 (Leiden, 1957), 242–258.

Idem
"The Names SHADDAI and ABRAM," *JBL* 54 (1935): 173–204.

Idem
"The Psalm of Habakkuk" in *Studies in Old Testament Prophecy presented to T. H. Robinson*, ed. H. H. Rowley (Edinburgh: Clark, 1950), 1–18.

Idem

"Recent Progress in North-Canaanite Research," *BASOR* 70 (1938): 18–24.

Idem

"The Seal of Eliakim and the Latest Preëxilic History of Judah, with Some Observations on Ezekiel," *JBL* 51 (1932): 77–106.

Idem

"What were the Cherubim?" *BA* 1 (1938): 1–3.

Alföldi, A.

"Die Geschichte des Throntabernakels," *NC* 1/2 (1949/50): 537–566.

Alt, Albrecht

"Gedanken über das Königtum Jahwes," in *Kleine Schriften zur Geschichte des Volkes Israel* 1 (München: Beck, 1953), 345–357.

Idem

"Höfisches Zeremoniell in Feldlager der Pharaonen," *WO* 1 (1947–52): 2–4.

Idem

"Jerusalems Aufstieg," *ZDMG* NF 4/79 (1925): 1–19; reprinted in *idem, Kleine Schriften zur Geschichte des Volkes Israel* 3 (München: Beck, 1959), 243–257.

Idem

"Judas Gaue unter Josia," *PJ* 21 (1925): 100–116; reprinted in *idem, Kleine Schriften zur Geschichte des Volkes Israel* 2 (München: Beck, 1953), 276–288.

Idem

Kleine Schriften zur Geschichte des Volkes Israel, 3 volumes, (München: Beck, 1953–1959).

Idem

"Megiddo im Übergang vom kanaanäischen zum israelitischen Zeitalter," *ZAW* 60 (1944): 67–85; reprinted in *idem, Kleine Schriften zur Geschichte des Volkes Israel* 1 (München: Beck, 1953), 256–273.

Idem

"Micha 2: 1–5 $\Gamma\hat{\eta}_S$ 'αναδασμός in Juda" in *Kleine Schriften zur Geschichte des Volkes Israel* 3 (München: Beck, 1959), 373–381.

Idem

"The Origins of Israelite Law" in *Essays on Old Testament History and Religion*, tr. R. A. Wilson (Garden City, New York: Doubleday, Inc., 1967), 101–171.

Idem

"Die territorialgeschichtliche Bedeutung yon Sanheribs Eingriff in Palästina," *PJ* 25 (1929 [1930]): 80–88; reprinted in *idem, Kleine Schriften zur Geschichte des Volkes Israel* 2 (München: Beck, 1953), 242–249.

Andrae, W. F.

Das Gotteshaus und die Urformen des Bauens im alten Orient, Studien zur Bauforschung, ed. by the Koldeway Society, Pt. 2 (Berlin: Schoetz, 1930).

Idem

Die jüngeren Ischtartempel in Assur, WVDOG 58 (Leipzig: Hinrichs, 1935).

Bach, Robert

Die Erwählung Israels in der Wüste, Unpub. Diss. (Bonn, 1951).

Badè, W. F.

"The Seal of Jaazaniah," *ZAW* 51 (1933): 150–156.

Baentsch, B.

"Pathologischer Züge in Israels Prophetentum, ' *ZWTh* 50 (1908): 52–81.

Baer, S. and Delitzsch, F.

Liber Ezechielis, Textum masoreticum accuratissime expressit, e fontibus Masorae varie illustravit, notis criticis confirmavit (1884).

Balla, E.

"Ezechiel 8: 1–9: 11; 11: 24–25" in *Festschrift Rudolf Bultmann zum 65. Geburtstag überreicht* (Stuttgart: Kohlhammer, 1949), 1–11.

Bardtke, Hans

"Der Erweckungsgedanke in der exilisch-nachexilischen Literatur des Alten Testaments" in *Von Ugarit nach Qumran*, BZAW 77 (Berlin, 1958), 9–24.

Idem

"Der gegenwärtige Stand der Erforschung der in Palästina neu gefundenen hebräischen Handschriften. 29. Die Kriegsrolle von Qumrān übersetzt," *ThLZ* 80 (1955): 401–420.

Barrois, A. G.

Manuel d'archéologie biblique 1 (Paris: Picard, 1939).

Barth, J.

"Zu dem Zauber des Umnähens der Gelenke," *MGWJ* 57 (1913).

Barton, George A.

"Danel, A Pre-Israelite Hero of Galilee," *JBL* 60 (1941): 213–225.

Baudissin, Wolf Wilhelm Graf

"Die alttestamentliche Bezeichnung der Götzen mit *gillūlīm*," *ZDMG* 58 (1904): 395–425.

Idem

"Alttestamentliches *ḥajjim* in der Bedeutung 'Glück' " in *Festschrift Eduard Sachau zum siebzigsten Geburtstag* (Berlin: Reimer, 1915), 143–161.

Bauer, Johannes

"Hes. xxiv 17," *VT* 7 (1957): 91–92.

Bauer, Hans and Leander, Pontus

Historische Grammatik der hebräischen Sprache des Alten Testaments 1 (Halle: Niemeyer, 1922).

Baumann, Eberhard

"Die Hauptvisionen Hesekiels in ihrem zeitlichen und sachlichen Zusammenhang untersucht," *ZAW* 67 (1955): 56–67.

Idem

"שוב שבות Eine exegetische Untersuchung," *ZAW* 47 (1929): 17–44.

Idem

"Die Weinranke im Walde. Hes. 15, 1–8," *ThLZ* 80 (1955): 119–120.

Baumgärtel, Friedrich
 "Die Formel nᵉ'um jahwe," *ZAW* 73 (1961): 277–
 290.

Baumgartner, Walter
 "Ein Kapitel vom hebräischen Erzählungsstil,"
 in *Eucharisterion für H. Gunkel*, FRLANT NF 19
 (Göttingen, 1923), 145–157.

Idem
 Die Klagegedichte des Jeremia, BZAW 32 (Berlin,
 1917).

Idem
 "Ugaritische Probleme und ihre Tragweite für
 das Alte Testament," *ThZ* 3 (1947): 81–100.

Beer, G. and Meyer, D. R.
 Hebräische Grammatik (Berlin, 1952–55).

Begrich, Joachim
 *Die Chronologie der Könige von Israel und Juda und die
 Quellen des Rahmens der Königsbücher* (Tübingen:
 Mohr [Siebeck], 1929).

Idem
 "Das priesterliche Heilsorakel," *ZAW* 52 (1934):
 81–92.

Idem
 "Die priestliche Tora," in BZAW 66 (Berlin,
 1936), 63–88; reprinted in *idem*, *Gesammelte Studien
 zum AT*, ThB 21 (München: Kaiser, 1964), 232–
 260.

Idem
 "Der Satzstil im Fünfer," *ZS* 9 (1933/34): 169–
 209; reprinted in *idem*, *Gesammelte Studien zum AT*,
 ThB 21 (München: Kaiser, 1964), 132–167.

Idem
 Studien zu Deuterojesaja, BWANT 4:25 (Stuttgart:
 1938).

Ben-Mordecai, C. A.
 "The Iniquity of the Sanctuary: A Study of the
 Hebrew Term עָוֹן," *JBL* 60 (1941): 311–314.

Berry, George Ricker
 "The Title of Ezekiel (1:1–3)," *JBL* 51 (1932):
 54–57.

Idem
 "Was Ezekiel in the Exile?" *JBL* 49 (1930): 83–
 93.

Bertholet, Alfred
 Die Stellung der Israeliten und der Juden zu den Fremden
 (Freiburg, 1896).

Bewer, Julius A.
 "Beiträge zur Exegese des Buches Ezechiel," *ZAW*
 63 (1951): 193–201.

Idem
 "On the Text of Ezekiel 7:5–14," *JBL* 45 (1926):
 223–231.

Idem
 "The Text of Ezek. 1:1–3," *AJSL* 50 (1934): 96–
 101.

Idem
 "Textual and Exegetical Notes on the Book of
 Ezekiel," *JBL* 72 (1953): 158–168.

Bin Gorion, M. J.

Der Born Judas 5 (Leipzig: Insel-Verlag, 1921).

Blank, Sheldon
 "Isaiah 52:5 and the Profanation of the Name,"
 HUCA 25 (1954): 1–8.

Blau, Josia
 "Adverbia als psychologische und grammatische
 Subjekte/Praedikate im Bibelhebraeisch," *VT* 9
 (1959): 130–137.

Idem
 "Zum angeblichen Gebrauch von את vor dem
 Nominativ," *VT* 4 (1954): 7–22.

Idem
 "Zum Hebräisch der Übersetzer des AT," *VT* 6
 (1956): 97–99.

de Boer, P. A. H.
 "The Counsellor" in *Wisdom in Israel and in the
 Ancient Near East*, ed. Martin Noth, VT Suppl 3
 (Leiden: Brill, 1955), 42–71.

Idem
 "De voorbede in het Oude Testament," *OTS* 3
 (1943).

Böhl, F.
 "ברא, bārā, als Terminus der Weltschöpfung im
 at.lichen Sprachgebrauch" in *At.lichen Studien
 Rudolf Kittel zum 60. Geburtstag*, BWAT 13 (Stuttgart, 1913), 42–60.

Böhl, M. T. de Liagre
 "Nebukadnezar en Jojachin," *NTS* 25 (1942):
 121–125; reprinted in *idem*, *Opera minora* (Groningen: Wolters, 1953), 423–429.

Bonnet, H.
 Reallexikon der ägyptischen Religionsgeschichte (Berlin,
 1952).

Borger, R.
 "Zu שוב שבו/ית," *ZAW* 66 (1954) [1955]): 315–
 316.

van den Born, A.
 Ezechiël—Pseudo-epigraaf? (1953).

Idem
 De historische situatie van Ezechiels prophetie, ALBO
 2 (Leuven: Bijbels Seminarie, 1947).

Idem
 *Profetie metterdaad. Een studie over de symbolische
 handelingen der profeten* (Roermond-Maaserk:
 Romen, 1947).

Idem
 *De symbolische handelingen der oud-testamentische
 profeten* (Nijmegen: Dekker & Van de Vegt, 1935).

Boström, G.
 Paronomasi i den äldre hebreiska Maschallitteraturen
 (Lund: Gleerups, 1928).

Bousset, Wilhelm and Gressman, Hugo
 *Die Religion des Judentums im späthellenistischen Zeit-
 alter*, HBNT 21 (Tübingen: Mohr [Siebeck],
 ³1926).

Brockelmann, C.
 Hebräische Syntax (Neukirchen-Vluyn: Neukirchener, 1956).

Brooks, Beatrice A.
"Fertility Cult Functionaries in the Old Testament," *JBL* 60 (1941): 227–253.

Broome, Edwin C., Jr.
"Ezekiel's Abnormal Personality," *JBL* 65 (1946): 277–292.

Browne, Laurence Edward
Ezekiel and Alexander (London: S.P.C.K., 1952).

Brownlee, William Hugh
"The Scroll of Ezekiel from the Eleventh Qumran Cave," *RQ* 4 (1963): 11–28.

Buber, Martin
Israel and Palestine: the History of an Idea (London: East and West Library, 1952).

Idem
"Zu Jecheskel 3:12," *MGWJ* 78 (1934): 471–473.

Idem
"Leitwortstil in der Erzählung des Pentateuchs" in Martin Buber and Franz Rosenzweig, *Die Schrift und ihre Verdeutschung* (Berlin: Schocken, 1936), 211–238.

Idem
The Prophetic Faith, tr. Carlyle Witton Davies (New York: Macmillan, 1949).

De Buck, A.
"La fleur au front du grand-prêtre," *OTS* 9 (1951): 18–29.

Budde, C.
"Das hebräische Klagelied," *ZAW* 2 (1882): 1–52.

Budde, Karl
"Zum Eingang des Buches Ezechiel," *JBL* 50 (1931): 20–41.

du Mesnil du Buisson, Le Comte
"Une Tablette magique de la région du moyen Euphrate" in *Mélanges syriens offerts à M. René Dussaud* 1 (Paris: Geuthner, 1939), 421–434.

Bultmann, Rudolf Karl
The History of the Synoptic Tradition, tr. John Marsh (Oxford: Basil Blackwell, [2]1968).

Burchard, Christoph
Bibliographie zu den Handschriften vom Toten Meer 2, BZAW 89 (Berlin: Töpelmann, 1965).

Burrows, Millar
"Daroma," *JPOS* 12 (1932): 142–148.

Idem
The Literary Relations of Ezekiel (Philadelphia: Jewish Publication Society, 1925).

Buttenwieser, Moses
"The Character and Date of Ezekiel's Prophecies," *HUCA* 7 (1930): 1–18.

Buzy, Denis
"Les symboles prophétiques d'Ezéchiel," *RB* 29 (1920): 203–228, 353–358; 30 (1921): 45–54, 161–194; reprinted in idem, *Les symboles de l'ancien testament* (Paris: LeCoffre, 1923), 157–264.

Cameron, G. G.
Persepolis Treasury Tablets, University of Chicago Oriental Institute Publications 65 (Chicago: University of Chicago Press, 1948).

Cardascia, G.
Les archives des Murašû, une famille d'hommes d'affaires babyloniens à l'époque perse (Paris: Imprimateur Nationale, 1951).

Cavaignac, E.
Les Hittites, L'orient ancien illustré 3 (Paris: Leroux, 1950).

Černý, Ladislav
The Day of Yahweh and Some Relevant Problems (Praze: Nákladem Filosofické Fakulty University, Karlovy, 1948).

Chantepie de la Saussaye, Pierre Daniel
Lehrbuch der Religionsgeschichte, 2 volumes (Tübingen: Mohr [Siebeck], [4]1925).

Cheyne, T. K.
"The Image of Jealousy in Ezekiel," *ZAW* 21 (1901): 201–202.

Cohen, A.
"Studies in Hebrew Lexicography," *AJSL* 40 (1924): 153–185.

Cowley, Arthur Ernest
Aramaic Papyri discovered at Assuan (London: A. Moring, Ltd., 1906).

Cross, Frank M., Jr.
"The Tabernacle: A Study from an Archaeological and Historical Approach," *BA* 10 (1947): 45–68.

Dalman, Gustaf
Arbeit und Sitte in Palästina, 7 volumes (Gütersloh: Bertelsmann, 1928–1942).

Idem
Jerusalem und seine Gelände (Gütersloh: Bertelsmann, 1930).

Danielsmeyer, Werner
Neue Untersuchungen zur Ezechiel-Septuaginta, Unpub. Diss. (Münster, 1936).

Daube, D.
"Über die Umbildung biblischen Rechtsgutes" in *Symbolae Friburgenses in honorem Ottonis Lenel* (Leipzig: Tauchnitz, 1935), 245–258.

Delitzsch, Friedrich
"Assyriologische Notizen zum Alten Testament. IV. Das Schwertlied Ezech. 21, 13–22," *ZK* 2 (1885): 385–398.

Idem
Die Lese- und Schreibfehler im Alten Testament (Berlin: Vereinigung Wiss. Verleger, 1920).

Dhorme, E.
Les Religions de Babylonie et d'Assyrie (Paris: Presses universitaires de France, [2]1949).

Dhorme, P. and Vincent, L. H.
"Les Chérubins," *RB* 35 (1926): 328–358; 481–495.

Diehl, W.
Das Pronomen personale suffixum 2. und 3. pers. plur. des Hebräischen in der alttestamentlichen Überlieferung, Unpub. Diss. (Giessen, 1895).

Dietrich, Erich Kurt

Die Umkehr im Alten Testament und im Judentum (Stuttgart: Kohlhammer, 1936).

Dietrich, Ernest Ludwig

שׁוב שׁבות. *Die endzeitliche Wiederherstellung bei den Propheten*, BZAW 40 (Giessen: Töpelmann, 1925).

Dold, Alban

Konstanzer altlateinische Propheten- und Evangelien-Bruchstücke mit Glossen, nebst zugehörigen Prophetentexten aus Zürich und St. Gallen, Texte und Arbeiten I. 7–9 (Leipzig: Harrassowitz, 1923).

Idem

Neue St. Galler vorheironymianische Propheten-Fragmente der St. Galler Sammelhandschrift 1398b zugehörig, Texte und Arbeiten I.31 (Hohenzollern: Beuroner Kunstverlag, 1940).

Driver, G. R.

Aramaic Documents of the Fifth Century B.C. (Oxford: Clarendon, 1954).

Idem

Canaanite Myths and Legends (Edinburgh: Clark, 1956).

Idem

"Difficult Words in the Hebrew Prophets" in *Studies in Old Testament Prophecy*, ed. H. H. Rowley (Edinburgh: Clark, 1950), 52–72.

Idem

"Ezekiel: Linguistic and Textual Problems," *Bibl* 35 (1954): 145–159; 299–312.

Idem

"Ezekiel's Inaugural Vision," *VT* 1 (1951): 60–62.

Idem

"Hebrew Notes," *JBL* 68 (1949): 57–59.

Idem

"L'interpretation du texte masorétique a la lumière de la lexicographie hébraique," *EThL* 26 (1950): 337–353.

Idem

"Linguistic and textual Problems: Ezekiel," *Bibl* 19 (1938): 60–69; 175–187.

Idem

"Linguistic and Textual Problems: Isaiah I–XXXIX," *JTS* 38 (1937): 36–50.

Idem

Semitic Writing from Pictograph to Alphabet (London: Oxford University Press, 1948).

Idem

"Some Hebrew Medical Expressions," *ZAW* 65 (1953): 255–262.

Idem

"Some Hebrew Words," *JTS* 29 (1928): 390–396.

Idem

"Studies in the Vocabulary of the Old Testament. 3," *JTS* 32 (1930/31): 361–366.

Idem

"Studies in the Vocabulary of the Old Testament. 8," *JTS* 36 (1935): 293–301.

Idem

"Three Notes," *VT* 2 (1952): 356–357.

Duhm, Bernhard

Die Theologie der Propheten als Grundlage für die innere Entwicklungsgeschichte der israelitischen Religion (Bonn, 1875).

Dupont-Sommer, A.

Les Araméens, L'Orient Ancien Illustré 2 (Paris: Maisonneuve, 1949).

Idem

The Essene Writings from Qumran, tr. G. Vermes (Cleveland: World, 1962).

Dürr, L.

Ezekiels Vision von der Erscheinung Gottes (Ez. c. 1 und 10) im Lichte der vorderasiatischen Altertumskunde (Würzburg: Richter, 1917).

Idem

"Hebr. נֶפֶשׁ = akk. napištu = Gurgel, Kehle," *ZAW* 43 (1925): 262–269.

Idem

Die Stellung des Propheten Ezechiel in der israelitisch-jüdischen Apokalyptik, AA IX 1 (Münster: Aschendorff, 1923).

Dussaud, R.

"L'idole de la jalousie," *Syria* 21 (1940): 359–360.

Ehrlich, Arnold B.

Randglossen zur hebräischen Bibel 5 (Leipzig: Hinrichs, 1912).

Eichrodt, Walther

Theology of the Old Testament 1, tr. J. A. Baker (Philadelphia: Westminster, 1961).

Eisler, Robert

"gśtj = Κάστυ τοῦ γραμματέως = קֶסֶת הַסֹּפֵר im Danielkommentar des Hippolytos von Rom," *OLZ* 33 (1930): 585–587.

Eissfeldt, Otto

"Das Alte Testament im Lichte der safatenischen Inschriften," *ZDMG* NF 29/104 (1954): 88–118.

Idem

Baal Zaphon, Zeus Kasios und der Durchzug der Israeliten durchs Meer, BRA 1 (Halle: Niemeyer, 1932).

Idem

"El and Yahweh," *JSS* 1 (1956): 25–37.

Idem

"Ezechiel als Zeuge für Sanheribs Eingriff in Palästina," *PJ* 27 (1931): 58–66.

Idem

"Hesekiel Kap. 16 als Geschichtsquelle," *JPOS* 16 (1936): 286–292.

Idem

Der Maschal im Alten Testament, BZAW 24 (Giessen: Töpelmann, 1913).

Idem

Molk als Opferbegriff im Punischen und Hebräischen und das Ende des Gottes Moloch, BRA 3 (Halle: Niemeyer, 1935).

Idem

The Old Testament; An Introduction, tr. Peter R. Ackroyd (New York: Harper and Row, 1965).

Idem

"Schwerterschlagene bei Hesekiel" in Studies in Old Testament Prophecy presented to T. H. Robinson, ed. H. H. Rowley (Edinburgh: Clark, 1950), 73–81.

Idem

"Zeilenfüllung," VT 2 (1952): 87–92.

Eitan, Israel

"The Bearing of Ethiopic on Biblical Exegesis and Lexicography," JPOS 3 (1923): 136–143.

Elhorst, H. J.

"Das Ephod," ZAW 30 (1910): 259–276.

Elliger, K.

"Chammanim = Maṣṣeben?" ZAW 57 (1939): 256–265.

Idem

"Das Gesetz Leviticus 18," ZAW 67 (1955 [1956]): 1–25.

Idem

"Ich bin der Herr-euer Gott" in Theologie als Glaubenswagnis, Festschrift für K. Heim (Hamburg: Furche, 1954), 9–34; reprinted in idem, Kleine Schriften zum A.T., ThB 32 (1966), 211–231.

Idem

Leviticus, HAT 4 (Tübingen: Mohr [Siebeck], 1966).

Idem

"Der Sinn des Wortes chammān," ZDPV 66 (1943): 129–139.

Elliott-Binns, L. E.

"Some Problems of the Holiness Code," ZAW 67 (1955): 26–40.

Erbt, Wilhelm

"Die Fürstensprüche im Hesekielbuche," OLZ 20 (1917): 270–274; 289–296.

Erman, Adolf

Die Religion der Ägypter (Berlin: de Gruyter, 1934).

Erman, Adolf and Ranke, Hermann

Ägypten und aegyptisches Leben im Altertun (Tübingen: Mohr [Siebeck], 1922–23).

Fahlgren, Karl Hjalmar

Ṣᵉdāḳā, nahestehende und entgegengesetzte Begriffe im Alten Testament (Uppsala: Almquist & Wiksell, 1932).

Falkenstein, A. and von Soden, W.

Sumerische und akkadische Hymnen und Gebete (Zürich: Artemis, 1953).

Fichtner, Johannes

"Jesaja unter den Weisen," ThLZ 74 (1949): 75–80.

Filson, Floyd V.

"The Omission of Ezek. 12:26–28 and 36:23b–38 in Codex 967," JBL 62 (1943): 27–32.

Finegan, Jack

Light from the Ancient Past (Princeton: Princeton University Press, ²1959).

Fink, E.

"Gedanken über die כרת-Strafe," Jeschurun 4 (1917): 383–393.

Finkelstein, Louis

The Pharisees; the Sociological Background of their Faith (Philadelphia: Jewish Publication Society, ³1962).

Fischer, A.

"Zur Siloahinschrift," ZDMG 56 (1902): 800–809.

Fischer, O. R.

The Unity of the Book of Ezekiel, Unpub. Diss. (Boston, 1939).

Flügge, T.

Die Vorstellung über den Himmel im AT, Unpub. Diss. (Königsberg, 1937).

Fohrer, Georg

Die Hauptprobleme des Buches Ezechiel, BZAW 72 (Berlin: Töpelmann, 1952).

Idem

"Das Symptomatische der Ezechielforschung," ThLZ 83 (1958): 241–250.

Idem

Die symbolischen Handlungen der Propheten, ATANT 54 (Zürich: Zwingli, ²1968).

Frankena, R.

Kanttekeningen van een Assyrioloog bij Ezechiël (Leiden: Brill, 1965).

Frankfort, H.

More Sculpture from the Diyala Region, OIP 40 (Chicago: University of Chicago Press, 1943).

Frazer, James George

Folk-lore in the Old Testament, 3 volumes (London: Macmillan, Ltd., 1918).

Idem

"Hunting for Souls," ARW 11 (1908): 197–199.

Fredriksson, Henning

Jahwe als Krieger (Lund: Gleerups, 1945).

Friedmann, M.

הציון הוא ביאור לנבואת יחזקאל (Vienna, 1888).

Galling, Kurt

Der Altar in den Kulturen des alten Orients (Berlin: Curtius, 1925).

Idem

"Archäologischer Jahresbericht," ZDPV 54 (1931): 80–100.

Idem

"Der Beichtspiegel. Eine gattungsgeschichtliche Studie," ZAW 47 (1929): 125–130.

Idem

"Der Ehrenname Elisas und die Entrückung Elias," ZThK 53 (1956): 129–148.

Idem

"Erwägungen zum Stelenheiligtum von Hazor," ZDPV 75 (1959): 1–13.

Idem

Die Erwählungstraditionen Israels, BZAW 48 (Giessen: Töpelmann, 1928).

Idem

"Die Halle des Schreibers," *PJ* 27 (1931): 51–57.

Idem

Textbuch zur Geschichte Israels (Tuebingen: Mohr [Siebeck], ²1968).

Gaster, Theodore

"Ezekiel and the Mysteries," *JBL* 60 (1941): 289–310.

Gehman, Henry Snyder

"The Relations between the Hebrew Text of Ezekiel and that of the John H. Scheide Papyri," *JAOS* 58 (1938): 92–102.

Geiger, Abraham

Urschrift und Uebersetzungen der Bibel in ihrer Abhändigkeit von der innern Entwicklung des Judenthums (Breslau: Hainauer, 1857).

Gemser, B.

"The Importance of the Motive Clause in Old Testament Law," *VTSuppl* 1 (1953): 50–66.

Idem

"The *rib*—or Controversy—Pattern in Hebrew Mentality" in *Wisdom in Israel and in the Ancient Near East*, ed. Martin Noth, VTSuppl 3 (Leiden: Brill, 1955), 120–137.

Gesenius, W.

Hebrew Grammar, E. Kautzsch (ed.) and A. E. Cowley (tr. and reviser) (Oxford, Clarendon, ²1910).

Gesenius, Walter and Buhl, F.

Hebräisches und aramäisches Handwörterbuch zum AT (Leipzig, ¹⁶1915).

Giesebrecht, Friedrich

Die Berufsbegabung der alttestamentlichen Propheten (Göttingen, 1897).

Idem

"Review of C. H. Toy, *The Book of the Prophet Ezekiel*, and Richard Krätzschmar, *Das Buch Ezechiel*," *OLZ* 3 (1900): 457–458.

Glasenapp, Helmuth von

Der Hinduismus (Muenchen: Kurt Wolff, 1922).

Goettsberger, J.

"Ez 7:1–16 textkritisch und exegetisch untersucht," *BZ* 22 (1934): 195–223.

Idem

"Zu Ez 9:8 und 11:13," *BZ* 19 (1931): 6–19.

Goetze, Albrecht

Kleinasien, Kulturgeschichte des Alten Orients 3 (München: Beck, ²1957).

Idem

"Short or Long *a*?" *Or* 16 (1947): 239–250.

Goldschmidt, Lazarus

Der babylonische Talmud neu übertragen durch L. Goldschmidt (Berlin: Biblion, 1929–1936).

Gordon, Cyrus H.

"Hos 2:4–5 in the Light of New Semitic Inscriptions," *ZAW* 54 (1936): 277–280.

Idem

Ugaritic Literature (Rome: Pontifical Biblical Institute, 1949).

Idem

Ugaritic Textbook, Analecta Orientalia 38 (Rome: Pontifical Biblical Institute, 1965).

Gordon, E. I.

"Of Princes and Foxes: The Neck-stock in the newly-discovered Agade Period Stele," *Sumer* 12 (1956): 80–84.

Graetz, H.

"Die Echtheit des Buches des Propheten Ezechiel," *MGWJ* 23 (1874): 433–446; 515–525.

Graf, Karl Heinrich

Die geschichtlichen Bücher des Alten Testaments (Leipzig, 1866).

Greenberg, Moshe

"Ezekiel 17 and the Policy of Psammetichus II," *JBL* 76 (1957): 304–309.

Gressmann, Hugo

"Der Festbecher" in *Sellin-Festschrift* (1927), 55–62.

Idem

"Josia und das Deuteronomium," *ZAW* 42 (1924): 313–337.

Idem

Die Lade Jahwes und das Allerheiligste des salomonischen Tempels (Berlin, 1920).

Idem

Der Messias, FRLANT 26 (Göttingen, 1929).

Idem

Der Ursprung der israelitisch-jüdischen Eschatologie, FRLANT 6 (Göttingen, 1905).

Grether, Oskar

Name und Wort Gottes im Alten Testament, BZAW 64 (Giessen: Töpelmann, 1934).

Grill, Severin

"Die Alten Versionen und die Partikeln lo', lô, lû, lî," *BZ* NF 1 (1957): 277–281.

Gronkowski, Walter

"De natura Ezechielis 'vinculorum'," *CT* 18 (1937): 374–412.

de Groot, J.

Die Altäre des Salomonischen Tempelhofes, BWAT NF 6 (Stuttgart: Kohlhammer, 1924).

Gunkel, Hermann

Schöpfung und Chaos in Urzeit und Endzeit (Göttingen, ²1921).

Idem

"Der Schreiberengel Nabû im A.T. und im Judentum," *ARW* 1 (1898): 294–300.

Gunkel, Hermann and Begrich, Joachim

Einleitung in die Psalmen (Göttingen: Vandenhoeck & Ruprecht, ²1966).

Gurney, O. R.

The Hittites (Harmondsworth: Penguin, 1952).

Haag, Herbert

Was lehrt die literarische Untersuchung des Ezechiel-Textes? (Freiburg in der Schweiz: Paulusdruckerei, 1943).

Haefeli, L.
Syrien und sein Libanon (Luzern: Raber & Cie,
1926).
Harford, John Battersby
Studies in the Book of Ezekiel (Cambridge: Cam-
bridge University Press, 1935).
Hejcl, Johann
*Das alttestamentliche Zinsverbot im Licht der ethnolo-
gischen Jurisprudenz sowie des altorientalischen Zins-
wesens*, BSF 12, 4 (Freiburg, 1907).
Heinisch, Paul
Die Trauergebräuche bei den Israeliten (Münster:
Aschendorff, 1931).
Hempel, Johannes
*Die althebräische Literatur und ihr hellenistisch-jued-
isches Nachleben* (Wildpark-Potsdam: Akademische
Verlagsgesellschaft Athenaion, 1930).
Idem
*Heilung als Symbol und Wirklichkeit im biblischen
Schrifttum* (Göttingen: Vandenhoeck & Ruprecht,
²1965).
Herntrich, Volkmar
Ezekielprobleme, BZAW 61 (Giessen: Töpelmann,
1933).
Herrmann, Johannes
Ezechielstudien, BWAT 2 (Leipzig, 1908).
Idem
"Zu Jer 22:29; 7:4," *ZAW* 62 (1949/50): 321–
322.
Herrmann, Siegfried
"Die Königsnovelle in Ägypten und in Israel,"
WZ 3 (1953/54): 51–83.
Idem
Die prophetischen Heilserwartungen im Alten Testament,
BWANT 85 (Stuttgart: Kohlhammer, 1965).
Hesse, Franz
Die Fürbitte im Alten Testament, Unpub. Diss. (Er-
langen, 1949).
Idem
Das Verstockungsproblem im Alten Testament, BZAW
74 (Berlin: Töpelmann, 1955).
Hilprecht, H. V. and Clay, A. T.
*The Babylonian Expedition of the University of Penn-
sylvania* 9 and 10 (Philadelphia, 1898–1904).
Hines, Herbert W.
"The Prophet as Mystic," *AJSL* 40 (1923): 37–
71.
Hoffman, Georg and Gressmann, Hugo
"Teraphim, Masken und Winkorakel in Ägypten
und Vorderasien," *ZAW* 40 (1922): 75–137.
Höhne, Ernst
*Die Thronwagenvision Hesekiels. Echtheit und Herkunft
des Vision Hes. 1: 4–28 und ihrer einzelnen Züge*, Un-
pub. Diss. (Erlangen, 1953/54).
Hölscher, Gustav
Das Buch Hiob, HAT 17 (Tübingen: Mohr [Sie-
beck], ²1952).
Idem
Geschichte der israelitischen und jüdischen Religion

(Giessen: Töpelmann, 1922).
Idem
Hesekiel, der Dichter und das Buch, BZAW 39
(Giessen: Töpelmann, 1924).
Idem
Die Profeten (Leipzig: J. C. Hinrichs, 1914).
Idem
Die Ursprünge der jüdischen Eschatologie (Giessen:
Töpelmann, 1925).
Honeyman, A. M.
"*Merismus* in Biblical Hebrew," *JBL* 71 (1952):
11–18.
Idem
"An unnoticed Euphemism in Isaiah ix 19–20,"
VT 1 (1951): 221–223.
Horst, F.
"Die Doxologien im Amosbuch," *ZAW* 47
(1929): 45–54.
Idem
"Der Eid im Alten Testament," *EvTh* 17 (1957):
366–384; reprinted in *idem, Gottes Recht*, ThB 12
(München: Kaiser, 1961), 292–314.
Idem
"Exilsgemeinde und Jerusalem in Ez viii–xi.
Eine literarische Untersuchung," *VT* 3 (1953):
337–360.
Idem
"Die Kennzeichen der hebräischen Poesie," *ThR*
NF 21 (1953): 97–121.
Horst, Friedrich and Robinson, Theodore H.
Die zwolf kleinen Propheten, HAT 14 (Tübingen:
Mohr [Siebeck], ³1964).
Horst, L.
*Leviticus xvii–xxvi und Hezekiel. Ein Beitrag zur Pen-
tateuchkritik* (Colmar, 1881).
Howie, Carl Gordon
The Date and Composition of Ezekiel, Journal of Bib-
lical Literature Monograph Series 4 (Philadel-
phia: Society of Biblical Literature, 1950).
Hulst, A. R.
"*Kol baśar* in der priesterlichen Fluterzählung"
in *Studies on the Book of Genesis*, OTS 12 (Leiden:
Brill, 1958), 28–68.
Humbert, Paul
"Emploi et portée du verbe bârâ (créer) dans
l'Ancien Testament," *ThZ* 3 (1947): 401–422.
Idem
"Die Herausforderungsformel 'hinnenî êlékâ',"
ZAW 51 (1933): 101–108.
Idem
La 'terou'a'; analyse d'un rite biblique, Université
de Neuchâtel: recueil de travaux publié par la
Faculté des lettres 23 (Neuchâtel: Secrétariat de
l'Université, 1946).
Ingholt, H.
"Le sens du mot ḥammān" in *Mélanges syriens
offerts à M. René Dussaud* 2 (Paris: Geuthner,
1939), 795–802.

Irwin, William A.

The Problem of Ezekiel (Chicago: The University of Chicago Press, 1943).

Idem

"*Hashmal*," *VT* 2 (1952): 169–170.

Jahn, Gustav

Das Buch Ezechiel auf Grund der Septuaginta hergestellt, übersetzt und kritisch erklärt (Leipzig: Pfeiffer, 1905).

Jahnow, Hedwig

Das hebräische Leichenlied im Rahmen der Völkerdichtung, BZAW 36 (Giessen: Töpelmann, 1923).

Janssen, Enno

Juda in der Exilszeit, FRLANT NF 51 (Goettingen: Vandenhoeck & Ruprecht, 1956).

Jenni, Ernst

Die theologische Begruendung des Sabbatgebotes im Alten Testament, ThSt 46 (Zollikon-Zuerich: Evangelischer Verlag, 1956).

Idem

"Das Wort ʿōlām im Alten Testament. III. Hauptteil," *ZAW* 65 (1953 [1954]): 1–35.

Jepsen, Alfred

Nabi: soziologische Studien zur alttestamentlichen Literatur und Religionsgeschichte (München: Beck, 1934).

Jeremias, Alfred

Handbuch der altorientalischen Geisteskultur (Leipzig: Hinrichs, 1913).

Jeremias, Joachim

Heiligengraeber in Jesu Umwelt (*Mt. 23, 29; Lk. 11, 47*) (Göttingen: Vandenhoeck & Ruprecht, 1958).

Jirku, Anton

"Eine hethitische Ansiedlung in Jerusalem zur Zeit von El-Amarna," *ZDPV* 43 (1920): 58–61.

Idem

Die magische Bedeutung der Kleidung in Israel (Rostock: Adler, 1914).

Idem

Materialien zur Volksreligion Israels (Leipzig: Deichert, 1914).

Johnson, Allan Chester; Gehman, Henry Snyder; and Kase, Edmund Harris

The John H. Scheide Biblical Papyri, Ezekiel (Princeton: Princeton University Press, 1938).

Johnson, Aubrey R.

The Cultic Prophet in Ancient Israel (Cardiff: University of Wales Press, ²1962).

Idem

"מָשָׁל," in *Wisdom in Israel and in the Ancient Near East*, ed. Martin Noth, VTSuppl 3 (Leiden: Brill, 1955), 162–169.

Idem

The Vitality of the Individual in the Thought of Ancient Israel (Cardiff: University of Wales Press, 1949).

Joüon, Paul

Grammaire de l'hébreu biblique (Rome: Pontifical Biblical Institute, ²1947).

Katz, Peter

"Septuaginta id est V.T. graece iuxta LXX," *ThLZ* 61 (1936): 265–87.

Idem

"Zur Textgestaltung der Ezechiel-Septuaginta," *Bibl* 35 (1954): 29–39.

Kautzsch, Emil

Die Aramaismen im Alten Testament untersucht. I. Lexikalischer Teil (Halle: Niemeyer, 1902).

Keil, Karl Friedrich

Biblical Commentary on the Prophecies of Ezekiel, 2 volumes, tr. James Martin. Biblical Commentary on the Old Testament (Grand Rapids, Michigan: Eerdmans Publishing Company, 1950).

Keller, Carl A.

Das Wort OTH als "Offenbarungszeichen Gottes" (Basel: Hoenen, 1946).

Kelso, J. L.

"Ezekiel's Parable of the Corroded Copper Cauldron," *JBL* 64 (1945): 391–393.

Kenyon, Frederic George

The Chester Beatty Biblical Papyri. Fasciculus VII: *Ezekiel, Daniel, Esther* (London: Walker, 1938).

Kessler, Werner

Die innere Einheitlichkeit des Buches Ezechiel (Herrnhut: Missionbuchhandlung, 1926).

Idem

"Aus welchen Gründen wird die Bezeichnung 'Jahwe Zebaoth' in der späteren Zeit gemieden?" *Wiss Z. Halle* GR 7 (1958): 767–771.

Kilian, Rudolf

Literarkritische und formgeschichtliche Untersuchung des Heiligkeitsgesetzes, BBB 19 (Bonn: Hanstein, 1963).

Kittel, Rudolf

Geschichte des Volkes Israel 3 (Stuttgart: Kohlhammer, 1927–29).

Klamroth, Erich

Die jüdischen Exulanten in Babylonien, BWAT 10 (Leipzig: Hinrichs, 1912).

Klein, F. A.

"Mittheilungen über Leben, Sitten und Gebräuche der Fellachen in Palästina (II)," *ZDPV* 4 (1881): 57–84.

Klein, Hugo

"Das Klima Palästinas auf Grund der alten hebräischen Quellen (Schluss)," *ZDPV* 37 (1914): 297–327.

Klinke-Rosenberger, R.

Das Götzenbuch Kitāb al-ʾaṣnām ibn al-kalbi, Sammlung orientalistischer Arbeiten 8 (Winterthur: Buchdruckerei Winterthur, 1941).

Klostermann, A.

"Beiträge zur Entstehungsgeschichte des Pentateuchs," *ZLThK* 38 (1877): 401–455; reprinted as "Ezechiel und das Heiligkeitsgesetz," in *idem*, *Der Pentateuch* (Leipzig: Deichert, 1893), 368–418.

Idem

"Ezechiel. Ein Beitrag zu besserer Würdigung

seiner Person und seiner Schrift," *ThStKr* 50 (1877): 391–439.

Knudtzon, Jørgen Alexander
Die El-Amarna-Tafeln, 2 volumes (1915 = Aalen: Zeller, 1964).

Koch, Klaus
"Zur Geschichte der Erwählungsvorstellung in Israel," *ZAW* 67 (1955 [1956]): 205–226.

Idem
"Gibt es ein Vergeltungsdogma im Alten Testament?" *ZThK* 52 (1955): 1–42.

Idem
SDQ im Alten Testament, Unpub. Diss. (Heidelberg, 1953).

Koehler, Ludwig
"Alttestamentliche Wortforschung. Beⁱdîl und *beⁱdîlîm," *ThZ* 3 (1947): 155–156.

Idem
"Archäologisches. Nr. 22. 23," *ZAW* 46 (1928): 213–220.

Idem
"Aussatz," *ZAW* 67 (1955): 290–291.

Idem
"Der Dekalog," *ThR* NF 1 (1929): 161–184.

Idem
Deuterojesaja (Jesaja 40–55) stilkritisch untersucht, BZAW 37 (Giessen: Töpelmann, 1923).

Idem
Hebrew Man, tr. Peter R. Ackroyd (Nashville: Abingdon, 1956/1957).

Idem
"Hebräische Vokabeln II," *ZAW* 55 (1937): 161–174.

Idem
"Hebräische Vokabeln III," *ZAW* 58 (1940/41): 228–234.

Idem
Kleine Lichter: fünfzig Bibelstellen erklärt, Zwingli-Bücherei 47 (Zürich: Livingli, 1945).

Idem
"Lexikologisch-Geographisches," *ZDPV* 62 (1939): 115–125.

Idem
Old Testament Theology, tr. A. S. Todd. Lutterworth Library 49 (London: Lutterworth, 1957).

Idem
"Syntatica IV," *VT* 3 (1953): 299–305.

Koehler, Ludwig and Baumgartner, Walter
Lexicon in Veteris Testamenti libros (Leiden: Brill, 1953).

Kopf, L.
"Arabische Etymologien und Parallelen zum Bibelwörterbuch," *VT* 8 (1958): 161–215.

Korošec, V.
Hethitische Staatsverträge. Ein Beitrag zu ihrer iuristischen Wertung, LRSt 60 (Leipzig: Weicher, 1931).

Kraeling, Emil G.
The Brooklyn Museum Aramaic Papyri (New Haven: Yale University Press, 1953).

Kraus, Hans-Joachim
Klagelieder (Threni), BK 20 (Neukirchen-Vluyn: Neukirchener, 1956).

Idem
Die Königsherrschaft Gottes im Alten Testament, BHTh 13 (Tübingen: Mohr [Siebeck], 1951).

Idem
Psalmen, 2 volumes, BK 15 (Neukirchen-Vluyn: Neukirchener, 1960).

Idem
Worship in Israel; a Cultic History of the Old Testament, tr. Geoffrey Buswell (Richmond, Va.: John Knox, 1966).

Kreipe, E.
Das literarische Problem des Buches Ezechiel. Programm des Wilhelmgymnasiums zu Hamburg (1913).

Kuhl, Curt
"Neue Dokumente zum Verständnis von Hosea 2:4–15," *ZAW* 52 (1934): 102–109.

Idem
The Prophets of Israel, tr. Rudolf J. Ehrlich and J. P. Smith (Richmond, Va.: John Knox, 1960).

Idem
"Der Schauplatz der Wirksamkeit Hesekiels. Ein Lösungsversuch," *ThZ* 8 (1952): 401–418.

Idem
"Die 'Wiederaufnahme'—ein literarkritisches Prinzip?" *ZAW* 64 (1952): 1–11.

Kuschke, Arnulf
"Die Lagervorstellung der priesterschriftlichen Erzählung. Eine überlieferungsgeschichtliche Studie," *ZAW* 63 (1951): 74–105.

Idem
"Die Menschenwege und der Weg Gottes im Alten Testament," *StTh* 5 (1951): 106–118.

Lagarde, Paul de
Prophetae chaldaice (Lipsiae: Teubner, 1872).

Landsberger, Benno
Materialien zum sumerischen Lexikon. Vokabulare und Formularbuecher (Rome: Pontifical Biblical Institute, 1937).

Landersdorfer, Simon
Der ΒΑΑΛ ΤΕΤΡΑΜΟΡΦΟΣ und die Kerube des Ezechiel, Studien zur Geschichte und Kultur des Altertums 9, 3 (Paderborn: Schöningh, 1918).

Latte, Kurt
Heiliges Recht; Untersuchungen zur Geschichte der sakralen Rechtsformen in Griechenland (Tübingen: Mohr [Siebeck], 1920).

Lauha, Aarre
ZAPHON, Der Norden und die Nordvölker im Alten Testament (Helsinki: Der Finnischen Literaturgesellschaft, 1943).

van der Leeuw, Gerardus
Religion in Essence and Manifestation, tr. J. E. Turner (New York: Harper and Row, ²1963).

Lehmann, Eduard
"Die Perser" in *Lehrbuch der Religionsgeschichte* 2, ed. Alfred Bertholet, Pierre Daniel Chantepie de

la Saussaye, Eduard Lehmann (Tübingen: Mohr [Siebeck], [4]1925), 199–279.

Levy, Jacob
Wörterbuch über die Talmudim und Midraschim, 5 volumes (Berlin: Harz, 1924).

Lewy, J.
"Nāḫ et Rušpān" in *Mélanges syriens offerts à M. René Dussaud 1* (Paris: Geuthner, 1939), 273–275.

Lindblom, Johannes
"Wisdom in the Old Testament Prophets" in *Wisdom in Israel and in the Ancient Near East*, ed. Martin Noth, VTSuppl 3 (Leiden: Brill, 1955), 192–204.

Loew, Immanuel
Die Flora der Juden, 1 and 2, Publications of the Alexander Kohut Memorial Foundation 4 (Wien: Löwit, 1928).

Loewe, Raphael
"Jerome's Treatment of an Anthropopathism," *VT* 2 (1952): 261–272.

Lotz, W.
"Das Sinnbild des Bechers," *NKZ* 28 (1917): 396–407.

Löwinger, S.
"Tel Abib—til Abūbi (Ezek. 3:15)" in *Études orientales à la mémoire de Paul Hirschler* (Budapest, 1950), 62–72.

Lucas, Alfred
Ancient Egyptian Materials (New York: Longmans, Green, 1926).

Maag, Victor
Text, Wortschatz und Begriffswelt des Buches Amos (Leiden: Brill, 1951).

Maisler, B.
"Canaan and the Canaanites," *BASOR* 102 (1940): 7–12.

Malamat, A.
"Jeremiah and the Last Two Kings of Judah," *PEQ* 83 (1951): 81–87.

Marmorstein, A.
"1 Sam 25:29," *ZAW* 43 (1925): 119–124.

Masterman, E. W. G.
"Hygiene and Disease in Palestine in Modern and in Biblical Times," *PEQ* (1918): 13–20; 56–71; 112–119; 156–171 [(1919): 27–36].

May, Herbert Gordon
"The Departure of the Glory of Yahweh," *JBL* 56 (1937): 309–321.

Meissner, Bruno
Babylonien und Assyrien, 2 volumes (Heidelberg: Winter, 1920).

Idem
Könige Babyloniens und Assyriens (Leipzig: Quelle Meyer, 1926).

Idem
Das Märchen vom weisen Achikar, AO 16, 2 (Leipzig: Hinrichs, 1917).

Mendenhall, George E.
"Covenant Forms in Israelite Tradition," *BA* 17

(1954): 50–76.

Idem
"Puppy and Lettuce in Northwest-Semitic Covenant Making," *BASOR* 133 (1954): 26–30.

Menes, A.
"Tempel und Synagogue," *ZAW* 50 (1932): 268–276.

Merx, A.
"Der Wert der Septuaginta für die Textkritik des Alten Testamentes, am Ezechiel aufgezeigt," *JPTh* 9 (1883): 65–77.

Messel, Nils
Ezéchielfragen (Oslo: Dybwad, 1945).

Michaelis, Wilhelm
"Zeichen, Siegel, Kreuz. Ein Ausschnitt aus der Bedeutungsgeschichte biblischen Begriffe," *ThZ* 12 (1956): 505–525.

Michel, Diethelm
"Studien zu den sogenannten Thronbesteigungspsalmen," *VT* 6 (1956): 40–68.

Miller, John Wolf
Das Verhaeltnis Jeremias und Hesekiels; sprachlich und theologisch untersucht (Assen: Van Gorcum, 1955).

Molin, Georg
"Die Stellung der Gᵉbira im Staate Juda," *ThZ* 10 (1954): 161–175.

Montgomery, James A.
"Hebraica," *JAOS* 58 (1938): 130–139.

Moore, George Foot
Judaism in the first centuries of the Christain era, the age of the Tannaim, 2 volumes (New York: Schocken, 1971).

Moortgat, Anton
Tammuz (Berlin: de Gruyter, 1949).

Moran, William L.
"Gen. 49:10 and Its Use in Ez 21:32," *Bibl* 39 (1958): 405–425.

Morgenstern, Julian
"Additional Notes on 'Beena Marriage (Matriarchat) in Ancient Israel'," *ZAW* 49 (1931): 46–58.

Idem
"The Gates of Righteousness," *HUCA* 6 (1929): 1–37.

Idem
"Jerusalem—485 B.C.," *HUCA* 27 (1956): 101–179.

Moritz, Bernhard
"Edomitische Genealogien. I," *ZAW* 44 (1926): 81–93.

Mowinckel, Sigmund
Le Décalogue (Paris: Alcan, 1927).

Idem
He That Cometh, tr. G. W. Anderson (Nashville: Abingdon, 1956).

Idem
"Der metrische Aufbau von Jes 62:1–12 und die

neuen sog. 'kurzverse'," *ZAW* 65 (1953): 167–187.

Idem

"Zum Problem der hebräischen Metrik" in *Festschrift Alfred Bertholet* (Tübingen: Mohr [Siebeck], 1950), 379–394.

Idem

Prophecy and Tradition (Oslo: Dybwad, 1946).

Idem

Psalmenstudien. II. Das Thronbesteigungsfest Jahwäs und der Ursprung der Eschatologie (Kristiania: Dybwad, 1922).

Mülinen, Eberhard v.

"Galgal. Hesekiel kapitel 10:13," *ZDPV* 46 (1923): 79–107.

Müller, David Heinrich

Biblische Studien 4: Strophenbau und Responsion in Ezechiel und den Psalmen (Wien: Hölder, 1908).

Idem

Ezechiel-studien (Berlin: Reuther & Reichard, 1895); reprinted as *idem, Biblische Studien 1* (Wien: Hölder, 1904).

Idem

"Der Prophet Ezechiel entlehnt eine Stelle des Propheten Zephanja und glossiert sie," *WZKM* 19 (1905): 263–270; reprinted in *idem, Biblische Studien 3* (Wien: Hölder, 1907), 30–36.

Müller, Werner Ernst

Die Vorstellung vom Rest im Alten Testament (Neukirchen-Vluyn: Neukirchener, ²1973).

Néher, A.

"Le symbolisme conjugal: expression de l'histoire dans l'Ancien Testament," *RHPhR* 34 (1954): 30–49.

Neufeld, E.

Ancient Hebrew Marriage Laws (London: Longmans, Green, 1944).

Neuss, Wilhelm

Das Buch Ezechiel in Theologie und Kunst bis zum Ende des XII. Jahrhunderts, Beiträge zur Geschichte des Alten Mönchtums und des Benediktinerordens 1–2 (Münster: Aschendorff, 1912).

Nöldeke, Theodor

Beiträge zur semitischen Sprachwissenschaft (Strassburg: Trübner, 1904).

Nöldeke, Theodor and Schwally, Friedrich

Geschichte des Qorāns 1 (Leipzig: Weicher, ²1909).

Noth, Martin

"Die Einnahme von Jerusalem im Jahre 597 v. Chr.," *ZDPV* 74 (1958): 133–157.

Idem

The History of Israel, tr. Stanley Godman (New York: Harper & Row, ²1960).

Idem

A History of Pentateuchal Traditions, tr. Bernhard W. Anderson (Englewood Cliffs, N.J.: Prentice-Hall, 1972).

Idem

"The Jerusalem Catastrophe of 587 B.C., and its significance for Israel" in *The Laws in the Pentateuch and Other Studies*, tr. D. R. Ap-Thomas (Philadelphia: Fortress, 1967), 260–280.

Idem

"The Laws in the Pentateuch: Their Assumptions and Meanings" in *The Laws in the Pentateuch and Other Studies*, tr. D. R. Ap-Thomas (Philadelphia: Fortress, 1967), 1–107.

Idem

"Noah, Daniel and Hiob in Ezechiel xiv," *VT* 1 (1951): 251–260.

Idem

"Num. 21 als Glied der 'Hexateuch'-Erzählung," *ZAW* 58 (1940/41): 161–189.

Idem

"Office and Vocation in the Old Testament" in *The Laws in the Pentateuch and Other Studies*, tr. D. R. Ap-Thomas (Philadelphia: Fortress, 1967), 229–249.

Idem

The Old Testament World, tr. Victor I. Gruhn (Philadelphia: Fortress, 1966).

Idem

Die israelitischen Personennamen im Rahmen der gemeinsemitischen Namengebung, BWANT 3, 10 (Stuttgart: Kohlhammer, 1928).

Idem

"The 'Re-presentation' of the Old Testament in Proclamation" in *Essays on Old Testament Interpretation*, ed. Claus Westermann. Tr. James Luther Mays (Richmond, Va.: John Knox, 1963), 76–88.

Idem

Das System der zwölf Stämme Israels, BWANT 4, 1 (Stuttgart: Kohlhammer, 1930).

Nyberg, H. S.

Die Religionen des alten Iran, tr. (into German) H. H. Schaeder. MVÄG 43 (Osnabrück: Zeller, ²1966).

van Nuys, Kelvin

"Evaluating the Pathological in Prophetic Experience (particularly in Ezekiel)," *JBR* 21 (1953): 244–251.

Oesterley, W. O. E. and Robinson, Theodore H.

An Introduction to the Books of the Old Testament (New York: Meridian, ²1958).

Oort, H.

"Ezechiël 19; 21:18, 19v., 24v.," *ThT* 23 (1889): 504–514.

Oppenheim, Max Freiherr von

Der Tell Halaf; eine neue Kultur im aeltesten Mesopotamien (Leipzig: Brockhaus, 1931).

Orelli, Conrad von

Das Buch Ezechiel und die zwölf kleinen Propheten, Kurzgefasster Kommentar zu den Schriften des Alten und Neuen Testaments (Nördlingen, ²1896).

Östborn, Gunnar

Tora in the Old Testament: a Semantic Study (Lund: Ohlsson, 1945).

Parker, Richard Anthony and Dubberstein, Waldo H.

Babylonian Chronology 626 B.C.–A.D. 75, Brown University Studies 19 (Providence: Brown University Press, 1956).

Parrot, André

Babylon and the Old Testament, tr. B. E. Hooke. Studies in Biblical Archaeology 8 (London: SCM, 1958).

Idem

Nineveh and the Old Testament, tr. B. E. Hooke. Studies in Biblical Archaeology 3 (London: SCM, 1955).

Idem

Samaria, the Capital of the Kingdom of Israel, tr. S. R. Hooke. Studies in Biblical Archaeology 7 (London: SCM, 1958).

Payne, J. B.

"The Relationship of the Chester Beatty Papyri of Ezekiel to Codex Vaticanus," *JBL* 68 (1949): 251–265.

Perles, F.

"Babylonisch-biblische Glossen," *OLZ* 8 (1905): 125–130; 179–183.

Pfeiffer, Robert H.

Introduction to the Old Testament (New York: Harper and Brothers, ²1948).

Pidoux, Georges

"Encore les deux arbres de Genèse 3!" *ZAW* 66 (1954): 37–43.

Planas, F.

"El pan del profeta," *CultBibl* 12 (1955): 153–157.

Ploeg, J. van der

"La Règle de la Guerre, traduction et notes," *VT* 5 (1955): 373–420.

Press, Richard

"Die eschatologische Ausrichtung des 51. Psalms," *ThZ* 11 (1955): 241–249.

Procksch, O.

"Die Berufungsvision Hesekiels" in *Beiträge zur alttestamentlichen Wissenschaft, K. Budde zum 70. Geburtstag überreicht*, BZAW 34 (Giessen: Töpelmann, 1920), 141–149.

Quell, Gottfried

Wahre und falsche Propheten, BFChrTh 46, 1 (Gütersloh: Bertelsmann, 1952).

Rabast, K.

Das apodiktische Recht im Deuteronomium und im Heiligkeitsgesetz (1949).

Rabenau, K. von

"Die Entstehung des Buches Ezechiel in formgeschichtlicher Sicht," *WZ* 5 (1955–56): 659–694.

Idem

"Die Form des Rätsels im Buche Hesekiel," *Wiss. Z. Halle* GR 7, 5 (1958): 1055–1058.

Idem

"Das prophetische Zukunftswort im Buch Hese-
kiel" in *Studien zur Theologie der alttestamentlichen Überlieferungen*, ed. R. Rendtorff and K. Koch (Neukirchen-Vluyn: Neukirchener, 1961), 61–80.

Rad, Gerhard von

"Erwägungen zu den Königspsalmen," *ZAW* 58 (1940/41): 216–222.

Idem

"Faith Reckoned as Righteousness" in *The Problem of the Hexateuch and Other Essays*, tr. E. W. Trueman Dicken (New York: McGraw-Hill, 1966), 125–130.

Idem

"Die falschen Propheten," *ZAW* 51 (1933): 109–120.

Idem

"The Form-critical Problem of the Hexateuch" in *The Problem of the Hexateuch and Other Essays*, tr. E. W. Trueman Dicken (New York: McGraw-Hill, 1966), 1–78.

Idem

Der heilige Krieg im alten Israel, ATANT 20 (Göttingen: Vandenhoeck & Ruprecht, ⁵1969).

Idem

"Die Konfessionen Jeremias," *EvTh* 3 (1936): 265–276.

Idem

"Die Lobpreis Israels" in *Antwort. Karl Barth zum 70 Geburtstag* (Zollikon = Zuerich: Evangelischer-Verlag, 1956), 676–687.

Idem

Old Testament Theology, 2 volumes, tr. D. M. G. Stalker (New York: Harper & Row, 1962 and 1965).

Idem

Priesterschrift im Hexateuch literarisch untersucht und theologisch gewertet, BWANT 4, 13 (Stuttgart: Kohlhammer, 1934).

Idem

"The Promised Land and Yahweh's Land in the Hexateuch" in *The Problem of the Hexateuch and Other Essays*, tr. E. W. Trueman Dicken (New York: McGraw-Hill, 1966), 79–93.

Idem

" 'Righteousness' and 'Life' in the Cultic Language of the Psalms" in *The Problem of the Hexateuch and Other Essays*, tr. E. W. Trueman Dicken (New York: McGraw-Hill, 1966), 243–266.

Ranke, E.

Par palimpsestorum wirceburgensium (Vindobonae, 1871).

Ratschow, Carl Heinz

Werden und Wirken. Eine Untersuchung des Wortes hajah als Beitrag zur Wirklichkeitserfassung des Alten Testamentes, BZAW 70 (Berlin: Töpelmann, 1941).

Reichel, Wolfgang

Ueber vorhellenische Goetterculte (Wien: Hoelder, 1897).

Reider, Joseph
"Contributions to the Scriptural Text," *HUCA* 24 (1952/3): 85–106.

Idem
"Etymological Studies in Biblical Hebrew," *VT* 2 (1952): 113–130.

Idem
"Etymological Studies in Biblical Hebrew," *VT* 4 (1954): 276–295.

Idem
"Etymological Studies: ידע or ירע and רעע," *JBL* 66 (1947): 315–317.

Rendtorff, Rolf
"Zum Gebrauch der Formel *neʾum jahwe* im Jeremiabuch," *ZAW* 66 (1954): 27–37.

Idem
Die Gesetze in der Priesterschrift, FRLANT NF 44 (Goettingen: Vandenhoeck & Ruprecht, 1954).

Reventlow, Henning Graf
"Das Amt des Mazkir. Zur Rechtsstruktur des öffentlichen Lebens in Israel," *ThZ* 15 (1959): 161–175.

Idem
Das Heiligkeitsgesetz formgeschichtlich untersucht, WMANT 6 (Neukirchen-Vluyn: Neukirchener, 1961).

Idem
"Die Völker als Jahwes Zeugen bei Ezechiel," *ZAW* 71 (1959): 33–43.

Idem
Waechter ueber Israel: Ezechiel und seine Tradition, BZAW 82 (Berlin: Töpelmann, 1962).

Riessler, Paul
Altjüdisches Schrifttum ausserhalb der Bibel, übersetzt und erläutert (1928 = Heidelberg, 1966).

Robinson, H. W.
"The Hebrew Conception of Corporate Personality" in *Werden und Wesen des Alten Testaments*, BZAW 66 (Berlin: Töpelmann, 1936), 49–62.

Idem
Two Hebrew Prophets. Studies in Hosea and Ezekiel (London: Lutterworth, 1948).

Rohland, Edzard
Die Bedeutung der Erwählungstraditionen Israels für die Eschatologie der alttestamentlichen Propheten, Unpub. Diss. (Heidelberg, 1956).

Rost, Leonhard
"Die Bezeichnungen für Land und Volk im Alten Testament" in *Festschrift Otto Procksch*, ed. A. Alt, J. Herrmann, M. Noth, G. von Rad, E. Sellin (Leipzig: Deichert, 1934), 125–148.

Idem
Israel bei den Propheten, BWANT 4, 19 (Stuttgart: Kohlhammer, 1937).

Idem
Die Vorstufen von Kirche und Synagoge im Alten Testament, BWANT 4, 24 (Stuttgart: Kohlhammer, 1938).

Rost, Paul

"Miscellen I," *OLZ* 7 (1904): 390–393; 479–483.

Rubinstein, A.
"A Finite Verb continued by an Infinitive Absolute in Biblical Hebrew," *VT* 2 (1952): 362–367.

Rudolph, Wilhelm
Jeremia, HAT 1, 12 (Tübingen: Mohr [Siebeck], ³1968).

Scharff, Alexander and Moortgat, Anton
Ägypten und Vorderasien im Altertum (München: Bruckmann, 1950).

Schäfers, J.
"Ist das Buch Ezechiel in der Septuaginta von einem order mehreren Dolmetschern übersetzt?" *ThGl* 1 (1909): 289–291.

Schiffer, Sina
Die Aramäer: historisch-geographische Untersuchungen (Leipzig: Hinrichs, 1911).

Schmidt, H.
"Kerubenthron und Lade" in *Eucharisterion für H. Gunkel*, FRLANT 36, 1 (Göttingen, 1923), 120–144.

Schmidt, H. and Gunkel, H.
Das Märchen im Alten Testament (Tübingen: Mohr [Siebeck], 1921).

Schulthess, Friedrich
"ריפות 2 Sam. 17:19, רפות Prov. 27:22," *ZAW* 25 (1905): 357–359.

Schwarzenbach, Armin
Die geographische Terminologie im Hebräischen des Alten Testamentes (Leiden: Brill, 1954).

Scott, R. B. Y.
"Meteorological Phenomena and Terminology in the Old Testament," *ZAW* 64 (1952): 11–25.

Seeligmann, I. L.
"Voraussetzungen der Midraschexegese" in *Congress Volume: Copenhagen*, VTSuppl 1 (Leiden, 1953), 150–181.

Seinecke, L.
Geschichte des Volkes Israel, 2 parts (1884).

Selbie, J. A.
"Ezekiel 13:18–21," *ET* 15 (1903/1904).

Selle, Fridericus Philippus
De Aramaismis libri Ezechielis (Halis Saxonum: Formis Kaemmererianis, 1890).

Sellin, Ernst and Fohrer, Georg
Introduction to the Old Testament, tr. David E. Green (Nashville: Abingdon, 1968).

Silbermann, Samuel
Das Targum zu Ezechiel nach einer südarabischen Handschrift (Strassburg, 1902).

Simons, Jan Jozef
Jerusalem in the Old Testament; researches and theories (Leiden: Brill, 1952).

Slotki, Israel W.
"Ezekiel XVI 4," *JTS* 27 (1926): 271–272.

Idem
"Ezek. 18:10," *AJSL* 43 (1926): 63–66.

Smith, James
The Book of the Prophet Ezekiel; a new interpretation (London: S.P.C.K., 1931).

Smith, Louise Pettibone
"The Eagle(s) of Ezekiel 17," *JBL* 58 (1939): 43–50.

Snaith, N. H.
"The Dates in Ezekiel," *ET* 59 (1947/48).

Snijders, L. A.
"The Meaning of זר in the Old Testament. An Exegetical Study," *OTS* 10 (1954): 1–154.

Soden, Wolfram von
Grundriss der akkadischen Grammatik, Analecta Orientalia 33 (Rome: Pontifical Biblical Institute, ²1969).

Idem
Herrscher im alten Orient, Verständliche Wissenschaft 54 (Berlin: Springer, 1954).

Speier, Salomon
"Alttestamentliche Wortforschung. Ṭārāf, Genesis 8, 11," *ThZ* 2 (1946): 153–154.

Sperber, Alexander
The Bible in Aramaic 3: The Latter Prophets according to Targum Jonathan (Leiden: Brill, 1962).

Spiegel, Shalom
"Ezekiel or Pseudo-Ezekiel?" *HTR* 24 (1931): 245–321.

Idem
"Noah, Daniel and Job, Touching on Canaanite Relics in the Legends of the Jews" in *Louis Ginzberg Jubilee Volume* (New York: Amer. Acad. Jewish Research, 1945), 305–355 (English section).

Idem
"Toward Certainty in Ezekiel," *JBL* 54 (1935): 145–171.

Sprank, Siegfried and Wiese, Kurt
Studien zu Ezechiel und dem Buch der Richter, BWANT 3, 4 (Stuttgart: Kohlhammer, 1926).

Sprey, Th.
"Review of W. Zimmerli, *Erkenntnis Gottes nach dem Buche Ezechiel, eine theologische Studie*," *VT* 5 (1955): 445–447.

Stade, Bernhard
"Das vermeintliche aramäisch-assyrische Aequivalent der מלכת השמים Jer. 7.44," *ZAW* 6 (1886): 289–339.

Stamm, Johann Jakob
"Review of *Ezechielfragen* by Nils Messel," *ThZ* 3 (1947): 304–309.

Stein, Bernhard
Der Begriff Kᵉbod Jahwe und seine Bedeutung für die alttestamentliche Gotteserkenntnis (Emsdetten: Lechte, 1939).

Steinmann, Jean
Le prophète Ézéchiel et les débuts de l'exil, Lectio Divina 13 (Paris: Cerf, 1953).

Steuernagel, Carl
"Jahwe, der Gott Israels" in *Studien zur semitischen Philologie und Religionsgeschichte Julius Wellhausen zum siebzigsten Geburtstag*, ed. Karl Marti, BZAW 27 (Giessen: Töpelmann, 1914), 329–349.

Idem
Lehrbuch der Einleitung in das Alte Testament (Tübingen: Mohr [Siebeck], 1912).

Stoebe, Hans Joachim
"Gut and Böse in der jahwistischen Quelle des Pentateuch," *ZAW* 65 (1953): 188–204.

Idem
"Seelsorge und Mitleiden bei Jeremia," *WuD* NF 4 (1955): 116–134.

Strack, Hermann L. and Billerbeck, Paul
Kommentar zum Neuen Testament aus Talmud und Midrasch, 6 volumes (München: Beck, ²1956–1961).

Stummer, F.
"אֲמָלָה (Ez xvi 30 A)," *VT* 4 (1954): 34–40.

Sukenik, E. L.
The Dead Sea Scrolls of the Hebrew University (Jerusalem: Hebrew University Press, 1955).

Sutcliffe, Edmund F.
"Effect as Purpose: a Study in Hebrew Thought Patterns," *Bibl* 35 (1954): 320–327.

Tallquist, Knut
Himmelsgegenden und Winde, StOr 2 (Helsinki, 1928).

Teicher, J. L.
"The Christian Interpretation of the Sign x in the Isaiah Scroll," *VT* 5 (1955): 189–198.

Thackeray, H. St. J.
"The Greek Translators of Ezekiel," *JTS* 4 (1903): 398–411.

Torrey, C. C.
Pseudo-Ezekiel and the Original Prophecy (New Haven: Yale University Press, 1930 = New York: KTAV Publishing House, 1970).

Tournay, R.
"Review of *Die Hauptprobleme des Buches Ezechiel*," *RB* 60 (1953): 417–419.

Tsevat, Matitiahu
"The Neo-Assyrian and Neo-Babylonian Vassal Oaths and the Prophet Ezekiel," *JBL* 78 (1959): 199–204.

Turner, N.
"The Greek Translators of Ezekiel," *JTS* 7 (1956): 12–24.

Ungnad, A.
Die Religion der Babylonier und Assyrer (Jena: Diederich, 1921).

Usener, H.
"Milch und Honig," *Rheinisches Museum für Philologie*, NF 57 (1902): 177–195.

Vincent, Albert
La religion des Judéo-Araméens d'Éléphantine (Paris: Geuthner, 1937).

Vincent, Hugues
Jerusalem de l'Ancien Testament; recherches d'archéologie et d'histoire, 2 volumes (Paris: Gabalda, 1954–56).

Virolleaud, Charles
  Mission de Ras-Shamra 1: *La légende phénicienne de Danel* (Paris: Geuthner, 1936).
Idem
  "Sur l'idole de la jalousie du temple de Jérusalem," *RES* 1 (1945): 59–63.
Vischer, W.
  "Jerusalem du hast deine Schwestern gerechtfertigt durch alle deine Greuel, die du getan hast. Hesekiel 16" in *Versöhnung zwischen West und Ost*, ThEx NF 56 (München, 1957), 16–38.
Vogt, E.
  "Ioiakîn collari ligneo vinctus (Ez 19:9)," *Bibl* 37 (1956): 388–389.
Volz, Paul
  Der Geist Gottes und die verwandten Erscheinungen im Alten Testament und im anschliessenden Judentum (Tübingen, 1910).
Vriezen, Theodorus Christiaan
  "'*Ehje* '*ašer* '*ehje*" in *Festschrift A. Bertholet* (Tuebingen: Mohr [Siebeck], 1950), 498–512.
Idem
  Die Erwählung Israels nach dem Alten Testament, ATANT 24 (Zürich: Zwingli, 1953).
Wagner, Max
  Die lexikalischen und grammatikalischen Aramaismen im alttestamentlichen Hebräisch, BZAW 96 (Berlin: Töpelmann, 1966).
Wanke, Gunther
  "אוֹי und הוֹי," *ZAW* 78 (1966): 215–218.
Idem
  Die Zionstheologie der Korachiten in ihrem traditionsgeschichtlichen Zusammenhang, BZAW 97 (Berlin: Töpelmann, 1966).
Watzinger, Carl
  Denkmäler Palästinas, 2 volumes (Leipzig: Hinrichs, 1933–35).
Weidner, E.
  "Hof- und Haremserlasse assyrischer Könige," *AfO* 17 (1956): 257–293.
Idem
  "Jojachin, König vons Juda in babylonischen Keilschrifttexten" in *Mélanges syriens offerts à M. René Dussaud* (Paris: Geuthner, 1939), 923–935.
Weiser, Artur
  Das Buch Jeremia, ATD 20–21 (Göttingen: Vandenhoeck & Ruprecht, [5/6]1969).
Wellhausen, Julius
  Reste arabischen Heidentums gesammelt und erläutert (Berlin: Reimer, [2]1897).
Idem
  Der Text der Bücher Samuelis (Göttingen: Vandenhoeck & Ruprecht, 1871).
Wernberg-Møller, P.
  "'Pleonastic' *Waw* in Classical Hebrew," *JSS* 3 (1958): 321–326.
Westermann, Claus
  Basic Forms of Prophetic Speech, tr. Hugh Clayton White (Philadelphia: Westminster, 1967).

Wevers, John W.
  "Septuaginta-Forschungen," *ThR* 22 (1954): 85–138.
Widengren, Geo
  Literary and Psychological Aspects of the Hebrew Prophets, UUÅ (Leipzig and Uppsala: Harrassowitz, Lundequists, 1948).
Wiesner, J.
  Fahren und Reiten in Alteuropa und im alten Orient, AO 38, 2–4 (Leipzig: 1939).
Wildberger, Hans
  Jahwewort und prophetische Rede bei Jeremia (Zürich: Zwingli, 1942).
Idem
  "Israel und sein Land," *EvTh* 16 (1956): 404–422.
Winckler, H.
  "Die Zeit der Ezechielprophetie," *Altor. Forschungen* 3, 1 (1902): 135–155.
Wiseman, Donald John
  Chronicles of Chalaean Kings (626–556 B.C.) in the British Museum (London: The British Museum, 1956).
Idem
  The Vassal-treaties of Esarhaddon (London: British School of Archaeology in Iraq, 1958).
Wolff, Hans Walter
  "Die Begründungen der prophetischen Heils- und Unheilssprüche," *ZAW* 52 (1934): 1–22; reprinted in *idem*, *Gesammelte Studien zum AT*, ThB 22 (München: Kaiser, 1964), 9–35.
Idem
  Hosea: A Commentary on the Book of the Prophet Hosea, tr. Gary Stansell. Hermeneia (Philadelphia: Fortress, 1974).
Idem
  "Das Thema 'Umkehr' in der alttestamentlichen Prophetie," *ZThK* 48 (1951): 129–148; reprinted in *idem*, *Ges. Stud. zum AT*, ThB 22 (München: Kaiser, 1964), 130–150.
Idem
  "'Wissen um Gott' bei Hosea als Urform von Theologie," *EvTh* 12 (1952/53): 533–554; reprinted in *idem*, *Ges. Stud. zum AT*, ThB 22 (München: Kaiser, 1964), 182–205.
Idem
  Das Zitat im Prophetenspruch, BhEvTh 4 (München: Kaiser Verlag, 1937); reprinted in *idem*, *Ges. Stud. zum AT*, ThB 22 (München: Kaiser, 1964), 36–129.
Worden, T.
  "The Literary Influence of the Ugaritic Fertility Myth on the Old Testament," *VT* 3 (1953): 273–297.
Wünsche,
  "Die Räthselweisheit bei den Hebräern," *JPTh* 9 (1883): 422–460.
Würthwein, Ernst
  Der 'amm ha'arez im Alten Testament, BWANT 4,

17 (Stuttgart: Kohlhammer, 1936).

Idem

    "Amos 5, 21–27," *ThLZ* 72 (1947): 143–152.

Idem

    The Text of the Old Testament; an Introduction to Kittel-Kahle's Biblia Hebraica, tr. Peter R. Ackroyd (Oxford: Basil Blackwell, 1957).

Yadin, Yigael

    "Hyksos Fortifications and the Battering-Ram," *BASOR* 137 (1955): 23–32.

Ziegler, Joseph

    "Die Bedeutung des Chester Beatty-Scheide Papyrus 967 für die Textüberlieferung der Ezechiel-Septuaginta," *ZAW* 61 (1945/48): 76–94.

Idem

    Ezechiel, Septuaginta. Vetus Testamentum graecum 16, 1 (Göttingen: Vandenhoeck & Ruprecht, 1952).

Idem

    Susanna, Daniel, Bel et Draco, Septuaginta. Vetus Testamentum graecum 16, 2 (Göttingen: Vandenhoeck & Ruprecht, 1954).

Idem

    "Zur Textgestaltung der Ezechiel-Septuaginta," *Bibl* 34 (1953): 435–455.

Zimmerli, Walther

    Das Alte Testament als Anrede, BEvTh 24 (München: Kaiser, 1956).

Idem

    "Die Eigenart der prophetischen Rede des Ezechiel. Ein Beitrag zum Problem an Hand von Ez. 14:1–11," *ZAW* 66 (1954): 1–26.

Idem

    Erkenntnis Gottes nach dem Buche Ezechiel, ATANT 27 (Zürich: Zwingli, 1954); reprinted in *idem, Gottes Offenbarung*, ThB 19 (München: Kaiser, 1963), 41–119.

Idem

    "Ich bin Jahwe" in *Festschrift für A. Alt* (Tuebingen: Mohr, 1953), 179–209; reprinted in *idem, Gottes Offenbarung*, ThB 19 (München: Kaiser, 1963), 11–40.

Idem

    " 'Leben' und 'Tod' im Buche des Propheten Ezechiel," *ThZ* 13 (1957): 494–508; reprinted in *idem, Gottes Offenbarung*, ThB 19 (München: Kaiser, 1963), 178–191.

Idem

    "Planungen für den Wiederaufbau nach der Katastrophe von 587," *VT* 18 (1968): 229–255.

Idem

    "Der Prophet im Alten Testament und im Islam," *Kreuz und Halbmond* 5 (1943): 3–8.

Idem

    "Sinaibund und Abrahambund. Ein Beitrag zum Verständnis der Priesterschrift," *ThZ* 16 (1960): 268–280; reprinted in *idem, Gottes Offenbarung*, ThB 19, (München: Kaiser, 1963), 205–216.

Idem

    "Das Wort des göttlichen Selbsterweises" in *Mélanges bibliques rédigés en l'honneur de André Robert*, Travaux de l'Institut Catholique de Paris 4 (Paris, 1957), 154–164; reprinted in *idem, Gottes Offenbarung*, ThB 19 (München: Kaiser, 1963), 120–132.

Zorell, Franciscus

    Lexicon Hebraicum et Aramaicum Veteris Testamenti (Rome: Pontifical Biblical Institute, 1946–1954).

Zunz, L.

    "Bibelkritisches II. Ezechiel," *ZDMG* 27 (1873): 676–681.

Pictured on the endpapers is a fragment of the Book of Ezekiel from Cave Four, Qumrân (4Q Ezᵃ) dating from the first century B.C. The text includes portions of Ezekiel 10:17–11:11.

1. The Contents of the Book of Ezekiel

The book named after the prophet Ezekiel 𝔐 (יְחֶזְקֵאל
𝔊 Ιεζεκιηλ 𝔖 חזקיאל 𝔙 *Ezechiel*)[1] begins with a dated
call narrative, told by the prophet himself in the first
person.[2] After a broad introductory description of a
theophany, this tells of the sending and commissioning
of the prophet (1:1–3:15). Seven days later his office
is further clarified by the image of the watchman (3:16–
21). In a fresh confrontation with Yahweh's glory
the prophet is commanded to perform a series of symbolic actions by which, as the appended interpretation explains, he is to announce the siege of Jerusalem
and the subsequent exile (3:22–5:17). In two further
thematic statements, the message of judgement upon
the mountains and valleys of Israel (6:1–14) and of the
impending end (7:1–27) is proclaimed.

8:1, with a new time reference, then introduces the
account of a great visionary experience, which showed
the prophet, after being transported to Jerusalem, the
abominations practiced in the temple there and the
divine punishment of them which has its climax in the
departure of God's glory from the temple (8:1–11:25).
To it there is appended a command to perform a symbolic action, which is to signify the removal of the
inhabitants of Jerusalem into exile (12:1–16). A further
symbolic action dramatizes the horror at the imminent
desolation of the land (12:17–20). What then follows up
to 14:11, is described by the catchword "prophet."
Two short sayings emphasize, in polemical address
against the attitude of his compatriots, the validity
(12:21–25) and imminent fulfillment of the prophetic
word (12:26–28). After a broad treatment of the false
prophets and prophetesses (13:1–23) there follows the
threat that the prophet who communicates God's
oracle to an idolatrous people will undergo God's
judgement (14:1–11). Not unintentionally there follows an oracle which gives assurance that even the
righteousness of the most pious man of God can no
longer bring about any change in the fate of the sinful
people (14:12–23).

With ch. 15 there begins a series of allegories,
although there are two breaks in this. The short section
15:1–8 compares Jerusalem to a useless vine, and the

complex 16:1–63, which has been considerably elab
orated by additional motifs, with an unfaithful wife.
17:1–24, with its mysterious imagery of an eagle, the
cedar and the vine, to which has been added an interpretation, has in mind the concrete contemporary even
of Zedekiah's disloyalty to his Babylonian overlord.
The end of the Judean royal house is lamented by the
allegory of the lioness, and its expansion with the allegory of the vine (19:1–14). In this series one would
like also to include 23:1–49, the allegory of Samaria
and Jerusalem as two unfaithful women, which has
similarly been expanded by additional elements. Just
as ch. 17 is separated from ch. 19 by the didactic exposition of the freedom to repent (18:1–32) which comes
between them and is casuistically formulated, so there
appears between chs. 19 and 23 a variety of differently
formulated units: the presentation of Israel's sinful
history from its departure from Egypt and the promise of a new exodus, which is formulated without
any metaphorical image and is again freshly dated
(20:1–44); a group of announcements of judgement
composed of several sayings which are in form variously
formulated but which in content are connected by the
catchword "sword" (21:1–12, 13–22, 23–37); and
finally three units, the first of which attacks the "bloody
city" of Jerusalem (22:1–16), the second of which
describes the coming judgement with the image of a
smelting furnace (22:17–22), and the third of which
in a sermon once again shows the utter corruption of
all classes in the land (22:23–31).

Ch. 24, which is put together from two separate units,
brings a final climax to the declaration of judgement.
By a date reference at the beginning it is established
that the siege of Jerusalem has now begun (24:1–2).
The besieged city is described under the figure of a pot
brought to white heat in a fire (24:3–14). The sudden
death of the prophet's wife and the paralyzing numb-
ness brought about by it become a proclamation of the
now imminent end of Jerusalem. Its occurrence will
be announced to the prophet in its time by a "survivor"
coming from Jerusalem (24:15–27).
There then follows in chs. 25–32 a very different section
between this harsh threat and the first subsequent

---

1   For the name, see pp. 110f.
2   On 1:3a, see pp. 100f.

information in ch. 33 of the fall of Jerusalem that has ensued. In units of unequal length judgements are announced against seven nations: Ammon, Moab, Edom and the Philistines in a comprehensive first section in 25:1–17, Tyre in three broadly set out compositions (26, 27, 28:1–19), in part formulated in metaphorical images and set out as laments (27:1–36; 28:11–19; cf. also 26:17f). At the beginning of the first of these a date is given (26:1). After a short saying against Sidon, coming as an appendix, and a general conclusion to chs. 25–28 (28:20–26) there follows in chs. 29–32 seven large compositions against Egypt, of which no less than six bear their own dates (29:1, 17; 30:20; 31:1; 32:1, 17) and which in part are also formulated in metaphorical images. In the accusations against Egypt which take up half of the section chs. 25–32 against foreign nations, the most important hostile nation is obviously mentioned.

The continuation in ch. 33 then follows, although remarkably a fresh date reference is not given until the short section 33:21f, the only purely narrative unit formulated without any announcement. This tells what we are led to expect from ch. 24, in mentioning the fall of the city and the report of this to the prophet. This is preceded in 33:1–20 by a section which, in its appointing of the prophet as watchman recalls 3:16–21, and ch. 18 in its didactic affirmation about the freedom to repent. For the first time we find in this a clear correspondence between the section beginning with ch. 33 and the introductory section chs. 1–24. After a double unit, which is directed against the lack of repentance and misplaced assurance of those in the homeland and those in exile (33:23–33), there follows in chs. 34–37 oracles announcing the coming salvation. Starting from reproach against the wicked shepherds, 34:1–31 announce the coming faithful care of the flock by God and his princes. 35:1–36:15 proclaims, on the basis of a judgement against Seir, the homeland of Edom which has taken possession of Israel's land, salvation for the mountains of Israel. In it is to be found ∴ counterpart to the earlier oracle of judgement, the threat against the mountains of Israel in 6:1–14. In the announcement of the free saving history of God for his people (36:16–38) we can probably find echoes of distant elements of the history of woe in 20:1–31. Quite clearly there are correspondences with 11:14–21.

In the vision of the awakening of the dead bones (37:1–14) the new life of the people is proclaimed. Once again the vision is followed directly by a symbolic action. By means of it the prophet can promise a new unity to the people who before the exile were divided (37:15–28). In chs. 38 and 39, however, the promise of salvation is extended to a yet further event. A mighty assault by the enemy from the North, in the last days, under its great prince Gog will confront the reoccupied land. Its inhabitants will move out afterwards in order to bury the corpses of the enemy army who will have been mysteriously struck down by God.

A vast vision, in which the prophet is transported to the temple mount in the land of Israel and is shown the new temple area arranged symmetrically, concludes the book (40–48) and is introduced by a new date reference. Once again the correspondence with earlier material is not to be overlooked, when the prophet sees the return of God's glory to the new temple. Further the prophet is not only shown the new ordinances of temple worship, but, after the vision of the temple spring which mysteriously becomes a river and waters and heals the land around, he is shown the new division of the land. The new name of the city, "Yahweh is there," concludes the impressive vision of the coming sanctuary and its blessing.

In coming from the other prophetic books, one is struck by the impression of great order in the book of Ezekiel. The three major sections can clearly be separated from one another. The slight oscillations from oracles of woe to salvation (promises of salvation at the close of some oracles of woe in 11:14–21; 16:53–61; 17:22–24; 20:32–44; beginning with threats of woe in oracles of salvation in 33:23–33; 34:1–10) are not very prominent. On the other hand, features which correspond appear all the more clearly: the commissioning of the prophet as a watchman 3:16–21/33:1–9, oracles of weal and woe upon the mountains of Israel 6/36:1–15, a vision of destruction with the departure of Yahweh's glory and a vision of restoration with the return of Yahweh's glory to the temple chs. 8–11/40–48. Further the date references show in the overall compass of the work a regular advance in time. Deviations (anticipation in 26:1; 29:17; 32:1) do not destroy the overall impression of good order, but appear rather to confirm the rule because they are exceptions.

2. Critical Work on the Book of Ezekiel

After what has been said it is not surprising that critical work on the book of Ezekiel only began very hesitatingly and late, but then finally came in sharply so as to attack the very foundations of the book.

The words of Rudolf Smend about the book of Ezekiel, which are indicative of the pre-critical phase, are often quoted: "The whole book is . . . the logical development of a series of ideas in accordance with a well thought out, and in part quite schematic, plan. We cannot remove any part without disturbing the whole structure."[3] Already in 1841 Ewald had said of the prophet, "that he was more an author than a prophet, and his great book arose almost entirely out of literary effort."[4] Granted that according to him the words of the prophet, "who lived mainly at home,"[5] were not all written down at the same time. The book must "first have arisen, gradually out of several strata."[6] Nevertheless, as a whole, including the section 40–48, which shows "the coloring of an anxious priestly mind and expresses ideas which are quite foreign to the rest of the book," it owes its form to the hand of the prophet himself. As a final touch he inserted 29:17–21 "in the book which was otherwise quite complete."[7] Subsequent displacing of sections is only recognizable in 46:16–18, which belongs after 45:8, and in 46:19–24, which belongs after 42:14.

According to Smend Ezekiel, who was "essentially not a prophet . . . but a pastor and lawgiver,"[8] wrote his book as a "literary unit." In it he "wrote down in the eventide of his life his whole view of the current position of Israel, as well as its past and future."[9] "Most probably therefore the whole book was written down in a single effort, and we can regard the date of 40:1 as roughly the time of its composition. The appendix in 29:17ff, which is dated two years later, already presupposes its publication."[10] Unlike Ewald nothing is said by Smend about earlier stages of composition. Regarding the text of the book Smend establishes that it belongs among the worst preserved of the Old Testament.[11] At this point critical work then first began. Cornill published a careful study of the text on the basis of the versions[12] and thereby carried further the work of Hitzig[13] and Merx.[14]

He says of the book as a whole: "His (i.e. the prophet's) book was not written down in a single effort in a study but although it was undoubtedly set out by the prophet himself according to a comprehensive and skilful plan, it is a composition, the separate parts of which were conceived at quite distinct times."[15] For Cornill the text of 𝕲 was consequently particularly important for the emendation of 𝔐. A similar work was undertaken by Jahn with a passionately one-sided partiality for the Greek over against the Hebrew text tradition: "There is scarcely a book in the whole of world literature which has been so mishandled as has Ezekiel by the Soferim, and it will remain a characteristic typical of literalistic belief that even in the most recent times this text is held to be original. The Soferim have removed the fangs of the most passionate prophet, and they have made him into a senile pulpiteer."[16] Besides Cornill and Jahn, Toy[17] also and Rothstein[18]

---

3   Rudolf Smend, *Der Prophet Ezechiel*, KeH (Leipzig, ²1880), xxi.

4   Heinrich Ewald, *Die Propheten des Alten Bundes erklärt*, volume 2, "Jeremja und Hezeqiel" (Göttingen, ²1868), 207.

5   Ewald, 209.

6   Ewald, 207.

7   Ewald, 217.

8   Smend, vi.

9   Smend, xvi.

10   Smend, xxii.

11   Smend, xxix.

12   Carl Heinrich Cornill, *Das Buch des Propheten Ezechiel* (Leipzig, 1886).

13   Ferdinand Hitzig, *Der Prophet Ezechiel erklärt*, KeH 8 (Leipzig, 1847).

14   A. Merx, "Der Wert der Septuaginta für die Textkritik des Alten Testamentes, am Ezechiel aufgezeigt," *JPTh* 9 (1883): 65–77.

15   Cornill, vi.

16   Gustav Jahn, *Das Buch Ezechiel auf Grund der Septuaginta hergestellt, übersetzt und kritisch erklärt* (Leipzig, Pfeiffer, 1905), iii.

17   C. H. Toy, *The Book of the Prophet Ezekiel*, SBOT 12 (New York: Dodd, Mead, 1899).

18   J. W. Rothstein in *BH²* (1913).

undertook further work on the text. Among more recent commentators Cooke stands out for his particularly careful work on the text.[19]

Bertholet in his commentary of 1897 pleads for the original unity of the book in spite of the fact that individual parts of the book of Ezekiel have probably been introduced late into their present context (11:1–21; 24:22f; 27:9b–25a; 33:23–29).[20] Thus at about the turn of the century a critical examination of this unity of the book began. It was at first by means of source criticism, which was used successfully in the study of the Pentateuch, that scholarship sought to unlock the puzzles which could not be wholly overlooked in the book of Ezekiel. Starting from the observations that in 1:3 Ezekiel is referred to in the third person, whilst in 1:4ff the prophet himself speaks in the first person, Kraetzschmar in his commentary believed that he was able to establish the phenomenon of parallel recensions, and he finds this repeated elsewhere in the text.[21] Kreipe subsequently examined in detail the texts which Kraetzschmar had explained by his theory of doublets, and showed convincingly that this method could in no way remove the actual obscurities in the texts dealt with.[22] Nevertheless the theory of doublets continued to find supporters right up till Bertholet's second commentary, although in a partially modified form.[23]

Without the scheme of a fixed theory J. Herrmann undertook to examine the rifts in the literary structure of the book of Ezekiel.[24] He came to the conclusion, which may appear from a distance as a continuation of proposals of Ewald and Cornill, that behind the present book the composition of parts of it by the prophet himself was discernible. The individual units were therefore carefully examined by him. Herrmann regarded it as possible that "Ezekiel's own editorial hand had often broken up originally connected sayings and had introduced inconcinnities." Therefore in individual texts we must also accept "the interventions of alien hands."[25] The picture of a planned overall composition is here softened into that of a collection of separate oracles such as we have in the other literary prophets. The view of Ezekiel as an introverted, "bookish" prophet, such as Hitzig set out, is here given up.[26] J. Herrmann expressly turns against the formulation of Reuss: "There is not a single page in the whole book which we must suppose to have been read or proclaimed publicly. Ezekiel was not an orator; he was a writer. What he gives us are literary reflections, the product of private study and the fruit of retirement and contemplation. We should have to shut our eyes to the evidence to arrive at the view that he had ever had occasion to interfere actively in affairs, and to go out from his retreat to appear on the scene where passions are aroused and events take place."[27] In opposition to such a view Herrmann sees in Ezekiel a preacher, not a litterateur, however much the character of his preaching among the exiles may have been modified by the change of place compared with the older prophets.

When J. Herrmann published his long awaited commentary on the whole book, there began the much

---

19   G. A. Cooke, *A Critical and Exegetical Commentary on the Book of Ezekiel*, ICC (Edinburgh: Clark, 1936).

20   Alfred Bertholet, *Das Buch Hesekiel erklärt*, KHC 12 (Freiburg: Mohr, 1897), xx. "We must either accept it or reject it as a whole" xxii.

21   Richard Kraetzschmar, *Das Buch Ezechiel*, HKAT (Göttingen: Vandenhoeck & Ruprecht, 1900).

22   E. Kreipe, *Das literarische Problem des Buches Ezechiel. Programm des Wilhelmgymnasiums zu Hamburg* (1913).

23   Alfred Bertholet and Kurt Galling, *Hesekiel*, HAT 13 (Tübingen: Mohr [Siebeck], 1936). Cf. Johannes Hempel, *Die althebräische Literatur und ihr hellenistisch-juedisches Nachleben* (Wildpark-Potsdam: Akademische Verlagsgesellschaft Athenaion, 1930), 170; Carl Steuernagel, *Lehrbuch der Einleitung in das Alte Testament* (Tübingen: Mohr [Siebeck], 1912), 596f.

24   Johannes Herrmann, *Ezechielstudien*, BWAT 2 (Leip-zig, 1908).

25   J. Herrmann, *Ezechielstudien*, 6.

26   Hitzig: "At first Ezekiel wrote his book, perhaps solely for himself and his own satisfaction. Thus he was not seeking to tell others that God had revealed the hidden future to him, or only so after he himself had been filled with the faith with which he encouraged them" (xiv).

27   *La Bible, traduction nouvelle . . . Ancient Testament II, Les Prophètes II* (1876), 10.

sharper attack, which Hölscher subsequently carried on against the acceptance of the relative unity of the tradition preserved in the book of Ezekiel.[28] Hölscher's book examined in its extensive first part the psychological phenomenon of prophecy and seeks to understand it from the double roots of ecstacy and divination. He strongly emphasized the ecstatic character of the genuine prophecies of Ezekiel and expressly ascribed to the prophet, as his own authentic material, visions and oracles (mostly formulated in poetry).[29] In his *Geschichte* he then distinguished clearly the presentation of the prophet himself (§51) from the presentation of the book of Ezekiel (§60), the formation of which was ascribed by him to the Babylonian exile in the period between 515 and 445 B.C.[30] "The genuine Ezekiel stands with both feet in line with the older prophetic era; he first became a lawgiver and ancestor of the later nomism by the author of the book which is named after him, which was written in the fifth century."[31] The full basis for his view was published by Hölscher, immediately after the appearance of Herrmann's commentary.[32] As he himself says in the introduction, he was not so much concerned to set out a new analysis, complete in all its details, as rather to make the problem clear. According to him the problem lies in the fact that in the book of Ezekiel the genuine picture of the poet-prophet has undergone a subsequent prosaic retouching. We can see without difficulty in Hölscher the characteristic picture of a prophet that was already drawn in his book on prophecy. The prophet is a divinely-filled religious personality, who clothed his words in poetry under the power of Yahweh's spirit. "By freeing the poetry of Ezekiel from the dry prosaic pattern in which the redaction has woven his poems, the poet Ezekiel appears once again in a clear light, with his brilliant, imaginative and passionate rhetoric. From a religio-historical point of view also the picture of Ezekiel changes completely: he is no longer the stiff priestly

writer and pathfinder of a legalistic and ritualistic Judaism, for which he has been held, but a genuine prophet of Jewish antiquity, a spiritual companion of the authentic Jeremiah."[33]

The new picture is only gained at the price of a radical reduction of the present material in the book of Ezekiel. Hölscher would only find authentic material up to ch. 32. Within this range chapters 6f, 10, 12–14, 18, 20, 25f fall out completely. Of the remaining chapters smaller or larger sections are recognized as genuine. Only in chs. 8, 16, 23 and 27 does the genuine material extend to more than ten verses. In all the other chapters it amounts to fewer than this number of verses. Of the total of 1273 verses in the book only 144 at the maximum, either whole or in part, are recognized as genuine.

Hölscher's analysis, even though it found few unreserved followers, had a very stimulating effect on further study of the book of Ezekiel.[34] A breach had been made in the dogma of a book of Ezekiel which was completely, or almost completely, free of problems. Thus subsequently questions arose from various sides. No longer were scholars afraid to try out extremely bold interpretations in order to reach a consistent picture, not only of the literary deposit, but also of the person behind this deposit, and his contemporary and historical background.

In method we can but put alongside Hölscher the study by Irwin.[35] Irwin believes he can find in Ezek 15 a discrepancy between parable (vv 1–5) and adjoining interpretation (vv 6–8). With the criteria gained from this it is possible to distinguish the genuine (251 verses) from the non-genuine material. By this a very much paler and less convincing overall result appears than with Hölscher. According to Irwin we can find in Ezekiel a thirty-year-old prophet, who received his call in the days of Jehoiakim, and who was exiled after the downfall of the state in 587.

In the latter fact a point is touched upon which had

28 Johannes Herrmann, *Ezechiel, übersetzt und erklärt,* KAT (Leipzig: Deichert, 1924).

29 Gustav Hölscher, *Die Profeten* (Leipzig: Hinrichs, 1914).

30 Gustav Hölscher, *Geschichte der israelitischen und jüdischen Religion* (Giessen: Töpelmann, 1922).

31 Hölscher, *Geschichte,* 114.

32 Gustav Hölscher, *Hesekiel, der Dichter und das Buch,*

BZAW 39 (Giessen: Töpelmann, 1924).

33 Hölscher, *Hesekiel, der Dichter,* 5f.

34 Thus M. Haller, *RGG¹,* 2.

35 William A. Irwin, *The Problem of Ezekiel* (Chicago: University of Chicago Press, 1943).

strongly influenced Ezekiel study in the period between Hölscher's and Irwin's examinations. Many utterances of Ezekiel give the impression that the prophet had spoken directly to the population of Jerusalem. Thus Herntrich questions very emphatically whether we have not then to reckon with the genuine activity of the prophet in Jerusalem.[36] After an argument with Herrmann and Hölscher on the one hand, and with Kessler and Kittel on the other, he sets out the thesis: the group of exiles around Jehoiachin cannot have been Ezekiel's audience.[37] Ezekiel was a Jerusalem prophet. It can no longer certainly be made out when he was taken into exile. Was it in 587? However, in any case the preaching of the Jerusalem prophet, who had spoken no more after 587, was afterwards edited by one of the exiles of 597. This editor wanted to show that the true word of prophecy was with the exiles of 597. To this editing we owe the whole revelatory apparatus, with the phenomenon of transportation which seeks to harmonize the exilic and Jerusalem standpoints. Here also the didactic assurances of deliverance were added.

Herntrich's thesis, which deals with the question already raised by Berry, although the solutions proposed are different, found a strong response.[38] For one thing the thesis invited development. Do we not also in Ezekiel occasionally see an exilic background for his preaching? Must the material which points to this simply be removed as secondary elaboration? Thus Oesterley and Robinson modified the thesis so that Ezekiel worked in Jerusalem from 602–598 (597),

but was then deported and continued his activity in exile.[39]

Bertholet also, in his commentary of 1936, which took up Kraetzschmar's thesis of doublets, came to a similar compromise theory. A period of activity in Jerusalem, which was introduced by the vision of the scroll (Ezek 2f), and a temporary stay in the proximity of Jerusalem (12:1ff) were followed by a period of activity in exile to which the visions of the throne-chariot of ch. 1 belongs. The manner of his being transported from Jerusalem into exile (of his own will, or forcibly?) must be left open.[40]

However is this differentiation of two periods of activity sufficient to remove completely all the tensions? In his dissertation O.R. Fischer proposed the yet further varied thesis that Ezekiel was deported with Jehoiachin, returned to Jerusalem as a result of his being sent to the house of Israel, where he saw the abominations of ch. 8 and proclaimed the destruction of Jerusalem. Finally, under a new commission, he returned again to the exiles.[41] This further development of the thesis that Ezekiel preached in Jerusalem raises very forcibly the question whether the apparently precise adaptation of the message of the prophet to the people to whom he spoke, in which the decisive features of a change of place find no support in the book of Ezekiel itself, does not lead in a fundamentally false direction.

It is a clear indication of the impossibility of removing all the tensions in the book of Ezekiel that critics entering into this discussion have proposed extreme

---

36 Volkmar Herntrich, *Ezekielprobleme*, BZAW 61 (Giessen: Töpelmann, 1933).

37 Werner Kessler, *Die innere Einheitlichkeit des Buches Ezechiel* (Herrnhut: Missionsbuchhandlung, 1926), and Rudolf Kittel, *Geschichte des Volkes Israel* 3 (Stuttgart: Kohlhammer, 1927–1929), defend the unity of Ezekiel's prophecy.

38 George Ricker Berry, "Was Ezekiel in the Exile?" *JBL* 49 (1930): 83–93. Cf. John Battersby Harford, *Studies in the Book of Ezekiel* (Cambridge: Cambridge University Press, 1935); I. G. Matthews, *Ezekiel. An American Commentary on the Old Testament* (Philadelphia: Judson, 1939); Curt Kuhl, "Der Schauplatz der Wirksamkeit Hesekiels. Ein Lösungsversuch," *ThZ* 8 (1952): 401–418; and others.

39 W. O. E. Oesterley and Theodore H. Robinson, *An Introduction to the Books of the Old Testament* (New

York: Meridian, [2]1958), 328f. Cf. Shalom Spiegel, "Toward Certainty in Ezekiel," *JBL* 54 (1935): 145–171.

40 Bertholet-Galling. This view was further presented by P. Auvray, *Ezéchiel*, Témoins de Dieu (1947); A. van den Born, *De historische situatie van Ezechiels prophetie*, ALBO 2 (Leuven: Bijbels Seminarie, 1947); H. W. Robinson, *Two Hebrew Prophets. Studies in Hosea and Ezekiel* (London: Lutterworth, 1948); and with some variation, Herbert G. May, "The Book of Ezekiel" in *The Interpreter's Bible* 6 (Nashville: Abingdon, 1956), 41–338.

41 O. R. Fischer, *The Unity of the Book of Ezekiel*, Unpub. Diss. (Boston, 1939). A similar three-stage thesis was presented by Robert H. Pfeiffer, *Introduction to the Old Testament* (New York: Harper & Brothers, [2]1948).

solutions. These completely deny the entire book to the prophet Ezekiel, as he presents himself in it and affirms this with dates, and endeavor to find in it instead a pseudepigraph. Such voices were already to be heard sporadically and without any thorough detailed substantiation, quite early, long before the beginning of the main phase of critical work on the book of Ezekiel.[42]

In *Pseudo-Ezekiel* C.C. Torrey sought to show that we have in the book of Ezekiel a pseudepigraph from the period c.230 B.C. In this work which was composed in Jerusalem, the fiction was maintained that it had arisen in the time of Manasseh, in the period before Josiah's reform. The 30th year of 1:1, which can only be fitted in as a regnal year of Judah in the long reigns of either Manasseh or Josiah, must be ascribed to the former. To this period also points the dissertation of M. Burrows, worked out under Torrey.[43] According to this the prophecy of Ezekiel, in the light of the evidence of its literary dependence, was later than the conclusion of the Pentateuch, and also I and II Kings, Haggai, Zech Obadiah as well as Is 13, 23, 34, 40–55, 56–60. It was perhaps also later than Joel, the Aramaic Daniel and Zech 9–11, but was certainly older than Ecclesiasticus (Ben Sirach). The original Ezekiel pseudepigraph was then, according to Torrey, reworked with a Babylonian setting 30 years later (c.200 B.C.) by an anti-Samaritan redactor who regarded the true Israel as coming from Babylon.

When Torrey's work appeared that of J. Smith was already in print. Smith attempted in this study to go in the other direction to show that Ezekiel's prophecy was the work of a North Israelite who had addressed the "House of Israel," understood as North Israel after the downfall of the Northern Kingdom, first in the land itself and then in the diaspora.[44] The transformation of the book into the work of a Judean exile was, according to Smith, the work of a later redactor.

With yet further variations Messel attempted to show in an analysis of all the parts of the book of Ezekiel that the book was written c.400 B.C., after Nehemiah's governorship, and had in mind the enemies with whom Nehemiah had also had to deal. Since at that time in Jerusalem there existed a community which had returned from exile, we can understand that Ezekiel addressed exiles, but was at the same time present in Jerusalem. The basic text, which was composed c.400 B.C., then underwent a far-reaching expansion by a redactor between 361 and 344 B.C. He introduced especially the extensive oracles against Egypt, which can be fixed chronologically in the later Persian period. L. E. Brown seeks to ascribe the pseudepigraph to the age of Alexander the Great on the basis of the references to Tyre.[45] A. van den Born again finds the book of Ezekiel to be the pseudepigraph of a well-read author of the period of Ezra-Nehemiah, with arguments which rather recall those of Burrows.[46]

Withal, the negative criticism of the book of Ezekiel's own claims has gone too far. In place of the carefully balanced unity of the whole book, which was spoken of above, there has entered here the picture of a variety of oracles, riddled with tensions. What had previously been taken as straightforward statements in the book were then made questionable. It could not remain for long, in view of this critical questioning of all the statements of Ezekiel, that the question of the validity of what the book claims for itself should be freshly put.

A critical reaction against such unrestrained hypercriticism and its unproved new reconstructions followed from two sides. In his dissertation C. G. Howie,

42 Thus L. Zunz, "Bibelkritisches II. Ezechiel," *ZDMG* 27 (1873): 676–681; L. Seinecke, *Geschichte des Volkes Israel*, 2 parts (1884); H. Winckler, "Die Zeit der Ezechielprophetie," *Altor. Forschungen* 3, 1 (1902): 135–155; Berry, "Exile" had put forward arguments in this direction, with detailed variations. These theses claimed a wider audience through the works of C. C. Torrey, *Pseudo-Ezekiel and the Original Prophecy* (New Haven: Yale University Press, 1930 = New York: KTAV Publishing House, 1970); James Smith, *The Book of the Prophet Ezekiel: A New Interpretation* (London: S.P.C.K., 1931); Nils Messel,

Ezéchielfragen (Oslo: Dybwad, 1945).
43 Millar Burrows, *The Literary Relations of Ezekiel* (Philadelphia: Jewish Publication Society, 1925).
44 See Excursus 2.
45 Lawrence Edward Browne, *Ezekiel and Alexander* (London: S.P.C.K., 1952).
46 A. van den Born, *Ezechiël—Pseudo-epigraaf?* (1953).

who belongs to the school of W. F. Albright, in dependence on the works of Albright and other scholars, adduced a considerable amount of archaeological and historical material in order to illuminate the statements in the book of Ezekiel itself about the prophet's abode, the date of his activity, the Aramaisms of his language, etc.[47] On the other side, Fohrer subjected to a careful and penetrating examination the critical arguments about the book of Ezekiel, and the time and place of the prophet's activity. He came to the conclusion that we can certainly no longer speak in the old manner of the complete unity of the book of Ezekiel, but that the work on this book has first to start from its own claims as to the time and place of Ezekiel's activity.[48] So the most recent commentaries have undertaken afresh to understand the words of the prophet from what the book itself says in evaluating the various critical arguments that oppose this.[49]

In this way new questions have been raised, and valuable new light shed on many statements of the book. The book of Ezekiel offers, by the formal and material variety of its contents, which clearly mark it out as a late work of written prophecy, rich material for form-critical and traditio-historical investigations. In preliminary studies to the commentary set out here I have endeavored to show some of these. In a careful study K. von Rabenau put questions along these lines.[50] In all this we undoubtedly need to keep constantly in mind the limits of form-critical and traditio-historical work, as Fohrer has rightly reminded us.[51] H. Graf Reventlow's monograph, which points to close connections between Ezekiel and the Holiness Code and emphasizes questions of the form-critical and traditio-historical matrix of the two documents, at the same time provides an example which warns us just how unhistorical such criticism threatens to become if it is used one-sidedly.[52]

S. Herrmann in his study has sought to claim, from a redaction-historical viewpoint, in regard to Ezekiel's oracles of assurance a Deuteronomistic editing of the book.[53] This redaction-historical method of study will undoubtedly need to be examined further and its acceptability tested. Besides the contacts with the Holiness Code those with Deuteronomy must be carefully studied.[54]

The storm of critical analysis, which has blown across the book of Ezekiel and appeared at times to scatter its parts in all directions, makes it appear probable in its (provisional?) results that we should pay serious regard to the date and time references of the book. This will be done in §3. After this we must consider what we can deduce from the statements of the book about the person Ezekiel (§4). After an examination of the language and form of the oracles of the prophet (§5) we must look into the question of the traditio-historical and literary dependence of the book, which has played so important a role in the critical study of its origin (§6). On the basis of these questions an attempt can be made to outline Ezekiel's preaching (§7) and to say something about the development from the prophet's sayings to their incorporation in a book (§8). Finally we must deal with the transmission of the book (§9).

47 Carl Gordon Howie, *The Date and Composition of Ezekiel*, Journal of Biblical Literature Monograph Series 4 (Philadelphia: Society of Biblical Literature, 1950).

48 Georg Fohrer, *Die Hauptprobleme des Buches Ezechiel*, BZAW 72 (Berlin: Töpelmann, 1952).

49 See Joseph Ziegler, *Ezechiel* (Würzburg: Echter, 1948); Walther Eichrodt, *Der Prophet Hesekiel*, ATD (1970); Carl Gordon Howie, *The Book of Ezekiel; the Book of Daniel*, The Layman's Bible Commentary 13 (Richmond, Va.: John Knox, 1961); John W. Wevers, *Ezekiel*, Cent-B (London: Nelson, 1969).

50 K. von Rabenau, "Die Entstehung des Buches Ezechiel in formgeschichtlicher Sicht," *WZ* 5 (1955–56): 659–694. Questions which have been raised by Alt, Noth, and von Rad in relation to legal and narrative material have been fruitful in connection with many of Ezekiel's sayings. Cf. E. Rohland, *Die Bedeutung der Erwählungstraditionen Israels für die Eschatologie der alttestamentlichen Propheten*, Unpub. Diss. (Heidelberg, 1956).

51 Georg Fohrer, "Das Symptomatische der Ezechielforschung," *ThLZ* 83 (1958): 241–250.

52 H. Graf Reventlow, *Wächter über Israel; Ezechiel und seine Tradition*, BZAW 82 (Berlin: Töpelmann, 1962).

53 Siegfried Herrmann, *Die prophetischen Heilserwartungen im Alten Testament*, BWANT 85 (Stuttgart: Kohlhammer, 1965).

54 See below, pp. 46–52.

3. The Date and Historical Background of the Book of Ezekiel

a. The Dates in the Book of Ezekiel. The book of Ezekiel does not leave its readers in the dark about the time at which his words were uttered. We find in it no fewer than fourteen precise dates for individual oracles, visions or reports of the prophet's experiences. Of these the reference "after 7 days" of 3:16 is a simple appendix to the date of 1:1f in which the 7 days of 3:15 are taken up. It is not to be reckoned among the independent date references. The date of 24:1 again shows itself on closer observation to have been taken over from 2 Kings 25:1.[55] It does not belong to the original substance of the prophet's words. In 32:1 we must read, with some textual witnesses, 11 years instead of the 12 given by 𝔐.[56] The same is true for the date of 33:21, in accordance with the considerations set out there.

Thus we must reckon with the following twelve original dates:

1) 5th day of the 4th month in the 30th year (1:1), which is clarified by the further definition "the 5th day of the month in the 5th year (after) the deportation of king Jehoiachin" (1:2).[57] The continuation "after 7 days" in 3:16 (15) follows on from this.[58]

2) 5th day of the 6th month of the 6th year (8:1).

3) 10th day of the 5th month of the 7th year (20:1).

4) 1st day of the ? month of the 11th year (26:1).[59]

5) 12th day of the 10th month of the 10th year (29:1).

6) 1st day of the 1st month of the 27th year (29:17).

7) 7th day of the 1st month of the 11th year (30:20).

8) 1st day of the 3rd month of the 11th year (31:1).

9) 1st day of the 12th month of the 11th year (32:1).[60]

10) 15th day of the ? month of the 12th year (32:17).[61]

11) 5th day of the 10th month of the 11th year "after our deportation" (33:21).[62]

12) At the beginning of the year, i.e., on the 10th of the month (= the beginning of the month of the cultic year) of the 25th year "after our deportation." This year is defined further as the 14th year after the fall of the city (40:1).[63]

By his exact dating of a considerable number of prophetic oracles the book of Ezekiel stands closest perhaps to the prophetic books of Haggai and Zechariah. Whilst pre-exilic prophecy shows an increasing precision of dating,[64] this is no longer to be found after the time of Haggai and Zechariah (so in Malachi and Joel). In the apocalyptic book of Daniel we find in chs. 7–10 a dating only according to the year. So from the dates that are given in the book of Ezekiel itself we can accept as appropriate a position in the period between Jeremiah on the one hand and Haggai-Zechariah on the other.[65] It is further striking how often the date references occur in the oracles against the nations, and in particular in the oracles against Egypt. No less than half of the genuine dates are to be found in chs. 29–32. Besides these it is especially the great visions which are introduced with exact date references, cf. 1:1 (and 3:16a, 22ff); 8:1 and 40:1.[66] It is easy to see the reason for a date reference in 33:21, at the arrival of the first exiles after 587, an event which loosens the prophet's tongue after a period of dumbness. In 20:1 a date prefaces the reception of a message, which is introduced by a description of the situation (but cf. 14:1).

The sequence of the dates and the disturbances in the order of their strict chronological placing will be dealt with when we come to deal with the formation of the book.[67] However, in the present connection something must be said about the two references where a double dating of oracles occurs and about the era according to which the book of Ezekiel is dated.

The meaning of the double dating in 40:1 occasions no difficulty. Besides the normal dating after the

---

55 See p. 498.
56 See note a to 32:1.
57 See pp. 112–115.
58 See note a to 3:16 and p. 157.
59 See note b to 26:1.
60 See note a to 32:1.
61 See note b to 32:17.
62 See note a to 33:21.
63 See note b to 40:1.
64 See p. 112.
65 Some considerations are expressed on pp. 112f about the reasons for the precise dating of the occasions of receiving a message.
66 For what is possibly the secondary omission of a date reference in the vision of 37:1–14, see note b to 37:1.
67 See below pp. 72–75.

deportation of 597, we find here, where the text deals with the vision of a new temple, a reference back to the destruction of Jerusalem in which the old temple was lost. However the mention of the 30th year 1:1, which is clarified in v 2 by a synchronism with the era of Jehoiachin, remains obscure.[68]

However the observation is more important that in the dates of the book of Ezekiel the first deportation under Jehoiachin represents the starting point for the reckoning of the years. In 33:21 and 40:1 this date is defined in speeches by the prophet himself as the time of "our deportation." 1:2 formulates objectively "(the time of the) deportation of king Jehoiachin." Jehoiachin was, as will be shown, deported shortly before the new year of 597/6 (reckoning the year from the spring). Since he (according to II Kings 24:8) ruled in Jerusalem for only three months, his first regnal year would have been 597/6. This coincides with the first year of the deportation and also with the first year of Zedekiah, who ruled in Jerusalem (II Kings 24:18). It is then noteworthy that in the book of Ezekiel there is no dating according to the years of king Zedekiah, who actually ruled in Jerusalem after 597, but only in accord with Jehoiachin, who was among those deported in 597. This fact will have to be considered more closely in the presentation of the historical background.

Furthermore the series of dates found in the book of Ezekiel does not at all show a uniform distribution over the period of time covered by them. Rather the dates cluster together in the time from the 10th to the 12th years of Jehoiachin's deportation. No fewer than seven of the twelve dates fall in this period. Three dates come before it (5th, 6th and 7th years), two follow it at a long interval (25th and 27th years). The period with the greatest number of dates corresponds to the period of the last struggle for Jerusalem and the time immediately after its fall—a time which also figures very prominently in the prophet's preaching.[69] The reference to the 25th year in 40:1 is closely connected with the account of the rebuilding in chs. 40–42, in which the number 25 is prominent. The question arises whether the visionary description of the rebuilding has not been formulated directly from the number given in the date. The date of 29:17ff in the 27th year, within the section of chs. 27–33 in which the numbering from the 10th–12th year predominates, appears to be quite incomprehensible. The acceptance of a noticeable disturbance of the order of the series of dates can be most easily explained if the redactor who introduced the section 29:17–21 into its present place for thematic considerations felt himself to be bound to its date simply because of its presence in the tradition which he had received. The overall result of these considerations can only lead to the conclusion that the dates of the book of Ezekiel deserve our basic confidence.

These dates cover the period between the 5th day of the 4th month of the 5th year (1:1f) and the 1st day of the 1st month of the 27th year after the deportation of Jehoiachin (29:17). *The Chronicles of the Chaldean Kings* edited by D. J. Wiseman have made possible an identification of the precise day of the capture of Jerusalem which was followed by Jehoiachin's deportation, by their references to the 7th year of Nebuchadnezzar.[70] B.M. 21 946 Rev. 11–13 run: "In the 7th year, in the month Kislev, the king of Akkad mustered his troops, marched to Ḥatti-land (=Syria–Palestine) and pitched camp against the city of Judah, and on the 2nd day of the month Adar he captured the city and took the king prisoner. He installed there a king of his

---

68   The various possibilities which have been proposed in order to understand the number are referred to on pp. 113f. The conjecture is there accorded some weight that we are faced here with a number which has been subsequently manipulated and which displaced the original reference which is now restored in v 2. We cannot, however, go beyond the scope of this conjecture.

69   The thesis that these numbers are a later fiction (p. 112) thus appears to bear little probability.

70   Donald John Wiseman, *Chronicles of Chaldaean Kings (626–556 B.C.) in the British Museum* (London: The British Museum, 1956).

own choice (*šarra ša libbišu*), imposed heavy tribute upon him and sent (him) to Babylon." According to Parker-Dubberstein the capture of Jerusalem is accordingly to be dated March 16, 597 B.C.[71] The call of the prophet (1:1ff), according to the same reckoning, took place on July 31, 593,[72] and the date of the latest oracle (29:17) on April 26, 571.[73]

b. The Historical Background. The years 593–571, in which the prophet was active, fall in the period of the rule of Nebuchadnezzar II, the great king of the Neo-Babylonian dynasty (605–562). Under Nebuchadnezzar the contemporary Babylonian power had once again taken control of the area of the land routes from Africa to Asia, after an interval in which Egypt, the power in the south, had sought to play a decisive role again, as it had once before in the period of the great pharaohs of the Middle and New Kingdoms.

Before this there had been stirring times in which it appeared possible for a few years that the small kingdom of Judah could rise once again to the greatness of the days of David. The power of the Assyrian empire, which, since the days of Isaiah had conquered one after the other the minor states of Syria and Palestine, and to which Judah also had submitted without opposition under the long reign of Manasseh (c.696/5–642/1), began to weaken with the start of the last third of the seventh century B.C. Inner conflicts weakened the kingdom in the later part of the reign of its great king Ashurbanipal. In the Iranian mountains the Median king Cyaxares prepared to strike against the Assyrian kingdom. From Southern Babylonia the Chaldean element raised its head, which had given the Assyrians a great deal of trouble at the end of the eighth century under Merodoch–Baladan (cf. Is 39:1). In the year 626 the Chaldean Nabopolassar ascended the throne in Babylon. The pressure in the east gave the provinces and satellite princes in the west freedom to move. Thus at this time Judah, under its king Josiah, dared to raise its head again. In a peculiar movement of restora-

tion, which both in the political and religious spheres sought to return back to an earlier blessed age, it took stock of itself. 2 Kings 22f tell of the reform of worship, of the cleansing of the temple from Assyrian idols and other symbols of its dominion—together with the cleansing of the Yahweh cult from all kinds of Baalistic nature worship which had grown up in the land itself—and of the concentration of the cult at the one sanctuary of Jerusalem. Less easy to describe, but yet not to be overlooked is the attempt which was connected with this to recover the form of a united greater Israel, as it had existed under David. Josiah entered the province of *samerina*, the heartland of the early North Israel, which was still under Assyrian rule. He destroyed the sanctuary of Bethel, which was relatively close to the border. Further, the fact that in the summer of 609 he went to battle against the Pharaoh at Megiddo, when the latter was marching north, shows that the Ephraimite–Manassite mountain region was firmly under his hand. We can also see in the book of Ezekiel that the hope of reunion, awakened afresh by these events, was not quickly silenced again. The clash with Josiah took place in his thirty-first year (summer 609) when the latter sought to bar the way to Pharaoh Necho II (609–595) and his army at Megiddo. Josiah fell in this battle. In Jerusalem the land-owning nobility passed over the eldest son of Josiah and raised his younger son Jehoahaz to the throne. After a three month reign he was compelled to appear before Pharaoh in his camp at Ribla and was there taken prisoner by him and deported to Egypt (II Kings 23:33f).[74] These events, which aimed at breaking the movement for independence in Judah and making it pliable to Egyptian politics, are echoed not only by Jeremiah (22:10–12), but also in a lament from Ezekiel (19:2–4).[75] In place of the deported Jehoahaz Necho put Eliakim, the eldest son of Josiah who had been passed over by the land-owning nobility. He took the regnal name Jehoiakim. The accounts about him show that

71 Richard Anthony Parker and Waldo H. Dubberstein, *Babylonian Chronology 626 B.C.–A.D. 75*, Brown University Studies 19 (Providence: Brown University Press, 1956).

72 P. 115 is accordingly to be corrected.

73 The date of 8:1 is, according to Parker-Dubberstein, to be identified as September 17, 592 (against p. 236); the second reference of 24:1 is then to January 15, 588 (p. 497 is to be corrected accordingly).

74 See pp. 191f to 6:14.

75 See pp. 393–395.

the pro-Egyptian line of Palestinian politics found in him an active representative.

The period of Egyptian power was only of short duration. As early as the year 605 the change came. In this year the Babylonians under Nebuchadnezzar decisively defeated the Egyptians, who had attempted in the previous year to uphold the waning Assyrian power under its last king Assuruballit II, at the city of Carchemish on the Euphrates (Jer 46:2), and forced their way through into Syria. The Wiseman Chronicle gives very precise information about the exciting events of this year. Although the Babylonians had still to fall back under the attacks of the Egyptians, who crossed the Euphrates at Carchemish in the twentieth year of Nabopolassar (606/5), yet in his twenty-first year, in which Nabopolassar no longer took the field himself but handed over command to the crown prince Nebuchadnezzar, they delivered the counter blow. The Egyptians were so thoroughly defeated that they fell back into the region of Hamath in Central Syria and were then destroyed by Nebuchadnezzar's army. In the midst of his victorious advance news reached Nebuchadnezzar of the death of his father, who had died on the 8th day of the month Ab (August 15, 605 B.C.) By the 1st of Elul (September 7, 605) Nebuchadnezzar was already in Babylon to take over the kingdom. Without delay, however, he returned immediately to Syria, to his army, in order to harvest further the fruits of his victory, and to collect the tributes of countries and provinces of Ḥatti-land. Until the month Šebat (February 2—March 2, 604 B.C.) and therefore deep into the winter season, he remained in Ḥatti-land in order to return to Babylon to "take the hand of Bel (Marduk)" by the beginning of the year (April 12, 604), in accordance with royal custom. In the first year of his reign (604/3) he moved westwards again with his troops in order to continue his advance in the south of Palestine. In the month Kislev (November 24—December 23, 604 B.C.) Ashkelon, in Philistine territory, fell to him. Its king was taken prisoner and the city plundered and destroyed. Campaigns into Ḥatti-land, where the situation required to be more fully cleaned up, are then also mentioned for the two

following years. In his fourth year he attempted a breakthrough from Palestine into Egypt, but appears to have failed in this. The Wiseman Chronicle narrates: "In the month Kislev (November 23—December 20, 601) he took command of his army and marched towards Egypt. The king of Egypt heard of this and mustered his army. In open battle they struck, each one the breast of the other, and inflicted great injury on each other. The king of Akkad and his troops turned and returned to Babylon." The fact that in his fifth year (600/599) Nebuchadnezzar did not move westwards but "assembled his chariots and horses in great number" in Babylon, i.e. reorganized his army, confirms the failure of the 4th year. Then in his sixth year Nebuchadnezzar was again in Ḥatti-land, although it appears to have included only minor undertakings against groups on the desert fringes. "He sent his troops out of Ḥatti-land, and when they passed through the desert they took rich booty from the Arabs, their possessions, their animals and their gods."

Judah was brought fully under the power of the Babylonian king by the events of 605. According to 2 Kings 24:1 Jehoiakim was subject to Nebuchadnezzar for three years. We should identify these three years with the first three years of Nebuchadnezzar's reign, in which the Babylonian king directly compelled the submission of the princes of Phoenicia and Palestine by his presence in Ḥatti-land. The withholding of payment of tribute by Jehoiakim, which then took place, must be dated in the fourth year of Nebuchadnezzar, in which the defeat at the border of Egypt occurred. We shall hardly be wrong if we conjecture that behind the withholding of tribute there lay Egyptian promises of help, as these determined the subsequent history of Judah in an unhappy way and as they make the passionate oracles of Ezekiel against Egypt intelligible. II Kings 24:2 asserts that Yahweh had sent raiding parties of Babylonians, Arameans, Moabites, and Ammonites against Jehoiakim.[76] We must then see in this the events of the 5th and 6th years of Nebuchadnezzar in which he claimed the reorganization of his army and preliminary actions against the Arabian border areas. The battle itself then followed in the seventh

---

76 According to Martin Noth, "Die Einnahme von Jerusalem im Jahre 597 v. Chr.," *ZDPV* 74 (1958): p. 146 note 35, Nebuchadnezzar was the original subject of the clause.

year (598/7), the eleventh and last year of Jehoiakim, which 2 Kings 24:12 designates wrongly as Nebuchadnezzar's eighth year (or by reckoning from the inclusion of Nebuchadnezzar's year of accession?). The references of the Wiseman Chronicle about this year have been cited above. They speak of the installation of a king favorable to Nebuchadnezzar and the collection of a heavy tribute. The biblical narratives expand this short account by the note that Jehoiakim himself had already died and had been replaced on the throne by his son Jehoiachin. According to Noth, this form of succession had directly occasioned the speedy intervention of Nebuchadnezzar.[77] In place of Jehoiachin Nebuchadnezzar set in Jerusalem Mattaniah, the king's uncle and the third son of Josiah, who took the throne name Zedekiah. The tribute paid included some of the temple utensils, which had originated in Solomon's time, as well as treasures from the royal palace (2 Kings 24:13). The whole event deeply grieved the population of Jerusalem (Jer 27f). Unmentioned in the Chronicle of the Babylonian king, but referred to in 2 Kings 24:14–16, is the deportation not only of Jehoiachin (hence the lament of 19) and his mother and his wives, but also of a not inconsiderable number of representatives of the classes who were politically and economically important in Jerusalem. Ezek 17:13bβ raises the possibility that they were deported to the east in the status of hostages. This could actually explain the fact that they are not mentioned in the Wiseman Chronicle.[78] The number of those deported is given in 2 Kings 24:14 (in a secondary addition?) as 10,000. 2 Kings 24:16, however, gives this differently as 7,000 warriors and 1000 craftsmen and smiths, and this points to a slightly smaller number. Against this, however, we have in Jer 52:28, in a note that is above suspicion, the very much smaller number of 3023 "Judaeans." Are we to add to this the men of Jerusalem, who alone are mentioned in 2 Kings 24? Or are we to regard this as the total number of those deported?[79]

The book of Ezekiel makes some references to the settlement of those deported in the year 597 to which Ezekiel, who came from a priestly family, belonged. These will be dealt with later in connection with the person of the prophet. What we can learn about the treatment of Jehoiachin personally is particularly important. The archaeological finds from Babylon and Palestine, which show that even in the decades before his release from imprisonment at the accession of Amel-Marduk 561 B.C. (2 Kings 25:27–30) he was not denied royal status, are dealt with in detail.[80] It follows from this (while it cannot be perceived from the brief notices of the Babylonian Chronicle) that Zedekiah took up a kind of governorship and was deputy of the legitimate king. How far we should see behind this a skillful calculation by the Babylonian king, who could then play off Jehoiachin against Zedekiah at any time, may be left open.[81] In any case the fact that the book of Ezekiel never reckons from the reign of Zedekiah, but throughout according to the era of Jehoiachin, receives from this a valuable illumination.

As important, however, is the fact that the position of those who remained in the land, if those deported really all had the status of hostages (see above) thereby falls into a peculiar uncertainty. Should they accept the events of 597 as definitive and enter fully into the new situation of the kingship of Zedekiah? Or should they merely acknowledge inwardly the provisional situation and look beyond this to the time when it would cease? The struggle between these two views determines the whole period of Zedekiah's reign with its disastrous outcome. Against those groups who were determined upon the reversal of the situation brought about in 597 B.C. stood other voices who urged the acceptance of the disaster which had come upon the people as a blow from Yahweh's hand. They urged obedient submission to it, until Yahweh was pleased to heal the wound. Jeremiah, who, since 605 had proclaimed the coming of Nebuchadnezzar as Yahweh's

---

77   Noth, "Einnahme."

78   See further the details on pp. 365f.

79   See further, besides Noth, "Einnahme," Enno Janssen, *Juda in der Exilszeit*, FRLANT NF 51 (Göttingen: Vandenhoeck & Ruprecht, 1956), 25–39.

80   See pp. 114f.

81   A. Malamat, "Jeremiah and the Last Two Kings of Judah," *PEQ* 83 (1951): 81–87.

decree and had preached this message without change in the following years, was the strongest proponent of this latter view. Ezekiel also, although caught up himself in the deportation, stood with the same undeviating firmness for this view.

It was inevitable that these basic attitudes should be carried over into concrete political policy. The groups who were committed to the restoration of Jehoiachin's kingship must have been forced by their innermost inclination into an anti-Babylonian policy. There were, further, not lacking among Judah's neighbors powers which longed for the removal of the Babylonian yoke. Above all the Egyptians presented themselves continually as instigators with their promises of help in the background. Those men, however, who saw in Nebuchadnezzar's intervention and the catastrophe of Jehoiachin's deportation Yahweh's hand at work in judgement were appealing for loyal submission to Nebuchadnezzar; i.e. seen from the outside they appeared as representatives of a pro-Babylonian, and sharply anti-Egyptian, policy.

These questions dominated the period of Zedekiah's reign. The picture of this era can be reconstructed in its major features with the help of narratives from the books of Jeremiah and Ezekiel, in combination with the references of the Wiseman Chronicle, the parts of which that are so far known unfortunately break off in the eleventh year of Nebuchadnezzar (594/3). Jer 27, the dating of which in v1 is to be corrected in accordance with 28:1aβ, shows that in the fourth year of Zedekiah emissaries from Edom, Moab, Ammon, Tyre and Sidon came to Jerusalem. The theme of their deliberations was the planned revolt against Babylon. Jeremiah opposed them, with a yoke upon his neck, with the intention of commanding a halt to such plans. Jer 28 shows further how the prophet, with this unmistakeable summons to submission under the yoke of Nebuchadnezzar, encountered in the temple, in the midst of his own people, the opposition of other prophets, who held a view of the future clearly supported by the sympathy of the general public, "In two years all the temple utensils which Nebuchadnezzar, the king of Babylon, took away from this place and brought to Babylon will be returned, and Jehoiachin, the son of Jehoiakim, the king of Judah, and all the population of Judah deported to Babylon will return to this place" (Jer 28:3–4). All of this was not merely formulated as a political prognosis, but as an authoritative saying of Yahweh's which takes a clearly anti-Babylonian turn: "I have broken (perfect) the yoke of the king of Babylon. I will bring back . . . I will break (imperfect) the yoke of the king of Babylon" (Jer 28:2–4). In this fourth year of Zedekiah there was a wave of expectation of liberation sweeping Jerusalem. The Wiseman Chronicle clarifies very usefully the political background of this year of conspiracy of the Palestinian—Phoenician powers. It shows that Nebuchadnezzar, who had appeared again in the west in the first year of Zedekiah, was in his second year (= Nebuchadnezzar's ninth year) preoccupied with battles against Elam on the eastern border of his kingdom and was concerned in his tenth year with a revolt among his own troops in Babylon. When we then read again of campaigns into Hatti-land for the end of his tenth and his eleventh years, these clearly have the aim of restoring his shattered authority in these western territories. His eleventh year corresponds to the fourth year of Zedekiah, which, according to Jer 27f, saw the unrest in Jerusalem. It appears that Nebuchadnezzar in the outcome of things regained a firm hand in the west. The mission to Babylon in the fourth year of Zedekiah, in which according to Jer 51:59 the king himself participated, must probably have had to do with dispelling the suspicion that had (justifiably) been aroused in Babylon and have contained a fresh declaration of loyalty by Zedekiah.[82]

We cannot make out with certainty whether the letter of Jeremiah to the exiles of 597 (Jer 29:1ff) was written in connection with the events of the fourth year of Zedekiah. In this letter Jeremiah appeals to the exiles to bid a final farewell to the provisional nature of their position (and the anti-Babylonian attitudes associated with it) and to adjust themselves to a long stay in Babylon. With all clarity he thereby opposed the prophetic message which had become current among the exiles, which promised a speedy return. The angry reaction of spokesman for the exiles, who

---

82   But cf. Wilhelm Rudolph, *Jeremia*, HAT 1, 12 (Tübingen: Mohr [Siebeck], [3]1968), 317.

demanded of the chief priest in Jerusalem the arrest and punishment of Jeremiah, shows how little the exiles were prepared to see themselves under the judgement of Yahweh.

In the year after the stirring events of Jer. 27f (and 29?) the call of Ezekiel to be a prophet among the exiles took place (1:1f).

Unfortunately it is not possible to follow exactly the movements in Jerusalem and among the exiles between the fourth and the ninth years of Zedekiah. Does the visit of the elders of Judah, which called forth the great vision of the sin and judgement upon the Jerusalem temple in his sixth year (chs. 8–11) and the reply to a further visit in the seventh year (20:1ff) by the proclamation of Israel's sinful history, indicate new waves of hope among the exiles? Cf. possibly the undated piece 14:1–11.

It is clear in any case that the internal strife in Jerusalem, with which the king Zedekiah was incompetent to cope, led finally to defection from Nebuchadnezzar and the withholding of tribute. On the 10th day of the 10th month of Zedekiah's ninth year (2 Kings 25:1; Ezek 24:1) Nebuchadnezzar stood at the gates of Jerusalem.[83] That Egypt had a hand in this revolt is clear from the numerous oracles of Ezekiel against Egypt from the tenth to the twelfth years of Jehoiachin's (=Zedekiah's) reign in Ez 29–32. It is further expressly attested by the account of Jer 37:5, according to which, during the siege of the city, an Egyptian task force sent by the Pharaoh Hophra-Apries (588–570), who is mentioned by name in Jer 44:30, advanced towards the city and compelled the Babylonians to lift the siege temporarily. Cf. Jer 34:21f. Isaiah's reference to Egypt as a reed which, if a man leans on it, will break and pierce his hand (Is 36:6), which is cited in Ezek 29:7, proved relevant again at this time. Egypt had no real power to help. The arm of the Pharaoh was broken beyond healing, as Ezek 30:21,proclaims. Ezek 21:23ff, which reflects the advance of the Babylonian army from the viewpoint of the exiles, shows further that the Ammonites were also implicated in the defection so that Nebuchadnezzar could consider whether his first blow should be against Rabbath Ammon or Jerusalem.

In Ezek 17 we can see further the sharpness with which the prophet regarded the seduction by Egypt which led to the defection from Babylonian suzerainty as a breach of an oath sworn before Yahweh.

The fate of Jerusalem was accomplished in the ensuing events with an inner logic. The city, ravaged by famine (Ezek 4:9–11; also 5:10) was ready for assault on the 9th day of the 4th month of Zedekiah's eleventh year (2 Kings 25:3f).[84] King Zedekiah accompanied by some of his troops fled into the Jordan valley, but was there overtaken by pursuing forces and sentenced with his sons in Nebuchadnezzar's headquarters at Ribla (2 Kings 25:6f). In the elaboration of Ezek 12:1–16 the horror of these events is echoed.[85] A mere month later, after waiting for instructions from Nebuchadnezzar, the city and the temple were reduced to ashes on the 7th day of the 5th month (according to Parker-Dubberstein—August 25, 587). According to Jer 52:29 a further 832 persons were deported eastwards in this year, the eighteenth year of Nebuchadnezzar (587/6), from the population of Jerusalem which had been decimated by famine, the ravages of war and executions (2 Kings 25:18–21). Whether they were settled in the same areas as those deported in 597, and therefore in Tel Abib (Ezek 3:15), is not stated. We cannot therefore decide whether the places of exile mentioned in the lists of those who returned in Ezra 2:59 (Neh 7:61) are to be ascribed to the first or second deportations, or are to be applied to both. Jer 40f tells how a last attempt of the Babylonians to try once again with an independent administration in Judah under Gedaliah, the grandson of Shaphan, the chancellor in the time of Josiah's reform, failed. No echo of this latter event is to be found in the book of Ezekiel.

Unfortunately all further historical information about the life of those deported ceases, as also does that regarding the life of those remaining in the land. That Jer 52:30 notes for the twenty-third year of Nebuchadnezzar (582/1) a further group of deportees of 745 Judeans suggests that there occurred again in this year a further attempt at independence on the part of those in the land. The connection of this deportation with the Gedaliah episode, is however excluded by the dates

---

83 See pp. 498–499, where instead of December 17, 589, we must correct, according to Parker-Dubberstein, to January 15, 588.

84 See p. 175.

85 See pp. 273f.

given in Jer 40 f.

From Josephus we have an account that for thirteen years Nebuchadnezzar then besieged the city of Tyre, under its King Ithobaal, which is mentioned in Jer 27 among the conspirators against Babylon. Considerations regarding the date of this event and the result of this siege, which occasioned the latest of all Ezekiel's dated oracles in 29:17–21, are set out in the commentary there.

The situation is not much better with the sparse accounts by Josephus which deal with the further undertakings of Nebuchadnezzar against Egypt, the great enemy which always lay in the background. A conquest of Egypt, such as Ezekiel's oracles against Egypt lead us to expect, did in any case not materialize. We can only hope that further finds of a similar nature to the Wiseman Chronicle will, in the future, improve our knowledge of this dark period of history.

Also in regard to the fate of the smaller nations which bordered on Israel in Palestine, with which Ezek 25 (and 35) deal, we cannot go beyond conjectures. Thus Noth conjectures, on the basis of Josephus, *Antiquities* X:9, 7, that Moab and Ammon lost their national independence five years after the fall of Jerusalem.[86] Nothing at all can be made out about Edom. The end of the remnants of Philistine independence also remains obscure. Under Darius the Philistine territory belonged to the fifth satrapy of the Persian Empire (Herodotus III:91).

4. The Personality of Ezekiel

The correctness of the reference that Ezekiel, the son of an unknown man named Busi was a priest (1:3), or at least the son of a priest, need not be doubted.[87] His interest in the temple, his knowledge of sacral ordinances, as well as the closeness of his language to that of the Code of Holiness and the Priestly Document (cf. §6), provide sufficient external support for this.

Thus, as the member of an influential family in Jerusalem, he was deported in 597 B.C. 3:15 states that he lived in a settlement of the exiles. Its name, Tel Abib, meaning "a mound of ruins from the time of the flood," points to a location which had once been abandoned and which had then subsequently been assigned as a settlement.[88] About its position all we can make out is that it must be sought by the "River Chebar" (נְהַר כְּבָר) (1:1, 3; 3:15, 23; 10:15, 22; 43:3), the "Grand Canal(?)," probably the *šaṭṭ en-nîl*, not far from the city of Nippur.[89] By this canal, possibly at the place of prayer used by the exiles settled here, Ezekiel was overtaken by the manifestation of Yahweh and called to become a prophet.

From the book we can make out very little of his personal circumstances. According to 24:15ff he was married and lost his wife by her sudden death, roughly at the time in 587 B.C. when Jerusalem fell to the armies besieging it and lost its existence and honor. The situation, which is recorded on three occasions, that he was sitting in his house and received a visit from the elders of Judah (8:1), or Israel (14:1; 20:1), who expected to receive through him a word from God, gives the impression of being stereotyped and already has its counterpart in the narratives of Elisha's disciples (2 Kings 4:38; 6:1, and especially 6:32). Also the "survivor" of 33:21f must have visited Ezekiel, who had been unable to speak, in his house. Also mentioned in 33:30–33 is the visit of the people, who came to the prophet in order to hear him proclaim a divine word, but which they then (after 587) regarded as a purely aesthetic enjoyment. The stereotyped manner of speech appears to be dropped in 3:24. When the prophet is commanded here to shut himself up in his house, we may ask whether this shows something of a prophetic hermitage.[90] Otherwise the book of Ezekiel avoids any description of outward circumstances. Only in the visionary descriptions do we see the prophet moving in external realm: through the temple area in Jerusalem (chs. 8–11, 40ff), through the field full of dead bones (37:1ff), into the plain where God appeared to him (3:22f). Thus at no point do we read of an express confrontation with his Babylonian surroundings.

The information that Ezekiel was put to death in Babylon by the prince of the people, since the prophet blamed him for his idolatry, lacks any support in the tradition and is in itself improbable.[91] The grave of the prophet is venerated today in *kifil*, south of ancient

---

86   Martin Noth, *The History of Israel*, tr. Stanley God-
      man (New York: Harper & Row, ²1960), 292f.

87   See p. 111.

88   See p. 139.

89   See pp. 111f.

90   See p. 159.

Babylon.[92]

Sparse as the references to the outward circumstances of the prophet's life are, there is a confusing mobility in what is told of his life and suffering on account of his divine message. The elements of vision and of drastic symbolic actions, which must be dealt with more fully where the forms of the prophetic messsage are to be discussed, appear very much more strongly in Ezekiel than in the other great writing prophets. Clapping the hands (6:11; 21:19), stamping the feet (6:11), the performance of actions the outward accomplishment of which is often hardly conceivable, and above all the dramatic endurance of translation to Jerusalem and other places and long-range vision, as well as bodily paralysis and inability to speak, give to this prophet a strangeness of psychic experience, which has repeatedly given offense.

Thus, even before the more particularly critical analysis of the book of Ezekiel and the questioning of its origin from a prophet in exile had begun, there were not lacking interpretations which endeavored to understand by the categories of modern medicine the detailed forms of expression of Ezekiel's prophecy as pathological phenomena. A. Klostermann attempted to rescue the true inspired humanity of the prophet.[93] He finds in Ezek 3–24 the diary of a sick person, over against which in chs. 33–48 the utterances of the person when recovered, are to be found. Already chs. 2f, the narrative of eating the scroll, show traces of sick feelings in his throat. For seven days afterwards he was unable to speak. The vision 3:22ff shows clearly that his place of work was the sick room. According to 4:4ff for 390 days he lay down "on his right side, half-paralysed," followed by a 40 day period of anesthesia on his left side.[94] The features of groaning and handclapping which are mentioned later also belong to this picture of illness. His wife's death leads to his complete loss of speech. He is healed only at the arrival of the messenger with the account of the fall of Jerusalem. Thus 33:21f form the turning point in the physical progress of the prophet, which in general is to be diagnosed as catalepsy. However, behind the sickness we must "recognize an idea, implanted in his soul by God, as the effective cause."[95]

In a somewhat broader framework B. Baentsch sets out "pathological features in Israel's prophecy" and therewith regards Ezekiel as a figure in whom such features are to be found particularly frequently.[96] He comes to the following conclusion: "These actions, in all their details, are so precisely calculated, and directed to their purpose, that we cannot speak here of a mental disturbance."[97] Hölscher sought to understand the abnormal phenomena in prophecy on the basis of ecstasy.[98] H. W. Hines sought to understand the prophetic experience under the catchword of mysticism, concerning himself in detail with the experience of Ezekiel.[99] E. C. Browne referred the prophet directly to the sphere of psychological illness. He endeavors to understand the various traits of illness which appear in the symbolic actions by Freudian categories, but also discerns directly schizophrenic features.[100] K. Jaspers also asserted this latter diagnosis. In the

91 For this information, which is found in the pseudo-Epiphanian *Vita* and in the *Menologium* of the emperor Basilius II (976–1025), see Wilhelm Neuss, *Das Buch Ezekiel in Theologie und Kunst bis zum Ende des XII. Jahrhunderts*, Beiträge zur Geschichte des alten Mönchtums und des Benediktinerordens 1-2 (Münster: Aschendorff, 1912), 87 note 2.

92 Joachim Jeremias, *Heiligengräber in Jesu Umwelt* (*Mt. 23, 29; Lk. 11, 47*) (Göttingen: Vandenhoeck & Ruprecht, 1958), 112f. Also M. J. bin Gorion, *Der Born Judas* 5 (Leipzig: Insel, 1921), 41ff.

93 A. Klostermann, "Ezekiel. Ein Beitrag zu besserer Würdigung seiner Person und seiner Schrift," *ThStKr* 50 (1877): 391–439. This essay includes a polemical attack against regarding Ezekiel as a decayed and dying form of true prophecy, as in Bernhard Duhm, *Die Theologie der Propheten als Grundlage*

für die innere Entwicklungsgeschichte der israelitischen Religion (Bonn, 1875), where Ezekiel appears as a cold dogmatician and the father of a religion of law.

94 Klostermann, "Ezekiel," 422.

95 Klostermann, "Ezekiel," 439.

96 B. Baentsch, "Pathologischer Züge in Israels Prophetentum," *ZWTh* 50 (1908): 52–81.

97 Baentsch, "Pathologischer," 79f.

98 Hölscher, *Profeten*.

99 Herbert W. Hines, "The Prophet as Mystic," *AJSL* 40 (1923): 37–41.

100 Edwin C. Broome, Jr., "Ezekiel's Abormal Personality," *JBL* 65 (1946): 277–292.

sequence of the actions and words of Ezekiel he sees the typical course of a process of schizophrenia: from an initial phase of disturbance, in which visions and colorful poems are given, it passes over, as Jaspers believes he can demonstrate by the dating of Ezekiel's oracles, into a later phase of relaxing of the disturbance, which is marked by greater calm and the detailed plans of the coming temple and its organization (chs. 40–48).[101]

In any attempt to interpret the personality of Ezekiel and his mental structure two basic facts must be set before all others. It is first of all to be noted that the book has undergone a considerable later editing and, in its present form, cannot simply be derived from the figure of the prophet himself. This is true in a special measure for the evaluation of Ezek 40–48. But it is also true for the call vision in which, for example, the editorial reworking concerning the eyes on the wheels cannot be regarded as evidence for a nightmare of the prophet in which the eyes pursue him and stare at him.[102] It is true also for the symbolic actions where, in 4:4–8, an element subsequently added to the composition of three signs, the different reckoning of the time spent lying on the right and left sides, has certainly only been added later.[103] The interpretation in regard to the prophet himself must keep soberly to the results worked out in a critical analysis.

To this we must add as a second point the fact that already the basic text of the visions and symbolic actions shows a strongly stylized form. It is certainly not appropriate to regard and read it simply as a description of a biographical situation. The visions and symbolic actions are undoubtedly set out in regard to the message to be heard and seen in them. They are stylized in a reflective way so that the underlying experience and action is often no longer clearly recoverable. Difficulties are just as much present in the symbolic actions of Ezekiel as they are in the reconstruction of the "biography" of Hosea in the history of his marriage.[104]

The biographical element is repeatedly integrated into kerygmatic considerations and by this estranged from its customary context. Thus it is not to be denied in chs. 40ff (basic text) that the apparent experience of a tour through the temple has been stylized out of an underlying temple sketchplan. So also the tour through the temple at the time of its sinfulness, with its four stations, has clearly been stylized with the number four as the number of totality. In Ezek 37 the pattern of man's creation in Gen 2:7 determines the division of the vision into two. Any direct evaluation of the situation regarding visions and signs which does not take account of this feature of stylizing in the service of the message is completely lacking.

Yet, for all this, it is still not said that in Ezekiel's visions and symbolic acts we have to do with a pure literary fiction. This interpretation, which was much favored in the pre-critical phase of Ezekiel study—and beyond it—is out of place. Everything which recent study of the prophets has brought to light of the true experiential background of prophecy renders it inappropriate to deny to Ezekiel, the younger contemporary of Jeremiah in whom the submission to the divine power is certainly not to be overlooked, a genuine experience underlying his prophetic preaching. Although the elements of stylizing in Ezekiel are to be found very much more strongly than they are with Jeremiah, yet we cannot put Ezekiel on the same level with the much later apocalyptists, with whom the suspicion of literary fiction and a concentration on the scholarly expositions of older traditions (cf. Dan 9) is very much more justified.[105]

What then, allowing for this double caution, are we to make of the distinctive character of Ezekiel? We shall still have to come to some statement about this, even allowing for this recognition that Ezekiel's personality is hidden by stylized forms and traditions more deeply than any other of the great prophetic figures.

In Ezekiel's prophecy we are first of all struck by the

---

101 K. Jaspers, "Der Prophet Ezechiel. Ein pathographische Studie" in *Arbeiten zur Psychiatrie, Neurologie und ihren Grenzgebieten* (1947). See also Dieckhoff, "Der Prophet Ezekiel," *Z Rel Psych* 1 (1908): 193–206; Kelvin van Nuys, "Evaluating the Pathological in Prophetic Experience (particularly in Ezekiel)," *JBR* 21 (1953):244–251.
102 Thus Broome, "Personality." See p. 129.
103 See pp. 163–168.
104 As is argued on pp. 156f.
105 See also Geo Widengren, *Literary and Psychological Aspects of the Hebrew Prophets*, UUÅ (Leipzig and Uppsala: Harrassowitz, Lundequists, 1948), 10.

number of broadly formulated visions (1:1–3:15; 3:16a, 22ff; 8–11; 37:1–14; 40–48). Visionary experiences are also to be found in earlier written prophecy (Am 7:1–8; 8:1–2; 9:1–4; Is 6; Jer 4:23–26; 24:1–10). The distinctive feature of Ezekiel's visions lies in the fact that the prophet himself is, in large measure, active and shares strongly in the event. We are at once reminded of Amos when Ezekiel, like the former in his first two visions (Am 7:2, 5), bursts out to Yahweh with a cry of intercession for his people (9:8; 11:13). Or of Isaiah, when in a vision Yahweh, in handing over the scroll, deals with the prophet in a similar way to that in which he acted towards Isaiah through the seraphim. However, it goes beyond this when Ezekiel himself, after he has expressly been warned to be obedient (2:8), eats the scroll offered to him (3:2f). Similarly when, in a vision he is transported by the spirit, or by Yahweh's hand (3:12–15; 8:3f; 37:1; 40:1–3), sees events at a great distance,[106] or walks through the old (ch. 8) or the new temple (40ff), or through a field of dead men's bones (37:2), in order to prophesy there (11:4; 37:4, 9) and could even bring about the death of a man through his prophesying (11:13), and another time bring the dead back to life (37:7f, 10).[107]

To this drama, in which the prophet himself shares, and in which he not only "sees" the vision, but acts within it, we must add the prominence given to the prophet's symbolic actions and gestures. Symbolic actions, in which the preached message may itself be anticipated as an event by being symbolically enacted beforehand, is also found in earlier prophecy, both before Amos, and then from Hosea through Isaiah to Jeremiah.[108] In Ezekiel we find such actions much more frequently than in Jeremiah. Further, we find with

him, as something distinctive, gestures such as the specific turning of the prophet's face when he prophesies,[109] clapping the hands and stamping the feet (21:22; 22:13 also said of Yahweh).

All this betrays an unusually strong, and even physical, participation of the prophet in the experience of receiving his message in vision and word. This "auto-dramatic" element in Ezekiel can further be seen in a distinctive feature which is not otherwise found in any prophet. We several times find that a metaphor which he has derived from elsewhere is transformed in Ezekiel's prophetic experience into a dramatic reality. In one of Jeremiah's confessions (15:16) in a metaphorical statement we read: "Thy words were found, and I ate them, and thy words became to me a joy." In Ezekiel's experience this saying is changed into an event which occurs at his call: he eats the scroll given to him by Yahweh, containing the divine message, and it becomes in his mouth as sweet as honey.[110] In Is 7:20 we have the threat of Yahweh that he, "will shave with a razor that is hired beyond the river the hair of the head and body, and will also cut off the beard"—a bold metaphor for the Assyrians, the rod of the divine anger, brought from Mesopotamia, with which Yahweh will chastise Judah. In the symbolic action recounted in Ezek 5:1f this metaphor takes on a dramatic reality: at Yahweh's command Ezekiel is to cut off his hair with a razor in order to proclaim in this act of destruction, in which his hair is divided into three parts, the coming destruction of the inhabitants of Jerusalem.[111] In 37:11 the lament of the stricken people is expressed: "our bones are dried up, our hope is destroyed, we are cut off." For the third time we find here that the metaphor at the beginning of this lament, which has its analogies in other metaphorical usage of the Old Testament, takes

---

106 This is already found in 2 Kings 5:26. See below p. 42.

107 The particular linguistic stylizing of these events will be dealt with further in connection with the question of the form of the prophetic word. We are concerned here simply with the strikingly dramatic emphasis which characterizes the visionary experiences of the prophet, however they are stylized in detail.

108 The material is to be found in Georg Fohrer, *Die symbolischen Handlungen der Propheten*, ATANT 54 (Zürich: Zwingli, ²1968).

109 For the eight references see p. 182.

110 See pp. 136f.

111 See p. 172.

on a dramatic reality—here again in connection with a visionary experience. Ezekiel sees a field full of dead men's bones and preaches his messages towards it.[112]

The number of these examples, which are clear and quite independent of each other, supports the view that Ezekiel was a prophet of particular sensitivity and dramatic power, for whom a metaphor could become a fully experienced event, however strange in itself this might be. In this connection we can perhaps also mention in Ezekiel a preference for a broad elaboration of particular themes which earlier prophets touch upon. We may note how fully, and sometimes even drastically, the pictures of the Last Day (7), of the Shepherd (34), of the Unfaithful Wife (16), and of the two unfaithful sisters (23) are elaborated with unusual visionary power, right down to small details.

To this sensitivity also belong the features which have been regarded in the prophet as features of a sick constitution: shocked dumbness throughout the whole week which followed his call (3:15), and also later at least one occasion of loss of speech, which in the redaction of the book has been made a sign of the whole early preaching period of the prophet (3:26f; 24:25–27; 33:21f).[113] Also the immobility which overcame the prophet at his wife's death (24:15ff) comes into this picture.

We cannot determine with certainty what stands behind the statement of 3:25, in which mention is made of Ezekiel's being bound with cords, probably the words of the prophet's disciples. The possibility is not to be ruled out that here reference is made to attacks by those close to the prophet, even though the book of the prophet says nothing further about such hostility. In the continuation in 4:8 this binding, of which Yahweh is now the subject, relates clearly to what is said in the addition in 4:4–7. There appears here, in a section that has been added later, a period of the prophet's being bound which can best be understood as being bound through illness.[114] Such physical weakness appears also in the strange command to the prophet to eat his bread with quaking and to drink his water with trembling (12:18). What is imposed upon the prophet as a bodily weakness becomes here an element of his message,[115] just as in 24:15ff his paralysis at the death of his wife was.[116]

All these traits of physical weakness, which were necessary in the senses of a man who was overwhelmed by images and visions up to the point of actual physical emotional participation, are scarcely sufficient for arriving at a specific diagnosis of illness for the prophet, on the basis of a key of "normal illness" current in medicine. This is even less so since otherwise with Ezekiel it has repeatedly been affirmed that his message, even in its frightening harshness, possesses a marked clarity of direction. How much all Ezekiel's preaching was determined by the knowledge of the exalted majesty of the Lord who was jealous for his name must be dealt with later. We can find here again, in a special measure, the priest who was familiar with the holiness and majesty of the God who is jealous for his name. All the warm personal features which are so clearly recognizable in Jeremiah, whose spiritual world was molded by the Psalms, fall into the background in Ezekiel, who came from the sphere of worship and exaltation of Yahweh.

There are only a few places at which we can trace in Ezekiel, behind the strong stylizing, the personal experience, and even the pulsebeat of the prophet's immediate feelings. Where, in the face of the impending judgement from God, he breaks out with the horrified cry: "Ah, Lord Yahweh, will you destroy the remnant of Israel, when you pour out your wrath upon Jerusalem" (9:8, cf. 11:13), we can trace, as in the early visions of Amos (7:1ff), the prophet's horror at the inevitability of judgement upon the remnant of Israel. So in 21:11f, where we hear again the prophet's groaning, but only wrapped up in a command from God, we must question whether the direct restraint of the

---

112 See p. 173 to 5:3.

113 See pp. 160, 508.

114 That the reckoning of the periods of Israel's and Judah's sin and punishment and the system of calculation employed with the unnatural lying on each side is a later stylizing is argued on pp. 163–168. There can, however, scarcely be any doubt of the fact of such lying immobile and its interpretation as a symbolic action commanded by Yahweh.

115 See pp. 227f.

116 Cf. further 21:11.

prophet, which we surmise in the personal realm behind his behavior at his wife's death, is discernible behind the cloak of the marked stylizing.[117] We gain the feeling that we can see in the prophet's horrified outcry when he is commanded to eat unclean bread: "Ah, Lord Yahweh, behold, I have never been unclean, and I have never eaten the flesh of dead and torn animals from my youth up till now, and no *piggul*-flesh has entered my mouth" (4:14), the elementary reaction of a person for whom the priestly idea of cleanness was the very element in which he lived. Finally the lament in 21:5: "Ah, Lord Yahweh, they say of me: does he not speak mysterious figures," allows us to see something of the temptation of the prophet, who proclaimed his message in figurative language with the result that he was not understood.

There are only a few passages in which the prophet reveals his personal feelings, even for a moment. As a rule his own feelings are forced into the background in the service of the high task which he fulfilled in the vigorous forms of his prophetic office. We must now go on to deal with the language and form of the prophetic message.

5. The Language and Form of the Prophecies of the Book of Ezekiel

A. Notes on the Vocabulary and Language of the Book of Ezekiel. In his *Hauptprobleme* Fohrer has summarized "Examples for Determining the Age of the Language of the Book of Ezekiel."[118] Even if not all the material adduced has the same power of conviction, the

result to which Fohrer comes is acceptable. Nothing opposes the acceptance of the book's own claim that its language comes from the sixth century B.C.

Even the claim of an unusually strong Aramaic coloring of the language, which we should not expect for the sixth century B.C., must be very limited on closer examination.[119] The excessive exaggeration with which Selle concludes his Halle dissertation does not stand up to examination.[120] It has then been retaken up by E. Kautzsch in its proper proportion.[121] Of the 153 words which Kautzsch examines as Aramaisms, Ezekiel has 16, perhaps 17, examples. Further to the considerations set out by Fohrer[122] we can now point to the study by M. Wagner.[123] Of the total of 371 words which Wagner studies as possible lexical Aramaisms,[124] only 28 are to be found in Ezekiel. In the statistics of individual references Ezekiel with 49 "more or less certain" and 3 "uncertain" Aramaisms, is at first seemingly very markedly distinguishable from Isaiah with 32 (+10), Jeremiah with 22 (+4) and Deutero-Isaiah with 26 (+1).[125] From this comparative table Wagner adduces that, "among the post-exilic [*sic!*] writing prophets only Ezekiel and Joel are notable for greatly increased number of Aramaisms."[126] Thus viewed in the number of words appearing, it emerges that in the 48 chapters of the book of Ezekiel there are 25 (+3) words against the 14 (+8) words of the 39 chapters of Isaiah, which is a scarcely noticeable increase. The overall statistics of occurrences undergoes a certain distortion by the 8 occurrences of בִּנְיָה/בִּנְיָן in Ezek 40–42 and the 9 occurrences of חזה in Ezek 12f

---

117 See pp. 506f.

118 Fohrer, *Hauptprobleme*, 127–134.

119 Such a claim has been raised by Torrey, *Pseudo-Ezekiel*, 84–90.

120 Fridericus Philippus Selle, *De Aramaismis libri Eze-chielis* (Halis Saxonum: Formis Kaemmererianis, 1890): "If I wished to enumerate all [all the Aramaisms], time would run out on me, unless it had been necessary that I write down nearly all the vocabulary of Ezekiel." (Si omnia [scil. omnes Aramaismos] velim enumerare, dies me deficiat, nisi fere totum lexicon Ezechielicum scribi necesse fuerit [47]).

121 Emil Kautzsch, *Die Aramaismen im Alten Testament untersucht*. I. *Lexikalischer Teil* (Halle: Niemeyer, 1902). He concludes in comparison with Isaiah and Jeremiah: "That Ezekiel has been influenced some-

what more strongly (although in no way strikingly) has already been recognized, and is conceivable in consideration of the circumstances of his life" (102).

122 Fohrer, *Hauptprobleme*, 122–127.

123 Max Wagner, *Die lexikalischen und grammatikalischen Aramaismen im alttestamentlichen Hebräisch*, BZAW 96 (Berlin: Töpelmann, 1966).

124 The number 333, which is given on p. 121, is to be emended because of omissions and intervening additions. See p. 17 note 12.

125 Wagner, *Aramaismen*, 140.

126 Wagner, *Aramaismen*, 144.

and 21f. In detail, among the Aramaisms in Ezekiel, the words קֹר[וֹ]בִים, מֶלַח, כחל represent the borrowing of Akkadian vocabulary stock. The words בקר, אַרְיֵה, תְּכֵלֶת, קַנְיָן, מְדִינָה, יְקָר, חֹסֶן, חִידָה, חזה (verb), (?) are already to be found before Ezekiel in Old Testament writings, whilst גְּדוּפָה (5:15 with emended text), כְּתָב, שַׁלְהֶבֶת, מֶלַח, מחא are not to be found previously, but reappear in later writing. Only found in Ezekiel within the Old Testament are חוֹב, חַד אֶת חַד, גֵּבֶל, בִּנְיָה/בִּנְיָן,[127] קרם, קֹר[וֹ]בִים, קְבֹל, פרח, סַרְעַפָּה, מְחִי, כפן, כחל, טעה. Further we must add to this the Aramaized form of writing certain words, which is to be put down to the account of later glossators of the book. So the גֻּבְהָא of 31:5, or the וְאַתּוּקֶיהָא of 41:15. The Aramaic קַיָּם of 13:6 belongs to a later addition.[128]

Beside this there are not lacking in the vocabulary of Ezekiel Babylonisms, mediated by Aramaic. Fohrer adduces 9 examples: כֶּסֶת, כסם, חַשְׁמַל, גֻּלָּב, אֵילָם, אֲנַף, עִזְּבוֹנִים, סוּגַר, סֵמֶל.[129] To these must be added the expression בְּלֵב יַמִּים dependent on a Babylonian form of speech.[130] However, we hardly need to bother with the Gilgamesh Epic for the address of the prophet as בֶּן־אָדָם. The title is fully intelligible from the antithesis אָדָם־אֵל, which is already to be found in Isaiah (31:3).[131] R. Frankena in his Utrecht Inaugural Lecture has particularly pointed to connections between Ezekiel's language and that of the Babylonian Irra-Epic, from which the particular usage of the expressions פרש רֶשֶׁת, הָמוֹן, עשה שְׁפָטִים and שאט can be illuminated by Ezekiel.[132]

Further the language of the book of Ezekiel is noteworthy both in the absence of central terms and verbs of other Old Testament writings as well as by the use of a specific vocabulary, which is not attested in other writings. Without claiming completeness both aspects may be illustrated in the following. It may help the clarity of the presentation when first of all the gaps in Ezekiel's vocabulary usage are noted in confrontation with other Old Testament writings.

At once it is striking that missing in Ezekiel are certain terms of the language of the Psalms, the influence of which on Deutero-Isaiah is particularly strong, and which are not altogether lacking in Isaiah and Jeremiah. We miss תְּהִלָּה "hymn of praise" (the verb הלל is found only in 26:17 in reference to a city famous among men), רִנָּה as also the verb רנן and the verbs עלז, עלע and גיל, which are closely related in meaning, and the nouns derived from them; similarly מִזְמוֹר and its verb. There is similarly lacking the word for "lament, petition" תְּפִלָּה, and הִתְפַּלֵּל, which is related to it (the root פלל is only used in 16:52 in the pi'el with a quite different meaning). We miss in Ezekiel the whole group of words from the root חנן (חֵן, תְּחִנָּה, חַנּוּן, תַּחֲנוּנִים, חֲנִינָה) with the exception of the very general adverb חִנָּם. There is also lacking any positive use of בטח, apart from the adverbial לָבֶטַח. In 29:16 there is an attack on false trust (מִבְטָח) in Egypt, and in 16:15 on the trust (בטח) of the unfaithful wife in her beauty, corresponding to 33:13 against the (false) trust of the righteous man in his righteousness. In this connection we must note the lack of the expressions מַחְסֶה "refuge" (and the verb חסה), צוּר "rock" (which also never appears in its proper meaning), which are at home in the language of trust, as also מָעוֹז, which is only found in a negative usage, expressing in 24:25 and the secondary 30:15 the insecure places of human "protection." The language of "crying out" to God is further missing: שׁוע and צעק are lacking זעק is only used twice (9:8; 11:13) in this way, of the prophet's crying out. In 21:17 and 27:30 it describes the aimless outcry of despair. Apart from the statement about conduct in a lawsuit in 18:8 (מִשְׁפָּט, אֱמֶת יַעֲשֶׂה), the whole family of words deriving from אמן is completely missing (אֱמֶת, אָמֵן, אֱמוּנָה, הֶאֱמִין).[133] Nouns deriving from the root ישע: יֵשַׁע, יְשׁוּעָה, תְּשׁוּעָה never appear in Ezekiel. Nevertheless the verb הוֹשִׁיעַ is three times used to denote saving action, but in a special context (34:22; 36:29; 37:23). It is wholly in line with this that the root צדק, with its derivatives,

---

127 Note a to 18:7 conjectures a reading חַיָּב.
128 See page 293.
129 Fohrer, *Hauptprobleme*, 240.
130 Fohrer, *Hauptprobleme*, 239.
131 See pp. 131f.
132 R. Frankena, *Kanttekeningen van een Assyrioloog bij Ezechiël* (Leiden: Brill, 1965).
133 The אֱמֶת in v 9 is a textual error. See note c.

22

unlike in Deutero-Isaiah, never appears as an expression to describe Yahweh's saving action. The verb גאל, which is likewise important for Deutero-Isaiah, is also completely lacking in Ezekiel, as is the related פדה. Mention is made in a quite institutionalized sense of the אַנְשֵׁי גְאֻלָּתֶךָ (11:15). There are further lacking, not only the verbs האזין and הקשיב, but also יָשָׁר (מֵישָׁרִים) in the description of the righteous man; יָשָׁר in 1:7, 23 is only used in a quite technical sense. It is also a striking fact that the verb ברך "to bless" is totally absent (the noun בְּרָכָה appears in 34:26; 44:30), which is hardly favorable to a connection of the prophet with a covenant festival. Similarly the opposite "to curse" ארר (and אָרוּר), pi'el קלל (nip'al participle נָקֵל in 8:17; hip'il "to despise" 22:7, pilpel "to shake" 21:26) is not found. There is also lacking the word of praise אַשְׁרֵי. אָוֶן appears only once in 11:2. נֵצַח is lacking.

When we compare the vocabulary of Ezekiel with that of pre-exilic prophecy, and especially to that of Hosea and Jeremiah who stand close to Ezekiel, the absence of בַּעַל is noteworthy.

אֲשֵׁרָה מַצֵּבוֹת are only mentioned in 26:11 for Tyre; is also lacking, and even the אֱלִילִים mentioned in Isaiah only appear in the secondary sections of 30:1ff in v13. We also miss the term בגד, popular with Hosea and Jeremiah as a designation of unfaithfulness. Still more striking is the fact, that for the conduct of the people towards God, both אהב "love" (only in 16:33, 36f, 23:5, 9, 22 for "lovers," or the false love of the people), as also רַחֲמִים חֶסֶד (the verb רחם is only found in the late redactional 39:25), and דַּעַת אֱלֹהִים are completely lacking.[134] Mention has been made of the word families אמן and צדק in the comparison with the Psalter.

In what has been said some differentiation in regard to the vocabulary of Deuteronomy has become recognizable. Beside the lack of reference to love for Yahweh and love on his part (אהב, חֶסֶד), the lack of any mention of the fear of God is also striking (ירא 1:22; 2:6; 3:9; 11:8 in other connections). The use of the תּוֹרָה-concept shows nothing of the Deuteronomic expansion into a comprehensive term for law. תּוֹרָה (the verb הוֹרָה is lacking) is used in 7:26; 22:26; 43:11f; 44:5, 24 consistently in its priestly emphasis. The term מִצְוָה, which

is significant for Deuteronomy, is completely missing in Ezekiel, although the verb צוה is used in 9:11; 10:6; 12:7; 24:18; 37:7, consistently for a command of Yahweh. The verb בחר, which is so important for Deuteronomy is only found in Ezekiel in 20:5. We further miss in Ezekiel's vocabulary אוה (תַּאֲוָה), מְנוּחָה, נסה.

On the other side Ezekiel is distinguished in its usage of vocabulary from P and H in some things, where otherwise so much relationship exists. Thus there are lacking in Ezekiel נדר, לְבֹנָה, אִשֶּׁה, קְטֹר (noun and verb), נזה, עֲצֶרֶת, עֵדָה and עָמִית, עֵדוּת, עֵדָה (עֲצָרָה).

We also find a lack of important concepts of the language of Wisdom, as, for example, בין and all its derivatives, and דַּעַת in use for the "knowledge" of the wise. יסר is found only in 23:48 in a section which certainly does not come from Ezekiel himself. מוּסָר is added secondarily in 5:15; otherwise it is absent. So also כְּסִיל, the word families נָבָל, לִיץ, לֵץ לָצוֹן (a textual error in 13:3), מְזִמָּה—although the term זִמָּה, with a different emphasis, frequently appears—, אֱוִיל אִוֶּלֶת.

From legal language we miss דִּין (verb and noun), ריב (verb, the noun רִיב is only found in later priestly law 44:24).

Further to this we must also note the absence of the expressions יצר, זֵכֶר, דּוֹר, דְּבִיר, בְּלִיַּעַל and its derivatives, עתר, אֱנוֹשׁ, מִלָּה and מלל (35:13 text error), (נָקִי) נקה פעל (פֹּעַל) (verb and noun). God is called אֵל only in the mouth of the king of Tyre (28:2, 9; אֵל־שַׁדַּי in 10:5; 1:24 uses simply שַׁדַּי). Among the predicates of Yahweh we miss the title מֶלֶךְ (used verbally of Yahweh only in 20:33), as also עֶלְיוֹן and צְבָאוֹת (יהוה).

Over against these notable absences there stands the plus of vocabulary peculiar to Ezekiel, which is not found elsewhere. Only in Ezekiel do we find the verbs סחה, נקע, כפן, כסם, כחל, טעה, חתל, חדר, דלח, בתק, שׂשׂא, קרם, קסס, צרב, עוג. Out of more than 130 words found only in Ezekiel, of words used more than once we can particularly note בְּנִיָה/בִּנְיָן, אַתִּיק, אֶלְגָּבִישׁ, אַגַּפִּים, מִכְלוֹל, מְכוּרָה, כֶּסֶת, חִתִּית, חַשְׁמַל, חֶלְאָה, חֲבֹל, זִרְמָה, (עֲנָבִים, סַלּוֹן, מֶשִׁי, מַשְׁטוֹחַ, מָשׁוֹט, מִקְסָם, (מַכְלְלִים), שָׁאָט, רְכֻלָּה, קֶסֶת, צַמֶּרֶת, צוּרָה, פַּתָּחוֹן, פֵּאָרָה, עִזְּבוֹנִים, עֻנָה תָּכְנִית, תַּזְנוּת, שְׁפַתָּיִם.

---

134 In spite of the rich use of the recognition formula. See below.

23

We shall deal later with the reception formula, which appears very prominently in Ezekiel.[135] Characteristic of Ezekiel is the designation of idols as גִּלּוּלִים which is admittedly found outside Ezekiel (39 times) in Lev, Dtn, 1 Kings, 2 Kings, and Jer in isolated references (a total of 9 times).[136] We further note expressions compounded with עָוֹן: מִכְשׁוֹל עָוֹן (7:19; 14:3f, 7; 18:30; 44:12), הַזְכִּיר עָוֹן (21:28f, 29:16), עֵת עֲוֹן קֵץ (21:30, 34; 35:5).

The observations made here, from a concordance, of the vocabulary of the contents of the book of Ezekiel must be carried further in an examination of the traditio-, and literary-critical, setting of Ezekiel's prophecy (§6).

B. The Form of the Book as a Whole. In its overall formation the book is distinguished from other prophetic books in that it is throughout composed in the I-style. The sole text which contradicts this observation (1:3) can be easily recognized as a superscription to the book added later. In 24:24 Ezekiel is mentioned in the third person in a divine speech, which is introduced by the prophet in the first person (24:15, 20). This stylizing, which reappears at its closest in Proto-Zechariah, where only 1:1–6 and the introductory superscriptions 1:7 and 7:1–3 deviate from it, gives to the book of Ezekiel the character of a continuous first person account. A style form, which is used only occasionally in the older prophetic books, is here used continuously for the whole book.[137]

It is to be seen in the sole short narrative passage in 33:21f, which contains no explicit divine word. It appears particularly fully in the broad vision narratives 1:1–3:15 (3:16a, 22ff), 8–11; 37:1–14; 40–48, which, with the exception of 37:1–14 where a date may have fallen out at the beginning, are all dated. However, it also dominates the remaining sections, which, with the exception of ch. 19 are all introduced with the personal narrative form וַיְהִי דְבַר־יהוה אֵלַי.[138] In 14:1 and 20:1 we find a further short description of the situation, to which is added in second place a reference to the date. Such date references are otherwise prefaced to individual sections only within the oracles against foreign nations, once regarding Tyre (26:1), six times regarding Egypt (29:1, 17; 30:20; 31:1; 32:1, 17). In 24:1 the original date appears to have been suppressed. The וַיְהִי דְבַר־יהוה אֵלַי can also occasionally appear a second time within a section (12:8; 17:11; 21:6). First person narrative sections are further found in 12:7, which concerns the performance of a symbolic action, as well as in 24:18–20, where uniquely instead of the usual formula for the receipt of a message, the prophet tells in a narrative saying (imperfect consecutive) to those around him that the word of Yahweh had come to him (perfect).

Beside this, after the first appearance of an autobiographical structure to the whole book of Ezekiel, we must go on to mention a second, opposite feature. It is striking how, throughout the entire book of Ezekiel, the activity is set almost exclusively in the words and actions of Yahweh. Events which are narrated by Ezekiel in the first person are repeatedly regarded as the acts and words of Yahweh upon him, God's creature, who is throughout addressed by Yahweh as בֶּן־אָדָם.[139] This is also the case in 33:21f, where, behind the fall of the city, which is here told by the prophet, Yahweh's action must be seen as the truly decisive reality.

In the vision narratives this does not need to be particularly developed. Here it is already clear that everything that is narrated, even the strongly dramatic involvement of the prophet in the event,[140] is experienced within the overall framework of Yahweh's control. In the sign-actions also, with the exception of the two narratives in 12:1–16 and 24:15ff, in Ezekiel's presentation, everything is subsumed in the word of Yahweh. The performance of the action by the prophet is not described, only Yahweh's word which commands the action.[141] Thus it can happen that the words with which the people question in astonishment the action

---

135 See pp. 37f.
136 See below pp. 186f.
137 As in the visions of Amos (7:1–8; 8:1–12; 9:1–4), the second account of Hosea's marriage (Hos 3), the call of Isaiah (Is 6), also Is 8, and some other passages of Jeremiah (1, 2:1ff; 13:1ff; 16:1ff; 17:19ff; 24).
138 See p. 391.

139 See pp. 131f.
140 To which reference is made on pp.19f.
141 We have also mentioned (pp. 20f) the few cases in which a sign-action (4:14), a vision (9:8; 11:13), or a parable (21:5) come from a spontaneous impulse of the prophet.

of the prophet are also incorporated into a divine word. Yahweh himself communicates to the prophet the reaction and the questions which come to him from the people (12:9; 21:12; 37:18). This is particularly striking in the discourses which are sparked off by sayings which are current among the people: nowhere does the prophet himself tell that these sayings came to him from the people. In every case it is Yahweh himself who informs the prophet of the saying which is current among the people and which the prophet is to answer with God's word. This is further true not only of the conversations which take place within the framework of a vision, where it is quite understandable 8:12; 9:9; 11:3; 37:11), but also in independent sayings in which the prophet answers sayings of the people (12:22, 27; 18:2, 19, 25, 29; 20:32; 33:10, 17, 20, 24; 36:13). Also 11:15, which did not originally belong to the visions of chs. 8–11, must be included here. Naturally this is then also true of the sayings of the nations which are taken up in the oracle against foreign nations (25:3, 8; 26:2; 28:2, 9; 29:3, 9; 35:10, 12; 36:2, also 38:11, 13).

It is to be seen particularly clearly in 33:30–33 how a circumstance which would in Jeremiah have been given the form of a confession in a Psalm-style, is, in Ezekiel, incorporated into a word of Yahweh. Even here, where we are concerned with the suffering of the prophet at the misunderstanding of the men around him, who regard the prophet's word simply as a pleasant love song, we hear nothing of the prophet's private grief. Here also his suffering is subsumed in the divine word, which tells of this suffering and sets against it the unshakable validity of the divine word.[142]

Thus the lamentations which are found extensively throughout Ezekiel are not set out as laments, such as men raise over the circumstances of their suffering and are so regarded in the book of Lamentations.[143] These laments also are always either set in the prophet's mouth by Yahweh (chs. 19; 27; 28:12ff; 32:2ff), or it is said in the framework of a speech by Yahweh that men raise them (26:17ff; 27).

Apart from some legal sections in chs. 40–48 which have their own prehistory, it is not possible in the book

of Ezekiel to remove the stylizing which has been outlined, as a dress that has been put on subsequently, and find beneath it a basic material which has been composed differently. This necessitates the view that, not only behind the book in its present form, but also behind the composition of its individual parts, there stands a definite plan which itself points back to a particular hand. Ezekiel's own hand has given his message this characteristic stamp. The school, whose later work on the book of Ezekiel is not to be overlooked, has formed its additions and later interpretations along the basic line drawn by the prophet himself.

The forms which are recognizable in the individual sections must now further occupy our attention.

C. The Form of Prophetic Speeches. The book of Ezekiel offers no particular difficulties for a primary delineation of its speech units. In the first place the dates mentioned in §2 show where new units begin. As a rule the formula for the coming of an oracle דְּבַר־יהוה אֵלַי וַיְהִי is connected with the dates, where no vision is introduced, and no short account of what happened follows as in 33:21. This formula, even where no date follows, delineates the introduction of a new speech unit, which is thereby marked out as possessing the character of an event.[144] In a few sections this formula is found a second time within the same speech unit. Thus in 12:8 the divine interpretation of the symbolic action performed by the prophet in vv 1–7 occurs on the following day as a second event besides the event of the previous day. In 17:11 and 21:6 it is the interpretation of an earlier figurative speech in 17:10 and 21:1–5 which is explained to the prophet and his hearers as a further event.

Only in two references are the two introductory features mentioned missing in sections which, by their content and form, clearly stand out as independent entities from what precedes: so at the introduction of the lament of ch. 19, which has no connection with the preceding exposition of ch. 18,[145] and again in the vision of 37:1–14, which in the present text is undated and which doubtless represents a section separate from ch. 36.[146]

With the criteria mentioned the book of Ezekiel

---

142 Cf. 21:1–12, pp. 421f.
143 For קינה see below.
144 See pp. 144f.

145 See, however, pp. 391f and 397.
146 But see note b to 37:1.

divides up into fifty speech units, which must be taken into account within the exegesis. That there are units of very varied length raised difficulties for Jerome, who would have liked to divide his exposition into similar sections.[147] What a difference there is between the short section of two verses in 33:21f and the great vision extending through nine chapters of 40–48!

By way of an appendix we must add here that, in addition to the fifty units to which the following commentary keeps, by use of the criteria mentioned basically two further sections are to be added which appear now as parts of the great temple vision of chs. 8–11. Here 11:1–13, although now built into the context of chs. 8–11, is striking as an independent vision. Also 11:14–21, which is introduced by its own formula for the coming of an oracle, has nothing to do in form and content with the vision of chs. 8–11. Thus in all we could list fifty-two units.

We must now immediately add that the units found by use of the clear criteria mentioned cannot be regarded as separate entities, complete in themselves, which derive from one single occasion. Rather a great number of them show on closer examination that they have had their own history of development and tradition. Not only can we see at many points how glosses and interpretative additions have been introduced into many texts (in some sections whole layers of subsequent elaboration can be separated off, as in chs. 1; 10; 12:1–16 and elsewhere), but we can also see how individual sayings in their basic content have already undergone a continuing elaboration and fuller unfolding of the theme dealt with, sometimes by the prophet himself.

An external help towards a more penetrating analysis of the sections, behind which such a process of growth lies hidden, is to be found in the formulaic material of the prophetic sayings. Its consideration can occasionally (but by no means always) point to seams and gaps in the text. Beside the addressing of the prophet as son of man, which we have already mentioned, there belongs to this formulaic material the introductory messenger formula, which shows that he knew himself to be someone sent, which derived from the receiving of a message.[148] To this there also belongs the formula for a divine saying, which possibly stems from the old utterances of seers, and which appears eighty-five times in the book of Ezekiel, both as context-formula and as concluding formula for a unit.[149] A help towards recognizing the structure is also to be found in the affirmatory oath formula, found sixteen times in the mouth of Yahweh, and which thirteen times is emphasized (if we also reckon 20:3 to this, fourteen times) by the formula for a divine saying.[150] This formulation, which appears twice in Jeremiah and once each in Deutero-Isaiah and Zephaniah, is particularly important for Ezekiel. The same is true of the formula הִנְנִי אֶל (עַל) which introduces a threat (once in 36:9 a promise also). Against the fourteen occurrences of this formula in Ezekiel stand two in Nahum and six in Jeremiah.[151] The sign of the conclusion of a speech section is the formula for the conclusion of a divine saying אֲנִי יהוה דִּבַּרְתִּי which is particularly characteristic of Ezekiel

147 "What do I do when some prophecies are short, others long: so that often by necessity we are compelled both to compress many into one section, and to divide one into many?" ("Quid faciam cum aliae prophetiae breves sint aliae longae: ut saepe necessitate cogamur et plures in unum librum coarctare, et unam in multos dividere?" [MPL xxv 107, in the introduction of the 4th book]).

148 See p. 133 and for the divine names Excursus 1.

149 See Rolf Rendtorff, "Zum Gebrauch der Formel *neʾum jahwe* im Jeremiabuch," *ZAW* 66 (1954): 27–37, and Friedrich Baumgärtel, "Die Formel *neʾum jahwe*," *ZAW* 73 (1961): 277–290.

150 See p. 176 to 5:11. Also, Baumgärtel, "Formel."

151 According to Paul Humbert, "Die Herausforderungsformel 'hinnenî êlékà'," *ZAW* 51 (1933): 101–108, we can see in this a formula of summons to a duel. K. von Rabenau, "Das prophetische Zukunftswort im Buch Hesekiel" in *Studien zur Theologie der alttestamentlichen Überlieferungen*, ed. R. Rendtorff and K. Koch (Neukirchen–Vluyn: Neukirchener, 1961), 61–80, speaks more cautiously of a formula of encounter.

and which appears six times asyndetically, twice introduced by כִּי and three times with the omission of the name of Yahweh. That this very speech of Yahweh has power to bring about its realization as is already shown in the overall structure of the book[152] is brought out by the prophet in the lengthening of this formula to: "I, Yahweh, have spoken it, and I will do it" which occurs three times.[153]

After these preliminary remarks regarding the help towards a further analysis of the larger complexes, we must deal now with the most important forms of the prophetic preaching in the book of Ezekiel and outline their formal characteristics.

Every reader is immediately struck by the visions which the prophet describes. In all there are four fully elaborated visions (1:1–3:15; 8–11; 37:1–14; 40–48). To these we must add the briefly described introduction to the complex 3:16a, 22–5:17, which is surrounded by many problems, and the scene 11:1–13, which has been subsequently added to the great vision. The visions are usually introduced by a quite stereotyped vocabulary. By the intervention of "Yahweh's hand" upon the prophet— 8:1 speaks even more harshly of the hand of Yahweh "falling" upon the prophet (said in 11:5 of the spirit)—he is removed from the everyday world and introduced into the vision given by Yahweh. So 1:3b; (3:14); 3:22; 8:1; 37:1; 40:1. In 11:1, where according to the present context the prophet is already experiencing a divine vision, this introduction is lacking. We have already spoken of the particularly mobile character of Ezekiel's visions. These experiences of ecstatic transportation are described in the visions as the working of the spirit.[154] Thus the prophet is carried off by the spirit from the place at which the manifestation of the divine glory came to him (3:12, 14). The spirit takes him from his abode in exile to Jerusalem, so that he can see the abominations in the temple (8:3). According to 11:24 it brings him back again from there. In 11:1 also, in the visionary element which is intro-

duced, the spirit brings him to the East Gate of the temple. He is brought "in the spirit of Yahweh" into the field full of dead bones (37:1). In 40:1 there is no mention of the spirit in the transportation to Jerusalem. First in 43:5 is this mentioned as the moving force in the removal into the inner court. The unusual connection of the receiving of the spirit and the word in 11:5 cannot be original.[155] The mention of "seeing," which we immediately expect in a vision, appears very much in the background, although in detail everything which the prophet saw is introduced with the typical וָאֶרְאֶה (רָאִיתִי) וְהִנֵּה. מַרְאוֹת אֱלֹהִים are only mentioned in 1:1; 8:3; 40:2, simply מַרְאֶה in 11:24. It is particularly unusual that in 8:3, alongside the spirit as the power which transports the prophet, the mysterious figure of a supernatural being appears, like a man, who grasps the prophet by his hair in his removal to Jerusalem (v 3a masculine), although the transportation itself is then again described as the work of the spirit (v 3b feminine). At the place of removal Yahweh himself then takes over the action (from v 5 on). The transportation is different in the vision of chs. 40-48. Here the supernatural figure of a man, which admittedly is described in 40:3 without such clear colors as in 8:2, appears first at the place to which the prophet is transported, but then takes over the whole task of guiding him through the sanctuary—right up to the movement within the temple in 43:5, where the spirit appears. In the man of ch. 40ff the *angelus interpres* is undoubtedly prefigured, who then appears as a firmly defined figure in the night-visions of Zechariah. In the other visions and parts of visions we learn nothing of this manlike figure. The vacillation in the intrusion of a mediating figure, which is no longer to be seen in Zechariah, speaks in favor of the view that the chronological ordering of Ezekiel's visions before those of Zechariah deserves confidence.

Whilst accordingly the introduction of the visions shows certain stereotyped forms, the composition of

---

152 See above section b.

153 We must deal later, in the larger context of the so-called proof-saying, with the recognition formula, which can also be connected with this concluding formula and which is one of the most significant features of Ezekiel's language. See also pp. 175f to 5:14f.

154 See Excursus 3.

155 See p. 258 to 11:5.

the conclusion is more variable. Only twice is an express conclusion of the vision described. According to 3:12–15 the prophet returned under the compulsion of the spirit from the place where he had received his call, after he had experienced the departure of the glory, to his fellow-exiles. 11:(22) 23–25 tells of the return of the prophet, who had been transported to Jerusalem, to his exilic surroundings in Babylon. The movement out of the temple into the surrounding country blessed by the temple stream of 47:1–12 can certainly not (as von Rabenau suggests) be regarded as the conclusion of a vision, since this event does not bring the prophet back to his Babylonian surroundings, from which he had been transported according to 40:1ff.[156] In the conclusion of the call vision the complete overwhelming of the prophet by his call is emphasized, rendering him unable to speak for a week. It is quite different in 11:25, where the prophet, immediately after his return to his exilic surroundings, reports to his fellow exiles what he has seen. Von Rabenau rightly points out that by this any idea of a visionary's secret knowledge and experience is removed.[157] This clearly distinguishes Ezekiel from the later apocalyptists, in which, according to Dan 8:26; 12:4 (cf 7:28), the visionary is commanded to keep secret what he has seen. What Ezekiel sees must enter into his preaching. Thus the vision of 37:1ff passes over in vv 12–14 into an explicit command to preach. Similarly 40:4 emphasizes that the new temple seen in the vision must be the subject of a proclamation to the house of Israel. So also 44:5f.

In detail the visions are variously composed according to their different content. In the great visions of 1:1–3:15 (3:22ff); 8–11; 40–48 we find a vision of the glory of Yahweh. In ch. 1 it introduces the prophet's call, and also in the fragmentary text of 3:22ff it similarly stands at the beginning, whilst in the two great temple visions it first appears in the course of the action (in chs. 10 and 43).[158] We had better not speak of a

series of visions stylized by the prophet himself.[159] The formulas of reference back to the description given of the manifestation of the glory of Yahweh (3:23; 8:4; 10:15, 20, 22; 43:5) underscore the strong suspicion of their being composed in the course of the final redaction of the book.[160] In any case the vision of the field full of dry bones in 37:1–14 is marked out as different. What the prophet sees here has the function of a magnificent pictorial sign-action, which is then affirmed in the message to the people in the address which follows, which is set out as a discussion-dialogue.[161] In contrast to this the two temple visions enable the prophet to see the present and future reality of the Jerusalem temple. The fragment 11:1–13 is fitted into the vision of chs. 8–11. Finally the appearance of Yahweh's glory in the call vision is concerned with the preparation for a particular speech from Yahweh (with ordination in the form of sign-action), as also in the fragment 3:22ff.

As a second feature, particularly characteristic of Ezekiel, we must stress the accounts of the sign-actions which the prophet is commanded to perform. G. Fohrer adduces the following twelve texts for Ezekiel: 3:16a + 4:1–3, 4–8, 9–17; 5:1–17; 12:1–11, 17–20; 21:11–12, 23–29; 24:1–14, 15–24; 3:22–27 + 24:25–27 + 33:21–22; 37:15–28.[162] Among these we must divide up 4:9–17 into the two parts vv 9–11 (basic text, symbolism of siege) and vv 12–15 (expansive addition, symbolism of exile; vv 16f are a later elaboration of vv 9–11), whilst we can more correctly see in the kernel of 24:1–14 a work song. The large composition 3:22–27 + 24:25–27 + 33:21f, which Fohrer accepts, must be reduced to the kernel element 33:21f[163] However, in what is reported here we cannot be dealing with a sign which the prophet is commanded to perform for his message but about a description of the divine seizure of his person, as in the dumbness after his call (3:15), under which, after a period of dumbness, a period when he can again speak follows.

---

156 Von Rabenau, "Zukunftswort."
157 Von Rabenau, "Zukunftswort."
158 For 8:4 and 9:3a see p. 232.
159 Von Rabenau, "Zukunftswort."
160 See pp. 156, 232.
161 See below pp. 36f.
162 Fohrer, *Handlungen*, 35–47.
163 See pp. 160, 508f.

The particular stylizing of these narratives of the sign-actions in Ezekiel, in which they are almost entirely comprehended by the word of divine command and the performance of the action is not described, was already pointed out in an earlier context. Only in 12:1ff and 24:15ff do we find elements of an account of the carrying out of the action, in which 12:8 dates the performance and interpretation of the action on two successive days. In 24:18f mention is made further of the inquiry of the people regarding the unintelligible action of the prophet. This inquiry by the people about the meaning of what the prophet has symbolically performed is mentioned in 12:9 and 37:18 by Yahweh himself in his message to the prophet. In 4:14 the objection of the prophet to the divine command which requires of the priest something unthinkable is quite unique.

The purpose of the prophet's sign-actions is to set forth in a visible action the event announced by Yahweh as something already begun.[164] This means that from the start sign-actions bear their rightful importance in the performance of the action. The type of speech suitable for this kind of prophetic proclamation was accordingly the narrative. That in Ezekiel almost all the sections which deal with sign-actions are reduced to the introductory divine word which commands the prophet to perform the action appears therefore as a process of formal transposition into another medium. The legitimacy of this transposition lies in the fact that the sign-action never arbitrarily becomes a meaningful didactic "pictorialization" by the prophet himself, but possesses its legitimacy solely from the fact that it is a part of the (coming) divine action. In this measure the divine command to perform the action becomes an integral part of it. In concentrating on this part, which is evident in the form of the great majority of the sections, we see afresh the fundamental importance of Yahweh's word in the preaching of Ezekiel, to which we have pointed already in considering the overall structure of the book.

In details the actions which the prophet is commanded to perform are of various kinds, showing a quite varied degree of prophetic activity. The three actions of seige symbolism, which are compiled into a three-sign composition in the basic text of chs. 4f, originally composed rhythmically, set out an action to be undertaken positively by the prophet.[165] Similarly the addition in 4:12–15, the section "an exile's baggage" in 12:1ff, the action at the road junction 21:23ff, and the joining of the two sticks in 37:15ff make mention of prophetic deeds. At other places, however, we gain the impression that the prophet, quite outside his own willing them, must become a "preacher" by events which overtake him and which make him appear to be overpowered by these experiences. So 24:15ff, where he is stunned by the tragic loss of his wife and is no longer capable of active mourning, but also in 12:17–20, where he is commanded to eat his bread with shaking.[166] Possibly this is also the case in 21:11f, where the shaking could quite similarly be an event which overtakes the prophet and not one that he "mimes." From this we can understand the basis of 4:4–8. A binding of the prophet, which must then subsequently have been recast in the interpretative calculation of days, is understood here as the representation, actively undertaken, of "bearing guilt." The prophet's whole life, both in its active possibilities as well as in what was passively experienced by him, has thus become the vehicle of a divine message.

To the sign-actions we must add the gestures and expressive movements of the prophet. Here we are no longer dealing with independently formulated actions, which are separate from each other and which conveyed their own message within themselves, but with stereotyped actions of a secondary kind, which gave emphasis to the prophet's word or qualified it in a particular way. This element appears therefore formally, only as the introduction to a section. Thus the oracle against the mountains of Israel in 6:2ff is introduced by the call to the prophet to turn his face towards these mountains. Something similar is commanded in 21:2 in the direction of "the forests in the south" (21:7 interpreted of Jerusalem), 25:2 against Ammon, 28:21 against Sidon, 35:2 against the mountains of Seir. Instead of a geographical location persons can appear: the false prophetesses 13:17, the pharaoh 29:2.[167]

---

164 This is dealt with further on pp. 156f.
165 See p. 156.
166 See p. 277f.

167 See pp. 182f.

If we are concerned here with a kind of *Qibla*,[168] it is in another place simply the underscoring of the dynamic character of the word, which is manifested by the movement of the prophet's action. Thus in 6:11 is found the summons to the prophet to smite with the hands and stamp with the feet. The former is also mentioned in 21:19 and according to 22 is to be understood as a reflex of the movement of Yahweh. The two gestures are connected in 25:6 in the introduction to an oracle against Ammon.[169] These expressive actions reveal an expressly "archaic" character.

Among the prophet's speech forms there appear especially the great metaphorical discourses. These show a characteristic distinctiveness, which is clearly different from the rich metaphors and similes in Jer 2–6. In these early oracles of Jeremiah one metaphor presses up against another and goes beyond it. There is a rich fullness of brief sketches which catch the eye. It is quite different in Ezekiel. Here we mostly have broad elaborate pictures, from which we get the impression that the elaboration is often more than adequately done. The patterns of imagery however, are unshakeably firm.

In detail the composition of the figures goes its own way and is joined with other variable elements. In the figurative discourse of the vine in Ezekiel 15 the figure (vv 2–5) and its interpretation (vv 6–8) are clearly divided. The figurative discourse is first opened up in the style of a discussion through a series of questions (vv 2–3) to which the prophet himself, still within the figure, gives the answer which emerges with compelling force. Further the brief description of the vine is still skillfully formulated as a historical parable, in which the period between the two "burnings" which the vine undergoes is made evident. The interpretation is then stylized as a "proof-saying."[170]

While ch. 15 is throughout formulated as a word to the prophet and the command to preach is first given in the interpretation, in ch. 16 on the other hand,

the great figure of the ungrateful foundling child, which Yahweh has brought up and taken in marriage, shows a quite different form. The entire figurative discourse, which is afterwards not further classified by an explicit interpretation, is stylized as an address to Jerusalem. After the introduction in v 2 it concerns an oracle to Jerusalem about a "revelation of abomination," i.e., an accusation.[171] From v 35 the speech passes over into an announcement of judgement, prepared for by the accusation. From v 44 we can see a further formal peculiarity which is important for the history of the development of the prophetic word in Ezekiel. Here the theme of the unfaithful wife Jerusalem is set under the new perspective of a comparison with her mother and sisters (Samaria, Sodom). It is clear that we are not dealing here with a new, independent oracle, but that we have a further elaboration of the theme of vv 1–43. Such development of a theme which is tacked on in a fresh, and almost separate, section, with a new point of view, is also to be seen in other places in the book of Ezekiel and can be regarded as a distinctive feature of this prophetic book. To the question about the setting in life of this process we must note that here we no longer have the free oracle, proclaimed publicly, as in earlier prophecy, but rather a kind of school treatment of preaching material which has already undergone a literary fixation.[172]

Chapter 23 is thematically very closely related to ch. 16, containing the figurative discourse of the two immoral sisters Oholah and Oholibah. In its formal dress it recalls still more the figurative discourse of ch. 15; a broadly elaborated first part, which contains the accusatory history of the two immoral sisters, is directed to the prophet himself. From v 22 on the divine announcement of judgement follows in direct address to Oholibah, behind which is hidden the Judean remnant of Israel. However any explicit interpretation is lacking, unlike ch. 15. It has first been added subsequently in the simile of v 4b by a glossator. In this also the for-

---

168 The meaning of which is shown by Numbers 24:2, that is, optical contact with the person addressed.

169 For the illumination of the dynamistic character of these two gestures we can point to 2 Kings 13:18.

170 For which see below.

171 That the same form of introduction is found again in 20:4; 22:2 (and imitated in the secondary section 23:36ff) makes it probable that there was in

Israel's process of law a quite definite situation of accusation of a crime. See p. 335.

172 In § 8 the phenomenon will be considered more fully.

mation of ch. 23 recalls ch. 15, that here a great deal of historical allusion has been woven into the figure. The Egyptian episode of the beginning of Israel is connected with the unhappy contemporary history of Judah with Egypt, with all its deceitful enticements. This is outlined against the background of Northern Israel's adultery with Assyria. When the two great metaphorical discourses of the faithless women in chs. 16 and 23 are sometimes qualified simply as allegories, then their true nature is not rightly understood. In the figures of the women we have before us personifications of nations, and they can therefore be better understood under the category of corporate personality. In the individual figures within the discourse the reality of the national entity is personally embodied.[173]

We can more correctly speak of allegorical traits in the figurative discourse of ch. 17. The history of the two eagles, the cedar, and the vine makes use of features of the wisdom fables of plants and animals mixed in an unconcerned (but not necessarily fortunate) way.[174] As in chs. 15 and 23 the whole is intended as an actual accusatory proclamation of judgement. Behind the figures of the animal fable there lie hidden the kings of the two great rival powers, and behind those of the plant fables the two Judean kings Jehoiachin and Zedekiah. In particular Zedekiah's apostasy from Nebuchadnezzar is represented. Ch. 17 is formally so stylized that after the description of the history of those represented by the vine (vv 3–8) the question about the consequences which the action of the vine will produce is set out—a question which is to be answered by the hearers. From this the more precise meaning of the term מָשָׁל ("proverb"), with which the fable can be designated, is given meaning by the preceding "riddle" (חִידָה).[175] When the interpretation, which leads up to the announcement of judgement, is added to the allegory in vv 11–21, this again recalls ch. 15. When, however, in vv 22–24 a promise of salvation follows, compared with the images of vv 3–8, then we have here

again the process, already seen in ch. 16, of the further development of a theme under a new light. This concluding element is stylized as a proof-saying, as in ch. 15 and in the promise of salvation which is developed in 16:53ff out of the oracle of accusation and judgement (and as in the section 23:36–49, which is certainly not authentic).

In a quite different sphere we find the figurative discourse of ch. 19. It is composed as a קִינָה "a lament for the dead". Here also we can recognize at once figures of the animal world and of the plant world in the appendix vv 10–14. It speaks of a lioness and her two cubs and then of a vine. This connects ch. 19 with ch. 17, with which it must have been directly connected before the insertion of ch. 18. The attitude of accusation and judgement, which also dominates 17:1–21, is softened here to an attitude of lament over a misfortune that has happened. For the formal composition of the lament the medium of a lame five-beat meter is used, with a descriptive contrast between then and now.[176]

It is striking how richly this form of the lament is used further in the book of Ezekiel. So in the broadly elaborated figure of Tyre as a noble ship in ch. 27. In this, in a series of twelve, or perhaps thirteen distichs, again in the Qinah meter, the erstwhile glory of the ship and then the catastrophe of its destruction is described. The presentation of an earlier glory has subsequently undergone an elaboration, very different in the formal nature of its language, by a prosaic list of the trade relations of the commercial seaport. The poetic basic text shows, in an artistically self-conscious heightening of its lament character, that the lamentation of the surrounding nations also over the end of the proud ship is made vital by the express citation of the lament voiced by these nations (vv 32b, 34a)—a lament for the dead within a lament for the dead. 28:11–19, the lament over the king of Tyre, is also formulated as a lament for the dead. The Qinah meter and the contrasting of then and now mark here also the formal

---

173 Thus in ch. 23 the legal accusation can be addressed directly to this person. See pp. 334f.

174 See p. 362 to 17:7.

175 In the sphere of the sayings of the wise the riddle has repeatedly had a part to play. Thus Wünsche, "Die Räthselweisheit bei den Hebräern," *JPTh* 9 (1883): 422–460, followed by K. von Rabenau, "Die Form des Rätsels im Buche Hesekiel," *Wiss. Z. Halle* GR

7, 5 (1958): 1055–1058, have ascribed Ezek 17 to the form of the riddle.

176 See pp. 391f and the fundamental study of Hedwig Jahnow, *Das hebräische Leichenlied im Rahmen der Völkerdichtung,* BZAW 36 (Giessen: Töpelmann, 1923).

composition of the oracle, which textually can only be restored to its original form leaving many gaps. This is further distinctive in its use of highly mythological material about the primal man driven out from the garden of God. Further examples of the lament are to be found in 26:17f, where the fall of Tyre (with no metaphorical dress) is lamented by the surrounding nations (in this case by their kings) in a first section against Tyre, exactly as in 27:32ff. So also in 32:2–16. While the formal marks of the lament for the dead, which have been mentioned above, can also be seen in 26:17f, so in 32:3–15 a quite differently constructed pronouncement of judgement, which finishes in a proof-saying, is introduced within the framework of a קִינָה.

In this connection we must also say something about 32:17–32, where the lament over the humbled pomp of Egypt is elaborated under the catchword נְהִי. Here the Qinah meter is lacking. The motif of then and now can only be traced on the fringe. The presentation is dominated by the motif of the journey to the under-world of the mighty prince, which is also used elsewhere in the book of Ezekiel. Egypt goes down into the under-world where the recently destroyed empires of Assyria, Elam and Meshek-Tubal lie in their graves. In the mention of the "heroes, who fell in olden days" (32:27) we can see here beside a historical reference the use of mythological material. However, more important is the fact that the motif of the journey to the underworld of the mighty prince is also used elsewhere in the book of Ezekiel, so that here in the final word about Egypt it reaches a final, climactic end. It is found again in 26:19–21, in an appendix to the קִינָה over the downfall of Tyre at the conclusion of ch. 26, which must again have been composed in accordance with the principle laid down in ch. 16 of the further development of a theme. However, in the judgement upon the prince of Tyre also (28:1–10) it is introduced towards the end of the oracle (v 8), whilst in 31:14, 15–18, in a striking way, it concludes the judgement upon Pharaoh.

Ezek 31 belongs to the great figurative discourses of the book. Just as in the lament over the king of Tyre (28:11–19) mythological material is here taken up and unfolded without any contemporary historical allusion. The Pharaoh is compared to the great world tree, the roots of which go down into the depths of the Primal Ocean. For the rest the formal distinctiveness of this figure lies in the fact that the description of the erst-while glory of the tree (vv 2–8) is composed in an elevated metric style, which however changes into prose in the threat of divine judgement (vv 10ff). If the divine threat of vv 10–13 (14) that the tree will be felled is completely intelligible from the figure, the con-clusion, which speaks of the descent of the tree into the underworld, is not very clear. It can only be under-stood from a principle of composition which is evi-dent in ch. 26; 28:1–10; and ch. 32, which conclude announcements of doom upon the great neighboring powers and their rulers wherever possible with the motif of the descent into the underworld. In this we can see a definite direction of the further development, especially in Ezekiel's oracles against foreign nations.

Besides the larger elaborate figures there are found also shorter parable-like oracles. Thus in the indepen-dent literary unit 22:17–22, in an oracle to the prophet (v 18), Israel is compared to dross. Then in the adjoin-ing declaration of judgement developed with an inner logic and addressed directly to the people, it is affirmed that Israel is condemned to the furnace. The image, which is taken over from Is 1:21–26, is described one-sidedly as a process of judgement through fire. The declaration of judgement is thereby formulated as a proof-saying. In 23:32–34, in the course of the develop-ment of the story of the two immoral women, we find in a small, and relatively independent, song the image of the cup of judgement, which the younger sister must now also drink. We may also mention in this connec-tion the image of the broken arm of Pharaoh, which is at first set out briefly and which must originally have been spoken of in a concrete situation, but has then undergone a further exposition in two phases and has been formulated as a proof-saying. When, in 29:17–20, the inconclusive siege of Tyre and a promise of the conquest of Egypt are set out in the image of the un-rewarded baggage carrier, this veils a historical descrip-tion in a colorful word picture. So also in 29:1–6a, where the judgement upon Pharaoh is presented, in a proof-saying, in the image of the killing of the Nile crocodile. The image content of the oracle which fol-lows, concerning the broken reed, was taken over by Ezekiel from Isaiah.

In the kernel of the section 24:1–14 we can see in

vv 3–5 a short work-song, which accompanied the task of cooking meat and bones in a cauldron.[177] The song, which is first given without any interpretation, is then actualized and interpreted historically in comprehensive additions, and a motive given for its message of judgement. The whole is a particularly instructive example of scholastic interpretation and subsequent history of a particular prophetic oracle. As the exposition of the short song, which at first appears as the accompaniment for a simple everyday occupation, makes plain the fearful background of the siege of Jerusalem, so also is it clear in the two-strophe song of the sword in 21:13–22 that the "work" of the weapon that is here called forth cannot be peaceful. In this song the prophet is first of all called to give a description of the sword and its purpose. Then, in the conclusion of the saying (v 21), he turns to address the sword directly and personally, and calls upon it to fulfil its work thoroughly and with a ghastly independence. This song also, which is textually not so clearly worked out as the song of the cauldron in 24:3–5, has subsequently undergone expansion.[178]

In the figurative discourses of chs. 15, 16, 17, 19 and 23 it has become clear how repeatedly a historico-theological narrative is woven into the figure. In ch. 20 we have besides this a great example of a historico-theological narrative which has completely abandoned any metaphorical dress. The closeness of its content to the message of the figures of chs. 15, 16, and 23 makes it appear as an error to deny this address to the prophet because it is composed prosaically and without any metaphorical image.[179] Like ch. 16 it is introduced as an accusation. In its original text it covered the verses 1–26bα, 30–31. This complex, which is limited to the recounting of the historical events comprised in the exodus-credo of the beginning of Israel in a sharply negative light, shows particularly clearly certain formal peculiarities, which then reappear in certain prose pieces of Ezekiel. There is the distinctive structuring of the narrative into phases: the period of the preparation for the exodus in Egypt, the period of the first generation in the desert, the period of the second generation in the desert. With this almost casuistic structuring into historical phases there goes also a stereotyping of the language, which leads to the repetition of similar usages in the description of all three phases and becomes particularly impressive in its monotony. With this is connected here again the moment of heightening, which is to be seen in another way also in ch. 15 (conclusion *a minori ad majus*) and ch. 23 (Oholibah is more sinful than Oholah, v 11).[180] Yahweh's threats of punishment also become harsher and harsher in three phases and lead up in vv 23 and 25 to the threat of scattering among the nations and the gift of evil laws. Ch. 20 also has subsequently not only undergone the expansion in vv 27–29, but also a further development in the section vv 32–44, which is closely related to vv 1–31. As in chs. 16 and 17, in this later elaboration, which is composed as a discussion-oracle and is stylized by a threefold proof-saying as its conclusion, there has been added after 587 a glance at the coming era of salvation. There is no reason for denying this development to the prophet himself, with its distinctively formulated message of the new exodus, which was so important for the future as the preaching of Deutero-Isaiah shows.

A casuistic schematizing of the prophet's oracle is also to be found in the section 14:12–23. Here it is not a sequence of several phases of the sinful history of the people that is set out, but a series of four possibilities of divine judgement, and mention is made of the impossibility of averting this judgement by the piety of an exemplary righteous man. The four cases are treated in a parallel stylization. In the number four we can perceive a declaration of totality, which is also freely used by Ezekiel in other passages for a stylizing of his assertions.[181] The historical actualizing is to be seen here first in the conclusion, which is composed as a proof-saying. As an example of the descriptive language, formed by the repetition of stereotyped expressions, we can mention finally 32:17ff, with its descriptions of the grave sites of Assyria, Elam and Meshech-Tubal.

As in the speeches so far discussed the people, the capital, or the king are addressed as representatives of the community, so we also find beside this an individualizing. Thus we see in the center of the section

177 For the work-song see Hempel, *Literatur*, 19.
178 For the possibilities regarding the origin of the song and its elaboration see p. 432.
179 So Hölscher.
180 See p. 318 to 15:5.
181 See pp. 120f.

22:23–31 a sermon against ranks in society. After an introduction, which addresses the land as a whole, there follows in vv 25–30 a rebuke against five groups among the people, whose specific offences are listed. The concluding announcement of judgement in v 31 then again is addressed to the people as a whole. Closer examination shows that this form appears here in a secondary usage, in which the detailed sketch of the group is preserved in the form of a retrospective review, which offers a motive for the judgement that has already occurred. In ch. 13 we have besides this a direct declaration of judgement against an individual group in the people. Prophets and prophetesses are attacked in a double oracle, the two parts of which are divided symmetrically into two proof-saying sections. More detailed analysis shows that here we can see not only a subsequent redactional composition of originally separate and independent units, but an overall structure, which has from the beginning been intentionally built up. Both initial strophes are thereby similarly composed as woe-oracles.[182]

The form of the larger unit, which is thematically arranged and in which a specific theme is dealt with, usually with a harsh repetition of a particular catchword, is found in the book of Ezekiel even more often. It is most clearly evident in Ezek 7. In two shorter units and a more broadly developed one, which are all composed in the style of a proof-saying, the horror of the last day is pictured in the present text, starting from the frequently repeated and somber בָּא הַקֵּץ of Amos 8:2.[183] We may be inclined immediately to speak of a sermon upon the Amos text, which is here expounded around the "day of Yahweh." The motif of the יוֹם יהוה in the oracle against Egypt in 30:1ff, which is questionable as to its originality, takes on a still greater breadth. Ezek 6 is also dominated by a thematic catchword, where the judgement upon the mountains of Israel is proclaimed in two sections which are introduced by gestures and which are stylized as proof-sayings. In the

complex 35:1–36:15 there stands over against it a contrasting oracle, built up in two parts, which proclaims judgement upon the mountains of Seir and salvation upon the mountains of Israel, with frequent use of the structure of the proof-saying and introduced by a command to perform a gesture. If the thematic connection here is due to a somewhat later phase of the collecting and compiling together of the oracles (otherwise than in ch. 13), yet the combined prophecy corresponds in its structure to the other thematic prophecies of Ezekiel. In this connection we should mention also the long drawn out saying against the shepherds of Israel in ch. 34, which starting from a woe-oracle, develops the theme in two statements (vv 1ff, 17ff) in distinct ways. The structure as a proof-saying is found here only in vv 25–30, a passage in which the shepherd theme falls into the background before a more general promise of salvation for the land.

However, our treatment of the range of themes which have determined some sections of the book of Ezekiel in a very characteristic way still lacks the sphere of law. The section 22:1–16, which is introduced as an "accusation," holds up before the bloody city of Jerusalem its crimes. Subsequently, in vv 13–16 there has been added to it an announcement of judgement formulated as a proof-saying. In distinction from the accusation in ch. 20, the sin of the defendant is not made evident here in the course of its earlier history. Rather there occur, as a declaration of this sin, throughout vv 6–12 a series of apodictic clauses, which declare the rejection of each of these laws by the city of blood. We are certainly not dealing here with a list of offenses added by the prophet from his own observations. Rather Jerusalem's total rejection of the whole series of laws, which the prophet already has listed before him, is brought to expression. In ch. 18 we can see even more clearly the taking up of a series of sacred laws from the entrance-liturgy of the temple worship. The first part, which at its beginning is stylized as a disputation oracle,

---

182 See pp. 290f. The form of the woe-oracle is used frequently in earlier written prophecy within the framework of reproach, particularly in Isaiah and Habakkuk. It appears more in the background in the book of Ezekiel, and besides being found in ch. 13, it is used only in the attack on the evil shepherds in 34:2. Gunther Wanke, "אוֹי und הוֹי," *ZAW* 78 (1966): p. 216, note 5 (see also p. 217, note 7), draws

attention to the linguistically deviant form of the woe-oracle in Ezekiel.

183 For vv 3–11 see the preliminary remarks pp. 193f.

shows at once the division of the description into three phases, which is also found in Ezek 20 and which must be understood here, not concretely and historically, but as generally didactic. It speaks in an exemplary way of a righteous man, his unrighteous son, and in turn of this man's righteous son. Each of these three figures is characterized, in the manner of 22:6–12, by running through a series of laws. In the description of the first figure in vv 5–9, which is set out in the casuistic style of the sacral law (אִישׁ כִּי), the individual clauses of the description of his righteousness are immediately followed by the declaratory צַדִּיק הוּא of the priestly language, followed in turn by the promise of life. This reflects the ritual of the entrance-liturgy, by which the admission or turning away of the pilgrim is decided.[184] The conventional priestly language is not to be overlooked in this description of the righteous man in ch. 18, and then of the unrighteous man, which is throughout aimed at the call to repentance in vv 30–32. A short fragment of the same kind reappears also in the description of the righteous man in 33:14f. 33:10–20 also is directed towards the scope of the call to repent, which precedes here in v 11. The sections ch. 18 and 33:10–20, marked out by these series of laws and which both appear as disputation-oracles, are explanatory didactic prophecies.[185] To this category also belong the units 33:1–9 and 3:17–21 which copies this. In these oracles, which contain a striking second description of the prophet's office, there is formally connected the metaphor of the watchman, which is fully worked out in 33:1–6 with a legalistic explanation of the responsibility of the prophet. The dependence on ch. 18 in 3:20f makes clear how repentance is possible for men. Here also the call to repentance dominates the whole composition, although hidden in the background. Finally the same also is true of the section 14:1–11, which is worked out formally entirely on the basis of a legal formulation in the manner of the sacral ordinances set out in Lev 17.[186] The interesting feature,

from the form-critical point of view, of 14:1–11 consists in the fact that here a casuistic legal text, which in its formal structure is quite clear, has been made the vehicle of the prophet's message and is broken up formally by this message. It is remarkable that this legal explanation also reaches its climax in a call to repentance (v 6). The form-critical consideration that all five of the last-named examples of the incorporation of a legal argument into the prophetic preaching lead up to a summons to repentance shows clearly that a single formative will of a prophetic nature lies behind the various forms of the adducing of the legal text. We can therefore hardly deny these sections to the prophet on the grounds of considerations of form.

This is not so with the legal material which is incorporated in the great vision of Ezek 40–48. Here in 43:18–27; 45:18–20a (see also 46:2, 12) we find priestly rituals. 44:17–31 in part contains apodictic priestly laws, which have many counterparts in the Holiness Code. In 45:21–46:12 instructions for the temple worship of the prince and regulations for sacrifice in the style of P are incorporated. At no point here can we see the recasting of the original legal form under the prophetic call for repentance. In all the legal material found in chs. 40–48 we are dealing directly with borrowings from extra-prophetic legal material, which is incorporated without formal change and which does not carry the signature of Ezekiel's hand. The same is also true of the description of the borders of the land in 47:15–20, which formally has its exact counterpart in Nu 34, and the same is similarly true of the order for the division of the land in ch. 48 with its reworked excerpt in 45:1–8a.

In the details just set out our interest has especially been directed to the formation of the large sections and the form-critical influences which underlay them. The question can further be put whether certain specific peculiarities are to be found in the formation of the smaller units in Ezekiel. K. von Rabenau has studied

184 Gerhard von Rad, "'Righteousness' and 'Life' in the Cultic Language of the Psalms" in *The Problem of the Hexateuch and Other Essays*, tr. E. W. Trueman Dicken (New York: McGraw-Hill, 1966), 243–266. Cf. pp. 374–377.
185 See below.
186 W. Zimmerli, "Die Eigenart der prophetischen Rede des Ezechiel. Ein Beitrag zum Problem an

Hand von Ez. 14:1–11," *ZAW* 66 (1954): 1–26.

the formulations which deal with Yahweh's action (in judgement and salvation) promised for the future. He has examined it according to the various aspects of the description: 1) the motive of the divine intervention, 2) the action of the divine intervention, 3) the carrying out of the divine intervention, 4) the outward consequences of the divine intervention, and 5) the inner consequences of the divine intervention. This shows that in Ezekiel's words the description of the "action" clearly stands at the head, then "the outward consequences," at a greater distance a description of "the inner consequences," and finally the "carrying out" follows, whilst the "motive" theme is often only added adverbially to the "action" theme.[187]

In this connection we must above all consider the two formulations which have already been encountered incidentally and which are particularly characteristic of Ezekiel's prophecies: the forms of the disputation-oracle and the proof-saying.

We can see frequently in the book of Ezekiel that the prophet answers sayings which were current among those around him by a disputation-oracle (counter-argument). This phenomenon makes it probable that the prophet spoke his prophecies outside the narrow circle of his disciples. His prophecy is formulated as an answer, or as a rule even more sharply, as an attack upon sayings voiced either by those around him, or more distantly, by the survivors of Israel in the old homeland.[188]

The quotations consist as a rule of short statements. In 25:3 it is simply a bald exclamation of delight over the misfortunes of others, which is put in the mouth of the enemy (הֶאָח), whilst in 26:2 and 36:2 this exclamation is explained by an appendix. Most frequently we find two clauses in synonymous (12:27; 26:2[?]; 28:2; 29:3, 9; 36:13), or continuous (11:15; 12:22; 18:2) parallelism of the members. Besides this we also find a further formulation in three clauses (11:3; 20:32; 33:10; 37:11), of which the two last-named

references show the heavy rhyming conclusion (-ēnū/ānū) of the lament.[189] Concerning them we can speak directly of quotations from the laments of the people. The quotation of Ezek 33:24 is formulated most fully, containing two clauses in (continuous) parallelism, in which those who remain in the land take assurance from a conclusion *a minori ad majus* out of the history of the promise to Abraham.

The sequel, in which the prophet polemically declares his message against the statements of the people, is introduced in four, perhaps five, cases (18:3; 20:33; 33:11; 35:11. Cf. 33:27 after 33:24) as a passionately expressed oath by חַי־אָנִי, which (besides 33:27 where the introductory messenger formula precedes) is emphasized by the formula for a divine saying and continued by the oath-particle אִם (differently in 35:11). This oath form is found again outside the quotation passages in 5:11; 14:16, 18, 20; 17:16, 19; 34:8; 35:6. In 20:3, 31 no explicit quotation precedes but instead the desire of the elders of Israel for a word from God, which is refused vehemently with the same speech form.

Besides the adducing of quotations at the beginning of a section we find once in 18:25, 29 and the parallel 33:17–20, its inclusion into the context of the explanation. The purely illustrative quotations, which we find in 8:12; 9:9; 27:32b, 34a; 33:30; 36:20, 35; 38:11, 13, do not belong to the speech form being studied here, nor do the citing of questions of the people (in 12:9; 18:19; 21:12; 24:19; 37:18, also 21:5), already mentioned earlier.

The discussion-oracles give to the prophet's words, which are so decisively stylized throughout as divine sayings, a noticeable vitality. This speech form makes it certain that there was in the prophetic message not only a majestic divine monologue, but a process of real encounter with the men of Israel to whom the prophet was sent.

In contrast to this the form of the proof-saying, which is found still more frequently in the book of Ezekiel,

---

187 Von Rabenau, "Zukunftswort."

188 The quotation of sayings of the people in the book of Ezekiel is an invaluable help for the reconstruction of the situation surrounding the prophet, which is otherwise so little described. See Hans Walter Wolff, *Das Zitat im Prophetenspruch*, BEvTh 4 (München: Kaiser, 1937); reprinted in *idem, Gesammelte Studien zum AT*, ThB 22 (München: Kaiser, 1964),

36–129.

189 Cf. Jer 3:25a; 14:7.

190 Hölscher.

affirms that the purpose of all this encounter of Yahweh with his people can be none other than the self-disclosure of the Lord of Israel to his people, and beyond this to the wider world of nations.

It is well known that the stereotyped recognition formula "you will know, that I am Yahweh" is a particularly characteristic element of the book of Ezekiel. In the phase of critical doubt regarding the direct assertions of the book, Hölscher came to the conclusion that in this formula, which is not composed poetically, we can see the hand of a later editor.[190] This leads to the further conclusion that so unique an element as the vision of the reviving of the dead bones must be explained as secondary. Even those who do not follow Hölscher have been inclined to see in the recognition affirmations simply an easily detachable concluding formula.[191] Closer examination, however, shows that this recognition formula is connected in a characteristic way with the preceding context and represents part of a larger structure.

The formula is clearly distinguished by the manner of its speaking of the knowledge of Yahweh (introduction of the content of such knowledge by a following object clause introduced by כִּי) from the Hosea and Jeremiah passages which speak of the knowledge of God (ידע with accusative). It consists of two parts, which from a form-critical viewpoint each have a different origin and setting in life.

The verbal element "you will know that . . .", which points to a fact from which this knowledge is to be gained, is found first in the profane sphere and belongs to the process of proving and demonstrating. This can be very well seen in the story of Joseph. According to Gen 42 the sons of Jacob tell their father what has happened to them in Egypt. They report that the master of the land suspected them of being spies, and when they contested this, he had said to them: "Bring me your youngest brother, that I may know that you are not spies, but reliable men" (v 34). The fetching of

Benjamin is to be the sign that they have not lied to Joseph. The preceding verse shows at the same time that this proof can be connected in yet another way with the verb "to know." Then the brothers say: "The man, the master of the land, said to us: By this I will know (בְּזֹאת אֵדַע) that you are reliable people . . ." Then follows the demand to fetch Benjamin. By the fetching of Benjamin, which would be expressed by בְּ with the infinitive, but which is here anticipated by the pronoun (בְּזֹאת), the proof was to be brought. The ידע–formulation therefore belongs to the sphere of legal examination in which a sign of truth was demanded.

To the verbal assertion of recognition there then appears in the Ezekiel formula as a second element the object clause כִּי אֲנִי יהוה. This also has a clearly recognizable setting in life. The conjecture of Th. Sprey that we should see in it an elliptical statement, which stands in place of a fuller אֲנִי יהוה הוּא, is not convincing.[192] The closeness of Ezekiel to the Holiness Code, which is noted in the following section, does not make it appear likely that we should separate this formula from the אֲנִי יהוה which is repeatedly found there in connection with the legal stipulations. From its origin, however, we must see in this a formula of self-introduction, as we still find it quite fully set out in the Decalogue preamble, which is intentionally set at the head of the divine proclamations on Sinai.[193] Self-introduction is the form of self-revelation of a person in his name—a self-revelation in which all other possible qualifications fall into the background before the unchangeable uniqueness of the person who lays himself open to call by his name. Because it concerns this free self-communication of a person, there belongs to this process of self-introduction an unchangeable tendency. This tendency remains with the formula of self-introduction, even where it concerns a fresh appearance of a person already known through an earlier encounter. In the repetition of the self-introduction, the one

---

191 So Ernst Sellin and Georg Fohrer, *Introduction to the Old Testament*, tr. David E. Green (Nashville: Abingdon, 1968), who find in it an "interpreting formula," which "is dependent on other forms."

192 Th. Sprey, "Review of W. Zimmerli, *Erkenntnis Gottes nach dem Buche Ezechiel, eine theologische Studie*," *VT* 5 (1955): 446.

193 The linguistic shift from the אָנֹכִי used there to the אֲנִי, which is usual in the priestly vocabulary, need not divert us.

who introduces himself actualizes his freedom afresh—even where it may recall an earlier knowledge and may recall fresh to the mind of the hearer this already known fact.

In the combined formula we are therefore dealing with the recognition of this person who introduces himself thus in his freedom.

In the book of Ezekiel this formula is found in its pure form fifty-four times. If we count the eighteen further passages in which it is added to by a finite verb, a noun, a participle, or a prepositional expression, there are all told seventy-two occurrences. To this must be added six further ידע-references in the wider circle of this formula, and the passages 21:4 and 39:21 in which the ידע is replaced by the synonym ראה.[194]

From what has been added here it is clear that the formula is only meaningful in connection with the mention of facts which have the function of proving what is said in the object clause—as in the Joseph story the fetching of Benjamin serves as proof for the claim of the brothers. Closer examination of the text passages from this point of view shows that the formula is always connected with the account of an action of Yahweh. In the first half of the book and in the oracles against foreign nations the judging and punishing action of Yahweh stands in the foreground. In the following chapters there appears also his saving action (this is found already, however, in the additions to the earlier chapters with a message of salvation, cf. 17:22–24; 20:32–44). This action, in which closer examination shows that Yahweh is always the subject, even when it is mentioned that his action is mediated by men, fulfils the function of a sign of proof that he is who he claims to be in his name. I have suggested the name "proof-saying" (*Erweiswort*) for this prophetic structure which appears so uncommonly frequently in Ezekiel.[195] All the announcements of coming divine action, where they are couched in the recognition formula, appear in the light of a divine self-evidencing. In his action in history Yahweh sets himself before his people and the world in his own person. All that which is preached by the prophet as an event which is apparently neutral in its meaning has its purpose in that Israel and the nations should come to a recognition, which in the Old Testament also always means an acknowledgement, of this person who reveals himself in his name. All Yahweh's action which the prophet proclaims serves as a proof of Yahweh among the nations.

It is appropriate now to consider more exactly the formal peculiarities of the structure of the proof-saying and to look at its distribution in the book of Ezekiel. For the composition of a proof-saying it is sufficient simply to have a connection of the divine announcement (von Rabenau's "Zukunftswort") with the recognition formula. This form of the two-part proof-saying is to be found, for instance, in 12:19aβ–20. Frequently, however, the divine announcement of judgement is preceded by a motivation.[196] In this connection there arises the three-part proof-saying, which is to be found in the first utterances against Israel's closest neighbors in Ezek 25 in a particularly pure form. The motivation, introduced by יַעַן, follows the announcement of judgement, introduced by לָכֵן, to which the recognition formula is attached. The connection יַעַן-לָכֵן is found particularly frequently in the book of Ezekiel in motive clauses and announcements of judgement. We also find frequently in Ezekiel the introduction of the proof element with בְּ, already evident in Gen 42:33ff, from which the recognition is to be gained. The generalized anticipation with the pronominal בְּזֹאת has completely

---

194 The material is summarized in detail in my study *Erkenntnis Gottes nach dem Buche Ezechiel*, ATANT 27 (Zürich: Zwingli, 1954); reprinted in *idem, Gottes Offenbarung*, ThB 19 (München: Kaiser, 1963), 41–119. For the formula of self-introduction see my contribution "Ich bin Jahwe" in *Festschrift für A. Alt* (Tübingen: Mohr [Siebeck], 1953), 179–209; reprinted in *idem, Gottes Offenbarung*, ThB 19 (München: Kaiser, 1963), 11–40. Also, K. Elliger, "Ich bin der Herr-euer Gott" in *Theologie als Glaubenswagnis, Festschrift für K. Heim* (Hamburg: Furche, 1954): 9–34; reprinted in *idem, Kleine Schriften zum*

AT, ThB 32 (München: Kaiser, 1966), 211–231.

195 Walther Zimmerli, "Das Wort des göttlichen Selbsterweises" in *Mélanges bibliques rédigés en l'honneur de André Robert*, Travaux de l'Institut Catholique de Paris 4 (Paris, 1957), 154–164; reprinted in *idem, Gottes Offenbarung*, ThB 19 (München: Kaiser, 1963), 120–132.

196 Hans Walter Wolff, "Die Begründungen der prophetischen Heils- und Unheilssprüche," *ZAW* 52 (1934): 1–22; reprinted in *idem, Gesammelte Studien zum AT*, ThB 22 (München: Kaiser, 1964), 9–35; Claus Westermann, *Basic Forms of Prophetic Speech*,

disappeared here in favor of the infinitive construction. Rarely this element comes before the recognition formula, as in the terse בְּבֹאָה וְידַעְתֶּם "when it comes, you will know . . ." (24:24) or, with clearer mention of the divine subject: "When (or: because) I execute judgement . . ., you will know . . ." More frequently this element is placed later, which then forms directly a further reference back to the preceding declaration of judgement after the recognition formula. Thus in 5:13: "And my wrath will be fully poured out, and my anger will be fully vented upon them . . ., and they will know that I, Yahweh, have spoken in my zeal, when I spend my anger upon them." Here we can see at once how the object clause can be extended in the recognition formula. In place of the simple Yahweh name we have here the verbal clause "I have spoken in my zeal." The later positioning of the infinitive with בְּ after the recognition formula is also found in 6:13; 12:15; 15:7; 20:42, 44; 25:17; 28:22; 30:8; 33:29; 34:27; 38:16; 39:28. The expansion of the object clause by דִּבַּרְתִּי (אֲנִי יהוה) in 17:21 (cf. 6:10); by various other verbal statements in 22:22; 35:12; 36:36; 37:14; by a suffixed אֱלֹהִים in 28:26; 39:28 (cf. 39:22); by a קְדוֹשׁ בְּיִשְׂרָאֵל in 39:7; by a participle in 7:9; 37:28; by a prepositional expression and an addition echoing the covenant formula in 34:30. A solemn heightening of emphasis must be intended by the doubling of this with an infinitive introduced by בְּ in 32:15. Similarly a certain pretentious fullness of expression is intended where a second recognition formula follows on an earlier one, which is extended by a recapitulation of the divine action (with infinitive and בְּ), as in 30:25–26 and 37:13–14. In 6:13–14; 11:1–12; and 28:23–24 this duplication must be explained as due to the redaction. In 17:24 the expanded proof-saying is significantly finished off in a different way by the divine assertion אֲנִי יהוה דִּבַּרְתִּי וְעָשִׂיתִי. For the divine speech to run beyond the recognition formula with a declaration of purpose (16:62–63) or a simple extension of the message (36:11) is a less common breakup of the original structure. The same is true of the addition of the recognition formula with the cumbersome לְמַעַן אֲשֶׁר instead of the simple consecutive perfect, in 20:26. However, this

later breakup of the form is not unimportant for an understanding of the form itself. Thereby quite explicit expression is given to the final character of the divine action, which aims at a recognition by men.

Variations are also possible in the naming of the subject of the verbal recognition clause. The reason for the change between the addressing second person and the descriptive third person of ידע is certainly not intelligible in all cases. However, occasionally the subject which makes the recognition can be expressly added. According to 17:24, in dependence on the verbal imagery of the context, it is "all the trees of the field," whilst in 39:22 it is the house of Israel. According to 29:6 it is the inhabitants of Egypt, whilst according to 36:23, 36; 37:28 (38:16); 39:23 it is the nations, and most comprehensive of all in 21:10 it is "all flesh" which is to gain a recognition of God who reveals himself in his actions. It is unusual that the formula of recognition in 20:12, 20 is composed with the infinitive. The replacing of the object clause by a simple accusative in 38:16 recalls the language of Hosea and Jeremiah and belongs to a later addition, similarly the formulation with the object expressed by a relative clause in 11:12.

Of the texts which belong to the narrower circle of the pure recognition formula 2:5 and 33:33 deserve closer attention. According to 2:5 the meaning of the sending of the prophet to the people is that the people shall "know that a prophet is in their midst." Similarly Yahweh assures the oppressed prophet in 33:33 of his interventions: "When it comes (בְּבֹאָה)—behold it comes!—then they will know that a prophet has been in their midst." We must not separate this recognition very far from the recognition which is expressed in the pure formula. In the recognition that a prophet is, or has been, present, the reality of its God will become clear to the people, not as a being in the distant heaven but as one who is present among his people by his word.[197]

In accordance with the details set out, it is clear from the preceding text, as regards the distribution of the proof-sayings, this prosaic form can have had no place in songs of lament. Similarly it is lacking in the work-

---

tr. Hugh Clayton White (Philadelphia: Westminster, 1967).

197 Cf. the description of this divine presence in the

freer formulations in 14:23; 25:14; 39:21; also 39:23.

songs of the cooking pot and the sword. It can also have had no place in didactic legal texts. Thus the formula is lacking in 3:17–21; 33:1–9; also in ch. 18 and 33:10–20. In 14:1–11 the marked mixture of form of the cultic-legal formula with the prophetic pronouncement about the future shows that the recognition formula in v 8 has been able to penetrate into a part of the announcement of punishment (formulated in a cultic-legal way). In the accusations of 22:1ff it has only entered into the sphere of the threat of judgement in vv 13–16, which has been added secondarily. In the figurative sayings it has entered where these are expressly interpreted of the coming divine action, so 15:7; 17:21. Whilst it is completely lacking in the great figurative oracle ch. 31, it has entered into the final elaborations of 16:62 and 17:24, which point to the coming salvation. Also in the great oracle of accusation, giving a theological interpretation to past history, in ch. 20 the pure proof-saying is first found in the promise of salvation, which has been added. The formulations with the infinitive, which regard the sabbath as a sign of the relationship of Israel as a holy people to its God, are set out somewhat differently. In the great visions also proof-sayings are only to be found where the divine action is announced. Thus in the call-vision it is only found in the formulation of 2:5, which is related to the mission of the prophet. It is altogether lacking from the original text of the great temple-vision of judgement.[198] In the vision of the new temple the proof-saying is similarly totally lacking. However in the vision of the dead bones, with its dramatic gift of new life from God, it has entered into the prophecy which announces the new life (37:6) and also into the message of vv 13f, addressed by the prophet to the despairing people. With the sign-actions it similarly appears where the coming divine action is explicitly announced (5:13; 12:15, 20; 24:24; 37:28), but not in the instructions to perform the sign-action proper. That the form of the proof-saying is found relatively frequently in the somewhat later additions promising salvation (but certainly not only there, and not in chs. 40–48) can only be interpreted as showing that a stylized feature was provided by it, which could have been current particularly easily in the prosaic language of the school. However, in many places it clearly goes back to the prophet's own language and can in no way be denied to him.

For the rest this particular element has strongly determined the character of Ezekiel's preaching and has given expression to a basic direction of his prophecy. The whole direction of the prophetic preaching is a summons to a knowledge and recognition of him who, in his action announced by the prophet, shows himself to be who he is in the free sovereignty of his person.[199]

In connection with a consideration of the form of Ezekiel's prophetic preaching we must now say a word in conclusion regarding its metric structure. One example of this is certainly to be found in the frequent songs of lament, described by the prophet himself as קִינָה. Only in ch. 32 it finishes sharply with v 3. In 28:11–19 it appears to offer direct help towards the restoration of the original text.

Besides these, however, we must reckon in Ezekiel with further sections in elevated language. The thesis suggested by E. Balla and Fohrer of a metric short verse is certainly not convincing.[200] However, we may reckon at many points in Ezekiel with an elevated prose, which does not move in a rough meter, but allows free variation. It has some metrical features, aiming to run in double twos and double threes.[201] The Song of the Sword 21:13–22 is composed in two

---

198 11:9f and 11f are later additions to the section 11:1–13, which has been added later to the great vision.

199 See § 7.

200 E. Balla, "Ezechiel 8:1–9:11; 11:24–25" in *Festschrift Rudolf Bultmann zum 65. Geburtstag überreicht* (Stuttgart: Kohlhammer, 1949), 1–11. Fohrer, *Hauptprobleme*, 60–66; Georg Fohrer and Kurt Galling, *Ezechiel*, HAT 13 (Tübingen: Mohr [Siebeck], ²1955), viiif. Cf., for instance, the remarks p. 334.

201 Thus in the description of the יום יהוה (see pp. 201f) and also in the figurative discourses of chs. 15 (p. 318), 16 (p. 334), 17 (p. 359), 23 (p. 481), and especially ch. 31.

rhythmic strophes.[202] Also behind the short Song of the Cup in 23:32–34 we may discern a rhythmic structure,[203] and the same is true of the work-song in 24:3–5. In the prophecies against the nations also of chs. 26, 28:1–10, and ch. 29f, we cannot deny the presence of rhythmic sections.[204] Besides this we can also undoubtedly find straightforward prose sections. So—apart from the factors regarding the קִינָה—we must give up any firm metric theory. We must also affirm under this perspective that Ezekiel belongs to a later phase of prophecy, which is no longer determined throughout by the spoken word, delivered publicly.[205]

6. The Tradition-Historical and Literary-Critical Background of the Book of Ezekiel

In considering the age of the book of Ezekiel, the question about its dependence on other Old Testament literature has repeatedly played an important role. Millar Burrows in his dissertation, the results of which were taken up by Torrey, believed he had been able to demonstrate in the book of Ezekiel, that it pointed beyond the age of exile.[206] When, in what follows, we examine the problem stated, it is best to deal with the purely literary-critical question of the dependence of the prophet on written documents after the tradition-historical question, and first to examine the traditions in which Ezekiel's preaching stands.

A. In his dissertation, E. Rohland examined the prophetic writings from the point of view of the presence of the three great circles of tradition: Exodus from Egypt, Election of Zion, and Election of David and his dynasty. G. von Rad also follows this line of examination.[207] From these studies it has been shown that the North Israelite Hosea is quite onesidedly familiar only with the first-named circle of tradition, whilst the Jerusalemite Isaiah just as onesidedly is determined by the second and third circles, which were particularly important in Jerusalem. What are we to

make in this regard of the position of Ezekiel?

Ezekiel shows himself clearly to be a prophet of the later period, since the one-sided adherence to one of the three tradition streams is no longer found with him. The traditions have begun to be mixed. Thus the tradition of the exodus dominates the theology of ch. 20, which in the first half speaks of the first exodus and in the second half of the second exodus in a typological fashion. The memory of Israel's origin in Egypt is also evident in the great figurative discourse of ch. 23, with a new emphasis, quite distinctively coming from Ezekiel. The David tradition is found in 34:23f and 37:24f.[208] In 17:22–24 also, without mention of the name of David, there is a reference to the Davidid of the future. The specifically Ezekielian character of this element of tradition is to be seen in 37:22, where the future unity of Israel is particularly stressed in preparation for vv 24f, which promises the coming David as the one shepherd. The Zion tradition also appears strongly in Ezekiel—admittedly with the striking peculiarity that the name Zion is avoided throughout. Instead reference is made to the mythical motif of Jerusalem as the center of the world (5:5; in 38:12 the conception of the navel of the earth is related to the whole land) or to the (historicized) motif of the world mountain as "the high mountain of Israel" (הַר מְרוֹם יִשְׂרָאֵל) (17:23; 20:40 cf. 40:2 and the plural use for the land in 34:14). Besides this the idea of the new temple of the future has an important and central place; the "holy mountain of Yahweh" (Ezek 20:40) is the goal of the new exodus. By the establishing of his abode among his people Yahweh makes visible to the nations that he sanctifies Israel, i.e., separates it for himself, according to 37:26–28. This expectation is also found in the great vision of 40–48 in the center of which stands the return and the final residence of Yahweh in the sanctuary of his people.

It is not so clear how far the tradition of the election of Israel through the patriarchs was important for

---

202 See pp. 431f.

203 See pp. 490f.

204 For 32:17ff see the commentary to these verses.

205 This fact will be repeated in another form in connection with the question of the tradition-historical background of the book of Ezekiel.

206 Torrey, *Pseudo-Ezekiel*, 91ff. See for this Fohrer, *Hauptprobleme*, 135–164.

207 Gerhard von Rad, *Old Testament Theology* 2, tr. D. M. G. Stalker (New York: Harper & Row, 1965).

208 See the commentary to these verses.

Ezekiel. Abraham is only mentioned in a saying of the people, which is cited polemically by the prophet (33:24). Israel is called in 20:5 the "seed of the house of Jacob." When mention is made in 39:25 of the turning of the destiny of Jacob, the collective entity Jacob is meant. In the formulation of the statements of 28:25 and 37:25, which belong to material added later, and in which it is said that Yahweh has given the land to his servant Jacob, a reference to the patriarchal history may be intended. However, we cannot altogether exclude a collective interpretation of this, which in any case scarcely comes from Ezekiel's own hand. Thus there is lacking in Ezekiel any positive and explicit mention of the patriarchal history.

However we find in 14:14 a mention of exemplary pious men of the past: Noah, Daniel and Job.[209] 32:27 knows of the heroes (גִּבּוֹרִים) of the mythical past (cf. Gen. 6:4; 28:11f the mythical story of the First Man in the Garden of God). Behind 47:1ff we can see the tradition of the river of Paradise, and ch. 31 paints the picture of the world-tree in brilliant colors (cf. 17:22f). In all this Ezekiel makes use of mythical material much more strongly than we see in the earlier writing prophets and uses it for his particular message.

B. If it remains an open question where we are to place Ezekiel's particular position in relation to these mythical traditions, things are clearer when it comes to Ezekiel's position within the prophetic tradition.

Here also we gain immediate confirmation that Ezekiel is a prophet of the later period. His preaching shows a not inconsiderable familiarity with the message and speech forms of earlier prophecy. Admittedly we only find the comprehensive statement that Yahweh had spoken in earlier days through his servants the prophets of Israel who prophesied in those days, first in a later addition to the Gog-pericope (38:17). It then became a fixed feature in the Deuteronomist and in the early post-exilic Zechariah (1:6). However, it is clear from Ezekiel's words that his preaching repeatedly took up material from earlier prophecy, and this not only on the fringe, and recast this with his own emphasis. In this regard it is immediately striking that Ezekiel, in the composition of his oracles, is connected much more closely than the writing prophets who preceded him with the traditions and forms of pre-classical prophecy. This appears particularly strongly in the stylizing of the visions which are recounted by him. Admittedly we find also in Isaiah (8:11) and Jeremiah (15:17) an occasional reference to the "hand of Yahweh," which removes the prophet from the everyday world by its powerful intervention (היה) or "falling" (8:1) upon him, as he describes it.[210] Similarly 1 Kings 18:46 tells how the hand of Yahweh came upon Elijah, so that he was able to run furiously beside Ahab's chariot from Carmel to Jezreel. 2 Kings 3:15 tells of Elisha that, under the sound of the music of a player, the hand of Yahweh came upon him so that he was able to declare the oracle expected of him by the king. Ezekiel's closeness to pre-classical prophecy is even clearer in his references to the spirit. Whilst the writing prophets before Ezekiel apparently avoid the use of the theologoumenon of the spirit of Yahweh— perhaps because it was connected with all the questionable and extreme mighty acts of "the men of the spirit" (Hos 9:7)—the "spirit" is spoken of fully and quite uninhibitedly in Ezekiel's descriptions of his visions. This again corresponds to the pre-classical prophecy. We hear there that the disciples of Elijah conjectured after his disappearance that the spirit of Yahweh had taken him up (נשׂא, as Ezek 3:12, 14; 8:3; 11:24; 43:5) to a high mountain, or cast him into a valley (השׁליך 2 Kings 2:16). A distinctive feature of the formulation in Ezekiel is only to be found in the fact that רוּחַ is used absolutely in the references given, without the addition of the name Yahweh.[211] The phenomenon of farsightedness, which is also characteristic of Ezekiel's visions, has no counterpart in classical prophecy prior to him, but does appear in the Elisha stories, when the prophet sees there how Gehazi overtakes Naaman and asks a gift of him, at a place lying beyond the range of his eyesight. "Did not my heart go with you (cf. 𝔊), when the man got down from his chariot to meet you?" said Elisha to Gehazi, according to 2 Kings 5:26. Similarly Ezekiel's heart goes to Jerusalem, by which the process is described in a way that differs markedly from full physical transporting.

---

209 See pp. 314f.
210 As is mentioned on pp. 117f.
211 See further Excursus 3.

Three times in the book of Ezekiel the markedly stereotyped situation is described in which Ezekiel experiences the coming of a vision or of the divine word in his house, whilst the elders are sitting before him (8:1; 14:1; 20:1). This also is a feature which is not found in any of the older prophetic books, but which has an exact counterpart in 2 Kings 6:32 in the narrative of Elisha. We are tempted here to speak of a typical account of an inquiry of a prophet in the "schoolhouse."[212] The וְדִבַּרְתָּ בְדְבָרַי of 3:4, which has its counterpart in the prophetic narratives of 1 Kings 13 (in vv 2, 5, 9, 17, 18, 32) and 20 (in v 35), also points to a connection with the formulations of pre-classical prophecy.[213]

We can further point out in this connection that the gesture of turning the face towards the persons addressed again has its clearest counterpart, not in the classical prophets, but in the old narrative of the seer Balaam. The establishing there of a visual contact between the seer and those addressed is clearly shown in Num 22:41; 23:13; 24:1f. Thus in Ezekiel full visual contact has been weakened into a simple turning of the face in the direction of those addressed. The more emotional actions of clapping the hands and stamping the feet, which contain a dramatic emphasizing of the power of the prophet's word, can be compared to the striking on the ground with arrows in the symbolic action of the Elisha story in 2 Kings 13:18.

In this connection we must also set the very prominent form of the proof-saying.[214] This has so clear a counterpart in the prophetic narrative of 1 Kings 20:13, 28 that it has been suggested that we have in these two sayings against the Syrians a subsequent insertion in the style of Ezekiel.[215] This is precluded by the fact that we find a close parallel of a similar kind in the Elisha narrative of 2 Kings 5. Here the prophet says to the king, who has been shocked by the appeal first directed at him to heal the leprous Naaman: "Why have you rent your garments, let him (i.e., Naaman) come to me, that he may know (וְיֵדַע) there is a prophet in Israel" (v 8). The recognition formula in Ezekiel's call narrative (2:5) corresponds exactly and is also formulated in Yahweh's personal word of encouragement to the prophet in 33:33: "They will know (וְיֵדְעוּ) that a prophet has been in their midst," at the appearance of the prophet and the fulfilment of his word. In the continuation of the narrative, Naaman's confession, "See, now I know that there is no God in the whole earth but in Israel" (v 15), corresponds to the message concerning the prophet. The fixed anchorage of this repeated recognition formula in the prophetic narrative of 2 Kings 5, which in no way permits its removal, makes it appear probable that the two proof-saying formulations of 1 Kings 20 should be kept in the text. We can further point to the formulations 1 Kings 17:24; 18:36f in pre-classical prophecy and 2 Kings 19:19 in the Isaiah legend. The comparison of 1 Kings 20:13, 28 with Ezekiel in which we find the purest, short three-part, proof-saying, which agrees most closely to the reference of 1 Kings 20 in the oracles to the nations of Ezek 25, raises the question whether the original setting in life of the proof-saying lay in oracles against foreign nations in the holy war.[216] Its entry into oracles against Israel, in which it now has a large place in the book of Ezekiel, must then be understood as a later development. The prophecies against the nations in Amos 1f appear to show a quite analogous development with a different type of foreign nation oracle. Overall we can in any case affirm that the connection through the proof-saying provides further important evidence of the tradition-historical connection between Ezekiel and the pre-classical prophecy. Over against the classical prophecy which preceded him, his preaching thereby contains an archaic character.

C. Besides these contacts with pre-classical prophecy, which become especially evident in the forms and in the framework of the words and visions, there also

---

212 We must not overlook the relationship of the formulation to the "story of the king," echoed in 2 Sam 7:1. See Siegfried Herrmann, "Die Königsnovelle in Ägypten und in Israel," *WZ* 3 (1953/54): 51–83. This relationship raises the question whether stylistic material or historical connections existed between the typical situation of a king making a decree and the prophetic preaching.

213 See note a to 3:4 (pp. 92f).
214 See above pp. 36–40.
215 Fohrer.
216 See my considerations in "Wort."

appears a strong tradition-historical contact of the prophet with the earlier literary prophets, penetrating deeply into the special themes of Ezekiel's preaching. The connection in Ezek 7 with the catchphrase בָּא הַקֵּץ of the fourth vision of Amos (8:1f) is not to be overlooked. As mentioned earlier, this catchphrase has become the special text of the broadly worked out message of the day of Yahweh in the whole of ch. 7.[217]

Similarly we can scarcely overlook the fact that the theme and details of the treatment of Ezek 16 were suggested by Hosea (1:2 and especially 2:4–15). The question may be asked whether it is sufficient here to accept a familiarity of Ezekiel with the preaching of Jeremiah, in which the picture of the unfaithful wife appears behind Jer 2:2 and with Jer 3:6ff has undeniably influenced the theme of the two unfaithful women in Ezek 23. However, the full description of the gifts which Yahweh gave to his bride at their marriage, which is not found in Jeremiah, but is found in Hos 2 as well as Ezek 16, makes probable Ezekiel's familiarity with the preaching of Hosea himself. We cannot claim with the same confidence that the theme of ch. 15, with its polemical message about the vine, has been influenced from Hosea (10:1ff). The image had a wide currency, as Isaiah's song of the vine and also Ps 80 (certainly composed after 721 B.C.) show.[218]

That Ezekiel knew Isaiah's preaching, is shown by the symbolic action of 5:1f, which has grown out of a metaphor used by Isaiah.[219] Behind Ezekiel's call vision Isaiah 6 may be traceable.[220] So also the metaphor of dross, which Ezekiel uses so arbitrarily in 22:17ff, strongly recalls Is 1:22ff.[221] That Isaiah's oracle of the "Day of Yahweh" in Is 2 may also have influenced Ezekiel is not to be excluded.[222]

In Ezek 7:19, a verbal quotation from Zephaniah (1:18) has probably been introduced later.[223] However, the sermon against sections of the community in 22:23ff, which develops somewhat freely the theme of Zeph 3:3f and which echoes exactly the conclusion of Zeph 3:8b in Ezek 22:31, points to a knowledge of Zephaniah's preaching by Ezekiel himself.[224]

The very marked connection between Ezekiel and Jeremiah offers a special problem. Already Smend pointed to this in his commentary and identified sixty-two passages as "borrowings from Jeremiah."[225] J. W. Miller in 1955 came to the following conclusion: "Ezekiel had read avidly a manuscript of the . . . scroll of Baruch [which the author finds in the prose sermons of Jeremiah]—probably in the form in which it existed before 597 . . . Ezekiel most probably also knew a copy of the promises of salvation in Jer 30 and 31, and had studied them carefully . . . It is correct, therefore, to include the letter of Jeremiah (29:1–23) in this judgement."[226] The material in question is set out in detail in this monograph.[227]

Here also the points of contact penetrate very deeply into the theme of Ezekiel's preaching. As regards the call-narrative it is shown that, in chs. 2–3, it shows close connections with the Jeremianic type of call-narrative.[228] Above all, however, in the distinctive episode which tells of Ezekiel's eating a scroll, we cannot mistake the dramatic recasting of the metaphorical image of Jer 15:16 into an actual experience—a phenomenon which is particularly significant for Ezekiel.[229] Since Jeremiah's saying occurs in connection with one of his most personal utterances, which, as his "confessions" we cannot think of having been proclaimed on the streets, but simply handed on in the circle of his intimates and written down there, we are compelled here to move out of the sphere of oral tradition, to think

---

217 Amos 5:18–20 also speaks of the day of Yahweh.
218 See p. 319.
219 See p. 172.
220 See pp. 108–110.
221 See p. 462.
222 See further in the oracles against the nations Ezek 29:6b–9a and 30:9.
223 See note b to 7:19 (p. 199).
224 See David Heinrich Müller, "Der Prophet Ezechiel entlehnt eine Stelle des Propheten Zephanja und glossiert sie," *WZKM* 19 (1905): 263–270; reprinted in *idem, Biblische Studien* 3 (Wien: Hölder, 1907),

30–36.
225 Smend, xxiv.
226 John Wolf Miller, *Das Verhältnis Jeremias und Hesekiels sprachlich und theologisch untersucht* (Assen: Van Gorcum, 1955), 118f.
227 S. Herrmann, *prophetischen Heilserwartungen*, explains the particular relationship of the expectations of salvation in a different way, by a Deuteronomic school tradition which underlies both books.
228 See pp. 97f.
229 See p. 19.

instead of a written form of mediation. Other references also support this view of written transmission, although less compellingly. Thus the watchman metaphor, by which in 33:1–9 and 3:17–21 the prophet interprets his own office, could have come orally from Jeremiah's preaching (Jer 6:17).[230] The theme of the false prophets, which is dealt with in Ezek 13, is also found in Jer 23:9ff (cf. Jer 27–29) with statements which are in part not very far removed from Ezekiel's. In Ezek 13 the setting in parallel of the prophets and prophetesses is distinctive of Ezekiel. In the explanation of the inevitability of judgement, which cannot be averted even by the presence of three exemplary pious men, we can again probably see a freely remolded sketch of Jer 15:1. In place of the great Israelite intercessors, Moses and Samuel, we find in Ezek 14:14 the three righteous men, Noah, Daniel and Job. When immediately afterwards in Jer 15:2 (and vv 3f) a casuistic development of the four different possibilities of judgement follows, although there are again differences of detail, we must reckon here also in Ezekiel on a very precise knowledge of Jeremiah's oracle. That Ezek 23, the figurative account of the two immoral women who are given names, is a development of the history of the two women in Jer 3:6ff, who are similarly mentioned with characteristic names, has already been shown.[231] Whilst the similarity, with an independent development, in Ezek 23 against the earlier saying is striking, we can only compare the significant conduct of Ezekiel at the loss of his wife in Ezek 24:15ff with Jer 16:1ff with some reservation.[232] On the other hand, the influence of Jer 23:1ff on the great shepherd discourse of Ezek 34 is quite clear. Here once again in Ezekiel a broad development, with its own emphases, has arisen out of the terse saying of the original.

In addition to these contacts in the larger themes there also appear further connections in individual verses. Admittedly the quotation from Jer 18:18, which we have in Ezek 7:26b, has been added to the text later by way of comment.[233] However, the fleeting saying in which only a brief rebuttal is made in Jer 31:29f has been taken up in the exile also, because of its vividness and suggestive content. In Ezekiel 18 it is

the cause of an elaborated discourse on the topic of freedom to repent. Jeremianic influence may also account for the description of the land of Canaan by the catchword צְבִי in 20:6, 15 (cf. Jer 3:19). The reference in 12:2 to the eyes which do not see and the ears which do not hear goes back through Jer 5:21 to Is 6:9f. Similarly the picture of the cup of judgement which we have in 23:32–34 can hardly have first been known from Jer 25:15ff.[234] After considering all the contacts, for some of which we must reckon simply with the similarity of certain formulations in the current language of the time, as Miller and Fohrer rightly stress, we come to the conclusion that Jeremiah's preaching was known to Ezekiel. Some of this supports the further view that words which Jeremiah did not proclaim publicly came to him in a written form. However, (against Miller) to fasten on the prose sermons of the prophet as the content of the scroll of Jer 36 is not satisfactory, since the reference which most strongly points to a written transmission, Jer 15:16, cannot have been in the scroll.

Ezekiel's closeness to Jeremiah is also further supported by certain basic features of his preaching: submission to the Babylonians, the decidedly anti-Egyptian attitude, the expectation of a new future for Israel among the exiles and not among those left in the land, the condemnation of the action of Zedekiah, statements about the inner transformation of the people in the promised age of salvation.

The establishing of the fact of Ezekiel's familiarity with the sayings of Jeremiah must straightaway be connected with the fact of the deep differences between the two figures, which can be seen at many points—even into details of language. For the latter we may point to the minor fact that instead of מַעֲלָל "act," which appears almost twenty times in Jeremiah, we have in Ezekiel עֲלִילָה (eight times), which is altogether lacking in Jeremiah. The one exception is in Ezek 36:31, in a doubtful section.[235]

Why then has Ezekiel never mentioned the earlier Jeremiah in his book, when he was so clearly influenced by so much of his preaching? We can see here a marked difference between the Jeremiah and the Ezekiel tradi-

---

230 See Volume 2.
231 See pp. 481f.
232 But cf. Miller, *Verhältnis*, 93f.
233 See pp. 212f.

234 Further references are dealt with by Miller, *Verhältnis*, and Fohrer, *Hauptprobleme*, 135–140.
235 See Volume 2.

tion that, apart from Ezek 11:1–13, which from this point of view also shows itself to be a distinctive section, no person from the prophet's circle is mentioned by name in the book of Ezekiel. This is true also of the prophets among the exiles, whose names are known from Jer 29:21ff, but not from the preaching of Ezekiel. If we question more generally whether Ezekiel knew anything at all of a preaching similar to his among those who were not exiled in 597, then Ezek 9:4, with its instruction to the man clothed in a linen garment to put a sign "on the foreheads of the men who sigh and groan over all the abominations which are committed in its [the city's] midst," gives room for such a knowledge on the part of the prophet. Even though nothing more of this is to be seen in the sharply stylized accusations of sin against Jerusalem (chs. 16, 22:1ff) and in the sermon against sections of the community (22:23ff), this reference shows the prophet's consciousness that in Jerusalem also there were men who suffered over Israel's sins. Jeremiah belonged to these men.

D. Scholars have also pointed to the influence of Deuteronomy on Ezekiel.[236] It is undeniable that Ezekiel 6 presupposes the polemic against the high places which was acted upon in the Deuteronomic reform. For the rest, however, it is striking how the most important elements and formulations of the Deuteronomic language and preaching are absent in Ezekiel. Thus there is no reference to love for Yahweh, and of the love of Yahweh, and of the fear of God. The term מִצְוָה is completely absent, and תּוֹרָה is never used for "the law" in general, as is characteristic of Deuteronomy. There is no well-defined convenant theology with its twofold patriarchal and Horeb covenants. The key word בחר of Deuteronomy appears only in Ezek 20:5, and the term שׁכח, which is important for the Deutero-

nomic understanding of sin, appears only in 22:12 and 23:35 in incidental passages, and the term זכר which corresponds with it is found as a description of right conduct only in 6:9, which is a later addition. Overall the smallness of the contact of Ezekiel with the language and ideas of the well-defined world of Deuteronomy is striking.

It is very different, however, in regard to the relationship between Ezekiel and the complex Leviticus 17–26, which has been called the Holiness Code (H) since Klostermann's article.[237] Already K. H. Graf had affirmed the connection between Ezekiel and Leviticus 18–23; 25f and had regarded it as necessary to accept that Ezekiel was himself the author of Lev 18–23; 25f.[238]

R. Smend listed a large number of detailed contacts, but under the impact of the distinctiveness of both corpora, he denied an origin of Leviticus 17–26 from Ezekiel, and like Wellhausen accepted a later date of composition for Leviticus 17–26.[239] Against this, L. Horst modified the thesis of Graf to see in Leviticus 17–26 Ezekiel at work as the collector and redactor of older legal material which was already extant: "First of all he put the laws collected by him into the mouth of Moses, according to his usual custom and probably he found them already in existence. Later, however, when he set out a new legal order for the land and people, he worked himself, as a prophet, under the direct influence of Yahweh. Here he was an author in the full sense of the word; there only a redactor. This must be the most natural solution of a riddle, which in part dominates Pentateuchal criticism."[240] With greater caution J. Herrmann saw Ezekiel as contributing "at least to the composition of Leviticus 26."[241] This dating of H either contemporary with, or later

236 So Burrows, *Relations*, 19–25; Fohrer, *Hauptprobleme*, 140–144; Fohrer-Galling, xxiii; also S. Herrmann, *prophetischen Heilserwartungen*.

237 A. Klostermann, "Beiträge zur Entstehungsgeschichte des Pentateuchs," *ZLThK* 38 (1877): 401–445; reprinted as "Ezechiel und das Heiligkeitsgesetz" in *idem, Der Pentateuch* (Leipzig: Deichert, 1893), 368–418.

238 Karl Heinrich Graf, *Die geschichtlichen Bücher des Alten Testaments* (Leipzig, 1866), 81.

239 Smend, xxv–xxvii.

240 L. Horst, *Leviticus xvii–xxvi und Hezekiel. Ein Beitrag*

zur Pentateuchkritik (Colmar, 1881), 96.

241 J. Herrmann, xix.

than, Ezekiel was passionately opposed by Kloster-mann, and, after a penetrating examination of all the comparable material, he defended the thesis that the dependence was wholly on the side of Ezekiel. The latter was so familiar with the public proclamation of law, in which H had its place, that the manifold closeness of the prophet to the formulations of H can be completely explained as a quite unconscious dependence on this legal proclamation. It is a continuation of the thesis of Klostermann when Graf Reventlow regards H as fundamentally a cultic document, which was at home in the old Israelite covenant festival, and sought to trace "the individual stages of the development of the law from the beginnings of the apodictic series up to the final form of the entire corpus in the framework of the cult."[242] In his understanding of the prophet himself as the representative of an amphictyonic office, at home in the place where the law was proclaimed and the warnings and preaching of woe and weal that were connected with this, he goes far beyond the intention of Klostermann.

Klostermann's solution, in spite of the many penetrating and valuable perceptions which he made, is not entirely satisfying with its well-rounded answer. Thus the question must be carried further. In his examination of the most important relevant texts, Fohrer came to the conclusion that H (or the redactor of H) and Ezekiel must have used a common source.[243] Rejecting a conjecture of Cazelles, who would see in H the scroll of Ez 2:9, L. E. Elliott-Binns came to a differentiated view of the Holiness Code which consisted in its pre-priestly compilations from various documents so that it must already have been available to Ezekiel.[244] R. Kilian came to the conclusion that Ezekiel (who must himself first be critically analysed, which Kilian does

not attempt) was dependent in his laws on proto-H. On the other hand the redactor of H (Rh) was, for his part, dependent on Ezekiel in style and language: "If Ezekiel, in his preaching appealed to proto-H and gained support from it, then it is only natural that one of his school and circle of traditionists (Rh) should have been concerned in a particular way with Ur-H and developed this."[245] From this circle of traditionists there emerged especially Leviticus 26. Elliger came to quite different conclusions, believing that he could find behind Leviticus 26, as well as behind parts of Ezek 34:25–31 which are closely connected with it, a liturgy of the Autumn Festival which was used by both.[246]

The methodical way to further progress in the study of "Ezekiel and H" must be indicated by the last-named works. Even if we exclude the view that Ezekiel was the author of H as improbable from the start, we will have to abandon the sharp alternatives: Ezekiel was dependent on H or vice-versa; or there was a common source for Ezekiel and H. Instead we must make a carefully detailed comparison. The contacts must be carefully studied in detail as well as the frequent direct interruptions of contact and the undeniable distinctiveness of the two corpora, each of which has its own tradition—and redaction—history. The overall document H, even when we disregard the final editing by the Priestly author, is no more free of problems than is the overall document 'Ezekiel'. Thus the heavy reworking of the extensive final vision in chs. 40–48, of which the laws added later (especially the regulations for the priests in 44:6ff) have repeatedly played an important role in characterizing and dating Ezekiel, must first be clearly defined and considered independently of the rest of the book, when we are examining the relationship between H and Ezekiel.

242 H. Graf Reventlow, *Das Heiligkeitsgesetz formge-schichtlich untersucht*, WMANT 6 (Neukirchen-Vluyn: Neukirchener, 1961), 30.

243 Fohrer, *Hauptprobleme*, 144–148. For the possibility that it was the redactor of H see Fohrer-Galling, 155.

244 H. Cazelles, *Le Lévitique* (1951), 16; L. E. Elliott-Binns, "Some problems of the Holiness Code," *ZAW* 67 (1955): 26–40.

245 Rudolf Kilian, *Literarkritische und formgeschichtliche Untersuchung des Heiligkeitsgesetzes*, BBB 19 (Bonn: Hanstein, 1963), 185.

246 Karl Elliger, *Leviticus*, HAT 4 (Tübingen: Mohr [Siebeck], 1966).

The question needs further intensive study in monographs. In the present context we can only collect some observations which may be helpful for such a task. The comparison may therefore follow the chapter sequence of Leviticus 17ff.[247]

In regard to the question of the relationship of Leviticus 17 to the many-sided complex of H, we may note that in Ezek 14:1–11 we find a striking analogy to the formulation of the first four "cases" of Leviticus 17, which has a parallel in Lev 20:2–6 (and again also at least in the heading section 22:18). The relationship does not concern the subject matter of the cases of Ezek 14:1–11, with which we could at best compare the מֶלֶךְ-saying of Lev 20:2–6. It concerns solely the very characteristic form of the formulation of the sacral law.[248] Further contacts in detail cannot be regarded as specific connections between H and Ezekiel (זנה אַחֲרֵי v 7, also 20:5/Ezek 6:9; 20:30; 23:30; eating blood v 10/Ezek 33:25; נשא עָוֹן v 16, also 20:17, 19; 22:16/Ezek: 4:4–6; 14:10; 44:10, 12, also 18:19f; חֻקַּת עוֹלָם v 7/Ezek 46:14; טְרֵפָה-נְבֵלָה v 15/Ezek 4:14. 44:31; גֵר-אֶזְרָח v 15/Ezek 47:22).

In a comparison with Leviticus 18 Klostermann already noted that the feature of the divine self-affirmation אֲנִי יהוה or more fully אֲנִי יהוה אֱלֹהֵיכֶם, which is characteristic of this and the following chapters of H, is only to be found in this separate form in Ezekiel in ch. 20 (here in the longer form). Here also it stands in a connection which has to do with the divine gift of the law in Israel's history (20:5, 19 as the introduction to a proclamation of law, in 20:7 as a concluding emphasis). Otherwise these formulations are found in Ezekiel only in the context of proof-sayings, which, so far as their form is concerned, belong not to the proclamation of law, but to prophetic pronouncements. The saying about the laws by which men live if they keep them (v 5/Ezek 20:11, 13, 21, cf. v 25) also points to the sphere of the communication of law. There is a particularly strong connection in the formulas of the

parenetic framework, which speak of "walking" (הלך) in the commands (חֻקּוֹת) or laws (מִשְׁפָּטִים) of God and keeping (שמר) and doing (עשׂה) them with a changing order of the elements.[249] On the other hand the noun מַעֲשֶׂה, as a designation for religious conduct, which in the parenetic framework is used with emphasis, is found in Ezekiel at best in the מַעֲשֵׂה אִשָּׁה זוֹנָה שַׁלָּטֶת of 16:30. Otherwise in Ezekiel the word has a very technical meaning (workmanship 1:16; useless works 6:6; products 27:16, 18; work 46:1). We must also establish that the anti-Canaanite tendency, which appears in the framework of Leviticus 18 and 20, and which speaks extensively of the conduct of the previous inhabitants of Israel's land and its reaction to their uncleanness (18:3b–4, 24ff; 20:22ff), is completely lacking in Ezekiel. The parallel anti-Egyptian tendency found in Lev 18:3a has a certain counterpart in Ezek 20 and 23. We must further establish that there are close contacts in the two frameworks distinguished by Elliger in Lev 18 in vv 3f and 5. Of the kin relationships in which sexual relationships are prohibited Ezekiel mentions only sister and daughter-in-law (22:11) in an analogous connection. To this we may add a woman in the time of her monthly period (18:6; 22:10). Beyond this, נִדָּה appears in 7:19f; 36:17, as in Lev 20:21, as a general term for uncleanness.

Contacts with Ezekiel are surprisingly weak in the central chapter of H, Lev 19. The concept of holiness is important for Ezekiel in a different way than for H. Only once, in 39:7, which does not belong to the basic material of the Gog-pericope, can Yahweh be described as "holy." Otherwise mention is made (with the noun קֹדֶשׁ) of his holy name (20:39; 36:20–22; 39:7, 25; 43:7f), of his holy mountain (20:40;28:14), and also with the verb that he shows himself holy in his actions (20:41; 28:22, 25; 36:23; 38:16, 23; 39:27). Otherwise in the vocabulary of the book of Ezekiel, even in the additional concluding vision, there stands evident in the first line the sphere of the holy (land, sacred

247 Klostermann, "Heiligkeitsgesetz," 386–401, follows the chapters of Ezekiel. He comes to the right conclusion "that the connections are not all on one side and do not exclude certain constant differences" (402).

248 How a prophetic style (and content) penetrated it in Ezek 14 was detailed above, p. 35. See also Zimmerli, "Eigenart."

249 For the statistics see Elliger, *Leviticus*, p. 236 note 3 and p. 237 notes 6 and 7.

gifts, temple area, sanctuary—so 42:13—the second appearance of the adjective קָדוֹשׁ in Ezekiel—and the holy offerings), in which the gradations between holy and very holy gain increasing importance. In this connection the consecration and sanctifying of oneself, used of men, has its importance. The late addition 48:11 speaks of the "consecrated priests." Most closely linked with H is Ezek 20, since not only is the sanctifying of the sabbath commanded here (v 20, cf. Lev 19:3, 30; 26:2 with the verb שׁמר), but v 12 lays down that Yahweh makes it known by the gift of the sabbath that he has sanctified his people. The closest connection to this reference is certainly to be found in Ex 31:13 (P). The connection of the demand for holiness from the people with the whole range of social and human conduct in Israel, which is characteristic of H and particularly of Leviticus 19 and which is emphasized against the background of Yahweh's holiness, is completely lacking in Ezekiel. There emerge then in the concrete individual demands of Leviticus 19 connections here and there with statements of Ezekiel and his followers (honoring of parents Lev 19:3 / Ezek 22:7; keeping the sabbath Lev 19:3 / Ezek 20:12, 20; 22:8; protection for aliens Lev 19:33f / Ezek 22:7, 29, also 47:22f in a later section; here also just weights and measures Lev 19:35f / Ezek 45:10–12). Wide areas of law which are characteristic of Leviticus 19 find no echo in Ezekiel (Lev 19:9f harvest regulations; vv 11f property offences, perjury; v 14 offences against the defenseless; vv 17ff love-hate for one's neighbor; v 19 "prescriptions" [כִּלְאַיִם]; vv 23–25 laws regarding the use of fruit trees; v 31 consulting of the dead; v 32 reverence for elders). There are lacking not only the terse concluding formula of Yahweh's self-affirmation, but also the conjunction of a prohibition with a positive command to fear God (Lev 19:14), which is particularly characteristic of Leviticus 19, or to love him (Lev 19:18).[250] Even where connections of subject matter are present, as in the instructions for conduct in a court of law (Lev 19:15f, cf. Ezek 18:18)

or in the prohibition of magic (Lev 19:26b, cf. Ezek 13:17ff), in language they each go their own separate ways that we should scarcely reckon on a closer relationship of Ezekiel to H from Lev 19 itself.

This is rather the case in Lev 20, where the contacts of the form of vv 2–6 with Ezek 14:1–11 have already been mentioned in connection with ch. 17, and the contacts of subject matter appear prominently with Leviticus 18. For the formula of vv 3a, 5a and 6b cf. Ezek 15:7aα and bβ; for v 4 הֶעְלִים עֵינַיִם, Ezek 22:26; for v 3 טַמֵּא מִקְדָּשׁ, Ezek 5:11 (8:6; 9:6f; 23:38). The מוֹת יוּמַת, which is furthermore significant in Leviticus 20, is only to be found in Ezek 18:13; the formula affirming responsibility דָּמָיו בּוֹ v 9 and elsewhere, in Ezek 18:13 (cf. 33:4f).[251]

However, שָׁכַב אֶת ("to lie with") in the sexual sense (vv 11–13, 18, 20) is only found in Ezek 23:8, and the נתן שְׁכָבָה of v 15 is completely lacking in Ezekiel as is the חֶסֶד (shame) of v 17 and the description of Israel's separation by election through הבדיל in vv 24, 26. This we should properly expect with Ezekiel.[252]

Contacts with the priestly regulations of Leviticus 21f are only found, as can be quickly seen, in the later passage regarding the priests in Ezekiel 44. For Lev 21:1–3(4) we must compare Ezek 44:25, in which, however, the term "flesh" (שְׁאֵר), which also plays an important part in the additions to the basic text of Lev 18 [Elliger], is lacking, as in the whole book of Ezekiel. For Lev 21:5–6 cf. the regulation in Ezek 44:20, which is admittedly formulated quite differently. The marriage regulations in Lev 21:7–8(9) are also quite differently formulated than in Ezek 44:22. Once again we miss here the theology of sanctification which is so characteristic of H. The figure of the priest, which is so prominent in Lev 21:10–15, "who is greater than his brothers," is completely lacking in Ezekiel, as is any mention of physical blemishes which would exclude a person from priestly service as in Lev 21:16–24. For Lev 22 also we can adduce only sparse contacts besides

---

250 See also the summaries in Lev 19:32 and 34.

251 For the formula of sanctification v 8, see the comments on Lev 19. For the כרת-formulation found in Lev 20 (as already Lev 17:4, 9f and 18:29) and the נשׂא עָוֹן of vv 17, 19 (v 20 נשׂא חֵטְא), see pp. 302–305 to 14:8 and 10.

252 Cf. the use of the verb in 22:26 and 42:20, and see further the comments on Lev 18.

the presence of certain formulations (כרת-formula v 3; שָׁמַר מִשְׁמֶרֶת v 9, cf. Ezek 44:8, 16; 48:11; אֲנִי יהוה מְקַדְּשָׁם said of the priests in vv 9, 16(32) / Ezek 20:12 of the people; the formula of introduction Lev 22:18b / Ezek 14:4, 7): the designation of a sacrifice to Yahweh as לֶחֶם אֱלֹהִים in Lev 22:25 / Ezek 44:7. The prohibition in Lev 22:8 has a counterpart in Ezek 44:31, which is a quite late addition and which again certainly lacks the characteristic conclusion of the formulation of H. Thus there is lacking in Ezekiel the predication of Yahweh as the God who brought up Israel out of Egypt, which found in Lev 22:33 as also in 19:36 and later in 25:38(55); 26:45.

Lev 23, with its regulations for the great festivals, is connected thematically with the late passage Ezek 45:18–25 (46:1ff). In substance, however, the two passages go quite different ways. Nothing is mentioned in Ezekiel of natural features of the first sheaf (Lev 23:9–14), the offering at the feast of weeks (Lev 23:15–21), the celebration in booths in memory of the exodus (Lev 23:39–43). Also the terms which are important in the schematic accounts of the festival regulations, עֲצָרָה, אִשֶּׁה, מִקְרָא קֹדֶשׁ, שַׁבָּתוֹן (used in Lev 23:1–3 of sabbath, vv (4) 5–7 of Passover-Unleavened Bread, v 21 feast of Weeks, v 23 New Year's feast, vv 26–32 Day of Atonement, vv 33–36 feast of Tabernacles) are completely lacking in the book of Ezekiel. The appearance of the כרת-formula in Lev 23:29 (cf. the variation in v 30) does not by itself indicate a relationship of H and Ezekiel.

The same is true of Lev 24, which must represent a late insertion within H. That in vv 15–22, which is now set in the context of a narrative exemplifying blasphemy, we find formal elements which also appear in Ezekiel (v 15 נָשָׂא חֵטְא vv 16f מוֹת יוּמַת) has already been mentioned earlier and does not point to a literary connection with Ezekiel.

Also the extensive chapter Leviticus 25, with its complex origin, does not point to a literary relationship with Ezekiel. The sabbath year ordained in Lev 25:1–7 is unknown in Ezekiel. The fiftieth year as the year of release, however, appears to be presupposed by the later addition 46:16–18 under the name שְׁנַת

הַדְּרוֹר.[253] Lev 25:9 has further preserved the old new year date, which is mentioned in Ezek 40:1. On the other hand there is lacking in Ezekiel the name יוֹבֵל as a title for the year of release, which occurs four times in Lev 25:10–13 and is firmly established in the text. In the language there is nothing to support a view that Ezekiel had before him the formulations of Lev 25:8–19 (with the appendix in vv 20–22). Lev 25:17f introduce the regulations in the parenetic style which is usual in H. Over against the formulations of Lev 25:18 (cf. Lev 18:5; 19:37; 22:31) which are attested in Ezekiel, יָשַׁב לָבֶטַח / Ezek 28:26; 34:25, (27), 28; 38:8, 11, 14; 39:6, 26 and הוֹנָה found in Ezek 18:7, 12, 16; 22:7, 29; 45:8; 46:18, there are the reverse: עָמִית which is unusual in Ezekiel, and the mention of the fear of God. Ezekiel never mentions the law of redemption which is given in Lev 25:23–34. The אַנְשֵׁי גְאֻלָּה of Ezek 11:15 certainly shows that the prophet knew something of the duty of redemption within the family.[254] For the rest, however, the passage points in a quite different direction, as well by its concise style in which twice a major case introduced by כִּי (vv 26, 29) is followed by a subordinate case introduced by אִם. Only in the survey of the right of redemption in respect to the land of the Levites are we led to see a remote connection with the regulations for the division of the land in Ezek 48:14.

The prohibition of interest, which is expressed in Lev 25:35–38 in connection with a reference to lending to the poor, is regarded as close to Ezek 18:8, 13, 17; 22:12, yet here also the idea of brotherhood defined by Deuteronomy, is totally lacking in Ezekiel. The vocabulary of the Leviticus passage which is unusual for Ezekiel (גֵּר וְתוֹשָׁב, נָטָה יָדוֹ, מוּךְ fear of God) and the motivation in a saving history forbid us to think of an influence on the text. A similar conclusion must be reached concerning the regulations for those who have become slaves in payment of debt in Lev 25:39–54 and the conclusion in v 55: פֶּרֶךְ, תּוֹשָׁב, שָׂכִיר and other words are lacking in Ezekiel.

However it is quite different with the concluding chapter Leviticus 26. After two of the regulations set out here (Lev 26:1f) in the manner of the individual commands of Leviticus 19, there follows a short assur-

---

253 Concerning this it is conjectured in the commentary that the date of 40:1 presupposes a knowledge of the fiftieth year as the year of release.

254 See p. 261.

ance of salvation which is to repay obedience and a broader threat of woe which is to follow disobedience. The whole is concluded by a glance at a possible repentance after the time of judgement. It is above all Leviticus 26 which made one consider seriously the similarity of authorship of H and Ezekiel. Here also, however, closer examination leads to the recognition that close connection stands alongside striking independence of formulation.

First of all the relationship: for close connections between Lev 26:4–13 and Ezek 34:25–31 (also 36:9, 11; 37:26–28) we can point to the careful analysis by Elliger.[255] It does not reach to Lev 26:5a, 7f, 10. With the declarations of woe in Lev 26:14ff we may compare נתן פָּנִים בְּ in Ezek 14:8; 15:7; for גְּאוֹן עֻזְּכֶם cf. Ezek 7:24 (with emended text); 24:21; 30:6, 18; 33:28— the expression appears in the Old Testament only in H and Ezekiel. For the sending of wild animals in Lev 26:22 cf. Ezek 5:17; 14:15; for pestilence Lev 26:25 cf. Ezek 14:19; the trilogy of sword, pestilence and famine Lev 26:25f/Ezek 5:12, 17; 6:11f; 7:15; 12:16; 14:21 (it is found even more frequently in Jeremiah); the breaking of the staff of bread Lev 26:26 / Ezek 4:16; 5:16; 14:13; eating bread by weight Lev 26:27 / Ezek 4:16; cannibalism in the besieged city Lev 26:29 / Ezek 5:10 but also Dtn 28:53; Lam 2:4, 4:10; destruction of the high places and the altars of incense Lev 26:30 / Ezek 6:3–6. גִּלּוּלִים only here in H (and P), frequent in Ezekiel;[256] הֵרִיק חֶרֶב Lev 26:33 only here in H (and P) / Ezek 5:2, 12; 12:14; יִמַּקּוּ בַּעֲוֹנָם Lev 26:39 / Ezek 4:17; 24:23; 33:10; מַעַל מַעַל Lev 26:40 / Ezek 14:13; 15:8; 17:20; 18:24; 20:27; 39:26; Yahweh's turning graciously "to remember" (זכר) Lev 26:42, 45 / Ezek 16:60; יַעַן וּבְיַעַן Lev 26:43 / Ezek 13:10 (36:3).

Beside this, however, there are striking differences, which are found immediately beside the element of the stylizing of the groups of plagues. First of all it is striking that in the headings of the announcements of salvation (Lev 26:3) and woe (Lev 26:14f) מִצְוָה is found (already in 22:31), which is completely lacking in Ezekiel —an important difference in vocabulary. Instead of בֶּהָלָה (v 16) we find in Ezek 26:21; 27:36; 28:19

בַּלָּהָה. To denote punishment, which in the present text is set out in five stages of severity, there appears in Lev 26:18, 23, 28 the verb יסר, which appears in Ezekiel only in the section 23:36ff, which is undoubtedly a secondary and linguistically confused passage, in v 48. Still more distinctive is the use of the noun קֶרִי "(evil) encounter" (Lev 26:21, 23, 24, 27, 28, 40f) in introducing the stages of punishment. It is lacking in all the rest of the Old Testament including Ezekiel. Also unusual is the connection of the sword with the idea of covenant in the expression חֶרֶב נֹקֶמֶת נְקַם בְּרִית in Lev 26:25. This distinctive phraseology is lacking in the book of Ezekiel, which otherwise has so much to say of the sword as the instrument of Yahweh's judgement (cf. Ezekiel 21). The absence of the sabbath year in Ezekiel has already been mentioned in connection with Lev 25:1–7. Similarly there is lacking in Ezekiel any counterpart to the threat which appears in Lev 26:34f, 43 that the land (after the removal of the people into exile) will be left to enjoy the hitherto neglected sabbaths (sabbath years). The verb used here רצה, besides the five occurrences in Lev 26, is otherwise only found in Is 40:2; 2 Chron 36:21. Lev 26:36f is striking for the words מֹרֶךְ, מְנֻסָה and תְּקוּמָה which are not found in Ezekiel, and Lev 26:40 for הִתְוַדָּה "to confess (guilt)" which is found in P but not in Ezekiel. Above all, however, one does not find anywhere in Ezekiel the conception of a covenant of Yahweh with Jacob, Isaac and Abraham (in this order Lev 26:42), with which Leviticus 26 ended and which is expanded in Lev 26:45 into the statement of the "covenant with the ancestors" (בְּרִית רִאשֹׁנִים) whom Yahweh brought up out of Egypt in order to be their God.

Thus a comparison of Ezekiel with Lev 26, the concluding chapter of H which is closely related to Ezekiel in many features, offers a confused and many-sided picture, which in any case forbids a hasty formula for the mutual relationship of H and Ezekiel. We must make careful distinctions. Elliger's view of the liturgy of the Autumn Festival, which underwent a different editing in Ezek 34:25ff and Lev 26, may be appropriate to explain a series of connections. Similarly Elliger may be right when he locates the threats against the high

255 Elliger, *Leviticus*, 364–367.
256 See pp. 186f.

places and incense altars primarily in the prophetic preaching, whence it has entered later into Leviticus 26. Finally it is quite clear that Leviticus 26 again contains a series of partially later elements (celebration of the sabbath year; stylizing of series of plagues of increasing severity with the words קְרִי, יֹסֵר; also the heightening as in numerical verse forms: seven times worse punishment in Lev 26:18, 21, 24, 28), which have no further contact with Ezekiel.

What we have established about the relationship of Ezekiel to Leviticus 26 is true more widely for the whole of the Holiness Code. It cannot be denied that Ezekiel has been influenced by detailed material built into H, or which already underlies it. This dependence appears in regard to the speech forms of Leviticus 17, the series of laws of Leviticus 18 (and 20), but less strong in regard to those of Leviticus 19, but then again in strong measure in regard to the underlying text used by Leviticus 26. Against this there are other parts, as Leviticus 21–25, in which the contacts are much less. On the other hand it can be seen most clearly in parts of Leviticus 26 that the prophecy of Ezekiel has exercised a reciprocal influence on the development of H, even though the theological basis of H is clearly different from that of Ezekiel. The circles which must have given to H its (pre-P Document) form must not be sought too far from the circles which transmitted the book of Ezekiel.

In what has been said it is already quite clear that we cannot speak of a dependence of the original words of Ezekiel on the Priestly Document (P), into which H in its present form has been worked. Smend has collected a multitude of connections between Ezekiel and P.[257] However, he rightly concludes that we cannot demonstrate any "certain traces of a use of the Priestly Code by Ezekiel."[258] After Burrows and Torrey had defended such a dependence of Ezekiel on P, in the context of a late date for Ezekiel, H. Haag took up again the thesis of such a dependence in the context of a

fresh early dating of P.[259] However, it is not to be overlooked that the specific theological ideas of the historical outline of P: creation (with man made in God's image, and a sabbath instituted at creation), the fixed systematizing of a covenant theology, whereby the tradition of a covenant at Sinai is eliminated in a revolutionary way, find no echo in Ezekiel.[260] Should we not look for at least an echo of them in Ezekiel 20? The law of the priesthood in Ezekiel 44, which is certainly secondary, knows of the Zadokites, but nothing of the Aaronids. We learn nothing at all here of a high priest. The undoubted contacts, in language and subject matter, between Ezekiel and P can be sufficiently explained from the view that P drew from the great stream of priestly tradition, from which also the priest-prophet Ezekiel (at an earlier point of time) had also been nourished. The narrative of P represents a later development of the priestly material.[261]

7. The Message of Ezekiel

A. The form-critical analysis of the book of Ezekiel has shown that it is stylized as a first-person account by the prophet, which derives throughout from God's actions and speaking. Thereby the etiology of the prophet's preaching is determined: he speaks because, and when, the acts and words of Yahweh come to him and send him on his mission.

However, Yahweh and his action is also in substance the great central theme of the prophetic preaching. The frequent use of the recognition formula of the proof-saying shows that this preaching of the prophet has to do above all with Yahweh's great self-revelation.

In view of the strong emphasis on the knowledge of Yahweh, it is striking that in Ezekiel a "theology" in the sense of a description of the attributes of Yahweh is almost completely lacking. Only in a later addition (39:7) do we hear once that Yahweh is holy in Israel. The adjective קָדוֹשׁ (holy) is otherwise used in the book of Ezekiel only in 42:13 for a designation of the priestly

---

257 Smend, xxviif.

258 Smend, vif.

259 Herbert Haag, *Was lehrt die literarische Untersuchung des Ezechiel-Textes?* (Freiburg in der Schweiz: Paulusdruckerei, 1943).

260 Walther Zimmerli, "Sinaibund und Abrahambund. Ein Beitrag zum Verständnis der Priesterschrift," *ThZ* 16 (1960): 268–280; reprinted in *idem, Gottes*

Offenbarung, ThB 19 (München: Kaiser, 1963), 205–216.

261 Fohrer, *Hauptprobleme*, 148–154.

rooms. Holiness (with the noun קֹדֶשׁ) is mentioned of the name Yahweh (20:39; 36:20–22; 39:7, 25; 43:7f), of his mountain (20:40).[262] The temple and its sacrifices are designated as "holiness" (קֹדֶשׁ). Never otherwise, however, is Yahweh named "the Holy One." Also he is never called great (36:23 said once of the name), the high or most high, the strong, the fearful, or "the faithful" (חָסִיד), "the righteous" (צַדִּיק), "the merciful" (חַנּוּן) "the compassionate" (רַחוּם). He is never described by the adjective "the zealous" (קַנָּא), although more than once his zeal (קִנְאָה 5:13; 16:42; 23:25; 36:5f; 38:19) is spoken of. However, the style of the hymnic description, using the participle, which characterizes the language of Deutero-Isaiah and the Psalms and also occasionally colors that of Isaiah and Jeremiah, does not appear in Ezekiel. Where statements about Yahweh are made the finite verb dominates. The expansions of the recognition formula, which as a rule sets the person of Yahweh, as indicated by his name, in the center of what is known ("know, that I am Yahweh") and which could easily lead directly into a hymnic predication, almost exclusively move in the same direction: "know that I Yahweh have spoken (in my zeal)" (5:13, see further 6:10; 17:21; 37:14); "that I, Yahweh, have brought down the high tree, but have raised up the low tree" (17:24); "that I, Yahweh, have kindled it" (21:4, where the ידע of the recognition formula is replaced by ראה); "I have drawn my sword from its sheath" (21:10); "have poured out my anger upon you" (22:22); "have heard all thy slanders" (35:12); "I build what has been torn down, and plant what has been uprooted" (36:36). Only rarely is there a participial formulation, that Yahweh strikes (7:9), sanctifies Israel (20:12; 37:28). Yahweh wills to be known, not in his being, but in his action. Thus the sole text in which a royal title is ascribed to Yahweh is formulated verbally. By his deed of the new exodus Yahweh will become the king of his people (אֶמְלוֹךְ עֲלֵיכֶם 20:33). By his action Israel may know him as "its God" (אֱלֹהֵיהֶם 28:26; 39:28). That Yahweh will deal with his people, in whose sphere his holy mountain lies (הַר קָדְשִׁי 20:40) and to whom his holy name is pledged (20:5,.7, 19f, cf. 36:20), is a presupposition

of the preaching of Ezekiel, even though the full "Yahweh god of Israel" (יהוה אֱלֹהֵי יִשְׂרָאֵל) appears only in 44:2, and the shorter "god of Israel" (אֱלֹהֵי יִשְׂרָאֵל), with the exception of 10:20, only in the phrase "glory of the god of Israel" (כְּבוֹד אֱלֹהֵי יִשְׂרָאֵל [mostly in secondary passages]), and the technical vocabulary of election only in 20:5. Ezekiel's preaching concerns this, divine activity.

Having said this we must not be misunderstood to say that for the prophet Yahweh himself lay wholly in obscurity. Rather at the beginning of the prophet's book there is an account of the encounter in which Yahweh comes to the prophet in an unprecedented vision and commands him to preach. The account of this encounter in his call has become a constituent part of the prophetic message of the book because it contains the legitimation of the entire message.

The detailed study of the original text of Ezekiel 1 shows how much the prophet, in his description of what he saw, stands in the older traditions of Israel. We cannot deny a relationship to the encounter with God of which Isaiah 6 tells with its commissioning of Isaiah in the temple of Jerusalem. On the other hand, Ezekiel 1 cannot be separated from the later Priestly Document's descriptions of the appearance of the "glory of Yahweh" (כְּבוֹד יהוה) in the desert. Whilst Is 6:3 still uses the "glory" (כְּבוֹד) concept in the seraphs' song in a general way to describe the worldwide glory of Yahweh, in Ezek 1:28 (3:12, 23 [8:4; 9:3]; 10:4, 18; 11:22f; 43:2, 4f [44:4], differently 39:21) as in P "glory of Yahweh" (כְּבוֹד יהוה) is a designation of the appearance of Yahweh's splendor. Like Isaiah, Ezekiel, even though he avoids the title "king," experiences Yahweh as the one who is enthroned in majesty. Isaiah's encounter, however, as his subsequent preaching shows, was dominated by faith in the one who was enthroned in Jerusalem the city of God (Psalms 46, 48, 76), the "one who abides in Mount Zion" (שֹׁכֵן בְּהַר צִיּוֹן) (Is 8:18), whereas Ezekiel appears at the same time both archaic and revolutionary in that he speaks of the manifestation of the glory of Yahweh in a remote place of exile. What earlier narratives tell of the God of Sinai (Horeb), that he came to the help of his people who

---

262 Cf. the קֹדֶשׁ (holy) added in 𝔐 to the mythical "mount of God" (הַר אֱלֹהִים) of 28:14, where see note c.

had settled in Canaan, Ezekiel experiences in a surprising way of the God who, meanwhile, had, according to Israel's faith so far as it lived in Judah, made his abode on Zion. Should we regard as an archaism or as a revolutionary innovation the fact that Ezekiel in his entire message both avoids the name Zion for Jerusalem and also any mention of the God who dwells on Zion by his name יהוה צְבָאוֹת?[263] In any case it must be regarded as a surprising fact for a person stemming from a priestly family to have seen Yahweh's glory at a place far from Jerusalem, where man ate "unclean bread" (4:13). Also that for Ezekiel's faith Jerusalem was the proper place of the divine dwelling is clear from the two texts in which he tells in chs. 10f (8:4 and 9:3 are additions assimilating to chs. 1–3) and 43 of the vision of the glory of Yahweh.

The school of Ezekiel has then filled out the picture of the appearance of Yahweh's glory. It has supplied the mobility of the throne-manifestation by the addition of wheels (1:15–21), which make the whole thing appear as a chariot. By the addition of ch. 10 it has explicitly interpreted the "living creatures" as cherubim or the like. The original description by the prophet, in contrast to this, is much more restrained. Like the prophet himself his school has been afraid to describe the appearance of the person of Yahweh (who is enthroned above the sapphire firmament [Ex 24:10] in brilliant light), giving only hints of a description. The message of the visionary scene does not lie in the elaboration of the visible figure of God, but in the unexpected event of the presence of the One who is enthroned in Jerusalem with the exiled and lost son of a priest in his remote exile, and through him, with his people. In this place of loneliness, at which Yahweh is no more than "a little sanctuary" for his people, he makes this man his mouthpiece.[264] The prophet proclaims this event as the legitimation of his office.

Similarly the figure who is introduced in the visions of chs. 8–11 and 40–48 with various functions in the course of the vision is not a strongly emphasized feature. "The man" of 8:2 (note b) shares in a way that is far from clear in the act of transporting in 8:3 and then disappears again. "The man" of 40:3 at the conclusion of the act of transportation is the prophet's guide and the interpreter of his vision more extensively. Neither the one nor the other takes on an independent importance. The same is true of the 6 plus 1 men of ch. 9, who represent the long arm of Yahweh's judgement and his protection, and who disappear as soon as Yahweh's will is accomplished. The message that is proclaimed has to do with judgement and protection, not with those who help to perform this. Ezekiel proclaims this message in his account to the exiles (11:25).

B. The prophet himself and the office to which he is called have a greater importance. Admittedly he himself is no more than any other creature. He is addressed as a "son of man," i.e., one of the genus "man," who is made essentially as a creature of Yahweh, his creator (the vocabulary of creation, however, is surprisingly nowhere fully elaborated by Ezekiel, ברא in the nip'al in 21:35; 28:13, 15).[265] This man, however, who, besides the heading of the book which has been added later (1:2), is only once called by the proper name Ezekiel (in 24:24), is sent by Yahweh (שלח 2:3), so that Yahweh's message to the house of Israel may be given by his mouth. By his preaching he is a נָבִיא of the message and thereby a part of the event which comes from Yahweh. Thus in 2:5 and 33:33 he can be directly introduced into the recognition formula: "They will know that a prophet has been in their midst." The historical concreteness of God's action becomes inseparably tied to the figure of the divine messenger.[266] The person of the prophet himself is described in 12:6, 11; 24:24 (27) quite expressly as "a sign" (מוֹפֵת) for the people. By his action what Yahweh is about to bring upon his people is already present. The prophet belongs inseparably to the "message."

---

263 See Werner Kessler, "Aus welchen Gründen wird die Bezeichnung 'Jahwe Zebaoth' in der späteren Zeit gemieden?" *Wiss Z. Halle* GR 7 (1958): 767–771; Gunther Wanke, *Die Zionstheologie der Korachiten in ihrem traditionsgeschichtlichen Zusammenhang*, BZAW 97 (Berlin: Töpelmann, 1966), 40–46.

264 11:16, see pp. 261f.

265 See pp. 131f.

266 See Zimmerli, *Erkenntnis*, 67.

The passages just referred to at the same time make clear that the word of Yahweh, which the prophet has to proclaim, is not a doctrine about the essential nature of God, which can be described to men apart from any events, but an announcement of Yahweh's action towards Israel. Time and again the prophet, in his own being, enters with all his physical activity into the event between Yahweh and Israel and has to proclaim this event through his actions and feelings, sometimes quite actively and sometimes passively.[267] He actively sets forth the events of the enemy's advance, the siege and conquest of the city, and the deportation of the population, by the brick which he besieges, the meager rations which he eats, the shaving and destruction of his hair (4:1–2[3], 9–11; 5:1–2[3–4a], always introduced by "Take for yourself," [קַח־לְךָ]), but also by his bringing out of the exile's baggage (12:3ff, introduced by "prepare for yourself," [עֲשֵׂה לְךָ]), by the sign of the two ways (21:24ff, introduced by "set for yourself," [שִׂים־לְךָ]). This is no mere play but an anticipatory sharing in what is about to happen. So also the putting together of the two sticks is to be understood in regard to a promise of salvation (37:16ff, again introduced by "take for yourself" [קַח־לְךָ]).[268] At the same time, however, what happens to him to make him more the passive sufferer; his lying bound (4:4–8), his quaking (12:17–20) and his groaning (21:11f), his paralysis under the divine blow which robs him of his wife (24:15–24, described by "Behold I take . . ." [הִנְנִי לֹקֵחַ] in v 16 clearly as an event coming from Yahweh) becomes a message of what will come from Yahweh upon Israel. Because the message which the prophet has to announce means a real historical action, the preacher is not only called upon to preach with his mind and mouth, but with all his personal being, both body and spirit.

It is thus clear that Ezekiel is not a puppet, with Yahweh pulling the strings. He is called by Yahweh as a person, summoned to obedience by stern commands, warned openly not to be rebellious (2:8), and not to be afraid (2:6; 3:9). In this connection he is equipped by Yahweh for his service, the temptations of which he is not left in doubt from the start (2:6; 3:5–7), with the hardness necessary for the task (3:8f). Constantly, and in a very striking way, the addressee of this task is the "house of Israel."[269] In 3:10f, in the conclusion of the call narrative, as the specific addressee the "Exiles" (גּוֹלָה) is once mentioned. Also in 11:24f it appears as the recipient of the message. In 8:1; 14:1; 20:1 the elders are mentioned, and in 33:30–33 the people of the prophet's immediate environment appear. On the other hand, in 11:14–21; 33:24–29 those who have been left in the land are clearly addressed. Throughout (apart from the foreign nation oracles which must be dealt with separately) the book constantly deals with the fate of all Israel, the judgement upon Israel, and the possibility of a future for the house of Israel.[270]

Within this framework there takes place a distinctive movement, which leads finally—a development unique in the prophetic literature—to a second explicit definition of the prophetic office. The call narrative of 1:1–3:15 constantly shows Israel as a whole as the addressee of the prophetic preaching, in which 3:10f adds further the more specific reference to the sphere of the גּוֹלָה surrounding him. In 33:1–9, however, and the insertion 3:17–21, which has been added directly to the call narrative, in a fresh way the individual within the house of Israel is in view. The office of "watchman," which is already known from prophecy before Ezekiel (Jer 6:17), is here turned towards individuals within Israel. It must be the final destruction of the political structure of the remnant of Israel in Judah / Jerusalem and the empowering of the prophet by Yahweh to declare an open future which made the prophet turn so decisively to the individual. From this we must raise the question whether Ezekiel's priestly origin, which was already familiar with the priestly entrance liturgies and also the purity–תּוֹרוֹת, had encouraged this turning to the individual. In this new connection the prophet's own responsibility was also determined. As it is said in the introductory call narrative, in regard to the people as a whole, that he had to preach, "whether they hear or whether they forbear" (2:5, 7; 3:11 [27]), so it is now said that the prophet must warn the individual sinner. If he neglects to do so "then I will demand his blood at your hand" (3:18, 20; 33:8, cf. v 6). If, in spite

---

267 See above pp. 28f.
268 In this connection we must also mention the active gestures. See above pp. 29f.
269 See Excursus 2.
270 For the references to Judah see Excursus 2.

of this warning, the wicked does not turn away from his sin, then "you will have saved your own life" (3:21; 33:9). In both texts we see a widely developed reflection upon the limits of prophetic responsibility. The announcement of God's action comes from the office of the prophet. However, the process of repentance and obedience, and the responsibility for it, lie wholly with those addressed. In the first call-narrative these latter are Israel as a whole, and in the second the individuals within Israel.

C. The call-narrative contains no concrete clarification of the prophet's message. Rather it is noteworthy here, as is simply reflected in 2:4 (3:11), that the latter is simply commanded to preach: "Thus has the Lord Yahweh spoken." His preaching is above all to show that it derives from his receiving a message.[271] His speaking must derive from the hearing (2:8), in which Yahweh's word comes to him (דְּבָרַי v 7), and which he is to proclaim to a rebellious Israel. In the call-narrative 1:1–3:15 all emphasis rests on this description of the "rebellious house." When the prophet is then given a scroll to eat, this "was written on both sides," and what is written contains "laments, sighs, and woes" (2:10), then we can see in this that Ezekiel also belongs to the prophets identified by Jer 28:8 as those truly sent by Yahweh, who speak "of war, famine and disease." A description of Ezekiel's prophetic preaching will accordingly first have to set forth the future judgement announced by Yahweh, from which emerges the "laments, sighs and woes," and, joining on to this, make clear the prophet's picture of the "rebellious house" to whom this message is sent and whose conduct justifies the announcement of judgement.

1) The intervention of the divine judgement is described in ch. 7 in the widest field. The catchword of the "end" which has come, stemming from Amos 8:1f, is connected here with elements of the description of the day of Yahweh.[272] In the basic text of the long section vv 5–6aα, 10–27, this day is described in an impersonal style, with all its horror and despair. The horror of the bad news of judgement is also made clear by the symbolic action of 21:11f, in similar words. As a rule the message of judgement is expressed with a clearer aim.

The introductory sections announce to the land of Israel the threatened day of Yahweh in direct address. 6:1–7 threaten the mountains and valleys of Israel with imminent devastation by war. In the section 6:11–14 (cf. 5:12) the devastation is made specific by the *tria* sword, famine, and pestilence (as in Jer 28:8). The scheme of the four divine plagues, which we now find in two variants in Jer. 15:1–4, is to be seen most clearly in 14:12ff.[273]

There appears most fully in Ezekiel's words of doom a threat against Jerusalem, which as ch. 15 shows, already suffered the first flames of judgement in the events of 597 B.C. and is now threatened with complete destruction. In the three-sign composition of chs. 4f, which possibly go back to the earliest parts of the prophet's preaching, siege, famine and the destruction of Jerusalem and its population are dramatically set out. The interpretative saying in 5:5, which speaks of Jerusalem as the city which Yahweh has set in the midst of the nations, makes clear how much this event is an event in the center of the divine history.[274] The nations are to be witnesses of this history of Yahweh (5:8 [14f]). 21:23ff speaks with great vividness of the advance of the besieger, who is now named openly as the king of Babylon, and of his decision to direct the spearhead of his attack directly against Jerusalem. The sword which lies in his hand, and which is in reality the sword of Yahweh's judgement, can be addressed directly as an independent person in the grim sword-song of the original text of 21:13–22 and encouraged to perform its bloody task. The siege of the city, with all the suffering which it brings to the besieged, is dramatically portrayed in the work-song of the cooking-pot filled with pieces of meat (24:1–14), which has similarly been subsequently expanded. This picture was possibly suggested by Jer 1:13f and is apparently echoed in 11:3, 7. With the adoption of Isaiah's picture of the smelting process (Is 1:25, also Jer 6:29), which Ezekiel uses in a bold way, this is portrayed as a burning heat (22:17–22).[275] In 21:1ff the threat of the sword which turns against Jerusalem and its sanctuary is then set out metaphorically with the picture of fire which rages in the forests of the south. However, fire is also the destroy-

---

271 See p. 133.
272 See pp. 201f.
273 For this connection see Miller, *Verhältnis*, 86.

274 See pp. 174f.
275 See pp. 462–464.

ing element which the prophet sees in the vision of chs. 8–11 as the instrument of the divine judgement. First, men with weapons of death are sent out of the temple into the city, according to 9:5ff, in order there to cut down without pity "the old man, the youth, the young woman, the child, and the women." The priestly figure who is then sent by Yahweh to put a sign on "the foreheads of the men who sigh and groan over all the abominations which have been committed in its [i.e., the city's] midst" and so to rescue them, receives the order to scatter fire from the most holy place around the city (10:2). The fire of judgement goes out from the sacred center of the very temple in Jerusalem, the dwelling place of Yahweh. It is then simply the fulfilment of this action when the glory of Yahweh abandons this dwelling place and thereby also empties the temple, making it a house given over to destruction.

The fate of the citizens of Jerusalem, however, who have survived this raging of the sword, will be deportation. Once again Ezekiel, in a visible symbolic action, has to portray the packing up of an exile's few belongings and to signify the departure from the homeland in a dramatic way (12:1ff). The horror of desolation will lie over the land, which the prophet announces by his quaking when eating his food (12:17–20). He has to proclaim in a sign-action, which offended the deepest feelings of a son of a priest, how the Israelites would have to eat their food in an unclean way among the nations (4:12–15). According to 4:4–8 his own bodily immobility is to serve to show the guilt and punishment which will lie upon his people. The paralysis which befalls him after the grievous death of his wife proclaims the paralysis which will numb the minds of the people when it loses the glory of Jerusalem.

Any minimizing of his message and any lighthearted disregard of it as something which is still a long way off the prophet opposes by the harsh word that Yahweh will not neglect to fulfill his word (12:21–25, 26–28).

With his preaching of judgement Ezekiel stands in the succession of Jeremiah, who similarly saw in the Babylonian king Nebuchadnezzar the agent of Yahweh's judgement and who had consistently opposed any attempt to resist this agency. However, whilst we

can see in Jeremiah what a depth of personal suffering the preaching of this message meant for the prophet himself and how deeply he felt compassion for his people, Ezekiel's preaching has a bitter harshness, which only quite exceptionally reveals his personal feelings. Nowhere does he betray anything of his compassion for the fate of the house of Israel, even where he lies personally bound, or where he quakes at eating his food, or where he is left stunned by the death of his wife. Only the cry at the departure of the destroyer into the city (9:8, cf. 11:13) appears to break through this harsh reserve of the prophet. Should we similarly understand the addition of 21:17, where the prophet is commanded to cry out at the raging of the sword? That the form of the lament (קִינָה) appears especially in the oracles against foreign nations as a stereotyped feature warns us against interpreting the lament over the princes of Israel in ch. 19 too hastily as a warm personal feeling of the prophet over the fate of the kings.[276] Ezekiel's preaching of the coming judgement remains hard and fearfully "objective." What undoubtedly permeates all his preaching is above all a knowledge of the majesty of the God of Israel, who has been so humiliated by the actions of his people that his harsh judgement for the sake of the holiness of his divine name becomes unavoidable. Thus we must now speak further of what the prophet has to say in his preaching by way of accusation against the dishonoring of the divine name and will by the house of Israel.

2) The call-narrative already makes clear how harsh is the accusation which Yahweh has to raise against his people by the mouth of the prophet, where the very name "house of Israel" can be immediately replaced by "house of rebellion."[277] Similarly the call-narrative already shows that Yahweh's accusation concerns not only a passing sin of Israel, which with a good will can be left alone, but that it has in mind the people in the whole breadth of their history: "They and their fathers" have been rebellious "up to this very day" (2:3).

This claim receives a full elaboration in the preaching of the prophet which follows. Already Hosea, Isaiah, and Jeremiah are familiar in their preaching with the

276 See further pp. 396f.
277 See p. 134.

feature of a survey of the past history of the people. In no other prophet, however, do we find a similar total verdict upon Israel's entire history from its beginnings, as is now formulated in Ezekiel with unsurpassable severity. In all three of the above-named predecessors of Ezekiel a bright beginning of the history of Israel or Jerusalem, is contrasted with the subsequent corruption (Hos 2:17; Is 1:21, 26; Jer 2:2). Ezekiel, however, recognizes only the offenses of his people from their beginnings in the great historical sketches, which in a particular way, are characteristic of him. Thus in 20:1–31 the beginnings of Israel's history, which it confesses in its credo-like formulations (von Rad) as the proper basis of its salvation as the people of Yahweh, are unfolded as a history which denotes the rebelliousness of the house of Israel (מרה) already at the initial phase of its existence in Egypt. Even at that time it had become stained with the worship of idols. Already in the period in the wilderness, when Yahweh had given to the people his sabbaths as a special sign of its relationship to him (v 20) and as a sign of the separation from the nations which makes it holy (v 12), Israel had desecrated this sacramental pledge. Thus there occurs then the divine resolve to punish and to scatter his people among the nations, already in the wilderness period, before the people have entered into the land, although Yahweh has at first held back the heat of his anger "for his name's sake." More fearful still, and unique in the entire Old Testament, is the statement that Yahweh had included in the laws which he gave to Israel in order that it might have life through them (vv 11, 13), evil laws and "laws, by which it could not live" (v 25). The deep mystery of blinding by God himself, which is touched upon in 14:9 in regard to the disobedient prophets and in 3:20 in connection with the righteous who come to disaster, has been introduced here into the early history of Israel with God, which was described by Ezekiel's predecessors so brightly.

With the picture of the two unfaithful women, which derives from Hosea through Jer 3:6ff and distinguishes the two parts of the house of Israel, Ezekiel 23 expresses the same message of the radical corruption of the nation. The two women are described, who already committed immorality in Egypt, in dependence on the credo of the exodus. Beyond what is said in ch. 20,

that immorality becomes the prototype of the immorality with the Egyptians in the present, the final episode of the history of the state of Judah. The זנה is thereby carried over, in dependence on earlier usage, to apply to political pacts with foreign powers. Egypt, as already in the days of Isaiah and also in the preaching of Jeremiah, is the great temptress in the background, who entices Judah to break out of the punishment imposed by Yahweh and to rebel against the eastern power, which is Yahweh's instrument of punishment (especially Jer 27–29; cf. especially Ezek 17). Ezek 16 turns the metaphor of the unfaithful wife, which is here expanded by the motif of the foundling child who owes all its life including its clothes and its jewelry to Yahweh, against Jerusalem, which here becomes the proper representative of sinful Israel. The radical corruption of this city is illustrated in a surprising use of historical elements from the biological ancestry of the city: "From your origin and your derivation you are from the land of the Canaanites. Your father was an Amorite and your mother a Hittite" (v 3). It is in agreement with this insult about its Canaanite origin that the sin in Ezek 16 is not seen to lie in the political sphere, but in the cultic. In line with Hosea the "playing of this harlot" (זנה) here is interpreted of the Baalized cults of the land, against which Hosea and the Deuteronomic reform stood—although in Ezekiel the name of Baal is not mentioned. The word בַּעַל ("Baal") is absent in the entire book of Ezekiel.

In another way chs. 15 and 22:1ff give expression to the radical corruption of Jerusalem. Ezekiel 15 uses the metaphor of the vine, which had a place of honor in Israel's religious language. The prophet, in an unexpectedly new direction, asks a question about the value of the wood of the vine. As a piece of burnt vine wood (cf. the event of 597 B.C.) he deduces directly from this metaphor the essential uselessness of Israel. Like the burnt vine wood, it is suitable only for burning. Ch. 15 is frightening in its directly ontological judgement about the essential uselessness of Jerusalem. In 22:1–16, on the other hand, Jerusalem becomes the "city of blood," measured against a series of laws and found guilty, point for point, under the comprehensive category of "blood." Here also an overall judgement is expressed on the basis of what is set out, not a picture made of little sections in a sequence of individual offenses.

Besides this, however, there are not lacking accusations against those immediately responsible in Jerusalem. In ch. 8, where the prophet in a visionary tour through the temple is shown the abominations in this special section of Jerusalem, we can see again in the adducing of four abominations an element of stylizing. Also we cannot avoid the impression that here four particularly gross sins are set out together in a single scene, so that we may question whether they all took place at the same time in the temple or whether notorious offenses from various periods of the temple's history have been drawn upon. In the individual offenses— the image of jealousy at the North Gate of the city, the wall carvings to which worship is made, the women weeping for Tammuz, and finally the solar features in the worship of Yahweh—we are dealing with facts which the prophet knew as features in Jerusalem. Most clearly we can see the invective which ch. 17 raises against the king of Judah over Zedekiah's breach of treaty. For the priest-prophet Ezekiel the most grievous aspect of the offenses is not that of arrogant pride, as with Isaiah, nor opposition to Yahweh's purpose of judgement, but the breach of the oath sworn in the name of Yahweh. We may also understand the attack on the sacrilegious king of 21:30–32 "Evil one, about to be slain" (חָלָל רָשָׁע) in this context. We find in ch. 34 (and 45:9) more general attacks against abuse of the law by the heads of the administration. In 43:7–9 offenses against the regulation for the complete separation of the holy from the profane are attacked by Yahweh at his entrance into the new temple. These had occurred through the (Solomonic) interlocking of the temple and palace areas, and the setting up of steles *pro memoria* in the sacred area.

The attacks against the prophets in Ezekiel 13 are also formulated more generally, rebuking them for their neglect of the task of exercising a critical watchfulness. Beside them stand the prophetesses, whose crude magical practices make them a subject for reproof. Particular attacks against the priests are lacking, once we look away from the criticisms of the Levites, who, previous to the time of judgement, misled the people into idolatry, but which do not derive from the prophet himself (44:10–14). The priests only appear in the sermon against sections of the community in 22:23ff, beside

the other sections of the princes, the officials (שָׂרִים), the prophets, and the "people of the land" (עַם הָאָרֶץ). Here they are accused of neglecting their typical duties (cf. 44:23, and 7:26). We may certainly also look for the priests among the figures mentioned in ch. 8. It is striking, however, that there they are not expressly mentioned as such.

We must still mention two groups of men against which the prophet's accusations are directed. These are first of all the representatives of the exiles. When, according to 8:1, these sit down before Ezekiel in his house, and then, according to 11:25, are told the prophet's vision of the events in the sinful temple of Jerusalem, no mention is made at first of an offense on the part of these men. In the analogous scene of 20:1ff, where they seek a divine oracular decision, this is refused them (vv 3, 31) with a reference to the sinful history of the people, in which they also are concerned. The refusal in the similar situation of 14:1–11 is quite clearly motivated by the addiction to idols (גִּלּוּלִים literally "pellets of dung") which also existed among the exiles. 33:30–33, on the other hand, has in mind the aesthetic disregard of the prophet's message by the exiles (certainly after 587 B.C.)

The prophet's accusations against those who remained in the land and did not go into exile is, however, consistently sharp. According to 11:15 the reproach is levelled against them that they thought of themselves as the owners of the land and therewith as the people who were still close to Yahweh. In 11:13 the same reproach appears to be raised against Pelatiah. 33:23–29 turns against those who were still left in the land after 587 B.C. and against their seemingly pious confidence, in the reference back to Abraham. They are accused of clinging to sins which are opposed to God's laws (eating blood, idolatry, bloodshedding, violence, sexual extravagance) and therefore are threatened with further judgement.

In the accusations of the prophet, by which his threats of judgement are justified, the reference recurs repeatedly that Israel clings to idols (גִּלּוּלִים). It appears that for Ezekiel so significant a word summarizes in a comprehensive way what the prophet must attack as infringement of Yahweh's absolute sovereignty and his holy purity.[278]

D. The prophet's threats of judgement in chs. 25–32 (and 35) turn against a number of neighboring nations to the house of Israel. In turning from the prophet's call-vision this is surprising because there (unlike in Jeremiah 1) nothing is said of the prophet's task to be a prophet to the nations, but on the contrary in 3:6 the nations with a foreign language are held up to Israel as an example: "If I were to send you to them, they would listen to you." Thus the task of preaching against the nations does not appear from the start to have been in the prophet's commission.

Closer examination shows that a half of the collection in chs. 25–32, which is directed towards seven foreign nations (or cities), is aimed at Egypt and its ruler (29–32). Again of the seven sections aimed against Egypt and its ruler, all are dated, with the exception of 30:1–19, a section which arouses much doubt about its origin from the prophet himself on the grounds of content and language. Apart from what is clearly a later insertion in 29:17–21, the dates of all the other Egyptian oracles which are dated point to the period in the tenth to the twelfth years after Jehoiachin's deportation. In the eleventh year Jerusalem fell and was destroyed by Nebuchadnezzar. Undoubtedly the oracles against Egypt surround this event. The preaching against foreign nations which we find in them has therefore first arisen in connection with the events of 588–586 B.C.

From these events it is certainly intelligible that Ezekiel's threat of judgement must turn directly against Egypt. Ezekiel 17, as also 23, has made clear how Egypt became the seducer of Judah and enticed it to treason against the oath sworn to Nebuchadnezzar and to political immorality (זנה). Thus it lies in the extension of the message committed to the prophet that he announced the coming judgement of Yahweh upon this power. 29:1ff and 32:1ff speak of Pharaoh as the crocodile (תַּנִּין) of the Nile which is destroyed,[279] and 31:1ff, with the broadly elaborated picture of the world-tree which is felled. The motif of the descent into the underworld of the pride of Egypt, which is set out in 32:17ff in an independent oracle, has also entered

into the conclusion of the oracle of the world-tree (31:15ff). In 30:1ff, which is an addition, the school of Ezekiel has added still further the motif of the "Day of Yahweh" coming upon Egypt. Besides these figures of judgement there appears in another place the plain announcement that the land will be devastated (29:12). 30:20ff; 32:11 mention the king of Babylon as the one who will break the arm of Pharaoh and knock the sword out of his hand. The appended saying in 29:17ff can speak directly of Yahweh's payment of wages to Nebuchadnezzar and his army: the reward which eluded the king of Babylon in the case of Tyre will be awarded to him by the handing over of Egypt.

The striking calculation of the divine judgement on Egypt in 29:9b–16 as a forty year period of punishment and the announcement of a subsequent restitution as a minor kingdom ("a humble kingdom"), which assimilates Egypt's period of punishment to that of Judah in 4:6, must derive from the school of the prophet.[280]

When we consider the outburst of preaching against Egypt in the period from 588–586 B.C., it is striking that in 29–32 the motivation which we should expect from chs. 17 and 23 is only echoed in 29:6b–9a. Here, in a metaphor familiar from Is 36:6, Egypt is described as a fragile staff, which breaks when anyone leans on it. In this way Egypt has become a cause of destruction to Judah. Otherwise the judgement upon Egypt in chs. 29–32 is declared either without any motive, or in a quite general way there is mentioned the *hybris* of the great power (29:3, 9; 31:10), its proud pomp (הָמוֹן 29:19; 30:4, 10, 15; 31:2, 18; 32:12, 16 and elsewhere), or in 32:17ff the fact that it spreads fear on the earth. This, however, is undoubtedly a stereotyped feature of prophetic oracles against foreign nations, which have their own history and, in their motifs, have not simply grown out the line of preaching of the other classical prophets.

This is also evident in the preaching against Tyre, which represents in 26:1–28:19 the second largest complex of the oracles against foreign nations. The sole reference to the date, which is found in 26:1 at the head of a collection comprising three units, similarly points to the year of Jerusalem's fall. Here also only

278 See pp. 186f.
279 See note d to 29:3.
280 See Volume 2.

the introductory oracle in 26:2 shows an explicit relationship to the fate of Jerusalem. Here judgement is announced against Tyre on account of its selfish, calculating gloating over the fall of Jerusalem with its rival trade. Also here Nebuchadnezzar is mentioned as Yahweh's assistant in judgement (26:7). In ch. 27, the great lament over Tyre, represented metaphorically as a beautiful ship, which suffers shipwreck, no special accusation is expressed which justifies the downfall. First in the legal pronouncement of 28:1–10 upon the prince of Tyre is the accusation of *hybris*, and the pretension of behaving like God, raised against the king. The allegory of 28:11–19 which, for all that remains obscure about it, reveals the myth of the first man thrown out of the garden of paradise, adds to the charge of pride a reference to violence and guilt over corrupt trading. The impression that we find in the oracles against foreign nations—in the frequent use of the קִינָה,[281] in the use of the motif of the descent into the underworld,[282] as well as in the charge of *hybris*, typical forms of address against nations, in which the prophet varies independently patterns used elsewhere (cf. Isaiah 14)—can only be strengthened by the oracles against Tyre.

On the other hand, the oracles against the immediate neighbors of the house of Israel: Ammon (cf. 21:33), Moab, Edom, the Philistines in ch. 25 (and 35) are fully related to the prophet's own message about the house of Israel. The type of the three-part proof-saying is formally dominant here throughout.[283] All these oracles, which lack any reference to date, are to be dated to the time after the fall of Jerusalem. They undoubtedly represent a later group of oracles against foreign nations. The judgement which is proclaimed here upon neighboring peoples is justified throughout by their conduct towards the remnant of Israel left in Jerusalem after its judgement. Because Ammon gloated (25:3, 6) over the desecrated sanctuary of Yahweh and Israel's devastated land, Moab taunted that the house of Judah had suffered like all other nations, Edom and the Philistines showed themselves to be revengeful and full of contempt (25:12, 15), they will in their turn become the prey of the enemy (25:4f, 7, 9f), and they

will suffer the devastation and vengeance of Yahweh (25:13f, 16f). Edom, which took an active part in the devastation of Jerusalem (35:5) and which claimed possession of part of Yahweh's land (35:10, 12, cf. 36:2 and 5), is threatened most severely. When here the threat against the mountains of Seir (ch. 35) is connected directly with a promise of deliverance for the mountains of Israel (36:1ff), it is clear that the judgement upon the gloating neighboring peoples means at the same time the heralding of a new act of mercy by Yahweh towards his people and his mocked and despised land (36:13). Overall, however, there is a reference here to Yahweh's glorifying himself who will not abandon his honor which he has pledged to his people, but will demonstrate who he is in his judgement upon his people's enemies. This purpose of demonstrating his holiness then dominates quite exclusively the short oracle against the city of Sidon (28:21–23), which is added lastly to bring the number of foreign nations or cities addressed up to seven. The sayings against Israel's immediate neighbors are concluded in 28:24 with Yahweh's promise to remove the prickly thorns and useless briers from the house of Israel. An added appendix in vv 25–26 glances further forward still to the saving gathering together and restoration of Israel in its land.

Before this side of the message of Ezekiel is fully dealt with we must note three facts which emerge from the study of his preaching against the nations.

In Jeremiah 25 we can see how the threats of doom upon enemies round about are brought together in an overall judgement upon the nations. In Ezekiel we seek in vain for such an overall judgement or indeed for any summary announcement of a general judgement upon the nations (cf. Is 45:20).

This is related to the second fact. The collection of seven oracles against the nations is also illuminated by the nations which do not appear in it. That Damascus, the immediate northern neighbor of "the house of Israel" (47:16; 48:1), no longer appears, as in Amos and Isaiah, can be explained from the downfall of this Aramaean state and erstwhile enemy of Israel in the Assyrian period. It is even more noteworthy that in the

---

281 See above p. 31.
282 See above p. 32.
283 See above pp. 36–40.

book of Ezekiel there is no oracle against the empire of the Babylonians, the particular opponent of Israel in the days of Ezekiel. The sole passage in which we can perhaps see a polemic against Babylon, expressed in a veiled way without mention of the name (in 21:33ff), certainly does not derive from Ezekiel himself. This fact is certainly very striking when we compare it with the preaching of Deutero-Isaiah, from the late exilic period, and also the position of the book of Isaiah (with ch. 13) and Jeremiah (with ch. 50f). It speaks in favor of the view that for the final redaction of the book of Ezekiel we must not go too much later. It is, however, also evidence of how decisively the prophet's own preaching and that of his school held fast to the line of Jeremiah's own preaching with its view that Israel had to see in Nebuchadnezzar in any case the arm of Yahweh's judgement and to acknowledge it without opposition.

As a third fact we must note finally the striking message of the Tyre-Egypt oracle in 29:17–21, which is added to the collection of oracles against Egypt and which has the latest date of any of Ezekiel's oracles. Here there is a transition from the oracles against Tyre to those against Egypt in a way that is quite unique for Ezekiel. Even more noteworthy, however, is the fact that here Yahweh changes the message himself in the freedom of the Lord who sends the message, which he has first entrusted to his prophet. The reward which was first promised to the Babylonian soldiers in Tyre is now granted to them in Egypt. The message of the prophet Ezekiel may appear at a distance simply as dogmatically fixed assertion with a specific programme. In this oracle against a foreign nation it becomes evident that the prophet, within the context of his message of judgement, was conscious of Yahweh's freedom to change the concrete historical pronouncement and yet still to retain its content.[284] Categories such as the "grandeur" of the prophet, "in being able to confess openly the non-fulfilment of his message" completely miss what is intended here.[285] We are not dealing with the liberality of the person of the prophet, but with the message of the freedom of Yahweh, who has the power to send out his messenger with a fresh charge, and yet who in this freedom remains faithful throughout to his purpose.[286]

E. In the message of salvation, to which we must now turn, the knowledge of Yahweh's freedom and faithfulness towards the house of Israel comes most fully to expression. With biting severity the prophet had proclaimed to the sinful house of Israel the inescapable necessity of judgement. Nowhere among the people in their conduct and behavior was there a sound basis from which a new people could be built up. Yet we find in the book of Ezekiel, as has already become evident in a glance at the oracle against Edom and again in the redactional conclusion of the earlier sayings against foreign nations in 28:25f, a richly developed message of salvation, above all in chs. 34, 36–48 and earlier in 11:14–21; 16:42, 53–63; 17:22–24; 20:32–44. Radical critics have denied all these oracles to the prophet himself, and have sought to ascribe them to the later history of Ezekiel's message.[287] It is not to be denied that Ezekiel's school has played a considerable part in the development of the future expectation, especially in chs. 40–48. Here as elsewhere, however, they have built upon the prophet's own words and have carried his ideas further. In individual cases it is particularly difficult here to recognize the borderline where the prophet's own words end and the development by the school begins.

We must first of all raise the question at what point of time in the prophet's preaching the promises of salvation emerged. The date of the fall of Jerusalem in 587 B.C. offers itself here in a special way. The book in its overall structure shows clearly enough how great a break the redactor of the whole book had believed he was able to see in this event (cf. the conclusion of the "pars destruens" of chs. 1–24 in 24 and the narrative of 33:21f within the "pars construens" of chs. 33–48).

---

284 This is unlike the legalistic Jonah who, according to Jonah 4, complains against God's apparent change-ableness.

285 See commentary to 29:17–21.

286 The awareness of the freedom and faithfulness of God is at the same time expressed in another way in chs. 38f, which will be dealt with at the conclusion of the sketch of the prophet's message of salvation.

287 So, for example, Hölscher, *Hesekiel, der Dichter*. In quite another way now also S. Herrmann, *prophetischen Heilserwartungen*.

However, the prophet's preaching before 587 B.C., with its intense interest in the fall of Jerusalem, raises the question whether a new prophecy is not to be expected after this event, if the prophet is not then to be wholly dumb.

Certainly the section 11:14–21, in which the quotation in 11:15 appears to reflect a situation of things in Jerusalem between 597 and 587 B.C., seriously raises the question whether already before 587, alongside his message of judgement against Jerusalem which was still standing, there was also expressed a word of salvation for the exiles—a message of salvation which could then be directed fully at the finally stricken house of Israel after the end of Jerusalem and the remnant of Israel in Judah in the year 587 B.C. We cannot certainly exclude this possibility.

There then emerges the further question whether in the prophet's preaching something of the inner reasoning of the emergence of a promise of salvation can be seen or whether we must be satisfied simply with pointing to the freedom of Yahweh asserted in 29:17–21, which now turns to a new message of salvation which has no deeper motivation.

It is first of all noteworthy that the great divine promise of a new future and new life in 37:1–14, and the expansion of the extensive oracle of judgement of ch. 20 in 20:32–44 are expressed as an antithetical message against sayings of the people expressing total resignation. "Our bones are dried up, our hope is finished, we are cut off" runs Israel's complaint in 37:11. 20:32 also is to be understood as an oracle of Israel's resignation to the fact of its total political destruction: "We shall become like the nations, like the families of the heathen lands, and worship wood and stone." The message of salvation answers such despair on the part of Israel, which no longer has any possibility of existence of its own, to say nothing of a righteousness of its own which could give it a claim to life: "Our offenses and our sins are upon us, and we are pining away because of them; how can we live?" (33:10). The message of salvation is the divine answer to Israel's confession of its failure.

In 37:1ff it then becomes clear how in God's answer the people's failure is not contested with a word. The field full of dried out bones, which proclaim utter death, for which there is no further hope of life, is shown to the prophet in a vision by God. In this death God enables the prophet to speak the word of command by which, in an event which recalls the initial creation of man in the Yahwist's narrative in Gen 2:7, living men are created. In them Israel is promised the salvation of new life, deliverance from its graves, a return to its homeland, and the gift of the divine spirit (vv 12–14). Even though the actual vocabulary of creation is not used, we cannot overlook that here a new beginning is proclaimed which belongs to the category of awaking to new life from death. We can only rightly speak of a future salvation under this category of a divine act, which begins completely afresh.

In 20:32ff it is made clear from yet another side what the new promise of salvation means. In a sovereign answer to the despair of the people, who are resigning themselves to the heathen world and giving up their own uniqueness, a new exodus is proclaimed which is to bring back the house of Israel into its land, through the "desert of the nations," after it has been gathered together from the lands where it had been scattered. Once again Yahweh goes back to the beginnings of the people, which were described in the first half of the chapter, which is earlier than the rest of the chapter. He thereby reaffirms his original will for Israel and for the historical creation of this people. God's faithfulness to the history which he had once begun with Israel, and which Israel had so hopelessly abused by its disloyalty, is thereby proclaimed. 36:16ff emphasizes this assertion of Yahweh's faithfulness in a way characteristic of Ezekiel. Nothing is said here of God's merciful tenderness towards those who were lost in exile (cf. Is 40:1f). It is simply said that God suffered on account of his holy name which the house of Israel had profaned among the nations to which it came (36:21). "Not for your sake will I act, O house of Israel, but for the sake of my holy name, . . . I will sanctify my great name which has been profaned among the nations" (36:22f). Yahweh had pledged his name to Israel when he had sworn to it, according to 20:5: "I am Yahweh, your God." From then on, when Yahweh is mentioned Israel is mentioned. A reversal of this connection was clearly never for a moment considered. In his faithfulness Yahweh remains loyal to the pledge that he had once given. On the basis of this faithfulness he now promises to restore the dead to life, to bring Israel once again out of the world of the nations, and to restore it to its land. On account of this faithfulness the "turning of the fate" (שׁוּב שְׁבוּת in the late texts 16:53; 39:25) of Israel occurs and, as it is formulated in 16:60, Yahweh "remembers" (זכר) his covenant. The theologoumenon of the covenant of Yahweh in Israel's earlier history is to be found in the prophet's own words only in 16:8, in the context of the marriage metaphor. Otherwise in the actual words of the prophet it is unmentioned. Breach of covenant is mentioned in the late texts 16:59; 44:7.

For the sake of his faithfulness Yahweh will bless the land and make it fruitful in a new way.[288] In the land Yahweh will also restore to the house of Israel its original unity. The sign-action of joining together two sticks, which carry the inscriptions "Judah" and "Joseph" (37:15ff), makes this clear. In this we can see how tendencies of the period of Josiah's reform, which are reflected in the preaching of Jeremiah, also color the future hope of Ezekiel.[289] The "one shepherd," which the prophet expects as a result of his particular emphasis of the old Nathan prophecy of 2 Sam 7 as a new David, also belongs to the unity of the house of Israel. 34:23f sets him as the good shepherd over against the evil shepherds of Israel's past history. With these events justice will return for the weak and also peace and security even in regard to the wild animals in the land. Yahweh, by his actions, will conclude a covenant of peace with his people (34:25–30; 37:26). If 17:22–24, as the present exposition accepts, concerns the coming king of the house of David, then once again in a particular way the picture of the coming protection of men in the shadow of his rule is illustrated by the imagery of the world-tree. Above all this reference emphasizes strongly the message of the exaltation of the humble, which alone lies in the hand of Yahweh.

The new salvation, which the prophet has to proclaim, is especially illuminated by him and the school which followed him from two sides. The Israel of the period before the judgement was shattered by its disobedience. The act of revival by Yahweh will consequently consist in his creating his people as an obedient and law-abiding people. This new situation, which

Jer 31:31–34 describes as a setting of the commandments on the hearts of the people, is set out in Ezek 11:19 and 36:26 as the gift of a new heart and a new spirit. The heart of stone will be taken from the body and replaced by a heart of flesh. 36:27 (37:14; 39:29) adds to this Yahweh's promise of the gift of his spirit. With imagery stemming from cultic ritual, this inner cleansing of men is described in 36:25 by the picture of sprinkling clean water on them.

This inward renewal of men in the house of Israel is, however, for the priest-prophet Ezekiel only one side of God's saving action. Beside it, and shedding light upon it, stands Yahweh's promise to come to his people and that the latter will be close to the God who so comes to them. It was the temptation of those who had been deported into exile in 597 B.C. that those who remained in Jerusalem, and to whom the land was now left, said of them apparently rightly: "They are far from Yahweh" (11:15). When Yahweh's glory met the prophet in his remote exile and when his word repeatedly came to him in exile, yet it remained that Israel's God was still only "a little sanctuary" (11:16) to those who sought to pray to him at a distance.[290] According to chs. 10f this fulfilled the judgement upon Jerusalem, which had even been spared in 597 B.C., that Yahweh's glory now left the temple in Jerusalem. The salvation of the new age could therefore only be complete when Yahweh appeared once again in the midst of his people. This is exactly what the prophet proclaims that the new exodus will bring the newly gathered people, which is made ready in the desert to return by a visible judgement to the holy mountain of Yahweh (הַר קָדְשִׁי), the high mountain of Israel, where it will give true worship to its God in acceptable gifts (20:35ff). Even more fully 37:26–28 say that Yahweh, in connection with his enduring covenant, will again set up his dwelling in the midst of his people. When his sanctuary stands once again in the midst of his people, the nations will know that Yahweh sanctifies Israel (in 20:12 this was said in regard to the sabbath). In this the major theme is introduced, which dominates the great vision of chs. 40–48.

At the basis of this rather unwieldy visionary section,

---

288 In the description of the salvation the connection with the concluding chapter of H is particularly strong, as mentioned above pp. 50f.

289 See Volume 2.
290 See pp. 261f.

which cannot with certainty be denied to the prophet himself, the new sanctuary of the age of salvation is shown to him. It is to be built of noble proportions and separated from everything that is unholy. The prophet is led through its gates and courts up to the threshhold of the most holy place. According to 43:1ff he sees the return of the glory of Yahweh to this place and hears the divine promise that Yahweh will now take up his dwelling here for all time. He sees the East Gate, which is now to be closed for all time with no human foot again to pass through it, and the river, which spreads mysteriously, starting out from the place of God's presence and making the land around fertile, healing the waters of the Dead Sea to the east. In the elaboration of this vision, which is ascribed to the prophet in the twenty-fifth year of exile, halfway towards a "year of release,"[291] we can clearly trace how the focus is directed very definitely towards the architectural realization of things to come. The message of the new age, which the prophet sees, is at the same time an instruction for the proper architectural construction of the place at which Yahweh promises his people that he will come to them again.

These features become stronger in the additions which have been made to the vision in the tradition of the school. The possibility of a fresh return becomes more and more concrete.[292] The question which first occupied the school of Ezekiel in regard to the structure of human relationships is the position of the prince to his people in this place of Yahweh's cultic presence. The political importance of the "prince" (נָשִׂיא), which is given expression in the promise of a shepherd—the new David (chs. 34, 37)—is here left wholly in the background, and the question is simply raised about his place in Israel's worship in the temple. The sacred center also dominates the considerations of the new division of the land, with the holy place in the center of the land. Not only are the sacrificial rites oriented towards this center, but also orders of priests and Levites are instituted, which have been added later, at a clear distance from the message of the prophet himself. The further distinctions of degrees of holiness for the sacred objects shows obvious advances here. The des-

cription of the city itself in 48:30–35, which is so clearly out of line with the previous reservation of everything holy to the temple area, shows in the new name of the city "Yahweh is there" a decisive connection with the center of the prophet's message of salvation, in speaking of Yahweh's coming to his people.[293] The salvation is that Yahweh will take up his abode in the midst of the house of Israel. This message also permeates through in the complicated later history of the vision-narrative of chs. 40–48 in individual additions to the basic text.

F. At this point we must still take a look at Ezek 38f. The basic text of this oracle of the attack of Gog from Magog, which has been heavily elaborated in the later work of the prophetic school, tells of the final major threat to the land of Israel, which however no longer falls under the category of Yahweh's judgement upon the house of Israel. In this regard the oracle, which goes on to speak of the destruction of this last enemy, belongs close to the prophet's oracles against foreign nations. In that it no longer concerns here an individual prophecy against a people which is judged in its land because of its offenses, but the invasion by a coalition of nations into the land of the center ("the people who dwell at the navel of the earth" which is what the interpretation of the school very pertinently says), we find here something of the general assertion of a comprehensive judgement of the nations which is missing in chs. 25–32. It is certainly not correct to find behind the sayings against Gog a threat against the Babylonians which is missing in chs. 25–32. In this regard the prophecy is rightly separated from the other oracles against the nations as something distinct. This is also correct insofar as we are dealing here with a threat to Israel which has received from God the gracious gift of being gathered together again and brought back to its land, "a land which has been restored from the sword, has been gathered together again on the mountains of Israel out of many nations" (38:8). On the other hand, however, it is a threat which is certainly no longer conceivable after Yahweh has finally taken up his abode in the rebuilt temple. Thus, in a striking way, in chs.

---

291 See Volume 2.
292 Walther Zimmerli, "Planungen für den Wiederaufbau nach der Katastrophe von 587," *VT* 18

(1968): 229–255.
293 See Volume 2.

38f both the temple and the holy city play no part, and the section has rightly been introduced before, and not after, chs. 40–48.

When we examine the inner direction of the message declared in chs. 38f, we find here, as in 29:17–21, although in a quite different development of content, a connection of the message of the faithfulness of God, who remains loyal to his word, with the knowledge of his freedom, which permits things that have been preached earlier to be realized in a new form. For the prophet, Jeremiah's message of the foe from the north and Isaiah's promise of the destruction of the enemies of the city of God on the mountains of Israel remain in the air without fulfilment. Will Yahweh keep these promises? That this victory over the nations on the mountains of Israel is now connected with Gog and the peoples of the north, which conveyed a threatening tone in the Mesopotamian mind,[294] reveals Yahweh's freedom, as does the view that the attack of these nations will follow on the return of Israel to its land. Yahweh will fulfil his word, whenever and however it fits in with his own plans.

With the announcement of an ultimate event after the saving return of the house of Israel into its land, the prophet certainly opens up a new path. He starts out on the way which leads in apocalyptic to a fuller description of a final course of historical events. Thus it is not surprising that this oracle is subsequently elaborated and interpreted with the apocalyptic features of a cosmic event (38:18–23) and that Gog also becomes an important figure in the apocalyptic of the New Testament period. This universal extension is still far from the thoughts of the original text.

That Babylon is not mentioned is also true of chs. 38f. The question is left unanswered in the book of Ezekiel what will happen to this imperial power, which was currently so important for Palestine, in the future age of Israel's salvation which is announced. The message of the prophet Ezekiel lacks a completely universal interest. "The nations" can sometimes (mostly in sayings from the school) be mentioned in the Recognition Formula as witnesses (36:23; 37:28; 38:16; 39:7, 21, 23). Unlike Deutero-Isaiah, the prophet of the late exilic age, Ezekiel lacks a fully-developed message about the world of the nations.[295]

G. Ezekiel 40–48 reveal the plans of the prophet and his school for a future in Jerusalem, made possible by Yahweh and expected at a not too distant time.

For the prophet, however, there was also a present spent in exile. Was it enough to address men who were groaning under this experience with the announcement of a future which was to begin miraculously with a new exodus brought about by Yahweh alone, and for the rest simply to encourage them to await this new creative act of Yahweh? The question arose immediately for Ezekiel, the prophet in the midst of his fellow exiles: what must we do today? In the outline we have given so far of the prophet's preaching we have omitted any attention to that part of his preaching which was concerned with answering this very question.

We must first of all point out in this connection that the prophet expected from those who were to be overtaken by the judgement an unlimited recognition of God's righteous judgement upon Israel. From those who escaped alive out of the catastrophe and were to join those who were already exiled he expected that they will "remember me . . . and they will be filled with loathing . . . because of all their abominations" (6:9). 14:22f speaks further of the accounts told by those who have just come from Jerusalem to those already in exile: "they will see their conduct and their deeds . . . and they will know that I have not done without reason all that which I have done to it [i.e., Jerusalem]." (Cf. 12:16.) That honor is given to God by those who are judged and his righteousness as Judge is recognized is the first thing. This attitude is not to change among those to whom the coming message of salvation belongs. The assertion that the receiving of the divine message and acts of salvation leads to an even deeper sense of shame belongs in a special way to the book of Ezekiel.[296]

The summons to a recognition of guilt is not the last word, however. When in 14:1–11 the elders of Israel who expect to receive from the prophet a divine message are refused it and their attention is drawn to the idolatry in which they are caught up, the prophet's

---

294 See commentary to 32:26.
295 Henning Graf Reventlow, "Die Völker als Jahwes Zeugen bei Ezechiel," *ZAW* 71 (1959): 33–43, gives

a somewhat different emphasis.
296 See the commentary on 16:62f and 36:32.

message in 14:6 finishes up with a summons to return as its true purpose: "Repent and turn away from your idols, and turn your faces from all your abominations." Ch. 18 and the shorter presentation in 33:10–20 show further that this call to return is not left in broad generalities, but becomes concrete in specific ways. It is significant that these two sections also are formulated as impassioned answers to statements made to the prophet by the people who have been overtaken by judgement. We may be inclined in a special way here to speak of a pastoral purpose in the prophet's answer. In the two quotations expression is given to the two fundamental reactions to the divine judgement of those who have been judged. In the saying in 18:2, which is familiar from Jer 31:29, people express a cynical rejection of a confession of guilt: "the fathers have eaten sour grapes, and the teeth of the children are set on edge!" It is formulated in 18:25, 29 and 33:17, 20 as a direct attack on God himself: "The way of Yahweh is not just!" In 33:10, on the other hand, it is the paralyzing depression of utter despair under the burden of guilt: "Our offenses and our sins lie upon us, and in them we pine away; how then can we live?" In both cases we see the prophet concerned to rebut the fatalism of the cynics as well as of the despairing, in giving voice to a call to return. Behind this call, however, he shows at the same time the open future of God: "As I live, says the Lord Yahweh, I have no pleasure in the death of the wicked, but that the wicked should turn from his ways and live. Repent, turn from your evil ways! Why will you die, O house of Israel?" (33:11, cf. 18:23, 30–32). In this call the future and a new possibility of life given by God are included. Indeed, in 18:31 in an unexpected development, it is the new heart and the new spirit, which the great message of salvation had mentioned as the special act of Yahweh's renewal, which are held out before men in the call to return as that which they themselves should take hold of with full alertness: "Cast away all your offenses, by

which you have offended against me, and make for yourselves a new heart and a new spirit." In particular in ch. 18 the prophet rebuts the paralyzing and cynical despair in a two-part speech. In concrete detail (vv 5–20) he makes clear that the son is not bound by the sins of the father. Then vv 21–30 proclaim further that, even in the life of the individual, man's past does not bind his present. The call to return sounds out as God's call into the freedom of the present. In this connection we can see that the prophet does not remain simply with a general call to return, but very definitely unfolds in a number of individual cases from real life how this return can take place in concrete obedience.[297] From this concrete commandment he offers to the exiles in their existing surroundings life from God and summons them out of their despair to renewed loyalty to God. In 33:14f also we can see a small part of such a concrete pointing to life.[298]

Ezekiel enables the exiles, in their existing situation, not to wait idly for the fulfillment of the great promises to the house of Israel. He shows them how to face up to this future in immediate decisions about the specific affairs of everyday life.

In this we come back to what was said at the beginning about the prophet's office: In his situation in exile the messenger who announces Yahweh's action towards the house of Israel, both in destruction and then salvation for his name's sake, becomes a watchman and guardian. He calls to return and watchfulness before the God who has disclosed himself through his prophet to warn the sinner from the way of death (3:17–21; 33:1–9).

This is the message of the prophet Ezekiel.

---

297 The traditio-historical examination makes it probable that the prophet here uses series of laws which he had before him by which entry into the sanctuary and so into its blessings, or "life," was decided.

298 Walther Zimmerli, " 'Leben' und 'Tod' im Buche des Propheten Ezechiel," *ThZ* 13 (1957): 494–508; reprinted in *idem, Gottes Offenbarung*, ThB 19 (München: Kaiser, 1963), 178–191.

8. From the Prophet's Word to the Prophetic Book

A. The few texts which reveal clearly anything of the prophet's activity among the exiles show that he addressed those around him verbally (11:25 besides 8:1 and 14:1ff; 20:1ff), except where silence was expressly imposed upon him (3:15, 26; 33:22, cf. 24:27), or where he was commanded to perform a sign-action (as 24:15ff and other sign-actions). From the call-narrative (2:4) up to the great vision of the new temple (40:4) we find repeatedly the explicit command to preach. By his words the prophet becomes a watchman (3:17ff; 33:1ff), he fulfils his task of legal accusation (20:4; 22:2), he becomes "one who reproves" אִישׁ (מוֹכִיחַ [3:26]) before dumbness silences his mouth. We read of a command to write down (כתב) parts of his message only in 43:11 in the plan for building the new temple, in the marks of possession on the sticks in the symbolic action of 37:15ff (in vv 16 and 20), and for the date of the beginning of the siege in 24:2.[299] He is never otherwise commanded to write down the spoken word, unlike Isaiah (Is 30:8; also 8:16?) and Jeremiah (ch. 36), although a "scroll" is already of importance at the call of the prophet (2:9–3:3).[300]

In the study of Ezekiel the picture of the writer—prophet has, however, played an important role at times.[301] Thus the question must be raised here: can we still recognize in the book of Ezekiel the oral, spoken word of the prophet, or is the book a piece of later literary work, which has subsequently collected together and revised the oral work of the prophet, which we cannot dismiss as a fiction?

The strongest argument that we can reckon at certain passages in the book of Ezekiel with the unaltered deposit of spoken address must be seen in the presence of rhythmic sections. Rhythm is for the ear, and not for the eye and the reflective spirit. Metrical speech is intended to be heard, and we must fully reckon with this for the time of Ezekiel. Thus especially in the קִינָה sections of the book of Ezekiel, with its limping rhythm, we can find primarily the spoken word. But also the two-beat, hammerlike rhythm, which is to be seen in chs. 7 and 21 and also in the elevated narrative prose

of chs. 16 and 23, was primarily intended for the ear, as well as the two-strophe song of the sword, which is found in 21:13–32.[302] That the terse three-part proof-saying, which is to be seen at its purest in the oracle against the nations in ch. 25, belonged originally to oral prophetic address may be clear from 1 Kings 20:13 and 28.[303] Here, however, where the rhythm does not emerge so directly, a secondary usage, which was simply written, is more possible. Thus we can affirm with certainty that we find elements in the book of Ezekiel which are the direct deposit of oral delivery. We must therefore reckon in Ezekiel with the phenomenon of the collection of already fixed units, which were first minted in oral delivery.

On the other hand, however, there are elements in the book which cannot be overlooked and which clearly cannot have been delivered orally. The concluding verse of the first great temple vision chs. 8–11, which states that the prophet recounted his vision to the exiles (11:25), is, like the conclusion of the call-narrative in 3:15, certainly not a part of a spoken address. The same is true of the narrative passage in 12:7, concerning the sign-action of the exile's baggage, and of the link section, in 24:18f in the sign-event of the death of the prophet's wife. We cannot therefore accept the simple explanation of the book as a straightforward collection of oral speeches of Ezekiel. We must reckon with a process of literary editing.

The subsequent development must at first have been due to the general narrative introductions to the prophecies, as well as to the narrative elements which have just been mentioned. In this connection still further considerations emerge, which are characteristic of the transmission process of the book of Ezekiel.

B. It is then noteworthy in the book how speeches which are well-defined and clearly marked-off by their introduction (by the formula for the coming of a message or a date in an earlier context) appear as sections which seem to have had their own tradition history.[304] We must now deal with the process of tradition which is discernible within these sections.

Such units of tradition can be speech units which are complete in themselves and have only been altered by

---

299 See pp. 498f.
300 See pp. 135–137.
301 See above pp. 3f.

302 For ch. 7 see p. 201; for ch. 21, pp. 440f; for ch. 16, pp. 334f; for ch. 23, p. 481; for 21:13–32, pp. 431f.
303 Cf. the metrical evidence for the two-part proof-

minor glosses. Thus, for example, 12:17–20; 12:21–25; 12:26–28; 14:1–11; 14:12–23; 18:1–32; 21:1–12; 22:17–22; 22:23–31; 33:21–22. Relatively seldom do we find in such sections two independent speeches put together (= collected together), as for example, in 33:1–20; 33:23–33. Much more characteristic for many parts of the book is the distinctive process of "development" of a section. Thus the basic prophecy of Ezek 16:1–43 (we shall deal later with the additions which this complex has further undergone in rich measure) describes the evil history which had taken place between Yahweh and the foundling-child who had been brought to honor by him. To this complex clearly separable additions have been made in vv 44–58 and 59–63, which cannot be regarded simply as independent units of tradition and which have not therefore simply been added in a process of "collection." On the contrary, they undeniably follow in new directions the theme set in the basic oracle. This indicates a process of successive development of a kernel element, which has been developed further in new additions at a somewhat later time.[305] The same phenomenon is to be seen in the related ch. 23, which tells of the two unfaithful women. To the basic material of vv 1–27, further elaborations have been made in vv 28–30 and 32–34, and then still later in the complex vv 36–49, which neither in style nor content are to be derived from Ezekiel.[306] Such development is also to be affirmed for the first sections of the oracles against Tyre and Egypt. The basic oracle against Tyre in 26:2—6 is followed by an elaborative exposition in vv 7–14, by the addition of a קִינָה in vv 15–18, and the further addition of the motif of the descent into the underworld in vv 19–21. A similar succession of additions is also to be conjectured in 29:1–6a / 6b–9a / 9b–16.[307]

In this successive elaboration of speech units we must not overlook that in many cases the further development moves beyond the threshold of the fall of Jerusalem. Thus in the example from ch. 29 which has

just been mentioned, the first addition in vv 6b–9a belongs to the time after the fall of Jerusalem. This process is to be seen very beautifully in the oracle about the broken arm of Pharaoh in 30:20–26. The very concrete announcement of the failue of the Pharaoh's attempt to help in vv 20f is followed in vv 22–24 by a more general oracle against the Pharaoh, and in vv 25f by the addition of a general saying against Egypt.[308] Quite clearly this "development" beyond the time of the catastrophe of 587 B.C. is to be seen also in 20:32–44 after 20:1–31.

Beside this development in the addition of new speech units the phenomenon also appears of the re-working of existing units in the light of subsequent events. Thus the symbolic action of the exile's baggage in 12:1–16 has clearly been reworked in the light of the personal fate of Zedekiah, so that a good deal of obscurity has come into the text. The same thing is to be said of the reworking of the work-song which lies at the basis of 24:1–14. In the first mentioned reference we can doubtless recognize the hand of the school at work on the text. We must understand the "updating of tradition" in ch. 17 in another way: the riddle of the two eagles, the cedar, and the vine, which are formulated metrically, are followed in vv 11–21 by an interpretation composed in prose, which is introduced by a new formula for the receipt of a message and which must have had in mind the events of 587 B.C. In vv 22–24 there is added to this a promise which takes up the initial figure with a new beginning and formulates a prophecy from its imagery. In the קִינָה of ch. 19, which must once have followed directly in ch. 17, we can probably trace in the "updating of tradition" of vv 10–14, which also seeks to introduce the fate of Zedekiah, the direct influence of the preceding oracle of ch. 17.

However, it now becomes very questionable in the "updating of traditions" whether throughout it all we have a process of the writing down of the oral preaching of the prophet. Much must undoubtedly be regarded

---

saying in Is 49:22f and 24–26.

304 See above pp. 25f.
305 See p. 334.
306 See pp. 480f.
307 See Volume 2. See further the chapter on the shep-
      herds in 34, in which the concluding verse (31) seeks
      to round off the various developments of the whole
      by a return to the beginning.

308 See Volume 2.

as the further scholarly development of prophecies which were already extant in writing.

This further development shows up in yet another way. We cannot overlook in 16:1–43 that the text has undergone additions under the influence of ch. 23 and vice versa. We can also see in this section that it has undergone "biblicist" additions under the influence of the related details of Hos 2. In the secondary elaboration of the great oracle of the day of Yahweh in 7:19 a complete quotation from Zephaniah has entered into the text. The pictorial detail in 16:27 possibly contains a direct allusion to contemporary experiences with the Philistines.[309] In 27:12–25 a detailed trading list has been worked into the great picture of the "ship of Tyre."

The consequences of the reworking in the great complexes of the call-narrative in 3:16a, 22–5:17, the Gog pericope, and the two great visions in which the prophet is transported are particularly penetrating. In the call-narrative the description of the manifestation of God has undergone a considerable reworking, which certainly reached its limits in the description of the form of God.[310] There is reflected in it an interest in the more precise elaboration of features of the appearance of the "glory of Yahweh" (כְּבוֹד יהוה). The most prominent element is the addition of the wheels which make the throne-vehicle borne by the heavenly creature into a throne-chariot. The intense interest in the phenomenon of the appearance of God shows itself secondly in the extensive additions to ch. 10, where we clearly have a later edition of the work. The creatures who bear the throne are here expressly identified with cherubim. In the list of the four faces of the creatures the face of a bull in 1:10 is replaced by that of a cherub (10:14). The conception of Yahweh's dwelling in the temple from which he then moves out in order to abandon it, which is discernible in the original text, has been modified in the reworking. Yahweh now comes from a distance to the temple (8:4), only then to leave it again. Behind all this redrafting we can see a deep theological reflection upon Yahweh's dwelling place and the manner of his appearance. On the other side, the insertion of the scene concerning Pelatiah and the

promise oracle in 11:14–21, which contrasts with the threat of woe implicit in this scene, must represent the redactional composition of already extant material.

The motives which have led to the reworking of the complex of the sign-actions in 3:22–5:17 are less clear in detail. In any case the intention of expanding the symbolic announcement of the imminent overthrow of Jerusalem by a reference to the period of guilt and punishment of the house of Israel (Judah) and to the uncleanness of life away from the sanctuary (4:12–15) is evident. In the interpretative section 5:4ff there then enter undeniable reminiscences of the horror of the time of Jerusalem's fall, which have been incorporated also in Leviticus 26. It would be wrong to dismiss the symbolic actions of 4:4–8 and 4:12–15, which have been inserted and of which the first still shows clear traces of the developmental interpretation as pure fictions of the tradents of Ezekiel's preaching. In spite of their markedly later styling both texts point back to original symbolic actions of the prophet. We may ask how far the reworking of the original three-sign complex may be derived from the prophet himself. The connection of the theophany scene in 3:22–24 with the complex of sign-actions in chs. 4f is very obscure.

The reworking in the Gog pericope is very fully evident. It moves in the direction of a strengthening of the apocalyptic features of this part of the prophet's preaching. Most clearly, however, there is reflected a historical process of the further cumbersome development of a basic text in several phases, in the final vision of the new temple in chs. 40–48, with its disconnected additions. Here it seems quite obvious that we have to assume as a background of these additions the near approach of the hour of a return to the land, and the necessity that thereby arose for the realistic planning of the reconstruction.[311]

In all this we cannot overlook the phenomenon of a "school of the prophet," which edited the prophecies of Ezekiel, commented upon them, and gave them a fuller theological exposition.[312] It needs still further study in order to work out more fully the features of this "school of Ezekiel." The general conclusion of S. Herrmann that we are dealing with the message of salvation

---

309 See p. 345.
310 See pp. 124f and 131f.
311 Zimmerli, "Planungen."

312 See Sigmund Mowinckel in his general consideration of the transmission process of the prophetic

of a Deuteronomic editor really does not fully cover the features of this school.[313] It overrates the Deuteronomic element over against the features that are expressly distinctive of Ezekiel in this school. In individual cases it is often not possible to define the borders at which the prophet's own work passes over into that of the school. The possibility that a great part of the transmission in the "school" and the "updating of tradition" of many oracles took place in Ezekiel's house by the prophet himself is not to be dismissed out of hand. That the prophet himself knew something of school instruction, which is phenomenologically very different from the older prophetic preaching in public, is made very clear by passages such as chs. 18; 33:1–9, 10–20. Thus besides the oral proclamation of rhythmically composed sayings, which continued the manner of preaching of the earlier prophets, we must reckon that the prophet himself undertook the secondary work of learned commentary upon and further elaboration of his prophecies, i.e., with a kind of "school activity." This is so even though the short autobiographical statements of the prophet never present a clear picture of this circle of disciples (unlike Is 8:16–18). On the basis of 3:24[314] and 33:30–33 (also 8:1; 14:1; 20:1) it must simply be conjectured that there took place on the prophet's part a preaching to the wider circle of his community from his house—in which archaizing features of pre-classical prophecy appear to be taken up.[315]

C. Undoubtedly the present book of Ezekiel stems from the hand of the "school." What then can we say about the process of redaction which has led from the individual unit to the book as a whole?

First there are not lacking some, although few, factors which make clear that the process of comprehensive redaction cannot properly be separated from the process of "updating tradition" and the further interpretation of the separate units. Thus we cannot deny that the last phase of the "updating" of the unit ch. 16 is connected already, by the adoption of the

double catchword "oath" / "covenant" (אָלָה/בְּרִית) (16:59), to ch. 17 where this pair of concepts plays a fundamental role in the sphere of the political treaty of Zedekiah in the interpretation of vv 11–21 in vv 13, 16, 18f. Similarly we have raised in the foregoing the question whether the "updating" of the קִינָה of ch. 19 in vv 10–14 is a consequence of the connection with ch. 17, which at one time directly preceded it. Similarly, in the "updating" of the section 24:15–24 in vv 25–27, which takes up afresh the material of vv 15ff, it is probable that we should see the intention of linking up with 33:21f. The narrative of 33:21f must once have followed directly on 24:15 in an earlier redaction phase. From this we may ask the question whether in the difficult passage 3:25–27 we cannot also see elements of such a redaction phenomenon of providing a link with the complex of chs. 4f, which is now not introduced by an independent formula for the receipt of a message.

In what we have said we have already noted that, in the present book as a whole, we can see passages which have been inserted at particular points, which break up earlier connections, and the introduction of which belongs to a late phase of the process of redaction, and which therefore appears as a process broken up into phases. At four points it has been thought possible to recognize with certainty such insertions which break up older connections:

1) 3:16b–21 break up the original connection of 3:16a, 22ff.[316] The section that has been introduced here shows itself in its content to have been a late composition, which connects material from 33:1–9 with other material from ch. 18.[317] It has been inserted at this point directly adjoining the original call-narrative in order to explain the prophet's understanding of his office which is to be ascribed to a later phase of his activity.[318]

2) Ch. 18 breaks up the earlier connection of chs. 17 and 19, which is shown by the lack of a separate formula for the receipt of a message in 19:1, as also in the refer-

oracles in *Prophecy and Tradition* (Oslo: Dybwad, 1946).

313 S. Herrmann, *prophetischen Heilserwartungen*.
314 See p. 159.
315 See above pp. 42f.
316 See note a to 3:16 p. 142, and p. 144.
317 See pp. 142–146.
318 See pp. 55f.

ence of 19:10–14 to ch. 17.[319] In the didactic elaboration of ch. 18 we can see again an element of the later phase of the prophet's preaching. The figurative discourse of ch. 17 and the קִינָה of ch. 19, which is formulated as a figurative discourse, have clearly been put together in an earlier phase of the "redaction." The insertion of ch. 18 at this point may belong together with the fact that ch. 17, as 19, shows the judgement on a succession of kings. Ch. 18, on the other hand, seeks to destroy any fatalistic misunderstanding of the course of judgement.

3) We have already pointed out the breaking up of the connection of 24:25–27 with 33:12f, the news of the fall of Jerusalem. That the great complex of oracles against the nations in chs. 25–32 was inserted here belongs together with the view that in the judgement upon the nations the turning point of Israel's destiny is reached—a view which also appears to be reflected in the arrangements of the books of Isaiah, Jeremiah (according to 𝕲) and Zephaniah. Reference to the dating of the oracles against foreign nations, which point to the period around 587 B.C., may also have supported this arrangement.

But then before 33:21f there was inserted 33:1–20 —a passage in which the new definition of the prophet's office (vv 1–9) is connected with a brief comment about the freedom of Yahweh who calls his broken people to return—a relevant arrangement in regard to the preaching phase after 587 B.C.

4) From the date reference it is quite clear that 29:17–21 is a late insertion in the series of prophecies against Egypt, which is otherwise well-ordered in its sequence of dates. Why the section has been inserted here can hardly be made out. At best we may think of the intention of arranging it directly before the oracle about the broken arm of Pharaoh (30:20–26). It then arises that the undated section of 30:1–19, which is in part obscure in its origin, has also broken up this connection somewhat later. However certainty cannot be reached here.

For further questions about the earlier stages of the redaction of the book we must mention first of all the complex of the Egyptian oracles in chs. 29–32. Apart from the insertions that have been mentioned, we have here a self-contained corpus of prophecies, which is clearly arranged in a sequence of dates. 29:1–16; 30:20–32:32 form a quite independent little book of sayings against Egypt and the Pharaoh. A particular redactional introduction to, and conclusion of it is not evident. It can at most be noted that the detailed oracle of the descent into the underworld stands appropriately at the conclusion of the whole.[320]

Since the editor who added 29:17–21 already had before him the collection of the five dated sections, which all show in a greater or lesser measure the phenomenon of "updating of tradition" or "commenting," we will have to date their completion before the twenty-seventh year of Jehoiachin's deportation. The complex 30:1–19, which is not dated and which is also not unified, must have been made up somewhat later to make up the total of seven oracles against Egypt.

The oracles against Tyre 26:1–28:19, i.e., the three sections directed against Tyre and its king, also once formed an independent collection. This is also to be deduced from the similar sounding concluding sentences of redactional origin in 26:21 (expanded by an addition) 27:36b and 28:19b. Unlike the collection of oracles against Egypt we find here only one date at the beginning of the whole collection. It points to the year of the fall of Jerusalem.[321] Of the three sections the first shows the phenomenon of "updating," the second is expanded by a prosaic trade list, and in the third two independent oracles are joined together, of which the first seeks to provide a motive for the judgement upon the king of Tyre proclaimed in the second.

This small collection of oracles against Tyre has then later been expanded by the placing of oracles against four of Israel's Palestinian neighbors in front of it in ch. 25. These have all originated after the fall of Jerusalem in 587 B.C. and possibly also once existed as an independent collection. The whole complex 25:1–28:19 has then been rounded off with an oracle against Sidon and a redactional conclusion which looks beyond the separate oracles against foreign nations. The idea that the judgement upon the nations is connected with salvation for the house of Israel is clearly expressed in this

---

319 See p. 397.
320 Cf. the sections 26 and 31 which finish up with the same motif.

321 But see Volume 2.

redactional conclusion. We should properly expect this summing-up at the end of the whole collection of oracles against the nations in 25–32. Since the saying against Sidon has clearly been added in order to make up to seven the number of oracles against foreign nations or cities, which the inclusion of the oracles against Egypt also presupposes, the question arises why the oracles against Egypt have not been put at the beginning, so that the redactional conclusion in 28:25–26 would then have had its appropriate place. To answer this question we may point to the series of dates in chs. 29–32. To be sure 29:1 goes back once again to the tenth year, where 26:1 has already mentioned the eleventh year. May not the intention of building up to a climax play a part, in which the short oracles against the small neighboring states are put at the beginning in order to come to a climax in the oracles against the empire of Egypt by way of the oracles against Tyre, to which the oracle against Sidon was also attached for obvious reasons?

When, after the removal of the collection of oracles against foreign nations in chs. 25–32 and the other recognizable additions, we examine the remaining parts of the book, we notice in 39:23–29 a second redactional conclusion, which recalls 28:25f. Here, however, the reference back to the action of Yahweh towards his people, both in judgement and mercy, is more fully elaborated. Whereas in 28:25f we can see a summing-up of the preceding collection of foreign nation oracles, 39:23–29 offer a summing-up of the entire preaching of the prophet. This points to an edition of the book of Ezekiel which lacked chs. 40–48.[322] The question may be raised, even though we cannot answer it with certainty, whether the statement of Josephus that Ezekiel had left two books presupposes the existence side by side of the two complexes of chs. 1–39 and 40–48.[323] In the tradition available to us we only have the single whole of chs. 1–48.

If we then question further about the principle of arrangement which has led to the formation of the remaining material of Ezek 1:1–3:16a, 22–17:24; 19:1–24:27; 33:21–39:29, some general considerations may be mentioned which admittedly do not il-luminate the entire process of redaction in all its details.

First of all it is clear that the dated sections 1:1–3:15 (16a, 22ff); 8:1–11:25; 20:1–44; 24:1–14;[324] 33:21f are set out in proper sequence. The chronological order is followed without interruption. Is it further of importance that the accounts of visions are always followed by a section which speaks of sign-actions? Thus the sign-actions of chs. 4f, in the basic text of which the siege and conquest of Jerusalem are announced, are joined on to the great opening vision (and its echo in 3:22ff). The two sections 12:1–16 and 17–20, which describe the deportation and horror of the time of devastation, join on to chs. 8–11, the vision of judgement upon sinful Jerusalem. The vision of the resurrection of the dead bones in 37:1–14 is followed in 37:15ff by the sign-action of uniting the two divided parts of Israel. We can see with great certainty that the announcements of doom in chs. 1–24 are followed in ch. 33 onwards by promises of salvation. This latter principle, however, is not so strictly kept that the promises of salvation which have been added to individual sayings of judgement in the process of addition or "updating of tradition" (11:14–21; 16:53–63; 17:22–24; 20:32–44) have been taken out of these units. Nor in the other direction have the threats of judgement in ch. 34 or the element of oracles to the nations in 35:1–36:15 been taken out of the section in which they are now still to be found. Two sections of a more general content have been added to chs. 1–5: the threat against the mountains of Israel and the announcement of the day of Yahweh. The complex of visions and symbolic actions in 8:1–12:20 is followed by a group of oracles which are grouped around the theme of "prophets." 14:12–23, which speak of the impossibility of a deliverance of the land by a man of exemplary piety, are joined loosely to this. There then follows in chs. 15–17, 19 a series of figurative sayings which must have been put together on account of their formal similarity. The connection of chs. 17 and 19, which existed before the insertion of ch. 18, and which has been established above, raises the question whether in this block of figurative sayings we can see an older collection later incorporated in a larger whole. Since we could readily

---

322 That the concluding vision of chs. 40–48 had its own redaction history is shown also in the exposition of this complex in the commentary.

323 *Antiquities* x 5 1.
324 But see pp. 498f.

regard the figurative saying of ch. 23, which is closely related to ch. 16, as connected with this block, why is it now separated from it by chs. 20–22? In this intervening section we find after the great theology of history in ch. 20 three sections grouped together in ch. 21 under the catchword "sword." In ch. 22 no connecting title for the three sections is to be found. It is then readily understandable that the two sections of ch. 24, which point directly to the fall of the besieged city of Jerusalem, have been set at the conclusion of the series of announcements of judgement. According to 33:21f an eye witness to the city's fall reached the prophet. In the two prophecies which are joined to this, about the position of those who were left in the land after 587 B.C. and of the exiles who misunderstand the prophet's message of salvation, a transitional introduction is reached for the prophet's proclamation of salvation, to which the extensive promises of deliverance in 36:15–37:28 appropriately form a conclusion. Chs. 38f, in the prophecy about Gog, contain once again a message of the assurance of salvation in a final threat from the nations. Then the redactor concluded the book with the comprehensive summing-up in 39:23–29, which ignores altogether the Gog episode.

The promise and program of a new beginning (chs. 40–48), which appear very prominently halfway to the time of the year of release, have then been added to Ezekiel 1–39 in a final phase of the redaction. The tradition which is available to us in the basic text and in the versions, and which we shall deal with in the following paragraph, knows only of the book of Ezekiel in the totality of its forty-eight chapters.

This history of the successive formation of the book of Ezekiel, in which in part fully independent sections have been added together and to which additions have been appended which break up the earlier units, makes fully intelligible the deviations from the proper sequence of dates noted in the list above. It does not indicate a subsequent breaking up of what was originally a better arrangement of the book, which we could attempt to recover, but is rather an impressive witness to the painstaking care with which the extant material was arranged into a book. The final redactor has preferred to accept disturbances of the given sequence of dates rather than change the statements of the text which he had. The thesis of the prophet as a scribe who

composed the whole book (Smend and others) becomes impossible from these considerations just as does the understanding of the book as a pseudepigraph of a later biased author.

9. The Later History of the Book and Its Text

A. The final book of Ezekiel became a part of the canon of the Synagogue. The anecdotal note in b. *Menahot* 45a appears to point to an argument over its canonical status on account of the deviations from the cultic regulations of the Pentateuch which are found in it: "R. Yehuda said in the name of Rab: that man is remembered for good, by name Hanina b. Hezekiah, for but for him the book of Ezekiel would have been hidden because its words contradict the words of the Torah. What did he do? He brought three hundred measures of oil to his room, sat down there and explained it." After that the canonicity of the book of Ezekiel was no more contested.

Whilst in modern times Ezekiel has been placed third among the great "latter prophets," b. *Baba Batra* 14b points to the sequence: Jeremiah, Ezekiel, Isaiah. This order, which was also striking to the rabbis, is justified in the text mentioned by the following consideration: "the book of Kings concludes with destruction, Jeremiah contains only destruction, Ezekiel begins with destruction and concludes with a promise of consolation, and Isaiah contains only promises of consolation: we thus join destruction to destruction and consolation to consolation." We note further that directly after this reference in b. *Baba Batra* 15a the writing of Ezekiel is ascribed to the men of the Great Synagogue. In considering this reference we must certainly not overlook the fact that also the book of Isaiah (unlike Jeremiah) does not derive from the prophet himself, but is ascribed to "Hezekiah and his college." This text, however, can scarcely support critical conclusions about a genuine recollection retained here of a process of editing the book of Ezekiel.[325]

The book of Ezekiel must have been held in high regard in the Qumran community, as the not inconsiderable quotations from it in their writings show.[326] According to the Damascus Document 390 years after the destruction of Jerusalem the community of the new covenant arose.[327] Here the reckoning of the period of sin of Ezek 4:5 reappears. In the War Scroll we find right at the beginning the "desert of the nations" of Ezek 20:35.[328] In correspondence with this, mention is also made of a "desert of Jerusalem." The name Gog reappears in the War Scroll.[329] A description of the new Jerusalem, preserved in fragmentary form, in which the new temple is described with exact measurements, shows the influence of Ezek 40ff.[330] A similarly fragmentary description of the divine chariot is not to be understood without a knowledge of Ezek 1 and 10.[331] It is all the more striking therefore that so far only few fragments of the book of Ezekiel have become known: from Cave 1 a fragment with Ezek 4:16–5:1; from Cave 3 a fragment with Ezek 16:31–33. In Cave 4 the remains of three manuscripts of Ezekiel have been found. W. H. Brownlee mentioned a scroll from Cave 11, which is only legible in small fragments and which is no longer capable of being unrolled.[332]

The book of Ezekiel was of great importance for apocalyptic, as is to be seen in the Old Testament in the book of Daniel. Jewish and Christian apocalypses draw from the imagery and material of Ezekiel.[333] We must further note the wall paintings of the synagogue of Dura, where Ezekiel has also influenced synagogue art.[334]

B. The text tradition of the book of Ezekiel offers particular problems. Critical scholarship was first aroused by them.[335] It is at once noticeable in 𝔐 how different things are in the separate complexes. Besides sections such as chs. 3, 6, 18, 20:1–31, 28:1–10, which are largely free from textual difficulties, as also the figurative discourse of ch. 15 and parts of other figurative sayings, other texts appear badly disturbed, as in chs. 7, 21, 28:11–19 and elsewhere. These are certainly not always only sections which have a content that is difficult to understand, such as the elaborate description of the vision in ch. 1 or the building description of chs. 40–42. Rather the question arises whether already at the initial phase, before the redactional composition of the prophet's words into a book, the individual sections were extant in differing qualities of preservation.

The versions offer some help towards a recognition of corruptions that have entered later, among which the Septuagint (𝔊) naturally stands first. Even if we do not emphasize their value for the reconstruction of the text as strongly as Cornill, or so enthusiastically as Jahn, they yet remain at many points a help that is not to be undervalued for the recovery of a better text.[336]

In the discussion about 𝔊 the question of the number of translators has motivated research. H. St. J. Thackeray has endeavored to show for Ezekiel, as in the Greek book of Jeremiah, that the hands of two translators have been at work in 𝔊, on the basis of an examina-

---

325 So Steuernagel, *Lehrbuch*, 579.

326 See the list of references in A. Dupont-Sommer, *The Essene Writings from Qumran*, tr. G. Vermes (Cleveland: World, 1962), 452.

327 Dupont-Sommer, *Essene*, 135.

328 Dupont-Sommer, *Essene*, 186.

329 Dupont-Sommer, *Essene*, 204.

330 Dupont-Sommer, *Essene*, 355f.

331 Dupont-Sommer, *Essene*, 360f.

332 William Hugh Brownlee, "The Scroll of Ezekiel from the Eleventh Qumran Cave," *RQ* 4 (1963): 11–28. For the whole see Christoph Burchard, *Bibliographie zu den Handschriften vom Toten Meer* 2, BZAW 89 (Berlin: Töpelmann, 1965), 325.

333 See L. Dürr, *Die Stellung des Propheten Ezechiel in der israelitisch-jüdischen Apokalyptik*, AA IX 1 (Münster: Aschendorff, 1923).

334 See commentary to 37:14. For the later history in Christian theology and art see especially Neuss, *Buch*. See further M. D. Beck and W. Werbeck, "Ezechielbuch—Das Ezechielbuch in der Kunst," *RGG*³ 2, 850f, for other literature and for the history of the book's interpretation.

335 As noted on p. 3.

336 For the state of the 𝔊-tradition one should refer to Joseph Ziegler, *Ezechiel*, Septuaginta. Vetus Testamentum graecum 16, 1 (Göttingen: Vandenhoeck & Ruprecht, 1952), 7–88 (the introduction). See also Joseph Ziegler, *Susanna, Daniel, Bel et Draco*, Septuaginta. Vetus Testamentum graecum 16, 2 (Göttingen: Vandenhoeck & Ruprecht, 1954), 77f (appendix); and *idem*, "Zur Textgestaltung der Ezechiel-Septuaginta," *Bibl* 34 (1953): 433–455. Also Peter Katz, "Zur Textgestaltung der Ezechiel-Septuaginta," *Bibl* 35 (1954): 29–39.

tion of the writing of some formulae, place-names, prepositions, conjunctions, and particular word counterparts.[337] According to him the book was divided up into three complexes which comprised Ezek 1–27 / 28–39 / 40–48. Thus, according to Thackeray, chs. 40–48 also must derive from the translator of chs. 1–27. The translation of the name of Tyre provides a particularly striking piece of evidence. The Hebrew צֹר ("Tyre") is translated in chs. 26f (in all ten times) with Σορ, but in chs. 28f (three times) by Τύρος. The translation of the sacred name in 𝔊 also points to different translators. In consequence Schäfers, J. Herrmann, Danielsmeyer, and Turner have attempted to show that in chs. 40–48 also we must see a third, independent, translator at work.[338]

The argument from the various translations of the sacred name has subsequently undergone a noticeable weakening by the introduction of Papyrus 967 into the discussion.[339] In this the text of 𝔊 in the relevant passages appears considerably different. Parts of this papyrus were first known by the publication of the Chester Beatty Papyri of the British Museum in London.[340] We find in them the text of Ezek 11:25 (end) —12:6, 12–18, 23–13:6, 11–17, 20–14:3, 6–10, 15–20, 23–15:7; 16:5–11, 16–22, 28–34, 39–45, 48–53, 57–17:1, 6–10, 15–21, which is probably to be dated to the first half of the third century.[341] There then appeared a further part of 𝔊[967].[342] It covers Ezek 19:12–20:16 (beginning) 20:40 (end)–44; 21:4(9)–25:5 (beginning) 26:10–28:18; 29:12–32:30; 34:6–36:23; 37:1–4 (beginning) 38:1–39:29 on twenty-one pages, written

on both sides, the last of which contains the text in the sequence Ezek 38f; 37:1–4 (beginning). Besides the detailed variants, which are in places quite marked,[343] the two striking omissions of 12:26–28 and 36:23b–38 have given occasion for explanation.[344] Subsequently still further parts of 𝔊[967] to Ezekiel have appeared. In Cologne there are a further ten complete, and three almost complete, pages. To this must be added ten fragments of various sizes, by which some of the gaps which have so far existed can by either partially or completely closed. The entire Cologne collection will be edited and prepared for publication by L. Jahn. It covers 12:6–7, 18–19; 13:8–9, 18; 14:3–4, 10–13, 21–22; 15:7 (end)–16:3, 11 (end)–14 (beginning), 23 (end)–26, 35 (end)–37, 45–46, 53–55; 17:1–5, 11–14, 21–19:12 (beginning); 20:5–8, 13–16, 21–25, 31–41 (beginning) 44 (end)–21:3; 25:5–26:10 (beginning) 43:9–48:35. The parts of chs. 12–15 are thus only preserved in a very fragmentary condition. Through the friendly assistance of Prof. Merkelbach in Cologne a copy of the Cologne Fragments was made available to me in transcription.

Besides this a further ten pages (twenty sides) of Papyrus 967 have subsequently appeared in Madrid. Through the friendly permission of Prof. M. Fernández-Galiano I personally saw these Papyri Biblici Matritenses, which belong to the "Fondo Photiadès," in the spring of 1967, and I have been able to use them for the text of the commentary to chs. 40–48. They cover Ezek 28:19–29:12; 32:30–34:6; 37:4–28; 40:1–43:9.[345] In regard to the papyrus as a whole,

337 H. St. J. Thackeray, "The Greek Translators of Ezekiel," *JTS* 4 (1903): 398–411.

338 J. Schäfers, "Ist das Buch Ezechiel in der Septuaginta von einem oder mehreren Dolmetschern übersetzt?" *ThGl* 1 (1909): 289–291; Werner Danielsmeyer, *Neue Untersuchungen zur Ezechiel-Septuaginta*, Unpub. Diss. (Münster, 1936); N. Turner, "The Greek Translators of Ezekiel," *JTS* 7 (1956): 12–24.

339 Joseph Ziegler, "Die Bedeutung des Chester Beatty-Scheide Papyrus 967 für die Textüberlieferung der Ezechiel-Septuaginta," *ZAW* 61 (1945/48): 76–94, especially 93f.

340 Frederic George Kenyon, *The Chester Beatty Biblical Papyri. Fasc VII: Ezekiel, Daniel, Esther* (London: Walker, 1938).

341 Ziegler, *Ezechiel*, 10.

342 In Allan Chester Johnson, Henry Snyder Gehman,

and Edmund Harris Kase, *The John H. Scheide Biblical Papyri, Ezekiel* (Princeton: Princeton University Press, 1938).

343 See Excursus 1 on the names of God.

344 For these omissions see the commentary. Also see Henry Snyder Gehman, "The Relations between the Hebrew Text of Ezekiel and that of the John H. Scheide Papyri," *JAOS* 58 (1938): 92–102; Floyd V. Filson, "The Omission of Ezek. 12:26–28 and 36:23b–38 in Codex 967," *JBL* 62 (1943): 27–32; J. B. Payne, "The Relationship of the Chester Beatty Papyri of Ezekiel to Codex Vaticanus," *JBL* 68 (1949): 251–265; John W. Wevers, "Septuaginta-Forschungen," *ThR* NF 22 (1954): 85–138; and the publications of Joseph Ziegler.

345 Since on one page here 37:22–28 connects with 40:1–3, the question raised in note a to 36:23 has

in its contents now only 1:1–11:25 (beginning); 12:8–11, 20–22; 13:10, 19; 14:5, 14; 16:4, 15, 27, 38, 47, 56 are missing. The surprises of recent times justify the hope that the missing parts also may appear sometime in the hands of a dealer. Discussion about the importance of 𝕲[967], however, in view of this newly recovered material, will no doubt continue.

The tradition of the Vetus Latina (𝕷) is of importance for the reconstruction of 𝕲. The Old Latin texts of Ezekiel, as a rule, follow closely that of 𝕲. Only rarely are they of importance beyond this for the restoration of older forms of the original Hebrew text.[346]

For the translation of the Vulgate (𝕭) the commentary of Jerome offers a useful guide.[347]

The Targum (𝕿), which generally keeps closely to the Hebrew original, offers a valuable help towards correcting later scribal errors. At many points it offers, through its paraphrastic interpretations and also those motivated by a desire for dogmatic improvement, a glance into the understanding of the text of the Judaism of its day. The Targum Jonathan (𝕿[J]), which is what concerns us on Ezekiel, must have received its final written form in the fifth century in Babylon. Doubtless, however, it used older material.[348]

In contrast to this the Peshitta (𝕾) shows a freer text translation and betrays at many points a tendency towards stylistic improvements and is also not afraid to transpose parts of the text. At difficult passages of the Hebrew original, which were not understood by 𝕾, we find also simple abbreviations which avoid the difficulties. Since 𝕲 must have exercised (later?) a not inconsiderable influence on 𝕾, the latter cannot overall be regarded without caution as a witness to the Hebrew original. However, it can at many points offer valuable help regarding 𝕲.[349]

---

unexpectedly received a quick (negative) answer. It can now be said definitely that 36:23bβ–38 are missing in 𝕲[967].

346 The basic text of 𝕷 is found in P. Sabatier, *Bibliorum sacrorum latinae versiones* (1739–1749). In addition there are available for use on Ezekiel the fragments of the Codex rescriptus wirceburgensis in E. Ranke, *Par palimpsestorum wirceburgensium* (Vindobonae, 1871). For the Constance and St. Gall fragments see Alban Dold, *Konstanzer altlateinische Propheten- und Evangelien-Bruchstücke mit Glossen, nebst zugehörigen Prophetentexten aus Zürich und St. Gallen*, Texte und Arbeiten I. 7–9 (Leipzig: Harrassowitz, 1923); *idem, Neue St. Galler vorhieronymianische Propheten-Fragmente der St. Galler Sammelhandschrift 1398b zugehörig*, Texte and Arbeiten I. 31 (Hohenzollern: Beuroner Kunstverlag, 1940).

347 *MPL* 25 (1884), 15–490.

348 It is cited from the edition of Paul de Lagarde, *Prophetae chaldaice* (Lipsiae: B.G. Teubner, 1872). The new edition by Alexander Sperber, *The Bible in Aramaic* 3: *The latter Prophets according to Targum Jonathan* (Leiden: Brill, 1962), is specifically indicated where it is used.

349 In the present commentary the 1823 edition of Lee is used, which rests essentially on the *London Polyglot* of 1657.

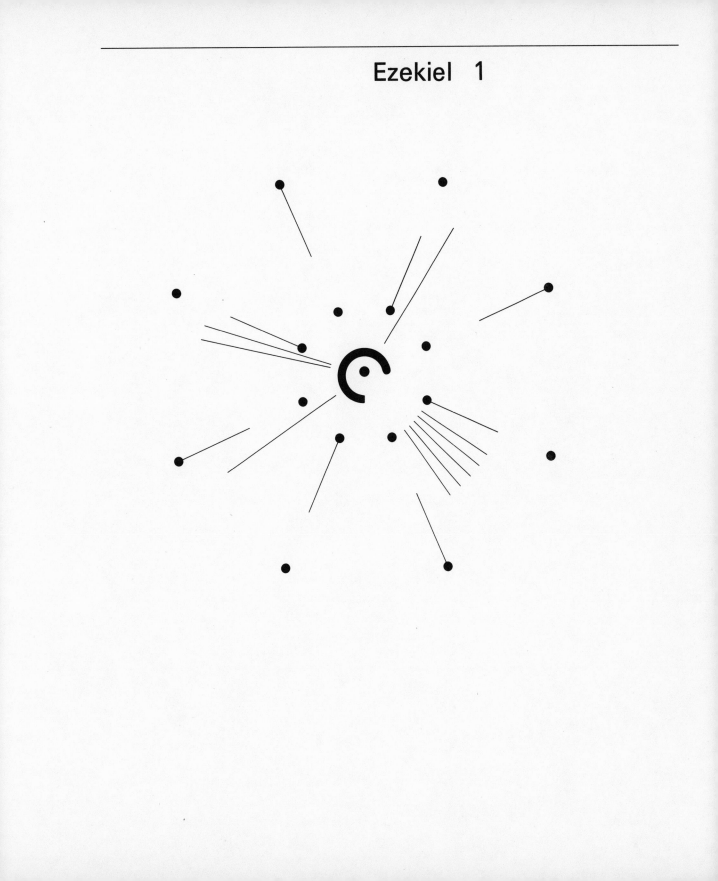

The Call

Bibliography

G. R. Berry
"The Title of Ezekiel (1:1–3)," *JBL* 51 (1932):
54–57.

J. A. Bewer
"The Text of Ezekiel 1:1–3," *AJSL* 50 (1933/34):
96–101.

K. Budde
"Zum Eingang des Buches Ezechiel," *JBL* 50
(1931):20–41.

H. M. Orlinsky
"Where Did Ezekiel Receive the Call to Prophesy?" *BASOR* 122 (1951):34–36.

A. Alföldi
"Die Geschichte des Throntabernakels," *La nouvelle
Clio* 1/2 (1949/50):537–566.

G. R. Driver
"Ezekiel's Inaugural Vision," *VT 1* (1951):60–62.

L. Dürr
*Ezekiels Vision von der Erscheinung Gottes (Ez. c. 1 und
10) im Lichte der vorderasiatischen Altertumskunde*
(Würzburg:Richter, 1917).

E. Höhne
*Die Thronwagenvision Hesekiels. Echtheit und Herkunft
der Vision Hes. 1:4–28 und ihrer einzelnen Züge*, unpub.
Diss. (Erlangen, 1953–54).

S. Landersdorfer
*Der ΒΑΑΛ ΤΕΤΡΑΜΟΡΦΟΣ und die Kerube des
Ezekiel*, Studien zur Geschichte und Kultur des
Altertums 9, 3 (Paderborn:Schöningh, 1918).

O. Procksch
"Die Berufungsvision Hesekiels," *in Beiträge zur alttestamentlichen Wissenschaft K. Budde zum 70. Geburtstag überreicht*, BZAW 34 (Giessen:Töpelmann, 1920):
141–149.

H. Schmidt
"Kerubenthron und Lade," *in Eucharisterion für H.
Gunkel*, FRLANT 36, 1 (Göttingen, 1923):120–144.

S. Sprank
Studien zu Ezechiel, BWANT III 4 (Stuttgart:Kohl-
hammer, 1926), 26–73.

1

1 And it happened[a] in the thirtieth year, in
the fourth (month), on the fifth (day)
of the month, when I was among the
exiles by the river Chebar, that the
heavens were opened, and I saw divine
visions.[b] 2/ On the fifth (day) of the
month—it was the fifth year (after) the

1:1 1:1a The sentence construction: 1) Introductory
ויהי, 2) reference to the date, 3) apodosis, is frequent
in the book of Ezekiel, cf. 3:16; 8:1; 20:1; 26:1;
29:17; 30:20; 31:1; 32:1, 17; 33:21, also 16:23f.
In 1:1; 8:1 a circumstantial clause (introduced in
8:1 without ו) is inserted between 2) and 3), which
describes in more detail the circumstances of the
prophet. In other passages (9:8; 10:6; 11:13) the
description of the accompanying circumstances, or
of a subordinate action, can stand in place of a reference to the date. The apodosis is introduced in
nine cases by the simple perfect without ו (1:1;
20:1; 26:1; 29:17; 30:20; 31:1; 32:1, 17; 33:21),

deportation of king Jehoiachin—3/ [ ]ª
the word of Yahweh came to Ezekiel,
the son of Buzi, the priest, in the land
of the Chaldeans by the river Chebar.ᵇ
And the hand of Yahweh was upon meᶜ
[there].ᵈ

4 And as I looked, behold, a storm wind
came from the north, a great cloudª and
flashing fire [with brightness round
about it]ᵇ and out of its midst (it
shone) as it were the appearanceᶜ of
electrum [from the midst of the fire].ᵈ

five times with the imperfect consecutive (3:16, see
on text; 8:1; 9:8; 10:6; 16:24), whilst only in 11:13
is a nominal clause found. This form of speech is
found in the prophetic books, also in the Deuteronomistic parts of the book of Isaiah (Is 7:1, cf. 2 Kings
16:5, and Is 36:1; cf. 2 Kings 18:13), in the narrative parts of the book of Jeremiah (13:6; 20:3;
26:8; 28:1; 35:11; 36:1, 9 and other passages) and
in Zechariah (7:1). See Gesenius-Kautzsch § 111g
and Koehler, "Syntactica IV," especially 304: *Hy-
pertropher Gebrauch von uajᵉhī*.

b 𝕲 translates literally ὁράσεις θεοῦ, 𝕲ᴸᵘᶜ ᶜᵃᵗ more
freely ὅρασιν; Σ Θ ὀπτασίαν (see Ziegler, *Ezechiel*, 45).

3 3a The infinitive absolute of היה in the form הָיֹה
is found again in 1 Kings 13:32, and with the form
הָיֹו Gen 18:18; Nu 30:7; Jer 15:18; Ezek 20:32.
In all these references the strengthening of the assertion becomes intelligible. In Ezek 1:3 it is noteworthy in view of the lack of emphasis which is otherwise found in Ezekiel in the formula for the receipt
of a message. The καὶ ἐγένετο of 𝕲 as little appears
to presuppose the emphasis as the (פיתגם נבואה
מן קדם יהוה הוה) of 𝕴 and the *factum est* (*verbum
domini*) in 𝕭. By its inclusion of the copula 𝕲 seems
to be assimilated to 1:1 and does not point to a ויהי
in the original text. 𝔐 must be regarded as dittography. A simple היה is read by Varᴷᵉⁿ ³⁸⁴.

b 𝕲 Χοβαρ 𝕭 Chobar.

c 𝔐 עליו "above him." One has to read עלי
"upon me" with thirteen MSS 𝕲 𝕾 𝔄, see below
p. 108.

d The שם of 𝔐 was not found by 𝕲, neither here
nor in the related texts 3:22; 8:1. From 40:1f,
where the secondary expansion of 𝔐 can be seen
particularly clearly, it appears likely that the שם of
𝔐 in all the references mentioned is to be ascribed
to subsequent redaction.

4 4a 𝕲 reads καὶ νεφέλη μεγάλη ἐν αὐτῷ. The local
placing of the cloud in the storm, which 𝕲 thereby
affirms, is not very convincing and is to be regarded
as a subsequent assimilation to the מתוכה of 𝔐,
which follows in verses 4 and 5. The connection by
καί, also followed by eight MSS and 𝕭, which
changes the explicative apposition to סערה into one
member of a series in a looser list, shows the tendency, which is often to be seen with 𝕲, of softening
asyndetic constructions by insertion of the copula,
cf. 1:12; 3:1, 8, 22, and other passages.

b ונגה לו סביב, both grammatically and concep-
tually, can only be related to ענן, from which, however, it is separated in 𝔐 by ואש מתלקחת. Hence 𝕲
transposes and reads καὶ φέγγος κύκλῳ αὐτοῦ καὶ
πῦρ ἐξαστράπτον. The clumsy introduction of the
sentence in 𝔐 shows that it is a secondary addition
stemming from 1:27.

c 𝕲 ὅρασις, 𝕲ʰ ὁμοίωμα, Ἀ ὀφθαλμός, Σ εἶδος, 𝕭
species.

d מתוך האש is a clarification made necessary by
the addition established in note 4b. The translation

5/ And from the middle of it (there appeared) the form of four living creatures. And this was their appearance: they were shaped[a] like men. 6/ But each had four faces and each had four wings. ( )[a] 7/ Their legs were straight, and the soles of their feet were like the sole of a calf's foot; and they sparkled like burnished bronze.[a] 8/ And human hands[a] (appeared) under[b] their wings on their four sides, and their faces ( )[c]

in 𝕍 *id est de medio ignis* brings out very well this character of an additional comment. It has subsequently entered into 𝕲 also, together with a further gloss obelized according to Jerome, where v 4 ends ἐν μέσῳ τοῦ πυρὸς καὶ φέγγος ἐν αὐτῷ.

5   5a The translations of 𝕲 ὁμοίωμα ἀνθρώπου ἐπ' αὐτοῖς and 𝕍 *similitudo hominis in eis* do not compel us to depart from 𝔐 (תָ דמות אדם להנה) אינשא להין and to read עליה instead of להנה (so Cornill, Herrmann). After זה מראיהן we expect a description of the living creatures and certainly not a mention of the enthroned figure of God already (Herrmann, see below p. 95).

6   6a להם is lacking in 𝕲 𝕍 and is to be deleted as a clumsy repetition of להנה of v 5. For the form of the suffix cf. v 7. 𝔗 here comes to the fantastic reckoning of 16 faces and 64 wings for each creature; cf. Cornill, 128f. In its own way 𝔗 is a witness to the assiduous editorial activity on the text.

7   7a The versions show many difficulties. There appears in them a transition into the masculine suffix form, which is already to be seen in the gloss to v 6. The feminine suffixes of some MSS and of 𝕲 may be a subsequent smoothing over of this unevenness. 𝕲 not only read כנף πτερωτοί (οἱ πόδες αὐτῶν) instead of כף, but also lacks any equivalent for רגל עגל, of which עגל was read by 'A (στρογγύλον, according to Jerome *rotundas*) and 𝔗 (סגלגלן) as עָגֹל (or עֲגֻלָּה) 'round.' At the end of the verse the reading of 𝕲 καὶ σπινθῆρες ὡς ἐξαστράπτων χαλκὸς καὶ ἐλαφραὶ αἱ πτέρυγες αὐτῶν points to a taking over of the וכנפיהם (which is lacking in 𝕲) from v 8b of 𝔐, and a Hebrew original ונצצים כעין נחשת וכנפיהם קלות (which Cornill reads). The addition of נצצים, taken by most commentators as a qal participle from נצץ (Gesenius-Buhl, Koehler-Baumgartner) or a po. participle from נוץ (Zorell), to what precedes is difficult. It cannot be joined smoothly either to חיות or to the feminine רגל, and in what precedes only כנים exists as a possible masculine noun to which it could relate. Dan 10:6, however, shows a connection with the legs of the phenomenon (מרגלתיו expanded by זרעתיו), already rendered probable by the 𝔐 of Ezek 1:7. The suspicion that here a strong reediting of the Ezekiel text has taken place is great.

8   8a Instead of the unintelligible K וידו we must read Q ויד. The singular text of 𝕲 (𝕾 𝕍) is to be explained by reference to 10:21, which in 𝕲 is also harmonized and assimilated to 10:8.

b 10:8 reads simply תחת instead of the מתחת of 𝔐. This could have originated through dittography of מ from אדם. However 𝔗 reads מתחות.

c וכנפיהם "and their wings" of 𝔐 is lacking in 𝕲, which does however read an additional כנפיהם in v 7. We must question, however, whether וכנפיהם is not rather the original beginning of the gloss v 9a; see below.

d לארבעתם is clumsy, but is an explicating gloss

[on the four of them].[d] 9/ [<But their wings> touched one another ( )];[a] they did not turn when they[b] went, each one went straight forward. 10/ This was the appearance of their faces: the face of a man, with the face of a lion on the right side on all four, and the face of an ox on the left side on all four, and the face of an eagle on all four.[a] 11/ [And their faces][a] And their wings were spread out upward. On each of them two wings touched one another[b] and two covered their bodies.[c] 12/ And each went straight forward. Wherever the spirit would go they went. They did not turn,[a] as they went. 13/ And <between>[a] the living creatures there appeared,[b] as it were coals burning in a fire. Something like torches[c] moved[d] to and fro between the living creatures. And the fire blazed, and out of the fire

which is already attested by 𝕲.

9   9a 𝔙 9a is lacking in 𝕲 𝔎[Bo] and is shown as a secondary intrusion into 𝔐 by its breaking up the section vv 8/9b. The וכנפיהם from v 8 of 𝔐, which is lacking in 𝕲, must therefore once have formed the subject of the sentence. After its inclusion in v 8 its repetition by the awkward כנפיהם at the end of the gloss was clearly necessary in 𝔐. For the origin of the gloss cf. v 11 note b.

   b This means the living creatures בלכתן.

10   10a Masculine and feminine forms of the suffixes לארבעתם – לארבעתן alternate here in a remarkable way within the verse, which has also occasioned attempts at alteration in the directions given for the faces. The insertion of מקדם (Cornill, Bertholet) or לפנים after אדם and מאחור after נשר (Toy) is quite without support in the tradition, as also is Jerome's translation *et facies aquilae desuper ipsorum quattuor.*

11   11a The disturbing ופניהם at the beginning of the verse is to be deleted with 𝕲 and 𝕷. The connection with v 10, conjectured by Smend by a change to לפנימה, is improbable in spite of 40:22, 26. The two words פניהם and כנפיהם appear to have exerted a strong mutual attraction. Already in v 8 we find this doubling wrongly appearing.

   b The eliptical חברות איש, in which חבר appears to be construed with an accusative, is striking beside 1:9; Ex 26:3; 28:7, where it is construed with אל, and Ex 39:4, where it is construed with על. The gloss v 9a has clearly retained the original text, which is also to be restored here. Read חברות אשה אל אחותה. V 9a as a gloss has possibly been added with the intention of improving the corrupt text of v 11, but has entered at the wrong place in the text.

   c The suffix form גויתיהֶנָה is found only here in the Old Testament. See Diehl, *Pronomen,* 42.

12   12a MSS (𝕲 𝕾 𝔙) ולא; read with 𝔐. Cf. v 4 note a.

13   13a With 𝕲 καὶ ἐν μέσῳ read ובינות instead of 𝔐 ודמות "and the likeness." Cf. the usage מבינות לכרבים in 10:2, 6, 7 and בינות הכרבים 10:7, which is related to the text here.

   b 𝔐 מראיהם; according to 𝕲 ὅρασις we should read מראה. In consequence of the scribal error of דמות for בינות 𝔐 arose as an attempt at making the text intelligible: "And the form of the creatures—their appearance was like. . . ."

   c According to 𝕲 לפדים should be read without the article. The article arose by dittography from the preceding מראה.

   d 𝕲 appears not to have read the היא and to connect לפדים מתהלכת, λαμπάδων συστρεφομένων. This is followed by Cornill and others who read לפידים מתהלכות. The connection of the masculine לפדים with the feminine participle, however, is not possible. Rather we should then have to consider the replacing of הוא by האש, to which the 𝔗 אשתא בעוריא could point; cf. Cornill, 129. More correctly, however, we should keep 𝔐, connecting היא to האש.

there went forth lightning. [14/ And the living creatures <darted> to and fro, so that it appeared like <lightning>.]ᵃ

15 And as I looked [at the living creatures],ᵃ behold, there was a wheel on the ground beside the living creatures, with all four of them ( ).ᵇ 16/ And the appearanceᵃ of the wheels [and the manner in which they were constructed]ᵇ was like the gleaming of chrysolite, and all four had 'a single'ᶜ form, and they [appeared and]ᵈ were so constructed, as though one wheel were within another.

17 They went inᵃ one of their four directions.ᵇ [when they went,]ᶜ They did

14 14a The verse is lacking in 𝕲, and we must read with 𝖁 (*ibant*) יצוא instead of the erroneous רצוא (Bauer-Leander, 405), and with 𝖳 (ברקא) 𝖁 Σ הברק instead of the mysterious הבזק (against Cohen, "Studies," 163). Jerome is of the opinion that 𝕲 has deliberately suppressed the verse, which speaks of a return (שוב) of the living creatures *ne legenti scandalum faceret* because it is previously claimed explicitly that the creatures did not turn as they went (vv 9, 13). He adds to this a very modern sounding warning to the text critic: *melius est . . . in divinis libris transferre quod dictum est licet non intelligas quare dictum sit, quam auferre quod nescias. Alioquin et multa alia quae ineffabilia sunt, et humanus animus capere non potest hac licentia delebuntur.* In the present text we must see in 𝕸 a later textual addition, still not found in 𝕲 and composed of catch phrases from v 13, which mixes the picture of the living creatures and of the lightning. The latter could have arisen from a wrongly written secondary form of 𝕸 in v 13, which likewise compares the form of the creatures to blazing fire. V 14 would then have entered after the scribal error of v 13.

15 15a החיות is lacking in 𝕲 and is a later attempt at clarification wrongly introduced. It breaks up in a clumsy way the stereotyped phrase וארא[ה] והנה, which introduces a new feature into the account of a vision. So 1:4; 8:2; 10:9; Zech 2:1, 5; 5:1; 6:1, also 4:2. A date has been introduced into Zech 1:8, but there is never an object, which would destroy the atmosphere of mystery about the declaration. Confirmatory proof of the secondary character of החיות is given by a comparison with 10:9, which is dependent on 1:15, in which the text appears still without any gloss.

b 𝕸 לארבעת פניו "on its four faces." Σ τετραπρόσωπος and 𝖁 (*rota*) *habens quattuor facies* are hopeless attempts at getting a meaning from 𝕸. 𝕲 suggests that we should delete פניו and then read the first word as לארבעתם (or לארבעתן?) and the following (v 16) as ומראה. Cornill offers a penetrating explanation of the scribal error, but we must question whether the middle letters of the original text ו[מראה] [ארבעת]ם became ניו, which could easily have happened graphically and which was then expanded by the addition of a פ to make the reading פניו of 𝕸.

16 16aומראה cf. v 15 note b.

b 𝕸 ומעשיהם is in place in v 16b, but in 16a it is an awkward gloss, which is lacking in 𝕲 and in 10:9, which is dependent on 1:16.

c Instead of the אחד of 𝕸 we should expect אחת.

d מראה or ומראיהם is in place in 16a where the impression of light and color is described. Here, where we are dealing with the technical construction, the right word is מעשיהם, and 𝕲 only attests τὸ ἔργον αὐτῶν. 10:10 displays a noticeable abbreviation of the statement.

17 17a 𝕸 על. In vv 9 and 12 אל is used in a similar

not turn, when they went. 18/ [And their rims] However they had rims. Then ⟨I saw that their rims⟩[a] on all four were full of eyes round about. 19/ And when the living creatures went, the wheels (also) went beside them and when the living creatures rose up from the earth, then the wheels (also) rose. 20/ Wherever[a] the spirit would go, they went, ( )[b] and the wheels rose along with them, for the spirit of the living creatures[c] was in the wheels.

phrase, which is what we should expect according to well-established Hebrew usage. However, the book of Ezekiel shows throughout a quite surprising blurring of the distinction between על and אל, which can be interchanged without fixed rules. We must see in this the influence of the Aramaic language (on Ezekiel or his exilic tradents?). In Aramaic it is true that "על . . . covers also the Hebrew אל, which only appears sporadically" (Koehler-Baumgartner, Aramaic part, see under על).

b 𝔐 רבעיהן. The clear underlying correspondence of vv 17 and 12 shows that רבע must correspond in meaning to the עבר of v 12. Do we then have in רבעיהן a scribal error, dependent on the sequence of consonants, for the preceding ארבעת (so BH)? Or, since the phrase ארבעת רבעיהם reappears with remarkable tenacity in 1:8, 17; 10:11; 43:16, 17 (with a change in the suffix), should we not rather think of an assimilation to the preceding ארבעת, brought about in the living language, so that the meanings of עבר and ארבעה coalesce? On the possibility of this play on ambiguity in the biblical language see Seeligmann, "Midraschexegese."

c That 𝔐 בלכתם appears beside the similarly used בלכתן and רבעיהן does not necessarily justify the deletion of the word since similar phenomena appear in this chapter quite frequently (cf. v 10). However, since it is superfluous beside ילכו and is lacking in 𝔊, it must be a subsequent addition. Nevertheless, the editor of 10:11 already had it before him. He smoothed the uneven text in which he read בלכתם twice and transferred the expression at its first occurrence to the beginning of the verse, away from its proximity to ילכו.

18   18a The text of the verse is undoubtedly badly disturbed in its first half. 𝔐 וגביהן וגבה להם ויראה להם "and their rims, and they had height and fear" is unintelligible. 𝔊, with its οὐδ' οἱ νῶτοι αὐτῶν καὶ ὕψος ἦν αὐτοῖς καὶ εἶδον αὐτά (cf. 𝔖) appears to have read the first three words of 𝔐, the first of which it connects with v 17, in the present form. However it must have had the first person singular qal imperfect of ראה, which deserves our attention. Can we then restore ואראה להם "I looked at them" (i.e., the wheels); their rims were full of eyes"? Or should we conjecture (as Cornill), with the uncertain support of a formulation in Θ, ואראה והנה which is graphically more drastic? The preceding וגבה להם can only be given a forced interpretation and has to be interpreted as a scribal error from וְנַבֹּת להם (Cornill). Is then the preceding וגביהן, which is noteworthy for its masculine plural construction and the feminine suffix which is out of place here, a variant of this? The גבהם of 𝔐 from 10:12 appears to support the masculine plural form, but is nevertheless probably a scribal error from גבתם. See on the text there. With considerable reserve we may then read [וגביהן] וגבת להם ואראה להם גבתם מלאת.

20   20a aα corresponds to 12bβ. אל-על cf. v 17 note a.

21/ When these went, these went; and
when these stood still, these stood still;
and when these rose up from the
earth, then these [the wheels]ᵃ rose up
like them, for the spirit of the living
creaturesᵇ was in the wheels.

22 And over the heads of the living creaturesᵃ
was something like a fixed platform,
shining like [awesome]ᵇ crystal, spread
out above their heads.ᶜ 23/ Under the
fixed platform their wings were
'stretched out',ᵃ so that one touched
the other (and) each creature covered

Instead of שׁם we should read שׁמּה, as is shown by
v 12 and the subsequent dittography in v 20aβ. Does
the unusual reading of 𝕲 οὗ ἂν ἦν ἡ νεφέλη ἐκεῖ τὸ
πνεῦμα τοῦ πορεύεσθαι point to the particular theologoumenon, that the phenomenon of the creatures
always strives toward the cloud (of the theophany)
from which it was loosed according to v 4? We must
certainly not follow Jahn, *Buch*, in correcting 𝕸 in
accordance with 𝕲.

b The words שׁמּה הרוח ללכת have been written
twice in error and are lacking in MSS 𝕲 and 𝕊.

c The singular form חיה, which is nevertheless
affirmed by the tradition of 𝕲 (πνεῦμα) ζωῆς and 𝕭
(*spiritus*) *vitae* and can therefore scarcely be changed,
is striking. We can either interpret it collectively for
each of the four creatures or find in it a form of
speech which consciously indicates comprehensively
the whole phenomenon as a חיה.

21 21a האופנים, which is dispensable, is lacking in 𝕲.
b Cf. v 20 note c.

22 22a 𝕲 reads ὑπὲρ κεφαλῆς αὐτοῖς τῶν ζῴων which
the later text witnesses seek to smooth over by assimilation to αὐτῶν (𝕲ᴸᵘᶜ ᶻᵛ and others), or τοῖς
ζῴοις (𝕲¹⁰⁶), or by complete accommodation to 𝕸
(𝕬ᴮᵒ 𝕬 Arm). τῶν ζῴων gives the impression of being
a subsequent addition in 𝕲. Has the החיה of 𝕸 also
come in late from vv 20f.?

b הנורא is lacking in 𝕲 and must be considered a
part of the later interpretation.

c The translation of על ראשׁיהם in 𝕸 by ἐπι τῶν
πτερύγων in 𝕲 must rest on a subsequent combination of 𝕲 on the basis of v 23.

23 23a 𝕲 reads καὶ ὑποκάτω τοῦ στερεώματος αἱ
πτέρυγες αὐτῶν ἐκτεταμέναι πτερυσσόμεναι ἑτέρα τῇ
ἑτέρᾳ, ἑκάστῳ δύο ἐπικαλύπτουσαι τὰ σώματα αὐτῶν.
The πτερυσσόμεναι points, according to the evidence
of 3:13, to a משׁיקות in the original text. The ישׁרות
of 𝕸 may have its origin in a scribal error (the falling out of an initial מ through haplography, the
transposition of י and שׁ, and ק wrongly written as ר).
It has then subsequently been understood in the
sense of ישׁר "straight, upright" from v 7. The reading of 𝕸 is first attested by Σ ὀρθαί and Θ εὐθεῖς 𝕭
rectae. The connection ישׁרות אשׁה אל אחותה of 𝕸
in any case evokes little confidence. ישׁר gives expression to a complete inner determination and is
therefore used absolutely in v 7. It is not a relation
as it appears in אשׁה אל אחותה. The ἐκτεταμέναι of
𝕲 points to a פרדות which is added in 𝕲 from 1:11.
However, the second ולאישׁ שׁתים מכסות of 𝕸 still
not read by 𝕲, must be a subsequent elaboration. It
has called forth the introduction of a repeated להנה
to divide up the expanded text. Both occurrences of
להנה, with their feminine suffix forms determined
by v 5, are to be deleted. The verse-section b, cleaned
up in this way following 𝕲, represents a simple repetition of 11bβ, and what remains difficult is the
change of the full feminine suffix גויתיהנה v 11 to
גויתיהם in v 23. The odd use of אשׁה and אישׁ to

its body with two of them (　).ᵃ 24/ And I heard the sound of their wings (and it was) like the sound of great waters, [like the voice of the Almighty,]ᵃ when they went, [the sound of a tumult like the sound of a camp,];ᵇ whenᶜ they stood still, they lowered their wings. [25/ And there came a sound from the place above the fixed platform, which was over their heads. When they stood still, they lowered their wings.]ᵃ 26/ And ⟨behold⟩ᵃ above the fixed platform over their heads there appeared something like sapphire—something like a throne; and above what appeared like a throne, [on it]ᵇ there was something to see, which looked like a man. 27/ And I saw a brightness like electrum [appearing like fire, which is enclosed round about]ᵃ upwards from what appeared to be his loins; and downwards from what appeared to be his loins I saw something which looked like fire. And he was surrounded by brightness.

denote the same creatures was noted by Jerome: *Ideo post mulierem virum posuit in persona eadem ne sexum in coelestibus putaremus.*

24   24a The כקול שדי is lacking in 𝕲 and has been introduced as a gloss from 10:5, where 𝕲 also has it. Beside the כקול מים רבים, found only in 43:2, it is superfluous and disturbs the order of the clause which is oriented to בלכתם. 10:5 and 43:2 are satisfied with a single comparison.

b aβ קול המלה כקול מחנה is lacking in 𝕲 here, whereas it has been introduced in a clumsy way in 𝕲 in 43:2. This third comparison of 𝔐 is perceptibly out of place and belongs again to the later interpretative work on the text. In another formulation 𝔗 has introduced here, in place of the third comparison, a reference to the heavenly praise of God by his servants, "when they praise and exalt their Lord, the Everlasting, the Eternal King"; the comparison with the sound of the camp it has taken as "like the sound of the camp of the angels in the height."

c 𝕲 𝕾 𝖅 smooth the text by the introduction of the copula, cf. v 4 note a.

25   25a The whole verse, which uses the catchword קול in a different direction, is missing in 9 MSS 𝕲ᴹˢ. 𝕲, which reads καὶ ἰδοὺ φωνὴ ὑπεράνωθεν τοῦ στερεώματος τοῦ ὄντος ὑπὲρ κεφαλῆς αὐτῶν, but then passes over vv 25b and 26aα (the reference of BH v 25 should be corrected accordingly), appears at first at least to support v 25a. However, Cornill rightly noted that the φωνή is an assimilation to 𝔐 and that the remaining text of 𝕲 is the counterpart of v 26aα of 𝔐. φωνή must certainly no longer be interpreted as "a Hexaplaric fragment" (Cornill), if Ziegler, *Ezechiel*, 28, is right in his assertion based on a reference to 𝕲⁹⁶⁷ that "already in the pre-Hexaplaric period the text of Ezekiel was corrected in accordance with the Hebrew text." (See Gehman, "Relations," and contrast Wevers "Septuaginta-Forschungen," 124f.) Thus 𝕲 also becomes an important witness for the elimination of 1:25, which is also shown not to be original by the emendation of Coppens, who relates the beginning of the verse, in the reading וַיְקַלּוּ מעל הרקיע, to the wings of the creatures (*Muséon* 47 [1934]: 259–261). 𝔗 gives here, as also in v 24, a broader exposition of קול when it says at the beginning of v 25 "And at the time when he was pleased to cause his servants, the prophets of Israel, to speak the voice went forth (הוי קלא) and was heard over the fixed platform, which was above their heads. . . ."

26   26a With 𝕲 (cf. to v 25) one has perhaps to insert here הנה and to read והנה ממעל.

b עליו is to be excised as a later superfluous elaboration with 3 MSSᴷᵉⁿ 𝕲 and 𝖅.

27   27a 𝔐 כמראה אש בית לה סביב (instead of בֵּית we could better vocalize with Smend as בַּיָת) is not attested by 𝕲. It must be removed since it introduces the appearance of fire which belongs to the

28 Like the appearance of the bow which is
in the clouds on a rainy day, so was the
appearance of the brightness round
about. This was the appearance of the
likeness of Yahweh's glory. And when
I saw it, I fell upon my face.

2

And I heard the voice of someone
speaking. 2:1 And he said to me: Son
of man, stand upon your feet, and I will
speak with you.[a] 2/Then the spirit
came into me [when he spoke to me,][a]
and he set[b] me upon my feet, and I
heard 'him', as he spoke to me.[c]
3/ And he said to me: Son of man, I
send you to the house[a] of Israel, [to
nations,][b] to the rebellious,[c] who have
been rebellious[c] against me; they and
their fathers [have turned away from

lower half of the body into the description of the
upper half also. The question may be raised whether
it is an interpretation of the assertion of v 27bβ ונגה
לו סביב which has entered the text at the wrong
place.

2:1 2:1a 𝔐 reads אֹתָךְ instead of אִתָּךְ which is what
we should expect. See Bauer-Leander § 81 o′: "In
the later books, particularly in Kings and constantly in Jeremiah and Ezekiel, we find forms borrowed
from the sign of the accusative: אוֹתִי 'with me' (properly a false tradition)."

2 2a The words כאשר דבר אלי of 𝔐 are not attested by 𝔊 𝔈 𝔖 𝔄. They represent a clarification of
the material which stands out linguistically through
their use of כאשר which is otherwise unusual in Ezekiel (Cornill).

b 𝔊 here offers no less than three variant texts:
καὶ ἀνέλαβέ με καὶ ἐξῆρέ με καὶ ἔστησέ με. The expansion must stem from 3:14.

c In את מדבר אלי it is striking that את appears
before the participle without the article. Ought we
to follow 𝔊 (ἤκουον) αὐτοῦ λαλοῦντος πρός με and
read אתו מדבר? The hitpaʻel מְדַבֵּר (for the form
see Gesenius-Kautzsch § 54c) is found again in 43:6;
Nu 7:89 to denote Yahweh's speaking; and in 2 Sam
14:3 to denote the king's speaking. In all four passages it is used to give expression to especially important addresses. In Nu 7:89 it is added to הקול.
The parallelism of מְדַבֵּר Ezek 1:28 and מְדַבֵּר 2:2
certainly raises the question whether we do not have
here a late Masoretic distinguishing of the forms.

3 3a 𝔐 בני ישראל with 𝔊 𝔈 𝔖 𝔄 is to be read as
בית ישראל, which agrees with the customary usage
of Ezekiel and which also forms the starting point
for the following בית מרי in v 5 and elsewhere. 𝔐
represents a weakening of the expression due to a
scribal error. See Excursus 2.

b אל גוים of 𝔐 is lacking in 𝔊 𝔏 𝔈 𝔖. The reading of 𝔖 attempts to accommodate the form, which
is impossible in the context, by changing to the singular. On the grounds of subject matter also we
ought not to follow this reading of 𝔖 (against BH).
גוי is only used in the book of Ezekiel for Israel in
36:13–15; 37:22 in a quite different connection.
The gloss of 𝔐, which does not quite fit syntactically, perhaps was intended to divert to the nations, the
indictment of Israel which was felt to be too severe.
This would be in line with Geiger's comments on
2 Sam 12:14 (Urschrift, 267). Or is it a simple marginal gloss, which would assert that Ezekiel had also
spoken against the nations? The lack of the article
in any case represents a difficulty.

c 𝔊, in its repeated use of παραπικραίνω for the
translation of מרד of 𝔐, appears to presuppose in
its original the verb מרה and thus to anticipate the
following בית מרי of vv 5 and elsewhere. (𝔊 οἶκος
παραπικραίνων). A change of 𝔐 to המרים or מרו,
which Cornill (cf. Jahn, Buch) proposes, does not
reckon with the fact that the verb is only found in

me]^d to this very day, 4/ [to the children with impudent faces and hardened hearts, to them I send you]^a And you shall say to them: Thus has [the Lord]^b Yahweh said; 5/ [and they,]^a whether they hear or refuse to hear^b—for they are a house of rebellion—will know^c that a prophet has been in their midst. 6/ And you, son of man, do not be afraid of them ⟨nor be afraid of their faces⟩,^a when ⟨thorns surround you⟩^b and you sit upon^c scorpions. Do not be afraid of their words nor be dismayed at their faces, for they are a house of

the hip'il in Ezekiel (5:6; 20:8, 13, 21, see also 5:7, with emended text). We would have to interfere with the text more profoundly. In this case such a change becomes orthographically more difficult. Since, on the other hand, מרד occurs in 17:15 in its proper sense and in 20:38 in a secondary religious sense, it is best to adhere to 𝔐. 𝔊 has simply translated in a more sophisticated way.

d פשעו בי of 𝔐 is missing in 𝔊. Its deletion gives a demonstrable improvement to the sentence structure. 𝔊 has attempted, by inserting the copula, to bring about an improvement in its own way.

4   4a This part of the verse according to 𝔐 is lacking in 𝔊 and is a secondary expansion of the text. בנים is never otherwise used absolutely in Ezekiel for the position of the people before Yahweh (Ezek 20:21 refers to the children of the Exodus generation, see on the text). It is a favorite expression in Isaiah (1:2, 4; 30:1, 9) and Jeremiah (3:14, 22; 4:22). קשי פנים and חזקי לב, however, are to be regarded as free variations of the formulations of 3:7f. 2:4b best joins on to v 3.

b אדני is missing in 𝔊, see Excursus 1.

5   5a והמה was lacking in the Hebrew *Vorlage* of 𝔊 and has entered into the text later. It creates a caesura in the sentence structure, which originally ran from vv 3 to 5 (I send you . . . and you shall say . . . and they shall know), and divides off v 5 from v 3 as an independent element. The insertion is a consequence of the glossing of vv 3f, which has overloaded the sentence and made it obscure. It is also lacking in the parallel in 3:11.

b 𝔐 יחדלו. 𝔊 (πτοηθῶσι) 𝔏 𝔖 𝔄 have clearly read here by mistake the Aramaic דחל, which does not occur in Biblical Hebrew and which offers no clear antithesis to שמע. The free interpretation of 𝔗 also removes the antithesis of 𝔐. 𝔗 reads אם יקבלון אולפן ואם יתמנעון מלמחטי

c The reading of 𝔊 (καὶ γνώσονται ὅτι προφήτης εἶ σὺ ἐν μέσῳ αὐτῶν) 𝔏 𝔖, which has אתה instead of the היה of 𝔐 is to be rejected (against Cornill). Cf. 33:33, 2 Kings 5:8 and the exposition.

6   6a The reading of 𝔊 μὴ φοβηθῇς αὐτοὺς μηδὲ ἐκστῇς ἀπὸ προσώπου αὐτῶν points to an original אל תירא מהם ומפניהם אל תחת. This avoids the awkward duplication of אל תירא in the first half of the verse, displays a parallel structure for aα and bα, and deserves every confidence. In 𝔐 6a has been wrongly influenced by 6b.

b 𝔐 כי סרבים וסלונים אותך "for rebellious people and thorns are with you (אותך to be understood as אתך cf. 2:1 note a?)" is unsatisfactory. 𝔊 διότι παροιστρήσουσι καὶ ἐπισυστήσονται ἐπὶ σὲ κύκλῳ is mysterious. The κύκλῳ points to an occurrence of the root סבב in the Hebrew original. Scribal considerations permit us to conjecture in סרבים a scribal error for סבבים. The reading סבבים אותך gives a satisfactory equivalent for the ἐπισυστήσονται ἐπὶ σὲ κύκλῳ of 𝔊. In it the אותך of 𝔐 also has a meaning-

rebellion. 7/ And you[a] shall speak my words to them, whether they hear or refuse to hear;[b] for they are a <house>[c] ( ) of rebellion.

8　But you, son of man, hear what I say to you. Do not be rebellious[a] like that house of rebellion. Open your mouth and eat what I give you. 9/ And when I looked, behold, a hand was stretched out towards me, and in <it>[a] was a scroll. 10/ And he unrolled it before me; and it was written upon on the front and the back, and upon[a] it there were written lamentations[b], words of mourning and <woes>.[c]

ful place. Then, however, the סלונים of 𝔐 (only found again in the Old Testament in Ezek 28:24 "thorns") is to be connected with the expression παροιστρήσουσι ("to unsettle by stings") standing in the first place. 𝔊 rephrases it verbally. Beside the עקרבים of the parallel statement we can better keep the noun. As the more original text we must then read סלונים סבבים אותך. The corruption of 𝔐 rests on the fact that the sequence סלונים סבבים has been reversed. This is an easy scribal error, with the meaning not at first being affected. Then, beside the error of סבבים into סרבים the copula was erroneously inserted. This made the original reading completely unintelligible, but is already attested by 𝔊, which has for the rest kept the original order of the words.

c על – אל cf. 1:17 note a.

7　7a The introduction of a new address "son of man," attested by 𝔊[Luc V] 𝔄 Arm[P] Thdrt, is not original here.

b Cf. v 5 note b.

c 32 MSS Edd 𝔊 𝔖 (𝔗 עם) make it probable that we should add a בית to 𝔐, which has fallen out. A particular reason for the abbreviation of the motive clause כי בית מרי המה, which is found another seven times in Ezekiel (2:5, 6; 3:9, 26, 27; 12:2, 3), cannot be found in the present text. Cf. again to 44:6.

8　8a מרי is not to be changed to מֹרֶה (against Ehrlich, *Randglossen*, Bertholet, BH). Cf. 2:3 note c.

9　9a The second הנה is lacking in 𝔊 𝔖 𝔙. It should be deleted. In what follows we expect בה or ובה. It is, however, striking that the vocalized Targum also reads the masculine form; cf. Silbermann, *Targum*. How are we to understand the masculine in the tradition?

10　10a על – אל cf. 1:17 note a.

b קנים of 𝔐 is unusual. Cornill wants to change, following 𝔊 θρῆνος, to קינה and to understand the plural as a subsequent alteration in regard to the frequent appearance of a קינה in the book of Ezekiel (19:1, 14; 26:17; 27:2, 32; 28:12; 32:2, 16). Why, however, do we have the unusual masculine plural form which has misled 'Α into regarding it as a derivation from קנה κτίζω and translating as κτίσις? Does the masculine plural express a totality of laments, analogous to the תהלים of the heading of the book of Psalms? Or should we understand the plural as an intensification, in accordance with Gesenius-Kautzsch § 124e? We may keep 𝔐.

c Gesenius-Kautzsch § 19h would understand הי of 𝔐 as a subsidiary form of נהי (Am 5:16; Jer 9:9 and elsewhere) formed by aphaeresis of נ. The οὐαί of 𝔊, however, makes us think rather of a defective writing of הוי. Or was there a word הי "cry of woe" (Koehler-Baumgartner; also Driver, "Ezekiel," 146, who thinks that he can find a היה "wailed" in Is 37:17 [so read instead of 36:17] and Ps 102:8)? A change of the text to נהי (Cornhill, Ehrlich, *Rand-*

3:1/ And he said to me: Son of man, [eat what you find]ᵃ eat this scroll, and go, speak to the houseᵇ of Israel. 2/ Then I opened my mouth, and he gave me the [this]ᵃ scroll to eat, 3/ and said to me: Son of man, make your body eat, and fill your stomach with this scroll, which I giveᵃ you. Then I ate it;ᵇ and it was in my mouth as sweet as honey.

4   And he said to me: Son of man, get up, go to the house of Israel and speak (with the authority of) my wordsᵃ to them.

glossen) is not necessary. 𝔗 elaborates further that there was on the scroll, written on both sides "what was from the beginning and what is prepared to happen at the end. On it there was written that, if the house of Israel transgressed the law, the nations would obtain power over them, but when they observed the law, laments, woes and sighing would come to an end."

3:1   3:1a The words את אשר תמצא אכול of 𝔐 are lacking in 𝔊 and should be deleted as a gloss, which does not agree well in its content with the sentence and which stylistically overloads it (cf. the awkward clash of אכול in 1a and 1b). The scroll has already been shown to the prophet. He has nothing more to "find" (Cornill). We expect a command which would relate to what has just been shown. This begins in 1b with the imperative of אכל, which demands of the prophet something new and additional. The gloss, however, is valuable because it is clearly influenced from Jer 15:16, where Jeremiah says of himself נמצאו דבריך ואכלם. Ezekiel's action is therefore particularly illuminated from Jeremiah. See further the exposition. In the reading of 𝔗 ית דמיתיהב לך קביל מא דכתיב במגלתא הדא not only is the smoothing of the roughness caused by the gloss instructive, but also the slight softening of the content of the statement. According to it Ezekiel was not to eat "the scroll," but "what was written on the scroll."

    b 23 MSS Ed 𝔊 𝔖 𝔙 𝔄; בני see Excursus 2.

2   2a הזאת of 𝔐, which is lacking in 𝔊, is an ill-fitting repetition of the demonstrative pronoun, which is appropriate to the divine speech in vv 1 and 3.

3   3a 3a is not a simple repetition of the command of 1b. The priority of the object, which deviates from the normal order of a verbal sentence (Gesenius-Kautzsch § 142f), shows that the emphasis here plainly lies on בטן and מעים. The inside of the prophet must be ready to receive the word of Yahweh. Jer 4:19 shows how the involvement of the מעים means the deepest inward involvement.

    b 𝔐 וָאֹכְלָה must be pointed as וָאֹכְלָה following 𝔊 𝔙.

4   4a The בִּדְבָרַי, which is not recognizable in the text of 𝔊 (καὶ λάλησον τοὺς λόγους μου) 𝔏 𝔖 𝔙, is unusual. The revocalization to בְּדַבְּרִי, which then states that the prophet must speak to his people not immediately but only when Yahweh has spoken (Ehrlich, *Randglossen*, with reference to 3:27; considered by BH), overloads the text too much. However, by comparing with 1 Kings 13:(1), 2,5, 9, 17, 18, 32; 20:35, we must question whether the formula of the stereotyped language of prophetic schools, which is certainly found in the extant prophetic teaching narratives, "to do something בדבר יהוה" has exercised an influence here, of course in accommodation to the speech of Yahweh in the first person (should we vocalize the singular בִּדְבָרִי?). The

5/ For you are not sent to a people of foreign speech [and a hard language]ᵃ [to the house of Israel]ᵇ and ᵃ**6/** not to many nations [with difficult languages and hard tongues]ᵇ whose words you cannot understand. <If>ᶜ I were to send you to such, they would listen to you. **7/** But the house of Israel are not willing to listen to you, for they will not listen to me. The whole house of Israel are of a hard foreheadᵃ and a stubborn heart. **8/** Behold,ᵃ I am making your face hard like their faces, and your forehead hard like their foreheads. **9/** Like diamond,ᵃ harder than flint [I have made your forehead].ᵇ Do not be afraid of them nor dismayed before them, for they are a house of rebellion.

5   expression דַּבֵּר בדבד יהוה then conveys the conception of speaking Yahweh's word "in a prophetic commission, officially," which is hard to recapture in translation.

5a וכבדי לשון of 𝔐 is to be deleted following 𝔊ᴮ (which Ziegler, *Ezechiel*, does not regard as a witness to the original 𝔊 text) 𝔆 Lucif. The text of 𝔐 in vv 5f is much too overloaded. The original parallel statement to 5a is found in 6a. The gloss must have arisen from Ex 4:10. It uses the expression used there of Moses' awkwardness of speech, but in a new connection.

b אל בית ישראל of 𝔐 is omitted by Ephrem "with true feeling" (Cornill) and is a later interpretative addition, attested by all the remaining text tradition, but which breaks up the parallelism of 5a/6a.

6   6a 𝔐 לא. With 𝔊 𝔏 𝔖 𝔙 we should read ולא. The suppression of the copula is a later consequence of the insertion of 5b.

b 𝔐 עמקי שׁפה וכבדי לשׁון repeats the predicate of the (expanded) text of v 5, and is to be deleted as a subsequent addition, following 𝔖. A still more heavily expanded text is attested here by 𝔊 ἀλλοφώνους ἢ ἀλλογλώσσους οὐδὲ στιβαροὺς τῇ γλώσσῃ ὄντας. The first two expressions were replaced according to 𝔊⁸⁶ (Barberinus) by the τρεῖς ἑρμηνεῦται, i.e., Ἀ Σ Θ, in favor of 𝔐 by βαθυχείλους. The hands of the various glossators are also shown by the various translations in 𝔊 of the similar sounding double statement of 𝔐 in vv 5 and 6.

c The translation of the introductory אם לא by "but" and the relating of 6b to Israel ("but I have sent you to them," Hitzig, Cornill) is improbable on grammatical grounds. The subject set at the beginning of v 7 ובית ישראל shows that the antithetical assertions about Israel first begin there. Thus 6b is still concerned with the nations. 𝔊 reads καὶ εἰ, cf. 𝔏 𝔙. Should we accept for the original text an אלו, attested by 𝔖 𝔗, but only found in biblical Hebrew rarely and late (Eccl 6:6; Est 7:4)? Or are we to presuppose אלו, secondarily glossed by לו, on account of the parenthetic clause? Also in 14:15, the only place in which לו is found in the book of Ezekiel, the suspicion of a secondary origin of the word arises. For the possibility of introducing an unreal conditional clause by אם, see GeseniusKautzsch § 159m. In the conjunction of אם לו the corruption into אם לא is easily intelligible. Or are we to understand (as *ultima ratio*) the formation of לא as a simple dittography and corruption of the letters of the following אלהים? There is scarcely any doubt about the translation of the verse.

7   7a The view that the φιλόνεικοι of 𝔊 points to a reading מַצָּה instead of מצח (Schleusner, Cornill) is more probable than Hitzig's view of an inner Greek miswriting of φιλόνεικοι out of φιλόνικοι. The error reappears in v 8 𝔊.

8   8a 𝔊 καὶ ἰδού, cf. 1:4 note a.

9   9a The reading of 𝔊 καὶ ἔσται διὰ παντὸς [κρα-

10	And he said to me: Son of man, all my words, which I speak to you, receive in your heart and hear with your ears. 11/ Now get up, go to the exiles, to the members of your people, and speak to them and say to them: Thus has [the Lord]ᵃ Yahweh said. Whether they hear or whether they refuse to hear.ᵇ
12	Then the spirit lifted me up, and I heard behind me the sound of a great earth-quake, when the glory of Yahweh ⟨arose⟩ᵃ from its place, 13/ andᵃ the sound of the wings of the living creatures, which touched one another, and the sound of the wheels with them, and the sound of a great earthquake.ᵇ 14/ And the spirit lifted me up and took me away, and I went [in bitterness]ᵃ in the heat of my spirit, the hand of Yahweh being heavy upon me, 15/ And I came to the exiles at Tel-abib,ᵃ [who dwelt by the river Chebar,] ( )ᵇ where they dwelt. And I sat there over-whelmedᶜ among them seven days.

ταιότερον πέτρας] can be explained (Hitzig, Cornill) from a scribal error of כשמיר into ותמיד.

b 𝔊 𝔈 appear not to have had נתתי מצחך, which the simile of v 9a, joined on to v 8, takes as an independent clause. Is it a later addition? Or, on the other hand, ought we to reckon with a free abbreviation of the clause in which 𝔊 has not properly understood the מצח of 𝔐 according to the evidence of vv 7f (cf. note a to v 7)?

11 11a אדני is lacking in 𝔊, see Excursus 1.

b 𝔊 here has ἐὰν ἄρα ἀκούσωσιν ἐὰν ἄρα ἐνδῶσιν, differently 2:5, 7 and 3:27,

12 12a The conjecture made by Luzzato (Cornill) and later independently by Hitzig of reading ברום instead of the hardly acceptable ברוך of 𝔐 (which, however, was already read by 𝔊) deserves every confidence. Merx, "Wert," 75, believes that he can find in 𝔐 a dogmatic correction. A simple scribal error is more probable. רום is found with the meaning "to rise up" in 10:4. 𝔗 shows already, in its slight paraphrase, an understanding of the text which was already in error. V 12b runs here דמש בחין ואמרין בריך יקרא דיהוה מאתר בית שכינתיה. Cf. *b Ḥag.* 13b and 𝔗 to Ezek 1:24f. Buber, "Jechesk-kel 3:12," wants to hear in 𝔐 an original cry of praise from the prophet himself,

13 13a The καὶ εἶδον of 𝔊, which 𝔊ˢ³⁴·²⁶ ⁼ ᶜᵒᵐᵖˡ changes into the more appropriate ἤκουσα, is (against Hitzig and Cornill) not original in spite of Rev 1:12, but a new point of connection which became necessary after the scribal error in v 12.

b גדול is lacking in 𝔊. The whole expression וקול רעש גדול, which is noticeably out of place after לעמתם, in which the two preceding statements are connected, is awkward and is therefore regarded by many as a summarizing conclusion adjoined asyn-detically (BH ZB, cf. Ehrlich, *Randglossen*). By its repetition of 12aβ does it intend to link up with v 12 again after a digression?

14 14a מר of 𝔐 is lacking in 𝔊 (see Ziegler, *Ezechiel*, 26) 𝔖 ℭᴮᵒ 𝔈. The subsequent explanation "in bitterness" must clearly make certain the right under-standing of the bold expression "in the (angry) heat of my spirit."

15 15a 𝔊 did not recognize the place name תל אביב and renders it at random, which 𝔚 translates: acer-vus novarum frugum. The 𝔊 translation μετέωρος καὶ περιῆλθον appears to presuppose in תל a deriva-tion from תלל "to be high" (μετέωρος means both "high" and "anxious, stirred up, afraid") and to have read אביב in the form אָסֹב or אָסוֹב. That תל אביב is a place name cannot be doubted (against Löwinger, "Tel Abib," who wants to connect תל אביב "hill of desolation" with הגולה) in view of the list of places in Ezra 2:59.

b V 15a is clearly disturbed further, as is shown by the embarrassment of the Masoretes with the ואשר. The conjecture of Q וָאֵשֵׁב is not satisfactory. We can best retain the reading of K and place the dividing accent before וָאֵשֵׁב. Then it appears that the clauses אשר המה (aα²) (על =) הישבים אל (נהר כבר and יושבים שם (aβ) are to be identified as doublets. Of these the first, formulated with a participle (aα²) does not fit well after the geographical reference תל אביב, which in this case comes too early, whilst the second (aβ), as a relative clause, can be smoothly appended once the וֹ, which now connects the two doublets, is removed. That aα² is a secondary addition is also supported by its undoubted reference back to 1:1, 3. The geographical reference there, which does not in reality give the abode of the exiles but the location of the theophany, must plainly have been added here. The omission of aβ, found in 2 MSS 𝕊, is then, like the text of 𝕲 which passes over the second יושבים, a subsequent attempt at smoothing the overloaded text by the omission of a part of it.

c The hip'il formation משמים of 𝔐 is taken by Koehler-Baumgartner as a strong causative interpretation of the hip'il "one who brings consternation (to others)," since the simple intransitive meaning (accepted by Gesenius-Buhl, Zorell), which is otherwise proper to the stem in the qal, is difficult with the hip'il form. We must, however, seriously consider whether with Ezra 9:3f we should not vocalize the polel form מְשׁוֹמֵם.

Form

The section 1:1–3:15 must undoubtedly be understood in its present form as a complete unit. Ezekiel, who was among the exiles of his people in Babylon (1:1, 3), was surprised by a powerful vision of God. Through the divine word which this brought, and an accompanying symbolic experience, he was called to be a prophet for the house of Israel. When the event had passed from him he returned under the compulsion of what he had experienced to Tel Abib, the place where the exiles dwelt, without first being able to express the message in speech. 3:16 marks the beginning, with a new introduction, of an event which took place seven days later.

The section contained within the introductory and concluding framework was regarded by earlier commentators as quite free from difficulty.[1] Although the introductory verses 1:1–3, with their striking change from the first to the third person, provoked critical analysis and led Kraetzschmar to his thesis of the two recensions of the book of Ezekiel, no one was at first struck by the parallelism between the great vision of chapter 1 and the divine speech of ch. 2f.

It was first certain small textual observations which led to the questioning of this view. J. Herrmann, however, had established that verses 14–28a "belong in the section in which they stand."[2] This led to a difficulty for him in his commentary when he emended להנה to עליהן in 1:5, following the 𝕲 ἐπ' αὐτοῖς. If the meaning here is "a being in human form was over them," then this appears directly to presuppose the description of the human forms above the living creatures in 1:27f. The description of the vision in 1:6–26, which is textually badly preserved, therefore represents according to Herrmann a subsequent expansion, deriving from Ezekiel himself, of the original text of the vision which was contained only in verses 4–5, 27–28. Against this interpretation Sprank rightly objects that to signify 'over above' Ezekiel was accustomed to use a more explicit expression than simple, על and that most particularly v 27 cannot be separated from v 26 without becoming unintelligible. Furthermore without v 22 these verses remain obscure.[3]

Hölscher is more radical in his judgement, cutting out verses 5–27, 28aβ, and seeing the whole description of the throne-chariot as a subsequent addition, alien to Ezekiel's own account, and derived from literary pro-

1   So Smend, Hitzig, Bertholet, and J. W. Rothstein, *Das Buch Ezechiel*, HSAT (Tübingen: Mohr [Siebeck], ⁴1922).

2   J. Herrmann, *Ezechielstudien*, 8.

3   Siegfried Sprank and Kurt Wiese, *Studien zu Ezechiel und dem Buch der Richter*, BWANT 3, 4 (Stuttgart:

totypes such as Ex 24:10 and Is 6. Can, however, 28aα be isolated in this fashion from 27 (Sprank)? Must not those who follow Herrmann and Hölscher eliminate the theophany even more radically?

Finally, therefore, in connection with the thesis that Ezekiel was originally connected with Jerusalem, a radical division has been made which regards the vision of chapter 1 as having nothing to do with the call narrative of ch. 2f. Herntrich rightly declares, "We cannot cut out the description of the throne-chariot from the vision."[4] His further conclusion is that the genuine prophetic call narrative is to be found in 2:6–3:9, with its original introduction now set in 3:22–23a. In the vision of Yahweh's glory which is now connected with the beginning of the book in 1:1–3, we have a different voice, in which we no longer hear the sound of a truly prophetic experience: "Chapter 1 is solely a display."[5] Unlike the voice of the genuine Jerusalem prophet Ezekiel, which we hear in 2:6–3:9, the description of Yahweh's glory in chapter 1 comes from a time when the temple was no longer standing.

Bertholet, in 1936, further modified Herntrich's view. He endeavored to connect the assumption of an initial activity of Ezekiel in Jerusalem with the traditional view of the prophet in exile. Like Herntrich he found in the scroll-vision of 2:3–3:9, which he divides into two recensions, the account of the prophet's original call to be a prophet of doom in Jerusalem. The vision of the throne-chariot in chapter 1 was then not denied to the prophet. Rather it set forth in its "more reflective and scholarly visionary style" the great experience which overtook the prophet in his later years, when, after 587 B.C., he was living in exile.[6] It showed him that Yahweh had survived the destruction of the temple and was able to appear to his own people also in a foreign land. Because it is unthinkable that such an event should have contained no message, Bertholet connected the Yahweh speech of 3:10–11 and the conclusion 3:12–15 with the vision of the throne-

chariot 1:1–2:2.[7] In this fragment of a divine message there arises, according to him, a close connection with the account of the vision of the scroll, which we have not dealt with in the present discussion. Thus the question directed against Herrmann and Hölscher must be raised again here in a different form. Can we separate 3:10f from the preceding and regard these verses which are related in vocabulary to 2:4f, 7 as a later section which is distinguished from the earlier material by its "more reflective and scholarly style"?

Van den Born rejected verses 3:10f as a secondary addition by an editor who noticed the lack of a specific sending of the prophet to the exiles.[8] Is, however, the Yahweh speech of 2:1, with the note in 2:2 that the prophet had heard the voice of someone speaking, a sufficient basis for regarding the section 1:1–2:2, 3:12–15 as a second call vision when it contains so little divine speech? Van den Born's reference to the section 3:16a, 22–23 (par. 37:1), 37:2–14, which he regards as following chronologically directly upon this call vision, does not help to get round the fact that there is for Ezekiel a surprising lack of divine words in such a basic section of his prophecy.

The same objection applies to the variations proposed by Auvray and Kuhl, according to whom 2:3–3:10 gives the Palestinian and ch. 1 the Babylonian inaugural visions.[9] 3:11, 14b–15, "however, is to be understood as the command to the prophet to go from Palestine away to the exiles, with its consequence."

In another way Messel gave a variant to the thesis of Bertholet when he connects the throne-chariot vision (1:1, 4–2:8) and the scroll vision (1:2–3, 2:9–3:8), but refuses to see in the throne-chariot vision a second call vision occurring on Babylonian soil. Following Berry, who wanted to place a critically refined groundwork of chapter 1 (vv 1*, 4–14, 22–28) after 43:3,[10] he saw in the throne-chariot vision the original introduction to the promulgation of the law 45:1–46:18. Finally Irwin regards only 1:1aα, 2:3aα, 4b, 5a* as

---

       Kohlhammer, 1926), 28ff.

4   Herntrich, *Ezekielprobleme*, 75.

5   Herntrich, *Ezekielprobleme*, 79.

6   Bertholet-Galling, 9.

7   In this he is followed by Jean Steinmann, *Le prophète Ézéchiel et les débuts de l'exil*, Lectio Divina 13 (Paris: Cerf, 1953).

8   Van den Born, *De historische situatie*, 170.

9   Kuhl, "Schauplatz," 413f.

10   Berry, "Title."

authentic to Ezekiel.

In all these analyses of the text the picture of a unified composition in 1:1–3:15 is broken up. To the literary-critical arguments must be added the serious considerations of the quite different nature of the contents of the visions of the throne-chariot and the scroll. These sometimes give an almost categorical validity to the division into two separate sections. "These two entities have such an inner dissimilarity that every attempt to unite them literarily with each other and to see them as the written deposit of not quite contemporary experiences of the prophet must be regarded as resulting from obvious lack of refined sensitivity to distinctions of spiritual subjects."[11]

In the face of these facts every exposition of 1:1–3:15 must, more than anything else, reach a decision on the basic question of whether the connection of the vision of the throne-chariot with that of the scroll is original or solely the product of a subsequent redactional bringing together of two quite different parts.

For the clarification of this question it is as well first to set aside Ezek 1:1–3:15 and to ask more generally: is such a connection between an account of the commissioning of a prophet in the strict sense and an elaborate vision of God to be found elsewhere? Can we in general discover anything about certain customs of style and given traditions in the presentation of the prophetic experiences of being commissioned? However personal the call experience of the individual prophet may have been, we cannot in advance rule out the possibility that, as in other forms of prophetic speech, here also a certain stereotyped form in the presentation of the call experience may have been at work.

The Form Criticism and Tradition-History of the Prophetic Call Narratives

The call narrative of Jeremiah (Jer 1:4–10), an older prophetic contemporary of Ezekiel with whom there are many connections, shows at first glance a type of account very different from that of Ezek 1:1–3:15.

The event is described through the introductory statement (v 4) as the coming of the divine word, as in Ezekiel (3:16; 6:1; 7:1 and elsewhere). Yahweh's pronouncement of Jeremiah's (election and) his appointment (v 5) dominates the content of the whole occurrence. From this statement the rejoinder of the prophet arises (v 6), which is set aside by the unfolding commission of Yahweh (v 7). At the same time the prophet is consoled by an exhortation to fearlessness and the promise of deliverance (v 8, see also vv 17–19). Only then the ordination proper follows, with the touching of the mouth through the mysteriously outstretched hand of Yahweh. This simple detail alone has been taken over from the realms of the spectacular and oddly crowded in at the end. This is connected with a declaration of the giving of the word of God to Jeremiah and with a further statement of appointment indicating also now the content of the message (vv 9f).

The particular significance of the account of Jeremiah's call is to be seen in the firm subordination of all its features to the word of Yahweh. We may question whether this is a unique and previously unknown formulation by Jeremiah, whose rejection of any emphasis upon mysterious phenomena accompanying the divine word is shown in 23:25ff, or whether Jeremiah is here giving an account of his call in a manner which he has taken over from elsewhere. Hosea, the prophetic predecessor to whom Jeremiah stands particularly close in many points, can be adduced as evidence for this, with his complete passing over of visionary elements, not only in chapters 1 and 3, but in his whole book. However, Hosea, like Amos and Micah, gives no detailed account of a call.

Jeremiah 1 can best be compared with the account of the call and commissioning of Moses, the account of which exists in three versions. According to J (Ex 3:1–4a, 5, 7–8, 16–22, 4:1–9 with additions)[12] and E (Ex 3:4b, 6, 9–15, 4:17) its beginning is linked with an account of a divine manifestation on the mountain of God, in which the ἱερὸς λόγος of the place may be preserved. In the Priestly Code (Ex 6:2–12, 7:1–7) this section is eliminated and once again everything is centered on the divine message. The account of Jeremiah's call is most of all brought to mind by the description of features of the recipient's struggle and

---

11 Bertholet-Galling, 2.
12 See Martin Noth, *A History of Pentateuchal Traditions*, tr. Bernhard W. Anderson (Englewood Cliffs: Prentice-Hall, 1972).

resistance, which Yahweh has to counter by special measures of assurance and promise. In the Elohistic version it is first Moses' reference to his own weakness (3:11, the same motif also occurs in the call narratives of Gideon Judg 6:15f and Saul 1 Sam 9:21), which Yahweh counters with the promise, "I am with you" (cf. Jer 1:8, 19) at the mention of a 'sign'. The second objection of Moses (3:13) provides the occasion for Yahweh to reveal himself under the name of Yahweh. In the Yahwist version it is Moses' reference to his incompetence in speech (4:10). After a reminder of his power as creator Yahweh answers with the promise, "I will be with your mouth, and will teach you what to say" (4:12). Nothing is said here of a symbolic touching of the lips, which in Jeremiah 1 accompanies this promise. At Moses' second stubborn refusal Yahweh orders Aaron, Moses brother, to accompany him, and once again he affirms to both, "I will be with your mouth and with his mouth, and will instruct you what to do" (4:15). The further equipping of Moses with the miraculous rod (4:17 [Elohist]), and the empowering to work "signs" with rod and hand and the water of the Nile (4:1–9 [Yahwist expanded?]) is to be seen in connection with the equipping of the reluctant envoy. The fixity of the feature of reluctance in the account of Moses' call and subsequent equipping by Yahweh is shown by the fact that it is not omitted by the Priestly Code, who otherwise so arbitrarily smooths over his narrative. 6:12 (repeated in v 30) gives Moses' objection, and 7:1–7 gives the commissioning of Aaron and his being equipped with the power to work signs.

When we seek to put together the features which connect the accounts of Moses' (Gideon's, Saul's) and Jeremiah's calls and to see in them a particular type of account, then we find that peculiar to all of them is the character of a very personal encounter between Yahweh (or a representation of Yahweh in his messenger) and the one who is called. In this dialogue there is room for reluctance and even objection by the one who is called, which Yahweh overcomes by personal promises and the granting of signs (I am with you; I have set my words in your mouth; this will be a sign for you).

When we turn from this form of call account to Ezekiel 1:1–3:15, we undoubtedly find connections with the contents of Ezekiel 2f. Here also the word is put in the mouth of the prophet. He hears the exhortation: "Do not be afraid" and is furnished with a hard forehead against his opponents.[13] At the same time, within the framework of these similarities, we must notice the much greater distance which separates Yahweh from his envoy in Ezekiel 2f. No room is left here for an opportunity of refusal. With Ezekiel 1 there are no connections at all. The throne vision, in its awesome loftiness, stands as an element to which there is nothing similar in the parallels we have considered. Thus tradition-historical study seems to support the separation of Ezekiel 1 from 2f.

There is, however, in the Old Testament a second, expanded type of call narrative of which Isaiah 6 is the most impressive example. It has rightly been pointed out that Is 6, in its basic elements, stands very close to the prophetic narrative of 1 Kings 22 and particularly to verses 19–22.[14] The prophet Micaiah son of Imla justifies his message of woe, which differs from the message of salvation given by the 400 prophets of Ahab, through an account of what he has experienced. The text contains no call narrative in the strict sense. It deals with an act by which the word of God is sent "into the mouth of the prophet" (v 22). In clear distinction from the first type of call narrative which we have outlined, the word is given to the messenger without any personal dialogue between Yahweh and him. The word given to the prophet is pictured as the result of Yahweh's taking counsel with his divine court, which is far removed from men, and, as befits the servants of the lord, the prophet stands reverently before the enthroned Yahweh. The distance between the royal lord and his earthly messenger can be seen not only in the fact that "the spirit" represents a mediator of the divine will, but also in that Yahweh uses the 400 prophets as impersonal tools and makes them bearers of a lying message. Only a single one is granted the grace to see clearly into the mysteries of the divine council (Jer 23:18–22; Am 3:7). Thus he could help to bring salvation, while the others became instruments

---

13 See the details of the exposition.
14 David Heinrich Müller, *Ezechiel-studien* (Berlin: Reuther & Reichard, 1895), 9f; reprinted as *Biblische Studien* 1 (Wien: Hölder, 1904); and Albrecht Alt, "Gedanken über das Königtum Jahwes" in *Kleine Schriften zur Geschichte des Volkes Israel* 1 (Mün-

of blindness.

Isaiah 6 shows the same elements in a noticeably different connection. There are various close contacts between this account, given in the first person from the hand of Isaiah, and the account in the third person in 1 Kings 22 of the promulgation of the divine decision. Here, as there, the message comes from the sphere of the heavenly council of God, in which Yahweh sits on his exalted throne, his court surrounding him as servants. Here, as there, we can recognize the element of deliberation, which is introduced by Yahweh's question to those about him: "Whom shall I send, and who will go for us (לנו)?" (Is it accidental that also elsewhere in Isaiah's message the council of Yahweh, the עצת יהוה, plays a great role?) Here, as there, the mediating servants are mentioned through whom God deals with men (spirit, seraph). Here, as there, however, the grace is given to a chosen person to hear the divine council directly and so to become God's instrument. Here, as there, also we are concerned with Yahweh's secret purpose to harden and blind men. The verbal connections extend to details of the formulation:

1 Kings 22:19–21		Is 6:1–8	
19	ראיתי את יהוה	1	ואראה את אדני
	ישב על כסאו		ישב על כסא רם ונשא ....
	וכל צבא השמים עמד עליו	2	שרפים עמדים
	מימינו ומשמאלו		ממעל לו ....
20	מי יפתה	8	.... את מי אשלח ומי ילך לנו
	ויאמר זה בכה וזה אמר בכה	3	.... וקרא זה אל זה ואמר
21	אני אפתנו	8	הנני שלחני

The strong connections which justify us in speaking of a type of commissioning narrative, which underlies Isaiah 6 and which influenced the prophet in his account (and in his experience?), are all the more striking because the distinctive character of Isaiah's account can be clearly seen. Whilst the divine court in 1 Kings 22 is to be sought in Yahweh's heavenly palace, with Isaiah of Jerusalem the background is set in the sphere of the Jerusalem temple and its symbolism. Yahweh sits enthroned over the ark in the most Holy Place. Isaiah smells the incense smoke of the temple in his nose. He sees with his own eyes the innermost room of the temple with the (ark-) throne of Yahweh (Ps 132:7f, 13f), and

the seraphim, of which a bronze image still existed in the temple in Uzziah's time (2 Kings 18:4, Nu 21:8f). He heard with his own ears the sound of the door pivots in their sockets; he heard the Trishagion of the seraphim, which echoed the threefold proclamation of divine holiness by the temple congregation (Ps 99). He heard from their mouths the honorific title "Yahweh of Hosts" addressed to the God of the Ark in Jerusalem. In the sanctuary in which men saw (In Ps 42:3 read וְאֵרָאֶה) the "face of God," he was overwhelmed by the power of the Holy One, whom no unclean person could see and remain alive. Then he experienced the grace of cleansing in an act of purification performed by the seraphim, in a fashion similar to that which may have been used by the priests at the temple over against worshippers who made their confession of sin.[15]

Furthermore with Isaiah the scene of the heavenly council has undergone a particular development. In the words "who will go for us" we can still hear Yahweh taking counsel with a number of counsellors, while in the description of the scene these heavenly aides are relegated to a quite different position. They cannot even look upon Yahweh himself, and their conversation in which "one called to another" has changed into the praise of the King around whom they stand and fly. The most striking change from 1 Kings 22 consists in the fact that the prophet, who has been allowed to listen to the divine council, after the shock of being cleansed by the seraph intervenes in the heavenly deliberations and volunteers for service. This is a privilege which is reserved in 1 Kings 22 for the "spirit."

It is not the place here to go into further details, but it is now possible to establish a second point in regard to the form-criticism and tradition history of the prophetic call narrative: the parallelism of the prophetic narratives of 1 Kings 22 and Is 6 provides us for the period of the ninth-eighth centuries with a form of prophetic commissioning account in which the words of the prophetic commission arise out of the description of a vision of the divine court. At the same time the differences between the two prophetic accounts serve to make clear that we are not dealing with a fixed formula for such commissioning narratives. Rather

---

chen: Beck, 1953), 352.

15 Georges Pidoux, "Encore les deux arbres de Genèse 3!" *ZAW* 66 (1954): p. 42 note 3.

the call narrative of Isaiah 6, combining together the throne vision and commission, has been formed with a remarkable freedom, which serves as a means of gaining new perceptions.

We may, by way of an appendix, point to a later development of this form of call narrative in the account in Acts 9:3ff; 22:6ff; 26:12ff of the call of Paul. Once again there is much here that is different. In place of Yahweh's appearance in the temple, there is a manifestation of the glory of the exalted Christ; instead of the prophet's being overwhelmed by his uncleanness in the sanctuary, Paul, the persecuter of Christ, is thrown to the ground while en route to further persecution. The connection, however, of the commission with a manifestation of glory in Acts 9, 22 and 26 shows a type of call-narrative similar to that in Isaiah (and Ezekiel) and unlike Paul's testimony in Gal 1:15ff, which is oriented towards Jeremiah 1.

These observations provide an important background for the understanding of Ezekiel 1:1–3:15. Besides the Jeremian type of call-account, there already existed in the period before Ezekiel another type in which the commissioning of the prophet took place through a manifestation of God in a throne vision. Accordingly on the basis of tradition-history, an original connection between the throne-vision of Ezekiel 1 and the act of commissioning in Ezekiel 2f (the vision of the scroll) can in no way be prematurely excluded. It must be regarded as entirely possible. At the same time, however, the comparison of 1 Kings 22 with Is 6 (and Acts 9, 22, 26) shows that this type of commissioning account can appear in its later context with various developments of its separate elements. If this "type" of call-account is really found with Ezekiel, we must therefore reckon from the start with the possibility of a very free reminting of its individual features occasioned by the particular experience of the prophet.

The considerations of form and tradition which we have set out above have simply been able to show the possibility of an original connection between the vision of God and the commissioning (the visions of the divine throne and of the scroll) in Ezekiel 1:1–3:15. Whether this possibility was actually the case can only be decided from the text itself.

The translation and textual emendation of 1:1–3:15, with the help of the versions, has shown that even in the time of the versions all kinds of additions to the original text had been made. The question is justified whether this further work on the text only took place in the period which we can trace with the help of the versions. A number of perceptions render it probable that even the critically established text given at the beginning represents the result of a considerable expansion of its original form. To endeavor to trace this original form of the text will therefore be our next task.

The original text of 1:1–3:15

1:1–3   Introduction and Heading

The three introductory verses of the book plainly fulfil a double function: they introduce the following great vision of the prophet. Like other similar visions (8:1ff; 40:1ff) or experiences of receiving of the divine word (20:1ff 26:1ff) this vision is chronologically established by the reference to a date. At the same time the three introductory verses give certain biographical information about the prophet, which is similar to that found in the headings of other prophetic books. This double content is connected with a striking imbalance in form in the verses. After the plain introduction in the first person (v 1), which agrees with the style of the further description in v 4ab f there is an unexpected change into the third person in verse 3 (verse 2 contains a date reference which is neutral as regards both forms of style). The uncertainty of the text tradition, in which 𝕲 already in v 3b, while 𝔐 𝔗 𝔙 first in v 4 revert back to the first person, betrays the fact that here a literary splicing lies before us.

Closer examination shows the following position: verse 1 gives the date in the first person, a reference to the locality, and the beginning of an autobiographical account. Verse 2 contains simply a date reference. Verse 3a is in the third person, as is unanimously supported by the text tradition.[16] It mentions the receiving of the divine word, gives the name of the prophet (otherwise also in 24:24), his father's name, his (father's?) vocation, the name of the place, which

---

16   It is not to be rephrased in the first person as Bewer, "Text," p. 100 note 8, considers.

partly repeats verse 1. Verse 3b speaks of the coming of Yahweh's hand upon the prophet and closely corresponds with 3:22 (the introduction of a commandment of Yahweh) and 8:1 (the introduction to a visionary translation). In both cases the sentence is there preserved in the first person. 8:2 continues as in 1:4 with וארא והנה. However, an analogy to the succession of the coming of the hand of Yahweh (3b) after the receiving of the divine word (3a) is otherwise not found in the book of Ezekiel. This encourages us to regard the 𝔊 reading of 1:3b as original. V 3b is accordingly not a part of the superscription of 1:3a, but belongs in connection with the introduction to the vision. 1:1, 3b are to be conjoined with 1:4ff.

Can we then regard the remaining verses 2, 3a as a connected entity and claim it with Kraetzschmar as a part of a special dated source? Closer examination shows that verse 2 does not contain a complete date reference. It lacks any note of the month. This is also the case in 40:1, although there the reference "at the beginning of the year" leaves no doubt that it concerns the first month of the ecclesiastical year. In 26:1 and 32:17, however, as the 𝔊 tradition also shows, we have reason to assume that the name of the month has accidentally fallen out. In 1:2 this is improbable and is in no way supported by 𝔊. However, the appearance here of היא directly after the mention of the day in verse 2 shows that verse 2 is to be understood as an additional remark to verse 1 connected by the catchword בחמשה לחדש. This additional remark seeks to provide an explanation of the date of verse 1. The date given in verse 1 is to be more fully interpreted through that of verse 2 and above all is to be related to a known era. Accordingly verse 2 is not to be separated from verse 1 and is certainly not to be connected with v 3a. V 3a represents a type of book heading in a pure form such as was subsequently prefixed to the individual writings in the collection of the prophetic books. So Hos 1:1; Joel 1:1; Mic 1:1; Zeph 1:1; (Jer 1:1 𝔊). In these instances, however, the heading is regularly placed at the beginning of the collection in the form דבר יהוה אשר היה אל, which Jer 1:4ff also gives in the first person. It appears as it does in Ezekiel because of the desire to avoid removing from the heading the date reference (1:2) and has been introduced into the text which already was expanded by v 2 as an interpretative remark. Verse 2 therefore has become an introduction to verse 3, and the text of the heading itself has, unlike Hos 1:1 and the other passages, undergone the simple syntactical accommodation to the form היה דבר יהוה אל. Perhaps the miswriting at the beginning of verse 3 (cf. note a to 3) gives evidence of secondary literary activity.

We find in Ezekiel in the uneven literary joins of 1:1–3 evidence of a two- or three-phase process with the secondary introduction of verse 2. This process is further developed in Hag 1:1; Zech 1:1 (1:7; 7:1) to a smooth introductory formula. The date takes its position at the head, and there is a complete syntactical reordering of the phrase which narrates the receiving of the divine word. Can we, however, go further and conjecture that the hands which redacted the books of Haggai and Zechariah, and which we must see in close proximity to these two prophets, were also those which introduced the heading of Ezekiel 1:3a and thereby introduced the book to the canon of the prophetic writings?

1:4–28 The Manifestation of the Glory of Yahweh

In verse 4, $a\beta$ and the concluding "out of the midst of the fire" have been excluded in the textual notes as a gloss. Hence also the words remaining in 4b "and out of its midst it shone like the appearance of bright gold" are striking through their relation to 1:27 and especially through the clumsy anticipation of the מתוכה which follows in verse 5. In the (emended) text of 1:27 the expression is in place. Here, however, it disturbs the connection of $4a\alpha$ and 5 and is to be regarded as a later expansion.

The description of the living creatures adjoined in vv 5–12, which rise out of the storm phenomena, raises serious questions. First of all in its outline it is not really clear. After an introductory summary of the human form of the creatures in verse 5, verse 6 describes their faces and wings, verse 7 their feet, verse 8 their hands. Verse 9 describes (after the removal of the gloss referring to the wings) the manner in which the creatures moved. Verse 10 then repeats a fuller description of their faces, verse 11 mentions the position of their wings and verse 12 finally describes once again the manner in which the creatures moved, with the verbal expressions of verse 9 repeated literally with reordering and expansion. If we may find in vv 6–8 a tolerable order of the listing of the bodily parts, then the account of v 9ab jumps from one to the other, returns to what has already been mentioned (faces, wings), and is not afraid of word by word repetitions. Do we really have the original order of the text before us in all this?

In this connection we find here and in vv 15ff a quite peculiar confusion in the use of the suffixes. That feminine plurals are represented with masculine plural suffixes is often to be seen in Ezekiel (cf. suffixes used for חקות in 5:6; 18:19; 20:16; 37:24; for ארצות in 20:34, 41; for עצמות in 37:2, 4, 6, 8, 10, and other passages). W. Diehl regarded this phenomenon as a sign of late Mishnaic linguistic usage.[17] The arbitrary change in gender of the two forms of the third plural suffix is particularly striking in connection with one and the same word (חיות) in Ezekiel 1. The references in 13:19–21 and in ch. 34, where masculine and feminine suffixes are mixed, form a special problem.[18] In 16:45–55, where altogether about fifteen plural suffixes refer to the godless mother and daughter, the feminine form of the suffixes is preserved throughout. Clearly in 23:3f, 13 in the original text of Ezekiel the pure feminine form is preserved, whilst in the undoubtedly secondary conclusion of vv 39ff masculine suffixes begin to be mixed. These distinctions in the book of Ezekiel are not considered by Diehl. They leave open the questions whether or not also in the underlying basis of chapter 1 a unified usage once appeared. E. Höhne deals with the problem in a special section "the mystery of the suffixes" and rightly points out that the use of the masculine suffixes in 1:5–12 is determined by the masculine כרובים of ch. 10, whilst the feminine suffixes wrongly used in 1:15–21 are determined by 1:5–12.[19] However, he does not use these correct observations at the decisive moment for critical analysis, but sees in them a scribal error, which first occurred in the later transmission of the text.

When we turn to the text seeking elucidation with the help of the criterion of the use of the suffixes, then it appears that in the opening of the description in verse 5, as well as in the authentic material of chapter 23, the grammatically regular feminine suffix is used twice. Concerning verse 6, where the להם is shown by the versions to be an addition, nothing need be said. With verse 7 however, there begins a massive use of the masculine suffix, which is broken up by v 9b, the verse which again is found in v 12. Was v 9b once directly joined to v 5(6)? Verse 10, with its variation in suffixes for the same word (לארבעתן/לארבעתם), is very mysterious. V 11a shows once again the use of the masculine suffix, whilst in v 11b the full feminine suffix appears. Also as regards its content, verse 11 appears to fall into two halves, which in their conceptional background do not belong together. Verse 11a mentions quite generally that the wings of the creatures were spread out upwards, while v 11b gives a differentiated picture with two wings touching one another, while two, which must be thought of as stretched downwards, covered the bodies of the creatures. These references to the two pairs of wings with their special functions join without difficulty on to v 6b. V 6b would then be suitably continued by this, rather than by v 11a where the content and its conceptional background does not fit. The connection then runs: "Each one had four wings. On each of them two touched one another (spread out upwards), and two covered his body (spread out downwards)." Is it wholly misleading to conjecture that in fact in the sequence vv 5, 6, 11b we reach an original connection?

It is not without considerable weight that the prophetic throne-vision of Isaiah 6 gives support in this regard. Is 6:2 describes the seraphim: "Each one had six wings. With two he covered his face, with two he covered his feet, and with two he flew." Here the proper connection is given without disturbance, which in Ezekiel 1 is obtained by connecting vv 6b with 11b. The common connection with a fixed descriptive scheme of the throne scene then becomes clear, apart from individual variations here and there.

The result that is obtained can now be considered in regard to verses 7–11a, which have been cut out. It can be seen that the descriptions of the feet (v 7) and hands (v 8) of the creatures represent subsequent elaborations. A mention of the hands could have been felt to be necessary from 2:9, where the stretched out hand must certainly be related to Yahweh himself.

17 Diehl, *Pronomen*, 57f.
18 See the exegetical notes.
19 Höhne, *Thronwagenvision*, 80–84.

More probably however we must look to the reference in 10:7, which undoubtedly had as a consequence two references to the hands of the cherubim in 10:8 and 10:21.[20] The gloss v 9a has, as we have already mentioned, anticipated what is said in v 11bα. The כנפיהם, with the masculine suffix, shows once again that v 10a, in its present text, belongs to a later stratum. In an analogous way v 9b anticipates what is said in v 12, but was, since it is attested in the versions, taken up into the text earlier than v 9a. The description of the four faces in v 10 also belongs to a subsequent interpretation. In chapter 10, also, as the counterpart of chapter 1, there is reference to the four faces of the cherubim. That the detailed listing of the faces in 10:14 differs from 1:10 can, in this connection, be an indication that the naming of the four faces was not so firmly fixed that it could simply be inferred from chapter 1.

The recognition of the secondary character of the reference in 1:10 possibly leads to a still further conclusion. Is it conceivable that the original text mentioned in verse 6 the four faces of each creature without, however, giving any further reference to their form? If the more detailed description in verse 10 is secondary, then could not also v 6a, which anticipates verse 10, here been secondarily introduced into v 6 as a preparation for this verse? The multiplicity of wings of the divine servants is already shown by their appearance in Isaiah to have been in the older tradition. The multiplicity of their faces, hence, has no recognizable precedent in the Old Testament conceptual world. It is therefore improbable that it has been introduced by a brief reference solely in v 6a (without 10). Rather v 6a has been introduced by the editor of the text, who also added verse 10, in exact formal correspondence to v 6b, which, for its part, is supported from Is 6:2. A certain problem is offered by the forms לארבעתן with their feminine suffixes in v 10b. Sprank wants to reconstruct a three-phased formation of verse 10: 1) a reference belonging to the original text: "all four of them had human faces"; 2) an expansion to two faces of men and eagles in line with the importance of men and eagles for the representation of mixed human-animal creatures in Babylon as shown by Dürr; 3) an

expansion to four, occasioned by 10:14, whereby the cherub, already deliberately avoided by Ezekiel himself in chapter 2, was replaced by a bull.[21] Although this reconstruction of the formation of verse 10 is highly questionable, yet it may perhaps be right insofar as it sees present in the לארבעתן with the feminine suffix an element of the original text. The possibility of secondary elaboration is certainly also not excluded, as the analogy of the secondary section 23:36ff shows. However we should then rather assign לארבעתן and לארבעתם to two distinct phases of expansion. V 11a finally has, within the framework of vv 7–11a, the function of returning to the description of the wings which had been dropped since v 7. This takes place by a vague generalizing reference to the position of the wings. V 11b then takes up the original text.

The elaborated detail of the interpolation vv 6a, 7–11 leads us to expect in the following section also that elements of expansion will be found. In verse 12 there follows a reference to the movement of the creatures. This has at the conclusion the feminine suffix form in בלכתן which is also found in verses 9b and 17, which are determined by verse 12. Of the subject matter a note about the movement of the creatures would not be out of place here. Since the introduction with the distributive איש connects directly with the לאיש of v 11b, one is inclined to find in the verse an element of the original description. The fact that the "going" (הלך) of the creatures is mentioned arouses suspicion, since according to the introduction 1:4ff and the conclusion 3:12, we are led rather to think of flying. Unless from texts such as Gen 3:14, Ex 9:23, Jonah 1:11, where הלך can describe the crawling of snakes, the descent of fire, and the currents of the sea, we are prepared to find in הלך a description of motion in a broad sense, we must, with Sprank see in verse 12 a very early piece of reworking.[22] One is also able to point to the masculine verb forms ילכו and יסבו as grounds for suspicion. However, an element of uncertainty remains here since these verb forms could be determined by the more neutral איש which is also found in v 11b. The central clause v 12bα, however, "wherever the spirit directed to go, they went" can scarcely here belong to the original

---

20   See the exegetical notes.
21   Sprank, *Studien*, 38–51; Dürr, *Ezekiels Vision*, 25.
22   Sprank, *Studien*, 70.

text. The two texts vv 9b and 17, which are directly dependent on v 12, made the reference of this central verse out of place. It could very well have been subsequently introduced into v 12 from v 20, which gives the details of the wheels.

Also the description of the fire between the creatures vv 13f gives the impression of being an expansion. Verse 14 of 𝔐 is dependent on v 13, as its absence from 𝔊 makes clear. The clause v 13aβ, introduced with היא, is shown as a gloss in which the connecting word אֵשׁ is so strangely out of place that it not only gives trouble to modern commentators, but already did so to the translators of the ancient versions (cf. 𝔗). The ceaseless movement of the phenomenon, which this sentence like v 14 introduces into the description, does not correspond with the original text. It is then striking that in v 13 the phrase "which looked like burning coals of fire" is expanded by a second comparison "like torches." This second comparison must be a later addition to the text. The double glossing of v 13 has obviously been influenced by Gen 15:17.[23]

With v 15 there begins a new section which introduces features that have previously not been mentioned and which extends as far as v 21. It deals with the wheels in the manifestation of the creatures and their relation to what has been described in vv 5–14. The introductory formula וארא והנה, which already introduces the description of the whole vision in 1:4, here begins a subsection. It is found again in 2:9; 8:2, 7, 10; 10:1, 9; 44:4, (cf. Zech 1:8; 2:1, 5, and other passages). It confers on what follows the significance of a new special theme. In considering the whole chapter we note with some surprise that this important new introduction is found here with the description of the wheels, yet is not repeated with the much more exciting and important description of the one being enthroned over the chariot (1:26). Does this not indicate a certain lack of proportion in the emphasis given?

A glance at the use of the suffix forms, made possible by the analysis of vv 5–12, shows in vv 15–21 again an apparently irregular interchange. Indeed the obscurity appears here even to increase in that not only in relation to the feminine חיות are masculine suffixes used (v 19 אצלם; vv 20f לעמתם; 21 בלכתם, ובעמדם, ובהנשאם),[24] but in relation to the masculine אופנים feminine suffixes appear (vv 15? [cf. note b on 1:15], 16, 18 לארבעתן;

גביהן (?); 18 בלכתן, רבעיהן; 17 (?). This fact is all the more surprising since in 10:9, 13, 16–17, where 1:15–21 reappear in an abbreviated form, this phenomenon has completely disappeared. Admittedly we can point to the fact that there the masculine cherubim appear in place of the חיות of ch. 1 so that the relation becomes unequivocal. Nevertheless, with the feminine suffixes which relate to חיות, the feminine suffixes which in ch. 1 relate to אופנים have disappeared there. To the question which text gives us the more original state of affairs we must decide solely on the basis of the grammatical phenomenon and argue with the majority against Sprank that the more original form of the text appears in ch. 1; ch. 10 then represents a smoothed over version of the strangely obscure form of ch. 1.

Can we go a step further in making judgements about the confused situation in chapter 1? It is striking that the feminine suffixes which relate to the masculine אופנים are found in 1:10 in ארבעתן, relating to the creatures (vv 15?, 16, 18), and again in v 17 which is heavily dependent on v 12. בלכתן derives directly from 1:12; אל רבעיהן paraphrases the אל עבר פניו.[25] We can scarcely avoid the conclusion that in these forms we are dealing with an echo of the correct formulations given to the description of the four creatures. In the גביהן of v 18, if it can be textually supported, as in the רבעיהן of v 17, we can therefore establish an arbitrary assimilation to the context.

The concern of the section 1:15–21 is to describe the wheels, which in their movement are directly parallel to the creatures. This description 1:15–21 is closely dependent on the corresponding statements of 1:5–12 and thereby completely overlooks that the statements of vv (10 and) 12, which relate to the living creatures and which use the feminine suffix form with complete grammatical propriety in the description in 1:15–21, should have been changed into the masculine in relating to the אופנים. The formulations which were already fixed were then taken over *tale quale*. Where they occur independently of these fixed formulations the masculine suffix form is found even where the feminine form should properly appear in reference to חיות.

These formal considerations lead directly to a critical evaluation of the content of the whole section. In this section we do not find the correct use of the suffixes discernible in the basic text of vv 5, 6b, 11b, 12, 13 aαb.

Rather it betrays a) a slavish dependence on the contents of the text which lay before it, which is only explicable as a secondary formation; and b) shows the same freedom in the use of the suffixes in the independently formed parts as is found in the secondary section 1:7–11a. This agrees with the observation made at the beginning, that v 15 gives a new emphasis through its fresh introduction to the vision, which is out of balance with the actual importance of its individual parts. It is therefore shown up as an introduction to an addition which was not present in the primary composition of the text.[26] Thus the whole section vv 15–21, which describes the wheels, may be recognized in chapter 1 as a piece of subsequent expansion.[27] Against Sprank, however, the observations on the text have made clear that the addition has not been introduced from chapter 10; but on the contrary, chapter 10 represents a polished up adaptation of the section first added to chapter 1.

When the secondary character of 1:15–21 is recognized, then the striking discrepancy found in the description of the wheels is also explained. The mention of the wheels appears somewhat unexpectedly after the full description of the phenomenon, even extending in v 13 to the area between the living creatures which it regards as full of fire. It also makes intelligible the discrepancy that the wheels are to be seen "on the earth" (v 15, cf. 19, 21), while what has been said before leads us to expect a descent from heaven. Here two circles of concepts are connected which at first had nothing to do with one another.[28]

The question can now be put whether 1:15–21 form a unity in themselves. The beginning of v 18, which comes somewhat late after the theme of the similar movement of the wheels and creatures has been introduced (in v 17) and which gives a description of the outward appearance of the wheels, is awkward and would join better to v 16. It suggests a successive elaboration of the addition, and this is supported by the

fact that v 21 simply contains a summary of vv 19–20, which is both strained, yet slightly enlarged by the addition of ובעמדם יעמדו. It is no accident therefore that the verse is lacking in a group of text witnesses.

In v 22 the original text of the vision is undoubtedly found once again. This reveals, however, a certain discrepancy in that v 22a uses the singular חיה (as also vv 20f), whilst v 22b, with its masculine plural suffix, points back to the living creatures. Thus in v 22b a subsequent explanatory addition can be recognized. The original text in this place, where it referred to the throne over the living creatures and the manifestation of God himself, had summarized the multiplicity of creatures collectively as "the creature."

After the mysterious reference to the "fixed platform," we expect the description to go higher and to describe what was borne above this platform, which itself simply had a utilitarian purpose. V 26 gives this anticipated continuation and undoubtedly once joined directly on to v 22a. V 26 is separated from v 22a in the present text through vv (22b) 23–25, which add a description of what was to be seen and heard beneath the platform. It is as though the description could not do enough to describe with details and interpretation, the things below the platform in striking contrast to the caution in the description of what was to be seen over it.

The addition of vv 23–25 is again not out of one mold. V 23 describes once again the wings of the creatures whereby v 22a varies what has been said in v 11aα and v 22b repeats the description of v 11bβ with a change of the feminine for the masculine suffix form. In a still later expansion the feminine suffix form from v 5 appears.[29] V 24 adds the audible impressions which arose from the movement of the wings, in which the textual evidence shows that subsequent additions have elaborated the text very heavily by repeated comparisons.[30] The brief statement in v 24b, which is repeated in v 25b, describes, within the framework of the subsequent

---

23 See the exposition for the causes of uncertainty regarding the remainder of v 13aαb.
24 See above p. 102.
25 Cf. note b to 1:17.
26 We shall show later that the important introductory formula of the vision is also used in other places in order to introduce insertions into the text (as 10:1, 9).
27 So also Sprank, *Studien*; Berry, "Exile," 85.
28 The exposition will deal more fully with them.
29 Cf. note to 1:23.
30 Cf. notes a and b to 1:24.

interpretation, the wings at rest.

If v 26 joins directly on to v 22a, then אשר על ראשם which stands out because of its masculine suffix form, becomes superfluous, since it has been introduced into 𝔐 to join up the broken connection with v 22a. Similarly in the second half of the verse the עליו, which is lacking in some texts, is to be removed as a subsequent attempt at clarification.[31] For the rest we find in vv 26–28, with the exception of the addition in v 27a, the original text.

2:1–3:11   The Commissioning of the Prophet

2:1 begins a long address containing the prophet's call, which extends to 3:11 and which is only broken up by small narrative sections in 2:9–3:3. The complicated problem of the glosses in ch. 1 recedes into the background here. The text is clear, and small additions can be recognized with the help of the versions. Can we then pronounce this whole address as original? Or do the undoubted length of the speeches and the appearance of repetitions in them point to the conclusion that here also subsequent expansion lies before us?

The section 2:1–3:11 is broken into a number of speeches which begin with the address בן אדם 2:1, 3; 3:1, 3, 4, 10, or the fuller ואתה בן אדם 2:6, 8. Such a text invites critical separation into sections when such repetition of individual sayings appears. We must still examine the question whether in fact we can recognize superfluous, or misplaced, passages.

2:1f contains the summons of Yahweh to get up, addressed to the prophet who has fallen down before him. This is not to be separated from ch. 1 (against Messel).

2:3–5 follow with the speech of commissioning from Yahweh. After the removal of additions, the very roughly-formulated clauses are related together by the catchword שלח, which is decisive for the prophet's understanding of his work and which continues into a formula of acknowledgement.[32] The whole section makes a most impressive presentation of the sending of the prophet to Israel, so that one can only wonder that it has been proposed to eliminate it as a redactional addition (Hölscher, *Hesekiel*, Messel).

2:6–7 adds an admonition to fearlessness, which Jer 1:8 (17) shows to be an essential part of a call-narrative. It in no way contradicts the genuineness of these verses that v 7 repeats sayings which can already be found in v 5. The element of encouragement and strengthening, which is also found in a different form in the calls of Moses and Gideon, follows naturally upon the oracle of commissioning.

Verse 8 forms a transition to the giving of the word of God in the form of a scroll. The acceptance of the word by ear and mouth is embedded in a sharp summons to obedience, which is clearly formulated against the background of the preceding saying about the disobedient people. This is decisive evidence against the view that the episode of the scroll first begins with 2:9 (Messel), or even with 3:1 (Hölscher, *Hesekiel*). It is clearly prepared for in what precedes. In detail this event of the giving of the scroll and its acceptance by the prophet is told in a particular order under the thrice repeated command of Yahweh (2:8; 3:1, 3). Since the commands move in a clear progression,[33] it is out of place to break off any one part of the series, however involuted and circumstantial the narrative may appear in detail.[34] The feature of the giving of the divine word, which is here firmly conceptualized in the form of a scroll, is already found as an established element in Jer 1:9, where the hand of Yahweh touches Jeremiah's lips, while the call of Moses formulates the whole event in words only and is not elaborated into a visible act (Ex 4:12 "I will be with your mouth"). In this connection we may question whether the particular feature of the touching of Isaiah's lips with the coal from the altar (Is 6:6f) represents a reworking of an element that was indispensable to a call-narrative. The giving of the Word of God by means of the touching of the lips is in Is 6 transformed into the preparation and consecration of the lips to receive the divine word. So the Isaianic account may also show the form of a call-narrative in which the preparation of the messenger's mouth is not left unmentioned. In contrast we may compare the remarkable putting of a lying spirit into the mouth of the prophet in 1 Kings 22:22.

In 3:4–9 a longer speech by Yahweh is added, which

---

31   Cf. note b to 1:26.
32   See the exposition.
33   See the exposition.

34   A similar, somewhat difficult elaborateness can also be found elsewhere in Ezekiel (37:1ff).

takes up and develops ideas from 2:3, 5 and which makes plain once again the hardening of the heart of the house of Israel to which the prophet is sent. Although nothing is said directly, as in 1 Kings 22 and Is 6, of an official task of the prophet of bringing about this hardening through his preaching, yet this negative description of Israel connects very closely with features of Is 6. Even at a quick glance the text of the formulations shows close contact with the Isaianic formulations. It is all the more surprising that at the conclusion of this speech, which tells of the prophet's being toughened for his task, there also occur features which have a very close connection with Jeremianic formulations. In the framework of the call-vision, Ezek 3:4–9 corresponds in theme and arrangement to Jer 1:17–19, which likewise follows an act of ordination, except that in the present form of Jer 1 it is separated from the act of ordination proper of 1:9–10 by the two visions of 1:11–12 and 13–16, which serve to make clear the content of the prophet's message. Accordingly in the overall framework of the call-narrative Ez 3:4–9 appears as a necessary part.

We are left with 3:10–11, verses which have recently aroused strong suspicion of belonging to another section or of being a section subsequently introduced by Ezekiel himself.[35] It is at once quite clear that 3:10–11, in their context, are dependent on what has already been said. 3:10 repeats 2:8aα, and 3:11 repeats the commissioning with a saying from 2:4f. To this may be added the emphatic repetition of ויאמר אלי, which is also found in 2:1, 3; 3:1, 3, 4, but not 2:6, 8. Above all the specific naming of the exiles in a divine speech arouses suspicion.

Those who accept the presupposition of a double activity of Ezekiel in Jerusalem and Babylon, and who see in chs. 2f the original call-narrative, are compelled to separate 3:10f, with its reference to the exiles, from what precedes it. On the other hand, those who look at the divine speech of 2:1–3:11 without such presuppositions will in no way feel compelled to make such a division. The phenomenon of repetition has frequently been shown in what precedes (cf. 2:5 with 2:6f, 3:9; 2:6 with 3:9). It is not necessary to cut out the repetitions because they sometimes appear within the framework of a speech which, as a whole, possesses a distinctive theme of its own throughout, and because through the verses a progression of thought from the theme of the one group to that of the other can be seen. This is also the case with 3:10f. The new theme, to which the repeated sayings in 3:10f are related, is the specific sending of the prophet to the small remnant of Israel, which was exiled in the near locality of the place at which he was overwhelmed by the vision of God. The whole section of the commissioning speech in 2:3–3:9 had simply spoken previously of the house of Israel. It can further be shown that Ezekiel often addresses the "house of Israel," which in his day was no longer united at one place, as those to whom he speaks. The undoubted generalizing and vagueness of many parts of his preaching are explicable from this. Ezekiel knew himself to be a prophet of "Israel." Beside this there are sections which are clearly directed at particular groups within this Israel, which had been torn apart in Ezekiel's day (such as those in which the message is addressed to the people "in the land of Israel" [18:2]). It is not at all surprising therefore that the conclusion of the speech of Yahweh in 3:10–11, which is marked as an independent saying by its fresh introduction, turns from the general act of commissioning to the concrete task of preaching to those who had been deported. The contents then echo once again what has already been expressed in the preceding speeches. In view of the uncertainty which attaches to the metrical thesis of "short verse," also the argument from meter is insufficient reason for cutting out the verse as an addition.[36] The verses 3:10f, as the conclusion of Yahweh's commissioning address to the prophet, are not seriously to be questioned.

3:12–15 The End of the Vision

If the preceding analysis is correct then v 13, which shows by its masculine suffixes referring to the חיות that it belongs to an editorial addition, must be deleted. After v 12 it is also in any case superfluous. The repetition of the קול רעש גדול from v 12a clearly marks it out as a repetition which, in its last word, connects up with the catchword from v 12.

---

35   For the former view see Auvray, Kuhl, "Schauplatz;" for the latter, Fohrer, *Hauptprobleme*, 78.

36   See Sigmund Mowinckel, "Der metrische Aufbau von Jes 62:1–12 und die neuen sog. 'Kurzverse'," *ZAW* 65 (1953): 167–187; Fohrer, *Hauptprobleme*, 65, 78.

The call-narrative of the prophet Ezekiel, after the removal of all editorial additions, thus runs:

And it happened in the thirtieth year [in the fifth year, see the exposition] in the 4th month, on the 5th day of the month, when I was among the exiles by the River Chebar, that the heavens were opened and I saw divine visions. And the hand of Yahweh was upon me. When I looked, behold, a violent storm came from the north, a great cloud and flashing fire. And from the middle of it there appeared the form of four living creatures. And this was their appearance: they were shaped like men, but each of them had four wings. With all four, (?) each had two wings which touched one another and two covered their bodies. Each went straight forward, they did not turn as they went (?). And between the living creatures there appeared as it were coals burning in a fire. The fire blazed, and out of the fire there went forth lightning. Over the heads of the living creatures was something liked a fixed platform, shining like crystal. Behold, above the fixed platform was something looking like sapphire—something like a throne; and above what appeared like a throne, there was something to see which looked like a man. And I saw a brightness like electrum upwards from what appeared to be his loins; and downwards from what appeared to be his loins I saw something which looked like fire. He was surrounded by brightness. Like the appearance of the bow which is in the clouds on a rainy day, so was the appearance of the brightness round about. This was the appearance of the form of Yahweh's glory.

When I saw it I fell upon my face. Then I heard the voice of someone speaking, and he said to me: Son of man, stand upon your feet, and I will speak with you. Then the spirit came into me, and he set me upon my feet, and I heard him as he spoke to me. He said to me: "Son of man, I send you to the house of Israel, which rebels against me, they and their fathers to this very day, and you shall say to them: Thus has Yahweh said. And they shall know, whether they hear or refuse to hear—for they are a rebellious house—that a prophet has been in their midst. And you, son of man, do not be afraid of them, nor be afraid of their faces, when thorns surround you and you sit upon scorpions. Do not be afraid of their words, nor be dismayed at their faces, for they are a rebellious house. You shall speak my words to them, whether they hear or refuse to hear—for they are a rebellious house. Open your mouth and eat what I give you." I looked, and behold, a hand was stretched out towards me, and in it was a scroll. He unrolled it before me, and it was written upon on the front and the back, and upon it there were written lamentations, words of mourning and woes. He said to me: Son of man, eat this scroll, and go, speak to the house of Israel. Then I opened my mouth, and he gave me the scroll to eat, and said to me: Son of man, eat, and fill your stomach with this scroll, which I give you. Then I ate it, and it was in my mouth as sweet as honey. And he said to me: Son of man, get up, go to the house of Israel and speak my words to them. For you are not sent to a people of foreign speech, and not to many nations, whose words you cannot understand. If I were to send you to such, they would listen to you. But the house of Israel will not listen to you, for they will not listen to me. The whole house of Israel are of a hard forehead and a stubborn heart. Behold I am making your face hard like their faces, and your forehead hard like their foreheads, like diamond, harder than flint. Do not be afraid of them, nor be dismayed before them, for they are a rebellious house. And he said to me: Son of man, all my words which I speak to you, receive in your heart and hear with your ears. Now get up, go to the exiles, to the members of your people, and speak to them and say to them: Thus has Yahweh said— whether they hear or whether they refuse to hear. Then the spirit lifted me up, and I heard behind me the sound of a great earthquake, when the glory of Yahweh arose from its place. Then the spirit lifted me up and took me away, and I went in the fervor of my spirit, whilst the hand of Yahweh was heavy upon me, and I came to the exiles at Tel Abib, where they dwelt. And I sat there overwhelmed among them seven days.

We can now proceed to attempt an answer to the question put at the beginning about the original relationship of the throne vision to the vision of the scroll. Our form-critical analysis has shown that beside the type of prophetic call-narrative which placed all its emphasis upon the divine speech (Jeremiah, Moses) there was a second type of narrative in which the commissioning speech arose out of a well-defined throne vision. This latter type is shown as a separate form by the similarity of 1 Kings 22 and Is 6. The critical analysis of Ezek 1:1–3:15 has revealed an underlying text of the Ezekiel call-narrative which enables us to recognize the connection with Is 6 more strongly than the heavily reworked text of 𝔐, especially in Ezek 1, makes possible. In Ezek 2f the relationship with Jer 1 appears even more strongly. Here also, however, there are not lacking connections with Isaiah. All of this makes the conclusion probable that in Ezek 1:1–3:15 we have a quite distinctive form of a prophetic call-narrative of the type of Is 6. Just as in Is 6 the throne vision and the commissioning cannot be separated, so also in Ezek 1:1–3:15 any such separation of the visions of the throne and the scroll would be wrong. Without the continuation in Ezek 2f, Ezekiel ch. 1 remains a torso. The adducing of a part of 2:1–3:15 as a conclusion of ch. 1 is not possible because a division of the speeches of 2:1–3:15 into two recensions has nothing to support it from the text.

We may conclude the examination of the form of Ezek 1:1–3:15 with a comparison of the structure of Ezek 1:1–3:15 with Is 6, showing both the relationship and distinctiveness of the two accounts. Both prophets describe, after a reference to the date, how they were overwhelmed by the glory of Yahweh. Isaiah experienced this event in the temple in Jerusalem, made sacred by ancient tradition, whilst Ezekiel encountered it in the remoteness of exile, where he had been cut off from his homeland and where worship itself seemed impossible.[37] The God whom he encountered was not seated peacefully on his throne, but was seen coming in a thundercloud, as had been the case in the older period. The divine council, which Isaiah had overheard in the most holy place in its deliberations, was no longer heard by Ezekiel. The supernatural creatures, which in Isaiah, unlike 1 Kings 22, had already taken on a new function as servants, have in Ezekiel become completely silent figures. The praise of the Holy One, which had been heard in the temple of Jerusalem, was no longer audible by the waters of Babylon (Ps 137). In the entire manifestation, apart from the earthshaking noise which accompanied the storm in which God appeared (Ezek 3:12), only the voice of Yahweh was heard by the prophet. The four creatures which accompanied Yahweh had no other function than to carry the throne of their Lord. That they were four in number pointed to the completeness of Yahweh's glory, of which the seraphim had sung. We can see particularly in this how a feature of the earlier description of the divine court disappears into the background from 1 Kings 22, through Is 6 to Ezek 1. In 1 Kings 22:20 the interplay of speech is still recognizable in the full vitality of debate "one spoke thus and so and the other thus and so" (ויאמר זה בכה וזה אמר בכה), while in Is 6:3 this is molded into the more rigid form used for worship in

which the divine praise is proclaimed "and one cried to the other" (וקרא זה אל זה). In Ezek 1 the only corresponding feature is the silent gesture of the beating of the wings "each turning toward the other" (חברות אשה אלאחתה v 11 [see the text]). By means of the reordering of the "living creatures," the whole picture of the enthroned figure is heightened by Ezekiel into an artificial, almost baroque structure. Isaiah speaks simply of Yahweh sitting upon a high and exalted throne, in which he may have in mind the ark-throne of the most holy place, while Ezekiel sees at once four creatures, the description of which recalls the seraphim of Is 6, but which cannot be separated from the cherubim of Ps 18:11 which carry Yahweh. Over these living creatures a fixed platform, with the transparency of crystal, is to be seen. Ex 24:10 gives rise to the conjecture that here there is present the imagery of the Lord who is enthroned above the firmament. Above this platform there is the throne upon which Yahweh sits in his glory.

In contrast with Is 6 it is noteworthy that in Ezekiel the third pair of wings of the creatures is missing, with which, according to Isaiah, they covered their eyes. We can look for the explanation of this in the great importance attached to the number four by Ezekiel. We can further consider that it was not necessary for the creatures, who upheld the divine throne from underneath the platform, to protect their eyes before the divine splendor. At the same time it then becomes clear that the scene of Is 6 is most of all distinguished from Ezek 1 in that everything in it is determined by the "Holy One." This is surprising for a priest like Ezekiel, but we must consider that Is 6 tells of an experience in the temple, Ezek 1, however, of an event far away from the temple. "Holiness" for the priest Ezekiel was something strongly determined by the order and sphere of the temple. For life in exile, even in its worship, Yahweh became for his people למקדש מעט (11:16).

The second act of the encounter is also different. Like Isaiah Ezekiel was thrown to the ground by the impact of the divine manifestation. However, with Isaiah it was the despairing collapse of an unclean person before

---

37 See the exposition.

the Holy One, whereas with Ezekiel it was the humiliation of the creature before its Lord. Ezekiel's being set on his feet by Yahweh is not, as with Isaiah, a removal of guilt, but the restoring of strength to one who had collapsed in weakness. In the commissioning, in which, as we have mentioned, the connection with Jeremiah is more clearly to be traced, instead of the touching of the lips we have the more concrete eating of the scroll. With Isaiah this feature was included in the experience of the removal of guilt which freed the prophet to present himself to the divine court for service. With Ezekiel this feature had scarcely any place. Instead of the Holy One there stands here the Lord who demands obedience with words of command. Like Isaiah the unwillingness of the people to hear is strongly emphasized. However, there is no explicit charge to the prophet to bring a message that is to lead to a hardening of the people.

By the addition of a concluding appendix, which tells of Yahweh's departure, Ezekiel is distinguished from both Isaiah and Jeremiah.

According to its stylistic form, 1:1–3:15 is a firsthand account given by the prophet. This agrees with the content of what is narrated which, for all its dependence on the traditional form and content of a call-narrative as it had become established, must be understood in its kernel as the outcome of a deeply personal experience. This firsthand form is further preserved throughout the whole book and also in the later additions, with the exception of the superscription of 1:3a (in 24:24 Ezekiel is referred to within the framework of a divine speech).

Setting

The basic text of the call-narrative may have been composed by the prophet himself in exile. How close the time when the account was composed lay to the actual day of the call cannot be made out. Nor can we make out whether the composition of the detailed account was preceded by the composition of shorter notes which were then worked up into the larger narrative in a second phase.

The basic text, especially in ch. 1, has later under-

gone a far-reaching process of further interpretation and comment. This reworking stems from the circle of the "school" which preserved Ezekiel's words, redacted the book, and elaborated upon his words by way of comment and addition.[38] For the chronological order of these additions, which were certainly not completed all at once, the relative sequence can be established that the editors who added 10:1, 9ff, 21 must have had before them ch. 1 in its enlarged form, with mention of the faces, hands, and wheels, as also the author of Daniel 10–12 must certainly have had the expanded text before him. We must therefore not date the expansion too long after Ezekiel. It could well have taken place in Babylon.[39]

The heading in 1:3a was added to the text when 1:1–3:15 had become the opening section of a collection of the prophet's words and when this collection had been included in a series of the other prophetic books. The close relationship of the heading to that of the books of Haggai and Zechariah makes it probable that it must have taken place at a time, and even in the circles of early post-exilic prophecy, since in the short book of Haggai the heading appears to have arisen stylistically out of the language of the prophet himself.[40] This points us to Jerusalem at the end of the sixth century.

Interpretation

The heading 1:3a, which is related syntactically to 1:2 which in turn has been secondarily introduced into the call-narrative, gives the prophet's name, his father's name, his (or his father's) professional status, and the location of his call as a prophet.

The name יחזקאל is mentioned again in the book only 24:24, in the mouth of Yahweh. It occurs elsewhere in the Old Testament in 1 Chron 24:16 as the name of a representative of the twentieth among the twenty-four priestly classes who shared in the temple worship. Although Chronicles regards the division of the priestly classes as having taken place in David's time, it is possible that we have here the name of a post-exilic priestly class. Unfortunately it cannot be established with certainty whether Ezekiel, who came from a

---

38 See the introduction.
39 See further the detailed exposition.
40 See above p. 101.

Jerusalem priestly family, was closely related to this priestly class. The name יְחֶזְקֵאל is clearly a name formed from the verbal imperfect יְחַזֵּק אֵל, expressing a wish for the newborn child (by the father or the mother) "may God make strong."[41]

The name of Ezekiel's father בּוּזִי, which appears in this form only here, is found in Job 32:2, 6 as the gentilic of Elihu "who was of the family of Buz." This connects Elihu with the mention in Gen 22:21 of the second child of Nahor who is named Buz. Jer 25:23 mentions בוז beside דדן and תימא as North Arabian groups. Neither can we rule out an Arabian origin for the Gadite בוז mentioned in 1 Chron 5:14, in view of the settlement of Gad east of Jordan. Whether, however, anything about the ultimate origins of Ezekiel's family is to be deduced from this is questionable, since it must certainly have regarded itself as belonging to the Zadokite priesthood.

The predicate "the priest" can syntactically be related either to the name of the prophet or to the name of his father. The loose מן הכהנים of Jer 1:1, which affirms Jeremiah's relationship to a priestly family, contributes nothing to the elucidation of our text. We could rather consider the זכריה בן ברכיה בן עדו הנביא of Zech 1:1, where the apposition certainly relates to Zechariah (cf. Hag 1:1), and not to his ancestors. There is nothing in the content of the book of Ezekiel which forbids the assumption that he was himself a priest. However, a measure of uncertainty remains, which is not as serious as it would be in the modern western world where a son's vocation cannot be construed from that of his father. This is not the case with Ezekiel. Whether Ezekiel himself had previously accepted priestly service in Jerusalem (which is the only place that can be considered) is beyond our knowledge, as also is the age at which Ezekiel was called to his prophetic ministry five years after the deportation from Jerusalem.[42]

Whilst the author of the heading could only have

learned the references to the parentage and status of Ezekiel from a tradition preserved orally, the references that follow in v 3a to the location derive from the call-narrative. The heading of the book is consequently not properly a heading for the whole book, but strictly speaking only for the scene of the prophet's call which immediately follows. Exactly the same can be said for the headings of the books of Haggai and Zechariah. The reference to the date connects it simply with the passage which immediately follows (so also in the case of v 2 which is secondarily related to v 3a).[43] The custom which is discernible in the older prophetic books of describing the entire period of activity of the prophet in the heading (Is 1:1; Jer 1:1–3; Hos 1:1; Mic 1:1; Amos 1:1 and Zeph 1:1 are also to be understood in this way) is no longer found here.

The word of Yahweh came to Ezekiel "in the land of the Chaldeans by the River Chebar." The mention of this river, which is further found in the book of Ezekiel in 1:1; 3:15, 23; 10:15, 22; 43:3, always with reference to the prophet's call, is preceded by the general reference "in the land of the Chaldeans," which agrees with the introductory character of the heading. כַּשְׂדִּים (Akk. *kaldu*, Greek Χαλδαῖοι) was originally the name of an Aramaean group who forced their way into Southern Babylonian territory about the turn of the first millenium.[44] They were first brought into subjection by the great Assyrian kings Shalmaneser III (858–824 B.C.) and Tiglathpileser III (745–727 B.C.), and then took over the kingship of Babylon with the neo-Babylonian dynasty of Nabopolassar (626–605 B.C.) and Nebuchadnezzar II (604–562 B.C.).[45] The mention of the "land of the Chaldeans" presupposes this process of gradual subjugation, followed finally by the taking over of the kingship, and points to the Southern Babylonian plain, which was the true center of Babylonian civilization. In this territory the River כְּבָר (𝕲 and 𝔚 suggest that the word was pronounced with a *u* or *o* vowel in the first syllable)

---

41 Martin Noth, *Die israelitischen Personennamen im Rahmen der gemeinsemitischen Namengebung*, BWANT 3, 10 (Stuttgart: Kohlhammer, 1928), 202.

42 See on 1:1.

43 See pp. 100f.

44 See Wolfram von Soden, *Grundriss der akkadischen Grammatik*, Analecta Orientalia 33 (Rome: Pontifical Biblical Institute, ²1969), § 30g, for the con-

sonantal change of *šd* to *ld* in Middle/Late Babylonian and Middle Assyrian.

45 Alexander Scharff and Anton Moortgat, *Ägypten und Vorderasien im Altertum* (München: Bruckmann, 1950), 400, 404, 426f, 445ff.

is to be sought. Excavations in Mesopotamia have in fact brought to light the name of a *nâr kabari* on two contracts from the time of Artaxerxes I (464–424 B.C.).[46] This "great canal" (?), called by the Sumerians "the Euphrates of Nippur" (Zorell), is to be sought in the broad *šaṭṭ en-nîl*, which leaves the Euphrates east of Babylon.[47] It flows through the site of ancient Nippur and then subsequently enters again into the Euphrates. That Jewish exiles were settled in this region is confirmed by the fact that in the documents of Murašû and sons, the great Babylonian trade and banking house, from the fifth century B.C. a number of Jewish names as men having business connections are found.[48] So we may think of numbers of Jewish exiles as settled not too far from Nippur, near to the canal. This confirms very well the reference of Ezekiel. Here therefore the word of Yahweh came to Ezekiel. The formula of the address, which is found here, as in the headings of the books of Jeremiah, Hosea, Joel, Jonah, Micah, Zephaniah, Haggai and Zechariah, and which here indicates the giving of the first message to the prophet, will be more fully dealt with in connection with 3:16b.

Dating

■ **1:1f** dates Ezekiel's call on the fifth day of the fourth month of the thirtieth year (v 1), which is the fifth year after the deportation of Jehoiachin (v 2). Here we encounter the first of the thirteen (fourteen) dates, precisely noted to the day, of the book of Ezekiel (1:1f; [3:16]; 8:1; 20:1; 24:1; 26:1; 29:1, 17; 30:20; 31:1; 32:1, 17; 33:21; 40:1). What are we to make of these dates? Some have regarded them altogether as a fiction and literary embellishment.[49] However, it is in order first of all to examine them carefully and to make an overall picture of the appearance of dates in written prophecy. In Amos, Hosea, and Micah no dates are discernible except for the references included editorially in the headings about the period of the prophet's

activity. Isaiah twice gives dates by referring to the year of a king's reign (Is 6:1, the year of king Uzziah's death; 14:28, the year of king Ahaz's death). "In the days of Ahaz" (7:1) is secondarily taken over from 2 Kings 16:5. In the book of Jeremiah dates become more numerous, and besides the simple mention of the year (25:1; 26:1; 27:1; 32:1; 36:1; 45:1; cf. 46:2; 49:34) dates are also given according to months (28:1; 36:9; 41:1). The dates in 39:1f are lacking in 𝕲, and probably, like those of ch. 52, they have been introduced from the historical books. Nevertheless, we must notice that in the basic collection of prophecies dictated by Jeremiah no dates are to be found. The reference to the year given in 1:2, which is now included in the editorial heading, may once have stood before the call-narrative (Rudolph, *Jeremia*). As for dating precisely to the day, apart from the book of Ezekiel, we find in Haggai, which contains only two short chapters, no less than five days specifically referred to (1:1, 15a, 15b; 2:10, 20), and in Zechariah there are specific references to a month (1:1) and twice to days (1:7; 7:1). We can therefore see in prophecy an increasing precision in the date references. Ezekiel stands in this progression in his rightful place, after Jeremiah and alongside the two latest of the writing prophets, where dates are to be found. If we wish to deny altogether to Ezekiel the originality of the dates, we cannot also avoid denying them also to Haggai and Zechariah. This, however, cannot be so simply done, particularly with Haggai. Unless there is doubt about the particular dates and the contents of the sections concerned, we must accept tentatively that these dates belong to the original form of the text, although their inclusion or exclusion in particular oracles does not betray any specific system.

What can have given rise to the dating of prophetic sayings? Certainly we cannot see behind it a subjective biographical interest on the part of the prophet. The unimportance of the prophet's own "life" [βίος], in contrast to the importance of his preaching, is clearly

46   H. V. Hilprecht and A. T. Clay, *The Babylonian Expedition of the University of Pennsylvania* 9 (Philadelphia, 1898), pp. 26ff nos. 4, 84.
47   Guthe, *BA*² 5, iv.
48   Hilprecht-Clay, *Expedition* 9 and 10; see also the economic and historical analysis of G. Cardascia, *Les archives des Murašû, une famille d'hommes d'affaires babyloniens à l'époque perse* (Paris: Impr. Nationale, 1951).
49   So Torrey, *Pseudo-Ezekiel*; Zunz, "Ezechiel"; Jahn, *Buch*; Berry, "Title"; Moses Buttenwieser, "The Character and Date of Ezekiel's Prophecies," *HUCA* 7 (1930): 1–18.

shown by other references.[50] More seriously we must consider the view of Fohrer, who sees here an influence upon the priest Ezekiel of the habit of exactness in matters of law and practice, and in noting all important events in temple annals chronologically.[51] He believes that this habit has led to this exact dating. Since, however, the incentive to give exact dates for prophetic sayings can be found outside of Ezekiel, it remains to be questioned whether there was not a genuine prophetic interest in the exact dating of oracles. This may indeed be the case as we can conclude from certain observations. Is 8:1f tells of the revelation to the prophet of a mysterious, unintelligible oracle. This is received with the summons to inscribe the message with the assistance of two witnesses upon a form of contract. A similar situation of an inscription commanded by Yahweh is to be found in Hab 2:1–3, where the prophet is commanded "Write down the vision (חזון), and inscribe it on a tablet, so that it can readily be read. For there is still a period of time allotted for the vision, which yet presses towards its conclusion and does not deceive." Although nothing is said here of witnesses we have the impression that we are dealing with a writing, similar to a contract, which is to be redeemed at a predetermined time. Such contractual arrangements are known from Babylon where the use of contracts underwent its classical development: "The chief claim for the validity of a legal transaction is its fixation in writing and the appeal to witnesses ... All important transactions are followed by an oath ... together with an exact reference to the date."[52] We can scarcely think otherwise therefore than that when the divine word was inscribed on a "large sheet" גליון גדול (Is 8:1f), witnesses assisting, and also on the לחות of Hab 2:2, there was a reference to the date. From this manner of inscribing the divine word, which is admittedly not common, the custom of giving an exact date for the receipt of a message could have gained general acceptance as a consequence. In any case in the dating there is expressed unmistakably the conviction that the word of Yahweh, which was given to the prophet and communicated by him, was not a timeless truth, but represented a message of God for a particular occasion.

There are great difficulties over the double dating, which includes two references to the year in vv 1f, and especially over the way in which the year is identified in v 1. The reference to the year in v 2 is immediately clear. The numbering of the fifth year "of the exile of the king Jehoiachin" לגלות המלך יויכין, i.e., after the year 598 B.C., points to an era which is also utilized in the dates of 33:21; 40:1, where it is abbreviated to "of our exile," לגלותנו. It agrees with the later references according to which the beginning of the siege of Jerusalem took place in the ninth year (24:1), and the fall of it in the eleventh year (33:21; where see) after the deportation of Jehoiachin. Further the date given in 1:1 fits smoothly into the series of other dates given (1:2 the fifth year; 8:1, the sixth year; 20:1, the seventh year; 24:1, the ninth year). The incompleteness of the date given in v 2, which, apart from the mention of the day which is repeated from v 1, only mentions the year, is explicable from the character of the verse in which it appears.[53] This now purports to be simply a further elucidation of v 1. Verse 2 gives us therefore a date which fits well into the whole series of dates in the book of Ezekiel, referring to the year by way of an additional remark. From this we may conjecture that it must at one time have stood in the first verse, coupled with the mention of the month and the day.

The reference to the year which is now to be found in v 1, however, presents what is in every way a riddle. What does the number thirty mean here? Why is it not referred to any particular era? All the other years mentioned in the book of Ezekiel, even where the era is not specifically referred to, are oriented towards the date of Jehoiachin's deportation. Are we to see in v 1 an isolated date which begins a prophetic oracle, but of which the message itself has been lost, and which has mistakenly been set at the beginning, outside the remainder of the series?[54] Or is the year referred to in v 1 to be ascribed to a regnal period? Torrey thought of the era of Manasseh. Budde, "Eingang," has shown the impossibility of this view on good grounds. We can as little accept with J. Smith, *Book*, a dating from the conquest of Samaria. A reckoning from the beginning of the reform of Josiah (𝔗, Jerome, J. Herrmann, Ziegler)

50 See the exposition of 3:16a, 22—5:17.
51 Fohrer, *Hauptprobleme*, 105.
52 Bruno Meissner, *Babylonien und Assyrien* 1 (Heidelberg: Winter, 1920), 154.
53 See above.
54 So Merx, "Wert," 72f.

is nowhere else to be found in the Old Testament and has little probability in itself. Kimchi and Hitzig think of a reckoning of a year of Jubilee, but for the time of Ezekiel this hangs completely in the air. The reckoning with the era of Nabopolassar (from 626 B.C.) does not agree chronologically, nor does that which starts from the year of Jehoiachin's birth.[55] The view that it concerns the time of the publication of the prophetic book in the framework of a reckoning of Jehoiachin's era fits better with a modern publishing custom than with the mentality of a prophet.[56] The conjecture made by Origen that it referred to the age of the prophet at the time of his call (so also Kraetzschmar who wants to insert "son" בן [or "I" אני] "when I was" בהיותי after "and it came to pass" ויהי; Budde, "Eingang," who wants to change שנה into שני and so forth) leaves the decisive point of reference in the dark. So also does the view that here two references to the duration of the exile, the seventy years of Jeremiah (25:11f; 29:10) and the forty years of Ezekiel (4:6), are reckoned together.[57]

We can scarcely avoid the conclusion therefore that an editorial hand has been at work here, and the date which originally stood in v 1, and which now stands in the later gloss v 2, was displaced by the insertion of the thirty years (Fohrer). In view of the considerable reediting which ch. 1 has undergone from the school of Ezekiel this view is not absurd.[58] In the context of such subsequent exegesis by a school, the number thirty may have had a meaning along the line of recent conjectures (harmonizing the references to the duration of the exile or to the age of the prophet, who would in this case have reached the stipulated age for the priesthood according to Nu 4:30). We cannot obtain certainty on this point. For the prophet's own particular message, however, the number has no importance.

The book of Ezekiel is dated according to the era of Jehoiachin. This fact must be regarded, in the light of recent knowledge, as more than simply a pious gesture of attachment to the unfortunate young king, whose fate Ezekiel himself had shared. From two quarters archaeology has brought new light to bear on this question. In his essay W. F. Albright has directed attention to three inscribed pottery fragments which were found in 1928 and 1930 in Tell Beit Mirsim, and in 1930 in Beth Shemesh, all in a stratum of Iron Age II (900–600 B.C.).[59] The last-named find undoubtedly derives from a stratum which belongs directly to the time of the great destruction of the place c. 600 B.C. All three fragments bear the inscription לאליקם נער יוכן.[60] The name here must be that of king Jehoiachin. Can we claim, however, that all three pots belong to the brief three months of the reign of a king who was soon besieged in Jerusalem by the Babylonians? The pottery sealings, which have been found at three sites, raise the question whether the exiled Jehoiachin was not rather regarded as the legitimate king of the land right up to the end in 587 B.C., so that Zedekiah was simply his representative.

This conjecture can be strengthened by a second observation from another side. E. F. Weidner has interpreted a find of about 300 cuneiform tablets which had been placed in a vault by the Ishtar gate in Babylon and which are to be dated in the period from 595–570.[61] The tablets contain references to the rations which were given to prisoners from Egypt, Philistia, Phoenicia, Asia Minor, Elam, Media, Persia, and Judah. K. Galling has given the four references from the texts Babylon 28122, 28178, 28186, 28232 (Weidner) in which Jehoiachin is named.[62] Of the measures named in them

---

55 For the former view see Smend, Toy, and Conrad von Orelli, *Das Buch Ezechiel und die zwölf kleinen Propheten*, Kurzgefasster Kommentar zu den Schriften des Alten und Neuen Testaments (Nördlingen, ²1896); for the latter, N. H. Snaith, "The Dates in Ezekiel," *ET* 59 (1947/48): 315f.

56 W. F. Albright, "The Seal of Eliakim and the Latest Preëxilic History of Judah, with Some Observations on Ezekiel," *JBL* 51 (1932): 97.

57 Duhm, *Theologie*; Bertholet-Galling; Hölscher, *Hesekiel*. See also Fohrer, *Hauptprobleme*, 110–116.

58 See above p. 110.

59 Albright, "Seal of Eliakim."

60 See *BRL*, 486 illustration no. 24.

61 E. F. Weidner, "Jojachin, König von Juda in babylonischen Keilschrifttexten" in *Mélanges syriens offerts à M. René Dussaud* (Paris: Geuthner, 1939), 923–935.

62 Kurt Galling, *Textbuch zur Geschichte Israels* (Tübingen: Mohr [Siebeck], ²1968).

1 PI = 36 Sila, 1 Sila = 0.4 litres.[63] They read: A) ... to *ia-'-ú-kinu*, the king of the land of Judah (written: *ia-a-ḫu-du*) B) ½PI to *ia-'-ú-kinu*, the king of the land of Judah ... 2½ Sila to 2 plus 3 sons of the king of the land of Judah ... 4 Sila to 8 Judeans, each ½ Sila. C) ½PI *ia-a-ú* ... 2½ Sila to 5 sons ... ½PI to *ia-ku-u-ki-nu*, the son of the king of *ia-ku-du* (sic!) in the hands of Qana'ama. D) ... of *ia-'u-kinu*, of the king of the land of Judah ... 5 sons of the king of the land of Judah in the hands of Qanāma (in some places extended). One of the lists referred to is expressly dated in the year 592. Since Jehoiachin carries the royal title in these Babylonian texts we can conclude from this that he was still recognized as such by the Babylonians, which also strengthens the conjecture from that side that in Jerusalem Zedekiah was solely a regent for the absent Jehoiachin. From this political arrangement not only does the passionate expectation of the citizens of Jerusalem that those who had been deported would soon return (Jer 28:3) come to stand in a new light, but also the method of dating in the book of Ezekiel. It names quite correctly the king of Judah who, although he had been deported, had not been stripped of his royal dignity, and does so, not simply with his royal name, but reckons his years in regard to his deportation.[64]

When Jehoiachin came to the throne in the summer of 598, by reckoning the date from the following spring the year spring 598/spring 597 was still counted as the last year of Jehoiakim and the year spring 597/spring 596 was counted as the first year of Jehoiachin.[65] The date given in 1:1f falls therefore in the time towards the end of June in the year 593.

Reference to the Place

In the reference to the place which follows the date, "when I was among the exiles by the River Chebar," the words "in the midst of the exile" בתוך הגולה give the impression that Ezekiel was among a group of exiles when the vision came to him. This shows a situation similar to that of 8:1 (14:1f; 20:1f). Since, however, 3:15 states that he went after the event "to the exiles at Tell Abib, where they dwelt," and sat there stunned for seven days "in their midst" (בתוכם), the "in the midst of the exile" בתוך הגולה of 1:1 must be a general reference to the place. Nothing else in the call-narrative points to the direct presence of eyewitnesses.

The localizing of the event "by the River Chebar" raises some further considerations. Acts 16:13 ἐξήλθομεν ἔξω τῆς πύλης παρὰ ποταμὸν οὗ ἐνομίζομεν προσευχὴν εἶναι shows that the Jewish diaspora of the New Testament period established its places for prayer preferably beside water. A decree of the city of Halicarnassus, which Josephus has preserved, describes the prayers on the sea-shore as "a custom derived from the fathers" (πατρῷον ἔθος).[66] According to the *Letter of Aristeas* 304f, the translators of the Greek Bible began their daily work by washing their hands in the sea and praying to God "according to a general Jewish custom" (ὡς δὲ ἔθος ἐστὶ πᾶσι τοῖς Ἰουδαίοις). In the rabbinic literature this custom is not mentioned,[67] although even in the Old Testament itself Ps 137 seems to point towards such a custom, especially in the case of deportees to Babylon, when it mentions reflectively "By the streams (canals) of Babylon, we sat down and wept ... On the willows beside them we hang up our lyres. Then those who brought us asked songs of us ...: Sing us one of the songs of Zion!—How could we sing Yahweh's song in a foreign land!" Here also the custom of meeting for worship beside water (where it was possible to carry out the prescribed washings) appears to be referred to. Perhaps here the singing of the songs of Zion (Ps 46, 48, 84, and 42f?) was first practised and subsequently stopped when it began to be a sensation for the local population.

We must therefore guard against any romantic interpretation of the place referred to in 1:1. The prophet did not come there because he sought solitude

---

63 According to *RLV* 8, 60f.

64 On the whole problem see F. M. T. de Liagre Böhl, "Nebukadnezar en Jojachin," *NTS* 25 (1942): 121–125; reprinted in *idem*, *Opera minora* (Groningen: J. B. Wolters, 1953), 423–429; Malamat, "Jeremiah"; Martin Noth, "The Jerusalem Catastrophe of 587 B.C., and its significance for Israel" in *The Laws in the Pentateuch and Other Studies*, tr. D. R. Ap-

Thomas (Philadelphia: Fortress, 1967), 260–280; Jack Finegan, *Light from the Ancient Past* (Princeton: Princeton University Press, ²1959), 188–189.

65 Joachim Begrich, *Die Chronologie der Könige von Israel und Juda und die Quellen des Rahmens der Königsbücher* (Tübingen: Mohr [Siebeck], 1929).

66 Josephus, *Antiquities*, 14, 10, 23.

67 Herman L. Strack and Paul Billerbeck, *Kommentar*

and hoped to experience nature beside the flowing water, nor as a symbol of transitoriness (Eccl 1:7). Rather, like Isaiah, he must have been surprised by the presence of Yahweh at a place used by the faithful of the community for worship. So also afterwards we read directly of the receiving of visions and of divine manifestations above the waters (Dan 8:2, 10:4; *Enoch* 13:7 —does Mt 3:16f also belong here, even though other features have entered in?).

The introduction of the prophet's vision is given in vv 1b and 3b with different imagery. V 1b "The heaven opened and I saw divine visions," speaks first of all in terms of an objective world. It leads to the conception of a massive heavenly vault (רקיע) which was normally firmly sealed in all its openings. In this the main interest is not taken up with the idea found in Gen 7:11 that by this sealing the world was made safe from the cosmic catastrophe of the heavenly ocean breaking in, so much as the idea that by this sealing the God of the heavens was hidden from all earthly view, seated in the secrecy of his celestial throne. Is 63:19 refers to the anxious cry of those who felt deprived by this hiddenness of God: לוא קרעת שמים ירדת.

Ezek 1:1 is the only text in the book of Ezekiel which presupposes so clearly the heavenly dwelling place of Yahweh. Far more frequently, on the other hand, we find references in Ezekiel to Yahweh's dwelling at the holy place, in Jerusalem (cf. 8:1ff; 43:1ff; 48:35). References to the heavenly and earthly dwelling places of Yahweh, occurring side by side, correspond in some measure to the parallelism of the dwelling-temples and the theophany-temples of Mesopotamia.[68] They are significant for the whole Old Testament.[69] The occurrence of such references side by side is occasioned by the necessity to guard both the freedom of Yahweh and also the contingency of his revelation.

The statement about the opening of heaven is only found here in the Old Testament, whilst the opening of the windows of heaven (or of the height) for punishment (Gen 7:11; Is 24:18) and blessing (Mal 3:10; cf. 2 Kings 7:2) is mentioned more than once. The language of Ezek 1:1 later became of great importance in late Judaism (3 *Macc* 6:18; *Apoc of Baruch* 22:1; *Test of Levi* 2:6, 18:6, cf. 5:1; *Test of Judah* 24:2) and in the New Testament (Mt 3:16 et par.; Acts 7:56; 10:11; Rev 4:1). The opening of heaven can then have as a consequence that human beings on earth can see directly into the heavenly mystery (Acts 7:56; Rev 4:1) and also that a heavenly figure leaves heaven and comes down to earth in order to meet man, such as is described in Ezek 1:4ff.

The statement that Ezekiel saw "heavenly visions" leaves all further eventualities quite open. The feminine noun מַרְאָה (plural מַרְאוֹת), which is found eleven times in the Old Testament (Ex 38:8 with the meaning "mirror"), describes a particular experience of prophetic revelation (Nu 12:6), which 1 Sam 3:15, however, can also describe as an event solely concerned with the receiving of a message. References such as Ezek 11:24; 43:3; Dan 9:23; 10:1, where the masculine מַרְאֶה occurs in a similar usage, show that uncertainty existed in the Massoretic definition of the two forms. Dan 10:7 says of the מראה: "I, Daniel, alone saw the מראה, but the men who were with me did not see the מראה. Great fear, however, fell upon them, so that they fled in order to hide (with emended text)."[70] A מראה accordingly is clearly raised above the perception of ordinary men. It is a supernatural vision, only given to someone especially chosen. The opening of heaven is therefore, through the use of the term מַרְאָה, also distinguished from ordinary everyday events and subordinated to the prophetic experience.[71] In Ezekiel it is also striking that the word only appears in the plural, and apart from the textually uncertain reference in 43:3, only in the combination מראות אלהים (1:1; 8:3; 40:2). As in the term "night visions" (מַרְאֹת הלילה Gen 46:2), which likewise only appears in the plural, it seems to represent a fixed usage. אלהים appears in the

---

zum Neuen Testament aus Talmud und Midrasch 2 (München: Beck, ²1957), 742.

68   W. F. Andrae, *Das Gotteshaus und die Urformen des Bauens im alten Orient*, Studien zur Bauforschung, ed. by the Koldeway Society, Pt. 2 (Berlin: Schötz, 1930).

69   See Gerhard von Rad, *TWNT* 5, 501–509; T. Flügge, *Die Vorstellung über den Himmel im AT*, Un-

pub. Diss. (Königsberg, 1937).

70   Cf. Acts 9:7.

71   Cf. Mark 1:10 against Luke 3:21.

book of Ezekiel, apart from the covenant formula (יהוה] אלהי ישראל] 8:4; 9:3; 10:19f; 11:22; 43:2 [44:2]; 11:20; 14:11; 34:24; אהיה [והייתי] להם לאלהים 37:23[26]; 36:28 אהיה לכם לאלהים; the suffixed form of the second person plural 20:5, 7, 19, 20; 34:31; the third person plural 28:26; 34:30; 39:22, 28), only in formulas of a pre-Yahwistic stamp (גן אלהים 28:13; 31:8f; 28:2a מושב אלהים; 28:16 הר אלהים; הר קדש 28:14 רוח אלהים; 11:24 אלהים) or in language which is mythologically colored (28:2b, 6). In free formulations of his own Ezekiel uses the name Yahweh. Hence, in the references to seeing visions of God or of being caught up in "divine visions," we are dealing with a technical expression of an old school of seers.

■ **1:3b** The formulation with Yahweh in the statement of v 3b "And the hand of Yahweh came upon me" must also have belonged to the language of the prophetic schools. Besides the vivid description of the rending of the heavens and the vision thereby made possible, we also find here the description of a more personal experience in the prophet's being seized by the hand of Yahweh.

In about 200 references the Old Testament speaks of the hand of Yahweh, either with the construct formation יד יהוה, or with the suffixed or absolute use of יד. Besides the simple description of a gesture such as "to raise the hand" = "to swear an oath" (cf. 20:5f) these are especially references which point to particular acts of Yahweh. In this connection the references to the deliverance wrought in the exodus from Egypt ביד רמה (cf. to 20:33f alongside ביד חזקה ובזרוע נטויה Ex 14:8) belong to the old religious language of Israel. We may question whether the strong emphasis of the Old Testament references to the hand and arm of Yahweh took their origin in the exodus narratives in which the outstretched arms of Yahweh and Moses are so important. The hand is the means by which Yahweh demonstrates the power of his promises in history (cf. the double reference דבר בפיו and בידו מלא 1 Kings 8:15, 24; 2 Chr 6:4, 15). So this form of speech reappears in a more somber tone in the prophetic threats (Is 5:25; 9:11, 16, 20; 10:4). It is voiced in a number of verbal formulations. First of all Yahweh himself is named as subject. He "puts his hand" (נתן ב Ex 7:4), "stretches out his hand" (נטה על Ezek 6:14), "brings back his hand" (השיב על Is 1:25), waves it (הניף על Is 11:15, as a noun Is 19:16). The hand of Yahweh can be an entity by itself and accorded a vitality of its own. It is active in the great works of creation: it stretches out the sky (Is 45:12), establishes the earth (Is 48:13), pierces the dragon (Job 26:13, cf. Is 51:9 of the arm of Yahweh). It acts in history, where it "strikes" (נגע ב 1 Sam 6:9), "takes" (לקח Amos 9:2), "comes upon" man (יצא ב Ruth 1:13, היה ב Ex 9:3; Dtn 2:15). In this connection emphasis may be given to the force with which it comes upon man. It may "lie heavy upon" man (כבד אל 1 Sam 5:6); its "removal" (סור מן 1 Sam 6:3) means "the removal of a burden" (הקל מן 1 Sam 6:5, said of Yahweh). Besides these there are positive references which show the power of this hand to protect (Is 49:2 כסה בצל יד, בצל ידו החביא Is 51:16). In the fifth century the references to "the good hand of God upon me" become a formula of pious speech (Ezra 7:6, 9 and other passages; Neh 2:8, 18).

From these general expressions the more particular prophetic form of speech arises which seeks to describe Yahweh's taking hold of the prophet and empowering of him by reference to the coming of Yahweh's hand upon him. Since, in these formulations the name of יהוה is always used, and never that of אלהים, unlike in the earlier reference to מראות אלהים, we are undoubtedly faced with a genuinely Israelite formulation. This may support the conjecture that the origin of this striking form of speech lies in the imagery of the exodus tradition. According to 1 Kings 18:46 Elijah was empowered by Yahweh's hand to run from Carmel to Jezreel alongside Ahab's chariot, which was clearly an unprecedented achievement.[72] 2 Kings 3:15f is the first reference to Yahweh's hand empowering a prophet to give an oracle (ותהי עליו יד יהוה ויאמר כה אמר יהוה). The text is particularly striking on account of its reference to the coming of the hand and word of Yahweh as though they were aroused in an almost technical way by the playing of a musician. Being seized by the hand of Yahweh and the disclosure of the word of God are also connected in Is 8:11, a text which clearly shows in

---

72 "And the hand of the Lord was on Elijah" (ויד יהוה היתה אל אליהו). Should על be read? 𝔊 ἐπί.

its formulation (בחזקת היד ויסרני מלכת) something of the fearful strength of the divine grip which shook the prophet. Most of all the direct physical pain of isolation from other men under the hand of Yahweh is given expression in the confessions of Jeremiah (Jer 15:17). At the same time it is clear that what it meant for a person to be held "by the hand of Yahweh" lay in the receipt of Yahweh's word (cf. Jer 15:16), which, because it was a message of judgement, prohibited any spontaneous freedom of conversation with other persons (מפני ידך בדד ישבתי כי זעם מלאתני Jer 15:17). A comparison with the reference in the Psalms to the weight of Yahweh's hand (32:4), which appears to be closely related, clearly shows the distinctive character of the prophetic experience of the hand of Yahweh.[73]

Besides these four references outside the book of Ezekiel, which although few in number are in each case important, describing the experience of Yahweh in terms of his hand, there are in the book itself no less than seven passages which use this form of expression (1:3; 3:14, 22; 8:1; 33:22; 37:1; 40:1).[74] We immediately notice the comparatively greater freedom with which Ezekiel uses the language of earlier prophetic schools. Five times Ezekiel formulates his message with the use of the verb היה על. In 3:14 the heavy pressure of Yahweh's hand is emphasized by the use of the root חזק, which also occurs in Is 8:11. When we find a reference in 8:1 to the hand of Yahweh "falling" (נפל) upon the prophet we are reminded of the language used of Yahweh's spirit, which, according to 11:5, falls upon the prophet. The two ways of speaking of men being seized by the power of God, which have different origins, come in substance very close to each other.[75] Judg 3:10 and 11:29 speak of the coming of the spirit in a way which is otherwise used of the hand of Yahweh (היה על).

In content we can see that the reference to Yahweh's hand coming upon the prophet is found in the introduction to the accounts of the four great visions of the book (1:3; 8:1; 37:1; 40:1), and also in 3:14 at the end of such an account. 3:22, where a short command to the prophet follows his being seized by Yahweh's hand, introduces, according to 𝔐, a vision.[76] 33:22 separates the coming of Yahweh's hand from the actual receiving of his word. In all this it is quite clear that for Ezekiel being seized by the hand of Yahweh meant more than simply his reception of the divine message. It was a submission in which among other things the receiving of the divine word took place, but which, as in 3:14f, could also have as a consequence a week long period of dumbness. The receiving of a message in which visionary and trance-like features are lacking is never introduced by the reference to the hand of Yahweh. From this fresh support is given for the separation of v 3b from the formula for the receiving of Yahweh's word in v 3a and for its connection with the account of a vision which follows in 1:4ff.

The reference to seeing divine visions (1:1) before the reference to being seized by Yahweh's hand (1:3b) may arouse suspicion. 40:1f shows exactly the reverse sequence; also in 8:1f what is seen follows the seizure by Yahweh's hand. If this difficulty is not removed by accepting the explanation of a subsequent expansion of the text, we can point to the fact that 1:1 certainly has the function of a superscription. Thus the objective statement about the opening of heaven and the seeing of visions of God stands at the beginning, and the reference to the coming of the hand of Yahweh, which is subjective to the prophet, follows after. In 8:1ff and 40:1ff, which do not have this significance as an introduction and so say nothing about the rending of the heavens, there is a more natural sequence of the two statements. Under the hand of Yahweh which comes upon him, the prophet sees 'divine visions' which are recounted in what follows.

■ **1:4** For the divine vision of the prophet we have shown in the preliminary remarks that a throne scene is described, which is followed by the commissioning

73 Gerhard von Rad, "Die Konfessionen Jeremias," *EvTh* 3 (1936): 265–276.

74 Dürr, *Apokalyptik*, 23f; Paul Volz, *Der Geist Gottes und die verwandten Erscheinungen im Alten Testament und im anschliessenden Judentum* (Tübingen: Mohr [Siebeck], 1910), p. 70 note 1.

75 Volz, *Geist Gottes*, speaks of entering into a trance-like state.

76 But see on the text.

of the prophet.[77] The introductory words "And when I looked, behold, a storm came from the north, a great cloud of flashing fire. And out of its midst there appeared the form of four living creatures . . ." clearly show that not everything had been said in the account of the throne-vision, which itself arose out of the occurrence of a storm.

O. Procksch, "Berufungsvision," believed that it was possible to find the basis of Ezek 1 in a natural experience. On a midsummer evening after a thunderstorm, the sun breaking out from behind a bank of clouds formed for Ezekiel the picture which he describes in ch. 1. Such a reference to the natural basis of the experience, however, certainly does not cover the emphasis which the prophet himself makes in the narrative. We must rather recognize that Ezekiel, in recounting the visionary experience of a storm that came to him and in which God's glory appeared to him, uses the language of early Israelite tradition in order to give expression to the unprecedented experience which overtook him.

The throne-vision of 1 Kings 22 leads us to think of Yahweh's sitting on a throne in heaven. Is 6, however, proclaims the mystery of Yahweh's throne in the chosen sanctuary in Jerusalem, at the place where the ark was kept (Ps 132). In this tension between the heavenly throne and the chosen earthly throne we see a vital tension of Old Testament faith.[78] Within the framework of this faith there is not properly room for a manifestation of Yahweh's throne at a distance from the place of the ark, in the midst of an unclean land (Amos 7:17, cf. the comments on Ezek 4:12–15).

However, we must consider whether the belief in Yahweh's dwelling on Zion is a late feature in the faith of Israel. It first became effective as a consequence of the belief in the election of David and his house, which was proclaimed in the prophecy of Nathan (2 Sam 7).[79] In its early history Israel knew of a period of wandering during which Yahweh had accompanied his people

in a cloud, and when they had encountered him at the mount of God in storm and thunder (Ex 19f). When Israel settled in Canaan it could describe the manifestation of Yahweh in a storm cloud from the south, occurring at a time of great danger (Judg 5:4f; Ps 68:8f; Dtn 33:2). Still in David's time Israel experienced Yahweh's coming in a storm wind to help his people fighting against the Philistines (2 Sam 5:24). This belief in the manifestation of Yahweh in a storm cloud also remained alive when the memory of Mount Sinai as the mount of God became less strong. Ps 18:10–12 describes Yahweh's help for his king: "He bowed the sky and came down, with dark clouds under his feet. He rode on a cherub and flew; he came swiftly on the wings of the wind, round about him as his tent were dark water and clouds."

The book of Ezekiel makes it sufficiently clear that the prophet came from a circle of faith which, like Is 6, knew of Yahweh as enthroned in the temple of Jerusalem. The unprecedented feature of this faith in Yahweh's appearing at a place of prayer in an unclean land of exile could only have become real for him through the form of a storm-theophany. In this way the appearence of God granted to him takes on the features of the great divine appearances recorded in the venerable earlier tradition. Babylonian tradition need not have come into it here.[80] The divine encounter in a storm is an old Israelite feature, and the vision of the enthroned deity, with features which strongly recall Is 6, derives from Jerusalem.

We must still question the derivation of the references to Yahweh's coming "from the north," which is in opposition to all Israelite tradition. It has been pointed out that the journey made by those taken into exile led first into Northern Syria, from there across to the Euphrates, and then along the Euphrates southwards (more precisely southeastwards). Thus Yahweh's coming followed this direction exactly (Bertholet-Galling). Procksch, however, in connection with his par-

---

77 See pp. 108f.
78 See above p. 116 and see also the statement in Solomon's dedicatory prayer for the temple in 1 Kings 8, and in another way Ps 50:1–3.
79 Hans-Joachim Kraus, *Die Königsherrschaft Gottes im Alten Testament*, BHTh 13 (Tübingen: Mohr [Siebeck], 1951).
80 Contra Dürr, *Ezekiels Vision*, 8–13.

ticular interpretation, thought of the sun breaking through the clouds in the northwestern sky. More correctly, however, we must think here of a belief in the mountain of God in the north, which ultimately stems from Babylonian mythology.[81] This is to be found in the Old Testament, not only in the geography of paradise (Gen 2:10ff), but also Is 14:13 and possibly in the historicized reference to the enemy from the north summoned by Yahweh in Jeremiah, Zephaniah and Ezek 38f. It had led, in the Jerusalem temple theology, to the formula "Mount Zion far in the north" (Ps 48:3). This formulation shows more clearly than any other that the concrete geographical conception in the reference is quite secondary. A direct influence upon Ezekiel from his Babylonian surroundings must be ruled out in this reference, since it must already have been current in the time when Ezekiel was still in Jerusalem. That the manifestation came "from the north" says nothing more, therefore, than the reference to the opening up of the sky. The phenomenon came from Yahweh's abode.

■ **1:5** From the cloud-covered fire of the storm theophany (cf. Ex 24:16f, 40:34f?) the glory of the enthroned deity appeared, which the prophet begins to describe from the bottom upwards. He first of all saw "something like four creatures. And this was their appearance: they looked like a human being." חיה used in the singular usually signifies "a dangerous animal, untamed, living free, and usually large" (Koehler-Baumgartner). So 5:17; 14:15; 34:25 חיה רעה; 29:5 חית הארץ; 31:6 and elsewhere חית השדה. The plural usage with this meaning is rare (only Is 35:9; Ps 104:25; Dan 8:4) and in any case cannot be adduced for Ezek 1–3. Rather the use of חיות in Ezek 1–3 is to be regarded as a general designation for living creatures, deliberately left vague, and the fuller definition of them consists in the reference to their human form.

As is shown by what follows, the creatures had the task of bearing Yahweh's throne (although this is never actually said in explicit terms). None of the accounts of the appearance of Yahweh's glory in the desert era (Ex 16:7, 10; 24:16f; 33:22; 40:34f; Lev 9:6, 23; Nu 14:10; 16:19; 17:7; 20:6—mostly P) mentions the presence of creatures who bear the divine throne. Ps 18:11, however, mentions the movement of Yahweh upon the cherubim. This is plainly close to what is said in Yahweh's divine title ישב הכרבים, which points back to the tradition of the ark (1 Sam 4:4; 2 Sam 6:2 and elsewhere). In Ezek 10 the later editorial work of the "school" takes up this tradition and in 10:20 expressly identifies the living creature(s) with the cherubim. Ezek 1, on the contrary, is striking for its careful avoidance of any such closer definition of the creatures who bear the throne. Any further speculation about the place of such mediating creatures, which became prominent in later Judaism, is far removed from the reference here.

Nevertheless, a definite stylizing in the presentation of these mediating creatures cannot be denied, any more than can the dependence upon the description of the seraphim of Is 6, which we have already established. Where Isaiah spoke of an indefinite number of seraphim, each of which had six wings, we can see clearly in Ezekiel the importance of the number four. This also appears elsewhere in Ezekiel (ch. 8 four acts of sin; 14:12ff four plagues; 47:1ff a fourfold measurement). Four is the number of totality: from the four points of the compass the breath of Yahweh's power comes, which restores the dead to life (37:9). The four horns of Zech 2:1ff are symbols of the power of earthly empires, and the four smiths who are summoned against them represent the totality of opposition appointed by Yahweh. The four world eras of Dan 2 and 7 represent the whole of human history which is still to run, from Nebuchadnezzar to its end. The Priestly Document, in its outline of world history, has in mind a scheme of four periods, such as is to be found in the framework of cyclic thought and in its most elaborate form in the Hindu doctrine of the four Jugas of a Kalpa.[82] In Ezekiel therefore the four creatures who bear Yahweh's throne give expression to the omnipotence of Yahweh which is effective in every direction, like the four chariots from "the Lord of the whole earth" of Zech 6:5.

■ **1:6b** In this way Ezekiel also gives expression to the importance of complete equilibrium which is expressed in the number four, in that he sees the creatures as

81 See Aarre Lauha, *ZAPHON, Der Norden und die Nordvölker im Alten Testament* (Helsinki: Der Finnischen Literaturgesellschaft, 1943).

82 See Helmuth von Glasenapp, *Der Hinduismus* (München: Kurt Wolff, 1922), 231f. For the number four see also Knut Tallquist, *Himmelsgegenden und Winde,*

having four wings, unlike those in the vision of Is 6. Later presentations, such as that given in the Vatican Kosmas manuscript, have not always preserved this distinction.[83] The visualizing of the four-winged creatures was certainly anticipated by some representations in the religious art of Mesopotamia.[84] In the Solomonic temple, however, the cherubim which protected the ark appear to have had only two wings.[85]

In the positions of the two pairs of wings there are connections with Is 6, but also some differences. The statement that each seraph covered "his feet" with two of them shows us how the heavenly servants hid their private parts from the Holy One. The euphemistic use of the word רגל for "private parts" is also found in Ex 4:25; Is 7:20 and in the usage הסך רגלים Ju 3:24; 1 Sam 24:4 (Gesenius-Buhl, Zorell; Koehler-Baumgartner differently). For the covering of the "private parts" before the Holy One cf. Ex 28:42 (cf. 20:26). Ezek 1:11, however, speaks of the covering of the entire body to hide the whole creature from the Almighty. Does this reflect the covering of the faces of Is 6? Throughout the whole account in Is 6 there is a tension between holiness and uncleanness, whilst in Ezekiel, as 1:28 and 2:1 show, the tension is that between creator and creature, master and servant. According to Is 6:2 the pair of outstretched wings were used normally for flight. Ezek 1, in its more elaborate statements, avoids any open affirmation of the flight of the creatures, although 1:24 and 3:13 mention the beating of the wings and 1:24b (25b) adds a reference to the lowering of the wings. The movement of the wings has become hardened into a particular ceremonial attitude, even in the basic text. This attitude characterizes the two-winged cherubim over the ark of the temple of Solomon, according to 1 Kings 6:27 נגעת כנף אל כנף. Admittedly we cannot deny that Ezekiel must have had in mind the forms of the temple furnishings in his description of the exalted throne. The stylizing into four creatures with four wings must then be pecul-

iar to him. The description of the divine phenomenon breaking through the clouds in full movement thereby takes on an aspect of hieratic rigidity and ornamental fixity which distinguished it from the lively mobility of the figures of Is 6. It is altogether unthinkable therefore that one of the creatures could deal directly with the prophet, as the seraph does in Is 6.

■**1:12** This aspect of solemn and mysterious rigidity reappears again in the description of the movement of the creatures: "And each went straight-forward; they did not turn in their movement." This statement, if it really belongs to the original text,[86] is not an attempt to explain the method of the creatures' forward movement, since such general references, which are not directly concerned with the situation but which are interested in the nature of the whole phenomenon, belong to the interpretative editorial work. In its original connection this statement must relate closely to the immediate event and describe the approach of the theophany towards the prophet. Each of the four creatures had its face turned towards him; each travelled straight forward, and none of them turned from the path which led directly to the prophet. Irresistably they came towards him, so that in the overall picture of the phenomenon no creature moved out of its proper position.

■**1:13** V 13 adds more precisely a feature which has already appeared in the summary description at the beginning (v 4): "and between the living creatures it appeared as if fiery coals were burning. And the fire glowed, and out of the fire appeared flashes of lightning." The elements of this description are already found in Ex 19: fire (Ex 19:18); lightning (Ex 19:16). The burning coals appear in Ps 18:9 (2 Sam 22:9) in what is perhaps a secondary addition to the fire of the divine manifestation. We cannot, however, ignore the fact that not all the objections against the originality of v 13aαb can be refuted. The exact position of the fire, which is described more precisely as burning coals,

---

StOr 2 (Helsinki, 1928), 105–185; Dürr, *Ezekiels Vision*, 58f.

83 Neuss, *Buch*, figs. 11f.

84 Cf. the reliefs from Nimrud (*AOBAT* 380; *ANEP* 651, 656), the Assyrian bronze statuette of the storm demon Pazuzu (*AOBAT* 383; *ANEP* 659), and the form on the right-hand side of the tree of life (*ANEP* 654) from Tel Halaf.

85 1 Kings 6:24, 27—under the influence of Egyptian practice? Cf. *AOBAT* 391, 497.

86 See above pp. 103f.

between the living creatures appears somewhat pedantic beside the statement in v 4 and recalls the more technical interest of the additions. Further it is relevant that 1:13 cannot be separated from 10:2 where there is a reference to the scattering of the burning coals which were between the cherubim. The analysis of 10:2 (see below) shows it to be an older part of ch 10 which has been much expanded by elements drawn from ch. 1. The relation between chs. 10 and 1 has clearly been established by means of the bridge 1:13/10:2. In this connection the question arises from ch. 10 whether the connecting reference in 1:13 already existed before the elaboration of ch. 10 into its present form or whether it was not first introduced for the purpose of establishing a bridge to 10:2 in ch. 1. Thus in the examination of ch. 10 we must refer back to 1:13, which simply repeats the statements of 1:4 in a more concrete form and introduces nothing that is particularly new into the description of the divine manifestation.

■ **1:22** "Over the heads of the living creatures was something like a fixed platform, shining like crystal." Once again the original text, unlike the expansion in v 22b which thinks of the fixed platform as resting on the heads of the living creatures, refuses to enter into a more detailed description of the technical disposition of the creatures and the throne which was set over them. In רקיע there lies the idea of compactness, firmness, from the etymology of the root (רקע = "to stamp, beat hard"; piʿel "to hammer flat" [of metalwork]). In all the other Old Testament references (Gen 1 *passim*; Ps 19:2; 150:1; Dan 12:3 [Sir 43:8]) the noun is related to the vault of heaven.[87] Thus here also the conception of the deity enthroned upon the splendor of the floor of heaven has entered into the description of the glory of Yahweh's appearing. קֶרַח signifies in Job 6:16, 37:10 "ice"; in Ps 147:17; Job 38:29 "hail"; Gen 31:40; Jer 36:30 "frost." The word, however, must also have signified crystal, as 𝕲 translates κρύσταλλος which is more suitable here as a description of the heavenly splendor. Ex 24:10 supports the view that the reference to Yahweh's being enthroned above the splendor of heaven represents a very

ancient Israelite tradition.

■ **1:26** The mention of the actual throne follows in v 26 (cf. Ex 24:10f, unlike 1 Kings 22 and Is 6 where it is missing): "And behold, above the fixed platform there was an appearance like sapphire stone, something like a throne." The comparison with sapphire or more accurately perhaps lapis lazuli (Koehler-Baumgartner), which was reckoned in antiquity by the Greeks and Romans as sapphire, is connected in Ex 24:10 with the ground under Yahweh's feet. (Does this mean that Yahweh was thought to be seated with "a footstool beneath his feet," as in the Jerusalem conception? Cf. Ps 99:5; 132:7; and also Is 66:1). Ezek 1:26 makes the comparison with the throne itself. Above the transparent crystal of the heavenly platform was the light blue of the divine throne.

On the throne a human figure was to be seen. The restraint in the description can be seen in the succession of phrases denoting approximate similarity (דמות כמראה אדם).

■ **1:27** The following description, giving just outlines and impressions of color, is to be understood against the background of ancient Near Eastern imagery, such as we find very impressively in the colored ceramics of the god Asshur from Qalʿat Šerqāt (the period of Tukulti-Ninurta II, 890–884 B.C.).[88] The form of god is seen emerging from the flaming disc of the sun and appears from the waist upwards with well-defined contours. The rays and flames of the sun's disc are shown in a mixture of yellow and blue tones, and the whole is framed by the edge of the sun's disc and its rays. Similarly in the description of Ezek 1 the upper half of the figure, from the waist upwards, is different from the lower half. Whether only the upper half was clearly recognized is not entirely clear in the original text of Ezek 1. Undoubtedly the addition of 27aα, which is still lacking in 𝕲, was intended to supplement this. In doing so it cut across the difference in the appearance of the two halves of the body in that it introduced fire, which belongs to the lower half of the body, into the upper half. The original text spoke of the splendor of חשמל, which 𝕲 translates by ἤλεκτρον-electrum. This refers to a bright mixture of gold and silver.[89] G. R.

---

87   Cf. to 1:1.
88   Cf. *AOBAT* 333; *ANEP* 536.
89   Koehler-Baumgartner, following Alfred Lucas,

Ancient Egyptian Materials (New York: Longmans, Green, 1926), 84–86.

Driver, however, conjectures that חשמל is to be connected with the Akkadian *elmešu* and is to be understood as brass.[90] Less probable is his connection of the following כמראה אש בית לה סביב with the dome of a brassfounder's furnace, comparing it with the Akkadian *bît kûri*, out of which the glowing metal could be seen. Since Driver starts uncritically from 𝔐, which is not supported here by 𝔊, and since nothing in the text points to a comparison with metal in a molten state, the interpretation as electrum still appears as the more probable. This is also true on the other hand against the interpretation cited by W. A. Irwin from G. G. Cameron, which takes חשמל as inlay, or overlay, from the Elamite *is-malu*; Old Persian *išmaruv*; Akkadian *ešmaru*.[91] In particular the interpretation of the preceding עין as "eye," in which the appearance of the inlay which stands out from its setting is compared to the brightness of an eye looking out from its socket, falls down in that עין in the (secondary) verses 7 and 16 is used directly in contexts which preclude such an interpretation.

■**1:28** The whole figure, in which the lower half merges into the background without clear delineation, like that of the figure of Asshur on the illustration referred to, is surrounded by a rainbow-colored circle (half-circle?) of light, like the latter. That this reflects something of the idea of the beneficent significance of the rainbow, shown in Gen 9:12–17 (P), is improbable.[92] With a conclusion which is almost didactic in tone and which recalls the ending of certain legal formulations regarding priests (Lev 7:37; 11:46; 12:7b; 13:59; 14:32, 54ff; 15:32f; 26:46; 27:34) the description of the theophany which the prophet saw is rounded off: "This was the appearance of the form of Yahweh's glory." This leaves the way open for the reaction of the

prophet, which corresponds with that which also occurs frequently in descriptions of the Priestly Document of the appearance of the כבוד יהוה to the wandering people (Lev 9:24; Nu 16:22; 17:10; 20:6; cf. Ex 34:8[J]): "Then I fell down upon my face." This act of abasement is that of a person who is overwhelmed by the divine majesty, in a way rather different from Is 6, where it is that of a person who is conscious of his impurity and sin and who is overwhelmed by the splendor of the divine holiness.

The expression כבוד יהוה, which is the technical term for the appearance of Yahweh in light, is used here for the first time in Ezekiel.[93] The word כבוד, which appears overall nineteen times in the book of Ezekiel, basically means "weighty, heavy" in a quite objective sense, and so the weightiness of a person or thing. Thus it can have a quite secular meaning. כבוד is wealth (Gen 31:1—the cattle of Jacob), or honor (Gen 45:13—the high position of Joseph). Ezek 31:18 is the only reference in the book where כבוד occurs in this secular sense, where it denotes the position of honor of the king of Egypt, represented by the form of a tree of paradise.[94] However, כבוד can also be used of Yahweh, and we must examine whether the transition to this way of speaking has taken place primarily from the direct meaning of the word כבוד as something weighty, powerful, as in Ps 29 where we see quite impressively the power of the coming of the כבוד יהוה in thunder, fire and earthquake (cf. Ezek 43:2b), or whether the transition has taken place from the metaphorical use of the word. In this case the expression must point to the glory and honor manifesting themselves in history and creation. In the book of Ezekiel this extended meaning is only to be found in 39:21, where Yahweh, through his power (ידי) and judgement (משפטי), dem-

90   Driver, "Inaugural."
91   William A. Irwin, "Hashmal," *VT* 2 (1952): 169–170; G. G. Cameron, *Persepolis Treasury Tablets*, University of Chicago Oriental Institute Publications 65 (Chicago: University of Chicago Press, 1948), 129–130.
92   Cf. Meinrad Schumpp, *Das Buch Ezechiel übersetzt und erklärt*, Herders Bibelkommentar (Freiburg: Herder, 1942): "Its appearance was surrounded by the sign of peace, the rainbow..."
93   See Bernhard Stein, *Der Begriff kᵉbod jahwe und seine Bedeutung für die alttestamentliche Gotteserkenntnis* (Ems-

detten: Lechte, 1939), especially 265–290 for Ezekiel; Gerhard von Rad, "δόξα (c כבוד im A.T.)," *TWNT* 2, 240–245.
94   Cf. the verbal usage in 27:25.

onstrates his glory to all the nations by punishing Israel, and then delivering and rescuing it from the threat of destruction by Gog.[95] The innermost kernel of the כבוד sayings, however, is represented in the tradition which we possess almost exclusively in references of a priestly character (P and Ezekiel), which speak of the כבוד יהוה and in which כבוד is not used as an attribute of Yahweh, but where the כבוד יהוה denotes the personal presence of the deity in light. The characteristic feature of the view of the Priestly Document, according to which the כבוד יהוה has the form of a fiery manifestation of light, has already been referred to in connection with 1:4. This manifestation of light was reflected in the shining face of Moses when he descended from the mountain (Ex 34:29–35), but was normally veiled from the eyes of men by means of the cloud which hid it. The human form of the כבוד יהוה is never mentioned in the Priestly Document. In the book of Ezekiel, which refers to the appearance of this glory of Yahweh in sixteen further passages (כבוד יהוה 1:28; 3:12, 23; 10:4 twice, 18; 11:23; 43:4f; 44:4; כבוד אלהי ישראל 8:4; 9:3; 10:19; 11:22; 43:2; הכבוד used absolutely 3:23), we must question, on the basis of the statement in 1:28, whether the glory refers to the entire manifestation which is described in v 5ab. 3:12 (23? cf. on the text); 8:4; 11:23, which refer briefly to the standing still or the rising up of the כבוד יהוה, may point to this understanding. Besides these, however, there are other references, all belonging to later additions, which mention the presence of the כבוד אלהי ישראל above the creatures which are described as cherubim (10:19; 11:22) or of a rising up of the כבוד יהוה (or אלהי ישראל) from his chariot (9:3; 10:4). It is not impossible, even though it cannot be demonstrated with certainty, that the original presentation by the prophet intended the whole phenomenon to be understood by the term כבוד יהוה. If an ultimate uncertainty remains here, it is at least clear from Ezek 1 that the prophet, in his encounter with the glory of Yahweh in the land to which he had been exiled, experienced something which shattered all his expectations and which also, of necessity, decisively determined his subsequent preaching. No vague presence of deity passed him by, but Yahweh, the God of Israel, in the glory of the כבוד יהוה met him as he had met with Israel in the great events of the wilderness period, as recalled in the related Priestly view of the nation's past history. Thus the whole of Ezekiel's preaching necessarily became a witness to the God of Israel who encountered his people in his own freedom.

The Expansion of the Account of the Vision of God by the School of Ezekiel

The account of the divine manifestation is now preserved for us in a form which has been heavily commented upon and which has been expanded in the circles of the school who transmitted Ezekiel's words. The catchphrases "redaction" or "gloss" do not rightly describe this elaboration. In this process it is not literary tendencies or simply attempts at artistic embellishment which have been at work. Rather we must see here a serious effort to grasp the meaning of what was revealed to the prophet by Yahweh and an attempt at further clarification. This further development of the "tradition" of the message in the prophetic book itself is an indication of its genuinely historical character, which continued to be influential in the "school" of Ezekiel. It was not something accomplished all at once, but clearly took the form of a gradual expansion of the text, accomplished in separate phases, of which the last remnants can be traced in the period of the translation into Greek.[96]

The study of ch. 1 shows that further interpretation has taken place by means of very broad additions to the description of the phenomena underneath the divine throne, in contrast to which any description of the divine form itself is completely lacking, apart from the brief comment in v $27a\alpha^2$. This latter additional comment also contains some slight clarification regarding color. This distinction between the broad commentary upon the features underneath the manifestation and the complete reserve regarding further elaboration of the actual figure of God and his throne, is illuminated significantly by the following statement in the Talmud: "R. Aha b. Jacob said: there is another heaven, which is found over the heads of the creatures, for it says: and above the heads of the creatures there was something

---

95 Cf. the verbal usage in 39:13 and also 28:22, where Yahweh glorifies himself in his judgement upon Tyre.

96 On this whole process see especially Mowinckel, *Prophecy*.

124

like a platform, like awesome crystal. This much it is permitted to you to say, but to speak further is not permitted to you, for it says in the book of Ben Sira: Seek not after that which is hidden from you, meditate not upon that which is veiled from you. Apply yourself to things which are permitted to you, and do not concern yourself with mysteries." [97] The nature of the expansions in Ezek 1 shows that even the elaboration of the prophetic word, even though it appears quite free in its detailed references, consciously stood within an order which it could not easily overstep.

■ **1:4b** First of all the whole picture of the storm theophany has been expanded in v 4b by the remark "out of its midst (there shone) something like the appearance of electrum," which is dependent on the feminine אֵשׁ. This comment plainly intends to point, in the first account of the theophany, to the divine figure in the midst of it whose upper body shone like electrum (v 27) and so also to connect the flaming fire of v 4 with that of v 27. The artistic structure of the original description, which intentionally moves from the lesser features of the divine manifestation to its center, is thereby disturbed. The concern in the addition to point as quickly as possible to the center and subject of the manifestation is therefore unmistakable. At a later time the reference to the surrounding (rainbow-like) splendor has been taken over word for word from the description of the divine appearance in v 27 and related to the masculine עָנָן. The aura surrounding the human figure has become that surrounding the cloud. The purpose of this addition lies along the same line as that mentioned first.

■ **1:6a** The expansions which are to be found in vv 6a, 7–11a, in the description of the living creatures of vv 5–12, have gone deeper and have broken up the related statements of the original text about the four wings (vv 6b, 11) in an awkward way. The entire disordered listing of the features (6a faces, 6b wings, 7 feet, 8a hands, 8b faces [wings], 9a disposition of wings, 9b

manner of movement, 10 faces, 11 disposition of wings) makes it impossible that this took place all at once. We must rather reckon with successive stages of growth. The latest features (v 9a which anticipates v 11b and isolated words in vv 6, 8, 11) can be recognized with the help of 𝕲. For the rest no chronological stratification can now be given. The features are therefore only referred to according to their content.

The most striking expansion lies in the statement about the four faces of the creatures, which is made in v 6a and which is developed in v 10 remarkably late. How is it to be understood? Unlike the features of the original throne vision no genuine Israelite tradition which could have led to this can be recognized. S. Landersdorfer has sought to adduce proof that the creatures with four faces had their precursors in the illegal cult images of Micah (Judg 17f) and Manasseh (2 Chr 33:7), with which we must connect the representation of the Phoenician Baal which Elijah opposed. [98] The small textual basis of the Peshitta tradition of 2 Chron 33:7, however, together with some accounts of Talmudic and post-Christian Greek evidence, is certainly not sufficient to support the far-reaching conclusions of Landersdorfer.

In the comparative material from the ancient Near East set out by Dürr, he shows that divine beings with four faces cannot be shown to have existed in Mesopotamia before Ezekiel. [99] The closest to it are certain Egyptian representations of the sun as a four-headed ram, the four heads of the god of the North Wind, and of the he-goat from Mendes ("Thou who hast four heads on thy neck"). In 1929 in the excavations of robbers at Ištšali near to ancient Ešnunna two bronze statuettes of a god with four faces and a goddess were discovered. The statuettes, which according to H. Frankfort stem from the time of Hammurabi, represent deities, the god standing and the goddess seated on a throne, with a human face on each side. [100] In Ezek 1 it is significant for biblical thought that speculative

97 *b Ḥagigah* 13a to Ezek 1. After Lazarus Goldschmidt, *Der babylonische Talmud neu übertragen durch L. Goldschmidt* (Berlin: Biblion, 1929–1936).

98 Landersdorfer, *Der BAAΛ*.

99 Dürr, *Ezekiels Vision*, § 5 "The Motif of the 'Four Faces' of the Cherub," 54–60.

100 H. Frankfort, *More Sculpture from the Diyala Region*, OIP 40 (Chicago: University of Chicago Press,

1943), pp. 21f to numbers 338 and 339, plates 77–81.

elaboration has taken place only on the creatures who bear the throne and not on the figure of Yahweh himself.

If v 12 abβ is reckoned as a statement of the original text, which, however, has a certain amount of linguistic evidence against it, then perhaps we can see in this verse the starting-point for the elaboration. We regarded the sentence as properly understood in the context of the original text as a description of the "direct" approach of the entire phenomenon towards the prophet. If this was so, then the reflection of the "school" may have found in it a general remark, which was unrelated to the immediate situation, about the manner of the creatures' movement. On the assumption that they each had four faces, one pointing in each direction, each moving straight forwards, the question of the manner of its movement was answered. The still later interpretation given in 10:11 shows how a further factor arose almost of necessity to subsequent reflection, viz. the idea of a "leading face" (הראש), which as chief undertook to lead the faces depending on the direction in which they were to go. The idea of four faces always going straightforwards thus led to a peculiar manner of movement in which the direction was always towards one of the four points of the compass and in which a diagonal direction could only be achieved by negotiating a right-angled bend. This is not developed further, however. The method of movement conjectured by D. H. Müller was certainly far-removed from that of the author.[101]

■ **1:10** V 6a is more fully interpreted by v 10, which comes strikingly late. Whoever is inclined to accept v 6a as an original statement from Ezekiel (which certainly cannot be ruled out as a possibility) then must suppose that originally four human faces were simply in mind here. This is what we find in the old Babylonian statuette referred to, as also much later in the Roman figure of Janus. V 10, however, mentions four different faces: man, lion, bull, eagle. Obviously here the strongest and most regal of animals and birds, together with man, are adduced in order to strengthen the expression of the all-embracing divine power which is reflected in the creatures which bear the throne.

Dürr has collected much material for the interpretation of the four figures in ancient oriental symbolism.[102] Here we must also note that the features of this symbolism which express the divine power are introduced in the creatures beneath the throne platform, but not in the figure seated on the throne. In the order of listing the four faces: in front that of a man, on the right a lion's, to the left a bull's, and (behind?) an eagle's, we see a hidden scale of values. In Christian interpretation there developed quite early a connection of the four faces with the four evangelists, and since Jerome this has penetrated into western exposition.[103]

■ **1:7** The addition of the feet (v 7) and hands (v 8a) to the creatures, which originates with the desire for a more complete description of the vision and the latter also perhaps to the adjustment to 2:9; 10:7, differs from what precedes by a greater vagueness in the references. The original text clearly shows the number and position of the creatures' wings (as in Is 6), whilst an uncertainty remains in the reference to the feet whether each creature had two feet or whether each of them was thought of as having a single foot like a pillar. The former may be indicated by the plural (or dual) רגליהם "their feet (two to each)," whilst the second possibility is suggested by the singular רגל ישרה which follows and which suggests that the body ended in an unjointed limb like a post. It is clear that such a foot would not permit real movement, such as is presupposed by v 12. Rather it already appears to be wholly regarded as an ornamental feature and to presuppose the combination of the whole with a metal support (vv 15ff).[104] This is the direction to which the comparison of the end of the foot with a calf's foot also points, which was possibly still not read by 𝕲. Does the reference to the shining of the feet like burnished bronze, the fomulation (כעין) and content of which (comparison with a metal) are determined by the כעין חשמל (v 27, secondarily v 4), show that with this part of the description no longer was the figure of a living creature in mind, but that of a throne-chariot cast in metal? V 7 accordingly entered the text at the earliest with 1:15ff.

■ **1:8a** The reference to the hands also remains obscure. Are we to think that each creature had two hands, as

101 Müller, *Ezechiel-studien*, 14.
102 Dürr, *Ezekiels Vision*, 31–54.
103 For details see Neuss, *Buch*.

104 See the reconstruction of Schmidt, "Kerubenthron."

with the human figure (v 5)? Is it presupposed that a hand appears on each side which has a face (under a wing?) Or is the "according to their four sides" to be understood from the whole description so that there was only one hand on each creature? The somewhat fuller formulation in 10:8 also contains a certain obscurity regarding all these questions, which contrasts with the clarity of the basic details.

■ **1:8b, 9** Vv 8b and 9 expand the statements about the faces and wings of the creatures. V 9a, which is still lacking in 𝕲, gives the impression of being a peripheral remark which seeks to preserve the statement about the wings (by the introduction of the catchword כנפיהם which is unnecessary in v 11), which is mutilated in v 11bα, but which does stand in its proper connection with the text of v 11bβ. The remainder of vv 8b and 9b takes up the statement about the forward movement of the creatures, which is made in v 12, and carries it over without any change to the faces of the creatures. This leads to the statement that each of the faces which were set on four sides, each looking in its own direction, always went straight-forwards. This is an impossibility which, as we have already remarked, has led in 10:11b to the introduction of the idea of a leading face.

■ **1:11a** Finally v 11a has the function of linking up again with the original text in v 11b, which had become broken off. Closer examination shows in this a slight variation of the picture. The statement "their wings were spread out above" is clearly determined by the recollection of the cherubim above the ark, of which Ex 25:20 says: "And the cherubim spread their wings above (פרשׂים) so that they covered the ark-cover with their wings." In the description of the cherubim with two wings this is quite in place, but with the four-winged creatures it needs to be added by way of correction that this concerns the upper pair of wings, since it cannot be said of the lower pair which cover the body. Thus v 11a is shown to be a piece of later interpretation determined by the temple cherubim.

■ **12b** The additional remark in v 12b "wherever the spirit would go, they went" represents again a reflection arising out of the immediate situation. It no longer has in mind the undeviating advance of the phenomenon, but describes quite generally the mystery of the strange coordination of movement in the four creatures with the aid of a statement about the "spirit." This has been introduced in dependence on v 20.

■ **1:13** That parts of v 13 belong to the original account of the divine manifestation cannot be claimed with complete certainty. On the other hand, subsequent additions can clearly be recognized. That there was fire between the creatures "like torches" and "moving to and fro between the creatures" are statements which must be determined by Gen 15:17. There, in the framework of the covenant with Abraham narrated by J, Yahweh appears in fire at night and passes (עבר) between the pieces of the sacrifice. In this later interpretation by the school of Ezekiel the appearance of Yahweh to the prophet contains something of the importance of that great covenant of the early period. The second addition (v 14), which is lacking in 𝕲, threatens to destroy completely the picture of the manifestation. In its sublime majesty, the phenomenon, which moves steadily towards the prophet, develops into a fiery will-o'-the-wisp in which the creatures who bear the throne share in the restless movement of the lightning which shoots out of the fire. For the method of later interpretation this carrying over of the movement of the lightning on to the creatures is instructive. For a proper understanding of the text, however, it is misleading.

■ **1:15–21** In the passage vv 15–21 the interest in the technical description of the manifestation and its details has predominated. The ascending order of the description of the mysterious nature of the creatures who bear the throne to an ever greater glory and exaltation of appearance is broken up by the reversion to the lowest features, the wheels, which are below and beside the creatures "on the earth," and to a consideration of the method of their construction, their mechanical form, and the synchronization of their movement to that of the creatures. The vitality of the creatures who bear the throne, in which we notice already in the original text an initial stylizing and a certain rigidity, falls into the background here and gives way to the picture of a "chariot," a throne furnished with wheels. Thus a later age could speak of a מרכבה (1 Chr 28:18; 𝕲 of Ezek 43:3; Sir 49:8 in the praise of the ancestors "Ezekiel saw a vision and made known the creatures of the chariot" [Smend]). The Judaism of the period of Johanan ben Zakkai and Akiba could describe the secret teaching about the nature of God, his dwelling, and the spirits who surrounded him as מעשׂה מרכבה.[105]

What is the origin of this reference to the throne-chariot, which is first found in the "school" of Ezekiel? Bertholet has put forward the thesis that the description of the throne-chariot had in mind the mobile stands of the temple (1 Kings 7:27–39) as a model. It is not clear, however, how the changeover could have been made from the various utensils on the mobile stand to the unique form of the divine throne. This view lacks any transitional stages. Against it Schmidt, "Kerubenthron," supposed that in the most holy place of the pre-exilic temple there already stood such a chariot, interpreted as an empty throne.[106] In the Priestly Document's presentation of the objects in the most holy place Schmidt believes that he can see in the כפרת of Ex 25:17–22 and elsewhere this mobile throne of God. The ark, which was underneath the כפרת, accordingly has the position of the footstool which lay beneath the feet of the occupant of the throne (Ps 99:5, 132:7). Even if we do not agree with this view, we cannot overlook the fact that in the ancient Near East the form of a mobile throne was not unknown. Dan 7:9, with its incidental reference to the wheels on the throne of God, is not simply to be understood from Ezek 1, but derives from a widespread ancient oriental custom.[107] Thus the Israelite throne conception (1 Kings 22; Is 6), even though no throne-chariot actually stood in the temple, could readily be enlarged upon without difficulty into becoming a mobile throne. This elaboration was particularly likely in the circle of Ezekiel's disciples, since they were aware through Ezekiel not only of the God who was seated in his sanctuary in heaven or on the earth, but of the One who appeared in his majesty to distant exiles. The event of which Ezekiel had to tell went beyond that of Isaiah and could well have been an important basis for the further elaboration of the throne conception which followed. What had been described by Ezekiel himself with the aid of old Israelite tradition (Yahweh's appearing in

a storm in the manner of Ps 18) has been reflected upon by the school of Ezekiel in regard to the throne phenomenon and described with an almost technical detail. Thus the necessity to seek a prototype for the מרכבה in the pre-exilic temple disappears. In the static nature of life in the settled land there was no necessity to speak of a mobile throne. Divine chariots and divine horses were at that time primarily non-Israelite divine symbols (2 Kings 23:11). The ancient Israelite ark of Yahweh was portable.[108]

The removal of the ark from Philistine territory (1 Sam 6:7ff) does not point to a sacred vehicle in continued use, as the burning of the cart which followed immediately after shows. When the ark was brought up from Kiriath-jearim to Jerusalem on a cart a mysterious accident took place (2 Sam 6:3ff). At its removal under the divine blessing into the city of David, the ark was carried (2 Sam 6:13), as already also in 1 Sam 4:4 where it was brought by two priests into the camp. Even when the ark was permanently set in the temple of Solomon, the carrying poles remained fixed to the ark and were visible from the holy place (1 Kings 8:8). The Priestly tradition also knew of the ark only as a portable sanctuary. Thus the reference to the throne-chariot in Ezek 1 points to an approximate parallel with the Mesopotamian type of mobile processional sanctuary, an idea first conceived after the loss of the actual ark.

Vv 15–21 avoid express mention of the "chariot," and it is obvious that the terminology was first taken up in the additions. These verses are restricted to making clear the appearance of the chariot in the description of the wheels.

■ 1:15 The phenomenon is described here as resting on the ground. Beside each creature there stood an individual wheel. The pattern of the four-wheeled chariot underlies the description. The stylizing of the number four has a further consequence here and connects easily with the appearance of the chariot.

105 Wilhelm Bousset and Hugo Gressmann, *Die Religion des Judentums im späthellenistischen Zeitalter*, HBNT 21 (Tübingen: Mohr [Siebeck], ³1926), 355–357.
106 Wolfgang Reichel, *Ueber vorhellenische Goetterculte* (Wien: Hoelder, 1897), has put forward analogies from the history of religion for the phenomenon of such an empty divine throne.
107 See the material in Dürr, *Ezekiels Vision*, 13–21.

There is considerable doubt, however, about the one-sided derivation of Ezekiel's picture of the throne from the Persian canopied chariot with its two-story stages which ultimately comes from the Eurasian nomadic world. Alföldi, "Throntabernakels," attempts to show such a derivation.
108 In dependence on an Egyptian custom? See Adolf Erman, *Die Religion der Ägypter* (Berlin: De Gruyter,

■ **1:16** In what follows the wheels are described in appearance, construction, and manner of movement. The wheels also share in the shining splendor of the whole phenomenon. Once again the language of the "splendor" (עין), which comes from the end of v 27, is used. The wheels gleam like תרשיש (𝕲 Chrysolith), a precious stone, which according to Koehler-Baumgartner cannot be more precisely defined. All four appear as though one wheel were in the other. In spite of the references by Alföldi to the chariot of Mithras (Avesta) and to that of the sun-god (Veda), we cannot here think of the four wheels inside each other, merging into a single wheel.[109] Rather the account intends to describe the appearance of each individual wheel. This is to be conceived as a disc, drawn with concentric circles or decreasing in thickness from the center outwards, so that its thickness formed concentric rings. Does this reflect a particular archaic type of wheel still retained when the spoked wheel had become normal?[110] Should we see in this description a subtle opposition to forms used by the pagan world?

■ **1:17** A certain conceptual difficulty arises in v 17. This states that the wheels could move on their four sides without turning. Again it is important to keep in mind here that the picture of the wheels is formed from statements about the creatures, to which it is completely assimilated. In v 17 the feminine suffixes which agree with חיות reappear from v 12 in reference to the masculine אופנים. Thus the necessity for assimilation is paramount and not the description of their appearance. Whereas with the forward movement of the creatures this was first intended to indicate their approach towards the prophet and was subsequently understood as a general statement about their movement, with the wheels the statement is intended from the very begin-

ning to be general. Thus "on all four sides" is added explicitly (lacking in v 12). The whole description therefore must be firmly understood from its character as a secondary assimilation. A wheel stood beside each creature and was clearly thought to be facing in the same direction. Thus when the creatures moved forward, so also did the wheels, and, as the leading face undertook to guide the creatures, making movement possible in all four directions, so the idea of a leading wheel which acted as guide was introduced, in order to make the whole thing to some extent conceivable.

■ **1:18** Behind the statement about the eyes which were on the rims (bosses?) of the wheels, we should probably picture a particular form of wheel decoration or strengthening, which is here interpreted as eyes. Should we think of nailed fitments? Galling mentions a wheel with nail fitments as current in the seventh century, where we must think of fitments to the outside of the wheel.[111] What may have been a special decoration is then interpreted in a deeper sense. In these eyes we have an indication of the all-seeing power of the Rider of the throne-chariot.[112] The mysterious description of the wheels could not fail to arouse much later reflection. In later Jewish speculation the Ophannim are raised to the level of independent angelic beings.[113]

■ **1:19–21** Vv 19–21 describe the complete coordination of movement between the wheels and the living creatures. The verses are heavily overloaded with repetitions and variant expressions. The rising up of the wheels is mentioned no less than three times (vv 19b, 20b, 21b). Twice a statement is connected with the assertion that the spirit of the creatures (creature) was in the wheels (vv 20b, 21b). In the repetition in 10:16f, vv 20 and 21aα of ch. 1 are passed over. Since the text of ch. 10 appears also in this repetition as a more pol-

---

1934), 180.

109 Alföldi, "Throntabernakels," 544.

110 Cf. *AOBAT* 78, 137, 278, 363, 538, 548, beside the disc wheel on Gudea's chariot *AOBAT* 479b, or the old Babylonian divine chariot, Dürr, *Ezekiels Vision*, p. 20 illustration 4. Cf. also the bronze model from *Tell Aqrab* in J. Wiesner, *Fahren und Reiten in Alteuropa und im Alten Orient*, AO 38, 2–4 (Leipzig, 1939), table 1, illustration 2; Meissner, *Babylonien* 1, 249 and illustration 205; for the Philistines, cf. *AOBAT* 111.

111 *BRL*, 423.

112 Cf. the illustrations of the god Bes covered with eyes in *AOBAT* 567; Dürr, *Ezekiels Vision*, 59f; also Zech 4:2, 10b.

113 Cf. *Enoch* 61:10, 71:7; *b Ḥagigah* 12b, 13a; *b Roš Haššanah* 24b.

ished account, we cannot draw certain conclusions from this about the original form of the text of ch. 1. In any case vv 19 and 21 of ch. 1 give the impression of being variants of the same. V 21 is formulated tersely with simple suffixes related to the creatures (לעמתם); v 19 is more broadly developed and expressly names the creatures and the wheels (אצלם). Added to this there are also further signs of unevenness in subject matter; whilst v 20a speaks of הרוח as the mysterious guiding power in the movement, vv 20b and 21b make explanatory reference to "the spirit of the creatures." Whilst v 19 speaks freely in the plural of the creatures, in vv 20f the singular החיה appears. The latter may be explained from the necessity of giving expression to the unity of the creatures, which becomes evident in the collective designation rather than in the plurality, where the united movement of the wheels is referred to. Thus here we must reckon with a process of gradual overlaying of the text through additions, without being able to distinguish the stages of growth in detail.

The movement of a chariot takes place through the movement of its wheels. It is striking, however, that in v 19 the exact identification of the phenomenon as a chariot is not made. Rather the creatures beside the wheels retain their own movement. The movement of the wheels remains parallel to the movement of the creatures and is coordinated to this. Can we regard this fact as a further indication that the expression concerning the wheels first entered after the appearance of the creatures had already acquired a vitality of its own?

The identity of movement between the creatures and the wheels is brought about by means of the רוח. This concept is first used absolutely in the addition to v 12 and refers to the mysterious underlying power which permeates the whole phenomenon, and which cannot be understood apart from the will of the One who is enthroned above the creatures. When we read in vv 20f of "the spirit of the creatures" we must see in it a process of rationalization. Different aspects of the will of Yahweh, who works through the רוח, which is referred to absolutely, are thereby isolated, and a particular power to determine their movements is ascribed to the

creatures. This is then carried over to the wheels.[114]

■1:22 In v 22 the original text continues with a description of the fixed platform above the creatures. The aspect of the *tremendum*, which radiates from the splendor of the platform, is added by a later hand through הנורא.[115]

■1:23–25 Then a feature which we certainly miss in the overall description has been introduced into the editorial work on the text: the audible impact of the phenomenon. The unfortunate introduction of a feature which relates to what lay underneath the platform at a point where the general description had already got beyond this makes the secondary character of the statements of 1:23–25 particularly noticeable.

■1:24 In v 24 the text of 𝔗 shows that attempts were made in the later editorial work to assimilate the description of Ezek 1 to Is 6 and to introduce a hymn of praise by the creatures (cf. also 3:12 𝔐). The expansion which we find in 1:23ff does not go so far, but speaks only of the impersonal sound of movement, in line with the original text of 3:12. In particular we can connect this with the description of the wings. The statement of 1:11 about the positions of the two pairs of wings is repeated with a change of verb (השיק c. 𝔗 instead of חבר, and then subsequently further glossed in 𝔐), although in the description of the beating of the wings (v 24) only a reference to the upper pair of outstretched wings would have been necessary. There then follows a reference to the lowering of the wings to a position of rest, which basically presupposes a picture of a creature with two wings, as in v 11a, since in a creature with four wings the lowering of the upper pair would lead to an ungainly overlapping when they were lowered to cover the body. The reference is subsequently introduced again in v 25.

The statement about the sound of the wings is made clearer by some analogies. The comparison with the voice of Shaddai, which is not found in 𝔊 and obviously represents a very late element of interpretation, stems from 10:5.[116] The comparison with the noise of a military camp, which is likewise lacking in 𝔊 and the syntax of which shows it to be late, has possibly entered by association with the simile of the sound of many

114 For רוח see Excursus 3.
115 Cf. Gen 28:17; Ju 13:6; and of Yahweh himself
     Dtn 7:21; Ps 47:3 and other passages.

116 See on the text.

waters, which stands beside it. Is 17:12 shows a connection between the roaring of the sea and the noisy camp of the army of the great king, filled with shouts in different languages and the din of weapons. The ancient oriental mind heard in the roaring of the sea the continued rebellion of the armies of the monster of chaos (Ps 46:4, 7 and elsewhere). This association is more likely than a reference to the armies of supernatural beings (Herrmann). There is very noticeably lacking in Ezekiel, as in the entire Priestly literature, any mention of Hosts (יהוה צבאות). The oldest feature of the interpretative additions is the comparison of the beating of the creatures' wings with the roaring of mighty waters, a feature which has plainly been taken over from 43:2 where the return of Yahweh's glory into the temple is described in terms of light and the noise of water. The gloss in Is 17:13aα, which takes up the מים כבירים, used in parallel with ימים, from 17:12 with מים רבים, leads us to think here of the noise of the sea. Cf. Ps 18:17; 29:3; 93:4; Hab 3:15 (also Ps 77:20; 107:23; Ezek 27:26). The entrance of Yahweh (43:2), and of the creatures who bear his throne (1:24), is to be compared with the mysterious sound of water, with all its supernatural associations. The catchword קול, which appears in all five times in v 24 and points, as in v 25 in another connection, to what is above the platform, is also related to this. It prepares for v 26, where the original text was joined on to v 22.

Although the editorial work of the "school" was so heavy in the description of what was beneath the platform, it was silent about the description of what lay above it. Only in the remark of v 27aα[1] "the appearance of fire round about" is there a comparison by way of comment which properly had the intention of affirming the sharp outline of the upper half of the enthroned figure. No notice appears to be taken of the fact that the antithesis intended in the original text between חשמל (upper half of the body) and אש (lower half of the body) is broken by the addition.

■ **2:1ff** As the analysis has shown, the commissioning of the prophet, after the preparatory introduction in 1:28bβ–2:2, is divided into a series of five units, each beginning with an address to the prophet (2:3–5, 6–7; 2:8–3:3; 3:4–9, 10–11). Each of them has its own particular theme. The middle section 2:8–3:3, however, undeniably has a special emphasis, in that it narrates Yahweh's action towards the prophet similar to an ordination.

■ **2:1** A voice addresses the prophet, who falls on his face before the appearance of the divine glory. For the first time Ezekiel's ears are also involved, not with an impersonal roaring as the additions in 1:24f state, but with a message addressed to him personally. That Yahweh's name is not mentioned in this, although "the voice of someone speaking" is referred to cautiously, helps to preserve the mystery of the deity, hidden in the manifestation of his glory. The address בן אדם occurs in all ninety-three times in the book of Ezekiel (twenty-three times strengthened to ואתה בן אדם). Whereas in the visions of Amos (7:8; 8:2) and Jeremiah (1:11; 24:3) the prophet is addressed by his proper name, here this is completely displaced by this stereotyped formula "son of man," in spite of an incomparably more frequent use of personal address (24:24 is a saying of Yahweh about the prophet). Since אדם can also be used collectively (Gen 1:26), the individual of the type is expressed by the preceding בן: you individual man. This is a good Hebraic form of speech[117] and is certainly not to be described as an Aramaism.[118] The emphasis, however, does not lie on the note of individuality, but on the אדם, to which the unexpressed counterpart is אל (Is 31:3; Ezek 28:2). In this summons the prophet was not being addressed in the uniqueness of his particular personal being, as would be expressed by his proper name, nor according to his office, but as an individual within the created order, the servant, who is summoned by his master in an act of unprecedented condescension by his divine Lord. We ought to avoid the weak translation "child of man," in which Dürr wants to see a note of tenderness.[119] It is certainly wrong to seek to find here use of a custom of Babylonian speech by a reference to Gilgamesh ix, 38, where Ea addresses the hero of the flood as "man" (*amelu*).[120] Ezekiel's background in the realm of priestly language, which often uses אדם as the subject of a ruling (Lev 1:2; 13:2; Nu 19:14) in its legal formula-

---

117 See Paul Joüon, *Grammaire de l'hébreu biblique* (Rome: Pontifical Biblical Institute, ²1947), § 129 j.
118 So Hölscher, *Hesekiel*, 10; Fohrer, *Hauptprobleme*,
239.
119 Dürr, *Apokalyptik*, 40.
120 Hölscher, *Hesekiel*, 9f; Fohrer, *Hauptprobleme*, 238.

tions, is quite sufficient to explain Ezekiel's usage.

■ **2:2** The form of address also corresponds to the content of the introductory divine speech. At once it lifts the prophet up and makes him capable of perceiving the divine word. The command to get up is strengthened by reference to the efficacious power of the רוח. This leaves some obscurity as to how far the רוח, which lifts the prophet up, is his own vital power and how far it is seen as the divine רוח acting under the divine command.[121] In any case the introductory scene serves to make clear that, before the power of the divine appearing, man's power to hear is no longer an obvious fact. He must first be prepared for it.[122]

■ **2:3–5** The first part of the commissioning speech (2:3–5), which has been considerably expanded in 𝕸 by additions, shows a clear division into three units in its basic structure: "I send you . . . and you shall say . . . they will know." From the words of the canonical prophets it becomes increasingly clear that the fact of being sent by God forms the basic authorization of the prophet. Neither the mastery of a mantic technique nor the possession of a particular psychic disposition distinguishes a man as a prophet, but only the fact of being sent by Yahweh. Thus the word שלח appears at the decisive point in the call-narratives (Is 6:8; Jer 1:7). It is the most serious form of opposition to a prophet when someone says to him: "Yahweh has not sent you" (Jer 28:15; 43:2; cf. 14:15; 27:15; 29:9; Ezek 13:6). We hear something of this asserted passionately in subsequent additions to Zechariah's prophetic word: "You will know that Yahweh of Hosts has sent me" (2:13; cf. 2:12, 15; 4:9; 6:15). The use of the messenger formula (see above) as an introduction to a prophet's speech also shows that the title "sent one" best fits the prophet's consciousness of his office.[123] It is therefore entirely to the point that the first divine word to Ezekiel should contain the statement of sending.

Sending, however, is always something concrete, directed towards specific persons. Ezekiel was from Judah, and he lived in the midst of a company of exiles from Judah. Thus we can expect him to be sent to the exiles from Judah. Instead of this, however, when 2:3 says: "I send you to the house of Israel," we must bear in mind first of all that Israel was the proper name for the people of God in their twelve tribes who consciously belonged to God through the covenant. As far as the people's spiritual character was concerned, the name Israel did not fall into disuse even when, historically speaking, it only concerned the remnant of Israel which could be defined in political terms as Judah to distinguish it from the political kingdom of Israel (North Israel). We can therefore see that the name Israel was carried over to Judah after the overthrow of the Northern Kingdom.[124] With the earlier classical prophets the political designation may have been loosely used, whilst with Ezekiel, who shows a pronounced theological reflection, we can see that he directs his preaching with unmistakable intention to Israel, the people of God. This Israel existed in Ezekiel's days in various remnants, both in exile and in the "land of Israel." We cannot deny that Ezekiel knew that he had been sent to the "house of Israel," though this occasionally shows a striking remoteness from the immediate situation in which he found himself.[125] It thus becomes clear that the words of 3:10f, which mention his being sent to his fellow exiles, are not simply a repetition of the statement of commissioning given in 2:3–5. 2:3–5 represents a comprehensive commissioning in all its breadth; 3:10f represents his being sent to the remnant of Israel closest to, and directly accessible by, him.

In this light we can also understand what follows. When in 2:3 the house of Israel to which Ezekiel is sent is described as rebellious, this does not refer to a particular hardening which Ezekiel had noted in his immediate surroundings, so that his preaching was simply built upon direct personal experiences. Instead he stands in a line of prophetic proclamation to "Is-

---

121 See Excursus 3.
122 In Dan 10:8–12 we find a stylized heightening of this feature.
123 The title "sent one," "apostle," however, came to be consciously preferred only in the time of the Arab prophets. Walther Zimmerli, "Der Prophet im Alten Testament und im Islam," *Kreuz und Halbmond* 5 (1943): 3–8.

124 See Leonhard Rost, *Israel bei den Propheten*, BWANT 4, 19 (Stuttgart: Kohlhammer, 1937).
125 See Excursus 2.

rael." This becomes quite clear through the extension of the assertion of sin back to Israel's ancestors. The whole of Israel's history, not only in its geographical extension over its scattered members, but also in its temporal extension in history, beginning with the exodus from Egypt (chs. 20, 23; ch. 16 goes back to the origin of Jerusalem) and reaching down to Ezekiel's own time, is set before the prophet's eyes. There lie behind this the judgements made by the prophets upon the entire national history from Hosea (11:1ff), through Isaiah (1:21ff, related to Jerusalem), up to Jeremiah (2:4ff).

In the אל גוים added in v 3 someone has noted the fact that Ezekiel would also have to address the nations, as exemplified in his oracles against foreign nations. Before this time Jeremiah had been named "a prophet for the nations" at his call (1:5, 10). This is followed in Ezekiel by two reaffirmations of the negative judgement upon Israel. The verb פשע primarily denotes the defection of a vassal in the political sphere (2 Kings 1:1; 3:5, 7 and other passages) and was then used to express a religious judgement upon Israel in the earlier classical prophets (Am 4:4; Hos 7:13; 8:1; Is 1:2; Jer 2:8; 3:13). It is here used to underline again the rebellion of Israel against Yahweh.

■ **2:4a** 4a, which repeats again the statements of the sending but with inversion of the syntax, perceptibly disturbs the syntactical arrangement of the sentence. Further it uses an Isaianic form of speech[126] in its description of Israel as "sons," and the statement about hardening has a close parallel in the קשה ערף of Ex 32:9; 33:3, 5; 34:9; Dtn 9:6, 13.

The prophet, who is sent by Yahweh, receives the charge: "Thou shalt say to them: Thus has Yahweh spoken." The very stereotyped character of this formula is striking. Nothing is said about the content of what Ezekiel is to preach. Only the introductory formula is mentioned which usually precedes the prophetic proclamation and points to the Lord who has commissioned the prophet. L. Koehler has emphasized that this introductory formula describes the situation of a messenger entrusted with a message.[127] It points back to the moment when he received the message and was used at the time of delivery in order to appeal back to this moment. From this the perfect tense of the messenger formula becomes intelligible. At the moment of delivery of his message the messenger identifies himself with the time when he was entrusted with it by the person who commissioned him. That the prophet, at the time when he was sent, was commanded simply to declare this messenger formula once again shows the striking distance of Ezekiel from the immediate situation in which he spoke and the peculiarity which this reflects upon him. He was capable of considerable abstractions. His office is here described in its basic definition, quite apart from any concrete elaborations of his message. This office did not rest on any one particular message, with a circumscribed content, as an administrator might commit himself to a specific program on taking office and derive his legal position from adherence to it. Rather the prophet's office rested solely on his personal connection with the sender, who retained in his own power the content of every message with complete freedom.

■ **2:5** From this formulation we must also understand the third element of the passage of 2:3–5: the declaration of purpose "they will know that a prophet has been in their midst." For the first time we encounter here an example of the recognition formula, which is especially characteristic of the book of Ezekiel. It is not sufficient that Yahweh's action should be stated, which consists according to the present text in his sending Ezekiel. In addition to this it is made clear that a recognition by Israel is attached to this action of Yahweh's. More precisely a recognition will be awakened in Israel. This form of speech about recognition is rooted in the proceedings by which a fact is ascertained through specific things or events ("signs").[128] Thus, in his being a messenger sent by Yahweh, Ezekiel takes the place of a sign by which the lawsuit between Yahweh and Israel will be brought to a conclusive understanding. When the substance of this recognition is described by the words "know that a prophet has been in their midst" (so also 33:33; cf. 2 Kings 5:8), this may at first appear tautologous. The sending of Ezekiel, who arrives with the messenger-formula, will become a sign

---

126 Cf. note a to v 4.

127 Ludwig Koehler, *Deuterojesaja (Jesaja 40–55) stilkritisch untersucht*, BZAW 37 (Giessen: Töpelmann,

1923), 102–109.

128 See Zimmerli, *Erkenntnis*, 49–57.

bringing about a recognition that a prophet has been present. However, the parallel in 2 Kings 5:9 and 15 makes clear that this "recognition that a prophet has been present" contains a fuller reference to a recognition of God, who works in history through his prophets. Accordingly the statement is not very different from the formula which is more frequently used by Ezekiel "they will know that I am Yahweh." The mystery of the person of Yahweh, who is present in Israel through the mouth of his prophet, summoning the people in a time of crisis, rather than the hidden mystery of God as he is in himself, will be made known through Ezekiel's being sent as a prophet. This recognition will be incontrovertible and self-authenticating. The opposition, which will almost certainly arise aong the people of Israel who are three times described as rebellious, will not be able to hinder the fact of this recognition. In the parenthesis "whether they hear, or refuse to hear, for they are a rebellious house" there is expressed the irrefutable nature of this recognition (cf. 2:7; 3:11, 27), and at the same time the unconditional nature of the commission of Ezekiel, who is not to hold back because of opposition. In the phrase "rebellious house" (2:5–8; 3:9, 26f; 12:2f, 9, 25; 17:12; 24:3; cf. 44:6) we have a counterpart to the expression "house of Israel" which occurs frequently in Ezekiel. The total submission to sin, which is made clear in the speeches of chs. 15f, 20, 23, and elsewhere in similes or historical surveys, is here sharply defined in a new name. In this we must remember that in the Old Testament the name is no mere sound or label, but expresses the essence of a thing or person. By renaming the house of Israel as a "rebellious house" full expression is given to Israel's strange submission to rebellion.[129]

■ **2:6, 7** The unconditional nature of Ezekiel's commission, which permits no holding back on account of Israel's rebellion, evokes a word of personal admonition to the prophet not to be afraid. Jer 1:8 (17b) shows that such an admonition may already have belonged to the form of the prophetic call-narrative before Ezekiel. In 2:6f this feature appears in Ezekiel. A comparison with the references in Jeremiah serves to make very clear the distinctive aspects of Ezekiel's experience.

We find with Jeremiah the encouraging "Fear not, for I am with you" (1:8), said to the despairing prophet, and the admonitory "Do not be afraid of them, lest I give you cause to fear them" (1:17b), uttered against the prophet's desire to evade his commission. In Ezekiel the admonition to be fearless is quite abruptly set within the message of Israel's unreadiness to repent, which is basically neither an argument intended to encourage nor a threat intended to preclude any evasion. Twice the admonition not to be afraid is formulated using two expressions (חתת – ירא). In the second (v 6b) there are various references to the reactions of the prophet's hearers of which men might well be afraid (introduced in 𝔐 in v 6a also). In the second formulation the reference to the hardening of the people is made with the formula taken from v 5 "for they are a rebellious house." In order to grasp fully the logical progression of thought we must add here, as in v 6a, a thought which is unexpressed: "Do not be afraid of them—though there is good cause to fear them—for they are a rebellious house." The causal clause does not in fact provide a motive for fearlessness, but establishes that fear might well be aroused. This is even clearer in the causal clause of v 6a: "though thorns are round about you, and you sit on scorpions." In the first statement two ideas are connected: 1) Danger surrounds the prophet on all sides, so that no escape is possible from this encirclement. The impossibility of evasion is given expression by the words "round about." 2) In the saying about thorns, which suggests a field fenced with a thorn hedge, we can see the complete hostility, even to the point of torture and bloodshed, of those to whom God's messenger is sent. Even stranger is the second simile of sitting on scorpions, which Ezekiel is to encounter in the fulfilment of his prophetic office. The command to the prophet to speak, which is repeated in v 7, is quite harsh, and gives no personal encouragement.[130] Finally the words of v 7, which repeat those of v 5, reaffirm the obligation to speak with no consideration of success or failure even more sharply.

■ **2:8–3:3** The call-narrative of Jeremiah shows the following sequence in its structure: a) call to be a

---

129 Cf. the similar renaming of בית אל to בית און Hos
     4:15 and other passages, and Amos 5:5.
130 But cf. on 3:8f.

prophet 1:5, the dialogue which follows in vv 6ff is Jeremiah's particular variation of this feature. b) admonition to fearlessness 1:8. c) act of ordination 1:9. This latter is formulated briefly: "Then Yahweh stretched out his hand and touched my mouth, and Yahweh said to me: Behold I have put my words in your mouth." In Ezekiel we have the sequence: a) call to be a prophet 2:3–5. b) admonition to fearlessness 2:6–7, and c) act of ordination 2:8–3:3. This is broadly elaborated into a three-part divine address in which the narrative details are inserted.

■ 2:8 An initial word from God in 2:8 prepares for the act of ordination and sets this against the background of a command to be obedient. Following the address there then comes in a personal address to the prophet, a summons to be attentive, which is common in the sayings of the prophets (Am 3:1; 4:1; Is 1:2; Jer 2:4; Ezek 6:3). Then follows the admonition not to be rebellious like the house of Israel, which connects up with the preceding details. Can we see in this (as in Is 50:5?) a surreptitious side glance at the possibility of a personal resistance such as appears in Jer 1:6? What other motive could the summons to obedience have had, made as it is with such surprising sharpness?

■ 2:9 The further element of the vision is introduced with the formula for recounting a visionary experience ואר(אה והנה), which has already appeared in 1:4 (15). The great reserve in simply mentioning "a hand stretched out towards me" is noteworthy and differs from Jer 1:9. The formulation is parallel to the קול מדבר of 1:28, which similarly avoids any mention of Yahweh and is clearly quite deliberate. In both texts the avoidance of the name of Yahweh is determined by what has been said in ch. 1. 2:9 also seeks to preserve the mystery of God, which is hidden in the manifestation of his glory, and consequently avoids any direct visible connection between the divine manifestation of glory and the hand which touched the prophet. In Is 6:6 we find the hand of a seraph in place of Yah-

weh's hand (the explanatory addition of Ezek 1:8 is to be understood as a preparation for the corresponding appearance of the hand of the creatures in 10:7). The original text of Ezekiel undoubtedly refers in 2:9 to the hand of Yahweh, as in Jer 1:9, and Yahweh not only remains the subject of ויפרש in 2:10 but also of ויאמר in 3:1.

■ 2:10 The hand which was stretched out towards the prophet held a scroll, which was first rolled up, but which was subsequently unrolled before his eyes. This was particularly unusual in that it was written on both sides, which was contrary to the normal practice.[131] This is clearly intended to make plain the distressing superabundance of the divine message. Besides its fullness, the content of what was written was also distressing: lamentation, mourning, and woe. K. H. Fahlgren and K. Koch have suggested the term "synthetic view of life" (*synthetische Lebensauffassung* or *Lebensanschauung*) for the close connection between cause and effect which is current in Old Testament thought.[132] We find this here in that the contents of the scroll are described by the effects which the words which it contains and which the prophet is to preach will have. We are not to think of laments which are written on the scroll, but of threats of divine judgement which the prophet had to proclaim. When they were uttered they would arouse lamentations, mourning, and woe on the part of those to whom they are addressed.

■ 3:1–3 This scroll was offered to the prophet for food. Its acceptance by him is divided into two phases. Twice the prophet receives the command to eat (3:1, 3a); twice his obedience to this command is mentioned 3:2, 3b). The fact that the revitalizing of the dead bones in 37:4–10 takes place in an analogous double act, in a twice-given command from Yahweh to prophesy, a twice-given carrying-out of the command, and two phases in the return of the bones to full life, warns us against simplifying the two phases here by postulating a double recension (Bertholet) or any other such critical

---

131 See Emil G. Kraeling, *The Brooklyn Museum Aramaic Papyri* (New Haven: Yale University Press, 1953), 127; G. R. Driver, *Aramaic Documents of the Fifth Century B.C.* (Oxford: Clarendon, 1954), plates 1ff outside/inside. Only letter notices are on the outside.

132 Karl Hjalmar Fahlgren, *Ṣᵉdāḳā, nahestehende und entgegengesetzte Begriffe im Alten Testament* (Uppsala:

Almquist & Wiksell, 1932), 50–54; K. Koch, *SDQ im Alten Testament*, Unpub. Diss. (Heidelberg, 1953), 85–102.

operations. Rather we must see in this a peculiarity of Ezekiel's manner of speech.[133] The first command of Yahweh in 3:1b mentions side by side what the prophet was commanded to do in his visionary experience (אכול) and what he was to accomplish outside this (לך דבר). The eating of the scroll was the prophet's preparation for preaching. At this command the prophet opens his mouth and accepts the scroll which was offered to him to eat (ויאכלני). The second of Yahweh's commands places the emphasis upon taking what has been eaten into his stomach (בטנך תאכל ומעיך תמלא cf. Jer 4:19), so that the prophet goes away filled (cf. מלאה in Eccl 11:5) with the divine message. After mention of Ezekiel's obedience to this second command, when the prophet himself states that he has eaten it (ואכלה), there follows a reference to the taste of the scroll.

"It was in my mouth as sweet as honey." This reference is not to be understood as a description of the content of the divine message, in which a promise of salvation follows after the announcement of judgement.[134] In the language of the Psalms the statement that Yahweh's word is sweeter than honey is used several times (Ps 19:11; 119:103). In general Ezekiel shows little contact with the language of the Psalter, whereas W. Baumgartner has demonstrated that in his laments the prophet Jeremiah is strongly influenced by the Psalms.[135] In these laments we find the prophet's statement in Jer 15:16 that "thy words were found, so I ate them, and thy words became to me a joy."[136] The sweetness of God's word is mentioned here without the simile of honey. Has Jeremiah been the mediator of the idea of the sweetness of the divine word, which Ezekiel has taken up and strengthened into a directly physical sensation?

The reference in Jer 15:16 has possibly, however, been influential to an even greater extent upon the whole ordination act of Ezek 2:8–3:3. That this relation was already consciously present to an earlier age is

shown by the fact that the addition in 3:1a, which is lacking in 𝕲, describes the event of ordination with the vocabulary of Jer 15:16a, but already presupposes for that reference the text of 𝔐.[137] The question arises of the derivation of the image of the eating of a divinely written scroll in the act of ordination, since it has no analogy in the other call-narratives. Although each prophet's call possessed its own undoubted uniqueness, and with this an element of mystery which cannot be illuminated by mere human reckoning, it also made use of images and concepts which had their own history and setting, as the whole account of Is 6 shows very clearly.[138] What then are we to say about the material used in Ezek 2:8–3:3?

Elsewhere in the Old Testament we hear of the eating of the divine word only in the simile of Jer 15:16. Since the sweetness of the divine word had already been mentioned earlier (Ps 19:11; 119:103; of Wisdom teaching Prv 16:24; 24:13f), this development of the metaphor was not a great step. Undoubtedly it is this metaphor which underlies the prophet's experience with the scroll. In the light of other close contacts between Ezekiel and Jeremiah we cannot rule out the possibility that Ezekiel was directly influenced here by the saying of Jeremiah. If this view is held to be too bold it must be assumed that the idea came from a third source on which both Jeremiah and Ezekiel are dependent. In a whole series of references (particularly 5:1f; 37:1ff, also 4:3, 4ff; 47:1ff) we find in Ezekiel the remarkable feature that images which occur in visionary experiences, as well as in symbolic actions, quite unexpectedly take on a dramatic realization and become transformed into actual events. This phenomenon is also to be seen in the ordination act of 2:8ff. The reference to eating the word of Yahweh, by which Jeremiah in one of his most personal sayings gave expression to his complete subordination to the word of God, is transformed in Ezekiel into a physical reality. It becomes a part of the experience by which Ezekiel

---

133 Cf. the division into four acts in 14:12ff; 47:2–5.
134 Th. Kliefoth, *Das Buch Ezechiels übersetzt und erklärt* (Rostock, 1864/65), according to Karl Friedrich Keil, *Biblical Commentary on the Prophecies of Ezekiel*, 2 volumes, tr. James Martin. Biblical Commentary on the Old Testament (Grand Rapids, Michigan: Eerdmans, 1950).
135 Walter Baumgartner, *Die Klagegedichte des Jeremia*,

BZAW 32 (Berlin, 1917).
136 The text is not to be emended in accordance with 𝕲, following Duhm, *Theologie*; Baumgartner, *Klagegedichte*, since 𝕲 is here smoothing the text.
137 Cf. note to 3:1.
138 See above pp. 98–100.

became aware of his being entrusted with the word of Yahweh. What happened to Jeremiah as a result of his own heart's irrepressible desire became for Ezekiel something imposed upon him by the firm command of Yahweh at the hour of his call. By his obedience to this command the prophet became an obedient servant, in contrast with the rebellious Israel (2:8).

We must still ask where the conception of the scroll has come from. By experiencing it in this form Ezekiel gives voice to a relatively late conception of the form of a prophet's work. No longer is the word of Yahweh simply something given in a personal address by God. It has become a book, and this undoubtedly presupposes a knowledge of the prophetic word written in a book. We may recall the historical analogy of Mohammed. Can we, however, learn anything of the historical process by which the prophetic word came to be preserved in book form? Once again our question brings us back to Jeremiah. A careful analysis of Jer 36 shows that the author of the account of Jehoiakim's burning of Jeremiah's scroll describes not so much Jeremiah's suffering as the rejection of God's word given in a book. The scroll, which contains the word of God, is in the very center of the account. Not for one moment is it left out of sight. In this regard we must bear in mind that the event of Jer 36 took place in the temple and the adjoining palace building in Jerusalem. According to Jer 36:9 this was in the 9th month of the fifth year of Jehoiakim's reign; i.e., in the winter at about the turn of the year 603/602, a good four years before the first deportation of 598, which Ezekiel experienced most likely as a full adult. The event of 603/602 would have been on the lips of all Jerusalem and particularly of the priests, of whom Ezekiel was one, as something over which opinions were divided. In view of the clear dependence of Ezekiel on Jeremiah in other places,[139] is it wholly out of place to ask whether Ezekiel could have been influenced by this event, during which he might even have seen the scroll of Jeremiah with his own eyes? On that unhappy day in the winter of 603 many people were present in the temple, including several priests. The fear shown by the minister (36:16) and the rough rejection by Jehoiakim (36:23, 29) make it appear not

unreasonable to believe that the image of the prophetic word as a scroll, "written with lamentation, mourning and woe," had imprinted itself so indelibly on the mind of the young onlooker that when he himself received a call from God, it took this form as a visible experience. We cannot prove this, but the reference to this background for an understanding of certain features in Ezekiel's world of thought should not be underestimated.

■ **3:4–9** After the act of ordination there follows in Jer 1:10 (17–19) d) a recapitulation of the sending, which repeats features of the divine speech which preceded the ordination. An analogous recapitulation is found in Ezek 3:4–9.

■ **3:4** Once again the sending is to the house of Israel (cf. 2:3), and the command to speak "in the word"[140] of Yahweh is given (cf. 2:4). In fresh language the hopeless hardening of the house of Israel is expressed again with greater sharpness (cf. 2:3aβb).

■ **3:5** This takes place through a comparison with the surrounding world. Ezekiel is not sent to a "people of foreign speech" (literally, "deep, unintelligible in its speech"). Is 33:19, which is secondary in the book of Isaiah but nevertheless might come from the Assyrian period, describes with similar words the unintelligible speech of the Assyrian overlords who govern Judah and who oppress it by their collectors of tribute and valuation officers (ספר – שׁקל Is 33:18). Ezekiel had in mind the speech of those immediately round about him.

■ **3:6** When mention is made in the parallel v 6 of the "many peoples, whose word you do not understand," this must reflect directly the very large number of groups of deportees which were here and there around Ezekiel's own place of exile.[141] The reference to unintelligible speech is strongly emphasized again in the addition in 3:5f. It is evident that these references of Ezekiel's would have been very well understood by his fellow exiles because they reflect the very immediate experience of not being able to understand the language of those round about. The mention of these experiences, however, in Ezek 3:5ff must directly have served to strengthen the prophet's rebuke. Those who speak a foreign language, with all their difficulty in under-

---

139 Cf. to 16:23.
140 Cf. note a to 3:4.
141 Cf. the ration list of Jehoiachin and the names of his

fellow prisoners above pp. 114f.

standing, would be more willing to hear than the house of Israel, for whom no such external difficulty existed (cf. Mt 11:21, 23).

■ **3:7** In a further echo of a phrase from Isaiah (Is 28:12; 30:9 "will not hear"; 1:19; 30:15 "are not willing," used categorically; by Ezekiel again in 20:8) Yahweh asserts that Israel will not listen to Ezekiel because it will not listen to him. The prophet sees himself set alongside God in an impressive solidarity of suffering. Beside the phrase "are not willing," which comes from Isaiah, we also find the catchword "hardening," which has been introduced in 2:4 with a slight change of wording by later editorial activity. The frequent reference in the Deuteronomic writings to Israel's being "stubborn" (Dtn 31:27; 9:6–13, but earlier in Ex 32:9; 33:3, 5; 34:9; Judg 2:19 where it refers to a way of life, and more categorically in Dtn 9:27) becomes in Jer 3:3 a reference to a "harlot's brow," which has no sense of shame (cf. Jer 5:3; Is 48:4). The statement about the stubbornness of the people strongly recalls Is 6:9f and 1 Kings 22. With Ezekiel, however, the hardening of the people is already an established fact, corresponding to the finality of his preaching. No room is left therefore for the Isaianic concept of the hardening being brought about by the prophet's preaching.[142]

■ **3:8** By way of conclusion a final summing up repeats the injunction to fearlessness which has already been expressed in 2:6 (cf. Jer 1:8, 17). Now, however, by being connected to the description of the hardening of Israel it is enlarged slightly. As Israel had hardened its brow against Yahweh, so Yahweh will harden the prophet's brow against Israel. We might expect that a comforting reassurance would be given to the prophet here, which we have missed in the reference in 2:6. In fact what we find is that any soft personal touch is totally lacking, even the "for I am with you" of Jer 1:8 (19). Everything has a metallic harshness and objectivity.

■ **3:9** Ezekiel's brow must be as hard as a diamond[143] and harder than flint (felspar, from which ancient knives for circumcision were made according to Josh 5:2f; Ex 4:25). Whereas in Jeremiah's similes of the fortified city and the wall of bronze we can trace in-

directly a reference to the protection of the prophet by divine power, with Ezekiel the hardening is introduced into the personality, and even onto the face, of the prophet. Ezekiel's whole prophetic message of judgement will prove that he is characterized by a thoroughgoing hardness, which permits of no soft feelings and leaves no way of escape, quite unlike Jeremiah.

■ **3:10, 11** *The final specific sending* in 3:10f, in which Yahweh sends the prophet directly to the exiles in whose midst he dwells, at first appears to contain no new elements apart from the specific address, but simply to repeat formulations from 2:4f, 7; 3:4. Two observations, however, can be made.

In the introductory formula of this closing speech "all my words . . . which I shall speak to you, receive in your heart" it is striking that it is not formulated with the perfect tense "all which I have spoken," although in the scroll Yahweh's word to the prophet appears to have been given once and for all. This shows clearly that the commission and ordination of the prophet were in no way such conclusive events that he became a kind of master of the word of Yahweh and could speak on the basis of possessing it. He had to continue to be a hearer and to receive it in his heart. Thus in the chapters that follow he can speak repeatedly of acts of receiving God's word. As Isaiah and Jeremiah had been continual hearers, mastered by the word (Is 8:11) and yet repeatedly awaiting it (Jer 28:11f; 42:7), so Ezekiel also was to live by the word which proceeded from Yahweh.

Lastly we may raise the question whether it is more than accidental that the words "for they are a rebellious house," which appear so strongly in the sending to Israel (2:5–8; 3:9), are not repeated in the sending to the exiles. Could this be because Yahweh's threat was more restrained in the sending to the exiles, who had already experienced the divine judgement, than where the prophet addressed all Israel, of which the remnant in Jerusalem had still not experienced that judgement?

■ **3:12–15** *The Conclusion of the Call*. 3:12–15. The dismissal of the prophet after all that he had seen and heard is set under the sign of the working of the divine רוח.

---

142 See Franz Hesse, *Das Verstockungsproblem im Alten Testament*, BZAW 74 (Berlin: Töpelmann, 1955).

143 So Gesenius-Buhl; Zorell; Galling, *BRL*, 140; Koeh-

■ **3:12** In particular we have a mention here of the prophet's being "lifted up" (נשא = "to raise, carry off") by it.[144] We must compare this with the mention in the earlier prophetic narratives of the fear of Ahab's steward Obadiah, who says to Elijah, "As soon as I have gone from you the spirit of Yahweh will carry you (ישאך) whither I know not—and so he will kill me" (1 Kings 18:12; cf. Is 40:24; 41:16 for a similar reference to being carried away by the stormwind). The particular nuance of the statement, which ought not to be removed by text-critical procedures, consists in the prophet's not being allowed to become simply a 'spectator' of the departure of the divine manifestation. The spirit carries the prophet away so that he hears the sound of Yahweh's departure only in the mysterious roaring (of an earthquake?) behind him.

■ **3:13** Later interpretation has then unveiled in v 13 the vague and mysterious mention of the רעש in v 12 by reference to the beating of the wings of the creatures (1:24) and the sound of the wheels (expanded from 1:15ff). In the original text the departure of the glory of Yahweh ברעש corresponds to his coming in the thundercloud and lightning (1:4). The added details of the sound effects in 1:24(25); 3:13 merely serve to weaken the great assertions of the original description.

After the departure of Yahweh's glory the final return of the prophet to his people is narrated.

■ **3:14** The statements of v 14, in the first half of which the word for removal לקח (Gen 5:24; 2 Kings 2:3; cf. Amos 7:15; Ps 49:16; 73:24) appears alongside the verb נשא, must not be broken up under the pressure of logical questioning (Was the prophet carried off or did he go to his house of his own accord?). Plainly the two halves of the verse describe one and the same event under different aspects. What is described by the reference to the prophet's being lifted up and carried off by the spirit is his personal experience of returning home with his spirit aglow under the pressure of Yahweh's hand laid upon him. The objective language describes a subjective experience. A later interpreter has added to this the explanatory words "in bitterness."

■ **3:15b** The experience weighed so heavily upon him, inhibiting all free activity, that he remained for seven days completely overwhelmed (cf. Acts 9:8f).

■ **3:15a** In connection with this the location of the exiles to whom Ezekiel belonged is mentioned for the first and only time. They dwelt in Tel Abib. In its form the name is undoubtedly to be connected with the settlements of the exiles תל מלח and תל חרשא mentioned in Ezra 2:59; Neh 7:61. W. F. Albright suggests an interpretation of the name תל מלח from the Akkadian malāḫu as "Hill of Sailors."[145] To ears familiar with Hebrew this would have been interpreted as "Salt Hill." Tel Abib would have been understood from the Hebrew as "Hill of Ears." However, the name is scarcely to be separated from the Akkadian word til abūbi, mentioned in Codex Hammurabi xvii r line 79f ("He might transform his land into a til abūbim") and in the Annals of Tiglath-pileser III, line 208f ("591 towns . . . from the sixteen regions of the land I destroyed as a til abūbi.") (cf. AOBAT 347). In these examples it means a "(ruin) hill of the flood"; i.e., a very ancient hill. What must have been, in the mouths of the Babylonian population, a description of one of the uninhabited mounds of an old city was understood as a proper name by the exiles to whom the place was assigned as a settlement by the Babylonian administration. The locality must be sought near to the canal Chebar, in the vicinity of Nippur.

Aim

When questioned about the message of Ezek 1:1–3:15 we must answer that the account of Ezekiel's call, like all the other prophetic call-narratives, is first of all a witness to the word of God which came unexpectedly to this particular individual. The actuality of this event forms the basis of all further utterances of the prophet. Within the people of God the prophet had importance not simply as a man to whom information had been entrusted, in the way that a great thinker may have importance among a people. In his person he was a witness to a divine history which took place, breaking in upon man in the form of an address from God. It called men, took possession of them, and commissioned them to service.

But Ezek 1:1–3:15 does not narrate a free religious

ler–Baumgartner "emery."
144 See further 8:3; 11:1, 24; 43:5.
145 Albright, "Seal of Eliakim," 100f.

experience of a pious man, but rather in itself contains a claim to stand within a continuum of divine history—besides being a free act of intervention from outside. The description of the theophany in the storm, surrounded by light, shows that the prophet encountered God as the Lord who had already earlier revealed himself to his people Israel in storm and light (Ex 19:1ff; 24:9–11) and who was now calling him. Even if we object that the event clearly stands in direct relationship to visual elements of the surrounding world, it is nevertheless clear from the word of God addressed to the prophet out of the midst of the manifestation that the relationship to what had earlier happened to Israel is of a very different kind. The coming of Yahweh to Ezekiel and the sending of the prophet to Israel show that God was still concerned with his mysterious and special purpose for "the house of Israel." This was the community with which he had been dealing since he had first encountered them in the beginnings of the wilderness period in a particular and exclusive way. The continuity of history which becomes evident in this call, and in the prophet's preaching which follows (cf. especially chs. 16, 20, 23), is therefore something quite different from the continuity of an accidental historical sequence or a geographical nearness. It is the continuity of divine faithfulness, which persevered with the people Israel and continued to deal with it, now also through the sending of the prophet Ezekiel. This even takes place in the remoteness of exile, where Israel was only present in a very reduced way. As the book of Ezekiel shows, this faithfulness would still be effective even when the remnant of Israel which—historically speaking—still had a life of its own in Jerusalem, was to be shattered. Ezek 1:1–3:15 thus recounts an event which actualizes in a remarkable way the story of God's faithfulness to his people Israel under new circumstances.

We must add to this that Ezek 1:1–3:15 proclaims an exciting freedom of God. The old Israel knew the territory of Palestine as the land of its God (1 Sam 26:19; 2 Kings 5:17). Amos could describe death in exile as dying "in an unclean land" (Amos 7:17). How much more must such a belief have been present to Ezekiel the priest, who had been carried off from his homeland and whose words show clearly enough how much he was conscious of the particular nearness of

Israel's God to his people in the sanctuary in Jerusalem. But now this Jerusalem priest encountered the coming of Yahweh in exile. As Is 6 told of the nearness of the Holy One of Israel to the person he called in the Jerusalem temple, so the narrative of Ezekiel's call proclaims the freedom of the divine appearing in an unclean land, and this of the very God of Israel. The special connection with his chosen sanctuary in Jerusalem is not denied, but beyond this connection (in bold recollection of earlier statements about Yahweh's appearing from afar, Judg 5), God reveals the sovereign freedom of his appearing, when and where he wills, even in an unclean land of the dead (37:1ff). God's coming to keep faith with his people knew no barriers. In the full splendor of his regal glory God met his people in the midst of a heathen land.

God's freedom, however, is not only to be seen in the place of his appearing. Incomparably more powerfully and threateningly it was revealed in his word given to the prophet. To what has been said about the continuity of God's faithfulness to the 'house of Israel', we must add that Ezekiel, in agreement with earlier written prophecy, was conscious of the prophetic reasoning in regard to Israel's election by the Holy One (Amos 3:2). As the free and holy Lord, the god of Israel had bound himself to his people. For the messenger of God's word, this meant for Ezekiel not simply that he was himself summoned to unremitting obedience (2:8), but that judgement was to be proclaimed over the rebellious people of God, which would inevitably lead to "mourning, lamentation and woe" (2:10). It meant that in facing this Holy One, from whom Israel could not cut itself free, the people would be shown up in the strongest possible light as more stubborn than all other peoples (3:6) and as "a rebellious house" (2:5–8; 3:9). Where the light shines brightest the shadows are strongest. Where God in his faithfulness comes really near to his people there his people's sinfulness becomes plain.

From this it also becomes clear what this is to mean for the life of the messenger of the word. His life was intended by God to be recognized by his people. It was to witness vitally to the historical advent of God to his people as a "sign" which men had to acknowledge as a proof of judgement and was therefore to be a hidden means of grace for the people.[146] Because of the rebelliousness of the people, however, he would be attacked on all sides. Thorns would tear the prophet's flesh, and he would sit upon scorpions (2:6). The life of the messenger would be overwhelmed. Its outward result would be failure because he was to encounter stubborn men.

Yet in all this he was himself to be equipped with a brow, made hard by a power other than his own, so that through everything it will become clear that he will overcome. All this is expressed very clearly in Ezekiel. Through this hardness, however, it was to become evident that the deepest consequence for Ezekiel, as God's messenger, was not to be a petrifying hardness, which could only be death, but the gracious blessedness of the word, which was to be in his mouth sweeter than honey (3:3).

Thus Ezekiel was called to be a witness to a history which the Christian Church believes has its center in Jesus Christ.

---

146 Cf. on 2:5.

3

The Office of Watchman

16   [And it happened after seven days], and the word of Yahweh came to me:[a] 17/ Son of man, I have made you a watchman for the house of Israel. Whenever you hear a word from my mouth, you shall give them warning before me.[a] 18/ If I say to the wicked: You shall surely die,[a] and you [have not warned him, and][b] have not spoken in order to warn the wicked[c] from his ' '[d] ways [in order to save his life][b] then he, the wicked, shall die on account of his guilt, but his blood I will require at your hand. 19/ But if you have warned the wicked, and he has not turned away from his wickedness, and his ' '[a] ways, then he shall die on account of his guilt; but you will have saved your life.

16   16a For the construction of the entire verse 16 𝔐 ויהי מקצה שבעת ימים ויהי דבר יהוה אלי לאמר cf. 1:1a. 𝔊 smooths the text by the omission of the second ויהי and joins it more closely to 3:15 by the introduction of the article in μετὰ τὰς ἑπτὰ ἡμέρας 3:16. The harsh sequence of the twofold ויהי is without parallel in Ezekiel (but cf. 1 Chr 17:3). An emendation of the second ויהי to היה (Cornill, BH, following 𝔊) may be supported by the analogy of the passages 26:1; 29:17; 30:20; 31:1; 32:1, 17. However the unified tradition of the Hebrew textual evidence, the fact that the sequence ויהי ... היה otherwise appears only in the oracles against the nations, and especially the striking פסקא באמצע פסוק of the Masoretic division of the text raises the question whether 𝔐 owes its unusual structure to an early redactional manipulation. Vv 16b–21 appear to break up an original connection of 16a/22. The fact that outside the oracles against foreign nations only oracles in the book of Ezekiel are dated which contain a certain description of the situation (1:1ff; 8:1ff; 20:1ff; 24:1ff; 33:21ff; 40:1ff), the further fact that the parallel 33:1–9, which is not to be separated from 3:16b–21, is undated, whilst conversely a date is prefaced to the ותהי (ותפל) עלי ... יד יהוה in 1:3; 8:1 (40:1; for 37:1 see on the text) supports the view that we should regard vv 16b–21 as a secondary addition on grounds of form. Considerations of content point in the same direction.

17   17a V 18 (33:8) supports the interpretation of הזהיר מן "warn before." The expression was already understood in this way by 𝔗 in v 17, in which 𝔗 lessens the harshness of the statement by its own free interpretation ותזהר יתהון מלמחתי קדמי. Against Cornill ("you shall warn them from me"), Herrmann, Bertholet, Gesenius-Buhl, Koehler-Baumgartner, Zorell, and with Ehrlich, we must preserve here the strong "before me," even though this was no longer tolerated by 𝔊 παρ' ἐμοῦ and 𝔙 ex me. In this it is supported by the section 33:1–9, see on the text.

18   18a Against 𝔊 θανάτῳ θανατωθήσῃ (so Cornill תומת) we must keep the text of 𝔐. Cf. the comments on 33:8 and 18:13.

    b This is missing in the parallel 33:8 and must be regarded as a subsequent expansion.

    c For the additional ἀποστρέψαι read here by 𝔊, we must compare the addition מדרכו לשוב ממנו in 33:9, which is certainly to be regarded as an addition. Did 𝔊 have in front of it a text glossed by לשוב?

    d הרשעה (from his) wicked (way) of 𝔐 is to be deleted here and in v 19. Cf. v 19 note a.

19   19a רשע is not otherwise found in the Old Testament in an adjectival usage. The apparent excep-

20/ Again if a righteous man turns away from his righteousness[a] and commits iniquity, and I cause him to stumble, he shall die. If you have not warned him, then[b] he will die on account of his sin, and his righteous deeds which he has done will not be remembered; but his blood I will require at your hand. 21/ Nevertheless if you have warned the righteous man,[a] not to sin ' '[b], and he does not sin, then he shall live,[c] because he took warning; and you will have saved your life.

tions אדם רשע Prv 11:7; Job 20:29, מלאך רשע Prv 13:17, and אנשים רשעים 2 Sam 4:11 are to be understood as nominal appositions. Ezek 21:30; 33:15, cf. on the text. 𝔊 read הרשעה neither in vv 18 nor 19. It clearly read in v 19b הוא רשע ὁ ἄνομος ἐκεῖνος (in 33:9 simply οὗτος). Has a marginal (וא)ה רשע entered at the wrong place in the text, been assimilated as a feminine form, then been introduced in v 18 from 19a? In the parallel text 33:8f it is lacking in both verses. Undoubtedly it was not part of the original text.

20 20a Instead of the noun צדק, which is otherwise only found in Ezekiel in 45:10 in a quite different connection, we should read מצדקתו following the evidence of the parallel texts 18:24, 26; 33:18, which is otherwise quite consistent.

b The words אשר עשה must be original, although they are missing in 𝔊^B 𝔐^{Ken 96}. Cf. 18: (21f) 24, 26, 27, 28.

21 21a 𝔊 supports the reading הזהרת, as in 3:19. The הזהרתו of 𝔐 must be regarded as an unintentional echo from v 20.

b The second צדיק is to be deleted. 𝔊 had it before חיו יחיה. It could be an explanatory gloss, which has been taken up at different places in the text.

c The form חיו is found again in 18:28; 33:15f, beside the regular form חָיָה in 18:9, 17, 19, 21; 33:13; 2 Kings 8:10, 14. The reason for the distinction is not clear.

Form

After the formula for the receiving of God's word in v 16b there follows in 3:17–21 an address directed personally to the prophet, in which Yahweh explains the responsibility of his office. Vv 17–19, apart from two additions in v 18 which are easily recognizable as subsequent expansions, reappear word for word in 33:7–9. There they are closely connected with 33:1–6. The possibility cannot be altogether ruled out that 33:7–9 may have formed the primary saying in the whole section 33:1–9.[1] 3:20–21 are also related to ch. 18 (cf. also 33:10–20). From that chapter, which is set out as an address from God to the people, these verses describe the case of the righteous man who turns away from his righteousness. In defining this person and his fate they show close contacts with 18:24, 26 (33:18). Obviously we are dealing here in all these cases with a well-established didactic form of speech. 33:1–9 and ch. 18 (33:10–20) in their theme form a self-contained unit, which refers to the office and obligation of a watchman (33:1–9) and the question of divine retribution (ch. 18). 3:17–21, however, in its theme and literary dependence, appears to be a fusion of earlier elements. 3:20–21 relate the responsibility of the watchman, i.e., the theme of 33:1–9, very closely to the case of the righteous man who turns away from his righteousness, which originally belonged to ch. 18. The details of the watchman's office, taken over from 33:7–9, are thereby elaborated by the taking up of a question from ch. 18. Thus it is clear that we cannot regard 3:17–21 as the original text to which 33:1–9 and ch. 18 made further elaborations, but conversely 3:17–21 presupposes the other two passages. Fohrer's view of a displacement of vv 16b–21 from an original position after 33:1–6 does not agree with the actual nature of 3:16b–21.[2]

1 See on the text.

2 Fohrer, *Hauptprobleme*, 30. For a more detailed consideration of the form reference must be made to the two underlying passages referred to.

Location

Note a on 3:16 shows that 3:16b–21 breaks up an original connection of vv 16a and 22ff. On the other hand, considerations of form have shown that 3:17–21 represents an expansion of the watchman oracle of 33:7–9 with material from ch. 18. So, in regard to the question of the composition of the section, it is probable that we are dealing in 3:16b–21 with an expansion of the call-narrative at the stage of the final redaction of the book, on the basis of material from Ezekiel, either simply collected or partly reformulated. The final redactor of the book felt a lack at the beginning of the basic statement of 33:7–9 regarding the prophet's office. To have introduced such a statement in the call-narrative proper of 1:1–3:15 would have broken up the character of this account in an unacceptable way. Hence it was not inserted there (this is indirectly a not unimportant argument against the view of large insertions in the divine speech of 2:1–3:11). Thus the addition was made in the form of the insertion of 3:16b–21 immediately after the end of the call-narrative and before the details of the prophet's message begin to become evident in 3:22ff.[3]

Interpretation

The unit is introduced by the formula for the receiving of God's word and is set out as an account from the prophet in the first person, which is highly characteristic of the book of Ezekiel.

■ **3:16b** The formula ויהי דבר יהוה אלי appears in the book of Ezekiel forty-one times in a pure form, and in 12:8; 24:1 a more precise date is introduced into it. In 24:20 it is set within an address to the people by Ezekiel in the perfect tense. To this may be added seven further passages, all of which belong to the oracles against foreign nations (26:1; 29:1, 17; 30:20; 31:1; 32:1, 17), in which the formula has undergone a slight change through the introduction of a date. 1:3 comes from the hand of the redactor of the book. As a rule

the formula introduces a new speech section and consequently is one of the essential helps towards defining the individual units of the book.

The formula was certainly not originally coined by Ezekiel, but rather belongs to a larger group of passages in the Old Testament, totalling 113, in which this formula occurs. No other book, however, surpasses Ezekiel's total of fifty occurrences of the construction of דבר יהוה with היה אל in reference to the prophet who receives the word.[4] With ביד (of the prophet) and אל (of those addressed by the prophet) the saying is also used in 1 Kings 16:7; Hag 1:1; cf. 1:3; 2:1. Finally outside the prophetic literature proper we must also compare Gen 15:1; 1 Kings 6:11; 18:31. Undoubtedly the expression had its roots in the language of prophecy and is used very frequently in the narratives of the prophets of the early monarchy, which must be regarded as having been preserved in the bands of prophets (Samuel, 1 Sam 15:10; Nathan, 2 Sam 7:4/1 Chr 17:3; Gad, 2 Sam 24:11; Shemaiah, 1 Kings 12:22/Chr 11:2; 12:7; the prophet of Bethel, 1 Kings 13:20; Jehu, 1 Kings 16:1[7]; Elijah, 1 Kings 17:2, 8; 18:1; 21:17, 28). It is absent in the actual oracles of the older classical prophets and first appears in the redactional headings (Hos 1:1; Zeph 1:1, also Joel 1:1), and the narrative traditions of the schools of the earlier prophetic books (Is 38:4/2 Kings 20:4). Even among the thirty occurrences in the book of Jeremiah a considerable proportion are found in secondary texts (46:1; 47:1; 49:34) or sections preserved by the disciples of the prophet (Baruch?). Nevertheless, with Jeremiah the use of the formula in the prophet's actual words is certainly not to be denied (1:4, 11, 13; 2:1 and other passages). From there it has a firm place in Ezekiel, Haggai (2:10, 20; cf. 1:1, 3; 2:1) and Zechariah (1:1, 7; 4:8; 6:9; 7:1, 4, 8; 8:1, 18). In later writings see also Jonah 1:1; 3:1; Dan 9:2.

As regards the content of this formula we must see in it a derivation from a very well developed conception

---

3 See Curt Kuhl, "Die 'Wiederaufnahme'—ein literarkritisches Prinzip?" *ZAW* 64 (1952): 1–11, on this feature of introducing summarizing repetitions.

4 See the summary in Oskar Grether, *Name und Wort Gottes im Alten Testament*, BZAW 64 (Giessen: Töpelmann, 1934), 67f, to which we must add Hag 2:10, which Grether wrongly includes in the following group.

of the "word of Yahweh." We can, perhaps, speak of a prophetic "theology of the word," which emerged in prophetic circles. Instead of a direct encounter by the personal address of God, the "word" is understood almost as an objective entity with its own power of entry.[5] Furthermore there lies in the mention of the coming of Yahweh's word a reference to its eminently historical character and its relation to events. The frequent connection of the formula with a date, especially in Ezekiel, clearly shows how little the "word of Yahweh" was a kind of timeless knowledge and how much it was actualized in a historical event. Thus C. H. Ratschow seeks to understand the verb היה, in its basic meaning, as "becoming effective."[6] What is the significance of the formula then, when it is used in the book of Ezekiel exclusively with the preposition אל and not the stronger על, which is preferred in references to the hand of Yahweh coming upon man,[7] especially bearing in mind that אל and על often interchange in the book of Ezekiel? Is 9:7 shows that Yahweh's word, like his hand (Ezek 8:1) could be said to "fall" upon man.

In his use of these current ways of describing the reception of the word of God Ezekiel stands in the old tradition of the prophetic schools more strongly than Jeremiah, where they do not appear so prominently, especially in genuine sayings of the prophet, and in sharp contrast to earlier written prophecy. It is quite mistaken to follow Hölscher, *Hesekiel*, in denying altogether the use of these formal expressions to Ezekiel. On the other hand, we cannot follow Irwin and see in them a unique coining by the prophet. Ezekiel adopted them from the language of the prophetic circles without giving a particularly strong accentuation of his own to them.

Only in one place can the distinctiveness of Ezekiel be seen in the use of the formula. Jeremiah already shows the introduction of the first person into the formula.[8] This personal form is throughout dominant

in Ezekiel.

■ **3:17–19** For details of the interpretation of vv 17–19, cf. on 33:7–9. In these words from Yahweh the prophet is called to be a watchman for the house of Israel. By being conceived as the office of a watchman the prophet's role is brought close to the members of the house of Israel, as regards their conduct and their life or death in obedience or disobedience to God, which is quite different from the very objective commissioning of the prophet with the word of God (2:3ff). The life or death of the individual is related to the prophet's neglect (v 18) or watchfulness (v 19) in his task as a watchman, thus bringing a new note of urgency into prophecy. Even without detracting from the self-determination of man, held prisoner in his own ungodliness, the unfolding of various possibilities through the prophet's conduct (vv 18f) sharply underscores his share of responsibility for the life or death of men. The two additions in 3:18, which go beyond the text of the parallel statement in 33:8, stress the importance of God's speaking to the prophet; the prophet's duty is to warn and the possibility which it includes of "saving his (the wicked man's) life" are both important parts of the saying.

■ **3:20, 21** In addition in 3:20f the same position is taken up once again. Beside the wicked the case of the righteous man who turns away from his righteousness is considered, in dependence on 18:24, opening out the possibility of his being saved. In their alternative formulation vv 20–21 are dependent on vv 18–19. Besides the reference to the responsibility of the prophet, there is also great stress here upon Yahweh's will to save the lives of men. The man who dies with no warning, as well as the man who turns away from righteousness, brings the negligent prophet to destruction. Over the prophetic office there stands the divine will to save life, and this is the will that the prophet is to serve.

This basis appears to be contradicted by v 20a, which

---

5   See the comments made by Grether, *Name*, 150ff, under the heading "Dabar as Hypostasis."

6   Carl Heinz Ratschow, *Werden und Wirken. Eine Untersuchung des Wortes hajah als Beitrag zur Wirklichkeitserfassung des Alten Testaments*, BZAW 70 (Berlin: Töpelmann, 1941). See especially pp. 34f: "*Hajah* signifies the commanding force of this word, from which Jeremiah seeks to flee and under which Eze-

kiel endures great physical suffering."

7   See above pp. 117f.

8   Hans Wildberger, *Jahwewort und prophetische Rede bei Jeremia* (Zürich: Zwingli, 1942), 19.

is without parallel in ch. 18 ("If the righteous . . . turns away and does iniquity, and I cause him to stumble," or more literally "put a stumbling block before him.")

Of the fourteen occurrences in the Old Testament of the word מכשול no less than eight are found in the book of Ezekiel. The word first of all signifies concretely an obstacle on the road, which can make a blind person fall (Lev 19:14) or which can prevent the free passage of people (Is 57:14). Quite early on, however, it took on a metaphorical significance. In 1 Sam 25:31 we find in Abigail's speech to David the metaphorical phrase מכשול לב "conscientious objection." The word otherwise always carries with it the idea of an outward failure (as a consequence of someone's misconduct). In Ps 119:165 מכשול, used absolutely, is the antithesis of the שלום רב of the man who loves the law. In prophecy before Ezekiel the word occurs only in a very characteristic formula in Isaiah and Jeremiah: in Is 8:14 in the harsh threat that Yahweh himself will become to the two houses of Israel a stone of stumbling and a rock on which to fall; in Jer 6:21 it occurs in the more objective statement that Yahweh will lay stumbling blocks (נתן מכשלים) before "this people," so that fathers and sons will fall against them. The latter text is particularly close to Ezek 3:20, but lacks the specific emphasis which Ezek 3:20 gives. Here מכשול is plainly not related to an external failure under divine judgement. This is first expressed in the ימות of the apodosis. Rather, as its position in the protasis shows, this is a part of the erstwhile righteous man's becoming sinful. This turning to sin already implies a punishment, in accordance with the "synthetic view of life" (Fahlgren) of the Old Testament and is set out in two acts: a) the turning away of the righteous man from his righteousness, which is virtually a preparation for b) the act of sin proper which brings about his downfall. This act of sin, which means falling to a particular temptation, is set out as the action of Yahweh: "I cause him to stumble." Behind this assertion, which has a slightly differently formulated parallel in 14:9, there lies the insight of biblical faith that even a man's downfall is not simply the result of his own freedom, but that behind it there may already be the overriding decree of Yahweh. The prayer "lead us not into temptation" is a true petition, from the point of view of the Old Testament as well as the New Testament. At the very moment of entering into temptation, which is to provide the occasion for sin, there may lie the judgement of God.

Besides 21:20, where the text is corrupt, the noun מכשול is only otherwise found in the book of Ezekiel in the combined formula מכשול עון (7:19; 14:3, 4, 7; 18:30; 44:12). In this formulation it becomes clear that מכשול is the occasion through which guilt passes from being potential into becoming actual through the committing of an offense at a particular place and moment.

Ezek 3:20 has probably been formulated by disciples of the prophet and mentions Yahweh's intervention in the guilt of the righteous man who turns away from his righteousness. It makes use of a current speech form to commission the prophet for his office and was not intended to make a new emphasis in which Yahweh's mercy no longer sought the sinner's salvation. Rather the prophet's obligation to warn is given fresh urgency in view of the depth of sin to which men may sink. How mysterious is the divine action which provides warning when destruction threatens to take over![9]

Purpose

We touch here upon the purpose of the addition in 3:16b–21. The disciples of Ezekiel who gave the book its final form have taken over from the fuller treatments in 33:1–9 and ch. 18 the conception of the prophet's task, as it is there described, and set it at the beginning of the prophet's mission. When Yahweh sent his messenger he impressed upon him with great urgency his responsibility for the lives of sinners. God's purpose in sending his prophet to Israel possessed an urgency, hitherto unknown, for every individual hearer. The prophet bore a responsibility for every life, even to the point of his own life or death. Without lessening the urgency of the divine demand, which called for obedience in every part of life, the prophet affirms that there lies behind it a burning love of God, which seeks the salvation of the ungodly, even when he has turned away from his life of righteousness.[10]

---

9 Cf. further on 33:1–9.
10 Cf. further on 33:1–9 and ch. 18.

The Siege of Jerusalem
and the Exile of Israel
in the Prophet's Symbolic Actions

Bibliography

A. van den Born

*De symbolische handelingen der oud-testamentische prof-
eten* (Nijmegen: Dekker & Van de Vegt, 1935).

A. van den Born

*Profetie metterdaad. Een studie over de symbolische han-
delingen der profeten* (Roermond–Maaserk: Romen,
1947)

D. Buzy

"Les symboles prophétiques d'Ezéchiel," *RB* 29,
(1920): 203–228; 353–358; 30, (1921): 45–54;
161–194: reprinted in *idem, Les symboles de l'ancien
testament* (Paris: Le Coffre, 1923), 157–264.

G. Fohrer

"Die Gattung der Berichte über symbolische Handlungen der Propheten," *ZAW* 64 (1952): 101–120.

G. Fohrer

Die symbolischen Handlungen der Propheten, ATANT 54
(Zürich: Zwingli, ² 1968).

W. Gronkowski

"De natura Ezechielis 'vinculorum'," *CT* 18
(1937): 375–412.

H. W. Hines

"The Prophet as Mystic," *AJSL* 40 (1923/24): 51–
56.

H. W. Robinson

"Prophetic Symbolism," in *Old Testament Essays.
Papers Read Before the Society for Old Testament Study*
(1927): 1–17.

3

And the hand of Yahweh was upon me
[there];[a] and he said to me: Arise, go
forth[b] into the plain, and there I will
speak with you. 23/ So I arose and went
forth into the plain; and, behold, the
glory of Yahweh was there. It stood
there like the appearance of glory,[a]
which I had seen by the river Chebar;
and I fell on my face. 24/ Then the
spirit entered into me and (the spirit)
set me upon my feet; and he (Yahweh)
spoke with me[a] and said to me: Go,
shut[b] yourself within your house.

25 And you, son of man, behold, cords will
be placed[a] upon you, and you shall be
bound with them, so that you can no
more go out in their midst. 26/ And I
will make your tongue stick to the roof

3:
22

3:22a The שָׁם of 𝔐 is lacking in 𝔊 𝔙. Origen and
Jerome had it in their Hebrew text tradition. Cf.
note d to 1:3.

b 𝔊 softens by the insertion of the copula. Cf. note
a to 1:4.

23 23a 𝔊 interprets the harsh כבוד of 𝔐 by the
double statement καθὼς ἡ ὅρασις καὶ καθὼς ἡ δόξα.

24 24a For the אֹתִי of 𝔐 cf. note a to 2:1.

b As in v 22 𝔊 improves the text here also by the
introduction of καί.

25 25a 𝔊 δέδονται 𝔙 data sunt presuppose the nipʻal
form נִתְּנוּ. 𝔗 here, as in 4:8, gives the free interpretation הא גזירת פיתגמי עלך כאיסור גדילן "behold the
ordinance of my word lies upon you like the bond of
a firmly tied knot." 𝔗 then understands 3:25 and
4:8 in a similar way, but does not, however, point
with certainty in 3:25 to an original נתתי, since the
continuation ואסרין בהין undoubtedly points to
ואסרוך as the original text of 𝔐. So we must keep
the נָתְנוּ of 𝔐. For the translation of נתנו as a future
see Hölscher, *Hesekiel*, 55 n. 1: "We are dealing here
with a perfect consecutive, which can be used after

of your mouth,[a] so that you shall be dumb and no longer a man who reproves—for they are a rebellious house. 27/ But when I speak with you,[a] I will open your mouth, and you shall say to them: Thus has [the Lord][b] Yahweh spoken. Whoever hears it, let him hear; whoever refuses it, let him refuse—for they are a house of rebellion.

4

1   And you, son of man, take a brick and lay it before you and draw upon it a city [namely Jerusalem];[a] 2/ and lay siege to it; and build siegeworks against it and set up a siege wall against it; and set camps against it also and establish battering rams [against it][a] round about. 3/ And you, take an iron plate and place it as an iron wall between you and the city; and set your face against it, and let it be besieged, and you shall besiege it. This is a sign for the house[a] of Israel.

4   And you, lie on your left side and "bear"[a] the guilt of the house of Israel ( )[b] according to the number of days that you lie on it, (so shall) you bear their guilt. 5/ And I am making[a] the years[b] of their guilt for you (to correspond with) the number of days—390 (𝕲 : 190).[c] And you shall bear the guilt of the house of Israel. 6/ And when you have completed this (time), you shall lie down on your right[a] side [a second time][b] and bear the guilt of the house of Judah, for 40 days, a day for each

the proclitics אז, הנה, ראה, etc., exactly similarly as after ו." So also in 4:8; 21:12; 39:8.

26a 𝕲 abbreviates τὴν γλῶσσάν σου συνδήσω.

27   27a For the אותך of 𝔐 cf. note a to 2:1.
b אדני] is lacking in 𝕲, see Excursus 1.

4:1   4:1a את ירושלם is generally attested, but is certainly an early interpretative gloss in the manner of Is 7:17, 20.

2   2a The final עליה is lacking in 𝕲 𝕭. Its secondary introduction in assimilation to the preceding statements can be more easily explained than its subsequent suppression. Also the structure of the heaped up short clauses in metrical three beats, which is otherwise closely kept in vv 1f, supports the omission of the final עליה.

3,4   3a 𝕲 τοῖς υἱοῖς Ισραηλ.
4a The tradition here uniformly supports the reading of 𝔐 ושמת את עון בית ישראל עליו "and you shall lay the guilt of the house of Israel upon it." This can only be given a very forced interpretation. Is the action of the prophet to be understood from the imagery of the high priest's action on the Day of Atonement? As the high priest there lay the guilt of the people on the head of the scapegoat by laying his hands upon it (formulated in Lev 16:21 ונתן אתם על ראש השעיר), so Ezekiel is to lay the guilt of the house of Israel on the left side of his body. This gives the quite impossible picture that Ezekiel is at one and the same time the bearer and the transmitter of the guilt, and further that he lays the guilt on the side of the body on which he is lying. The continuation in vv 4b, 5, 6 supports the conjecture advocated by Cornill, Ehrlich, Toy of reading ונשאת in place of ושמת, and (with Cornill and Toy) of deleting עליו as a subsequent attempt at assimilation (depending on the following תשכב עליו). An emendation to ושמתי and עליך (Wellhausen, Smend, Bertholet) is less satisfactory because Yahweh's action is first introduced in v 5 with an emphatic ואני and the perfect נתתי.
b 𝕲 introduces here the number 150.

5   5a The perfect נתתי expresses the idea that the event is already a reality through Yahweh's decision. See Gesenius-Kautzsch § 106m.
b 𝕲 τὰς δύο ἀδικίας αὐτῶν has misunderstood שני. Has 𝕿, with its ואנא יהבית לך על חד תרין בחוביהון "I have placed double upon you on account of your offences," in mind Is 40:2, 𝕿 לקת על חד תרין בכל חטאהא?
c For the different numbers in 𝔐 and 𝕲 cf. the exposition.

6   6a The form of K, ימיני beside the gentilicium ימיני Nu 26:12 and בן ימיני (passim), is otherwise only found in 2 Chr 3:17. The regular form demanded by Q reads יְמָנִי; cf. the priestly references Ex 29:20; Lev 8:23f; 14:14, 16f, 25, 27; and again in Ezek 47:1f.
b The שנית of 𝔐 is lacking in 𝕲 𝕾 𝕮 𝕮 𝕬 and is a later attempt at clarification.

year do I set[c] upon you. 7/ And you shall turn your face towards the siege of Jerusalem and make bare your arm,[a] and you shall prophesy[b] against it. 8/ And behold, I place[a] cords upon you, so that you cannot turn from the one side to the other until you have[b] completed the days of your oppression.

9 And you, take wheat[a] and barley and beans and lentils and millet and spelt, and put them into the same pot, and make bread of them for yourself [for the number of days during which you lie upon your side, 390 (𝕲: 190)[b] days, you shall eat it].[c] 10/ And your food which you eat shall be 20 shekels a day, exactly weighed out.[a] At regular times you shall eat it. 11/ And water you shall drink by measure, a sixth of a hin. At regular times you shall drink. 12/ And, in the form of barley cakes[a] you shall eat it,[b] and you shall bake it in pieces of human dung in their sight. 13/ [And Yahweh said:[a] Thus shall the Israelites eat [their bread][b] unclean among the

c For the perfect נתתיו cf. note a to v 5.

7 7a 𝕲 misunderstood the action, which is quite clear from Is 52:10, and in its τὸν βραχίονά σου στερεώσεις it has adopted a derivation from חזק. 𝕶 ודרעך תתקף follows the same track.

b Cf. the exposition for the secondary character of v 7.

8 8a For the perfect נתתי cf. 3:25 note a and 4:5 note a.

b The translation in 𝕲 ἕως οὗ συντελεσθῶσιν αἱ ἡμέραι τοῦ συγκλεισμοῦ σου in which the suffix of כלותך is not represented, must be regarded as a free translation and does not point to a different Hebrew original. The difficulties of v 8 cannot be removed by introducing changes into the text, which is uniformly attested. Cf. the exposition for its evaluation.

9 9a חטין is an Aramaizing plural; cf. Bauer-Leander § 63t; Gesenius-Kautzsch § 87e; Joüon § 90c.

b Cf. to v 5.

c Cf. the exposition for the secondary character of v 9b.

10 10a Literally: according to weight. מִשְׁקוֹל is found only here instead of the more usual מִשְׁקָל (so v 16; Lev 16:26). Cf. Bauer-Leander § 61eη besides 61zε. An emendation is not necessary.

12 12a The ἐγκρυφίας (cakes baked in hot ashes; ash-cakes) and the following ἐγκρύπτειν of 𝕲 are clearly intended to express the view that the food had wholly entered into the unclean realm. The Hebrew עוג (noun עגה) does not usually bear this emphasis. The word appears here simply to express the round form of the flat cakes (cf. Arabic ʿāǧā "to be curved"). However, in the construction of the verb with ב (unlike the עשה על of 4:15, which mentions the softening concession of Yahweh's), the same idea must be present.

b The feminine suffix has been inaccurately influenced by עגת. Strictly the relationship is to the masculine לחם or מאכל, as in vv 9f.

13 13a The introduction ויאמר יהוה is not otherwise found in Ezekiel. The slightly expanded ויאמר יהוה אלי is found in 9:4; 23:36; 44:2, 5; cf. on the text. 𝕲 has expanded the beginning of the verse to the fuller expression καὶ ἐρεῖς Τάδε λέγει κύριος ὁ θεὸς τοῦ Ἰσραηλ. It supports rightly the view that in v 13 we have a complete section of the interpretation of the sign-action (to be proclaimed to the people). The whole verse, which is unusual for its introductory formula and which anticipates the interpretation of the sign-action in a clumsy way, breaks up the close connection of vv 12/14. It is suspicious for its בני ישראל (cf. note a to 2:3), and also, as notes b and c indicate, it shows in its tradition-history the addition of further elements. It must therefore be regarded as a secondary addition to the text. Cf. the exposition.

b 𝕲 did not have the את לחמם of 𝔐, which completely assimilates the account of the interpretation to the description of the sign-action, in its Hebrew

nations, [to which I am driving them].c]
14/ And I said, Ah, [Lord]a Yahweh, behold, I have never been unclean, and from my youth up till now I have never eaten the flesh of what dies of itself or was ravaged, and nob *piggul* flesh has come into my mouth. 15/ Then he said to me: Behold, I granta you cow's dungb instead of human dung,c and you may prepare your food ond it. 16/ And he said to me: Son of man, see, I am breaking the staff of bread in Jerusalem, and they shall eat bread by weight [and with fear]a and drink water by measure [and with shaking].a—17/ Therewitha they shall have a shortage of bread and water, and one shall shake like another, and they shall waste away in their guilt.

5

1 And you, son of man, take a sharp sword; use it as a razora and pass it over your head and your beard. And take a balance and divide it (i.e., the hair). 2/ One thirda you shall burn in the city

original.

c The אשר שם אדיחם of 𝔐 is a phrase which reappears in different variations more than ten times in the book of Jeremiah (Jer 8:3; 16:15; 23:3, 8; 24:9; 29:14, 18; 32:37; 40:12; 43:5; 46:28; cf. Dtn 30:1; Dan 9:7, abbreviated in Jer 27:10, 15). It is otherwise completely lacking in the book of Ezekiel. הדיח appears again only in Ezek 34:4, 16 in another connection. The addition was still lacking in the Hebrew original of 𝔊.

14 14a 𝔊 κύριε θεè τοῦ Ισραηλ. See Excursus 1.
b Does the πᾶν κρέας of 𝔊, *omnis caro* of 𝔅 point to a כל in the Hebrew text or are we faced with a very free translation in 𝔊 𝔅?

15 15a For the perfect נתתי following רָאֵה cf. note a to 3:25, also note a to 4:5.
b It is not possible to decide certainly between K צפיעי and Q צפועי.
c For the form גֶּלְלֵי cf. Bauer-Leander § 70e′.
d Cf. note a to v 12.

16 16a The words בדאגה and בשממון of 𝔐 are uniformly attested by the tradition. However, since they are out of line with the correspondence to 4:10f, which is otherwise strongly maintained, and they introduce a new idea rather late and only in connection with the interpretation of the sign-action, they must be regarded as an intrusion from 12:19.

17 17a The final למען is here, as in 12:19, related to Yahweh and points to the consequence willed by him, and certainly not by the hungry men mentioned immediately previously in 4:17a; 12:19aβ as the subject. The statement consequently takes on a harsh objectivity.

5:1 5:1a The reading of Θ (𝔖 𝔏) ὥσπερ ξυρὸν κουρέως, in which Ziegler, following a conjecture of Katz, wants to find the original reading of the unusual ὑπὲρ ξυρὸν κουρέως (sharper than a razor?) of the 𝔊 tradition, must be regarded as a subsequent smoothing of the sharp transition from aα¹ to aα².

2 2a 𝔊 reads both in vv 2 and 12 τὸ τέταρτον. The renumbering must have originated from v 12, see on the text there. It has, as a consequence, led in v 2 to the separation of the two verbs ולקחת and תכה to two different actions performed each with a quarter of the hair. Thus the ולקחת is freely expanded by 𝔊, in line with the first act of destruction, καὶ λήμψῃ τὸ τέταρτον καὶ κατακαύσεις αὐτὸ ἐν μέσῳ αὐτῆς. For the following תכה the object has to be expanded καὶ τὸ τέταρτον κατακόψεις. 𝔐 undoubtedly gives the original form of the text with its divisions of the action into three. However, the text of 𝔐 is also not without difficulty. ולקחת ... תכה is "an unbearable construction" (Cornill). Both vv 2a and 3 (cf. also 1) show the usual construction of ולקחת with a following verb form in the perfect consecutive. Further the interpretation of the symbolic act in v 12 shows syntactically a closely parallel action to the threefold שְׁלִישִׁית. This is also achieved in v 2 by the bracketing of לקחת as a subsequent addition (Cornill, Toy,

with fire,[b] when the days of siege are completed; and one third you shall [take and]ᵃ cut up with the sword around it, and one third you shall scatter to the wind. [And I will draw the sword after them]ᶜ 3/ And you shall take from there a small number and bind them in the skirt of 'your' garment.ᵃ 4/ And you shall take (some) of them and throw them into the fire and burn them with fire.

'And you shall say'ᵃ to the whole house of Israel: 5/ Thus has [the Lord]ᵃ Yahweh said: This is Jerusalem! I have set it in the midst of the nations, with 'the' lands round about it.ᵇ 6/ But it was rebelliousᵃ against my laws, in that it was more wicked than the nations, and against my statutes, more than the lands which were around it [, for they rejected my laws and did not walk in my statutes,].ᵇ 7/ Therefore thus has [the Lord]ᵃ Yahweh said: Because you are more rebelliousᵇ than the nations which are around you, and you have not walked in my statutes and have not obeyed my laws, and have notᶜ even obeyed the laws of the nations which are around you, 8/ therefore thus has [the Lord]ᵃ Yahweh said: Behold, thus will I also (now) do to you! And I will execute judgementᵇ in your midst before the eyes of the nations. 9/ And I will do to you what I have never done before, and will not do again, because of all your abominations. 10/ Therefore fathers will eat their sons in your midst, and sons will eat 'the' fathers,ᵃ and I will execute judgement within you, and scatter to the winds any of you that are left. 11/ Therefore, as I live, says [the Lord]ᵃ Yahweh because you have made my sanctuary unclean [with all your detestable things and]ᵇ with all your abominations, I will cut

Bertholet) or לקחת את (Ehrlich, Herrmann). Read והשלישית.

b The באור, which is unique in Ezekiel, is striking. The reading of MSᴷᵉⁿ ¹⁸² באש is a smoothing of the text, which Cornill would restore. The emendation to בעור, conjectured by Herrmann, however, makes the expression too heavy and is not probable after the preceding object. Since Is 31:9; 47:14 (44:16?) attest the extension of the meaning אור, which basically denotes "light," to make it a synonym of אש, we must keep the text of 𝔐. אור is preferred here to אש on account of its similarity of sound to תבעיר.

c The verse section by, which introduces too soon the interpretation into the description of the symbolic action and introduces Yahweh as speaking in the first person, stems from v 12.

3   3a Instead of 𝔐 בכנפיך we should read בכנפך. 𝔊 τῇ ἀναβολῇ σου 𝔙 in summitate pelli tui.

4   4a The ממנו תצא אש of 𝔐, which does not fit grammatically, is an addition (from 19:14?) still not attested by 𝔊. In its place the *Vorlage* of 𝔊 appears to have had ואמרת. Accordingly v 4b was originally the introduction to vv 5ff.

5   5a אדני is lacking in 𝔊, see Excursus 1.

b The continuation in v 6 leads us to expect here הארצות instead of ארצות without the article, as in 𝔐. So we must follow 𝔊 in reading the article, which has fallen out through haplography.

6   6a καὶ ἐρεῖς sees in the ותמר of 𝔐 the verb אמר, Σ ἀντικατηλλάξαντο the verb מור, so also Θ 𝔖 𝔗.

b The transition to the third person plural betrays another hand in v 6b.

7   7a אדני is lacking in 𝔊, see Excursus 1.

b The המנכם (your raging?) of 𝔐 was certainly already attested by 𝔊 ἡ ἀφορμὴ ὑμῶν. However, with Böttcher, Cornill and others we should certainly emend to הַמְרֹתְכֶם. Cf. the related transitions with יען and a following infinitive with suffix in 13:8; 21:29; 25:3, 6; 28:6.

c The omission of לא in 30 MSS Edd 𝔊³¹¹, ⁶¹³ 𝔖, Arm is an attempt to soften the severity of the original statement in line with 11:12, which is omitted in 𝔊.

8   8a אדני is lacking in 𝔊, see Excursus 1.

b The parallel texts 5:10, 15; 11:9; 28:22, 26; 30:19 support the reading here of שפטים instead of משפטים.

10   10a 𝔐 אבותם. We can clearly see in the development of the text tradition (𝔊ᴸ 𝔖 𝔗 𝔙) the softening of the harsh formulations "fathers' sons" by the introduction of a pronominal back reference. It has also entered into the corresponding phrase "sons of their fathers" in 𝔐. The original 𝔊 text in both references preserved the harsh formulation without the suffix.

11   11a אדני is lacking in 𝔊, see Excursus 1.

b 𝔊 did not read בכל שקוציך ו. As in 7:20 it may be a subsequent addition to 𝔐.

you[c] up, and my eye will not show pity, and I shall feel no compassion. 12/ The third part of you[a] shall die of pestilence and be destroyed by famine in your midst, and a third part will fall by the sword round about you, and a third part I will scatter to the winds and will draw the sword after them. 13/ And my anger will be fully spent, and my fury will I vent[a] upon them [and I shall exhaust my anger (or: compassion?)],[a] and they shall know [b]that I, Yahweh,[c] have spoken in my zeal, when I spend my anger upon them. 14/ And I will make you a place of ruins [and a reproach][a] [among the nations which are round about you][b] before the eyes

c The אגרע of 𝔐 offers difficulties. 𝔊 ἀπώσομαί σε may point to a derivation from גרש (cf. Jonah 2:5 𝔊); the *confringam* of 𝔅 points to גדע 𝔗. אקטוף תקוף דרעיך "I take away the power of your arms" could point in the same direction as a free interpretation. Hitzig conjectures אֶפְרַע "Thus will I also let (my desire) go (its course)"; Ewald אפרע "I will not let go (neglect)"; Cornill אתגרה "I will go in." Possibly the other passages, Is 15:2; Jer 48:37, which support the technical meaning of גרע as "to shave," enable us to keep to the text of 𝔐 here, regarding it as an absolute use of the verb without an object. Then it is no longer v 12 which first goes back to the images of the symbolic action of 5:1ff, but this already takes place in v 11.

12   12a שלשתיך of 𝔐 is wrongly written from שלשיתך, cf. MSS[Ken]. 𝔊 here, as in v 2, lists four groups. The appearance of the two verbs in aα, the separate treatment of pestilence and hunger in 14:12ff and elsewhere, and the frequent importance of the number four in Ezekiel may have provided an encouragement to elaborate the text further. The text is a particularly good example of the far-reaching interpretative work on the text right up to the time of its translation into Greek. 𝔊 further changes the order of aβ and bα, since they clearly seek to bring together into close proximity statements connected by the catchword חרב (Cornill).

13   13a 𝔊 καὶ συντελεσθήσεται ὁ θυμός μου καὶ ἡ ὀργή μου ἐπ' αὐτούς does not translate (ו)הנחותי and והנחמתי of 𝔐. Loewe, "Anthropopathism," 266, seeks to understand the lack of והנחמתי as a tendentious change to soften an anthropopathism regarding God. The graphic similarity of the hitpaʻel verbal form of נחם with the assimilated נ, which is only found here (Gesenius-Kautzsch § 54c; Joüon § 53e, cf. also § 29f), to the preceding הנחותי makes it appear possible that we should see in והנחמתי a simple erroneous scribal repetition of והנחותי. In support of the originality of והנחותי we may note that the phrase הניח חמה ב is found again in 16:42; 21:22; 24:13. We find חמתי and אפי in parallel clauses again in 7:8; 13:13 (20:8, 21), and as a simple double statement only in the adverbial expressions formed with prepositions באף ובחמה 5:15; כאפי וכחמתי 22:20; באפי ובחמתי 25:14.

b 𝔊 καὶ ἐπιγνώσῃ assimilates the recognition formula of the insertion vv 12bβ, 13 to the original text of vv 12abα, 14, formed with the second person singular feminine. Cf. the exposition.

c Undoubtedly the formula of self-introduction אני יהוה is echoed in the phrase כי אני יהוה דברתי, so that if it did not sound too clumsy we could translate: "that I, I Yahweh, have spoken." Cf. Zimmerli, "Jahwe," 185 and the exposition.

14   14a The ולחרפה of 𝔐 anticipates in a clumsy way the language and ideas of the following verse. It is lacking in 𝔊 and is a gloss.

b The בגוים אשר סביבותיך, which reappears

of everyone who passes by. 15/ And 'you will become'ᵃ a reproach and an object of scornᵇ to the nations which are around you, [a warning and a horror],ᶜ when I execute judgement upon you [in anger and fury and]ᵈ with furious punishments. I, Yahweh,ᵉ have spoken 16/ to the effect that I am sending against 'you'ᵃ 'my' arrows of destruction [of famine],ᵇ which bring destruction [, which I am sending in order to destroy you, and I will bring yet more famine upon you]ᶜ and break

word for word in the next verse, disturbs the clear connection of aα/b and should be cut out as a gloss (Herrmann). 𝕲 (𝕷 𝖀 𝕰) καὶ τὰς θυγατέρας σου had before it in its Hebrew original the בגוים wrongly written as בנותיך.

15   15a Instead of 𝔐 והיתה "and she will be" we should read וְהָיִית. ה is a dittography of the following ה.

b 𝔐 גְדוּפָה is to be vocalized according to Koehler-Baumgartner as גְדוּפָה with Is 51:7.

c 𝕲 στενακτὴ καὶ δηλαϊστή (Jerome: cuius verbi notitiam non habemus) is not altogether clear. When Θ (Jerome's reference to the reading of Θ is to be corrected, see Ziegler, Ezechiel, 64) adds παιδεία καὶ ἀφανισμός it is in any case clear that it seeks to add thereby the equivalent of מוסר ומשמה = "for a warning (?) and a horror." Accordingly these words must still have been lacking in the Hebrew original of 𝕲 and should be cut out.

d באף ובחמה ו "in anger and wrath and" is not attested by 𝕲 and is a subsequent addition, as the clumsy repetition of חמה in 𝔐 shows.

e Cf. note c to v 13.

16   16a 𝔐 בהם "against them." The parallel clause bβ, as also the addition aβbα point to an original בכם. Or should we delete בהם altogether with 𝕾?

b 𝕲 ἐν τῷ ἐξαποστεῖλαί με τὰς βολίδας μου τοῦ λιμοῦ ἐπ' αὐτούς appears not to have known the Hebrew הרעים. Should we regard it as an incorrect repetition of הרעב which stands beside it? Or is it the other way round, that הרעב should be regarded as a scribal error for an original הרעים, which would be likely in this context? In any case הרעב in spite of being supported by 𝕲, is highly questionable in aα. In 𝕲's τὰς βολίδας μου there appears a tradition of interpretation which knows nothing of the construct relationship of 𝔐 חִצֵּי הָרָעָב, but seeks to understand חצי as the suffixed form חִצֵּי "my arrows," beside which no genitive is in order. Of the contents we can say that the Old Testament often mentions the "arrows of God" (Dtn 32:23, 42; Hab 3:11; Ps 18:15; 38:3; 144:6), but never "arrows of hunger." In the present text of Ezekiel the addition in aβbα (cf. note c) shows that the arrows sent for destruction and the famine represent two different misfortunes. The הרעב of v 16aα anticipates in a clumsy way the only statement made in bβ. It is to be deleted as a gloss. חצי is to be read with 𝕲 as a suffixed form and understood in the manner of v 17aβ (cf. Ex 12:23 המשחית) as a pestilence moving among the people.

c aβbα is lacking in 𝕲 𝕰 𝖀 and clearly has the purpose of explaining the verse section aα (and bβ), which had become obscure by glossing. The insertion keeps to the original formulation in the second person plural of the appendix vv 16–17—beginning (note a to v 17). 𝕲 has assimilated the whole to the preceding section in the second person singular feminine. אֹסֵף is to be regarded as a remnant of an orig-

your staff of bread. 17/ And famine I will send upon you, and wild animals, and they will make you (?) childless, and when pestilence and blood shall pass through you (?) and I bring the sword upon you (?).ᵃ I, Yahweh,ᵇ have spoken.

17

inal i-imperfect qal of יסף according to Gesenius-Bergsträsser II § 14h(a).

17a The second person singular feminine, which has imposed itself upon the whole section of vv 16–17 in 𝔊, is only to be found in 𝔐 in the concluding statement of v 17 from ושכלך on. The use of the verb שכל suggests the picture of a mother who has no children, and the use of the feminine singular for Jerusalem, which is found in the original part of vv 5–17, appears appropriate. The degree of flux in the text tradition of this addition is shown by the translation of ושכלך in 𝔊 by καὶ τιμωρήσομαί σε, as well as the κυκλόθεν introduced after ἐπὶ σέ. Vv 16–17 are a late addition which concludes with the solemn אני יהוה דברתי analogous to v 15.

b Cf. note c to v 13.

Form

The beginning of the section 3:16a, 22–5:17 is now obscured by the redactional insertion of 3:16b–21 and the unfortunate placing of the chapter division between chapters 3 and 4. No doubt, however, can exist about its conclusion on account of the concluding formula 5:15, 17 and the fresh formula for the receipt of an oracle in 6:1. Its structure follows a scheme which is frequent in the book of Ezekiel (for example 14:1ff; 20:1ff): a) Introduction narrated in the third person 3:22–24bα. The description of the situation which is given in this introduction is here enlivened in a special way by a command from Yahweh which sends the prophet into the plain. b) Yahweh's address to the prophet 3:24bβ–5:4a. This is broken up in 4:14f by a short dialogue between Yahweh and the prophet. c) Summons to preach to the house of Israel 5:4b–17. Yahweh's address to the prophet which stands in the center is characterized, like the call address in 2:1–3:11, by a number of sayings which are introduced by the address ואתה בן אדם (3:25; 4:1; 5:1), בן אדם (4:16) or simply ואתה (4:3, 4, 9). The renewed narrative introduction ויאמר אלי is also striking (4:16, in the preceding verse a change of person in the conversation is necessary).[1]

At first sight the section 3:16a, 22–5:17a shows in the order and formal introduction of its parts a significant outline. On closer examination, however, all kinds of difficulties arise which cast doubt on the originality of this overall structure in its present form. The problem of the reference to the situation (part a) can best be

dealt with in relation to the detailed exposition. The conclusion of the preaching (part c) appears as a much elaborated passage with interpretative additions.[2] In the remaining section vv 4b–15 it is striking that, after the introductory invective against Jerusalem (vv 5f), in 5:7ff sentences are pronounced no less than four times with לכן-clauses, twice with repetition of the messenger formula (vv 7, 8), once with the emphatic context formula נאם יהוה (v 11). These lead us to expect a declaration of judgement (vv 7, 8, 10, 11). Verse 7 is easily recognized as an addition since it repeats in a clumsy way the reproach of v 6 (introduced with יען) and does not get to a formula for the declaration of judgement. Similarly v 10 appears as a clarification of v 9. So also v 11 introduces (with a יען-clause) the reproach once again. In content it points back to the sign-action of 5:1–2, but cannot be the original continuation of 5:1–2 since it defines afresh the details of the carrying out of judgement in three ways. So also the section 5:11–13 (which is not a unit in itself), which clearly comes to a fresh conclusion in the recognition formula of v 13, must belong to a secondary interpretation of the text. The original text of part c must therefore be found in vv 4b–6a, 8–9, 14–15 (freed from small additions).[3]

But even part b, which constitutes the kernel of the section, does not on closer examination hold together as a complete unity. Study of the text, both in regard to its content and form, strengthens this position and offers a welcome aid to analysis.

Already Cornill noted that the sign-actions which the

---

1 For v 13 cf. note a on the text.

2 On the doubling of the conclusion in vv 16–17 cf. note a to 5:17.

3 Cf. the notes.

prophet was commanded to perform sometimes have in mind the siege of Jerusalem and sometimes the lasting condition of the Exile, and so he sought in his exposition to make a strict separation between the two on these grounds. Hölscher, *Hesekiel*, connected this with the formal consideration that some of the commands of Yahweh to the prophet begin with the stereotyped קַח לְךָ, and that in these sections we are faced with the symbolism of siege. So he believed that he could find the basic material of the whole section in (3:16a, 24bα[1]) 4:1–2, 9a, 10–11; 5:1–2, "a poem of three regular strophes," which had then been filled out by another hand and the introduction of the symbolism of exile.

Buzy and others attempt to come to a better sequence of the sign-actions by transposing them or giving them a forced interpretation, in contrast with these other attempts.[4] However, Hölscher, with his perceptions, appears to have shown the right way. As with chapter 1 we can recognize behind the present confused form of the section 3:24b–5:4a a clear and simple original form of a series of instructions to perform sign-actions. By the gradual addition of new elements, through the addition of connectives which relate the actions to each other, and through other interpretative additions, the text has grown to its present form. Beyond Hölscher, nevertheless, we must examine carefully the areas in which this expansion took place. The simple reference to a "redactor" is no longer a sufficient answer to the question of the text in an age when we have a very much sharper insight into the living process of the tradition that lies behind it. We must therefore consider the whole living process of the development of the message, from the moment when it was first proclaimed, initially by the prophet himself and then through the circle of disciples who followed him.

The introductory words קַח לְךָ, holding together 4:1f, 9–11 to 5:1f, are also to be found in 4:3, a symbolic action which is clearly related to the siege of Jerusalem. So we may question whether we can see in 4:3 a fourth unit of the original text. However, the recognition of the formal structure of the verse is to be set against the three units mentioned. Certainly Höl-

scher's description of the whole as "a poem in three regular strophes" is somewhat exaggerated. The balance of the three units consists solely in the fact that they (excluding the address) each appear to consist of eight lines. These eight lines show in 4:1ff a consistent rhythm in three beats (Sievers meter). In 4:9*–11 the first four lines can be read with four beats, whilst the second half shows an alternation between threes and overlong lines (which Hölscher reduces to four beats by exclusion of במשורה v 10 and אשר תאכלנו במשקול v 11). Finally in 5:1f the four last lines can be read with three beats, whilst the first half shows an irregular line structure. We cannot therefore speak of a fixed meter, and even a reckoning of short verses (Fohrer) cannot change the picture. In this regard 4:3 gives a series of only six lines. The fact that the symbolic actions first of all clearly stood beside one another as independent, self-contained units speaks more sharply against regarding 4:3 as an independent unit in the original build up of text. Yet 4:3 is clearly dependent on 4:1f. Further it appears that the three "strophes," 4:1–2, 9*–11 and 5:1–2, describe the sign-action without any interpretation, whilst 4:3 presents an obvious *applicatio*. So we are left with the conclusion that the original series only covered the three sign-actions mentioned first. The original material of 3:25–5:4a[5] must therefore have had the following text:[6]

> And you, son of man—take a brick
> and lay it before you
> and draw upon it a city
> and lay siege to it
> and build siegeworks against it
> and set up a siege wall against it
> and set camps against it
> and establish battering rams round about.
>
> And you—take wheat and barley
> and beans and lentils and millet and spelt
> and put them into the same pot
> and make bread of them for yourself
> and your food shall be 20 shekels a day;
> at regular times you shall eat it.
> And water you shall drink by measure, a sixth of a hin;
> at regular times you shall drink.

---

4   Buzy, "symboles," 217–228: "État littéraire des symboles."

5   See the exposition for 3:24b.

6   See the exposition for the justification of the excisions which this implies.

And you, son of man—take a sharp sword
and pass it over your head and your beard;
and take a balance
and divide it (the hair)
One third you shall burn with fire;
and one third you shall cut up with the sword
and one third you shall scatter to the wind.

The three actions stand in a clear succession: 4:1f shows the beginning of a siege; 4:9*–11 the food shortage during the course of the siege; and 5:1f finally shows the end in the catastrophe breaking in on the inhabitants of Jerusalem. Should we also see a conscious form at work in the repeated emphasis upon the number three? There are three pictures of the fate of the city, of which the third shows the threefold fate of its inhabitants. Throughout the prophet's action portrays the coming fate of Jerusalem.

In the use of sign-actions as a form of preaching Ezekiel stands in line with earlier prophetic practice. Already in pre-classical prophecy we can see how Ahijah of Shiloh hands the kingship over ten of the tribes of Israel to Jeroboam in the ten parts of his torn cloak (1 Kings 11:29–31; cf. 1 Sam 15:27f). Zedekiah assures Ahab of victory over Syria by the iron horns on his head (1 Kings 22:11). Elisha enables Joash to gain victory over Syria by means of "the arrows of Yahweh's victory" which Joash shoots through the open window towards the east and with which he strikes the ground (2 Kings 13:14–19). The wide range of possibilities, from the simple gesticulation supporting what has been said up to the strange obsessive action carried out deliberately, can already be seen here. It is more important to recognize the specific function which the sign-action fulfils. It establishes the character of the prophetic word as event. By this action, which is more than mere symbolism, the prophet prefigures as an event what he proclaims through his word. More precisely this event is brought into effect by the prophet and is commanded to happen. By accomplishing this action the prophet guarantees the coming event.

Classical prophecy did not put an end to this feature. Both in Hosea and Isaiah the prophet's message is given visible form in his children and their names, which convey messages (Hos 1; Is 7:3; 8:1–4, also 7:14?). Isaiah's going about naked prefigures the catastrophe coming upon the Ethiopians (Is 20). Jeremiah's unmarried state, and his withdrawal from all joyful activity as a mourner, is a prefigured realization of the disaster coming upon Jerusalem (Jer 16:1–9). His shattering of a jar prefigures the shattering of Judah in judgement (Jer 19). The yoke worn by him is a part of the realization of slavery under Babylon (Jer 27f; cf. further Jer 32; 43:8–13; 51:59–64). Even in early post-exilic prophecy Zechariah announces the coming glory of the Davidic line by the crown which he puts on Zerubbabel's head (Zech 6:9–15, cf. the commentaries).

In what has been said it appears that the answer to the oft-quoted question whether the sign-actions were actually carried out can only be that the accomplishment is essential to a true sign-action.[7] Even where, in this connection, the idea of a sign (אות) is used, this is clear.[8] In the concept of an אות a fact is made visible and recognizable to the senses which is not at first immediately intelligible. A sign-action which was not actually performed but only narrated must be regarded as a late and weakened form.

A glance at the literary structure of the narratives of sign-actions (it is preferable not to speak of a "genre") shows that in the course of time there was a clear change of form.[9] We find the simple narrative form in which a) an explanation of the circumstances is followed by b) an account of the action followed by c) the interpretation (1 Kings 22:10f; 2 Kings 13:14–19; Jer 28:10f). Later on the explanation (a) is replaced as it happens by the divine command (Jer 13:1–11; 32:6–15; Ezek 12:1–16; 24:15–24). Into this divine command, however, the interpretation may also enter (Hos 1:3). This leads on to a type of narrative in which the carrying out of the action is no longer narrated, but everything is swallowed up in Yahweh's command. This is frequently to be seen in Jeremiah (16:1–4, 5–7, 8f; 19:1f, 10f; 43:8–13). This type also dominates in Ezekiel (besides 3:25–5:4a; cf. 12:17–20; 21:11f, 23–29; 24:1–14; 37:15–28). This concentration of the account on the word of Yahweh expresses the fact that the sign-action is not to be regarded as an "actualizing" of the prophet's message which he has ingeniously devised, but that it is wholly

7   See Fohrer, *symbolischen Handlungen*, 49–69.
8   See Carl A. Keller, *Das Wort OTH als "Offenbarungszeichen Gottes"* (Basel: Hoenen, 1946).
9   See Fohrer, *symbolischen Handlungen*.

given through God's sending and empowering him. Furthermore the sign-action is throughout only a living manifestation of the word of Yahweh. It is itself a form of preaching and is in no way separable from the other words of the prophet.

We must add a further preliminary consideration to what has already been said about the interpretation of Ezekiel's sign-actions. To the modern mind, interested in biography, the sign-actions take on a rather arbitrary value as a disclosure of the life and personality of the prophet. The extensive debate about Hosea's marriage in Hos 1 and 3 can be adduced as an example of this. Yet the peculiar difficulty into which biographical questions about Hos 1 and 3 fall makes it clear that such biographical questioning moves in a direction which is far removed from that of the text itself. The βίος of the prophet is recorded in his message, only so far as it is capable of expressing the word of Yahweh. The whole style of the narrative is directed towards preaching. The prophet is unaware of any need to complete a full and connected biographical picture of his experience within the framework of the sign-action and to show it in its actual setting. (Compare, for example the death of Ezekiel's wife ch. 24.) The desire for completeness and full clarification of the circumstances is restricted solely to the preaching aspect of the action. In evaluating Ezekiel's sign-actions it is constantly necessary to keep in mind these limits of the intention of the text.

The place and date of the section 3:16a, 22–5:17 will be fully dealt with in connection with the detailed study of the section.

Interpretation

A) *The Situation.* After the removal of 3:16b–21, vv 3:16a, 22–5:17 connect up with the call-narrative. Following on this encounter, in which the prophet received his call to the prophetic office and in which he learned of the harshness of the message entrusted to him in the eating of the scroll, he went home without receiving any more specific message to preach and remained there, dumb, for seven days. A fresh experience of the hand of Yahweh upon him shakes him out of this,[10]

and we now expect that what he is to preach will be made clear to him.

■ **3:16a, 22** The prophet hears a summons to go out into "the plain" because Yahweh wishes to speak with him there.[11] More precisely the wide alluvial plain of Babylon is referred to here. The בקעה is mentioned again in 8:4 (in a secondary reference back to 3:22)[12] and 37:1f. Is exactly the same locality intended by 3:22 and 37:1ff or does the former refer only to the region surrounding Tel Abib, bordering the river Chebar? One thing in any case is clear from the reference in v 23a, that the locality is to be distinguished from the place of prayer by the river where Ezekiel received his call. The summons into the plain occurs within the context of the general remark that Yahweh wants to speak with him there (cf. 2:1). A similar summons to a place, without first knowing what is to happen there, is found in Acts 8:26, as the result of divine guidance. There an angel says to Philip, "Rise and go at noon to the road that goes down from Jerusalem to Gaza. This is a lonely road. And he arose and went—and behold . . ."

■ **3:23–24a** In Ezek 3:23 the encounter in the plain is also introduced by והנה "Behold, the glory of Yahweh . . ."

It is further striking how briefly and incidentally the vision of God is referred to, with only a terse reference to what was seen "by the river Chebar." In comparison with the violent storm of 1:4 and 3:12, the way in which the כבוד יהוה stands in the plain appears wooden and static where it waits the coming of the prophet.[13] It is further striking that the prophet's reaction is described in literal dependence on 1:28 and 2:2, with a short quotation from these passages. The brief description of the glory of Yahweh, with a reference back to what has already been said, is found again in 8:4, where it has doubtless been added later.[14] Here, as in the other passages which refer back (10:15, 20, 22; 43:3), we are clearly dealing with statements which

---

10   Cf. on 1:3.
11   By בקעה a shallow valley is intended, in distinction from a mountain or mountain range. So Armin Schwarzenbach, *Die geographische Terminologie im Hebräischen des Alten Testamentes* (Leiden: Brill, 1954), 35f.
12   Cf. on the text.
13   "to stand" (עמד)—Are we to think of the כבוד יהוה

without the throne as Cooke does?
14   Cf. on the text.

were first introduced at the stage when the whole book was put together to serve as connectives. Closer analysis of the section chs. 8–11 shows that besides the attempt to elaborate in greater detail the appearance of Yahweh (ch. 10), which is already evident in ch. 1, there was a tendency to follow up the appearance of Yahweh's glory in as many passages as possible, as a second interest on the part of those who transmitted the text. We must question whether this attempt was already operative in the formation of 3:22–24, and whether an earlier form of the passage did not have vv 23 (from והנה) to 24a, which would then have been added later in dependence on chs. 1f.

It is more difficult to answer the question whether vv 22b–23aα[1], the command to go out into the plain and its sequel, are also to be regarded as a later addition (Hölscher, *Hesekiel*). Was this removal of the prophet from the midst of the exiles necessary (3:15) because of his encounter with the divine glory, which could not have been seen by everybody? 8:1ff (37:1ff); 40:1ff would certainly support the introduction of ecstatic transportation in a trance for such an addition. Hence it is not impossible that the summons into the plain, and the address by Yahweh which takes place there (with no mention of the appearance of the glory), is an original part of the Ezekiel tradition. The fact that 37:1ff narrates a similar summons into the בקעה (admittedly in a text which is very different) does not altogether speak against this. In no case is 3:22–24a to be understood as the introduction to 37:1ff, as Bertholet suggested and Steinmann adopted. 3:16a, 22ff, which is dated early, does not belong to 37:1ff, which is certainly to be dated after 587 b.c. However, the short introduction of the late passage 37:1 may have been formulated with a brief allusion to the circumstances of the earlier experience of 3:22ff.

B) *Yahweh's Message to the Prophet* 3:24b–5:4a. Yahweh's commission to the prophet begins with the brief command, "Go, shut yourself within your house." The command leads immediately into the difficulties of interpretation of 3:24b–27, which is one of the most difficult passages in the whole book. We cannot deny that this introductory command stands in some sort of relationship to the statements which immediately follow about the binding of the prophet and about his being unable, or not permitted, to speak. The statement about binding is connected with 4:8, which must be considered in relation to the section 4:4–8. On the other hand, the reference to the prophet's inability to speak points forward to 24:27, the promise that his dumbness will come to an end, and to 33:21f, the account of its ending at the time of the confirmation of the fall of Jerusalem. How are we to understand this broad web of statements spread throughout the whole book?

Various interpretations have been attempted. Gronkowski, "De natura," finds in 3:15, where משמים should be emended to משובב in accordance with 𝔊 ἀναστρεφόμενος, a reference to a first week-long action of the prophet which made clear to him the total hostility of his people. Thereafter, in the vision of the plain, Yahweh commanded him to shut himself in and no longer to go out among the exiles with their threats. The fall of Jerusalem then lifted the ban and proved to the people that he really was a prophet. So the dumbness ceased after 33:21f, which, like the binding, is to be understood metaphorically. From then on the prophet became a *pater spiritualis, magister consolatorque*. Following Heinisch, the prophet's dumbness was not primarily a consequence of his lack of success.[15] Rather Yahweh forbade the prophet to speak on account of the rebelliousness of Israel which he had predicted. Heinisch also understands the prophet's binding and inability to speak in a metaphorical sense. Against this we have the interpretations of Bertholet, Kraetzschmar and Jahn, according to which we must reckon with a real difficulty of speech on the part of Ezekiel and with periods of intermittent dumbness, since the prophet spoke frequently between the time seven days after his call and that of the arrival of the fugitive from Jerusalem. The difficulty of speech disappears completely after the event narrated in 33:21f. In a different way Herrmann thought of a prevention of Ezekiel's speaking by the exiles, but not of a literal binding. Real imprisonment (such as Jeremiah suffered in the last months of Jerusalem) is conjectured by van den Born, who is fol-

---

15   Paul Heinisch, *Das Buch Ezechiel übersetzt und erklärt* HSAT 8 (Bonn: Hanstein, 1923).

lowed by Steinmann. This imprisonment was then
understood by Ezekiel as a restriction imposed by
Yahweh, and as an atonement for the sins of Israel,
according to 4:4–8. Thus an action which was originally not voluntary and was occasioned by outward
circumstances becomes on reflection an act ordained
by Yahweh and containing a symbolic meaning. This
latter view is followed by Knabenbauer, who understands what is narrated in 3:24b ff as a sign-action
performed voluntarily by the prophet.[16] He had himself bound by his compatriots in order to portray the
siege of Jerusalem thereby, which is clearly referred to
in 4:1ff.

In view of this confusing multiplicity of interpretations it is necessary to proceed step by step.

■ **3:24b** There then emerges first of all the fact that the
command 3:24b (as already 3:22b) is formulated
without an address to the prophet. This then follows in
3:25. This raises the question whether 3:25 really
represents the original continuation of 3:24b, which
is not at all obvious from its content. Rather the command to the prophet to shut himself in his house stands
as a quite independent announcement and is not related
directly to the references to binding and dumbness.
We can look for an understanding of 3:24b in two
directions.

If we put together the references in the book of
Ezekiel (apart from 1:1ff and 3:22f) which show us
something of the location of the prophet's activity,
then nowhere do we learn of any public appearances,
such as are shown in Amos 7:10–17; Is 7; Jer 26, 28 and
other passages. Where reference is made to the location
of Ezekiel's activity, it is to his house. Here he is visited by the elders of his people (8:1; 14:1; 20:1; cf.
33:30f); from here he is transported in the spirit (8:1ff;
thereafter 37:1ff; 40:1ff?). The sign-action of 12:1ff
also begins at home. The question arises whether the
command in 3:25 has to do with this unusual prophetic activity at home. It is anticipated in 2 Kings
6:36 (and Is 37:5f?) in connection with Elisha, although without the exclusiveness with which it occurs
in Ezekiel. Was there a type of prophetic restriction
(עצור Neh 6:10; Jer 36:5; should we also include Jer

16:1ff?) imposed upon Ezekiel right at the beginning
of his ministry by command of God (Hölscher, *Hesekiel*)?[17]

The second consideration need not stand in opposition to the first, but can possibly complement it. 3:24b
is the beginning of a series of symbolic actions which the
prophet is commanded by Yahweh to perform. The
kernel of these commands is the announcement of the
siege of Jerusalem, which is proclaimed in the symbolic
actions. The idea is not far away that the introductory
command to the prophet, to operate while staying in
his house, with emphatic use of the verb סגר, may be
seen in the light of the symbolic actions. What is mentioned in 2 Kings 6:32 and Jer 36:5 as a (traditional?)
prophetic style of life, without any interpretation as a
message, becomes with Ezekiel a revelation of his
message of the imminent siege of Jerusalem, through
Yahweh's command regarding it. The prophetic
κάτοχος (Hölscher, *Hesekiel*) assumes the function
of a sign-action and a prefiguring of the siege facing
Jerusalem.

An element of uncertainty remains about this interpretation, since this explanation of Ezekiel's shutting
himself in is not made explicit in 3:24. However, we
may consider that in 4:1f, 9*–11 and 5:1f the sign-
action is simply commanded without any further
interpretation.

■ **3:25–27** In 3:25–27 there is added a further series of
sayings which raise questions regarding their relationship to v 24b. As regards form, it is striking that the
address ואתה בן בדם first appears here. In its content
we must note that after the clear command of v 24b
which the prophet was to obey (further commands
follow in 4:1f, 9*–11; 5:1f) things are mentioned in
vv 25–27 which have nothing to do with the prophet's
own choice, but are simply to be suffered by him; viz.
binding v 25; inability to speak imposed by Yahweh
v 26, which is only lifted by Yahweh's intervention v 27.
Verses 25 and 26 are formulated in parallel: v 25 binding so that he can no longer go out in the midst of the
people; v 26 inability to speak so that he can no longer
warn the people. Do the verses refer to one and the
same thing (in a kind of poetic synonymous parallel-

---

16   Joseph Knabenbauer, *Commentarius in Ezechielem
       prophetam*, CSS (Paris, 1890).
17   The הסגיר performed by the priest (Lev 13:4f and

other passages, accordingly Nu 12:14f) is rather
different.

ism)? Or do the binding and the dumbness concern two different circumstances?

■ **3:26** Of the two statements v 26, as the clearer, must first of all be considered more closely. Here an action of Yahweh towards the prophet is certainly referred to. It has already been mentioned that this action of Yahweh cannot be separated from what is announced in 24:27 and the event reported in 33:21f. The passage 33:21f, which is dated, shows that the prophet's recovery of speech concerned something that happened shortly after the fall of Jerusalem and was connected with this event. The precise dating even to the day points to an understanding of the passage as an actual loosening of the tongue in the full sense, unlike the plainly metaphorical reference in 16:63, 29:21, which are sometimes adduced as evidence. The precise interpretation of the dumbness and the renewal of the ability to speak after the announcement of Jerusalem's fall must be dealt with in the study of 33:21f, which is the most precise of the three relevant passages. With 3:25 the question arises whether this dumbness of the prophet, which ended after the fall of Jerusalem, did in fact begin seven days after his call. The entire message which is contained in Ezek 4–24 forbids such a view. Ezekiel did speak during this time, even if in his activities he was restricted to his house.

So scholars have come, on the balance of the references, to the thesis of an intermittent speech difficulty of the prophet. 3:27 appeared to be a reference to the fact that Ezekiel was not continually dumb, but whenever Yahweh spoke to him he recovered the power to speak. Hölscher, *Hesekiel,* who regarded the whole section as a redactional connection, believed v 27 should be understood as a harmonizing verse in this sense. From 24:27 and 33:21f, however, which affirm that at a quite specific point of time Yahweh opened Ezekiel's mouth, the iterative interpretation of ובדברי אותך in 3:27 becomes improbable. It is more likely that in 3:26 also we have a hint of what is narrated in 24:27 and 33:21f.

■ **3:25** Beside dumbness there appears in 3:25 a reference to the prophet's being bound with cords. This points to 4:8, which concludes the section 4:4–8. The analysis of this unit shows that 4:8 already has 3:25 in mind and should be understood as a counterpart to it. The connection of the statement with Yahweh himself,

which is found there, is to be understood as an intentional assimilation to the situation of 4:4–8 and is certainly not to be introduced into 3:25, with 𝕲.[18] So it is better at first to look away from 4:8 for an interpretation of 3:25. But if Yahweh is not the subject of the action in 3:25 the verse is not to be understood simply as a parallel to v 26, but must be regarded as an independent saying. Cords are frequently referred to in the Psalms as metaphors of submission and oppression. Ps 2:3 uses it to express the dependence of vassal kings; 129:4 for the oppression of the wicked (Ps 119:61 uses the word חבל, cf. also Ps 18:5; 116:3 חבלי מות 18:6 חבלי שאול). However, since we believe that v 26 should be understood in a literal sense, we must reckon seriously with the possibility of a literal interpretation in v 25 also. Jer 20 shows that Jeremiah was put in stocks. Jer 29:26 shows, with desirable clarity, that the tendency to put unwelcome prophets in stocks was also present among the exiles. Are we to think of a kind of imprisonment of the prophet? Or ought we, in accordance with Mk 5:3f, to think of binding on account of illness? The only people who come into the question as the cause of this action, without forcing the grammatical construction, are those referred to in the suffix of the following בתוכם, i.e., the exiles, in whose midst Ezekiel will no longer be allowed to go. 3:25 could well point to active hostility which the prophet experienced from those immediately around him. Such hostility is not explicitly referred to elsewhere in the book of Ezekiel, although 2:6 might suggest it.

In the light of these detailed considerations how are we to interpret the section 3:25–27? It points to a hostility towards the prophet from those around him, and to a dumbness imposed upon him by Yahweh, from which it becomes clear that this dumbness cannot have lasted from his call up to the fall of Jerusalem, when it ended.

Two considerations may be enlarged upon in this regard. We must first establish that vv 26f are formulated with clear dependence on the call address. Exactly as in chs. 2f there appear here the words כי בית מרי המה, added twice, which originate in a quite different piece of reproach.[19] In the remainder of the book it is only found in 12:2f and it is lacking altogether in chs. 4f. The renewed possibility of preaching is stated in v 27, with the formula familiar from 2:4f and 3:11, which is slightly varied in its second part. 3:25–27 therefore betrays a dependence on the formulations of the call-narrative, which is absent in the following section chs. 4f.

For the rest it is clear that 3:25–27 must be understood as the continuation of v 24b. The prophet's shutting himself in is defined in the statement that he no longer was to go out among the exiles (v 25) and was no longer to be לאיש מוכיח to them (v 26).[20]

All these considerations point to the view that we are faced in 3:25–27 with a piece of late interpretation in the framework of the tradition of the prophetic word in the circle of Ezekiel's disciples. It is inadequate here to speak, with Hölscher, *Hesekiel*, of a redactor, since more than a purely literary editorial intention is present in the addition. In 3:25–27 we can see the desire for a fuller unfolding of the word and for an exposition on the basis of what was otherwise known about the prophet. If the original divine saying to the prophet in v 24b dealt with his isolation, and the command to this was at the same time a sign-event signifying Jerusalem's being shut in, then the subsequent interpretation by the prophet's "school" added this reference to the prophet's being bound by his hostile fellow exiles. This "school" also added the reference to the prophet's dumbness, which was regarded as brought about by Yahweh and occurred at the time of the fall of Jerusalem. These were events in the life of the prophet in which Yahweh himself further interpreted the first command to him to isolate himself, by the sufferings he brought upon the prophet. This secondary tradition cannot be adequately classified by the category of genuine or non-genuine. Rather it testifies to the continuing vitality of the prophet's word among his disciples. These sought to understand the message afresh at a later time on the basis of the whole word of God given through Ezekiel. This interpretation of the origin of 3:25–27 solves at once the difficulties regarding the chronological placing of the prophet's dumbness immediately after his call,

which have led to all the tantalizing efforts at interpretation and the removal of non-genuine material. 3:25–27 contains statements which were placed there in view of the prophet's whole life and which originally had nothing to do with the date of 3:16a.

■ **4:1, 2** *The Sign-action of Besieging the City.* 4:1f has been shown in the introductory analysis to be a part of the original composition of three signs. Eight independent verbal clauses, preserved in three acts, follow each other in a peculiarly rigid form. The first and last are formulated in the imperative and those in between with perfect consecutives, each containing Yahweh's instructions to the prophet. No further interpretation is added to the instructions in these eight clauses. The interpretative gloss את ירושלם, which anticipates the summarizing interpretation of v 5, is undoubtedly a later insertion.[21] The action speaks for itself.

The form of the brief command recalls 3:24a, which introduces the entire divine speech. However, against the smooth connection of 4:1 with 3:24b the same formal objections arise as with the joining of 3:25 to 3:24a. Why does the address ואתה בן אדם not follow in 3:24b, but first in 4:1? Although the three-sign section joins well to 3:24a in its content, where all three signs can be thought of as performed in the prophet's house, an awkwardness remains in the transition. Can this be explained by regarding the three-sign section as having already been combined into one before being subordinated to the narrative introduction?

The command comes from Yahweh to Ezekiel to take a clay brick and to draw upon it the plan of a city. C. G. Howie has pointed out that we can see local Babylonian coloring here.[22] לבנה Akk. *libittu* (from *labānu* "making flat") refers to an air-dried brick and not to one that has been fired. Gen 11:3 shows that to the Israelite mind such a type of brick belonged in a special way to the Babylonian plain. Against this C. Kuhl has pointed out that clay bricks are referred to, apart from Gen 11:3, in regard to the forced labor in

---

18 Cf. note a to 3:25.

19 See above p. 134.

20 In Amos 5:10; Is 29:20f those who rebuke in the gate are referred to by this title. See Victor Maag, *Text, Wortschatz und Begriffswelt des Buches Amos* (Leiden: Brill, 1951), 152–154.

21 Cf. note a to 4:1.

22 Howie, *Date*, 18.

Egypt and also in connection with building in Palestine.[23] We must not overlook, however, that drawing the outline of houses, temples, and boats on bricks and tablets is attested in Babylon from an early period.[24] Among the half dozen or so city plans there is actually one for the city of Nippur, which was not far from Ezekiel by the River Chebar.[25] In Palestine we know nothing of such a use of clay bricks nor of the form of city plans. Here ostraca and papyrus were the usual writing materials. Thus the assertion of a Babylonian coloring for 4:1f is still valid.

■ **4:2** The city which Ezekiel had sketched in the soft clay he was now to begin to besiege. In the ancient orient the art of siege was especially developed by the Assyrians.[26] Ezek 4:1f shows us something of its technique. A siege was primarily the surrounding of a city to cut off any escape (מצור "shutting up"). Siege works, דיק Akk. *dājiqu* (from דוק "to examine carefully, to consider" Koehler-Baumgartner), permitted a measure of control (2 Kings 25:1, Jer 52:4 against Jerusalem, similarly used with the verb בנה; otherwise only in Ezek 17:17; 21:27). Artificial constructions, especially a roughly heaped up wall (סללה) cut the city off from the outside world.[27] Ramps, thrown up and planked with boards, were also brought against the city wall in order to bring the assault weapons against them (so in 2 Sam 20:15 against the city of Abel-beth-Maacah; 2 Kings 19:32 = Is 37:33; Jer 6:6 mentions the cutting down of trees to provide wood for the planks of the ramp; plural Jer 32:24; 33:4). The battering ram (does כר derive from the animal or from כרה "to dig"?), which is only otherwise mentioned in the Old Testament in Ezek 21:27, was an invention of the Assyrians and was brought to the West by the Phoenicians–Carthaginians.[28] They were brought against the wall under a protective cover in order to attack it.[29] A feature of unusual emphasis is found in the picture of 4:2, where it portrays the battering rams brought against the city on all sides.

■ **4:3** The action portrayed by Ezekiel, with its perfectly clear meaning, has received an addition in v 3, in a very terse formulation with a new beginning (ואתה) and a similar introductory קח לך. This later addition is similar to the first action in its character, although it is not so obvious in its meaning.[30] There is no decisive objection to the view that this addition was later made by the prophet himself, so that the account tells of a second action performed by the prophet in his own home at a later time against the Jerusalem he had placed under siege.

Lev 2:4–7 names three distinct kinds of home-baked מנחה: 1) That which was baked in an oven מאפה תנור, 2) that which was baked on a griddle מנחה על המחבת, 3) that which was cooked in a pan מנחת מרחשת. Since only in the case of 2) is there a prescription to break what has been baked into pieces, what was baked on a griddle must have been of larger size than those which were prepared in other ways. The griddle itself, therefore, cannot have been very small.[31] The griddle (מחבת) belonged to the usual cooking equipment of a home. The Beduin still use today the *sāǧ*, the baking griddle, which is placed on stones so that a fire can be lit under it.[32] The excavations in Megiddo and Taanach show that the older period used clay bricks for baking.[33] The explicit instruction to Ezekiel to take an iron griddle may therefore point to the fact that clay bricks were also in use. The prophet was to set up such a griddle between himself and the brick with the city drawn on it, as a "wall," and in this way to set his face against the city and to press the siege.

23   Kuhl, "Schauplatz," 405f. For Egypt Ex 1:14; 5:7f; 16:18f; cf. Adolf Erman and Hermann Ranke, *Ägypten und aegyptisches Leben im Altertum* (Tübingen: Mohr [Siebeck], 1922–23), 507f; for Palestine, Is 9:9; 65:3.

24   Meissner, *Babylonien* 1, plates 154, 159; cf. 1, p. 290. Also A. Falkenstein and W. von Soden, *Sumerische und akkadische Hymnen und Gebete* (Zürich: Artemis, 1953), 142f; Meissner, *Babylonien* 1, 250.

25   Meissner, *Babylonien* 2, plate 54.

26   Meissner, *Babylonien* 1, 110; Galling, "Belagerung," *BRL.*

27   Meissner, *Babylonien* 1, plate 65.

28   Athenaeus (c. 215 A.D.) thought that battering rams were invented by the Carthaginians on the occasion of the siege of Gades.

29   Meissner, *Babylonien* 1, 108f.

30   Cf. pp. 154f.

31   Cf. further Lev 6:14, 7:9; 1 Chr 23:29.

32   A. G. Barrois, *Manuel d'archéologie biblique* 1 (Paris: Picard, 1939), 319 illus.

33   *RLV* 1, 318; *BRL*, 76 illus.

Through this elaboration of the siege the whole oracle concerning it takes on a very definite character. The iron griddle set against the city makes clear the severity with which Yahweh deals with it. The impenetrable and unbreakable nature of the griddle represents the corresponding features in Yahweh's action.

What is the origin of this elaboration of the sign-act? For the second time we can see here in Ezekiel that imagery of earlier prophecy has taken on an unusual objective reality.[34] According to Jer 1:18 Yahweh says to Jeremiah, in an expansion of the call-narrative which we have already noted influenced Ezekiel, "And behold, I make you this day a fortified city, an iron pillar, and bronze walls against the whole land." If this saying to Jeremiah was intended to affirm the prophet's protection from his enemies and was therefore meant defensively, it has undergone a change of meaning here and taken on an offensive character. It has become a picture of the severity of the divine assault on Jerusalem. Whereas with Jeremiah it was simply a metaphor, in Ezekiel's sign-action with the iron griddle it has assumed a visual realization, even though still only symbolic.[35] The shocking everyday character of the utensil used for the sign shows that this additional action of the prophet's was also carried out in his own home.

The concluding remark of 4:3 is fresh and goes beyond the style of the remainder of the three-sign section: "This is a sign for the house of Israel."[36] What occurs in Jerusalem concerns the house of Israel. The city of David had become the place of decision for Israel, which had once been a tribal federation. Here in Ezekiel's time the history of Israel was to be summed up. Judgement was to come to this city, represented symbolically by the simple utensils of a private home.

■ **4:4–8** *The Prophet Bears the Guilt of Israel (and Judah).* Between 4:1f, the announcement of the beginning of the siege of Jerusalem, and 4:9*–11, showing the height of the distress brought by the siege, there is inserted in 4:4–8 a section which has quite a different purpose. 4:1–2(3) demands of the prophet the active performance of a series of actions bearing a special

significance. This is also true of 4:4, where we have an imperative form "Lie upon your side." In its content, however, the prophet's action here is rather something that he must suffer, as in the interpretation of v 8 in which Yahweh makes the prophet into a sign by his being bound by an alien power, recalling 3:25–27.

We may add to this further questions regarding the content. "The house of Israel" has up till now been the designation of the whole people of Israel, which was represented in Ezekiel's day by Judah, forming the remnant of Israel with Jerusalem as its sacred center. In 4:3 the symbolic action regarding Jerusalem is interpreted as a "sign for the house of Israel." In 4:4–6, however, the "house of Israel" and the "house of Judah" stand side by side quite unexpectedly, so that Jerusalem indeed is no longer representative of "the house of Israel." We should therefore expect that in this oracle regarding the two kingdoms all the emphasis would be placed on the saying about Judah (and Jerusalem), as in the oracle against the two kingdoms in ch. 23. Here Oholah, who represents the Northern Kingdom and its fate, is dealt with briefly at the beginning (23:5–10), and all the emphasis then rests on the description of the actions and experiences of Oholibah, who represents Judah (and Jerusalem). Instead of this, in 4:4–5 the action of the prophet concerning the house of Israel is given in detail, whilst the house of Judah is dealt with briefly in v 6. The question arises whether here an oracle regarding Israel, in which "house of Israel" as usual stood for all Israel, represented by Judah and Jerusalem, has subsequently been changed so that "Israel" has taken on a quite different and unexpected meaning.

It is further striking that in 4:4–8 the siege of Jerusalem, which is the dominant theme of the context, is only discernible in v 7 and at the conclusion of v 8 incidentally, whilst the rest of the statements run in quite another direction. This already touches upon the further difficulty that 4:4–8 does not give the impression of unity in itself, so that any attempt to make completely clear what is described by these verses comes up against great difficulties. Whereas 4:4–6, 8a show the prophet lying bound and altogether passive,

---

34 Cf. to 2:8f and also 5:1f.
35 For the sign-act's previous history, cf. A. Alt, "Hic murus aheneus esto," *ZDMG* 86 (1932): 33–48;

"Neues aus der Pharaonenzeit Palaestinas," *PJ* 32 (1936): 10 n. 3.
36 For אות see above p. 156.

verse 7 reveals a strong positive activity, with threatening speech and attitude. How also are we to understand the ימי מצורך at the end of v 8? Are we to understand the "oppression" actively, in accordance with 8:3, as the days in which the prophet performed the symbolic siege of Jerusalem on behalf of Yahweh, or passively as days of suffering and bondage brought about by Yahweh, in accordance with v 8a which immediately precedes? Plainly neither of the two possibilities is right by itself, but it appears that both had to be brought together in a conscious ambiguity by a connecting saying, which stands at the end and opposes the suggested division of the whole section in which v 7 seems to be a doublet of v 3 (Bertholet, Steinmann).

4:4–8, like 3:25–27, is to be regarded as made up of additions and later interpretations of the prophet's words in the tradition of the school. With this we must accept, as with 3:25–27, that this addition worked with genuine elements of the Ezekiel tradition, even though their use in the present connection belongs within the secondary expansion. Similarly it appears probable that we are not dealing with one single addition, made at one time, but that several phases of such activity are discernible. In the different numbers given in 𝔐 and 𝔊, which are not simple scribal errors, we can follow still further the interpretative work which molded the text.

■ **4:4** The kernel of the entire section 4:4–8 is to be found in 4:4, in which originally השמאלי must have been lacking, as v 9b also confirms: "Then lie upon your side, and bear the guilt of the house of Israel. For as long as you lie upon it you shall bear the guilt of the house of Israel." Undoubtedly "house of Israel" here is primarily to be understood in line with Ezekiel's other preaching to God's people Israel, who were currently represented by Judah. In its content this saying may possibly refer back to what has been said in 3:26f. Clearly there was a period in Ezekiel's life when he was bound, which here seems to mean more than simply a time of restricted ability to speak, and which is also said here to have been commanded by Yahweh. According to 33:21f it took place about the time of the fall of Jerusalem. 4:8 goes back to the image

of binding with cords, which was used in 3:25 for the hostile action of outside enemies. Here it is related to Yahweh, and the lying on one side is interpreted as a result of the prophet's being bound by Yahweh himself.

Here also, however, the text is not concerned with speculations about biographical features of the prophet's life, which is left in obscurity. All that is important is the clear setting forth of the message which lay in the acts and sufferings of the prophet. This suffering is interpreted by the expression נשא עון, which is repeated several times in these verses with a certain fixity, and is regarded as intended by God. I have examined the use of this phrase in the Old Testament.[37] Of the thirty-five occurrences of נשא [ב]עון in 𝔐 of the Old Testament, eight of them, which occur outside the Priestly Document and Ezekiel, point to a meaning "to forgive guilt." Of the remaining twenty-seven occurrences, eighteen are found in the Priestly Document and nine in the book of Ezekiel. We are undoubtedly therefore dealing with a central expression of the priestly language. We can distinguish more precisely three ways in which it is used in priestly literature:

1) In the sphere of sacral law it is used in concluding formulations to establish a condition of guilt.[38]

2) In a weaker usage the expression can take on the meaning "to be responsible for something" (such as the sanctuary, Nu 18:1).

3) In substitutionary acts it can express the "guilt bearing" of the substitute. Thus the scapegoat bears the guilt of the people on itself into the desert (Lev 16:22). The scapegoat is ordained by Yahweh "to bear the guilt of the community, in order to make atonement for them" (Lev 10:17). Does the fact that Aaron bears on his gold headband "the guilt relating to the holy offerings" (Ex 28:38) also belong here?

Ezek 4:4 is clearly to be understood from the third circle of ideas. Ezekiel's lying bound is regarded as an event of substitutionary sin-bearing. We must not be too hasty here in introducing an elaborate theory of substitution, especially since Ezek 4:4 is not a primary statement about the priestly נשא עון, but is an attempt at interpreting an event of the prophet's life in a new way, making use of this phrase drawn from the priestly

---

37 Zimmerli, "Eigenart," 9–12.
38 In this connection more will be said with reference to Ezek 14:10.

vocabulary. Nevertheless two things can be said: in this proclamation of the binding of Ezekiel as an event in which he bore "the guilt of the house of Israel," the idea is expressed that Ezekiel portrayed publicly, in a meaningful sign, a condition of guilt. Guilt and punishment, however, are not to be held apart, according to the faith of the Old Testament, as we have already mentioned.[39] Ezekiel, by lying bound, became a revealer of guilt, an accuser, as he had been previously in threatening punishment (4:1–2 [3]). We must add a further consideration to this. In the prophet's עון guilt-bearing there occurs at the same time an act of public identification. His own life is brought into the עון (guilt-punishment) of the people. He brings together in his symbolic bondage the guilt of Israel as a burden in his own life. We can scarcely deny that ideas are set in motion here which were to be more fully worked out in Is 53, again probably in a prophetic figure.[40] Is it a mere accident that not only in the use of נשא עון, which also dominates the oracle of Is 53 (although the formulation appears there with greater variety in a much looser use of the form), but also in the לא יפתח פיו . . . כרחל . . . נאלמה ולא יפתח פיו (Is 53:7) there are undoubted contacts with Ezek 3:26 (24:27; 33:22)? The Ezekiel tradition thus appears to have made its contribution to the formation of the picture of the Servant of Yahweh who bears the guilt of the many. Does this point to a connection between the school of Ezekiel and that of Deutero-Isaiah in Babylon?

■ **4:7** The elaboration in Ezek 4:4 is closely connected to what precedes by the saying in vv 7f. Verse 7 is the connection to v 3, to which it adds the idea that the prophet's lying bound is to be connected with his threats against Jerusalem, in a way which breaks up the original picture of v 4. This emphasizes the accusatory aspect of the prophet's symbolic action in v 4. The instruction to the prophet to set his face (threateningly) against Jerusalem is then repeated from v 3, to which is added that he must stretch out his bared arm against the city. Whereas in Is 52:10 this baring of the arm is used of Yahweh as a demonstration of his great saving power over the world, it is intended here to be a dangerous threat. Ezekiel has to "prophesy" against

Jerusalem (cf. 6:2; 11:4; 13:2; 21:2, 7 and other passages).

■ **4:8** 4:8 connects up with 3:25, defining further the image of the prophet's being bound by the mention of cords which Yahweh himself will place upon him. If by this is meant that the prophet is to be unable to turn from one side to the other, it shows that the author of this addition still did not have v 6 in the underlying text, since this commands the prophet to turn from one side to the other. In v 7b, as we have mentioned already, the reference to the siege of the city and the oppression which the prophet is to experience are brought together inseparably by the ambiguity of מצור.

■ **4:5** The reference to the prophet's bearing of guilt has undergone a further scribal interpretation of a detail in v 5. This recalls in its particular character the rationalizing elaboration of the vision of God in the additions to ch. 1 and belongs to a later phase of the tradition. The מספר of v 4 can very well be construed without any thought of a definite number of days (the number of days which you lie = as long as you lie). Verse 5, however, takes the מספר quite literally "I have made the years of their punishment to be for you the number of days: 390 (𝕲 190) days." This reveals a clear interest in a detailed reckoning of the guilt and a correspondence between the scale of the guilt and the length of the substitutionary sin-bearing. The scale of reckoning runs: a day for a year. The Priestly Document shows very clearly the presence of such a scale in its own view of history. Nu 14:34 recounts, in the context of the narrative of the spies, the divine punishment on the people who complain. The J tradition already included the idea that the people had been compelled to remain in the desert as a punishment until the generation of the exodus had died out (Nu 14:22f, J). This covered a period of forty years (Amos 2:10; 5:25). The precise method of calculation in P, however, is distinctly priestly, and in the reference to the spies who have demoralized the people with their story, we read: "According to the number of the days in which you spied out the land, forty days, for every day a year, you shall bear your iniquity, forty years, and you shall know my enmity. I, Yahweh, have spoken." A dis-

---

39   See above pp. 145f.
40   See Walther Zimmerli, "παῖς θεοῦ A: Der עבד יהוה im AT," *TWNT* 5, 654–677.

tinctive scheme of divine reckoning is made use of here, which can be seen to be operative in Ezekiel's symbolic action in the reverse direction (from the years of guilt to the days of the נשׂא עון), but nonetheless by God's command (אני נתתי לך). We may question whether such a calculation had in mind a specific point of reference in some form of priestly action, as in a rite of absolution.[41]

According to 𝔐 Ezekiel was to lie on his side for 390 days, corresponding to the 390 years of the guilt of the house of Israel. There can scarcely be any doubt that for these 390 years we must refer back to Israel's past, since these were the years of her offence. According to the chronological reckoning of Begrich, Solomon's accession took place in the year 975/4. That is 387/8 years before the destruction of Jerusalem, and this is presupposed as the lower starting point for the reckoning of the text of Ezekiel. We must certainly question therefore whether this late calculation is in agreement with the reckoning of the temple chronicles, which must have been authoritative in the priestly circles around and after Ezekiel. We must certainly allow for some deviations. A glance at the royal chronology of the Deuteronomic History leads us to caution, since the reigns of all the Judean kings from Solomon on, by a simple addition, give a total of $433\frac{1}{2}$ years, instead of the 387/8 years reckoned by Begrich. The question arises therefore whether there lies in the number given by 𝔐 a calculation which reckoned with a round figure of 390 years for the period from the dedication of the temple under Solomon up to its destruction. Ezek 8 shows that Ezekiel himself saw the sin of the people, which led up to the destruction of the city and the departure of Yahweh's glory from Jerusalem, in the abominations which took place in the temple. From this we could well understand that, in the school of Ezekiel, the years of the first temple's existence (calculated as 390) were regarded as the proper period of the עון בית ישראל. That other views of

Israel's sinful past are also found in Ezekiel's own words in chs. 16, 20, 23 (which do not entirely agree among themselves) need not oppose this view.

■ 4:6 What then are we to conclude from the reckoning of 𝔊? It cannot be understood apart from the subsequent expansion which has taken place in 4:4–8 by the addition of v 6 and the השמאלי in v 4. In this further exposition of the message in the tradition of the school the symbolic action is explained in regard to the two kingdoms of the house of Israel. The long allegory of ch. 23, and also 37:15–28, may have encouraged further interpretation in this direction. In this development a distinction is made between the guilt of the Northern Kingdom and that of Judah. That this introduced some obscurity into the reference to the "house of Israel" was not taken into account. The connection with the Northern Kingdom by lying on the left side, and with the Southern Kingdom by lying on the right side, is determined by the custom of taking an orientation from the rising of the sun.[42] With an orientation to the east the left becomes a designation of the north and the right the south. To this may be added the further aspect that the right is the side of honor. Judah, with its honored center in the sanctuary of Jerusalem, lay on the side of honor.

𝔊 and 𝔐 clearly attest for the house of Judah a period of guilt of forty years. According to the analogy of the Israel oracle, we should see in this a period of guilt of the Southern Kingdom analogous to the time of the Northern Kingdom's guilt. Accordingly, in interpreting the forty years we must start from the year 587 B.C. and work backwards. By reckoning in this way, however, we cannot see how we can arrive at an intelligible result. Thus we appear to have here a shifting of meaning which has its eminent consequences for the interpretation of the oracle. The narrative of the spies shows that from an early period the round number of forty years had a place as a period of punishment, in which one generation of grown men passed away and

---

41 That the process of such calculation was of importance in priestly activity has been shown by Gerhard von Rad, "Faith Reckoned as Righteousness" in *The Problem of the Hexateuch and Other Essays*, tr. E. W. Trueman Dicken (New York: McGraw-Hill, 1966), 125–130.

42 Tallquist, *Himmelsgegenden*, 123–129: "Die Ostqibla."

a new generation arose, who were not twenty years old before the beginning of the forty years or who were still unborn then. There is everything in favour therefore of the view that the forty years of Ezek 4:6 are to be understood in accordance with this pattern. They represent the period of punishment which Judah must expect for its guilt. Whilst עון, in the context of the original address which understood the "house of Israel" to mean the entire people, referred to the period in which guilt had been incurred, in the forty years of the later interpretation, which made special reference to Judah, it was changed to mean the period of punishment following on the guilt. What appears as a logical contradiction is not in fact so in view of the Hebrew way of thinking of עון. Besides meaning "wrongdoing," and the guilt this incurs, it can also denote the punishment consequent upon such guilt (cf. Koehler-Baumgartner).

A considerable obscurity has entered into the meaning of the original oracle by the addition of v 6. When regarded as the period of sin of the "house of Israel," meaning the whole nation with its center in Jerusalem and with its sins evident in the Jerusalem temple, the 390 years were intelligible. They lost their intelligibility, however, when they were made to apply to the "house of Israel" regarded as the counterpart of the "house of Judah" and were thereby referred to the Northern Kingdom. The parallelism is only to be regarded in the context of the subsequent addition of Judah to an oracle originally concerning all Israel.

We can perhaps illuminate the intention of these calculations from a calculation in the Priestly chronology. According to the reckoning so far the years of atonement and punishment, referred to under the catchword עון, are to be added together to make a period of 430 years for the whole period of the עון, from the time of the foundation of the temple to the time of the expected punishment, i.e., the end of the exile. This same number is found in P (Ex 12:40f) as a reference to the period of the sojourn in Egypt: ". . . at the end of 430 years, on that very day, all the hosts of Yahweh went out from the land of Egypt." In Ezek 20:33ff we see that the second half of ch. 20 looks forward to a new exodus of Israel after the period spent in exile. This is to progress from the scattering among the nations to the "desert of the nations," just

as the exodus from Egypt led to the "desert of Egypt," and from there into the "land of Israel" through a further judgement and sifting by Yahweh. We may then question whether we ought to relate the round number 430 in the two passages. In both passages an exodus event forms the end of the 430 years. We must then interpret the mysterious reckoning of this number from its appearance in the book of Ezekiel. The Priestly tradition shows a use of the number in a way which indicates that it had already become fixed. Perhaps then we can see in at least this one place something of the Priestly calculation of time, which is otherwise largely obscure. We should then have here the clear development of a stylizing of the earlier history after the pattern of the later history leading up to the second exodus.

The form of the text given by 𝔐, which we have been interpreting so far and which arose by the combination of two distinct phases of interpretation, contains an unsatisfactory feature at one point. The reckoning of the עון of the house of Judah, which was added later to the עון of the house of Israel in the view we have set out, must have been arranged in parallel to it, not one after the other, by a more detailed reflection on the situation. We must regard the figure given in 𝔊 of 190 years for the עון of the "house of Israel" as an attempt to smooth the unevenness, in interpreting the reference to the "house of Israel" as applying to the Northern Kingdom. In 𝔊 the עון is clearly interpreted as a period of punishment both for the house of Israel and the house of Judah. Ezekiel's being bound expresses the years of punishment of the two kingdoms, recalculated into days. The difference of 150 years between the punishments (Northern Kingdom 190; Southern Kingdom 40) expresses the fact that the Northern Kingdom came to an end politically 150 years before the Southern Kingdom. Are we then to reckon the beginning of the 150 years from the subservience of Menahem to Assyria in 738 B.C., or to the downfall under Pekah in 733 B.C., or to the final defeat of what was left of the state of Ephraim under Hoshea in 722 B.C.—the latter under a different chronology? There are many uncertainties of detail here also. It is in any case clear that there was still in mind for both the Northern and Southern Kingdoms a period of punishment of forty years from 587 B.C., equalling the period of punishment of those who wandered through the desert. The two calculations meet in this immediate expectation of a period of punishment for Jerusalem of forty years. This calculation from the school of Ezekiel, where we cannot be sure whether the number goes back to Ezekiel himself, stands in the Old Testament alongside the expectation of the disciples of Jeremiah who calculated the period of Babylonian dominion as seventy years (Jer 25:11; 29:10). In consequence the reckoning in the book of Jeremiah, which is given much more explicitly and which comes much closer to the actual period whether we reckon from 605–539 (Babylonian rule) or from 587–521/517 (destruction and restoration of the temple), came to be regarded as the prophetic message regarding the duration of the exile in the minds of the community (Zech 1:12; Dan 9:2).

Starting from the experience of being bound, which is certainly to be traced back to the life of the prophet, the section 4:4–8 shows several phases of interpretation in which we cannot certainly make out in detail how much goes back to actual statements from Ezekiel. The dating of the separate phases is scarcely possible. Only for the latest stratum of interpretation do we have a firm *terminus post quem non*. The expectation of the forty years of exile for the "house of Judah" must in any case be placed before 547 B.C., i.e., the effective end of the forty years following the destruction of Jerusalem, since after this time it would scarcely have remained explicable in its composition and outline. This somewhat surprising fact warns us, in a way which appears to be well-founded, that, with the "tradition" of the school of Ezekiel, we are not very far from the words of the prophet himself, which are last attested in the year 571 B.C., according to 29:17. Thus a large part of the expansion of the present text could have taken place during the lifetime of the prophet himself.

■ **4:9–11** *The Scarcity of Food During the Siege.* In 4:9–11 we again come up against a part of the original three-sign composition from the hand of the prophet himself.

Of this v 9b, which has the purpose of connecting the symbolic action with the preceding act of the prophet's being bound like vv 7f, is certainly to be cut out. The preparation of rationed food is ascribed in this half-verse, which derives from later editorial activity, to the time when the prophet lay bound, with which it originally had nothing to do. Verse 9b, therefore, presupposes the composition of vv 4f, before v 6 had been added to them, which mentioned only the 390 days when the prophet lay on one side.

According to v 9a the prophet was commanded to take six kinds of vegetables and cereals and to mix them for food in a bowl. This shows that it cannot concern the preparation of food for 390 days, which would be out of the question in view of the food's liability to decay. The sign-action was originally to take place for a much shorter time. No definite local background can be seen in the different kinds of food named, which are as follows:

1) Wheat (חטין singular חטה).[43]
2) Barley (שערים singular שערה).[44] For Palestine, as for Babylonia, wheat and barley were the most important cereals. Herodotus, 1, 193 and Strabo 16 1, 14 praise the richness of Babylonia, "This land produces barley like no other, for it yields three hundredfold, according to reports."[45]
3) Beans (פול).[46] According to 2 Sam 17:28 they were among the means of sustenance brought to David in East Jordan.[47]
4) Lentils (עדשים only found in the plural).[48] 2 Sam 23:11 refers to a battle in a field of lentils during David's Philistine wars. Cf. also Gen 25:34; 2 Sam 17:28. In this latter reference, as in Ezek 4:9, the items are listed in pairs: wheat/barley, beans/lentils.
5) Millet (דחן).[49] דחן is only mentioned here in the Old Testament. For Mesopotamia it is known not only through literary reference (Akk. *duḫnu*), but also directly through a find of millet seeds in a late Assyrian sarcophagus.[50]

43 Immanuel Loew, *Die Flora der Juden* 1, Publications of the Alexander Kohut Memorial Foundation 4 (Wien: Löwit, 1928), 776–798: *triticum sativum*; Gustaf Dalman, *Arbeit und Sitte in Palästina* 2 (Gütersloh: Bertelsmann, 1932), 243–246.

44 Loew 1, 707–723: *hordeum*; Dalman, *Arbeit* 2, 251–255.

45 Meissner, *Babylonien* 1, 184f, 197f.

46 Loew 2, 492–505: *vicia faba*; Dalman, *Arbeit* 2, 265–268.

47 For Babylonia see Meissner, *Babylonien* 1, 199.

48 Loew 2, 442–452: *lens lens*; Dalman, *Arbeit* 2, 264–265.

49 Loew 1, 738–740: *panicum*, 740–746: *sorghum vulgare*; Dalman, *Arbeit* 2, 258–259, also 260–261.

50 Meissner, *Babylonien* 1, 198.

6) Spelt (כסמים singular כסמת).[51] It takes its name from its cropped (כסם) beard (Koehler-Baumgartner). In Ex 9:32 it is mentioned in Egypt, together with wheat, as a crop that ripens late in comparison with flax and barley, which ripen early. Is 28:25 shows that spelt was planted as a border to wheat and barley in the fields.[52]

Ezekiel was to mix together these different cereals and vegetables in a bowl and bake them into bread (עשה ללחם). In Lev 19:19 (cf. Dtn 22:9) there is a prohibition against sowing a field with two kinds of seed. From this it has been concluded that the idea of the uncleanness of what Ezekiel is to bake stands in the forefront of the action that he is commanded to perform (Smend), so that here, as in vv 12ff, there is a pointer to the uncleanness of life in exile. Nowhere, however, even in the Mishnah tractate *Kil'ayim* where we might expect it, do we find that the prohibition of the *perturbatio sacrorum* was related to the mixing of different kinds of cereal in food. Ezekiel's action is intended rather to make clear that the prophet is to sustain himself with food baked from all kinds of scraps. It is what we should call in modern speech "compulsory admixture." Again this leads to the idea of a city under siege, in which food begins to become scarce and has to be eked out in every possible way.

Verses 10f point in the same direction and speak of the rationing of food and drink. At regular times (מעת עד עת found in late usage "at fixed intervals of days")[53] he is to take a specific, carefully rationed amount per day. This is to be 20 shekels of food, i.e., c.230 gr. Barrois reckons with a shekel of 11.424 gr., which would correspond to the middle of the three demonstrable shekel weights of 12.2, 11.5, 9.82 gr. (*BRL*).[54] According to Koehler-Baumgartner the name of the volume measure hin comes from the Egyptian *hnw* "pot." In P this measure is still often used for the measurement of oil (Ex 29:40; 30:24 and other passages) and wine (Lev 23:13; Nu 15:5 and other pas-

sages). It comprises one sixth of a bath (בת) and, according to Barrois, is to be reckoned at 6.56 liters (*BRL*, 6.6).[55] However, on the basis of a fragment of a jug from *Tell Beit Mirsim* and the upper part of a jug from Lachish which carry respectively the inscriptions בת and בת למלך, W. F. Albright also considers a calculation of only 3.83 liters.[56] Ezekiel's ration therefore contains at least 1.1 liters per day. The circumstances of the siege of Jerusalem in 589–587 are illustrated by Jer 37:21: "They committed Jeremiah to the court of the guard; and a loaf of bread was given him daily from the bakers' street until all the bread of the city was gone." Alongside this we must reckon that the water supply of a besieged city was no less a problem than the supply of bread. The account of Jeremiah's sufferings also shows a cistern that was almost empty (Jer 38:6).

What Ezekiel was commanded to do and the actions performed in his house portray visibly the imminent assault on Jerusalem at the climax of the siege, without any further interpretative comment (as previously in 3:24b; 4:1f). There now appears to follow in vv 16f an interpretative comment on vv 12–15 in precisely this direction. The connection appears at first to be particularly clearly given in the catchwords found in both (במשקל) שתה במשורה/אכל במשקול. However, it seems that we must regard the catchwords במשקול and במשורה in 4:10f as later additions. Two further considerations tell against an original connection of vv 9–11. Why is 4:16f introduced by the narrative formula ויאמר אלי in a way which otherwise does not occur in the section 3:24b–5:4a?[57] Further, why does this word of interpretation, which is apparently so closely tied to 4:9–11, first appear after the later section vv 12–15? In fact we have in 4:16f an independent saying to the prophet which, in its content, stands close to the mention of the sign-action in 4:9–11. Besides this, in its syntactical structure and vocabulary it stands in clear relationship to 12:17–20, from which the interpretive

---

51 Loew 1, 767–776: *triticum sativum (dicoccum)*; Dalman, *Arbeit* 2, 246–248.

52 For Babylonia see Meissner, *Babylonien* 1, 198; for the brewing of beer from barley, spelt, and wheat see Meissner, *Babylonien* 1, 241, 417.

53 Jacob Levy, "עת," *Wörterbuch über die Talmudim und Midraschim*, 5 volumes (Berlin: Harz, 1924).

54 Barrois, *Manuel* 2, 252–258.

55 Barrois, *Manuel* 2, 247–252.

56 *The Excavation of Tell Beit Mirsim* 3 (1943), pp. 58f and note 7, according to Barrois, *Manuel* 2, 251f.

57 See above p. 154.

glosses ובדאגה and ובשממון have been taken.[58]

The saying of 4:16f is headed by a separate call to the prophet and informs him of the imminent action of Yahweh towards Jerusalem. In the threat that Yahweh will break the staff of bread in Jerusalem we may see a metaphor. Gen 18:5 and Judg 19:5, 8 show that the phrase סעד לב "to maintain the heart" had the meaning "to refresh oneself." From this it is not far to an allusion to the support, or staff of bread. Is 3:1 also points in this direction, where we read of the "staff of bread" and the "staff of water." Against this L. Koehler has pointed to the custom, still found in southern countries, of putting round loaves (חלה) on a staff and has raised the question whether the saying "to break the staff of bread" does not rest on this actual custom.[59] The phrase regarding "the staff of water" would then be understood as an analogous formation from a time when the objective meaning was no longer directly recognized. It would be a consequence of Yahweh's intervention that bread and water would be subject to severe rationing. The two glosses from 12:17–20 then make additional reference to the fear and horror with which all meals, which should be happy occasions, would be eaten in Jerusalem. The למען clause of v 17, which expresses the intention of Yahweh in his action in a clause which appears again in 12:19b, stresses the thorough disturbance and the total offense of the people in its guilt. The verb מקק appears again in 33:10 in a quotation of the words of the people (cf. 24:23; Lev 26:39).

■ **4:12–15** *The Unclean Food.* It now remains to consider vv 12–15 which we have hitherto passed over. V 12 joins smoothly on to vv 9–11 and mentions a further stipulation for the preparation of food by the prophet. It then leads to a short dialogue between the prophet and his God. Thus vv 12–15 appear as a genuine continuation of vv 9–11. Its content, however, as well as the novel form of a dialogue with Yahweh within a sign-action make it clear that we are dealing here with a passage which was foreign to the original three-sign composition.[60]

■ **4:12** The addition of vv 12–15 begins very skilfully with a closer interpretation of ועשית ללחם of v 9, taking up the תאכלנו, which appears in 𝔐 of vv 9f no less than three times. It is slightly changed to the form תאכלנה.[61] We gain the impression so far as language is concerned that we are simply faced with the continuation of vv 9f, but closer examination shows that the more precise elaboration is out of step, since v 11 has already extended the mention of food to cover drink. V 12 therefore passes over v 11 and rejoins v 10, or more precisely v 9. The לעיניהם is also striking. That the symbolic action should take place "before the eyes" of a circle of onlookers is not previously mentioned, however much the idea may be present that Ezekiel's actions were to be seen by others. This לעיניהם takes on a quite specific importance in the symbolic action of 12:3ff (cf. 21:11; 37:20). It is repeated no less than seven times in 12:3–7 𝔐. 4:12 therefore with its concluding לעיניהם has undoubtedly been formulated from the situation of 12:1ff, where its suffix has a clear reference, whereas in 4:12f it hangs in the air.

The prophet is commanded to eat his food "as a barley cake," i.e., to treat its preparation as for a "barley cake." Does this presuppose that the preparation is like that of ἐγκρυφίας?[62] He then receives a specific command to use human dung as fuel. Up to the present day animal dung, mixed with straw and dried, is an important fuel in the poorer countries of the East.[63] The substitution of human dung for that of animals is not otherwise known. Undoubtedly from the ritual standpoint of priestly regulations for purity it was a quite impossible action. The rule for the holy area of the camp of the people of God (Dtn 23:13f) shows clearly how "unclean" (ערות דבר Dtn 23:15) Yahweh's command to the prophet must have appeared.

■ **4:14** For the first time there then occurs a spontaneous

---

58 Cf. note a to 4:16.

59 Ludwig Koehler, *Kleine Lichter; fünfzig Bibelstellen erklärt*, Zwingli-Bücherei 47 (Zürich: Livingli, 1945), 25–27.

60 Cf. note a to v 13 for the secondary character of the verse.

61 Cf. note b to 4:12.

62 Cf. note a to 4:12.

63 Barrois, *Manuel* 1, 319.

reply from the prophet. It is significant that this first spontaneous outburst from the prophet who had grown up in the sanctuary occurred when he was urged to perform a crassly unclean act. Ezekiel's complaint, which begins with the painful interjection אהה (again in 9:8; 11:13; 21:5), contains a confession of his previous manner of life in which he had avoided all such crass uncleanness. The Book of the Covenant already forbade the eating of the flesh of mutilated animals (טרפה) with a reference to the holy character of the people (Ex 22:30). The flesh of dead animals (נבלה) is mentioned in Dtn 14:21; Lev 17:15 and other passages. Ezek 44:31 forbids the eating of both categories of meat, especially to the priests. The flesh of a sacrificial animal which had not been eaten by the third day, the holiness of which had become a dangerous uncleanness, is described as פגול in Lev 7:18; 19:7. The מרק פגלים (Q) of Is 65:4 could be a broth made with such meat, either cooked after the third day or itself kept until a third day. It is not quite clear whether פגול meant this meat from the very beginning, or whether it once had a more general meaning which extended beyond the case described in Lev 7:17f; 19:6f.

The prophet's words, which express a very definite ideal of purity, reveal as their background the formula of a negative confession of guilt, or rather a protestation of innocence voiced in negative statements which lists in a fixed series specific typical offences. We compare as a parallel the liturgical prayer of Dtn 26:13–15, which contains in v 14a a corresponding negative series of statements. A comparison with Ezekiel shows a certain freer mode of expression and a stronger personal note which sets more in the background the fixed summary formulations.[64]

■ **4:15** In the related scene of Acts 10:14ff the consideration of Peter's ritual antipathy is answered by an authoritative assertion of purity for what had hitherto been unclean by God. God's merciful answer to Ezekiel lies within the Old Testament order of cleanness. Ezekiel is permitted to do what is ritually pure and to bake his food in the usual way over (על) animal dung. Is this simply a personal concession to the prophet or is this act of alleviation also to be understood within the

framework of the declaratory sign-action? The gloss in v 13 seeks to interpret only the first of Yahweh's commands, which is not taken up in the sequel, as a sign (this is why it is inserted immediately after v 13 although it perceptibly disturbs the section vv 12/14): "Thus [ככה for the interpretation of a sign action is not otherwise found in Ezekiel, but cf. Jer 13:9; 19:11; 28:11] will the Israelites eat unclean things among the nations." This interpretation is faithful to the meaning of v 12. Earlier Amos had threatened the priest Amaziah, "You will die in an unclean land" (Amos 7:17). So also Hos 9:3, "Ephraim shall return to Egypt, and they shall eat unclean food in Assyria." A foreign land was the sphere of foreign gods (1 Sam 26:19). With the many rites of consecration which permeated life men could scarcely avoid entering into this realm of uncleanness when they ate the food of a foreign land, and thereby becoming unclean.[65] Daniel 1 also shows that in the conduct of life in exile there were possibilities of avoiding gross uncleanness, even in the heathen royal court. From this we must also understand the נפשי לא מטמאה of Ezek 4:14 as the assertion of an exile. In the מקדש מעט of 11:16 also we find that there was for those in exile a (reduced) possibility of a pure life. We cannot therefore exclude the the possibility that the lessening of the divine demand in 4:15 had a significance for the message preached. V 15 could, especially in the more original text which lacked the interpretative emphasis of v 13, point to the possibility which Yahweh graciously upholds of remaining untainted by any uncleanness. It could contain the veiled promise that, where a community did not turn aside from God's command, but asked for the grace of purity, Yahweh was willing to grant it.

From the symbolism of siege in vv 9–11, vv 12–15 pass over to the symbolism of exile. In the context of ch. 4 they are undoubtedly a later addition. The phenomenon of an expansion of a sign-action by the addition of a new feature which arose out of the original action was already evident in 4:3, and it recurs a third time in the third part of the three-sign composition. In 4:3 it is possible that we have an expansion by the prophet himself at a somewhat later time. This must

---

64   See Kurt Galling, "Der Beichtspiegel. Eine gattungsgeschichtliche Studie," *ZAW* 47 (1929): 125–130.

65   See further the New Testament discussion about the "weaker brother" and the εἰδωλόθυτον in 1 Cor 8.

also be conceded as a possibility in 4:12–15. In its content there is nothing which necessitates that the verse should be regarded as out of place in the mouth of Ezekiel. Otherwise we should have to see here an element of the later exposition within the framework of the school tradition. We must not place the addition too late since the expansion in 4:16f presupposes the fully-formed section 4:9–15 and does not permit this to be broken up further, although vv 16f must obviously follow after v 11.

■ **5:1, 2** *The Divine Shaving.* In 5:1f we have the third section of the three-sign composition of the siege of Jerusalem. It points to the end of the period of siege and shows the experience of the population of Jerusalem at this time. This third section also must originally have been formed as an independent symbolic action without relation to the series of actions in 4:1ff; 9–11. In the text which we now have there are obvious additions. The clause תער הגלבים תקחנה לך is a simple explanatory gloss (Hölscher, *Hesekiel*). We find stated here, with the purpose of echoing the message of Is 7:20, that the sword with which the prophet cuts off his hair fulfilled the function of a barber's razor. In v 2 the words בתוך העיר and סביבותיה are interpretative glosses which give a specific locality to the separate phases of the judgement. Bertholet would connect these statements with 4:1f. According to him Ezekiel was to burn a part of his hair on the brick carrying the sketch of Jerusalem and to take another part of it and to chop it with the sword in all directions. We should then recognize here, as in 4:7f and 9b, features which served to join together the individual sections. Perhaps, however, these additions project the interpretation back into the sign, since the reference to the time "when the days of the siege are completed," as a part of the interpretation, appears already to enter as a threat into the original text. The time referred to in 4:4–8 was not originally in mind here.

The action chosen to signify the final overthrow of Jerusalem is quite unusual. We must certainly not follow van den Born and Steinmann in interpreting it of Ezekiel's being imprisoned by his enemies and shaved as a convict, which he then interpreted as a sign concerning Jerusalem after it had happened to him. For an explanation of the sign we must turn rather to Is 7:20. There Isaiah had threatened the people, "In

that day Yahweh will shave with a razor which is hired beyond the River the head and the hair of the feet, and it will sweep away the beard also." Jer 41:5 (48:37; Is 15:2) mention the shaving of the beard (and hair of the head) as a sign of mourning. In Old Testament thinking mourning is not far removed from shame. 2 Sam 10:4f illustrates the humiliation of the compulsory shaving of a free man. There it was felt as a sufficient ground for a declaration of war. Fundamentally in Isaiah's opinion Yahweh was to take away his people's honor by means of Assyria, his razor hired in the East, and throw it into humiliation and mourning. Isaiah describes the judgement on Judah by means of the very forthright picture of the barber. In Ezekiel, however, we can see the process of the transformation of the word picture into a dramatic action, as we have already previously seen (2:8–3:3). The razor is the sword in the prophet's hand which he passes over his head. That Ezekiel should have had a חרב at hand in his place of exile need occasion no difficulty. In Judg 3:16 חרב denotes a dagger which could be hidden under a coat without difficulty. In Josh 5:2f it denotes flint knives used for circumcision, and in Ex 20:25 it denotes a chisel used for cutting stone. In the present text we must understand from the announcement of judgement occasioning threatening speech that Ezekiel describes the knife with which he cuts his hair as a חרב and deliberately avoids the more innocuous תער of Isaiah's prophecy. The addition then continues this. That Isaiah's saying undergoes such a remarkable development with Ezekiel shows once again how deeply this prophet was rooted in the sayings of earlier prophecy.

Strange as the event described in 5:1f is in its accomplishment, its message is nonetheless obvious. With a peculiar mixture of features, the prophet sets out two things by his action and suffering: Yahweh has drawn the sword against Jerusalem, and by a threatening act of shaving with it he foretells that Jerusalem will be stripped of its honor and its joy.

Ezekiel's action adds to the imagery given by Isaiah a further elaboration which heightens the strangeness of the whole event. The hair is divided into three parts, in line with Ezekiel's frequent delight in precise numbers and measurements. Is this meticulousness a priestly inheritance? Here the separate portions of hair are weighed on scales. We must ask whether accurate scales were available at that time or whether Ezekiel was making do with improvised weights. The text offers no answer to such questions about the details of the action. All that is important for it is the message for Jerusalem. The population of Jerusalem is to be divided, numbered into three parts, and weighed. Division, numbering, and weighing are all acts of judgement (Dan 5:26ff). The later interpretation of 𝔊 goes still further in introducing here the scheme of four plagues found later in 14:12ff in a free elaboration. In this judgement one third perish in the burning of the city.[66] A third are to be overtaken by the sword in attempting to escape in the region round about the city (2 Kings 25:4–7), and the other third are to be scattered to the winds. As individual fugitives they are to be scattered among neighboring countries or are to be carried off as prisoners to the land of the enemy. Such different fates become evident in Jer 40:1; 41:15; 43:5–7.

In 5:2bβ a glossator has endeavored to affirm explicitly that these latter have not excaped the judgement. The divine sword is then to be unsheathed over them also (הריק from "to empty," of the scabbard). The gloss is wholly in line with the original intention of the text, since, in describing a scattering to the winds, this was certainly not intending to affirm the possibility of deliverance but simply a third way of destruction.

■ **5:3** We now find repeated in the third part of the three-sign composition the phenomenon established in the first two parts, that the imagery has undergone a subsequent expansion by the addition of a further feature: "And you shall take from these a small number and bind them in the skirts of your robe." The addition is entirely drawn from the imagery of vv 1f, but is formally betrayed as a gloss by its disturbance of the statement about the three equally weighed parts of v 2 in favor of the last of them. This leads on to a change of subject in that v 3 interprets the three kinds of judgement mentioned in v 2 as the basis for a further, sub-

sequent event in which a "remnant" is preserved. This certainly goes beyond what was intended in v 2.

This preservation of a remnant is again referred to by the device of developing an earlier metaphor into a visible event, in what appears to be a common practice with Ezekiel. According to 1 Sam 25:29 Abigail says to David, "If a man rises up to pursue you and to seek your life, then may the life (נפש) of my lord be bound up in the bundle (צרור "pouch") of life with Yahweh thy Lord; and may the lives of your enemies be slung out as from the hollow of a sling." The antithesis: sling out = to hand over to destruction/to bind = to preserve alive, is quite clear here. This binding is further strengthened by the "bundle" (Luther) of life, which is derived from the same root and is not therefore to be translated as "pebble" with A. Marmorstein.[67] In Sir 6:16 a true friend is described as a צרור חיים (Smend "magic for [protecting] life,") "whoever fears God, obtains him." The saying has become fixed as an expression for something that brings good fortune. In Ezek 5:3, however, the image is used in a fully real sense. The action of binding is a gesture of hiding. We must ask whether there lies behind this picture of "binding in the hem of one's garment" an ancient conception of a particular power in the hem of a garment.[68]

■ **5:4a** There follows immediately in v 4a a reference to a further judgement brought upon a part of those who have escaped: "And of these again you shall take (some) and throw them into the fire, and burn them with fire." Those who have escaped, which undoubtedly refers to those preserved alive in exile in Babylon, will have to undergo a further division in which some will fall to Yahweh's judgement. This idea of dividing in judgement taking place at a new exodus from exile is unfolded more fully in 20:33ff. The mention of fire again here, as previously in v 2, can no longer refer to the destruction of the city by burning. The threat of Jer 29:22, according to which the king of Babylon

---

66 Cf. Ju 9:49; 1 Kings 16:18; Meissner, *Babylonien* 1, 112.

67 A. Marmorstein, "1 Sam 25:29," *ZAW* 43 (1925): 119–124; see also James George Frazer, *Folk-lore in the Old Testament* 2 (London: Macmillan, 1918), 503ff.

68 Mt 9:20, 14:26; Anton Jirku, *Die magische Bedeutung der Kleidung in Israel* (Rostock: Adler, 1914).

"burnt the prophets Zedekiah and Ahab with fire," raises the question whether this saying has in mind a literal punishment by burning at the hands of Babylonian captors (cf. the "fiery furnace" of Dan 3). However, it is just as possible that fire is a general metaphor for judgement here, leaving open the details of how it was actually carried out. The gloss in v 4b, which is lacking in 𝕲, again uses the catchword "fire" without making clear whence the fire came. Is this given by 19:14?

The one thing that can be said with certainty about the origin of the gloss is that it stems from the time after the fall of Jerusalem. It knows of the deliverance of a remnant with whom Yahweh still has a continuing history in exile. It also knows, however, that this hoped-for future can only be expected by a fresh sifting. If 20:33ff stems from Ezekiel,[69] nothing stands in the way of the view that we hear Ezekiel's preaching in this gloss also (after 587 B.C.), whether the formulation of it derives from his own hand or is to be ascribed to the circle of his disciples.

A final conclusion in this regard can scarcely be avoided. We have accepted that the sign-action which Ezekiel was commanded to perform was actually carried out by him. What is related in 5:1f is a brief action which could not, by its nature, have extended over a long period. The continuation reported in 5:3, 4a, however, shows the circumstances of a time some years later (after 587 B.C.). We cannot then avoid the conclusion that 5:3–4a was never actually carried out. Thus we have in 5:3–4a the form of a sign-action which was simply preached (and described), and which we have already been compelled to regard as a late break-up of the form.[70] We must clearly reckon this form within the framework of the later history of the prophet's preaching. Is this true of 4:12–15 also?

■ **5:4b–17** C) *The Commission to Preach to the House of Israel.* The symbolic actions which the prophet was commanded to perform were not complete in themselves. They were a proclamation. Thus, as we might expect, there has been added directly to them a commission to preach to the house of Israel (v 4b).

Our analysis has pointed to vv 5–6a, 8–9, 14–15 as the original content of the section vv 5–17. This original material shows a clear outline:

a) The introductory v 5 mentions Jerusalem, which is referred to in all three symbolic actions, and describes its position of honor.

b) V 6a, in clear dependence on v 5, formulates reproach against the disobedient city and thereby establishes

c) The threat of judgement, vv 8–9, 14–15. The transition from reproach to threat is not only made through the introductory לכן and the repetition of the messenger formula (v 8; cf. v 5), but is also strongly emphasized by the change from the description in the third person (vv 5–6a) to the direct address in the second person (vv 8–9, 14–15). In a concluding formula, common in Ezekiel, the threat reaches its goal in v 15bβ.

■ **5:5** The original text of the three-sign composition avoided any element of interpretation. 5:5 first reveals the intention of the symbolic actions. We find the assertion, "this is Jerusalem," which is decisive for the interpretation of the symbolic action, in a clause which recalls in its brevity the terse explanation of the guide through the new temple (40:45f; 41:4b, 22b). This city is then described with its rise and fall, and the judgement which it is to undergo.

"I have set her in the midst of the nations, with countries round about her" describes its exaltation. The linking of גוים (or עמים) with ארצות, which we could properly translate "heathen peoples—heathen lands," is particularly characteristic of Ezekiel (5:5f; 6:8; 11:16; 12:15; 20:23, 32; 22:4, 15; 29:12; 30:23, 26; 36:19, 24; cf. 20:34, 41; 25:7; 34:13). It is used here in an elevated style as a saying in *parallelismus membrorum* in order to stress the uniqueness of Jerusalem as the locality of the "center" of the entire world of nations. This idea of the "center" is expressed still more clearly in 38:12 with the metaphor "navel of the earth." Just as in the Roman Empire all roads led to the golden milestone in Rome itself, marked with the *umbilicus urbis,* the navel of the earth, in the Forum,[71] so according to Ezek 5:5 the world of nations and lands had its center in Jerusalem.[72] The reference to

---

69   Cf. on the text.
70   See above pp. 156f.
71   Alfred Jeremias, *Handbuch der altorientalischen Geistes-*

kultur (Leipzig: Hinrichs, 1913), 34.
72   Cf. further on 38:12 for the idea of the omphalos.

the "center" provides the possibility of stressing the special position of a people in regard to the geographical plan of the world. Thus Imperial China, in which the "Son of Heaven" annually restored the world to order by his sacrifice on the altar of the sky, was designated the "Kingdom of the Center." By this mode of expression, which appears to contain a dangerously static element, the election of Jerusalem was affirmed. However, it is significant that a proper biblical perspective is given immediately afterwards in the words spoken by Yahweh "I have set it (שמתיה)." In the final analysis the position of Jerusalem as the place of the center is not describable in purely geographical terms as something "naturally" given. It rests on a free divine affirmation, and it cannot be upheld without this affirmation or in contradiction to it. We are tempted to speak of an adoptionist motif which appears here, similar to that in Ps 2:7 affirming the divine sonship of the Davidic kings. In no place is election conceived as at man's disposal in a purely objective way.

■ **5:6a** Against the background of this divine election, which exalted Jerusalem over other peoples and countries, reference is now made to the sinfulness of the city, in that it had become more rebellious than other peoples and countries. In the formal dependence of the declaration of sin (v 6) on the declaration of election (v 5), a strong emphasis is given to the assertion that the sin of Israel exceeds the sins of the nations which has already been made in 3:6. In its conduct Jerusalem has trampled underfoot its election by Yahweh and changed its honor into disgrace. In a summarizing statement its sin is described as rebellion against (את) the laws and statutes of Yahweh.[73] The double expression משפטי – חקותי shows the coming together in Israel's sacred law of both the casuistic (משפטים) and apodictic (חקות) types, which have been analyzed by A. Alt, and which is already apparent in the Book of the Covenant.[74] This double expression is found in Ezekiel again, besides 5:6f, in 11:20; 18:9, 17; 20:11, 13, 16, 19, 21, 24; 37:24 (with the masculine plural of חק in 11:12; 20:18, 25; 36:27). Jerusalem's sin is not something vague, but an affront to the clear, revealed

law of God. This is shown in a particular way in ch. 22.

■ **5:6b–7** The two additions of vv 6b–7 seek to emphasize again the reproach of v 6a in somewhat more precise language.

■ **5:8, 9** Yahweh's judgement on Jerusalem will go beyond anything previously reported. In the הנני עליך, which introduces the direct address to Jerusalem which now begins, P. Humbert, "'hinnenî êlêkâ'," believed he could trace a formula of summons to a contest, which (with variation of אל and על) is to be understood as an abbreviation of an original הנני בא אליך. Of the twenty-two Old Testament occurrences of this formula two are found in Nahum (Na 2:14; 3:5), six in Jeremiah (Jer 21:13; 23:30–32; 50:31; 51:25) and the remaining fourteen in Ezekiel (5:8; 13:8, 20; 21:8; 26:3; 28:22; 29:3, 10; 30:22; 34:10; 35:3; 36:9; 38:3; 39:1). Accordingly the saying only occurs in prophecy at about the turn of the seventh/sixth centuries B.C., and, apart from Ezek 36:9, it always has a threatening meaning. It is also regularly (with the exception of 29:10) connected with the messenger formula or an oracle-formula. Thus in its present connection it contains a wholly threatening divine announcement.

■ **5:10** The threat of a hitherto unheard of judgement, left undefined in v 9, has been given a fuller explanation in v 10. Do actual experiences of the siege of Jerusalem in 589–587 B.C. lie behind the references to the appearance of cannibalism in the city, or are we simply dealing with a stereotyped feature? In any case the statement of 5:10, alongside the parallels in 2 Kings 6:29; Jer 19:9; Lev 26:29, is striking on account of the emphasis that children will also abuse their parents, which is doubly horrible in view of the strict Old Testament demand of respect for parents. The scattering of the remnant to the winds is plainly intended to explain 5:2.

■ **5:14–15** The basic text continues in vv 14f and speaks only of the destruction of the city. For the third time this clearly underscores the contrast with the nations. Jerusalem, which is exalted "in the midst" of the nations, but which has become more sinful than they, will be destroyed "before the eyes of everyone who passes by." It will become a reproach "among the nations round about." Jerusalem's political downfall is to be

---

73 Hip'il of מרה again in 20:8, 13, 21 directly related to Yahweh by ב.

74 Albrecht Alt, "The Origins of Israelite Law" in

Essays on Old Testament History and Religion, tr. R. A. Wilson (Garden City, New York: Doubleday, 1967), 101–171.

a sign of the judgement of God. In this judgement the city is to lose its honor, which it possessed by dint of the fact that it rested on God's promise. This deprivation of honor will become evident in the reproach of the surrounding nations. The "I, Yahweh, have spoken" is found again, tacked on asyndetically, in 5:17; 21:22; 24:14; 30:12; 34:24; appended with כי 21:37; 26:14 (with the omission of the divine name 23:34; 26:5; 28:10; 39:5). The fact that this formula can appear in the conclusion of the recognition formula in place of the formula of divine self-introduction (17:21; 37:14) clearly shows that it does itself contain an element of divine self-presentation.[75] Thus the concluding formula "I, Yahweh, have spoken" also understands the judgement upon Jerusalem as the effect of a divine message in which Yahweh reveals himself in the mystery of his person. This divine revelation, however, is in no way merely a word (6:10 𝔐 וידעו כי אני יהוה לא אל חנם דברתי). It is a word which effects an event. This concluding formula therefore can still be expanded with a fuller explanation אני יהוה דברתי ועשיתי (17:24; 22:14; 36:36b; cf. also 5:13 and 12:25). The importance of this formal language should not be undervalued for an understanding of the prophetic word.

■ **5:11–13** The two longer additions in vv 11–13 and 16–17 seek in their own way to give stronger coloring to the declaration of judgement, which is only given in general terms in the basic text. Vv 11–13 take up the last symbolic action of 5:1f and announce a threefold manner of punishment. This later interpretation by the school is formally distinguished by the fact that it returns once again in v 11a to describe the sin of Jerusalem and so once more prefaces the declaration of judgement with invective. This has in mind the desecration of the sanctuary which is decribed in detail by the prophet in ch. 8. With the threefold division of punishment, stemming from 5:1f, four forms of punishment (pestilence, famine, sword, dispersion) are combined in a clumsy way which gave 𝔊 occasion for rearranging the text.[76] The whole is clothed in the form of an oath, introduced by חי אני (which is in turn emphasized by the oracle-formula נאם יהוה). This oath form is found

no less than sixteen times in the book of Ezekiel (5:11; 14:16, 18, 20; 16:48; 17:16; 18:3; 20; 31, 33; 33:11; 34:8; 35:6, 11; in 17:19; 20:3; 33:27 without נאם אדני יהוה). The final recognition formula, expanded by the repetition of the declaration of judgement, delineates the whole as a prophetic proof-saying.[77]

■ **5:16–17** The second addition, which is not uniform in itself and which further increases the number of the misfortunes (arrows—of pestilence?, famine, wild animals, pestilence, blood, sword), imitates the basic text in its conclusion (v 13). Both additions draw upon other biblical material. A relative independence appears only to be found in the picture of the destructive arrows of evil in v 16.[78]

Setting

The question of the location and date of the formulation of the whole section 3:16a, 22–5:17 cannot be answered by any one reference. The basis of the section has been shown to consist in the three-sign composition of 4:1f, 9*–11; 5:1f, introduced by 3:16a, 22, 23aα (23aβb–24a?) 24b and concluded by a commission to preach in 5:4b–6, 8f, 14f. The possibility that the three-sign composition may represent an earlier unit within this whole (with its conclusion to preach in 5:4bff?) is not to be excluded altogether in view of the harsh formal transition 3:24b/4:1f. A clear date is given for this basic unit in 3:16a: seven days after the call. How should we evaluate this?

In the call-narrative it is striking that the prophet was given the scroll, with lamentation, mourning and woe, to eat, but was not called to any specific message. After this we should certainly expect a definite charge to the prophet to preach. Jer 1 offers an analogous situation. There also the call-narrative in the narrower sense (Jer 1:4–10) only commands the prophet to preach in general terms. The two visions, Jer 1:11f, 13–16, which may once have been independent and unattached to the call-narrative, but which are now undeniably built into the whole call account by the conclusion Jer 1:17–19, first contain the anticipated specific message about the "foe from the north." With Ezekiel it appears that the three-sign composition at

---

75 For details see Zimmerli, "Jahwe" and *Erkenntnis*.
76 Cf. note a to 5:12.
77 See Zimmerli, "Wort." Also what we have said to

v 15 for the expansion of the formula of self-introduction contained in it.
78 For the rest cf. to 14:12ff.

the end of the call-narrative had to fulfil the same function. Here, however, the actual situation is clearly removed chronologically from the call-narrative by the date given in 3:16a. According to this Ezekiel seven days after his call received the charge to shut himself in his house and to proclaim the imminent siege and fall of Jerusalem there by symbolic actions.

Jer 29, which is unfortunately not dated to a particular year, offers the fullest information about the domestic situation of the exiles from 597 B.C. According to this there had continued among the exiles an open attitude which regarded the situation as provisional. Men expected the speedy possibility of a return. A letter from Jeremiah which warned men to prepare for a longer period of exile led to an inflammatory letter of protest to Jerusalem in return. The event recorded in Jer 28, dated in the fourth year of Zedekiah, i.e., the year before Ezekiel's call, shows that in Jerusalem also at this time people reckoned on a speedy return of the exiles. It is in this situation that Ezekiel had to announce by his symbolic actions the imminent siege and fall of Jerusalem.

We must note that Ezekiel's message was harsher than the contemporary message of Jeremiah in Jerusalem who, according to Jer 38:17, appeared to regard the sparing of Jerusalem as possible even at the time of the final siege in the case of a voluntary capitulation by the people. Jeremiah's whole effort consisted in seeking to move the citizens of Jerusalem to a willing acceptance of the yoke of Nebuchadnezzar which had already been placed upon them. That these features are completely lacking in Ezekiel speaks decisively against transferring the performance of the symbolic actions to Jerusalem with Herntrich, Bertholet and others, and seeing in Ezekiel a prophet who worked in the same situation as Jeremiah. Rather, in the extreme severity of the message as it is contained in the three-sign composition and its interpretation, we hear the voice of the prophet in exile, who knows of the imminent accomplishment of the judgement upon all Israel, including Jerusalem. Since 597 B.C. he had himself come to share in the bitter experience of exile. He did not live at a place where the rightness of political decisions could be fought over, but outside such a sphere, in exile where he formulated the harsh and final prophetic message of judgement without any direct contact with the deci-

sions of the inhabitants of Jerusalem.

The additions to the basic text in 3:25–27; 4:3, 4–8, 12–15, 16f; 5:3–4a also point to the exile. 4:3 belongs to a time before 587 B.C., and 4:16f was also formulated before the fall of Jerusalem and was then later set in its present position. 5:3–4a certainly, and 3:25–27; 4:4–8, 12–15 probably, were first formulated as additions developing the message after 587 B.C. 3:25–27; 4:4–8 appear to look back on events which are to be dated in the life of Ezekiel about the time of the city's fall. However, the date of these interpretative additions, within the framework of the tradition either of the prophet himself or of his school, remains essentially uncertain. Composition in Jerusalem is in no way probable here.

Aim

The three-sign composition and its introduction in 3:24b proclaim the impending encirclement and destruction of Jerusalem. The interpretation which follows in 5:5ff sets this event in a larger context. What happens in Jerusalem does not take place in a corner, but is an event in the center of the world, and therefore possesses a worldwide exemplary meaning. So serious is the judgement of God—so this section avows—that it does not cease to apply to the very city which has been chosen by God and distinguished above all the world. It is to be plunged into humiliation and shame in the sight of the whole earth. Further this does not happen in a secondary and discreet way, brought about by a third party, but is ordained by God himself for Jerusalem, his city.

In this event the mysterious truth is revealed, which, when rightly considered, must disturb all mankind. Human rebelliousness is nowhere so clearly visible as sin as in the place which God has uniquely chosen to be the special place of his presence. Consequently the judgement of God is never so fully visible as in the very place where his love has come particularly close to men. The concluding verses 5:13, 15, 17 stress emphatically that in the judgement upon the city of God there is a divine message which reveals the hiddenness of God in the most personal mystery of his name. In this way God is to be recognized.

The question about the nature of the divine judgement is answered by two additions to the original symbolic actions; 4:3 says that where judgement occurs an iron wall appears between the face of God and man, so that the latter no longer enjoys God's looking upon him. 4:12 (with the interpretative gloss 4:13), however, speaks in priestly language of the dwelling in an unclean, God-forsaken land of those who are judged.

There then appears to be evident in two places a faint reference to the fact that the judgement of God upon his people shows a strange restraint. 5:3f shows a gesture of men being hidden by God, who preserves some of those condemned in the judgement in order to give them room for a renewal of loyalty. 4:14f makes the prophet recognize that when a man cries in distress to God he is spared being thrown into a state of uncleanness with its isolation from God.

In all the sign-actions the figure of the prophet enters into a prominent connection with the message of God. In the original three-sign composition it was the prophet himself who received the scant rations of siege to eat. The sword, which represents the judgement upon Jerusalem, passes over the prophet's own head. In a quite personal way he is threatened by the horror of unclean food in the gloss in 4:12. His personal confinement to his house (3:24b), his suffering at the hands of his enemies (3:25), and his physical bondage, clearly meant literally, became vehicles of his message. In using the priestly language of נשא עון to describe his suffering he himself became a representative and revealer of the guilt of the people of God, and a representative of the bondage in exile of the house of Israel. Starting from the priestly terminology of the נשא עון we must, however, hear a stronger accent of priestly identification in this bearing of guilt. The double reckoning of numbers and the process of reckoning days for years, which is added in the later interpretation of this bondage, presuppose such identification. Such assertions do not reach the full extent of those made by Isaiah 53. However, it is not to be denied that in Ezekiel's role as a messenger of the word a clear identification of the message-bearer with his message is attested. We can see from Ezek 4:4–8 that both the word and work of those who declare God's word can be interwoven with each other in a more than merely symbolic way.

6

1 And the word of Yahweh came to me:
2/ Son of man, set your face toward the mountains of Israel and prophecy against[a] them, 3/ and say: You mountains of Israel, hear the word of [the Lord][a] Yahweh! Thus has [the Lord][a] Yahweh said to the mountains and hills,[b] to the ravines and valleys:[c] Behold I will bring a sword upon you and destroy[d] your high places. 4/ Your altars shall be destroyed and your incense altars shall be broken;[a] and I will make your slain fall before your idols, 5/ [And I will lay the corpses of the Israelites before their idols][a] and I will scatter your bones round about your altars. 6/ In all the places where you dwell the cities shall lie desolate and the high places shall be ruined,[a] so that your altars shall lie waste [and ruined],[b] your idols broken [and brought to an end],[c] your incense altars cut down [and your works wiped out].[d] 7/ And the slain shall fall in the midst of you, and you shall know that I am Yahweh.

8 [And I will leave],[a] When there are[b] some of you among the nations who have escaped the sword, when you are

6:
2a עַל־אֶל cf. 1:17 note a.

2, 3
3a אדני is lacking in 𝔊, see Excursus 1.

b 𝔊 breaks up the grouping of the word-pairs by the insertion of the copula.

c BH³ וְלַגֵּאָיֹת (BH² Q וְלַגֵּאָיֹת K וְלַגְּיָאֹות, cf. also the variants in Ginsburg). The form גֵּאָיֹות, which is found again with plene writing in 7:16; 31:12; 32:5; 36:4, 6 "is perhaps falsely pointed for גֵּאָיֹת, formed by metathesis from גְּיָאֹות," according to Bauer-Leander § 72 v′. Cf. also 2 Kings 2:16. Ezek 35:8 also attests a plural formation גֵּאָיֹות, which has arisen from the contracted singular form גַּיְא.

d The piʿel form וְאִבַּדְתִּי is to be preferred to 𝔊 ἐξολεθρευθήσεται (hence Cornill, Herrmann וְאָבְדוּ). Cf. Dtn 12:2.

4
4a 𝔊 simplifies by bringing the first two verbs together καὶ συντριβήσονται τὰ θυσιαστήρια ὑμῶν καὶ τὰ τεμένη ὑμῶν.

5
5a The half-verse, which is lacking in 𝔊 ℭ (cf. Jerome) and which formally does not fit in with the style of the address, must be influenced by Lev 26:30.

6
6a Instead of the תִּישַׁמְנָה of 𝔐 (Var^G תֶּשְׁמְנָה) we should expect תֵּשַׁמְנָה. Can תישמנה be explained as a (later) plene writing or a derivative of a root ישׁם? Bauer-Leander § 58 p′.

b 𝔐 יֶאְשְׁמוּ is to be understood as a scribal error for וְיֵשַׁמּוּ, following Σ 𝔊 𝔗 𝔙 (hinting at the root אשׁם either deliberately or accidentally). It is lacking in 𝔊 and is probably a later addition following v 4a.

c ונשבתו is not attested by 𝔊 and creates a further repetition (cf. note b) of the verbal clause, which is alien to the clauses which precede and follow. The similar sound of the verbs ונשברו ונשבתו may have encouraged such repetition. For the content of the statement cf. 30:13.

d 𝔐 ונמחו מעשׂיכם is not attested by 𝔊. Since the clause is unusual on account of the vagueness of what it asserts (cf. the exposition), as also through its unusual vocabulary (מחה "wipe away" is otherwise lacking in Ezekiel, as also the use of מעשׂה as a designation for a cult object), it must belong to the later interpretative additions.

8
8a The והותרתי of 𝔐, which does not fit syntactically and which is not attested by 𝔊, is an addition from a later hand, dependent on 12:16, and is of not inconsiderable theological importance. Cf. the exposition. To emend to הזהרתי and to connect it with v 7 is not preferable. See Bewer, "Exegese," 193.

b Driver, "Linguistic Problems," 61, would find in בהיות vv 8, 13, the verb היה = הוה "to fall," following Job 37:6; 1 Sam 1:18. In order to obtain a connection with what precedes he conjectures a reading בְּהֻיָּתוֹ or בְּהָיָתוֹ (cf. Job 6:2 K "to fall

scattered[c] in the countries, 9/ then those of you who escape among the nations where they are carried off will remember me, when I have broken[a] their heart which lusted [which has departed][b] from me, and their eyes which lusted after their idols, and they will become loathsome in their own sight [on account of the evil deeds which they have done][c] on account[d] of all their abominations 10/ and they will know that I, Yahweh, have spoken [not in vain to do this evil to them].[a]

11 Thus has [the Lord][a] Yahweh spoken:
     Clap your hands and stamp your foot

down"), in which the suffix would relate to חלל v 7. However, if the secondary character of והותרתי (note a) is recognized and it is cut out, פליטי חרב stands in the position of subject to בהיות. Driver's interpretation thus becomes impossible for v 8 and indeed also for v 13.

c Instead of 𝔐 בהזרותיכם we should read בהזרותכם. The infinitive ending is wrongly understood in 𝔐 as the ending of a noun in the feminine plural. Gesenius-Kautzsch § 91 1; Diehl, *Pronomen*, (see above p. 102) 60.

9   9a 𝔐 אשר נשברתי *A Σ Θ 𝔗 𝔅* point to a reading אשר שברתי. In 𝔊 the preceding ἐκεῖ (שם) is followed immediately by the verb ὀμώμοκα, which points to a Hebrew original נשבעתי, but which cannot be original. Since 𝔊 does not presuppose אשר should we postulate an original (י)שברתי (כ) which then, after being corrupted to נשברתי, demanded the introduction of אשר in order to join on to what precedes? The difficult suggestion of a mixed form from שברתי and נשבר (Herrmann) would then be avoided, and the superfluous אשר is then shown to be secondary. The usage שבר לב is otherwise lacking in Ezekiel, but is found in Ps 69:21; Jer 23:9 and has then entered into pious vocabulary, Ps 34:19; 51:19; 147:3; Is 61:1. The reference to a breaking of the heart disappears if J. A. Bewer is right in his conjecture (cf. note a to v 8) that in אשר נשברתי we should find an original reading אשר שביתי as a repetition of the preceding את לבם אשר נשבו. then becomes the direct object of וזכרו. The originality of this reading could be supported by the fact that זכר, which is used in all twenty-one times in Ezekiel (10 in the qal) only appears here with a personal object, although in the closely related passages 20:43; 36:31 a material object appears. But since v 9 also shows besides this a striking peculiarity (two-fold expression heart—eyes, use of שבה only here in Ezekiel), the conclusion is not compelling.

b 𝔐 אשר סר is a clumsy attempt at clarification, which was still lacking in the Hebrew original of 𝔊 and which disturbs the parallel construction of the repeated participle of זנה.

c אל הרעות אשר עשו is lacking in 𝔊 and appears to be an addition influenced by 20:43. על – אל cf. 1:17 note a.

d 𝔐 לכל is striking. 𝔊 (ἐν) 𝔅 (in) 𝔖, as well as the parallel in 20:43, would lead us to expect בכל. Or should we conjecture, after 36:31, an original על כל, which has then been softened to לכל in view of the preceding addition?

10 10a The short text of the recognition formula attested by 𝔊, which can be compared to the addition in 17:21 (5:13; 37:14), has received two additions which may have been influenced by 14:23.

11 11a אדני is lacking in 𝔊; see Excursus 1.

b 25:3; 26:2; 36:2 read the exclamation as הֶאָח. We may question whether the shorter form אָח, attested by 𝔐 in the present text, also existed (Koeh-

180

and say: Ha!ᵇ because ofᶜ all the [evil]ᵈ
abominations of the house of Israel! ' 'ₑ
they shall fall by the sword, through
famine and pestilence. 12/ He that is far
off shall die of pestilence, and he that
is near shall fall by the sword, ' 'ᵃ and
he that is left shall dieᵇ of famine; and
I will pour out my fury upon them,
13/ and youᵃ shall know that I am
Yahweh—when their slain shall lieᵇ
among their idols round about their
altars uponᶜ every high hill, [on all the
mountain tops]ᵈ and under every green
tree [and under every leafy terebinth]ᵈ
at the place where they offered to all
their idols a sweet-smelling sacrifice.

ler-Baumgartner) or whether here we have to reckon with an erroneous abbreviation of an original האה to אח (so Ehrlich, Herrmann, Bertholet, Fohrer). אח is found besides here in the textually corrupt passages 18:10; 21:20. The εὖγε εὖγε of 𝕲 may point to a repetition of the exclamation in its Hebrew original. Cf Ps 35:21 (differently in 25); 40:16; 70:4.

c על – אל cf. 1:17 note a, also 25:3.

d רעות, which is not attested by 𝕲, is syntactically unrelated to the context. To be grammatically correct it would have to run כל תועבות הרעות בית ישראל. Furthermore תועבות does not require a pejorative adjective. The sole adjectival strengthening which is demonstrably free from textual objection elsewhere in the book of Ezekiel (the הרעות of 8:9 is also not attested by 𝕲) runs: [תועבות] גדלות 8:6, 13, 15.

e 𝕲 supports the rougher order of the text without the (clumsy) connecting אשר of 𝔐. Cf. also note a to v 9.

12   12a 𝕲, which transposes the first two cases (clearly in order to obtain the sequence of v 11 where famine and pestilence are transposed by it), leaves out the והנשאר of 𝔐 in the third case. This is an addition securing the right understanding of והנצור. הנצור is not to be interpreted with 𝕲 ὁ περιεχόμενος as "the besieged," but, following Is 49:6, as a reference to those who surprisingly escape the first two eventualities. In this way the assertion takes on its full severity. Driver, "Linguistic Problems," 61, interprets differently.

b 𝔐 ימות seemingly echoes the ימות of aα. For such echoes cf. the יחליפו of Is 41:1 alongside 40:31. 𝕲 συντελεσθήσεται seems to presuppose a derivative of כלה; e.g., יכלה in its Hebrew original, cf. 5:12 and also 4:6, 8; 5:13 and other passages. יתם, which is graphically closer, is less probable because the qal of תמם is translated by 𝕲 in the book of Ezekiel with ἐκλείπειν (24:11; 47:12; cf. also 22:15. Differently in 𝕲 Dtn 34:8; Josh 3:17; 4:1, 10, 11; cf. Jer 14:15).

13   13a 𝕲⁵³⁴ 𝕾𝕮 Arm assimilate the unusual second person plural to the third person speech of the context. 𝕲 goes in the reverse direction and assimilates the following statements of v 13a to the second person plural of the beginning of the verse, but in vv 13b, 14a goes back to the third person plural with 𝔐. These contrary attempts to improve an apparently uneven text favor the reading of 𝔐 as the *lectio difficilior*.

b For 𝔐 בהיות cf. note b to v 8.

c על־אל cf. 1:17 note a.

d The additions are lacking in 𝕲 and seem to be secondary expansions of the text. The fact that we are dealing in the second place with a distinctive addition, whilst the original text which is supported by 𝕲 shows the more usual formulation (Dtn 12:2; 1 Kings 14:23 and other passages), does not permit us (against Cornill) to explain offhand the elements

14/ And I stretch out my hand against them and make the land a terrible waste[a] from 'the wilderness to Riblah'[b] throughout all their habitations. Thus they[c] will know that I am Yahweh.

14

which are lacking in 𝕲 as original.

14a Literally "a ruin and desolation," a double expression formed with two derivatives from the root שמם in which there echoes a strong note of horror.

b 𝔐 מִמִּדְבָּר דִּבְלָתָה "from the desert of Diblatha" (so also 𝕲 ἀπὸ τῆς ἐρήμου Δεβλαθα 𝖁 *a deserto Deblatha*), or "more than the desert of Diblatha"? Already Jerome draws attention here to the possibility of a confusion of ד and ר, and we must read with Var[P] 3 Var[G] רבלתה, and this must be separated from ממדבר with Michaelis (Cornill), which is then to be vocalized, with 6 Var[G] 4 Edd, as an absolute מִמִּדְבָּר. Reference to two border regions is then found in מִמִּדְבָּר רִבְלָתָה for the devastated land.

c 𝕲 assimilates the recognition formula here to the formulation of v 13a and reads the second person plural.

Form

The narrative formula for the coming of a message introduces the section 6:1–14.[1] The end of this is clearly marked off by 7:1, which forms an analogous introduction to the following section. Twice in this section the prophet receives a summons to perform an expressive gesture (vv 2, 11) with a specific accompanying message. That the messenger formula in v 3 follows the command to the prophet, whilst in v 11 it introduces an address of Yahweh to the prophet with a breakup of the original messenger situation, is not an important variation of the speech form for what follows.[2]

Thus we must distinguish two sections, vv 2–10 and 11–14, each introduced by an expressive gesture. The expressive gestures of the prophet undoubtedly belong in close proximity to the prophetic sign-acts. Whereas the sign-actions of chs. 4f were originally performed in silence and carried the prophetic message within themselves, the expressive gestures take on the role of simple accompanying actions, besides which the preached word appears as more important. They underscore, reinforce, and clarify the preached word as features which point to real life and history. However, once we recognize the connection between the gestures and sign-actions (in 6:2f there is also a clear connection in subject matter with ch. 4) we must be warned against devaluing the former into simple reflex gestures. Rather there still exists in them something of the same power to effect their realization as in the sign-actions. They establish a reminder of the character of the word as event.

In vv 2f the prophet receives the command to turn his face to the mountains of Israel and, with this physical movement, to prophesy. The prophet is commanded to perform this gesture a further eight times in the same words, in connection with a definite injunction to preach: 13:17 against the false prophetesses; 21:2 against the יער הנגב, which is interpreted as against Jerusalem in 21:7; 25:2 against Ammon; 28:21 against Sidon; 29:2 against the Pharaoh of Egypt; 35:2 against the mountains of Seir; and 38:2 against Gog. The formulation שִׂים פָּנֶיךָ דֶּרֶךְ תֵּימָנָה of 21:2 shows that the expression first of all means a simple turning in the particular direction which is to be addressed, so that the עַל in 29:2 and 35:2 has undoubtedly replaced an original אֶל.[3] The following (הטף ו . . .) הנבא is construed with אל in only three of the nine occurrences (6:2; 21:2, 7). Here the adversative על may be in place. More important is the question about the initial origin of this gesture which accompanied the prophet's speaking. In the additions to the sign-actions of ch. 4 we find a command to the prophet to turn his face (with the formula הכין פנים) in v 3, as a silent accompaniment to the threatening siege action. In 4:7 it is connected with the threatening gesture of baring the arm and the command to prophesy, in which the prophet's spoken word was not performed. The reduction of a feature that was once an independent part of a sign-action to an accompaniment of the spoken word can be clearly followed in the parallelism of the three texts 4:3, 7; 6:2. We must point to the Balaam narrative, however, for the original objective meaning of

---

1 See above pp. 144f.
2 See above p. 133.
3 Cf., however, note a to 1:17.

182

the action. According to the final form of 𝔐 Balak attempted no less than three times, from three different places, to obtain a proper curse against Israel from the seer. It is said of each of these places that Balaam could see the camp of Israel (Nu 22:41; 23:13; 24:2). In Nu 23:13 we can see the belief of Balak that Balaam could not curse properly because he could not see the entire people, but only a part of it. Nu 24:2 appears to say that the spirit of Yahweh came upon Balaam at the moment when he saw Israel with his own eyes. The eye to eye contact of the man of God with those who were to face him through his word of power is regarded as necessary in every case. Old ideas of the effectiveness of contact through direct vision, as they have been preserved through the ages in the belief in the evil eye, are plainly still effective here.[4] We may question further whether there is also a connection between this prophetic action and God's "turning of his face" against someone, which is mentioned in Israel's sacral law.[5]

When, according to 29:2, Ezekiel has to turn his face against Pharaoh this can no longer mean a direct visual contact, but simply the turning of the face in a particular direction (דרך 21:2). A saying which was once meant very objectively has become weakened and only used improperly.[6] From this saying in Ezek 6:2 therefore we are in no way compelled to accept the necessity of Ezekiel's physical presence in sight of the mountains of Judah (Herntrich). Rather the saying betrays a certain remoteness. For the particular type of Ezekiel's prophesying it is significant that in distinction from the other great writing prophets, in his preaching the expressive gesture has assumed such a large place. In this Ezekiel is again more archaic, and in a certain sense closer to the early prophets (and to the seers) than the other great classical prophets.

The section, vv 2–10, introduced by the first gesture, contains the recognition formula in vv 7 and 10, which is often the mark of the conclusion of an address. Since

in its content a different theme is evident in vv 8–10, over against vv 2–7, we must recognize two separate sayings in vv 2–7 and 8–10.

But are vv 2–7 to be regarded as a single unit? 𝕲 suggests in vv 5f the removal of some later additions. The late appearance of the address "mountains and hills, ravines and valleys" in v 3b, after mountains only are mentioned twice in vv 2, 3a, raises the question whether here we have a subsequent expansion (Fohrer). Since, however, there is no objection against them as regards their content and they are certainly presupposed by 36:4, they may well be original. More difficult is the fact that in vv 2–4, 5b–7 a displacement of the addressees appears to have taken place. If we think first of all of the actual mountains of Israel (your high places, your altars, your incense altars) then in what follows these are displaced by the men of Israel as the addressees (your slain, your bones, your dwelling places, in your midst). We must add to this the awkward reappearance of similar expressions (במות vv 3, 6; מזבחות 4, 5, 6; חמנים vv 4, 6; חלל vv 4, 7; גלולים vv 4 [5] 6 and others). Do we not have to reckon with additions here? On the other hand, the imperceptible transition from the address to the mountains of Israel to the address to the men who dwell there, which does not occur at the place where the repetitions begin, makes the separation difficult. The removal of vv 5b–7 (Fohrer) is therefore precluded since v 5b cannot be separated from v 4b as its parallel (in 𝔐 this is obscured by the gloss in v 5a, which is not found in 𝕲). We should also be unwilling to destroy the clear conclusion of the section in v 7b. So we shall have to accept the change of address as original. In vv 6, 7a there appears to be a second formulation of the whole movement of thought, which can easily be removed as a subsequent expansion of the original saying. In its particular use of the למען-clause it recalls the saying in 5:16f.

In their form vv 2–4, 5b (6–7a) 7b represent a prophetic proof-saying (cf. Zimmerli, "Wort"). With the

---

4 Pierre Daniel Chantepie de la Saussaye, *Lehrbuch der Religionsgeschichte*, 2 volumes (Tübingen: Mohr [Siebeck], [4]1925), index s.v.

5 Cf. to 14:18.

6 Cf. the analogous development in the imprecatory turning of the worshipper towards the sanctuary, which at one time meant a real looking towards the most Holy place, still actually visible in the act of

worship, and developed from this, through 1 Kings 8:44 and Dan 6:11, to the Muslim *Qibla*.

emphatic הִנְנִי אֲנִי Yahweh announces in the first person his judgement as his own personal action. The section then fluctuates between general description in the third person and address in the first. The addition in vv 6–7a is given wholly in the form of description. The final recognition formula refers to the goal of the personal demonstration of Yahweh, which is present throughout the entire action.

Vv 8–10, which relate the event to the times in which the sword will have accomplished its work, represent a simple development of this type of proof-saying. The consequence of the judgement for men is described here without the use of an announcement begun in the first person (for וַהֲוֹתֵרֹתִי see note a to v 8). The recognition of the power of Yahweh's word is declared as the content of the recognition which will take place then, in an expansion of the recognition formula, which does not, however, go as far as in 5:13.

Vv 11–14 are introduced by a command to perform a second expressive gesture. Clapping the hands (הַכֵּה בְכַף) appears in Ps 47:2 (תִּקְעוּ כָף) in a royal celebration. In Ps 98:8 it proclaims the eschatological jubilation of nature at the ascension of Yahweh, and in Is 55:12 the return home of his people (מָחֲאוּ כָף). In Na 3:19 it expresses the triumph of the nations over the fall of Nineveh (תָּקְעוּ כָף). In Ezek 21:19, where, with a different order of the verbs, the same expressive action (הַכֵּה כַף אֶל כָּף) is used in connection with a command to preach, it is clear from its repetition in the saying itself (21:22, cf. הַכֵּה כָף in 22:13) that a triumphant gesture over the vanquished is in mind here. At the same time, however, 21:19/22 show that the prophet was not expressing by his action a gloating gesture of an onlooker, but was giving expression to the action of Yahweh himself in which he triumphantly settled accounts with his enemies, and "vented his fury" on them (21:22; cf. 5:13).

From this we must also interpret the second gesture of foot stamping (רְקַע בְרֶגֶל). In 25:6 this, together with the מַחֲאֵי יָד, accompanies the mocking delight of the Ammonites over the catastrophe of the land of Israel. This action also is not to be interpreted as though Yahweh implants in the prophet the subjective feeling of gloating pleasure over the coming judgement. We are not concerned here with a feeling and an inner attitude, but with a physical expression of unrelenting

anger which proceeds from Yahweh upon the house of Israel and is signified in the prophet's gestures, both visible and audible. Thus, in the prophet's stamping on the ground there appears something of the strangeness of the bringing to objective expression what God has said (the word "magic" is best avoided). We may recall here the striking on the ground with a sheaf of arrows in 2 Kings 13:18 (הַךְ אַרְצָה). It is quite clear that this action simply expresses the pathos of God, standing in judgement over Israel, and not his gloating satisfaction.[7] This is shown by Yahweh's later gracious words (e.g. chs. 36f). Yet we cannot deny that there is a discernible distinction from Jeremiah's declarations of judgement in which the "compassion" of Yahweh is evident (12:7ff; 45:4f). Ezekiel's message is, in its theme of judgement, one of great harshness ("Like adamant, harder than flint" 3:9).

Verses 11–14 are also striking through the repeated use of the recognition formula (vv 13a, 14b). Once again we can recognize in the divisions created by this a slight change of theme. Vv 11f appear to start from the distress coming upon a besieged city (cf. 5:12), whilst vv 13f, in line with 5:2–7, start from the desolation of the high places and of the land. Since however vv 13aβ–14 are syntactically closely dependent on what precedes and the clause beginning with בִהְיוֹת at first looks like a subsequent expansion of the recognition formula, we have to reckon in vv 13aβ–14 not with a saying which was originally independent, but with a (subsequent?) elaboration of vv 11–13aα, which seeks to bring to a final conclusion the theme of the first half of the chapter.[8]

The basic text of vv 11–13aα and the expansion in vv 13aβ–14 are shaped to the form of the prophetic proof-saying. The announcement of judgement in vv 11f is more exactly stylized as a threatening exclamation which is closely related to the הוֹי-oracle found more frequently in prophecy (Amos, Isaiah, Habbakuk). The exclamation הָאָח usually expresses mockery or delight in other's misfortunes (25:3; 26:2; 36:2; Ps 35:21 and other passages). In Job 39:25 the snorting of war horses is denoted by it. In Sir 41:2 it is clearly parallel to הוֹי in v 1, as the introduction to a woe saying without any particular emphasis on delight in other's misfortunes. It is in this direction that the present text is to be understood. We may question whether the variant form of the interjection (אח instead of האח, more familiar in Ezekiel) was especially chosen at the end with the intention of setting in the background the note of delight in other's misfortunes which would be very unsuitable beside the motivating (על =) אל כל תועבות. From this also the twofold gesture of v 11aα is further illuminated.

Setting

The comparison with 29:2 makes clear that the performance of the gesture in vv 2f in no way demands the location of Ezekiel in Palestine. Also the הרחוק – הקרוב of v 12, as the exposition will show, is not to be regarded in this sense as biographical information regarding Ezekiel's place of residence. Ezekiel uttered the words in exile. The two basic sayings, vv 2–5, 7b and 11–13aα, undoubtedly stem from the time before the fall of Jerusalem. Of the additions, vv 8–10 belong in the time after 587 B.C. The remaining additions are conceivable either before or after this time. However, from the literary development their derivation is more probably from the later period of Ezekiel's ministry or the editorial work of his school.

Interpretation

■ **6:2–7** *Death upon the mountains of Israel*. The prophetic oracle in vv 2–7 is directed against "the mountains of Israel." The designation הרי ישראל, which appears fairly often in the book of Ezekiel, but only in this book (6:2, 3; 19:9; 33:28; 34:13, 14 bis; 35:12; 36:1 bis, 4, 8; 37:22; 38:8; 39:2, 4, 17), is not to be understood without bearing in mind that Ezekiel's preaching was addressed to "the house of Israel," meaning the whole Israelite people.[9] It therefore expresses more than the profane fact that the Palestinian mountain region was the abode of the political entity Israel. There echoes in it something of the value of the particular land which was given to the people of God. Thus the expression stands closer to the Isaianic הָרַי in Yahweh's mouth

(Is 14:25; cf. 65:9; less certainly Is 49:11; Zech 14:5) than to the reference to the הרי שמרון (Jer 31:5, less certainly Amos 3:9). The expression "mountains of Israel" is not to be understood narrowly; i.e., the mountains, but not the valleys of Israel. "Mountains of Israel" means the whole land and is to be understood synonymously with אדמת ישראל in 7:2. It contains, however, an archaizing echo in which the mountains are named as the true land of Israel. A. Alt has clearly demonstrated this fact in his works on the Israelite settlement.[10] This fact is revealed not only in the old, credo-like predication of Yahweh as the God "who brought you (us) *up* from the land of Egypt" (Dtn 20:1; Ps 81:11; Lev 11:45; Josh 24:17 and other passages), but also in the logic of the Arameans, after their defeat at the hands of Israel, who say "Yahweh is a God of the mountains and not a God of the valleys" (1 Kings 20:28, cf. v 23), thereby denying his true nature. We should not ignore this solemn archaizing note in the reference to the "mountains of Israel," to which the references to the "tents of Israel" in the summons to go out (2 Sam 20:1; 1 Kings 12:16) may be set as an analogy.[11] The nomenclature, which is important in Ezekiel far beyond ch. 6, must not be too hastily limited to the particular theme of ch. 6.

Thus no objection can be raised against the more precise definition of the הרי ישראל, which is first added to the messenger formula in the commission to preach, as הרים וגבעות אפיקים וגאית. It describes excellently the revered land of Israel in its heights and depths.[12] On the distinction between הר and גבעה Schwarzenbach establishes, "גבעה describes undulations of lesser height, הר such which were sometimes of considerable elevation. גבעה describes only an isolated rise, הר an isolated rise in the ground and a chain of hills."[13] According to Koehler-Baumgartner אפיק means "the central watercourse of a valley," גיא, the root of which גיא is interpreted by Schwarzenbach as a by-form of גאה which can mean both "to be high" and "to be

---

7   See especially

8   Zimmerli, *Erkenntnis*, 14–16.

9   See above pp. 132f and Excursus 2.

10 Albrecht Alt, *Kleine Schriften zur Geschichte des Volkes Israel* 1 (München: Beck, 1953), 89–125, 126–175.

11 Gerhard von Rad, *Der heilige Krieg im alten Israel*, ATANT 20 (Göttingen: Vandenhoeck & Ruprecht, ⁵1969), 14.

12 See Schwarzenbach, *Terminologie*.

13 Schwarzenbach, *Terminologie*, 10.

low." [14] Thus גיא signifies the valley lying between a chain of hills or mountains, the slopes of which are gentler than those of a נחל. The surface of the great plains, which 1 Kings 20:28 describes as עמקים, is plainly therefore not in mind. Thus none of the thirteen more precise localities given by Koehler-Baumgartner under גיא is relevant here.

Over this land of Israel the prophet announces the coming of the sword (cf. 5:1ff). No human arm wielding it is mentioned. It appears to be commissioned as an independent power, which is doubly strange since it is Yahweh himself who is dealing with Israel by it. In 21:7–10; 13–22; 33–37 the sword is spoken of more fully.

The reference to the mountains, however, would convey a second, and quite different, emphasis for the ear of a pious priest in the decades around the Deuteronomic reform. As the high mountains and hills were, for Isaiah, still generally places which displayed the *hybris* of God's creatures towards him and were therefore destined for judgement on the day of Yahweh (Is 2:14), so Ezekiel thinks more specifically of the places at which idolatrous sacrifices were made. In the list of the marks of the righteous man we find at the beginning, "He does not eat upon the mountains or lift up his eyes to the idols of the house of Israel" (18:6). Thus the announcement of judgement mentions three elements of worship which will be in the first line of destruction when the sword comes against the mountains of Israel: 1) במות 2) מזבחות 3) חמנים.

The basic meaning of במה is shown by the Ugaritic *bmt* as "back." [15] In a derived sense it then can describe a "high place" or "ridge." Schwarzenbach seems to be wrong in his argument against a non-cultic use of במה in the Old Testament in the face of such texts as Mic 3:12; Amos 4:13; Hab 3:19 and other passages. The occurrences where it has the meaning "cultic high place" are numerous, cf. 1 Sam 9:12ff. Since Jer 7:31; 32:35 can also speak of a במה down in the valley of

Hinnom, this shows that the element of height could be entirely absent, leaving only the idea of a cult place. In other references a further development to denote cult buildings can be discerned. The fuller בית במה (1 Kings 12:31 and other passages) can become, in ellipse, simply במה. Thus it can be said that man builds a במה (1 Kings 14:23), makes it (2 Chr 21:11), or destroys it (Amos 7:9). In this latter meaning we must include Ezek 6:3, which speaks of destroying (אבד, v 6 שמם) a high place. Ezek 16:16 may lead us more particularly to think of the colorful tents which were set up at the cult place.

■ **6:4a** The altar naturally belonged especially to the cult place. As the name מזבח shows, this was the place at which the slaughter of sacrificial animals took place (1 Sam 14:32–35).

The exact meaning of חַמָּן, which is mentioned only rarely in the Old Testament and probably not before the time of Ezekiel (Is 17:8; 27:9; Ezek 6:4, 6; Lev 26:30; 2 Chr 14:4; 34:4, 7), was clearly not properly intelligible already to the early translators. 𝕲 τεμένη, 𝕭 *simulacra, delubra*. Since Rashi its meaning has been sought as "sun pillar" through its etymological closeness to חַמָּה "sun." However, K. Elliger has shown that more correctly we can find in it a connection with the meaning conjectured in the *Annotationes* of Grotius, "incense altar." [16] This could be set up as an ornamental altar on the great altar of burnt offering. Perhaps this found entrance into Israel (Judah?) from Arabia in the later pre-exilic period. [17] To the pious Israelite mind it was therefore an unacceptable innovation. Yahweh's judgement would shatter (שבר) this novelty and cut it off (גדע) from the altar.

■ **6:4b, 5b** "And I will cast down your slain before your idols, and scatter your bones round about your altars." Are the mountains still being addressed here or are they not rather the men who dwell on the mountains of Israel? It is clearly part of the intentional strangeness of the saying that it passes directly from the one to the

14   Schwarzenbach, *Terminologie*, 32f.
15   W. F. Albright, "The Psalm of Habakkuk" in *Studies in Old Testament Prophecy presented to T. H. Robinson*, ed. H. H. Rowley (Edinburgh: Clark, 1950), 18.
16   K. Elliger, "Chammanim = Maṣṣeben?" *ZAW* 57 (1939): 256–265, and "Der Sinn des Wortes *chammān*," *ZDPV* 66 (1943): 129–139.
17   See H. Ingholt, "Le sens du mot ḥammān" in *Mé-*

langes syriens offerts à M. René Dussaud 2 (Paris: Geuthner, 1939), 795–802. Also see Ingholt's remarks in G. Ernest Wright, " 'Sun-Image' or 'Altar of Incense'," *BA* 2 (1938): 9–10.

other. By the sins of the mountains of Israel in reality the sins of its inhabitants are meant. 4:14 has made clear that to the priestly mind what has to do with death and the corpse represents the most repulsive uncleanness. Now in the judgement the sword will bring down its victims at the most holy place and leave corpses lying around about the altars (cf. Jer 8:1f). The feeling of the uncleanness of the land through corpses lying about is given fullest expression in 39:14f. As a deliberate means of destroying cultic holiness it could happen, at its most extreme, that corpses were burnt on the altar—the most unholy in place of the usual קֹדֶשׁ as in 2 Kings 23:16; cf. 1 Kings 13:2.[18]

For the first time in the book of Ezekiel the גלולים are mentioned here as features of the sanctuaries of the high places. The close connection between "eating on the mountains" and "lifting the eyes to the גלולי בית ישראל" in the list of 18:6(15) which is cited above, as well as the content, forbids the conclusion that the mention of the גלולים is a secondary element in a section in which the theme is the sin of the "mountains" of Israel. The noun גלולים is used in a quite particular way in Ezekiel's vocabulary. Of the forty-eight occurrences in the Old Testament no less than thirty-nine are found in the book of Ezekiel (otherwise Lev 26:30; Dtn 29:16; 1 Kings 15:12; 21:26; 2 Kings 17:12; 21:11, 21; 23:24; Jer 50:2). In the Old Testament it is always used very polemically (parallel to שִׁקּוּצִים) and in the plural (only Sir 30:18 in the singular). It always refers in a hostile way to heathen cult objects (Jer 50:2 parallel to עֲצַבִּים). We must think of a large divine image set up at the holy place, rather than an amulet worn on the heart (Ezek 14:3), as is conjectured by du Mesnil du Buisson.[19] Lev 26:30, which mentions פִּגְרֵי גִלּוּלִים, clearly leads us to think of human or animal-shaped images. In the book of Ezekiel we find in the foreground the idea of abominable uncleanness (גלולי תועבותיך 16:36), which was brought into Israel by the representatives of a non-Yahwistic cultic holi-

ness and which rendered the Israelites who used them unclean (20:7; 23:7 and other passages). If the word is connected, not with גַּל "heap of stones," as Gesenius-Buhl and Zorell conjecture,[20] but with the word גֵּל (construct plural גֶּלְלֵי) which appears in Ezek 4:12, 15 in connection with the mention of extreme impurity, then this characteristic of uncleanness could be echoed in the name itself. The word may then be a term of reproach, "things of dung," which is vocalized similarly to שִׁקּוּצִים, which is used in parallel to it in Dtn 29:16. Since Isaiah and Jeremiah refer to idols with a completely different terminology, we may ascribe the formation of the term to the sphere of life to which Ezekiel belonged; i.e., to the circles of the Jerusalem priesthood. Since it is used in the book of Ezekiel without any closer definition, Ezekiel must have taken it up as a term already coined. Was it formed in the period of the reform?

The judgement which Yahweh brings upon the land by the sword has, by a deep inner logic of righteousness, the consequence that the cult places of the mountains of Israel, which are outwardly places of venerable sanctity, although in Yahweh's eyes they are places of abomination, are to be publicly desecrated by the dead of Israel lying there.

■ 6:5a (The addition in v 5a stresses this declaration in its own words still further.) The second formulation in vv 6, 7a repeats, partly in the same words, the same line of thought from the destruction of the cities to the desolation of the apparently holy places of the land. Only what is meant by ונמחו מעשיכם remains obscure. If we hold the words to be original, against 𝕲, we shall be inclined to interpret the מעשים/חמנים as parallel to the preceding גלולים/מזבחות and to understand the idols as the "work" of men (as in Jer 10:3, 9; Hos 13:2 and other passages).[21] However, if, by looking to 𝕲 and the linguistic peculiarity of the clause (note d to v 6), we regard it as a subsequent insertion, we have the possibility of interpreting it according to Is 17:8 as a

---

18 See also Otto Eissfeldt, "Schwerterschlagene bei Hesekiel" in *Studies in Old Testament Prophecy presented to T. H. Robinson*, ed. H. H. Rowley (Edinburgh: Clark, 1950), 73–81.

19 Le comte du Mesnil du Buisson, "Une Tablette magique de la région du moyen Euphrate" in *Mélanges syriens offerts à M. René Dussaud* 1 (Paris: Geuthner, 1939), p. 421 note 3. Cf. Sir 30:18 "Good

things poured out upon a mouth that is closed are like a food offering (תנופה) which is set before a גלול" (Smend).

20 Following Wolf Wilhelm Graf Baudissin, "Die alttestamentliche Bezeichnung der Götzen mit *gillūlīm*," *ZDMG* 58 (1904): 395–425.

21 So Elliger, "Chammanim," 259.

reference to the altars. The proof-oracle in vv 2–7 comes to an end with the declaration of its purpose in v 7b, in which Yahweh demonstrates the mystery of his name by this action which convicts the people of their unholiness.

The whole section vv 2–7 leaves a historical question. According to 2 Kings 23:8 King Josiah had removed all the high places of Judah in his great reform, together with those of the province of Samaria according to 2 Kings 23:19. He must thereby have removed the abominations which Ezekiel mentions. How then can Ezekiel refer in his early preaching here, dated between 593 and 587 B.C., to a judgement coming upon the altars and idols on the mountains of Israel? For an answer to this question we can point to the fact that in many matters Josiah's reform was plainly inconclusive. A. Alt conjectured this in regard to the transfer of local priests to Jerusalem.[22] It has repeatedly been pointed out that under Jehoiakim a sharp counterblow against Josiah's policy took place, which must have brought back much that had been removed in 622 B.C. These facts alone, however, are still not fully adequate to explain Ezekiel's preaching. Rather we must consider here also the particular generalizing outlook of the prophet with his all-Israel viewpoint. As is made clear in the great "trial through history" oracles of Ezekiel in chs. (16), 20, 23, this constantly had in mind the history and conduct of Israel as a whole, with all its vicissitudes and errors. Thus here also, where he proclaims a comprehensive judgement upon "the mountains of Israel," he must have had in mind not only a Judean situation of roughly 590 B.C., which he knew from direct reports from the homeland, but the whole of Israel's history (including that of the Northern Kingdom), with its sinning on the mountains of Israel. In his oracle he announces a total judgement of Yahweh upon the land to take place in his own days. Ezekiel is less bound than the prophets before him to a concrete situation. In his distant place of exile he is particularly the "theologian" among the prophets, who proclaimed the total action of Yahweh towards Israel.

Aim

It is in regard to this that the purpose of the oracle in vv 2–7 is to be determined. Ezekiel proclaims the coming historical self-disclosure of God, which is to take place upon the "mountains of Israel." This is the territory of the chosen people who have been called in grace and endowed with salvation, and to whom God has made himself known in the mystery of his being.

This self-disclosure is to be quite other than what the people think, who lift their eyes to the mountains on which they have set up the symbols of their prayerful worship, and from which they look for help. They believe that their salvation rests upon the mountains of Israel, whereas the prophet announces the coming of a fearful death upon them. The historical forces which are to accomplish this death are not important in this oracle, and the simple catchword "sword" is sufficient for Ezekiel to point to it as wrought by God.

In the face of this death all that Israel has built up politically (the cities of v 6a) will be devastated, and the entire outward life of individual Israelites will be threatened (the slain of vv 4, 7). Even more it will embrace everything which Israel has regarded with esteem, and by which it has sought to glorify the high places of the "mountains of Israel" (cultic high places, altars, incense altars, divine images), making them instead into places, the uncleanness of which is evident to all. The inner lie of the "idols of the house of Israel" (8:10 and other passages) will be judged by this death brought by Yahweh himself and made plain to the world.

Judgement is of such a nature that God does not deal with the remote people of the world, the heathen and the Turks, but with those who have been called by him. It unmasks what this people have built up in piety, with the intention of giving both holiness and religious splendor to everything throughout its land, and reveals it in its idolatrous and unclean nature. It is said unmistakably that God is not in these places of devotion at which his people seek his righteousness and his religious support. His name is disclosed rather in the judgement in which this "religious nature" of his people is destroyed.

If the people say that this is for the "high places," but not for Jerusalem, then Ezekiel 8 demonstrates that Jerusalem also lies on the "mountains of Israel," with which Ezek 6 deals.

6:8–10 *The recognition of God by those who are broken.* The saying which follows in vv 8–10 asserts that some will survive this disaster. The Hebrew פליט and the

related פְּלֵטָה are preserved in the German word
pleite (bankruptcy). פליט is one who has passed through
bankruptcy. The והותרתי (note a to v 8) added at a
later time betrays something of the astonishment
felt at the survival of some from this disaster (7:2 speaks
of the "end") and asserts quite categorically that
Yahweh himself ordained that there should be survivors from the sword of judgement. They no longer
live on the mountains of Israel, but among the nations,
scattered in the (heathen) lands as exiles (נְשַׁבּוּ v 9).

A threefold new event is to take place among these
survivors through the harshness of their experiences: a
remembering (וזכרו), a loathing (ונקטו) and a recognition (וידעו). We find mixed with the description of
this event ideas of what had already become true for the
exiled prophet after 587 B.C with the expectation of
what was undoubtedly still not a completely realized
eventuality. His word is both summons and description.
20:43f speaks of the same threefold event; the two first
steps are mentioned in 36:31 (16:61 ונכלמת – וזכרת;
16:63 ובשת – תזכרי; the saying in Jer 51:50f about
those who survive the sword also belongs here).

In the Old Testament זכר means more than a sad and
romantic turning back to what once was, with some
enjoyment of the recollection and regret at the ills of
the present. In the Old Testament "to remember" is a
genuine grasping of a reality which then becomes a new
living and present fact. Thus זכר can be used of God
(Gen 8:1; Ex 2:24; in the book of Ezekiel 16:60; also
the הזכר of the righteous or godless deeds before God
3:20; 18:22, 24; 33:13, 16 is to be understood from
this). We must similarly understand זכר as used of men
(cf. Ps 77:4, 12; in Ezek 16:43; 23:19 in the context
of a reproach which points to more than simply forgetting the "days of one's youth"), especially where it
concerns man's "remembering" God, who, even when
he is remembered for his past acts, can never, by reason
of his very nature, be thought of as simply active in the
past.[23]

We must also add to this immediately that this
biblical "remembering" of God is never without an
element of "recollection" (formulated in the perfect)
of an action of God towards man accomplished in
history. Thus the remembering of Yahweh by fugitives
of Israel scattered among the nations was directly a
remembering of the God who had destroyed those
whose "heart had turned away from him and whose
eyes had lusted after their idols." The death which
Yahweh had brought upon the mountains of Israel by
the sword of judgement would from now on be a part
of the "remembering" which determined Israel's faith.

This death concerned the whole man, which is
described as in Nu 15:39 by a twofold reference, heart-
eyes, since it was in this totality that man had sinned.
It is good biblical anthropology that man's responsibility is described not only by his inner being (לב), but
also by an organ which opens the inner life of man to
the external world and which gives access from the
physical world to the inner life (עין). It was in this
totality of heart and eye that Israel had sinned. This
shows a genuine awareness that it is the eyes in particular which turn in faithlessness to idols, flattered by
a sense of their beauty. It is through the gate of the eye
that temptation comes to man (Gen 3:6; Mt 5:28f;
6:22f), so that the heart, which should not only be
regarded as the center of feeling but as the center of
man's thought and will, breaks faith with Yahweh.
The זנה of eye and heart which is referred to here means
first of all immoral conduct between the sexes without
any rule or faithfulness, and then, from the time of
Hosea, religious disloyalty (cf. Ezek 16:23). So here
where the word appears it has been interpreted subsequently by the gloss אשר סר.

Therein lies the meaning of the judgement sent by
Yahweh, that this attitude on the part of Israel is
dealt with. The oft repeated reference in the Old
Testament to the breaking of the heart is here related
to the eyes also (Jer 23:9; Ps 34:19; 69:21; 147:3;

---

22 Alt, *Kleine Schriften* 2, 300.
23 For הזכיר עון cf. exposition of 21:28f. See Martin
    Noth, "The 'Re-presentation' of the Old Testament
    in Proclamation" in *Essays on Old Testament Inter-
    pretation*, ed. Claus Westermann. Tr. James Luther
    Mays (Richmond, Va.: John Knox, 1963), 76–88.

Is 6:11).[24] In both formulations there is the idea that a human attitude of stubbornness (3:7f חזקי מצח, קשי; cf, 2:4 קשי פנים, חזקי לב) must be broken like a stout stick.

A deep loathing (ונקטו) over the horror of the past was to grow out of this "remembering" of Yahweh as the one who had brought such a great destruction (Zerbrechen) in the history of his people. תועבה, which is already found in 5:9, 11, and 117 times in the Old Testament as a whole, 43 of them in Ezekiel (4 times in the singular), is a comprehensive term for all sins of cultic impurity, to which the evils on the mountains of Israel belonged in a particular measure. According to W. F. Albright it is derived from the Egyptian w'b "to be pure, to purify oneself" in a contrary meaning.[25] Loathing (נקוט again in 20:43; 36:31; Job 10:1; qal in Ps 95:10; hitpo'lel in Ps 119:158; 139:21) is an act of the most direct, pre-logical rejection, which among other things may express itself spontaneously by the act of "vomiting" (Brechen). Lev 18:25, 28; 20:22 show that priestly thought could use this word to describe the response of the land to what is unclean. This elementary rejection of all "abominations" would occur where those who had passed through the judgement actually reflected upon the action of Yahweh. In the נקטו בפניהם (again 20:43; 36:31) there must lie the recollection of shame over what has happened, which shows in men's faces. Cf. 16:61, 63; 36:31f.

The way which leads from remembering Yahweh's action to horror at sin ends finally again in the recognition of Yahweh. The formula of recognition is modified to the extent that Yahweh's speaking, which is the decisive feature for the prophetic proclamation, is emphasized: "They will know that I, Yahweh, have spoken." In 5:15, 17 the saying is rounded off by the emphatic "I, Yahweh, have spoken." What is simply stated there is here made the purpose of the recognition. In the knowledge of God, which also always means the acknowledgement of him who guides history by his word, the "remembering" reaches its goal.[26] When a later hand has further defined this speech of Yahweh by the addition that Yahweh has not spoken "in vain," i.e. ineffectively, this is a thoroughly relevant clarifica-

tion.

The saying of vv 8–10 about those who escape the sword undoubtedly presupposes the threat of the sword in vv 2–7. It deals with what happens (or should happen) when the sword has raged. It thereby presupposes that the catastrophe of 587 B.C. has occurred. Analogous expansions of the prophetic word after the crisis of 587 B.C. can be seen in 5:4; 12:16 (14:21–23?); 20:32ff. There is no decisive objection against the view that also the expansion of these sayings is from Ezekiel himself.

Aim

The statement of vv 8–10 thus seeks to make clear that the death brought about by Yahweh with the sword upon the mountains of Israel is not his final goal. God's purpose is not completed in bringing death upon the sin of his people, since there are survivors from it. The והותרתי added in v 8 is concerned to emphasize that God himself wills such survivors and ordains that they should exist. He wills that through them that which first began in the judgement in the will of God does not lead to oblivion. It is not a way of being lost among the nations and of escaping into the broad desert of the world. Rather it is—again by the will of God—a new way "before God." "They will remember me."

Under the harsh intervention of God which destroys every wanton desire (זנה), even the pious wantonness of his people, both in their experience of the world of the senses (עין) and in their inner life (לב), the latter are called to his way. They will not easily escape the judgement of God and forget about it, since this judgement also includes its continued proclamation in the history of his people as a reminder of his continuing presence with them. On the contrary, they must face up to it (זכר). This contains a promise that a loathing of the old nature will arise, and through this loathing, a new understanding. At the end of this there will no longer be the elaborate worship of self-chosen deities, flattering men's eyes but leading their hearts away from God. Rather there will be the recognition of God as one who directs the world by his word.

6:11–13a *God's Disclosure by Sword, Famine, and Pesti-*

24   Richard Press, "Die eschatologische Ausrichtung des 51. Psalms," *ThZ* 11 (1955): 247f, would interpret Ps 51:19, where the breaking of the heart is mentioned in parallel with a broken spirit, as a reference to the exile on the basis of Ezek 6:9.

25   William Foxwell Albright, *From the Stone Age to Chris-*

lence. We have dealt above with the gesture which introduces the threat of vv 11f, as well as with the opening words of the threat.[27] In both something of the passionate triumph of the judge accomplishing his destructive task can be heard. The "house of Israel" is now expressly mentioned as the addressee of the judgement, and its guilt is described in a brief invective with the catchword "abomination." The main content of the saying, however, consists of the threat which, like the symbolic action of 5:1–3, mentions three ways of judgement. There they were fire, sword and dispersion, whilst here they are sword, famine and pestilence, a group of three which is frequently to be found in Ezekiel (7:15; 12:16; cf. 5:12; 14:12ff) and even more often in Jeremiah (fifteen times). As in 5:1ff we find expressed here the idea that no one can escape the judgement. This is shown in 5:1ff by the dividing up of the prophet's hair into three, whilst here it is affirmed by the reference to "he that is far off and he that is near." This is also found in Is 57:19, and in the reverse order in Jer 25:26; Ezek 22:5; Est 9:20; Dan 9:7. It means "everybody." Analogous descriptions of totalities by reference to two things which exclude a third are "heaven and earth" (Gen 1:1; 2:4a) and "earth and heaven" (Gen 2:4b); "man and woman" (Gen 1:27; 6:19; 7:16). It is certainly not true that the use of such a word-pair, which receives no closer definition, shows that Ezekiel was resident in Jerusalem (Herntrich, Bertholet). Why could the prophet not have used such an antithetical expression in a saying spoken in exile, but applying to the besieged Jerusalem? Essentially the combination of two things to express a totality, with a threefold form of judgement, is not particularly skillful. It has made necessary the addition of the third group of the "survivors," which was not foreseen in the antithesis of "far and near" and which basically robs it of its character of comprehensiveness. Through the surprise effect which it achieves, it may however bring a certain emphasis to the saying: even if, as you do not expect, there should be yet a third alternative beside "far and near," yet here also the judgement will catch up with the survivors.

In the apportionment of the three forms of judgement among the three groups we can trace the tension between the two viewpoints. The three plagues are conceived from the situation of the besieged city. If those who are far die through pestilence and those who are preserved die through famine, the arrangement is determined by the combination of the two forms of speech, not by the actual viewpoint.

6:13aβ–14. Further to the recognition formula of v 13aα, which gives an element of divine demonstration to the event of vv 11f, the saying of vv 13aβ–14 has undergone an expansion which undoubtedly goes back to the theme of the beginning of ch. 6, the idolatrous worship on the mountains. It thereby seeks to round off the chapter as a unit. The picture which is given there, of the slain lying between the idols and the altars, also reappears. In this there reappear expressions which take up the Deuteronomic-Jeremianic formulations about the worship on the high places, sometimes verbally (תחת כל עץ רענן Dtn 12:2; 1 Kings 14:23; 2 Kings 16:4; 17:10; Jer 2:20; 3:6, 13; 2 Chr 28:4), and sometimes slightly varied (אל [= על] כל גבעה רמה cf. 20:28; 34:6; beside על כל גבעה גבהה 1 Kings 14:23; 2 Kings 17:10; Jer 2:20). In the description of sacrificial worship as an offering of a "pleasing odor" we can discern priestly language (again in Ezek 16:19; 20:28, 41). Since the literary connection with 20:28 is strikingly close, and 20:27–28(29) belongs to a subsequent expansion of ch. 20, we may also regard 6:13aβ–14 as a later addition. The fact that with these verses the redactional rounding off of the whole chapter is intended points in the same direction.

The concluding v 14 is strikingly stereotyped in its first half, as is confirmed by a comparison with 35:3, which is almost verbally identical. In it the description of the land devastated by the divine judgement "from the wilderness to Riblah" is found only here in the Old Testament. "The wilderness" must refer to the southern border desert, dividing Egypt from Palestine, which is described in 20:36 as מדבר ארץ מצרים. In the description of the southern border in 47:19 and 48:28 mention of the desert is surprisingly absent. Riblah, (present day *rable*) on the Orontes, referred to as the most northerly point, is mentioned in the Old Testa-

tianity (Baltimore: Johns Hopkins University Press, ²1957).

26 Zimmerli, *Erkenntnis*, 39–47.

27 See above pp. 184f.

ment in 2 Kings 23:33 as the place where Pharaoh Necho's army encamped, when the latter removed Jehoahaz from the kingship after the death of Josiah. In 2 Kings 25:6, 20f, however, it was the location of Nebuchadrezzar's camp where the bloody execution of the king and nobles of Jerusalem took place. Since, according to 2 Kings 23:33; 25:21 it lay בארץ חמת, seventy-five kilometers south of חמת (present day *ḥama*), we must see in Riblah the contemporary substitute of Ezekiel's day for the ideal northern border of Israel לבוא חמת (47:15f with emended text; 48:1; Amos 6:14; 2 Kings 14:25 and other passages). After 587 Riblah remained alive in the mind of every Judean as the place of judgement. The all-Israelite viewpoint of the judgement on the mountains of Israel in Ezekiel, and in the circle around him, is again confirmed.

Aim

The saying in vv 11–14, built up in two stages vv 11–13aα, 13aβ–14 and couched in the form of a prophetic proof-saying, proclaims as in vv 2–7 the inescapable divine judgement upon the house of Israel. We have mentioned a *tria* of instruments of judgement (sword,

famine, pestilence vv 11f) instead of only the sword (v 3). Beside the cultic desecration of the high places in v 13, mention is made of the destruction of the entire land in v 14, extending across all Israel. In the surprising reference to Riblah, instead of the more familiar לבוא חמת, there is echoed a name grim with misfortune and catastrophe for the ears of the generation of 609 and 587 B.C. Modern analogies of such geographical names of woe come easily to mind. The twice repeated recognition formula in vv 13, 14 shows here also that God is active in this scourge of war and slaughter, which particularly concerns the places where the abominations of God's people were concentrated. This makes plain that God himself lies hidden in such judgement. In all its parts (do we have in the וידעתם of v 13 the prophet's reference to his fellow exiles and in v 14 his reference to those in the land itself?) the people will become aware of God. In God's blazing anger, which is expressed in the prophet's passionate gestures (v 11a), they will recognize the revelation of his mystery.

Bibliography

J. A. Bewer
  "On the Text of Ezekiel 7:5–14," *JBL* 45 (1926):
  226–231.
T. H. Gaster
  "Ezekiel and the Mysteries," *JBL* 60 (1941): 289–
  310, esp. pp. 297–304, Ezekiel's Satire on the Mys-
  teries.
J. Goettsberger
  "Ezek. 7:1–16 textkritisch und exegetisch unter-
  sucht," *BZ* 22 (1934): 195–223.

Preliminary Remarks

The content of 7:3–11 poses problems which have
so far not been satisfactorily explained. Vv 3f are
repeated word for word, with a slightly changed beginning, in vv 8f. Also between vv 6f and 10f there
exist striking verbal similarities, although less close.
To this must be added that 𝕲 puts the section vv
3–6aα of 𝔐, which it translates literally apart from
some abbreviations, after v 9. Vv 6aβ–7a, which
then follow directly on v 2, are found in 𝕲 only in a
considerably abbreviated form. A comparison of the
parallels of vv 3f and 8f within 𝕲 raises questions in
yet another direction. The variants τὰς ὁδούς σου
and ἔσονται v 6 𝕲, beside τὴν ὁδόν σου and ἔσται v 8
𝕲 may appear inconsiderable. More striking is the
change of κρινῶ v 5 𝕲 to ἐκδικήσω v 7 𝕲 in the translation of שפט (ἐκδικέω also v 27; there is further
variation in the translation of the qal of שפט ἐκδικέω
16:38; 20:4 and κρίνω 18:30; 21:35; 22:2; 24:14
and other passages). Most important, however, is
the change in the translation of the recognition formula. In this כי אני יהוה is in 𝕲 of Ezek 1–26 translated in about forty occurrences by διότι (ὅτι) ἐγὼ
κύριος. Roughly thirty occurrences in the second
half of the book, beginning with 28:22, show quite
consistently (cf. on the text for the single exception
of 36:[36] 38 in the passage 36:23bα–38 missing in
𝕲 ⁹⁶⁷ vid.) the translation ὅτι ἐγώ εἰμι κύριος. Thus
7:6 𝕲 (= 7:9 𝔐) stands out as the sole text in the
firm translation tradition of Ezek 1–26 𝕲. Accordingly we must accept a quite particular translation
hand for 7:6 𝕲, which then means also for the whole
passage of vv 6aβ–9 𝔐 ± vv 3–6 𝕲 when set against
𝔐. Against the view of Hölscher, *Hesekiel*, 67, who
sees in 7:2b–4 an "addition from a later hand which
gives the text a different interpretation," on grounds
of content (subsequently also Bertholet), we are
forced to recognize for 𝕲 that the passage vv 3–6,
corresponding to 𝔐 vv 6aβ–9, is secondary in the
text of 𝕲. Can we carry this perception over un-
changed to 𝔐?

A further consideration leads to an additional

complication of the position. If we compare the text
of 𝕲 with that of 𝔐, after the removal of 𝕲's vv 3–6,
then it is striking that this points back to an original
text in which the messenger formula of v 5a (= 𝕲 v
9) introduces the section vv 6aα, 10ff (= 𝕲 vv 10ff)
after the self-contained section 𝔐 vv 2–4 (𝕲 2, 7, 8).
(It was therefore once separated from v 5b, which is
not found in 𝕲 and the הנה באה באה הצפירה אליך
of vv 6f and the corresponding הנה באה יצאה הצפרה
of v 10). 𝕲 undoubtedly therefore witnesses to a text
in which not only the messenger formula introducing the saying in vv 10ff, but also a short fragment
of the saying itself, has been attached. This is supported by the fact that 𝕲, with its ἰδοὺ τὸ πέρας ἥκει
ἰδοὺ ἡμέρα κυρίου in v 10, binds together the two
elements v 6aα and v 10aα 𝔐, surely in a slightly
expanded textual form connecting parallels to a
twofold saying. Here we appear to have an original
section before us, which has been broken up in 𝔐
by vv 6aβ–9, which in itself is a well-rounded parallel to vv 2b–4. Through this disturbance the messenger formula of v 5a and the short phrase v 6aα,
which opens the saying and which forms one half of
the periods 6aα, 10aα according to 𝔐, have been
torn off from their original position.

Thus the following view emerges of the formation
of the present text of 𝔐: 1) The earliest basis which
is recognizable on text critical grounds is found in
the section vv 1–6aα, 10ff (without the additions
which are throughout lacking in 𝕲 and which are
mentioned below under v 5). – 2) This basic text
was taken up in the Greek (𝕲 without vv 3–6). –
3) After this time the Hebrew original text was enlarged by the parallel formation of vv 6aβ–9 by
which the original connection of vv 5a, 6aα, 10ff
was broken, and the messenger formula which originally introduced vv 6aα, 10ff became the introduction to the parallel saying which has been inserted. – 4) Thereupon 𝕲 was again assimilated at a
later time to the Hebrew text. The Greek translation
of vv 6aβ–9 was taken over, first as a marginal note.
Through a slip, perhaps aided by the catchword

πέρας ἥκει, this additional note was inserted directly after v 2 so that 𝔊 emerged in its present form. However this slip in 𝔊 had the favorable consequence for an understanding of the text history that in vv 9f (= 𝔐 5a, 6aα, 10) the old connection remained recognizable, which had been broken in 𝔐 by the insertion of the parallel saying at a clumsy position. – 5) After the conclusion of this whole process yet further additions were made in 𝔐 (5b, cf. note c to v 5; הנה באה באה הצפירה vv 6/7, cf. note c to v 6, note a to v 7; 10aβbα, cf. note a to v 10, etc.). These were not then introduced into 𝔊.

---

1 And the word of Yahweh came to me: 2/ And you,[a] son of man, 'speak' (?):[b] Thus has [the Lord][c] Yahweh said to the land of Israel: (The) end 'has come,'[d] the end has come upon the four[e] corners of the earth.

3 Now the end is upon you[a] and I will let loose[b] my anger upon you, and will judge you according to your ways and will bring upon you all your abominations.

7:2 2a Introduction of the speech to the prophet with ואתה directly after the formula narrating the receipt of the word is found again in 21:24; 22:2; 27:2; 37:16.

b 𝔊 𝔖 supports the addition of אָמֹר, which is materially desirable, cf. 12:10, 23, 28 and other passages. Since the introduction of the divine speech with the messenger formula without an express command to speak is also found elsewhere occasionally (5:5; 15:6; 22:19; 23:22; 26:3 and other passages, yet never with a directly preceding address) the possibility must be left open of a subsequent filling out in the versions of an original ellipse. (Cf. also 𝔊 to 15:6; 22:19).

c אדני is lacking in 𝔊, see Excursus 1.

d 𝔊, with its reading πέρας ἥκει, τὸ πέρας ἥκει which appears to be confirmed by 𝔙 *finis venit venit finis* and also קיצא מטא פורענות קיצא למיתי 𝔗, appears to presuppose a second בא like 𝔐 v 6, which must have fallen out in 𝔐 through haplography. The sole consideration which could speak against this appears to lie in the fact that בא הקץ in v 6 (= 𝔊 v 3) is translated with exact preservation of the sequence of words with ἥκει τὸ πέρας. Since, however, 𝔊 vv 3–6 = 𝔐 (5b) 6–9, as our preliminary remarks have made clear, must stem from another translator's hand, the argument loses its force. The beginning of the saying therefore runs קץ בא בא הקץ.

e K ארבעת is striking. Q reads with Dtn 22:12; Is 11:12 more correctly ארבע, Bauer-Leander § 79d. Ehrlich, *Randglossen*, however, on the basis of 2 Chr 3:11f sees in כנף a *nomen utriusque generis*.

3a The עתה הקץ עליך is by no means "an impossible saying" (Goettsberger, "Ez 7:1–16"), as can be shown clearly by the parallel פלשתים עליך Ju 16:9, 12, 14, 20. The terseness of the saying, which has led to the omission of the verb, has arisen from the intention of making a parallel to the following three-member formulation. Cf. also the corresponding saying in v 6.

b שָׁלַח בְּ also in 5:16; 7:3; 28:23; 39:6, cf. 14:13. It is neither, with 𝔖 (Graetz, Toy), to be replaced by שָׁפֵך, which in Ezekiel is always connected with עַל of the person, nor assimilated to v 9 (Goettsberger, "Ez 7:1–16"). Cf. the exposition.

4 And my eye will not spare [you][a]
  nor will I have pity;
  but will bring upon you your ways
  and your abominations shall take effect
    in your midst,
  and you shall know[b] that I am Yahweh.

5 Thus has [the Lord][a] Yahweh spoken:[b]
  [Disaster 'upon' disaster! See it has
    come].[c]

6 (The) end has come,[a]
  The end has come,
  'the end'[b] upon you [See it has come,[c]
  7/ has come . . .[a] upon[b] you],[c] O
    inhabitant of the land!

4a עָלֶיךָ is lacking in 𝕲 (and in v 9) and is a subsequent prosaic addition.

b 𝕲 𝕾 assimilate the verb to the singular of the context.

5a אֲדֹנָי is lacking in MS^Ken 𝕲 𝔄, see Excursus 1.

b Cf. the preliminary remarks for the connection of the messenger formula with vv 10ff, introduced in 𝕲 by the syntactically flexible διότι.

c The אַחַת of 𝔐 "one disaster" is not properly clear. Hence opinion differs whether we should read with 𝕾 (Ehrlich, Toy) תַּחַת or with 30 MSS Edd 𝕋 אַחַר. In meaning both come roughly to the same thing. We can certainly not find in this saying, which depicts objectively a coming disaster, the idea of retribution, with Bewer, "Exegese," 195, and therefore an element of reproach. The whole of v 5b is lacking, however, in 𝕲 and must be a subsequent addition.

6a The introductory בָּא קֵץ is, as 𝕲 shows, the first half of the present divided parallel saying vv 6aα, 10aα. Cf. the preliminary remarks.

b הֵקִיץ of 𝔐 may be understood as hip'il of קיץ ("it is awakened," 𝕲^Q ἐξηγέρθη, 𝔙 evigilavit). Driver, "Ezekiel," 148, with reference to 𝕾 𝕋, thinks of a denominative verbal form from קֵץ. Bewer conjectures after Amos 8:2 the noun קָיִץ. More plausible is the view of a simple orthographic variant of קֵץ. This הקץ (אליך) (for על־אל cf. note a to 1:17), which has a support in the parallel הקץ עליך (עתה) v 3, is lacking in 𝕲. The omission can easily be understood, however, from the purpose of 𝕲 of avoiding the repetition of three clauses in succession with קֵץ, which would otherwise have arisen.

c The division of the verses here breaks up connected material. The feminine בָּאָה is only intelligible in reference to the following הַצְּפִירָה. Cf. v 10.

7a הַצְּפִירָה, which is repeated in v 10, cannot satisfactorily be interpreted, especially since 𝕲 lacks both texts. See Koehler-Baumgartner. The interpretation "garland," crown," which appears in the only other Old Testament occurrence Is 28:5, is not acceptable in spite of Θ πλοκή. The etymological basis for the contritio of 𝔙 is not clear. The translation by מלכותא in 𝕋 must be determined by Is 28:5. Should we think of a meaning "fate" (Smend) from the Arabic ṣafara "to twist"? Gaster, "Mysteries," by reference to the Arabic ṣafara, Ug. ṣpr "to turn, make a circle," finds here a synonym for תקופה "the cyclic point (day and night) has come," in the context of his whole interpretation of the chapter as related to the Autumn Festival. Reider, "Studies," 279, finds here a word for the setting of the sun, which would be a picture of the end. Bewer, "Ezek 7:5–14," 226, conjectures an emendation to הַבָּצִיר "vintage" (parallel to קַיִץ "autumn"), and in "Exegese," 194f, הַפְּצִירָה "extortion." In any case the context leads us to expect a (metaphorical?) synonym to קֵץ.

b על־אל cf. note a to 1:17.

The time has come,
  the day is near. . . .[d]

8 Now I will soon pour out my wrath upon
    you
    and spend my anger against you,
    and judge you according to you ways
    and bring upon you all your
      abominations.

9 My eye will not spare, nor will I have pity,
    'but'[a] will bring upon you your ways
    and your abominations shall take effect
      in your midst,
    and you shall know,[b] that it is I,
      Yahweh, 'who smites'.[c]

10 Behold, the day,[a]
    [behold, it has come, come forth . . .][a]
    'injustice'[b] has blossomed
    pride has budded.

11 [Violence has arisen][a] . . . to the rod of the
    wicked[a] . . .[b]

c The bracketed text in vv 6/7 is without counterpart in 𝕲 and is probably a later addition. Cf. also
v 10.

d 𝔐 מהומה ולא הד הרים, 𝔙 (*dies*) *occisionis et non
gloriae montium* may, if need be, be interpreted: "assault, and not rejoicing [הֵידָד = הַד "cry of the
wine-presser," Jer 25:10; 51:14; Is 16:9f] on the
mountains." Driver, "Linguistic Problems," 61f,
with a slight textual emendation יום מהומה ולא
הידד, holds to an interpretation along this line. However 𝕲, with its reading οὐ μετὰ θορύβων οὐδὲ μετὰ
ὠδίνων appears to have read a לא at the beginning,
which appears to be supported by the collection of
variants in v 11. Its θόρυβος points to a המון (Dtn
10:6 𝕲), ὠδῖνες to a derivative of הרה (or חול?). So
Goettsberger, "Ez 7:1–16," reconstructs לא בְּהֲמֹנָם
וְלֹא בְּהֶרְיֹנָם "not with noises, nor with birth cries."
Bewer, "Ez 7:5–14," reconstructs differently and
points to Σ *dies festinationis et non resurrectionis* (according to Jerome), then to v 11 and Hab 2:3: לא
מְהַר וְלֹא, מתמהמה ולא מאחר; in "Exegese," 194f,
אַחַר הַיֹּום. A really convincing interpretation of the
saying is still lacking.

9a 𝔐 כדרכיך "according to your conduct (will I
bring it upon you)." Reference to the parallel passage makes it probable, with v 4 and 𝕲, that we
should give preference to the reading כי דרכיך. Cf.
also the usage found in 9:10 (11:21; 16:43; 22:31)
דרכם בראשם נתתי.

b Cf. note b to v 4.

c 𝔐 מכה 𝕲 (𝕊) ὁ τύπτων makes it probable that
we should add the article which has fallen out
through haplography. הַכָּה used without an object,
also 9:5, 7f, is more fully elaborated by 𝔗 (אנא יהוה)
אייתיתי עליכון מחא.

10a In 𝔐, which puts the dividing accent on בָּאָה,
we are struck by the grammatically impossible coupling of the masculine היום with the feminine בָּאָה.
The *athnach* belongs to the היום. Then, however, it
appears that in the הנה באה יצאה הצפירה which is
now connected, the הנה באה באה הצפירה of vv 6/7
reappears, slightly varied by the replacing of the second באה by יצאה. The passage, however, is lacking
in 𝕲 here also and must be regarded as a later addition. Cf. the preliminary remarks and note b to v 6
for the connection (supported by 𝕲 ἰδοὺ τὸ πέρας
ἥκει, ἰδοὺ ἡμέρα κυρίου) of 𝔐 vv 6aα and 10aα. In
the הנה which follows היום we are not to find an
original יהוה of the basic Hebrew text (Cornill,
Bertholet, Fohrer), since it would imply also the
further change of היום into יום. This conflicts with
the other usage of ch. 7, which also offers the simple
היום in vv 7, 12. 𝕲 must be regarded as a (correct)
theological unfolding of the shorter basic text.

b הַמַּטֶּה (the staff) of 𝔐 (𝕲 ἡ ῥάβδος, 𝔙 *virga*, 𝔗
interprets: שֻׁלְטָנָא) in the parallel to הַזָּדֹון is more
correctly read in accord with 9:9 as הַמֻּטֶּה.

11a 𝔐 would be translated as: "violence has exalted itself to the staff of godliness," which could be

12 The time has come,
   the day has arrived.[a]
   Let not the buyer rejoice,
   nor the seller be mournful
   [, for wrath comes upon[b] all his pomp].[c]

13 For the seller shall not return to what he
   has sold,
   [whilst their life is still among the
   living (?) (, for 'wrath' comes upon
   all his pomp), 'they will' not return][a].
   And no one will 'be able to preserve'[b]
   his life [because of his iniquity ?].

understood as an explanatory remark to v 10bβ (Fohrer). 𝕲, however, καὶ συντρίψει στήριγμα ἀνόμου clearly did not have החמס קם which can easily be recognized as a further elaboration to the saying of v 10bβ. This could therefore be a later addition. The reversal of the order subject–predicate distinguishes this clause from v 10bβ. Where the καὶ συντρίψει of 𝕲 comes from, which would go back to a וְשָׁבַר, is not clear.

b 𝔐 לא מהם ולא מהמונם ולא מהמהם ולא נה בהם is quite unintelligible. 𝕲 καὶ οὐ μετὰ θορύβου οὐδὲ μετὰ σπουδῆς simply allows the double assertion that the four expressions of 𝔐 probably concern an original text with two expressions subsequently expanded with two (corrective?) additions, and that this must stand close in content to the similarly obscure v 7bβ. Cf. note d to v 7.

12 12a 𝔐 הגיע. If 𝕲 in its ἰδού preserved the original reading, then we have here a close parallel to v 10aα. Cf. note a to v 10. Linguistically nothing can be raised in objection against הגיע, cf. Song 2:12; Eccl 12:1.

b על – אל cf. note a to 1:17.

c 12b is lacking in 𝕲 𝔏ˢ 𝕮. We are struck here not only by the awkward doubling of the motive clause vv 12b/13a, but also by the ill-fitting third feminine singular suffix in המונה. This seems to point back to the heading of the chapter (v 2a) and concerns the connecting phrase אדמת ישראל. The use of the noun חרון, which otherwise does not appear in Ezekiel apart from 7:12–14 (cf. to vv 13, 14), also points to a strange hand (it is found in Jer 4:8, 26; 12:13; 25:37f; 30:24).

13 13a αβbα is without counterpart in 𝕲 𝔏ˢ 𝕮. The fact of the doubled לא ישוב at the end of v 13aα and 13bα raises the question whether we have in the versions a textual omission as the result of homoioteleuton, in which in v 13aβbα the parallel to v 13aα was lost. This is improbable because the corresponding expression to v 13aα must lie in 13bβ. Above all, however, the text of v 13aβbα itself speaks decisively against this view. From it there emerges first of all in bα the motive clause כי חזון אל כל המונה, although the חזון is already witnessed by 𝔗 ... ארי נבייא מתנבן על, 𝔙 visio, 𝕲ʰ ὅρασις in which we can see a miswriting of the addition כי חרון אל כל המונה (על =) v 12b (14b), which is distinguished from its entire context by its suffix as well as from v 13aβ. V 13aβ is textually unsatisfactory. The conjectures to change חַיָּתָם into חַיָּתוֹ (Toy) or הֲיָתוֹ (Bertholet, Fohrer) bring no real alleviation of the objection. The לא ישוב which concludes bα is either to be changed to a plural reading (יָשֻׁבוּ instead of יָשׁוּב of 𝔐, cf. the miswriting of ויבוא in 14:1; 36:20) and accepted as the conclusion of aβ, or regarded as a marginal gloss to aα, falsely brought into the text.

b Instead of 𝔐 יתחזקו "they mustered their strength," we must read יחזיק. Cf. 𝕲, which, apart from the miswriting of עונו in עין, had before it bβ

14 'Blow the trumpet'[a]
    and 'prepare the weapons of war,'[b]
        [yet none goes into battle, for my
        wrath comes upon all his pomp].[c]
15 The sword is without[a]
    and pestilence and famine are within—
        he that is in the field will die by the
        sword,
        and he who is in the city, famine and
        pestilence will 'destroy'[b] him.
16 And if any of them escape, and they[a] are
    on[b] the mountains [like 'moaning'
    doves],[c] then will they all 'die,'[d] each
    one for his iniquity.

in the form of 𝔐, which 𝔅, however, did not rightly understand. A replacing of בעוגו חיתו by בעורגו חי (BH³) is not necessary, although we may question from the corresponding expression in aα whether the motivating בעוגו belonged to the text from the beginning.

14 14a 𝔐 תָּקְעוּ בַתָּקוֹעַ "they blow the horn" (?) is usually changed (Cornill, Toy, Bertholet, Fohrer) to תִּקְעוּ תָקוֹעַ. Is 6:9 can be pointed to for the position of the infinitive absolute. Herrmann and Goettsberger, "Ez 7:1–16," however, consider whether or not in תקוע of 𝔐 a wind instrument could be meant here. 𝔊 σαλπίσατε ἐν σάλπιγγι, 𝔅 canite tuba, 𝔗 נפקין באצוחת קרנא could point to the mention of an instrument. (For the absolute use of תקע Nu 10:7 [Koehler-Baumgartner] beside 10:5f is not a truly supporting reference.) The recollection of Jer 6:1 could have determined the choice of words.

b 𝔐 והכין הכל "and all equip" is undoubtedly corrupt. 𝔊 καὶ κρίνατε τὰ σύμπαντα points to a parallel to תקעו, which then in any case is to be read as an imperative. We can explain this either by regarding κρίνειν as a translation of הכין (Cornill cites Schleusner: "*Apud Hesychium κρῖναι inter alia exponitur τάξαι*"), or by seeing underneath והכין a wrongly written תדינו. If we reconstruct an infinitive absolute תקוע then we should also probably read the analogous הָכֵן beside הָכִינוּ. הכין is used absolutely again in 38:7. 𝔊 follows here with v 15 and has ὁ πόλεμος, which is not found in 𝔐. This seems to indicate an original reading והכינו כלי מלחמה (cf. 32:27). 𝔗 ומתקנין במני זינא has understood the text in this direction independently of 𝔊. Cf. also note c.

c v 14αβb is lacking in 𝔊 except ὁ πόλεμος, introducing v 15, in which clearly מלחמה appears from αβ. The מלחמה which originally concluded v 14 (see note b), and which 𝔊 has moved to v 15, has accordingly been enlarged in 𝔐 to the short clause v 14αβ. The reason for it is provided by the reference already gained from vv 12 and 13 to the coming חרון, which is here directly related to Yahweh by its suffix.

15 15a 𝔐 בחוץ. 𝔊 ἔξωθεν 𝔗 מלברא could commend the reading מבית better corresponding to the following מחוץ.

b 𝔐 יאכלנו "will eat him" is unusual, with famine and pestilence as the subject (it is used of fire in 15:4f, 7; 19:12, 14 and other passages). 𝔊 συντελέσει 𝔗 ישיצינה must point to the reading יכלנו, cf. 5:12.

16 16a Reider, "Etymological Studies," 119, finds here a verb היה "to go up," cognate to the Arabic *hwj*. The general use of היה "to be," however, is already seen in 6:8, 13, and is here used in a new direction. 𝔏ˢ elaborates: *errantes*.

b על־אל cf. note a to 1:17.

c 𝔐 כיוני הגאיות "as the doves of the valleys" (for the writing of גאיות cf. note c to 6:3) is lacking in 𝔊 𝔏ˢ 𝔗 and is clearly an interpretation of the wrong-

17 All hands[a] become feeble
 and all knees are dripping with water,[b]
18 and they put on sackcloth
 and horror covers them.
 Shame is upon[a] all faces
 and all their heads are shaved bald.
19 They throw their silver into the streets
 and their gold is like rubbish,[a]
 [their silver and their gold cannot
 deliver them on the day of Yahweh's
 anger].[b] They cannot satisfy their
 hunger
 nor fill their belly—for it has become a
 stumbling block to their guilt.
20 And 'his'[a] beautiful ornaments 'they have'
 used[b] for arrogance, and they have
 made their abominable images [their
 detestable things][c] of it. Therefore
 I have made it an unclean thing[d] to
 them.
21 And I will give it into the hands of
 foreigners for plunder, and to the
 godless of the earth[a] for a spoil.
 They will desecrate[b] it.
22 And I will turn my face from them, and
 they will desecrate my jewel.[a] And
 robbers[b] will enter it[c] and desecrate it[c]
 23/ and will execute a massacre (?),'[a]

ly written המות of the Hebrew original (note d).
𝕲[h] Θ ὡς περιστεραὶ μελετητικαί (Jerome translates:
meditantes), then Ἀ τῶν φαράγγων, Σ ἐν φάραγξιν,
𝔅 convallium. These translations commend the read-
in כְּיוֹנִים הֹגִיוֹת (Cornill) as the original text of the
addition. הגה "to murmur" Is 38:14; 59:11.
 d 𝔐 כֻּלָּם הֹמוֹת "they all groan." cf. Ps 55:18. 𝕲
πάντας ἀποκτενῶ, however, points to a derivative of
מות, which must originally have stood here. In v 13
also (cf. also 3:18f; 33:6, 8f) the אִישׁ בַּעֲוֺנוֹ is connected with a reference to dying. Driver, "Linguistic
Problems," 62, reads הֵמַתִּי, Goettsberger, "Ez
7:1–16," אָמִית; more probably we should read with
𝕲 ימותו in this literary connection where only the
addition of v 14b is preserved in the first person singular.

17 17a 𝔐 כל הידים parallel to ברכים. ידים without
the article would be preferable, cf. 𝕲 and 21:12.
 b Cf. Ehrlich, Randglossen, on the text for the
coarse expression which reappears in 21:12; Driver,
"Medical Expressions," 260.

18 18a על־אל cf. note a to 1:17.

19 19a נִדָּה in proper use 22:10. Cf. the exposition.
 b The bracketed section is lacking in 𝕲 𝔏[s] 𝕮 Spec.
and is an interpretation, cited with a slight change
of wording from Zeph 1:18. Cf. also Prv 11:4.

20 20a The suffix relates to כספם of v 19. Cf. עֲדִי זָהָב
2 Sam 1:24; Jer 4:30. A change to עֶדְיָם (Σ 𝕲 BH³,
Bertholet, Fohrer) is not necessary.
 b 𝔐 שָׂמָהוּ "he (man?) has used." This is better
vocalized with 𝕲 𝔏[s] 𝕮 𝔅 as שָׂמֻהוּ. On the form of
the verbal clause joined with a pronominal reference cf. Gesenius-Kautzsch § 143, Beer-Meyer, II,
§ 92, 4.
 c 𝔐 שִׁקּוּצֵיהֶם is not attested by 𝕲 and is shown by
its asyndetic construction to be a subsequent addition, cf. 5:11. The insertion of the copula in 20 MSS
Ed 𝔗 𝔅 is certainly an attempt to smooth this.
 d Cf. note a to v 19.

21 21a רִשְׁעֵי הָאָרֶץ is only found here in the book of
Ezekiel. Ps 75:9; 101:8; 119:119 show that it is an
expression familiar in the usage of the Psalms. 𝕲
τοῖς λοιμοῖς τῆς γῆς scarcely justifies the change to
לְעָרִיצֵי הָאָרֶץ by reference to 28:7; 30:11; 31:12;
32:12 (as Cornill, Toy).
 b With Q we should read וְחִלְּלוּהוּ.

22 22a צְפוּנִי literally "my hidden thing" is only
found here. 𝕲 τὴν ἐπισκοπήν μου, 𝔅 arcanum meum,
Ἀ τὸ ἀπόκρυφόν μου. 𝔗 interprets v 22a as "and I will
take away my glory (שכינתי) from them because
they have desecrated the land of my temple (ארע
בית שכינתי)."
 b What Hebrew original is presupposed here by
𝕲's ἀφυλάκτως?
 c We would like to vocalize the masculine here:
בּוֹ and חִלְּלוּהוּ.

23 23a 𝔐 עֲשֵׂה הָרַתּוֹק "make . . ." The root רתק is
found in Na 3:10 with the meaning "to bind" (Eccl
12:6 emended text), רְתֻקוֹת Is 40:19 as "bonds."

for the land is full [of lawsuits concerning]^b bloodguilt, and the city is full of violence.

24 [And I will bring the worst of the nations who will take possession of their houses.]^a And I will make an end of their proud 'might,'^{b} and 'their sanctuaries'^{c} will be desecrated.

25 Anguish^a 'has come'^{b} and one is seeking peace, but there is none.

26 Disaster^a follows disaster^a
and bad news follows after^b bad news.
One is seeking revelation by the prophets,
but instruction departs from the priests and counsel from the elders.

27 [The king mourns and]^a The prince is clothes with despair,
and the hands of the people of the land are paralyzed with fear.
On account of^b their conduct I will deal with them,^{c} and according to their manner of judgement^d I will judge them, and they shall know that I am Yahweh.

Accordingly 𝔗 עיביד שישלן "make bonds," 𝔅 *fac conclusionem* (ΣΘ καθήλωσιν "nailing"). The imperative, however, is suspicious. Thus 𝔊, which in v 23a continues the description of v 22, deserves acceptance. Its καὶ ποιήσουσι φυρμόν ("confusion, disorder"), 𝔊^{407} φρυαγμόν ("wild snorting"), favors the conjecture that behind הרתוק there lies a mention of a threatened punishment. Can we suppose a text ועשׂו הבתוק (Kraetzschmar, Bertholet, Koehler-Baumgartner, cf. בתק 16:40)? This is more in line with the context than Driver's conjecture of עשׂו הרתוק "fists are clenched" ("Ezekiel," 149), or the more radical textual changes of Cornill and others. In details the meaning remains obscure.

b 𝔐 משפט דמים. 𝔊 (διότι ἡ γῆ πλήρης) λαῶν presupposes first of all a scribal error of דמים as עמים. However, it clearly did not read משפט. Reference to 9:9 also encourages us to see in משפט a later interpretation and to restore the metrical balance of bα and bβ.

24 24a V 24a is lacking in 𝔊 𝔏^s 𝔆 Gild. and is to be regarded as a later addition since its content goes back behind vv 22f and possesses unusual features, both in its language and ideas.

b 𝔐 גְּאוֹן עַזִּים "the pride of the strong ones." 𝔊 τὸ φρύαγμα τῆς ἰσχύος αὐτῶν, 𝔐 of 24:21; 30:6, 18; 33:28 favor the reading גְּאוֹן עֻזָּם.

c 𝔐 מְקַדְּשֵׁיהֶם "those whom they have sanctified." It is better to read with 𝔊 𝔅 מִקְדָּשֵׁיהֶם.

25 25a קפדה is a hapax legomenon from the root קפד "to constrict": anxiety. 𝔊 ἐξιλασμός appears to think of a derivation from כפר. Σ ἀθυμία, Θ συνοχή 𝔅 *angustia*.

b The feminine subject demands the reading באה or תבוא.

26 26a הֹוָה again in Is 47:11. 𝔊 οὐαί points to הוי. Σ συμφορά 𝔅 *conturbatio*.

b על־אל cf. note a to 1:17.

27 27a The clause in brackets is lacking in 𝔊 𝔏^s 𝔆^{sa} 𝔄 and is a later addition, since Ezekiel uses the title נשׂיא for the king of Judah and the parallelism of נשׂיא and מלך in the present text presents a difficulty. Ezekiel's terminology was no longer clear to the glossator, so that he missed a reference here to the king.

b 𝔐 מדרכם. For the unusual מן "on account of" (or should we follow 𝔊 [𝔏^s 𝔊 𝔅] κατὰ τας ὁδοὺς αὐτῶν to read כדרכם?) we can compare the analogous use in 16:61; 35:11; 45:20 (Cooke); also Driver, "Linguistic Problems," 62, keeps 𝔐.

c אֹתָם – אִתָּם cf. note a to 2:1. The connection עשׂה את is often found in the book of Ezekiel, cf. 16:59; 22:14; 23:25, 29; 39:24, also 11:13; 20:17, 44.

d 20 MSS 𝔅 (*secundum judicia eorum*) read וכמשׁפטיהם, although already 𝔊 ἐν τοῖς κρίμασιν had before it the במשׁפטיהם of 𝔐.

Form

Ezek 7 is divided into two sections, vv 2–4, 5–27, through the repetition of the messenger formula in vv 2 and 5. The tradition of 𝔊 shows an older form of the text in which v 6aα had its immediate continuation in v 10, and v 5a appeared as the introductory messenger formula to vv 6aα, 10–27. The section vv 6aβ–9, which is thereby shown to be a subsequent insertion, represents, both in form and content, a slightly changed parallel to vv 2–4. Like vv 2–4 it is identified as a prophetic proof-saying by the concluding recognition formula. Vv 2–4, par. 6aβ–9, after some brief assertions about the coming end, have the form of a direct address of Yahweh to the land (אדמת ישראל) or the inhabitant of the land (יושב הארץ). The question arises therefore whether the relapse from the address to the inhabitant of the land in v 7 (second person masculine singular) to the address to the land in vv 8–9 (second person feminine singular) was originally intentional, or whether the whole saying (including אליך in v 6) was actually directed against the inhabitant of the land. The consonantal text of vv 8–9 also reads the masculine without any change of text.

However, an impersonal style dominates in the section vv 5–6aα, 10–27, which is identified as a proof-saying by v 27b. Apart from the imperative in v 14, which must be understood in a more general sense (cf. the exposition), no direct address appears (for v 23 cf. note a). Apart from the secondary חרוני in v 14, the "I" of Yahweh first appears clearly from v 20.

All three sections show an impressive descriptive style preserved in vigorous, and often quite brief, parallel clauses in the separate verses. It is least evident in the first section and most noticeable in the last. However, it is broken up in an irregular way by more formless elements of speech. In content these verses give a very objective announcement and description of the day of woe in a strikingly broad compass and without any precise motivation, and do not show the specifically Israelite or Jerusalemite features of the act of judgement. These can only be found in statements which break up (as in v 20) the strict stylistic buildup which has been described.

These formal considerations must now be directly linked to certain considerations of content. In the large section vv 5a, 6aα, 10–27 we are concerned with the day of Yahweh, whether in v 10 we read with 𝔊 the full יום יהוה or whether we keep the present היום with vv 7 and 12. The basis of the prophetic reference to the יום יהוה is to be found in Amos 5:18–20. The argument whether with H. Gressmann we should accept from Amos 5:18–20 the existence of an eschatological expectation in Israel prior to the time of Amos, or whether with G. Hölscher we should see here solely a reference to the epiphany of God in the cult, which could already be described in Babylonian prayers as a "fearful day," need not be decided here.[1] Amos 5 in any case makes clear that the prophetic reference to the day of Yahweh, even in its first appearance, was not a free formulation, but was a new development of an already existing expectation, which it actualized in a decisive historical way. From this adoption of a form of speech, which originally grew up in another sphere of concepts, we have an explanation for the fact that the prophetic preaching of Yahweh's epiphany in contemporary historical events, where this preaching is clothed in the form of an announcement of the יום יהוה, continually shows features which go beyond the direct historical situation and which demonstrably separate these sayings from the genuine prophetic declarations of judgement. In Amos 5:18–20, where it is simply announced in the images of light and darkness and with the example of the man who jumps out of the frying pan into the fire, this is not too obvious. However it can be seen very clearly in Is 2:9ff that the announcement of the יום יהוה goes beyond the immediate historical situation of Judah which the prophet addresses. Here the day of Yahweh is spoken of as one which encompasses all the cedars of Lebanon, all the oaks of Bashan, and all the ships of Tarshish. The man (אדם) who faces this event humbles himself and crawls, taking off his finery, including ritual finery, and throwing it away. That we may be dealing here with post-Isaianic additions in particular sayings does not change the basic facts about the style of the references to the day of Yahweh. Is 22:5 is more directly related to the histori-

---

1 Hugo Gressmann, *Der Ursprung der israelitisch-jüdischen Eschatologie*, FRLANT 6 (Göttingen, 1905), 141–158; idem, *Der Messias*, FRLANT 26 (Göttingen, 1929), 74–77. Gustav Hölscher, *Die Ursprünge der jüdischen Eschatologie* (Giessen: Töpelmann, 1925), 13, following Mowinckel.

cal situation. Zeph 1f, however, which is the most vigorous picture of events on the day of Yahweh, shows a particular connection of very concrete descriptions of historical doom (as in 1:10ff the shouts in the different parts of the city of Jerusalem) with a worldwide fate extending far beyond Judah which terrifies "men" (1:17) and consumes the whole earth (1:18). The tendency in references to the יום יהוה to look away from the concrete features of historical time and place and to describe in a more universal fashion the helplessness of men in the face of this overwhelming intervention of the divine presence is undeniable.[2]

From these considerations we must clarify certain features in the formal structure of the prophecy of the יום יהוה. This favors a strongly monotonous repetition (ten times [יום] על כל Is 2:12–16; יום six times with the genitive Zeph 1:15f; four times [פקד] על Zeph 1:8f; three clauses with בטרם Zeph 2:2; repeated twice [יום יהוה] קרוב Zeph 1:14). It describes not so much by broad general statements as by brief allusions and favors the nominal sentence. In this there arises a certain formal language. The repetition of the saying קרוב יום יהוה Is 13:6; Joel 1:15; 4:14; Obadiah 15; Zeph 1:7, 14; cf. Joel 2:1f; (יהוה) חרון אף Is 13:9, 13; Zeph 2:2; יום חשך ואפלה יום ענן וערפל Joel 2:2; Zeph 1:15; יום נקם Is 34:8; 61:2; 63:4, and יום נקמה Jer 46:10; the connection with the verb בוא, often formulated somberly in the perfect or with a participle Is 63:4; Joel 2:1; Zeph 14:1; Mal 3:19, imperfect Zeph 2:2 is undoubtedly to be traced back not only to an external literary dependence, but to a deeply rooted tradition of speech in references to the יום יהוה which endured through a long period.[3]

It cannot be denied that Ezek 7 stands wholly within these considerations. Here also we find in many statements the stylized forms of speech, simply set out and connected in doublets or triplets which describe in a general human way the horror of the day of Yahweh without making clear the uniqueness of the situation in Jerusalem in Ezekiel's day.

The traditional elements determined by the description of the יום יהוה are, however, not used straightforwardly in vv 5a, 6aα, 10–27, and more especially in vv 2–4, 6aβ–9, as was shown in the first survey of the formal structure. Rather in all three cases they are here introduced in the form of the prophetic proof-saying. This means, however, that the day of Yahweh, at first described impersonally, is afterwards shown as Yahweh's personal action at the end of the section by the form of Yahweh's speaking in the first person. It further means that place can be given here to an element of motivation for the day of judgement and of punitive rebuke to the sin of (the land of) Israel, which are both foreign to the genuine language of the day of Yahweh's epiphany. The personal feature of the divine appearance in the יום יהוה, which now further summons men to a recognition of this personal revelation of Yahweh, reaches its fullest expression in the concluding recognition formula.

We can best deal with the subsequent additions which the oracles, especially the last of the three, have undergone in connection with the detailed exposition.

Setting

In noticing the stereotyped language of the descriptions of the day of Yahweh (for details see the exposition), Herntrich's conclusion "that vv 10–14 are spoken directly from the point of view of the onlooker, who sees himself surrounded by the historical facts" cannot be regarded as compelling.[4] The view that Ezek 7 could have arisen in the exile encounters no serious objection.

Chronologically the announcement of the near "end" undoubtedly occurred in the years before 587. Whether the secondary passage vv 6aβ–9 and the other later additions could have derived from the prophet himself must be considered in relation to the exposition.

---

2 For the יום יהוה in the prophetic writings, cf. further Is 13:6, 9, 13; 34:8; 61:2; 63:4; Jer 46:10; 47:4; Joel 1:15; 2:1f, 11; 3:4; 4:14; Obadiah 15; Mic 7:4; Zech 14:1, 3; Mal 3:2, 19; and see Ladislav Černý, *The Day of Yahweh and Some Relevant Problems* (Praze: Nákladem Filosofické Fakulty University Karlovy, 1948).

3 Cf. the table of the "Characteristic Terms" in Černý, *Day of Yahweh*, Appendix 1.

4 Herntrich, *Ezekielprobleme*, 85.

Interpretation

The "land of Israel" is mentioned as the addressee of the whole unit of Ezek 7 after the introduction by the formula for the coming of a message, followed by the address and commission to speak (? cf. note b to v 2), in stylistic conjunction with the messenger formula (analogous to 6:3b).[5] The reference to the אדמת ישראל, which appears in all seventeen times in the book of Ezekiel (7:2; 11:17; 12:19, 22; 13:9; 18:2; 20:38, 42; 21:7, 8; 25:3, 6; 33:24; 36:6; 37:12; 38:18, 19), but not once outside it (אדמת יהודה in Is 19:17), means more than simply a geographical-political identification. אדמה, which according to L. Rost originally referred to the light-brown agricultural land without any political significance, is defined by the addition of the name of the people of Yahweh (all Israel).[6] There also lies in the expression אדמת ישראל a recollection of the splendor of the beloved land, the land "which Yahweh thy God gives you" (Ex 20:12; cf. Dtn 4:40f and other passages). It is essential to the understanding of the following declaration of judgement to notice this particular qualification of the addressee.

The first proof-saying, which ends in v 4, begins with the particularly important phrase קץ בא, in which קץ is without the article. In a reversal of the order of subject and predicate this is taken up again in a parallel formulation and expanded by a reference to the direction of the coming "end." The terse and formal speech, which appears more strongly in the second and third oracles, is limited in this first oracle to the introduction. V 3 then already introduces the personal attitude of Yahweh to the addressee. In v 2b, however, we must now recognize the further distinctive feature referred to in the introductory mention of the יום יהוה: the worldwide reference. It undoubtedly occasions a surprise and appears to create a logical contradiction when a saying addressed to the land of Israel refers to the end which will come upon "the four corners of the earth." The phrase ארבע כנפות הארץ is, as the parallels

Is 11:2; Rev 7:1 (cf. Is 24:16; Job 37:3; 38:13)[7] show and as is confirmed by the analogous use of the Akkadian *kippat irbitti*, undoubtedly originally to be understood not of the "land," which would then be identical with the אדמת ישראל (Kraetzschmar, cf. Bertholet), but of the whole world. The logical contradiction between vv 2a and 2b (Hölscher, *Hesekiel*) encourages only those who deny that Ezekiel here actualizes in prophecy a form which had arisen long before him, and which has been preserved ino ther aspects of the proclamation of the coming of God, to resort to critical textual surgery.

The designation יום יהוה does not yet appear in the section vv 2–4. Instead of this the coming day is described with the catchword קץ, which is used twice. This catchword, which also dominates the two further sayings (vv 6aβ to 6aβ–9; 6aα to 5–6aα, 10–27), is lacking in all the other prophetic oracles regarding the day of Yahweh (Hab 2:3 and other passages). Thereby we can fully apprehend the derivation of this expression from earlier written prophecy. In Amos 8:1f it arises directly out of the fourth vision of Amos. In an aural wordplay the announcement of the קץ: בא הקץ אל עמי ישראל appears here directly out of Amos's vision (which is characterized as כְּלוּב קָיִץ). It is significant that this radical prophetic threat, which Amos directs against the Northern Kingdom, is not further taken up by the other pre-exilic prophets of doom, apart from Ezekiel in whom such prophecy reached its most radical form (קץ in other usage by the prophets in Is 9:6; 23:15, 17; 37:24; Jer 13:6; 34:14; 42:7; 50:26; 51:13; cf. also Ezek 29:13). Ezekiel sets it in its fullest meaning in the center of his preaching. By it he describes the nature of the events of the impending day of Yahweh (7:2, 3, 6, six times altogether; further we must compare the particular saying, only found in Ezekiel, of the עֲוֹן קֵץ 21:30, 34; 35:5). An echo in the Priestly Document, and therefore in the sphere in which Ezekiel's saying arose and to which it first belonged, affirms the

---

5   See above pp. 144f, pp. 131f. For the messenger formula see above p. 133. For an understanding of this naming of the addressee we must refer back to the study of the "mountains of Israel," pp. 185f.

6   Leonhard Rost, "Die Bezeichnungen für Land und Volk im Alten Testament" in *Festschrift Otto Procksch*, ed. A. Alt, J. Herrmann, N. Noth, G. von Rad, E. Sellin (Leipzig: Deichert, 1934), 125–148, especially

125–130.

7   For the four sides of a garment see Dtn 22:12.

thoroughgoing exegesis of Ezekiel's use of קץ. Gen 6:13 formulates the divine sentence of judgement before the beginning of the flood, which for P has the significance of a fundamental threat to the cosmos and its greater order which God had created according to Gen 1, with the words: "The end of all flesh has come before me (קץ כל בשר בא לפני). G. von Rad calls it "a cosmic catastrophe of inconceivable proportions."[8] קץ is here undoubtedly more than a simple definition of time. It is a complete "annihilation." This must therefore be expecially noteworthy because in the second half of the book of Daniel, which has certainly been influenced by Ezekiel, there is again a significant use of the word קץ in which it loses its threat and tends to become an apocalyptic category of time. Within Daniel 8–12, in which it occurs no less than fifteen times, there is mention of the עת קץ (8:17; 11:35, 40; 12:4, 9), מועד קץ (8:19), and קץ הימין (12:13). Hab 2:3 also belongs in this connection. Here קץ has become a time scale of apocalyptic reckoning and has lost its threatening content. Ezekiel in his oracles stands on the nearer side of the weakened meaning of the word. With him the accent lies not primarily on the time element of what happens at "the absolute end," but on the element of death under the wrath of Yahweh, and of the annihilation of the honor and vitality of the אדמת ישראל.

■ **7:3** This threat is expressed in v 3 in a direct address to the land. In a silent transition, which recalls our comments on 6:2–7,[9] the population of "the land of Israel" is addressed in what follows with an oracle of doom, and its guilt is affirmed. As was once shouted at Samson "the Philistines are upon you," this land now hears "the end is upon you."[10] The parallel makes clear that in this "end" the wrath of Yahweh falls upon Israel. Just as 5:16 speaks of "sending" (שלח) deadly arrows against the people, so in this formulation of Yahweh's wrath, the destruction almost becomes a personal assistant to Yahweh, which he brings upon

the land without any feeling (v 4a).

■ **7:4** The style of the description of the day of Yahweh is completely abandoned in vv 3b and 4. The judgement of Yahweh is announced in formulations such as reappear in a stereotyped way in the prophetic threats of the book of Ezekiel, and which also immediately point to the justification for this judgement in the evil conduct of the land (and people) and in their abominations. The motive clause in v 4ba again makes clear that what is in one way the wrath and action of Yahweh is in another shown to be merely the full outworking of the evil conduct of the land itself (and its inhabitants). In that Yahweh makes the conduct of the land "come upon it," and its abominations "take effect in its midst," he leaves it to an act of destruction which is apparently quite indwelling and which arises out of its ways and abominations.[11] This whole event is shown to be an act of divine demonstration over the land by the concluding recognition formula. In this event Yahweh appears in the mystery of his name. We may therefore question whether the וידעתם of v 4 was addressed to the individual inhabitants of the land, who have previously been addressed in the second person singular feminine, or to Ezekiel's fellow exiles, who are already living in the death of exile and who will then become witnesses of this event.

Aim

"Israel" is addressed as "the land of Israel," although in Ezekiel's day the people were only living in the Judean remnant of the land. The address "land of Israel" shows that this Israel was an entity which possessed its secret in its divine election (Ezek 20:5), but which could be described not only as a phenomenon preserved by a purely spritual bond, but also as a land. Thus conversely this land also defined Israel because it was the physical pledge of the people's election by God.[12]

The "end" was proclaimed to this Israel, signified

8   Gerhard von Rad, *Priesterschrift im Hexateuch literarisch untersucht und theologisch gewertet*, BWANT 4, 13 (Stuttgart: Kohlhammer, 1934), 172.
9   See above pp. 183f.
10   Note a to v 3.
11   Klaus Koch, "Gibt es ein Vergeltungsdogma im Alten Testament?" *ZThK* 52 (1955): 1–42.
12   Martin Buber, *Israel and Palestine; The History of an* Idea (London: East and West Library, 1952).

by the land to which it was historically and geographically rooted. In the announcement of the day of Yahweh, which extended beyond the world, a radical threat against the people of God was made, since it had preserved in the pledge of the land some measure of sacramental assurance of its calling. This threat could not be expressed more sharply than by the word "end," which here has a considerable meaning.[13]

The prophet's preaching shows that the announcement of the "end" had come to the people with whom God was concerned on account of their sins. It thereby deprives the people of God, who continued to find in the land the pledge of God's presence with them (with the saying: "to us the land is given for a possession" more than once Ezekiel is opposed, 11:15; 33:24; cf. also the unjust claim of heathen neighbors in 26:2; 35:10, 12; 36:2), of everything, even this very pledge. The threat of the "end" stood directly over the land of Israel. All optimistic contentment, which expected the cheerful light of God's coming to his people on his day (Amos 5:18–20), is thereby rejected without pity. There is no obvious continuity into the distant future, of which the people whom God had called could be assured, but only a day when God would come to the world to bring destruction and an "end" for every sinful creature. God's coming brings a crisis to his people from which there is no way out. Yet even this coming is a special demonstration of God through his holy name. That God comes and that this coming means an end for sinful man, leaving no way of escape, is at one and the same time God's revelation.

Interpretation

■ **7:6aβ–9** The section in 7:6aβ–9, which has been introduced later into the section of vv 1–6aα, 10–27, represents an extensive parallel variant to vv 2–4. Here also it begins with ponderous phrases which announce the coming of the end. It then passes over into direct address which mentions explicitly the inhabitant of the land as the object of the "end": "The end has come, the end upon you, O inhabitant of the land." In this the word ארץ used here hovers ambiguously between the use of ארץ in v 2b with a worldwide meaning (as

in the close parallel Is 24:17) and the אדמת ישראל of the address in v 2a. V 7bβ, according to the usual interpretation, contains the same idea as Amos 5:18ff. All optimistic expectation of the day of God as a joyful festival occasion, on which people call out הידד, will be removed.[14] However the uncertainty of the text does not permit here more precise statements. The beginning before vv 8f is carried over from vv 3f, with the formulations at the beginning slightly varied and more discursive (cf. v 3aαβ with 8aαβ and the participial elaboration of the recognition formula in v 9), then v 7bα introduces again an element of general description of the day of Yahweh, and with it the traditional statements are given a somewhat larger space, "the time has come, the day is near." Here first of all we have the catchword "day (of Yahweh)." With this there enters the vital statement, found from Zeph 1:7, 14; Joel 1:15 right up to the ἤγγικεν ἡ βασιλεία τῶν οὐρανῶν of John the Baptist and Jesus (Mt 3:2; 4:17 and parallel passages) that the coming of God "has drawn near."

■ **7:6b, 7aα** Nothing more can be made out of the subsequent expansion of the oracle by the addition of v 6b, 7aα on account of the obscurity of the word צפירה.[15] The repetition of the addition in v 10, with slight variation, allows the conjecture that it must once again be a characteristic qualification (stemming from traditional language?) of the day of Yahweh.

Aim

When we question the particular situation of this slightly altered oracle it is immediately evident in the more concrete address to the inhabitant of the land. The addition endeavors to affirm still more emphatically the true understanding of the divine threat. The "end" is not to be regarded as a "misfortune on the land," understood in a neutral fashion as an act of fate, but as an act of "judgement" interpreted as a personal encounter between God an the inhabitant of the land.

Besides this the imminence of the day of Yahweh is more sharply emphasized in vv 6aβ–9 by the twofold עתה מקרוב v 7, קרוב היום v 8, which heightens the simple עתה of v 3. The "nearness" is full of threatening urgency. Behind this heightening of the prophetic

---

13 See above pp. 203f.
14 Cf. note d and Is 9:2.
15 Cf. notes c to v 6 and a to v 7.

word do we have a discussion such as can be found in 12:21–28? In this case the variants could still be ascribed to the time before 587 B.C., since they stand loosely in the context, and although v 8a, over against the parallel in v 3aβ, clearly shows a certain paraphrastic broadness.[16]

Interpretation

■ **7:5–6aα, 10–27** The third section vv 5–6aα, 10–27, again introduced by the messenger formula, appears to correspond in its overall structure to the two shorter units already dealt with. It also describes the coming end, first in impersonal statements, and finishes in v 27b in a threat, formulated personally of Yahweh, together with the recognition formula. Closer examination then shows that this clear basis is disturbed in three regards: 1) the speech of Yahweh in the first person does not first begin at the end of the oracle in v 27b, but already in vv 14b, 20b–22, 24, only to fall into the background behind the descriptive style. 2) The vigorous style of descriptive sentences, especially as they are found in vv 10bβ, 12a, 15a, 17f and other verses, is disturbed by the more formless expressions in vv 13, 16, 20 and other verses. 3) It is striking that the description of the coming day of the end, as in vv 20, 23, is prematurely broken up by elements of invective which anticipate the statements of the conclusion in v 27b.

The textual notes have already made clear that 𝔐 contains a series of oracles and also longer statements, which must have been unknown to the Hebrew original underlying 𝔊. In the section vv 5–6aα, 10–27 𝔊 supports the excision of more than ten longer or shorter passages of the text.[17] The text has undoubtedly been heavily commented upon during the period of its transmission up to the time of 𝔊. The question cannot be avoided therefore whether this commenting had not already begun at an earlier time and whether the elements which break up the clear structure in the three ways mentioned are not to be ascribed to it. In fact there appears to me to be much which speaks in favor of a development which has later changed the face of the text. We must also understand that the brief statements, sometimes merely allusions, of the original description of the coming day of the end must have provoked such additions in a special way. In this, as in other texts (as in 12:1ff), the actual historical course of the catastrophe of 587 B.C., which brought the fulfilment of what is threatened here, brought about an interest in more clarifications.

In accord with the points mentioned a critical analysis must point to the following text as the unelaborated basic form of the prophetic oracle regarding the bitter day of the end:

Thus the Lord Yahweh said:
The end has come,
    behold, the day,
injustice has blossomed,
    pride has budded.
. . . . (11b)
The time has come,
    the day has arrived.
Let not the buyer rejoice,
    nor the seller be mournful.
Blow the trumpet
    and prepare the weapons of war.
The sword is without
    and pestilence and famine are within.
all hands become feeble,
    and all knees are dripping with water,
and they put on sackcloth,
    and horror covers them.
Shame is upon all faces,
    and all their heads are shaved bald.
They throw their silver into the streets,
    and their gold is like rubbish.
They cannot satisfy their hunger
    nor fill their belly.
Anguish has come,
    and one is seeking peace—but there is none.
Disaster follows disaster,
    and bad news follows after bad news.
The prince is clothed with despair,
    and the hands of the people of the land are paralyzed with fear.
On account of their conduct I will deal with them,

---

16   The problem of the proclamation that the end is near must be considered further in connection with the exposition of 12:21–28, where this preaching itself becomes the object of attack by opponents of the word of God.

17   Cf. the notes.

and according to their manner of judgement
I will judge them, and they shall know that I am
Yahweh.

The oracle, in its unelaborated form, describes the
coming of the day of the end in a quite factual impersonal style, in which only at the end does Yahweh speak
in the first person. The imperatives of v 14, if they are
original to the text and not a scribal error for an
infinitive absolute, are not really intended to form an
address in dialogue.[18] They are a means of adding life,
pointing to the dread of the coming event. This event
is mentioned purely descriptively, without any direct
address by Yahweh to the people concerned, unlike the
sections vv 2–4 and 6aβ–9.

■ **7:6aα, 10aα** This latter oracle also begins in v 6aα
with the catchphrase קץ בא, which is varied in the
parallel v 10aα by the phrase הנה היום recalling v 7.
𝕲, which has certainly interpreted the passage and
smoothed it over, may point to a doubled triplet.[19]
More specifically, as has happened in vv 6f, the saying
deriving from Amos 8:2 of the "end" and the statement
about the "day of Yahweh" of Amos 5:18 are equated.

■ **7:10bβγ** The formula of the "day of Yahweh,"
quoted by Ezekiel in abbreviated form (rightly interpreted by 𝕲 as ἰδοὺ ἡμέρα χυρίου), gives expression to
the certainty of God's day of judgement very sharply.
Directly beside it there appears in v 10bβγ a statement
which describes the inevitable certainty of this day in
a metaphor taken from nature. The day of judgement
is the day on which human "injustice" and human
"pride" blossom in their fullness, and men are themselves completely destroyed by them. The language
of farming makes the metaphor of "fruit" for an evil
action appropriate. Fruit is clearly referred to in the
"blossoming" and "budding" or "breaking out."[20]
Judgement on the day of Yahweh is, in the last analysis,
not something strange to human activity. Whoever
sins has already entered into judgement. We must bear
in mind here also what K. Koch has said about the

power of an action to effect punishment.[21] Admittedly
for v 10, since Rashi, Kimchi and Calvin, the interpretation of "rod" (מַטֶּה) and "violence" in terms of
punishment by Nebuchadnezzar has been suggested.
The recollection of the mention of the rod of Assyria
(Is 10:5), together with the fact that in the post-
Jeremian threats against Babylon (Jer 50:31f) זדון
is the cover name for Babylon, appears to favor this
interpretation. It undoubtedly makes the reference to
the day of Yahweh very concrete and historical. Since
such symbolic cover names for Babylon are otherwise
not usual in Ezekiel (we could perhaps point for analogies to Oholah and Oholibah, 23:4), we should certainly have to question then whether the verse does not
come from a later hand. However, against this argument we must reckon its tight-fitting style and its
complete appropriateness to the basic text of chapter 7.

■ **7:11b** Unfortunately however its continuation in
v 11b, in which an original part of the text may be
hidden, is quite obscure so that no further help for an
understanding of the text can be derived from it.

■ **7:12a** In language reminiscent of v 7b, v 12a begins
afresh in terse couplets with a forceful statement about
the coming of the day and the arrival of the time. In
distinction from v 10bβγ, however, which shows in the
briefest formulation the inevitable "fulfilment" of the
evil of men, there now follows a more elaborate picture
of the consequences of the day of God. This is described
as a time of the cessation of all natural everyday feelings
and activities vv 12aβγ; of military threat vv 14a*, 15a;
of paralysis and uncontrollable lamentation vv 17–
19aα¹β; and horror vv 25, 26a, 27a. It thereby connects
with the style of description of the day of Yahweh which
puts concrete contemporary allusions into the background behind the more general human distress of this
time.

Thus it is scarcely appropriate to interpret the
statement "Let not the buyer rejoice, nor the seller be
mournful" as meaning that with the first deportation

---

18 Cf. note b.
19 Cf. note a to v 10.
20 פרח can also be used of the breaking out of skin
    disease, cf. Lev 13:20, 25 and other passages; צרעת
    "skin disease." See Ludwig Koehler, "Aussatz,"
    ZAW 67 (1955): 290–291. For the parallelism of
    ציץ and פרח cf. Nu 17:23; Is 27:6.
21 See above p. 204.

the exiled aristocracy had to sell off their possessions at any price (Bertholet, also Kraetzschmar, Cooke, Fohrer). Such purposeless selling of family property is historically very improbable in view of the provisional character of the state as to its constitutional status at the time of 597 b.c.[22] Beside this the deportees would scarcely have covered an entire family. Against it a comparison with Is 24:2 shows that the theme of buying and selling had its proper place in a general description of judgement, which overcame and removed all human distinctions: "Then the priest will be like the man among the people, the master like the slave, the mistress like the maid, the buyer like the seller (כקונה כמוכר), the lender like the borrower, the creditor like the debtor."[23] Further the antithesis rejoice/mourn (Is 24:7; cf. Eccl 3:4) must be interpreted from this formal style. This renders superfluous the forced attempts to find a historical situation in which the buyer rejoices whilst the seller mourns. Buying and selling are colorful signs of life in the Orient where every market is at the same time an occasion of calculated play, in a quite special way. Rejoicing and mourning are the two poles of human emotion. In both spheres which the saying brings together, the day of God breaks up the natural course of things, in that horror and paralysis take hold of men (cf. 24:1ff; Jer 16:1ff). Thus we have here not the idea of a threat to those who rejoice and a consolation for those who mourn, which would both be quite normal emotions and so signs of real life, but only a reference to the fact that an all-destroying terror would fall upon both the man who rejoices and the one who mourns.

■ **7:14a*, 15a** Vv 14a*, 15a lift the mystery a little at one point about the coming day; this day means war. The dramatic vigor of the imperatives must certainly be determined by earlier statements such as Hos 5:8; Jer 4:5; 6:1 (cf. also Joel 2:1). Here again we must not think of an active possibility for men to which they could be summoned. The wild and paralyzing call to hear is simply given: "It is war!" In a way that is customary in Ezekiel and Jeremiah this is clarified by a reference to the three plagues: sword, famine and pestilence.[24] In a less skilful way this *tria* is divided

between opposites: outside/inside. We may recall Ezek 6:12f. In our examination of the remarks in 7:16 this connection will become clear at a second point.

■ **7:17** The more detailed description of the manner of the divine judgement then breaks off again. The oracle returns to the description of the terror occasioned for those in the judgement. The indirectness of the description, which hides a strong element of vagueness within it and makes the actual course of the judgement obscure, increases the grimness of the uncertain expectation. The panic works itself out. Hands fall down in weakness. Men are no longer able to preserve the elementary aspects of self-control, like the infant and the dying man who passes water. Outwardly also men have the appearance of those facing death. In this again, when v 18 describes the performance of particular mourning rites: putting on rough clothing (Gen 37:34; 2 Sam 3:31; Is 3:24; Jer 4:8 and other passages), shaving the head (Ezek 27:31; Is 3:24; 15:2 and other passages),[25] we must not think of an active effort to action. All these statements are simply seeking to express the outward powerlessness and defenselessness of those concerned in the judgement. In the "fear" or "quaking" which "covers" them (as clothing), i.e., identifies their entire outward appearance, this weakness takes on a meaning for the world outside. In the shame which lies on their faces there is betrayed a humiliation which is more than the simple psychological reaction to the surrounding world. It is the specific loss of honor and all that this means in the way of righteousness, which alone makes life possible.

■ **7:19aα¹** There then follows the despairing rejection of all those things which normally give stability to life: silver and gold. Is 2:20 mentions in connection with a description of the day of Yahweh the same gesture of despairing rejection of silver and gold idols. It is again a specific priestly expression when Ezekiel says here that the gold of men becomes לנדה. נִדָּה denotes secretion, in particular a woman's menstrual flow (Lev 12:2; 15:19f and other passages, cf. also the Midrash tractate *Niddah*). From this it can occasionally in a more general usage be an expression for severe uncleanness, contact with which should be avoided uncondi-

---

22 See above pp. 114f.
23 Cf. also *Apocalypse of Elijah* 27:1, Riessler, 117.
24 See above pp. 190f.

25 For the whole subject see Paul Heinisch, *Die Trauergebräuche bei den Israeliten* (Münster: Aschendorff, 1931).

tionally. Severe loathing, in which what had previously seemed good becomes abhorrent and despised, finds a strong expression in this word.[26] With such loathing on the day of the end men will rid themselves of the gold which had previously seemed to them to be a very special asset. That day will show that nothing more remains for men by which to satisfy their appetite.[27]

■ **7:25** The description of unreasoning terror is continued by vv 25ff, in which the introductory קפדה באה (or תבוא?)[28] appears to modify the קץ בא of vv 2, 6 and thereby to have the effect of making a minor new beginning. Instead of a reference to the day, the time, the end, which is coming, we have here the word "anguish, oppression." The character of that fateful approaching event is thereby described by a very distinctive word. From this attack of anguish men grope for deliverance (שלום is the concept of completeness, of "wholeness" between man and man, or between man and God)—in vain! In language which may recall distantly Jeremiah's anguished saying in Jer 4:20, the unbroken assault of disaster after disaster, bad news after bad news (cf. Jer 51:46, also Ezek 21:12) is pictured. Job 1f illustrates such a situation.

■ **7:27a** Finally, in a deliberate transition to the concluding formula, which is again clearly addressed to the inhabitant of the land (cf. v 2), the hopelessness among the politically responsible circles of the people is shown.

נשיא, a title which is already found in the Book of the Covenant, Ex 22:27, was possibly in the period before the monarchy the title of the tribal representative at the amphictyonic sanctuary.[29] In the book of Ezekiel the title is used for lesser kings, whilst the מלך-title is mostly (not exclusively, cf. 17:12) kept for the emperors in Mesopotamia and on the Nile. For the עם הארץ see

E. Würthwein, who has shown that before the exile it was the designation of the land-owning full citizens of Judah with military responsibility.[30] Only after the exile did the title drop to becoming a deprecatory designation by the pious of the poorer part of the nation, who were despised for their unfaithfulness to the law. Thus on the day of the "end" complete confusion was to reign where normally in times of political crisis important counsel would have been given. By the metaphor of clothing, which both covers a man and determines his outward character ("clothes make people," cf. v 18), the despair of the prince is described: "The prince is clothed with despair." Where men's hands should have been raised to defend themselves they would be paralyzed with fear: "The hands of the people are paralyzed with fear" (cf. v 17).

■ **7:27b** Quite briefly a deeper significance is added to the description by v 27b. What appears according to v 10bβ to be the maturing of Israel's history in accordance with its own inner nature and what is according to vv 14f the outward consequence of the attack by the sword is shown in these concluding phrases to be the personal action of Yahweh. He deals with the nation; he judges it so that his very judgement confirms that he deals with Israel according to its own manner of dealing with the law. Thus there remains no possibility of its lamenting its strange unrighteous judgement. The entire judgement however is only a sign, a demonstration to the world, of the personal reality of Yahweh represented by his name.

The great oracle of the bitter day of the end has subsequently undergone a considerable amount of elaboration. This undoubtedly did not take place all at once. 𝕲 again allows a short indication of a time at which the elaboration had reached only a certain stage.

---

26   Cf. to נקוט, p. 190.
27   See Aubrey R. Johnson, *The Vitality of the Individual in the Thought of Ancient Israel* (Cardiff: University of Wales Press, 1949), especially 9–26 with references to fuller literature, for נפש, which developed from the objective meaning "throat" (Lor. Dürr, "Hebr. נֶפֶשׁ = akk. napištu = Gurgel, Kehle," *ZAW* 43 [1925]: 262–269) through the meanings "breath, soul, desire" to meaning "appetite, demand."
28   Cf. note b to v 25.
29   Martin Noth, *Das System der zwölf Stämme Israels*, BWANT 4, 1 (Stuttgart: Kohlhammer, 1930), Ex-

kursus 3: "Gebrauch und Bedeutung des Wortes נשיא," 151–162.
30   Ernst Würthwein, *Der ʿamm haʾarez im Alten Testament*, BWANT 4, 17 (Stuttgart: Kohlhammer, 1936).

Further possibilities for more precise chronological definition of this later work on the text are not available to us. Thus here the elaboration is reviewed simply in the sequence of the verses.

■ **7:5b** The addition of v 5b (note c), lacking in 𝕲, copies in its second half the difficult basic assertion of the whole oracle and in its first half recalls the formulation of v 26a. It contains a certain ambiguity, since רעה can denote on one side a disaster and on the other moral evil, as can be seen in the ambiguous saying of Jer 4:18. Thus the clause perhaps echoes a subtle element of accusation besides lamentation.

■ **10aβbα** The addition of v 10 (note a), which is lacking in 𝕲, is not to be separated from the additions of vv 6/7. The replacing of the second באה found there by יצאה is to be explained from the connection with the following v 10bβ and its metaphors of growth. Here also a growing up of the צפירה is expressed. Later v 10bβ appears to have been further elaborated by the first words of v 11 (note a), which are missing in 𝕲 and which are likewise preserved in a strict style of couplets. In Gen 6:11 in P חמס is the word which expresses comprehensively the entrance of sin into the world. It is found in v 23 (cf. also note c to 9:9) as a synonym for דמים (משפט) and appears again in 8:17; 12:19; 28:16; 45:9 in significant references. The connection by zeugma with שׁד and the contrast with משפט and צדקה in 45:9 show that it is an expression for brutal treatment of one's fellow men. The glossator of v 11aα has undoubtedly understood the מטה and זדון of v 10 in this direction. In its Massoretic vocalization, therefore, the text of v 11a must clearly be interpreted as an explanation of the מַטֵּה (𝔐) of v 10.

■ **7:12b, 13bα¹, 14b** In vv 12–14 there is found the addition of כי חרון אל (על =) כל המונה (so also v 13, cf note a), which reappears twice, but which is missing in 𝕲. Here the grim day of the end is described from its content as one of חרון "wrath," a root which is not found elsewhere in Ezekiel either as a noun or a verb (חרר in 15:4f; 24:10f), but which is often found as a noun in Jeremiah (Jer 4:8, 26; 12:13; 25:37f; 30:24; cf. 49:37; 51:45). It reveals distantly the person burning with anger who stands behind the historical judgement (the suffixed form חרוני appears in v 14). At the same time the thrice repeated gloss with its אל (על =) כל המונה, the suffix of which must relate

beyond the immediate context to the אדמת ישראל mentioned at the beginning of the chapter, summarizes the sin of those affected by the judgement with the catchphrase "pomp." This catchword המון is frequently found again, especially in Ezekiel's oracles against Egypt (Ezek 29:19; 30:4, 10, 15; 31:2, 18 and other passages). However, as the prophetic oracles from the wars against Syria show (1 Kings 20:13, 28), long before the time of Ezekiel it was a word which could denote presumptuous human *hybris* against the divine greatness. Not first the violent deed, but the insolent *hybris* which puffs itself up against God was seen by this glossator as the basic sin of the land of Israel, against which the divine anger burned.

■ **7:13** In v 13 the gloss bα¹ is set within an additional comment aβbα², which is also not found in 𝕲, which offers for its part a more detailed explanation to the double motive clause v 13aαbβ. This motive clause, which is to be found in 𝕲, "For the seller shall not return to what he has sold. And no one will be able to preserve his life (because of his iniquity?)" is undoubtedly a comment on the basic text of v 12aβ, "Let not the buyer rejoice, nor the seller be mournful." Admittedly it only takes up the second half of the two parts of this saying, which indicates the breaking off of all human activity with no return to commercial transaction because no one will be able to save his life. Since no less than seven of the ten occurrences of the noun מִמְכָּר occur in Lev 25 (Lev 25:42 has the hapax legomenon מִמְכֶּרֶת), Jerome may be right about the text when he conjectures that the author here has in mind particularly the law of the Jubilee year in which purchased property reverted back to its original owner. A second editor then later varied the same idea (in the form of a later marginal gloss which became incorporated into the text?) and added; "Whilst their life is still among the living they will not return." This variant, ending with לא ישוב, has entered into the text in connection with the לא ישוב of v 13aα. In a third phase the second כי חרון אל (על =) כל המונה, plainly without any meaningful consideration, was introduced into the text of the second gloss. The subsequent miswriting of חזון for חרון then finally changed the meaning of the clause to: "For the vision (= the prophecy) will not be made backward (i.e., remain unfulfilled) against all his pomp."

■ **7:14aβ** The addition in v 14 (note c) is again a witness to the later interpretative work on the text. The statements of v 14aα could, if they were originally read as imperatives (notes a and b), have led to the misunderstanding as though in face of the evil of the coming war an active opposition was still conceivable. Thus a later editor, with a bold reinterpretation and by taking the מלחמה which belongs to the basic text as a summons to those addressed, has added: "Yet none goes into battle," which (at the same or a later time?) was affirmed by a third gloss "for my wrath comes upon all his pomp." In another way C. Kuhl attempts to deal with the difficult text of vv 12–14, when he reckons with two phases of expansion in which first v 13a, then vv 13b–14 were added.[31] This explanation remains unsatisfactory, however, since it neglects the evidence for the text given by 𝕲.

■ **7:15b** In v 15b we should probably see a later piece of exposition in view of the circumstantial breadth of the statement, which stands out noticeably from the brevity of the basic text. In v 15a the traditional three-fold instruments of judgement: sword, famine, and pestilence were combined rather unskilfully with a group of two: those within and those outside, so that one weapon falls on "those within," but two on "those outside." In the related text of 6:12, where the three-fold instruments of judgement are connected with the antithesis of "far" and "near," we find the surprising device that beside these two, which apparently excluded a third, mention is made of "the preserved," which thus provides a particular group for the third instrument. In 7:16 also there now appears, within the framework of later interpretation which had obviously already noted the absence of such a group in 6:12, a third group of "the survivors." Since, however, the three instruments have already been divided in the original text between "those within" and "those outside," the solution of 6:12 was no longer possible and a more general statement was formulated for this last group: "And if any of them escape and they are on the mountains, then they will all die." In the additional "each one for his iniquity," which is similarly found in v 13, the concern is taken into account, which is then

fully unfolded in ch. 18: the divine judgement, even when it occurs without pity, is in every case, with every individual, a righteous judgement (cf., however, 21:8f). A later hand has then added a comparison with the moaning of doves, which is still not found in 𝕲 (note c), to the description of the men who flee to the mountains. Is 38:14; 59:11 also, where the simile appears again in connection with lamentation, intends by it the sound of an anxious, terrified bird.[32]

■ **7:19aα²** The mention of silver and gold which is thrown away as useless in v 19aα¹ because it cannot satisfy hunger in v 19aβ gives rise to a particularly extensive additional comment. A thoughtful reader, familiar with the prophetic message, has first added in 19aα² (note b) a phrase from the great announcement of the day of Yahweh by Zephaniah (1:18), in which the uselessness of silver and gold "on the day of Yahweh's wrath" (יום עברה also in Zeph 1:15, cf. Is 13:9) is expressed. 𝕲 still did not have the addition.

■ **7:19b, 20** The character as a commentary is much more clearly recognizable also in its stylistic aspect in vv 19b, 20. The comment, which is already found in 𝕲 and must therefore have been made at a time when the Zephaniah quotation still did not stand in the text, goes back beyond the intervening v 19aβ to the זהבם כי מכשול עונם היה in v 19aα¹. The singular עונם היה לנדה יהיה is related, beyond the plural v 19aβ, to זהבם. In this motive clause the strange treatment of the gold is explained. The gold has become a "stumbling block to their guilt" (מכשול עון is found again in 14:3f, 7; 18:30; 44:12. It is a characteristic expression of Ezekiel and his school, which is not otherwise found in the Old Testament.)[33] This claim is elaborated in v 20a. Israel has arrogantly misused its beautiful gold and made detestable images out of it. צלם is used by Ezekiel in 16:17 and 23:14 for figured images of men. Here images of gods must be in mind. The addition שקוציהם, which is not found in 𝕲 (note c), appears to interpret the expression in this direction (37:23 שקוציהם parallel to גלוליהם). After this invective, which describes Israel's sin with its gold, the addition returns to the basic text, taking up once again its starting point: "Therefore (על כן) I have made it an unclean thing to

31   Kuhl, " 'Wiederaufnahme'," 7f.
32   Already Babylonian laments were familiar with this simile. See A. Ungnad, *Die Relgion der Babylonier und*

Assyrer (Jena: Diederich, 1921), 220.
33   Cf. to 14:3f.

them." This is a prosaic addition, which is clearly marked out from the original harsh text, expressed with parallel clauses. It is therefore noteworthy how in this comment the basis of the original text is slightly changed and (anticipating v 27b) appears to be interpreted theologically. The event of despising gold, which in v 19aα was described quite impersonally, is indicated here as an event brought about by Yahweh (נתתיו).

■ **7:21–24** In this personal style (v 21 repeats the נתתיו of v 20) the explanatory comment continues through the following verses up to v 24. In the verses up to 23, which mentions bloodshed (דמים cf. especially 22:1ff) and violence (חמס see above to v 11a) as sins of the land and city in a stereotyped invective (cf. 8:17; 9:9), the coming judgement is announced. This announcement, in which v 24a is a yet later addition according to the evidence of 𝕲, is distinguished from the threats of the original text above all by the fact that it appears to have in view the fall, plunder, and burning of the city of Jerusalem and its sanctuary in a much more concrete way. Without doubt these comments were formulated after 587 B.C., with reference to the grim reality of this year, unlike the basic text which comes from before 587. We get the impression that we are still not very far from these events. The possibility of a (partial?) expansion of the text by Ezekiel himself is therefore not to be ruled out altogether in this text.

In these verses those who destroy Jerusalem are called "foreigners,"[34] "the godless of the earth" (רשעי הארץ cf. note a to v 21), "robbers" (פריץ in Ezekiel only again in 18:10 in a somewhat different meaning), and in the gloss v 24a "the worst of the nations" (רעי גוים not found again, but cf. רעים 30:12). They plunder the gold from which Israel has made its idols, desecrate it, so that what was once holy for

Israel becomes an abomination to it. They go further still and desecrate Yahweh's own sanctuary.[35] This is only possible because Yahweh has turned away his face from his people. The turning towards of the face would be a sign of honor, as is to be heard in the priestly blessing of Nu 6:26, and contrary to Ezek 4:3, 7; 6:2 where it is a sign of threats.

In all this the "proud might" (this phrase is found again in 24:21; 30:6, 18; 33:28 and nowhere else in Ezekiel) of the people is ruined and its sanctuaries are desecrated. The further gloss in v 24a (note a) mentions again the houses of the Israelites which now become the possession of foreigners.

■ **7:26b** With the saying of v 26b, split up into three parts, we may remain undecided whether it should be ascribed to the basic text or not. Its three sections distinguish it from the otherwise well-preserved series of parallel clauses. To this must be added the close connection with Jer 18:18 and the striking repetition of ובקשו, which just introduced v 25b. Thus it appears probable that we have here also a later comment with a more detailed description of the lost capacity of comprehension by the people. In dependence on Jer 18:18 the people's loss of all charismatic gifts is described: in vain men seek a "vision" (חזון) from the prophets (Jer 18:18 speaks of דבר). "Instruction" (תורה) departs from the priests. This clause is taken over word for word from Jer 18:18.[36] The elders lack "counsel" (עצה). Jer 18:18 mentions in place of the elders the wise men. This leads J. Fichtner to question "whether, in the period before the exile, the influential wise men who were important in diplomacy fell into the background and the elders took their place."[36a] The charismatic character of Wisdom is clear from 1 Kings 3:4–15.[37] Since v 27a returns to a description of the

---

34   Cf. 11:9; 28:7–10; 30:12; 31:12. G. R. Driver, "Ezekiel: Linguistic and Textual Problems," *Bibl* 35 (1954): 148f, would find here the Akkadian *zā'iru, zāru* and Arabic *zā'irun* "enemy," while L. A. Snijders, "The Meaning of זר in the Old Testament. An Exegetical Study," *OTS* 10 (1954): 1–154, especially 28–33, keeps the usual interpretation "foreigner."

35   For צפוני cf. note a to v 22.

36   Cf. Hag 2:10–14 for the concept of priestly torah, and see especially Joachim Begrich, "Die priesterliche Tora" in BZAW 66 (Berlin, 1936), 63–88;

reprinted in *idem, Gesammelte Studien zum AT*, ThB 21 (München: Kaiser, 1964), 232–260; and Gunnar Östborn, *Tora in the Old Testament: a Semantic Study* (Lund: Ohlsson, 1945). For Ezekiel see further 22:26.

36a   Johannes Fichtner, "Jesaja unter den Weisen," *ThLZ* 74 (1949): 77.

37   For the figure of the counsellor see P. A. H. de Boer, "The Counsellor" in *Wisdom in Israel and in the Ancient Near East*, ed. Martin Noth, VT Suppl 3 (Leiden: Brill, 1955), 42–71.

confusion of the people, which is here represented by the prince and the people of the land and connects quite smoothly with the reference to the terrifying reports in v 26a, v 26b must be under suspicion as an addition, also from the point of view of what follows.[38]

Aim

The great oracle on the terrible day of the end in vv 5–6aα, 10–27 stands fundamentally on the same base as the two shorter oracles about this day which precede it. Now, however, all direct personal address on the part of God, both to the land and its inhabitants, tends to disappear. Everything is described in a dispassionate way by God, who first appears in the first person again in v 27b. Everything that is to happen to men is first described as though it were unrelated to God and did not concern him, until in v 27b it becomes clear that it is he who is acting in his righteous judgement, revealing himself to the world by his name.

At a second point the announcement of judgement shows a certain fearful objectivity. What is made plain on the day of the "end" is not something that is foreign to man's nature and activity, but is in fact the ripening of his own deepest nature. Nothing of what God says has such grim irony as the description in v 10 of the judgement as the "blossoming" of human activity. Man's destruction is the "flowering" of his activity. In this very act God's judgement comes upon men, v 27b.

Furthermore this oracle makes especially clear that all human purposes are frustrated when God, in his judgement, fixes the day of the "end." Not only all commercial activity with which men fill their lives (v 12), nor the sparkle of gold which acts as a magic key to open closed doors and to satisfy life's needs (v 19), but even the powers of inner self-control, the very power of one's own hands (vv 17, 27), and the superiority of the politician who is normally well able to give advice (v 27) will fail. Paralyzing panic, which early Israel had praised as the great weapon of God in the holy wars against his enemies, would then be turned completely against the people under judgement.[39] After the summons to battle (v 14), terrifying

reports will be heard (v 26), and panic will paralyze every hand (vv 17, 27). For the men upon whom God's judgement falls there will be no way out and no help through which they might escape. They are given over to God's judgement with no way of escape. In this case there is only one who can help, and this is God himself, if in his grace he should set a limit to his wrath. With grim relentlessness the oracle of the day of the end opposes every cheap discounting of God's anger against his sinful people.

The additional comments further underscore the harsh features of the day of the end: its irreversibility (v 13), the fierceness of the divine anger which opposes all arrogant human boasting (vv 12–14), the personal accountability of the individual for his own guilt (vv 13, 16), the impossibility of armed defence against it (v 14), and the rejection of all "religious" remedies (v 26b).

Vv 21b–22 point beyond this to a further position regarding the inner righteousness of God which makes the gold which men have used for the sins of *hybris* and idolatry become loathsome to the sinner. In this regard it appears in vv 21–24 that from the experience of the year 587 B.C. individual features of the day of judgement have been drawn into the earlier oracle of the day of the end in a way which is very much more historically detailed. In modern exposition such later elaborations, under the influence of actual historical events, have been freely described as *vaticinium ex eventu* and dismissed as inauthentic and of little value. The special purpose and evidence of these additions has in this way certainly not been given. Such elaborations and clarifications of earlier oracles by the prophet himself (or his school) rather preserve the plain recognition that the judgement has actually taken place. God's word did not remain empty, but became a visible, painful event. The editor of vv 21–24 seeks to bring the reader (or hearer) with him under this meaningful event. We must not regard the intention of this closer historical definition in a modern way, which would have been foreign to the author of the text, of setting the announcement of the end in the past as history and so in this way making it less binding. This would

---

38 For the gloss v 27aα', which repeats the verb אבל from v 12, cf. note a.
39 von Rad, *Krieg*, 10–13.

be to thank God that the threatened disaster lay in the past. On the contrary, by introducing the historical details of what happened to the people into the proclamation of the end, the editor seeks to affirm the personal relevance of the event of 587 B.C. This catastrophe was not simply a past event and thus no longer of any account. It stood directly as God's threat against his people, as something that had really happened in history.

It belongs to the peculiarity of the Old Testament message that through such identification of the event of 587 B.C. with the Day of Yahweh the former acquired an ultimate validity, which the actual event does not altogether sustain and in which the announcement goes beyond the historical fulfillment. This is also found elsewhere in the Old Testament.[40] In a deeper sense it makes such oracles into a word of future promise.

---

40   See Gerhard von Rad, "Erwägungen zu den Königs-psalmen," *ZAW* 58 (1940/41): 216–222.

The Great Vision of the Sinful Worship in Jerusalem and its Judgement

Bibliography

W. F. Albright
Archaeology and the Religion of Israel (Baltimore: Johns Hopkins University Press, 1956).

E. Balla
"Ezechiel 8:1–9:11; 11:24–25," in *Festschrift Rudolf Bultmann zum 65. Geburtstag überreicht* (Stuttgart, Kohlhammer, 1949), 1–11.

E. Baumann
"Die Hauptvision Hesekiels in ihrem zeitlichen und sachlichen Zusammenhang untersucht," *ZAW* 67 (1955): 56–67.

T. K. Cheyne
"The Image of Jealousy in Ezekiel," *ZAW* 21 (1901): 201–202.

D. Daube
"Über die Umbildung biblischen Rechtsgutes" in *Symbolae Friburgenses in honorem Ottonis Lenel* (Leipzig: Tauchnitz, 1935), 245–258, esp. 245–248.

T. H. Gaster
"Ezekiel and the Mysteries," *JBL* 60 (1941): 289–310, espec. 289–297, "Ezekiel ch. viii. A Canaanite Liturgy from Ras-Shamra-Ugarit."

J. Goettsberger
"Zu Ez 9:8 und 11:13," *BZ* 19 (1931): 6–19.

R. Gordis,
"The Branch to the Nose. A Note on Ezekiel viii 17," *JTS* (1936): 284–288.

H. Gunkel
"Der Schreiberengel Nabû im A.T. und im Judentum," *ARW* 1 (1898): 294–300.

F. Horst
"Exilsgemeinde und Jerusalem in Ez viii–ix. Eine literarische Untersuchung," *VT* 3 (1953): 337–360.

H. G. May
"The Departure of the Glory of Yahweh," *JBL* 56 (1937): 309–321.

E. von Mülinen
"Galgal. Hesekiel Kap. 10:13," *ZDPV* 46 (1923): 79–107.

H. Torczyner
"Semel ha-qin'ah ha-maqneh (Ezek. 8:3, 5)," *JBL* 65 (1946): 293–302.

C. Virolleaud
"Sur l'idole de la jalousie du temple de Jérusalem (Ezek. 8:3–5)," *RES* 1 (1945): 59–63.
For ch. 10 cf. also the literature to ch. 1.

1 And it happened in the sixth year, in the sixth[a] month, on the fifth (day)[b] of the month, as[c] I sat in my[d] house, with the elders of Judah[e] sitting before me, that [there][f] the hand of [the Lord][g] Yahweh fell[h] upon me. 2/ And when I looked, behold there (appeared) a form [, in appearance like that][a] of a 'man,'[b] from [that which appeared][c] his hips downwards was fire, and from his hips upwards [like the appearance of a pure brightness][d] like the shining of

8:1 8:1a 𝔐 בַּשִּׁשִׁי 𝔊 ἐν τῷ πεμπτῳ μηνί. Although since Smend the reading of 𝔊 has repeatedly been preferred (Cornill, Hölscher, *Hesekiel*, Bertholet, Fohrer) on the basis that 𝔐 has replaced the 5th by the 6th month in order to leave room for the interval mentioned in 3:16; 4:4ff (𝔐), this view cannot stand closer examination. The 7 (3:16) plus 390 (4:5, cf. 9) plus 40 (4:6) equals 437 days (so rightly Hölscher, whilst Smend and Fohrer, by inaccurate calculation, reckon only 7 plus 390 days). These stand over against only 354 plus 60 (59) = 414 (413) days between the 5.IV.5 (1:1f) and the 5.VI.6, according to the lunisolar calendar system (*BRL*, 309f; Barrois, *Manuel*, 2, 171–175). According to the solar reckoning current in Egypt this would give 365 plus 60 = 425 days. It would impute to the tendentious editor too much mystery to accept the tacit reckoning of a leap month, as was commanded in the Old and New Babylonian empires from time to time by the king, and which appeared from 534 B.C. in a fixed order three times in an eight year cycle and since 381 B.C. seven times in a nineteen year cycle (Meissner, *Babylonien* 2, 397). Thus we must retain 𝔐 and regard the variation in 𝔊 as obscure. Cf. also the mysterious dating in the eighteenth year in 𝔊[407] (ninth century).

b Var[p] בְּאֶחָד. In view of 29:1 𝔊 can we speak of an inclination to place the dates at the beginning of the month?

c A circumstantial clause without introductory ו. Cf. note a to 1:1 and Gesenius-Kautzsch, § 156a.

d 𝔊 ἐν τῷ οἴκῳ, 𝔊[Zv, h, Luc] 𝔏[S] Arm 𝕮 = 𝔐.

e 𝔗 סבי בית יהודה cf. v 17.

f שָׁם is lacking in 𝔊, cf. note d to 1:3.

g אדני is lacking in 𝔊, see Excursus 1.

h 𝔊 (𝔏[S]) καὶ ἐγένετο MS[Ken 105] ותהי replaces the mention of the "falling" of Yahweh's hand, which appears only here, by the regular reference of 1:3; 3:22; 33:22; 37:1; 40:1, see above p. 118.

2 2a 𝔊 gives the text in a shorter form than 𝔐. The כמראה, which is not attested by 𝔊 (unlike in 1:26), must be regarded as a subsequent assimilation to 1:26.

b According to 𝔊 (𝔏[CS] 𝕮 𝕰 𝔄) (ὁμοίωμα) ἀνδρός we must vocalize as אִישׁ. Geiger, *Urschrift*, 343, rightly conjectures that 𝔐 has altered the original text out of reverence for the divine appearance.

c 𝔐 ממראה מתניו, 𝔊 (𝔏[CS]) ἀπὸ τῆς ὀσφύος αὐτοῦ, MS[Ken 96] ממתניו. The simple ממתניו, in parallel, makes it probable that the shorter 𝔊 text is correct over against 𝔐. The gloss, which has 1:27 as its basis, has occurred in an inconsequential way only with the ממתניו ולמטה and therefore the ממתניו ולמעלה is not relevant. The introduction of מראה in the second member makes an improvement at the wrong place (Toy).

d 𝔊 gives the concluding comparison of 𝔐 in an

'electrum'.ᵉ 3/ And he stretched out something like a hand and took me by the hair of my head;ᵃ and (the) spirit lifted me up between heaven and earth and brought me in divineᵇ visions to Jerusalem, to the entrance 'of the gate' ' 'ᶜ which faces north, where was the positionᵈ of the image of jealousy,

abbreviated form which overloads the line, and breaks the simile of the parallel descriptions. Its ὡς ὅρασις ἠλέκτρου (cf. 𝔏ᶜˢ 𝕮 Cyr Hierᵗᵉˢᵗ) appears to point to an original כמראה החשמלה. The comparison with 1:27, however, argues against splitting up כעין החשמלה. Thus 𝔊 must already have had the reading of 𝔐 and have abbreviated it arbitrarily (cf. also 𝔊 v 5). In this the strikingly vague כמראה זהר must be secondary.

e 𝔐 חשמלה is striking beside the חשמל of 1:4, 27. Hölscher, *Hesekiel*, believes he can find here an Aramaic emphatic ending.

3   3a 𝔊 takes בציצת ראשי together in a free translation in the one expression τῆς κορυφῆς μου. This is then later intentionally elaborated in the more exact translation of ’Α Θ τοῦ κρασπέδου τῆς κορυφῆς μου, Σ τοῦ μαλλου (τῆς) κορυφῆς μου.

b 𝔐 במראות אלהים is not to be changed to the singular in spite of seven MSS 𝔊 (ἐν ὁράσει θεοῦ) 𝔏ᶜˢ 𝕾 𝕿 𝕭.

c הפנימית is not attested by 𝔊 𝔏ᶜˢ 𝕮ᴮᵒ. With its feminine ending it cannot be related to שער, which is shown as masculine by the accompanying הַפּוֹנֶה. See also Albrecht, "Geschlecht," 86. Thus the expression must be understood either by changing to the masculine הפנימי (Cornill, Toy), or as an abbreviation of החצר הפנימית (Herrmann, Aalders, van den Born). However it must, since this abbreviation is otherwise not found and the reference also materially disturbs the outline of Ezek 8 (cf. the exposition), have been foreign to the original text. This will have read השער, and subsequently the article has fallen out through haplography beside the preceding ה.

d מושב, which appears only here with the meaning "position" (Ehrlich, *Randglossen*, would deduce the image of a seated deity), is not directly attested by 𝔊 𝔏ᶜˢ 𝕾. However, since 𝔊 elsewhere permits abbreviations (cf. note a), it is very possible that its στήλη loosely translates the סמל מושב of the original.

e 𝔐 סמל הקנאה המקנה. Against this 𝔊 reads ἡ στήλη τοῦ κτωμένου; 𝕾 𝔏ᶜˢ *lapis titulus ipsius possidentis* can only point to one single expression formed from the root קנא (= קנה). 𝔊 𝔏ᶜˢ point rather to a מקנה in their underlying Hebrew original, 𝕾 to קנאה. Are קנאה and מקנה originally variant readings? Or does the expression מקנה deriving from קנה = קנא, as צלם קינאתא דמרגזין 𝕿 and 𝕭 *idolum zeli ad provocandam aemulationem* have understood, seek to underline the idea of Dtn 32:16? The attempt of Driver, "Linguistic Problems," 62, to read a hopʿal מְקֻנָּאה or מְקֻנֶּה in analogy with the הָעֵצָה הַיְּעֻצָה of Is 14:26 as "(image of jealousy) which is made zealous" carries as little conviction as his later conjecture in "Ezekiel," 149. Here, in dependence on Virolleaud's interpretation of קנאה as אֶקְנֶה "lapis lazuli" (Akk. *uqnû*; Ugar. *iqnu*; also Dussaud, "L'idole"), he would read הַקֳנָּאָה הַמָּקְנֶה and compare for קֻנָּא Syr. *qûnāʾāh* "sky blue," and for מקנה Sab. *hqny* =

which provokes to jealousy (?).ᵉ 4/ And behold, the glory of the God of Israelᵃ was there, exactly like the vision which I had seen in the plain. 5/ And he said to me: Son of man, raise your eyes northwards. And I raised my eyes to the north, and behold, in the north of the gate there stood 'an altar'ᵃ—the image of jealousy itself stood in the entrance.ᵇ 6/ And he said to me: Son of man, do you see,ᵃ what theyᵇ are doing? [The] great abomination [, which the house of Israel (are committing here)]ᶜ they commit here, by which they depart from my sanctuary.ᵈ But you will see still greater abominations. 7/ And he brought me to the entrance of the forecourt [and when I looked, behold,

Min. *sqny* "to consecrate."

4 4a 𝕲 (𝕷ᶜˢ) δόξα κυρίου θεοῦ Ἰσραηλ appears to point to an original text כבוד יהוה אלהי ישראל also attested by two MSS. Since, however, the book of Ezekiel otherwise only shows the parallelism of the forms כבוד יהוה (1:28; 3:12, 23; 10:4, 18; 11:23; 43:4, 5) and כבוד אלהי ישראל (9:3; 10:19; 11:22; 43:2), and this distinction is also elsewhere completely adhered to by 𝕲, we must see in 𝕲 8:4 a secondary mixture of two formulations and keep 𝔐 as the original reading.

5 5a 𝔐 לשער המזבח "of the altar gate." 𝕲 (𝕷ᶜˢ 𝕾) ἐπὶ τὴν πύλην τὴν πρὸς ἀνατολάς point to a reading לשער המזרח. An "altar gate" is not elsewhere mentioned. On the other hand, the mention here of an east gate is quite impossible, since Ezekiel is led to the north gate and the path from the north is also discernible in v 14. So we must read לַשַּׁעַר (with article) and connect this with the preceding מצפון. In the following word we can consider whether it is to be read with 𝕲 as מזרח (or המזרח) and connected: "north of the gate, towards the east." Since such combinations of two directions for that which lies between them are not otherwise found, even in the frequent remarks on directions of Ezek 40ff, we can more correctly keep the מזבח of 𝔐, perhaps without the article, in construct with what follows (Bertholet, Fohrer). Or should the article be regarded as original (cf. to הנשים v 14), in accordance with Gesenius-Kautzsch § 126q?

b The whole of bβ (not only the last two words; BH³ is therefore to be corrected) has no counterpart in 𝕲 𝕷ᶜˢ, but it is scarcely to be dispensed with. The בָּאָה, which is only found here in the Old Testament and which was already read by 𝕿 מעלנא, 𝖁 *in ipso introitu*, and Σ ἐν τῇ εἰσόδῳ as "entrance" and is to be regarded, according to Tournay, "Review," 419, as a Babylonian expression from Akkadian *bi'u*, clearly means a place inside the entrance. bβ is to be regarded as a descriptive nominal clause pointing back to v 3.

6 6a 𝔐 הראה אתה is translated by 𝕲, like the הראית of vv 12, 15, 17, by ἑόρακας, which makes Cornill, Herrmann, Balla also read הראית here. However, the deviation here can be connected with the preceding בן אדם, which does not occur in that sequence in vv 12, 15, 17.

b מהם of 𝔐 = מה הם.

c The interpretative gloss אשר בית ישראל was not yet before 𝕲 𝕷ᶜˢ Hierᵉᵖ ¹⁰⁰﹐⁶.

d We must not reckon here with 𝖁 (*ut procul recedam*), Herrmann, Cooke, Fohrer, and Jahn, *Buch*, on the departure of Yahweh from his sanctuary, but with the setting up of an altar outside the sanctuary by men, following 𝕲 (τοῦ ἀπέχεσθαι ἀπὸ τῶν ἁγίων μου) 𝕷ᶜˢ, Hölscher, Bertholet, Balla. Cf. the exposition.

7 7a The second half of the verse, which is fully set out in the style of a vision (ואראה והנה see above

there was a hole in the wall].ᵃ 8/ And
he said to me: Son of man, dig through
the wall.ᵃ And I dug through the wall.ᵃ
And behold, there was an entrance.
9/ And he said to me: Go in and see the
[evil]ᵃ abominations which they are
committing here. 10/ Then I went in
and saw. And behold, all kinds of
[images of reptiles and beasts]
abominationsᵃ and all kinds of idols of
the house of Israel were cut as
engravingsᵇ in the wallᶜ round about.ᵈ

p. 104), is lacking in 𝕲 𝔏ᶜˢ Hierᵗᵉˢᵗ and anticipates
v 8, the command to the prophet to dig a hole in the
wall.

8a 𝕲 𝔏ᶜˢ בקיר is unattested in both places (otherwise 12:5, 7, 12). Since the same phenomenon appears in 𝕲 to v 10 (note c to v 10) in a section in
which 𝕲 can scarcely have the original text, here
also 𝔐 is to be retained. Does all this point to a particular translator who has not understood קיר? Cf.
the introduction. Balla, Fohrer twice read the verb
חפר instead of חתר and understand it as "to spy,
look around." 𝕲 has interpreted it falsely as ὀρύτ-
τειν "to dig." This reading, which would undoubtedly smooth the text, is however textually very uncertain. The text remains difficult, cf. the exposition.

9a The attributive הרעות is not attested by 𝕲 𝔏ᶜˢ
𝕮ᴮᵒ and is superfluous beside תועבות. Cf. note d to
6:11.

10a For the shorter reading of 𝕲 (𝔏ᶜˢ 𝕮ᴮᵒ Hierᵗᵉˢᵗ)
ἰδοὺ μάταια βδελύγματα over against 𝔐 Cornill has
expressed the conjecture that the unusual use of
μάταια (11:2 translation of און, 13:6–9, 19 translation of כזב, 21:29 [= 𝔐 v 34]; 22:28 of שוא) arose
from an inner Greek miswriting of πάντα τά (ΠΑΝ-
ΤΑ ΤΑ) so that the כל of 𝔐, which can scarcely be
dispensed with on account of the parallel, also had
its counterpart in 𝕲. The Hebrew original of 𝕲 accordingly runs והנה כל שקץ. The שקץ, which is
prominent in Lev 11, is not elsewhere found in Ezekiel. However a change to שִׁקוּצִים, found in 5:11,
7:20 and other passages (Cornill, Toy), is not necessary. The explanatory gloss of 𝔐 תבנית רמש ובהמה,
which has been added in a clumsy way before, instead of after, שֶׁקֶץ, which now appears awkwardly
subordinated as an apposition (Cooke), must be
determined by Dtn 4:17f. Whereas, however, the
Ezekiel text thinks primarily of the cult of unclean
creatures, Dtn 4:17f has in mind creatures, images
of which represent an infringement of the second
commandment of the Decalogue.

b Since מְחֻקֶּה appears to demand a singular related word, Hölscher, Hesekiel, Balla, Fohrer delete
וכל גלולי בית ישראל as a gloss. מְחֻקֶּה is, however,
certainly used as a noun in two other passages in the
Old Testament: 1 Kings 6:35. Ezek 23:14. Thus
the possibility exists here of regarding מחקה as a
nominal predicate, with Ehrlich, Randglossen, and
connecting it with a plural subject. To this לפניהם
of v 11 demands a related expression in the plural.

c 𝕲 ἐπ' αὐτοῦ, which for the third time leaves a
קיר of 𝔐 untranslated (note a to v 8, cf. also v 7b),
is therefore particularly striking because in the text
of 𝕲 no related word is discernible for αὐτοῦ. 𝔏ᶜˢ
in ea appears to relate it in a strange way to the accompanying "domus istrahel" [sic]. If we accept an
actual עליו in the Hebrew original of the difficult
reading of 𝕲 𝔏ᶜˢ, then we must understand it as a
neutral "therein, thereto." However, we should be

11/ And seventy men of the elders of the house of Israel [' 'ᵃ, Jaazaniah, the son of Shaphan, was standing among them,]ᵇ stood (as servants) before them, each one with his censer in his hand, and the scent [of the cloud]ᶜ of incense went up. 12/ And he said to me: Have you seen, son of man, what the elders of the house of Israel are doing [in the darkness],ᵃ each one in 'his room of pictures'?ᵇ For they say:

slow to depart from 𝔐 here.

d 𝔐 סביב סביב. The simple κύκλῳ of 𝔊, which only the later textual witnesses (𝔊ᴮᶜ, ⁸⁸⁻⁶²' 'Α Θ) duplicated or (Σ) expanded by δι' ὅλου, does not point (against Hölscher, *Hesekiel*, Balla, Fohrer) to a simple סביב in the Hebrew original. Only 37:2 𝔊, which derives from the hand of another translator (cf. the introduction), offers the fuller translation of the expression with κυκλόθεν κύκλῳ. From 40:5 up to 43:12 the double Hebrew expression is translated in twenty-three cases in 𝔊 by a single word.

11 11a In 𝔊 𝔏ᶜˢ and also in 𝔊Q, which as an exception here deviates from the Hexaplaric witnesses, the copula is missing; cf. note b.

b The conjunction of עמד and עמדים, separated only by one word in 𝔐, is hardly acceptable syntactically. In 𝔊 also only a single word counterpart is evidenced. Certainly therefore in the older texts the singular form (εἱστήκει) appears where 𝔐 has the plural. First 𝔊ʰ, ᴸᵘᶜ, ᶻᵛ 𝔆ᴮᵒ 𝔈 Thdrt change, plainly as an assimilation to 𝔐. Cornill, in close dependence on 𝔊, wants to put עמד in the place of עמדים and to translate: "And seventy men . . . and Jaazaniah in their midst, standing before them, had each his censer in his hand." However since what 𝔊 already did not understand, עמד לפני, had the meaning "to stand as a servant before someone" (before the ark Ju 20:28; 1 Kings 3:15; before Yahweh 1 Kings 17:1; 18:15 and other passages; cf. also the לעמד לפני העדה לשרתם of Nu 16:9 P), whilst "to lead (others)" was expressed by עמד על (Nu 7:2), this reading does not meet the sense of 𝔐. This plainly says that the whole group of men stood in cultic service before the images (𝔙 elaborates correctly: *ante picturas*), in which Jaazaniah participates (standing among them). Most commentators therefore (see BH³, Ehrlich, *Randglossen*, Herrmann, Bertholet) delete עמד by appeal to 𝔊. This appeal to 𝔊, however, is not accurate. Rather 𝔊 arouses the strong suspicion of offering a compromise rendering of the difficult text of 𝔐 which it had before it. 𝔐 therefore becomes quite clear when we recognize in the passage [ו]יאזניהו בן שפן עמד בתוכם a subsequent addition, which disrupts the flow of the sentence. The asyndetic introduction in 𝔊 (note a) may be shown thereby to be the more original form of the text.

c ענן is a superfluous gloss, lacking in 𝔊 𝔏ᶜˢ, which may have arisen from Lev 16:13.

12 12a 𝔐 בחשך is not attested in 𝔊 and is an elaborative gloss. A further gloss, arising from v 9, of עשה used absolutely is shown by 𝔊ᴹˢˢ of the Alexandrian text type and the Cat-group, with their inserted ὧδε. The ὧδε ἐν τῷ σκότει of 𝔖ʰ connects the two additions. The original text corresponds to v 6a.

b 𝔐 איש בחדרי משכיתו. 𝔊 ἕκαστος αὐτῶν ἐν τῷ κοιτῶνι τῷ κρυπτῷ αὐτῶν 𝔏ˢ *unusquisque eorum in cubiculo* (𝔏ᶜ + *occulto*) *suo*, 𝔗 גבר באידרון בית משכביה 𝔙 *unusquisque in abscondito cubiculi sui*, 𝔖 אנשא בתוונה

220

"Yahweh does not see [us],[c] Yahweh has forsaken the land." 13/ And he said to me: You shall see still greater abominations which they do. 14/ And he brought me to the entrance of the gate of the house of Yahweh, which lies toward the north,[a] and behold, there were women[b] who were sitting down and weeping for Tammuz.[c] 15/ And he said to me: Have you seen, son of man?[a] You shall see still greater abominations than these. 16/ And he brought me into the inner court of the house of Yahweh, and behold, at the entrance of the temple of Yahweh, between the entrance room[a] and the altar, (stood) 'about twenty'[b] men, with their backs to the temple of Yahweh, and their faces turned toward the east, prostrating themselves and worshipping[c] [towards the east][d] before the sun. 17/ And he said to me: Have you seen, son of man? Is it too slight a thing for the house of Judah[a] to commit the abominations which they have committed here—for they have filled the land with violence—[and have provoked me further,][b] behold, now they stretch out to me . . . on 'my'

כסיא clearly have the singular חדר before them. 𝔐 is accordingly to be emended. However, משכית the meaning of which as "image, figure" is unquestionably fixed by Lev 26:1 אבן משכית "stone cut in relief"; Nu 33:52, was clearly no longer understood by the versions. 𝔗 presupposes משכב. Do the others point to a derivation from כסה (Cornill) or חשך? On the question of the originality of the passage, which Cornill and Fohrer doubt, cf. the exposition.

c 𝔐 אתנו is lacking in 𝔊, as also is the parallel 9:9 (which has a different order). The shorter text is more compact.

14   14a For הצפונה cf. Gesenius-Kautzsch § 90e.

b 𝔐 שם הנשים, in which Bertholet, Hölscher, *Hesekiel*, Fohrer, following 𝔊, read הנשים without the article, could be read as שמה נשים by a different word division without any further graphic change. שמה "there" is found also in 23:3; 32:29f; 48:35. However, the possibility cannot be excluded that the definite הנשים is original here and is to be interpreted according to Gesenius-Kautzsch § 126q. See above note a to v 5.

c 𝔊[Qmg] τὸν Ἀδωνιν, 𝔙 *Adonidem*.

15   15a 𝔊[MSS] of the Alexandrian text type 𝔏[CS] 𝔄 add here what follows in v 17a after בן אדם.

16   16a 𝔐 הָאוּלָם. This word only otherwise appears in the book of Ezekiel in chs. 40f, 44, 46 (thirty-two times in all). It varies in chs 40ff in its writing between the forms אֻלָם (אֻלָּם) and אֵילָם (אֵלָם). 𝔊 takes it throughout as a loan word in the form αιλαμ. According to F. Delitzsch (Baer-Delitzsch), Gesenius-Buhl, Fohrer, *Hauptprobleme*, 240, it is a technical building term, also a loan word in Hebrew, and is to be derived from the Akkadian *ellamu*, "front."

b 𝔐 כעשרים וחמשה. Two MSS 𝔊 𝔏[CS] Hier[test] read the number as twenty. Since the כעשרים (𝔊 ὡς εἴκοσι) points to a round number, 𝔐 must be regarded as a subsequent assimilation to 11:1.

c 𝔐 משתחויתם (𝔊 προσκυνοῦσι, 𝔗 מתחברין סגדין, 𝔙 *et adorabant*) is undoubtedly a scribal error for משתחוים.

d The superfluous second קדמה, which repeats what has been said, is lacking in 𝔊 𝔏[CS] ℭ[Bo] ℭ Arm and is rightly regarded by most commentators as a subsequent clarification.

17   17a 𝔊[MSS] of the Alexandrian text type and the Cat. group 𝔄 Arm read "House of Israel." 𝔏[S] connects the two readings: *domui ihl [sic] et iuda*. 𝔐 is to be retained as the *lectio difficilior*.

b וישבו להכעיסני is lacking in 𝔊 𝔏[S] ℭ[Bo] and is to be deleted. The addition has the purpose of joining the preceding beginning part of bα, against the originality of which serious doubt arises in spite of good textual evidence (cf. the exposition), better with the statement of bβ. Also grammatically it appears that the use of the hip'il of כעס, with the meaning "to provoke (Yahweh)," which is very common in the Deuteronomic writings (Jer, Kings), is completely

nose.^{c} 18/ Therefore I also will deal^a in wrath, my eye will not spare, and I will have no pity. [And they will cry out with a loud voice in my ears, but I will not hear them.]^b

9

1 And he cried in my ears with a loud voice: The woes of punishment^a for the city have drawn near [each with his weapon

absent in the book of Ezekiel up to 16:26 (cf. on the text). It occurs in another usage in 32:9 (*qal*); 16:42.

c זמורה cannot be interpreted with certainty. 𝕲 καὶ ἰδοὺ αὐτοὶ ὡς μυκτηρίζοντες gives here, as already in the description of the sinful acts in vv 3, 5, an abbreviation of the statement: "And behold, they are like those who turn up their noses," or "snort through their noses." Σ is clearly to be understood as a rewriting of the same sense, standing closer to the text: καὶ ὡς ἀφιέντες εἰσὶν ὡς ᾆσμα διὰ τῶν μυκτήρων αὐτῶν which Jerome translates: *quasi emittentes sonitum in similitudinem cantici per nares suas.* Is this the reticence of a person who has understood the text and does not wish to translate it, or the slip of a person who no longer fully understood the text? 𝔐 *tiq soph* (Wuerthwein, *Text*, 20) אפם instead of אפי, which must have preserved an older form of the text and given a meaning which was unacceptable to later ears. Does the objection in this lie simply in the anthropomorphic allusion to God (שלחים א . . . אל אפי) or beyond this to a particular coarseness in the expression? זמורה denotes in Nu 13:23; Is 17:10; Ezek 15:2; Na 2:3 the shoot of a vine, without any doubt. Thus Jerome translates here (𝔙): *et ecce applicant ramum ad nares suas* and in his commentary thinks of a palm branch (*quas graeco sermone βαία vocant*), which was held in the hands in idolatrous worship. 𝔗 והא אינון מיתן בהתא לאפיהון, by its translation of זמורה by בהתא (shame, disgrace), shows that in its view זמורה was something shameful. Thus already in the old translations a starting point is given for the more recent attempts at translation which will be dealt with in the exposition.

18 18a 𝔐 אעשה. 𝕲 ποιήσω αὐτοῖς appears to support the addition of a בהם, which could easily be regarded as having fallen out through haplography beside בחמה. However the absolute use of עשה in 𝔐 could have been chosen in deliberate correspondence with the use of עשה in the description of the sin in the temple (vv 6, 12, 17). 𝕲 could not have brought out this emphasis by a ποιήσω standing alone. Thus it adds αὐτοῖς. The absolute use of עשה in the mouth of Yahweh is found again in 20:9, 14, 22; 36:22, 32.

b V 18b is lacking in 𝕲, and its ideas fit better in the thought of Jeremiah than Ezekiel (Jer 11:11; 29:12, cf. also Ex 22:26; Zech 7:13). The sentence is an addition formed in dependence on 9:1aα.

9:1 9:1a The translation of קרבו is uncertain. Should it be regarded (by removal of the *metheg*) as qal imperative, with Ehrlich, *Randglossen*, Herrmann, Balla, Cooke and others (for the form cf. Ps 69:19 and Gesenius-Kautzsch § 46d), and the following פקדות taken as a personal address? ZB: "Draw near, you who have to carry out judgement on the city"; Hölscher, *Hesekiel*: "Draw near, you overseer of the city." Or is it to be regarded as pi'el imperative, construed impersonally? "Let men bring forth the

222

of destruction[b] in his hand].[c] 2/ And behold, six men[a] came from the upper gate,[b] which faces[c] north, each with his tool of destruction[d] in his hand, and in

punishments of the city." 𝕲 ἤγγικεν ἡ ἐκδίκησις τῆς πόλεως and 𝖁 *appropinquaverunt visitationes urbis* have regarded קרבו as qal perfect. פְּקֻדּוֹת is found again in the book of Ezekiel in 44:11 as a designation for the office of watchman at the gate. In this direction 𝔗 interprets פקדות as דממנן על קרתא "which have come upon the city." פקדה, however, is also a catchword for the prophetic preaching of woe. It is then as a rule bound with a temporal reference: יום פקדה Is 10:3; cf. Hos 9:7; Mic 7:4; עת פקדתם Jer 10:15; 46:21; 50:27; 51:18; שנת פקדתם Jer 11:23; 23:12; 48:44. In this connection the announcement, formulated in the perfect, that the punishment has come appears to be a fixed usage of the prophets of doom: Hos 9:7 באו ימי הפקדה cf. Mic 7:4. The free development of the expression in the hip'il imperfect is found in Jer 11:23; 23:12 שנת פקדתם . . . אביא. In content all these usages belong closely to the קרוב היום of Ezek 7:7 or the קרבו הימים of 12:23 and therefore also in the wider sphere of reference to the יום יהוה. See above pp. 201f. From this it becomes probable that also in 9:1 we must understand the word as a divine declaration. 9:1 therefore appears as a more concrete assertion alongside 7:7 and 12:23. A change of the plural פקדות into the singular (Toy, Bertholet with reference to 𝕲) is therefore not probable because in the plural פקדות clearly already, with its double meaning, hints at the plurality of the executioners which subsequently appears. Also elsewhere Ezekiel frequently makes reference to a number of judgements (14:12ff and other passages). Hos 9:7 ימי הפקדה shows another possibility of the plurality of judgement.

b 𝔐, כְּלִי 24 MSS (𝕲 𝔏ˢ 𝕲 𝖃) כְּלִי.

c V 1b is a well-attested, but secondary addition, which already presupposes the personal interpretation of the פקדות (and the imperative understanding of קרבו?), but which anticipates the assertions of v 2 in a disturbing manner. Also the fact that 𝕲 translates the כלי משחתו in a literal manner with τὰ σκεύη (plural cf. note b) τῆς ἐξολεθρεύσεως, but the כלי מפצו of v 2 in a summarizing way with πέλυξ (singular), points to two distinct translation hands and therefore to a secondary position of v 1b in 𝕲 also.

2a 𝔗 (Reuchlinianus) paraphrases the simple אנשים of 𝔐: מלאכיא מחבליא בדמות גברין.

b The שער without the article is striking beside העליון, but is supported by 2 Chr 23:20. We must therefore think of an abbreviation from שער בית יהוה העליון 2 Kings 15:35 (Ehrlich, *Randglossen*) or from שער בנימן העליון (Jer 20:2). Consequently the expression can then be understood by analogy with the names of other gates (שער הדגים, שער האשפת, שער הגיא) as a construct expression. Cf. the analogous phenomenon in Zech 14:10 שער הראשון, also שער הישנה Neh 3:6; 12:39.

c 𝔐 מָפְנֶה. The hop'al of פנה, however, is only found in Jer 49:8. To denote the direction of a gate

their midst a man, clothed in linen,[e] and with a scribe's instrument[f] at his side. And they entered and stood beside the bronze altar. 3/ And the glory of the God of Israel went up[a] from the cherubim,[b] on which[b] it was, (and went) to the podium[c] of the (temple-) house. And he called to the man clothed in linen,[d] who carried the instrument of a scribe[e] at his side, 4/ and [Yahweh][a] said to him: Go through the city [through Jerusalem][b] and draw a sign on the foreheads of the men who sigh and groan over all the abominations which are committed in their[c] midst. 5/ And to the others he said in my hearing: Go behind him through the city and smite. Your eye[a] shall not[b] spare, and you shall show no pity.

the book of Ezekiel otherwise uses the qal participle of פנה (8:3; 11:1; 44:1; 46:1, 12; 47:2; cf. 43:1) or the noun formula אשר פניו (40:6, 20, 22 and other passages). In 9:2 מפנה could be a scribal error for הפנה and have been made intelligible by the subsequent addition of אשר.

d 19 MSS 𝔊 read the plural here also. Cf. note b to v 1.

e 𝔐 בדים (לבש), 𝔊 (ἐνδεδυκὼς) ποδήρη (cf. Rev 1:13), 'A ἐξαίρετα (= praecipua, trans. Jerome), Σ λίνα, 𝔙 lineis.

f 𝔐 קסת, according to Eisler, "gśtj," a loan word from Egyptian gśtj. It is misunderstood by 𝔊 ζώνη σαπφίρου (perhaps קֹשְׁרֵי סַפֵּר?) ἐπὶ τῆς ὀσφύος αὐτοῦ, by 'A Θ corrected to καστυ γραμματέως by transliterating the unintelligible קסת; Σ πινακίδιον γραφέως, 𝔗 פינקס. A scribe's tablet is in mind here, so with 'A (2nd ed.) μελανοδοχεῖον, 𝔙 atramentarium of an ink pot. Cf. Jerome on the text.

3   3a The nip'al of עלה is found again in Ezekiel 36:3 with a quite different meaning. 10:4 uses the verb רום in a similar expression. However, the nip'al of עלה corresponds to the usage of P, which speaks in Ex 40:36f; Nu 9:17, 21f; 10:11 of the ascent of the cloud of Yahweh from the tent abode. Thus in spite of 𝔊 (𝔏ˢ 𝔖 𝔄) ἀνέβη it is not to be changed to the qal.

b The singular כרוב and עליו of 𝔐, which are confirmed by 10:(2) 4, are to be left. 𝔊 assimilates to the plural of 10:5, 7ff.

c 𝔊 τὸ αἴθριον (open space), 'AΣ τὸν οὐδόν, 𝔗 סקופא (the threshhold), 𝔙 limen. Cf. the exposition.

d 𝔐 הלבש הבדים. Ehrlich, Randglossen, would read לבש הבדים as in 9:11; 10:2, 6.

e 𝔊 τὴν ζώνην possibly did not have הספר, which is then also lacking in v 11 of 𝔐, in its Hebrew original.

4   4a 𝔐 יהוה is not attested by 𝔊 𝔏ˢ 𝔆ᴮᵒ. It has entered from the expansion of the text by v 3a (cf. the exposition). The reference to the כבוד יהוה made it appear advisable that Yahweh should be mentioned again at the beginning of the divine speech. Cf. also note a to 4:13.

b The repeated בתוך העיר בתוך ירושלם of 𝔐 is striking. In 𝔊 בתוך העיר is unattested. Cornill, however, rightly remarks that a ירושלם standing in the text could scarcely have been glossed by העיר. So בתוך ירושלם must be cut out as an explanatory gloss, which is supported by the word order, and 𝔊 must be regarded as a secondary abbreviation of a text already glossed. Cf. also 4:1.

c 𝔐 בתוכה is to be preferred to the ἐν μέσῳ αὐτῶν of 𝔊.

5   5a with Q, mlt MSS 𝔗 𝔙 עינכם is to be read. K, (𝔊 𝔏ˢ) עיניכם. Cf. 8:18.

b Instead of K על we must read with Q mlt MSS אל (𝔊 𝔏ˢ 𝔖 𝔗 presuppose וְאַל). The scribal error could be connected with the frequent interchange of the prepositions אל and על (note a to 1:17), which

6/ Old men 'and'ᵃ youths and young
women and infants and women you
shall kill and destroy.ᵇ But you shall not
come near anyone who carries the
mark. At my sanctuary you shall make
a beginning. So they began with the
men [, the elders,]ᶜ who stood in front
of the (temple-) house. 7/ And he said
to them: Desecrate the (temple-)
house and fill the courtsᵃ with slain.
'Then go out and slaughter' in the city.ᵇ
8/ Then it happened that when they
smote [and I was left (alone)]ᵃ I fell
downᵇ on my face and cried out and
said: Ah, [Lord]ᶜ Yahweh, will you
destroy the [entire]ᵈ remnant of Israel,
when you pour out your wrath over
Jerusalem? 9/ And he said to me: The
guilt of the house of Israel [and Judah]ᵃ
is very very great, andᵇ the land is full
of bloodguilt,ᶜ and the city is full of
injustice.ᵈ For they say: "Yahweh has
forsaken the land, and Yahweh does
not see (it)." 10/ So then my eye will
not spare, and I will show no pity.
Their ways have I brought upon their
own heads. 11/ And behold, the man
clothed in linen, who carried the
writing instrument at his side, brought
a message and said, I have done asᵃ you
commanded me.

10

1   And when I looked, behold, overᵃ the
fixed platform, which was above the
heads of the cherubim, there was
something like a sapphire, something
[resembling]ᵇ a throne [, which was

would then have been carelessly carried over here
to the negative אל.

6   6a With 𝕲 𝕷ˢ 𝕊 the copula is to be added in 𝔐,
which has fallen out through haplography beside
the preceding ן.

b Literally "to destroy."

c The הזקנים, which is asterisked by 𝕲ʰ, but is
only actually missing in 𝕲¹⁰⁶ 𝕮, is to be deleted as
an explanatory gloss. The "elders" stem from 8:11.
The text, according to Ziegler, *Ezechiel*, 19, 40f, is
evidence that 𝕲ᴮ has also undergone some hexaplaric influences. Cf. the introduction.

7   7a 𝕲 (𝕷ˢ) τὰς ὁδούς points to the reading החוצות,
which is, however, not to be preferred to 𝔐 (against
Cornill, Toy).

b 𝔐 צאו ויצאו והכו בעיר "Go out, and they went
out and smote in the city" is not in order. 𝕲 (𝕷ˢ)
ἐκπορευόμενοι καὶ κόπτετε clearly presupposes only a
single derivative of יצא. 𝕲 (𝕷ˢ), however, because
of its misreading of החצרות as החוצות (note a), is
forced to take the form of יצא as a participle to the
preceding. We must read with 𝕲 צאו והכו בעיר.
The בעיר, which is not attested by 𝕲, cannot be
easily given up because of the antithesis of בית and
עיר, which appears to be the basis of this verse (cf.
the exposition).

8   8a 𝔐 ונאשאר appears to be a mixed reading from
ונשאר and ואשאר, cf. Gesenius-Kautzsch § 64i. Read
וְנִשְׁאָר. "The finite verb is not in place; that he could
not likewise be struck down is obvious, and he had
no need to say so" (Hitzig). Since the whole circumstantial clause is lacking in 𝕲 𝕷ˢ, it must be
regarded as a subsequent addition by a tidy-minded
reader.

b 𝔐 ואפלה, cf. Gesenius-Kautzsch § 49e.

c אדני is lacking in 𝕲 𝕷ˢ 𝕮ᴮᵒ, see Excursus 1.

d 𝔐 כל is lacking in 𝕲 𝕷ˢ, cf. 11:13.

9   9a For "Judah," cf. *VT* 8 (1958):82.

b 𝕲 ὅτι ἐπλήσθη cf. 7:23.

c 𝔐 דמים, 𝕲 λαῶν πολλῶν, a striking continuation
of the scribal error of 7:23, cf. on this text. The edition Soncino 1485/6 (Prophets), 1488, Neapel 1491–
93, Brescia 1494 and Baer-Delitzsch read here חמס,
most likely under the influence of Gen 6:11, cf.
Ginsburg, Baer-Delitzsch on the text.

d מֻטֶּה is only found here in 𝔐, but cf. on 7:10.
𝖅 אסטיות דין (waiving of justice), 𝕭 *aversio*. 𝕲 offers
a double translation ἀδικίας καὶ ἀκαθαρσίας. Its second element could point to a variant טֻמְאָה.

11   11a Q ככל אשר, read with K Vers כאשר.

10:1 10:1a על – אל. Cf. note a to 1:17. 𝕲 ἐπάνω (τοῦ
στερεώματος) scarcely compels us to change to ממעל
(cf. 1:26 ממעל לרקיע) with Cornill, however.

b כמראה of 𝔐 stands appropriately in 1:26 before אבן ספיר. It is not attested by 𝕲 and is plainly
secondary, a gloss wrongly placed in the text from
1:26, cf. also 8:2.

c 𝔐 נראה עליהם 𝕲ᴮ, ⱽ ἐπ' αὐτῶν 𝕲ᴸᵘᶜ ἐπ' αὐτό
𝕲¹⁴⁷ ἐπ' αὐτοῦ 𝕲ʳᵉˡ ἐπ' αὐτῷ. In the Hexaplaric texts

visible]ᶜ over them. 2/ And he spoke to the man clothed with linenᵃ [and said]:ᵇ Go in to the place between the *galgal*ᶜ to the place underneath the cherubimᵈ and fill your hands with burning coals from the place between the cherubim, and scatter (them) over the city. And he went in before my eyes. 3/ Now the cherubim were standing on the right of the (temple-) house, when the man went in.ᵃ And the cloud filled the inner court. 4/ Then the glory of Yahweh went up from the cherubimᵃ to the podiumᵇ of the (temple-) house, and the (temple-) house was filled with the cloud, and the forecourt was filled with the brightness of the glory of Yahweh. 5/ And the sound of the wings of the cherubim was heard as far as the outer court—(a sound) like the voice of El Shaddai when he speaks. 6/ And it happened that when he commanded the man clothed in linen:ᵃ "take fire from the place between the *galgal*, from between the cherubim," he went in and stood beside the wheel. 7/ And the cherubᵃ stretched out his hand [between the cherubim]ᵇ to the fire,ᶜ which was between the cherubim,ᵈ and he lifted (it) and put (it) in the hands of the man clothed with linen,ᵉ and he took it and went out (into the city).

there appears an asterisked ὤφθη. The נראה of 𝔐 appears therefore, in any case, to be an addition. However, it is not necessary, in spite of Jerome's *super eam*, 𝔙 *super ea*, to change with Cornill the עליהם to עליו, by appealing to 1:26, since עליו in 1:26 is related differently.

2 2a 𝔊 reads here τὴν στολήν (differently in 9:2f, 11), 𝔊¹³⁰ (ℭᴮᵒ ℭ) τὸν ποδήρη, 𝔏ˢ (Armᵖ) *stolam scam* (= *sanctum*). Cf. note a to v 6.

b The second ויאמר, which is not attested by 𝔊, is superfluous and must have entered into the text as a result of the strong secondary editing of ch. 10 (cf. the exposition).

c 𝔐 אל בינות לגלגל, 𝔊 εἰς τὸ μεσον τῶν τροχῶν. For גלגל cf. the exposition.

d 𝔐 (Jerome) לכרוב, 𝔊 (𝔏ˢ 𝔗 𝔙) τῶν χερουβιν. After the pattern of 𝔊, 𝔐 is almost universally assimilated by commentators to the context, which speaks elsewhere except in 9:3, 10:4, 7aα¹ of כרובים. The formulation תחת לכרוב is, however, too peculiar over against the בינות לכרובים, which is found elsewhere (vv 2aβ², 6f), for us to smooth it away hastily. It should certainly be retained as the *lectio difficilior*, especially with the support of 9:3, 10:4, 7aα¹. Cf. the exposition.

3 3a 𝔐 בבאו has arisen from a careless transposition of א and ו and is to be emended in accordance with 𝔊 𝔏ˢ 𝔗 𝔊, to בבוא. Such misplacing of ו (י) and א with the verb בוא is surprisingly to be found no less than eight times in the book of Ezekiel (10:3; 14:1; 20:38; 22:4; 23:44; 33:22; 36:20; 44:25).

4 4a 𝔐 (𝔗 𝔙 𝔊) הכרוב, 𝔊 (𝔏ˢ) τῶν χερουβιν, cf. note b to 9:3, note d to 10:2 and the exposition.

b על – אל, cf. 9:3 and note a to 1:17. For מפתן cf. note c to 9:3.

6 6a 𝔊 (τῷ ἐνδεδυκότι) τὴν στολὴν τὴν ἁγίαν interprets the linen garment as sacred priestly clothing in accordance with Ex 28:4 בגדי קדש (𝔊 στολὰς ἁγίας). Has this interpretation entered secondarily in 𝔏 𝔊 Armᵖ? Or is there also in τὴν στολήν of 𝔊 the remnant of a fuller original reading τὴν στολὴν τὴν ἁγίαν?

7 7a הכרוב is not attested by 𝔊 𝔏ˢ ℭᴮᵒ. It raises the question whether the word represents an addition drawn from Is 6:6, giving expression to the view that the man clothed with a linen garment did not himself take the holy fire, but was given it by a divine creature. The final decision can only be made in the context of the exposition.

b 𝔐 מבינות לכרובים is lacking in 𝔊 𝔏ˢ and is a superfluous addition.

c 𝔐 אל האש. 𝔊 (𝔏ˢ) εἰς μέσον τοῦ πυρός strengthens the assertion in dependence on related formulations of the context.

d With vv 2 and 6 (and the addition, cf. note b to v 7) 17 MSS we could better read here בינות לכרובים.

e The verse section aβ, in which only the cherub can be the subject, was also read by 𝔊, although it

8/ And by the cherubim there appeared[a] something like a human hand[b] under their wings. 9/ And when I looked, behold, there were four wheels beside the cherubim, each[a] wheel beside a cherub,[b] and the appearance of the wheels was like the brightness of chrysolite. 10/ And as for their appearance, all four had the same[a] form, as though one wheel were inside another. 11/ When they went, they went on to the four sides[a] which they faced. They did not turn as they went, for in the direction which the front wheel faced, they followed behind it. They did not turn when they went. 12/ [And their whole body][a] And their rims (or backs)[b] [and their hands, their wings and their wheels][c] were all four full[d] of eyes round about [their wheels].[e] 13/ The wheels were called in my hearing *galgal*. [14/ And each one had four faces. The face of the first was that of a cherub, and the face of the second that of a man. And the third had the face of a lion, and the fourth that of an eagle.][a] [15/ And the cherubim went up.[a] These were the living creatures,[b] which I saw by the river[c] Chebar.][d] 16/ And when the cherubim went, the wheels (also) went beside them, and when the cherubim lifted their wings, in order to rise up from the earth, the wheels did not turn from beside them. 17/ When they stood still, then these stood still, and when they rose up, then these[a] rose up with them,[b] for the spirit of the living creatures[c] was in them.

does not attest the הכרוב in aα, and the clause aβ consequently becomes unintelligible. Cf. note a. In content it is striking that the messenger of doom can be designated as לבש הבדים, without the preceding האיש of vv 2 and 6. Cf. the exposition.

8   8a 𝔊 (𝔏ˢ 𝔖) καὶ εἶδον, 𝔊ᴬ 𝔄 καὶ ἰδού cf. v 9.

b 𝔐 תבנית יד אדם, 𝔊 (𝔏ˢ) ὁμοίωμα χειρῶν ἀνθρώπων. The singular יד of 𝔐, which is certainly the more original, may have led to the subsequent introduction of the hand of the cherub mentioned in v 7. 𝔊 harmonizes in accordance with 10:21. The reverse has happened in 1:8.

9   9a Gesenius-Kautzsch § 134q.

b הכרוב אחד Gesenius-Kautzsch § 134 l.

10   10a אחד. Cf. note c to 1:16.

11   11a Cf. note b to 1:17.

12   12a 𝔐 וכל בשרם is not attested by 𝔊 𝔏ˢ; cf. note c.

b 𝔐 וגבהם, read וְגַבֹּתָם, cf. note a to 1:18.

c The וידיהם וכנפיהם of 𝔐 is certainly attested by the versions, but undoubtedly belongs to a secondary elaboration of the text like the וכל בשרם of 𝔐, which is lacking in 𝔊. As in what precedes the wheels are mentioned and the original in 1:18 had in mind here also only the wheels, the elaboration relates the assertion to the cherubim, whose body, back (וגבתם is to be understood in this way), hands, and wings are now unexpectedly also covered with eyes. Since the גבתם originally related to the wheels, but is now additionally referred to the cherubim, it became necessary to mention the wheels (והאופנים) again at the conclusion.

d 𝔐 מלאים is related to the והאופנים, which directly precedes it in 𝔐. In the unelaborated text (note c) מְלֵאֹת will have stood, as in 1:18.

e The אופניהם of 𝔐, which goes beyond 1:18 and is not adapted syntactically, is clearly a marginal catchword which seeks to relate back to the wheels the statement about the cherubim in the later additions (note c). It is only unattested in 𝔏ˢ. 𝔊 harmonizes τοῖς τέσσαρσι τροχοῖς.

14   14a V 14, which is lacking in 𝔊 (𝔊ᴮ Hierᵗᵉˢᵗ, but not 𝔏ˢ), gives a variant form of 1:10 and undoubtedly belongs to the later parts of the text. Cf. the exposition.

15   15a 𝔐 וַיֵּרֹמּוּ is a nipʿal of רום, formed on the analogy of verbs ע״ע, cf. Gesenius-Kautzsch § 72 dd. Cf. further vv 17, 19; Nu 17:10.

b החיה, cf. note c to 1:20.

c בנהר occurs again in v 20 in the sense of על נהר of v 22.

d V 15a comes too soon before v 19. V 15b anticipates v 20. The whole of v 15, which together with vv 13, 14 and the additions in v 12 breaks up the section taken over from 1:15–21, is a later part of the text similar to these sections.

17   17a 𝔐 ירומו, cf. note a to v 15.

b אותם = אַתָּם, cf. note a to 2:1.

c 𝔐 החיה, cf. note c to 1:20.

18 And the glory of Yahweh went out from the (temple-) house [from the podium of the (temple-) house]ᵃ and mounted on the cherubim. 19/ And the cherubim lifted their wings and rose upᵃ from the earth before my eyes as they went away, and the wheels were beside them. And itᵇ went to the entrance of the east gate of the house of Yahweh, with the glory of the God of Israel over them. 20/ These were the living creatures,ᵃ which I had seen beneath the God of Israel by the riverᵇ Chebar. And I knew that they were cherubim. 21/ [Each]ᵃ had four faces and fourᵇ wings each. And under their wings was something like a human hand. 22/ And the form of their faces—they looked like the faces which I had seen by the river Chebarᵃ [their appearance]. 'They'ᵇ went every one straight forward.

11

1 And (the) spirit lifted me up and brought me to the east gate of the house of Yahweh, which faces east. And behold, at the entrance of the gate were twenty-fiveᵃ men. And I saw in their midst the rulers of the people, Jaazaniah, the son of Azzur, and Pelatiah, the son of Benaiah. 2/ And heᵃ said to me: Son of man, these are the men who plan iniquity and who plan evilᵇ in this city, 3/ who say: "Do not . . . build houses,ᵃ it is the pot, and we are the flesh." 4/ Therefore prophesy against them, prophesy, son of man. 5/ Then the spirit of Yahwehᵃ fell upon me, and he said to me: Say:ᵇ Thus has Yahweh spoken, Thus have you spoken, house of Israel, and what arisesᶜ in your spirit, I know (well). 6/ You have made numerous your slain in this city, and have filled its streets with slain.ᵃ

---

18 18a 𝔊 𝔏ˢ 𝔖 point to a Hebrew original which had simply מן הבית in place of the מעל מפתן הבית of 𝔐. From this the preceding ויצא, where we should have expected a nipʿal of רום, נשא or עלה in 𝔐, becomes intelligible.

19 19a וירומו, cf. note a to v 15.
b 𝔐 ויעמד. The subject is כבוד יהוה of v 18; 𝔊 (𝔏ˢ 𝔖) smooth the difficult text, but cf. the analysis on p. 232.

20 20a 𝔐 החיה, cf. note c to 1:20.
b 𝔐 בנהר כבר, cf. note c to v 15.

21 21a The doubling of ארבעה, which is not found in the parallel v 21aβ and is also not attested by the original in 1:6, is scarcely authentic, cf. 𝔊 𝔏ˢ 𝔙.
b 𝔊 (𝔏ˢ) ὀκτώ. Was the doubling of ארבעה (note a) read in reference to the wings? 𝔠ᴮᵒ 𝔄 sex (in accordance with Is 6:2).

22 22a 𝔊 𝔏ˢ add ὑποκάτω τῆς δόξης θεοῦ Ισραηλ, cf. v 20.
b 𝔐 מראיהם ואותם. 𝔊 καὶ αὐτὰ (ἕκαστον κατὰ πρόσωπον αὐτῶν ἐπορεύοντο) appears only to have had והם, which could, by a scribal error, lie in the otherwise unintelligible וא[ותם. In the מראיהם (𝔊ᴸ, ³¹¹, ⁴⁶, ⱽ, cf. Σ τοῦ εἴδους αὐτῶν, Θ τὴν ὅρασιν αὐτῶν), which is admittedly already attested by 𝔏ˢ et aspectum earum; et ipsa (singula contra faciem suam ibant), we must see a subsequent interpretative remark.

11:1 11:1a 𝔊 introduces, as in 8:16, a ὡς. Since the number twenty-five gives the impression of being precise, unlike the round figure of twenty in 8:16 (note b), preference must be given to 𝔐.

2 2a 𝔊 (𝔏ˢ 𝔖) clarifies by the insertion of κύριος, cf. note a to 4:13.
b עצת רע, literally "counsel of evil," cf. עצת שלום Zech 6:13.

3 3a For the translation cf. the exposition. 𝔊 interprets the quotation as a question: οὐχὶ προσφάτως (Σ ἀρτίως) ᾠκοδόμηνται αἱ οἰκίαι "Have not the houses been built recently?"; 𝔏ˢ nonne inrecentia aedificatae sunt domus? 𝔙 nonne dudum aedificatae sunt domus?

5 5a 𝔐 יהוה is not attested by 𝔊 𝔏ˢ.
b 𝔐 אמר is lacking in 𝔊 𝔏ˢ Arm Thdrt (for 𝔊ᴮ, which was here influenced by the Hexapla, cf. Ziegler, Ezechiel, 41).
c In the plural מעלות, to which the singular suffix of 𝔐 ידעתיה relates, the verbal components could be so strong that it was taken up as a neutral statement in the third singular feminine. However, since 𝔊 𝔏ˢ 𝔙 have no hint of a suffix in their underlying original, the subsequent formation of the suffix through dittography of the following (רביתם)ה is more probable (Cornill). For the usage מעלות רוחכם cf. the related formulations in 14:3; 20:32; 38:10.

6 6a The variations of the repeated חלל of 𝔐 in 𝔊 νεκρούς – τραυματιῶν, 𝔏ˢ mortuos- vulneratis does not point to a different Hebrew original (against Herrmann, Bertholet). Cf. also 𝔙 and 𝔊 in 11:7.

7/ Therefore thus has [the Lord]ª Yahweh spoken: Your slain, whom you have laid in its midst, they are the flesh, and it is the pot. But Iᵇ will bring you out from its midst. 8/ You have feared the sword—and I will bring the sword upon you, says [the Lord]ª Yahweh. 9/ And I will bring you out from the midst of it,ª and give you into the hands of foreigners, and execute judgements upon you. 10/ You shall fall by the sword; by the bordersª of Israel I will judge you, and you shall know that I am Yahweh. [11/ It shall not be the pot for you, so that you become the flesh in it.ª By the borders of Israel I will judge you, 12/ and you shall know that I am Yahweh (, according to whose statutes you have not walked and whose ordinances you have not fulfilled; rather you have acted according to the laws of the nations which are round about you).]ª 13/ However when I prophesied then it came about that Pelatiah, the son of Benaiah, died. And I fell on my face and cried with a loud voice and said: Ah,ª [Lord]ᵇ Yahweh, will youᶜ completely destroy the remnant of Israel?

14 And the word of Yahweh came to me: 15/ Son of man, all your brethren,ª the members of your familyᵇ and the whole house of Israel, all of them,ª of whom the inhabitants of Jerusalem say: "They are farᶜ from Yahweh, to us ' 'ᵈ has the land been given for a possession"—

7

7a אדני is lacking in 𝔊 𝔏ˢ, see Excursus 1.

b 𝔐 הוציא. With 33 MSSᴷᵉⁿ 7 MSSᴿᵒˢˢⁱ 𝔏ˢ 𝔗 𝔊 𝔙 אוציא is to be read.

8

8a אדני is lacking in 𝔊 𝔏ˢ, see Excursus 1.

9

9a Vv 8–9aα is lacking in 𝔊⁵³⁴⁻⁸⁶·¹⁰⁶ (v 8 also in ℭᴮᵒ), through homoioteleuton. So Ziegler.

10

10a 𝔊 ἐπὶ τῶν ὁρίων is wrongly written in 𝔊ᴮ and the majority of 𝔊ᴹˢˢ (cf. also v 11) as ἐπὶ τῶν ὀρέων (influenced by 6:2; 36:1?), thence 𝔏ˢ *in montibus*.

11

11a 𝔊 (cf. note a to v 12) 𝔏ˢ 𝔊 𝔙 expand the negation in aβ (according to the sense). 𝔐 treats the quotation from v 3 as a whole and makes the introductory negation suffice.

12

12a Vv 11–12aα are lacking in 𝔊ᴮ·⁴⁶·⁴³⁴⁻⁸⁶ ℭᴮᵒ 𝔄. The relative clause in v 12aββb, giving the motive, first appears in the latest (Hexaplaric and Lucianic) phase of the Greek text tradition and is missing also in 𝔏ˢ. Ziegler ascribes vv 11–12a to the original 𝔊 text and conjectures that it fell out through homoioteleuton in the first mentioned group of witnesses. However, since the verses are, in their entire construction, a briefly summarized repetition of vv 7–10, it must be strongly questioned whether the first mentioned text group, in which vv 11f are completely missing, offers the original text of 𝔊. In the later history of the text we can see clearly its elaboration in two phases.

13

13a 𝔐 אהה. The double οἴμμοι οἴμμοι (𝔏ˢ *heu me* [h]eu me) of 𝔊 is striking, but may not point to a different Hebrew original in view of the parallels in 4:14; 9:8; 21:5 and the fact that אהה in 𝔐 never appears doubled. 𝔙 gives it three times *heu heu heu*.

b אדני is lacking in 𝔊 𝔏ˢ ℭᴮᵒ, see Excursus 1.

c The versions and the analogy of 9:8 support the addition of a ה-interrogative before 𝔐 כלה, which has disappeared through haplography.

15

15a The doubling of אחיך, which is not attested by 5 MSS 𝔊 𝔏ˢ 𝔖, is striking. However, the fact that also in the כָּל־בֵּית יִשְׂרָאֵל כֻּלֹּה (for the usage of the emphasizing of an expression formed with כל by a second כל with suffix, which is peculiar to Ezekiel, cf. further 20:40; 35:15; 36:10) a similar underscoring of the parallel ישראל is found points against the deletion of one אחיך. The doubling gives the idea of "every, all," according to Gesenius-Kautzsch § 123c.

b 𝔊 οἱ ἄνδρες τῆς αἰχμαλωσίας σου, 𝔏ˢ *viri captivitatis tuae* have not understood 𝔐 אנשי גאלתך (unlike 𝔗 איניש קריבך and 𝔙 *viri propinqui tui*) and have interpreted it as אנשי גלותך, which is not to be followed (against Cornill, Toy, Bertholet, Fohrer). Cf. the exposition.

c 𝔐 רַחֲקוּ "Go away" is to be vocalized with Hitzig (following Abarbanel and Jarchi) and most modern scholars as the perfect רָחֲקוּ.

d In 33:24b, where the expression reappears, the unusual היא is lacking. It is perhaps a subsequent addition of emphasis. We ought not to delete הארץ (Herrmann), since היא has otherwise no word to

229

16/ Therefore say:[a] Thus has [the Lord][b] Yahweh said: Indeed, I have removed them far away among the nations, and I have scattered them among the countries, and I have been a sanctuary to them (only) a little in the countries to which they have come [. 17/ Therefore say:[a] Thus has (the Lord)[b] Yahweh spoken, I will gather you[c] from the peoples and bring you[c] together from the countries in which you[c] have been scattered, and give you[c] the land of Israel. (18/ And they will come there and remove from it all its detestable things and all its abominations.)],[a] 19/ but I will give them another[a] heart and put a new spirit within them,[b] and remove the stone heart out of their body and give them a heart of flesh, 20/ so that they may walk in my statutes, and keep my laws and do them; and become my people, and I shall be their God, 'says Yahweh' (?).[a] [21/ 'These, however, in their hearts have gone after'[a] their detestable things and abominations. I will bring their ways upon their head.][a]

22 Then the cherubim lifted their wings, with the wheels beside them, whilst the glory of the God of Israel stood over them. 23/ And the glory of Yahweh rose up from the midst of the city and stood upon the mountain,[a] which is on the east side of the city. 24/ And (the) spirit lifted me up and brought me to Châldea, to the exiles, in the vision[a] by the spirit of God. Then the vision[a] which I had seen went up away from me.[b] 25/ And I told the exiles all the words of Yahweh, which he had shown me (in the vision).

16
16a אמר is lacking in 8 MSS 𝔊 𝔙, but is, how-ever, attested by 𝔊 𝔏ˢ 𝔗 (against BH³).
b אדני is lacking in 𝔊 𝔏ˢ ℭᴮᵒ, see Excursus 1.

17
17a אמר is lacking in 10 MSS 𝔊ᴬ, ²³³ 𝔄 (𝔏ˢ *dicit*). It would clearly have been regarded as superfluous beside v 16.
b אדני is lacking in 𝔊 𝔏ˢ ℭᴮᵒ, see Excursus 1.
c 𝔊 𝔏ˢ assimilate throughout to v 16 and read the third plural instead of the second plural of 𝔐. How-ever, v 17 stems, as is shown by the slight change of the parallelism ארצות – גוים v 16 to עמים – ארצות v 17, from another hand than that of v 16. There exists no necessity therefore to assimilate it stylisti-cally to v 16.

18
18a The renewed break in the style (transition to third plural) shows that v 18 cannot be the original continuation of v 17. In its content it presupposes the statement of v 17 and is thus to be regarded as a further late interpretation of v 17, which falls back into the style of the impersonal speech of the original text.

19
19a Instead of the difficult אחד of 𝔐 (𝔙 *cor unum*, 'ΑΣΘ καρδίαν μίαν), 𝔊 καρδίαν ἑτέραν (𝔏ˢ *cor aliud*) presupposes אחר. 3 MSS 𝔊 and 𝔐 in 36:26 (18:31) raise the question whether חדש is to be read, which could then have been expanded to אחד by a muti-lated writing as חד. 𝔊 could then be understood as a subsequent attempt at interpretation of the לב אחד, which is also found in Jer 32:39. 𝔗 interprets as לב דחיל ורוח דחלא.
b 𝔐 בקרבכם is (under the influence of v 17 and 36:26, or through simple dittography of the כ–ב) a scribal error and is to be read as בקרבם with Or MSS Edd Vrs.

20
20a The λέγει κύριος found in 𝔊ᴬ, ᶜᵃᵗ (𝔊ʰ 𝔏ˢ ℭᴮᵒ 𝔄) could point to a concluding נאם יהוה as original here, cf. note a to v 21.

21
21a 𝔐 וְאֶל־לֵב. The beginning of v 21, which is quite clearly an addition, is mutilated. The versions offer no help for a restoration of the text. Cornill's conjecture of ואלה אחרי may come close to the ori-ginal meaning. Cf. 20:16.

23
23a 𝔗 interprets more fully טור זיתא.

24
24a מַרְאֶה here and in 43:3 is synonymous with מַרְאָה, see above pp. 116f.
b 𝔊 (𝔏ˢ) recasts in the first person καὶ ἀνέβην ἀπὸ τῆς ὁράσεως, which does not, however, point to a different Hebrew original (against Hitzig, Cornill).

Form

Ezekiel 8–11 describes a great vision experienced by the prophet in a state of ecstasy. In his exilic abode the hand of God falls upon him. By a figure which recalls in its appearance the divine figure of ch. 1, he is brought to Jerusalem. In four stages he sees there four abom-inations on a route which brings him to a place directly in front of the temple. 8:4 then affirms quite incidental-ly the presence there of "the glory of the God of Israel." Equally incidentally 9:3 then notes, in a description of the judgement which goes out from the temple upon the sinful city, that the glory of the God of Israel has gone up from the cherubim chariot. The judgement itself is carried out by six agents of destruction, beside whom a seventh figure is given the commission to mark with a sign those who are to be spared the judgement. The initial killing in the temple forces from the prophet a despairing cry, which is, however, sharply cut short by Yahweh and is answered by a charge to the separate figure to throw fire upon the city. In the drama of these events the glory of Yahweh, described remarkably lengthily with statements from ch. 1, begins to depart from the temple, at first only as far as the east gate of the temple area. Then it vanishes. Rather surprisingly we find ourselves in 11:1ff facing an assembly of men who clearly know nothing of the destruction of the temple and city which is already in course of accomplishment. They are first concerned in it through the word given to the prophet himself of an initial blow which kills one of their number and which serves as a sign. The divine word, which answers the renewed cry of the prophet, deals with the difference between those who remain in Jerusalem (how are we to understand this from vv 9f?) and those who are deported. Only then follows in 11:22f the final departure of the divine glory from the city and the return of the prophet to his situation in exile.

Ezek 8–11 is intended, as is shown by the reference back to the beginning in the conclusion, to be understood as an account of a connected visionary experience. The narrative unevenness, which our brief survey has already encountered, raises the question whether we must reckon here also with a later development of the text which has altered its original form. Thus a literary analysis must precede all form critical considerations.

Quite directly 11:1–21 is marked out as a foreign element in the surrounding section. The meeting of the men at the east gate in vv 1–13 is in no way to be expected after the departure of the destroying figures in 9:7f and the setting out of the seventh man with fire to burn the city in 10:7. Also the judgement, which according to 11:13 happens as a sign to one of them at the word of the prophet, is in substance of quite a different kind from the total judgement of chs. 9f, accomplished by the divine destroying figures. The unexpected ignoring of the divine glory of Yahweh (according to 10:19 present at the east gate) by the whole assembly and by the prophet himself may be noted as well. Since further the sins mentioned in 11:2ff deviate completely from the direction of ch. 8 (cultic abominations), the direct connection of 11:1ff with ch. 8, conjectured by Herntrich, Harford, and Bertholet, which also breaks up the close connection of chs. 8–9, is in no way likely.

On the contrary, the theme of 11:1ff leads directly into the divine speech of 11:14–21, which it considerably broadens by the confrontation between Jerusalem citizens and exiles. Thus the divine speech, which is introduced by a fresh formula for the coming of a message, must be understood in the same temporal connection as the divine answer to the prophet's cry in 11:13.[1]

Even more difficult questions arise in ch. 10. Three facts quickly emerge on a closer examination of the text:

1) The description of the glory of Yahweh shows a remarkable disorder in its detailed assertions. V 1 begins quite abruptly with a description of the divine throne above the platform. However, this theme is then immediately dropped. V 5 describes the sound of the wings, v 8 the putting forth of a human hand under the wings of the cherubim. The assertion reappears with slight changes in v 21. In vv 9–13 the wheels and their movement are introduced. V 14 then speaks of the four faces of the creatures bearing the throne. Then v 21 again comes back to this. V 15 speaks of the going up of the cherubim and thereby anticipates v 19, so that v 15b reappears, with a slight addition, in v 20a. Vv 16f describe the movement of the wheels and cherubim. The reference to the movement of the faces straight ahead in v 22b stands in marked contrast to this.

2) This diffuse description of the glory shows strong verbal contacts with ch. 1 in its details. Cf. v 1 with 1:26; v 5 with 1:24; v 8 with 1:8; vv 9–12 with 1:15–18; v 14 with 1:6, 10; vv 16f with 1:19–21; v 21 with 1:6, 8; v 22b with 1:9b. Exact comparison of the text has already shown earlier that the parallels in ch.

---

1   See above pp. 144f. The formula is strange in the context of a description of a vision, and essentially unrelated.

10 show a text which has been subsequently worked over so that it no longer preserves the unevenness in the use of suffixes which was characteristic of ch. 1.[2]

3) The relationship to ch. 1 finally hardens into definite assertions of identity. The repeated references back in vv 15, 20 to the divine manifestation by the River Chebar have their prototype already in 3:23 (cf. further 8:4; 43:3). More peculiar is the emphatic identification in v 15 of the creatures bearing the throne, which throughout ch. 10 are designated as cherubim, with the "creatures" (חיה) of 1:20b, formulated quite personally, "And I knew that they were cherubim." Finally and instructively the reader is told here that the cherubim and the "creatures" are one and the same. The strength of the emphasis allows the conjecture that things have been subsequently brought together here which at first had a quite separate existence. The same process is found in v 13 at a second point. "The wheels were named in my hearing גלגל." The peculiar term גלגל, used in vv 2 and 6 in Yahweh's speech, is identified with the אופנים of ch. 1. Again this expresses what was clearly not obvious from the start. We must therefore consider that the hand of a commentator freely introduced the כרובים, which are not mentioned in ch. 1, into the additions which are drawn from that chapter and only mentioned the term חיה of ch. 1 in the two parentheses of vv 15 and 20. Conversely, however, the term גלגל, used in the basic text of ch. 10, could not displace the term אופנים in the additions drawn from ch. 1.

When we attempt, in accordance with these general considerations, to separate off the individual elements of the secondary expansion, 10:1, which breaks up the sequence of 9:11/10:2, immediately falls out of its context. The complex dealing with the wheels in 1:15–21 is found again in a slightly varied form in 10:9–12, 16–17. Then 10:13–15, which breaks up this connection, is clearly a still later addition.[3] 10:8, which precedes the section 10:9–17, comments rather belatedly upon the hand of the cherubim referred to in v 7 by the use of statements from 1:8. The description in vv 20–22, which comes late in the sequence of the initial departure of the divine glory, is in parenthesis. V 20(22a) is a subsequent definition (parallel to v 15). The description of the four faces (also in v 14) and four wings in v 21a derives from 1:6. That of the hands (also in v 8) comes from 1:8, and of their movement in v 22b from 1:9.

In 10:18f, which is left as a transition to 11:22ff, it is striking that beside the simple כבוד יהוה of v 18a there stands the fuller כבוד אלהי ישראל in v 19bβ, a repetition which reappears in the reverse order in the concluding 11:22f. In both places the fuller reference is connected with the appearance of the glory of Yahweh enthroned above the cherubim. In 10:19 the unusual change of subject (plural-singular-plural) is further noteworthy. At one time it presupposes the action of the cherubim and at another that of the glory of Yahweh (the parallel ויעמד of 11:23 supports this understanding). This leads to the recognition that we have here two different conceptions of the movement of the glory of Yahweh: a simpler one which speaks of the כבוד יהוה and leaves it to move by itself (10:18a, 19bα, 11:23), and a much more complicated one. In the former there is always a connected statement about movement (ויצא 10:18; ויעל 11:23a) and an immediately following reference to standing still (ויעמד) at the new resting-place (10:19bα; 11:23b). The latter is already shown by the fuller כבוד אלהי ישראל, according to which the divine glory is seated upon its cherubim chariot and is transported by it. 10:18b, which anticipates the ויעמד of v 19bα, skillfully achieves a redactional transition from the simpler to the more complicated conception. The original conception can accordingly be seen in 10:18a, 19bα, 11:23, and the secondary elaboration in 10:18b, 19abβ; 11:22.

The removal of the elements which are identified by the fuller description of the divine glory as the כבוד אלהי ישראל also involves the two references to the presence of the glory of Yahweh in 8:4; 9:3a, which were already noted in the first survey because of their lack of connection with the context. They stem either from the same or a later hand, which was oriented to the stratum of interpretation outlined above.

In the remaining vv 2–7 of ch. 10 it is at once striking

---

2   See above p. 104.
3   Cf. further the notes to vv 14, 15.

that, after the brief command of Yahweh to the man clothed in linen (v 2a) and the account of its initial execution (v 2b), the appearance of the throne is described again. There then follows a further, slightly varied repetition of the content of v 2 (in v 6) of the final accomplishment of Yahweh's command by the man clothed with linen (v 7). With this there is the substantial consideration that in vv 2—7 there undoubtedly stood in strong tension a view which presupposes one cherub (singular) against a second view which speaks of cherubim (plural). V 4, which speaks of a cherub in the singular, uses the simple כבוד יהוה, which also belongs in vv 18f to the basic text which had not yet been elaborated from ch. 1, with its plurality of throne-bearers. The basic text, which is to be seen in vv 2 (without מבינות לכרבים), 4 and 7 (without אשר בינות הכרבים and מבינות לכרובים), spoke in the singular of a cherub. The assimilation has multiplied this in accordance with ch. 1.[4]

With the anticipation of some further excisions from chs. 8f (8:2, 7b, 8, 17bα; 9:7), which will be justified in the detailed exposition, the basic text of chs. 8–11 runs accordingly:

> And it happened in the sixth year, in the sixth month, on the fifth (day) of the month, as I sat in my house, with the elders of Judah sitting before me, that the hand of Yahweh fell upon me. And when I looked, behold, there (appeared) a form of a man. And he stretched out something like a hand and took me by the hair of my head; and (the) spirit lifted me up between heaven and earth and brought me in visions of God to Jerusalem, to the entrance of the gate which faces north, where was the position of the image of jealousy. And he (i.e., Yahweh) said to me: Son of man, raise your eyes northwards. And I raised my eyes to the north, and behold, in the north of the gate there stood an altar—the image of jealousy itself stood in the entrance. And he said to me: Son of man, do you see what they are doing? Great abomination they commit here, by which they depart from my sanctuary. But you will see still greater abominations. And he brought me to the entrance of the forecourt.

And he said to me: Go in and see the abominations which they are committing here. Then I went in and saw. And behold, all kinds of abominations and all kinds of idols of the house of Israel were cut as engravings in the wall round about. And seventy men of the elders of the house of Israel stood (as servants) before them, each one with his censer in his hand, and the scent of the incense went up. And he said to me: Have you seen, son of man, what the elders of the house of Israel are doing, each one in his room of pictures? For they say: "Yahweh does not see (it); Yahweh has forsaken the land." And he said to me: You shall see still greater abominations which they do. And he brought me to the entrance of the gate of the house of Yahweh, which lies towards the north, and behold, there were women who were sitting down and weeping for Tammuz. And he said to me: Have you seen, son of man? You shall see still greater abominations than these. And he brought me into the inner court of the house of Yahweh, and behold, at the entrance of the temple of Yahweh, between the entrance room and the altar, (stood) about twenty men, with their backs to the temple of Yahweh, and their faces turned toward the east, prostrating themselves and worshipping before the sun. And he said to me: Have you seen, son of man? Is it too slight a thing for the house of Judah to commit the abominations which they have commited here—[for they have filled the land with violence(?)] behold, now they stretch out to me . . . on my nose. Therefore I also will deal in wrath, my eye will not spare, and I will have no pity.

And he cried in my ears with a loud voice: The woes of punishment for the city have drawn near. And behold, six men came from the upper gate, which faces north, each with his tool of destruction in his hand, and in their midst a man, clothed in linen, and with a scribe's instrument at his side. And they entered and stood beside the bronze altar. And he (i.e., Yahweh) called to the man clothed in linen, who carried the instrument of a scribe at his side, and said to him: Go through the city and draw a sign on the foreheads of the men who sigh and groan over all the abominations which are committed in their midst. And to the others he said in my hearing: Go behind him through the city and smite. Your eye shall not spare, and you shall show no pity. Old men and

---

4   The question how far thereby the original understanding of the text has been changed must be examined in the detailed exposition. Similarly the question, whether or not we should follow Hölscher, *Hesekiel, der Dichter*, J. Herrmann, *Ezechielstudien*, Fohrer and others in regarding the original basis of ch. 10 as separate from the vision of chs. 8f must be examined there.

youths and young women and infants and women you shall kill and destroy. But you shall not come near anyone who carries the mark. At my sanctuary you shall make a beginning. So they began with the men who stood in front of the (temple-) house. Then it happened that when they smote I fell down on my face and cried out and said: Ah, Lord Yahweh, will you destroy the remnant of Israel, when you pour out your wrath over Jerusalem? And he said to me: The guilt of the house of Israel is very very great, and the land is full of bloodguilt, and the city is full of injustice. For they say: "Yahweh has forsaken the land, and Yahweh does not see (it)." So then my eye will not spare, and I will show no pity. Their ways have I brought upon their own heads. And behold, the man clothed in linen, who carried the writing instrument at his side, brought a message and said: I have done as you commanded me. And he spoke to the man clothed with linen: Go in to the place between the *galgal* to the place underneath the cherubim and fill your hands with burning coals, and scatter (them) over the city. And he went in before my eyes. Then the glory of Yahweh went up from the cherubim to the podium of the (temple-) house, and the (temple-) house was filled with the cloud, and the forecourt was filled with the brightness of the glory of Yahweh. And the cherub stretched out his hand to the fire, and he lifted (it) and put (it) in the hands of the man clothed with linen, and he took it and went out (into the city).

And the glory of Yahweh went out from the (temple-) house and went to the entrance of the east gate of the house of Yahweh. And the glory of Yahweh rose up from the midst of the city and stood upon the mountain, which is on the east side of the city. And (the) spirit lifted me up and brought me to Chaldea, to the exiles, in the vision by the spirit of God. Then the vision which I had seen went up away from me. And I told the exiles all the words of Yahweh, which he had shown me (in the vision).

The Traditio-Historical Background. Ezekiel narrates a great ecstatic experience. Features of similar ecstatic experiences under the "hand" or the "spirit" (of Yahweh) are to be found already in 3:12, 14, 22f; cf. further 37:1. In these references the account of the experience describes mysteriously the internal aspect of an outwardly normal activity of the prophet.[5] In 8:1ff (and 40:1ff) the ecstatic occurrence is heightened in that the prophet is removed over great distances on a route which he could certainly not have traversed at the same time on foot from Babylon to Jerusalem. 8:1ff, in contrast with 40:1ff, further contains a stronger coloring in that the feeling of physical removal is described quite objectively as a lifting by the hair

between heaven and earth.

First of all we must affirm that, as the texts cited show, so far as a definite vocabulary is discernible, we are certainly not dealing with a cliché-like stereotyped conception. The intensity of the exceptional physical experiences is clearly heightened from 3:23; 37:1, over 3:12, 14 to 40:1ff, and finally to 8:1ff. In every case the ecstatic phenomenon not only meant a physical experience, but spiritually the crossing of the threshold dividing normal objective perception from the underlying reality which is not discernible in the sober light of day. Certainly Ezek 8 is full of objective facts which everyone in Jerusalem was similarly capable of perceiving. However, ch. 8 is also dominated by the voice and guidance of Yahweh which was not discernible to the uninitiated ear. In ch. 9 supernatural figures appear who enter before the prophet's eye into the temple area. 40:1ff presents a reality which in the future will be an element of faith, but for Yahweh in any case is already real. 37:1ff presents a situation in a vision of something which is purely symbolic and which never happens in such a way on earth, nor will do so in the future.

When we inquire about the earlier history of such ecstatic prophetic experiences the result is that we sometimes find with the great pre-exilic writing prophets accounts of a visionary seeing of hidden realities (Amos 7:1–8; 8:1–2; 9:1; Jer 1:11–16; 4:23–26). In Is 6:6f; 8:11; Jer 1:9 there is also mention of being physically touched by a supernatural hand. A full experience of ecstatic transportation is looked for here in vain. However, within the older prophetic narratives there is again mention of such. The fear of Obadiah, Ahab's steward, and the prophet-pupil's inquiry for Elijah in Jericho: "Perhaps the spirit of Yahweh has taken him (נשׂאו) and cast him (וישׁלכהו) on a mountain or in one of the valleys" (2 Kings 2:16), betray an awestruck faith in the possibility of such mysterious ecstatic transportations which a "man of the spirit" could experience.[6] These are regarded as quite physical happenings, separate from any visionary revelation (cf. 1 Kings 18:46). Furthermore these prophetic narratives also speak of the supernatural seeing of contemporary earthly (2 Kings 6:32f) and heavenly (1 Kings 22:19; 2 Kings 6:14ff) realities, as also of those that are imminent in the future (2

Kings 8:7ff). The closest parallel to Ezek 8, where the prophet sees in his ecstatic experience the sinful activity of the citizens of Jerusalem with his own eyes, is found in 2 Kings 5:26. Here Elisha discloses to Gehazi, coming along the road with an innocent bearing, that he has seen how the latter has accepted a reward from the restored Naaman, contrary to the express command of his master, "Was not [read הלא] my heart present when a man turned back from his chariot to meet you?" Ezek 9, however, the seeing of a commission to a heavenly assistant of Yahweh, recalls 2 Kings 6:16f, a text which certainly lacks the element of ecstasy. In any case it allows no doubt that Ezekiel, even in his most marked ecstatic experiences, stands in line with an older tradition, which otherwise bypasses classical prophecy and which connects him directly with the prophetic traditions of the Elijah-Elisha period. The undervaluing of these features as mere redactional material intended to maintain the fiction of the prophet's exile (Herntrich and others) undoubtedly denies the weight of this connection with an older tradition.[7]

Ezekiel stands in the line of this tradition not only as a pupil, but as a unique creator. The fact that afterwards the features of Ezek 8:3 entered into the style of the descriptions of ecstasy (Bel and the Dragon, 36; *Gospel of the Hebrews Frag.*, 2a) must not hide the vital variations of the experiences in 3:12, 23; 8:1ff; 37:1; 40:1ff, with all their use of traditional language. Above all we must say that the miraculous substantiation of the ecstatic experiences, as is seen in 1 Kings 18:2; 2 Kings 2:16, is not found with Ezekiel. The transportation is here the threshhold to a vision and the word of Yahweh contained in the vision, which is proclaimed to the exiles after the ending of the vision (11:25).

On closer examination the vision of chs. 8–11 shows in its original form a quite clear structure in accordance with the scheme of a two-part prophetic oracle. The word of the prophet appears in the order: 1) motivating reproach, 2) declaration of judgement.[8] A comparison with the prophetic sayings of 1 Kings 20 shows further that, in place of a motive clause introduced by יען אשר (v 28), a question can appear introduced by הראית (v 13), which points to the evident fact of the sin of those involved in the declaration of judgement.[9] What is seen by Ezekiel in his ecstatic transportation is clearly stylized according to this pattern of the prophetic message. Ezek 8 shows the sinful conditions in Jerusalem which occasion the judgement. Chs. 9f speak of the judgement arising from this. The motivating first part (ch. 8) further undergoes a particular stylizing when there is brought before the eyes of the prophet not just a single sin committed in Jerusalem, but four of them, which are underscored by the divine question הראית or הראה אתה. We have established earlier of the number four that it expresses the totality of an event or sphere.[10] Accordingly, by the four sins Ezekiel is shown the whole fullness of sin in Jerusalem. It is therefore highly improbable that in 11:1ff we have a fifth sin, separated from its original position after ch. 8. Ch. 8 presents the reasons for the judgement, which are not introduced in any accidental way, but which represent a significant series of four, set out according to a definite plan.[11]

Setting

By this refusal to separate the assertions of chs. 8–11 from their setting in an ecstatic experience, which is implicit in the preceding, we have already arrived at a decision regarding the locality of the event (against Herntrich, Bertholet). For the original text of chs. 8–11 there exists no reason for mistrusting the claim of the text itself when it speaks of the prophet's experience in his place of exile.

---

5   See above p. 139.
6   See above p. 139.
7   For the psychological problem of the experiences, see the Introduction.
8   See Hempel, *Literatur*, 60f; Wolff, "Begründungen."
9   Zimmerli, "Wort."
10 P. 120.
11 See the detailed exposition for a fuller development of the description.

Interpretation

■ 8:1 The situation in which the experience comes to the prophet, dated on the fifth day of the sixth month of the sixth year, i.e., on the seventeenth day of the ninth month in the year 592 B.C., is undoubtedly set out as a typical situation.[12] No less than four times is it mentioned in the book of Ezekiel that men who are waiting for a (reassuring) word from God to the prophet sit down before him (8:1; 14:1; 20:1; 33:31). The same situation is found again, significantly, in narratives regarding Elisha. 2 Kings 4:38; 6:1 mention that prophetic disciples of Elisha "were sitting before him (ישבים לפניו)." 2 Kings 6:32 leads still closer to Ezekiel where Elisha is sitting in his house.[13] The elders (of Samaria) sit beside him (ישבים אתו). During the siege of the city they seek counsel of the prophet. In a mysterious vision he recognizes the approach of the royal messengers and hears behind them the steps of the king himself, who then becomes a direct witness of the reassuring word of God which comes (7:1). In this connection we must also compare the royal messengers sent to the prophets (Is 37:2ff; Jer 21:1ff; 37:3ff).[14]

Elders are also mentioned among the exiles in Jer 29:1 as the recipients of a letter from a prophet. They are there, however, expressly described as זקני הגולה, i.e., as leaders established by the new sociological structure of the גולה. Here they are זקני יהודה (14:1; 20:1 זקני ישראל, see Excursus 2), which points to the origin of these men from the political sphere of Judah. Undoubtedly a certain continuity of office was dominant here.

■ 8:2 The hand of Yahweh which fell upon the prophet first of all opened up for him a vision in the manner of 1:3f (otherwise 3:22; 37:1; 40:1f).[15] In the heavenly figure which Ezekiel came to see, the close connection with the description of the enthroned figure of 1:27 is striking. Since in ch. 10 there is no doubt regarding the later elaboration of the text with figures of the introductory theophany, the suspicion of subse-

quent contamination also arises for 8:2. Considerations of content also support this view. The similarity of the description in 1:27 and 8:2 appears compellingly to lead to the view that in 8:2 also Yahweh must be intended (Cooke, Herrmann, Fohrer). However, since Yahweh otherwise only encounters the prophet visibly in the form of the כבוד (cf. also the Priestly Code), the "man" here must refer to the figure of a heavenly messenger. If we are unwilling to avail ourselves of the explanation that a cliché-like description of a heavenly being is used in 1:27 for Yahweh and in 8:2 for a heavenly messenger, we must regard v 2aβb as a subsequent elaboration. So Hölscher, *Hesekiel*, Sprank. In substance the introduction of a heavenly mediator who lifts the prophet up between heaven and earth (Zech 5:9) must be regarded as a development of the assertions of ecstatic transportation in earlier prophecy, which mention only the רוח. Behind the seizure of the hair we may conjecture a basis in the experience of actual bodily pain (and giddiness) felt by the person concerned. The merging together of the subjects of the action: 1) the man 2) the spirit 3) Yahweh himself, who determines the further course of the experience from v 5 on by his word to the prophet, must not be separated in a logical division and torn apart by literary criticism. The one divine intervention is here experienced by the prophet under various aspects.

Through this intervention the prophet sees himself placed at the north gate of the city of Jerusalem. The temple area is first mentioned in v 14. Here begins the vision of the four abominations, which are each marked by the divine question, "Have you seen?" In 1 Kings 20:13 this question leads up to an everyday fact available to anyone, whilst in Ezek 8 it moves into an ecstatic vision. Thus the simple הראית is set in the narrative in a formal scheme, of which Horst rightly establishes that "much recalls formal elements of a definite type of vision description."[16] After an intro-

---

12   According to Parker-Dubberstein.
13   Is there any relation here to the form of the *Königsnovelle*, where "the sitting down of a king in his house is ... in 2 Sam 7 a canonical introduction"? See S. Herrmann, "Königsnovelle," 58.
14   For the "sitting in the house" see also what has been said above (p. 159) regarding the possible confinement of Ezekiel. For ישב לפני as a technical term

in the priestly sphere, cf. Zech 3:8, more loosely Gen 43:33, also Ps 61:8 (140:14); Ju 20:26, 21:2; 1 Chr 17:16.
15   Pp. 117f.
16   Horst, "Exilsgemeinde," 345. Cf. Zech 2:1, 5; 5:1; 6:1.

ductory reference to being transported and to mention of the place (vv 3bα, 7a, 14a, 16aα[1]) it moves on to the perception of an idolatrous cult in which as a rule the place, the persons participating in it, and the nature of it are mentioned (vv 5b 10f, 14b, 16aα[2]βb). In the first two parts of this there is an explicit divine summons to look (vv 5a, 9), and in all four cases there is an introductory והנה. Through a further ויאמר אלי the affirmative question of Yahweh to the prophet, known from 1 Kings 20:13, is introduced (vv 6a, 12, 15a, 17). The connecting remark, which concludes the section and which prepares the prophet for something worse (vv 6bβ, 13, 15b, imitated in the disclosure of heavenly mysteries in [Greek] Baruch 2:5; 5:3)[17] is appropriately absent in the last section.

The four assertions of sin, in order of their seriousness, follow, taking the prophet along a route which leads correspondingly from the outer gate of the city to the inner part of the sanctuary. When Hölscher, *Hesekiel*, sees this route as one from the east gate of the surrounding wall to the west gate in the interior of the temple, by cutting out אשר אל הצפונה of v 3 and הפונה צפונה of v 14, he has certainly been unconsciously determined by the course of movement in 40:6ff. His radical alterations to the text do not deserve serious acceptance.

Nevertheless, Hölscher's recognition that we are dealing here with the pre-exilic temple is important. Although the narrative of 1 Kings 6f sheds little light upon the total building complex of Solomon's temple, yet it is clear however that the temple, as a royal sanctuary (cf. Amos 7:13), was a constituent part of the whole palace edifice, set wall by wall against the secular buildings of Solomon (Ezek 43:7ff).[18] A single wall divided the *temenos* (temple and forecourt) from the palace area (1 Kings 6:36). The whole palace

area, including the slightly raised temple platform (40:26aα), was further surrounded by a wall (1 Kings 7:12).[19] The northern part of the חצר גדולה mentioned in 1 Kings 7:12 must have been related in the course of time to the temple more closely and have become attached to it as "an outer forecourt." 2 Kings 21:5; 23:12 clearly speak in the time of Manasseh and Josiah of the שתי חצרות בית יהוה. Ezek 40ff seeks to determine the order of the enlarged sacred area once for all. Furthermore it is not probable that the outer wall of the palace court, especially the exposed northern flank, simply coincided with the city wall. Between the northern fortification of the city, where many scholars would place the gate of Benjamin (Jer 37:13),[20] and the north gate which guarded the entrance into the palace area, we must set a further intervening area. Accordingly, whoever entered the city from the north would have passed through three gates on the way to the temple: 1) the city gate, 2) the gate of the original palace wall (1 Kings 7:12), 3) the gate of the temple court which was consequently distinguished as the "inner" court from the "outer" temple forecourt, in distinction from the earlier "great (palace) forecourt" of 1 Kings 7:12. Ezekiel appears to presuppose this layout.

After Hævernick had made the conjecture that the four sins of Ezek 8 concerned four acts of a celebration for Adonis, the interpretation of the text as a libretto of a *sacer ludus* at an agricultural festival has recently been attempted by Gaster with an appeal to the Ugaritic text of the birth of the gods *šḥr wšlm*.[21] The setting up of thrones for the gods (*mṯbt ilm*), a ἱερὸς γάμος in a secret cave, a lament for Tammuz and prayer to the sun are taken to represent the sequence of a traditional harvest festival carried out at the time

---

17   Riessler, 42, 45.

18   Carl Watzinger, *Denkmäler Palästinas* 1 (Leipzig: Hinrichs, 1933–1935), 88f, 95.

19   Cf. the levels in Guthe, *BA*², map 2a; Jan Jozef Simons, *Jerusalem in the Old Testament; researches and theories* (Leiden: Brill, 1952), figure 46.

20   With Gustav Dalman, *Jerusalem und seine Gelände* (Gütersloh: Bertelsmann, 1930), 234; Kurt Galling, "Archäologischer Jahresbericht," *ZDPV* 54 (1931): plate 6; *idem, BRL*, 302f; Hugues Vincent, *Jerusalem de l'Ancien Testament; recherches d'archéologie et d'histoire* 1 (Paris: Gabalda, 1954–1956), plate 61 (contra

Simons, *Jerusalem*, 342).

21   H. A. C. Haevernick, *Commentar über den Propheten Ezechiel* (1843). Gaster, "Mysteries," especially 289–297: 'Ezekiel chapter VIII. A Canaanite Liturgy from Ras-Shamra-Ugarit'; for the Ugaritic text see Cyrus H. Gordon, *Ugaritic Textbook*, Analecta Orientalia 38 (Rome: Pontifical Biblical Institute, 1965), 52; *idem, Ugaritic Literature* (Rome: Pontifical Biblical Institute, 1949), 57–62.

of the equinox. W. F. Albright, however, has pointed out the insupportability of Gaster's interpretation of the Ugaritic texts, which can only be brought into relation to Ezek 8 by a reordering of the action.[22] The interpretation of H. G. May, which takes up suggestions of J. Morgenstern, also finds here the separate phases of a celebration of the end of the summer solstice with the departure of Yahweh, but this too is unconvincing. So we must give up trying to find behind the four abominations of Ezek 8 a comprehensive cultic event and endeavor to understand each act for itself.

■ **8:4** The first abomination is encountered by the prophet at the north gate of the city (the gate of Benjamin of Jer 37:13?). Since in what follows undoubtedly Yahweh himself addresses the prophet (מקדשי v 6), a later editor, who already had before him the elaboration of the description of the theophany in Ezek 10, felt the need to assert in v 4 the presence of Yahweh in his glory. This had as a consequence that the seeing of a vision, introduced with והנה, now anticipates in v 4 in an awkward way the divine summons to look in v 5a and the following vision which is introduced by והנה in the right place in v 5bβ.

■ **3bβ** However one can ask if v 3bβ, which mentions the image of jealousy at the gate in connection with a reference to the prophet's position, does not already contain a similar premature statement when it mentions the abomination seen by him, before Yahweh has given the command to look (v 5a). This fact has led commentators (Cornill, Hölscher, *Hesekiel*, Herntrich, Bertholet, Fohrer) repeatedly to cut out v 3bβ. A closer study of the text, however, shows that the seeing in v 5, which takes place at the command of Yahweh, is directed not towards the סמל הקנאה, but to the altar (cf. note a), which catches the attention of the prophet, who is gazing northwards, at Yahweh's command, "north of the gate" (this northern direction is emphasized three times!), i.e., outside the gate of the city. From this the לרחקה מעל מקדשי of v 6, which elaborates the vision, becomes clearer. Following 𝔙 the verb here has been related by Ewald and Smend, through to Fohrer, to Yahweh, thereby seeking to find an allusion to the imminent departure of Yahweh from

his sanctuary. This is not only unsatisfactory grammatically, but also deviates from the line of the analogous statements in vv 12, 17, which further unfold the sins of the people and do not point to a punishment by Yahweh. The saying rather concerns those who are rebuked and "who have gone far from my sanctuary" (so Hölscher, *Hesekiel*, Bertholet, Aalders). That an altar stood outside the temple, or even outside the city, was a very serious offence to Ezekiel's priestly understanding, which is reflected also in the rebuke of the false direction of prayer in v 16. By it, according to Ezekiel's view, a commandment such as Lev 19:30 = 26:2 מקדשי תיראו must be impaired.[23]

■ **8:3bβ** If this understanding is correct, which finds the particular abomination in the altar outside the gate, then v 3bβ, which still does not mention the altar and also has no והנה pointing to the first glimpse of something unexpected, is no more than a simple local reference. This is supported by the use of the *nomen loci* מושב (note d), which should not be cut out. מושב literally denotes the "seat" of the king at the royal table, as in 1 Sam 20:25. In 2 Kings 2:19 מושב העיר means in a more general sense the position of a city. So here the "position" of the סמל הקנאה is referred to, without thereby specifically meaning the sitting posture of the figure shown (Ehrlich), or the installing of a throne (Gaster). Also the more concrete understanding of it as a "niche in the wall in which the figure was set up" (Albright) cannot be certainly demonstrated.

The סמל, which is found in the Old Testament three times besides Ezek 8:3, 5, stands parallel in Dtn 4:16 to פסל. As there this is more closely defined by תמונת כל (the *athnach* is to be placed under כל in accordance with the parallels in Dtn 4:23, 25), so סמל is defined by . . . תבנית זכר או נקבה תבנית כל בהמה. The use of the word in Phoenician also leads us to think of a figured representation.[24]

The general designation סמל receives a closer definition by the conjoined קנאה. The noun קנאה denotes in secular usage a jealous passion (Nu 5:14, 30; Prv 6:34; Song 8:6), then in a derived sense rivalry in work (Eccl 4:4), or simply becoming aroused quite generally (Prv 14:30; 27:4). Thus the conjecture has

---

22 W. F. Albright, *Archaeology and the Religion of Israel* (Baltimore: Johns Hopkins University Press, 1956), 165f.

23 Cf. the קדשי בזית of Ezek 22:8. The idea of a spatial separation from the sanctuary may also be echoed in the רחקו מעלי of 44:10.

been made that סמל הקנאה could mean an image of "passion" (Herrmann). However, in verbal and substantival usage קנא is repeatedly a designation for the jealous anger of Yahweh against everything hostile to him. One of the rare adjectival expressions predicated liturgically of Yahweh is derived from it (קַנָּא Ex 20:5; 34:14; Dtn 4:24; 5:9; 6:15; קַנּוֹא Josh 24:19; Na 1:2). It must not be overlooked that the further use of קנאה in the book of Ezekiel points almost exclusively in this direction (5:13; 16:38, 42; 23:25; 36:5f; 38:19, otherwise only 35:11; the verb is used in 39:25 of Yahweh; 31:9 of the trees of Eden). Thus it is most likely that the expression should be understood, in the context of Ezekiel's terminology, as a polemical one. Such cult-polemical terminology, used broadly, is otherwise frequent in the book of Ezekiel. He speaks of "dung" (גלולים),[25] of "abominations" (תועבות, שקוצים), of the "obstacle of guilt" (מכשול עון 14:3) in a way which repeatedly makes it difficult to see exactly what is meant. The polemical reference to the "image of jealousy, which provokes to jealousy (cf. note e to v 3)" must also belong in the realm of such language.

To the question which sin Ezekiel actually had in mind by this expression, attention has repeatedly been drawn to 2 Chr 33:7, where the Chronicler designates the פסל האשרה mentioned in 2 Kings 21:7 as פסל הסמל (v 15 simply as הסמל). Already Syriac *Baruch* 64:3 "He made a statue with five faces; four of them looked to the four winds; the fifth was on the top of the statue as though to provoke the jealousy of the Almighty" presupposes apparently this identification.[26] But apart from the question whether this image, which had already been removed by Josiah (2 Kings 23:6; according to 2 Chr 33:15 already by Manasseh), was

really restored under Zedekiah (or Jehoiakim), this view is clearly opposed by the reference to its position in Ezek 8:3, 5. The Asherah image set up "in the temple (area?)" (בית יהוה 2 Kings 23:6; cf. 21:7) cannot be identical with an image set up at the outer gate (Ezek 8:3) "in the entrance" (8:5). So we must seriously question whether Albright is right when he thinks of the analogy of the orthostats, with cultic or mythological representations, very richly attested from between the twelfth to the seventh centuries B.C. in North Syria as far as southeastern Asia Minor and northern Mesopotamia.[27] Further it is perhaps more correct to think of the full sculpture of a figure at an entrance gate, since Ezekiel speaks of the single סמל הקנאה and therefore chooses, not the word for relief (מחקה v 10), but סמל, which is synonymous with פסל.[28] These guardian figures may have been set up in the course of the assimilation to the surrounding culture in the northern entrance of the city or palace. Here it could have survived the age of Josiah, although it must have been a feature which would have "provoked to anger" the more rigorous temple circles. The reference to its position in Ezek 8:3 appears to speak of the סמל as a well-known phenomenon at the gate.

■ **8:5** The particular novelty which provoked the prophet was the altar which had clearly only recently been set up outside the gate before this figure. Ezekiel may have seen it before his deportation or have learnt subsequently of this innovation through accounts brought from Jerusalem. In the small temples of Nimrud there were two crenelated altars to the right and left of the *cella* entrance.[29] The tendency to set up new altars is not only testified by Hosea (8:11; 10:1) for the late period of the Northern Kingdom, but also by Jeremiah for the late period in Judah. It is clearly

---

24 Cf. the second century inscription on the marble base of two statuettes (*LidzEph* 2, 161): סמלם שנם אל יתן עב]ד ... "Ab[d ...] dedicated these two statues."

25 See above pp. 186f.

26 Riessler, 97.

27 Cf. the large number of illustrations in Max Freiherr von Oppenheim, *Der Tell Halaf; eine neue Kultur im aeltesten Mesopotamien* (Leipzig: Brockhaus, 1931).

28 Albright, *Archaeology*. Cheyne, "Image," came to a surprisingly similar view with his wholly unacceptable textual rendering למס כיון "Lamassu of Kai-

wan" (Amos 5:26). We may compare the gigantic lionesses in the walled passage shown in Oppenheim, *Tell Halaf*, plate 12; the hugh griffins in the second passage of the temple-palace, plate 15; or the gateway lions of Karatepe and the winged lions and bull figures in the doorway of Assurnasirpal's palace in Nimrud, *ANEP* 646f, *AOBAT* 381.

29 As is shown by Kurt Galling, *Der Altar in den Kulturen des alten Orients* (Berlin: Curtius, 1925), illustration 14, plate 9, and as was established by Layard *in situ*: "They stood in the openings in front of the entrance to the *cella*, flanked by giant lions" (45).

the same movement concerned with the multiplying of places for prayer, which is reflected in Jer 11:13: "For your gods have become as many as your cities, O Judah; and as many as the streets of Jerusalem are the altars you have set up . . . to sacrifice to Baal," and which has been at work here. It is also to be seen in the directly following second abomination in the temple in 8:10f.

■ **8:6** With Ezekiel, however, the abomination is seen in a particularly priestly light, especially in regard to the physical distance of the altar from the holy area. A particular group of men who worshipped here was not seen by the prophet. The altar, set at a distance from Yahweh and in front of the image of jealousy at the gate, is sign enough of Jerusalem's sin.

■ **8:7** On the way through "the gate to the forecourt," i.e., to the original palace forecourt Ezekiel encounters a second scene of cultic sin.[30] The way which leads to the sight is strangely obscure in its details, in spite of the endeavors of G. R. Driver.[31] Three times in 𝔐 a feature of the vision is introduced by the והנה of the vision form. Ezekiel sees 1) a hole (חר אחד) in the wall (of the gate-building?), v 7b. After he has broken through the wall at God's command he sees 2) an opening (פתח אחד), v 8. Only then follows directly on the divine command to (enter and) see, which recalls v 5, 3) the vision of the sin. 𝔊 clearly did not have the first element (v 7b) in its Hebrew original. However, the second element of the vision also, which precedes the divine summons to enter and see, is suspicious as regards its originality and, together with its introduction, the account of the digging through the wall, must be regarded as an addition dependent on 12:5, 7. This is supported by the related reference to the פתח in v 7a, which forms the antecedent for בא in v 9. The original section spoke simply of being led to the gate of the court (v 7a), of the divine summons (in the court) to enter and look, and the ensuing vision of the second abomination, introduced by והנה.[32]

■ **8:10–12** The event described in vv 10–12 originally took place in the forecourt, i.e., in the northern part of the old palace court after Ezekiel had crossed it to get to the gate of the temple area in the narrower sense (v 14).

■ **8:11** It is scarcely accidental that in this outer area the lay representatives of the people were to be found, "seventy of the elders of the house of Israel." It appears probable, from Ex 24:1, 9, where seventy of the elders of Israel (שבעים מזקני ישראל) were summoned, as the distinguished men of the people (אצילי בני ישראל, v 11), to see God and to eat the covenant meal before him on the mountain of God, and from Nu 11:16 (24f), where seventy elders (שבעים איש מזקני ישראל [העם] or הזקנים) share something of the spirit of Moses, that there was an institution, sanctified by ancient tradition, of seventy elders as the representatives of Israel.[33] What Ezekiel sees therefore is not a chance group, but the representatives of Israel, as they had once stood before Yahweh at the making of the covenant.

What Ezekiel sees them doing is all the more unheard of. The walls of the court are covered round with relief work (מחקה note b). The closer definition of this by כל גלולי בית ישראל does not make this very clear. The שקץ, subsequently filled out by "images of reptiles and beasts" (note a), speaks more plainly. This expression, which occurs eight times in Lev 11 and again in Lev 7:21 and Is 66:17, contains a ritual qualification. A comparison of Lev 11:10 (שקץ הם לכם) with 11:8 (טמאים הם לכם) shows שקץ as synonymous with טמא. Similarly Lev 11 shows that in the animal world everything which points to hybrid creatures is avoided as שקץ: creatures which live in water, which do not have scales and fins (Lev 11:10) like a normal fish; winged creatures which do not hop on two legs, as is normal for birds (Lev 11:20); above all small lizard-like creatures (Lev 11:29f). In the wall figures of Ezek 8:10 animals of these kinds appear to have been represented. Such creatures received the incense offering

---

30 See above p. 237.
31 Driver, "Ezekiel," 149–150.
32 So also Bertholet; Kuhl, "Schauplatz," 406.
33 Cf. for the later period the seventy translators of the Bible (*Letter of Aristeas* 46–50 seeks to connect the number seventy, which was undoubtedly originally intended, with the number twelve of the tribes and arrives at a number seventy-two by counting six

representatives for each tribe) and the sending of seventy disciples (Luke 10:1, beside the sending of the twelve in 9:1f). Cf. 1 Sam 9:22 𝔊.

of Israel's representatives.

The scene contains a summary of actions hostile to God. As in 8:3, 5, here also the rigid ordinance of no images is infringed. The close verbal connection of the additions with Dtn 4:16–18, particularly in the emphatic sharpening of the prohibition of images, is noticeable here. To the priestly mind it was especially offensive that creatures which were unacceptable for ordinary food and were classed as abominations were the object of pious worship here. Finally a comparison with 2 Chr 26:19, the only other text in the Old Testament in which the designation מקטרת "incense burner" is found and which relates the sinful intrusion by Uzziah upon the privileges of the priests (cf. also the Korah episode in Num 16), raises the question whether the priest-prophet Ezekiel saw in the incense offering of the elders a presumptuous intrusion into the cultic sphere which was prohibited to them.

How are we to regard the action of the elders? When Gaster finds here a mystery rite performed in a cave which celebrated the ἱερὸς γάμος of two deities, then the decisive features are not taken from the text itself.[34] Also if the actual references of the text scarcely suffice for an exact definition, then it must be pointed out that Ezek 23:14, in a quite different connection, refers again in polemical terms to the existence of wall carvings (מחקה) which seduce the people to destruction. The portrayals of men mentioned there (אנשי מחקה) are more closely described as חקקים בששר. The nominal מחקה is otherwise only found in 1 Kings 6:35 in the description of the carvings on the door surfaces in the sanctuary, the form of which must, according to Watzinger, have been the result of North Syrian-Phoenician influence, and thereby of indirect influence from Egypt.[35] The use of red lead (ששר) in the decoration of buildings is mentioned again in Jer 22:14. If the "windows" mentioned there in Jehoiakim's building may be regarded as intended for public royal appearances (cf. Rudolph, *Jeremia*), since Jehoiakim was king

of Judah by the power of Egypt (2 Kings 23:34f), then the Egyptian origin of this building and wall decoration may be recognized very clearly. The wall carvings, which among other things may have included mythological motifs (hybrid creatures) in which also older Canaanite traditions (idols of the house of Israel) became important again, certainly need not have been intended when they were originally put on the wall to be the object of cultic observance. Here also the contemporary movement which tended to multiply pious customs may have been influential, as in the setting up of the altar at the gate (v 5).[36] In all this we cannot exclude that the devotion of the elders had, in their own minds, a Yahwistic interpretation. Do we not find in the Psalms references to Yahweh as creator which make use of such mythological material?[37] In the eyes of the priest-prophet all this activity could only appear as a blasphemous abomination which denied any genuine obedience.

The mention of Jaazaniah, which has been added subsequently to the text (note b), is not clearly explicable. Behind his father's name we may readily conjecture the chancellor of Josiah's time, well-known from 2 Kings 22. That Jaazaniah does not appear in the book of Jeremiah, which mentions three sons of Shaphan by name, is no compelling argument against such a view. It is certainly noticeable then how far this son had departed from the conduct of Shaphan's family, which remained faithful to Josiah's reform and to Jeremiah.[38]

■ **8:12** The divine speech which concludes the account of the second sin shows that the action of the elders was not simply a misguided accretion to the Yahweh faith (as it may subjectively have been interpreted by the citizens of Jerusalem), but meant a departure from Yahweh. In a quotation which unveils completely the unspoken thoughts of the elders, he encountered the godless independence of an attitude which in reality no longer reckoned with the presence of Yahweh:

---

34 For a criticism of the parallels adduced by him, see Albright, *Archaeology*. Albright himself thinks of a syncretistic cult of Egyptian origin with features of Osiris worship.

35 Watzinger, *Denkmäler* 1, 94.

36 A splendid example of such subsequent reverence for a sculpture which was not originally intended to receive it has been shown by Erman, *Religion*, 144,

in the Sachmet relief on the pyramid of Sahure.

37 See the material in Hermann Gunkel, *Schöpfung und Chaos in Urzeit und Endzeit* (Göttingen, ²1921).

38 Cf. further to 11:1ff.

"Yahweh does not see (it), Yahweh has forsaken the land."[39]

If we do not ascribe the critical remark that "everyone commits abomination in his room of pictures" to later editorial glossing, then we must see in it the accusation that the sinful form of devotion which the prophet saw practiced in an assembly of the seventy elders took place also in individual houses. Had the movement towards the multiplication of cult places led also to the setting up of a wall of images or of a corner with an image in the houses of the citizens of high rank?

■ 8:8 The element of secrecy before God, which can be heard in the accusing quotation of the words of the elders, would then have led to the addition of the בחשך, which is not in 𝕲 (note a), and further to the setting of the entire scene with the elders in a hidden room which could only be reached by the breaking through of a wall, described after the pattern of 12:5, 7.

■ 8:7b In a second phase of elaboration, v 7b, which is missing in 𝕲, was finally added. By its mention of the prophet's finding of an opening, does this intend to show the basis and technical possibility of the breach in the wall, or is it, in the last analysis, an attempt to answer the question how the elders entered the hidden room?

■ 8:14f The third occasion of sin seen by the prophet is described very briefly and brings him to the temple area proper. At the north gate of the court (פתח שער בית יהוה), which the prophet first enters at the beginning of the fourth scene (v 16), he sees women sitting on the ground weeping for Tammuz. Was the entrance to the (inner) temple forecourt, which was later, according to the vision of Ezek 40ff, firmly reserved for the priests, already prohibited to women in the late pre-exilic period?

The Sumerian-Babylonian vegetation deity *dumu-zi* "proper child, proper son" (Akkadian *du'zu*) is only mentioned by name in the Old Testament here. Explanations about the name and the early history of the god have recently been set in motion again.[40] According to Falkenstein the worship of Dumuzi at the beginning pointed to the figure of the earthly lover of Inanna, who handed him over to the underworld, and is not to be identified with the goddess *dumu-zi-abzu*, the "lady of Kinunira" (against Meissner, Dhorme).[41] It was at first limited to Uruk, Kullaba, and Badtibira. His title, "the shepherd" must at first have been accepted simply as a human royal epithet. The relatively late subsequent penetration of his worship throughout the southern Babylonian region was the consequence of an enlargement of his characteristics into the image of a vegetation deity, particularly of the god of the dying summer vegetation. Hence the fourth month (June-July) gained the name Tammuz. As a dying youth he was lamented by his worshippers. The texts of such laments, which were sung in the dramatic ritual exactly like ordinary laments for the dead, especially by women, are still preserved for us.[42] It is very doubtful, however, whether in Ezek 8:14 we should go further and see in the ישבות the official name of the living Astartes to whom the קדשים served as opposite numbers, as the bearers as the role of fertility, as B. Brooks wishes to do, following J. G. Frazer.[43] The literal understanding of the ישבות (נשים) as women squatting down in lamentation (26:16; Job 2:13; Lam 2:10) is quite adequate to the present text.

The type of deity who sets out in his fate the dying (and rising) of vegetation was known to Israel in the earlier period of the monarchy in the form of the Phoenician Adonis, as the laments of Jer 22:18; 1 Kings 14:13 𝕲, also 𝕲 3Βασ 12:24m show. Cf. also נטעי נעמניב Is 17:10; מספד הדדרמון Zech 12:11; חמדת נשים Dan 11:37. So 𝔙 (cf. note c) could translate התמו freely as *Adonidem*, cf. Jerome, "*Quem nos Adonidem interpretati sumus, et hebraeus et syrus sermo Thamuz vocat.*" The introduction of the Tammuz name (does the article show that it was regarded as an appellative?) was undoubtedly a consequence of the inclusion of Palestine

39 Wolff, *Zitat*, 57–60.

40 In addition to Meissner, *Babylonien* 2, 23–25, see E. Dhorme, *Les religions de Babylonie et d'Assyrie* (Paris: Presses universitaires de France, ²1949), 115–119; Anton Moortgat, *Tammuz* (Berlin: de Gruyter, 1949); and especially the various contributions in *Compte rendu de la troisième rencontre assyriologique internationale* (28.6–4.7, 1952, Leiden) (Paris: Imprimerie nationale, 1954), 18–74.

41 Falkenstein-von Soden, 41–65.

42 See Ungnad, *Religion*, 231–239; *AOT*, 270–273; Falkenstein-von Soden, 185–187.

43 Beatrice A. Brooks, "Fertility Cult Functionaries in the Old Testament," *JBL* 60 (1941): 240.

in the Assyrian sphere of influence in the eighth and seventh centuries B.C. Through the Assyrian rulers, and even more through the communities from the East which were settled in what had once been the Northern Kingdom, the Tammuz figure set foot in Palestine and was given a place in certain city circles of Jerusalem. The prophet saw in his vision that it had penetrated to the threshhold of the sacred area. In this the custom of lamenting a dead god on the threshhold of Yahweh's sanctuary shows that the women who practiced it must have regarded it, not as something which would abolish the worship of Yahweh, but rather as something which was supplementary to it. The true faith in Yahweh, however, completely lacked this aspect of pious sympathy with the deity in the rhythm of nature, oscillating from life to death and then from death back to life. Did it not therefore call for some supplementation here? However, for the prophet it is clear that the intrusion of such creaturely features into the realm of Yahweh, who was known to Israel as the "living God" (Ps 42:3; 84:3), was an act of apostasy from this living Lord and bore the character of the worst abomination.

■ **8:16** The fourth sin moves completely into the sphere of the holy. In the temple court (חצר בית יהוה הפנימית), before the entrance to the temple building which is referred to as Yahweh's "palace" (היכל, using a loanword stemming from the Sumerian *e-gal*) there stood twenty (𝔐 twenty-five) men "between the entrance hall (cf. 40:48f) and the altar." This latter refers to the great altar of burnt offering, which according to *b. Middot* 5:1 stood in the Herodian temple twenty-two cubits distant from the vestibule. Its existence in the pre-exilic temple is referred to in 2 Kings 16:10ff. Joel 2:17 speaks, in a description of a major rite of penitence, of the weeping of the priests "between the temple and the the altar," and Mt 23:35 states that the dreadful murder of Zechariah took place "between the temple and the altar," whereas 2 Chr 24:21 mentions that it occurred בחצר בית יהוה. Matthew therefore noticeably heightens the statement. These references show the great importance of this position in the court. The question then arises whether the "men" refers to priests. The view set out by Lightfoot (cf. Keil,

Hitzig), that here the twenty-five men of 𝔐 were representatives of the twenty-four priestly classes (1 Chr 24:7–19) and the high priest, is a conjecture incapable of proof. So also is the view which reckons on the basis of the number twenty in 𝔊 that we have here the number of the sun god Shamash of Babylonian theology (Bewer). On the other hand, however, since the הזקנים of 9:6 is undoubtedly secondary (cf. note c to 9:6) there is also no compelling proof against the interpretation of the twenty men as priests. In the whole series of scenes disclosing Israel's sins, which so clearly reach their climax in the action in the sanctuary, it is in fact noteworthy that after the mention of the elders in the outer court and the women at the threshhold of the sacred area, the priests are not then mentioned in the sacred area itself. Thus the conjecture carries weight that behind the reference to the men "between the entrance hall and the altar" we have a specifically priestly circle, analogous to the circle of seventy elders. Was then the avoidance of the title "priest" intended polemically?[44]

The men stood with their faces turned toward the east in order to prostrate themselves in that direction to the (rising) sun. Commentators here have rashly worked with the assertion of a "cult of the sun god," in which Fohrer thinks of the worship of the Egyptian sun god, whilst others (Cooke, Bertholet, Ziegler, *Ezechiel*, Herrmann) conjecture oriental influences. The Jerusalem temple undoubtedly underwent under Manasseh strong intrusions of Assyrian star worship (2 Kings 21:5). Josiah attempted to abolish the features of this cult from the temple (2 Kings 23:5, 11f; cf. Dtn 4:19). It has further been conjectured that already with the building of the temple strong solar features were in play.[45] Here we should have to reckon with Egyptian influences mediated by Phoenicia. In the period of weakening and relaxation after the reform these tendencies must have reasserted themselves under Jehoiakim, whether we now think of them as established from the Assyrian period, or trace them back to Solomon, or even beyond this to reckon them as influences of the Canaanite Baal religion. Further to this it is also possible, and even probable, that here these ritual features were not regarded in the minds of those who

---

44   Cf. further to 44:6ff.
45   See Julian Morgenstern, "The Gates of Righteousness," *HUCA* 6 (1929): 1–37; May, "Departure."

practiced them as a betrayal of the Yahweh faith, but rather as elements of a possible solar interpretation of Yahweh.

It is once again significant for the priest-prophet Ezekiel how he describes the solarized Yahweh worship which he sees. He does not stress the fact that in such worship the sun appears as a second Lord beside Yahweh. Just as the first abomination consisted in the distance from the abode of Yahweh (v 6), so he sees here the particular abomination which offended Yahweh in the infringement of the ordained direction of prayer and the turning of men's backs to the Lord who dwelt in the היכל. Assertions such as we find in Jer 2:27; 32:33 ("they have turned their backs to me, not their faces"), and the later echoes which are to be heard in 2 Chr 29:6 in a metaphorical usage, take on a strikingly literal realization with Ezekiel.

■ **8:17** We must interpret v 17 from v 16. In analogy to vv 6 and 12 (there is no analogy for the third sin) a divine speech interprets the abomination seen by the prophet from the point of view of Yahweh. In a question v 17a, there is a look backwards to the first three sins, and the word תועבות, which reappears monotonously in vv 6a, 6b, 9, 13, 15, is taken up once again. Are all these abominations too slight a thing? The answer, which contains the final climax, follows in v 17bβ. It is now separated by the intervening clause v 17bα, which unexpectedly introduces into the great description of the cultic abominations of Jerusalem the mention of the social guilt of the land (cf. 7:23; 9:9; Gen 6:11). The וישבו להכעיסני, which is lacking in 𝕲 (note b), clearly endeavors to smooth the transition from this clause, which is of questionable originality in the text, to the following.

From this it is clear that we must not see in v 17 the mention of a further, fifth, example of sin, as Kraetzschmar, Bertholet and Schumpp do, which would immediately disturb the framework of four scenes. Rather v 17bβ clarifies what has been described in v 16. In turning their faces away from the place of the divine presence they bring about the iniquity mentioned in v 17bβ.

If these considerations are correct then a series of attempts at interpretation of the difficult word זמורה is not necessary. Elsewhere in the Old Testament (cf. note c) this means the (vine-) shoot. Accordingly attempts have been made to find in 8:17 a cultic rite performed with a vine branch. By retaining 𝔐 (אפם) reference has been made to the sacrificial branch used in the cult of Zarathustra, which is sometimes mentioned in the Avesta as "*baresman*" and which later is called "*barsom*," mentioned frequently as playing a role in the framework of rites of purification.[46] Apart from the difficulty of a connection in the history of religion, the exact nature of the performance of the rite is throughout very varied.[47] Fohrer therefore has sought to find an Egyptian rite, according to which flowers, or symbols of plants which in Palestine would have been the vine shoot, were held up to the rising sun.[48] Is it likely, however, that Yahweh, of whom we have just been told that the "men" turn their backs on him, now suddenly takes the place of the rising sun and then says that "they stretch out the branch to *my* nose"? Messel, who cuts out v 17 bβ as an addition and understands it as a loosely added reference to the vine branch which Yahweh hates, but which is held out to him, abandons any interpretation from the context of the original text.[49] However, if we hold to the originality of the connection of v 16 with 17bβ then we ought not to follow Zunz (according to Hölscher, *Hesekiel*), Jahn, and Hölscher in regarding זמורה as a term for the male *membrum*, and think of a phallic rite. Hitzig's reference to a pruning knife (reading זְמוֹרָה "they put the pruning hook to their nose," i.e., "they cut their own flesh") has only a curiosity value. Pure conjecture, such as Schmidt's "they throw their rebellion (מְרִיָּה) in my face," only leaves us in uncertainty. In regard to the whole situation we must question whether the interpretation of זמורה as "stench," suggested by 𝔗 (בהתא) and attested by later Jewish exegesis (cf. the drastic explanation in *b. Yoma* 77a), may not point in the right direction, even though it is etymologically obscure. We should not then think with Kraetzschmar and Schumpp of a reference to the cult of the high places in the surrounding countryside, which rises as a "stench" in Yahweh's

46   See Eduard Lehmann, "Die Perser" in *Lehrbuch der Religionsgeschichte* 2, ed. Alfred Bertholet, Pierre Daniel Chantepie de la Saussaye, Eduard Lehmann (Tübingen: Mohr [Siebeck], ⁴1925), 237, 240f; H. S. Nyberg, *Die Religionen des alten Iran*, tr. (into German) H. H. Schaeder. MVÄG 43 (Osnabrück:

nose, but understand this broad expression firmly
in the scene of adoration. The difficulty naturally
remains with this interpretation, which is supported
by Bertholet and van den Born, of the uncertainty
resulting from the lack of etymological explanation of
זמורה, which we must regard either as a crude metaphor
or as a euphemism.

This abominable insult to Yahweh, which is the
exact opposite of the "sweet-smelling savor" expected
on the altar of the place of his presence, represents the
unsurpassable height of blasphemy, over which Yahweh's wrath must break out.[50]

■ **8:18** This is asserted generally in v 18a in a formal
threat and made quite clear in ch. 9.[51]

In looking back over chapter 8 two things may be
said. The chapter has constantly been the chief witness
for the view that after Josiah's death "a formal reaction
must have arisen against the cult reform introduced by
Josiah," which led to a fresh introduction of foreign
cults into the temple of Jerusalem.[52] In this it must
always remain striking that little of this is to be discerned in the book of Jeremiah, which is otherwise a
rich contemporary source informing us of events in
the temple (Jer 26, 36). In Jeremiah's reproach against
Jehoiakim (22:13–17) his unrighteousness in the
administration of justice and his irresponsible greed
for buildings are mentioned with no word of his apostasy in cultic matters. Further the by no means meager
accounts of events in the time of Zedekiah show nothing
of an official return to the alien worship of Manasseh.
Thus Smith, Torrey, and others came to the radical
conclusion that Ezek 8 did not have in mind the time
of Zedekiah, but that of Manasseh.

Against this, however, careful study has shown that
Ezek 8 cannot refer to a return to the circumstances
of the time of Manasseh. A tendency to increase religious devotion can certainly be seen from Jer 7:1–15(26)
for the period of Jehoiakim. That, in this connection,
in the course of a certain relaxation after the rigid
period of reform all kinds of degraded cults (the building of altars, incense rites before carved images which
had previously been acceptable, the intrusion of
Tammuz rites into the temple area) could come freshly
into play, is in itself probable and is certainly not
excluded by the statements of Jeremiah, when we
consider simply the direction of the preaching of this
prophet and its difference from that of Ezekiel. Jer 7
shows us the prophet, (in the days of Jehoiakim!)
fighting against a false trust in the temple, in which
the effects of the period of reform can still readily be
seen. In the age of Zedekiah the political question of
the attitude towards the divinely ordained Babylonian
yoke is the most urgent interest of Jeremiah which let
him put aside other things. In Ezekiel, however, the
priest speaks with a feeling for the cultic purity of
worship before the Lord who dwells in the sanctuary.
From this he regards the iniquitous sins of Jerusalem
in quite another perspective and sets the accent in
quite different places in his stylizing of the vision.

This leads to a second assertion. Ezekiel tells of
things which were shown to him during his ecstatic
experience in the context of a vision from God. For all
those matters which belong to features of interpretation
and stylizing in his description he undoubtedly seeks
to point to things which really happened in Jerusalem.
Only so does the accusation which justifies the ensuing
judgement upon Jerusalem carry real weight. It is
therefore improbable, even when nothing is taken away
from the reality of the prophetic vision, that everything
which he saw should have become visible directly from
heaven, without any presupposition in his own mind
or through human communication.[53] Undoubtedly
there are embedded in Ezekiel's vision recollections
from the age of Jehoiakim, when he was himself still
in Jerusalem, and information which came by letter
(cf. Jer 29) or by word of mouth to the exiles. These
were brought together into an impressive picture of
the whole (four scenes) sin of Jerusalem, seen by him

Zeller, [2]1966), 367.

47 Cf. the arguments of Shalom Spiegel, "Ezekiel or
   Pseudo-Ezekiel?" *HTR* 24 (1931): 298–301.

48 By reference to A. de Buck, "La fleur au front du
   grand-prêtre," *OTS* 9 (1951): 18–29.

49 Messel, 58–61.

50 See above p. 191.

51 For the absolute use of עשׂה cf. note a. For the

double expression of v 18aβ see also 5:11; 7:4, 9;
9:5, 10; 16:5.

52 Bertholet, viii, repeated by Fohrer, *Hauptprobleme*,
   xiv.

53 Cf. what has been said above on pp. 99f regarding
   Isaiah's vision.

in a single event. In view of these demonstrable sources of information it is wrong to describe Ezek 8 as an impossible vision and to regard the visionary character regarding the particular sins of the citizens of Jerusalem which it contains as a product of a late fiction (Herntrich).

■ **9:1ff** Features of objective earthly perception demonstrably fall into the background in the visions of the impending judgement, to make way for the appearance of supernatural figures. Thus not only Herntrich, who contrasts sharply the "pictures formed out of the imagination" of ch. 9 with the "events of real life" found in ch. 8 (and 11:1–13), but also Horst want to see here a separate tradition-complex, originally independent of ch. 8.[54] The clear connecting features with ch. 8, however, do permit such a division. The same locality is preserved. Further the vision of ch. 9 takes place in the inner court entered by the prophet in 8:16, into which new figures also enter, once again from the north. The unity of the groups of persons is also kept insofar as the judgement, which must have its beginning at the sanctuary of Yahweh, begins with "the men in front of the (temple-) house" (9:6). Finally the thematic עשׂה תועבות of Ezek 8 echoes again when reference is made to the deliverance of those who groan על כל התועבות הנעשׂות בתוכה (9:4). All of this opposes a separation of ch. 8 from ch.9.

Into the area known from ch. 8 there now enters a quite new group of figures, "six men, each with his tool of destruction (כלי מפצו, in v 1 כלי משחתו) in his hand," and among them, clearly to be numbered as the seventh, a "man clothed in linen with the instrument of a scribe at his side."

Israel's ancient Passover tradition already knew of the destroying angel (משׁחית Ex 12:23 J, cf. v 13 P, further Ezek 9:8 [1]), in the form of which Yahweh himself passed through Egypt (עבר Ex 12:23 J, v 12 P, further Ezek 9:5 [4]) and struck (הכּה Ex 12:29 J, v 12 [13] P, further Ezek 9:5 [7], 8). Similarly Sennacherib's army was struck down by the angel during the night in order to deliver Jerusalem (2 Kings 19:35, cf. Jer 22:7; of lions Jer 2:30; 4:7). The narrative of David's census was aware furthermore that this fearful angel could, at Yahweh's command, turn against Israel itself (2 Sam 24:16f; 1 Chr 21:15). In Ezek 9 this destroying power appears differently as a group of seven figures, as we find again later in the angels of wrath of Rev 15:6 (cf. the seven evil spirits in Mt 12:45). We must look for an analogy to this, not so much in the seven great deities of the planets (Gunkel, "Schreiberengel," Fohrer), as in the seven evil spirits of Irra (Meissner) or the seven demons of the incantation text "Evil Monsters" (A. Ungnad).[55] Do we not today still speak of the evil seven? Although Ezek 9 is the first positive reference in the Old Testament, the possibility is certainly not to be excluded that earlier Israelite tradition already knew of a group of seven (evil) spirits. Whether Is 11:2f 𝔐, as 𝔊 𝔅, can be adduced as evidence for a reference to the sevenfold רוח remains uncertain.[56]

A greater antiquity of the tradition of a group of seven destroying angels appears to be attested by the fact that Ezek 9:2 already shows a clear development of the conception. The seventh figure is immediately separated here from the group of destroying angels by a special function. The linen garment, which according to Meissner was also worn in Babylon by the priests, identifies him as a priestly figure.[57] בַּד, originally "rag,"[58] is here used absolutely of an item of clothing, without further definition. In Ezek 9f and Dan 10:5; 12:6f, which are dependent on it, it occurs throughout in the plural, whilst in earlier references (1 Sam 2:18; 22:18; 2 Sam 6:14), in P (Ex 28:42; 39:28; Lev 6:3; 16:4, 23, 32) and 1 Chr 15:27 it is equally as consistently found only in the singular, whilst in Ezek 44:17f it is replaced by פשׁתים. The instrument of a scribe (which is denoted by an Egyptian loanword [note f]), which hangs from his girdle, further identifies

---

54 Herntrich, *Ezekielprobleme*, 86; Horst, "Exilsgemeinde," 346–350.

55 Meissner, *Babylonien* 2, 186; Ungnad, *Religion*, 62–65. Cf. further Meissner, *Babylonien* 2, index under the title: seven (evil spirits).

56 Cf. the commentaries of Fischer and Feldmann on the text.

57 Meissner, *Babylonien* 2, 55, 62.

58 Koehler-Baumgartner; differently H. J. Elhorst, "Das Ephod," *ZAW* 30 (1910): 266–268.

the figure as a scribe. In early Egypt the scribe's instrument consisted of a palette with two small containers for black and red ink, a small container for rushes, and a bowl with water. From the Middle Kingdom the container for rushes was fitted to the square, board-like wooden palette itself.[59] In Babylonia the stylus (*qan ṭuppi*—stylus for the [clay] tablet) was usually carried in a leather case "in the bands of the hips." In the divine world Nebo was particularly known as the scribe deity. His stylus may be illustrated among the emblems of the gods on boundary stones.[60] Since Nebo is identified on the stele of Adadnirari II as "he who holds the scribe's stylus," Gunkel "Schreiberengel," believed he could find in the god Nebo, in the group of the seven planet deities, the immediate prototype for Ezek 9f. The clear connection of priestly features with those of the office of scribe, a consideration of the technique of a scribe in which the painting of a sign on the forehead with a reed is more conceivable than the impressing of the scribe's stylus associated with Nebo, as well as the Egyptian derivation of the designation for a scribe's instrument, lead us to think of the possibility of an Egyptian origin. This Egyptian origin would have come to Jerusalem via Canaanite tradition. The task of this figure of marking those who were to be spared the judgement with a sign was undoubtedly given by earlier Israelite tradition.[61] Marking a person first of all identified him as the property of another (Ex 21:6). Daube raises the question whether or not the law of asylum, which in Palestine may have been influenced from Egypt, was familiar with such marks of possession placed on men by the gods or their representatives. Herodotus II:13 mentions a temple in Egypt in which the slave who fled there for protection was marked with the στίγματα

ἱερά, and so became untouchable.[62] The Cain narrative, which mentions in Gen 4:15 the putting of a mark (שִׂים אוֹת) on Cain and thereby offers an aetiology of the tribal mark of the Kenites, shows a clear knowledge of the protective character of such divine marks of possession. The sign which also seems to have been worn by the prophets was put, according to 1 Kings 20:38, 41 עַל עֵינָיו, and according to Zech 13:6 בֵּין יָדָיו. We may also question whether there were not, in the priestly atonement ritual in Israel, occurrences of such "marking" of someone to whom Yahweh had shown mercy, analogous to the mouth-cleansing rite which must lie behind Is 6:6f.[63]

If much is uncertain regarding the derivation of the pictures given to the prophet of the figures of the supernatural world who come upon the scene in the inner temple court, nevertheless it is quite clear for the present form of the text that all these figures enter at a particular authoritative word of Yahweh.

■ **9:1** Ezekiel's vision is the proclamation of an act of judgement. Over it there sounds in the prophet's ears the divine summons: "The woes of punishment for the city have drawn near." The vision which follows comes to stand in an uncanny light through this threatening summons, which has an evidently formal character and which recalls the threat of the day of Yahweh in 7:7 (cf. note a to 9:1). At the same time the plural פְּקֻדּוֹת הָעִיר points, rather ambiguously, to a number of servants of the divine judgement. (For 1b cf. note c).)

At the announcement of Yahweh the figures enter through the north gate. The more precise definition as the "upper gate" shows that it was the gate of 8:14, on the inner raised area of the most central part of the temple. According to 2 Kings 15:35; 2 Chr 27:3

59 Erman-Ranke, 378.

60 Meissner, *Babylonien* 2, 343; *Babylonien* 1, plate, illustration 19; cf. the Barrakub Stele, *Babylonien* 1, plate, illustration 34.

61 The verb תוה goes back possibly to the last letter of the Hebrew alphabet ת, which in the old Hebrew orthography was written in the form of a cross. See Gustav Hölscher, *Das Buch Hiob*, HAT 17 (Tübingen: Mohr [Siebeck], ²1952), on Job 31:35; differently in G. R. Driver, *Semitic Writing from Pictograph to Alphabet* (London: Oxford University Press, 1948), 209.

62 Cf. Kurt Latte, *Heiliges Recht; Untersuchungen zur Geschichte der sakralen Rechtsformen in Griechenland* (Tübingen: Mohr [Siebeck], 1920), 106–108.

63 See I. Engnell, *The Call of Isaiah* (1949), 40f. For the later history of Ezek 9:4 in the *Damascus Document* see J. L. Teicher, "The Christian Interpretation of the sign x in the Isaiah Scroll," *VT* 5 (1955): 196f, and in the New Testament Rev 7:2ff. That a reference to "bearing the cross" belongs here, as E. Dinkler in BZNW 21 (1954), 110–129, thinks, is improbable according to Wilhelm Michaelis, "Zeichen, Siegel, Kreuz. Ein Ausschnitt aus der

Jotham had built the שער בית יהוה העליון. It must be identical with the שער בנימן העליון אשר בבית יהוה in which, according to Jer 20:2, Jeremiah was put in the stocks. It was not, however, the same as the שער העליון which is mentioned in connection with the account of the revolution against Athaliah, 2 Chr 23:20.[64] In the bronze altar, beside which they stood, we must see the altar put there on the northern side by Ahaz, according to 2 Kings 16:14f. It is not the altar mentioned in 8:16 and installed by him directly in front of the temple entrance, nor that postulated by J. de Groot as the "small" altar deriving from the pre-Davidic age.[65] The figures stand on the "left" (oriented from the east), i.e., harmful, side of the temple—should we see in this their function hinted at?

■ **9:3, 4** First of all Yahweh gives an order to the priestly figure clothed in linen commanding him to mark the remnant which is to be preserved.[66] The existence of a pious remnant is surprising after the total assertions of sin in Ezek 8. Its mention appears once again to show earlier elements of tradition which go back behind Ezekiel to the Elijah narratives. Thus in the context of a great announcement of judgement (1 Kings 19:15–17), Yahweh spoke to Elijah of the 7000 who had not bowed the knee to Baal, and whose mouth had not kissed him, and who should therefore be spared (v 18). Ezek 9, in a clear reference back to Ezek 8, speaks of those "who sigh and groan over all the abominations which are committed in it (Jerusalem)." What are these groups who regard every abomination as such, without being able to change them? A glance at 44:15 (beside v 10) raises the question whether they were groups of the Zadokite priesthood, who must have seen the abominations but were strongly lacking in influence. Or does Ezekiel think of prophetic groups such as the group around Jeremiah? Or is it, as with Elijah, a small secret group, unknown to the prophet himself, but mentioned to him by Yahweh so that the prophet had to believe now that this group still existed.

In this group Yahweh would reveal the future of his elect people in Jerusalem. It is in any case striking how this promise of a pious remnant spared by the judgement in Jerusalem is left unutilized in the further preaching of Ezekiel, whilst room is given to quite different statements about the surviving remnant, cf. to 5:3f; 6:8–10; 12:16; 14:22f.[67]

■ **9:5** After the man clothed in linen the six executioners are commanded, like the destroying angel in Egypt, to pass through the city. In the merciless divine command there echoes as a *leitmotif* the unsparing nature of the divine command of 8:18. In all severity it is unfolded: no age, no sex escapes it. Only those marked with the sign of divine ownership must be spared. Indeed in a climax it becomes clear that there can be no flight into the sacred area of Yahweh itself for those fleeing from the judgement. Jeremiah's rejection of pious regard for the temple, which was proclaimed in an unholy trisagion: "The temple of Yahweh, the temple of Yahweh, the temple of Yahweh is this" (Jer 7:4) and which believed, in the depths of its own self deceit, to find security here: "We are delivered" (Jer 7:10) in order to go out afterwards to practice iniquity, is heightened in the mouth of the priest Ezekiel to unbearable sharpness: the slaughter will begin in the very sanctuary of Yahweh. As Ezekiel had shown the people's sins on the route from the city into the temple, so now the judgement takes the reverse way back from the temple into the city. Before the eyes of the prophet standing in the inner court the judgement begins with those who are standing there and who despise the presence of the Holy One (8:16–18).

■ **9:7** The following instruction, which is now found in v 7, to profane the house (בית "temple-house" as v 6b or "temple area" including the inner court as 8:16a?) and to fill the court with slain, comes rather late and is clearly separated from the context by the plural חצרות. It is to be cut out as an explanatory later addition. The disturbance of the text in v 7b (cf. note b)

Bedeutungsgeschichte biblischer Begriffe," *ThZ* 12 (1956): 505–525.

64 Cf. Kurt Galling, "Die Halle des Schreibers," *PJ* 27 (1931): 51–57.

65 J. de Groot, *Die Altäre des Salomonischen Tempelhofes*, BWAT NF 6 (Stuttgart: Kohlhammer, 1924), 29.

66 For the addition of v 3a see above p. 232 and also what is said on p. 238 to 8:4.

67 For the "Remnant" in the Old Testament see Werner Ernst Müller, *Die Vorstellung vom Rest im Alten Testament* (Neukirchen-Vluyn: Neukirchener, ²1973).

is plainly connected with the supplementary character of the whole verse.[68]

■ **9:8** When Ezekiel breaks out in a cry of intercession to Yahweh at this terrible event commencing in the midst of the temple then he is acting as a true prophet. According to the more recent interpretation of prophecy intercession for the community belonged especially to the office of the prophet.[69]

In the intercessions of Ezekiel it is striking that the prophet, even when he has been shown that the "remnant" of the pious will be saved (v 4), puts the question to his God: "Will you destroy the remnant of Israel, when you pour out your wrath over Jerusalem?"[70] We can answer this with a reference to the stereotyped formulation of such prayers of intercession (11:13, cf. also "the remnant of Joseph" Amos 5:15), but it must also be affirmed that a judgement which begins right in the sanctuary must necessarily raise the question whether a remnant of the people of God should at all find the possibility of protection with God once the center of life, the place of the divine presence, had been destroyed.[71]

For the third time there follows as a *leitmotif* on the cry of the prophet the affirmation of the mercilessness of Yahweh (8:18; 9:5), who now brings upon the people their own "ways" (cf. to 7:4, 9). This is established here by a prefatory remark about the guilt of the house of Israel, which is very very great (במאד מאד otherwise in 16:13, and only again in Gen 17:2, 6, 20; Ex 1:7 in P). This is here much more extensively described as it had become clear in the abominations in the temple of Ezek 8. The reference to the complete injustice in the land in 8:17bα (cf. also 7:23), which there appears too early and breaks up the connection, appears to have had its original place here. The land is full of bloodguilt (דמים cf. to 22:2ff) and the city full of injustice (cf. to 7:10). For the second time the blasphemous reference to Yahweh's forsaking the land, which occurred in 8:12 in the mouth of the elders

responsible for political life, is heard. Does this hint that here also Yahweh will take the sinners with their own words?

■ **9:11** Directly after this hard rejection there follows the notice of the return of the man clothed in linen, who announces the fulfilment of his orders. Since this notice comes remarkably late and for its own part certainly marks the transition to a second phase in the activity of the man clothed in linen, many have wanted to see in it already a redactional connecting element which joins the original conclusion of the prophet's vision to a second vision which was once independent of Ezek 9 (Messel, Fohrer, cf. also Horst, "Exilsgemeinde," Hölscher, *Hesekiel*). However, what is then left of this second vision (Fohrer: 9:3a, 10:2, 7, 18f; 11:22f) is so small, whilst the immediate return of the man clothed in linen in a second vision is otherwise so remarkable that this solution is unsatisfactory. A closer consideration of the section makes clear that the return of the man clothed in linen, on whose heels the six executioners immediately follow, could not have been narrated earlier. The complete sequence of the events and words of vv 5–10, which has no cracks, should not be broken up. Furthermore a strong positive concern can possibly be seen in the reserve of the notice in v 11. Precisely at the point where Yahweh, apparently in utter severity, has refused the prophet's intercession, the man clothed in linen returns and by his announcement recalls that in the judgement a remnant will be marked out. If this remnant is not apparent in the public scene of the inner court, in which the prophet is left alone (as the addition of v 8 aβ [note a], which is lacking in 𝔊, rightly affirms), yet it is there. God's judgement is not without a place of pity.

■ **10:2** However, this is left in a cautious hint. Yahweh's frank word is also full of harsh judgement even at the point where he sends out the man clothed in linen to a second task. That now, unlike 9:2f, 11, the instru-

---

68 For the profaning of what is holy by corpses see above pp. 186f.

69 Gerhard von Rad, "Die falschen Propheten," *ZAW* 51 (1933): 109–120; Aubrey R. Johnson, *The Cultic Prophet in Ancient Israel* (Cardiff: University of Wales Press, ²1962). Thus Amos 7:2f, 5f; Jer 27:18, beside the prohibition of intercession in Jer 7:16; 11:14; 14:11. See also P. A. H. de Boer, "De voor-

bede in het Oude Testament," *OTS* 3 (1943); Franz Hesse, *Die Fürbitte im Alten Testament*, Unpub. Diss. (Erlangen, 1949), 54–58.

70 A later hand has sharpened this further: "the entire remnant" (note d).

71 In no case is 9:8 to be deleted with Goettsberger, "Ez 9:8, 11:13," as a subsequent addition on the basis of 11:13.

ment of the scribe is no longer mentioned in the equipment of the man clothed in linen, need not give rise to critical operations. The second task is no longer that of a scribe, but yet remains in another way the work of a priest. Who other than a priest could undertake to take hold of the holy fire of God! The narrative of Korah's faction shows how the fire of Yahweh encounters one who is not a priest (Nu 16:35).

In details the understanding of the scene which follows is loaded with many uncertainties. The analysis has shown that in it references to a single cherub have been subsequently overlaid by a large number of references which speak of a plurality of cherubim in the form of the creatures of Ezek 1. According to 10:2 the man clothed in linen receives the commission to go in (בוא) to the place בינות לגלגל, under the cherubim, in order to fill his hands with burning coals from the holy fire. According to the present context this undoubtedly means the burning coals between the creatures of the throne-vision (1:13). By 8:4; 9:3, the reader is prepared for the presence of this appearance of the divine glory, which then immediately enters from the gate into the inner court of the temple (43:3 then rightly refers to a coming [בוא] of the glory of Yahweh for the destruction of the city). It became clear in the analysis that the references to the כבוד אלהי ישראל do not belong to the original text. If, therefore, the references which mention a coming of the glory of Yahweh into the temple are removed, the conclusion cannot be avoided that the original text at first reckoned with the presence of Yahweh in his holy place, and that undoubtedly means in the most holy place of the temple. Thus it was also presupposed by 8:16f. From this the following departure of Yahweh, which is not just a departure after a short stay but an abandoning of his own particular dwelling place, first gains its full weight.

The "entering" (בוא), which is commanded the man clothed in linen in v 2 and the "coming out"

(יצא) narrated in v 7 are therefore intended in the original text as an entering and coming out of the temple. According to 1 Kings 6:23ff there stood in the most holy place of Solomon's temple two cherub figures which covered with their wings the ark, which had been placed in this room (1 Kings 8:6f). The designation כרוב cannot be separated from the Akkadian *kāribu*, which is to be derived from *karābu* "to pray, to bless" and which denotes "a deity of the second rank, who especially speaks to the higher gods for men."[72] In Israel new conceptions must have been connected with the name, unrelated to polytheism. The position above the ark makes the cherubim appear in accordance with Egyptian prototypes as creatures protecting the ark.[73] This does not agree with the conception of Yahweh invisibly enthroned over the ark. In the predicate of Yahweh ישב הכרובים the cherubim have become Yahweh's servants who support his throne.[74] In the temple of Solomon the ark stood with its narrow end facing the exit (cf. the reference in 1 Kings 8:8 to the carrying poles). Since, according to Ex 25 18f which must also be valid for the positioning of the cherubim in the temple of Solomon, the cherubim stood at the ends (קצות) of the cover of the ark, which means also of the ark itself, the person who entered the most holy place found himself at once facing a cherub.

All these references make it probable that, by the command בא . . . . אל תחת לכרוב, the man clothed in linen was summoned by Yahweh into the temple in order to fetch the holy coals, which would then burn up the city, from a position under the cherub facing the door. As in 9:2 "the upper door" and "the bronze altar" refer to real features of the temple, as also clearly the cherub of 10:2. Except that here, unlike the two first-named things, it concerns in the prophet's vision not an object made by an artisan, but the living reality of Yahweh's throne-bearers, who then in v 7 also intervene actively in the event. That such is not

72 Herbert Haag, *BL*, 905. Cf. P. Dhorme and L. H. Vincent, "Les Chérubins," *RB* 35 (1926): 328–358, 481–495; W. F. Albright, "What Were the Cherubim?" *BA* 1 (1938): 1–3.

73 *AOBAT* 496; Hugo Gressmann, *Die Lade Jahwes und das Allerheiligste des salomonischen Tempels* (Berlin, 1920).

74 See above p. 120.

unheard of in a prophetic vision is raised beyond all doubt by Is 6 and the seraphim mentioned there.[75]

To the further question what is meant by גלגל, the present text leaves no doubt that it understood גלגל as the "wheels" under the cherubim in the sense of 1:15ff. Quite emphatically this identification is made in v 13 by Yahweh's own voice.[76] Does this identification, however, actually fit the original sense of the passage? Does the text presuppose wheels under the ark or under the cherubim which alone after 597 B.C. (Jer 3:16?) were left in the temple?[77] Or is גלגל a brazier for the incense offering, perhaps made movable with wheels, which was set before the ark? Or has this word—which denotes the wheels of a war chariot in Is 5:28; Jer 47:3; Ezek 23:24; 26:10; Ps 77:19, and in Eccl 12:6 the pulley wheel at the well, and in Is 17:13; Ps 83:14 in a derived meaning, the wheel-shaped thistledown driven by the wind—nothing to do with all this? Is it a fireplace like the אראל of 43:15? Should we then preserve בינות ל as the original text? All these questions can only be put, but not answered with certainty. If we are concerned here actually with a visible object seen with wheels, then this text could have given a considerable impulse to the elaboration of the wheel speculation of 1:15ff.

However we interpret גלגל, it is clear that the figure clothed with linen was to take some of the fire from the most holy place and scatter it over the ungodly city in whose area the temple stood. Again the metaphorical language (9:8 "pour out [coals of] fury") finds here its objective realization.[78] Then 10:7 describes how the cherub himself stretched out his hand to the fire and put some of it into the palm of the hand of the man clothed in linen, who then left the temple. B. Yoma 77a believes it can see in this a feature of unforeseen mercy: "If the coals from the hand of the cherub had not become cool in the hand of Gabriel, so would . . . no remnant and no survivors be left." That Ezek 10 no longer narrates expressly the carrying out of the con-

sumation need not point to a gap in the text (Balla, Fohrer). It is elsewhere demonstrable in Hebrew narrative style that a command alone is given, whilst its fulfillment is left untold as an obvious consequence.[79]

Within this event there arises something further, in which the "end" of Jerusalem occurs. Just as is stated in the Desert Narrative of P (Nu 14:10; 16:19), Yahweh appears suddenly at his dwelling place in his glory, coming before men out of the unseen. There, however, this occurs in order to introduce a revelation in word and judgement, whilst here it is in order to abandon his sanctuary without a word. We must certainly understand v 4 as the first act of this event. From his throne above the cherubim, from which hitherto he had invisibly accompanied the prophet with his word, he enters upon the מפתן הבית. In 1 Sam 5:4, a caricature of this event, the head and hands of the Philistine god are cut off and lie on the מפתן. Thus it is probable that we should seek the מפתן הבית in the inner part of the temple. Hitherto מפתן has usually been translated as "threshold" (cf. also note c to 9:3), though Koehler-Baumgartner (after Winckler) conjectures the translation "podium" (for the image). What the function was in Jerusalem of this "place of appearance" where the "seeing of God" took place, which the psalmists so earnestly desired (27:4; 42:3), can no longer be made out. It is clear, however, that by this entrance of Yahweh on to the מפתן of the temple, the house and court (singular) were filled with the cloud and glory, the attributes of the appearance of Yahweh. 1 Kings 8:10f is analogous.

■ 10:18a After the man clothed in linen has left the house with the fire, the glory of Yahweh abandons the sanctuary. V 18a mentions this, and at the same time confirms the fact that vv 2 and 7 concern events in the inner part of the house. The departure from the temple area does not take place immediately, however, so that the sacred regulations for the gate, which were also sacred law for human pilgrims as the entrance-liturgies

---

75 See above p. 99.
76 Mülinen's ("Galgal") translation of v 13: "And one wheel called out to the other the praise of his majesty" is quite erroneous.
77 Cf., however, above pp. 127f.
78 See above p. 136.
79 See Walter Baumgartner, "Ein Kapitel vom hebräischen Erzählungsstil" in *Eucharisterion für H.*

Gunkel, FRLANT NF 19 (Göttingen, 1923), 145–157, especially 145–150.

(Ps 15; 24:3–6 [cf. 7–10]) and the "entrance-law" (Ezek 40ff) show, were missed out.

■ **10:19bα** Thus, as a second station, the gate in the east is mentioned explicitly. For this we must think of the gate of the temple area proper (cf. בית יהוה 8:14), which led from the temple court into the original palace court. The east gate, and not the gate of evil in the north, is again in 43:1ff; 44:2 the gate of Yahweh, where we must think of the outer east gate corresponding to the extension of the sphere of holiness.

■ **11:23** From this gate the glory of Yahweh departs from the city area, to which the palace court also belonged, and went to the east of the city across the Kidron valley to the Mount of Olives. It is unnecessary here to discuss the Jewish tradition (*b Roš Haššanah* 31a) about the further whereabouts of the divine glory. It is sufficient that the prophet had seen the departure of Yahweh from his sanctuary, and therewith the completion of the judgement upon the city, over which the divine fire has been poured out.

■ **11:24** His vision finishes here. The spirit then took him back to his abode among the exiles.

■ **11:25** There the vision passed from him, and he became free to declare to the exiles what had come to him in his visions by the "word of Yahweh."

Aim

The men, who came before the prophet in his house, expect a divine word from him, which would comfort them in their being cast out. The vision which God grants to his prophet, and which he afterwards has to proclaim to his fellow exiles, contains a revelation of the depths of sin and of the judgement which falls upon it.

Throughout nothing is spoken in a cosmopolitan generality. The references to sin and judgement start from the fact, which is far from obvious and unheard of, that there is a place under the broad sky to which God has given his presence and his holy nearness to men out of undeserved grace. In this act he has summoned a people which is allowed to live round about this place and dwell with their faces toward Him—a people in whose midst he will dwell and whose God he will be. With these words the Priestly narrator in Ex 29:45f describes, wholly in line with Ezekiel's purpose and intention, the history which God had begun with the deliverance of his people from the slavery of Egypt.

This makes the reference to sin so very strange that it refers to the activity of those who have been deemed worthy of dwelling around the place of the divine presence—a sin of the people of God, in which the latter despise its "jewel" (7:22). In a fourfold series the prophet is shown the actuality of such sin. In this the totality of sinfulness, which cannot be further exceeded, is unmistakably given expression.

Outside the palace, or city, gate Ezekiel sees an altar set up, which must provoke God to anger. It is not enough for the people to remain near the presence of God, under the one name proclaimed in this presence. We can no longer see clearly whether it was the fascination of novelty, of change in the religious life, of the intriguing stimulus of what is strange, or of a once traditional connection stemming from Israel's ancestors, however questionable in the divine ordinance, which had zealously multiplied the religious institutions and had led to the setting up of this altar. It is sufficient that this was a second object of pious desire, frequented outside the place of the given presence of God.

Even so we can only question, without obtaining certainty, whether there lay behind the activity of the seventy elders, who carried responsibility for the political well-being of the city, forms of religious devotion which were influenced by specific political aims of the time. Thus too can sin entice men away from the place of the real presence of God, so that men are led following political modes into the dark recesses of religious custom, in which all genuine distinctions between clean and unclean, true and false were lost. Men behave as though the living God no longer saw them.

What the prophet found at the entrance of the inner court was quite different. The weeping for Tammuz, with its clinging to the rhythm of the withering and blossoming of nature, undoubtedly met a strong human need—both as regards sympathy with nature and also the bringing of the phenomenon of "death" into the world of religious feeling. Does faith in the God who encounters his people in historical summons, challenging them to responsibility under the law and placing them in the clear need for decision in daily life, not leave an essential sector of pious human need unsatisfied? Thus sin, which seeks to give room for human needs in the sphere of piety and which includes the creator of all creatures equally in a partnership with their death and departure (in order in this way quietly to obtain the hope of their own rebirth), itself enters into the proximity of the divine abode.

Then it is finally the prayer to the sun, which rises victoriously each day over the world for all to see, in which the sin of Jerusalem, at the place of the divine abode, blasphemes the living God in an unbearable way. Here also men are in flight from the hiddenness of God, who keeps himself from every selfish grasp and who will be worshipped only by belief in his promise and by observance of his commands (cf. 20:5–7). The power of what is preeminently visible, the sun, here leads men, standing before the very sanctuary of God, to turn their backs on him. Inside the sanctuary they stand amidst lies, however much they veil their lies from themselves with a beautiful solar temple-theology and liturgy.

In all this it is not the sins of the "nations," the sins of "the world" which are described, but the sins of those who stand in the elect city, indeed in the innermost room of the sanctuary before the place of the divine presence, and think that here they will find protection and security from the "nations" and the "world" (Jer 7:10). The prophet sees the people ruined by their worship of lies.

Here it is now shown to him that where this occurs the judgement of God must start from this very place. It is a great mistake when the people who live near the place of the divine presence think that they will find here special security. Nowhere is sin shown for what it is so sharply as in this presence. What could appear at a place far from the presence of the Holy One as a possible fringe affair and elaboration of piety, is here shown in the strongest light in its blatant incompatibility with the worship of the only God. Thus the place of the divine presence becomes the place of the establishing of judgement, in which the power of the divine holiness not only unfolds its burning fire, but where also abandonment by the divine presence becomes a bitter reality. Where men thought that God was near to them, it becomes fearfully plain that he is no longer there. But how can the people continue when God is no longer in their midst?

Here it must also be said that we are not concerned with judgement upon the nations who are "outside," but with the "judgement at the house of God" (1 Peter 4:17). That death is the reward of sin becomes evident here at the place which men regarded as especially full of "life." Judgement cannot be interpreted here in a harmless way or as an unlucky misfortune, which could be understood with a "who knows whence it comes?" It is the power which stems from the place of the presence of the Holy One. It is being forsaken by the presence of God.

It also becomes clear, however, through this severe judgement, that it is not the blind and uncontrollable anger of the Holy One. Within the scene of judgement it becomes evident that God has set a mark on men by a priestly figure—all "who sigh and groan over all the abominations which are committed in their midst." Even in the blaspheming of the Holy One by human abomination, when men begin to groan over the abominations of the self-willed devotion of the people, then a place of mercy may be seen within the burning of the divine wrath and at the point of abandonment by the divine presence. The prophetic word is reserved about any fuller description of this place of protection. It is sufficient that the mark of divine possession is placed upon those who groan by the priestly figure in whose consecrated hands also the coals of the fire of judgement lie, and the messengers of death lose their power before this sign.

The Editorial Work in Ezek 8–11 assimilating it to the Call Theophany (Ezek 1).

Interpretation

Yahweh, in the surpassing wonder of his glory, had appeared to the prophet in the hour of his call, far from his homeland. The great ecstatic experience Ez 8–11, a year later, enabled him to see how the Lord in Jerusalem abandoned his dwelling place there in order to leave the city and temple to their destruction. The details have attempted to make clear that it was not incompatible with the Old Testament faith to regard Yahweh as dwelling in Jerusalem as his own elect earthly sanctuary and then again to see him freely appearing in power from heaven.[80]

The final composition of Ezek 8–11 shows that the circle of Ezekiel's disciples, from whose hands we have received the book, could not grasp this two-sided tension but sought to bring it into a more uniform conception. They desired to express in 8–11 also a coming of Yahweh from his supernatural dwelling place to Jerusalem, parallel to his coming to the place of exile in 1:1–4. The place of departure in Ezek should be assimilated to that of Ezek 1.

■ **8:4** This is how the addition 8:4 is to be understood, which makes the glory of Yahweh appear to the prophet not in the sanctuary, but at the North Gate, whence it has plainly come from a distance.[81] The reference back to the manifestation in the plain (3:23) similarly betrays the hand of the redactor who joined the separate visions together so that each points back to the preceding vision (3:23 to 1:1ff; 8:4 to 3:23; 43:3a, where באו [c.T] clearly already presupposes the reworked text of 8–11, to 8–11; 10:15, 22 are tertiary additions, cf. further to 43:3b). The title "glory of the God of Israel," which is not found outside the book of Ezekiel (8:4; 9:3; 10:19; 11:22; 43:2), represents a fuller description alongside the simpler כבוד יהוה of the style of Ezekiel himself (1:28; 3:12, 23; 10:4, 18; 11:23; 43:4f; 44:4). According to C. Steuernagel, this introduces the divine title אלהי ישראל, which was originally localized at the (amphictyonic) sanctuary in Shechem, into the ascription of glory.[82]

■ **9:3a** In 9:3a, in agreement with the further movement of the prophet, the divine presence moves into the inner temple area. Thereby 10:4 of the original text, to which the singular כרוב is related, is so clumsily anticipated that we may at once question whether the same editorial hand is at work as in 8:3, in view of the consistent use of the plural cherubim in the following. For the latter view it could certainly also be claimed that through 9:3a the join with the statement of the original text in 10:4 is gained. The temple cherub to which 10:4 originally referred is thereby already interpreted in advance as the cherub of the mobile throne-chariot in the sense of Ezek 1. The awkward duplication of the mention of the descent

of Yahweh from his chariot (9:3a נעלה = 10:4a וירם) may be acceptable if 10:4a is understood as past perfect.

8:4 and 9:3a show the main interest of the later editorial interpretation in Ezek 10. This seeks to make clear that the God who is now departing from the temple is the same, in his attributes and glory, as the God who appeared to the prophet at his call. Therefore the reference to the single cherub, which is to be found in the original text of 10:2, is silently elaborated by the reference to several cherubim, which are described by words borrowed from Ezek 1. The original cherub is now only discernible with difficulty.

■ **10:1** In the style of a vision (וארא והנה)[83] the throne of Yahweh is then described with words from 1:26a. That the figure seated upon it is not also mentioned as in 1:26b has its basis in the fact that the throne was already empty according to 9:3a. The mention of several cherubim, which have only been incorrectly introduced through the singular כרוב of 9:3a, is then in many ways surprising.

■ **10:2, 3** Through the addition of מבינות לכרבים in the original text of 10:2, the place from which the fire comes, and which according to the original text was to be sought in the inner room of the temple, becomes identified with the place בין החיות mentioned in 1:13, i.e., a place outside the temple building, for the cherubim are standing "on the right of the house." Unlike the executioners of 9:2 who stood on the north (= harmful) side, the divine throne stands on the south (= beneficial) side of the temple building. In this way v 3b carries the reference to the cloud, which according to the original text in v 4 filled the temple building, out into the court. In the view of the later edition, Yahweh's chariot, which was a part of the manifestation of his glory, remained stationary here. The half verse is also distinct in its terminology from the original text through its mention of the "inner court," which in v 4b is simply referred to as the "court."

■ **10:5** V 3b is elaborated by v 5, which joins smoothly on to it, where the penetration of the noise of the wings into the "outer court" is mentioned (the term החצר החיצנה, which is frequently introduced in the presenta-

80 Pp. 116, 118–120.
81 See above p. 238.
82 Carl Steuernagel, "Jahwe, der Gott Israels" in *Stu-* *dien zur semitischen Philologie und Religionsgeschichte* *Julius Wellhausen zum siebzigsten Geburtstag*, ed. Karl Marti, BZAW 27 (Giessen: Töpelmann, 1914), 329–

tion of the eschatological temple, is not to be found in the original text chs. 8–11 at all). In place of the related הבית and החצר in the basic text (v 4, otherwise in 8:7, 16 and other passages) we have here as counterparts החצר הפנימית and החצר החיצנה (vv 3b, 5). In place of the glory entering the court (v 4) there is mentioned here the penetration of the sound of the wings into the outer court. If this is compared with the utterance of אֶל־שַׁדַּי, which has then been reflected back in a gloss on 1:24, then this קול אל שדי can be understood as thunder in the sense of the קול יהוה of Ps 29:3ff, which is connected there also with the אל הכבוד.[84]

■ **10:6** Also v 6, which goes back to v 2 of the original text, contains a subtle reinterpretation of earlier statements. Not only here is the בינות לגלגל, as also in the additions to v 7, immediately secured by a reference to "the place between the cherubim" in the sense of the manifestation of Ezek 1 (through the concluding remark that the man clothed in linen went אצל האופן), but at the same time the point of connection is created for the complex which describes the wheels and which is taken over as a whole from Ezek 1.[85]

■ **9:9–12, 16, 17** Vv9–12, 16–17, which correspond to 1:15–21, were certainly added as a connected whole. They presuppose, as was elaborated earlier, the expanded form of Ezekiel 1, added in 1:15ff. They refashion the text, in its details, with a certain freedom, remove the unevenness in the use of suffixes, offer explanatory additions (the ראש in the addition of v 11b), and abbreviate overextensive elaborations (cf. 10:16f with 1:19–21).[86] However, the extension of

the covering of the wheels with eyes on to the cherubim (and the wheels) belongs to a still later hand.[87]

■ **9:13** Whether the assertion of identity of the גלגל and the אופנים (v 13) had already been introduced by the first editorial hand cannot be decided with certainty.

■ **9:15** However, v 15, which speaks too soon in its first half of the departure of the cherubim and in its second half, within its explanation of the wheels, identifies the כרובים and the חיה, is undoubtedly the work of a later hand.

■ **9:14** So also is the statement regarding the appearance of the four faces of the cherubim (v 14), which is out of place in the passage about the wheels. From its basis in 1:10 it is distinguished by its smooth style, which no longer leaves any trace of the unevenness of 1:10, and still further by the replacing of the face of a bull mentioned in 1:10 in the third position by the face of a cherub, here set at the front. Since the entire form of the throne-chariot in Ezek 10 bears the name cherub this is very strange. Are we to think that this face of a cherub itself had four sides? What was then the first of its four sides? Clearly we have in mind here a cherub with one face which must then be distinguished from the cherubim of Ezek 10, which are identified with the חיות of Ezek 1. The replacing of the bull face must be understood from the fear of the bull form, which ultimately derives from anti-Canaanite polemic (cf. Ex 32:1ff; 1 Kings, 12:28–30; Hos 8:5f; 10:5; 13:2).

In vv 18a 19ba the basic text spoke simply of the departure of the כבוד יהוה, and not of an accompani-

349, especially 334f.

83 See above p. 104.

84 אל שדי must originally have been the name of a deity localized in pre-Israelite Canaan. Otto Eissfeldt, "El and Yahweh," *JSS* 1 (1956): p. 36 note 1, raises the question whether this may have been the local deity of Hebron. In the systematization of the Priestly Document it is the name behind which Yahweh hides in the patriarchal age. According to W. F. Albright, "The Names SHADDAI and ABRAM," *JBL* 54 (1935): 173–204, and *Stone Age*, it corresponds with the Akkadian *šaddā'ū* "Mountain-dweller." Cf. Koehler-Baumgartner. In the present interpretive addition, which stems from the priestly circle of Ezekiel's disciples, a noisy, destructive movement (echoing the Hebrew שדד) must be heard in the name.

85 For v 8 see above p. 232.

86 See above pp. 102, 104f. All these features are overlooked by Baumann, "Hauptvisionen," who wishes to see the "kabod-chariot vision" chs. 10f as more original than the "Spirit-chariot vision" of Ezek 1.

87 Cf. notes a and c to 10:12. For all the details of interpretation we must point to the comments on 1:15ff.

ment by the cherubim mentioned in 10:4 or by the גלגל. The movement away from the cherubim (10:4) was here directly the sign of the initial departure, which took place with an intervening stop at the מפתן, through the east gate and on to the Mount of Olives. Where the cherubim were regarded as the mobile throne chariot of Yahweh they must move with it.

■ **10:18b** So it became necessary that Yahweh should again go up onto the cherubim (v 18b).

■ **10:19a** On this chariot, with its wings and wheels, Yahweh departed from the place (v 19a), even though it first of all simply concerned the short journey to the east gate.

■ **10:19bβ, 20** The fact that Yahweh departs on the chariot is not to be taken for granted at all. One can trace the double emphasis affirming that the glory of the God of Israel remains over the cherubim (v 19bβ) (the suffix of עליהם goes back beyond v 19bα to v 19a) and the double identification of v 20, which has certainly been added subsequently by a later hand. Beside the prophet's direct recognition that it was the same manifestation as at the river Chebar, the recognition which follows to some extent logically from this that the creatures, or more precisely the individual figures of the חיה, were cherubim, is remarkably emphasized.

■ **10:21, 22** Why then there is added in v 21a the statement of 1:6, which is already partly taken up in v 14; in v 21b (besides 8) that of 1:8a; in v 22a once again an identification concerning the faces (cf. v 20a); and in v 22b the affirmation of movement of 1:9b, is not quite clear.

■ **11:22** Finally the addition which has been made in 11:22 to the account of the departure from the city area (11:23) has its formal analogy in the addition of 3:13 at the departure of the call-manifestation.

Aim

When we examine the hidden purpose of this considerable editorial work we are able to recognize first of all a special interest in the theological comparison of the conceptions of Ezek 1 and chs. 8–11, as it must have continued in the school of Ezekiel. In this we may

perhaps trace something of the zealous concern for the freedom of Yahweh. It should become clear that Yahweh came from afar, of his own free will, for judgement over Jerusalem, just as he had encountered Ezekiel in the hour of his call in the same freedom.

Furthermore, in the additions to Ezekiel ch. 10 we can trace the desire to make the description of Yahweh's presence in judgement, at the departure of his glory, no less splendid than was his appearance in Ezek 1. The glory of God was to be praised even in the midst of his active judgement. The people of God are accustomed to praise him, so that they give honor to him, even where human sin is great and the divine judgement severe.[88]

■ **11:1–21** *Those who remained and those who went into exile.* 11:1–21 stands out as a subsequent addition to the section chs. 8–11. What is narrated in 11:1–13 takes place at the point where the event of the departure of the divine glory in 10:19 has taken place. Also in content 11:13 recalls 9:8. However, in its particular substance 11:1–21 breaks up the clear progress of the departure of the glory from the sanctuary and introduces for the intervening period specific events of quite a new content.

In this, vv 14–21 stood out once again as an independent element. They tell of the simple receiving of a message, which is at first quite complete in itself and which had nothing to do with the event at the east gate of the temple area (vv 1–13). However, it is not by chance that vv 14–21 follow on vv 1–13. The oracle, which refers here to the hope set before the exiles, must undoubtedly be understood as a counterpart to the preceding narrative of the visions. These reveal the threat of judgement which stands over the inhabitants of Jerusalem, the blindness of whom is to be seen in v 15 also through a quotation of their own words. The link between the two elements is formed by the prophet's cry of intercession, known from 9:8, in view of the threatened position of the citizens of Jerusalem. The recognition of this intentional relation of ideas in the structure of the parts is important for a right understanding of the individual assertions, which sometimes are quite difficult, especially in vv 1–13.

---

88   Cf. F. Horst, "Die Doxologien im Amosbuch," *ZAW* 47 (1929): 45–54; Gerhard von Rad, "Die Lobpreis Israels" in *Antwort. Karl Barth zum 70 Geburtstag* (Zollikon-Zürich: Evangelischer-Verlag, 1956), 676–687.

Interpretation

■ **11:1** The declaration of judgement upon those who remain behind, in which the basic content must be found in vv 1–8 (without v 5a*α**), 13, takes place in the framework of what the prophet sees in a vision. By use of the affirmations of ecstasy of 8:3 (cf. ותשא אתי רוח ותבא אתי against ותשאני רוח ותביאני of 43:5) we are told how the prophet was brought to the east gate of the temple area. We must not think in this of an originally independent vision (Fohrer). The dependence on the language of 8:3 and the parallelism of the cry of intercession v 13 to 9:8, which (against Goettsberger, Fohrer) is to be preserved in both texts, on the contrary make it probable that 11:1 from the very beginning has been added directly on to 10:19bα as an expansion of the great visionary experience. It is likely that the expansion of ch. 10 had at that time not taken place. Since in content there is no compelling ground against regarding the basic content of vv 1–8 (without v 5aα*), 13 as from Ezekiel, and there are strong grounds for its composition in the time when Jerusalem was still standing (before the beginning of the siege 589 B.C.), an origin from Ezekiel himself is not to be excluded. Ezekiel would then have incorporated subsequently, with a surprising carelessness for exact placing in the narrative, into the older description of a vision one which he saw somewhat later and which is better described as a thematically displaced parallel to the original vision chs. 8–11 rather than as a continuation of it.

At the east gate of the temple area Ezekiel saw an assembly of 25 men, of which two are mentioned by name. The name Jaazaniah recalls the figure of the same name, to whom a reference was subsequently added in 8:11. Since, however, the names of their fathers are different, and the name Jaazaniah was at that time in no way singular, 8:11 cannot illuminate the figure here.[89] His father עזר is not to be identified with the father of the prophet coming from Gibeon, חנניה בן עזור, of Jer 28:1. For Pelatiah also further information is lacking. The title given to the two men שרי העם, which is only again found in post-exilic formulations (Neh 11:1; 1 Chr 21:2; 2 Chr 24:23;

Est 3:12), is scarcely to be compared with the single office of the שר העיר of Ju 9:30; I Kings 22:26; 2 Kings 23:8, but rather with the שרי יהודה of Jer 26:10; 29:2; 34:19; 52:10; Hos 5:10; Neh 12:31f. However, it is less precise than that title which mentions the administrative area of Judah (Jer 29:2 beside the sphere of the royal city of Jerusalem), and it simply designates the men as bearers of public responsibility among the "people." Does this betray the distance of the exiles from the concrete political relations of pre-exilic Judah? Cf. further the more general שרי ישראל, which is only to be found in 1 Chr 22:17; 23:2; 2 Chr 12:6; 21:4. Syntactically 1b fits well in its context, unlike the name reference in 8:11, so that its removal by Fohrer solely on the ground of uncertain metrical considerations is not acceptable, since without it v 13, which is not to be removed, hangs in the air. However, the mention of the name in 11:1 may have provided the impulse for the gloss in 8:11, just as the number 25 has subsequently influenced 8:16. Originally 11:1ff had nothing to do with the cultic offences of 8:16ff.

■ **11:2** The word of Yahweh, which comes to the prophet in 11:2 just as directly as in 8:5ff, describes the group seen by the prophet as "men who plan iniquity and who plan evil in this city." The חשבים און (חשב in the book of Ezekiel only again 38:10) may have its basis in the description of those who covet lands in Mic 2:1 (חשבי און). The יעצים עצה (עצה in the book of Ezekiel only in 7:26, cited from Jer 18:18; the verb יעץ is lacking in Ezekiel) points to a counsel in public matters (cf. to 7:26), which is clearly underscored by the בעיר הזאת.

■ **11:3** A decision about the city and its current affairs is clearly also the subject of the words quoted from the mouths of the men, in which the היא of v 3b undoubtedly means the city of Jerusalem. The reference in vv 6f expressly confirms this identification.

The second part of the men's speech, which alone is clearly taken up and answered in the following divine speech, shows in terse similes a specific self-understanding of this people and their relation to the city: "It is the pot, and we are the flesh." The simile of the pot is found again in 24:3ff. There also it is

---

89 W. F. Badè, "The Seal of Jaazaniah," *ZAW* 51 (1933): 150–156.

applied to the city (v 6, cf. 9). The event of the siege is interpreted as a cooking, i.e., heating up, of the pot. Here, as there, the contents of the pot are a metaphor for the population found in the city. Whilst, however, 11:3 speaks of the flesh, 24:3ff mentions beside the pieces of meat, the water and the best pieces of bone (מבחר עצמים), which are put in the pot. This opposes the view that the mention of the bones in 11:3 is an intentional antithesis: the good meat, by which the speakers are represented, in opposition to the useless bones, by which the exiles are meant, who are thrown out from the city. Rather the flesh must mean all the contents of the pot, which is described in 24:3ff by flesh and bones, and all the emphasis must lie on the אנחנו: we, the speakers, are the contents of the pot. It was the reckless claim of those who remained in Jerusalem after 598/7 B.C. that they were now the people of Jerusalem, so that in the intentionally added words of 14ff "the inhabitants of Jerusalem" claim, in regard to the whole land: "to us the land is given for possession." It is the declaration as definitive of a circumstance, which was to be looked at as a *provisorium* both by the exiles who hoped to return, as also by the prophet with his knowledge of an imminent judgement.

The formulation of v 3a, similarly roughly phrased in catchwords, must contain the specific plans of the men, which Ezekiel denotes as 'iniquitous plans' with the same words as Micah. A definite interpretation of v 3a has so far not been made. Since בנה בית, according to Dtn 25:9; Ruth 4:11; Prv 24:27, is used in the metaphorical sense of establishing a family (Ex 1:21 appears also to use it in the plural בתים in the sense of "families" and then possibly Neh 7:4 בתים בנוים is to be understood in a metaphorical sense [Horst, according to Haupt, Rudolph]), here also we may have this interpretation before us. It is very improbable, therefore, when Horst interprets the difficult לא בקרוב by reference to the family law in Holiness Code (Lev 21:2f; 25:25) concerning blood relationships and seeks to find here an arrangement which forbids, in the sense of Neh 7:4ff, the establishing of families with close relatives in the framework of the rules for a συνοικισμός. Would Ezekiel cite such an arrangement

polemically? Thus בנה בית can be understood in a literal sense. Are we then to take בקרוב in a temporal sense and interpret the clause as a heartless attitude of the rich who regard it as unnecessary that men should "soon" build houses for the poor (Fohrer)? Or should we see in it a despairing expression of anguish in face of the imminent danger (Irwin, van den Born), whereby, according to Irwin, we should particularly think of the bad policies of the leaders of Jerusalem which had brought about the danger? Or should we interpret the בקרוב, which is unique in the Old Testament, spatially, after the analogy of ברחוק in Ps 10:1, which likewise is only found once? So thus, as in Mic 2:1, people would have been referred to here who wanted to build houses for themselves, not only in the center, but in the outlying parts (Is 5:8) and so make it understood that they appeared as the lords and owners of Jerusalem?

■11:4 That Ezekiel received the commission to prophesy against this godless speech of the men seen by him in his vision has its closest parallel in the great vision 37:1ff, where, as here, the word of the prophet decisively controls the further vision.

■11:5 However, the expression that the spirit fell upon the prophet at the command of Yahweh is quite unique and contrary to all that is otherwise found in Ezekiel. There is, however, frequent reference to the falling (8:1) or coming (היה) of the "hand of Yahweh" upon the prophet.[90] The reference, which is likewise found in the earlier prophecy, of the coming of the spirit upon the prophet is otherwise not found in Ezekiel, where the "spirit," in the context of the prophetic experiences, shows a different character.[91] The assertion is also structurally quite out of place in 11:4 within a spirit-experience (v 1) and can only be understood as a clumsy addition by a later hand, which must have intended to explain the especially powerful effect of prophesying in the manner of earlier prophets through a fresh inrush of the spirit of Yahweh. The parallels 34:2; 37:4, 9 make it probable that we should make the command to speak אמר (34:2; 37:4, 9 ואמרת) follow directly the הנבא (בן אדם) and cut out v 5aα* (up to אלי).

---

90   See above pp. 117f.
91   See Excursus 3. 11:24; 37:1 cannot be adduced here.

In a surprising extension of the group addressed the prophet then addresses the "house of Israel," the most secret thoughts of which Yahweh knows, and which are expressed in the counsel at the east gate.[92] By "house of Israel" only part of the people remaining in the land can be intended (otherwise than in 11:15).

■ **11:6** The understanding of the section vv 6–8 is not immediately clear. It may first of all be probable that we have in v 6, just as in v 5aβb, a rebuke which refers to the sin of Israel, followed by Yahweh's threat of judgement in vv 7f introduced by לכן כה אמר יהוה. V 6 would then describe the brutal folly of the rulers of the city, which costs the lives of their victims. However, against this there stands the consideration that the word חלל, which occurs frequently in the book of Ezekiel (35 times, in a total of 93 occurrences in the Old Testament; verbal derivatives in 28:9; 32:26), never denotes those who are executed judicially, not even in the speech about the עיר דמים in 22:1ff. Also the formulations in 30:11; 35:8, which are related to that in v 6b, always mean death in battle.

■ **11:7** Thus we must already find in v 6 a part of the threat of judgement, which is then fully unfolded in the express announcement vv 7f and which opposes in a threatening way the speech of the men. As they had intended with their plans "to build houses" to secure their continual life behind the safety of the city walls, so it is revealed to them that they fill the city with people whose final destiny is not to be life, but death in battle. The dangerous existence of the "boiling pot," which is unfolded in 24:3ff, here also stands behind the metaphor used so undiscerningly by those addressed. The reference to "death in the pot" (מות בסיר) of the Elisha narrative, 2 Kings 4:38–41, thus receives a strange variation. The picture of the slain lying in the streets, which is sketched in v 6, was already well-known to earlier prophecy (Is 5:25; Jer 14:16; Na 3:10). The political authorities in Jerusalem, however, will be the subject of a special judgement outside the city and will be lost there to the sword which they fear.

■ **11:8** The concluding formula v 8bβ points to the fact that the original oracle had once ended with v 8.

Also the resumption of the אתכם אוציא מתוכה (v 7 c.T.; cf. note b) in the והוצאתי אתכם מתוכה (v 9) shows that in 9f a subsequent addition, which extends the divine speech into the form of a proof-saying, has been put in.[93] It must presuppose the event of the catastrophe of 587 B.C. narrated in 2 Kings 25:20f, according to which the leaders in Jerusalem were brought to the headquarters of Nebuchadnezzar at Riblah in Syria and were executed there "on the borders of Israel" (cf. to 6:14).[94] In the interpretative gloss vv 11f, which is still lacking in 𝕲, this same assertion has been added once again in the form of a proof-saying extended beyond the recognition formula. The addition v 12aβb states in a general formulation, verbally dependent on 5:7, the disobedience of the people, which has even left behind the actions of the "nations." The slight grammatical variation, which substitutes the masculine חקים for חקות which is otherwise usual in Ezekiel (cf. however, to 20:8, 25; 36:27), also possibly betrays another hand.

■ **11:13** At this prophesying there takes place in the prophet's vision the startling feature that Pelatiah falls down dead. Any fuller description of the event is lacking. The interpretation of this event, which we may certainly not simply delete (Fohrer—why should this event, which lies not at all in a simple straight line with the preceding threat, have been arbitrarily added?), is immediately clear. The destruction which has been announced takes place symbolically before the prophet's own eyes, upon one of the figures seen by him. In this sign the word of the prophet is demonstrated as a destructive reality.

The question has repeatedly arisen whether we must really reckon with such a farsightedness of the prophet, which then passes over directly into a long-range action. The question contains a clear overstepping of a limit. The prophet narrates his vision. A glance at the event of Jer 28, which appears to be parallel, cannot lead us to brush aside the peculiarity of Ezek 11. Just as Ezekiel according to 37:1ff sets in motion mighty events through his word, within the context of a vision, so also does he here. The difference from 37:1ff appears to lie in the fact that contemporaries of

---

92 For מעלות רוחכם cf. note e on the text. see above pp. 213f.
93 Zimmerli, "Wort."
94 For the problem of such interpretative later exegesis

259

Ezekiel from Jerusalem, who are mentioned by name, participate in the vision. As we have already stressed in connection with Ezekiel 8, the portrayal there, with all its concrete references, must be understood as a stylized vision, built up around a particular viewpoint. So also is this true here. The question whether at the moment of this vision Pelatiah died in Jerusalem cannot be answered from Ezek 11:1ff. It must therefore seriously be questioned whether it would really have been a temptation to Ezekiel if it had not happened at this moment. The validity of the prophetic word does not depend on its fulfillment according to the calender, as can be readily demonstrated from prophecy.[95]

Setting

The view that the whole scene, in the manner of Jer 28, was experienced by Ezekiel working in Jerusalem (Herntrich, *Ezekielprobleme*) is as exegetically arbitrary as the view of L. Finkelstein, who seeks to find in Pelatiah one of the elders of 8:1.[96] We may at once compare the genuine situation of a controversy in Jer 28 with the distant oracle of Ezekiel, which argues by the citing of words which have been brought to him from a distance and which may have stimulated his vision.[97] Ezek 11 contains no element of direct encounter.

Aim

The scene, which once again ends with a despairing cry of intercession by the prophet, is clearly distinct from the vision of Ezek 8f. Not the sanctuary (8:6, 16) and its cultic activity, but the city (9:3) and its political affairs are here the sphere of man's guilty actions. Thus the guilt which is here revealed to the prophet is not a turning away from the place and manner of the divinely given presence and order of worship among his people, but the disregard of the manner in which God encounters his people in history and will continue so to do. The year 598/7 B.C. had broken down assurances and left open wounds. The preaching of a Jeremiah and a Zephaniah which preceded that year had sought to make heard that in this destruction and wandering God spoke afresh to his people, to make

his presence felt by it and to call it to responsible action. Instead of this the prophet Ezekiel sees how the people, which had passed through this judgement, sought hurriedly to build up again a secure life behind the walls of its city. He saw how his brothers in the east, in the Babylonian plain, who were cut off from unity with their people, were swiftly struck out of their political reckoning, and how they praised themselves as the people who had escaped with their lives and had the sole right of survival in the city of God. "It is the pot, and we are the flesh."

Over such ungodly forgetfulness and unwillingness to repent the prophet sees judgement breaking in. Significantly it began in the death of an individual, who was responsible for this wrong attitude, coming as a thunderclap. What had been built behind such apparently safe walls was built for the slain. Death sits in judgement. The end of human unwillingness to listen, which closes hardened hearts against judgement and misunderstands the mercy received, can only be a new, and more severe, judgement.

The cry of the prophet reveals the deep menace of this severe threat of judgement by God. Must the destruction of the people of God to the very last remnant not then be the end of God's way? Goettsberger, "Ez 9:8, 11:13," would find this particular threat in the death of the man whose name means "Yahweh causes a remnant to escape."[98] The divine speech which follows in 11:14–21, and which was originally separate, is undeniably a part of the divine answer to this very question.

Interpretation

■ **11:14** *The divine word of grace to the exiles.* In distinction from vv 1–13, vv 14–21 are a message without vision or action. Yet here also it concerns the divine answer to a speech of the citizens of Jerusalem which is again given as a citation.

■ **11:15** Whilst the exiles were concerned in 11:3 without being mentioned, now v 15 expresses in brutal clarity the assessment of them by the citizens of Jerusalem.

In an anacoluthic opening clause, the group of exiles

95 In apocalyptic things begin to change. Cf. further to 12:21ff.

96 Louis Finkelstein, *The Pharisees; the Sociological Back-*

ground of their Faith (Philadelphia: Jewish Publication Society, ³1962), p. 688 note 27.

97 See above pp. 257f.

addressed by Yahweh is described: "All your brethren, your relations and the whole house of Israel, of whom the inhabitants of Jerusalem say . . . ." Only here is mention made in so unusually personal a way of Ezekiel's "brothers." The following אנשי גאלתך (only found with the suffix here) clearly points in the same direction. Of the fourteen occurrences of the word גאלה no less than nine come in the extensive law of the Jubilee Year in Lev 25 (vv 24, 26, 29[bis], 31, 32, 48, 51, 52), which regulates the redemption and return of close possessions. The two occurrences in Jer 32:7f and Ruth 4:6f apparently describe two legal matters which have to do with the right of the redeemer (גֹּאֵל), i.e., the close relative, to exercise primary right of purchase. Thus in the אנשי גאלה we must see "the circle of those from whom a man could be called upon to help his family, especially on an occasion incurring the law of redemption" (Horst, "Exilsgemeinde"). In this specific reference which points to those who with Ezekiel were interested in his family inheritance, it already becomes clear that the following divine oracle has to do with the question of a share in the ancestral land. The third reference is comprehensively to "the whole house of Israel," which goes beyond the circle of Ezekiel's close, and farther, relatives (the addition of an emphasizing כל with the suffix is a linguistic peculiarity of Ezekiel also to be found in 20:40; 35:15; 36:10). This includes those who were affected by the speech of the Jerusalem citizens, i.e., the whole circle of the exiles, which here quite intentionally receives the name Israel.[99] Through the repetition of אחיך and כל it is strongly emphasized that the word of God must address every single one of the exiles without exception, tempted by the words of the citizens of Jerusalem.

The saying of the people of Jerusalem: "They are far from Yahweh; to us the land is given for a possession" is not merely an argument about property. It is a contestation in the full sense. Admittedly there is first of all in it an objective claim to legal right. It is spoken of the land where the original owners had already been away for some years and which had been taken over by those who remained behind. No longer

was any reckoning made that old rights of redemption were still declared. Beside the burning expectation of the return of the exiles, which can be seen in Jer 27–29, there had entered a realism (subsequently— or at the same time in different circles?), which also out of very selfish motives reckoned upon the final removal of the exiles and finally settled itself in the vacated properties—a mockery of the genuine obedient realism which Jer 27–29 demanded. This is shown above all in the religious motive which this realism produced. Whilst Jeremiah, by his appeal to acceptance of the deportations of the upper classes as a real fact, called for obedience in a sense which accepted this act as a judgement from the hand of Yahweh upon those who remained behind as well, yet those who remained in Jerusalem excluded themselves from this judgement. They ascribed the realization of judgement to the exiles, whilst to themselves they ascribed grace and the renewed offer of the assurances of this grace. The statement: "They are far from Yahweh" is ambiguous. Beyond the literal fact that the exiles were far from Jerusalem, it hinted at the distance of the exiles from the place of the presence of God in a spiritual, and thus adverse, sense: those who have been deported are the sinners, who have gone far from Yahweh (cf. 8:6; 44:10) and who therefore have been literally put away by him and robbed of the assurances of his presence. The land was the sacramental assurance of the favor of Yahweh. Whoever lost the land had visibly lost the sign of his favor and was far from Yahweh's salvation.

The divine word, which basically must only have comprised those parts of vv 16, 19f which are formulated in the third person plural, goes out to those who are attacked by such judgements. Two things can be found in this:

■ **11:16** The first is a word of sharpened confirmation of the fact which the Jerusalem citizens affirmed. Whereas they had quite objectively said: "They are far from Yahweh," now Yahweh reaffirms this statement in the first person and declares that it is a condition which he himself has brought about (for כי "certainly" see Koehler-Baumgartner under כי;

---

98   פלטה, cf. 14:22.
99   For the counterpart in 11:5 see above pp. 258f.

Horst, "Exilsgemeinde"). The favored expression of Ezekiel of "removing among the nations and scattering among the countries," with its usual parallelism of the verbs הפיץ and זרה (12:15; 20:23; 22:15; 36:19; of Egypt 29:12; 30:23, 26) is varied here (and only here!), in clear dependence upon the saying of the people of Jerusalem, by replacing the זרה with הרחיק (coming first). Besides this, however, the unassailable reality brought about by Yahweh is described by a second very unusual formulation: "And I have been to them (only) a little for a sanctuary (למקדש מעט) in the countries to which they have gone."

This statement, with its striking speech form of Yahweh's personal address, cannot be understood without the counterpart of the covenant formulation אהיה להם לאלהים, which follows in v 20. It is a variation of that assertion, which is found nowhere else. In the Priestly history it is clear from the promise to Abraham (Gen 17:8), through the narrative of the call of Moses (Ex 6:7), right up to the (original) conclusion of the law-giving with the prescription for the Tent of Meeting (Ex 29:45), that the particular saving content of Yahweh's history with his people consists in the fact that God gives himself as God to his people (והייתי להם לאלהים). This is then expanded in the full covenant formulation by the counterpart that the people will become the people of God. Furthermore the Priestly history makes clear that this self-giving to the people was given concrete realization in that God established a sanctuary in Israel and dwelt there by his presence in the midst of his people. Ez 8 shows that Ezekiel also knew of this. So we are led to think directly of a priestly variation of the covenant declaration which was formulated אהיה להם למקדש. In the מקדש the divine presence was established in the covenant people. Thus the Holiness Code can directly demand מקדשי תיראו (Lev 19:30; 26:2), as though in מקדש the person of Yahweh was embodied, to whom the demand for ירא is otherwise related (Dtn 5:29; 6:24 and other passages; with מן Lev 19:14, 32; 25:17, 36, 43).

"They are far from Yahweh" say the citizens of Jerusalem. Yahweh takes up this saying: "I have carried them far off." In the complaint of the exiles

(37:11) this distance is described using the language of death. In the categories of the covenant formula it would run: "I am not their God" (is this to be read in Hos 1:9?), and in the priestly variation: "I am not a sanctuary to them." Against this it is now noteworthy that the divine saying in 11:16b is formulated ואהי להם למקדש מעט בארצות . . . . This is the divinely formulated saying regarding the position of the exiles: "A little sanctuary." The grace of a preservation of the exiles, almost completely obscured to men, is expressed in this formulation. We must interpret it from what is recognizable in Ezekiel himself: Where the exiles sat down at the site of their limited worship by the rivers of Babylon—there the prophet saw the manifestation of the divine glory. Where the elders sought instruction in the house of the prophet—there the prophet was gripped by the hand of Yahweh (8:1ff; cf. 14:1; 20:1). All of these events did not replace the reality of the sanctuary. Nevertheless it was certainly not a place abandoned by God. It was a form of the divine presence in the place of exile. 𝔗 "I gave them synagogues (בתי כנישתא), which were distinct from my sanctuary, and they were few in the lands wherein they were carried," undoubtedly introduces here anachronistically the later situation of the organized synagogue. What is in mind here is undoubtedly the limited forms of a worship practiced far from the sanctuary, which was accepted gracefully by Yahweh as a (reduced) possibility of a real life.

■ 11:19 Beyond this description of the restricted circumstances there now comes, as a second feature, the firm promise of a new being, which will transform the old evil one. The heart, the seat both of thought and of the will, must be changed.[100] Its hardness, described as a stony heart, must give place to a new genuine vitality, to a heart of flesh. The spirit must become new.[101] 36:27 mentions directly here the spirit of Yahweh (רוחי) as the new element; whilst 18:31, in an imperative formulation, offers to faith, as something to be taken hold of, what is promised as a gift in 11:19. The fruit of this new gift will be the keeping of the commandments (משפטים – חקות) of Yahweh. In such an event the forfeited reality of the covenant will once

---

100 Johnson, *Vitality*, 77–88.
101 רוח here used of men, Johnson, *Vitality*, 26–39.

again become a full reality for Israel by divine gift. Instead of למקדש מעט Yahweh will once again in the full sense become God for his people, and the people will once again in the full sense be God's people.[102]

The basic text of 11:14ff, in its central promise of the renewal of the covenant (the word ברית then 16:59–62) through the revival of heart and spirit, appears to have left it at that, without further pointing out what consequences this event would have for the outward conduct of the exiles.

■ **11:17** At a later time it has been expanded (still by Ezekiel himself?) in v 17 with the full promise of the future gathering from the nations and the new gift of the "Land of Israel," which represents the assurance of the covenant.[103] The fresh introduction to the saying, parallel to v 16a, betrays the later character of the promise, as does the form of the direct address in second person plural and perhaps also the slight incongruence between גוים (16) and עמים (17). In 20:34, 41; 34:13 it has very close parallels.

■ **11:18** V 18 offers a second addition, which, stylistically linking up again with the form of the basic text in the third person plural, expressly declares the removal of the cultic abominations after the return to the land. Does the declaration of v 21, which is also broken off in its beginning, stem from the same hand? Thus besides the promise of deliverance, this gives a threatening reference to the judgement upon those who do not reject their "abominations." Does this addition derive from the period of the exile or from the time after the return to the land?[104]

Setting

After 598/7 B.C. Jeremiah (Jer 27f) turns against those voices in Jerusalem which expected a hasty redress of the judgement of the first deportation. We hear nothing from him of statements by the citizens of Jerusalem which displayed a speedy forgetting of the deportees. It is certainly not accidental that it was from one of those carried east from the homeland that we hear particularly clearly about those other voices, when Ezekiel cites the words of the men of Jerusalem. The bitterness of being hastily forgotten echoes through quite clearly. We cannot rightly see here that the "attitude demanded of the prophet in favor of his relatives and those who shared their fate" must presuppose his presence in Jerusalem (Horst, "Exilsgemeinde").[105] Ezekiel does not speak as if he were really in Jerusalem, and he does not speak of the exiles as absent. Rather the "remoteness" both in the quotation of the words of the Jerusalem citizens as also in the divine word must be understood as "remoteness" from Yahweh, i.e., from his chosen place in Jerusalem. There is no decisive argument against the derivation of the oracle from the exiles, but rather much in favor of it.[106]

Chronologically the oracle undoubtedly goes back to the period when the Jerusalem sanctuary was still standing, i.e., before the year 587 B.C. A comparison with 33:24, where those who remained in the land after 587 B.C. are described as "the inhabitants of these ruins," speaks clearly enough in this regard.

Purpose

In this oracle God speaks about the group of those whom he had driven away from his presence in judgement and whom he had made to feel the heat of his anger quite directly. Later oracles will show how despairingly these circles must have viewed their position: "How can we live?" (33:10), "Our bones are dried up" (37:11). Life far from God was death.

God's word does not in any way render this situation harmless. God himself, in his judgement, has driven away the members of his community into this remote and hostile place. However, over the despairing situation of hostility and death he first of all proclaims: It is not death. Even for the departed God remains "a little sanctuary." Even in exile there was still room

---

102 Outside of the references in the Priestly Document and in Ezekiel (Lev 26:12; Ezek 11:20; 14:11; 34:24; 36:28; 37:23, 27, also Zech 8:8) the double- or single-sided repetition of the covenant formula is above all to be found in the Deuteronomic parts of Jeremiah (Jer 7:23; 11:4; 24:7; 30:22; 31:1, 33; 32:38).

103 See above p. 203.

104 For דרכם בראשם נתתי see above to 9:10, also 22:31. For vv 17–20 cf. the comments on 36:24–27. We must also consider the parallels with Jer 31:31–34, Miller, *Verhältnis*, 98f.

105 Cf. the related text 33:23–29.

106 The Jerusalem counterpart is to be found in Jer 24. See Miller, *Verhältnis*, 96f.

for prayer and for obedience to the law—even where there was no longer a sanctuary to proclaim his presence before men's eyes, and therefore where all prayer must be without the sign of God's listening, a blind leap into space to the hidden, but mighty, God.

Secondly, however, he makes his great promise to this place of exile and judgement, where there can only by prayer from a distance: Here, and not in Jerusalem, where God's temple still stood where he was still apparently a "sanctuary" for his people without restraint, there would take place that which really established the covenant of the future. Here, and not in Jerusalem, where men congratulated themselves on the possession of the land as the pledge of the divine presence, would the transformation occur. To those who had become poor and who had been robbed of every religious assurance, God would give a new heart and a new spirit. Here the strong hardness of human nature which closes men against God and their fellow men would be broken and made into a human heart of flesh, i.e., in every way human, capable of hearing, loving, seeing, and praying to God in truth. Thus here once again God would become God to his people, and they would truly become his people on the basis of a gift given to the exiles.

To this there has subsequently been added that only here can God be concerned to lead his people out of their exile back to the homeland, out of their abandonment into his presence, and so give to it the whole physical fulfillment of its being God's people: the promised land (v 17). Here then would also take place the open rejection of everything which had previously dishonored God (v 18)—whilst there, where such a rejection had not happened, God's judgement would be given a free hand to execute the death that lies hidden within sin (v 21).

This oracle, which first came at a definite point of time quite independently of other oracles and visionary experiences of the prophet, was connected, either by Ezekiel or his disciples, with the vision of judgement upon Jerusalem's politicians at the east gate of the temple. This ended with the despairing cry of the prophet and then further with the great prophetic vision of judgement upon the city and the departure of the glory of Yahweh, i.e., the end of the sanctuary. In this way this word of divine assurance is given a somber background which first fully brings it to light. Precisely where the judgement began, at the house of God and in the city of God, which appeared to possess all the guarantees and assurances of, and historical claims to, the divine presence, and where it became clear that the people of God had foundered because it had blasphemed God where it should have honored him, there the miracle of grace would be heard. This promises that a true people of God would be established where to man's view in face of complete disaster there no longer remained any life.

Beyond this impossibility that the people of God could hold on to God in his sanctuary on earth, this oracle asserts the free divine possibility that he would establish his covenant in that dark abyss in which men, even the men of God's own people, had been destroyed by their own works (even their pious works).

The Exile's Baggage.
A Visionary Sign for the Blind.

Bibliography

Cf. to 3:22–5:17.
F. Giesebrecht
Die Berufsbegabung der alttestamentlichen Propheten
(Göttingen, 1897), 166–171.

12

1 And the word of Yahweh came to me:
2/ Son of man, you dwell in the midst
of a rebellious house,ᵃ which has eyes
to see, but sees not, 'and'ᵇ ears to hear,
but hears not, for they are a rebellious
house. 3/ But you, son of man, prepare
for yourself an exile's baggage [and go
away]ᵃ in the (light of) day before their
eyes and go away from your place to
another place before their eyes.ᵇ
Perhaps they will see it, for they are a
rebellious house. 4/ And bring out your
baggage in the (light of) day before
their eyes asᵃ baggage for exile, and you
yourself shall go out at evening before
their eyes,ᵇ (just) as exiles usuallyᶜ go
away. 5/ Before their eyes, dig a hole
through the wall and bringᵃ (your
baggage) through it. 6/ Before their
eyes you shall liftᵃ (the baggage) upon

12:2 2a 𝔐 בתוך בית המרי. The reading of 𝔊 (𝔠 𝔊 𝔄
𝔊ʰ) ἐν μέσῳ τῶν ἀδικιῶν αὐτῶν points to an inner
Hebrew scribal error תועבותיהם(תוך)ב, which is
noteworthy for the lack of any antecedent for its
suffix and cannot therefore, with Cornill, be recognized as the more original text.

b The copula, attested by 16 MSSᴷᵉⁿ 𝔊 𝔗 𝔊 𝔙,
has fallen out by haplography in 𝔐 אזנים.

3 3a 𝔐 וגלה is not attested by 𝔊 𝔏ᶜ 𝔠. Since it anticipates awkwardly the following וגלית we must
regard it as having arisen through dittography of
the preceding גולה (for the transposition of ו with
the following consonant, cf. note a to 10:3). If we
retain it we must, with Driver, "Ezekiel," 150, understand the following bα as the protasis to bβ.

b bα is not attested in 𝔊⁸⁷ ᵗˣᵗ ¹⁰⁶, but is not to be
excised with Herrmann as "an explanation of the
previous clause." Cf. the exposition.

4 4a 𝔐 ככלי. 𝔊 (𝔏ᶜ) leaves כ untranslated.

b We should not miss here the לעיניהם, which is
not attested by 𝔊 (𝔏ᶜ) 𝔊, since v 3b has already so
clearly emphasized: אולי יראו. Nevertheless 𝔊,
which already through its change from ἐνώπιον
αὐτῶν (v 3) to κατ' ὀφθαλμοὺς αὐτῶν (v 4) betrays a
tendency to stylistic variation, must here have abbreviated out of regard for style.

c 𝔊 ὡς ἐκπορεύεται αἰχμάλωτος, 𝔙 sicut egreditur
migrans does not necessitate the revocalizing of the
כְּמוֹצָאֵי גּוֹלָה of 𝔐 גּוֹלָה) Cornill, Bertholet;
Fohrer, Koehler-Baumgartner, BH³). For the plural
use of מוֹצָא cf. Ps 65:9.

5 5a 𝔐 והוצאת. This hip̱ʻil, in spite of 𝔊 𝔏ᶜ 𝔊 𝔗 𝔙
which appear to point to a reading ויצאת, is much
too firmly attested in view of its reappearance in the
analogous statements of vv 6a, 7b, 12a (twice cf.
note c) for it to be simply changed to the qal in all
these texts (so the majority). It is determined by v 4a
(7a) and, in an elliptical formulation, it gives expression to the idea that the baggage also must be
taken through the opening in the wall. Driver, "Ezekiel," 150, would like to add in this ellipse a נפשך.
The analysis (p. 268) shows that all the texts with the
elliptical הוציא belong to the late interpretation.

6 6a 𝔐 תשא. 𝔊 ἀναλημφθήσῃ (ʼΑ ἀρθήσῃ) 𝔏ᶜ susci-
pieris, 𝔙 portaberis take the verb as passive and derive
from it a picture of the king being carried out. Only

your shoulder, in[b] the dark you shall carry (it) out;[c] your face you shall cover, that you may not see the land. For I have made you a sign for the house of Israel.

7 And I did as I was commanded. I brought out my baggage,[a] as baggage for exile, in the (light of) day. And in the evening I dug a hole in the wall [with my hands].[b] In[c] the darkness I brought out[d] (my baggage). I[e] carried (it) upon my shoulder before their eyes.

8 And the word of Yahweh came to me the (following) morning: 9/ Son of man, has not the house of Israel, the rebellious house, said to you: What are you doing (there)? 10/ Say to them: Thus has [the Lord][a] Yahweh said: This oracle concerns 'the prince'[b] in Jerusalem and all the house of Israel who are in 'its'[c] midst. 11/ Say: I am a sign for you.[a] As I have done, so shall it be done to them. They must go into exile [in the horde of prisoners].[b] 12/ And the prince, who is in their midst, shall lift[a] (his baggage) upon[b] his shoulders. In the dark 'he will bring (it) out';[c] they will make[d] a hole in the

Θ reads ἀρεῖς. The same phenomenon is also found in vv 7 and 12.

b 𝔊 (𝔏^C) adds the copula in an attempt to smooth the text, cf. note a to 1:4.

c 𝔐 תוציא. MS$^{Ken\ 150}$ 𝔊 𝔏^C 𝔗 𝔖 (𝔙 *effereris*, Jerome *effugies*) as in v 5. Cf. note a to v 5.

7 7a 𝔊 passes over the כלי of 𝔐. It therefore introduces the copula to smooth over the roughness. Cf. note b to v 6.

b The ביד "with the hand" of 𝔐, for which Ehrlich, *Randglossen*, conjectures ביתד after Dtn 23:14, is not attested by 𝔊 𝔖 ℭ. Since it is missing in the corresponding expression of the divine command (5) and sounds peculiar in its absolute formulation without the suffix (analogies Is 28:2, with the negative 2 Sam 23:6; Job 34:20?), it is probably to be excised as a gloss (or a scribal error for בקיר?).

c 𝔊 again adds the copula, cf. note a.

d 𝔐 הוצאתי. For the versions cf. note a to v 5.

e 𝔊 ἀνελήμφθην 𝔙 *portatus*, *Σ* 𝔖^h: ἐβάστασα. Cf. note a to v 6.

10 10a אדני is lacking in 𝔊, see Excursus 1.

b 𝔐 הנשיא המשא הזה. 𝔊$^{BQ.88.62}$ ὁ ἄρχων καὶ ὁ ἀφηγούμενος offer no help towards understanding the difficult text. The literal τὸ ἐπηρμένον τὸ ἄρμα τοῦτο of *'A* presupposes the text of 𝔐. However, we must question whether or not the remaining 𝔊—tradition given by 𝔊^A with its τῷ ἄρχοντι καὶ τῷ ἀφηγουμένῳ, which is strengthened by *Σ* to περὶ τοῦ ἄρχοντος τὸ λῆμμα τοῦτο, and supported by 𝔗 על רבא מטול נבואתא הדא and 𝔙 *super ducem onus istud*, points to an introductory ל or על, which has been lost in 𝔐 and which must certainly then be repeated before (ו)כל בית ישׂראל. Or should we leave 𝔐, with Herntrich, *Ezekielprobleme*, 123, and translate in accordance with Jer 23:33: The prince is this burden!"? For v 10 cf. also the analysis p. 268.

c The suffix of 𝔐 בתוכם, which is striking in the present context, could be determined by the והנשיא אשר בתוכם (v 12). The context demands the reading בתוכה.

11 11a 𝔐 מופתכם. A change to מופת לכם (Ehrlich, *Randglossen*) is not necessary. The inaccurate translation in 𝔊 (ἐγὼ τέρατα ποιῶ ἐν μέσῳ αὐτῆς), against which 24:24 also speaks, is certainly not to be followed with Bertholet.

b 𝔊 (𝔙) smooth the text by the insertion of the copula. Cf. note b to v 6. The disconnected בשבי of 𝔐 is a secondary interpretation of בגולה, as can still be seen from 𝔖.

12 12a 𝔊 ἀρθήσεται, 𝔙 *portabitur*, cf. note a to v 6.

b על־אל cf. 1:17 note a. In v 6 𝔐 has על.

c Uncertainty prevails in the division of the short verbal clauses, as a comparison of 𝔐 and 𝔊 shows. A comparison with the parallel formulation in v 6 shows that a new sentence begins with בעלטה. Again 𝔊 introduces the copula here (cf. v 6 note b). 𝔐 has misread an older (יוציא =) יוֹצִא (for the hipʿil cf. note a to v 5) as וְיֵצְא (for the interchange of

wall, in order to bring (the baggage) out through it.[e] He will cover his face, 'so'[f] that he may not 'be seen' by any eye[f] (𝔐 because he does not see with his eyes) [he—the land].[f] 13/ And I will spread my net over him, and he will be taken in my snare; and I will bring him to Babylon in the land of the Chaldeans. Yet he will not see it and will die there. 14/ And all those who are round about him 'as his helpers,'[a] and all his troops will I scatter to the winds, and I will unsheath the sword after them. 15/ And they shall know that I am Yahweh when I scatter them among the nations and disperse them throughout the countries.

16   And I will let a few of them escape from the sword, from[a] famine, and from pestilence, that they may recount among the nations to which they came all their abominations, so that they may know that I am Yahweh.

consonants cf. note a to v 3) and so brought about the confusion of sentence division, which then gave rise to further scribal errors.

d 𝔐 יחתרו. 𝔊, which again wrongly puts in a copula, by its singular διορύξει assimilates to the singular context. In 𝔐 we must recognize an older reading, which related the sign-act of the prophet, as in v 11, not to the prince, but to the citizens of Jerusalem. A similar significance of the change of subject is already found in 10:19. Cf. further the analysis.

e 𝔐 להוציא. For the versions (𝔗) לאסקותיה attests the hip'il here) cf. note a to v 5.

f 𝔐 bβ יען אשר לא יִרְאֶה לעין הוא את הארץ is scarcely to be interpreted satisfactorily. 𝔊⁹⁶⁷ reads ὅπως μὴ ὁραθῇ and points to a Hebrew original למען אשר לא יֵרָאֶה, in which the last words of 𝔐 (הוא את הארץ), which are already suspect on account of their fresh connective הוא, are lacking. The καὶ αὐτὸς τὴν γῆν οὐκ ὄψεται, which still follows in the other 𝔊ᴹˢˢ, can scarcely be used for a reconstruction of a further part of the original text והוא את הארץ לא יראה (Cornill, Bertholet). It is an attempt in free translation to deal with the addition in 𝔐. This is to be understood, as a result of the change to יען אשר and the vocalization יִרְאֶה, as an assimilation to v 6. Cf. also Giesebrecht, 167¹, Cooke, Fohrer.

14   14a 𝔐 עזרה is, on the evidence of 𝔊 𝔏ᶜ 𝔖 𝔗, a scribal error for עֹזְריו.

16   16a MSS 𝔊 𝔏ᶜ 𝔖 𝔙 add the copula.

Form

The more recent exposition (cf. Hölscher, *Hesekiel*, Cooke, van den Born, Fohrer) is agreed that the narrative of the sign-action 12:1–16, in which Ezekiel announces the deportation of the Jerusalem citizens, has undergone some reworking with features of a second action which dealt with the personal fate of Zedekiah at the downfall of Jerusalem (2 Kings 25:4–7; Jer 39:4–7; 52:7–11). Whilst Ezekiel first receives the command to portray in broad daylight (יומם vv 3, 4, 7) to the people, which refuses to see, the event of the departure of the exiles before their eyes (לעיניהם vv 3a, 3b, 4a, 4b, 5, 6, 7), so that it may perhaps thereby see at last, there are woven into the sequel ever clearer features which point to an action in the obscurity of a dark night, i.e., the events in the nocturnal flight of Zedekiah (בעלטה vv 6, 7, 12, corresponding to (ה)לילה 2 Kings 25:4; Jer 39:4; 52:7). The explanation is given in v 10, which joins together both actions, that the action of the prophet concerns both the prince and the house of Israel in Jerusalem.

Giesebrecht (followed by Cooke), after a careful consideration of the narrative, came to the conclusion that the twofold character of the text is to be understood from the time of the composition of the whole section. Since the prophet had first outlined this after the destruction of Jerusalem, arbitrary features of the actual event of 587 B.C. have been woven into it as later clarifications of the account of the original action. However, the tensions in the statements, which are discernible right up to the syntactical structure, oppose the view of a single writing down of the text. Thus Bertholet and van den Born have attempted to work out with the methods of source analysis two complete parallel accounts, which were subsequently woven together. Our considerations so far concerning the book of Ezekiel lead us, however, to reckon here with a later interpretative addition to the text, in which a narrative compiled soon after the performance of the sign-action has been expanded and actualized by subsequent additions regarding later events of the destruction of Jerusalem.

If we approach 12:1–16 in this way, then first of all v 16 is separated off as an addition which has nothing to do with the sign-action in the narrower sense. In the remaining vv 1–15 the double summons to interpret the action vv 10/11 introduced by אֱמֹר is striking. Besides the simple connection with the subject in the third person plural, by which the inhabitants of Jerusalem must be meant (v 11), there appears in v 10 an interpretation in respect of the prince and people in Jerusalem which is formulated clumsily and is grammatically awkward. מַשָּׂא, as a designation for a prophetic oracle, is not elsewhere found in Ezekiel; in 24:25 it has a quite different meaning. V 10 is formulated as a Yahweh saying with the whole weight of the messenger formula, whilst in v 11 Yahweh puts a prophetic I-oracle in the mouth of Ezekiel. This contains the direct answer to the question of the people in v 9, from which it is now separated in 𝔐 by v 10. The fuller original introductory formula אמר אליהם is subsequently taken up again in the shorter אמר of v 11. It may further be questioned whether the insertion of v 10 has not had as a consequence the abbreviation of a once fuller לישבי ירושלם to the להם of 𝔐 (v 11). The interpretation in regard to the prince and his followers is continued in vv 12–15. Whilst in vv 13–15, as in v 10, the divine speech predominates, with the personal-descriptive elaboration of v 12 we are not wholly free from the suspicion that here statements which were originally plural and which related to the citizens of Jerusalem according to v 11, may have subsequently here been related in the singular to the prince (for the revealing plural יחתרו cf. note d). This is not true of the בעלטה יוצא (= יוציא) (note c), which, like the corresponding בעלטה תוציא (6) and בעלטה הוצאתי (7), was from the beginning intended as a reference to the subsequent flight of Zedekiah and was therefore missing in the basic text.

However, the reference to breaking through the wall and the bringing out of the exile's baggage through the gap thus made, v 5, which hints at the breaches which will be made in the wall at the conquest of Jerusalem (וַתִּבָּקַע הָעִיר 2 Kings 25:4 and parallel passages), cannot have belonged to the basic text, but must represent a first phase of the additional comment (v 12 still plural). The assertion is marked off grammatically from the basic text not only by the striking elliptical use of the hip'il of יצא, which is not found there (note a to v 5), but also by the fact that it comes

late after v 4, which has already mentioned the bringing out of the baggage and the abandoning of his home by the prophet himself. In v 7 it has been subsequently connected with the בערב (cf. v 4) which belongs to the basic text.

The probable basic text of 12:1–16 thus runs:

> And the word of Yahweh came to me: Son of man, you dwell in the midst of a rebellious house, which has eyes to see, but sees not, and ears to hear, but hears not, for they are a rebellious house. But you, son of man, prepare for yourself an exile's baggage in the light of day before their eyes and go away from your place to another place before their eyes. Perhaps they will see it, for they are a rebellious house. And bring out your baggage in the light of day before their eyes as baggage for exile, and you yourself shall go out at evening before their eyes, just as exiles usually go away. Before their eyes you shall lift the baggage upon your shoulder. Your face you shall cover, that you may not see the land. For I have made you a sign for the house of Israel.
>
> And I did as I was commanded. I brought out my baggage, as baggage for exile, in the light of day. In the evening I carried it upon my shoulder before their eyes.
>
> And the word of Yahweh came to me the following morning: Son of man, has not the house of Israel, the rebellious house, said to you: What are you doing there? Say to them: I am a sign for you. As I have done, so shall it be done to them (or: to the inhabitants of Jerusalem). They must go into exile. (Their baggage they will carry upon their shoulders. Their faces they will cover.)

For the sign-action as a form of preaching, we must compare the study of Ezek 4f.[1] In the manner of its accomplishment 12:1–16 shows some divergencies from chs. 4f. After the divine command to perform the action (vv 3–6), which, as regards form, takes the place of an original exposition (Fohrer), there follows in v 7, in a terse statement, the narrative of the accomplishment of the action by the prophet. The element of interpretation, which follows in third position, is varied insofar as it (analogous to 21:[5], 12; 24:19; 37:18) has been accommodated to the form of an answer to the question of the people who do not understand the sign. Whereas, however, in 24:19 this question has been given in conjunction with the narrative of the performance of the action and is itself in narrative form, there appears again in 12:9 the tendency to incorporate the widest possible number of elements into the divine speech. In the framework of a further receiving of a message, Yahweh himself here mentions the question (as in 21:12 and 37:18) which the people raise. The interpretation given to the prophet by Yahweh is stylized in a manner unusual for Ezekiel, as a pure I-address of the prophet. In view of the clear text this must certainly not be altered arbitrarily with Bertholet (note a to v 11) into a divine address.

A further formal variation of the narrative concerning the sign-action appears in the fact that this is connected here with a preceding divine rebuke (v 2, further the related v 3bβ). The sign-action, performed before the widest public (the emphasis on this feature by the repeated יומם and לעיניהם cannot be overlooked), is a further attempt ordained by Yahweh himself finally to make his people see, in spite of their blinded vision. It is no departure from this when the subsequent interpretation regarding the prince in v 15 finishes up with the recognition formula, i.e., it is stylized as a proof-saying. It already concerns the demonstration of the true (judgement) history of Yahweh with his people, who will neither see nor hear, in the combined form of reproach and sign-action in the basic text.

Setting

When Herntrich lays down for 12:1ff: "This section shows us clearly the Jerusalem situation of Ezekiel's prophecy," then this assertion is only possible after altering the text of v 11.[2] With 𝕾 he reads here in b the second plural לכם and תלכו as the original text. According to him, in 𝔐 the editor who made Ezekiel into a prophet in exile has carelessly retained in מופתכם a remnant of the original text which shows us the immediate situation of the address to the citizens of Jerusalem; 𝕲 had first removed the inconsistency (cf. note a to v 11). In fact, however, 𝕾 and 𝕲 must be regarded as attempts to smooth over the difficulty in the two possible directions. The original text of 𝔐 (*lectio difficilior*) clearly distinguishes the immediate

addressees, for whom Ezekiel, by the action which he performs before their eyes, is a sign (מופתכם), from the men to whom what he symbolically portrays will happen. He speaks in exile about the fate of those who remain in Jerusalem, who are threatened by the divine judgement which the exiles, whose hope depends on the continued existence of Jerusalem, refuse to see. In the sign-action of carrying the exile's baggage Ezekiel addresses them with a portrayal which very directly reawakens the memory of their own experience of 598/7 B.C.[3]

The basic text, drawn up before 587 B.C., which told of Yahweh's command (vv 1, 8) and the prophet's actions (v 7), has subsequently after the events of 587 B.C. undergone an extensive interpretative elaboration.

Interpretation

■ **12:1, 2** After the introductory formula for the prophet's receipt of an oracle, in which Eissfeldt, without any compelling reason, conjectures the falling out of a date, and the address to the prophet as son of man, there follows immediately an accusatory designation of the people among whom Ezekiel dwells.[4] Four times in the present section (vv 2a, b, 3, 9) we hear its title as "house of rebellion," the title which in the call narrative denotes the entire people.[5] The group of exiles in whose midst Ezekiel lives is thereby regarded as representative of the whole people whose character it embodies. Thus there appears beside the בית המרי which is peculiar to Ezekiel, the description of Isreal (or Judah) as a people who have eyes to see, but see not, and ears to hear, but hear not, which we already find in prophecy before Ezekiel. It is, so far as we know, found first in the call narrative of Isaiah at the commissioning of the prophet to preach to harden the people's hearts (6:9f), subsequently in Jeremiah,[6] Deutero-Isaiah (43:8), also Dtn 29:3, and again in the New Testament Mk 4:12; 8:18 and other passages. That the late Ps 115:5f, 135:16f use this saying in a

---

1   Pp. 156f.
2   Herntrich, *Ezekielprobleme*, 99.
3   Cf. the exposition.
4   See above pp. 144f, 131f. Otto Eissfeldt, *The Old Testament; An Introduction*, tr. Peter R. Ackroyd (New York: Harper and Row, 1965), 376–377.
5   See above p. 134.
6   If 5:21 is authentic. See Rudolph, *Jeremia*, on the

text.

still broader characterization of the powerlessness of idols can scarcely justify the view that the prophetic rebuke of the people was a "quotation from the 'mocking of the gods' in the cult."[7]

The reference to the blindness and deafness of the people is related in Jer 5:21 to evidence of God in creation, and in Dtn 29:3 to the divine demonstration at the exodus. This may raise the question whether or not Ezek 12:2 also thinks of blindness and deafness as quite definite things, which must have stood plainly before the eyes of the men around Ezekiel. In the following symbolic act Ezekiel sets before the eyes of his fellows in a vivid way the event of preparing baggage for exile and the departure with a pack carried on one's back. He thereby stands once again with his symbolic action in the succession of Isaiah.[8] Just as this latter prophet, in the time of the Ashdod rebellion which ended in 711 B.C., was commanded to go for three years "naked and barefoot" (Is 20) in order to show visibly the blind and deaf people (Is 6:9f) how feebly the Egyptian and Ethiopian helpers, who looked so strong, would be put to flight by the Assyrians. Ezekiel varies Isaiah's imagery and unlike him relates it quite directly to the citizens of Jerusalem. By his sign-action he portrays not prisoners of war, carried off immediately from battle, who are robbed of clothes and often fettered,[9] but those who are compulsorily removed after the end of the battle and who go off, taking with them a small bundle of their belongings, (under military observation) to their new home. This situation also is not unknown to ancient oriental pictorial art. An Egyptian relief stemming from the old kingdom (5th/6th dynasty; c 2350 B.C.), from dešāše, shows a woman leading a child with her right hand and with her left hand carrying on her shoulder a bundle with her belongings.[10] Above all, however, those figures appear frequently in the pictures of the Assyrians, who elevated the method of transplanting the civil population into a system.[11] In that Ezekiel now sets this picture before the eyes of his companions in exile, he enters at the same time quite directly into their experience. They had themselves all lived through this making up of a small bundle, with all its previous painful considerations of what could be taken; they had lifted their baggage on their shoulders to the heedless cry to move on the part of the guards who led the removal in small groups of those marked out.[12] They had covered their heads at the grim anguish of departure. When now they are addressed by Ezekiel as a "rebellious house, who have eyes to see but do not see, and ears to hear but do not hear," this all points to the fact that Ezekiel opposes the conduct of Israel (also among the exiles of his environment) in which the so recently experienced catastrophe of 598/7 B.C. had already strangely faded into the background and had been removed from consciousness. Are they the birthpangs of the recently planned and carried out defection from Babylonian overlordship under Zedekiah, the siren songs of an imminent freeing of Jerusalem and a return of the exiles (cf. Jer 27:16; 28:3f, also 29:31 for the sphere of the exiles), in which Ezekiel must actualize afresh as firmly as possible in his own personal action the reality of exile?

■ **12:3** Thus Yahweh commands the prophet in broad daylight before the eyes of his neighbors to prepare the small bundle of an exile. The expression כלי גולה is found again in Jer 46:19 in a threat against Egypt. With this bundle Ezekiel must move from his abode in broad daylight. To define "the other place" (cf. Acts 12:17) is quite unimportant, since it simply

---

7 Artur Weiser, *Das Buch Jeremia*, ATD 20–21 (Göttingen: Vandenhoeck & Ruprecht, [5/6]1969), 54 (on Jer 5:21).

8 See above p. 172 to 5:1–2.

9 *ANEP* 1.

10 *ANEP* 311, lower left.

11 See for the time of Tiglath-pileser III *AOBAT* 133; *ANEP* 366, for the time of Sennacherib *AOBAT* 141, and for the time of Asshurbanapal *ANEP* 10; André Parrot, *Nineveh and the Old Testament*, tr. B. E. Hooke. Studies in Biblical Archaeology 3 (London: SCM, 1955), p. 47 figure 11; *idem, Babylon and the*

Old Testament, tr. B. E. Hooke. Studies in Biblical Archaeology 8 (London: SCM, 1958), p. 91 figure 34.

12 Erich Klamroth, *Die jüdischen Exulanten in Babylonien*, BWAT 10 (Leipzig: Hinrichs, 1912), 24f.

concerns the leaving of his usual abode. We certainly cannot think with Bertholet, Auvray of a place "in the area of the land of Judah," from which Ezekiel had watched the ensuing siege of Jerusalem at a safe distance, in order to settle in Babylon after this sojourn in the thirteenth year of Jehoiachin (so Bertholet reads 1:1)—"whether by compulsion or of his own free will cannot be established."[13] The fresh command of Yahweh, which follows in vv 8ff on the fulfillment of the action, clearly presupposes that Ezekiel is afterwards again at his old abode and interprets the event to those who saw his departure there. Bertholet wants then consequently to delete the אמר of v 11. When Auvray says, without being fully convinced of this deletion, that Ezekiel, in the interpretation, "addresses himself to his new compatriots to explain to them his sudden arrival and his curious baggage," this explanation is quite unconvincing since at the "other place" the strongly emphasized features of his departure could not have been seen.[14]

"Perhaps they will see it." The task of the prophet, though his message is so stern, is a summons of God calling to repentance, which may make men ready to see his activity.[15]

■ **12:4** The summarizing formula in v 3, which strongly emphasizes the character of the prophetic action as a plea, is followed in 4, 6 by a fuller unfolding. This goes back once again to the beginning of Ezekiel's departure. In the characteristic bundle, which can be seen on the ancient oriental representations mentioned, the belongings which are to be taken are brought out of the house. Thus would a man in Jerusalem in 598/7 B.C. have prepared his baggage at the door of his house for the moment when, in the evening, i.e., after the passing of the hot noonday hours, which were unsuitable for marching, the commander of the military guards would have commanded a departure. Then, clothed protectively for the long journey,[16] he moved out of the house (4b) at the command of the "driver"

(the שבט הנגש Is 9:3 could very well have in mind the Assyrian method of deportation), put his baggage upon his back, and, with the first steps which parted him from his homeland, covered his face. The shame (cf. the gesture of the prostitute, Gen 38:15; are we to think of additional ill-treatment on the journey, as appears in Is 47:2f; Nah 3:5f?) and suffering (cf. the gesture of the mourner, 2 Sam 15:30; Jer 14:4; Est 6:12; 7:8) of the deportation are shown by this gesture, which also plaintively hides the lost homeland from the view of the exiles. Thus Yahweh makes his prophet a sign to the house of Israel. Instead of אות, which is used in 4:3 and 14:8 (cf. also 20:12, 20), here (vv 6 and 11) the synonym מופת is used as in 24:24, 27.[17]

■ **12:7** The fulfillment of what the prophet is commanded is described in a stereotyped introductory clause, reappearing in 24:18; 37:7, in loose dependence on the statements of the divine command, without adding new descriptive elements. The public character of the event, open to every eye, is once again strongly emphasized.

■ **12:8–12** The interpretation of the prophet's action, which came on the following day in the framework of a second message, shows once again, by the mention of the people's helpless question (similarly in 21:5, 12; 24:19; 37:18), the inability of the people to see.[18] Thus then, the sign which they have seen is followed by the preaching which they hear (אמר אליהם v 10). This makes clear that the prophetic action, as little as the prophetic word, is an empty playing with ideas. It is an event already begun.[19] The citizens of Jerusalem, who are not directly present, and of whom the prophet therefore speaks in the third person, who also belong to the house of Israel to whom the message of the prophet is addressed, will experience what was seen happening to the prophet. The prophet's preaching has to do with them also. They will have to go through the departure into exile, to shoulder their

---

13 Bertholet 45; xvi.
14 Auvray, 64.
15 Cf. further the אולי of Jer 26:3; 36:3. To the prophet's displeasure (Jon 4:2), this merciful and hopeful אולי stands unexpressed over the declaration of punishment in Jon 3:4, which appears to be fixed so categorically. For the motive clause by, which is logically surprising, cf. what is said above p. 134

to 2:6. Here also we must read between the lines roughly what is said in v 2b.
16 "Their feet I set on the road" *Annals of Asshurbanapal* IX 8, according to Klamroth, *Exulanten*, 24.
17 See Keller, *OTH*, 60–61.
18 Cf. Mt 15:15f; Mk 7:17f.
19 Pp. 156f.

baggage and veil their faces. But what happens to them is, in its anticipation in the sign-action of the prophet, a direct message to those who are sitting down far from Jerusalem: "I am a sign *to you.*" Will those who are so addressed hear and recognize that their God, in enabling them to see the depth of his holy judgement, is appealing to them?

History, very shortly after this, began to speak. Jerusalem fell. 2 Kings 25:3–7; Jer 39:1–7; 52:6–11 tell how King Zedekiah, after the Babylonians had made a breach in the city wall and their commanders had established themselves at the "middle gate,"[20] broke out at night with his bodyguard through the "gate between the two walls."[21] Across the Jordan valley (ערבה), he tried to gain safety in the territory east of Jordan—just as, a few months later, another member of the royal house did after the murder of Gedaliah, with better success (Jer 41:1, 15). Zedekiah's attempt failed. Still this side of the Jordan, in the region of Jericho (בערבות ירחו) he fell into the hands of the pursuing Babylonians. The soldiers who accompanied him clearly no longer put up a serious fight, but abandoned the king to his tormentors. In Riblah on the Orontes, the Syrian headquarters of the Babylonian king, the latter passed sentence upon him.[22] After he had been forced to witness the execution of his sons, his eyes were put out, in accordance with the barbaric custom of military punishment, which Assyrian kings already knew and had announced on their monuments.[23] Zedekiah was taken off to Babylon blind. After an interval of nearly a month, in which the royal instructions had to be awaited from the Syrian headquarters, the fate of Jerusalem was sealed. The city and temple were plundered and reduced to ashes. The walls were demolished, and the inhabitants who were of importance for independent political life were deported, as Ezekiel had threatened (2 Kings 25:8–12; Jer 39:8–10; 52:12–16).[24]

How deeply these events engraved themselves in the consciousness of the people can be seen not only in the threefold repetition of the account in 2 Kings and Jeremiah and the number of the fast days which sought to keep alive the memory of it (Zech 7:3, 5; 8:19), but also Ezek chs. 12 and 17. In Ezekiel 12 the account of the prophetic sign-act of the exile's baggage has undergone an extensive additional interpretation. The possibility that parts of it may still derive from the prophet's own hand is not absolutely to be excluded.[25]

■ **12:5** A first "clarification" appears still within the framework of the interpretation concerning those who were deported. The divine command: "Before their eyes, dig a hole through the wall and bring (your baggage) through it" (v 5) appears to have in mind the breach in the walls or even the complete demolishing of the city walls of Jerusalem. It is conceivable that the sad group of exiles did not go out through the burnt-out gates (for such burning cf. Neh 1:3; 2:3, 13, 17; also Jer 17:27; 51:58), but through the ruined walls. Also among Ezekiel's neighbors knowledge of this would have been received. An interpretation of the breaking through the wall in terms of the disastrous flight of Zedekiah is not likely.[26] The לעיניהם unlike the בעלטה תוציא (v 6), appears to have in mind an event taking place in the daylight. The combination with בערב in v 7 does not point to an event in the dark of night and is besides scarcely original. Also the plural יחתרו, in the context of the interpretation (v 12), contains a further reference to the fact that here originally the crowd of exiles was in mind, and not the נשיא, who otherwise is the subject in v 12 𝔐. – In the conception of the breach in the house wall (קיר, not חומה "city wall"), C. G. Howie believes that he can discern once again with certainty Babylonian coloring.[27] The stone walls, which Albright has found in Tell Beit Mirsim and other cities of pre-exilic Judah, would have been broken down, rather than dug through in the manner described by Ezekiel. So, according to Howie, the text points compellingly to

---

20   שַׁעַר הַתָּוֶךְ; according to Rudolph, *Jeremia*, note a to 39:3, the northern gate of the old Jebusite city, gate 9 in *BRL*. Simons, *Jerusalem*, 276, who reckons with the pre-exilic extension of the city to the west hill, locates it in the middle of the northern wall.

21   According to *BRL*, 302, the most southerly gate, number 5; identified by Simons, *Jerusalem*, 127–129, with the "dung gate."

22   See above pp. 191f to 6:14.

23   Sargon II, according to André Parrot, *Samaria, the Capital of the Kingdom of Israel*, tr. S. R. Hooke. Studies in Biblical Archaeology 7 (London: SCM, 1958), p. 82 figure 23.

24   For the number of those deported see Janssen, *Juda*, 25–39.

25   For the basic evaluation of such editing on grounds

the view of clay brick walls, i.e., like the Babylonian. It is uncertain, however, in view of Is 9:10, whether this can be established with certainty.[28]

A second, more extensive, stratum of editorial interpretation deviates more markedly from the original line of the sign-action. In it the event of the exile of the people in Jerusalem, who appear in the preparation, bringing out and carrying of the exile's baggage, and the departure with covered faces, does not stand in the center, but the personal fate of Zedekiah. This was of a different character with a nocturnal escape, the scattering of his bodyguard, his being rendered blind and then carried off to Babylon. The connection with the original sign-act is achieved by the remark in v 6 that those who go out from the land will not see it. The fate of Zedekiah is here set in a twofold manner under the picture of darkness. The darkness of the night of the attempted escape from the beseiged city, which was intended to save him from the eyes of the pursuers, is connected with the thought of the darkness of the sightless eyes, which would no longer be able to see the land of the Babylonians into which he was led as a blinded captive.

■ **12:6** The later interpretative addition begins first of all here in quite a restrained way with the addition of a בעלטה תוציא in v 6. This takes up the elliptical והוצאת of the earlier addition in v 5, which echoes the (כליך) והוצאת of the basic text v 4a (note a to v 5) which has an object. The shifting of the event, which originally took place publicly in daylight, into the nightime, where no eye could see it (v 12b), links up with the fate of Zedekiah. The narrative of the fulfillment of what is commanded in v 7 shows the same expansion by בעלטה הוצאתי.

■ **12:10** The second addition first gains its full breadth in the sphere of the divine interpretation of the sign in v 10b, which is marked out as a divine saying by the introductory messenger formula v 10aβ, and which establishes in advance the expanded reference of the

sign-action in regard to the prince in Jerusalem and the house of Israel who dwell there. If the reading of 𝔐 is original, then there is a close connection with Jer 23:33. According to Herntrich, v 10 is an originally independent prophetic saying, which only entered its present position by error, in which Ezekiel answered in his own way the question raised by the people in Jer 23:33 מה משא יהוה "What is the message [= the burden] of Yahweh?".[29] Jeremiah answered: אתם המשא (c.T.) "You are the burden"; so Ezekiel הנשיא המשא הוה "The prince is this burden." From this, with its acute wordplay in Ezekiel's use for the first time of the נשיא title for Zedekiah, Herntrich believes that he can explain the later redactional suppression of the title מלך in favor of נשיא. Apart from the uncertainty of the text of 𝔐 (note b to v 10), it is also opposed by the fact that unlike Jer 23:33, where the question of the people (v 9) precedes the prophet's saying, Ezekiel does not record the word which then occasions the wordplay. Thus we shall be more correct here if we abstain from any far-reaching conclusions based on a connection with Jeremiah and simply affirm that here the word משא, which is nowhere else found in Ezekiel, was taken up as a designation of the divine saying because this could echo both the נשא of vv 6, 7 (cf. also v 12) as also the title נשיא.[30]

■ **12:12–15** The interpretation of the sign-action in terms of the prince and his followers is further unfolded beyond v 11 of the basic text in vv 12–15. The development takes place in the style of the two-part proof saying (declaration of judgement—recognition formula). The declaration of judgement is first of all given in v 12, as in v 11, in a purely descriptive picture. This raises the question whether elements of the basic text which had the exiles in mind have undergone here a subsequent reinterpretation in terms of the prince.[31] Vv 13f then first move into the style of the Yahweh address in the first person, in which the recognition formula is also preserved.

---

of events that have happened in the meantime, see what is said to ch. 7 (pp. 213f).

26 So Bertholet; Ziegler, 38f; "Perhaps this exit was made because a breach for the fleeing king had to be made first."

27 Howie, *Date*, 18.

28 Cf. Kuhl, "Schauplatz," 406.

29 Herntrich, *Ezekielprobleme*, 123; cf. Miller, *Verhältnis*,

p. 105 note 2.

30 For the problem of the נשיא title for the king in Jerusalem, cf. also the exposition of 17:12.

31 See above p. 268.

■12:12 Thus in v 12 𝔐, somewhat surprisingly (and therefore changed by 𝔊 𝔙, see below), the carrying of the baggage for exile is connected with the flight of the prince by night. For the third time בעלטה יוצא (cf. note c) is added. The breaking through the wall now concerns the breaking out of the southern gate by night. The plural subject of 𝔐 must have in mind the king and his followers who fled with him. The covering of the face must be understood in this new connection as a sign of the secrecy of those who fled. Then 𝔊, which still lacks the addition of 𝔐, has added here as a kind of catchphrase (note f) the idea of v 6 that those who leave the land cannot see, and has related this statement to the blinded prince.

■12:13 The threat of Yahweh, which begins in the first person in v 13, is dependent in its formulation on related texts. The metaphor of the king captured in a net must have its original basis in the simile of the lion in 19:8 (see below). It was then connected in 17:20f with the reference to bringing to Babylon and the scattering of Zedekiah's bodyguard. In the present text these statements have been further expanded by a reference to the blinded king, who can no longer see the land of Babylon, and to his death in exile (also 17:16). The latter is a valuable account which enlarges upon the narrative sources (2 Kings, Jeremiah).

■12:14 Where, however, 17:21 speaks of death by the sword for Zedekiah's guard and of the scattering of those who escape the sword, 12:14, in closer agreement with the events of Zedekiah's arrest, speaks of the scattering of his "helpers" and of the sword drawn in pursuit of those who flee. Accordingly 12:13f appears to have been formulated in dependence on 17:20f with assimilation to the particular situation of Zedekiah's flight. Here as there the action of Yahweh is proclaimed as the proof of his reality.

■12:15 Whereas 17:20f thinks of the divine demonstration to the exiles who were directly being addressed (וידעתם), 12:15 thinks of those around Zedekiah, who were directly concerned in the event being announced (וידעו).

It is instructive to notice how the process of secondary interpretation of 𝔐 has not yet come to an end, but has left certain rough edges which come from the reinterpretation of a text originally concerned with the exiles of Jerusalem in terms of the personal fate of Zedekiah, and which have needed subsequent smoothing. Thus in 𝔊, and the traditions which follow it, the יחתרו (12) is translated as singular and likewise directly related to the prince. So also the perfectly clear statement in 𝔐 of the "bringing out" of the exile's baggage by the prince, which is explained by the relation of the addition v 6aα[1] to v 5, and behind 5 to 4, has here had to be weakened to the simpler assertion of the "going out" of the prince (according to v 4b). The same difficulty in the reading of 𝔐 has led in 𝔊 (𝔏ᶜ) 𝔙 (note a to v 6) to a change of "carry (the baggage) on the shoulder" to "will be carried on the shoulder." This appears to be more appropriate for a king.

■12:16 V 16 is an addition of a peculiar kind, which under the impact of the events of 587 B.C., raises the question what the divine purpose could be in a small remnant (אנשי מספר cf. מעט במספר, 5:3) scattered among the people after the catastrophe of Jerusalem. Just as in 14:21–23 the existence of these survivors, who could not be designated as a "pious remnant" and who therefore appeared to contradict the firm order of divine retribution, is interpreted as a means of demonstrating the righteousness of Yahweh before all the world. Through them knowledge of the abominations of Jerusalem enters into the world of the nations, who thereby come to understand the righteousness of the divine punishment. The addition is preserved in the style of the proof-saying.

Aim

The prophet Ezekiel spoke to a people which had not been living without the divine message—that message which was never a "mere word," the communication of an idea, but was always an event, a gift of grace, and an experience of chastisement from the divine father's loyalty.[32] Where God's people were in danger of falling asleep or threatened to run away from him either by neglect or self-will, there he had spoken clearly to them, even taking a secure hold of them. Had this severe rebuke not been heard even in Ezekiel's day by the Israelites who had ears to hear and eyes to see, when they had been driven out from Jerusalem with their exile's baggage?

Nevertheless, although men stood within the oppression brought about by the severe summons of God in history, yet they had already quickly forgotten. They had paid no serious attention (Amos 4:6ff; Is 1:4ff), and they went on living, in Jerusalem, as in exile, making their own new plans and clinging to their own expectations. This is man's life, even when he belongs to the people of God. He wants to remember nothing in the present of the judgement of God which caught up with him yesterday.

With all his personal power and action Ezekiel had to set before this people, who were unwilling to see and hear and who sought to evade the seriousness of the truth of God, the reality of God's holy power. With brutal frankness he set before their eyes scenes which were familiar to each of them, but which had clearly been thrust out of consciousness. By the prophet himself there was given unexpectedly, as a new, compelling summons from God to his people in a foreign country, the picture of expulsion from home.

In that God commanded the prophet once again to attempt with this portrayal to awaken the people to the divine summons and to a recognition of him he reveals his hidden concern for his own. "Perhaps they will see it." Thus God waits even where he himself terrifies and passes judgement.

In the later interpretation, which continued after the year 587 B.C., the message of the basic text, which contained God's hidden summons to repentance, has been expanded and strengthened. By its reference to the breaking through the wall of Jerusalem (v 5), and the grim fate of the prince there (vv 12–14) which appears as darkness and horror, it reveals the God who must rightly be "known" by his people.[33] To make this God known in his absolute righteousness, which will not allow those whom he has called to profane his holiness, is the task of those who, at the downfall of Jerusalem, apparently escaped the righteous judgement of God by fleeing through the back door. By their reports of the end of Jerusalem and everything that happened there they are to make known the "abominations" which were practiced by the people of God. Although they neither wanted to be, nor regarded themselves as such, they are to become preachers of the God who has broken out in judgement in the history of his people, to demonstrate the power of his name before men.

32   See above pp. 144f.
33   Zimmerli, *Erkenntnis*, 39–47: "Das Ereignis der Erkenntnis."

The Trembling of the Prophet.
A Sign from God.

12

Bibliography

F. Planas
"El pan del profeta" *Cult Biblica*, 12 (1955): 153–157.

17 And the word of Yahweh came to me:
18/ Son of man, you must eat bread
with quaking[a] and drink water with
trembling [and in fear][b] 19/ and say to
the people of the land: Thus has [the
Lord][a] Yahweh spoken of[b] the inhabitants of Jerusalem in[c] the land of Israel:
They shall eat their bread with fear and
drink water with shuddering—in order
that[d] 'their' land[e] may be emptied of all
its contents[f] on account of the violence
of all who dwell in it, 20/ and the
inhabited cities[a] shall be laid waste
and the land made desolate, and you
shall know that I am Yahweh.

12:

18a ⅏ μετ᾽ ὀδύνης, ᾽Α ἐν σεισμῷ, Σ ἐν ἀκαταστασίᾳ,
Θ ἐν σάλῳ. Only here is רעש used of the quaking of
men. Otherwise it denotes an earthquake. This does
not, however, justify the change to כעש (= כעס; so
Koehler-Baumgartner, considered by Fohrer). The
meaning is guaranteed by the parallel רגזה. רגז can
also denote the quaking of the earth (1 Sam 14:15;
Amos 8:8) or the mountains (Is 5:25; Ps 18:8).

b The double expression ברגזה ובדאגה is striking
beside the simple ברעש of the parallel and the two
simple statements in v 19aβ, in the first of which
דאגה reappears as an element of the interpretation.
If we cut out בדאגה as an interpretative gloss with
Herrmann, Bertholet, Fohrer, which prematurely
expresses the interpretation of v 19aβ, then we not
only obtain in v 18 the double-triplets, which clearly
correspond to the interpretative clause, but also the
intentional distinction between the sign-action and
its interpretation: The sign-action shows the physical trembling (רגזה/רעש) which could actually be
seen. The divine word interprets this perceptible fact
in relation to the inner anxiety (שממון/דאגה) of the
citizens of Jerusalem. Cf. further the similar twofold
interpretative addition in 4:16 (note a on the text).

19 19a אדני is lacking in ⅏ ℭ, see Excursus 1.
b אמר ל "to speak about" also 11:15, also with a
similar meaning אמר על 26:2; 36:2.

c על־אל cf. 1:17 note a.

d For למען cf. note a to 4:17. We could paraphrase the sense: "I am doing it, so that." Cf. Sutcliffe, "Effect as Purpose."

e The suffix of 𝔐 ארצה could best be related to
the preceding ירושלם, which is, however, rather
forced. ⅏ ἡ γῆ does not appear to presuppose the
suffix (hence Bertholet הארץ, Cornill ארץ). It is
graphically more likely that we should read with 5
MSS^Ken 3 MSS ^de Rossi Edd ארצם. Cf., however,
note f.

f 𝔐 ממלאה. Herrmann, Bertholet, would (cf.
MS^Ken 224) change to ומלאה. The widely used expression ארץ ומל[ו]אה (Dtn 33:16; Jer 8:16; 47:2;
Mic 1:2) is also found in Ezekiel in 19:7; 30:12.
Beside this, however, we also find in 32:15 ארץ
ממלאה. Since ⅏ also, which translates in 12:19;
32:15 σὺν πληρώματι αὐτῆς, whilst in 19:7; 30:12
offering the simple copula, attests the unusual reading, we must keep 𝔐 here.

20 20a 𝔐 והערים. ⅏ καὶ αἱ πόλεις αὐτῶν must be a
free translation.

Form

12:17–20 narrate in a short composition a further sign-action of the prophet. The whole account is presented in the form of a divine address in the manner sketched above.[1] After the divine command to perform the action (v 18), there follows directly its interpretation (vv 19aβ–20) formulated as a proof-saying. Its proclamation is expressly ordered by Yahweh in v 19aα, an introductory clause which mentions incidentally the addressees of the message as those to whom the symbolic action applies. The addressees are therefore only addressed directly in the concluding recognition formula. That which is announced in the sign-action, however, is (vv 19aβ–20a) described in the third person as an event concerning another party. Those directly addressed by the prophet are therefore to be distinguished from the men to whom that which is proclaimed in the sign-action will occur. This formal consideration is also relevant if, with Cooke, Bertholet, Fohrer, we wish to cut out ליושבי ירושלם אל אדמת ישראל as a subsequent addition, which is, however, scarcely necessary.

The metrical structure of *parallelismus membrorum* (double threes) can clearly be seen in the divine command (v 18 without address) and the interpretation (vv 19aβ, 20a). In the whole oracle it has been enlarged in a prose style by additional speech formulae, the explanatory gloss v 19b and the recognition formula.

Setting

The prophet speaks to the עם הארץ and, in his symbolic action, portrays to these the experience of the population who are still in the land and who are described in the introduction as "inhabitants of Jerusalem in the land of Israel." He cannot therefore himself be staying in Jerusalem (against Herntrich, *Ezekiel-probleme*). Also the "other place" in the region of Judah conjectured by Bertholet on the basis of 12:3, cannot be intended here.[2] Rather in the עם הארץ,

following E. Würthwein, the exiles in Babylon must be intended, who were in 598/7 B.C. drawn from the upper classes.[3] The oracle was delivered in exile.

Fohrer follows Hölscher, *Hesekiel*, and accepts that by the population that were still in the land, whose condition is portrayed in the symbolic act, the remnant of the population left after 587 B.C. must be in mind, and the oracle composed after this point of time. This view rests on the presupposition that 12:17–20 belongs clearly with 12:1ff. "After the announcement of the deportation in 12:1–11 there follows the fate of those who are spared in it" (Fohrer). However, this presupposition is not proved in view of the new introduction of v 17, and is improbable in view of 33:24 where those who are left in the land are identified as ישבי יושבי ירושלם. By the החרבות האלה על אדמת ישראל we must, as in 11:15; 15:6, understand the citizens of Jerusalem in the period before the destruction of the city, which first appears to be threatened in v 20. The oracle must be dated in the period between 593 and 587 B.C.

Interpretation

■ **12:17** After the introductory formula for the coming of a message and the address as son of man, the prophet is commanded by Yahweh to eat his bread with trembling and quaking.[4]

■ **12:18** The relationship to 4:16f, which is particularly clearly emphasized by a gloss (note b to v 18), does not lead us, with Schumpp, Steinmann, Herntrich, Troelstra and others, to see in "bread and water" the scant food of a besieged city.[5] All the emphasis here lies on the eating "with trembling." In the quite unusual use of the word רעש for human quaking there lies a special emphasis.[6]

Hölscher regards this divine summons to quake, which has a parallel in the summons to "groan (אנח) before their eyes" in 21:11, as "a badly executed imitation of 4:9ff" and as poorly conceived sym-

---

1 Pp. 156f.
2 See above pp. 270f.
3 Würthwein, *'amm*, 43.
4 See above pp. 144f; pp. 131f.
5 Steinmann, *Le prophète Ezéchiel*; Herntrich, *Ezekiel-probleme*; A. Troelstra, *Ezechiël*, 2 volumes, TeU (Groningen: Wolters, 1931).
6 38:20 is not a full parallel; cf. note a to v 18.

bolism.[7] Hence he removes it as a clumsy addition. In this, however, he has as little understood the divine ordering of the symbolic action as Kraetzschmar, who speaks of a "mimetic talent" which called forth the performance of the action. More correctly we must think of phenomena of the kind which became evident in Jer 4:19–21, where the prophet speaks of the trembling (אחולה K) which befell him physically under the compulsion of the divine commission. References could easily be multiplied from the book of Jeremiah.[8] Behind the reference to the coming of the hand of Yahweh there must, with Ezekiel, lie similar experiences.[9] The seizure by the divine hand shakes the prophet physically in the very depths of this being. That events in which the prophet was first emotionally exposed to the divine control became features of the symbolism of his preaching has already become clear in connection with the study of 3:25–27 and 4:4–8.[10] Besides the prophet's being bound and dumb, which outwardly looked like an illness, there is apparently asserted here a quaking which also was almost pathological, and which made it difficult for him to put food in his mouth and made him spill his drink. Once again, however, this is not mentioned here out of a biographical interest in the prophet's personality and its peculiarities, but solely because this physical shaking of the prophet becomes, at the divine command, a commission to preach to his people.

■ **12:19** To the "people of the land" around him,[11] who awaited with passionate longing the restoration of Jerusalem, which would bring for the exiles the possibility of return, the prophet has to proclaim the terror which is coming upon the land, which will make the citizens of Jerusalem quake. Not the jubilation of victory, but anguish and "terror" (שממון) only

again in the gloss in 4:16 which has arisen from here) will prevail there. Because of the judgement of Yahweh, which is called forth by the violence of the people,[12] the land will be denuded of its wealth, the cities which (at the time of the prophet's action) were still inhabited would be devastated, and the land would be turned into a barren wilderness. The Jerusalem citizens are chiefly addressed in this oracle as the actual landowners.[13]

Aim

A "healthy" attitude likes to see the typically healthy preacher of the word of God. The prophet knew that with his sick and trembling body he was called to proclaim the will of God, and that he was defenseless before the mockery and jibes of the people. God's people, whose violent actions (חמס) trampled upon the weakness of their neighbors, sought to live in security. Yet they had to learn through the pitiable and quaking figure of the divine messenger, who was deprived of life's securities, where they really stood and the truth about their possession of home and safety. Ultimately, however, the quaking of the inhabitants of God's city, proclaimed by the trembling of his messenger, was to lead not only to men coming to know the truth about themselves, but also to a recognition of God breaking in upon them in his revelation. God demonstrates the mystery of his own greatness through the destruction of those who fall by his judgement.

---

7   Hölscher, *Hesekiel, der Dichter*, 82.
8   Cf. the agitated state which Islamic tradition records in connection with the revelatory experiences of Arab prophets. Theodor Nöldeke and Friedrich Schwally, *Geschichte des Qorāns* 1 (Leipzig: Weicher, ²1909), 24–26.
9   Pp. 117f.
10   Pp. 159–161; pp. 163–168.
11   For the עם הארץ see p. 209 to 7:27.
12   For חמס see above p. 210.
13   See Albrecht Alt, "Micha 2:1–5 Γῆς ἀναδασμός in Juda" in *Kleine Schriften zur Geschichte des Volkes Israel* 3 (München: Beck, 1959), 373–381.

12

And the word of Yahweh came to me:
22/ Son of man, what is this proverb,
which (you have) in the land of Israel:
The days grow long, and nothing
happens of all[a] the visions. 23/ Therefore
say to them: Thus has [the Lord][a]
Yahweh said: I will put[b] an end to this
proverb, and they shall no more repeat
it in Israel.[c] But say to them: The days
have drawn near and that which every
vision proclaims.[d] 24/ For there shall no
longer be any lying visions or flattering
divinations within the house[a] of Israel.
25/ For it is I, Yahweh, who speaks. The
word which I speak is fulfilled.[a] It will

12: 22a 𝕲 μακρὰν (𝕲ᴮ μακραὶ) αἱ ἡμέραι ἀπόλωλεν
ὅρασις offers a briefer summary of the proverb. Hitzig, Cornill, Bertholet would therefore delete the כל
of 𝔐 and explain it as an addition dependent on
v 23bβ. However the rhythmic correspondence of
22b (saying of the people) and v 23bβ (reply of the
prophet), which is clearly deliberate, opposes this
view.

23 23a אדני is lacking in 𝕲 𝕮, see Excursus 1.
b 𝔐 השבתי. 4 MSSᴷᵉⁿ 𝕲 Σ 𝕾ʰ point to a reading
והשבתי, with which also 11:17; 30:10 (13) are to be
compared.
c 𝕲 presupposes בית ישראל as subject and, like
MSᴷᵉⁿ ¹²⁴, has taken ב׳ ישראל as an abbreviation
and has written it out in full. Cooke further points
for this process to 𝕲 20:5; 44:28. For the retention
of 𝔐 we have the support of the reading of the parallel text 18:3, also attested by 𝕲.
d The well attested ודבר is neither to be changed
with Cornill, Herrmann, Jahn, *Buch*, Rothstein to
ובא; with Ewald to וְעָבַּד; with Bertholet, Ziegler,
Ezechiel, Fohrer to וגבר; or with Kraetzschmar and
Schmidt to ומהר. Σ καιρός understands דבר of 𝔐 as
"moment of occurrence."

24 24a MSS (cf. 𝕲 𝕾 𝕿ʷ 𝕭) read בני instead of the
בית of 𝔐.

25 25a The syntactical structure of 25a is not immediately clear. Before examining details it must be
said that those explanations which give an understanding of the abbreviated parallel formulation
28bα without further textual change deserve preference above all other interpretations. We are first
inclined to regard the את אשר אדבר as an object
clause to the preceding אדבר (so 𝕲 λαλήσω τοὺς
λόγους μου) and to find in it a formulation in the
manner of Ex 3:14; 33:19. So Ewald, Smend, Bertholet. A certain difficulty is then offered by the separated following דבר, which is consequently deleted
as dittography by Vriezen, "'Ehje," page 505 note
1. Ewald's translation "What words I speak" is not
convincing. Ehrlich, *Randglossen*, Bertholet, (cf. also
Fohrer) change to דַּבֵּר וְעָשֹׂה. On this understanding v 28bα would be a broken formulation. Thus the
interpretation already proposed by Hitzig, which
takes the את אשר אדבר with what follows, gains full
weight. In the אשר אדבר דבר we clearly have before us a formulation in the manner of Amos 5:1;
Jer 14:1; 46:1, and other passages, according to
which the relative clause qualifying a noun is placed
in front of it (Gesenius-Kautzsch § 138 e note 1). For
the stressing of the subject (דבר) by את cf. Brockelmann § 31b. The introduction of the apodosis by ו is
grammatically unobjectionable, especially since the
clause carries a temporal-conditional emphasis ("If
I utter a word, so it will happen"). The test of the

no longer be delayed,[b] but in your days,
O rebellious house, I will speak a word
and perform it, says [the Lord][c]
Yahweh.

rightness of this understanding must lie in the fact
that from it v 28bα becomes intelligible without any
change.

b The feminine formulation תִמָּשֵׁךְ must be understood as a neutral form. Cf. also note b to v 28.

c אדני is lacking in 𝕲 𝕮, see Excursus 1.

Form

In 11:1–13 the divine word of the prophet was given in
the framework of a visionary scene, whilst in 11:14–21,
in connection with a word of assurance, it is given as
an answer to a saying of the people which is cited.
This speech form shows that Yahweh's word, which
at first appears to be simply a message proceeding
from above, enters into full dialogue with those addressed and can take up the words of men.[1] Whilst the
words of the people in many references are simply
adduced as a clarification of the attitude attacked by
the prophet (Amos 6:13; 8:5f; 9:10; Is 5:19; 9:9),
in other places there arises from them a real disputation
in which Yahweh argues with the sayings of men
(Is 30:15f; Jer 2:23; Is 40:27ff; 45:9ff). In the book
of Malachi, where respectively a word of Yahweh
(1:2, 6; 3:6f, 13) or a prophetic oracle of reproach
(2:10–13, 17) gives rise to the dialogue, we can see the
beginning of the true doctrinal disputation which
became of great importance in Talmudic Judaism. Also
in Ezekiel the disputation which counters a citation
has an important place. It appears in two especially
clear examples in 12:21–25 and 12:26–28, and is to
be found beside 11:2ff and 11:15ff, also in 18:2ff
(19, 25, 29); 20:32ff; 33:17ff, 24ff; 37:11–14. In
form therefore Ezekiel is undoubtedly to be set before
Malachi, where, as a rule in the examples mentioned,
a false human utterance is given which Yahweh answers.
In Ezek 18:19, where a divine rule is put in question,
there is clearly outlined even from afar the possibility
of further development into a doctrinal disputation
in the manner of Malachi. For the rest the peculiarity
of Ezekiel's use consists in the fact that the statement
of men, which is countered by the word of Yahweh
(in a declaration of judgement or of assurance), is

wholly taken up within the divine speech, either so
that Yahweh draws the prophet's attention to a particular saying of the people or in 12:22 so that God
himself speaks to him in a question about the saying
of the people. Further there is found in Ezekiel very
frequently the third possibility, that the quotation is
built into a יען clause and simply illustrates the reason
for a following declaration of punishment, as is already
found in 1 Kings 20:28 (Ezek 25:8; 26:2; 28:2;
35:10; 36:2, 13).

Interpretation

■ **12:21, 22** Verse 22, which is introduced by the formula
for the coming of a message, is addressed to the "son
of man" and directs Yahweh's word against a proverb
which is current "in the land of Israel."[2]

According to O. Eissfeldt and A. R. Johnson, מָשָׁל
is derived from a basic meaning "to be like, similar,"
whilst J. Hempel, in dependence on G. Boström,
connects the word with משׁל "to rule" and regards
as its basic meaning "that which goes beyond what is
usual."[3] It covers a rich fullness of meanings. It ranges
from the folk proverb, the detached quotation, the
mannered proverb, to the doctrine of the wise men
and the oracle of the seer (Nu 23:7–18; 24:3, 15,
20f, 23). Also a mocking saying (Dtn 28:37; Is 14:4)
can be called a מָשָׁל. In the present text מָשָׁל means
a clever saying which in its concentrated diction gives
expression to an idea in the most poignant possible
way and is therefore repeated and believed by many—
a well-phrased saying is already half a truth!

The saying of the people deals with the prophetic
word, which here (vv 22–24, 27) and in 13:16, as
already in the slightly transformed Jeremiah quotation
of 7:26 (cf. note a to 7:13), is described as a חזון

1   See especially Wolff, *Zitat*.
2   See above pp. 144f; pp. 131f.
3   Otto Eissfeldt, *Der Maschal im Alten Testament*,
     BZAW 24 (Giessen: Töpelmann, 1913); Aubrey R.
     Johnson, "מָשָׁל" in *Wisdom in Israel and in the Ancient
     Near East*, ed. Martin Noth, VTSuppl 3 (Leiden:
     Brill, 1955), 162–169 (for further literature see there
     p. 162 note 1); Hempel, *Literatur*, 44; G. Boström,

Paronomasi i den äldre hebreiska Maschallitteraturen
(Lund: Gleerups, 1928).

"vision." In this description there is retained a recollection of the basis in visionary experience of older prophecy. In classical written prophecy it has largely fallen into the background behind the (auditive) receiving of a message: "The visual passes; the word remains."[4] From the "vision" (חזון) which Isaiah saw (חזה) 1:1 there emerged the "word" (דבר), which he saw (חזה) 2:1, cf. Amos 1:1; Mic 1:1. With Ezekiel also, in whose book the visionary element is again relatively strongly to the fore, the central position of the "word" in the description of the prophetic experience is incontestable, even in the present text. In the quotation we can therefore recognize the popular manner of speech.

This makes a pronouncement about the prophetic preaching first of all in a quite general way. The imperfect (הימים)יארכו precludes our regarding the saying as an assertion made at a specific moment, which looked back over a completed period: "a long time has now passed." Rather the statement expressed by the imperfect remains open and general. Indeed we must question whether or not a slight conditional accent lies in the first clause which would then become subordinate to the following main clause: "If now some time has already passed, then the whole prophetic message will fail completely." The saying therefore lies closer to Jer 5:12f, with its הנבאים יהיו לרוח, than to Is 5:19, with its challenge of Yahweh at a specific point of time. The threat of divine judgement is here comfortingly dismissed: nothing is eaten as hot as when it is cooked! Even for the word of God the actual wearing down of time will have its effect.

■ **12:23** Against this lighthearted dismissal Yahweh speaks immediately with a general threat, which is repeated in 18:3; suddenly he will put an end to the naive saying in Israel. Then follows a sharp and concrete antithesis to the saying of the people, formed in the perfect: "The days have drawn near and that which every vision proclaims." It is the message known from 7:7 and 9:1 in which the saying of the people is taken up, but at the same time altered in a threatening way: Against the timeless drawn out imperfect יארכו "become long" there appears the conclusive

angry perfect קרבו "have drawn near," and against the indefinite הימים "days," the days of fulfillment, הימים "the (judgement) days," determined by reference to the day of Yahweh.[5] Against the contemptuous ואבד כל חזון there appears the דבר כל חזון "that which was contained in the prophetic vision as the message (of Yahweh)," which clearly points to the expression דבר יהוה. Verse 25 elaborates it still further: "For I, Yahweh, I speak."[6]

■ **12:24** To this central message of the whole oracle there is added in v 24 a further statement of prophetic defense, which should not, with Fohrer, be dismissed as a later gloss. Regarding the word of God as harmless also touches upon the fact that in Israel from time to time many irresponsible sayings coined to please (Is 30:10, further Mic 2:11; 3:5) had been uttered by the mouths of prophets. 13:1ff deals with them further. But "what has straw to do with wheat?" Jeremiah (23:28f) puts this question to the prophets who confuse their dreams with the word of God, which is like a fire and a hammer shattering the rocks. We must regard the statement of v 25a in this way. It is a variation, in the imperfect, of the אני יהוה דברתי, which is often found as a concluding formula in Ezekiel's oracles and which can also be expanded to the fuller אני יהוה דברתי ועשיתי.[7]

■ **12:25** The continuation of v 25 serves as a paraphrase of this expansion. Because Yahweh himself—he who is exalted above all failure by his power—speaks in the words of the prophet, his word will not succumb to the wear and tear of age and decay, to which everything in this world is subject, but will endure in its reality and force.

Setting

The prophet was addressed by Yahweh about a saying which was current "in the land of Israel." 18:1–3 shows that this is a stereotyped introduction to a disputation oracle. In his reply Yahweh addresses directly the men who pass on the ungodly proverb as a "house of rebellion." Since there are no compelling reasons for locating the activity of Ezekiel in Jerusalem, we must either accept here that the information about

---

4   Ludwig Koehler, *Old Testament Theology*, tr. A. S. Todd. Lutterworth Library 49 (London: Lutterworth, 1957).

5   Pp. 201f.
6   Cf. note c to 5:13.
7   See above pp. 175f; p. 176.

what was said by those who remained in the land came to him in the manner of Jer 29, or that he had in mind the whole history of Israel and, in the general saying quoted in v 22, was thinking of the contemptuous way in which Israel had always responded to its prophets.[8] The prophet, living in exile but responsible by his word for the whole "house of Israel," declared to Israel not simply the disproving in his days of lying prophecy, but the near arrival of that which was declared by the true word of Yahweh.[9] The event of 587 B.C., before which the present oracle is to be dated, soon showed in an unmistakable way the reality of the power of Yahweh's word in history.

Aim

Against the impious confidence of his people who regard God's word, like all created things, as transient, the prophet has to proclaim its validity. God's word cannot be dismissed as part of the scheme of worldly realities and wisdom which are subject to the laws of age because in it God himself is present in person. In it the Lord is present who is not subject to any decay, but who rather forms with his own hands the stuff of transient things into his history. Statements such as became current in prophecy in Jer 1:11f; Is 40:8; 55:10f can here be heard directly before the fall of Jerusalem.

In this the prophet is not concerned with asserting a definite calendar of the course of history into which men could withdraw, either cynically or in resignation, as into a fixed process of fate. Rather he is concerned with a personal message coming directly from God, which cannot be isolated into a single conceptual area, but which encompasses life and history with all their realities and events. Where God's people are addressed by the prophetic word there can be only either a falling to judgement or a flight to deliverance in obedient repentance, but not the third possibility of a convenient awaiting of the day when this message, like so many human messages, would ultimately become dead.

---

8   Cf. Janssen, *Juda*, 87: "The proverb about the un-fulfilled prophetic message in Ezek 12:21f was directed against prophecy as a whole."

9   See above p. 132.

God's Word Does Not Refer
to "Distant Days."

Bibliography

F. V. Filson
"The Omission of Ezekiel 12:26–28 and 36:23b–
38 in Codex 967," *JBL* 62 (1943): 27–32.

Preliminary note. The section 12:26–28 is lacking in
the Chester Beatty Papyrus $\mathfrak{G}^{967}$. The loss of the
piece, which is certainly not simply a copy of 21–25
in spite of contacts in form and content, must be
explained with Filson as a scribal error as a result of
homoioteleuton.

12

26 And the word of Yahweh came to me:
27/ Son of man, see, the house of
Israel[a] says: The visions which he sees
are for many days hence, and he
prophesies of distant times. 28/ Therefore say to them: Thus has [the Lord][a]
Yahweh said: None of my words will
be delayed any longer.[b] The word which
I speak will be performed, says [the
Lord][a] Yahweh.

12: 27a $\mathfrak{G}$ + ὁ παραπικραίνων, which has been marked
with the obelus in $\mathfrak{G}^{Q.88}$, has been secondarily added
in dependence on v 25.

28 28a אדני is lacking in $\mathfrak{G}$ $\mathfrak{C}$, see Excursus 1.
b The formally neutral לא תמשך of v 25 has here
been expanded by a subject added later. The feminine formulation of the verb can be retained, but
this must, other than would be expected from the
context with its singular דבר, be formulated as plural. Cf. Gesenius-Kautzsch § 145 k. There is strong
influence of משך on the (preceding) subject in Is
13:22.

Form

The section vv 26–28, freshly introduced by the formula
for the coming of a message and the address as son of
man, is not to be regarded simply as a redactional
repetition beside vv 21–25 (Messel), nor as an appendix
which is shown to be such by the formal peculiarity of
the "resumption."[1] It is an independent disputation
oracle, introduced with a quotation and thematically
separate throughout.[2] In distinction from vv 21–25,
it does not introduce the quotations in the form of a
question to the prophet, but in a simple statement.
Instead of referring to the quotation as a משל (v 22),
we find, as in 37:11, הנה . . . אמרים, recalling the
French "On dit."

Setting

If vv 21–25 arise from a general assertion about the
word of prophecy, then vv 26–28 take their origin from
a judgement about the prophetic preaching of Ezekiel

himself. Thus here, unlike in v 22, we are not concerned
about a saying of the people "in the land of Israel."
The "house of Israel" (v 27) means the exiled community around the prophet, which, before the occurrence of the catastrophe of 587 B.C., gave expression
to these skeptical words about Ezekiel's preaching.
The saying must have been spoken before the beginning
of the siege of Jerusalem in the year 589 B.C.

Interpretation

■ **12:27** The prophet counters with a threat of disaster
(33:30–33 deals with a reaction to the later message
of the prophet) the confident evasions of his compatriots: "The visions which he sees are for many days
hence, and he prophesies of distant times."[3] This
does not express the fundamental distrust of the validity
of the divine word, which is heard in v 22. Rather
those who spoke thus were putting off the message
concerning them in another way and, in disobedience

---

1 See above pp. 144f; pp. 131f. Kuhl, "'Wiederaufnahme'," 8f.
2 See above p. 280.

3 Cf. Hezekiah's saying Is 39:8.

and indifference, were claiming for themselves a period of freedom, which allowed them to remain undecided. Sometime in a distant future the message may have its fulfillment, but they were not going to let their present be spoiled by it.

■ **12:28** The divine answer repeats the saying of v 25a, with the omission of the introductory assertion and a transposing of clauses. Yahweh is ready to fulfil his word without further delay. The similar repetition of the divine affirmation of v 25a, with slight variation of the order and length, is not to be explained away as a redaction, and shows something of the fixed validity of the divine word. The same message opposes the general disregard of the divine word by those who remain in the land, and the indecision of the exiles.

Aim

God's announcement of his action, given at a particular time, here suffers an apparently pious form of rejection by his people. The word of God is not completely dismissed, but is removed from the present and applied to a distant date. Obedience is changed into a pious view of the world which even has room for judgement—only a far off judgement some time, finally at the end of time. Examples of the putting off of the immediate threat of God's judgement in what was perhaps a very elaborate "eschatology" could easily be multiplied in Synagogue, Church, and Islam

In the last resort the prophetic word which counters this is not concerned with replacing a long-term reckoning with a short-term one, but with depriving men of their shield and defenses behind which they hide themselves from God. Their pious, or godless, "Après nous le déluge!" or their "Let us eat and drink for tomorrow we die!" (Is 22:13; 1 Cor 15:32) must be silenced. They must learn that where they encounter the living word of God all reckoning on obtaining security by postponement is at an end. They must face him, eye to eye, accepting his threat, and with nothing more nor less than his grace between them, summoning them to obedience. This is the reality of God, who comes to man by his word.

Against the False Prophets and Prophetesses

J. Barth
"Zu dem Zauber des Umnähens der Gelenke,"
MGWJ 57 (1913): 235.

W. H. Brownlee
"Exorcising the Souls from Ezekiel 13[17–23]," *JBL*
69 (1950): 367–373.

J. G. Frazer
"Hunting for Souls," *ARW* 11 (1908): 197–199.

G. Quell
Wahre und falsche Propheten, BF ChrTh 46, 1 (Gütersloh: Bertelsmann, 1952).

J. A. Selbie
"Ezekiel 13[18–21]," *ET* 15 (1903/4): 75.

13

1 And the word of Yahweh came to me:
2/ Son of man, prophesy against[a] the
prophets of Israel. 'Prophesy' (?)[b] and
say 'to them':[c] Hear the word of
Yahweh: 3/ Thus has [the Lord][a]
Yahweh said: Woe 'to those, who
prophesy out of their own hearts'[b] and
according to that which they have not

13: 2a על – אל cf. 1:17 note a.

2 b The הַנִּבָּאִים, standing absolutely, "those who prophesy" of 𝔐 is unusual. It is hardly original. 𝕲 καὶ προφητεύσεις suggests an emendation to הִנָּבֵא. The connection הִנָּבֵא וְאָמַרְתָּ is also found elsewhere in the book of Ezekiel (21:14, 33; 30:2; 36:3). Further the doubling of הנבא which then arises does not lack analogies (11:4; 34:2; 37:9). However, in view of the heavy glossing of the chapter, the question cannot altogether be dismissed whether or not we ought to see in the הנבאים of 𝔐 a subsequent addition (perhaps as part of an original הנבאים מלבם). Cf. also note c.

c 𝔐 לנביאי מלבם "to those (who are) prophets out of their own minds." This identification of those addressed, which anticipates the substance of the following invective, is noticeably awkward after the ואמרת and would certainly stand more correctly with נביאי ישראל, cf. note b. The shorter text of 𝕲 καὶ ἐρεῖς πρὸς αὐτούς deserves preference. Read אליהם, cf. 37:4 also 34:2.

3 3a אדני is lacking in 𝕲 𝕮, see Excursus 1.

b 𝔐 הוי על הנביאים הנבלים אשר הלכים אחר רוחם "Woe to the foolish prophets who follow their own spirit." 𝕲 οὐαὶ τοῖς προφητεύουσιν ἀπὸ καρδίας αὐτῶν points to the simpler reading הוי לְנְבָאֵי מלבם, which is probably more original. Through the glossing of v 2 (note c) the original reading of v 3 was anticipated. Thus it was replaced by the alteration which is now to be found in 𝔐. Conceivably there is also a scribal error changing an original מלבם to הנבלים which was then subsequently interpreted by the relative clause. In 𝔐 not only the unusual use of נבל is striking, but also the use of the phrase הלך אחר. אחר is otherwise found in Ezekiel only in 40:1, in the combination אחר אשר, and in 20:39 in an uncertain text. הלך is connected in 20:16; 33:31 with אחרי, which frequently appears in Ezekiel (6:9; 16:23; 20:24, 30; 23:30, 35; 44:10, 26; 46:12). Beside the gloss in v 2 also the parallel in v 17 speaks in favor of the reading of 𝕲.

seen. 4/ Like foxes among ruins are your prophets, O Israel. ''ᵃ./ 5/ You have not gone up into the 'breach'ᵃ and have not built the wall for the house of Israel, so that it might stand in the battle on the day of Yahweh. 6/ Theyᵃ seeᵃ falsehood and divineᵃ a lie, and then say: oracle of Yahweh, when Yahweh has not sent them—and yet theyᵇ expect that he will fulfill the word. 7/ Have you not seen delusive visions and spoken lying oracles [and said: oracle of Yahweh, when I have not spoken]?ᵃ 8/ Thereforeᵃ thus says [the Lord]ᵇ Yahweh: Because you have spoken delusion and seen lies, behold, therefore I will be againstᶜ you, says [the Lord]ᵇ Yahweh. 9/ And I will 'stretch' outᵃ my hand against the prophets, who see delusion and divine

c לבלתי is only here in the Old Testament construed with the perfect. According to Gesenius-Kautzsch § 152 x ראו לבלתי is "to be regarded as a relative clause governed by לְ." Driver, "Linguistic Problems," 63, and "Ezekiel," 150, questions whether or not ראו is to be understood analogous to the שׁחו of 47:5 as an abstract verbal noun. Just as much the vocalization as infinitive ראֹו (Koehler-Baumgartner) should also be considered.

4   4a 𝕲 can still not have had the היו at the end of the verse ("they have become"). It is lacking in MSᴷᵉⁿ ⁷².

5   5a Since פרץ in similar phrases is otherwise used in the singular (בפרץ עמד 22:30; Ps 106:23; Sir 45:23), and the plural, where it is attested (Am 4:3; 9:11; Is 28:21), shows a masculine formation, we must here read with the versions בפרץ. 𝔐 is a dittography. For the rest 𝕲 appears in v 5 to be translated from a strongly corrupted Hebrew original. Also it transposes the text into the third person in an effort to smooth it. 𝕋 paraphrases it to mean that the lack of good works (עובדין טבין) of the prophets consisted in neglecting prayer for the preservation of Israel and for the divine mercy (רחמין) on the day of distress.

6   6a 𝔐 חָזוּ שָׁוְא וְקֶסֶם כָּזָב "they saw delusion and lying oracles." 𝕲 translates as participles βλέποντες - μαντευόμενοι (𝕋 מתנבן and מלפין is not a surer witness since it also translates the following ויחלו with the participle מחצפין). This points to a Hebrew original חֹזֵי – קֹסְמֵי. So Ehrlich, *Randglossen*, Bewer, Fohrer, BH³. Cf. v 9. The reading חָזוּ – וְקָסְמוּ, apparently supported by 𝖁 (*vident vana et divinant mendacium*) and accepted by Toy, Herrmann and Bertholet, is not to be recommended in view of the perfect consecutive, otherwise understood of the future. Driver, "Ezekiel," 150, leaves the ראו understood as an abstract verbal noun analogous to שׁחו (cf. note c to v 3) and regards aα as an exclamation.

b Perfect consecutive for the continuation of a participle, cf. Gesenius-Kautzsch § 112 k.

7   7a V 7b is lacking in 𝕲 𝕮ˢᵃ Hierᵗᵉˢᵗ and is a later expansion making use of v 6aβ, 22:28 (Jer 23:21), as the clumsy addition of ואמרים shows.

8   8a 𝕲 + εἶπον.

b אדני is lacking in 𝕲 𝕮 Gild., see Excursus 1.

c אל - על cf. 1:17 note a. In the fourteen occurrences of "the challenge formula" (see above p. 175) in Ezekiel, it is ten times written with אל and four times with על.

9   9a With 𝕲 καὶ ἐκτενῶ, instead of 𝔐 והיתה "and (my hand) be against..." we must read ונטיתי. יד as subject of היה appears in Ezekiel only in the references to the prophet's seizure by the hand of Yahweh (see above pp. 117f), never as a description of Yahweh's punitive action. נטה יד על is, however, found with him no less than eight times (6:14; 14:9, 13; 16:27; 25:7, 13, 16; 35:3). For על – אל cf. note a to 1:17.

lies. They shall not come[b] into the
congregation[c] of my people, nor be
enrolled in the register of the house of
Israel,[d] nor shall they enter the land of
Israel. And you shall know[e] that I am
[the Lord][f] Yahweh.

10 Therefore, indeed therefore,[a] because
they have led my people into error,[b] in
that they have said: Peace! when there
is no peace—because they have built a
wall,[c] and behold they daub it with
whitewash[d]—11/ say to those who daub
with whitewash ' ':[a] 'when therefore'[b]
a deluge of rain comes and ' '[c] hailstones fall, and a storm wind breaks
out,[d] 12/ and the wall is thrown down,[a]
will they not then say to you: Where is
(now) the daubing with which you
daubed it? 13/ Therefore thus has [the
Lord][a] Yahweh said: I will make a storm
wind break out in my wrath, and a
deluge of rain will come in my anger
and hailstones will 'fall'[b] through (my)

b 𝔐 יהיו literally "(not) be."

c 𝔐 סוד "private conversation," Mishnaic Hebrew "secret," interpreted by 𝔗 eschatologically
ברז טב דגניז לעמי.

d 𝔗 ובכתב חיי עלמא דכתיב לצדיקי בית ישראל
לא יתכתבון again recalls the heavenly reward of
the righteous among the people of God.

e Just as 𝔊 has already attempted to smooth a
difficulty in v 4, so also the adaptation καὶ γνώσονται
(against Bertholet, Fohrer) here arouses little confidence.

f אדני is lacking in 𝔊 𝔠 Gild., see Excursus 1.

10 10a The doubling יען וביען recurs again in 36: 3;
Lev 26:43.

b טעה is an Aramaism only found here. However,
the Hebrew form תעה is found in 14:11; 44:10, 15;
48:11. Is a play of טעה on טיח intended?

c חיץ hapax legomenon; according to Ehrlich,
Randglossen, on the text it denotes a wall constructed
of loose stones. 𝔊 τοῖχον.

d 𝔐 תפל related to טפל "to smear, smear over."
It was not understood by 𝔊 πεσεῖται, but interpreted
as תָּפֵל. Is there intended an allusion to תפל II
"insipid, worthless" (Job 6:6)? 𝔊ᵠ ἀφροσύνη, ᾽Α
ἄναλον, Σ ἀνάρτυτον 𝔗 טין פטיר דלא תבן, 𝔙 *luto
absque paleis* paraphrase as an attempt at clarification.

11 11a 𝔊 εἶπον πρὸς τοὺς ἀλείφοντας πεσεῖται here
also misunderstands תָּפֵל as תָּפֵל. It does, however,
lack any counterpart to the following ויפל in 𝔐,
which should then be deleted as a subsequent interpretative addition (or as a wrongly written dittography for תפל?), the ו of which has made superfluous the copula which once stood with the next
word. Cf. the following note.

b 𝔐 היה. According to 𝔊 καὶ ἔσται, we should
read והיה; perfect consecutive for a new action also
in vv 9, 13.

c The ואתנה is certainly attested by the versions,
whether we read with 𝔊 καὶ δώσω, 𝔙 *et dabo* as
וְאֶתְּנָה; with 𝔊 אה אנא יהב as אֶתְּנָה; or with 𝔗 וית as
וְאֶת; but in any case it breaks up the parallel position of the three clauses of v 11 (cf. v 13). It must be
deleted as a dittography for ואבני. The copula is to
be connected with the correctly written אבני.

d 𝔐 תְּבַקֵּעַ. The pi'el of בקע is in its right place in
v 13; here we must vocalize nip'al תְּבָּקֵעַ with Is
58:8.

12 12a Literally: "and behold, the wall has fallen."

13 13a אדני is lacking in 𝔊 𝔠, see Excursus 1.

b 𝔊 appears to here read a text which did not
deviate from 𝔐 in spite of the added verb ἐπάξω in
the last stichos. The undeniable correspondence of
the three stichoi of v 13αβb to those of v 11b, whereby only expressions of the divine wrath are added,
raises the question whether the לכלה ("to destruction") of 𝔐, which comes too soon before v 14, is a
scribal error for תפלנה corresponding to v 11 (Cornill). This is accepted in the translation above.

wrath. 14/ And I will break down the wall, which you have daubed with whitewash, and bring it down[a] to the ground, so that its foundation will be laid bare [; and it shall fall, and you shall perish in the midst of it].[b] And you shall know that I am Yahweh. 15/ And I will pour out to the full my wrath upon the wall, and upon those who have daubed it with whitewash, and 'they will say' to you:[a] 'Where'[b] is (now) the wall and 'where'[b] are those who have daubed it—16/ the prophets of Israel who prophesied concerning Jerusalem and who saw visions of peace for her, when there was no peace? says [the Lord][a] Yahweh.

17 And you, son of man, set your face against[a] the daughters[b] of your people, who prophesy out of their own hearts, and prophesy against them 18/ and say: Thus has [the Lord][a] Yahweh said: Woe to those who sew bands for every 'wrist'[b] and make veils[c] for (people of) every stature,[d] in order to hunt for human lives. Will you[e] hunt down[f] lives among my people and keep alive lives for your own profit? 19/ You have profaned me among my people for a few handfuls of barley and for pieces[a] of bread, putting to death persons who should not die and keeping alive persons who should not live [, in that you have lied to my people, who listen to lies].[b]

20 Therefore thus has [the Lord][a] Yahweh

14 14a Literally: "I will make it touch the earth."

b The change of gender that becomes evident in ונפלה and בתוכה is remarkable. Ehrlich's conjecture to change ונפלה to ונפל (also BH³, Bertholet) and to understand בתוכה as neuter is not satisfying. As בתוכה is difficult to understand in connection with a picture of a wall collapsing (we would expect תחתיו or תחתיה), and the connection of bα to bβ raises difficulties (How could those who perish recognize anything?), thus we must see in bα a section which was added later and which must relate to the city Jerusalem (or its wall חומה?). From this בתוכה can be understood. Cf. Albrecht, "Geschlecht," 85.

15 15a 𝔐 וְאֹמַר "and I will say"—a theological interpretation, already attested by 𝔊, of an original neutral וְאָמַר (or יֵאָמֵר?). Cf. 𝔊 ותאמר לכון, 𝔗 ויתאמר לכון.

b 𝔐 ואין or אין "is no more." The restoration of איה or ואיה in agreement with v 12 is supported by 𝔊. 𝔐 is surprisingly flat.

16 16a אדני is lacking in 𝔊 𝔏ˢ 𝔆, see Excursus 1.

17 17a על–אל cf. note a to 1:17.

b בנות does not have in mind a particular age, but refers to individual women within the nation, cf. p. 131 to בן.

18 18a אדני is lacking in 𝔊 𝔏ˢ 𝔆ᶜᵒ, see Excursus 1.

b 𝔐 יָדָי "my hands" is doubtless a textual error. We must either read as יד, following 𝔊 ἐπὶ πάντα ἀγκῶνα χειρός (𝔏ˢ 𝔆ᴮᵒ 𝔙), in which י could be a dittography of the following (עשות)ו, or ידים, following MSS^{Ken 154.313 marg. 597} (𝔖, 𝔗) in which ם has fallen out from 𝔐 by error.

c The article in המספחות is remarkable beside the parallel כסתות, without the article. Is ה a dittography for the preceding ת, wrongly written?

d 𝔊 ἐπὶ πᾶσαν κεφαλὴν πάσης ἡλικίας (𝔏ˢ 𝔙 aetatis) rightly points to the particular degree of growth. Possibly it read a כל before ראש.

e The ה of הנפשות is to be vocalized as ה-interrogative, against the 𝔐 הַנְּפָשׁוֹת. Read הַנְפָשׁוֹת.

f תצודדנה undoubtedly stands here in antithesis to תחיינה. Cornill, Bertholet, Fohrer would consequently read תמותתנה in adaption with v 19. Since the root צוד is also a catchword in 20f, and the pilpel of מות is never used with Ezekiel, but only the hip'il (so in v 19) beside the qal, we must keep 𝔐. This is further supported by the fact that the text tradition offers no support for an emendation.

19 19a The feminine פתות, corresponding to the Arabic futāt, is here found for the more frequent פת. Cf. Schulthess, "ריפות," 358.

b 𝔐 בכזבכם is unusual for its masculine suffix form. Since also the pi'el of כזב and the formulation שמע כזב is not again found in Ezekiel, the question must be raised whether v 19b is not a subsequent addition, which seeks to relate the catchword כזב, which is related to the prophets in vv 1–16, to the prophetesses as well. However cf. note e to v 20.

20 20a אדני is lacking in 𝔊 𝔏ˢ 𝔆ᴮᵒ, see Excursus 1.

said: Behold, I will 'be against'[b] your bands, with which[c] you hunt human lives ' ',[d] and tear them[e] from your[e] arms; and I will let the people that you[e] hunt go free[f]...[g]. 21/ And I will tear off your veils[a] and deliver my people out of your hand, and they shall be no more in your hand as prey. And you shall know that I am Yahweh.

22 Because you 'have brought into distress'[a] falsely[b] the heart of the righteous, when I have not yet brought him into distress, whilst you have strengthened the hands of the wicked, so that he does not turn from his evil way and so that you might bring him to life,[c] 23/ therefore you shall no (more) see delusion nor divine a 'lie,'[a] and I will deliver my people out of your hand, and you shall know that I am Yahweh.

b עַל – אַל cf. note a to 1:17 and note c to 13:8.

c In the שָׁם of 𝔐, which is supported by 𝔊 ἐφ' ἅ . . . ἐκεῖ 𝔏ˢ quibus . . . illuc, there is a direct spatial reference: human lives have been caught in these magic bonds as in nets. However, the purely instrumental בָּהֶין of 𝔗, בהון of 𝔊 quibus of 𝔙 appear to represent a (subsequent) smoothing over.

d 𝔐 לִפְרֹחֹות was clearly not present to 𝔊 here and is to be deleted. Cf. further note g.

e In 20aβ–21aα¹, remarkably, masculine suffixes and pronominal forms appear throughout. These forms (מִסְפַּחְתִּיכֶם, אַתֶּם, זְרֹועֹתֵיכֶם, אֹתָם) then subsequently disappear. It cannot be made out with certainty whether this denotes a secondary text element (cf. note b to v 19), whether it shows a textual corruption in the course of transmission, as appears in considerable measure in Ezek 13, or whether it is an original mixture of forms. Cf. further the comments upon Ezek 1, see above p. 102.

f אֶת נְפָשִׁים of 𝔐 is certainly not correct. נֶפֶשׁ is usually formed with a feminine plural; it also lacks the article here, and further the whole expression is quite inappropriate after the preceding אֶת הַנְּפָשֹׁות. Cornill's conjecture, to read אֹתָן חָפְשִׁים (original feminine suffix? cf. note e), gives a clear meaning to the text. For שְׁלַח חָפְשִׁי cf. Ex 21:2, 5, 26f; Dtn 15:12f, 18; Jer 34:9–11, 14, 16, plural Is 58:6. A feminine formation is not found.

g 𝔐 לִפְרֹחֹת. 𝔊 εἰς διασκορπισμόν, 𝔙 ad volandum, Σ εἰς τὸ ἀναπετασθῆναι, Θ εἰς ἔκλυσιν (= לִפְרֹעֹות?), 𝔗 לְאַבָּדוּתָא. The meaning is obscure. By the occurrence of the Aramaic reference to פרח "to fly" are we to think of a picture of a bird escaping from a snare (Ps 124:7; Prv 6:5)? Is the whole saying a gloss, which was inserted after the corruption of the preceding words? The saying, which can scarcely be interpreted, would then remarkably also have been added again in v 20a, cf. note d.

21 21a Cf. note e to v 20.

22 22a 𝔐 הַכְאֹות from כאה, corresponding to the Syriac כאא "to intimidate"? Hip'il only here. 𝔊 διεστρέφετε, Ἀ διεταράττετε καὶ ἐχειμάζετε or ἠμαυρώθη (𝔊⁸⁶), Σ διὰ τὸ βασανίζειν, 𝔙 maerere fecistis. We may conjecture that the original text used the same verb for the action of men and Yahweh (aβ). However, we must then give preference to הכאיב which occurs again in Ezekiel in 28:24, rather than to the hip'il of כאה, which is otherwise never found Read הַכְאִיב.

b שֶׁקֶר is lacking in 𝔊 and is a clarifying addition.

c 𝔐 לְהַחֲיֹתֹו. The hip'il of חיה is not found elsewhere in Ezekiel, but is otherwise frequent in the Old Testament. Thus the emendation to לַחֲיֹותֹו (Cornill) is not compelling in spite of MS[Ken 115] 𝔊 𝔖 𝔙.

23 23a The analogy of vv 6, 7, 9, 19 leads us to expect here כָּזָב instead of קֶסֶם, which otherwise in Ezekiel nowhere means by itself "lying oracle."

Form

13:1–23 is identified as a self-contained section by the introductory formula for the coming of a message, which is then followed in 14:1 by a comparable introductory narrative element. The question arises, however, whether this was planned as a unit or whether it was first redactionally put together as a collection of individual sayings, theoretically related but originally independent.

Certain breaks can quickly be seen. The address בן אדם and the following commission to speak in v 2f and 17f mark formally the beginnings of two subordinate themes: prophets – prophetesses. That they both begin with the הוי cry, which is otherwise only found in Ezekiel in 34:2, is then certainly not an accident. The two halves vv 1–16 and vv 17–23 are intended to correspond like diptychs.

Within the two section we can recognize yet further structural parts. Of importance for distinguishing them are the recognition formulas, which are found twice in each of the two parts (vv 9, 14, 21, 23). In form these should give the purpose of the sections of the proof oracles. When we begin the analysis of Ezek 13 from the end, then it is immediately clear in vv 22–23 that we have here the clasic form of the proof oracle, which is already evident as a three-part formula in 1 Kings 20:13, 28.[1] After a) a motivation introduced by יען there follows b) the declaration of the divine intervention introduced in a vigorous style with לכן and c) the declaration of purpose in the recognition formula.[2]

1 Kings 20:13 has put in place of the motive clause introduced with יען a question introduced with הראית.[3] A further possibility of variation from the basic form in the first member is visible in Ezek 13 in the proof saying part, vv 18–21. In place of the motive clause introduced with יען we have here the woe-cry (הוי-cry), which already had an earlier history in the development of forms in prophetic speech. Prophetic sayings like Is 5:8–10; 11–13; Mic 2:1–3 show that the setting of the woe-cry first of all lay in reproach, which, as a special formulation of the prophet's, was intended as a motivation for the following divine word. Thus the reproach could also become independent as a shorter or longer "exclamation" (Am 5:18–20; Is 5:18f, 20, 21; 29:15; Hab 2:6b–8; 9–11, 12f, 15–17, 19).[4] However, this element of the motivation of the judgement was then included in the divine word (Is 10:1ff, 5ff; 29:1ff; 30:1ff; Jer 22:13ff; 23:1ff). The cry of woe and the following word of judgement were now formulated in the first person of Yahweh himself. This developed form of the woe-cry is presupposed by Ezekiel and worked into the proof-oracle 13:18f (also in 13:3; 34:2, the woe-cry stands in the shadow of the preceding formula for the receipt of a divine message).

Finally the element of the divine announcement undergoes a particular stylizing, when in v 20 the לכן, expanded by the messenger formula, follows a threat beginning with the challenge (note c to 13:8) הנני אל(על), known from 5:8.

It is then striking that a structure can also be seen in vv 3–16 which is quite parallel to the duplicated proof oracle vv 18–21; 22–23. Here also in vv 10–14, parallel to vv 22–23, we find the classic form of the proof oracle in a series of three parts: a) motivation with יען v 10, b) declaration of judgement introduced with לכן and the messenger formula, vv 13–14bα, c) formula of recognition v 14bβ. To this we certainly should add a twofold remark. First vv 15f, which conclude with a particular formula for a divine oracle, go beyond this. These verses, since they disturb the symmetry of the structure, are probably a later addition. Their content also, which appears as a fuller formulation of the declaration of v 12 (cf. the exposition), supports the view that we should see in them a later comment upon v 12. However, vv 11f are also already an element of secondary interpretation. They are distinctive not only on account of the unexpected fresh command to speak within a section of the proof oracle, but even more because of the premature mention of the divine threat, which would first be expected after the לכן of v 13. In their content vv 11–12a appear as a doublet of vv 13f. Thus the original content of the proof oracle, which corresponds to vv 22–23 in the second half, is to be found in vv 10, 13–14.

The question still remains, however, whether the

---

1   For details see Zimmerli, "Wort."
2   Cf. further the oracles against the nations 25:1ff.
3   See above p. 235.
4   See Hempel, *Literatur*, 60f.

first half of the oracle against the prophets (vv 2–9) corresponds to the first half of the oracle against the prophetesses. In fact we find here the parts we should expect: a) the element of motivation vv 3–7, formed as a הוי-cry, b) The declaration of judgement vv 8–9a, introduced with לכן, the messenger formula and the following הנני אל, c) The formula of recognition v 9b. Admittedly this unity shows certain irregularities in detail. Thus especially the change of address from the second to the third person was always striking. Fohrer, following Bertholet, has attempted, by connecting together the verses preserved in the second person, and those in the third person, to separate out two independent units which were later interwoven (vv 1f, 5, 7f, and vv 3f, 6, 9). The parallelism of the structure to vv 18–21 is thereby broken up, without giving two units which are really convincing in their form. This also raises the question why there should have occurred only here a subsequent weaving together of two oracles in the manner of the interweaving of sources in the Pentateuch. Bertholet is therefore more consistent than Fohrer when he utilizes the 'documentary hypothesis' of interwoven parallel strands in the continuation of ch. 13 and a number of other chapters. However, it is more correct to reckon here with the process of a gradually enlarged series of comments upon the text, as has already emerged in the earlier chapters. For the basic text we need not altogether fear the change from the second to the third persons. 26:3ff; 28:22ff also attest a transition to speech in the third person in direct conjunction with a very vigorous הנני עליך. We must then look for the basic text in vv 3, 5, 7a, 8f.

In the basic text of Ezek 13 which is thereby gained, are we faced with a composition of four originally separate sayings, cast in the form of a proof oracle, about prophets and prophetesses? Closer examination opposes this view. More detailed study shows that the second and fourth proof oracles (vv 10, 13f and vv 22–23) could never have existed by themselves, since they presuppose as already mentioned the subjects "prophets" and "daughters of Israel." They must from the start have been formed as a continuation of what precedes them. Each half of the chapter therefore is a two-strophe structure.

The considerable formal relationship of the first proof saying in each half to its counterpart suggests that these also were not initially separate sayings, but were composed from the start as related to each other. The bringing together of all four parts of ch. 13 under a single formula for the receipt of a message is therefore not the arbitrary act of a later collector, but the intention of the prophet himself. Since such phenomena of duplication (ch. 23), triplication (18:5–17; 20:5–26), or even quadruplication (14:12–20) of parallel statements are to be found also elsewhere in Ezekiel, this understanding of ch. 13 need not be regarded as strange. As regards tradition-history, Ezekiel, in his cry of woe against prophets and "prophetesses," appears particularly close to Jeremiah (just as he is also in ch. 34, the cry of woe against the shepherds). Hosea also (4:5), Isaiah (28:7ff) and Micah (3:5ff) occasionally speak polemically against the prophets (cf. Am 7:14). At the level of a central theme of prophetic preaching (of judgement), so far as we can see, the prophets first appear in Jeremiah (cf. Jer 27–29 besides the great collection Jer 23:9ff, which is set under the heading לנבאים). Since Jeremiah's influence on Ezekiel is elsewhere not to be denied (Miller), here also Ezekiel must have been influenced by Jeremiah. This conjecture will be confirmed in the detailed exegesis.

Therewith what is specific to Ezekiel is not only the full adoption of an earlier theme (the character of a detailed elaboration of an existent theme can be seen even more strongly in chs 16, 23, 34) and its recasting into Ezekiel's favorite form of a proof oracle, but above all the formal duplication of the presentation. Besides the prophets there appear the "prophetesses" (בנות עמך המתנבאות). Ezekiel's tendency towards architectonic stylizing and symmetrical elaboration becomes particularly strong, when we consider the difficulties which the material itself offers for rigid parallelism. Whilst vv 1ff may be drawn from the extant tradition, it is necessary for vv 17ff to go their own way. What, from the point of view of tradition-history, is new in the content of vv 17ff is particularly striking beside the contents of vv 1ff, which are fixed by tradition, because of the strong formal similarity of the two halves.

Interpretation

The introduction of the oracle against the prophets

(vv 1–16), which is made to follow on the formula for the coming of a message, the address to the "son of man," the command to prophesy, the summons to attention and messenger formula, recalls the introduction of 6:1ff.[5] The difference is only the omission of any command for a prophetic gesture, which here is introduced into the summons to address the prophetesses (v 17).[6] This makes a clear division in regard to the overall composition of the chapter. The intention that can be detected in the glossing of 𝔐 (note b to v 3), of identifying the prophets as false right at the beginning, is made stronger in 𝔗, where the simple נביאים of 𝔐 is regularly paraphrased as נביי שקרא. It was not present in the original text, which spoke of the "prophets of Israel." The Elijah narrative can speak of "prophets of Yahweh" (1 Kings 18:4, 13) and "prophets of Baal" (1 Kings 18:19, 22, 25, 40) and "prophets of Asherah" (1 Kings 18:19). Jeremiah speaks of the "prophets of Samaria" (23:13) and "prophets of Jerusalem" (23:14f). The phrase peculiar to Ezekiel נביאי ישראל (again v 16; 38:17), which recalls his הרי ישראל and אדמת ישראל, underscores again that Ezekiel is concerned with the state of affairs inside Israel, the people of God.[7] The question whether those referred to by Ezekiel were particularly those prophets in exile (Jer 29:15, 21ff) or those in Jerusalem (Jer 28) is to draw a too sharply contrasted alternative. Undoubtedly v 9 has the punishment of exile in mind. However the reproach refers to prophetic activities or at least claiming to be prophetic in the people of God as a whole. The immediate personal opposition against prophets mentioned by name, which characterizes Jer 28f and even cannot be hidden in Jer 23 where no name occurs, is not found in Ezek 13:1–16 in the same way. Here from a distance is given a comprehensive judgement about prophecy in Israel.

■ **13:3** The reproachful cry of woe is addressed first to the contumacy of these prophets. Prophecy is the profession of a messenger.[8] They stand and fall with their task, which emerges in the "vision."[9] Israel is the people of God, which has been repeatedly honored by his messengers endowed with such "visions," by which he declares the mystery of his counsel to his own people (Am 3:7). On account of sin Israel has also, in a special way, become the place where things which the prophets have not seen (ראה synonymous with חזה) and which do not have their origin in Yahweh, but in the human heart (לב),[10] are proclaimed (נבא) in full authority as prophecy. A later addition (or scribal error? note b to v 3), which is to be found in 𝔐, refers to these preachers as "fools" (נבלים). Their offense must not be regarded by this term simply as an intellectual defect, for which one can do nothing. "Folly" was already identified as responsible guilt in early Israel, which denoted as "folly in Israel" sexual sins (Gen 34:7; Dtn 22:21; Ju 20:6; Jer 29:23; cf. Ju 19:23f; 2 Sam 13:12) or the criminal transgressions of the law of cultic sanctity (Josh 7:15).[11] Thus the "following after their own spirit" of the prophets is a responsible offense. As men in ritual procession go after the image or symbol of their god's presence (Dtn 6:14; 8:19 and other passages), as warriors follow their captain (1 Sam 11:7), so the false prophets follow their own spirit as the master who leads them. By רוח here the same faculty is meant as the לב of the original text.[12]

■ **13:5** The stubborn resistance to the authority which is the source of any commission is shown quite directly in the prophet's refusal to accept responsibility in Israel. Prophecy in Israel was never a private experience, but a gift given by Yahweh for his people's good (Am 2:11). Ezekiel knows, as the written prophecy which preceded him, that Israel, in the time of its going astray (תעה 14:11; 44:10, 15; 48:11), stood under the serious threat of the coming "day of Yahweh" (ch. 7), which was to take on historical form in the impending war. Where, however, the enemy in war had already made breaches in the walls of a city

---

5   See above pp. 144f; pp. 131f.
6   For שים פניך אל see above pp. 182f.
7   See above pp. 185f; p. 203; and see Excursus 2.
8   Cf. what is said above (p. 131) regarding the prophetic commission.
9   See above pp. 280f for חזון.
10   See above p. 262.
11   Noth, *System*, 104–106.

12   Excursus 3.

(בקע 2 Kings 25:4), then it was the duty of those who were concerned for their city to go into these breaches (עמד בפרץ 22:30) and to climb up on the threatened places in the face of hostile fire (עלה בפרצות), or, if others were already there, to work feverishly for the setting up of a new defense wall hurriedly built from stones. גָּדַר גָּדֵר undoubtedly means here, and in 22:30, the same as גדר פרצים of Am 9:11 (cf. Is 58:12). By גָּדֵר is meant in Hos 2:8; Prv 24:31; Ps 80:13 the wall of a vineyard built with courses of stones (without mortar). Even this duty of defending the breaches and closing the threatened gaps the prophets have neglected towards their people.

To the question what is meant by these statements without metaphor, a twofold answer can be given: v 10 mentions that the prophets disobediently preached peace when they ought to have spoken of the coming judgement. The didactic story of Jonah shows in chs. 3f how a city could be saved by the giving of a threatening message of judgement. It is this saving function which the prophets of Israel have neglected for their people. Beside this there may be in mind the task of intercession, which was in a special way incumbent upon the prophets, as in Jer 27:18.[13] True prophecy had to know that in a time of danger it had to choose, like Moses, to fulfill the responsibilities of its task in complete disregard of its own concerns.[14] Instead of this the prophets of Israel had handed on uncritically their delusory visions (מחזה שוא) and spoken of them, perhaps personally quite sincere in their belief in their deceitful message (מקסם כזב). In the form of a question this is put to the prophets. Is it not so?

■ **13:4** At three points the description has been expanded by additions which were not made by a single hand. V 4 brings a comparison preserved in the style of a declaration. In it Israel is directly addressed. (The direct address to the prophets in v 5 can scarcely represent the original continuation of v 4.) The prophets of Israel are compared to "foxes among ruins." This can scarcely, with A. Jirku, be intended to regard the foxes as signs of coming disaster, a meaning traceable in a cuneiform letter from the Assyrian period and in a Babylonian omen text.[15] Rather we should

compare the Song of Solomon 2:15, where it is mentioned that foxes destroy (חבל) a vineyard. Quell considers whether "the fear felt by men, unfamiliar with animals, of the apparently cowardly behavior of the shy fox" is a picture of the cowardly behavior of the prophets who "go the wrong way seeking to escape."[16] Or does the jibe of the Ammonite Tobiah at the building of Nehemiah's wall: "Yes, what they are building—if a fox goes up on it (עלה) he will break down their stone wall (פרץ)!" (Neh 3:35) show that there was a saying about foxes jumping up on to the walls (of a vineyard) and breaking them down? The additional remark about the foxes could then have been provoked by the עלה בפרצות of the basic text of v 5. Instead of defending and closing the breaches, the false prophets make use of them like foxes in a vineyard, running about through the torn walls and damaging the vine shoots.

■ **13:6** The addition in v 6 explains v 7a of the basic text. The "seeing delusion and divining a lie," which was first cited from v 7a, transposed into the third person plural and with a slight variation in vocabulary, is more clearly defined. By using the formula for a divine message the false prophets apparently spoke with full authority, although in reality without any commission, and expected that their words would prove true. The יהוה לא שלחם clearly echoes in its language Jer 14:14; 23:21 and seems to have been influenced from there. The Aramaizing קַיֵּם (Bauer-Leander § 56 1') is not found again in Ezekiel, but occurs seven times in the book of Esther, and further in Ruth 4:7; Ps 119:28, 106. In its content the addition is in line with what Ezekiel meant.

■ **13:7b** V 6aβ is repeated with slight variations in v 7b (an addition still lacking in 𝕲), clearly with the feeling that the explanatory elaboration of v 7a should follow, and not precede, it.

■ **13:8** The divine declaration of punishment which follows in vv 8–9, if the whole section really belongs to the basic text, begins with a considerably developed introduction. After the introductory לכן and the messenger formula there then follows a יען-clause, giving a motive, which repeats v 7a with some changes.

---

13   See above p. 249.
14   Ex 32:9–14, 31–34; Nu 14:11–20; Ps 106:23, cf. the הפגיע of the servant of Yahweh, Is 53:12.
15   Anton Jirku, *Materialien zur Volksreligion Israels* (Leipzig: Deichert, 1914), 115; also Fohrer.
16   Quell, *Propheten*, 146.

Then a second לכן introduces the challenge formula.[17] Since otherwise in Ezekiel this is always a support for a detailed declaration of judgement (somewhat differently in Jer 23:30–32) which is mostly continued with perfect consecutive, the saying is certainly not, with Fohrer, to be accepted as original here. The desire to identify the false prophets once again in the threat also has thereby necessitated a change into the third person.[18]

■ **13:9** In the threat proper, which here continues with the perfect consecutive, there are added to an assertion, which is formulated personally and shows Yahweh at work in a very personal way, three negative clauses, undeniably formulated in parallel, which describe the consequences for the prophets. The gesture of the stretching out of the hand asserted directly of Yahweh against those who are threatened (again in 6:14; 14:9, 13; 16:27; 25:7, 13, 16; 35:3) recalls the threatening gesture which the prophet was commanded to make according to 4:7.[19] In its tradition-history the references to the "outstretched hand" clearly goes back to the oldest credo-like formulations of Israel's exodus from Egypt by Yahweh "with a mighty hand and outstretched arm" (cf. to Ezek 20:33f). Already in Isaiah, within written prophecy, it is found in a hostile way to express judgement: "For all this his anger is not turned away, and his hand is stretched out still" (5:25; 9:11, 16, 20; 10:4). Yahweh's gesture of deliverance, which helped to establish the existence of Israel in its origins, has here become a gesture which threatens Israel in its entirety.

In a threefold manner this threatening intervention of Yahweh will have its effect on the fate of the prophets. They are excluded from the סוד עמי, not enrolled in the כתב בית ישראל, and no longer allowed into the אדמת ישראל. These assertions show first of all that the deliverance (or destruction) of an individual in Israel was only possible as a participation in, or exclusion from, the salvation of Israel, which is designated in one of the three descriptions by Yahweh as "my people" (14:9 connects "my people Israel").[20] Further the salvation of Israel is understood quite concretely, in the reality of history: it exists as a people in which counsel is taken. סוד, which is related to the Syriac סודא "conversation," Arabic sāda "to speak privately" (cf. also note c to v 9), can denote the secret participation in the counsel of Yahweh (Jer 23:18; Job 15:8) as well as the ordinary deliberating circle of men, godless (Ps 64:3; Gen 49:6) as well as upright (Ps 111:1), or of youths (Jer 6:11) and merrymakers (Jer 15:17).[21] The word then denotes also the content of what is decided in private discussion, a secret (Prov 11:13; 20:19; 25:9). The בעל סודך, according to Sir 6:6, is the most intimate confident, who is to be distinguished from the wider circle of lesser friends (אנשי שלומך). The false prophets, who belonged through their office in the first place to those who know about the divine secret (Amos 3:7) concerning the people (R. Eleazar thinks here of the secret of knowledge of the calendar), would be excluded from the trusted circle of the people of God.

The "book of the house of Israel," denoted by the Aramaizing כְּתָב (again Ezra, Neh, Chr, Est, but also Ps 87:6 BH³), must first of all have referred quite objectively to the tribal roll of the people, as may have been established by David's census 2 Sam 24:2, 9. Jer 22:30 witnesses to the existence of such citizenship rolls for the pre-exilic period, and Ezra 2:62 illustrates the importance of their contents for the returning exiles. In the mouth of Yahweh there sounds the deeper truth that beyond the tribal rolls which existed on earth in the hands of Israel's leaders, there is also the enrollment given by Yahweh, which governs every aspect of life, which can then be denoted as the book of Yahweh (ספרך אשר כתבת Ex 32:32f), or as the "book of life" (ספר חיים Ps 69:29, cf. Is 4:3), or simply as "the book" (הספר Dan 12:1). The false prophets will lose the possibility of authorizing themselves as

---

17   See above p. 175.
18   See above pp. 290f.
19   See above p. 165.
20   See further the distinctive exposition of R. Eleazar
     b Ketubot 112a.
21   For these circles see Ludwig Koehler, *Hebrew Man*,
     tr. Peter R. Ackroyd (Nashville: Abingdon, 1956/
     1957), 99ff.

members of the house of Israel. (R. Eleazar believed that in his ordination this authorization was assured).

In this it is already determined that they are denied the possibility of claiming rights in the "land of Israel." A return to the land, without which a really living Israel could not be conceived, would not be granted to them. False prophecy was excluded from the "life" which stood as a divine possibility even over the people under judgement (11:14–21).

In such a judgement upon unauthorized and disobedient prophecy Yahweh would again make himself recognizable in his own mysterious nature—as the Lord who remained Lord and who did not suffer that his word should be mocked.

■ **13:10, 13f** The second saying against the prophets (10, 13–14) also gives expression in a new way to a feature of earlier prophetic polemic. Mic 3:5 already shows the prophets of the eighth century in conflict with prophets who lead Yahweh's people astray (מתעים את עמי, further Jer 23:13, 32), in that they proclaim "salvation" (שלום, further Jer 6:14; 8:11), when they are given something to eat. Jer 27–29 shows that in the last days of Judah the polemic about the prophetic preaching of salvation was very directly concerned with the question of "yes" or "no" to the dominion of Nebuchadnezzar II. The prophet of salvation, Hananiah, who according to Jer 28 was trying to break, by his oracle of salvation, Jeremiah's proclamation of the Babylonian yoke, was to become a victim of the iron yoke, which was subsequently to be set still more firmly on Judah. Furthermore Jer 23:17 shows that a false complacency could enter not only into the great political proclamation to the nation, but also in address to an individual. We may conjecture that Ezekiel, in whose preaching we can see clearly a turning from address to the whole nation to a pastoral concern for individuals, would have known both the facts of Jer 27–29 as also those of Jer 23:17. Ezekiel knows of the guilt which an illegitimate preaching of salvation would carry at the downfall of the house of Israel, no less than of the guilt which the prophet, called to be a watchman (3:17–21; 33:1–9), brings upon himself when he leaves the individual sinner,

unwarned, to rush on to destruction. Thus the saying of vv 10, 13–14, which points forward to Mt 7:24–27, proclaims the demonstration of Yahweh, which brings down everything that, through the preaching of salvation, is built upon unsafe ground, and so asserts the holy majesty of his name.

■ **13:10** Here also Ezekiel illustrates his message with a metaphor. Whereas in v 5 it was the picture of a city wall, which had to be rebuilt and protected where it had been broken through, here it is the picture of a (house) wall, which had to be built properly by its builder. The חיץ, only found here in the Old Testament, and the root of which is to be seen in חיצון, חוץ, denotes, according to Šebiʿit 3:8, a light partition wall, not filled in with dust (עפר), i.e., not firmly cemented with mortar.[22] Is there in mind here a loosely layered wall of Babylonian style made out of clay bricks?[23] The action of the false prophets, who by their oracles of salvation mislead (טעה note b) the sinner threatened by God into a false complacency, is compared to the action of a man who gives to a wall, built in loose layers, the outward appearance of a reliably built wall by a coat of whitewash, and so misleads those who live in the house into a feeling of security and pride.[24]

■ **13:13f** Yahweh, however, uncovers the simulated construction in its inner falsity. The image of the collapsing wall is already found in Is 30:13. Whilst there it was used for a collapse brought about, not by any outward pressure, but solely by the inner weakness of the wall, here it is used openly for the divine day of crisis coming in outward misfortune, which will reveal its hidden flaw. Yahweh destroys the work of his enemies by storm wind brought on (בקע) by him (there is an echo here of Jer 23:19), by a deluge of rain (38:22; cf. Is 28:2, 17), and by a bombardment of hailstones (אלגביש only here, 11, 13 and 38:22; cf. Akkadian *algamešu*, Egyptian *irqbs*,[25] which belong in earlier narratives to the divine intervention in the holy war (Josh 10:11). What is falsely built collapses to its foundations. A later hand has then thought in particular of the city of Jerusalem and its collapse, which buried its inhabitants beneath it, and added

---

22 Levy, *Wörterbuch*, s.v.
23 See above pp. 272f.
24 For the ambiguity of תפל cf. note d.

25 According to Driver, "Ezekiel," 151, crystals of emery.

v 14bα.[26] In such a revelation of the "truth" Yahweh asserts himself over the lies of the prophets.

A judgement which uncovers the lies also finds an echo in the speech of those who see it. Ridicule over a person's downfall is for biblical men always a direct part of the judgement (Is 14, cf. Luke 14:29f). So it is intelligible that a later hand has added further in vv 11f the express command of Yahweh to intensify the downfall, which is recapitulated in vv 11–12a in roughly the same words as in vv 13f, with the mocking question: "Where now is the whitewash with which you daubed it?"[27] The replacing by טיח of the noun תפל, used in the basic text in vv 10, 14, does not point to a variant conception, but is to be understood from a linguistic preference for a *figura etymologica*.

■ **13:15** A second redactor, however, had missed any express reference to those who daub with whitewash in the formulation of the mocking question of v 12; so he has later added it in an extended form (with the use of תפל of the original text) with a brief introduction which describes the event, in connection with v 13, as the outworking of the divine wrath.

■ **13:16** The concluding v 16, which once again identifies those threatened by the judgement with the words of v 10a, and further to what has so far been said mentions Jerusalem as the addressee of the prophetic word, may stem from him or from the hand of a still later editor.

■ **13:17–23** The two-part oracle against the prophets is followed by a two-part saying against the women who prophesy, introduced with a renewed address to the prophet, a fresh commission, which is expanded here by the command to perform an expressive gesture, and a renewed messenger formula.[28] Whereas the two-part oracle against the prophets has been strongly influenced by the older prophetic preaching in its content and even to the text of certain formulations, here the striking thing is the novelty of the content and the formulations. Not that the Old Testament does not otherwise know of women who prophesy. In Ex 15:20 Miriam, who sings with the daughters of Israel the saving action of Yahweh toward Israel, receives (as a singer?) the title of נביאה. Deborah, who "judged" Israel and became through her song (Ju 5:12) the source of the summons of the tribes against Canaanite oppression, is described in Ju 4:4 as אשה נביאה. Whilst with Isaiah's wife we do not know for what action she is described in Is 8:3 by the title נביאה (scarcely simply because she was the wife of a prophet, and we could better think of service as a temple singer), Huldah, the wife of a temple official (2 Kings 22:14; 2 Chr 34:22), appears as a נביאה in connection with the delivery of a divine decision of very great importance for the Judean state. Further Noadiah (הנביאה), exactly like the "remnant of the prophets" (Neh 6:14), appears to have been concerned with instructions to the political governor.

Nothing of all this can be found in the description given by Ezekiel. Rather there is noteworthy here not only the (intentional?) avoidance of the title נביאה and its replacing by the looser בנות עמך המתנבאות, in the hitpo'el of which Cooke would find a slight note of contempt ("who behave like prophets"), but also the concentration on private concerns in the actions of the women attacked here. Of the great question about the "house of Israel" (v 4) struggling for its existence, which can be seen in the images of the breaches in the wall and its endangering, nothing is to be seen here. It is concerned solely with the deliverance (or endangering) of individuals (נפשות vv 18–20), about the fate of the righteous and the wicked (רשע–צדיק v 22)—things which the exiled prophet knew in glancing at his immediate surroundings in a particular way as his responsibility. Not by chance do we find in this oracle formulations which recall by way of contrast the assertions about the prophet's role as watchman (3:17–21; 33:1–9) and the explanations of Ezek 18.

The twofold oracle of vv 17ff undeniably enters into a sphere of minor mantic acts and magic—a sphere which can only be put quite improperly under the catchword "prophetic." Dtn 18:9ff sets this mantic activity in opposition to the "prophets" (נביא) given to Israel, as a Canaanite counterpart, even in its terminology. When we examine the perspective which enables Ezekiel to set these lesser activities under the

---

26   Cf. note b to v 14.
27   For the formulation of a mocking question cf. **Ps** 42:4, 11; 79:10; 115:2.
28   See above pp. 182–185.

catchword "prophetic," then it is clearly the case that here also powers were employed which mediated "life" and "death." Just as the word of the prophet legitimately gives death (11:13) and life (37:4ff), so, in the activity of these women of Israel (המתנבאות מלבהן v 17), death and life were dispensed in an unauthorized manner, and so Yahweh's dominion was infringed upon.

■ **13:18f** In details much that is described here remains obscure in its exposition. The first saying, found in parallel to vv 3ff as a הוי cry, describes the women who give their oracle for the small payment of a couple of handfuls of barley and some pieces of bread. Cooke and van den Born would follow Kimchi, and the view already opposed by R. Aši (*b. 'Erubin* 64b), according to which barley and bread refer to the materials for magical practice, supporting this by references to barley (Nu 5:15) and pieces of bread (Lev 2:5f) as elements of sacrifice, and by the Greek ἀλφιτομαντεία and χριθομαντεία. However, more correctly, we must point here to the analogy of 1 Sam 9:7, according to which a seer gives his oracle for a small payment in bread, which could in an emergency be replaced by a gift of money. Nevertheless what is meant by כְּסָתוֹת, which were sewn and fastened on the wrists, and the מִסְפָּחֹת, which were worn on the head and were made in various sizes according to the stature of the wearer (note d to v 18)? For כסתות, which 𝕲 interprets as προσχεφάλαια "cushion for the head," but scarcely correctly, whilst Origen, according to Cod. Reg. (Field) prefers the translation φυλαχτήρια, reference has been made to the Akkadian kasû "to bind, ban," and it has been taken as "bandages" (Baer-Delitzsch XIIf: *fasciae*; Koehler-Baumgartner) or "cords" (van den Born). מספחות, which is translated loosely by 𝕲 as ἐπιβόλαια, is connected with the Akkadian *sapāḫu* "to scatter, spread out" and interpreted as an item of clothing set loosely on the head, as a veil or shawl.[29] Can we then see in the connection of the two items,

cords and veil, the process of binding and loosening which was certainly elsewhere important in the history of religion? Or do both features represent in their own way a "binding"? For binding and loosening all kinds of illustrative material has been adduced from excavations in Palestine, from Babylonian-Assyrian texts, especially the series of incantations *maqlū* and *šurpū*, as well as other ancient Near Eastern narrative sources.[30] An exactly relevant explanation of Ezekiel's statements, however, has so far not been advanced.

As a result of the magical action of the women, which was accompanied by certain sayings, there is mentioned in v 18aβbα the "hunting for souls." V 19aα expresses it more sharply as "putting to death persons who should not die." There stands out against this in v 18aβ and v 19aβ "keeping persons alive who should not live." By נפשות, as Selbie, "Ezek 13:18–21," rightly asserts against Frazer, "Hunting," we must think, not of the "souls" which were understood animistically to leave the body and which could be imprisoned by magicians, but simply of the person and his life.[31]

All dealing with "power" was only possible in Israel in the name of Yahweh. This name was invoked by the women who "prophesied." In this, however, according to the prophet Ezekiel, there lay their specific crime, in that they dispensed life and death according to the size of the payments which were given to them (Mic 3:5), thereby dishonoring the name of Yahweh among his people. They brought his majesty down to the level of their ungodly human decisions. A later hand has added in v 19b, in anticipation of the ideas of v 23, that, whereas Yahweh himself as sovereign Lord ought alone to dispense life and death in accordance with his righteous order, they have administered lies to his people.

■ **13:20f** Yahweh, however, brings judgement. With a bold anthropomorphism we now have the assertion that he himself will tear the magic bands and veils from the hands and heads of the women. He will thereby

---

29   See G. R. Driver, "Linguistic and textual Problems: Ezekiel," *Bibl* 19 (1938): 63f.

30   Cf. Herrmann, Cooke, van den Born, also Meissner, *Babylonien* 2, 198–241, ch. 17: "Die Magie." Barth, "Zauber," mentions the custom of the Abyssinian Tigre tribes, who, when a deformed child is born, make ropes of palm leaves, bast, or wool, in order to bind the limbs so that such misfortune may not oc-

cur more frequently.

31   See the literature mentioned above p. 209.

nullify their practices and deliver by his sovereign authority those whom they have thought to bind, so that they will escape from the magic spell like birds from a snare (Ps 124:7), if לפרחות is rightly so understood (note g to v 20). By such free saving action it will once again become plain who he is.

■ **13:22f** The second saying (vv 22–23) starts from the same circumstance, but emphasizes it from another aspect. The presumptuous actions of the women, who think that they can dispense life and death at their own will, disrupt the order which Yahweh has in his command, and according to which life is promised to the righteous, but death to whoever is not prepared to turn from his wickedness (ch. 18). Against such "afflicting" of the righteous and encouragement of the wicked (the formulation is clearly close to Jer 23:14, but must be understood here from the particular circumstances which Ezekiel has mentioned in what precedes), Yahweh will intervene and, by asserting his law, will deliver the men of his people from the hand of these women. In the והצלתי את עמי מידכן there echoes Israel's old language of deliverance (Ex 18:9f; Ju 8:34). Yahweh's deliverance, which once came to his people, is here promised fully to individuals.

Setting
V 9 shows, as L. Rost and others have strongly stressed, the future perspective of a return to the land.[32] This is the view of exiles. When Herntrich, in order to be able to maintain the thesis of Ezekiel's activity in Jerusalem for Ezek 13 also, removes v 9 as "a very late insertion by an exilic hand," then the arguments of J. J. Stamm must also be turned against him.[33] The threat of judgement in v 9 is an indispensable element in the symmetrical structure of Ezek 13.

The strong appearance of mantic actions by the women who prophesy is perfectly credible in the exile, where the attempts to fill up the vacuum left with the loss of the cult in a right way were made at first quite hesitantly.[34] The forms of this mantic activity could have been determined by "pagan religious influence."[35] The importance of what had been brought from the homeland, however, which now may unexpectedly have gained considerable possibilities of enlargement through the gap in worship, and which carried with it the special glow of something from home, must not be dismissed too hastily.

Since we cannot certainly see in Ezek 13 that Jerusalem was still standing, whilst the possibility of a coming return in v 9 is very clearly presupposed, we can, in seeking to fix the date of the oracle, easily look beyond 587. However, it is also possible that v 5, as well as the picture of the coming assault on the wall vv 13f and the imminent threat of the "battle on the day of Yahweh," could point to a time before the fall of Jerusalem. The question must therefore remain open.

Aim
God had not only delivered his people from the worship of hostile powers and called them into his presence (20:5f), but he had also repeatedly set men and women in a living position of responsibility within his community. He had entrusted to these watchmen (Ezekiel himself knows that his office is that of watchman 3:17–21; 33:1–9) his living word, which was not simply an idea, but an event which determined history and dispensed life and death.[36]

God had therefore moved, without protective guarantees, into an area where his gifts could possibly be endangered. Ezek 13 shows how God's power given to men could be despised and misused by them.

The men who should have watched over the protection of the community (Amos 6:6), to make clear the work of Yahweh (Is 5:12), and who should have been ready to help speedily, had been asleep. They had neglected to turn to God in ceaseless intercessions. They had not unsparingly shown up the gaps in the people of God, like a responsible builder, seeking

32   Rost, *Israel*, 79f.
33   Herntrich, *Ezekielprobleme*, 99; Johann Jakob Stamm, "Review of *Ezechielfragen* by Nils Messel," *ThZ* 3 (1947): 304–309, who firmly presents a methodical argument against such excisions in this review of the study of Messel.
34   See above p. 115 to 1:3 and p. 262 to 11:16.
35   Curt Kuhl, *The Prophets of Israel*, tr. Rudolf J. Ehrlich and J. P. Smith (Richmond, Va.: John Knox, 1960), 132.
36   Pp. 144f.

thoroughly to repair places that were in danger. They had scornfully misused the word of proclamation, which had been given to them by divine authority, in order to whitewash superficially (על נקלה Jer 6:14; 8:11) over the damaged places. God's word had been brought into disrepute in "beautiful-worship" and sentimental "assurances" (שלום). It had lost its condemning sharpness (Heb 4:12f; cf. Mt 5:13) and instead of leading, it had misled.

The women of God's people, however, had misused the authority to offer life and death through words and signs which God had entrusted among his people to human mouths and human hands. They had used conveniently for their own gain and for payment the life and death which God had bound to his own summons to righteousness and man's obedience. The secret of divine grace, empowered to bind and loosen, they had dishonored by the secret of magical practices of binding and loosening.

Against such debasing of his gifts God can only reveal himself in his truth as the judge. The dizzy world of splendid worship and misplaced assurances would collapse unexpectedly like a cracked wall in a storm. It would occasion deep disillusionment. Except through his judgement, however, the Lord who wills to gather his people afresh and to prepare his habitation for them (v 9) and to rescue them from the hand of their enemies (vv 21, 23), cannot meet them.

The Prophet and the Worshippers of Idols

D. Daube
"Uber die Umbildung biblischen Rechtsgutes" in in *Symbolae Friburgenses in honorem Ottonis Lenel* (Leipzig, Tauschmitz, 1935), 245–258:2. Die Karetstrafe, 249–255.

E. Fink
"Gedanken über die כרת-Strafe," *Jeschurun* 4 (1917): 383–393.

W. Zimmerli
"Die Eigenart der prophetischen Rede des Ezechiel. Ein Beitrag zum Problem an Hand von Ez. 14:1–11," *ZAW* 66 (1954): 1–26.

14

1 And some of the elders of Israel 'came'[a] to me and sat down before me. 2/ Then the word of Yahweh came to me: 3/ Son of man, these men have devoted themselves[a] to their idols and have set before themselves what is an occasion for iniquity. Should I then really[b] let myself be questioned by them? 4/ Therefore speak to them,[a] and say to them: Thus has [the Lord][b] Yahweh said: Everyone of the house of Israel who clings to[c] his idols, and sets up in front of him what is for him an occasion for iniquity, and (then) comes to the prophet, to him will I—I Yahweh —'myself' allow myself to give answer[d] because of his many idols,

14:1 1a 𝔐 ויבוא. The frequent interchange of א and ו in the book of Ezekiel (note a to 10:3) makes it probable that we should think also here (differently Joüon § 150 j) of a scribal error and read with 6 MSS (𝔊 𝔏ˢ 𝔗 𝔖 𝔙) ויבאו. The introductory אמר נביא of 𝔗 is clearly intended to lessen the harsh transition from the divine speech in 13:23 to the prophetic speech in 14:1.

3 3a Literally "cause to come into their heart." When du Mesnil du Buisson (see above p. 187) understands the העלו גלוליהם על לבם "à la lettre" of wearing an amulet above the heart ("The gillulim were undoubtedly worn underneath the clothing"), the parallels in 38:10; also 11:5; 20:32, where רוח stands instead of לב, clearly speaks against it. Cf. further Is 65:17; Jer 3:16; 7:31; 44:21.

b The unusual form of the infinitive absolute (הַ)אִדָּרֵשׁ rests, according to Gesenius-Kautzsch § 51 k, Bauer-Leander § 44a'; 50v, on the influence of the neighboring imperfect form.

4 4a 𝔐 אותם cf. note a to 2:1.

b אדני is lacking in 𝔊 𝔏ˢ �ℭᴮᵒ, see Excursus 1.

c Cf. note a to v 3; for the replacing of על by אל cf. note a to 1:17.

d 𝔐 נעניתי לו בה (ברב גלוליו). V 7 reads in a parallel context, נענה לו בי. The reading בי is firmly anchored there, since the formulation of v 7 is clearly related to the preceding ובא אל הנביא) לדרש לו) בי. However, against 𝔊 (𝔏ˢ), which assimilates verse 7 (ἀποκριθήσομαι αὐτῷ ἐν ᾧ ἐνέχεται ἐν αὐτῷ) to verse 4 (ἀποκριθήσομαι αὐτῷ ἐν οἷς ἐνέχεται ἡ διάνοια αὐτοῦ), we must rather correct verse 4 in accordance with 7 (cf. 𝔗) and read נעניתי לו בי. For the interpretation we must start from the clear antithesis (v 7), which rests on the connection of דרש with ענה and with which Ps 34:5 (דרשתי את יהוה) (ועלני is to be compared. The verb דרש can be construed with the meaning "to question (God)" with a simple accusative (20:1, 3; Gen 25:22 and other passages), with אל (Is 19:3 and other passages) or with ב. The last mentioned construction is

5/ that I may lay hold of the hearts of the house of Israel, which has completely (?)[a] estranged itself[b] from me with its idols.

6   Therefore say to the house of Israel: Thus has [the Lord][a] Yahweh said: Repent and turn away from[b] your idols; and turn away your faces from all your abominations! 7/ For everyone from the house of Israel, or from the protected aliens who reside in Israel, who separates[a] himself from me and clings[b]

found in the narrative of the prophets 2 Kings 1:2, 3, 6, 16, cf. further 1 Sam 28:7; 1 Chr 10:14; 2 Chr 34:26 (the parallel in 2 Kings 22:18 uses the accusative with את). It is clearly now also to be seen in Ezek 14:7. The preceding לו is then not to be related to the prophet but, as in 14:3 להם, 20:3, 31 לכם, 36:37 לבית ישראל, to those on whose behalf the inquiry is made. Accordingly v 7bα reads: "And he goes to the prophet in order to question me for himself." The assertion of Yahweh in v 7bβ is preserved with a strongly schematic parallelism (Ezekiel loves such heavy schematism, cf. 20:35f): "I, Yahweh, I myself [𝔙 v 7 *per me*, 𝔗 interprets במימרי] will allow myself to give answer to him [in regard to him]." The nip'al of ענה is difficult. The verb ענה is otherwise only found in Ezekiel in 22:10f in the pi'el with the meaning "to abuse (sexually)." The correspondence with דרש in 14:4, 7, however, leaves scarcely any doubt that here the verb ענה "to answer" must be intended, which is otherwise not found in Ezekiel. The nip'al, which is otherwise in the Old Testament only found in Job 11:2; 19:7 (9:15 c.T); Prv 21:13 with the meaning "to receive an answer," represents then an arbitrariness in the language of Ezekiel which seeks to give expression to the almost passive "to allow oneself to be forced to answer." But cf. Levy, *Wörterbuch*, under ענה nip'al "tune up, pronounce a saying; properly to be made to give answer, to be heard, *b. Qiddušin* 40b." The passive formulation stands in an intentional tension besides the sovereign authority of אני יהוה in the divine introduction. With the perfect נעניתי, v 4, we must compare the analogous פתיתי, v 9, which likewise follows on אני יהוה. It gives expression to the unwavering authority of Yahweh. The participle נענה v 7, represents a slight softening of the expression over against this.

5   5a 𝔐 כלם is not attested by 𝔊 𝔏ˢ. Against the connection with גלוליהם "with all their idols," already represented by 𝔊⁶² 𝔗 𝔖 𝔙 and taken up by Smend, Kraetzschmar, Auvray, ZB, Fohrer, speaks the fact that this expression is otherwise in Ezekiel always found with a preceding כל (8:10; 16:36; 20:31; 23:7; 36:25).

b 𝔐 נגזר must undoubtedly prepare for the וינזר of v 7, but must not, with Cornill, be assimilated to it. The usual derivation from זור "to turn oneself away, become strange" (Gesenius-Buhl, Koehler-Baumgartner, Snijders, "Meaning," 12) is opposed by Driver, "Isaiah," 36f, and "Linguistic Problems," 64, who proposes a derivation from זרר = Arabic *zarra* "to carry off, bring back."

6   6a אדני is lacking 𝔊 𝔏ˢ 𝔠ᴮᵒ, see Excursus 1.

b The rhetorical duplication שובו והשיבו, in which the hiph'il, unlike in b, must be simply a variation of the qal, is found again in 18:30 at the parenetic climax of the chapter. For such duplication cf. the יען וביען 13:10.

7   7a 𝔐 וינזר. The connection of the verb נזר, which

to his idols and sets up in front of him what is an occasion of iniquity, and (then) goes to the prophet in order to question me for himself, to him will I— I Yahweh—myself allow myself to give answer.[c] 8/ And I will set my face against that man and 'make him'[a] a sign and a byword[b] and cut him off from the midst of my people, and you shall know that I am Yahweh. 9/ However, if the prophet is befooled and speaks a word (from God), then I— I Yahweh—am befooling that prophet. And I will stretch out my hand against him and cut him off from the midst of my people Israel, 10/ and they shall bear their guilt, the inquirer and the prophet alike,[a] 11/ that the house of Israel may no more go astray from following me, nor make themselves unclean any more by all their sins, but that they may be my people and I may be their God, says [the Lord][a] Yahweh.

echoes the designation of the נזיר who is devoted to Yahweh by his acts of denial, with מאחרי gives a surprising oxymoron. Cf. Hos 9:10.

b Cf. note c to v 4.

c For the translation cf. note d to v 4.

8 8a 𝔐 והשמתיהו. Since the hip'il of שים, where it elsewhere appears to be found in 𝔐 (21:21; Job 4:20), is textually quite uncertain, it is best to follow most commentators in accepting the reading ושמתיהו, with the excision of the ה.

b ולמשלים of 𝔐 is certainly already attested by 𝔗 ולמתלין, but is scarcely to be retained beside the normal singular use of משל in this form of expression (Dtn 28:37; 1 Kings 9:7; Jer 24:9; Ps 69:12; 2 Chr 7:20). 𝔊 καὶ θήσομαι αὐτὸν εἰς ἔρημον καὶ εἰς ἀφανισμόν (𝔏^S et ponam illum in signum et in exterminium approximates to 𝔐) is to be understood as a free reconstruction of a Hebrew original unintelligible to 𝔊, like 6:14; 33:28f.

10 10a Literally: "Corresponding to the guilt of the inquirer shall be the guilt of the prophet."

11 11a אדני lacking in 𝔊 𝔏^S 𝔠^Bo, see Excursus 1. 𝔅 dominus exercituum.

Form

The section 14:1–11, which is clearly defined by its narrative introduction and the concluding formula in v 11, appears to stand in the usual form of the prophetic word. In an element of reproach Yahweh (v 3) points first to the idolatrous nature of the men who wish to question the prophet. That the reproach finishes with a question to the idolaters, according to which these must judge for themselves whether they are really worthy of the divine word, is a particular stylistic feature which vitalizes the reproach. There then follows in vv 4ff a command to the prophet, introduced in the usual way with לכן, and the messenger-formula then introduces the divine word which announces the action of Yahweh. The recognition-formula in v 8, at the end of a speech, appears to point to the three-part structure of a proof oracle.

However, closer examination reveals some form-critical considerations of quite a different kind. The oracle begins in the prophetic style. But in the place at which the direct announcement of the punitive divine action, in all its rigor, should begin, the oracle surprisingly breaks off. In a neutral formulation, which appears not to keep in view the idol worshippers sitting directly in front of the prophet, v 4 defines once again the fact of sin. Then Yahweh announces his

intervention against the sinners who are described in the third person. After a break in vv 5f, in which "Israel" appears in the foreground and is addressed in direct speech in v 6, we have then in v 7 the impersonal style, defining the nature of the offense, which takes up again word for word the declaration of v 4. Verse 9 speaks also of the prophets who are concerned with the divine word in this neutral style. This is very remarkable after Yahweh has first (vv 3f) addressed the prophet Ezekiel directly.

The different speech form, which appears so unexpectedly, is easily definable as a legal form. More precisely a comparison of its form with legal sections in H and P leads to the conclusive recognition that it is the characteristic style of particular sacral-legal formulations.[1]

The sacral-legal sphere is first of all indicated by the position of the conditional כי after the subject (v 9), which is also to be seen in 3:19; 14:13; 18:5, 18, 21; 33:2, 6, 9. It is customary in the casuistic form of the priestly regulations (Lev 1:2; 2:1; 19:20 and other passages). In the "civil" casuistic law כי precedes (Ex 21:2, 7; Dtn 22:23, 28 and other passages).

Even more evident is the relation to the sacral law in the introduction of the subject of the legal case, which we find in vv 4, 7, with the generalizing איש איש

מבית ישראל, which is expanded in v 7 by the addition ומהגר אשר יגור בישראל. This form of speech is found, with minor variations in the formulation, six times altogether in H (Lev 17:3, 8, 10, 13; 20:2; 22:18); in 17:3 in the shorter form corresponding to Ezek 14:4, otherwise in the expanded form of Ezek 14:7. The sequence of the four examples in Lev 17 shows that there were ordered collections of laws of this type. The explicit mention of the בית ישראל shows that it is a form of law orientated towards Israel as the people of God and its purity. The mention of the גר makes it probable that the formation of this type of law must be sought in the period of the pre-exilic settlement of Israel in the land, the period when settlement "in the midst (בתוך Lev 17:8, 10, 13) of Israel" still retained its quite objective meaning. At first the גר was "a man who had, by himself (or with his people), left the village and tribe to which he belonged on account of war, unrest, famine, disease, blood-guilt, or some misfortune, and fled elsewhere, where he sought to stay, being limited in his rights of land ownership, marriage and participation in lawsuits, cult, and war."[2] A. Bertholet rightly affirms that Ezek 14:7 displays the distinct intention of including the גר in the cult.[3] However, he has not seen clearly enough that Ezekiel uses a fixed form of expression, which he himself had received and which undoubtedly had already become stereotyped before the beginning of the exile.

The parallels in H show further that the formal correspondence not only concerns the words of introduction, which describe the punishable offence, but also covers the description of the punishment. The offenders mentioned are here, as there, threatened with a "cutting off" (הכרית Ezek 14:8 is varied in 14:9 to השמיד) from the sphere of the עם or the עמים. This elaboration has disappeared in H only in Lev 22:18, but in the five remaining occurrences it is clearly to be seen. Admittedly in this a great deal of variation

in the individual formulation is to be found. The formula of punishment is abbreviated in Lev 17:13f to the simple יכרת. In the law of Lev 20:2–5, which is formed in two parts (vv 2f, 4f), it similarly appears twice. The law of Lev 20:6, which is joined on to this, beginning with the simple הנפש אשר, shows further that this particular formula of punishment was certainly not limited to sentences introduced by . . . איש איש, but had a much greater usage. Besides Lev 20:6 and the texts already mentioned, it is demonstrable in twenty-one further passages, all of them in the priestly documents.[4] In this we have Lev 23:30, where האביד appears in place of הכרית, and Dtn 4:3, the only text coming from the Deuteronomic sphere, where השמיד appears. Here also we are dealing directly with infringements of sacred laws. When we examine more precisely the manner in which the punishment of the offense should be carried out according to this formulation, it appears at first as though the death penalty is demanded, especially where it comes next to מות יומת (Lev 20:2f). Closer examination, however, shows that the formula first of all has in mind a punishment executed by Yahweh himself upon men, which would take place through a sudden divine blow. This can be particularly clearly seen, even where the text appears to point to a man as the subject of הכרית. With the sharpening of the precautionary measures which are introduced for the Kohathites in carrying the holy vessels, Yahweh warns Moses and Aaron (Nu 4:18): אל תכריתו את שבט משפחת הקהתי מתוך הלוים. 2 Sam 6:6f, which tells of Uzzah's sudden death when he incautiously touched the ark, makes clear that what is meant here is: "Be careful therefore that the tribe . . . is not exterminated" (ZB). The הכרית itself occurs by the divine action.[5] Man's part in the act of punishment can therefore only consist in excluding the sinner from the community and thus precluding him from the possibility of reconciliation and of reentry into

---

1   For a detailed examination of the following conclusions see Zimmerli, "Eigenart."
2   Koehler-Baumgartner, s.v.
3   Alfred Bertholet, *Die Stellung der Israeliten und der Juden zu den Fremden* (Freiburg, 1896), 110–113.
4   To the references given in Zimmerli, "Eigenart," 14f, Ex 31:14 is to be added.
5   This is how later Judaism understood it, which fur-

ther distinguished two kinds of מיתי בידי שמים. Besides the כרת דיומא, sudden death without a sickness of five days duration, there was the כרת דשני, dying aged between fifty and sixty years (Fink, "Gedanken"). See for this *b Moʿed Qaṭan* 28a: "The rabbis taught: if any one dies suddenly, this is a sudden death; if he is sick for one day and then dies, this is a hasty death. . . . If he was [sick] for two days,

the sphere of "life."[6]

A glance at the change in form of the כרת statements may illustrate still more clearly the cases dealt with by them and may at the same time make clear at what point of the form-critical development Ezekiel stands.

Exact comparison of detail makes it probable that at the beginning of such development there stood the short saying, formulated impersonally ונכרתה הנפש ההיא מעמיה. This formulation was broken up and reformulated afterwords. As 1) so far as the verb is concerned, it is easily intelligible from the subject matter that there could appear in place of the impersonal-passive formulation a personal declaration set in the mouth of Yahweh. The figure who lay hidden behind the impersonal formulation then appears openly. In particular we must expect that with the adoption of the legal formula in a prophetic oracle, as is to be seen with Ezekiel, this alteration to the personal divine address was introduced. A further aspect of Ezekiel's license appears in the variation of הכרית, v 8, to השמיד, v 9 (as Dtn 4:3). 2) The impersonal subject of the original formula, with the change into the active formulation, appears in the position of the object. In the combination with the introductory איש this object takes the form of the masculine suffix. 3) The simple מן can be replaced by the fuller מקרב (Lev 18:24) or מתוך (Nu 19:20). Ezek 14 shows in both occurrences the full מתוך. Particularly important then is 4) the change in the reference to the sphere from which the offender is excluded. The plural עמים points back to an early stage in which the cultic community was represented by the clan (cf. 1 Sam 1:1ff; 20:29). The plural עמים is therefore, in its form, undoubtedly older than the singular עם. The latter is an assimilation to historical reality. It identifies the cultic circle with the people of God. Thus in two cases (Ex 12:19; Nu 19:13) the name Israel is referred to explicitly. That this really concerns the religious, and not the political, structure of Israel becomes clear in the later interpretation by עדת ישראל Ex 12:19 or קהל Nu 19:20, or now in the two suffix formulations עמי and עמי ישראל in Ezekiel (14:8, 9). The beautiful interpretation of Lev 22:3 points further in the same direction, where the formula is expressed as ונכרתה הנפש ההיא מלפני. Israel, the cultic community, "my people," is set "before my face." "To live" is to stay in the place looked upon by the face of God (Nu 6:25f; 1 Kings 8:29; Ps 80:4, 8, 15, 20; 104:29 and other passages). The punishment of the sinner consists in his being expelled from this position.

When we summarize the conclusions reached so far we can say that already at an early period Israel clearly knew a type of sacred law which protected certain orders of cultic taboo and which concluded with a pregnant formula of banishment. That the formulations preserved for us, with the exception of Dtn 4:3, belong exclusively to the priestly documents, which must be a sign of a late date for their final literary form, cannot obscure the fact that this type of law must go back to an early date, as the plural עמים especially shows.

From the wide range of those legal banishments there may be separated a smaller group of stipulations which introduce the offender, through whom the offense is defined, by the full formulation איש איש . . . מבית ישראל. This further elaboration of the formula is undoubtedly relatively late, since it presupposes in its introductory מבית ישראל a conception of the עם in relation to the saving history—even though in Lev 17:9 the plural עמים has been preserved as a firmly fixed relic of the older formulation. The high degree of formal development in the examples known to us of this narrower group of statements, which even extends to the complete displacing of the banishment formula, points to a formation at a later stage. However, on the other side, its formation is not to be dated within the period of the exile, since the inclusion in the introductory formula of the גר, who sojourns in Israel,

---

this is a quick death; if three [days], this is a death through shouting; if four [days], this is a death of reproof; five [days lying in bed and then death] is the death of every man." And later: "When R. Joseph was sixty years old, he established a feast for the rabbis in which he said: now I have escaped being cut off (כרת)."

6 von Rad, " 'Righteousness'." Cf. Daube, "Um-bildung."

7 What was only briefly outlined on p. 164 under 1) must here be carried further.

is explained most easily from the period of the settlement in the land. The reference in Ezek 14, belonging to the early exilic period, which appears as a prophetic secondary development of a speech form which was originally not prophetic, and the form of which was varied with great freedom, points in the same direction.

According to the evidence of Lev 17:10; 20:3, 5, 6 (26:17) the assertion: "And I will set (נתן or שׂים) my face against (that) person" (בנפשׁ [ההיא]) or "that man" perhaps also belongs to the form of the divine proclamation of banishment in the first person. With the appearance of this assertion in Ezek 14:8 (and again 15:7) Ezekiel has scarcely minted a new expression for the first time, but drawn upon an extant tradition.

With what has been noted so far the form adopted by Ezek 14 has not been fully described. The sign-action of 4:4–8 has already given occasion to consider the formulation נשׂא עון.[7] Assyrian legal texts show that the formula ḫiṭa našū, "to bring an offense upon oneself, to make oneself punishable," was already current in Mesopotamian legal tests.[8] ḫiṭītam našūm is already found in Old Babylonian.[9] To this must be added combinations of našū with other words for punishment such as arnu and šērtu. For the Old Testament I have shown that the formulation נשׂא עון is used outside of Ezek 14 in thirteen references (including Ezek 44:10, 12) exactly like the synonymous formula נשׂא חטא (in eight texts, including Ezek 23:49) in order to qualify decisively a sacral-legal offense.[10] The law regarding water of cursing in Nu 5, with its concluding ונקה האישׁ מעון והאשׁה ההיא תשׂא את עונה in v 31, shows this particularly clearly. It is also true here that the final saying does not anticipate a punishment carried out by men, but means a handing over to the judgement of Yahweh, which in Lev 20:20 simply takes the form of punishing a guilty marriage with childlessness. The human share in it must here also be limited to exclusion from the community, which again means exclusion from the place of the divine life. Only in the case of serious guilt, which endangered the welfare of the community by its חרם, do we see that additionally a human punishment is ordered—or is it more properly

here a protective measure? The man who blasphemes God is stoned according to Lev 24:15f.

Ezek 14:10 shows this formula precisely in the position which its form would lead us to expect, as the concluding summarizing statement about the worshipper of idols and the prophet questioned by him, when the legal aspect of the case has been dealt with in detail in vv 7f and 9.

The recognition of the broad intrusion of the language of sacred law into the prophetic preaching necessitates a fresh consideration of the whole structure of the oracle of 14:1–11.

Repeatedly the attempt has been made to correct the apparently disturbed structure of the oracle by critical operations. The repetition of similar statements (4/7; 8/9), the renewed summons to speak (v 6) appear immediately to call for textual surgery. Thus Jahn removes vv 1–5 as an addition and leaves only the section vv 6–11, introduced by the formula for the receipt of a message, as the original oracle. Bertholet distinguishes, after an introduction in vv 1–4a, two parallel recensions: A vv 7a, 8–10; B vv 4b–6, 7b, 11. In another way van den Born distinguishes two parallel texts in A vv 4–5 and B vv 6–8, whilst he finds in vv 9–11 an "appendix." Fohrer also believes that this last point is right and removes vv 3b, 6–7 as "variant glosses."

A careful consideration of the inner movement of thought, with regard to the insight we have obtained into the legal style, appears to me to oppose all of these operations and to favor the unity of the section (cf. Hölscher, *Hesekiel*). The question of the elders, who expect a prophetic oracle, is surprisingly countered by Yahweh in the detached style of the law, in which he now makes a very serious threat couched in the personal form of the divine sentence. However, before this reply has had time to elaborate upon this sentence in greater detail, by utilizing the traditional banishment formula in the style of the law, it turns in v 5 to disclose the hidden purpose which guides Yahweh's action and which is already echoed in the introductory formula of the law: *Israel* will be affected by it. Clearly this refers first of all to the addressee, to whom Yahweh's

---

8   E. Weidner, "Hof- und Haremserlasse assyrischer
    Könige," *AfO* 17 (1956): 257–293, see lines 9, 51,
    55, 109, further p. 270 to line 9; *Mittelass. Rechtsbuch*

1 § 32/Col. IV 54.
9   *Yale Oriental Series* 8, 105, 12.
10 Zimmerli, "Eigenart," 10–12.

action will be directed. It need not then be surprising, and lead us into critical surgery, that there is then immediately introduced here a full divine command, with the messenger formula, which calls upon Israel to repent. Jahn has rightly perceived that with v 6 the prophecy proper begins. In the shadow of this important address to Israel the oracle in v 7 then takes up the legal style, first noted in v 3 and then dropped again, in order to carry through the legal process with complete rectitude. In a casuistic distinction, the two partners who are involved in the case are dealt with: 1) the idol worshipper (vv 7–8), 2) the prophet (v 9). The concluding formula, corresponding to Nu 5:31, deals with both together (v 10). Then, however, the concluding v 11 emphasizes once again the application of the whole proceeding to Israel, first raised in vv 5–6. If we do not regard this forceful turning of a saying originally referring to an individual to the basic problem of "Israel," we shall not grasp the real intention of the oracle. However, if we recognize the formation of the Israel oracle out of the legal case, there is no longer any necessity for smoothing over the oracle by deletions.

Setting

The recognition of the formal language used by the prophet prevents us from concluding from the mentions of the גר at the end, that v 7 "certainly points to Jerusalem-Judah." Rather the complete indifference to the actual situation of Jerusalem and the individualizing of the divine judgement against specific idolaters and specific prophets speak strongly for the exilic situation. There the oracle, which strives for the obedience of the exiles, is conceivable both before and after 587. The consideration that idolatry first became a dangerous temptation for the exiles in the period after 587, when the hope of a speedy return to Jerusalem was finally destroyed, could point to that time. With uncertainty in the understanding of גלולים, however, this consideration is not compelling.

Interpretation

■ **14:1** The situation known from 8:1, according to which some of the elders come to the prophet, is here made still clearer by the divine reply (v 3) that the visitors want an oracular decision from the prophet.[11] Is it the expectation of a turning point for the "house of Israel," completely defeated after 587, which brings them to the prophet? Or do they expect, as in 8:1; 20:1, an assurance of deliverance for the still intact Jerusalem?

■ **14:2, 3** The message which the prophet then receives does not give him the information expected by them, but a revelation of the secrets of their hearts, in a way which recalls the working of the spirit in 1 Cor 14:24f.[12] They are men who have not broken free from idols, but have given them a place (literally, they have caused them to go up from a hidden depth) in their hearts. Indeed they have set up before their eyes what is a temptation to themselves. The heart and the eye (Gen 3:6; Mt 6:22ff) are the entrance points of temptation. This is denoted as מכשול עון.[13] The phrase מכשול עון, which only appears in the book of Ezekiel and here no less than six times, is an expression coined by Ezekiel (or of his priestly background).[14] It shows, exactly as the expression עון קץ, similarly only found with him (21:30, 34; 35:5), its origin from the sphere in which עון is the great problem upon which life turns. Of the 232 (or 228) Old Testament references to עון almost one fifth (44 or 42) occur in the book of Ezekiel alone. The "stumbling" (כשל) is therefore so hateful to Ezekiel because it occasions "guilt."

The man who "bears guilt" (נשא עון) is excluded from the cultic community, and thereby from 'life'.[15] The description of idolatry as מכשול עון enables us to see that the man who chooses idols chooses death. Ought then, so Yahweh first questions the prophet, these people to be given an oracular decision which would be the sign of a living communion with Yahweh?[16]

We should like to know what constituted the concrete offense of the elders of Israel who visited the prophet. The general term גלולים is used by Ezekiel in a very wide meaning for the whole sphere of those things which concern non-Israelite worship and its impurity.[17] It does not, in itself, satisfy the modern desire with its interest in religious history, for precise distinctions,

---

11 In distinction from 8:1 the "elders of Israel" are mentioned here, see Excursus 2.
12 See above pp. 144f.
13 For מכשול see above pp. 145f to 3:20.
14 See above p. 211 to 7:19b.
15 See above p. 305.

and leaves the offense of the elders more veiled than revealed. We should scarcely think of a cynical and blatant worship of figures beside Yahweh (Jer 44:15ff). Such people would scarcely come to Ezekiel in order to receive an oracular decision from him. Ought we then to think of a semi-private survival of superstitious forms of worship in the belief in magic and amulets? Or does it concern (cf. 20:32 but cf. the exposition) the attempt to establish a sacrificial cult to Yahweh in exile, which Ezekiel could only have regarded as an unclean devotion to idols? The text gives no certain answer. It simply enables us to see that for Ezekiel, in spite of the changed situation of exile, there could in any case only be the firmest adherence to the pure order of Yahweh worship, even though the exiled community could then only continue miserably with the lesser possibilities of the one worship which remained to it.[18]

■ **14:4** It is clearly now of importance that the divine announcement, which follows in v 4 on the introductory reproach, breaks off abruptly in the style of the law. This abrupt style was intended to catch the attention. For the men who seek Yahweh's oracle, with its attention-catching messenger formula (כה אמר יהוה) and its implied command: Silence, a word from God (cf. Ju 3:20), the way is completely blocked by the word of the law, known to everyone. With complete clarity the men who want a specific divine oracle are answered by the assertion: "It has been told to you, O man, what is good and what Yahweh requires of you" (Mic 6:6–8; Luke 16:27–31). Admittedly the legal formula, in its description of the occasion of guilt, bears features of Ezekiel's language (מכשול עון גלולים). However, it is certain that in its content it keeps wholly to the line of the laws which were known both in their form and content (as in the manner of Lev 20:2ff; for the subject matter cf. Ex 20:3; Dtn 13). It is a well-known law which is directed here so exactly to the situation of an inquiry of God by an idolater. At the same time, in the choice of the traditional introduction איש איש מבית ישראל, there is given a hint of that which is afterwards set unmistakably in the center: Israel! The people of God.

In place of the neutral declaration of punishment, which would be expected in accordance with the fixed style of the sacral law (Lev 17:4; 9:14, as well, however, as Lev 17:10; 20:2, 4f), there appears here the sharpest personal formulation. In the אני יהוה, which introduces the divine announcement of judgement, there echoes the formula of self-introduction, which not only begins the proclamation of the laws in the Decalogue, but also in H, from Lev 18 on, often concludes the individual series of laws (cf. to Ezek 20:7), and which must have had its place in specific acts of law proclamation.[19] Without any closer delineation of the threat, Yahweh counters with his frontal attack: I, I myself, allow myself to be moved to answer the inquirer (cf. also note d to v 4). Behind this answer, which says at the same time both little and much, there echoes menacingly the fullness of the divine punishment.

■ **14:5** However, the divine saying does not restrict itself with this threat of judgement to individual men, but shows immediately the deeper truth that this holy wrath has in mind "Israel" when speaking about the individual sinner. The "house of Israel" will be taken hold of in their hearts by the divine judgement against idolaters. The verb תפש otherwise means the forceful, even violent taking hold of a man as a prisoner (1 Sam 15:8; 1 Kings 13:4; in the nip'al Ezek 12:13; 17:20) or of an animal (19:4, 8; cf. to 21:28f) or the conquest of a city (Dtn 20:19; Josh 8:8; Is 36:1). Just as a father and mother lay hold (תפש) of their rebellious son and bring him before the elders at the gate (Dtn 21:19), so Yahweh, by judging individuals, lay shold of Israel which has gone astray through its idolatry. In this judgement upon the sinner there is made known who Yahweh is. In another formulation the development of thought of the proof oracle is expressed, for which the recognition formula, in the second person, is then introduced in v 8. The house of Israel is thereby involved as more than an onlooker being taught a lesson. Against it, it is asserted that it is concerned as a whole in the accusation because it has estranged itself from Yahweh with its idols. "All of them" is stressed by the כלם, which has perhaps been added to

---

16 Cf. the question in Dtn 13:2–6 of prophetic incitement to idolatry.

17 See above pp. 186f.

18 Cf. to מקדש מעט in 11:16 above pp. 261f.

19 Zimmerli, "Jahwe"; Elliger, "Ich bin."

the text subsequently (note a to v 5). Further consideration here must lead to the conclusion that the whole of Israel stands condemned by the law.

■ **14:6** From this it is surprising that Yahweh does not finish off fatalistically his action against Israel, but appeals in v 6, with a fresh command to the prophet and a further messenger formula, for repentance from idols and abominations (the parallelism shows again how comprehensively גלולים denotes the whole sphere of what is unclean and alien to Yahweh). The call to repentance, which is the most binding form of prophetic instruction and which could therefore be regarded by the post-exilic prophet Zechariah (1:4) as a proper summary of the prophetic message, is already found in Hosea (14:3) and Jeremiah (3:14, 22; 18:11; 25:5; 35:15). Cf. Amos 4:6ff, Is 30:15 and other passages. H. W. Wolff has pointed to the close connection between the call to repentance and the assurance of deliverance.[20] It must be noted in reflection upon the oracle 14:1–11 how strongly here, in the middle of a severely critical oracle, there emerges a call of invitation, which can only be understood against the background of a new divine act of deliverance.

The call is not to be regarded as a sentimental inconsequential saying of Yahweh. It is God's judgement upon sin which calls to repentance. Thus the oracle harks back directly to the clear remembrance of the sacred law, which is now unfolded in two parts.

■ **14:7, 8** Vv 7–8, like v 4, speaks first of the divine law, which stands over the man who, as a sinful idolater, wants to receive an oracle from the prophet: Yahweh himself will give his word to this man, who "devotes himself" (note a to v 7) away from him. In three clauses this divine word is now elaborated. The first and the third, the threat of turning away the face and of cutting off from the people, derive from the terms of the law, which was explained in the earlier section.[21] Further to this the idolater is threatened that Yahweh will make him a sign and a byword.

By the "sign," which consists in the judgement upon the idolater, what had previously been hidden is made clear to everyone, and in the "byword" the knowledge of this comes to the mouths of all people and is hardened into a fixed saying, stuck in every memory like a proverb.[22] Thus Yahweh demonstrates through his judgement upon idolaters, before the eyes and in the mouths of men, who he really is—quite involuntarily the law in vv 7f changes, by the addition of the recognition formula, into a prophetic proof oracle.

■ **14:9** Secondly Ezekiel takes the case of the prophet who is moved to give to the idolater, on his own authority, a message from God (דבר), where Yahweh, in a case already clearly covered by the sacral law, had himself refused to give a decision. The problem of the disobedient prophet, which is here given concrete form beyond the firm traditional statements of Ezek 13:1–16, in a way peculiar to Ezekiel, was of concern both to prophecy and the law-givers (Dtn 13:2–6; 18:20). That people knew of the possibility of a prophet being deceived (פתה) is shown by the narrative of the prophetic school in 1 Kings 13. With Ezekiel it undergoes a grim heightening in the statement that what at first appears to be an occasion of human guilt may be a serious involvement in divine punishment (cf. 1 Kings 22). The frightening mystery that man's sinning may not only be his freedom, which was first touched upon in 3:20, echoes here afresh.[23] Also against the prophet who became disobedient in this way there stood the threat of exclusion from the people of God mentioned in the sacral law. The hand of God stretched out for disaster would effect this punishment.[24]

■ **14:10** V 10 concludes, in the fixed legal style, the explanation of the two cases. The guilt formula ונשאו עונם once again has the force of consigning to an area far from Yahweh those whose lives could no longer be saved by any cultic act of reconciliation.

■ **14:11** The two cases dealt with by the sacral law

---

20 Hans Walter Wolff, "Das Thema 'Umkehr' in der alttestamentlichen Prophetie," *ZThK* 48 (1951): 129–148; reprinted in *idem, Gesammelte Studien zum AT*, ThB 22 (München: Kaiser, 1964), 130–150.

21 See above pp. 303f.

22 See above p. 156; pp. 280f, for illustration cf. Jer 29:22.

23 See Quell, *Propheten*, 99–102, who rightly emphasizes

that here, however, the possibility of recognizing a true obedience was given to the prophet through a reference to the clear word of Yahweh forbidding idolatry, as in Dtn 13:2–6.

24 See above p. 294 to 13:9.

were properly finished by the concluding formula in v 10. Once again, the continuation in v 11 shows that this twofold case had become for the prophet a part of a broader event. Once again the oracle returns to the "house of Israel," which is the object of this severe judgement and "the heart of which is to be taken hold of" by it. We hear further that Yahweh, in his severe judgement, is preparing for the deliverance of his people. In two negative statements and a concluding positive one, this final intention of Yahweh is expressed: 1) In the divine judgement upon idolaters and disobedient prophets Yahweh would free Israel from "going astray" from him.[25] The reference to Israel's "going astray" (תעות [בני] ישראל) later becomes an almost stereotyped expression for the pre-exilic period of the people's sin, cf. 44:10, 15; 48:11. 2) Yahweh would deliver Israel from the uncleanness of its offenses. פשע, which appears again in 18:22, 28, 30f; 21:29; 33:10, 12; 37:23; 39:24, according to L. Köhler, primarily denotes rebellion, insurrection, and then becomes a particularly sharp expression for sin against Yahweh, which contests his legitimate claim to lordship.[26] The specific usage of Ezekiel is to be seen in that rebellion is here described as a becoming unclean. Finally 3) Yahweh will again truly make Israel his people. The two-sided covenant formula, which expresses this most fully, has already been encountered in 11:20 in an important reference in an oracle of salvation.[27] Here, as the final goal of Yahweh's judgement, the restoration of the covenant is wholeheartedly affirmed.

Aim

The section 14:1–11 shows halfhearted men. They have experienced God's judgement, and yet they do not want to be cut off from him by it, but to await his salvation. So they come running to the prophet. Nevertheless they are wanting a new faith, without wholly giving up the old. The judgement had not completely broken their old nature, with the old trust in powers other than God, just as men always resist letting go the past completely, with all its particular helps. Who really wants to die completely?

To this half hearted piety, which prays for help from God before it is ready to give him his rightful place (cf. the inquiry of Zedekiah Jer 38:14ff), there is given instead of the anticipated word of God, a recollection of the divine law in all its sharpness, from which not a jot can pass away. The person who is half hearted must be excluded from the people of God. There is no alternative path of pious experiences and encouragements which bypasses the holy and clear will of God, which runs simply: "He has told you, O man, what is good. . . ."

Behind these preliminary considerations, which apply to every individual, there lies a still more mysterious depth.

God kills in order to save. In his judgement he is zealous for his people. The choice of the language of the sacral law brings to expression this will for the purity of his people—and this will is a zeal full of compassion. Nevertheless must he not assert against his entire people that they are all (כלם v 5) idolatrous, totally unfit (Ezek 15) and sinful from the beginning (Ezek 20, 23)? Must he not then banish them all with his curse from his people, in accordance with his holy law? What then would remain of his people? We cannot see how, from a human point of view, any possibility remains for the people. However, God's passionate zeal for Israel shows that for him this possibility remains. In the midst of his prophecy (v 6) he calls his people with all urgency to repentance, not on the grounds of a human possibility, but on that of his own mysterious, unfathomable will (cf. 11:17ff; 36f). There is an unresolved mystery behind the oracle of 14:1–11, with its righteous zeal against all halfheartedness and its confident zeal, going beyond all human possibilities, for the true people of the covenant seen afar off. This unresolved mystery is a promise.

In the light of this promise lying beyond all human despair and sin, which calls God's people to return to him and to turn away from all its halfheartedness, lies the ultimate purpose of the prophecy of 14:1–11.

25 For תעה cf. what is said above p. 295 to 13:10.
26 Ludwig Koehler, "Archäologisches. Nr. 22. 23," *ZAW* (1928): 213–218.
27 See above p. 263.

The Inevitability of the Divine Judgement

Bibliography

G. A. Barton
"Danel, a Pre-Israelite Hero of Galilee," *JBL* 60 (1941): 213–225.

S. Daiches
"Ezekiel and the Babylonian Account of the Deluge. Notes on Ez 14[12–20]," *JQR* 17 (1905): 441–455.

P. Joüon
"Trois noms de personnages bibliques à la lumière des textes d'Ugarit," *Biblica* 19 (1938): 280–285.

J. Lewy
"Nāḫ et Rušpān" in *Mélanges syriens offerts à M. René Dussaud* I (Paris: Geuthner, 1939), 273–275.

M. Noth
"Noah, Daniel and Hiob in Ezechiel 14," *VT* 1 (1951): 251–260.

S. Spiegel
"Noah, Danel and Job, Touching on Canaanite Relics in the Legends of the Jews," *Louis Ginzberg Jubilee Volume* (New York: American Acad. Jewish Research, 1945), 305–355 [English Section].

14

12 And the word of Yahweh came to me: 13/ Son of man, when a land sins against me by acting faithlessly, and I stretch out my hand against it, and break its staff of bread and send[a] famine upon it, and cut off man and beast from it, 14/ and if (then) these three men: Noah, Daniel, and Job were in its midst, they would be 'delivered'[a] for the sake of their righteousness ' ', says [the Lord][b] Yahweh. 15/ 'Or if'[a] I make wild animals pass through the land, so that it is depopulated and becomes a wilderness because no one will pass through it (any more) on

14:
13 13a 𝔐 והשלחתי. In vv 19, 21; 5:17; 28:23, in a related or similar statement, the pi'el of שלח is used. Herrmann and Bertholet therefore read here also שִׁלַּחְתִּי; cf. the scribal error in v 8 (note a). However the hip'il of שלח is also frequent in the Old Testament and appears every time in connection with the sending of plagues (gnats, Ex 8:17; wild animals, Lev 26:22; enemies, 2 Kings 15:37; famine, Amos 8:11). Thus the reading of 𝔐 is not necessarily to be altered.

14 14a 𝔐 ינצלו נפשם. The pi'el of נצל, which appears in the Old Testament only in Ex 3:22; 12:36; 2 Chr 20:25 with the meaning "to despoil," is at once striking beside the correct יצילו נפשם of v 20. Thus Bertholet, Fohrer, BH³ change to יצילו. This is not supported by 𝔊 σωθήσονται, 𝔏ˢ *salvi erunt*, which point to a simple יִנָּצְלוּ in their Hebrew original (cf. vv 16, 18). If we do not interpret נפשם with Ehrlich, *Randglossen*, following Jer 46:2, as "they themselves," we shall have to find in it an incompletely assimilated interpretative addition which seeks to make clear already in the beginning of the explanation that the pious only save "their own lives."

b אדני is lacking in 𝔊 𝔏ˢ 𝔆ᴮᵒ, see Excursus 1. 𝔅, as in v 11, *dominus exercituum*.

15 15a In לוּ, which is only found here in the book of Ezekiel (cf. note c to 3:6) and is scarcely defensible in spite of the reference by Toy to Gen 50:15 in a section which preserves the casuistic legal style, we must see an older textual error. Cf. 𝔊. Vv 17 and 19

account of the wild animals, 16/ 'and'[a] (if then) these three men were in its midst—as I live, says [the Lord][b] Yahweh, they would deliver neither sons nor daughters. They alone would be delivered, but the land would become a wilderness. 17/ Or if I bring a sword upon that land and say: Let a sword go through the land; and I cut off from it man and beast, 18/ though these three men were in its midst—as I live, says [the Lord][a] Yahweh, they would deliver neither sons nor daughters. They alone would be delivered. 19/ Or if I send a pestilence against[a] that land, and pour out my wrath upon it with blood, to cut off from it man and beast, 20/ and (then) Noah, Daniel and Job were in its midst—as I live, says [the Lord][a] Yahweh, they would deliver[b] neither son nor[c] daughter. They would (only) deliver their own lives by their righteousness.

21 Thus then[a] has [the Lord][b] Yahweh said: Indeed when I[c] have sent my four evil judgements, sword, famine, wild beasts, and pestilence, against[d] Jerusalem, in order to cut off from it man and beast, 22/ and there are still[a] in it some survivors, who 'bring out' (sc. from the destroyed city)[b] sons and daughters—behold,[c] they will come out to you, and you will see their ways and their deeds [and you will be consoled for the evil which I have brought upon Jerusalem, for[d] all that I have brought upon it. 23/ And they will console you, when you see their ways and their deeds,][a] and you will know that I have not done without cause all that I have done in it (sc. Jerusalem), says [the Lord][b] Yahweh.

support the reading אוֹ.

16   16a 𝔐 שְׁלֹשֶׁת, read וּשְׁלֹשֶׁת with 32 MSS 𝔊 𝔖 (in 𝔏ˢ vv 16f have fallen out by homoioarkton). Cf. vv 18 (20).

    b אדני is lacking in 𝔊 𝔆ᴮᵒ, see Excursus 1.

18   18a אדני is lacking in 𝔊 𝔏ˢ 𝔆ᴮᵒ, see Excursus 1.

19   19a על—אל cf. note a to 1:17.

20   20a אדני is lacking in 𝔊 𝔏ˢ 𝔆ᴮᵒ, see Excursus 1.

    b 𝔊 varies the translation of this clause in vv 16, 18, 20.

    c 𝔐 אם, Eb 22 ואם as in v 16.

21   21a 𝔐 כי is certainly not attested by 𝔊 (except 𝔊⁶²) 𝔏ˢ, but, against Cornill, Bertholet, Fohrer, is not to be deleted since it connects the general explanation of the righteous punishment of Yahweh with the concrete address to those condemned. ƵB "Indeed, thus says. . . ." Cf. the exposition.

    b אדני is lacking in 𝔊 𝔏ˢ 𝔆ᴮᵒ, cf. Excursus 1.

    c אף כי is here not comparative ("how much more than . . ." Ehrlich, *Randglossen*, Herrmann). אף is simply emphatic; כי introduces the conditional clause as in 15:5 (cf. Koehler-Baumgartner s.v. אף 6): "Indeed, if I. . . ."

    d על—אל cf. note a to 1:17.

22   22a In the והנה of 𝔐 there is a note of surprise in view of what is not to be expected after vv 12–20.

    b Instead of הַמּוּצָאִים we must read with 𝔊 οἳ ἐξάγουσιν (𝔏ˢ 𝔊 𝛴 𝔙) מוֹצָאִים. The article has arisen by dittography of the preceding final ה. Or should we see preserved in it the remnant of a lost ממנה (Cornill, Herrmann, following 𝔊 οἱ ἀνασεσωσμένοι ἐξ αὐτῆς), or בה (𝔏ˢ *residui in ea*)?

    c הנם introduces the apodosis and is certainly not to be emended with BH³ in accordance with 𝔖 or 𝔗.

    d 𝔐 את is very unusual. We would expect על. So Bertholet BH³. Driver, "Linguistic Problems," 65, understands את as "beside, in comparison with," as in 16:22.

23   23a Vv 22b–23a are lacking in 𝔊ᴮ,¹⁰⁸,⁵³⁸, which Ziegler, *Ezechiel*, explains as a scribal error resulting from homoioteleuton. Cf. Bertholet. The clumsily overloaded diction of the section, which is lacking in the textual witnesses referred to and which connects back again in v 23a with the assertions of the conclusion of v 22a in an awkward repetition of what is said in v 22b, seriously raises the question of whether we are faced here with a secondary textual addition. Vv 22a, 23b form a completely smooth section which is free from objection. Unfortunately the text occurs at a gap in 𝔊⁹⁶⁷ so that this important witness gives us no help here.

    b אדני is lacking in 𝔊 (𝔊⁹⁶⁷ ὁ θεός) 𝔏ˢ 𝔆ᴮᵒ.

Form

The section 14:12–23, which is independent of 14:1–11 (Hölscher, *Hesekiel*, differently) is divided into two halves by the messenger formula in v 21. In content also the explanation in vv 13–20, which treats of the punishment of the sin of the land in a quite general way, is different from the prophecy in vv 21–23, which explicitly names Jerusalem and is addressed to the exiles. Vv 13–20 set out, in the style of the sacral law, the example of the land struck by Yahweh with four possible judgements.[1] The four cases represent no necessary connected sequence. They also contain no element of heightening, such as appears to be intended in the series of punishments in Lev 26:14ff. These similarly include in Lev 26:22–26 wild animals, sword, pestilence, and famine. Instead the monotonous repetition of the cases, which are only slightly varied in details, has the intention of expressing the totality of the divine judgement through the use of four examples.[2] Beside them there is no possibility of a fifth punishment, and they imply the inescapability of the divine order. As in vv 1–11 (cf. Lev 17:10; 20:2–6) the legal style, initially with a neutral formulation, is vitalized by a change into an address by Yahweh in the first person. In this the הכרית of the old banishment formula is echoed in vv 13, 17, 19 (cf. 21).[3] Each individual case is then emphasized by the concluding formula for a divine address. However, from the second case (vv 16, 18, 20), this formula is displaced from its position at the end into the context. In the order which is already found in Ezekiel in 5:11 the oath חי אני, which introduces the apodosis and which reveals the force of the divine will, is given emphasis by this formula.[4]

The second part of the section (vv 21–23), which passes over into concrete speech about Jerusalem and the judgement hovering over it, echoes several formulations from vv 13–20 in vv 21f. Undoubtedly it must be understood as a continuation of those verses. However, since vv 13–20 speak of the complete destruction of the offenders, whilst vv 21–23 surprisingly appear to presuppose a group of the wicked who survive, the question has been put whether vv 21–23 really are the genuine continuation of vv 13–20. Bertholet would find in vv 21–23 an appendix, originating after the fall of Jerusalem, to the teaching about individual retribution which arose before this fall (vv 13–20). However, the independence of vv 13–20, which would then become a doctrinal section without any actual connection, is unsatisfactory. Not only the section 14:1–11, which grew out of the law, but also the apparently closely related "doctrinal sections" in 18; 33:1–9, 10–20 show that Ezekiel's word, even where it appears to be preserved in a strongly generalized and doctrinal fashion, is always directed to Israel in a very definite and concrete summons. Thus van den Born relates v 21 to vv 13–20 and considers only vv 22–23, which refer to a פלטה, as an "appendix." However can v 21 really be taken as a declaration which is self-contained, as van den Born conjectures? The further elaboration in vv 22f cannot be dispensed with after v 21. More precisely it appears to be that vv 21–22aα make clear the application to Jerusalem of the general rule of the righteousness of Yahweh, which was developed in vv 13–20, whilst vv 22aβ, 23b add a formula of recognition formulated in a particular way.[5] This is a familiar phenomenon at the close of Ezekiel's prophecies.

Thus in vv 12–23 two forms of oracle are bound together in the section in a particular way. In the structure of the oracle as a whole, however, the connection with the type of proof-oracle in three parts cannot well be denied.[6] Here, however, in place of the two first parts (motivating reproach-proclamation of judgement) a legal pronouncement in two parts has entered. This is first outlined quite generally in a fourfold casuistic affirmation of Yahweh's incorruptible righteousness (vv 13–20) and then makes an "application"

---

1 With the use of כי, see above p. 302.
2 For the importance of the number four see above pp. 120f.
3 See above pp. 303f.
4 See above p. 176. The case is similar in Jeremiah, see Rendtorff, "Gebrauch," 28.
5 For vv 22b–23a cf. note a to v 23.
6 See above p. 290.

of Yahweh's righteousness to Jerusalem (vv 21–22aα). In this legal pronouncement in two parts the features of reproach and judgement oracle are combined in a novel form. When Fohrer designates vv 12–23 as a "discussion oracle," he is characterizing the subject of the saying, but not its formal structure.

In order to pinpoint the location of vv 12–23 in the history of tradition we must finally point to Jer 15:1–3.[7] In the framework of a great liturgy for a day of penitence in time of drought (Jer 14:1–15:4), we have Yahweh's rejection of the solemn prayer of penitence by the community (Jer 14:19–22).[8] Not even Moses and Samuel, Israel's two great intercessors, could move Yahweh to be gracious. To the despairing question (from the temple?) of the rejected people as to where they should turn (אנה נצא), they are sent, in a saying which is in four parts, to the sentence of death that is hanging over them (מות "pestilence") and to the threat of sword, famine, and being taken prisoner.[9] The four families (משפחות) of destruction: sword, famine, birds, and wild animals, are summoned against them by Yahweh, in order to destroy them. The connection between the reference to the four powers of judgement and Yahweh's refusal to listen to prayer, even the prayers of great men of piety, sets Ezek 14:12ff in such a striking relationship to Jer 15:1–3 that we cannot regard it simply as accidental. Since Ezekiel's familiarity with sayings of Jeremiah is not to be denied in other places (especially ch. 23), we may conclude that here also he is dependent. The comparison which we can make within the context of the detailed exegesis will certainly then show the distinctive development in Ezekiel of what he has received.

Setting

With the assertion of the connection of vv 12–20 with 21–23 on the grounds of content, there can be no doubt about the formation of the oracle among the exiles

(against Bertholet, Herntrich). The fall of Jerusalem must already have taken place, according to v 21. However, the perfect consecutive וראיתם (also וידעתם) raises the question whether the company of those deported from Jerusalem after 587 B.C. had already arrived in Babylon. The oracle, which is certainly not to be explained away with Herntrich as a "simulated prophecy," seeks to show how the arrival of the new exiles serves to show afresh Yahweh's righteousness to the exiles of 598/7 B.C.[10]

Interpretation

■ **14:12, 13** Unlike vv 1–11, the prophecy of vv 12–23 shows a lack of any explicit command to prophesy. The explanation which follows after the formula for the coming of a message appears to presuppose that only the prophet hears, according to the address to him.[11] However, the messenger formula in v 21, which initially belonged to the realm of preaching and not to a dialogue between Yahweh and his messenger, turns to the circle of those addressed from the exiled community in vv 22f.

The casuistic explanation in vv 13–20 mentions first of all, as a prior matter to all the four examples given, the case of the sinfulness of the land before Yahweh. The word חטא, which at first denoted the missing of a norm or of an aim (Ju 20:16 of bowshots), is only here related to Yahweh by ל in the entire book of Ezekiel. In all the other cases it is used absolutely as a technical term (3:21; 18:4, 20; 28:16; 33:12; 37:23) or with the cognate object חטאת (16:51; 18:24; 33:16).[12] The use of the verb מעל with it to give a closer definition (Lev 5:21), is first (? Josh 7:1) found in Ezekiel (again 15:8; 17:20; 18:24; 20:27; 39:23, 26; with the exception of 39:23 always connected with the noun מעל), must derive from the priestly vocabulary and have originally denoted an offense against what was holy. Thus the infringement of the ban (Josh 7:1; 22:20), the breach of an oath (Ezek

---

7   Miller, *Verhältnis*, 93.
8   See Rudolph, *Jeremia*, on this passage.
9   See Rudolph, *Jeremia*, on Jer 14:12. He would delete this fourth member in regard to Jer 14:12.
10 Herntrich, *Ezekielprobleme*, 101.
11 See above pp. 144f; pp. 131f.
12 Cf. further to 43:20.

17:20), a breach of the marriage order (Nu 5:12) can all be described as מעל. Further the word appears then certainly to have outgrown the sphere of sacral law and to have become a more general designation for specific religious sins.

Ezek 14:13 does not define a sin any more precisely, but mentions God's positive reaction by the formulas already known from 13:9; 14:9 for "stretching out the hand" and for "cutting of"; i.e., in the saying והכרתי ממנה אדם ובהמה, which echoes the references to a total judgement from God.[13]

At this point, however, there begins a casuistic development. The four forms of annihilating judgement upon a land, which have already been listed in the appendix in 5:16f, in dependence on the present text, as a threat against the people of Jerusalem, are now dealt with in a series. In a bold development of the casuistic form of law, which normally dealt with "cases" concerning human behavior, "cases" of divine judgement are here listed in sequence. In each case the same situation of Yahweh's refusal to be entreated encounters man afresh. The casuistic form becomes a means for making a penetrating repetition of one and the same message.

■ **14:14** Jer 15:1, the prototype of Ezekiel's oracle, had referred to Yahweh's being entreated by his people on a specific occasion of penitence. In the passage there, his refusal of all such entreaty was emphasized by the statement that even the intercession of Moses and Samuel, the two great prophetic figures of Israel's past (cf. Ps 99:6; 1 Sam 7:9; Ex 32:31f), could no longer avert the punishment. In Ezek 14:12ff the actual situation has disappeared, and the reference is formulated generally and didactically. In place of the great intercessory figures of Israel we have three men marked out by their particular "righteousness." Ezek 9:8; 11:13; 13:5 show that Ezekiel also knew something of prophetic intercession. Nevertheless, the use of the language of sacral law, especially the legal formula of banishment, shows how strongly the prophet was rooted in the priestly sphere in which "life" was bound up with reliance on the sphere of the holy. Ezek 18:9 shows that the predicate צדיק is accorded to the man who relies upon God. Thus with Ezekiel the question about "life" is repeatedly a question about "righteousness" (3:17–21; 18; 33). Under this catchword there also

appears in the present text the question about the possibility of deliverance by a third party. However, just as Ezekiel knew from the priestly practice of the temple that only a decision given to individuals could give them permission to enter, and allowed no unclean person to come into the sanctuary along with a clean one, nor a leper with a healthy person (Lev 13), so also here he knew of the strongly personal decision of Yahweh concerning the righteous man. No unrighteous person could follow in behind the broad back of a righteous one, even though the latter may have been exemplary in his righteousness.

When Ezekiel adduces as the three exemplary righteous men Noah, Daniel, and Job, then in doing so he clearly moves consciously from the sphere of the covenant people into one of worldwide range. The continuation in vv 21–23 then refers to Jerusalem. Noah, who is mentioned outside of Genesis (and 1 Chr 1:4) in Is 54:9, in an allusion to the Flood story, is found in Genesis in two different roles: he is the hero of the Flood and the first vinedresser. Lewy, "Nāḥ," has recognized the Akkadian name *Mu-ut-na-ḫa*, *Na-aḫ-AN*, *Na-ḫi-lum*, *Na-ḫi-li* as theophorous and has deduced from this a divine name *Nāḥā*, or *Nāḥ* (deriving from a deified man? cf. Utnapishtim in the Babylonian Flood story). According to Noth, "Noah," the name belongs to the ruling class of the population living in the Middle Euphrates in the nineteenth/eighteenth century B.C., which stood in a certain relationship to later Israelite groups. The biblical name Noah could have been formed here. We may question whether yet more traditions of Noah were known to Ezekiel. Since in the P Document the description of Noah as a righteous man begins quite programmatically the Flood story (Gen 6:9 איש צדיק תמים) and is found even with J in an initial declaratory affirmation by Yahweh (Gen 7:1), it remains by far the most probable explanation that Ezekiel had in mind in his reference to Noah the tradition of the pious man who was delivered from the Flood, along with his family. As a figure of that earliest of human catastrophes he rightly stands at the beginning of the list.

The Daniel who is mentioned next cannot be identified with the leading figure of the book of Daniel, who appears as a contemporary of Ezekiel's from Judah.

Rather we must also think here of a well-known figure of ancient time. The mention of Daniel in Ezek 28:3, where the prince of Tyre is praised as being "as wise as Daniel," makes it likely that we should see in Daniel a figure who stood close to Phoenician tradition. This conjecture is given greater probability by the mythological texts from Ugarit. In the epic of *Aqht*, the son of *Dnil*, which Virolleaud first published under the title "La légende phénicienne de Danel," *Dnil* appears in the person of a righteous ruler.[14] Twice (II Aqht V 5–8; I Aqht I 20–25) his righteous judgement in the gate in the midst of persons of noble rank (*adrm*), which secures the rights of widows and orphans, is described in similar terms: *dn almnt ytpt tpt ytm*.[15] According to Spiegel, "Noah," the form דנאל in Ezekiel, in distinction from the דניאל of Daniel, points here to a form of the name Danel which corresponds to the Ugaritic. Can we go further and conjecture that Ezekiel knew a story of a miraculous deliverance of the righteous Daniel like that of Noah? G. A. Barton's view that we should see in the Ugaritic *Dnil* a "semi-mythical hero of Galilee" and an "eponymous ancestor of the Zebulonites" is scarcely supportable.

A story of the remarkable deliverance of a pious man is also found in the biblical accounts of Job (Job 42). The introductory framework of the book of Job similarly leaves no doubt in the very first verses that we are concerned in the case of Job with a non-Israelite man of piety, one of the "people of the East" (בני קדם Job 1:3), who are to be sought east of the Dead Sea. Can we conclude from the sequence of the three names that in Ezekiel's mind Job was the latest of the three? When Spiegel, "Noah," deduces from Ezek 14 a tradition in which Dan(i)el and Job redeemed their sons from corruption by their piety, he is schematizing the tradition much too strongly.

The mention of three pre-Israelite, or even non-Israelite, heroes makes clear that Ezekiel was here speaking in a universal way of the divine righteousness, which inevitably concerned every man, whether Israelite or not, in his own actions. By this emphasis Ezekiel stands in clear opposition to all the selfish assurances of Israel which sought to rely on the efficacy of its great men of piety.

■ **14:13–19** With great firmness this order of Yahweh's righteousness is now affirmed through all four forms of divine judgement in history.[16] The depopulation of the land through a plague of wild animals, in which the beasts of prey take over the only pathway through (עבר), is mentioned in 2 Kings 17:25f. The individualizing of the sword as a destructive force is repeated with grim emphasis in Ezek 21. Pestilence and blood were already connected in 5:17.

■ **14:21** The four examples of the inexorable righteousness of Yahweh which concerns "any land," like the "any land" in the parable of 33:1ff which sets up a watchman, becomes the background of the specific message from God which follows. Since the sternness of the divine righteousness upon "any land" is valid, how much more will it affect Jerusalem, the central place where the divine judgement falls in its fullness.[17] The four misfortunes are reiterated in a slightly different order and denoted as שפטים, a word characteristic of Ezekiel and P (Ex 6:6; 7:4; 12:12; Nu 33:4; Ezek 5:10, 15; 11:9; 14:21; 16:41; 25:11; 28:22, 26; 30:14, 19, also echoed in 2 Chr 24:24 and Prv 19:29, with emended text). Jer 15:3 speaks at this point of four "families."

■ **14:22a, 23b** The prophecy then takes a surprising turn. Yahweh's inexorable justice, which hovers over Jerusalem, will now, according to vv 22f, become clear to the exiles by a special sign so that they will "see and know" (the sequence וראיתם . . . . וידעתם, which is found again in 39:21f in the third person plural, whilst in 21:4 ראה has penetrated into the recognition formula and has suppressed the ידע, is broken up in 𝔐 by the insertion of vv 22b, 23a, going back in v 23a to 22a). A remnant is to escape from Jerusalem. To

---

13 See above p. 294; pp. 302ff.

14 Charles Virolleaud, *Mission de Ras-Shamra* 1: *La légende phénicienne de Danel* (Paris: Geuthner, 1936).

15 Gordon, *Ugaritic Textbook* 2, 182, 179; *idem*, *Ugaritic Literature* 88, 94; G. R. Driver, *Canaanite Myths and Legends* (Edinburgh: Clark, 1956), 52f, 58f.

16 For the description of famine by reference to the breaking of the staff of bread see above p. 170.

17 See above pp. 174f to 5:5.

315

argue that this means that unrighteous men will be "delivered" overlooks the fact that Ezekiel intentionally avoids the verb נצל at this point (the conjecture of Ehrlich and Bertholet to read המצילים instead of 𝔐's המוצאים spoils this subtlety) and simply speaks of those brought out (המוצאים), and of those who go out (יוצאים) to the exiles. Does the repetition of יצא echo Jer 15:1f: to go out from the sanctuary, to go out in death? This going into exile is in reality something different from the "saving his life" of 14:20 or the "being saved" of vv 14 (with emended text), 16 and 18.[18]

This remnant[19] will become, through its ways and deeds which will make clear the wickedness of Jerusalem to those far away in exile, a sign in a new way of the inexorable justice of Yahweh spoken of in vv 13–20. Thus every mouth which would accuse Yahweh of injustice in his action against Jerusalem will be put to silence. The parallel formulation "ways and deeds" recalls the parallelism of דרך and מעלל which is found nine times in Jeremiah (mostly plural, Jer 4:18; 7:3, 5; 17:10; 18:11; 23:22; 25:5; 26:13; 32:19).[20] With Ezekiel it reveals the variant usage דרך and עלילות (14:22f; 20:43, 44; 24:14; 36:17, 19), with only 36:31 standing out with its Jeremianic מעלל.

The surprising turn of vv 21–23, which applies the assertion of vv 13–20 to Jerusalem without formal identity, but with apparent illogicality, cannot be understood by those who found in vv 13–20 "a doctrine of just retribution," which now should be applied to Jerusalem. The whole oracle rather proclaims quite personally the justice of Yahweh who reveals himself afresh in his freedom by his actions. Thus the troop of "those who come out" from Jerusalem, which would be a counter argument against the validity of the doctrine of vv 13–20 if seen within the framework of a simple theoretical consideration, is in reality the physical sign of the historical actuality of Yahweh's righteous order.[21] The appearance of the remnant of the wicked citizens of Jerusalem among the exiles becomes a clearer proof of the righteousness of Yahweh than would the straight forward fulfillment of the destruction of Jerusalem, which would not have the same relevance and evidence for the exiles.

■ **14:22b–23a** The mention of this divine demonstration has undergone in vv 22b–23a a surprising later interpretation. The proof of the inexorable righteousness of Yahweh means for the exiles a "consolation" for the fall of Jerusalem. This idea can only have belonged to someone who had recognized that all salvation does not lie in the retaining of one's own property, but solely in the upholding of the divine righteousness. Once again this faith can only arise when it is recognized that God's righteousness towards man does not seek his death, but his life (18:23, 32; 33:11).

Aim

The prophecy proclaims the triumph of the righteousness of Yahweh, not with the proud sophistication of one who thinks he can look at the cards of God, but in the humility of an obedient hearer.

In this humility the prophet says here that God's righteous action leaves open no hiding place and so does not permit anyone to protect himself laughingly in his wickedness behind the back of those who are righteous before God. God looks everyone straight in the face and wills the repentance of each (Ezek 18). Saving faith is no mass-produced article, but something unique and individual, taking place in the full light of God's face.

In this humility the prophet also exerts himself to proclaim to those around him that God will accomplish a full demonstration of his righteous judgement precisely where a disobedient and presumptuous calculation would presume upon his unwillingness to assert his holy law. "Those who come out from it" will also become a shattering proof of God's holy judgement to those whose eyes are open to God.

Through all this, however, the latest addition of the divine message affirms finally that the horrifying confirmation of the righteous judgement of God means at the same time a strange consolation. Over this consolation there stands the recognition that only where God's holy judgement remains inexorable can man hope at the same time, without wavering, for the unchangeability of the divine covenant promise.

---

18 Cf. the comments on "life" to 18:9.
19 Failure, the German "Pleite," is derived from the Hebrew word *peliṭah*, slang for bankruptcy. See above pp. 188f to פלטה.
20 Miller, *Verhältnis*, 92.
21 Zimmerli, *Erkenntnis*, 49–57.

The Useful Vine

E. Baumann
"Die Weinranke im Walde. Hes. 15$^{1-8}$," *ThLZ* 80 (1955): 119–120.

15

1 And the word of Yahweh came to me:
2/ Son of man, how is the wood of the vine (different) from any wood,[a] which is among the trees[b] of the forest? 3/ Is wood taken[a] from it to make anything?[b] Or do men take a peg from it in order to hang any vessel on? 4/ Behold,[a] it is given to the fire for fuel. Its two ends the fire consumes, and its middle is charred. Is it useful for anything then?[b] 5/ Behold, (even) when it was (still) whole, it was not used[a]—how much less when the fire has consumed it and it is burnt; can it still be used then?

6 Therefore[a] [the Lord][b] Yahweh has said: Like the wood of the vine among 'the trees'[c] of the forest, which I have given to the fire for fuel, so will I give up the

15: 2a 𝔐, which divides עץ by its *athnach* from the following הזמורה, interprets הזמורה as a parallel taking up of עץ הגפן. So also 𝔊 𝔗. However, it is improbable (in spite of Driver, "Ezekiel," 151) that the feminine זמורה could be resumed by the masculine היה. 𝔊 𝔗 therefore change this to הות. Thus Hitzig attempts to get round it with the strained translation "the wood, which it (the vine) was" (cf. Smend), which is scarcely convincing. The fact that 𝔊$^{B txt}$ Cyr. reads the 𝔊 text ἐκ πάντων τῶν ξύλων τῶν κληmάτων without the words τῶν κληmάτων, raises the question whether הזמורה is a gloss that is alien to the original text (Jahn, *Buch*). Hölscher, *Hesekiel*, Cooke, Herrmann have gone still further and have explained all the words הזמורה אשר היה בעצי as a gloss, by appealing to v 6. Similarly Fohrer. 𝔊^{967} 𝔏^s, however, oppose the text of 𝔊$^{B txt}$ Cyr., the reading of which must rather rest on a scribal error arising through homoioteleuton (Ziegler, *Ezechiel*). So with 𝔊 𝔙 𝔏^s עץ הזמורה are to be connected and understood as a general designation, formed in dependence on עץ הגפן, for a vine branch and also for stems with weaker shoots. For the meaning of היה מן, the reading of 𝔗, with its שנא מן "to be different from," must point the way.

b The wordplay with עץ repeated four times in vv 2f, denoting both "wood" and "tree," cannot be fully translated into English.

3 3a 𝔊 (𝔏^s) εἰ λήμφονται, 𝔗 היסבון make it appear possible that for their Hebrew original they had a reading היקחו, analogous to v 3b.

b Literally "to make for work (a tool?)."

4 4a 𝔐 הנה. 𝔊 interprets freely πάρεξ "beyond it" (𝔏^s *excepto eo*).

b 𝔊 translates bα as τὴν κατ᾽ ἐνιαυτὸν κάθαρσιν αὐτῆς ἀναλίσκει τὸ πῦρ καὶ ἐκλείπει εἰς τέλος. Cf. 𝔏^s. It must have had in mind the annual "pruning" of the vine (John 15:2f) and the burning of the wild shoots (John 15:6). For the relation of 𝔊 to 𝔐 see Cornill.

5 5a 𝔐 imperfect לא יעשה. There is already an interweaving of a timeless expression with what is defined historically in the description of the parable. Cf. the exposition.

6 6a 𝔊 (𝔏^s) + εἶπον. Cornill, Herrmann, Fohrer accordingly add אָמֹר.

b אדני is lacking in 𝔊 𝔏^s 𝔆, see Excursus 1.

c 𝔐 בעץ, read בעצי with MSS 𝔊 𝔖 𝔗 𝔙; cf. 15:2.

inhabitants of Jerusalem. 7/ And I will set my face against them. Though they have escaped from the fire, the[a] fire will consume them, and you[b] will know that I am Yahweh, when I set my face against them, 8/ and make the land a desolation because they have acted unfaithfully, says [the Lord][a] Yahweh.

7   7a 𝔐 adds the copula.
     b 𝔊 (𝔏ˢ) assimilates to the context καὶ ἐπιγνώσονται as already in 5:13; 6:14; 7:4, 9; 13:9.

8   8a אדני is lacking in 𝔊 𝔏ˢ 𝔆.

Form

The section 15:1–8 divides, after the customary introductory formula in v 1, into a parable of the vine (vv 2–5) and an interpretation (vv 6–8), introduced by the messenger formula (𝔊 also adds a commission to speak) and rounded off by the concluding formula for a divine message. Hölscher, *Hesekiel*, endeavors to connect this with the further consideration that vv 2–5 form a poem in four strophes, whilst vv 6–8 are a prose appendix. In fact in v 3 the poetic feature of *parallelismus membrorum* can be seen, and in another way two affirmations are held together in v 5 in the sequence *a minori ad majus*. However, a full rhythmic structure cannot be obtained without considerable changes. On the other hand, since in v 7aβ we can see an element composed with very rigid parallelism, we shall be more correct in abandoning the distinction between a poetic and a prose part and recognize in both parts an exalted preaching style which here and there becomes poetic.

Irwin, who finds only two strophes in the more obliterated form of the parable in vv 2–5, then believes that he can demonstrate further a major discrepancy in content between parable and interpretation. Vv 2–5 affirm the uselessness of the vine wood, whilst vv 6–8 point to the declaration that Jerusalem will be burnt with fire. Accordingly we must find in the interpretation a different voice from that in the parable, so that vv 6–8 are to be isolated as a secondary comment. The arguments which Irwin makes regarding chapter 15 then serve him as a key to his whole analysis of Ezekiel. However, his objections are formed much too logically and formalistically and pass over the vital movement of Ezekiel's language (both here and elsewhere).

Undoubtedly vv 2–5 at first give a parable which emphasizes the idea of the uselessness of vine wood. In form it is identified by the fact that it not only begins the description with a question (we must also compare 19:2 for the introductory מה of a parable), but that it is also further broken up by questions which call upon the hearer for an answer. The parable is thereby stylized as a disputation saying. J. Lindblom conjectures here that we have influences drawn from the didactic literature of Wisdom.[1] To this we must add a clear element of a historical parable. The idea of the uselessness of the vine is not simply set out as a general truth. In the particular process of a first act of burning, which destroys the ends of the vine and scorches its center, there undoubtedly enters into the description an account of the history of Jerusalem which is not intelligible from the simple parable. To the assertion of uselessness (implied by the basic simile of the vine wood), a description of its destruction is added which introduces an element of historical movement.

At this point, however, the interpretation in vv 6–8 begins and relates to the citizens of Jerusalem the process of destruction which has already become apparent in the first part of the parable. What is said about the uselessness of the vine wood is thereby set before every hearer as the inescapable basis of this judgement. The assertion that the parable and its interpretation do not completely correspond (Hölscher, *Hesekiel*) is correct insofar as the interpretation only derives from the parable what concerns Jerusalem in the immediate announcement of a divine action and leaves the rest of the picture unexpressed, but not without significance, in the background. Irwin's claim, however, that the interpretation is "a false commentary" on the parable is a distortion of the real facts.[2]

In the explanation in vv 6–8 it is striking that the speech in vv 7bβ–8 continues after the recognition formula, which is otherwise usually found at the end of an oracle. The continuation is all the more unusual in that v 7bβ repeats the preceding phrasing of v 7aα with a different verb. This is clearly in order to introduce the further declaration of punishment, after

1   Johannes Lindblom, "Wisdom in the Old Testament Prophets" in *Wisdom in Israel and in the Ancient Near East*, ed. Martin Noth, VT Suppl 3 (Leiden: Brill, 1955), 201f.

2   Irwin, *Problem*, 35.

which there follows in v 8bα a further motive clause. Possibly, with Hölscher, *Hesekiel*, and others, it should be regarded as an addition. The text which we are then left with contains an explicit connection with the preceding parable in the assertion that Yahweh will make the inhabitants of Jerusalem like the vine wood (v 6). In v 7 a declaration of judgement follows, expressed without any metaphorical dress. It is expressed in v 7aα according to its personal character, and in v 7aβγ according to its actual content. The latter formulation is cast in a terse oracular style, a statement of intense impetus, and is rounded off by the recognition formula in v 7bα.

A review of the whole prophecy shows that it is set out in the structure of a complete proof-oracle, except that here, in place of the normal sequence: reproach (motivation)-declaration of judgement, the more artistic sequence of parable and interpretation is used. This contains within it elements of reproach and announcement of judgement.[3]

Setting

The text of the oracle in Ezek 15 distinguishes those addressed in the recognition formula (v 7bα) in direct speech from the inhabitants of Jerusalem, who are mentioned in the third person plural. The prophet is addressing his companions in exile as those who are summoned to acknowledge Yahweh's judgement upon Jerusalem. Since the final catastrophe upon Jerusalem is still to come, we must think of the period before 587 B.C.

Interpretation

■ **15:1, 2** After the formula for the coming of a message there follows first an address to the prophet.[4] The questions which follow, by their intention, turn already to the wider circle of men who are not addressed explicitly until the recognition formula in v 7. At the center of the question there lies a parable, the importance of which in the present connection can only be rightly gauged when we overhear in it undertones deriving from its place in the history of tradition. The narrative of the spies in Nu 13:23 mentions the vine

as the particular sign of the richness of Canaan. In Jotham's fable (Ju 9:12f) the vine, in contrast with the thornbush, belongs to the honorable plants which are truly worthy of the kingship. Gen 49:11 mentions the vine as a representative of the fullness of blessing to come in the messianic age. The description in Is 5:1ff of Israel in its relationship to Yahweh under the image of a vineyard in the hands of its owner has undoubtedly been influenced by love-song poetry, which delights to present the loved one under the metaphor of a vineyard (cf. Song of Solomon 7:13; 8:11f). At the same time, however, we must also find in this already the convention of the metaphorical language of the cult of describing the people of God under the metaphor of the vineyard or vinestock (cf. further the New Testament parables of the vineyard). In its most intact form this pictorial religious language is to be seen in Ps 80:9ff, where Israel is described as a noble vinestock, transplanted from Egypt, which grows up unexpectedly into the "world-tree."[5] However, Hos 10:1 also speaks of Israel as a luxuriant vine which bears much fruit. In the continuation the polemical accent is not to be overlooked, which comes out clearly in Jer 2:21 when it speaks of the degenerate vine.

Ezekiel stands in the line of these traditions, which were also familiar to his hearers. Yet with him we hear a brutal and offensive development in the conception. The earlier image of the vine, to which we must add with Ezekiel himself, Ezek 17:5ff; 19:10ff, and which has entered centrally into the preaching of Christ in John 15:1ff, had in mind the fruit of the vinestock. The critical estimates of the prophets point to the lack of fruit. Ezekiel now turns to consider the wood of the vine, in a surprising change of interest, and he knows that from this perspective he can destroy the dignity of the metaphor which has already come under attack. Who could now defend the honor of the vine wood? From royal dignity the vine sinks under this unsuitable perspective to a position of contemptible uselessness and is now no longer distinguishable from the useless brushwood of the forest.[6]

■ **15:3** The uselessness of vine wood is so evident that,

---

3 See above pp. 312f to 14:12–23.
4 See above pp. 144f; pp. 131f.
5 See also *b Hullin* 92a and, as a picture of the messiah,

Syriac *Baruch* 36–40; Riessler, 75–78.
6 When Baumann, "Weinranke," finds in Ezek 15 an antithesis between a vine growing in the forest and

by his question, God can rebut any reply on the part of the hearers. The soft vine shoot is of no use for any tool, not even for a light peg in a wall (יתד "tent peg"; also Is 22:23, 25 "wall peg").

One use for vine wood is doubtless to be conceded: its use as fuel. Quite smoothly the consideration of the vine leads on to the picture of burnt vine wood, which is yet again pulled out of the fire (in this the event willed by God obtrudes into the picture), with both ends burnt and its center scorched. Amos 4:11, which was not forgotten in the exile according to the evidence of Zech 3:2, may have been important for the formation of the picture. The question about the usefulness of scorched vine wood, which recalls in its phraseology Jeremiah's verdict upon the spoiled waistcloth (Jer 13:7, 10),[7] can be answered by the hearers even less than before.

■ **15:5** In spite of this the even greater uselessness of the wood is explicitly affirmed yet again in v 5 with even greater firmness.[8]

■ **15:6** In the interpretation of the parable, which is introduced as a messenger saying, v 6aβ once again takes up the theme of v 2. What is resumed in v 6aγ from v 4a, however, is clarified in that now Yahweh says openly that he himself has cast the vine wood into the fire. The judgement on the inhabitants of Jerusalem, who are now mentioned as those to whom the parable applies (v 6b), has been the work of Yahweh. Here, as often with Ezekiel, Jerusalem is representative of Israel (referred to under the cultic image of the vine). The first act of burning refers to the catastrophe under Jehoiachin. It is very doubtful that we should interpret allegorically still further, with Heinisch, Schumpp, and Bertholet, and see in the burning of the two ends the judgements on the Northern (721 B.C.) and Southern Kingdoms (the separation of the South following Jer 13:19?), with the scorched middle representing Jerusalem, involved in the first deportation. It is in any case clear that a judgement had already taken place.

When *b. Baba Batra* 79a relates the אש in מהאש יצאו, in agreement with Jer 23:29, to the fire of the word of *torah* and interprets: "whoever separates himself from the words of *torah* is consumed by fire," this is a de-historicizing of Yahweh's word, which is inappropriate since this word is very directly related to judgements in history. Then very directly a new judgement is announced. The preceding formula of Yahweh's setting his face against them as a threat makes the event that is described quite objectively by והאש תאכלם appear as a personal action by Yahweh.[9] However, the concluding recognition formula also affirms that this sequence of judgements is to reveal Yahweh in the mystery of his person to those whom the prophet addresses.

A later hand has sought to expand further the description of the judgement by taking up the formula of v 7aα, with a slightly altered wording (שום instead of נתן), extending the threat to the desolation of the land.[10] At the same time it mentions quite explicitly, in a tardily placed motive clause, the guilt of the people (in dependence on 14:13?), which until this point had remained veiled behind the metaphor of the useless vine, as the cause of the judgement.[11]

Aim

The prophecy in 15:1–8 argues, in a disputation saying, against the reassuring claim of the people of God who regard themselves as a noble vine, with royal fruit ripening upon them. In their being elect they believe that they are assured of this honor.[12] Although there may also be times when poorer fruit ripens, the vine stock, which God himself has planted (Ps 80), remains through it all the royal growth in the center of the world's history.

Against this security, however, God sends his word through the mouth of the prophet. Where God begins to put the question about the true nature of his people, then fearful depths open up. God's word affirms of

---

one growing in the vineyard, and interprets it of Israel being mixed among the nations, then he himself is first introducing the decisive factor into the text.

7 Miller, *Verhältnis*, 93.

8 In *b Šabbat* 20a the saying about the scorched wood is cited in an argument about what is permitted before the beginning of the sabbath.

9 See above p. 305 to 14:8.

10 Kuhl, "'Wiederaufnahme'."

11 For מעל see above pp. 313f.

12 For the distinction between election and being elect see Theodorus C. Vriezen, *Die Erwählung Israels nach dem Alten Testament*, ATANT 24 (Zürich: Zwingli, 1953), especially 109–116.

his people that they are useless; and this not simply on account of a passing defect which will quickly disappear. On the contrary, by its very nature it is useless. Again and again therefore it fails on account of its sinful human nature. "Though they have escaped from the fire, the fire will (again) consume them."

Wherever God's people think that they can dodge this divine judgement, by whatever form of piety they attempt to do so, then they are deceiving themselves. God's word summons the community to accept this judgement upon itself and to recognize that under the revelation of the living God all its honor will be turned into shame and all its righteousness, even its church-righteousness, will be destroyed.

"To live" is then only conceivable when the call to do so comes from the Lord, who seeks to reveal himself in judgement in all this destruction. However, where the life of the people of God would be lived solely in response to God's call, beyond this destruction of its righteousness, then undoubtedly all these barriers, by which men have fenced off their vineyards from one another in the self-righteousness of their consciousness of election, must fall.

The Unfaithful Wife

R. Bach
Die Erwählung Israels in der Wüste, Unpub. Diss. (Bonn, 1951).

O. Eissfeldt
"Ezechiel als Zeuge für Sanheribs Eingriff in Palästina," *PJ* 27 (1931): 58–66.

O. Eissfeldt
"Hesekiel Kap. 16 als Geschichtsquelle," *JPOS* 16 (1936): 286–292.

A. Jirku
"Eine hethitische Ansiedlung in Jerusalem zur Zeit von El-Amarna," *ZDPV* 43 (1920): 58–61.

E. Neufeld
Ancient Hebrew Marriage Laws (London: Longmans, 1944).

A. Néher
"Le symbolisme conjugal: expression de l'histoire dans l'Ancien Testament," *RHPhR* 34 (1954): 30–49.

W. Vischer
"Jerusalem, du hast deine Schwestern gerechtfertigt durch alle deine Greuel, die du getan hast. Hesekiel 16" in *Versöhnung zwischen West und Ost*, ThEx NF 56 (München, 1957), 16–38.

16

1 And the word of Yahweh came to me: 2/ Son of man, make known[a] to Jerusalem her abominations, 3/ and say, Thus has [the Lord][a] Yahweh said to Jerusalem: According to your origin[b] and your ancestry you come from the land of the Canaanites.[c] Your father was the Amorite,[d] your mother was a Hittite.

16:2   2a 𝔐 הודע. 𝔊 διαμάρτυραι (𝔏ˢ *testificare*) appears to point to a Hebrew original הָעֵד, but is probably a loose translation. It also appears in the parallel text in 20:4, whilst in 22:2 the same usage is translated by παράδειξον. Cf. 43:11; 44:23 γνωρίζειν.

3   3a אדני is lacking in 𝔊 𝔏ˢ, see Excursus 1.

b The מכורה, which is perhaps to be derived (Koehler-Baumgartner) from כור = כרה "to dig," is only found in Ezekiel (singular 29:14; plural 16:3; 21:35), always in closer or further connection with ארץ. 𝔊 translates here ρίζα, 𝔏ˢ 𝔙 *radix*; 𝔗 is noteworthy in connection with its reference to the patriarchs תותבתכון "your settlement." Σ (𝔖ʰ) ἡ δόσις σου.

c 𝔐 מארץ הכנעני. 𝔊 𝔏ˢ 𝔖 𝔙 read "land of Canaan." 16:29, 17:14, however, show that ארץ כנען for Ezekiel can have the meaning "land of merchants." The choice of the gentilic כנעני is clearly intended to avoid this ambiguity and at the same time to show forcefully that not only a geographical reference, but also a racial, and thereby also spiritual, condition of Jerusalem is intended.

d 𝔐 אביך האמרי. Driver's conjecture in "Linguistic Problems," 64, to read אביך (= אביכה) אמרי (cf. Toy, Bertholet, Fohrer, BH³) is given up by him in "Ezekiel," 151. האמרי may very well be original, though it was translated without the article by 𝔊.

4 As for your birth, it was in this manner. On the day when you were born[a] your navel string[b] was not cut;[b] you were not washed with water ' ';[c] you were not rubbed with salt nor wrapped with bands.[d] 5/ No eye[a] looked pityingly upon you, to do any of these things to you out of compassion for you; but you were thrown out on[b] the open field, for your life was disregarded on the day that you were born.[c]

6 Then I passed by you and saw you, weltering in your blood,[a] and said to you, as you lay in your blood, Live ' '[b]

The assertion is loosely repeated in v 45, as the rearrangement of the members already shows.

4   4a For the impersonal construction הוֹלֶדֶת אֹתָךְ cf. Brockelmann § 35d.

b For 𝔐 כָּרַת and שָׁרֵּךְ cf. Gesenius-Kautzsch § 22s. For כָּרַת further § 52q, 64e. 𝔊 (𝔏ˢ) οὐκ ἔδησαν τοὺς μαστούς σου, cf. Cornill for its explanation.

c 𝔐 לְמִשְׁעִי is not attested by 𝔊 and arouses the suspicion that it is an addition, since it disturbs the rhythmic balance of the four negative clauses. There is considerable uncertainty about its interpretation. 𝔊ᴬ τοῦ χριστοῦ μου introduces in a Christianizing interpretation a לְמָשִׁיחִי; 𝔊ᴼᴸ (Arm) εἰς σωτηρίαν; 𝔙 in salutem, point to a derivation from ישׁע; 𝔖ʰ εἰς ἐπιμέλειαν. Against Perles', "Glossen," 129, reference to an Akkadian mašā'u, Driver, "Difficult," 64, objects that this would correspond to a Hebrew משׁח. He wants to take it as an Aramaic infinitive of a Hebrew שׁעה (= Aramaic שְׁעָי), not found in the Old Testament, but corresponding to a Hebrew-Aramaic שׁעע "to smear over." The meaning remains uncertain.

d The last stichos, which could hardly be omitted, is significantly asterisked by 𝔊ᵠ·⁸⁸, denoting in 𝔊ᵠ that it belongs to ᾽ΑΘ. Had the passage fallen out in the Hebrew original of Origen by homoioteleuton? Ziegler, *Ezechiel*, 38. The connection of infinitive absolute hopʿal with a puʿal is striking. According to Cornill, BH³ חתלת would be a scribal error for החתלת. But cf. Gesenius-Kautzsch § 113w.

5   5a 𝔊 𝔏ˢ 𝔖 put the copula at the beginning. However, it is rightly lacking in 𝔐 before this sentence, which summarizes the preceding statements. Cf. also note a to 1:4. 𝔊 (𝔏ˢ) ὁ ὀφθαλμός μου further assimilates carelessly to the formulation of 5:11; 7:4, 9 and other passages.

b על – אל cf. note a to 1:17.

c For הֻלֶּדֶת (beside הוֹלֶדֶת v 4) cf. Gesenius-Kautzsch § 71; for the construction cf. note a to v 4.

6   6a 𝔐 reads here and in v 9, but not in v 22, the plural of דם. The plural דמים is used in the language of sacral law for bloodguilt, cf. 18:13; 22:2. Has the plural in the present chapter been brought in subsequently and inconsequentially, with the intention of hinting at the bloodguilt of Jerusalem, the עיר דמים of 22:2; 24:6, 9, already in the story of its youth? The exposition of Jerome, who describes Jerusalem here as *ream mortalium*, appears to emphasize this. Cf. the ambiguity of the דמים assertion in Is 1:15. The חתן דמים of Ex 4:26, the דמי טהרה of Lev 12:4f, and the "blood" clauses of Lev 20:18; Is 4:4 certainly reveal a further usage of the plural דמים in the context of cultic sexual ordinances, which could point to a legitimate original variation of the singular and plural דם in Ezek 16.

b 𝔐 has repeated v 6bα in error. Five MSS 𝔊 𝔏ˢ 𝔖 attest the original text without dittography. 𝔗 interprets the first בדמיך of the blood of circumcision

323

7/ 'and grow up'[a] like a plant of the field [did I make you].[b] And you grew up and became tall and came 'to the time of (monthly) periods'.[c] 'Your' breasts[d] became firm and your hair had grown; yet you were naked and bare.[e] 8/ Then I passed by you (again) and saw you. And behold, it was your time, the time of love. So I spread my skirt over you and covered your nakedness; I gave my promise to you and entered into a covenant with you,[a] says [the Lord][b] Yahweh, and you became mine. 9/ Then I bathed you with water and washed off your blood[a] from you, and anointed you with oil. 10/ I clothed you with many-colored garments and gave you shoes of fine leather;[a] I wrapped you with byssus, and covered[b] you with fine fabric.[c] 11/ I adorned you with jewelry, and put bracelets on your arms and a chain on your neck. 12/ I put a ring on your nose, and earrings on your ears, and a beautiful coronet upon your

(אדמא דמהולתא), with its saving significance, and the second בדמיך of the blood of Passover which delivers Israel (בדם פיסחא).

7   7a Following 𝕲ᴬ καὶ πληθύνου 𝕾 𝕰 𝔄 (𝕲ᴮ· ⁹⁶⁷ πληθύνου, 𝕷ˢ habundavit) we must read ורבי instead of the impossible 𝔐 רבבה (great crowd). With the חיי of v 6 this forms an imperative pair in the manner of פרו ורבו of Gen 1:22, 28; 9:1, 7; cf. Ezek 36:11.

b 𝔐 נתתיך is lacking in 𝕾. It became necessary after the erroneous writing of רבי, in order to bring out a meaning: "I have made you numerous as the plants of the field." However, it clearly breaks the connection in which the רבי of the word of God and the following ותרבי of the fulfillment are closely related to one another and do not permit any other word between them.

c 𝔐 בעדי עדיים "with the highest adornment" Θ εἰς κόσμον κόσμων. This is misunderstood by 𝕲 (𝕷ˢ) as the result of a confusion of ר and ד as εἰς πόλεις πόλεων. By cutting out the first עדי as dittography we must read ותבאי בעדים). Is 64:5 attests עדים as a designation for a woman's monthly menstruation. Cf. Arabic 'dd "to number." The construction בוא בעדים, which has an analogy in the usage בוא בימים of Gen 18:11; 24:1; Josh 13:1 (also בוא בשנים 1 Sam 17:12, with emended text?), is to be preferred to the clumsier בוא עד עדים (Cornill, following Michaelis). The two member ותבאי בעדים fits better into the two member clauses of the context than the ותבאי בעת עדים of Bertholet, which is graphically equally worthy of consideration.

d Following 𝕲 𝕷ˢ 𝕾 𝔅 we must read שדיך instead of the erroneous שדים of 𝔐, the miswriting of which is clearly dependent on the preceding עדי(י)ם.

e ערם ועריה understood substantively beside the feminine subject.

8   8a אתך – אתָך cf. note a to 2:1.
b אדני is lacking in 𝕲 𝕷ˢ 𝕮, see Excursus 1.

9   9a Cf. note a to v 6. V 9aβ is different from the surrounding two-beat descriptive clauses. Cf. the exposition.

10   10a 𝕲 (𝕷ˢ) ὑάκινθον, 𝔅 ianthino (violet colored), cf. the exposition.

b 𝔐 וָאֶכְסֵךְ in accordance with diqduqe hateamim § 71, is the sole example of the survival of the lengthening of the a-sound with ו of the first person singular of the imperfect consecutive, cf. Gesenius-Kautzsch § 49c.

c The translations have difficulty over the משי, which is only found here in Ezek 16:10, 13. 𝕲 τριχάπτῳ, or τρίχαπτα, ’Α in v 10 has the first reading ψηλαφήτῳ, second reading (after Jerome) florido = ἀνθίμῳ, so in v 13 ἄνθιμον; 𝔅 subtilibus or polymito, untranslated by Θ μεσσι. According to Koehler-Baumgartner it is an Egyptian loanword mśj, which denotes a fine cloth, which cannot be more closely defined. The rabbinic interpretation as silk must be rejected since the importation of silk (from China)

324

head. 13/ And you adorned yourself with gold and silver, and your clothing was of byssus[a] and fine fabric and many-colored cloth. You ate[b] wheat grits (semolina) and honey and oil,[c] and you became very, very beautiful [and you became fit for royalty].[d] 14/ And your reputation went out among the nations because of your beauty, for it was perfect through my splendor,[a] which I had bestowed upon you, says [the Lord][b] Yahweh.

15 But you trusted in your beauty, and played the harlot because of your reputation, and lavished your harlotries[a] upon every one who passed by; ['you

was first known in the Hellenistic-Roman period, cf. Barrois, *Manuel* 1, 470; 2, 231.

13 13a K שׁשׁ could be understood as (an otherwise unattested) nisbe-formation of שׁשׁ. More likely, however, we should read with Q[Occ] K[Or] שֵׁשׁ and understand K as an erroneous assimilation to the following מֶשׁי.

b K אכלתי displays here and often elsewhere the old vocalic ending of the second singular feminine perfect.

c 𝕲 𝕷[s] 𝕮 read the sequence of v 19: fine flour, oil, honey.

d V 13bβ is lacking in 𝕲 𝕷[s] 𝔄. It must be a later addition, provoked by v 12b, which points to Jerusalem as a royal city. The framework of the original image of Ezek 16 is thereby completely overstepped. Stade's correction of למלוכה to למלאכה ("Aequivalent," 337f) "you became capable for . . . work of love" is a despairing way out and cannot prove that this stichos is genuine. צלח ל again in 15:4; Jer 13:7, 10, cf. Miller, 93.

14 14a 𝔐 בהדרי doubly translated in 𝕲 by ἐν εὐπρεπείᾳ ἐν τῇ ὡραιότητι.

b אדני is lacking in 𝕲, see Excursus 1.

15 15a 𝔐 תזנותיך, this plural formation is found again in 16:22, 33, 34, 36; 23:7, 8, 11, 14, 18, 19, 29, 35, 43 (so. Edd. BH²), singular form in 16:26, 29; 23:8b, 17. Singular K, plural Q text in 16:20, 25; 23:43 (so BH³). For such plural formation of abstract nouns in ות–cf. further Nu 14:33; Is 54:4; Jer 3:8, and see Gesenius-Kautzsch § 91 1, Joüon 94j. Just as the fullness of bloodguilt is given expression by the plural (note a to v 6), so the totality of immorality is expressed by the plural of תזנות, which is grammatically a secondary formation. Also the similarity in sound and content to the frequently occurring תועבות may have had some influence. However, the lack of uniformity in the treatment of the word remains striking, and consistently the word is attested in the singular by 𝕲. Joüon 94j regards as possible a formation on the simple grounds of euphony.

b The concluding לו יהי of 𝔐 has no counterpart in 𝕲 𝕊. In 𝕲[o] there appears (asterisked 𝕊[h]) αὐτῷ ἐγίνου. 𝕲[AC] translate ὃ οὐχ ἔσται, followed by 𝕷[s] Arm. This uncertainty of interpretation continues up to the present. This undoubted secondary element in the text is interpreted by Halevy (Toy) as לוּ יְהִי "whoever he may be." Bertholet, Ziegler, *Ezechiel*, Fohrer, follow 𝕊[h] and read לו היית. Cornill adduces v 16b and reads לו באת ולו היית "you came to him and became his." Driver, "Ezekiel," 151, joins the statement to יפיך: "that it (thy beauty) might belong to him," and for the falling out of the ו, which is expected before the jussive, he points to the analogy of Job 9:33. Graphically the reading לויתי "(to every passer by) you clung" is particularly close. Must we then let it rest with Toy's description "unintelligible"?

clung to (him)' (?)].[b] 16/ And you took
some of your clothes, and made for
yourself colored high places (-tents?)[a]
and played the harlot on them[b] ' '.[c]
17/ And you took your adornments
(, which were made) of my gold and
silver, which I had given you, and made
for yourself images of men and played
the harlot with them; 18/ and you took
your many-colored clothes and covered
them (with them), and you set[a] my oil
and my incense before them. 19/ And
my food, which I had given you, [wheat
grits (semolina), oil and honey, which I
had given you to eat,] you[a] set before
them as a sweet smelling offering ' ',[b]
says [the Lord][c] Yahweh. 20/ And you
took your sons and your daughters,
which you had borne to me,[a] and you
sacrificed them to be consumed. Were
your harlotries[b] (still) so small a matter
21/ that you (also) slaughtered my[a]
sons and delivered them up as an
offering (by fire) to them? 22/ 'Such'[a]
are all your [abominations and][b]
harlotries.[c] You have not remembered[d]
the days of your youth, when you were
naked and bare, weltering in your

16   16a 𝔐 במות טלאות. 𝔊 εἴδωλα ῥαπτά "sewn up
(= patched up) idols." Ἀ ὑψηλὰ ἐμβεβολιασμένα or
ἐμβολίσματα, thence Jerome: *quod significat diversos
pannos* [patches] *hinc et inde consutos*, thence 𝔙 *excelsa
hinc et inde consuta*. 𝔗 במן מחפין פתכומרין "high
places, covered with colored material." Cf. the exposition.

b 𝔐 עליהם masculine suffix related to בגדים.

c 𝔐 לא באות ולא יהיה "not by the sign (not entering?), and it will not be" is certainly attested by
𝔊, but is not understood: καὶ οὐ μὴ εἰσέλθῃς οὐδὲ μὴ
γένηται, Σ ἃ οὐκ ἐγένετο οὐδὲ ἔσται. The section of
text, which must contain an addition, has not so far
been satisfactorily explained. G. R. Driver, who in
"Linguistic Problems," 64, conjectured a reading
אליו באת ולו היית (so also Ziegler, Grill, "Version-
en," 281), suggested in "Ezekiel," 151f, the reading
לו באת ולו יהיה "you went to him so that it (your
beauty) became his." Cf. note b to v 15. Even so
this is not convincing.

18   18a K נתתי, cf. note b to v 13.

19   19a 𝔐 ונתתיהו is harsh after the enumeration of
the individual gifts (𝔊 ἔθηκας αὐτά). The suffix must
refer to לחמי. The entire intervening list from סלת
to האכלתיך has then come into the text secondarily
as an interpretative addition after v 13. Cf. Cornill,
Herrmann, Fohrer. However, the perfect consecutive remains striking. So Cornill and Herrmann pro-
pose to change to נתת.

b 𝔐 ויהי is not to be connected with the following
ותקחי (Aalders), but is to be cut out as an addition,
following 𝔊. Cf. also vv 15, 16. Should it be understood as a (wrongly written) scribal dittography for
ניחח?

c אדני is lacking in 𝔊, 𝔏ˢ 𝔗, see Excursus 1.

20   20a In 𝔊 (𝔏ˢ) there is lacking the μοι as a counterpart for לי in 𝔐. It first appears in 𝔊ᴼ (sub as-
terisk) and 𝔊ᴸ. It could have been suppressed for
dogmatic reasons. In 23:17, however, it is certainly
translated by 𝔊. Cf. also note a to v 21.

b Cf. note a to v 15.

21   21a 𝔐 בני, 8 MSS (𝔊 𝔏ˢ) בניך, which must be an
assimilation to the בניך of v 20, as a dogmatic correction. Cf. also note a to v 20.

22   22a 𝔐 ואת, 𝔊 (𝔏ˢ) τοῦτο (παρὰ πᾶσαν τὴν πορνείαν
σου). Accordingly it appears that an original זאת
(as in 47:17ff) has, by a scribal error, become the
ואת of 𝔐. Behind παρά Cornill, Herrmann conjecture an על in the Hebrew original, although it
could also be a free correction of 𝔊. Driver, "Linguistic Problems," 64f, would keep 𝔐 and translate
את, following Ex 20:23, as "with, beside." So also
Bertholet, Fohrer and others.

b 𝔐 תועבתי ו is not attested by 𝔊 𝔏ˢ and is probably secondary. Further 𝔊 introduces the copula
again before the following לא-clause. Cf. note a to
1:4.

c For תזנתיך cf. note a to v 15.

d K זכרתי, cf. note b to v 13.

blood ' '.[e] 23/ Then after all your evil deeds[a] [woe, woe to you!][b] says [the Lord][c] Yahweh, 24/ you built yourself a platform (for immorality)[a] and made yourself high places[b] in every open square. 25/ At[a] every crossroads you built your high place,[b] and made your beauty into an abomination, and spread your legs for everyone who passed by, and multiplied your harlotry.[c] 26/ You also played the harlot with the Egyptians, your neighbors with the large[a] genitals, and multiplied your harlotry to provoke me. 27/ And see, I stretched out my hand against you, and I diminished your portion, and delivered you to the greed[a] of the Philistine women who hated you, but who were ashamed[b] of your immoral behavior.[c] 28/ You also played the harlot with the Assyrians,[a] because you had not had enough, and you played the harlot with them (?),[b] but were still not satisfied. 29/ Then you multiplied your harlotry[a] with the trading land of Chaldea,[b] and

e 𝔐 היית is to be deleted, following 𝔊 (Cornill, Herrmann, Bertholet, Fohrer). The ἔζησας (= חיית) of 𝔊 (𝔏[s]) refers back to v 6b.

23 23a 𝔐 רעתך, 1 MS (𝔊 𝔏[s] 𝔖) רעתיך. Since the singular רעה is used in the book of Ezekiel for a God-sent evil (6:10; 7:5; 14:22), but never for a human evil, although the plural רעות is used for the latter (6:9; 20:43), the plural is also preferable here.

b 𝔐 אוי אוי לך "Woe, woe to you!" is a passionate interjection of a reader, lacking in 𝔊 (and in the "vulgata editio" found by Jerome, Ziegler, *Ezechiel*, 36).

c אדני is lacking in 𝔊 𝔏[s] 𝔆, see Excursus 1.

24 24a 𝔐 גב, 𝔊 οἴκημα πορνικόν, 𝔏[s] *habitationem meretricum*, Ἀ βόθυνον ("pit"), ΣΘ πορνεῖον, 𝔙 *lupanar*. 𝔗 איגורין (*Dalman WB* "heap, hill, idolatrous altar"). Cf. the exposition.

b 𝔐 רמה, 𝔊 ἔκθεμα, 𝔏[s] *expositionem*, 𝔙 *prostibulum*, ἈΣΘ according to Jerome: *excelsum, sublime*, 𝔗 plural רמן.

25 25a אל – על cf. note a to 1:17.

b 𝔐 singular רמתך, accordingly 𝔙 *signum prostitutionis tuae*, 1 MS plural רמתיך. 𝔊 τὰ πορνεῖά σου. 𝔏[s] *lupanaria tua*, 𝔖 𝔗.

c Cf. note a to v 15.

26 26a The participial גָּדֵל, presupposed by the derivative גְּדָלִי, is to be found further in 1 Sam 2:26; 2 Chr 17:12. There it is used in connection with הלך "to become great" (cf. Bertholet).

27 27a 𝔐 בנפש. 𝔊 𝔖 𝔗 ביד "in the hand" replaces the singular text of 𝔐, confirmed by 𝔊, with a more usual expression.

b From the very difficult reading of 𝔊 τὰς ἐκκλινούσας σε (ἐκ τῆς ὁδοῦ σου) Cornill, with reference to Wellhausen, *Text*, page 10 note **, conjectures that 𝔊 has striven "to find a similar sounding Greek equivalent for the Hebrew words." The reading of 𝔊 דתכסן הוי לכי מן אורחתכי דזניותא, adopted by Bewer in BH³, "which will bring blame (rebuke) upon your shameful behavior," endeavors to smooth the text which contains an objectionable reference to the more developed moral sense of the Philistine enemy. Cf. however 3:6 also.

c For the construction דרכך זמה cf. 24:13 and Gesenius-Kautzsch § 132 r.

28 28a 𝔐 אשור, אל בני אשור, 𝔊 (𝔏[s]) ἐπὶ τὰς θυγατέρας Ασσουρ in false assimilation to v 27.

b 𝔐 ותזנים. The coupling of זנה with the accusative is only found again in Jer 3:1 (Is 23:17?). Thus Ehrlich, *Randglossen*, Herrmann, since 𝔊 𝔏[s] 𝔙 do not attest the object, believe they must accept an original ותזני.

29 29a Cf. note a to v 15. 𝔊 (𝔏[s]) καὶ ἐπλήθυνας τὰς διαθήκας σου (for the variations of the whole 𝔊 tradition, cf. Ziegler, *Ezechiel*, 80) interprets the image of 𝔐 of the intended reference to political treaties. Cornill thinks of an influence from v 30 (see text).

b 𝔊[B, 106] (𝔆 𝔈 𝔄) read πρὸς γῆν Χαλδαίων, 𝔊[967, A] (𝔏[s]) πρὸς γῆν Χαναναίων καὶ Χαλδαίων, 𝔊[L, 311] πρὸς

still you were not satisfied. 30/ How feverish is your heart (?),[a] says [the Lord][b] Yahweh, when you do all this, just as an arch-harlot[c] does, 31/ building[a] your platform (for immorality) at every crossroad, and making[b] your high place in every open square, yet unlike[c] an (ordinary) harlot you have scorned any

γῆν Χαναάν καὶ εἰς τοὺς Χαλδαίους. The remaining 𝕲ᴹˢˢ correspond to 𝔐, and Origen puts the Χαναάν in asterisks. In spite of the fact that the original 𝕲 clearly does not appear to attest כנען, we must keep 𝔐 (against Cornill, Fohrer), where the ה of כשדימה denotes this word as an independent apposition marked by the accusative of direction. In the construct relationship with ארץ the ה-locale would be expected with the subordinate word, cf. ארצה כנען Gen 11:31; 12:5 and other passages, ארצה הנגב Gen 20:1, ארצה בני קדם Gen 29:1, ארצה שעיר Gen 32:4, ארצה מצרים Ex 4:20. In 11:24; 23:16 כשדימה appears without ארץ. The abbreviated use of כשדים (feminine) for ארץ כשדים is found in Jer 50:10; 51:24, 35; Ezek 11:24; 16:29; 23:15f. The ארץ כשדימה conjectured by Cornill, Fohrer is grammatically impossible. If we were to reconstruct, following 𝕲, we should also then have to read with Jahn, *Buch*, ארץ כשדים, making a second text emendation.

30   30a 𝔐 מָה אֲמֻלָה לִבָּתֵךְ. 𝕲 τί διαθῶ τὴν θυγατέρα σου already appears to have before it the present consonantal text. Only it derives לבתך from בת and אמלה from מול and interprets the circumcision as a sign of the covenant. Σ τίνι καθαριῶ τὴν καρδίαν σου and subsequently 𝔙 *in quo mundabo cor tuum* understood the circumcision as a purification. The original meaning of the text, however, cannot be derived from מול. Driver, "Hebrew Words," 393, and "Studies. 3," 366, has attempted to interpret the לבתך by connecting it with the Akkadian *libbatu* (Knudtzon, *Amarna*, 7, 15, 32) and Aramaic לבא (Cowley, *Papyri* 37:11; 41:4) "anger." He reads אֲמֵלָה (מה אמלה) (or לְבָּתֵךְ "I am (how I am) full of anger against you"; cf. Koehler-Baumgartner. However, this reference to anger appears too soon in v 30. The interpretation accepted above, which adheres closely to 𝔐, has been argued in detail by Stummer, "אֲמֻלָה," and is more in line with the text. It takes אמלה with Zorell from Arabic *mll* "to be shaken with fever" and finds in לבה a feminine byform of לב (cf. חקה beside חק, and see also Aalders). However, the interpretation remains uncertain.

b אדני is lacking in 𝕲 𝔏ˢ 𝕮, see Excursus 1.

c 𝔐 שלטת is certainly to be understood in the sense of an inner raising. Ehrlich, *Randglossen*, points to *Midrash Rabba Genesis* paragraph 45, where the verb שלט is used of the daughters of Lot. Driver, "Ezekiel," 152, compares Arabic *salīṭatᵘⁿ* "loose-tongued, foul-mouthed," which appears to be clearly pointed to in 𝕲ᵠ. The original 𝕲 text has completely misunderstood the text and reads καὶ ἐξεπόρνευσας τρισσῶς ἐν ταῖς θυγατράσι σου. (Thus it repeats the זונה of its Hebrew original, takes over the first word from v 31, and understands שלטת as שלשת).

31   31a Instead of 𝔐 בבנותיך we should read בבנותך, cf. 𝕲 𝔗 𝔙. In 𝕲 ᾠκοδόμησας the word בבנותיך, which was first attached to v 30 (cf. note c), appears

payment.[d] 32/ The wife who[a] commits adultery[b] against her husband accepts gifts.[c] 33/ Men give payment[a] to all harlots, but you have given your gifts[a] to all your lovers and have bribed them to come to you from every side in your harlotry.[b] 34/ And with you it was the opposite[a] to what it ought to be with women, in your harlotry[b]—you were not sought after as a harlot,[c] and you gave gifts, while no gifts were given to you. So it was perverted[d] (with you).

35 Therefore, you harlot,[a] hear the word of Yahweh! 36/ Thus has [the Lord][a] Yahweh said: 'Because you uncovered your shame'[b] and 'made bare' your

again subsequently in its correct position.

b K עשׂיתי, cf. note b to v 13.

c K ולא הייתי. 𝕲 omits לא, undoubtedly wrongly.

d 𝔐 לקלס אתנן. 𝕲 (Σ + ἐν ἀξιοπιστίᾳ) συνάγουσα μισθώματα, 𝔏ˢ congregans mercedes, 𝔙 fastidio augens pretium. 𝕲 appears not to have understood the rare קלס (found again in Ezek 22:5 in the hitpa'el, otherwise Sir 11:4 in qal; 2 Kings 2:23; Hab 1:10 in the hitpa'el). Its reading, therefore, scarcely forces us to replace it by לקט (Cornill, Bertholet, BH³, Fohrer), which is otherwise lacking in Ezekiel, or כנס (Herrmann, Cooke) otherwise found in 22:21; 39:28, or קבץ (Toy). Ehrlich, Randglossen, פלט "to weigh out exactly."

32 32a The addition in 𝕲 ὁμοία σοι, which has no support in 𝔐, is clearly intended to connect the unattached v 32 (cf. the exposition) more closely with the preceding verse.

b נאף תחת "adulterously to choose one another in place of. . . ." Cf. further the זנה תחת of 23:5 and the שטה תחת of Nu 5:19, 29. The interpretation of תחת as "whilst she is under the command (of a man)" (Herrmann, Cooke, Aalders) appears, in spite of Rom 7:2, to be very forced.

c 𝔐 את זרים. The use of זרים without the article and the unusual use of לקח ("receive strangers") make it probable that we should see in the μισθώματα of 𝕲 the original reading, and in את זרים a scribal error from אתנגים. Driver, "Ezekiel," 152, conjectures a fuller text (תקח) אתנגים מאת זרים), shortened by homoioteleuton.

33 33a Two forms of the word "gift" are used here close together: נֵדֶה Arabic nadᵃⁿ (root ndy) and נדן(?) Akkadian nudunnū "dowry" (Koehler-Baumgartner).

b Cf. note a to v 15.

34 34a In 𝔐 הפך (only otherwise Is 29:16) there lies not only the idea of a "counterpart," but rather the idea of unnatural inversion of the human order, similar to the παρὰ φύσιν of Rom 1:26.

b Cf. note a to v 15.

c Pu'al of זנה only here. In 𝕲 the ואחריך לא זונה is not translated. However, the parallel structure of the statements appears to demand the clause (against Cornill, Herrmann, Fohrer).

d 𝔐 ותהי להפך, which is passed over by 𝕲 and following it (wrongly) cut out by Cornill, Herrmann, Bertholet, takes up the introductory words of the verse in a neutral formulation to round off the assertion once again.

35 35a Vocative without the article, cf. Gesenius-Kautzsch § 126e; Brockelmann, § 10.

36 36a אדני is lacking in 𝕲 𝔏ˢ, see Excursus 1.

b 𝔐 יַעַן הִשָּׁפֵךְ נְחֻשְׁתֵּךְ, which 𝕲 translates by ἀνθ' ὧν ἐξέχεας and 𝔙 by quia effusum est aes tuum, and which Jerome seeks to interpret by reference to the God-given gift of wealth, appears strange. Driver, "Linguistic Problems," 65, seeks to interpret it by

nakedness[b] in your harlotry[c] with[d] your lovers, and because of all your detestable idols, and because of the bloodguilt over your children, which you delivered up to them,[e] 37/ therefore behold, I will gather all your lovers for whom 'you have expressed desire',[a] and all whom you have loved, together with all whom you have loathed. And I will gather them from all sides against you, and I will uncover your nakedness[b] to them, that they may all see your shame. 38/ And I will judge you according to 'the law'[a] of adulterous and murderous (literally 'bloodshedding') women, and 'bring' wrath and zeal 'upon you'.[b] 39/ And I will give you into their hands, and they will tear down your platform (of immorality) and destroy 'your high place';[a] they will strip you of your clothes, and take your jewels, and leave you[b] naked and bare. 40/ They will summon an assembly against you, and stone you, and cut you to pieces[a] with their swords. 41/ They 'will burn you'[a] with fire and bring judgement upon you before the eyes of many women. And I will make you cease playing the harlot, and you

reference to the Akkadian *nuḫšu* "superfluity, luxury," according to which נחשת is understood as "sexual extravagance." However, the error chiefly lies in the striking השפך. With a slight graphic change to חָשְׂפֵּךְ we can find in it an infinitive of חשׂף "to uncover," which is found again in Ezek 4:7. This is used in Jer 13:26; Is 47:2 in a similar context, and in Is 47:2 in parallel with גלה. Is 47:3 develops it further by תגל ערותך. נחשת is understood by Koehler-Baumgartner from Akkadian *naḫšatu* as "menstruation." However, this is improbable from its context. For this we should question why נִדָּה, which is otherwise usual in Ezekiel, is not used. Geiger, *Urschrift*, 391–393, seeks to adduce a word נחשת "open bottom," used in later Hebrew. Cf. Levy, *Wörterbuch*, s.v. The paraphrase of the Targum חלף דאיתגלית בהתתיך points in a similar direction. As uncertain as the exact etymological explanation is, we can scarcely doubt that we have here a parallel to the following ערותך. We can then easily read וַתְּגַלִּי, following 𝕲, in order to complete the parallelism of the assertions.

c Note a to v 15.

d על – אל cf. note a to 1:17.

e 𝔐 וכדמי. MSS Edd 𝕲 𝕿 𝔚 recommend the reading ובדמי. For דמים cf. note a to v 6.

37   37a 𝔐 ערבת. For ערב אל "to be pleasing to someone," cf. Ps 104:34. Driver, "Linguistic Problems," 65, understands it from the Akkadian *erēbu* "to whom you have entered" and points to Ju 19:9; Is 24:11; Hos 9:4. More probably, however, we should read with Graetz, "Echtheit," Ehrlich, *Randglossen*, Herrmann, Toy, Bertholet, following 23:5, 7, 9, עגבת עליהם.

b 𝕲 τὰς κακίας σου, 𝔏ˢ *malitias tuas*, influenced by 𝔐 of v 57.

38   38a 𝔐 משפטי. 𝕲 ἐκδικήσει, 𝔏ˢ *vindicta*, and 23:45 recommend the reading of the singular משפט.

b 𝔐 ונתתיך דם חמה וקנאה gives the forced translation of 𝕲 καὶ θήσω σε ἐν αἵματι θυμοῦ καὶ ζήλου, which omits the ושפכת דם (apparently in error). If we accept in ונתתיך דם not simply a vertical dittography from v 39a (ונתתי אותך בידם), and see in bβ a closer definition of "in anger and jealousy," then it is best to improve the text in accordance with 23:25: ונתתי בך חמה וקנאה (Toy, Bertholet). Driver, "Linguistic Problems," 65, less convincingly, takes דמי as "a likeness, an example (of fury and jealousy)."

39   39a 𝔐 רמתיך. With 𝕲 𝔏ˢ and vv 24f, 31 we should read the singular רמתך.

b הניח, with personal object, denotes "that someone is left in the position in which he already is" (Stoebe, "Gut," 191).

40   40a בתק hapax legomenon. Cf., however, note a to 7:23.

41   41a In 𝔐 ושרפו בתיך באש the ultimate reference (the burning of Jerusalem) is brought into the image of the harlot. If, however, we give credence to the text of MSS^Ken 28, 30, 72 (בתוך האש), which is ex-

shall no longer give gifts. 42/ And I will satisfy my fury upon you, and my zeal shall depart from you; I will be calm, and will no more be angry. 43/ Because you have not remembered[a] the days of your youth, but have enraged[b] me with all these things [see ,][c] therefore I also have brought your conduct upon 'your own head,'[d] says [the Lord][e] Yahweh. Have you not committed[a] immorality in addition to all your abominations?[f]

44 See, everyone who makes a proverb about you says: Like mother,[a] like daughter. 45/ You are the daughter of your mother, who has driven away in disgust her husband and her children from her; and you are the sister of your sisters,[a] who have driven out in hatred their husbands and their children. Your[b] mother was a Hittite and your[b] father an Amorite. 46/ And your elder sister is Samaria with her daughters who lived to the left of you. Your younger sister, who lived on your right, is Sodom with her daughters. 47/ Have you not[a] walked in their ways and committed[b] abominations like them? (Indeed,) have you not already in a short while (?)[c] behaved worse than them in all your ways? 48/ As I live, says [the Lord][a] Yahweh, your sister Sodom, she and her daughters, have not done as you and your daughters. 49/ See, this was the guilt of your sister Sodom: she lived[a] with her daughters in pride, abundance of food, and careless ease. To the poor and needy she stretched out[b] no hand. 50/ They

panded in 𝔊 by the introduction of the suffix with the verb (וְשָׂרְפוּ), then v 41a remains wholly within the picture mentioning the further punishment of burning (Lev 20:14) beside the punishment of stoning (Lev 20:2, 27) and the cutting up (of the body?) in pieces with the sword.

43 43a K זכרתי and עשׂיתי. Cf. note b to v 13.

b 𝔐 qal "and you have aroused." The versions favor vocalizing as the hip'il וַתַּרְגִּזִי.

c הא of 𝔐 is found again in Gen 47:23 with a meaning of an equivalent to הנה. That a subordinate clause, beginning with וגם אני could be broken up by an exclamatory particle is very strange and is not to be expected from the parallels in Ezekiel (5:11; 8:18; 9:10; 20:15, 23, 25; 21:22; 24:9 cf. 5:8). Since הא is also not attested by 𝔗 𝔙, it must be a later addition.

d 𝔐 בראשׁ. With 3 MSS 𝔊 𝔖 𝔙 we should read בראשׁך; cf. 9:10; 11:21; 22:31.

e אדני is lacking in 𝔊 𝔏ˢ 𝔐, see Excursus 1.

f Vbβ is very difficult to explain, both in its meaning and its syntactical relationship, and is therefore frequently removed as an addition (Cornill, Herrmann, Toy). We can best understand ולא as an interrogative introduction. Since the same phenomenon is repeated in vv 47 and 56, we are scarcely justified in changing it to הלא (BH³, Fohrer). Cf. 𝔊 καὶ οὕτως ἐποίησας.

44 44a 𝔐 אִמָּה instead of אִמָּה; Bauer-Leander § 29 l. Literally: "like her mother – her daughter."

45 45a 𝔐 אחותך singular. The continuation in the plural אשׁר געלו makes it likely that we should read with 𝔊 𝔏ˢ 𝔙 (cf. 𝔖) אחותיך. For this form cf. note a to v 51.

b The plural of the suffix is unusual, even when it can be made intelligible by its reference to Jerusalem and her daughters or her sisters.

47 47a Cf. note f to v 43. Even Driver, "Ezekiel," 152, takes the clause as a question.

b K עשׂיתי, cf. note b to v 13.

c Since in what follows it is stated very clearly that Jerusalem has behaved worse than her sisters, the translation of כמעט by "almost, little less than" (ZB, Ziegler, Bertholet) is difficult. We could think with Fohrer of a subsequent glossing of the text, added to lessen harshness on dogmatic grounds. According to 2 Chr 12:7 a temporal understanding also appears possible. The קט which follows in 𝔐 has been explained from the Arabic qṭ; so A. Schultens, according to Gesenius, Thesaurus, 1202. Eitan, "Bearing of Ethiopic," 137f, compares Ethiopic quaṭiṭ "small" (Koehler-Baumgartner). However, it is probably to be removed as an incorrectly written dittography.

48 48a אדני is lacking in 𝔊 𝔗, see Excursus 1.

49 49a For the masculine הוה after שׁלות השׁקט see Blau, "Gebrauch," 14.

b The singular החזיקה of 𝔐 corresponds to היה לה which precedes. 𝔊 𝔖 𝔙 assimilate secondarily

were arrogant[a] and committed abominations before me. So I removed them, as you have seen.[b] 51/ Yet Samaria had not committed half your sins. But you have practiced more abominations than they, and have justified your sisters[a] through all your abominations which you have done.[b] 52/ So (now) you also shall bear your disgrace, which you have interceded[a] for 'your sisters,'[b] through your sins. Because you have acted more abominably than they, they are (shown to be)[c] more righteous than you. So be ashamed, you also, and bear your disgrace, for you have shown your sisters[d] to be more righteous.[e] 53/ But I will change their fortune[a]—the fortune[a] of Sodom and her daughters and the fortune[a] of Samaria and her daughters—and I will 'change'[b] your fortune[c] together with them,[d] 54/ so that you may bear your disgrace and be ashamed of all that you have done— thereby becoming a comfort to them.[a] 55/ As for your sisters,[a] Sodom and her daughters will return[b] to their former circumstances,[c] and Samaria and her daughters will return to their former circumstances,[c] and you and your daughters will return[b] to your former circumstances.[c] 56/ Was not[a] your sister Sodom a frightfully instructive example[b] for you on the day of 'your pride,'[c] 57/ before 'your nakedness'[a]

to the plural of v 50 (against Cornill, Bertholet, Fohrer).

50 50a The grammatically unusual תגבהינה is an (erroneous or deliberate?) assimilation to the adjoining תעשינה. Cf. Gesenius-Kautzsch § 47 1.

b for 𝔐 ראיתי cf. note b to v 13. The meaning "when I saw it" cannot certainly be excluded.

51 51a For אחותיך (to be read instead of 𝔐 אחותך, cf. note a to v 45) beside אחיותיך (52b), cf. Bauer-Leander § 78c; Gesenius-Kautzsch § 96.

b K עשׂיתי cf. note b to v 13.

52 52a פלל "to arbitrate, intercede for" was not understood by 𝔊 ἐν ᾗ ᾗ ἔφθειρας τὰς ἀδελφάς σου, 𝔙 quae vicisti sorores tuas. More correctly 𝔗 דבעית לאחתיך, in which התפלל is in mind.

b Instead of 𝔐 לאחותך we should read לאחותיך, cf. note a to v 51.

c 𝔊 more freely καὶ ἐδικαίωσας αὐτάς. The changing of 𝔐 to ותצדקין (Cornill, Herrmann, Bertholet) is not necessary.

d 𝔐 אחיותך is to be read with 3 MSS (Versions) as אחיותיך. Cf. note a to v 51.

e 𝔐 בצדקתך. An analogy to pi'el infinitive with lengthened feminine ending is given by שלכת Is 6:13.

53 53a K שבית[הן], Q שבות[הן], cf. Borger.

b 𝔐 ושבית is to be emended, following 𝔊 𝔏ᶜ 𝔗 𝔙, to ושבתי, which alone is meaningful in the context.

c 𝔐 שביתיך is to be emended to שבותך or שביתך with MSS (𝔊 𝔖).

d For the form בתוכהנה cf. Gesenius-Kautzsch § 91f; literally "in their midst."

54 54a 𝔊 (𝔏ᶜ) ἐν τῷ σε παροργίσαι με, following Cornill's inner-Greek interchange of παροργίζω and παρηγορέω. So Σ περὶ πάντων ὧν ἐποίησας παρηγοροῦσα αὐτάς. 𝔐 אֹתָן "The only example of a particle in ‍ךָ," Diehl, Pronomen, 43. Cf., however, note f to 13:20.

55 55a 𝔐 ואחותיך. The general sense and the support of 𝔊 𝔏ᶜ 𝔙 make it probable that we should read ואחותך (against Cornill, Bertholet, Fohrer, BH³).

b For an attempt at distinguishing the third plural feminine תשבן from the second plural feminine תשבינה cf. Gesenius-Kautzsch § 72k, Gesenius-Bergsträsser, § 28f; Joüon § 80b.

c קדמה plural 36:11. The singular is found again in Is 23:7 (Ps 129:6 with text emendation).

56 56a For ולוא cf. note f to v 43.

b שמועה, otherwise "rumor, revelation," must have a pedagogical emphasis here through its correspondence with חרפה (v 57). Cf. 𝔗 אולפן. An emendation to שבועה or שנינה (Ehrlich, Randglossen, Bewer, Bertholet) is not necessary. Somewhat differently Herrmann: "The name . . . was not in your mouth."

c Instead of the strange גאוניך we should read with 4 MSS^Ken (Versions) גאונך.

57 57a 𝔐 רעתך "your misfortune" or "your iniquity," cf. note b to v 37. The connection with גלה,

was uncovered, as now[b] the reproach
of the women of Edom[c] and all her
neighbors [, the Philistine women],[d]
who despise you,[e] sounds round about
you? 58/ You must (now) bear your
immorality and your abominations, says
Yahweh.

59 For[a] thus has [the Lord][b] Yahweh said: 'I
will do to you'[c] what you have done,
who have despised the oath and broken
the covenant. 60/ But I will remember
my covenant with you[a] (, which I made)
in the days of your youth, and I will
establish with you an everlasting
covenant. 61/ And you will remember
your behavior and be ashamed, when
'I' 'take'[a] your sisters,[b] who are older
than you, together with those who are
younger than you, and give them to
you as daughters[c]—though not as
participants in your covenant. 62/ I will
establish my covenant with you, and
you shall know that I am Yahweh,
63/ that you may remember and be
ashamed, and no more open your
mouth because of your shame, when I
make atonement for you for everything
which you have done, says [the Lord][a]
Yahweh.

however, makes it likely that we should read with
3 MSS[Ken] (Geiger, *Urschrift*, 390), and following v
37 𝔐 ערותך.

b 𝔐 כמו עת could, by reference to the temporal
use of כמו Gen 19:15 (before the verb!), be translated, if need be, as "in the time when." 𝔊 ὃν τρόπον
νῦν, 𝔏[c] *quemadmodum nunc*, 𝔅 *sicut hoc tempore*, however, favor a reading (ה)עַתָּ (so with Ewald, Cornill). Since 𝔊 preserves what follows in direct
speech, many scholars would emend still more radically. Ehrlich, *Randglossen*, כמוה את, Herrmann
כמוה עתה היית, Bertholet, Fohrer כמוה את עתה.
Cf. also Driver, "Linguistic Problems," 66.

c 𝔐 ארם, with MSS Edd 𝔊 we must read אדם.
For the idea cf. 35:10.

d 𝔐 בנות פלשתים is shown by its asyndetic position to be an addition (following v 27). When 𝔊
overlooks סביבותיה and 𝔅 translates this word by *in
circuito tuo*, these represent subsequent attempts to
correct the clumsily glossed text.

e For the form השאטות cf. 28:24, 26, where the
verb "despise" is found again alone. Cf. Gesenius-
Kautzsch § 72p. The noun שאט is found in 25:6, 15;
36:5.

59 59a כי is lacking in 𝔊, and the whole introductory
formula is missing in 𝔏[c].

b אדני is lacking in 𝔊 ℭ, cf. Excursus 1.

c K ועשית "and you (masculine) do." We should
read with Q and versions ועשיתי. For אתָּך – אותָך
cf. note a to 2:1.

60 60a אתָּך – אותָך cf. note a to 2:1.

61 61a Since לקח belongs with the following נתן,
following 𝔊 instead of 𝔐 בקחתך, we must conjecture an original בקחתי. So most commentators.

b For the plural אחותיך cf. note a to v 51.

c 𝔐 לְבָנוֹת is misinterpreted by 𝔊 as εἰς οἰκοδομήν
(לִבְנוֹת).

63 63a אדני is lacking in 𝔊 𝔏[c] ℭ[Bo], see Excursus 1.

Form

The section 16:1–63 is introduced editorially by the
formula for the coming of a message and makes an
unwieldy impression of constituting a unity.

In seeking an analysis the section vv 59–63, which
is introduced by the messenger formula and is concluded by the affirmation that God has spoken, is
straightaway marked off by its particular theme (the
new covenant) as a separate unit from what precedes.
The preceding section also, comprising vv 44–58, is
marked off from vv 1–43 by its obviously different
theme. It deals with Jerusalem and her sisters and is
rounded off by the formula that God has spoken.
Similarly the formula for a divine saying in v 43bα

appears to mark the original conclusion of the section
which precedes. The remaining clause v 43bβ has
subsequently been added as a transition from the
proclamation of judgement in vv 35–43bα to the fresh
reproach in vv 44ff. In the remaining material of
vv 1–43 the messenger formula in v 36 may serve for
further demarcation. However, since vv 1–34 and
35–43 are related to one another in the sequence
of reproach-declaration of judgement, it is better,
without prejudice to individual observations which
are still to be made regarding vv 1–43, not to separate
off vv 35–43.

Now, however, as a superficial examination shows,
the sections vv 44–58 and 59–63 are not simply to be

isolated from what precedes and identified as independent sayings. Rather v 44 takes up a catchword from v 3 and develops it in a different way. Vv 59–63 for their part treat the assurance which already begins in vv 53–58 under the catchword "covenant" with a clear reference back to the theme of the one woman of vv 1–43, beside whom the "sisters" (vv 44ff) are only mentioned later and from a different viewpoint (v 61). So already a quite general review of the editorial section vv 1–63 shows the development of tradition in the book of Ezekiel in a particularly clear way. The unit has not grown up in the manner of the collections of shorter independent oracles (cf. Amos 3ff) in which later material has sometimes entered between sayings. Rather it has been formed in a process of successive supplementation of a kernel element, the ideas of which have been developed and expanded. This development of a tradition may recall factors which have been noted in the growth of the tradition of the priestly laws.[1] How far the prophet himself may have contributed to this development must be examined in connection with the content of the material.

A further question must be raised about the comprehensive kernel element in vv 1–43. Does this section, will all its assertions, form an original unit, or can we distinguish here also parts of a later interpretative addition? If the latter is the case, by what criteria are these later elements to be distinguished?

Since Ezek 16 contains an allegorical image and shows an elevated style, especially in the opening verses, and since elements of parallelism are not lacking, Hölscher, *Hesekiel*, on the basis of his thesis of the "poet" Ezekiel, has sought to work out in vv 1–43 a poem with regular strophes. He believes that he can find its beginning in vv 3–12, 15, 24f, whilst the conclusion has been irretrievably lost in the later reworking. The clear strophic structure, however, is only attainable in the verses mentioned at the price of the removal of parts of the text, which in their content

are quite unobjectionable. So in vv 3aβ–5 the following text elements are cut out by Hölscher: v 3 וּמֹלַדְתַּיִךְ, לַעֲשׂוֹת לָךְ אַחַת מֵאֵלֶּה v 5, בְּיוֹם הֻלֶּדֶת אֹתָךְ ,וּמֹלְדוֹתַיִךְ v 4 בְּגֹעַל נַפְשֵׁךְ. In a different way Fohrer seeks to work out, by closer adherence to the text in vv 1–15, 22–25, 35–43, a series of twenty strophes, each with five short verses (*Kurzversen*). However, here also the division into short verses in order to obtain the strophes is often far from convincing. Can we really divide v 3 וְאָמַרְתָּ כֹּה אָמַר / יְהוָה לִירוּשָׁלַ͏ִם and split up the following passages into three short verses / מְכֹרֹתַיִךְ / וּמֹלַדְתַּיִךְ מֵאֶרֶץ הַכְּנַעֲנִי? The thesis of short verses also, for which the introduction is further to be compared, does not lead here to an illuminating strophic-metric explanation of the whole composition. Thus we shall have to reckon here in the basic material of Ezek 16 with a free treatment of an elevated narrative language, which is to be distinguished from pure prose and which occasionally shows the form of parallel clauses, but which does not follow any fixed meter. The mark of this elevated prose is above all the short clause, to be read with two or three accents, which is dominant at the beginning of Ezek 16, mostly in a paratactic sequence. Elements of later interpretation must then be conjectured where a more extended prose speech interrupts this characteristic style.[2]

Further, in the search to identify additions in vv 1–43, we must consider the parallel in Ezek 23. Here the history of the two kingdoms into which Israel was divided is described by the picture of two adulterous women. It must not be overlooked that the later interpretation of Ezek 16 has been influenced by features from Ezek 23, and conversely Ezek 23 has been influenced from Ezek 16.[3]

Ezek 16 and 23 are described as a rule as allegories (as also chs 17, 19, 31, 34). "An allegory in the proper sense is a portrayal, which in all its individual features, has a pictorial meaning."[4] Among the Old Testament prophets Ezekiel is regarded as the true father of

1   See Rolf Rendtorff, *Die Gesetze in der Priesterschrift*, FRLANT NF 44 (Göttingen: Vandenhoeck & Ruprecht, 1954).

2   Cf. the analysis of Ezek 7.

3   Both points of view must be considered in the analysis of vv 1–43, and this can best be done in connection with the detailed exegesis. For its results see below pp. 347f.

4   L. Goppelt, *RGG*[3] 1, 239. For what follows see also Rudolph Karl Bultmann, *The History of the Synoptic Tradition*, tr. John Marsh (New York: Harper & Row, [2]1968), 166–205.

allegory. However, with Ezek 16 and 23 we must notice how the developed form of the figurative discourse has nothing to do in the beginning with the allegory, but develops out of a way of picturing things in Israel and its contemporary environment. H. W. Robinson examined the phenomenon of "the conception of corporate personality," according to which a national group could be regarded as embodied in an individual person.[5] For this we should not only understand the singular address to Israel in the Decalogue (Ex 20:2ff) and in Deutero-Isaiah (Is 40:27; 41:8 and other passages), but also the popular Old Testament figure of speech of the "daughter of Zion" (Jer 4:31), "daughter of Egypt" (Jer 46:24), "virgin daughter of Egypt" (Jer 46:11), "daughter of Babylon" (Jer 50:42) and others. These figures of speech show that national groups or cities could readily be seen under the metaphor of a young woman. Thus Amos could lament for the "virgin of Israel" (Amos 5:2). On the basis of such metaphorical language it then came about, first with Hosea so far as we can see, that sinful Israel could be portrayed in its behavior under the figure of an אשת זנונים (Hos 1:2; cf. 2:4).[6] From Hosea the metaphor must also then have become familiar to Isaiah (Is 1:21, Jerusalem as זונה) and Jeremiah (Jer 3:6–25 משבה ישראל beside בגודה יהודה. Cf. also the faithful bride in Jer 2:2). Thus the reference to the unfaithful wife in Ezekiel is more than an allegorical image, simply chosen for aesthetic appeal. In it there lives the reality of the people. In Ezek 16 (and 23) the gap between the metaphor and the fact portrayed can easily disappear, and the reality referred to may arise directly out of the metaphor. The reality is not simply portrayed artificially, but is present with unusual power in the metaphor.

From this we must also understand the directness of the address in which the allegory is here presented. It is not cast in the artistic form of a חידה or a משל (Ezek 17:2), nor lamented in the style of a קינה (Ezek 19:1). From the very beginning everything is set within the realm of an address of accusation. The allegory is a "disclosure of abomination" (v 2), upon which the threat of judgement can follow in a direct address to the woman. Reference to the "disclosure of abomination" is found again in 20:4; 22:2 (הודיע, cf. 23:36 הגיד). In the three parallel texts the imperative is preceded by a stylized question appealing for judgement (התשפ[ו]ט twice in 20:4; 22:2). The stereotyped form of the usage raises the conjecture that there was in legal procedure a particular form (or situation) of "accusation," i.e., a form of accusation which was both revealing and condemnatory. If we connect this with the reference to the מוכיח, then 3:26 offers clear evidence that Ezekiel himself was conscious of being called to this office outside the period of his enforced silence.[7]

In summarizing the form of the central element of Ezek 16 we can say that the prophet, in the manner of legal processes at the gate (Amos 5:10; Is 29:21 מוכיח בשער), was summoned to accuse (הודיע, accordingly vv 1–34 are reproach) Jerusalem, out of which the judgement arises in accord with the inner circumstances of the situation (שפט, accordingly vv 35–43 are a declaration of judgement). As in Deutero-Isaiah the people, as a corporate personality, are addressed as the individual figure of the עבד Israel (Is 41:8), so Ezekiel speaks of the collective entity Jerusalem under the individual figure of a woman, which follows the prophetic tradition of Hosea, Isaiah, and Jeremiah. This woman is not given any personal name (as in ch. 23), and is apostrophized in v 35 as זונה. However, the allegory is repeatedly broken up by the immediacy of the condemnation, which mentions Jerusalem's sin openly by name. So then also (unlike in 17:1ff for which see below) a subsequent "interpretation" of the allegory is superfluous here, since this enters directly into the description itself and is understood within it.

We shall deal with the location and date of the basic

---

5   H. W. Robinson, "The Hebrew Conception of Corporate Personality" in *Werden und Wesen des Alten Testaments*, BZAW 66 (Berlin: Töpelmann, 1936), 49–62.

6   For details see Hans Walter Wolff, *Hosea: A Commentary on the Book of the Prophet Hosea*, tr. Gary Stansell. Hermeneia (Philadelphia: Fortress, 1974).

7   See above p. 161 to 3:26. For the (polemical) echo of priestly language which is found in the use of הודיע see below to v 2.

text of Ezek 16 after a detailed analysis and exposition.

Interpretation

■**16:1, 2** The formula for the coming of a message introduces the following broadly presented allegory, not as something to be considered, but as a summons from God to listen.[8] Through his prophetic messenger, addressed as a "son of man," Yahweh makes known to Jerusalem her abominations.[9] In this Jerusalem represents, just as in ch. 15, the center of the "house of Israel" which had hitherto been spared, as is shown by the following description, which works with traditional material common to the whole of Israel and which carries further Hos 1–3 (Jer 2). The "making known," which derives from legal practice, is described in the formulation and vocabulary of the priesthood (הודע את ירושלם את תועבתיה).[10] To the priestly office belonged the task of distinguishing (הבדיל) and instructing (הורה) in the sphere of the clean and the unclean (= abomination). הבדיל and הורה, however, are used parallel to הודיע in 22:26 and 44:23, which recalls the דעת of the priest.[11]

■**16:3–34** In distinction from 22:2ff, but in agreement with 20:4ff (cf. further the secondary 23:36ff), the judgement of the people in what follows is not kept in the form of a simple listing of sins, but in the style of a historical narrative. This is the specific language of Old Testament faith, according to which both the divine encounter and the human disclosure in the face of this encounter repeatedly occur in the sphere of a divine summons and a historical response on the part of Israel.[12]

For Hosea's view of history, which undoubtedly through Jeremiah influenced Ezekiel's preaching in chapters 16 and 23, the bright beginning of God's nearness to Israel lay in the period of wandering in the wilderness. At the entry into the land of Canaan the people first fell into the steep descent of sin at Baal Peor (Hos 9:10; 13:5f; Jer 2:1ff). So Jeremiah

and Hosea (cf. Is 1:21ff) make a contrast between the "beginnings" and the present. An echo of this way of speaking of the beginning on the part of his predecessors may be heard with Ezekiel in Ezek 16 in the presence of the "foundling motif." Bach has followed up in this section the striking forms of speech, according to which Yahweh had "found" (מצא) Israel in the wilderness, and he has endeavored to trace in it the special "Ur-tradition" of an Israelite group. This is certainly worthy of consideration. H. J. Kraus sees this established in a nomadic Autumnal Festival.[13] Thus according to Hos 9:10 Yahweh had found Israel "like grapes" in the wilderness. Similarly Dtn 32:10 and also more obscurely Jer 31:2f. Ezek 16 speaks of the newborn child, abandoned by its parents, whom Yahweh passed by as a foundling child (the verb מצא is lacking) in the open country (שדה, the noun מדבר is not used) and whom he had adopted.

The account of the happy beginnings and the subsequent somber history, which both Hosea and Jeremiah narrate, has now undergone with Ezekiel a further deep change. The whole story has been set out in a greatly extended form and elaborated in its details. Further the personification of the people who are addressed, which has its origin in the lawsuit (ריב) of the child against its adulterous mother in Hos 2:4ff, is rigidly carried through, and the "beginnings" of the woman's faithlessness are carried back to the very day when she was born naked into the world. This also may have been suggested by Hosea (cf. ערמה . . . כיום הולדה of Hos 2:5). Yet even more penetratingly we find that instead of the people of Israel with its desert tradition there appears the city of Jerusalem, and that it is made aware of its Canaanite inheritance (beyond Is 1:21ff), with the full anti-Canaanite feeling of Israel. This is certainly not an accident, but has taken place by deliberate intention, governed by the aim of the prophet's preaching. The decline into a Canaanite nature, which Hosea and Jeremiah narrate as an

---

8   See above pp. 144f.
9   See above pp. 131f.
10 See above p. 335.
11 For the דעת of the priest see Begrich, "Tora"; Rendtorff, *Gesetze*. For דעת in Hos 4 see Hans Walter Wolff, " 'Wissen um Gott' bei Hosea als Urform von Theologie," *EvTh* 12 (1952/1953): 533–554; reprinted in *idem, Gesammelte Studien zum AT*, ThB 22

(München: Kaiser, 1964), 182–205.
12 See further Néher, "symbolisme."
13 Hans-Joachim Kraus, *Worship in Israel; a Cultic History of the Old Testament*, tr. Geoffrey Buswell (Richmond, Va.: John Knox, 1966), 61–69, 128–134.

inexplicable event taking place in the course of history, is thereby introduced already into the very beginning of the history of the city which is addressed, and which represents Israel. Jerusalem, when it expresses its "Ur-tradition," must be seen as already held prisoner by its Canaanite corruption. Although Israel's roots may lie outside Canaan, those of Jerusalem could in no case be adduced from this sphere.[14] However, everything is covered with considerable obscurity. The "good beginning," which in Ezekiel's detailed picture consists solely in Yahweh's gracious action, from the human side lies under the shadow of a dark burden. The apple cannot fall far from the branch (16:44)! The assertion of the ancient iniquity of JerusalemIsrael, which is found in Ezek 15 in the image of vine wood, which is naturally useless, reappears in this recasting of the "history of the beginnings." It is found yet again in a new way in the marriage story of Ezek 23, which then dares to introduce fully the tradition of Israel in Egypt (cf. also ch. 20).

■ **16:3** In the terse style, which is reminiscent of a telegram, with three nominal clauses scanned in double-twos, v 3 presents the primitive history of Jerusalem's parentage. If the מכרת, which is peculiar to Ezekiel, in fact echoes the root "to dig" (note b), then we have clearly mentioned here the rock from which Jerusalem was hewn (Is 51:1). מ(ו)לד(ו)ת "place of birth," which is taken up again in v 4 with a slight change of emphasis ("event of birth"), belongs to the realm of anthropology and points to the human motherhood of Jerusalem. The surprising use of the designation כנעני (cf. note c) clearly is intended to emphasize further this origin from a particular racial stock, going beyond what is merely geographical.[15] For the religious consciousness of Israel what was "Canaanite" bore

a strongly negative emphasis, indicating that which was rejected by Yahweh and indeed was even cursed (Gen 9:25). Further the designation of the ancestral father as an Amorite points to the sphere of the settlement tradition of Israel. אמרי (which only appears as the name of a people) is not to be separated from the Akkadian *amurru* "West, West land." A concrete historico-geographical meaning is given to the word in the Akkadian texts only in the fourteenth/thirteenth centuries B.C., where in central Syria a land is described as Amurru "in the great plain of the *nahr el-kebîr*, between Lebanon and the Noṣeiriyeh mountain range."[16] In the Old Testament no definition of the name Amorite can be found for a specific political entity (not even in East Jordan).[17] Already the basic content of the old settlement tradition, followed by the Elohist and the Deuteronomistic History, uses this designation quite generally for the early population which Israel found in the land.[18] Thus the Gibeonites speak of "the kings of the Amorites who dwell in the mountain country" (Josh 10:6), among whom Adonizedek, the king of Jerusalem, is the leading power. The definite article in האמרי (note d) betrays here the generalized character of the "Amorite." The article is lacking in the designation of the mother as a Hittite. The Hittites were settled at first as a politically unified people in Asia Minor.[19] After the downfall of their empire, the name, as is seen in Assyrian inscriptions, was used for Northern Syria in which the Hittite ruling class were settled from the period of the Hittite empire. It could then, in a generalized way, have been carried over to Palestine and have emerged here in the listing of the seven peoples of Canaan which Israel expelled (Dtn 7:1; Josh 3:10; 24:11). However, when we notice that not only is David's soldier Uriah,

---

14 See Albrecht Alt, "Jerusalems Aufstieg," *ZDMG* NF 4/79 (1925): 1–19; reprinted in *idem, Kleine Schriften zur Geschichte des Volkes Israel* 3 (München: Beck, 1959), 243–257.

15 For כנען as a general designation of the land and כנעני as a designation of the pre-Israelite inhabitants of the land see Martin Noth, *The Old Testament World,* tr. Victor I. Gruhn (Philadelphia: Fortress, 1966), 49–53, 76–79; Albrecht Alt, "Völker und Staaten Syriens im frühen Altertum," *AO* 34, 4 (1936), 24–26. Further see also below pp. 361f to 17:4.

16 Martin Noth, "Amoriter," *RGG*³ 1, 328.

17 Martin Noth, "Num. 21 als Glied der 'Hexateuch' –Erzählung," *ZAW* 58 (1940/1941): 182–189.

18 Cf. A. Alt, "Völker und Staaten Syriens im frühen Altertum," 22–24.

19 See E. Cavaignac, *Les Hittites,* L'orient ancient illustré 3 (Paris: E. Leroux, 1950); O. R. Gurney, *The Hittites* (Harmondsworth: Penguin, 1952); also Albrecht Goetze, *Kleinasien,* Kulturgeschichte des Alten Orients 3 (München: Beck, ²1957).

who lived in Jerusalem, designated a Hittite (2 Sam 11:3ff)—cf., however, 1 Sam 26:6 for the pre-Jerusalem period—but that also a king of Jerusalem in the Amarna period was named Abdiḫepa after the Hittite (= Hurrian) goddess Ḫepa, then the question cannot be altogether evaded whether Ezekiel knew a special tradition of Jerusalem which preserved a recollection of the Hittite influence in the city.[20] It is then further not without importance for Ezekiel's tradition-historical position to see how later P has affirmed the Hittites as the previous population of the land, pure and simple (Gen 23:3ff; 27:46 and other passages). In the piling up of national names Ezekiel seeks to make unmistakably clear that Jerusalem, in its origin, stems from the circle of those peoples which the land had spewed out—to use the priestly terminology (Lev 18:24f)—for their uncleanness.

■ **16:4–14** This is the background of the early history of the city of God. It is now followed, as v 3 strongly foreshadows, in vv 4–14 by a section on the "happy childhood" of the divine city. Whereas Hosea and Jeremiah had spoken uninhibitedly of the early period as a time in which things went well between Yahweh and the people who had "followed Yahweh in the desert, in a land not sown" (Jer 2:2), now with Ezekiel we find a change of emphasis. In a way which recalls the creation narrative of Gen 1 the ascription "very good" belongs solely to the action of Yahweh, who calls the foundling child to life from the hopelessness of impending death. Ezekiel, with the thoroughness peculiar to him, introduces right at the beginning in his narrative what had only been mentioned incidentally in Hos 2:5, a reference to the nakedness of the girl at the hour of her birth (Ezek 16:4–5). On the basis of the hopelessness of that first day, the brightness

of the action of God, which is unfolded in two sections (vv 6–7, 8–14), begins to shine very brightly.

■ **16:4, 5** The stylizing of the beginning of the narrative (vv 4, 5) after that of the great prototype of the creation account can scarcely be overlooked. In the style of a heading (thereby recalling the P narrative form; cf. the תולדות headings and subheadings Gen 2:4; 5:1; 6:9; 10:1 and elsewhere) the account of the day of birth is preceded by the *casus pendens* ומולדותיך "Now the circumstances of your birth were."[21] There then follows the introductory time reference, anticipating in its triple stress the following negative description, which reappears at the end of the negative in v 5, forming a kind of framework: ה[ו]לדת אתך. The formulation (cf. Gen 40:20) recalls the normal type of time reference peculiar to the creation narrative in which it is followed by the negative description of the primeval "not yet" (so Gen 2:4b J ביום עשות יהוה אלהים ארץ ושמים). In Gen 1 the introductory ביום is replaced by a בראשית, since the creation then extends throughout a week, and the following word is to be read as the infinitive בְּרֹא. The traditional formulation then reappears in Gen 5:1 (P) ביום ברא אלהים אדם. After the time reference there follows in Ezek 16:4 the detailed description of the initial hopelessness of Jerusalem's beginning, in a series of negative clauses.[22]

In the hopeless state of the newly born girl child left to die, Jerusalem's history had begun.[23] None of the assistance which must be given to a newborn child if it is to live was given to the foundling child. Beside the cutting (and binding) of the navel, and the washing and wrapping in bands, as has always been practiced, the rubbing with salt conveys a specific Palestinian coloring. Masterman has found even in our time the

---

20 Jørgen Alexander Knudtzon, *Die El-Amarna-Tafeln 2* (1915 = Aalen: Zeller, 1964), 1333. Cf. Jirku, "Ansiedlung."

21 The word is certainly not to be cut out as a scribal error for ביום הולדת אתך with Israel W. Slotki, "Ezekiel XVI 4," *JTS* 27 (1926): 271–272.

22 Cf. the negative statements of the initial description in Gen 2:5; *Enuma elish* 1:1ff (*ANET*; *AOT* 109, 130); in a classical way also in the *Song of the Formation of the World*, *Rigveda* 10, 129 (*RGL* 9, p. 88). The description of the conditions of Gen 1:2 has become separate in form from that of the negative clauses.

23 Mohammed regarded himself as the defender of these helpless creatures among his people when he described the judgement as a day "when the [girl] who is buried alive is asked for whose sin she has been put to death" *Koran*, Sura 81, 8f.

Palestinian custom, possibly with an apotropaic purpose, of rubbing a newly born child with salt, water, and oil, and binding it tightly for seven days in bands, after which a further washing and rubbing with oil takes place.[24] Klein mentions a procedure, carried on through several weeks, in which the child is not washed, but simply rubbed with finely ground salt to protect it.[25] The omission of all these actions which were necessary for the life of the child is interpreted in v 5 in words which are common in Ezekiel (cf. 5:11; 7:4, 9; 8:18; 9:5, 10) as the lack of any merciful care for the child, which is thrown out into the open country (שדה counterpart of עיר in Gen 34:28) as unwanted.

Into this hopeless beginning Yahweh's pitying love has intervened. Twice, each at a decisive moment of life, this happens to the girl and brings a decisive change to her.[26] It would be needless pedantry to ask in detail what had happened between the two occasions. The figure of speech is not, as Schmidt and Gunkel would have it, an agreeably worked-out folk tale of the child of fortune, even though ancient folktale motifs play a part in it.[27] In all the breadth of all the subsequent description it is only a sketch and seeks above all to emphasize clearly the necessary message to be proclaimed.

■ **16:6, 7** At the first occasion of passing by (vv 6, 7, in the description of which a two-beat rhythm predominates, although at the beginning and conclusion three-beat lines are not lacking) Yahweh acts towards the newborn child, which he sees lying in the blood of its birth. In a clear concentration, which may again recall the Priestly creation narrative, all Yahweh's activity is directed through his word. It is at once both command (cf. Ps 33:9) and blessing. In an unconditional affirmation he gives command as the lord of life. In this there is recalled immediately and directly an escape from the hopelessness of imminent death. At the same time, however, there echoes in the word "life" for the Old Testament reader some-

thing incomparably greater: good fortune, fulfillment, the presence of God.[28] Certainly in the early phase of the sacred history described here the spiritual and personal blessing of God is simply a kind of promise which is yet to flower. Only at the second occasion of Yahweh's passing by does it become clearly visible. Nevertheless, already at the day of birth the חיי shows, by the closely parallel רבי (note a to v 7) and by the illustrative reference to the "growth of the field," that the command to live was not a call to mere existence but contained within it an even richer assurance. In the formulation of the blessing חיי ורבי we can sense an echo of the primordial blessing for all living creatures, according to P פרו ורבו Gen 1:22, 28; 9:1, 7, cf. the patriarchal narratives Gen 17:[2/6] 20; 28:3; 35:11). The רבה is then only further unfolded with the meaning "become great" (ותרבי parallel to ותגדלי). It denotes growing to the threshhold of maturity and childbearing in a woman. As regards bodily growth, the marks of adulthood (for עדים cf. note c to v 7; for שער "pubic hair" cf. Is 7:20) appear as signs of a future blessed fertility. All this, however, takes place at first still in a childhood ignorance and on a purely physical basis (cf. the analogous first phase of awakening to life in 37:7–8).

■ **16:8–14** After this there takes place the second occasion of Yahweh's passing by, introduced verbally exactly like the first. This calls the mature girl to the full honor of womanhood and to "life" in the full sense (cf. the analogous 37:9–10). We can see a subdivision of this description in that v 8 first describes the act of the divine marriage choice and vv 9–14 then tell in detail the subsequent gifts which follow from this.

■ **16:8** The second occasion of Yahweh's passing by is introduced like the first without a motive. The sovereign freedom of Yahweh, who is wherever he wills to be and who is therefore always present at the right time, is to be seen in this. Yahweh affirms what v 7 has described, on the basis of what he himself has seen, and

---

24 E. W. G. Masterman, "Hygiene and Disease in Palestine in Modern and in Biblical Times," *PEQ* (1918): 118f; cf. Jirku, *Materialien*, 16f.

25 F. A. Klein, "Mittheilungen über Leben, Sitten und Gebräuche der Fellachen in Palästina (II)," *ZDPV* 4 (1881): 63f.

26 Bach, *Erwählung*, would see in עבר a catchword of the "finding" tradition, by reference to Hos 10:11.

However, ought we to think of the עבר of Ex 33:19, 22; 1 Kings 19:11, behind which a form of cultic epiphany must lie hidden?

27 H. Schmidt and H. Gunkel, *Das Märchen im Alten Testament* (Tübingen: Mohr [Siebeck], 1921), 113–116.

28 See below pp. 376f to Ezek 18.

does not shrink from the view that he is waiting until the time is ripe. Then he affirms his choice. The election of the bride takes place under the protection of legal customs, as can also be seen elsewhere. For the spreading out of the skirt over the person chosen we must compare the request of Ruth to Boaz (Ruth 3:9). The "covering" of a person's nakedness is the opposite to the conduct of an adulteress and that of a disobedient son in a lifting up or removing of the skirt.[29] An oath of betrothal or marriage (the two are not distinguished here) is not elsewhere expressly attested, but is confirmed by the mention of the "covenant" which appears in the parallel statement here, in Mal 2:14 (אשת בריתך), or the "divine covenant" in Prv 2:17.[30] The purpose of the divine action is summarized, after the emphasizing, not separating, formula for a saying of God, in the terse ותהיי לי. Since this statement reappears in 23:4 and appears to be superfluous metrically, it is cut out by Hölscher, *Hesekiel*, as secondary. However the removal of this declaration of intention in v 8 should certainly not be followed. This has rightly been affirmed by Cooke, who, however, with as little justification, feels it necessary to remove the clause which precedes *metri causa*. The agreement of chapters 16 and 23 in this basic assertion must be original.

■**16:9** Yahweh's choice, in which he makes the girl his own and also thereby becomes hers, is not simply a legal action.[31] This is shown further in the rich fullness of gifts which are given to the chosen girl and which are described in vv 9ff. In this the action of Yahweh appears to tie up with the poverty of the girl, as it has been described in the preceding verses. Features of the first encounter are mixed with those of the second. Thus the references to washing and anointing clearly have in mind the circumstances of the initial helplessness and natural dependence of the child. Neufeld thinks differently and sees here ceremonies of fetching the bride.[32] He points to Ruth 3:3, Susanna 17, and later Jewish custom. Uncertainty surrounds the washing off (שטף for purification in Lev 15:11) of the blood, leaving it unclear whether we should think of the blood of birth (דמיך v 6, Aalders) or the blood of purification (עדים, v 7, Ehrlich, Cooke). However, there is suspicion here that we may have a subsequent insertion, intended in the second sense, which was oriented towards the ritual ordinance for the union of marriage. No one would miss the clause, which divides the clauses v 9aα and 9b which are parallel in form and content, if it were removed.

■**16:10** After the cleansing and renewal there comes the providing with clothes, which was already symbolically pointed to in the custom of covering with a skirt. This also is carried out sumptuously by Yahweh himself. רקמה "many-colored cloth" is mentioned in Ps 45:15 in connection with the dress of a queen; in Ju 5:30 among the booty desired by the royal women. The word is otherwise found only in Ezekiel, apart from 1 Chr 29:2 (Ezek 16:13, 18; 17:3; 26:16; 27:7, 16, 24). The participle רקם, in the Priestly sphere, denotes the weaver in colors in the making of the sacred tent; the verb occurs in the pu'al in Ps 139:15. תחש is undoubtedly to be connected with the Egyptian *ths* "to stretch hide, leather" (Erman-Grapow) and denotes a fine type of leather (imported along with its name).[33] The connection with the Arabic *tuḫas^un*, which denotes the great sea cow, a kind of dolphin (Koehler-Baumgartner), the skin of which is still used today by Beduin for the making of sandals (Cooke), is not uncontested. The name is otherwise found in the Old Testament only in Priestly texts as the name

29   Curt Kuhl, "Neue Dokumente zum Verständnis von Hosea 2:4–15," *ZAW* 52 (1934): 102–109; Cyrus H. Gordon, "Hos 2:4–5 in the Light of New Semitic Inscriptions," *ZAW* 54 (1936): 277–280; P. Koschaker, *FuF* 18 (1942): 246–248; Albrecht Alt, "Eine neue Provinz des Keilschriftrechts," *WO* 1 (1947–52), 87f.

30   Neufeld, *Marriage Laws*, 160f; also Friedrich Horst, "Der Eid im Alten Testament," *EvTh* 17 (1957): 366–384; reprinted in *idem, Gottes Recht*, ThB 12 (München: Kaiser, 1961), 292–314.

31   Cf. the covenant formula above p. 263 and the di-

vorce formula which is directly reflected in the formula of separation. See also the articles of Kuhl and Gordon referred to in n. 29 above.

32   Neufeld, *Marriage Laws*, 149.

33   So Galling, *BRL*; Frank M. Cross, Jr., "The Tabernacle: A Study from an Archaeological and Historical Approach," *BA* 10 (1947): 62.

of a kind of leather, with which the sacred tent and the sacred implements for its transport were covered (Ex 26:14 and other passages). In Nu 4:25 we read simply of תחש instead of the usual עור תחש, in an abbreviation similar to that in the present text. Along with Ex 29:9; Lev 8:13 חבש "to bind round," which is otherwise used with a different range of meanings, is related here to a head band. שֵׁש in Prv 31:22 is mentioned alongside purple, in Gen 41:42 as the material of Joseph's splendid coat, and again in Ezek 27:7 in a reference to "colorful byssus from Egypt." Otherwise it only occurs in the Priestly description of the sacred tent and the clothes of the priests. It must be related to the Egyptian šš as a loanword. It refers to fine linen which was later (Esther, Chronicles; cf. Ezek 27:16) designated as בוץ, and afterwards as βύσσος, which must have come, along with its name, from Egypt. מֶשִׁי (note c) means a fine garment, which similarly might come from Egypt along with its name.

■ **16:11, 12** To the rich clothing belongs rich jewellry: bracelets on the arms (the Old Testament says "on the hands"; cf. Gen 24:22, 47), a neck chain (רביד again Gen 41:42 for the honoring of Joseph), a nose ring ("deriving from Beduin custom" *BRL*; made of gold in Gen 24:22), earrings, the name of which, עגיל (again in Nu 31:50), must point to a round ring-shaped ornament.[34] A coronet (עטרה) is also mentioned and points to the adorning of a bride, who received a coronet on the day of her wedding (Song 3:11, said of the bridegroom).

■ **16:13** The conclusion in vv 13f is different from the transparent brevity of the description so far. It contains prosaic expressions and in v 13 repeats what has already been said. Thus we must reckon with a subsequent expansion. The connection of the two three-beat lines v 13aα[1] and bα "and you adorned yourself with gold and silver, and you grew very, very beautiful" must effectively have concluded the original description and at the same time have prepared for the counter-formulation in v 15a with which the next section begins.

The later interpretation in this section adds a feature which must have arisen from a reference back to Hos 2.

There, in the mention of the rich gifts of the fertile soil of Canaan, we have a reference to the food which Yahweh had given Israel, the mother, and which she had then subsequently given in her profligacy to her lovers. Thus here, in a prosaic narrative style, the gift of clothing is once again referred to from v 10 (in part), and to this is added that Yahweh gave her food: סֹלֶת "wheat grits (semolina)," very popular in P as material for sacrifice, cf. Ezek 46:14.[35] For oil cf. Hos 2:10 (honey and oil Dtn 32:13f). The glossator of v 14, however, appears to have had before him here an awareness of Jerusalem's political entanglements with the great powers, which are especially described in ch. 23. Thus he anticipates this involvement of "the nations" by the idea, connected by the catchword יפה, that the beauty of the woman allured the nations by her praise. The basic picture, as well as the horizon of the original scope of Ezek 16, is clearly left behind in this prosaic sentence, which otherwise uses Ezekiel's vocabulary and at the same time prepares for v 15a.

■ **16:13bβ** The gloss in v 13bβ, which is lacking in 𝔊, rounds off the idea by a reference to Jerusalem's (Israel's) transition to a monarchy. In this also the original picture is left behind.

■ **16:15–34** Vv 15–34 pass from the happy time of Yahweh's favor to the unhappy time of the abuse of his gifts by the one who received them so lavishly, which must then be followed in vv 35–43 by the divine punishment. Vv 15ff also begin with a series of descriptive clauses, already familiar from vv 3ff. We then find in increasing measure longer clauses with syntactical subordination (vv 17, 19, 26), leading on to pure prose (v 32). In content they become colorless repetitions and rephrasings (v 25aα beside v 24b, v 31a beside v 24). In v 27 there enters already a mention of divine punishment, which is not properly to be expected according to the outline structure until v 35. Furthermore in some passages contact with the basic material of Ezek 23 is traceable. Since the style of terse paratactic main clauses is clearly continued in vv 35–43, particularly in vv 39–41, those elements which deviate from this style are already formally

---

34 Cf. *BRL* 30–35; 398–402.
35 Dalman, *Arbeit* 3, 290–299.

suspect as later additions.

In content vv 16–23 speak of immoral actions and attitudes which belong together with the Canaanite cult practices of Israel and which lie in the same direction as the polemic of Hos 2(4). In vv 26–29 there enters further a polemic against political associations with foreigners, which is similarly regarded as immorality. Since a regard for the relationship to neighboring peoples undoubtedly belongs to the basic content of Ezek 23, and in its vocabulary also 16:26–29 contains many noted marks of secondary formulation, we must regard it as belonging to an interpretative addition which adapts this text to Ezek 23. However, the further description in vv 30–34 belongs to vv 26–29 and speaks of the senseless conduct of the harlot who pays a harlot's fee to her lovers. This detail similarly is a subsequent reflection, like the addition in vv 44ff. In the remaining section, vv 15–25, the two phases of adulterous behavior are striking. We may at once think of the occasional double actions of Ezekiel in his narratives.[36] However, the fussy way in which the second phase is introduced in v 23 here, the lack of clarity in distinguishing between the two phases of activity, which is otherwise unusual in Ezekiel in this form of speech, and above all the reference in the divine threat, expressed directly in v 39, to the removal of the גב and the רמה mentioned in v 24, whilst nothing is said of the removal of the במות טלאות of v 16 or the צלמי זכר of v 17, point to the conclusion that vv 24f certainly belong to the original text, but not vv 16f. However, vv 18f and 20 belong to vv 16f. They are introduced in a similar form and get a summarizing note in v 21. Thus the transition to a second phase of sin in v 23 also becomes superfluous. The basic content of the description of the offense is thus to be found in the terse statements of vv 15, 24f. (so also Hölscher, *Hesekiel*).

■ **16:15** The root of the sin of the woman who had been so lavishly favored by Yahweh lies in her false trust in her own beauty and the reputation gained from this. The gift replaces the giver. The verb בטח, which so often denotes a right attitude to Yahweh in the Psalms (Ps 13:6; 25:2; 26:1; 37:3, 5 and others),

is only used again by Ezekiel in 33:13, where it again denotes the false security (of the righteous). The sphere of trust of the divine majesty, plays a surprisingly small role in the classical prophets for whom obedience has first place.[37] The fruit of this "trust," which lies within one's own power, is an arbitrary dealing with physical endowments. The reference to immorality (זנה) dominates the accusations of Ezek 16 and 23 (the verb זנה twelve times in ch. 16, seven times in ch. 23; זנות in 23:27; זנונים in 23:11, 29; תזנות eleven times in ch. 16, and eleven times in ch. 23). Outside of chapters 16 and 23 this usage is rare in the book of Ezekiel (used in 6:9 twice in the metaphorical sense of heart and eye; otherwise 20:30; זנות 43:7, 9). It clearly does not belong to the widely used vocabulary of the prophet, but is wholly dependent on the simile of the unfaithful wife, which reached Ezekiel from Hosea and Jeremiah.

■ **16:24f** In the further image of lavishing adultery upon every passerby, which is only found again in 23:8 in the Old Testament, the unrestrained extent of wantonness becomes evident, and this is then unfolded in its fullness in vv 24f. In גב "swelling, hump, boss, pedestal" and the parallel רָמָה "high place," which recalls בָּמָה and is certainly interpreted in this direction by Ezek 16, we must be concerned with man-made structures, as is shown by the use of the verb בנה.[38] This formed the "prescribed" place for the immoral activity so shockingly described in v 25. The versions also presuppose an interpretation in this direction (cf. notes a and b to v 24). Thus Eissfeldt, "Kap. 16," pointed to the unique low altar structures built of brick, on which, according to representations on lead plaques from the Ishtar temples of Asshur, "the temple women sacrificed themselves in the service of the goddess."[39] This would then make clear, as is also possible for the אשת זנונים of Hosea, the action of individual members of the people without any metaphorical carrying over into the action of the figure of the simile, who represents the whole nation.[40] Hosea had thereby pointed to events which took place in the Northern Kingdom which were dictated by the many Baalized local sanctuaries. When we ask what Ezekiel, for whom the

---

36 See above p. 136, also the repeated ואעבר of vv 6 and 8.

37 See above p. 131.

38 See above p. 186.

39 W. Andrae, *Die jüngeren Ischtartempel in Assur*, WVDOG 58 (Leipzig: Hinrichs, 1935), plate 45a,

woman represented Jerusalem, had in mind, we are led most probably to the age of Manasseh. Here, beside the sacrifice of the firstborn (cf. to vv 20f), which must have corresponded in its inner motive to the sexual initiation rites of the newly betrothed, the same Ishtar ceremonies could have been at home in Jerusalem. Ezek 8 shows nothing of the sort in the Jerusalem temple of Ezekiel's time. We must therefore consider whether Ezekiel was addressing himself to a custom of the sacrifice of virginity by the women of Jerusalem, which had once particularly been practiced in the days of Hosea in the Northern Kingdom and which now applied metaphorically to the cultic apostasy of Jerusalem, but which was no longer properly carried out in the form of a cultic act. In this case we should have to affirm a sharper division between the metaphor and the actual sin referred to. The additional remark "in every open square," which is further altered in the secondary addition in v 25aα to "at every crossroads," may point to this interpretation. We must then think of a rural setting, rather than of the narrow street corners of Jerusalem.

The shameless immorality with which Jerusalem so disgracefully repaid (ותרבי את תזנתך) the רבה, which was addressed to her as a blessing in v 7 (רבי ... ותרבי), turns into a detestable uncleanness what was once a divine gift and therefore holy.[41] Thus the beauty of Jerusalem, which derived from Yahweh's own hands, had become an abomination and an uncleanness through its impious immorality with every passerby, just as, according to Dtn 7:26, the gold of the Canaanite idols became חרם and תועבה.

■ **16:16–21** The brief account of Jerusalem's sin has led to a fuller explanation and an expansion of the subject matter. Verses 16–21, which appear to contain also later additions, represent a first "interpretation," which is set closely within the framework of the outlook of the basic text. They add to the terse description of Jerusalem's adultery the idea that, for her iniquitous deeds, this city had misused the gifts which Yahweh had given to it. This is first set out in vv 16–20 in tight phrases, which are not far removed in style from the basic text. From the language there is no difficulty in finding here also the formulation of Ezekiel himself. The stylistic element of repetition of a similar clause, which is to be seen in the repeated ואעבר of vv 6 and 8, is here increased into four such statements (cf. 14:12ff). The fourth goes beyond the horizon of the original text, and this clearly opposes our regarding vv 16–20 as a part of the basic composition. Four times, marked by a repetitive ותקחי, one or other of the gifts of Yahweh is mentioned, which was then abused.

■ **16:16** In v 16 it is the clothes, which have been described in detail in v 10 (without the use of the word בגדים). From them במות טלאות were made in which the acts of adultery took place. The assertion must point to the sphere of the גב and the רמה referred to in the original text. W. F. Albright has sought to establish of the במות, which have already been mentioned in 6:3, 6, that they were primarily memorial places for the dead, on which a stone heap (cairn), or a memorial pillar, or something similar was set up, away from the grave proper.[42] The analogy with the Muslim *weli*-graves must then be mentioned. Subsequently many other features may have been connected with them, such as the rural fertility cult which was begun in the colored festival tents.[43] Or should we think of the "colored high place" (טלוא again in Gen 30:32f, 35, 39 as a color word for the herds of Laban) and of a colored piece of cloth such as is hung on the *weli*-graves and holy trees up to our own day? The mention of color would connect with the רקמה of v 10, which is, however, first cited word for word in v 18 in the mention of the clothing of the sacred images.

■ **16:17** The making of such images from the adornments given by Yahweh (v 11) is mentioned in the

---

b; also p. 103.

40   Wolff, *Hosea*.

41   תעב pi'el only here in Ezekiel; hip'il again in 16:52; for the noun תועבה see above p. 190.

42   W. F. Albright, "The High Place in Ancient Palestine" in *Volume du Congrès, Strasbourg 1956*, VT Suppl 4 (Leiden, 1957), 242–258; see above p. 186.

43   See also the remarks of Hugo Gressmann, "Josia und das Deuteronomium," *ZAW* 42 (1924): 325f, on 2 Kings 23:7.

second action (v 17). The strong emphasis מזהבי ומכספי אשר נתתי לך, however, may be a yet later elaboration. That sacred images or cult objects were made from ornaments (with the power of amulets) is clearly to be seen from Ex 32:2–4, 24 (also 33:4–6?); 35:22; Ju 8:24–27. Less clear is what is in mind with the צלמי זכר made of metal, with which Jerusalem carried on adultery (= idolatry) and which she clothed with the many-colored garments given by Yahweh.[44]

■ **16:18b, 19** Ehrlich, Herrmann, and Fohrer think that the צלמי זכר refers to a phallic symbol, citing Is 57:8. (Cf. further Ezek 7:20 and 23:14.) Prosaic diction and the subject matter make it likely that we should see a later addition in this reference to sacrifices which were brought to these images (vv 18b, 19). In this way Yahweh's gifts of food to Jerusalem, mentioned in the addition to v 13, augmented by the mention of קטרת and לחם, are added.[45] In the sacrificial worship given to these metal images are we once again to think of the age of Manasseh? Or have recollections from Israel's early period (Ju 8:17f) been incorporated into a bold picture of the history of Jerusalem (= Israel)?

■ **16:20** The fourth mention of the abuse of God's gifts in v 20, with its reference to child sacrifice, may also point to the age of Manasseh. This was undoubtedly particularly current in the Assyrian era (2 Kings 16:3; 21:6). With this reference to children (is the אשר ילדת לי a subsequent attempt at clarification?) the list of Yahweh's gifts in vv 10ff is exceeded. It doubtless concerns child sacrifice למלך, in which expression we may conjecture the designation of the recipient of the sacrifice as "king," and not a sacrificial term.[46] The fact that the prohibition of sacrifice למלך is found in H (Lev 18:21; again 20:2–5), in an appendix to a list of sexual regulations, supports Elliger's conjecture "that the Moloch worship was an immoral cult in the form that the newly born children, who were the result of immoral cultic intercourse, were

sacrificed again to the god."[47]

■ **16:21** After the question of v 20b, which would clearly round off the series of four (as a deliberate expression of the totality of sin?),[48] there follows in v 21 a subsequent mention of child sacrifice in which Yahweh's children are now openly mentioned. This is described as a form of offering, first denoted by the term שחט and then further by the technical term העביר (found again in 20:26; 23:37; cf. Ex 13:12; Lev 18:21; Jer 32:35, with באש 20:31; cf. Dtn 18:10; 2 Kings 16:3; 17:17; 21:6; 23:10; 2 Chr 33:6). V 22aα, which reads like a terminal summary (cf. the terminal summaries in P, Lev 7:37; 11:46; 12:7 and other passages), is followed *post-festum* by a reference to the forgetfulness of Jerusalem, which has been silently implied in the whole account, with a glance back at the "days of her youth" (cf. v 43 and Hos 2:17, arranged differently Ezek 23:19, also 16:60). ערם ועריה, cited from v 7, is found again in v 39 and 23:29.

■ **16:23** V 23 links up with the basic text by a general formula (Gen 15:1; 22:1).

■ **16:26–29** Whilst vv 16–22 in their subject matter keep within the framework of the basic text, vv 26–29 branch out in a new direction. They enlarge upon the description of the immorality of Jerusalem by taking up features concerning this immorality from ch. 23 and interpreting them of political relationships with foreign nations. The addition must be of a later date than vv 16ff. In its language also it no longer shows the tightness of vv 16 ff. Thus, in the three phases of political activity which are mentioned, both vv 26 and 28 are each introduced by a ותזני אל. In the third case (v 29) this is changed to ותרבי את תזנותך אל. In this the catch-word זנה is also used and has been suggested by the basic text in v 25bβ. This assertion reappears again in vv 26b and 29a. For the rest, the description, for the details of which we must compare Ezek 23, remains pale and clearly derives from recollections from elsewhere.

---

44 For the clothing of an image in Egypt see Erman, *Religion*, 172; for Mesopotamia see Meissner, *Babylonien* 2, 42ff, 85.

45 For ריח ניחח see above p. 191 to 6:13.

46 Contrary to Otto Eissfeldt, *Molk als Opferbegriff im Punischen und Hebräischen, und das Ende des Gottes Moloch*, BRA 3 (Halle: Niemeyer, 1935); H. Cazelles, "Molok," *DBSuppl* 5.

47 Karl Elliger, "Das Gesetz Leviticus 18," *ZAW* 67 (1955 [1956]): 17.

48 See above pp. 120, 235f.

■ **16:26** The גדלי בשׂר is a general summary quoted from 23:20. The reference to the Egyptians as "neighbors" (never elsewhere in the Old Testament) is original.[49] The pale description of the relationships with the Assyrians and Babylonians is set under the connective catchphrase of "never being satisfied." Here also we must see a reminiscence of Ezek 23 (formulated independently).

■ **16:27** V 27 is a description of punishment which comes too soon and which does not stand in any close relation to its context in vv 26, 28f. It therefore appears strangely out of place. Eissfeldt, "Zeuge," believed that he could find in this saying, which refers in retrospect to a deliverance of Jerusalem from the Philistines, a recollection of the events of the year 701 B.C. At that time Sennacherib, because of the continual unreliability of Judah and its political alliance with Egypt, reduced Judah's territory (ואגרע חקך) and joined parts of Judah to the Philistine territory.[50] Cornill and Toy (see also Herrmann) thought that here we have a reference to the period of Philistine oppression before the founding of the state. The addition (in line with Amos 4:6ff; Is 9:7ff?), which gives historical exemplification, bears the marks of the language of the school of Ezekiel.[51] Of the twenty-eight (twenty-nine with the inclusion of the uncertain text Job 17:11) Old Testament occurrences of זמה no less than fourteen occur in the book of Ezekiel (only in chs. 16; 22–24). The use of the word in the declaratory judgements of Lev 18:17; 20:14 shows that it was an expression of the sacral-ritual language for an offense which denoted uncleanness.[52] The usage in Ju 20:6 (זמה ונבלה בישׂראל); Jer 13:27; Job 31:11, like that in H (Lev 18:17; 19:29; 20:14 bis) and in Ezekiel, points to sexual offenses. A developed (metaphorical?) use appears in Hos 6:9; Ps 26:10; 119:150; Prv 10:23; 21:27; 24:9, and in the plural in Is 32:7. In the present text זמה appears in the sense of a permutative qualification of דרכך, expressing the evil of a

way of conduct of which even the "heathen" Philistine women would be ashamed.

■ **16:30** The mention of immorality with neighboring peoples leads to a further feature which is worked out in the image of the adulteress. Again it is in the form of an additional excursus, deviating from the original form of the simile. It is questionable whether v 30, the content of which is reinforced as an introduction by the formula for a divine saying, and which can no longer be interpreted with certainty (cf. note a), belongs to the introduction of this excursus. Its זונה שׁלטת could also be the emphatic conclusion of the section vv 26–29, governed by the catchword זנה.

■ **16:31a** However, v 31a clearly reveals itself as a connecting element, making a transition to a new theme by the circumstantial recapitulation of what has already been said (cf. vv 24f). Vv 31b–34 contain a development, complete in itself, of the idea of the senselessness of Jerusalem's immoral conduct. The normal, perhaps we might say "ordinary," prostitute receives a payment from the men to whom she gives herself. Jerusalem is so perverse (cf. note a to v 34) that she gives a payment instead of receiving one and seeks lovers instead of being sought after. So "extremely sinful" is Jerusalem that its sin is even turned against her own inner order and sense of honor. Throughout there is undoubtedly in mind the tribute which Yahweh's people paid to the great powers upon whom it was dependent (Hos 7:9; 8:9f; 12:2; Is 30:6f). The view of the basic text, according to which Jerusalem was dependent on foreign gods, is thus completely left behind. The references to immorality on the גב and the רמה are interpreted as places of political adultery in the sense of Ezek 23. The אתנן of vv 31, 32 (note c), 34 (cf. 41), designating the "gift," is always used elsewhere in the Old Testament for the payment of a prostitute (Hos 9:1; Is 23:17f, expressly אתנן זונה in Dtn 23:19; Mic 1:7). Beside this there appear in v 33 נדה and נדן (cf. note a), as well as the root שׁחד,

49 For הכעיס cf. note b to 8:17. For the mention of the land of the Chaldeans as a "trading land" we must compare 17:4.

50 See also Albrecht Alt, "Die territorialgeschichtliche Bedeutung von Sanheribs Eingriff in Palästina," *PJ* 25 (1929 [1930]): 80–88; reprinted in *idem, Kleine Schriften zur Geschichte des Volkes Israel* 2 (München: Beck, 1953), 242–249.

51 For נטה יד see above p. 294.

52 See below p. 376.

which is otherwise used in the nominal form שֹׁחַד
for a bribe, and as a verb again in Job 6:22. The
section must originally only have spoken of the זונה.
V 32, with its mention of אשה מנאפת, must be a subsequent definition which corresponds fully with the
whole outline of Ezek 16 which deals with the immorality of a married woman.

■ **16:35–43** Vv 31–34 also have further helped to prepare
for the following announcement of divine judgement
in vv 35–43. Both in form and content this section
again leaves a somewhat discordant impression. In
form vv 39–41a recall very closely the terse sentences
of the basic text (vv 3ff), arranged in sequence and
avoiding *hypotaxis*, with their two or three beat rhythm.
What precedes and what follows makes a discordant
impression over against this. In vv 36 and 43 the
יען-clauses cause surprise, once again pointing back
to the area of reproach (i.e., before v 35). Since vv 42f,
with their assurance of salvation, already anticipate
the subsequent assurances in vv 53ff, they must be
regarded as a summarizing addition made at the end.
However, vv 36–38 speak of a punishment directly carried out by Yahweh himself, whilst in vv 39–41a
Yahweh sets the punishment in the hands of helpers
whom he commissions (uncovering by Yahweh v 37,
by an enemy v 39). Since the suffix of ידם (v 39) has no
connection in v 38, but demands a mention of the
gathering of the enemy before it which is found duplicated in v 37, we must conjecture that the first clause
of v 39a (הנני מקבץ את כל מאהביך v 37a) has been
introduced in the addition in vv 36–38 and thereby
removed out of its original place. Accordingly the
concluding part of the basic text is to be found in
the passage vv 39–41a, to which has been added the
part of v 37a just mentioned. To this there belongs as
an introduction v 35 and the messenger formula
of v 36aα[1].

■ **16:35, 37aα*** In direct address, introduced by a summons to pay attention (6:3; 13:2; 18:25; 21:3; 25:3;
34:7, 9; 36:1, 4; 37:4), Yahweh announces to the
adulteress that he will again fetch (v 37aα*) the lovers
to whom she has given herself (vv 24f).[53]

■ **16:39–41a** Their vengeance, which is the anger of

Yahweh, clearly works itself out in two stages. In the
first, v 39, the individual enemies, who are the actual
witnesses of the misdeeds of Jerusalem, take action.
In the second, vv 40–41a, they act through an assembly
(קהל), summoned according to the law which existed
in Israel to deal with an adulterous woman. This
division into two stages illuminates once again the
conclusion reached earlier that in the basic text the
lovers did not refer to the nations, since they would
form quite directly the קהל which is entrusted with
the judgement. This will be stated then in 23:22ff.

■ **16:39** The case here is that the lovers whom Yahweh
has commissioned have no real love and pour out
their anger on the places used for immorality, tearing
down what has been built there (הרס again in 13:14;
26:4, 12; 30:4; 36:35, 36; 38:20, נתץ again 26:9, 12),
in order then to attack the adulteress herself, robbing
her of her clothes and jewelry, leaving her naked and
bare. In this way Yahweh accomplishes indirectly
the divorce whereby he declares that he "regards himself as free from the obigation to clothe the woman."[54]
At the same time the text makes clear that Yahweh
abandons the foundling child as naked as when he
had taken it up and bestowed his gifts upon it.

■ **16:40** In the second action, however, in which the
legally responsible community acts in accordance
with the law of adultery (Dtn 22:21, 24; John 8:1ff, cf.
Ezek 23:47), the adulteress is stoned and her body
cut in pieces as a punishment. This is not mentioned in
any Old Testament reference (Aalders regards it as a
feature deriving from the actual situation described).
Thereby Yahweh revokes his first action, the initial
call to life (v 6), through his servants and hands Jerusalem over to death. The burning that is then mentioned (cf. note a) is, according to Lev 21:9, the
punishment for an immoral daughter of a priest, and,
according to Lev 20:14, the punishment for a person
who marries at the same time both a mother and a
daughter.[55]

The entire punishment is rounded off by the (shameful) fact that it is public (cf. the conclusion of the
Tyre oracle 27:35f, also 28:19 and the threats against
the enemies in the Psalms).

53 Brooks, "Functionaries," 236–239, thinks she can
find in זונה the title of a fertility cult functionary.
54 Wolff, *Hosea*, on Hos 2:5; see also above p. 340.

55 Cf. earlier *The Laws of Hammurabi* 157.

■ **16:36–38** The declaration of judgement has then undergone an expansion as a result of later editorial interpretation in vv 36–38 (without the introductory messenger formula), first of all with a powerful theologizing. Here Yahweh himself acts. The assembling of the lovers, which is taken up in v 37b from what has been stated in the basic text, is reduced to the level of a secondary means of action before Yahweh's own intervention. The מאהבים of the basic text are described in an additional relative clause with the use of the verb עגב (note a to v 37), which is prominent in Ezek 23. The second description of the enemies as "those who love and hate" is determined by 23:28. Yahweh acts before these enemies and uncovers Jerusalem's nakedness before their eyes. Whilst in v 39 they form the arm of Yahweh, their part here is solely that of witnesses.[56]

■ **16:38** Yahweh himself here carries out the sentence of death, as was demanded in Israelite law against adulterers and murderers (23:25, 45 has exercised an influence here). In v 40 this has been described as the action of the קהל. In this way he will work out his zeal and wrath against Jerusalem (cf. 23:25).

■ **16:36** However, this action of Yahweh's, in accordance with the לכן . . . יען scheme of v 36 (without the messenger formula), is preceded once again by a reference to the city's guilt. Thereby the idea that the guilty act (the uncovering of oneself before lovers) which comes upon the wrongdoer as a curse in the form of punishment (uncovering by Yahweh) is connected with the corresponding reference in v 38a to the double crime of immorality and shedding of blood (child sacrifice). In the reference to immorality there appears at the same time both the metaphor (adultery with lovers) and the reality intended by this (immorality with detestable idols).

■ **16:41b–43** The intention of making clear that it is Yahweh who is wielding judgement upon Jerusalem's immorality is also clearly to be seen in the additions which follow in vv 41b–43 upon the basic text. Thus a redactor has first laid down in v 41b that Yahweh, with his final blow against the adultery of Jerusalem (cf. [זמה] השבתי זמתך 23:27, 48), also puts an end to the prostitute's unnatural payment. This presupposes the addition in vv 31–34.

■ **16:42** A second hand has then taken up in v 42 the catchwords חמה and קנאה of the (secondary) v 38 and has introduced the idea of the calming of the divine anger with the phrase הניח חמה ב already found in 5:13; 21:22 and 24:13. Within the description of judgement a note of assurance of salvation can be detected here, pointing beyond the judgement. Vv 59ff then take this up more fully.

■ **16:43** The third addition in v 43 finally shows the form of the יען . . . לכן scheme, slightly altered (לכן is replaced by וגם). Exactly as in the addition in v 22 there lies the presupposition that Yahweh's anger is provoked above all else by Jerusalem's forgetfulness of its beginnings and God's gracious action at that time.[57]

In order to be able better to draw conclusions about the location and date of the original basic text, we can now set out the prophecy against Jerusalem, without the additions, in what may be regarded as its original form.

According to your origin and your ancestry you come from the land of the Canaanites. / Your father was the Amorite, your mother was a Hittite.

As for your birth, it was in this manner: / On the day when you were born your navel string was not cut; / you were not washed with water; / you were not rubbed with salt / nor wrapped with bands. / No eye looked pityingly upon you, / to do any of those things to you / out of compassion for you; / but you were thrown out on the open field, / for your life was disregarded / on the day that you were born.

Then I passed by you and saw you, / weltering in your blood, / and said to you, as you lay in your blood: / Live and grow up / like a plant of the field! / And you grew up and became tall and came to the

---

56   For the וראו (v 37) cf. the וראו of 21:4, synonymous with וידעו, and the sequence וידעו־וראו in 39:21–23. See also Zimmerli, *Erkenntnis*, 7f, 49–57.

57   For זכר see above p. 189; for רגז cf. note b. It is found only here in Ezekiel and is quite unique in the Old Testament for the "excitement" of Yahweh. For the description of punishment in v 43bα cf. 9:10; 11:21; 17:19; 22:31; 33:4; the absolute

בראש is found only here. For 43bβ see above p. 333.

time of monthly periods. / Your breasts became firm / and your hair had grown; / yet you were naked and bare.

Then I passed by you (again) and saw you. / And behold it was your time, the time of love. / So I spread my skirt over you / and covered your nakedness; / I gave my promise to you / and entered into a covenant with you, / says the Lord Yahweh, / and you became mine. / Then I bathed you with water / and annointed you with oil. / I clothed you with many-colored garments / and gave you shoes of fine leather; / I wrapped you with byssus / and covered you with fine fabric. / I adorned you with jewelry, / and put bracelets on your arms / and a chain on your neck. / I put a ring on your nose, / and earrings on your ears, / and a beautiful coronet upon your head. / And you adorned yourself with gold and silver / and became very, very beautiful.

But you trusted in your beauty, / and played the harlot because of your reputation, / and lavished your harlotries / upon every one who passed by. / And you built yourself a platform (for immorality), / and made yourself high places in every open square, / and made your beauty into an abomination, / and spread your legs for everyone who passed by, / and multiplied your harlotry.

Therefore, you harlot, / hear the word of Yahweh! / Thus has the Lord Yahweh said: / Behold, I will gather all your lovers, / and I will give you into their hands, / and they will tear down your platform (of immorality) / and destroy your high place; / they will strip you of your clothes, / and take your jewels, / and leave you naked and bare. / They will summon an assembly against you, / and stone you, and cut you to pieces with their swords. / They will burn you with fire / and bring judgement upon you / before the eyes of many women.

Setting

Particular characteristics which point to a specific place of composition are not to be found in this basic text. From the address to Jerusalem in the second person an origin in Jerusalem is certainly not to be deduced (against Herntrich).[58] Rather the remarkable chronological summary of the history of Jerusalem, in which matters are referred to which may best be ascribed to the age of Manasseh, allows us to deduce a certain remoteness from immediate events in Jerusalem.

As to its date the basic text must be placed before 587 B.C. The threat of the summoning of lovers, which in the basic text refers to foreign gods, who then in turn summon the קהל to carry out the actual punishment, leads us to think of an event that is still in the future, on account of its vague metaphorical character. Only the interpretative expansions, which (in vv 36 and 43) subsequently elaborate the punishment very sharply, then do appear to have in mind the actual event of the final catastrophe and to be very much concerned about its significance. To what extent the hand of Ezekiel himself is to be seen in these additions cannot be determined with certainty, at least for the whole. In vv 26 and 43 the vocabulary speaks against it, whilst in vv 16–20 there is no compelling reason against such an origin.

Aim

In Ezek 16, just as in chapter 15, the prophet is speaking of Jerusalem, the place of the "center" (5:5), which contains within it the whole history of Israel's election. However, unlike chapter 15, it tells the history of the elect city from its beginnings. The prophet does not use the wrong categories if he starts in history with a clear beginning and a series of decisive moments chronologically determined. Although the people of God, in dealing with its Lord, are facing one who is beyond all time, yet it encounters life or death within history, in God's call and Israel's response to it.

The prophet does not shrink from making clear the deep questions about the people's historical origin. Against any vain boasting of a special election (see above to ch. 15), he sets out the harsh challenge that there is nothing to boast about in a sober reflection upon the actual earthly origin of Jerusalem: Canaanite, Amorite, Hittite—this is the human stock. Furthermore, so far as its "power to survive" is concerned, it began as a foundling child, left to die without help or hope.

The only feature worthy of praise is the unasked for mercy of God, who passed by the helpless child, which faced imminent death. Nor only did he pass by, like the priest and the Levite in the parable in Luke 10:29ff, but he took pity and immediately, with creative power, called the child back from death to life, from curse to blessing. Again he passed by, and now by promise and oath he called the girl who had grown up like a flower into fellowship with himself, making her honored status visible to all the world by gifts of clothes and jewelry. Thus the prophet sees the condition of God's people, which they themselves should never be

too tired to praise. Where God has called his people
there is beauty and honor, but all the praise for these
must consist in a humble giving of thanks.

However, the frightful thing is that God's people,
whom Ezekiel addresses, have willfully taken this
gift of beauty and honor into their own hands and have
used it as "plunder" (Phil 2:6 ἁρπαγμός) in their
own way, without noting how disgracefully they
thereby turn their honor to shame. When a person
takes possession of God's gift and no longer thinks
of the Giver, then the very beauty of the chosen ones,
which itself comes from the hand of God, becomes a
means of disgrace. This is not addressed to the "world,"
but to the people of God, the Church. Thereby it is laid
down that nothing is so holy, even the sacramental
inheritance of the Church, that it cannot become a
means of the worst abuse when it is used selfishly
(whether it belongs to the Church or the world of
individuals).

The announcement of judgement stands over such
degenerate behavior on the part of God's people, who
prostitute themselves to the religious (vv 16ff) or
political (vv 26ff) rulers of the world in order to gain
their own ends. The very powers from whom the community of God seem to profit will strike back and
execute God's judgement upon them. Once again the
prophet affirms that the attack of the powers of "the
world" upon the people of God is not a blind act of fate
and a failure on the side of God, but must be regarded
as a judgement, beginning at the house of God (9:6).
In such judgements, so the interpreters of the prophet's
school underline in vv 37f, 41b, 43, quite in the line
of the prophet's own thinking, God's people encounter
their own Lord and Husband. This Lord's power is
at work even in the deep shame and dishonor in which
his chosen one is regarded in the eyes of the world
(v 41a).

Another redactor of the prophet's school has noted
in vv 30–34 how senseless this sinful disobedience
towards the Creator appears in the eyes of natural
man, even though the people themselves do not notice
this. In its blindness it sacrifices its possessions even
where others, calculating more soberly, expect to be

paid. Thus it is even more despised by them. The
world in fact would have to question whether it had
ever seen anything like the disgraceful disobedience
of the people of God and shake its head in incompre-
hension. The perverseness of God's people in acting in
their own way had become something completely
strange in the world's history, even to worldly eyes—
corruptio optimi pessima.

The rabbis discussed whether Ezek 16 should be
read in worship as a haphtorah. Rabbi Eliezer addressed
someone who did so with the words: "When you
would examine the sins of Jerusalem, examine rather
the sins of your own mother," and pointed out to
the reader the stain of his own illegitimacy (*b. Megillah*
25ab). According to *b. Sanhedrin* 44b no less than the
"contending spirit" (Gabriel who contended for
Israel) dared to question God himself regarding Ezek
16:3b: "Lord of the world, if Abraham and Sarah
were to come and stand before you, would you tell
them this and put them to shame?" We can trace
throughout something of the amazement which people
felt at the righteous judgement of the divine word.
"Who then can be saved?" (Mt 19:25).

Interpretation

■ **16:44–58** Knowledge of the deep uncertainty surrounding the people of God also dominates the beginning of the further additions made in vv 44–58, which
are undoubtedly to be ascribed to the period after
587 B.C., since the judgement is clearly presupposed
and not just threatened. Furthermore vv 53–58 also
presuppose an (unusually far-reaching) promise of
restitution. Vv 44–58 compare Jerusalem to Sodom and
Samaria, the two sinful neighbors of Judah-Jerusalem.
Sodom, in early Israelite tradition, had already become
the type of the sinful city, and the judgement upon
Sodom had become the type of Yahweh's holy judgement (Gen 18f J; Amos 4:11; Is 1:9, 10; 3:9; 13:19;
Zeph 2:9; Jer 23:14; 49:18; 50:40; Dtn 29:22;
32:32; Lam 4:6). The ancient Sodom tradition saw
the corruption of the city in the typically Canaanite
sin of sexual perversion (Gen 19:5).[59] Thus the claim
that Sodom is better than Jerusalem, even if v 49 offers

---

58   Cf. the comments on Ezek 6 above pp. 183f, 185.
59   Noth, *Pentateuchal Traditions.*

a variant description of the sin of Sodom, is in any case an incomparably more offensive assertion than the comparison with the sister kingdom of Northern Israel, already outlined in Jer 3 and more fully elaborated in Ezek 23. From the theme of the chapter we then find that, beside the city Jerusalem, two cities, and not simply two lands, are mentioned as sisters.[60] The section comprising vv 44–52 expresses in a new form the ideas of 3:5–7; 5:6: the specially chosen one has sunk very deep in sin, more deeply in fact than the one who was not so chosen. It contains an impressive piece of reflective elaboration upon the theme of Ezek 16. In a still further sharpening of the assertion of Jerusalem's sins, the judgement, which is not more fully described in detail, is again emphatically justified. The very desire of the hour seems to have been to understand the inner meaning of the judgement under which one actually lives. Thus the reference to the coming transformation in vv 53–58 serves as an appeal to Jerusalem to be ashamed.

■ **16:44** The quotation of a proverb makes the connection between vv 44ff and what precedes.[61] Our "an apple does not fall far from the trunk" was current in Israel in the saying כאמה בתה.[62] Its quotation makes possible an adoption of the idea of v 3. Imperceptibly, however, this moves in a different direction, which has no anticipation there.

■ **16:45** The reference to the mother who repudiates (געל only here in Ezekiel, cf., however, Lev 26:11, 15, 30, 43f) both her husband (vv 15ff, without any further explicit mention of the husband) and children (v 20) is followed directly by a mention of the "sisters" among whom Jerusalem is not out of company. Vv 45bβ–46 present the whole notorious family. V 3b, to which the משל has already pointed, is then explicitly quoted. The mention of the mother, who alone was referred to in the proverb, is then put at the beginning, unlike v 3b. The second feminine singular suffixes are changed to refer to the enlarged circle of daughters

in the second person plural. In introducing the sisters Samaria appears historically as more important (in dependence on Jer 3 and Ezek 23?) and as the elder sister.[63] It is not properly clear why Samaria and Sodom are not mentioned alone, but with their daughters. Is this intended to obscure the fact that the repudiation of "husband and children" which was said in v 45 also about Samaria and Sodom and which needed to be explained is not further mentioned? Or has the ancient formulation עיר ובנותיה (cf. Ju 1:27 "Taanach and its daughters . . . Megiddo and its daughters") influenced it?[64]

■ **16:47** If, according to the expanded exposition of the משל, Jerusalem in its wickedness appears to be on a level with the two sisters, Samaria and Sodom, then v 47 adds the surprising new emphasis that Jerusalem is worse than the others. This goes beyond the introductory proverb.

■ **16:48** The accusation is reaffirmed in v 48 by an oath from Yahweh himself referring to Sodom—precisely Sodom which is known for its wickedness! In this we find the "daughters of Jerusalem" beside the city itself. It is then not quite clear why Sodom's guilt is described as pride, gluttony, complacency, and social irresponsibility which arises from it. This is surprising when compared with Gen 19. Are we to look for a variant tradition behind this, or should we regard it simply as a straightforward adaptation arising from typical social conditions in Israel? The latter is more probable. A parallel elaboration of the sins of Samaria is lacking. However, the accusation of sin against Jerusalem, when compared with Samaria, takes on a new emphasis. She has not committed half the sins of Jerusalem. Thus the misdeeds of the sisters, set against the background of Jerusalem's actions, are given a strange "justification" (צדק vv 51f), and Jerusalem, by its wickedness, unintentionally assumes something of the burden of their guilt. This gives a strange negative twist to a forensic act (פלל Koehler-

60   For the avoidance of the name Israel for the Northern Kingdom which this makes possible see Auerbach, *VT* 8 (1958): 9.

61   See above p. 333 for the link in v 43bβ.

62   See Hempel, *Literatur*, 46. For משל see above p. 280.

63   For left = north; right = south see above p. 166. Is there a further emphasis in that Sodom is on the right (= honorable) side of Jerusalem?

64   Albrecht Alt, "Megiddo im Übergang vom kanaanäischen zum israelitischen Zeitalter," *ZAW* 60 (1944): 80; reprinted in *idem, Kleine Schriften zur Geschichte des Volkes Israel* 1 (München: Beck, 1953), 268.

Baumgartner "to act as arbitrator for").[65]

The whole section finishes up with a passionate summons to Jerusalem, formulated in the imperative, to bear its disgrace, in view of the so unexpected and striking comparison with Sodom and Samaria. The phrase נשא כלמה, which is peculiar to the book of Ezekiel (beside the two occurrences in v 52 it is found again in v 54; 32:24f, 30; 34:29; 36:6f; 39:26 Q; 44:13; altered to נשא חרפה 36:15; Mic 6:16, cf; also to v 58), is undoubtedly formed in dependence on the legal formula for the declaration of guilt נשא עון.[66] This brings to expression the idea that guilt (through its punishment by Yahweh) is also a disgrace in the eyes of the people.[67] If the legal explanation of the fact of guilt should properly be set out in the indicative or jussive third person style (cf. the perfect v 58), the declaration in the prophet's speech here has been changed into an impassioned appeal, which demands the recognition of guilt and the acceptance of the disgrace attaching to it by those who are guilty and under judgement. Dependence of style and alterations to it can be seen here very clearly.

■ **16:53–58** The appeal to acknowledge the disgrace inflicted by Yahweh and to submit to it also dominates the further development in vv 53–58, which, surprisingly, points to a turning point. We may question whether it derives from another hand than vv 44–52.

However, the close connections in content between the two sections oppose such a division. Vv 53–58 are not intended to be understood as the first announcement of a coming transformation. This turning point is expressed by the phrase שוב שבו/ית, which is not peculiar to Ezekiel, but is already to be found from the time of Hosea (Hos 6:11, thence Amos 9:14; Zeph 2:7; 3:20; Jer 29:14; 30:3, 18; 31:23; 48:47;

Dtn 30:3; Ps 14:7; 53:7; 85:2; 126:4; again in Ezekiel 29:14, as well as 39:25 השיב שבו/ית, as also Jer 32:44; 33:7, 11, 26 Q; 49:6, 39 Q; Joel 4:1; Lam 2:4) and is clearly presupposed as already known.[68] Whether שבו/ית originally derived from שוב the idea of restoration or from שבה that of the lifting of a state of arrest on account of guilt has so far not been finally explained.[69]

■ **16:53, 54** The particular emphasis lies in the present text on the extent of the coming deliverance. Samaria and Sodom will also have a share in it. "In the midst of them" (בתוכהנה) Jerusalem will also receive favor, so that it (this final assertion of v 54 should not be overlooked!) may come to an acceptance of the disgrace that has come upon it and humble itself in the recognition of the peculiar "consolation" which this means for Sodom and Samaria. נחם here is to be understood as parallel to צדק and פלל vv 51f. As Vischer rightly affirms, there is therewith a particular forensic element in the נחם: "Paradoxically it means that the one who sinned more than Sodom and Samaria defends these two sisters before God's judgement of the world and effects their rehabilitation."[70]

■ **16:55** The return to their former state, which v 55 asserts of all three cities with circumstantial detail and fresh vocabulary, naturally does not mean a return to the old wickedness of Sodom and of the other cities, but their cleansing and restoration, although any more precise definition of this is lacking.

The prophecy then returns to the main theme: just as Sodom was once the city of exemplary disgrace and became proverbial as such (for לשמועה cf. note b), so now after the judgement (the "uncovering of nakedness" according to vv 37, 39) Jerusalem is to become an object of reproach among its neighbors (cf. notes

---

65   B. Gemser, "The *rīb*—or Controversy—Pattern in Hebrew Mentality" in *Wisdom in Israel and in the Ancient Near East*, ed. Martin Noth, VT Suppl 3 (Leiden: Brill, 1955), 124.

66   See above p. 305.

67   Cf. the mention of the women witnessing it in v 41, also vv 56f.

68   Cf., however, R. Borger, "Zu שוב שבו/ית," *ZAW* 66 (1954 [1955]): 315–316; note a to v 53.

69   The former is the explanation of Ernst Ludwig Dietrich, שוב שבות. *Die endzeitliche Wiederherstellung bei den Propheten*, BZAW 40 (Giessen: Töpelmann,

1925); the latter, that of Eberhard Baumann, "שוב שבות. Eine exegetische Untersuchung," *ZAW* 47 (1929): 17–44, especially 22–24; subsequently Koehler-Baumgartner.

70   Vischer, "Jerusalem," 33.

c and d).[71] Verse 58, formulated analogously to v 52, concludes the events of vv 44–52 and expresses the final judgement. The old legal formula, which is here used indicatively, unlike in v 52, is then appended, although the original עון is changed to the double expression זמה (cf. to v 27) and תועבות.[72] The statement about the connection between guilt and punishment becomes quite clear in its synthetic character: in carrying its punishment Jerusalem is carrying its own trespasses and its abomination.

Aim

In inexorable severity the addition in vv 44–58 emphasizes yet again the inescapable sinfulness of the city of God, which feels secure in its own election (יום גאונך v 56). Even less than Sodom and Samaria, the city's greatly despised "fallen" neighbors, is there anything worthy of praise in her. It is all the bitter fruit of the same tree. Indeed self-righteous Jerusalem, the chosen people of God, had fallen lower than her sisters, and had in this way unwittingly given them a strange "justification." In that God, in his righteousness, could not be less gracious to these sinners than to Jerusalem itself, the disgrace of those who were so proud of their election could only be complete when the pure light of the divine grace began to shine over those who were lost. Something of the truth which Paul (Romans 11) began to discern later is undoubtedly anticipated much earlier here, that God, in his grace towards those who are "outside," provokes his children who are "within" to a recognition of the grace of righteousness, even though to them belong sonship, the presence of God, the covenant, the law, worship, the promise, the patriarchs, and even Christ himself (Rom 9:4f).

Interpretation

■ **16:59–63** In conclusion a final explanatory oracle in vv 59–63 undertakes to set out fully the mystery of the divine faithfulness, which has already been introduced in the promise of the coming transformation. Once again it is clear that this concluding oracle is not to be regarded as an independent composition, but as a conclusion to the assertions which precede it. Within the framework of the marriage metaphor v 8 refers to the "covenant" which Yahweh entered into with the young girl. The reference to the covenant, which Israel used in its older tradition as a comprehensive expression for its relationship to God, appears in the book of Ezekiel as an independent part of the tradition, occurring occasionally in different sections (besides 16:8, 59–62; again in 34:25; 37:26; 44:7; cf. 17:13–19; 20:37 [textual error], and untheologically also in 30:5).[73] Its content in the covenant formulation is unfolded at several important points.[74] Even so the word itself does not belong to the specific theological vocabulary of Ezekiel. Thus, in the present text, the major emphasis lies on the זכר, which appears earlier in vv 22, 43.[75] Against Jerusalem's "not remembering" v 60 sets the gracious "remembering" by Yahweh, through which Jerusalem is to be brought to a right "remembering" (vv 61, 63), with a sense of its own shame.

In form the section is set out as a proof-saying in two parts.[76] The motive clause is missing for understandable reasons because especially here the inconceivable free act of Yahweh is expressed. This action will follow Jerusalem's recognition (v 62b). Once again Yahweh's purpose for Jerusalem is shown beyond that contained in the recognition formula.

■ **16:59–61** The mention of Yahweh's new action is preceded in v 59 by a recollection of the punishment inflicted by him (cf. 11:16 before vv 17ff). Jerusalem's faithlessness towards its divine partner is affirmed by the formulation which is used in 17:18 to describe the political breach of covenant by Zedekiah. This shows that Yahweh's punishment is, in reality, simply the righteous judgement foreseen in the covenant

---

71 For the mockery of the neighbors, among whom the Edomites, because of their participation in the destruction of Jerusalem, become the most hated, cf. 25:1–14.

72 See above p. 190.

73 Walther Eichrodt, *Theology of the Old Testament* 1, tr. J. A. Baker (Philadelphia: Westminster, 1961); von Rad, *OT Theology* 1, 129–135.

74 See above p. 263.

75 See especially p. 189.

76 See Zimmerli, "Wort," 163.

which imposes obligations on both parties. Yahweh does in judgement what his covenant partner has done in disloyalty. Over against this it is surprising that Yahweh remembers the covenant of Jerusalem's youth, and this remembering takes the form of his establishing (הקים) an everlasting covenant (again in 37:26; cf. 34:25) with them.[77] In this it becomes quite clear that this promise for Jerusalem's future does not mean a superficial and hasty glossing over of the past under the impact of a miracle of social and architectural reconstruction in Jerusalem, but that the shameful memory will continue to remain alive. In a glance back to vv 53ff, and at the same time in continuation of what is said there, the two sisters Sodom and Samaria are recalled, and it is asserted that they will be given to Jerusalem as "daughters." This may be meant in the sense of Ju 1:27 (cf. to v 46) and in any case asserts that the divine transformation of his elect city does not deny the truth about its origin, but rather adds a new gift to it. More concretely we may think of Jerusalem's being restored in the context of a greater Israel, in which Samaria, the capital of the Northern Kingdom, and Sodom, sought for at the bottom of the Jordan Valley, will not be missing. The new sketch of the division of the land in 47:13ff and the promise of the healing of the Dead Sea (47:8ff) point to the same view of things, without making any further reference to the formulation of 16:61. The ולא מבריתך is difficult to interpret. Does it mean that the two sisters will certainly be accepted, but not be made members of the same covenant, which would have in mind the permanent position of Jerusalem as the temple city (chs. 40ff)? Or is it to be understood as looking back so that Yahweh acts towards Sodom and Samaria beyond all that has hitherto been foreseen

in the covenant?

■ **16:62, 63** The recognition formula, which rounds off the proof-saying, also endeavors to express here that Yahweh discloses the mystery of his own being in his saving action. It asserts emphatically, in connection with this final addition, that such recognition will include Jerusalem's "remembering," its being ashamed, and its humble silence before God. The reconciliation which Yahweh will bring to his sinful people (for כפר cf. 43:20, 26; 45:15, 17) will effect such a recognition.

Aim

The last part of the later interpretative additions to the chapter, in which the disciples of Ezekiel carry further the lines of the prophet's preaching, points back to the heart of the basic text. Out of the affront to the free and gracious kindness of God towards the lost girl, the harsh accusations of the basic text grew. This free and gracious kindness, however, God now once again asserts as his valid "everlasting" intention, which will not be disregarded, even through the terrible judgement and Jerusalem's deserving of death. Through his judgement God will lead his people so that they will be made ashamed of the overplus of grace shown to them and will be pleased to accept as a daughter the Canaanite Sodom which they had hitherto rejected as too sinful. By such action they will come to recognize their God and know who he is.

---

77   See Ernst Jenni, "Das Wort ʿōlām im Alten Testament. III. Hauptteil," *ZAW* 65 (1953 [1954]): 21f.

The Eagle, the Cedar and the Vine
(Zedekiah's Breach of Covenant)

Bibliography

W. Erbt
"Die Fürstensprüche im Hesekielbuche," *OLZ* 20 (1917): 270–274, 289–296.

M. Greenberg
"Ezekiel 17 and the Policy of Psammetichus II," *JBL* 76 (1957): 304–309.

V. Korošec
Hethitische Staatsverträge. Ein Beitrag zu ihrer iuristischen Wertung, LRSt 60 (Leipzig: Weicher, 1931).

G. E. Mendenhall
"Covenant Forms in Israelite Tradition," *BA* 17 (1954): 50–76.

K. von Rabenau
"Die Form des Rätsels im Buche Hesekiel," *Wiss. Z. Halle* GR 7, 5 (1958): 1055–1057.

L. P. Smith
"The Eagle(s) of Ezekiel 17," *JBL* 58 (1939): 43–50.

17

1

ªAnd the word of Yahweh came to me:
2/ Son of man, declare a riddle, and
speak a parable to the house of Israel,
3/ and say: Thus has [the Lord]ª Yahweh
said:
The great eagle
with great wings,
with long pinions,
with full plumage,ᵇ
which had brightly colored feathers,ᶜ
came to Lebanon
and took the topᵈ of the cedar.
4/ He broke off the topmost shootª
and brought it to a land of traders,ᵇ
into the city of merchantsᵇ he set it.

5

And he took some of the seed of the land
and planted it in a fertile field,
' ';ª he placed it beside abundant waters

17:
1

1a 𝕲⁶²·⁴⁴⁹⁽⁴¹⁰⁾ preface with a heading: (ἡ) περὶ τῶν ἀετῶν παραβολή. 𝕲ᵠᵐᵍ περὶ τοῦ ἀετοῦ μεγάλου.

3

3a אדני is lacking in 𝕲 𝔏ᶜ 𝔗ᴮᵒ, see Excursus 1.
b 𝔐 נוצה is found again in v 7; Lev 1:16 (?); Job 39:13. 𝔐 מָלֵא is taken as a verb. Cf. Dtn 33:23 besides the nominal מְלָא יָמִים Jer 6:11 (Ehrlich). 𝕲 misunderstands as πλήρης ὀνύχων, 𝔏ᶜ *plena unguibus* (also in v 7).
c Driver, "Ezekiel," 152, because of the unusual article in 𝔐, suggests pointing as a verb הָרִקְמָה. 𝕲 misinterprets ἥγημα, 𝔏ᶜ *ducatum*.
d צמרת only in Ezekiel (17:3, 22; 31:3, 10, 14). 𝕲 ἐπίλεκτα, 𝔏ᶜ *electa*, in ch. 31 more correctly ἀρχή.

4

4a יניקה only found here in the Old Testament. 17:22 gives the more usual form יונקת; cf. Hos 14:7; Ps 80:12; Job 8:16; 14:7; 15:30; the masculine יונק Is 53:2. An assimilation of the forms should not be accepted since vv 22–24 ought not to be written in the same way as vv 1ff.
b Whilst 𝕲 interprets the כנען of 𝔐 as the proper name of Canaan and also translates the following בעיר רכלים in an unusual way with εἰς πόλιν τετειχισμένην (𝔏ᶜ *in civitate murata*), a part of the later tradition lifts the veil of the metaphor. 𝕲ᴬ Χαλδαίων, 𝕲²²ᶜ Βαβυλῶν. 𝔗 interprets as "land which has no worship" and "city into which the house of Israel has not come."

5

5a The unintelligible קח of 𝔐, which Driver, "Ezekiel," 152, would interpret according to the Syriac קוחא, Akkadian *qū*, as "shoot, stalk," is not attested by 𝕲 𝔏ᶜ 𝕾 𝕮 𝔄. How 𝔅 came to its *ut firmaret*

like a growth on a river bank,[b]
6/ 'that it should sprout and become'[a] a
    fast growing[b] vine,
spreading low,
and[c] its branches[d] turned towards him
and its roots remained under him.[e]
And it became[f] a vine
and put forth shoots
and stretched out branches.[g]

7 But there was another[a]
    great eagle,
with great wings
and many feathers;
and behold, this vine
bent[b] its roots towards[c] him

radicem remains obscure. The קיו of Bab. MS E 22 is a simple scribal error for קם. This must be explained as a vertical dittography for the ויק from a and is to be deleted (Cornill, Toy, and others).

b 𝔐 צפצפה hapax legomenon, Arabic *ṣafṣāfat^un* "pasture," so Gesenius-Buhl, Koehler-Baumgartner, Zorell. However, if we wish to defend the word as original here we must take it as a more general designation, *ℨB* "shore growth." G. R. Driver conjectures, from the Akkadian *ṣippatu*, a reading צפה "fruit tree." 𝔊 ἐπιβλεπόμενον, 𝔏ᶜ *recipientem*, 'ΑΣΘ ἐπιπόλαιον "on the surface," so 𝔙 *in superficie*. Jerome explains: *in superficie . . . nec potestatem eius alta imperii radice firmavit*. Cf. the discussion in *b Sukkah* 34a.

6   6a According to 𝔐 the growth of the vine is described both in a וַיִּצְמַח וַיְהִי לְגֶפֶן and in b וַתְהִי לגפן. Thereby the second half of v 6a (from לפנות), which ought clearly to express the purpose of the eagle in connection with the planting, is removed in a striking way from v 5, where the eagle is the subject. So we may conjecture with Ewald that already the beginning of v 6a belongs to the description of the purpose of the eagle and is to be read as וְיִצְמַח וִיְהִי לְגֶפֶן.

b סרח is only found again in the Priestly description of Ex 26:12 of the overhang of the curtains of the sacred tent.

c 𝔐 לפנות is subordinated.

d דליות according to Driver, "Ezekiel," 153, originally "roots," cf. דלה Ex 2:16, 19 "to draw," then secondarily "shoots." So Gesenius-Buhl, Koehler-Baumgartner "foliage." Outside the book of Ezekiel (17:6f, 23; 19:11; 31:7, 9, 12) the word is only found in Jer 11:16.

e 𝔐 תחתיו taken reflexively by Cooke, following Kimchi. Otherwise, following Rashi, mostly related to the eagle, i.e., Nebuchadnezzar.

f In the feminine ותהי there is influence from גפן. Differently in v 6a.

g פֹּארָה only in Ezekiel (17:6; 31:5f, 8, 12f). The form פֹּארָה "branch" in Is 10:33.

7   7a 𝔐 אחד. 𝔊 ἕτερος, 𝔖 אחרנא, 𝔏 𝔙 *altera* (𝔗 חד) are not compelling in pointing to אחר in the Hebrew original (differently in 11:19). The parallelism of 17:7; 19:5; 37:16 appears to point to a usage – אחד אחד "one-one" (= a second, another). The first אחד in this does not always need to be explicitly given.

b The verb כפן, attested in the Aramaic and Nabatean spheres with the meaning "to be hungry," is only found here in the Old Testament. The noun כָּפָן "hunger, famine," is found in Job 5:22; 30:3. Driver, "L'interpretation," 343f, conjectures for this a semantic development of the meaning "to turn, twist," which gives a satisfactory meaning in the present text. Cf. also 𝔊 περιπεπληγμένη, 𝔗 כפת "twisted itself." 𝔙 *quasi mittens* clearly presupposes the reading כְּפָנָה. To emend to כפלה (Ehrlich, *Randglossen*), or פנתה (Bertholet) is therefore unnecessary.

c אל – על cf. note a to 1:17.

and stretched out its branches[d] towards
    him,
that he might water it
—away from 'the bed,'[e] in which it was
    planted.
8/ In good soil
by[a] abundant water
it was planted,
so that it might put forth branches
and bear fruit
and become a noble vine.

9   Say: Thus has [the Lord][a] Yahweh said:
    'Will it thrive'?[b]
    Will some one not tear up[c] its roots
    and break off its fruit (?),[d]
    so that all its fresh shoots wither?[e]
    [It will wither][f] [and not with great
    power or many people][g] [to tear it
    out (?) from its roots].[h]

10   And behold, it[a] has been planted—will it
    thrive? When the hot wind strikes it,
    will it not utterly wither?[b] On 'the
    bed'[c] on which it sprouted it will
    wither[b].

11   Then the word of Yahweh came to me:[a]

8

9

d 𝔐 דליותיו certainly a scribal error from
דליותיה. Cf. 𝔊 𝔖 𝔗 𝔙.

e 𝔐 מערגות arose by a transposition of consonants
from an original מערוגת, cf. Eb 22, MSS (𝔊 𝔖).
עֲרֻגָה besides Ezek 17:7, 10, also is found in Song
5:13; 6:2.

8a על – אל cf. note a to 1:17.

9a אדני is lacking in 𝔊 𝔠Bo; see Excursus 1.

b 𝔐 תצלח. The reading of 𝔊 εἰ κατευθυνεῖ, 𝔙
ergone prosperabitur (𝔖 changes to the negative form
לא תכשר) and a comparison with v 10 make it probable that we should add, with some MSS, the interrogative particle which has fallen out through haplography.

c In 𝔐 ינתק, 𝔊 αἱ ρίζαι τῆς ἁπαλότητος αὐτῆς
wrongly finds a form of ינקת, following v 22 (4).

d 𝔐 יקוסס. 𝔊 σαπήσεται ("to rot"), 𝔖 correspondingly. Koehler-Baumgartner (following Loew)
"to make scaly." The parallel ינתק, however, leads
us to expect a violent destructive action brought
about by man. Accordingly the usual translation
"to tear off," which points etymologically in the
direction of קצץ. 𝔙 *distringet* (to scatter), 𝔗 יקטף
(to pluck).

e For the relationship of טרף "freshly picked" to
the Arabic *ṭarufa* see Köhler, "Hebräische Vokabeln III," 230, and Speier, "Wortforschung."

f 𝔐 תיבש is not attested by 𝔊. Is it a secondary
marginal correction to the syntactically incongruent
ויבש, which has entered into the text, as in v 10, on
גפן (but cf. Brockelmann, 50a)?

g bβ completely obtrudes from the allegory and
has entered in from the interpretation (v 17).

h 𝔐 למשאות אותה משרשיה. 𝔊 τοῦ ἐκσπάσαι αὐτὴν
ἐκ ριζῶν αὐτῆς, 𝔙 *ut evelleret eam radicitus*. משאות is
usually interpreted as an Aramaizing infinitive from
נשא. Gesenius-Kautzsch § 45e. Selle, *De Aramaismis*,
23, in contrast, wants to find in משאות a nominal
verbal form with the ending ות, after the pattern of
verbs ל"ה on the analogy of משא, 2 Chr 19:7. Koehler-Baumgartner emends to hip'il infinitive השאות
"to raise to the heights" (?), Cornill reads ליום שאת
"on the day when men raised it from its roots." Driver, "Linguistic Problems," 66, wants to take the
word as a *forma mixta* (ל"א – ל"ה) from a verb משא
Akkadian *masû* "be destroyed." No explanation is
completely satisfying. The whole of v 9bγ, which
does not fit in well syntactically, gives the impression of being a subsequent addition.

10

10a 𝔐 הִנֵּה would probably be better vocalized as
הֲנֵּה.

b The translation of יָבֵשׁ (for the infinitive absolute following the verb cf. Gesenius-Kautzsch
§ 113r) is lacking in 𝔊B 26, 967 𝔠Bo Arm 𝔖 𝔙, and
that of תיבש 2° in 𝔊A 𝔠Bo Arm 𝔖. Is this a free abbreviation of the text?

c 𝔐 עֲרֻגֹת. The plural vocalization has entered
secondarily from v 7.

11

11a V 11 is lacking in MSKen 4.

12/ª Say now to the rebellious house: Do you not know what this means? Say: Behold, the king of Babylon has come to Jerusalem[b] and has taken its king and its officials, and has brought them to Babylon. 13/ And he took (one) of the seed royal and made a covenant with him and made him swear an oath, and the noble men of the land he took away, 14/ that the kingdom might be humble and not exalt itself (and) keep the covenant with him,ª so that it might endure.[b] 15/ But he turned away from him in that he sent ambassadors to Egypt, that they might give him horses and a large army. Will he succeed? Can a man escape who does this?ª Can he break the covenant and still save himself?[b]

16 As I live, says [the Lord]ª Yahweh, in the place of the king who made him king, whose oath[b] he despised and whose covenant (, which the former had made) with him[c] he broke, in the midst of Babylon he will die. 17/ Pharaoh, with his mighty army and many soldiers,ª will not deal with him[b] in battle,[c] when a siege wall is set up and siegeworks built to cut off [many]ᵈ lives. 18/ He has despisedª the oath, and broken the covenant. And behold, he has (even) put out his hand and done all this. He will not (be able to) save himself.

12   12a 𝕲 adds the address "son of man," which is lacking here in 𝔐 (cf. 18:2; 19:1).

b 𝕲 misunderstands the whole section vv 12–15 as a prediction of coming events and translates as future.

14   14a 𝔐 בריתו, Eb.22 בריתי, cf. note b to v 16.

b The suffix in 𝔐 לעמדה may be related formally to ממלכה (van den Born, Aalders, and others). However the connection is more exactly with ברית. So clearly in 𝔙: *ut servet illud*. Besides this, already earlier a לעבדו, which smooths the expression, is found in bab MSS Eb 22, Eb 23 Q (𝔗 למיפלחיה). So BH³, Bertholet, Fohrer.

15   15a For the unusual writing הָעָשֹׂה cf. Gesenius-Kautzsch § 93rr. עשׂה without the article before אלה in Dtn 18:12; 22:5; 25:16.

b It is not necessary to change ונמלט to הימלט in view of the influence of the double appearance of the interrogative particle in bα (against Bertholet, Fohrer). Clearly a variation of expression is intended.

16   16a אדני is lacking in 𝕲 𝕮ᴮᵒ, see Excursus 1.

b The idea expressed in v 19 that in the treaty with Nebuchadnezzar we are also concerned with a treaty made with Yahweh is added in v 16 by 𝕲 (τὴν ἀράν μου; τὴν διαθήκην μου). With this, however, the meaning of the verse is changed, and the great king who attacks the king of Jerusalem becomes the covenant breaker. Cf. note a to v 14.

c The formulation of Lev 26:44 (להפר בריתי אתם in the mouth of Yahweh) makes it probable that we should follow 𝔙 here and, against the accentuation of 𝔐, relate אתו to בריתו.

17   17a For this interpretation of קהל cf. L. Rost, *Vorstufen*, 4f, 17. Ezekiel uses the word here without any particular theological accent (cf. 16:40; 23:24, 46f, and other passages).

b For עשׂה את "to act in punishment towards" cf. 7:27; 16:59; 22:14; 23:25, 29; 39:24 (also עשׂה כלה את 11:13; 20:17), beside 20:44 "to act in friendship towards," also Jer 21:2, Ps 109:21. For אוֹתוֹ – אִתּוֹ cf. note a to 2:1. However, Greenberg, "Ezekiel 17," page 308 note 17, draws attention to the fact that the two forms of vocalization in the book of Ezekiel (differently Jer 21:2) are divided between the two ways of interpreting עשׂה את. So we must reject the otherwise attractive conjecture of Graetz, "Echtheit," of reading יושׁיע "may rescue him," which is without the support of any textual evidence. Driver, "Ezekiel," 153, would accept here and in Prv 13:6 (cf. 12:23); 10:4; 26:28; Is 32:6, a meaning "protect" from the Arabic *ġaśiya*.

c 𝕲 𝔙 𝔗 make מלחמה the direct object of the harsh עשׂה (note b).

d 𝔐 is lacking in MSᴷᵉⁿ ¹⁸⁰ 𝕲. The comparison with 13:18f; 22:27 makes it probable that we should regard the 𝕲 text as the more original (Cornill).

18   18a 𝔐 ובזה. If we do not reckon with a weakening in the use of the perfect consecutive, such as is dis-

19 Therefore[a] thus has [the Lord][b] Yahweh said: As I live, my oath,[c] which he despised, and my covenant,[c] which he broke,[d] 'I will bring'[e] upon his own head. 20/ And I will spread my net over him, and he will be taken in my trap [, and I will bring him[a] to Babylon and enter into judgement with him there because of the disloyalty which he has shown towards me].[b] 21/ [And all his 'picked soldiers'][a] 'and'[b] all his troops will fall by the sword, and those who are left will be scattered to the winds, and you shall know that I, Yahweh, have spoken.

22 Thus has [the Lord][a] Yahweh said: I will take[b] (a sprig) from the [lofty][c] top of the cedar, [and will set it out][c] from its

---

cernible in later Hebrew (Ecclesiastes) (cf. Cooke note a on 13:6), we must accept here either that a descriptive subordinate remark is being made ("thereby was he . . ."), or we must emend to בזה (BH³).

19 19a 𝕲 adds εἶπον.

b אדני is lacking in 𝕲 𝕮ᴮᵒ, see Excursus 1.

c This means "the oath sworn by me (by invocation of my name)," i.e., "the covenant made by me."

d For הפיר cf. Ps 33:10; 89:34. The carrying over of forms from verbs ע″ע to those of verbs ע″ו is occasionally found, Gesenius-Kautzsch § 67v; Gesenius-Bergsträsser § 27q.

e 𝔐 ונתתיו. Since only the feminine אלה and ברית come into question as words to which the suffix relates, we must read ונתתיה; Driver, "Linguistic Problems," 66, ונתתין.

20 20a 𝔐 והבאתי אתו, in 12:13 והביאותיהו.

b V 20b is lacking in 𝕲 𝔏ᶜ 𝕮ᴮᵒ 𝔄; cf. the exposition. The construction of נשפט with a doubled accusative is harsh and should perhaps be smoothed with MS (cf. 𝕾) by the insertion of על, or with 9 MSS 𝔅 (*in praevaricatione*) by a ב (Herrmann, Graetz, "Echtheit"). Following 39:23 the replacing of מעלו by על is possible (Ehrlich, *Randglossen*).

21 21a Against 𝔐 (Q מברחיו) ואת כל מברחו "his company of fugitives" (Σ 𝕲ᵒ 𝔅 𝕮) there is not only the reading מבחרו of many MSSᴷᵉⁿ ʼA (οἱ ἐκλεκτοί following 𝕲⁸⁶) 𝔗 𝕾 and the fact that מברח in the Old Testament is otherwise never found, but also the context which leads us to expect first a word for a normal army and then a word about the fugitives as the "remnant" (והנשארים aβ). The analogy of 12:14 also, to which there is a relationship, suggests a reading מבחרו. Differently Reider, "Contributions," 90. The word is found in Ezekiel in 23:7; 24:4f; 31:16. The parallel references point to a singular vocalization מִבְחָרוֹ (plural only Dan 11:15 עם מבחריו). The introductory את is not unheard of with the subject (Gesenius-Kautzsch § 117m), although clearly from v 20a (cf. 12:14) the possibility of understanding the expression as object has been a primary influence; cf. Blau, "Gebrauch," 9. 𝕲 has also translated the יפרשׁ of 𝔐 in unconscious dependence on 12:14 with διασπερῶ and then, as in 17:20, made Yahweh the subject of the assertion. In 𝕲 admittedly the introductory ואת כל מבחרו is not attested; cf. note b to v 20.

b The introductory ב in 𝔐 בכל אגפיו is harsh, both as a connection with the beginning of the verse in 𝔐, which is lacking in 𝕲 (cf. note a), and as the beginning of a clause (so 𝕲 𝔏ᶜ). It is best to emend to a simple וכל with 12:14.

22 22a אדני is lacking in 𝕲 𝔏ᶜ 𝕮ᴮᵒ, see Excursus 1.

b 𝔐 ולקחתי. An initial clause with perfect consecutive also in 25:13; 36:6, 10; 32:3.

c 𝔐 הרמה "the exalted" is without a counterpart in 𝕲 𝔏ᶜ, and 𝔐 ונתתי "and I will set" is without a

358

highest branches.[d] I will break off a tender shoot,[e] and I myself will plant it upon a high and lofty[f] mountain. 23/ On the high mountain of Israel I will plant it, and it will put forth branches and bear fruit[a] and become a noble cedar. And under it 'all kinds of animals'[b] will make their abodes, and [birds of every sort],[b] all feathered creatures will nest in the shade of its branches, 24/ and all the trees of the field will know that I, Yahweh, have brought low the high tree, but have exalted the low tree, that I have made the green tree dry, but have made the dry tree put forth shoots. I, Yahweh, have spoken, and I will do it.

counterpart in MS$^{Ken\,252}$ 𝕲 𝔏^C 𝕾. The two words appear to be an addition. Since the predicate of height already lies in "the high mountain," the רמה, which is redundant in comparison with vv 3f, introduces a clumsy additional emphasis in the verse. ונתתי is perhaps a marginal gloss to ושתלתי, which sought to avoid the inelegant repetition of שתל in vv 22/23 (Ehrlich, *Randglossen*).

d 𝔐 רך is not attested by 𝕲 𝔏^C.

e 𝔐 ינקותיו cf. note a to v 4.

f 𝔐 תלול hapax legomenon, cf., however, note a to 3:15. According to Baer-Delitzsch, xvii, properly *aggeratus* "heaped up." It was misunderstood by 𝕲 (𝔏^C) as a verb καὶ κρεμάσω αὐτόν, which again made necessary the introduction of the copula before אשתלנו (v 23).

23   23a The reference to fruit in connection with the cedar is striking, but is determined by the parable previously given (v 8) and is therefore not to be emended to פארה (Cornill, Bertholet).

b 𝔐 ושכנו תחתיו כל צפור כל כנף בצל דליותיו תשכנה. 𝕲 καὶ ἀναπαύσεται ὑποκάτω αὐτοῦ πᾶν θηρίον (already assimilated to 𝔐 in 𝕲^{BOL}; 𝔏^C 𝕾: ὄρνεον) καὶ πᾶν πετεινὸν ὑπὸ τὴν σκιὰν αὐτοῦ ἀναπαύσεται καὶ τὰ κλήματα αὐτοῦ ἀποκατασταθήσεται. In the first half 𝕲 appears to have preserved the original text here, with its clear parallelism: animals-birds, confirmed by 31:6. Behind תחתיו we must add וכל חיה. In what follows כל כנף (Gen 7:14), or better still כל צפור since כנף appears to be supported by πετεινόν of 𝕲, is to be deleted as a gloss. The concluding clause of 𝕲, however, must be a double reading of the last words of 𝔐 in the form ודליותיו תשבנה.

Form

In form Ezek 17 at once recalls Ezek 15. A metaphorical saying, which appears to need an answer by the putting of a question to the hearers, is followed in nonfigurative language by a direct divine announcement of judgement. Whilst in 15:1–5 the whole parable from the first word onwards appears to be preserved in the form of a question it hardens here in vv 9f into a question put by Yahweh to the hearers which seeks to bring the Israel concerned to the inevitability of the divine judgement upon itself. The divine interpretation (vv 11–21) is then made into a second revelatory event through a new formula for the receipt of a message (analogous to the interpretation in 12:8ff, alongside the symbolic actions 12:1–7; in 21:6 again at the conclusion of a parable). The messenger formula in v 19 breaks the interpretation into two acts (vv 11–18, 19–21). In form the second of them (vv 19–21) is set out, like 15:6f, as a proof-saying.

This is true also of the reassuring appendix in vv 22–24, which is introduced by a new messenger formula, the broad conclusion of which in v 24 points to the form of an expanded proof-saying and recalls once again the recognition formula.

V 11 introduces a caesura in another way. The parable in vv 3–10, introduced by vv 1f, is undoubtedly a metrically formed unit, although it is scarcely possible to reconstruct metrically ordered lines or strophes. Hölscher's translation here goes far too arbitrarily over the unevenesses, and the reconstruction by Smith, "Eagle(s)," is in no way convincing throughout. Two beat rhythms interchange with threes. A rhythmic division of a distinctive kind is also favored by the התצלח of v 9a (the introductory formulae in vv 3 and 9 lie outside the metrical scansion), which introduces the question of vv 9f. A further artistic device is to be seen in 3bβ / 4a, 4bα / 4bβ (v 5), in the chiastic positioning of the clauses: a clause introduced by a verb in the imperfect consecutive corresponds to one in a parallel clause which concludes with a perfect. Against this the interpretation in vv 11–21, even though it is occasionally expressed more tightly (most clearly v 13 with double threes and chiasmus in b), and the use of parallelism is found in it, shows a broader dissolving prose style. In the appendix in vv 22–24 the speech again becomes tighter (cf. especially the two beautiful double threes in which the recognition formula in v 24a is added).

Thus, from the metrical aspect also, vv 3–10 form the kernel of Ezek 17, to which vv 11ff have been joined as a further exposition. This kernel must be examined in regard to the further question of form.

In the introduction in vv 1f, which cannot (with Hölscher *Hesekiel*) simply be deleted and set aside as materially unimportant, the prophet receives the commission to utter a "riddle" and a "saying." Apart from the separate משל "to rule" (19:11, 14) which does not fit here, the verb משל appears in Ezekiel in 12:23; 16:44; 18:2f for the "delivering of an utterance."[1] It denotes the prophetic (figurative) saying in 17:2; 21:5; 24:3 (cf. further Nu 23:7, 18; 24:3, 15, 20, 21, 23; Is 14:4). Beside it stands the parallel formulation חוד חידה. The verb חוד is otherwise found in the Old Testament only in Ju 14:12f, 16, where Samson sets his companions the task of solving a riddle. The noun חידה is found eight times in the Old Testament besides the eight occurrences in Ju 14:12–19. The prophetic usage is recalled in Hab. 2:6a, where F. Horst finds a redactional introductory reference, stating that the following woes are "mocking words in allegory."[2] Besides Ezek 17:2 and Dan 8:23 (Koehler-Baumgartner "utterance with a double meaning") the remaining five occurrences point clearly to Wisdom as the sphere in which חידה was at home. Prov 1:6 describes the Wisdom address as משל ומליצה דברי חכמים וחידתם. 1 Kings 10:1 (2 Chr 9:1) tells of the Wisdom debate between Solomon and the Queen of Sheba, who tested him "with riddles." Similarly the Psalm introductions in Ps 49:5; 78:2, which are preserved in the Wisdom style, denote their utterances as משל and חידה in parallel. In Wisdom speech the artistic cover of a saying in a metaphor plays a great part. The uncovering of the enshrouding metaphors, the solving of cunning riddles, is here a direct part of conventional usage in Wisdom speech, as is shown by the Aḥikar story besides 1 Kings 10.[3] Certain conventions of Wisdom, as, for example, the number saying, have also clearly grown up on this basis, as also proverbs in parallelism in which the first half gives the figure of speech or metaphor and the second its interpretation (especially Prv 25ff). So von Rabenau, "Rätsels," would then understand Ezek 17 exclusively under the form of the riddle.

However, in Wisdom animal and plant fables have also at all times played an important role.[4] In Ezekiel 17 (and 19) we encounter the prophetic adoption of this form, and its elaboration by elements taken from the riddle. Nevertheless, Ezek 17 combines elements of plant and animal fables. Besides the eagle, the royal bird, we have the cedar and the vine, both of which are found already in the satirical political fables of the period of the Judges (Ju 9:12f) and that of the monarchy (2 Kings 14:9).[5] If, in the sphere of Wisdom, the fable could at first communicate timeless truth, in Ezek 17 it has fully entered into the service of the prophetic preaching of history. Further the fable in Ezek 17 is already strongly penetrated with allegorizing features. Unintentionally, however, elements of the political reality pointed to by the fable may also have entered into the figurative speech, without any metaphorical dressing up (land of trade—city of merchants v 4). The view of Smith, "Eagle(s)," goes further, and according to her an older poem composed by Ezekiel which was unrelated to the contemporary historical scene, has been taken up and elaborated. This can only

1   See above pp. 280f, 308 for the noun מָשָׁל.

2   Friedrich Horst and Theodore H. Robinson, *Die zwölf kleinen Propheten*, HAT 14 (Tübingen: Mohr [Siebeck], ³1964). In the first edition he takes חידות as an explanatory gloss on מליצה, while in the second edition, following Paul Humbert, he changes to וְיָחוּדוּ.

3   See Bruno Meissner, *Das Märchen vom weisen Achikar,*

AO 16, 2 (Leipzig: Hinrichs, 1917).

4   Hempel, *Literatur*, 47ff; Meissner, *Babylonien* 2, 426ff; Spuler, *HO* I:2, 180f, 203.

5   See above p. 126 to 1:10; Dürr, *Ezekiels Vision*, 44–50; also Herrmann, 106f.

be obtained by deletions from the text which certainly do not recommend themselves.

Setting

The allegory in vv 1–10 presupposes the conspiracy of Judah with Egypt and Zedekiah's defection from Babylonian overlordship implicit in it. Greenberg has put together the accounts which appear to support an intervention of Psammetichus II (594–588) in Palestine. The Babylonian reaction, according to Ezek 17:1–9, has still not taken place. So we are led to the time before the beginning of the siege of Jerusalem (cf. 24:1f). Thus the literary placing of Ezek 17 between the dates of 8:1 and 20:1 would then be roughly the correct time, even if no compelling arguments can be brought in demonstration of it. Erbt's dating in the Persian era has rightly found no following. The allegory shows that its author clearly had a strong impression of Babylon as a "city of trade." Whether someone resident in Jerusalem, who expected a threatened intervention of the Babylonian military power, would have described Babylon from this perspective is questionable. An actual encounter with the metropolis of trade, i.e., the situation of the prophet among the exiles, may better explain this formulation.[6]

Interpretation

■ **17:1–3** The prophet, who is addressed as "son of man" in the formula for the coming of a message, receives a divine commission to address the house of Israel with a mysterious riddle and to recount to it a fable as a message from God.[7]

It deals with the eagle, the king of birds (see above). Its royal greatness, behind which the power of the Babylonian empire is cloaked, is described in brief statements of two units, taking up the introductory גדול, by reference to the great wings (כנף also in Gen 1:21 in the first explanatory definition of עוף), the long pinions (אבר again in Is 40:31 of the eagle, Ps 55:7 of

the dove, אברה in Dtn 32:11; Ps 68:14; 91:4; Job 39:13, echoes the root אבר "to be strong"), and the thick feathers (note b). אשר לו הרקמה is surprising, but is not to be deleted as an addition (Hölscher, *Hesekiel*) on account of its variant formal structure. Because of the paucity of adjectives in Hebrew the representation by the noun is not suspicious.[8] In this G. R. Driver thinks of a heavy stylizing of an eagle's feathers.[9] Among the commentators who interpret רקמה in the proper sense as "colorful" it has often been suggested that Ezekiel had in mind in his description a colored relief of an eagle's wings, "made with glazed tiles or other colored sculptures" (Herrmann).

The eagle takes action against the cedar, or more precisely its topmost branches. צמרת (note d to v 3) denotes "the topmost," following Arabic ṣumr^{un}, and is found in the parallel (v 4) as "the head (= uppermost) of its shoots" (note a to v 4). ארז, according to the opinion of many, does not refer to the gnarled *cedrus libani Barrel*, still found today in a few areas in Bsherreh, but rather to a kind of deal such as *abies cilicica*, used at one time for building (I Kings 6f) and for flagpoles (Ezek 27:5).[10] In the Old Testament it is always connected with Lebanon, the mountain range on the borders of Israel, which was so impressive and which ranged so high. That the eagle comes to Lebanon means in the allegory that the emperor attacks the "high one," i.e., the king who is honored by Yahweh himself through the election of the house of David (2 Sam 7). It is unlikely that we should see referred to in "Lebanon" the hill territory of Judah (Cooke) or the temple (so Jerome with reference to Zech 11:1f). Thus, as a bird plucks off the tender shoots of trees (the real enemy of such fresh shoots in Palestine is undoubtedly the goat), so in 597 B.C. Jehoiachin, the tender branch, was plucked off from the royal tree of Israel by the eagle. By the bringing of the branch to the city of trade, by which the deportation of Jehoiachin to Babylon, the trading center of the Babylonian empire,

---

6   For vv 11ff see below.
7   See above pp. 131f; pp. 144f; for the messenger formula see above p. 133.
8   For רקמה see above p. 340 to 16:10.
9   Driver, "Ezekiel," 152.
10 See L. Haefeli, *Syrien und sein Libanon* (Luzern: Raber, 1926), 190–204; Ludwig Koehler, "Hebräische Vokabeln II," *ZAW* 55 (1937): 163–165.

is meant, the allegory refers to the actual historical event. The exiles settled in the territory of Nippur must undoubtedly have kept a regular contact with king Jehoiachin, who was held in the capital according to the information contained in the ration lists.[11] Thus the reference to the land of trade and the city of merchants (cf. Rev 18:11–17) was also full of meaning for those living in Tel Abib.[12] The ארץ כנען (cf. note b) already referred to in 16:29, deriving from the Phoenician cities of (purple dye) trade, has here become a general designation for the land of trade, and thus כנעני has become a word for a trader (Is 23:8; Zech 14:21; Prv 31:24; Job 40:30).[13]

■ **17:5** In the description of a first phase of events nothing is told about any particular action or reaction of the one who was deported far away. Only the eagle is strongly emphasized. This is changed in the second phase, in which the vine appears as a counterpart to the eagle. This also was an ancient product of Canaan of royal dignity. It is first of all said of it quite vaguely that it had been taken from "the seed of the land" and planted by the eagle in fertile soil with abundant water. The זרע הארץ, compared with the description of the lofty cedar shoot, undoubtedly bears less emphasis. On the other hand, it gives expression to the fact that in Zedekiah, who is referred to here as the successor of Jehoiachin (2 Kings 24:17), the emperor did not set up a foreigner, but a native, as king. The great care and the full possibility of life, which the favorable treatment by the Babylonians allowed, is thereby strongly emphasized. If צפצפה is rightly interpreted as "growth on a river bank" (note b), then there is in this a reference to the good situation beside water which the Babylonians had granted. The image of the tree planted beside water was current in Israel's Wisdom tradition (Ps 1:3; Jer 17:8).[14] However, v 6 mentions directly the limitation which the overlord had placed upon the royal plant who should by the will of the overlord spread abundantly in breadth (for סרח cf. note b). He must remain humble. This has in mind the low growth of the vine, which even in Palestine today is not trained high, but grows low over the ground. The contrast is clearly discernible with the top of the cedar, the height of which is trebly stressed (the topmost branch of the tallest tree on the highest mountain of the land). At the same time it points to the relationship in which what is so planted stands to the one who plants it. The turning of the branches (or leaves? cf. note d) towards him, however inappropriate this feature is in view of the free movement of the eagle which is constantly free to change its position, rightly expresses the willing obedience to the superior ruler to whom Zedekiah owed his position. The picture becomes still more awkward if the תחת is to be interpreted in a similar line of thought of subordination to the overlord (cf. note e). Thus the vine grows up and bears shoots (בדים again in Ezek 19:14, frequently in Ex 25ff with the meaning "poles" in the apparatus for carrying the sacred objects of the tent) and branches (note g).

■ **17:7** The true counterpart of the first eagle appears in v 7 with the appearance of the second eagle, which refers to the Egyptian power represented by Psammetichus II. It is first mentioned with similar, although more briefly described, attributes to the first. The ארך האבר is lacking, the מלא הנוצה is slightly shortened to רב נוצה, and especially the mysteriously splendid רקמה of v 3 is lacking. We shall not go wrong in seeing in this an expression of a lesser regard for the Egyptian power. Thus no real activity of this second eagle is narrated, although the action of Psammetichus II could have given occasion for it (the march to Syria in 591 B.C.? Greenberg). The action of the vine therefore towards the second eagle remains completely mysterious. Like the first eagle this appears unrealistically to have a fixed "position," and the vine bends its roots and stretches out its branches (foliage?) in order to be nourished by it. According to the *Letter of Aristeas* 13 this may perhaps have in mind the sending of a contingent of troops to Psammetichus II's battle against the Ethiopians (Herodotus, II, 161).

■ **17:8** The mystery of this removal of the vine from its position, in which everything was properly given to it, is strongly emphasized again by v 8. In this it is surprising that only here, coming rather late, is there mention of the vine's bearing fruit; that the word עָנָף is used here for the first time for its branches (again in

11   See above pp. 111f; pp. 114f.
12   Meissner, *Babylonien* 1, 336ff.
13   See B. Maisler, "Canaan and the Canaanites,"
BASOR 102 (1946): 7–12.
14   Further *Amenemope* 4, see *ZAW* 42 (1924): 280. In Ezekiel further in 19:10; 31:4, 5, 7.

v 23; 31:3; 36:8; Lev 23:40; Mal 3:19; Ps 80:11; cf. עָנָף Ezek 19:10); and, above all, that after the somewhat surprising designation of the vine as שפלת קומה (v 6), it becomes a גפן אדרת. The expression is taken up in v 23 for the high cedar planted by Yahweh himself, where it fits better. So Giesebrecht sees in v 8a a marginal correction belonging to v 10 after the statement of the catchphrase היא שתולה and joins v 8b directly on to v 7.[15] V 8b would then express the presumptuous idea of the vine, which turns to the second eagle, in order by means of it to become a noble tree. However, it is questionable whether the whole of v 8 is not a subsequent addition, taking up the argument with the vine, in which its גפן אדרת, without its having noticed it, goes beyond the limits preserved by the original text. If we keep v 8 then the גפן אדרת must be understood from the גפן סרחת in v 6.

■ **17:9** The removal of v 8 from the original text is also supported by the fact that the question following in v 9 fits far better onto v 7 than to the assertion of v 8, which goes back to what was said earlier. Then in v 9, with the full weight of a word proclaimed by Yahweh (a fresh messenger formula!), the hearer is called into the events, as in the prophetic pictures of judgement (Hos 2:4ff; Is 5:3f).[16] The hearer must decide whether the conduct of the vine can be expected to prosper. The התצלח (note b), which disturbs the meter, forces an answer, the content of which cannot be in doubt. It is further set out in the form of a continued question by Yahweh himself. After what has preceded, it can scarcely be in doubt that the unnamed avenger who tears out the root and plucks off the fruit of the tree refers to the first eagle. He then hands the uprooted plant and its branches over to destruction. The interpretation which refers it to the second eagle (Hölscher, *Hesekiel*) can only be described as very forced, even though the mention of this second eagle is closer than the first.

In what follows all kinds of additions have been made to this clear conclusion of the fable. We should not include in it elements from v 10bα (כגעת בה רוח הקדים should be inserted after it after הלוא in v 9b), following P. Rost.[17] The suspicion is considerable that we are faced here with marginal glosses which have erroneously entered into the text.

■ **17:10** Finally v 10 is also an addition which formulates once again the reference to coming judgement by taking up catchphrases from what has already been said. In הנה שתולה (note a) the היא שתולה of v 8, which is thus already presupposed as a part of the text, is taken up in a new statement. התצלח takes up once again the question of v 9 in order to answer it with a further question, which in its content runs parallel to the original text of v 9bα. This suits well, for its part, the metaphor, since the hot sirocco, which comes from the desert and is particularly dangerous to plants (cf. Ps 103:15f; Is 40:6f), is introduced as the "avenger."[18] However, it deviates from the original plan of the fable in that it altogether leaves out of play the "avenger" referred to in v 4, to which the fable and its interpretation in vv 11ff point. Or does the east wind refer to the Babylonians? Under the scorching heat of the east wind the vine will be dried up in its soil.[19] ערגת צמחה varies the ערגות מטעה of v 7. Has v 10 been influenced by 19:12?

Aim

The allegorical fable of the two eagles, the cedar, and the vine, behind which the kings of the empires of Babylon and Egypt lie hidden, is told throughout as a secular tale, as is proper to the nature of a fable. Even though individual features of the story are given a strange twist by their allegorical reference (the eagle which brings a cedar twig into a city; the eagles standing on each side with a vine situated between them facing one side or the other; the uprooting of a vine by an eagle), the conclusion which the fable presupposes is "natural." This is no longer told in a neutral way but the hearers are brought into its inner logic by the

---

15 F. Giesebrecht, in his review of the commentary of Kraetzschmar, "Review of C. H. Toy, *The Book of the Prophet Ezekiel*, and Richard Krätzschmar, *Das Buch Ezechiel*," *OLZ* 3 (1900): 457–458.

16 See Gemser, "*rîb*," especially p. 131.

17 Paul Rost, "Miscellen I," *OLZ* 7 (1904): 392. For תיבש cf. note f: for bβ cf. note g. Greenberg, "Ezekiel 17," finds here the prophet's announcement

that Nebuchadnezzar could overcome the revolt with a small military force. For bγ cf. note h.

18 R. B. Y. Scott, "Meteorological Phenomena and Terminology in the Old Testament," *ZAW* 64 (1952): 11–25, especially 20.

19 See Hugo Klein, "Das Klima Palästinas auf Grund der alten hebräischen Quellen (Schluss)," *ZDPV* 37 (1914): 322–325; Dalman, *Arbeit* 1, 318–328.

posing of a question. To the התצלח there is only one answer possible: it cannot.

The questions at the end, with which the fable finishes, press upon the hearers the view that the unfaithfulness of Zedekiah will rebound upon him. At no point is God's action explicitly mentioned by the fable. By its being projected into the analogy of a worldly event, it does however become very clear how Zedekiah's disloyalty is seen simply from a human viewpoint as an act of folly which must bring down punishment upon his own head. The reference to the scorching east wind, which is to kill the vine, has been added subsequently. Its presence is not the result of the previous action of the vine, and it shows somewhat clearer that the Lord who makes even the winds his servants (Ps 104:4) stands as judge over the wrong act, so that while the fate is linked inextricably with the action, still the Lord is the judge.

Setting

■ **17:11–21** The interpretation which has been added in vv 11ff must have been formulated at a certain distance in time. The firmness with which the end of Zedekiah in Babylon is expressed by it supports the view that the events of the year 587 B.C. had already taken place. The close connection with the later section in 12:1–16 also points in this direction. In content there is no compelling ground against deriving the basic material from the prophet himself. That the intervening historical events are discernible in the interpretation cannot seriously be adduced as an objection against a derivation from Ezekiel. However, we naturally cannot exclude the possibility that it was formulated by Ezekiel's disciples.

Interpretation

The interpretation also seeks to be understood as a proclamation authorized as a divinely given message.[20] Its introduction by the question: "do you not know what this means?" with which we must compare 12:9; 21:5, 12; 24:19; 37:18 (cf. Mk 4:13), betrays something of the divine impatience over the lack of understanding which the prophet's word repeatedly en-

counters from the "rebellious house." (Cf. also 24:3 [21:5] and Mt 13:10–13.) Vv 12b–15 then at once interpret quite directly the allegorical fable and its individual assertions. To this there is joined in vv 16–18 a first direct divine announcement of judgement, preserved in the form of an oath, with a second announcement in vv 19–21.

The coming of the Babylonian king (the proper name נבוכדראצר first occurs in 26:7; 29:18f; 30:10) and the deportation of the king of Judah (Jehoiachin) and his officials to Babylon (2 Kings 24:15) is thereby foretold. When C. Kuhl interprets the repeated ויקח of vv 12 and 13 as a subsequent "resumption" and cuts out the mention of the deportation (v 12b from ויקח) as a secondary addition, this is opposed by the clear correspondence between the twofold ויקח in the allegory (vv 3 and 5).[21] Whether the parallel of king and officials is intended as an interpretation of the parallelism of צמרת and יניקות (vv 3b, 4a) may be questioned. That the title מלך is used so freely here both for Nebuchadnezzar and Jehoiachin must be connected with the historical narrative character of vv 12b–15a. It expresses the plain political institution. נשיא, however, in being used for the Davidic kings, contains a theological reflective character.[22] In v 13 the echo of זרע המלוכה in זרע הארץ (5) is clearly recognizable. It is then very strongly emphasized that the Babylonian king made a covenant with the king in Jerusalem and put him under oath. This becomes a basic motif of what follows. The repeated twofold reference to the covenant in vv 16, 18f as ברית and אלה, according to Korošec and Mendenhall, corresponds exactly to the Hittite and Babylonian terminology (Akkadian *rikiltu*, or *riksu u mamītu*; Hittite *išḫiul* and *lingaiš*) which clearly distinguishes the stipulations laid down by the overlord (in the vassal treaty) from the oath taken by the vassal.[23] The content of the covenant is seen by v 14, in a reference that clearly points back to v 6, in the king's subordination (Zedekiah), i.e., his position as a vassal, from which he must not raise himself (לבלתי התנשא).

■ **17:13bβ** V 13bβ, which speaks of the carrying away of the אילי הארץ (cf. 31:11, איל גוים 32:21, אלי גבורים 31:11), is striking in the present section. V 12 has told of the

---

20 See above pp. 144f.
21 Kuhl, "'Wiederaufnahme'," 5.
22 See above pp. 209, 273 and below to 37:22–24.

23 Korošec, *Staatsverträge*, 21–35; Mendenhall, "Covenant Forms," 57. In parity treaties both are under-

carrying away of the regent to Babylon. V 13 then tells of the making of the covenant, the content of which is unfolded directly in v 14. In its present position v 13bβ is only intelligible if it forms a constituent part of the covenant making. Thus the conjecture of Ehrlich, which has in mind here the hostages taken from the sons of nobles through whose deportation the treaty with Zedekiah was to be sanctioned, must be considered seriously and outlined more sharply in the light of recent knowledge. This shows us differences among those deported in 597 B.C.: 1) the small circle of the rulers who were directly guilty of a harmful policy and who were held in the city of Babylon in close proximity to the Babylonian king;[24] 2) the larger circle of those carried off as hostages and settled away from the capital along with others in Tel Abib (provisionally?), to which the prophet himself belonged. If they were regarded by the Babylonians as possessing the status of hostages, but were not among those who were permanently deported, this explains the lack of mention of a deportation in the Wiseman Chronicle, in which Rev. 13 only mentions the sending of heavy tribute (*bilatsa kabittu*). At the same time Zedekiah's breach of faith, which made the situation of the hostages a permanent one, is thereby further illuminated. Ezekiel's immediate concern with this breach of faith, as well as the concern of those around him, is then made incomparably deeper.

■ **17:15** V 15 tells of this breach of faith. Exactly as in the allegory, v 15 shows that Zedekiah sends to Egypt (the דליותיו שלחה לו of v 7 is then expounded by the לשלח מלאכיו מצרים of v 15) in order to secure help for himself from there. The mention of wanting equipment from Egypt (סוסים) recalls the similar desire for equipment in Isaiah's time (Is 31:1, 3), without bringing out the specifically Isaianic antithesis: human help— divine help.[25] The whole weight of Zedekiah's guilt and disloyalty is thus adduced.[26].

■ **17:16–18** The fact of this disloyalty, which is repeated twice for emphasis (vv 16, 18), now stands in the middle of a divine pronouncement of judgement, formulated as an oath, which declares quite concretely Zedekiah's death in Babylon.[27] The Egyptian help will be denied at the decisive moment, when the war reaches its climax in the siege of Jerusalem. This is described in a stereotyped expression as שפך סללה (4:2; 21:27; 26:8) and בנה דיק (4:2; 21:27). The covenant is mentioned in v 18 more precisely by the handshake which was customary in it (נתן ידו). (Cf. 2 Kings 10:15 [2 Chr 30:8].) In the refusal of Egyptian help we must think (against Greenberg, who deletes the פרעה in v 17 as a secondary addition and interprets v 17 in accordance with v 9 [see above to v 9bβ]) of the weak help of Apries, who followed Psammetichus II in 588, which events are mentioned in Jer 37:5ff.

■ **17:19–21** The second fulfillment of the divine threat of judgement is affirmed in the first part of v 19, which describes the guilt of Zedekiah in a strong theological concentration of assertions. As the despising of the oath and the breach of covenant are set out in vv 16–18 as guilt against the human partner, it is now most emphatically regarded as guilt against the oath and covenant of Yahweh. Behind this there stands a form of covenant according to which the partner taken into covenant by a superior affirmed his loyalty by appealing to his own gods. In the Hittite treaties, which are of the "suzerainty treaty" type, the deities of the suzerain, together with the deities of the vassals, are appealed to as witnesses.[28] With the Assyrians the deities of the vassal states are ignored.[29] According to Babylonian practice the vassals appear to swear by their own deities.[30] In the present oracle, the God of Israel, who is appealed to in the vassal's oath, stands as witness and turns against the treaty breaker. Even though his oath affirmed the servitude of the "House of Israel" to a foreign overlord, yet it was the oath of Yahweh which demanded undivided allegiance. That also ideas in line with Jer 25:9; 27:6 played a part, according to

---

taken by both parties (Korošec, *Staatsverträge*, 23–26).

24   Cf. the ration lists of King Jehoiachin dealt with above, pp. 114f. This circle is referred to in the Wiseman *Chronicles* as the *šarra iktašad* BM 21946 Rev. 12.

25   See von Rad, *Krieg*, 56–62.

26   See the remarkable story of Zedekiah's oath in *b Nedarim* 65a.

27   See above p. 176; p. 274 to 12:13.

28   Korošec, *Staatsverträge*; Johannes Hempel, "Bund," *RGG*³ 1, 1512–1516.

29   Mendenhall, "Covenant Forms," 60.

30   George E. Mendenhall, "Puppy and Lettuce in Northwest-Semitic Covenant Making," *BASOR* 133 (1954): page 30 note 16.

which Nebuchadnezzar was summoned by Yahweh as his servant (for a particular time) to be the instrument for judgement upon his people, is not to be seen. All that is expressed is a reference (important for priestly interest in the divine order) to the properly sworn covenant, any departure from which is to be punished by Yahweh. This punishment is described as the turning back of the evil deed upon the head of the doer, which is a common formulation in Ezekiel (Ezek 9:10; 11:21; 16:43; 22:31; 33:4).[31]

■ **17:20** The curses which are hypothetically expressed in the covenant against the oath breaker are given free rein. The judgement that then takes place is described in vv 20f with words slightly varied from 12:13–15. Like a wild animal (19:8) Zedekiah will be taken by Yahweh in a net and a snare, brought to Babylon, and there judged for his act of treason.[32]

■ **17:21** The king's army, however, will fall or be scattered in flight (פרשׂ nip'al, instead of זרה 12:14). In this painful event Yahweh will demonstrate (before the eyes of the exiles) the reality of the word declared by him (וידעתם second plural).

Aim

Jeremiah and Ezekiel (and his school) proclaim Yahweh's word on the question of Zedekiah's defection from his Babylonian overlord. (Cf. Jer 21:1–10; 27–29; 34:1–7; 37f.) Here and there this appears in a characteristically distinct light. Jeremiah points to the Lord of the history of nations who has given to Nebuchadnezzar power over the world, and wills that all people, including Israel, which has been prepared by the prophet's preaching to accept this period of judgement, should submit to "the servant of Yahweh" (Jer 25:9; 27:6; 43:10).[33] Ezekiels' allegorical parable does not speak of Yahweh's control of history. First of all (vv 1–10), from an external viewpoint, it points to the folly and ingratitude which has moved the King of Jerusalem to defect from the suzerain who had bestowed upon him his office and the possibility of life. The interpretation, in its first statement (vv 11–18), emphasizes the covenant as a valid institution. If Zedekiah has broken it then, without gaining anything by his

tactical concern for protection from Egypt, he will experience the punishment of the suzerain whom he has offended. He will suffer retribution in the very city of his overlord. The second part, however (vv 19–21), extends this to its full depth: in the covenant, God himself, who witnessed the oath, stands over Zedekiah.

Behind Zedekiah there were counsellors who also reckoned with the special election of Israel. The God who had chosen Israel to be his people could not will that they should lose their freedom. Thus in Jerusalem, even before Zedekiah's defection, Hananiah had declared an imminent deliverance in God's name (Jer 28). Also among those in exile some had reckoned on a speedy end of their deportation (detention as hostages?). By these pious people Zedekiah's treason was regarded as a legitimate attempt at regaining their lost freedom by his own determination, and even by doing so to increase God's honor on earth among his people. Ezekiel, however, knew that the covenant had brought God's people into a sacred obligation. In any case this obligation included the necessity of avoiding any misuse of the name of God (Ex 20:7) and the obligation not to break oaths sworn by it lest his name be dishonored (Lev 19:12; cf. Mt 6:9). This meant that a word which had been spoken under the watchful eye of God had to be kept for God's holy name's sake. In such honoring of the divine name the people of God would find life, not through a war of liberation or a crusade.

However, when the people of God, through its representatives, came to regard itself as able to take hold of life and freedom disregarding the word it had sworn before God, then he, whose name is holy, reveals himself in the tragic end of Zedekiah in the foreign city of Babylon and under the scorn of the Babylonians. God wills that nothing should come to honor except in the hearing of his word, which is holy law, and in obedience to it. Beside this all ecclesiastical concerns for honor and importance are secondary.

Interpretation

■ **17:22–24** In vv 22–24 an oracle of salvation is added to the declaration of judgement in vv 1–21. Like the

---

31 See above p. 204 to 7:4.
32 For מעל see above pp. 313f.
33 See *TWNT* 5, 655–672.

concluding oracle of salvation in 16:53–58, 59–63, it is dovetailed onto the preceding section by its use of images and its vocabulary. However, since it contains a quite independent statement, which is in no way contemporary with vv 1–21, it offers further strong evidence for the distinctive transmission and elaboration of the book of Ezekiel.[34]

■ **17:22** Against the "taking" (ויקח vv 3, 5; cf. 12, 13) by the eagle, i.e., the king of Babylon, there now appears a corresponding action of Yahweh (ולקחתי אני). By the emphatic אני, which is repeated again in the following ושתלתי אני, the antithesis between the free divine action and all human activity is set out very prominently. The theological character of the assertion, which is already discernible in a comparison of vv 19–21 with 16–18 within the declaration of judgement, is brought to a climax. Thus it follows naturally that this oracle of salvation should also conclude with the recognition formula. In this majestic action of Yahweh all the world will see who he is.

The action of Yahweh is, in detail, a lofty counter to the action of the eagle. With the vocabulary of vv 3f it is laid down, with a slight change of vocabulary, that Yahweh will take a young shoot from the top (מצמרת) of the cedar and from its topmost branches (מראש ינקותיו]). (Cf. vv 3f [את צמרת . . . את ראש יניקותיו].)

■ **17:23** Unlike the case with the eagle, however, this shoot is to be raised up, and not humiliated. It is planted on a high mountain, which is described in the continuation as "the high mountain of Israel" (again 20:40; plural 34:14). It is superfluous to question whether Yahweh then reestablishes the political status which is presupposed by vv 3f, or whether he is to bring Jehoiachin or his descendants back from Babylon, the city of trade where they are for the present a cut off and dried up shoot. Vv 22f would draw the opposite picture to the event of humiliation by using the same vocabulary. They thus take into account that the images of putting forth branches, bringing forth fruit, and growing up to be a noble plant are used of the vine in v 8b, to which fruit-bearing alone is really appropriate. In reality they have in mind neither the cedar nor the vine, but the divine tree, which is set in a most

prominent and glorious place and which bears all honor in itself. The description used of the mountain of God, the paradisal place of God's presence (cf. to 28:11ff), and the "world tree" under which all the creatures of the earth gather (cf. to 31:1ff) stems from the language of myth.

■ **17:24** By such an exaltation of the Davidic line, which is referred to as the shoot of the cedar tree, as in vv 3f, all the trees of the field, which in the language of the fable must mean the historical environs of Israel, would recognize the mystery of the person of Yahweh. In this it may be noted that the formulation has returned to a straightforward plant fable, which does not weaken the clarity of the image. The eagle plays no further role here. The mysterious nature of God is once again made plain by Yahweh's revealing himself in his actions, expressed in two parallel clauses which have a firm metrical structure, and which still keep to the imagery of the plant fable. For the faith of the Old Testament it is again significant that preference is given to a verbal, rather than an adjectival formulation. To humiliate and to exalt are also sovereign actions of Yahweh in 1 Sam 2:7; Ps 18:28; 75:8; 147:6. Appropriately the image is expanded here by the contrast between making green and making dry. The first pair of opposites was familiar in Israel's religious environment. In the Babylonian Inanna hymn there is a reference to the mysterious, wayward, and at time confusing, freedom of the divine Lady ("I provoke the wife against her consort, I make the child hostile to the mother . . . . I make the black white, and the white black").[35] In the Old Testament the assertion is an expression of the holiness of the Lord, who suffers none of his creatures to emulate his greatness and who proceeds as a storm against all that is "exalted" (Is 2:2–17), but who turns towards the poor and downtrodden (Is 57:15). Once he had begun his history with Israel when he had heard the cry of those who groaned under oppression in Egypt (Ex 2:24; 3:7, 9).

The expanded proof-saying concludes with a strong self-assertion, once again formulated verbally, which is in line with 12:25, 28 in asserting that Yahweh's word comes to pass (cf. 22:14; 36:36; also 24:14;

---

34 See above p. 334.
35 Falkenstein-von Soden, 228–231, especially 231: "The weak I cause to enter into the house, the strong I drive out . . . he who is honored I make a slave, and he who is despised, to him I am a counseling mother."

37:14).

Undoubtedly there is here a word of messianic promise, as is to be found again in 34:23f; 37:24f. Yahweh will again bring to honor in Jerusalem a member of the Davidic royal house, which has been temporarily humbled. He will achieve greatness and a dominion of great extent, in which men will find peace and protection. The portrayal of the messianic king under the image of the shoot is prepared for by the חטר of Is 11:1 and, with a slight change, in the צמח of Jer 23:5; 33:15; Zech 3:8; 6:12. That the allegory does not tell of the restoration of the vine stock, but the exaltation of the cedar shoot points to the fact that the promise of the new beginning was emphatically not seen as applying to the family of those ruling in the land after 597 B.C., but through the family of those deported in 597 B.C. Cf. Jer 24.[36] The fact that the language of exaltation and humiliation in Ezekiel is only found in the sharp attack on Zedekiah in 21:30–32 would also suggest an echo of a polemic against Zedekiah.[37]

Setting

Nothing speaks against an origin of the saying among the exiles. Chronologically it must be separated somewhat from vv 1–21. The sharp polemic against Zedekiah, as a comparison with 21:30–32 shows, is restrained. The positive content of the promise undergoes a very broad formulation. In its language the saying undoubtedly belongs to the circle of Ezekiel and his school (recognition formula v 24aα^1; concluding formula v 24b).[38]

Aim

The saying of vv 22–24 seeks to proclaim the faithfulness of God, in which he holds fast to his promises in his history. The old promise given through Nathan to David in the name of God in 2 Sam 7, that God would give to the people Israel a king from the house of David, was not to be allowed to die out through the catastrophes which Israel had suffered as a consequence of the self-determined action of the contemporary descendant of David.

In this it is unmistakably emphasized that the new event which was awaited as the fruit of the divine faithfulness was not the consequence of a new and clever human plan, but was to arise solely out of the new free act of God. God's majesty would thereby be revealed to the whole world. Because God, in his action, does not begin with a man who was seeking to express his own freedom, but with one who had been deeply humbled, his majesty would be revealed as that of one who opposes the arrogant, but who receives in mercy the humble and oppressed. Thus God would reveal himself when he gave to his people a king, in whose reign of peace all creatures would find protection.

---

36 Differently Noth, "Jerusalem Catastrophe." Did some sons of Zedekiah survive the catastrophe of 2 Kings 25:7? Cf. the "prince" Ishmael of Jer 41:1.

37 Cf. further to 21:30ff and see also Gressmann, *Messias*, 254–256.

38 For הר מרום ישראל see *VT* 8 (1958): 78f. For the problem of messianic expectation in Ezekiel cf. further to 34:23f; 37:24f, and the Introduction.

The Freedom to Repent

Bibliography

A. Alt
"The Origins of Israelite Law," *Essays in Old Test-
ament History and Religion*, tr. R. A. Wilson (New
York: Doubleday, 1967), 101–171.

K. Galling
"Der Beichtspiegel. Eine gattungsgeschichtliche
Studie," *ZAW* 47 (1929): 125–130.

H. Haag
*Was lehrt die literarkritische Untersuchung des Ezechiel-
textes?* (Freiburg in der Schweiz: Paulusdruckerie,
1943), esp. 80–93.

S. Mowinckel
Le Décalogue (Paris: Alcan, 1927).

G. von Rad
" 'Righteousness' and 'Life' in the Cultic Language
of the Psalms" in *The Problem of the Hexateuch and Other
Essays*, tr. E. W. Trueman Dicken (New
York: McGraw-Hill, 1966), 243–266.

G. von Rad
"Faith Reckoned as Righteousness" in *The Problem
of the Hexateuch and Other Essays*, 125–130.

R. Rendtorff
Die Gesetze in der Priesterschrift, FRLANT NF 44
(Göttingen: Vandenhoeck and Ruprecht, 1954).

W. Zimmerli
" 'Leben' und 'Tod' im Buche des Propheten Ezechiel," *ThZ* 13 (1957): 494–508.

18

1 And the Word of Yahweh came to me:
2/ What do you mean that you repeat
this proverb in the land of Israel:ᵃ the

18: 2a 𝕲 (𝕷ᶜˢ, cf. 𝕾) υἱὲ ἀνθρώπου τί ὑμῖν ἡ παραβολὴ
2 αὕτη ἐν τοῖς υἱοῖς Ισραηλ λέγοντες introduces at the
start an address to the prophet as son of man (see
above pp. 131f). In the parallel 12:22f there follows
quite correctly a command to address the people.
Since such a command is not found at all here
throughout the chapter it is not improbable that the
introductory בן אדם was not present from the beginning. 𝕲 will have introduced the address subsequently in conformity with custom (cf. 17:12;
19:1). Also in its lack of any counterpart for 𝔐's
אתם משלים את, 𝕲 must have smoothed over the
somewhat awkward formulation of 𝔐 in accordance with 12:22. The אתם is not a strengthening of
the suffix in לכם (Herrmann, following Gesenius-
Kautzsch § 135g), but the subject of an asyndetic
nominal clause related to לכם. Cf. the analogy in
Is 3:15, where מַלְּכֶם is carried on by a relative verbal clause. Also 𝕲's ἐν τοῖς υἱοῖς Ισραηλ is not to be
followed, since 𝕲 υἱοὶ Ισραηλ is also introduced in
other places (3:1; 4:3; 12:24; 27:17; 44:28; cf.
44:13; 47:13), over against the customary usage in

fathers eat[b] sour grapes, and the children's teeth are set on edge! 3/ As I live, says [the Lord][a] Yahweh, none of you[b] shall any more use[c] this proverb in Israel. 4/ Behold,[a] every person belongs to me: the person[b] of the father as well as the person[b] of the son. They belong to me. The person[b] who sins, he shall die.[c]

5   If a man is righteous and does what is just and right[a]—6/ if he does not eat upon[a] the mountains, nor lift up his eyes to the idols of the house of Israel, if he does not make his neighbor's wife unclean and does not approach a woman in the time of her uncleanness;[b] 7/ if he does not oppress any one, restores 'to the debtor his pledge,'[a] commits no[b] robbery, gives his bread to the hungry, and covers the naked with clothing; 8/ if he does not[a] lend (money)[b] at interest nor take any profit, keeps his[a] hand back from wrongdoing; upholds true justice between man and man, 9/ 'walks' [a]in [b]my statutes and

Ezekiel (see Excursus 2).

b 𝔐 יאכלו. The parallel in Jer 31:29 here reads the perfect, which appears to be confirmed by 𝔊 (𝔏ᶜˢ 𝔖). 𝔊, however, also translates the following תקהינה by an aorist. In the gnomic style both tenses are possible (Gesenius-Kautzsch § 107g beside § 106k). 𝔗 removes the image and formulates quite briefly אבהתא חטן ובניא לקן "the fathers sin, the children suffer."

3   3a אדני is lacking in 𝔊 𝔏ᶜˢ 𝔠ᴮᵒ, see Excursus 1.

b 𝔐 לכם is not attested by 𝔊 𝔏ᶜˢ 𝔖. A smoothing over?

c 𝔐 מְשׁל. Instead of the infinitive, which rarely appears as the subject of a clause in the Old Testament, (Ehrlich, *Randglossen*) it is possible to vocalize as a participle מֹשֵׁל. Does 𝔊 ἐὰν γένηται ἔτι λεγομένη interpret the form as a passive participle?

4   4a 𝔐 הן (= הִנֵּה, 𝔗 הא, 𝔙 *ecce*) is only found here in Ezekiel. 𝔊 ὅτι 𝔏ᶜˢ *quoniam*, 𝔖 מטל ד.

b For the translation of the Hebrew נפשׁ there is no satisfactory equivalent. נפשׁ denotes a person from the point of view of his vital force. See above at 7:19aβ.

c The Alexandrine text group of 𝔊 expands this, following Jer 31:30: "the teeth of those who eat sour grapes will be set on edge."

5   5a 𝔐 משפט וצדקה cf. v 19; 33:14, 16. 𝔗 paraphrases more fully, whilst 𝔊ᴮ (𝔏ᶜˢ) summarizes to a simple δικαιοσύνην.

6   6a על – אל cf. note a to 1:17. In v 15 𝔐 על.

b Literally "a woman who is uncleanness (through her monthly period)." A change from 𝔐 נדה to בנדתה (Cornill, Toy) or בנדה (Bertholet) is not necessary in spite of 𝔖 (בכפסה; cf. 𝔊 ἐν ἀφέδρῳ οὖσαν) and the formulation in Lev 15:20.

7   7a 𝔐 חבלתו חוב ישׁיב "his pledge, guilt he gives back" (Aalders: zijn voor schuld ontvangen pand) is hardly correct. The parallels formulate more briefly חבל לא ישׁיב v 16, cf. v 12 חבל לא חבל (said of the wicked). None of these uses the feminine form חבלה which appears only here, whilst the masculine חבל is found again in 33:15. 𝔊 ἐνεχυρασμὸν ὀφείλοντος ἀποδώσει appears to point to a Hebrew original חבל חיב ישׁיב. The feminine form of 𝔐 and its suffix must have arisen as an erroneous scribal dittography of the following חי (= תו). The root חוב, current in later Hebrew, is first certainly found in the Old Testament in Dan 1:10 (Sir 11:18), but is possibly also found in 1 Sam 22:22. The emendation from חוב to שׁוב (Cornill, Toy), which is often recommended, is orthographically attractive, but makes the expansion too heavy in the context of otherwise similarly formed legal clauses.

b 𝔊 adds the copula, cf. note a to 1:4.

8   8a 𝔊 adds the copula, cf. note a to 1:4.

b The καὶ τὸ ἀργύριον αὐτοῦ, found in 𝔊 (𝔏ᶜˢ) must be a free paraphrase.

9   9a 𝔐 יהלך is striking, not only beside the parallel perfect שׁמר, but also beside the simple qal הלך of

observes my laws, to do 'them'ᶜ—he is righteous, he shall live, says [the Lord]ᵈ Yahweh.

10 However, if he begets a son who is a robber, who sheds blood and ' ' does 'any of these'ᵃ (things), 11/ [when he (i.e., the father) had not done all this]ᵃ —ᵇhe eats uponᶜ the mountains and makes his neighbor's wife unclean, 12/ he oppresses theᵃ poor and needy, commitsᵃ 'robbery,'ᵇ does not giveᵃ backᶜ a pledge, and lifts up his eyes to idols, commits abomination, 13/ lends (money) at interest, and takes a profit— he shall 'certainly not'ᵃ live. He has done all these abominations. He shall

the similar expression in v 17. 𝕲 πεπόρευται presupposes a simple הלך. It should therefore be read. The imperfect prefix of 𝔐 has arisen by a dittography.

b 𝕲 𝔏ᶜˢ add the copula, cf. note a to 1:4.

c 𝔐 אמת. 𝕲 (τοῦ ποιῆσαι) αὐτά and the parallel text in v 19 render the reading אֹתָם probable. So most scholars since Ewald.

d אדני is lacking in 𝕲 𝔏ᶜˢ 𝕮ᴮᵒ, see Excursus 1.

10 10a 𝔐 ועשה אח מאחד מאלה, where Delitzsch (Baer-Delitzsch, x) would interpret the second half, in accordance with Assyrian parallels, as *unum de uno*, h.e. *aliquidpiam harum rerum*, is clearly corrupt. A correction, following 𝕲 (𝔏ᶜˢ) καὶ ποιοῦντα ἁμαρτήματα, to ועשה עול (Cornill) is improbable because the analogy of the transition to the next generation in v 14 leads us to expect a comparison of the actions of the son with those of the father. Thus in 𝔐 we must conjecture a dittography with a subsequent scribal error and read as the original text, following 𝕲 ונעבד. ועשה אחד (?אחת) מאלה: חדא מן הלין. The addition in v 11a also reflects a reading which contains the words עשה אלה. P. Rost, "Miscellen," 480f, sees in the superfluous אח 'מ' an abbreviation of an original אחד מאלה. This would introduce, as a kind of catchphrase, the explanatory gloss in vv 11b–13a, which repeats secondarily the list of vv 6ff. Cf. Slotki, "Ezek. 18:10."

11 11a The addition in v 11a, which is lacking in 𝕲, is clearly intended to set the original assertion of v 10b once again in its right context. P. Rost (note a to v 10) also sees in the half verse 11a, which according to him belongs to the beginning of v 15, the heading of a gloss (vv 15–17a). 𝕲 shows in v 11 an addition of a unique kind: ἐν τῇ ὁδῷ τοῦ πατρὸς αὐτοῦ τοῦ δικαίου οὐκ ἐπορεύθη. The Deuteronomistic הלך בדרך (1 Kings 16:2, 19, 26, and other passages), which is presupposed by this, is only found in Ezekiel in 23:31 (cf. on the text). The usage is missing in Ezek 18, which would have offered an excellent opportunity for its employment.

b For the adversative גם Ehrlich, *Randglossen*, points to 2 Sam 12:14. Toy, Kraetzschmar, Cooke change to כי אם.

c Cf. note a to v 6.

12 12a 𝕲 adds the copula, cf. note a to 1:4.

b The plural גזלות, which deviates from the formulation in vv 7, 16; 33:15 and does not reappear in the Old Testament, is not supported by 𝕲 (𝔏ᶜˢ) ἅρπαγμα and is certainly a scribal error for גזלה.

c Although the tenses change in the series of commandments (see below), the single imperfect formulation ישיב is striking between the surrounding perfects, and the suggestion of Cooke to read השיב must be seriously considered.

13 13a Instead of 𝔐 וחי, which must be understood as a question (Aalders), we must read חיו and place the *atnaḥ* under יחיה. Cf. 𝕲 𝔏ᶜˢ. For the interchange of consonants cf. note a to 10:3.

be put to death.[b] His blood shall be upon himself.

14 And behold, if he begets a son, and he sees all the sins of his father which he has done, and, because he sees them,[a] he does not do likewise—15/ he does not eat upon the mountains, does not lift up[a] his eyes to the idols of the house of Israel, does not make the wife of his neighbor unclean, 16/ and does not oppress any one; does not take[a] a pledge and commits no robbery; gives his bread to the hungry and covers the naked with clothing; 17/ he keeps[a] back his hand 'from what is wrong,'[b] accepts neither interest nor profit; carries out my laws and walks in my statutes—he shall not die for the guilt of his father. He shall live. 18/ If[a] his father practiced extortion, committed robbery[b] ',[c] and[d] did what is not good[e] among his relatives,[f] behold, then he shall die for his own guilt. 19/ Yet you say: Why does the son not bear the guilt[a] of the father? When the son does what is just and right,[b] observes all my statutes and

b 𝔐 יומת (מות), 𝔊 (θανάτῳ) θανατωθήσεται. Ehrlich, *Randglossen*, Herrmann, Bertholet, Fohrer would read ימות, as in vv 17, 21, 24, 28, for which Eb 22 𝔊$^{A-26-544, 106-410}$ (ἀποθανεῖται) 𝔏^{CS} 𝔗 𝔖 may be adduced. The change is prohibited, however, because of the conjoined דמיו בו יהיה. Since this formula turns away any guilt from the executioner in sentences carried out by men, the formulation cannot be presupposed here, which points to the divine carrying out of the punishment. Cf. the exposition.

14 14a 𝔅 (= BH²) K וירא, Q ויראה; L (= BH³), Baer-Delitzsch ויראה is derived from ירא by 𝔊 καὶ φοβηθῇ, 𝔏^{CS} *et timuerit*, 𝔅 *timuerit*, and by 𝔗, as in 𝔐, from ראה. In 𝔖 there is no equivalent for it. Most commentators emend, following 𝔊. The usage elsewhere in Ezekiel, in which ירא plays a strikingly small part (2:6ter; 3:9 in the traditional warning not to be afraid in the call-narrative; 11:8 of fear of the sword; and in the secondary נורא 1:22), whilst ראה appears more than seventy-five times and "seeing" is undoubtedly of great importance in Ezekiel's message, leads us to retain 𝔐. For the form cf. Gesenius-Kautzsch § 75t. Cf. further v 28 and also v 19.

15 15a 𝔊 𝔏^{CS} add the copula, cf. note a to 1:4.

16 16a 𝔊 𝔏^{CS} add the copula, cf. note a to 1:4.

17 17a 𝔊 𝔏$^{(C)S}$ add the copula, cf. note a to 1:4.

b With 𝔊 𝔏^{CS}, corresponding to v 8, מעול is to be read instead of the impossible מעני. The עני used adequately in v 12 may have influenced this scribal error.

18 18a 𝔊 adds δέ, 𝔏^{S} *autem*.

b 𝔊 𝔏^{S} 𝔅 add the copula, cf. note a to 1:4.

c The את of 𝔐 is not attested by 𝔊. Since in Ezekiel 18 otherwise only the feminine גזלה is found (vv 7, 12, 16, also 33:15, differently 22:29), we must see in את the wrongly written ending of a preceding גזלה (instead of 𝔐 גזל). In v 12 (cf. note b) there is another scribal error of the same ending.

d 𝔊 𝔏^{S} suppress the copula.

e 𝔊 strangely ἐναντία ἐποίησεν, 𝔏^{S} *contraria fecerit* (𝔏 *fecit*).

f M עמיו. 𝔊 (𝔏^{S}) τοῦ λαοῦ μου. The plural עם in the sense of "relatives" is otherwise not found in Ezekiel, but is common in the priestly literature, see above p. 304. The glance at the circle of the family is not out of place in this explanation, which is so strongly concerned with the question of corporate guilt in a family. 𝔊 presents a secondary application to the people of God, which is also found in 𝔐 in 14:8f.

19 19a נשא בעון twice again in v 20. ב- *pretii*? Otherwise in Ezekiel only נשא עון, see above pp. 164f. In view of the threefold occurrence in vv 19f it is wrong to enforce uniformity.

b 𝔐 צדקה. 𝔊 ἔλεος shows the beginning of the reinterpretation of the צדקה concept towards the meaning "alms"; cf. Strack-Billerbeck 1, 386–388, on Mt 6:1f.

has kept them,^{c} he shall live. 20/ The person^a who sins, he shall die. A son shall not bear the guilt^b of his father, nor shall a father bear the guilt^b of his son. The righteousness of the righteous shall be upon him (i.e., the righteous), and the wickedness of the wicked^c shall be upon him (i.e., the wicked).

28 But if the wicked turns from all his sins^a which he has committed, keeps all my statutes, and does what is just and right,^{b} he shall live and not die. 22/ None of the offenses which he has committed shall be remembered against him.^{a} On account of the righteousness which he has done he shall live. 23/ Am I really pleased 'in' the death^a of the wicked,^{b} says [the Lord]^c Yahweh, and not rather that he should turn from his way^d and live?

24 But when a righteous man turns away from his righteousness and does what is wrong, just like all the abominations which the wicked has done, [if he does this—shall he live?]^a then all his righteous actions^b which he has done will no more be remembered. For the disloyalty which he has committed and his sin^b which he has done—on their account he shall die.

25 But you say: the way of 'Yahweh'^{a} is not just. Hear then, O house of Israel, is my way not just? Are^b not (rather) your ways^b not just? 26/ When a righteous man turns away from his righteousness and does what is wrong and ' '^{a} dies, then he dies on account of his wrongdoing which he has done. 27/ But if the wicked turns away from the wickedness which he has committed^a and does what is just and right,^{b} then he will save his life. 28/ [He has seen it.]^a He

c For the form וישׂה cf. וירֹאה vv 14, 28, and note a to v 14.

20   20a Cf. note a to v 4.
   b Cf. note a to v 19.
   c 𝔐 רשׁע. Q Eb 22 would read הרשׁע parallel to הצדיק. In none of the words does 𝔊 add the article. Did it also read צדיק without the article? A glance at the related texts 3:18–21; 13:22; 18:24, 26f; 33:12 shows the use of both forms of expression.

21   21a חטאתיו with Q Eb 22; cf. 𝔊 𝔏^S 𝔗 𝔖 𝔙, K חטאתו.
   b 𝔊 as in v 19, cf. note b.

22   22a 𝔊^B μνησθήσεται (𝔏^S erunt in memoria), 𝔊^A μνησθῶσιν, Θ μνησθῶ, thence 𝔙 recordabor. First 𝔊$^{O L}$ (𝔗 𝔖) give an equivalent to לו in αὐτῷ. The expression is found again in 𝔐 in 3:20; 18:24; 33:13 without לו, in 33:16 with לו (also lacking here in 𝔊).

23   23a 𝔐 מות. The בשׁובו in v 23b and the parallel in v 32; 33:11 make it likely that we should read here במות, with 20 MSS.
   b רשׁע without the article. In 33:11 (cf. 18:32) the article is found. Cf. note c to v 20.
   c אדני is lacking in 𝔊 𝔏^S, see Excursus 1.
   d 𝔐 (= Q) מדרכיו. K (𝔊^S 𝔏 𝔖 𝔗) must, however, be correct with the singular reading מדרכו. Cf. the closely related text 33:11 and also 13:22; 33:9. 𝔊 adds τῆς πονηρᾶς (𝔏^S male) in assimilation to 13:22; 33:9b.

24   24a The וחי יׂעשׂה, which breaks the flow of thought and is not used by 𝔊 𝔏^S (differently in 𝔏) 𝔊 𝔄, must be deleted as a gloss. וחי can, as 𝔗 Reuchlinianus האיתקים and 𝔙 numquid vivet rightly show, only be understood as a question.
   b K צדקתו. The following תזכרנה, however, demands the plural reading of Q (and Eb 22 𝔊 𝔏^S). Cf. 3:20; 33:13. However, in the following חטאתו we must keep the singular of 𝔐 against 𝔊 𝔏^S because of the parallel to מעלו.

25   25a 𝔐 here, in v 29 and 33:17, 20 אדני. MSS Eb 22 𝔗 read יהוה יוי 𝔗 here; also MSS 𝔗 in 33:17, 20. The versions translate the divine name so their witness is no help. Since the mention of the divine name in a hostile saying was undoubtedly more repugnant than its paraphrase with אדני, the reading of 𝔐 must be understood as a softening for dogmatic reasons. See further Excursus 1.
   b 𝔊 𝔏^S read the singular.

26   26a 𝔐 עליהם. The word, which is not attested by 𝔊 𝔏^S 𝔖, appears to be an addition, the suffix of which is related to the "disloyalty" and "sin" of v 24. It anticipates the thought of v 26b. An emendation of ומת (also not attested in 𝔖) to ימות (so Ehrlich, Randglossen, Bertholet, BH^3) is not necessary, either here or in 33:18.

27   27a Attention may be drawn to Mal 3:15, 19 (Prv 16:12) for the striking עשׂה רשׁעה.
   b 𝔊 here κρίμα καὶ δικαιοσύνην as in v 5; differently in vv 19, 21; cf. note b to v 19.

28   28a 𝔐 is not supported by 𝔊^B 𝔏^S 𝔗 𝔄 and must

has turned away[b] from all the offenses which he has done. He shall live, and not die. 29/ But the house of Israel says: the way of 'Yahweh'[a] is not just. Is 'my way'[b] not just, O house of Israel? Are not (rather) your ways not just? 30/ Therefore[a] I will judge you, each according to his ways,[b] O house of Israel, says [the Lord][c] Yahweh.

Repent and turn[d] from all your offenses, so that they may not become[e] an occasion of guilt for you. 31/ Throw all your offenses away from you, by which you have offended against 'me,'[a] and get yourselves a new heart and a new spirit. Why will you die, O house of Israel? 32/ For I have no pleasure in the death of those who are its victims, says [the Lord][a] Yahweh. [So turn away, that you may live.][b]

have been taken over from v 14 since its content does not fit well here.

b K וישוב, Q וישב. Is there a connection with the two unabbreviated imperfect forms ויראה (vv 14, 28) and ויעשה (v 19)?

29 29a Cf. note a to v 25.

b הדרכי . . . יתכנו. We can better read the singular here, as in v 25bα, with the support of 𝕲 𝔏ˢ.

30 30a לכן is lacking in 𝕲 𝔏ˢ.

b 𝕲 𝔏ˢ singular, cf. v 29.

c אדני is lacking in 𝕲 𝔏ˢ 𝕮, see Excursus 1.

d 14:6 makes it likely that we should add to השיבו the unexpressed object פניכם. An assimilation to the שובו שובו of 33:11 (Bertholet, BH³) is not likely in view of the parallel in 14:6.

e In the singular יהיה we must see the influence of מכשול. The plural of 𝕲 is a smoothing over. Cf. 7:19.

31 31a 𝔐 בם. 𝕲 (𝔏ˢ) εἰς ἐμέ. Thus, with MS^Ken 154 we must read בי. The scribal error may have been caused by the directly preceding ם.

32 32a אדני is lacking in 𝕲 𝔏ˢ 𝕮, see Excursus 1.

b The striking והשיבו וחיו, which is lacking in 𝕲 𝔏ˢ 𝕮 𝔄, comes too late after the concluding formula and otherwise only appears in the double assertion שובו והשיבו (14:6; 18:30), is certainly a subsequent expansion. The Lucianic text group of 𝕲 has further enlarged the gloss in dependence on v 23b.

Form

The external limits of the section 18:1–32, which is introduced by the formula for the receipt of a message, are perfectly clear. Although the lament of 19:1–14 is not freshly introduced by this formula (see below to 19:1), yet it is so separated by its metrical form and concrete political content from chapter 18 that there can be no doubt of the break after 18:32.

More strongly contested is the inner division of the section. Fohrer finds two independent sections in vv 1–20 and 21–32. When, in order to be able to answer this question, we inquire after any external signs of connection, the chapter entirely lacks the formula commanding the prophet to speak and the messenger formula.[1] The formula for a divine saying in v 3 is used in the context to emphasize an oath.[2] In v 23 it appears also as a context formula, which makes possible a slight pause between two related questions. In vv 9 and 30 it

denotes the end of a section of the oracle, which is certainly not to be separated from what follows. So, on the basis of form, there is no indication of a join at vv 20/21. In subject matter v 21 undoubtedly begins a new sequence of ideas. A glance at the closely related section in 33:10–20, in which (against Fohrer) vv 11f are certainly not to be isolated as a separate unit in spite of the fresh introduction in v 12 (cf. on the text), forbids in my opinion the separation of vv 1–20 from vv 21–34. Considerations of subject matter lead to the same result. This shows that in the call to repentance, which is anticipated in 33:10f and which is set at the end in 18:30b, the scope of the oracle is to be found. Without a connection with this aim vv 1–20 remain an academic explanation.

As a whole Ezek 18 shows the form of a disputation saying which answers a saying of the people quoted at the beginning.[3] Beside the initial quotation in 18:2, which in its content introduces the whole oracle, the opponents speak again in v 19 in a question, and in vv 25 and 29 in expressing doubt about the righteousness of God. To cut out vv 26–29, as suggested by Herrmann, following Kraetzschmar (parallel text), is unlikely in view of 33:10–20. Instead a comparison with this related section, which is formulated quite distinctively, shows that the statements of Ezek 18 are at home in the area of scholarly discussion which has coined its own stereotyped vocabulary. 3:17–21 and 33:1–9 also show the characteristic vocabulary of this didactic language.

The formal elements, the scholarly language of which is used in ch. 18, need further careful consideration. In this, the section vv 5–17 (20), which deals with the causal nexus of guilt and punishment between generations in the form of a review of three generations, stands out in a particular way. It is irrelevant here to inquire after the historical figures which could have been intended in the sequence: righteous—unrighteous—righteous.[4] The entire sketch is not drawn from history, but from case law. For this we can best point quite generally to the genealogical lists within the priestly tradition and affirm that thinking in genealogical series, where generations are bound together by הוליד (18:10, 14 beside Gen 5:6ff; 11:10ff P), lay close at hand in the priestly sphere. So in Ezek 18 a legal case is worked out which is concerned with the problem of the divine justice through several generations, in the framework of a list (itself drawn from legal practice). From this it is then not surprising that in the elaboration of the individual cases, as already in 3:19; 14:9, 13 and other passages, the sacral law style is to be seen, which was at home in this sphere with its sequence of conditional clauses after the subject (v 5 איש כי; v 18 אביו כי; v 21 והרשע כי).[5]

Far more important, however, is the fact that the distinctive complex of vv 5–9, which is altered in vv 10–13 and 14–17, with its successive series of legal

clauses describing the righteous man, points to a declaratory formula affirming the righteousness of the man (v 9 צדיק הוא), which was at home in the temple rites. The concluding promise of life also undoubtedly points to such a sphere.

So far as the series of legal pronouncements is concerned, which is repeated in vv 10ff, 14ff and which is quoted in 33:15 in a connecting clause describing the righteous (or unrighteous) man, in their form such pronouncements undoubtedly belong to the sphere of legal commands of which the classic form is to be seen in the Decalogue (Ex 20: Dtn 5). Alt has been able to show further such series in the legal material of the Pentateuch, either as a whole or in fragmentary form.[6] For their setting in life he has supposed the great assemblies of the covenant people for a covenant renewal ceremony. The evidence of this solemn assembly of Israel is supported by references in Ps 50 and 81, as well as the self-introduction of Yahweh which introduces the Decalogue, with its citing of the Israelite credo of the exodus.[7] However, beside these there must have been other occasions for formulating series of sacred pronouncements of the divine law directly and firmly aimed at individual worshippers coming to a feast. H. Gunkel and J. Begrich have recognized the form of a *torah*-liturgy, in which worshippers coming up to the sanctuary were told the rules of the sanctuary by a priest.[8] S. Mowinckel and L. Köhler have raised the question whether the formation of the classical Decalogue is connected with this from the point of view of form criticism.[9] Somewhat differently Galling, *Beichtspiegel*, has questioned whether this list of rules to be observed by pilgrims is not rather to be sought in a "confession of integrity" (German "Beichtspiegel") expressed by the pilgrim rather than the priest. However we decide this question, it is certain that in the entrance liturgy, after a declaration by the worshipper (evoked by a question from the priestly gatekeeper?) in which he gave information about his conduct towards the

---

1 See above p. 133 to 2:4b.

2 See above p. 176 to 5:11.

3 See above p. 280 to 12:21–25.

4 Hölscher, *Hesekiel, der Dichter*, 103f: Josiah; his three wicked sons Jehoahaz, Jehoiakim, Zedekiah; his pious grandson Jehoiachin. Cooke considers the sequence Hezekiah–Manasseh–Josiah.

5 See above p. 302.

6 See also K. Rabast, *Das apodiktische Recht im Deuteronomium und im Heiligkeitsgesetz* (1949).

7 Zimmerli, "Jahwe."

8 Hermann Gunkel and Joachim Begrich, *Einleitung in die Psalmen* (Göttingen: Vandenhoeck & Ruprecht, ²1966), 408f, see also 327–329.

9 Sigmund Mowinckel, *Le Décalogue* (Paris: Alcan, 1927), especially 141–156; Ludwig Koehler, "Der

stipulations of the law, there followed a pronouncement by the priest which gave a decision either permitting or refusing entry.

The צדיק הוא, which is found in v 9 at the end of a series of descriptive clauses and which appears rather tautologous beside the איש כי יהיה צדיק, which introduces the whole series in v 5, belongs most probably to the priestly sphere. R. Rendtorff, *Gesetze*, in his examination of the laws in P, has noted a form of regularly repeated short nominal clauses, built up from the pronominal third person singular as a predicate. For these G. von Rad, "Faith," has conjectured the title "declaratory formulas." These clearly reflect certain priestly diagnoses in their content. Such diagnoses concern themselves first of all with factual circumstances. In the laws governing leprosy, in the case where the sickness is evident to the priest, the diagnosis is expressed: נגע צרעת הוא—or if the case is harmless: מספחת היא (Lev 13:3, 6). Of a properly offered sacrifice it is said: עלה הוא (Lev 1:17), מנחה הוא (Lev 2:15). In both cases it concerns not simply an inconsequential (analytical) judgement, but a thoroughly consequential (synthetic) declaration which concerns permission, or refusal, to enter the sanctuary, and the validity or otherwise of sacrifice. It is an act of "reckoning, acknowledging" (von Rad). Thus the judgement about the physical condition of a sick person in the priest's concern with leprosy passes over directly into a more comprehensive personal judgement about the man upon whom the judgement טמא הוא or טהור הוא now lies (Lev 13:11, 13). This judgement corresponds to the preceding diagnosis of sickness. In this judgement the act of טמא or טהר takes place. We must regard as in line with this the logically striking צדיק הוא of Ezek 18:9. In it there is echoed the priestly declaration customary in the gate-liturgy, which was pronounced regarding the pilgrim, whether in the form of a "confession of integrity" regarding his conduct towards a code of laws set out before him, or whether he answered the reading of the commandments by the priest with the saying "all these have I kept" (cf. Mt 19:20). The partial diagnosis reckoned against individual laws, and oriented towards individual "works" as accomplished acts, is characteristically raised by the priest to the level of a comprehensive diagnosis about the person. The pilgrim is declared to be צדיק, and the process of צָדֵק takes place. Or can we formulate with Gen 15:6 that it was "reckoned" to him as righteousness (von Rad)? By the sequence: recapitulation of the laws—declaratory judgement, Ezek 18 reflects a real action which used to be performed in the sanctuary (in Jerusalem) at the temple gate.

The third element of Ezek 18:5–9, the promise of life, also points to an event in the sanctuary. "Life" is especially the gift given in the sphere of the sanctuary as the place of God's presence (von Rad, "Righteousness"). This becomes clear behind the polemical *torah* of Amos: "Seek me, and you will live, but do not seek Bethel . . ." (Amos 5:4f). Behind it there echoes the priestly *torah* "Seek Bethel, and you will live." [10] In the current *torah* of the priests the reference to the sacral law which was proclaimed at the temple gate, only by observance of which was there granted a way into "life" at the sanctuary, was improperly given second place to the simple admonition to come to the sanctuary (Ex 23:17). Against this "cheap" offer of life (cf. D. Bonhoeffer's "cheap grace") Amos upheld the divine law which he describes comprehensively in 5:14 as "good" (דרשו טוב ואל רע למען תחיו cf. the אשר לא טוב of Ezek 18:18) and thereby recalls that "life" is only given where the divine covenant law is obediently listened to. In the light of Amos's assertions we can understand Jeremiah's temple sermon, which polemically sets the keeping of the commandments (cf. the background in the Decalogue of Jer 7:9, also vv 5f) over against the people's blind assurance in the temple. The word ח׳ה (חיים) is admittedly not found in Jer 7 (or 26). What the worshipper actually seeks in order to have "life," which he expects to find in the sanctuary, is clear enough in the repetitive words of confession "The temple of Yahweh, the temple of Yahweh, the temple of Yahweh is this" (Jer 7:4), which recall the trisagion of the liturgy (Is 6:3). This becomes even clearer in the נצלנו of Jer 7:10 (Ezek 33:12 varies חיה with הציל). [11] "To live" is to be delivered by the divine presence. (According to Amos 5:14 "to live" can be

---

Dekalog," *ThR* NF 1 (1929): 161–184.

10   See Begrich, "Tora."

11   See Zimmerli, " 'Leben' und 'Tod'," 496.

described by the worshipper's assertion "Yahweh is with us" (יהוה אתנו.) The explicit mention of "life" is only found in Jeremiah in the (secondarily formulated?) narrative parts in connection with particular historical instruction by the prophet. If the חיה of Jer 21:9; 38:2, 17 is understood physically of simple survival under the acute threat of siege, the advice given in the face of this threat in Jer 27:17 (cf. v 12), "Submit to the king of Babylon, and you will live," clearly echoes the temple formulation recognizable in Amos. Further the classical prophets are striking for their frequent avoidance of promises of "life," with their overtones of the temple *torah*.[12] This is indirectly evidence which should not be overlooked of the connection between the strictly formulated promise of life and what took place in the sanctuary.

In conjunction with the Psalm references given by von Rad, " 'Righteousness'," the texts referred to are sufficient to demonstrate that the worshipper, who was permitted to enter the sanctuary and to share in the worship of the community on the basis of his confession of obedience, could expect by doing so to enter into the promise of life, honor, and deliverance given by Yahweh. The question may be asked whether this gift of life was only expressed in the form of the blessing of the community, or whether beyond this it was also given as an individual promise to a person. Passages such as Ezek 33:13 (with a negative parallel in 3:18; 33:14, see below to 33:13f) make it likely that there was also an individual promise.

From this language formed around the liturgy of the temple worship the description of the righteous in 18:5–9 (with an abbreviated repetition in vv 10–13, 14–17) also undoubtedly comes. The dramatic action at the temple gate (and the subsequent action in the temple) is here recast into a simple narrative. From the keeping of the commandments and the confession of obedience (cf. Ps 50:16 for the listing of the commandments following spontaneously upon the "con-

fession of integrity"), the priestly declaration which follows it, and the promise of life given in the sanctuary, there arises here a general description of the righteous and the promise of life given to him.

A knowledge of the background of the prophet's words is indispensable for an understanding of the hidden emphasis of his message.

Setting

From the reference in v 2, according to which the prophet inveighs against a saying current "in the land of Israel," Herntrich and Bertholet adduce that in the prophet's reply we must also be dealing with a prophecy uttered in Jerusalem "in regard to the catastrophe" (Herntrich).[13] In the succession of generations in vv 5–17 Herntrich sees the succession of the reigns of Josiah, Jehoiakim, and Zedekiah. The latter king is then regarded as being presented here with a call to repentance and the possibility of life which it brings.

Against the connection of the scheme of three generations with specific kings, however, we may adduce, as already noted, the didactic character of the details which avoid any precise individualizing of the three periods and also any precise chronological allusion. For the quotation of a saying current "in the land of Israel" we must note what has been said above regarding 12:22, which is introduced similarly, that the explicit localizing of the saying "in the land of Israel" rather favors the view that the speaker was not himself in that land.[14] Chronologically the saying quoted points rather to the situation after the great collapse of 587 B.C. That Ezekiel reacted to sayings which circulated after the collapse in Palestine is clearly shown by ישבי החרבות האלה על אדמת ישראל of 33:24. The book of Lamentations, which certainly belongs to the region of Palestine, expressly mentions in 5:7 the presence in the land of similar assertions.[15] Jer 31:29 can scarcely be claimed for the period before 587 B.C.[16] Such pregnant metaphorical sayings as Ezek 18:2 (=Jer 31:29)

12 Cf. Hab 2:4, a משל, so Friedrich Horst in the second edition of Horst-Robinson, *kleinen Propheten*, 179f; Is 55:3, in the style of Wisdom address according to Joachim Begrich, *Studien zu Deuterojesaja*, BWANT 4:25 (Stuttgart, 1938), 53f.
13 Herntrich, *Ezekielprobleme*, 102f; Bertholet, 69.
14 See pp. 281f; see *VT* 8 (1958): 77f, and Excursus 2 for the nonhistorical and theological character of

this title.
15 Janssen, *Juda*, 9–12; Hans-Joachim Kraus, *Klagelieder (Threni)*, BK 20 (Neukirchen-Vluyn: Neukirchener, 1956), 11–13.
16 See Volz and Rudolph, *Jeremia*, on the text.

undoubtedly became a temptation and danger for many exiles whose ears they reached. Thus an argument with a saying current "in the land of Israel" was quite directly intended for the exiles also. 33:10–20, which relates to a complaint by those who were lost in exile, then shows the clear application of the content of Ezek 18 to the exiles.[17]

Interpretation

■**18:1, 2** After a brief introductory remark about the coming of the message, there follows immediately, in a way that is unusual for Ezekiel, a disputation oracle without any further address to the prophet and without any explicit commission to speak (cf. note a to v 2).[18] Does this relate further to the fact that we have before us here an oracle of the prophet's which was formulated relatively late? The citation of a saying of the people in "the land of Israel," introduced by the formulation used in 12:22, clearly carries the formal characteristics of a משל. Those who are left in the land, according to Lam 5:7, complain in personal contrition: "Our fathers have erred; they are no more, and we must bear their sins." H. J. Kraus rightly contends that this assertion had the tone of indignant revolt, so that the saying cited by Ezekiel, in its metaphorical dress, is different in its purpose and has become an expression of cynical disillusionment.[19] Whether the "teeth being blunted" points to a popular superstition according to which the teeth of those who ate unripe sour grapes (בסר cf. Is 18:5; Job 15:33) quickly decayed (Eccl 10:10 קהה pi'el of the blunting of an axe),[20] or in a derived sense of the teeth becoming "on edge, bitter" (Jewish-Aramaic קהה of grapes becoming sour), it is in any case clear that we can see in it a mocking at the divine "righteousness" which lays the guilt of the fathers upon the children. The ancient liturgical predication of Yahweh as the God who punishes sins until the third and fourth generations (Ex 20:5f; 34:7; Nu 14:18; cf. further the revised formulation in Dtn 7:9f)

could give rise to such reactions. The actual intervention of judgement, after the threat of it by prophets proclaiming God's punishment upon the people who had sinned throughout the generations (Hos, Jer, Ezek 16, 20, 23), had clearly brought this out in all its sharpness. The winged word, which must have enjoyed a wide currency (Jer 31:29), cannot have remained unheard by the exiles, as a word of human self-assertion over against the judgement of God. As such Ezekiel set against it the message of Yahweh which concerned all Israel in all its historically separated parts.

■**18:3** The passionate form of an oath in which the answer is given shows that Yahweh had well understood the indignant attack by the house of Israel.[21] In sharp antithesis to the popular saying he asserts that such an insolent accusation would have no place in the future.

■**18:4** Instead the statement of Yahweh's fundamental righteousness would be upheld: "The person who sins, he shall die." H. Haag correctly points out the close verbal connection of this statement with the formulation of the priestly law (cf. the נפש כי תחטא Lev 4:2; 5:1, 17, 21; further Nu 15:27).[22] This verbal connection is also true of the directly related assertion of lordship in which Yahweh appears as Lord of the life of every individual (for נפש cf. note b to v 4), both father and son. In a similar way Moses and Aaron cried out in the knowledge that the sovereign Lord of life is also righteous toward every individual: "God, the Lord of the spirits of all flesh (אל אלהי הרוחת לכל בשר), wilt thou be angry with the whole congregation because one person has sinned?" (Nu 16:22). Modern ideas are inclined to connect the idea of unlimited power directly with those of arbitrariness and of submission on the part of the person ruled. Over against this the quite different point of view of the priestly assertions should be considered. This ideal stands also behind the Noah covenant of Gen 9:1–7. If life were to remain in the hands of men, then it would be given over to unrighteousness, but because the Lord of all life has set bounds to each

---

17 For the reasons which may have led to the insertion of this late prophetic saying into the first half of the book, see the Introduction.
18 See above pp. 144f.
19 Kraus, *Klagelieder*, 84.
20 See Loew 1, 77; see above pp. 168f.
21 See above p. 176 to 5:11.
22 Haag, *Untersuchung*, 84f.

individual's life, man can live joyously under the reassuring sign of a covenant of grace. In this way life is protected.

■ **18:5ff** Ezek 18 proclaims the message of Yahweh's righteousness towards men who, in cynical nihilism (and then also in the despair of Lam 5:7; cf. Ezek 33:10), are condemned to the rigid nexus of guilt and punishment in the solidarity of the generations and who give in fatalistically to this. Ezekiel's preaching, however, does not remain in the form of a general statement, but takes on a concrete immediacy for the individual. The scheme of a series of generations, which was familiar to the priests,[23] permits the linking together of three cases: 1) the case of the righteous man, apart from any question of his "inherited burden;" 2) the case of the unrighteous son of a righteous man; 3) the case of the righteous son of an unrighteous man. The listing of two righteous men, of which the first could satisfactorily be left out since it has nothing to do with the particular father-son problem that is in hand, shows clearly that the cases: righteousness—life, unrighteousness—death are not set equally beside each other, but that the emphasis lies on righteousness—life. On the side that demands attention the promise is painted very brightly. The introductory description of the righteous man (vv 5–9), which is preserved in the style of the sacral law and which very strongly echoes the movement of the old temple rite which led to the promise of life, gives expression to the fact that we are not dealing with a static "doctrine of life," but with the situation of a promise of life which demanded a personal decision on the part of the person addressed. The repetition of this in vv 10–13, 14–17 show, by their omission of the declaratory formula, a marked weakening of the form.

The slight logical tension which is noticeable in the description of the righteous man in vv 5–9, with its tautological repetition of the צדיק of the protasis (v 5) in the apodosis (v 9), goes back to the secondary connection of two originally separate speech forms.[24] The form of the old temple rite presupposes that the pilgrim who passed the inquiry at the temple gate about obedience to the commandments was then assured that this

was reckoned as righteousness, expressed in the declaratory judgement, and was promised "life." The antithesis of the righteous and the wicked, set out in the structure of Ezek 18, however, demands a reference to the "righteous" at the very beginning and understands the history of the commandments as a subsequent explication of the righteousness that has been mentioned previously. The omission of the declaratory judgement in vv 11–13 and 14–17 then becomes intelligible on the basis of the inner tension between the two speech forms.

■ **18:5** Thus the description of the righteous man in v 5 begins with a thematic mention of the צדיק, who is formally described as one who does משפט וצדקה.

■ **18:6–8** The listing of specific laws through which the righteous man's obedience is assured in the practical situations of life begins with v 6. It is concluded in v 9a with a general reference to keeping the statutes and commandments of God. In vv 6–8 the individual ordinances are set out in thirteen short clauses (eight of which are formulated negatively). The clauses are set out in pairs, and only in v 7a is a threefold group given. Since a positive formulation has entered here between two negatively formulated clauses, we may conjecture that the former is later from the point of view of the history of tradition. Quite generally we may accept that the two positively formulated pairs, vv 7b and 8b contain the later formulation, since the negative formulations belong at the beginning of the whole course of the apodictic legal tradition (Alt, "Origins"). Whether finally a decalogic, or a dodecalogic, formulation stands behind the series cannot certainly be decided since the series is plainly given by Ezekiel in what was already a "worn out" form. Does the גלולי בית ישראל (v 6), which is peculiar to Ezekiel, also belong to this broken form? Or does the use of this polemical term belong to the language of the temple liturgy?[25]

Further it is not to be denied that the listing of the clauses of the sacral law is set in an order which recalls the classical Decalogue. The first pair of clauses (v 6a) mentions the ordinances of right worship of God, whilst the second (v 6b) concerns ritual regulations. The ordinances of social life and legal activity which then follow in three groups of couplets and triplets

23   See above p. 375.
24   See above p. 376.
25   See above pp. 186f.

(vv 7, 8aα) are also concluded by a pair of expressions which refer to the sphere of law (v 8aβ bα). In many of these short legal rulings there are clear echoes of laws of the Book of the Covenant, of Deuteronomy, and especially of the Holiness Code. Over against this the verbal contacts with the classical Decalogue are surprisingly small.

■ **18:6** The position of primacy given to the prohibition of eating on the mountains enables us to see once again quite directly the struggles of the eighth and seventh centuries, which came to a decisive point in the reform of Josiah. This decision could not be reversed in the long run in spite of some backlashes. In Hos (4:13) we first hear the polemic against sacrifices (זבח) on the mountains. Deuteronomy raises a polemic against the places of sacrifice "upon the high mountains and hills, and under every green tree."[26] With Trito-Isaiah sacrifices (קטר) upon the mountains appear again as the particular sin of the ancestors (Is 65:7). The summary formulation אכל על ההרים, which emphasizes the community meal accompanying the sacrifice, is a formulation peculiar to Ezekiel (18:6, 11, 15; 22:9). It is in line with the cultic-ritual sins of 8:6 (driving away from the sanctuary) and 8:16 (and 17bβ?) (the turning of one's back upon the most holy place).[27] The listing of these offenses clearly attests the Palestinian origin of the traditional formula. Since Ezekiel's oracle arose directly out of an argument with "those in the land of Israel," the citing of this peculiarly Canaanite-Palestinian offense is in no way out of place.

The "lifting up of the eyes to the idols of the house of Israel" is formulated wholly in Ezekiel's terminology. גלולי בית ישראל is found beside 18:6, 15 also in 8:10. נשא עינים אל is found in 18:6, 12, 15; 23:27; 33:25. The statement refers in a quite general formulation to giving attention (8:5, as Gen 13:10, 14; 18:2 and other passages), being conscious of an attraction (Gen 39:7), and looking trustfully (Ps 121:1; 123:1), to powers whose very title (גלולים) indicates their uncleanness.[28]

The prohibition against adultery, which the Decalogue (Ex 20:14; Dtn 5:18) and the Holiness Code (Lev 20:10) express by the verb נאף, is here set under the perspective of ritual uncleanness, like the ritual prohibition of intercourse with a woman in the time of her menstruation.[29]

■ **18:7** Oppression (הונה) is forbidden in the Book of the Covenant towards a foreigner (Ex 22:20), and in Dtn 23:17 towards a slave. Lev 25:17 (H; further Lev 19:33; 25:14) is particularly close to Ezekiel's formulation (cf. further 22:7, 29). Robbery (גזל) is not mentioned either in the laws of the Book of the Covenant or those of Deuteronomy, but is found in H in Lev 19:13. The priestly law of sacrifice is concerned in Lev 5:23 (גזלה 5:21, גזל) with robbery. The positive statement, introduced between the mention of oppression and robbery, about the restoring of a pledge looks back to older rulings in Ex 22:25f; Dtn 24:10–13, 17. It is clearly intended to clarify the general reference to oppression by giving a concrete example.

The laws nowhere command the giving of food to the hungry and the clothing of the naked in such specific terms, although quite early they already encourage the showing of pity to the needy (Dtn 15:7–11; Lev 19:9f; cf. the description of the attitude of Yahweh described in Dtn 10:18f).[30] Further the positive formulation points to a late presentation of the demand within the legal tradition.

■ **18:8** Against this the doubly formulated prohibition against taking interest belongs to the ancient order of sacral law. In the Book of the Covenant it is mentioned in Ex 22:24; in Deuteronomy in Dtn 23:20; and in the Holiness Code in Lev 25:35–37 (cf. Ps 15:5; Prv 28:8). In the parallelism of נשך (properly "bitten off, deduction") and תרבית (properly "multiplying, addition"), which reappears in 22:12, Ezek 18:8 stands particularly close to H in the wording of its formulation.[31]

The final pair of pronouncements is concerned with

---

26 See above p. 191 to 6:13.
27 See above p. 238; pp. 243–245. See also the polemic against the "mountains" in Ezek 6.
28 See above p. 187.
29 For נדה see above pp. 208f to 7:19; in H Lev 18:19; cf. 20:21.
30 Cf. Is 58:7; Job 31:16–20; Mt 25:31–46, and Strack-Billerbeck 4, Excursus 23: "Die altjüdischen Liebeswerke," pp. 559–610.
31 For the question of usury in the ancient Orient and in Israel see Johann Hejcl, *Das alttestamentliche Zinsverbot im Licht der ethnologischen Jurisprudenz sowie des altorientalischen Zinswesens*, BSF 12, 4 (Freiburg, 1907).

conduct in courts of law. The first clause, although it is formulated positively like the second, allows the negative form of speech to show through: מעול ישיב ידו could easily be changed into לא יעשה עול. That עול must be interpreted here of unlawful action in a court of law is supported not only by the parallel statement, but also by the related לא תעשו עול במשפט in Lev 19:15, 35. The word אמת, which is completely absent in P and H (Haag), is only found here in Ezekiel (for 𝔐 of v 9 cf. note c on the text). The related expressions in Jer 2:21 זרע אמת "true seed," Jer 14:13 שלום אמת "true salvation," Jer 42:5 (Prov 14:25) עד אמת ונאמן "a true and reliable witness," and Mal 2:6 תורת אמת "true teaching" point to the meaning "true law." (Cf. further Zech 7:9.) The inculcation of right conduct in the administration of law was already a foundation of Israel's early law. (Cf. the "Judge's Code" [Alt "Richterspiegel"] in the Book of the Covenant [Ex 23:1–3, 6–8; further Dtn 16:18–20; 24:17; 27:19].) The formulations of the Holiness Code in Lev 19:15, 35 are also very close in language here.

■ **18:9** The same is true of the concluding statement which demands obedience to Yahweh's laws and statutes, which has quite close counterparts in Lev 25:18; 26:3.

The declaratory צדיק הוא which then follows, has lost its original weight in the present connection. In the shadow of the איש כי יהיה צדיק (v 5) set at the beginning, it can only appear as a repetition. The forensic force of this personal judgement, which "reckons" the marks of obedience to Yahweh's law given in what precedes and then affirms authoritatively the "righteousness" of the person before Yahweh, is now only heard in the background.

The particular emphasis of the legal affirmation now lies in the following חיה יחיה. If this was spoken by the priest in the temple, who clearly had behind him the whole weight of the sacred temple instruction for everyone, then this saying has been set here in the mouth of the exiled prophet in a situation where all these assurances have gone, leaving no guarantee. Thus the question arises unavoidably as to what the prophet meant by the promise of life to the righteous.

Scholars have felt it necessary to interpret Ezekiel as the preacher of a general doctrine of righteous retribution. By his obedience the individual is to receive "life," i.e., blessing and prosperity, beside which the "life" of Israel properly sinks to a level of secondary importance.[32] "People can also 'live' in Babylonia, i.e., they can lead a full, long, and happy life if they will only walk spiritually, and in accordance with the will of God. Not the outward situation, but the conduct within it is decisive."[33] This separation of the promise of life to the individual from the promise of life to Israel-Jerusalem, for which dwelling in the land and the right worship of God were indispensable elements, as the preaching of Ezekiel elsewhere shows, can in the long run not be wholly satisfying. Thus Bertholet, who places Ezek 18 before 587 B.C., would interpret "to live" as pointing to the survival of the pious in the imminent destruction of Jerusalem and to membership of the remnant which was to be preserved (in the land; cf. also 9:4): "The question is in fact simply this: who is to remain alive when the great killing takes place?"[34] However, can the parallel saying in 33:10ff be set before 587 B.C.? Kraetzschmar, who places Ezek 18 after 587 B.C., thinks of the "killing" of the wicked, and of "dying under God's judgement, which excludes participation in the coming messianic glory. The latter alone is the concern here, and in so far the chapter deserves the description 'eschatological'."[35] However, where in Ezekiel is there mention of this judgement on the eve of the "coming messianic glory"? Haag attempts to make the answer historically specific: "The exiles are all summoned to return to the land of their ancestors and to participate in the life of the age of salvation. The sinner, however, who has not returned by then will not experience this; he will die beforehand

---

32 W. von Baudissin, "Alttestamentliches *ḥajjim* in der Bedeutung 'Glück'" in *Festschrift Eduard Sachau zum siebzigsten Geburtstag* (Berlin: Reimer, 1915), 143–161.

33 Fohrer, 18:21–32.

34 Herrmann, 113, cited Bertholet, 69.

35 Kraetzschmar, 162.

(cf. Ezek 20:35ff)."[36] In view of this interpretation, which connects the promise of life to the individual much more closely with the promise of life to Israel, we cannot avoid the question why in Ezek 18, unlike the clear statement of 13:9, there is no word of the future decisive end of the new settlement, nor even any allusion to it.

To answer this question we shall have to take seriously the results gained from our form critical investigation. The promise of life, like the preceding description of the demands of righteousness and the declaratory affirmation, stems from the sphere of the sanctuary and echoes all that goes on there. Several Psalm references make clear, however, that the salvation promised there was not primarily the promise of a specific, and materially defined, gift, but more broadly a promise "God will be with you." Amos 5:14 shows that even in the worship of the Northern Kingdom this יהוה אתנו stood at the center.[37] We may also refer here to the structure of the oracle of salvation ("Heilsorakel"), identified by J. Begrich.[38] In this there is promised to the worshipper by the priest, at first in a quite general formulation in the perfect tense, the assurance that Yahweh has heard (cf. the reflection of this in the שמע of Ps 6:10), helped (עזרתיך Is 41:10, 14), redeemed (גאלתיך Is 43:1; 44:22). There then follows, couched in the imperfect, the concrete unfolding of the saving activities that are to be expected. The assurance of help that "God is with you" (so Is 41:10, parallel to the following גאלתיך) is thus here set out in the perfect tense as something already achieved. Ps 73:25f shows that the gift of this "Yahweh is with you" or "Yahweh is my portion" (it could also easily have been expressed as "Yahweh is my life") can be set in many fuller formulations in direct antithesis to all outward blessings. This does not arise from any indifference to the world and its gifts, marking a retreat into inwardness, but from the knowledge that in this affirmation about Yahweh all other gifts are included, however little they can be seen at the present. Yahweh will certainly receive the man with whom he is "into his glory" (Ps 73:24). This is the "life" which belief in Yahweh's promise expects, even where it has still not

become tangible in his gifts.

Ezekiel lived in exile. The immediate reality of the sanctuary, its blessing, and promise of life had vanished for him. Ezek 37:1ff shows that he was conscious of the free promise of a new life beyond the realm of death. This was the case besides death which meant the exile with its remoteness from the place where the priest promised life. This new life meant for Israel as a whole the promise of a return to the land (37:12–14), to "the high mountain of Israel" (Ezek 20:40) with its sanctuary, which would become once again, through the miracle of Yahweh's action, the place of his presence and thus of life (Ezek 40ff). By the receiving of the divine word (v 1) the prophet receives authority to proclaim the promise of life as a pure gift, even at his remote place of exile where that promise had not altogether been extinguished and where Yahweh had become a מקדש מעט.[39] The reference to "life" is thus left pending in a peculiar balance and remains open. It is left (unlike in 13:9) without any specific explanation, in a restraint which is comparable with the way in which the promise of life was given also in the temple liturgy. That God promises his "Yes," and therewith his assurance of "life," to the man who confesses obedience to him and his commands is here also the only important factor. This "Yes" would undoubtedly have been made known also in outward signs in which, from the perspective of the exiles, a return to their land would have been included along the lines of the promise of 13:9. However, nothing in the text entitles us to reduce this "Yes" of Yahweh, given to his "righteous ones," to this one hope of a return. This would be to say both too much and too little.

■ **18:10–13** Cynical resignation (v 2) had pointed to the "righteousness" of Yahweh which allowed evil to befall the children whose fathers had sinned. Thus the giving of life to the righteous, which is expressed quite generally in vv 5–9 in the picture of the "righteous" man, is further clarified in vv 10ff, with a glance at the paralyzing fatalism of the linking together of the generations. Vv 10–13 then unfold the first case of the problem of the generations, that of an unrighteous son of a right-

---

36   Haag, *Untersuchung*, 92.
37   See above pp. 376f.
38   Begrich, *Studien*, 9; Joachim Begrich, "Das priester-

liche Heilsorakel," *ZAW* 52 (1934): 84f; reprinted in *idem*, *Gesammelte Studien zum AT*, ThB 21 (München: Kaiser, 1964), 217f.

eous man. Here also the negative overall judgement is formulated in advance and is then unfolded in a list of offenses.

■ **18:10** The overall predicate צדיק in v 5 (v 9) surprisingly does not correspond to a simple רשע, which is otherwise the usual antithesis to צדיק in Ezekiel (3:17–21; 13:22 and other passages), but to a double qualification of פריץ and שפך דם. The word פריץ is only found again in the Old Testament in Ezek 7:22;[40] Jer 7:11; Dan 11:14; Is 35:9 (of animals); Ps 17:4 (inc.) and comprehends all violent deeds which individual laws prohibited into one overall personal judgement. שפך דם points again to a distinctly priestly mode of evaluation. It reappears in Ezekiel with a clear emphasis as a technical term in 22:3ff, where it dominates the whole context, and in 23:45; 33:25. Lev 17:4 says of the man who does not bring his slaughtered animal to the sanctuary: דם יחשב לאיש ההוא דם שפך. Non-cultic slaughter is "reckoned" as "shedding blood," which thereafter becomes a fixed category of guilt. With this we must take the P account of the order of the world after the Flood (Gen 9:1–7), where cultic offenses concerning the blood of a slaughtered animal and the shedding of blood in society are summarized as "blood" offenses. An evaluation of this kind must be in the mind of Ezekiel, both here and in the other references given, where the שפך דם, which P sets out so prominently, appears as a fixed term. Ultimately is פריץ also a similar technical term, as Jer 7:11 would support?

The detailed description of the unrighteous son is introduced by a general connection with assertions already made about the righteous father: "He does one of these things." The positive formulation shows how obviously the normal description of the righteous man moves in a negative way: "He has *not* done this."

■ **18:11** Thus the addition in v 11a (note a) adds this in respect of the righteous father. The list of commands in vv 6–8 is then freely repeated with some abbreviations and slight changes and an occasional change of tense. In this way the offense against the laws is made clear. From the first pair of commands, which demand right worship of God, the regard for the idols of the house of Israel has come in after the threefold group of crimes of violence, listed in third place.

■ **18:12** In the second pair, which deal with the cultic order, the rendering of a woman unclean in the time of her menstruation is passed over. The threefold group, set in third place, merely repeats the earlier formulation in all three of its assertions, and the only change is the transposing of the second and third items. The formulation is slightly modified in that "the poor and needy" are now explicitly mentioned as the objects of oppression (הונה). The linking of עני and אביון, which is frequent in the Psalms, is found in the legal literature only in Dtn 15:11 and 24:14. In the restoring of a pledge the חיב, mentioned in v 7 (admittedly in an uncertain text), is not mentioned again. The fourth pair of statements which deals with helping the hungry and naked is missing, as also is the sixth which concerns conduct in a court of law. The fifth (the taking of interest) is adduced in exact correspondence to v 8. In accordance with the analogy of vv 5–9 we should expect to find a declaratory judgement upon the wicked in this place, but it appears to be lacking. Thus the guilt of the wicked between the refusal of life (v 13bα[1]) and the explicit threat of death (v 13bβ) is again indicated by the clause את כל התועבות האלה עשה. From the form-critical viewpoint this is now certainly not to be separated from the declarative qualifications which are to be found in Lev 18 and 20 in various formulations at the end of a list of prohibitions. The terse declaratory תועבה הוא (Lev 18:22; cf. further זמה הוא Lev 18:17; 20:14; תבל הוא Lev 18:23; חסד הוא Lev 20:17; נדה הוא Lev 20:21) is thereby changed into a verbal clause with עשה. This development is already anticipated in Lev 20:13 (תועבה עשו, in v 12 תבל עשו). It appears therefore that in the description of the wicked also the declarative qualification (which is admittedly already in a broken form here) is not altogether lacking. It is simply that in place of the personal רשע the word תועבה, which usually diagnoses a physical condition, is used.[41] Lev 18 and 20 certainly suggest that תועבה, beside the qualification זמה which appears there, חסד, תבל, and נדה, belongs to the sphere of uncleanness according to the priestly mode of reckoning.[42]

We must also see the influence of stereotyped lan-

39 See above pp. 261f to 11:16.

40 See above p. 212.

41 Cf. further what is said above on p. 376 regarding

Lev 13.

42 For זמה see above p. 345 to 16:27; for נדה see above pp. 208f to 7:19f.

guage in the concluding sentence of death. Over against the חיה יחיה of the promise of life (v 9), the מות ימות must be set as a fixed counterpart as is also found in fact in the free formulations of vv 17, 21, 24, 28. This is then also read here by many commentators, who refer to certain textual variant readings (cf. note b). The change of reading, however, demands also the excision of the connected דמיו בו יהיה, which they have not seen. As Leviticus shows, this is the formula with which the persons who are to carry out a death sentence affirm that no bloodguilt rests on them because the unrighteous dies on account of his own guilt. Where Yahweh himself inflicts the punishment such an affirmation of assurance for the men who carry out the law becomes pointless. Thus in Lev 20 the דמיו בו (and דמיהם בם) always stands after the passive form מות יומת, or יומתו, which points to the death of the wrongdoer by a human judgement (Lev 20:9, 11, 12, 13, 16, 27). It is lacking in Lev 20:17–21, where the excommunication formula or the formula of bearing guilt points to a judgement from God.[43] Lev 20:2 also, where execution by the people is only mentioned late, after the excommunication formula, must be interpreted from this.[44] We can then establish that the casuistic description of the sinner, especially in its first part, is clearly set out as a counterpart to the description of the righteous man, whereas in its conclusion we can see the influence of a different law which was certainly not rooted in the gate-liturgy. It is certainly also probable from the nature of the case that life and death were not proclaimed at the gate equally. The sanctuary was the place of life. Undoubtedly there were occasions, even in the worship of Israel, when the law of God, threatening the penalty of death, was proclaimed (cf. Alt). Further to this there were occasions in which a sentence of death was declared quite personally to an individual.[45] For an understanding of the content of Ezek 18 it is important that the prophet, when he speaks of the death of the wicked, does not avoid

echoing the idea that the community itself was actively responsible for the removal of the disobedient. The major emphasis certainly lies in the whole section on the assertion that the son of the righteous man is personally punished by God for his own actions. There is no "inherited stock" of righteousness.

■ **18:14–17** The main point of the first part of Ezek 18 is reached in the third case (vv 14–17) which deals with the righteous son of an unrighteous father.

■ **18:14, 15** The terse narrative statement (הוליד בן), taken over from the style of official lists, is expanded slightly by the addition of a third "case." The son's turning away from evil is inwardly motivated by having seen the wickedness of his father. This is then followed again by a detailed description of the righteous behavior of the son. The stronger emphasis, which the reference to the righteous man and the life that he receives carries, is noticeable over against vv 10–13 in the fuller elaboration of the individual clauses (in the perfect tense throughout here). Even so, even here there is not the comprehensiveness of the thirteen clauses of vv 6–8. The first pair of statements about right worship repeat word for word the statements of v 6a. In the cultic prescriptions the conduct towards a woman in the time of her menstruation is passed over.

■ **18:16** In the group of three which then follows and which mentions the avoidance of violence, the middle clause, which in v 7 is formulated positively, is changed into the older negative formulation (חבל לא חבל). The two rules of charity correspond to the pattern of v 7, apart from their change into the perfect. However, the twofold saying about right conduct in law is reduced to a single statement which precedes the fifth pair of statements in the pattern. In this way the parallel twofold saying of this fifth pair is summarized in a single statement (נשך ותרבית לא לקח). The formal twofold saying about keeping the laws and statutes of Yahweh concludes, as in v 9a, the detailed description of the righteous, which is now followed immediately by

---

43   See above pp. 303–305.

44   It is not clear why the formula for bloodguilt is lacking in Lev 20:10, 14f. Is it because burning by fire (v 14) is not regarded as the shedding of blood? Should we then accept that the same is true in v 2 in regard to stoning? What are we to make then of 10:15? There is much that needs clarification here.

45   See further Zimmerli, "'Leben' und 'Tod'," page

497 note 7, page 500 note 12 (= *Gottes Offenbarung*, page 181 note 7, page 184 note 12).

the promise of life, with the omission of a declaratory pronouncement that the man is righteous. This is given a strong emphasis by the preceding rebuttal of the death sentence, which is formulated here in parallel with the promise of life, unlike v 13.

■ **18:18** V 18 also adds emphasis with a glance back at the case of the sinful father (vv 10–13), and it is once again laid down that in any case the sinful father must die for his sins (violence and robbery are particularly stressed, cf. 22:29). That the sins are described comprehensively as "that which is not good" (cf. 36:31) recalls the summaries of the *torah* in Amos 5:14f; Jer 7:3, 5.[46]

■ **18:19** With the connection to the basic theme which is thereby reached and with which the whole wide-ranging explanation started in v 4, there occurs a further occasion for debate with the person being addressed. If he should ask why the son does not share the father's guilt, there is no further treatment of the question. The evidence of the righteousness in the personal answer by God is simply held up to him. In this the generalizing formulas reappear which formed the comprehensive summary of the description of the righteous man in vv 9 and 17: the man who has practiced righteousness will live.

■ **18:20** The thesis of v 4 is then repeated immediately in a didactic formulation in two parallel clauses: 1) it is denied that the generations are bound together, and 2) a clear responsibility in regard to righteousness and ungodliness is expressed. Righteousness and ungodliness, according to the formulation of the concluding sentence of the first speech in vv 2–20, are not only causes, but powers, which carry life and death within themselves.

■ **18:21–29** The cynical fatalism which has been expressed in the מָשָׁל of v 2 has been attacked in the sharpest way by the considerations so far adduced and has led to a call for responsibility addressed to each generation. Yet it is not formulated as an imperative. A second line of paralyzing thought must first be removed before the imperative can properly be formulated in vv 30f. It is certainly conceivable, and even very probable for Ezekiel's day, that his generation had

in mind its own sinful past for which the "fathers" were not particularly to be blamed. In view of this unrighteousness wrought by their own hands, how could life be possible for them after they had been punished, especially if everyone must be judged according to his own deeds?

Secondly the prophet, with a striking didactic objectivity, deals with the treatment of the two "cases" that are possible under this aspect.

■ **18:21f, 24** In a parallel formulation vv 21f consider the case of the wicked man who turns away from his wickedness to keep the commandments, and in v 24, the case of the righteous man who turns from his righteousness to do what is wrong (cf. further *b Berakot* 29a). In regard to both cases the prophet proclaims the free righteousness of God, which man encounters in his immediate present and which either deals graciously with him or judges him, granting him life or sentencing him to death, in accordance with his present state.

■ **18:23** In v 23 a quite different type of saying breaks into this objective casuistic order: the question of God's concern for man. That it is attached to the case of the wicked man who repents shows that Yahweh does not stand coolly indifferent to either possibility, but proclaims to the erstwhile wicked man that the gateway of repentance stands open for him in the present. In his penetrating ... הֶחָפֹץ אֶחְפֹּץ "Do you really think then that I am pleased with the death of the wicked?" he uncovers his own heart, his hope, and his strong bias for the *life* of man.

■ **18:25–29** Space is then given also in this second treatment of the theme to the sayings of the opponents with whom the entire discussion began. The renewed discussion is given an unusual framework, with an almost literal repetition (vv 25 and 29) covering the central section in vv 26–28. This repeats the consideration of the two cases of vv 21f and 24 in briefer form. In the מָשָׁל cited in v 2 the people in the land of Israel had made a mockery of Yahweh's slow-moving justice by a cynical characterization of it. In the saying in vv 25 and 29 any artistic-satirical covering is dropped. In a frontal attack Yahweh's activity (literally דֶּרֶךְ "way, behavior") in his ordering (תכן) of the world is set in

---

46   For the reference to the עמים, which was undoubtedly sanctified by ancient usage, we must compare note f.

question totally and without any restriction to the sequence of generations.[47] Equally sharply, however, Yahweh points to the arrogance and lack of insight in such strictures by his question about the rightness of the people's actions. When in v 25 the divine answer precedes the call to pay attention directed to the "house of Israel," and in v 29 the quotation is put in the mouth of the "house of Israel" so that Yahweh's answer is expressly directed to them, the emphasis is on the fact that Yahweh is not calling a few dissatisfied individuals to take note, but his people as a whole. He wants to separate it as a whole from the temptation posed by such questions, which threaten to put it beyond the pale.

■ **18:26–28** The order that is set out once again in vv 26–28 seeks to show the way of life to every member of the people. Over against vv 21f and 24 the sequence of cases is changed again. Here the fuller details of the description (which follows in second place here) of the repentance of the wicked man makes it clear where the greatest emphasis lies. The description of the change of heart in vv 27f recalls the turning away of the son from the wickedness of his father in v 14.

■ **18:30–32** In all this a path is cleared for the open proclamation of what has previously lain hidden underneath the earlier consideration. Accordingly it is once again affirmed that Yahweh, in his judgement of every individual, makes an urgent call to repentance, as is already to be found in 14:6.[48] In Ezekiel repentance is not, as with Amos and Isaiah (Wolff, Dietrich), described as a return to Yahweh, but as a turning away from wickedness. Here it is a turning away from rebellion.[49] Rebellion is the occasion for falling into guilt.[50] Hence Yahweh commands the casting away (for השליך cf. Mt 5:29f) of the rebellious acts like a dangerous object and the determined acceptance (עשׂו לכם, cf. the ποιήσατε of Mt 12:33) of a new heart and a new spirit. The entire casuistic ruling of individual laws (vv 5ff) is completely and finally subordinated here to an appeal to men to be renewed inwardly and to return to obedience, such as is to be found again in 11:19 and 36:26. It is not a matter of a more resolute keeping of individual laws, nor the increase of their number, but of man's turning completely to God. When we find commanded in the imperative here what is promised in the indicative in 11:19,[51]

then it is made clear in this doubling of clauses, with their logical tensions, that in the divine salvation man never appears simply as a vague object, but always as the purposeful subject of grace for a new beginning. Overall, however, there lies the appeal, stemming from God's hidden faithfulness, which poses the question: "Why will you die?" This is now not simply a question (so v 23), but a wholly positive call to life, addressed to those who are otherwise destined to death (הָמֵת) on account of their wickedness.

It is probably a later hand which has rounded off in v 32b (note b) the declaration of the purpose of the whole chapter appropriately in the style of the priestly *torah* (Amos 5:4, 6, 14) with the terse הָשִׁיבוּ וִחְיוּ.[52]

Ezek 18 does not set out a "doctrine of righteous retribution," but seeks to make plain, through all its didactic-casuistic details, which make extensive use of older formulations, the prophet's passionate appeal to those who are lost to repent. The strict formal rigidity of the first speech and the harking back to this in the formal aspects of vv 21ff show that Ezekiel here comes fully to the expression of his prophetic message.

Aim

The purpose of the whole section has already been touched upon. Ezekiel was speaking in a time of great crisis for his people. The bitterness of the outward suffering of the "house of Israel" is mixed with the despair, and then the cynicism, of a feeling of hopelessness which could no longer see God's righteousness in face of all that they had suffered. The old solemn praise of God as one who punished the guilty to the third and fourth generations (Ex 20:5) and the insistent prophetic proclamation (particularly in Ezekiel) of the judgement of God which extended over a long history of sin (Ezek 16, 20, 23) could only serve to strengthen this feeling of hopelessness. Was there a righteous Governor of the universe? Or was there only meaningless catastrophe?

God's word through the prophet counters these voices. Against the rebellious doubting of God's righteousness it places a counterquestion about the righteousness of the rebellious questioners (vv 25, 29). Have those who raise the question a legitimate right to do so? Does God's thunder really roll against his people who are living righteously and at peace?

The particular feature of Ezek 18 lies in the fact that this question, as an audit looking backwards, really only stood at the fringe. Admittedly it was not an unimportant question. Embarrassment at the revelation of one's own evil ways plays no small part in the book of Ezekiel.[53] However, it is not the urgent message for the hour of despair (33:10) and for Israel's cynical resignation (18:2).

At the center of Ezek 18 (and 33:10–20) stands the message of life. It is clear that the prophet was not therewith introducing something wholly new, but was simply authorizing the fresh acceptance of a message which had previously been expressed by the priests of the temple. The true prophetic word for the hour of Israel's collapse, which came to him as an event (v 1), lay in the fact of its attempt to affirm afresh the possibility of "life" for those who stood condemned in the fearful present. This took place at the very time when such "life" had lost all its pledges and support from the temple service, together with all that was to be seen, heard, and experienced in Jerusalem. God willed the proclamation of his "Yes," and with it to grant his power of life.

It is not therefore something new, but the free application of the ancient faithfulness of God, when he couples this promise of life with the proclamation of the divine law as it had once been heard at the gates of the sanctuary. The "conditions of life" (so further 33:15) for individuals are then proclaimed to the present generation, which stands under judgement, as its own possibility of life. Against a fateful expectation of death Ezekiel sets, not a simple expectation of life, but the living word of God which calls men and demands of them obedience, and only therein promises life. This had once been proclaimed to individuals in the temple. Now it was to be heard in the call to life through acceptance of the demand for "a new heart and a new spirit" (see on v 31), which removed the curse of guilt from Israel's ancestors. God is always concerned with my generation; his word concerns me, without the way being blocked by those who have gone before.

Furthermore he is so directly concerned with my own present that even my own past does not stand in the way of it. Any fatalism which sees the scales to be hopelessly weighed down by the burden of past sins is broken by the call to enter the open door to life. Any ponderous "doctrine of righteous retribution" is broken through by this unheard of freedom of God to promise life, which itself penetrates into every guilty and rebellious person's experience.

All this has nothing to do with a theology of decision which only considers the present and where God could be, so to speak, only a "God of the present day." The call of God in the present is the expression of an unchangingly valid will of God to save, even those who have already been condemned to death (הַמֵּת v 32). In a reproachful question God rejects any notion that he might be pleased at the death of the wicked (v 23). When this is repeated in v 32, we have a firm assurance in place of a question. God's call to life in the present derives from his initial free call to life (16:6) and extends to his final act in which he transforms the death of his people into life by his free, sovereign, and creative word (37:1–14). In this assurance of divine faithfulness, which compasses both beginning and end, Ezekiel 18 carries the summons into the present.

This summons also has nothing to do with a simple invitation to a beautiful idea which those who are addressed must think. It is rather an invitation to life, in which God's command must be master, and hearing the assurance of life must never be separated from a turning to this new life.

This is the turning to life which must be proclaimed wherever God declares his faithfulness to his people who are living under judgement.

47 See Arnulf Kuschke, "Die Menschenwege und der Weg Gottes im Alten Testament," *StTh* 5 (1951): 106–118.

48 See above p. 308 and Erich Kurt Dietrich, *Die Umkehr im Alten Testament und im Judentum* (Stuttgart: Kohlhammer, 1936), especially 137–152.

49 For פשע see above pp. 308f.

50 For מכשול עון see above pp. 211, 306.

51 See above pp. 362f, also 36:26.

52 See above p. 376.

53 See above p. 190.

Lamentation over the Lioness and the Vine (The End of the Judean Royal House)

Bibliography

W. Erbt
"Die Fürstensprüche im Hesekielbuche," *OLZ* 20 (1917): 270–274, 289–296.

H. Jahnow
Das hebräische Leichenlied im Rahmen der Völkerdichtung, BZAW 36 (Giessen: Töpelmann, 1923), esp. 197–210.

M. Noth
"The Jerusalem Catastrophe of 587 B.C. and its Significance for Israel," *The Laws in the Pentateuch and Other Essays*, tr. D. R. Ap-Thomas (Philadelphia: Fortress, 1967), 260–280.

H. Oort
"Ezechiël 19; 21:18, 19v., 24v.," *ThT* (1889): 504–514.

E. Vogt
"Jojakîn collario ligneo vinctus (Ez 19:9)," *Biblica* 37 (1956): 388–389.

19

1 But you,[a] raise a lament over the princes[b] of Israel 2/ and say:
What a lioness[a] was your mother among lions!
She made her lair[b] among young lions, her cubs grew big.
3 And she raised[a] up one of her cubs; it became a young lion.
And he learnt to seize his prey; he devoured men.

19:1 1a 𝔊^A (𝔖^h Cat ℭ 𝔄 Arm 𝔖) adds the address here also *υἱὲ ἀνθρώπου*. However, it is lacking in 𝔊, as also 𝔐 and 𝔗. Cf. note a to 17:12.

b 𝔐 נשׂיאי. 𝔊 𝔏^S read the singular, which may have fallen out in the Hebrew original through haplography or through a later connection of the word with Zedekiah (Hölscher, *Hesekiel*). The content of the two laments that follow requires the plural.

2 2a 𝔐 לְבִיָּא is an artificial secondary vocalization of the usual לָבִיא, which wants to bring out the feminine gender clearly and which should properly be לְבִיאָה. 𝔊 *σκύμνος*, 𝔏^S *catulus leonis*, 𝔖 גוריא דאריא, 𝔗 ליתא felt no need to make clear the feminine element in their translation. However, cf. 𝔊^Qmg, L, V Thdrt *λέαινα*, 𝔅 *leaena*.

b The *qinah* meter, which is undoubtedly present in 19:2ff, requires that רבצה is related to what follows, against the accent of 𝔐. It becomes unnecessary to accept with C. Budde, "Klagelied," 16, the omission of a second רבצה before רבתה.

3 3a 𝔊 relates the ותעל of 𝔐, taken as a qal, to the young lion: *καὶ ἀπεπήδησεν* (𝔏^S *et exiliit*) "and he went out," 𝔊^A *καὶ ἀπεδήμησεν* "and he went out of the land." 𝔖 ורבא "and he grew big." The third feminine singular, however, demands the mother as subject. Against the usual interpretation as "to bring up, to rear" (Gesenius-Buhl, Koehler-Baumgartner, the commentaries), which repeats what has already been said in v 2b, Driver, "Ezekiel," 154, conjectures עלה hipʿil as "to raise." This understanding is especially supported by the parallel שׂמתהו of v 5.

4 Then 'they levied' nations against[a] him;[b]
   he was caught in their pit.[c]
   And they brought him with hooks[d] to
   the land of Egypt.

5 When she saw that she 'was disgraced'
   (?),[a] her hope was lost,
   she took another[b] of her cubs and made
   it[c] a young lion.

6 It went about among the lions, became a
   young lion and learnt to seize prey;
   he devoured men.

7 And he 'did evil' to their 'palaces' (?),[a]
   and made ruins of their cities,
   so that the land, and all that was in it,
   was (horrified) stunned at the noise of
   his roaring.

8 Then they turned[a] nations against him
   from the lands[b] round about; they
   spread out their net against him, he
   was caught in their pit.

4

4a עַל – אֶל cf. note a to 1:17.

b 𝔐 וַיִּשְׁמְעוּ "and they heard," so 𝔊 𝔏ˢ 𝔖 𝔙 𝔗. However, the connection requires a vocalization as hipʻil (Hitzig, Cornill, and others). For הִשְׁמִיעַ "to command, levy" cf. 1 Kings 15:22; Jer 51:27 with עַל, Jer 50:29 with אֶל. Since in all these cases an object of the command is mentioned, so here also the גוים must be seen as the object. The subject remains mysteriously indefinite. Cf. v 8.

c 𝔐 בְּשַׁחְתָּם, strangely misunderstood by 𝔊 (𝔏ˢ) here and in v 8 ἐν τῇ διαφθορᾷ αὐτῶν, which 𝔙 then freely interprets non absque vulneribus suis. 𝔗 בסריגתהון "in their nets."

d 𝔊 ἐν κημῷ "with a nose bag," ᾽A (𝔊⁸⁶) (ἐν) πέδαις "in fetters." 𝔙 in catenis, 𝔗 בְּשִׁישְׁלָן "in chains." Cf. further note b to v 9.

5

5a 𝔐 נוחלה cannot meaningfully be derived from יחל "to wait." The roots חלל (᾽A ἐτρώθη), חיל, חלה, חול (Σ ἠσθένησεν, 𝔙 infirmata est, 𝔖 אתכרהת) do not help towards a satisfactory sense. 𝔊 ὅτι ἀπῶσται ἀπ᾽ αὐτῆς "that he was carried off from her," similarly 𝔊ᴬ ἀποσπᾶται, is etymologically obscure, like the פסק "come to an end" of 𝔗. Perhaps we should read with Cornill נואלה and translate this by reference to Is 19:13; Jer 50:36 "to become foolish = to be ashamed." Driver, "Linguistic Problems," 67, points to Arabic wḥl "to be uncertain" ("that her hope became uncertain"). Bewer, "Textual Notes," 158f, reads וַתֶּאֱרַךְ תּוֹחֶלֶת "and hope was delayed."

b 𝔐 אחד, 𝔊 ἄλλον, 𝔏ˢ alterum, 𝔖 𝔗 𝔙 = 𝔐. Cf. note a to 17:7.

c Cf. note a to v 3.

7

7a 𝔐 וידע אלמנותיו "and he recognized his widows" is unintelligible and is first attested by 𝔊 𝔙 (didicit viduas facere). 𝔊 καὶ ἐνέμετο τῷ θράσει αὐτοῦ and ᾽A καὶ ἐκάκωσε χήρας (αὐτοῦ), also 𝔗 וְאַצְדִי בִּירְנִיָּתֵיהּ point in different ways to a reading of the verbal element as וירע, which is to be vocalized as וַיָּרַע and is to be interpreted as hipʻil of רעע ("to do evil"). Reider, "ידע," 316, reads וַיֵּדַע "and he broke, shattered," whilst Driver "Hebrew Notes," 57f, by keeping the consonants of 𝔐, vocalizes it as וַיְדַע, or better וַיָּדַע, and would derive it from a verb דעה = Arabic daʻā "to strike down." Behind the mysterious אלמנותיו we must conjecture a counterpart to the עריהם of the parallel expression. Should we then think of אלמנות = ארמנות (Is 13:22) and read this as אלמנותיהם (or graphically better אלמנותם, cf. Gesenius-Kautzsch § 92n)? Cf. Baer-Delitzsch, xi. Or should we, with Hitzig, break it up into אל מעונתיו and also change the suffix here? Both solutions remain very uncertain, as do the more radical conjectures.

8

8a With the impersonal understanding of the verb (analogous to v 4) the ויתנו of 𝔐, which is already attested by 𝔊, is quite acceptable. For the use of נתן על cf. Neh 5:7 ואתן עליהם קהלה. נתן is one of the verbs most frequently used by Ezekiel.

b מדינות, properly "administrative areas, prov-

9 And they put him into a wooden collar [with hooks]ᵃ and brought him to the king of Babylon [where they brought him in custody (?)],ᵇ that his voice might not be heard [again]ᶜ onᵈ the mountains of Israel.

10 Your mother 'was equal'ᵃ to a vine, which has been planted beside water. It became full of fruit and fresh growth because of the plentiful water.

11 And it grew strong branchesᵃ (fit) for royal scepters [and its growth went

inces," is only found here in Ezekiel. An alteration to מצודות (Ehrlich, *Randglossen*, Herrmann, Bertholet) is not necessary, in view of the clear text tradition and the suitability of the content. The word is already attested in 1 Kings 20:14f, 17, 19.

9 9a 𝔐 בחחים is lacking in 𝔊 and must be a subsequent addition from v 4.

b The unusual asyndetic imperfect clause exceeds the meter and, like בחחים (note a), represents a later addition. 𝔐 במצדות "(whilst they brought him) into a net" (?) is very questionable. 𝔊 εἰς φυλακήν, 𝔙 *in carcerem*, 𝔖 לבית חבושיה appear to point rather to a derivation from צרר or נצר. So Ehrlich, *Randglossen*, would read במצורות "in close custody" (from נצר), similarly Bertholet. Noth, "Jerusalem Catastrophe," considers among others the reading מַצֶּרֶת which is to be compared with Akkadian *maṣṣartu* "supervision." Driver, "Ezekiel," 154, מְצֶרֶת or מַצָּרָה "prison, guardhouse." P. Rost, "Miscellen," 392f, finds in bα a catchword gloss to v 4bα, which adds the third word which has fallen out there.

c 𝔐 עוד is not attested by 𝔊. Its deletion is also supported by the meter.

d אל – על cf. note a to 1:17.

10 10a 𝔐 בְּדָמְךָ "in thy blood" is certainly not original, in spite of 𝔊 כדמך, 𝔙 *in sanguine two*, Σ Θ ἐν τῷ αἵματί σου. The reading of MSᴷᵉⁿ ³⁵⁶ כרמך, which is graphically close, creates difficulties by its suffix. Toy, Hölscher, *Hesekiel*, Bertholet, Fohrer would read כברם, whilst Cornill, Ehrlich, *Randglossen*, following MSᴷᵉⁿ ³⁹⁹,⁴³¹, would simply delete בכרם. Already Rashi and Kimḥi favor a derivation from דמה, which is probable. However, we can scarcely read with BH³ תִּדְמֶה, since the qal of דמה in Ezekiel is always otherwise construed with אל (31:2, 8ᵇⁱˢ, 18). The reference 27:32 (32:2?), which is unfortunately not textually certain, could however point to nip'al with כ. 𝔗 דמיא should not be adduced as a compelling witness for a דמה of the original, since this participle can also be used as a variant for the simple כ (cf. vv 2, 13), but it does not in any case oppose the view accepted. Should we then read a participle נדמה or a perfect נדמתה, which has been written incorrectly as in 27:32? Bewer, "Textual Notes," 159, conjectures, with a simple change of the word division: אמך כגפן בד[י]ם כן]על מים שתולה.

11 11a The plural ויהיו לה מטות עז is striking in view of the singular continuation in aβb (דליותיו, בגבהו, קומתו). However, the singular reading of 𝔊 (𝔏ˢ 𝔄) καὶ ἐγένετο αὐτῇ ῥάβδος ἰσχύος ἐπὶ φυλὴν ἡγουμένων, which gives a smooth text, arouses the suspicion of a secondary harmonization. 𝔖 has gone the opposite way of harmonizing by a continuation of the plural reading of 𝔐 vv 11aα–12aα. Thus Noth, "Jerusalem Catastrophe," must be correct in his view that v 11aβb is a subsequent addition, which does not relate to מטות, but (with strained grammar) to גפן, which both before and after is treated as a feminine.

12 up[b] as high as the clouds, and it became conspicuous for the multitude of its shoots because of its height].[c]

12 But it was torn up in anger,[a] thrown to the ground, and the east wind shrivelled up its fruit;[b] [they were torn up and scorched][c] its strong branch—the fire consumed it.

13 And now it is planted[a] in the wilderness, a dry [and thirsty][b] land.

14 [And fire went out from its branch, it devoured its own shoots [[its fruit]][a]][b] and no strong branch remained on it (fit) for a royal scepter. This is a lament and it has become a lament.

In its formulations it is clearly determined by 31:3, 9. Whether we should also argue on the grounds of meter (Noth) is questionable, cf. note a to v 12. The ἰσχύος of 𝕲, corresponding to 𝔐 עז, has fallen out in 𝕲^BV (𝔏 𝕮)^s by homoioteleuton (Ziegler, *Ezechiel*). In vv 12, 14 it remains.

b על – אל cf. note a to 1:17. For עבותים cf. 31:3.
c For the secondary character of aβb cf. note a.

12 12a Bertholet's and Noth's desire to change the clearly attested and meaningful ותתש בחמה for metrical reasons to והיא התשה is excessive and is not justified. Since also in v 12aβb double twos predominate, we shall have to be content with the change of meter. Vv 13f first return to the *qinah* meter.

b 𝔐 פְּרִיָה. 𝕲 τὰ ἐκλεκτὰ αὐτῆς, Cat. τὰ κλήματα αὐτῆς appear to presuppose בדיה. So Cornill, whilst Ehrlich, *Randglossen*, would read פֹּארְיָה, Fohrer פארותיה, Bertholet even בדיה את פריה "their growth with their fruit." But since v 10b introduces likewise fruit and branches together, the same two together in the account of the destruction is in no way out of place.

c 𝔐 התפרקו ויבשו is syntactically unrelated to the context. 𝕲 ἐξεδικήθησαν (presupposing hitpaʿel of צדק?) καὶ ἐξηράνθη has assimilated the second verb to the singular context, whilst 𝕲 again, on the other hand, puts the following word, understood as the subject, in the plural. However, the two words are to be understood as a later interpretative addition, which relates to the royal scepters, taken as a plural relating to v 11a. וְיָבֵשׁוּ being no longer felt as a perfect consecutive seems to attest late usage.

13 13a 𝔐 שתולה. Cornill, Herrmann would follow 𝕲 πεφύτευκαν αὐτήν and read שְׁתָלוּה.
b 𝔐 וצמא "and thirsty" is lacking in 𝕲 𝔏^s. Its deletion is also supported by metrical considerations.

14 14a 𝔐 פריה is noteworthy for the lack of the copula. It is not attested by 𝕲 𝔏^s, which otherwise deviate slightly, and must be understood as a subsequent assimilation to v 12.
b aα comes strangely late after v 12. Cf. the exposition.

Form

19:1–14, although it is not introduced by a fresh formula for the receipt of a message, stands out both in form and theme as a separate section from Ch. 18. We may question whether ch. 19, at an earlier stage of its redactional history, without being introduced by a fresh formula for the receipt of a message, was joined directly on to ch. 17 and then subsequently split off from this connection by ch. 18, which is introduced by its own introductory formula.[1]

The heading and closing rubric designate 19:1ff as קינה "lament for the dead." This designation is confirmed by the metrical structure in which the lament meter demonstrated by Budde can be clearly seen.[2]

---

1 See further below p. 397.
2 C. Budde, "Das hebräische Klagelied," *ZAW* 2 (1882): 1–52.

Periods such as 2a/2b (for the delineation cf. note b), 3a/3b make it probable that we should read five beats (3:2) in accordance with Sievers' accentuation system.[3] In the addition in vv 10–14 (see below) we can find a stronger intrusion of double twos.

The literary form of the lament, the use of which by Ezekiel is prepared for by the קנים of 2:10, occurs again in 26:17 (17–18); 27:2 (3–36); 28:12 (12–19); 32:2, 16 (2–15). H. Jahnow has described in detail the original setting of the lament in the rites for the dead. Hempel has further shown that the distinctive character of Old Testament laments lies in their complete separation from any mythological connection with events in the sphere of belief in the dying and rising god.[4] Only in connection with this complete desacralization was the particular Old Testament development of the lament possible in the sphere of political preaching and imagery, as Old Testament prophecy shows. This usage appears in the lament for the "fallen virgin of Israel" in Amos 5:2 in a genuine prophetic prediction at a time when no one expected the "fall of Israel." The great lament of Is 14 and even more clearly the laments in the book of Lamentations point to a time when the political events which were the subject of the laments had already taken place. At the same time Is 14 shows how, in an atrocious contrast, the characteristics of the lament begin to be mixed with those of a mocking song.

Ezek 19 shows nothing of the mixture of the lament and the mocking song. Nevertheless, here the lament is connected with the element of narrative metaphor, which is found in chs. 15–17 and reappears in chs. 23, 31, cf. 27:3ff; 28:12ff; 32:2ff also in the קינה. Jahnow speaks of the "epic character" which the originally lyric lament for the dead thereby receives.[5] The original situation of the lament in the presence of the dead (2 Sam 3:33f, also Amos 5:2) is weakened. In its place the metaphorical account of the fall of the lamented appears.[6]

The question of the original unity of Ezek 19, which in its present form is clearly marked off as a unit by vv 2 and 14 (analogous to 32:2, 16), has often been dealt with. The unit divides up according to its content into three sections: 1) vv 2–4 deal with the story of the lioness with her first cub, 2) vv 5–9 with the story of her second cub, 3) vv 10–14 with the growth of the vine and its royal shoots.

Accordingly van den Born believes we should accept three originally separate units, which were first joined by the redactional insertion of v 5a, whilst the third originally comprised only vv 10, 12f. However, the splitting up of the first elements (vv 2–4, 5–9), which are clearly related together through the same image and also in details, is scarcely to be accepted. Nevertheless, the break between vv 1–9 and 10–14 is much sharper. Not only does the image change here from that of a lion to that of a vine, but also in details vv 1–9, with their complete transparency, appear much clearer than the section vv 10–14, which also in meter does not show the consistency of vv 1–9 and which has been subsequently worked over (note c to v 12, note b to v 14).

On the other hand the introductory אִמְּךָ v 10 appears clearly to be connected with v 2. Thus most commentators would take Ezek 19 as a unity set out in three strophes from the beginning (Ewald, Bertholet 1897 and 1936, Heinisch, Noth and others), in which the concluding section vv 13f (Bertholet 1936), or perhaps only v 14b (Schumpp, Ziegler, *Ezechiel*), may be regarded as an addition. Noth believes further, on the grounds of meter, that he can reconstruct the pattern of three similar strophes.

The undeniable break after v 9, however, is still left unexplained. This view necessitates therefore, in analogy to the first two strophes which interpret the lion cubs as royal figures who are offspring of the "mother," that also in vv 10–14 we find an offshoot of the "mother." Yet an examination of the text points rather to the view that here originally the fate of the vine, i.e., the

3   For an attempt at an alternating reading of the קינה see Sigmund Mowinckel, "Zum Problem der hebräischen Metrik" in *Festschrift Alfred Bertholet* (Tübingen: Mohr [Siebeck], 1950), 379–394; Friedrich Horst, "Die Kennzeichen der hebräischen Poesie," *ThR* NF 21 (1953): 97–121. For the phenomenon of *enjambement* in v 9 see Joachim Begrich, "Der Satzstil im Fünfer," *ZS* 9 (1933/34): 169–209, especially

179f; reprinted in *idem, Gesammelte Studien zum AT*, ThB 21 (München: Kaiser, 1964), 132–167, especially 141f.

4   Hempel, *Literatur*, 29; see above pp. 242f.
5   Jahnow, *Leichenlied*, 201f.
6   The use of the images of the lion and the vine will be dealt with in the detailed exposition.

mother herself, is what is signified. Noth's reference to 2 Kings 24:12 and Jer 22:26, according to which the royal mother Nehushta had suffered the same fate as her royal son Jehoiachin, which Noth finds referred to here, does not help since it renders impossible a unified understanding of אִמְּךָ in vv 2 and 10.

The difficulties are solved, if here also we reckon with a successive composition of the text. To an original section vv 1–9 there has been added in a somewhat later phase (once again the events of 587 appear to be drawn into it) the section vv 10–14. This addition has taken up the catchword אִמְּךָ from v 2 and added, with a new simile, a further strophe (metrically less tightly composed). For its part this has then, as a result of the endeavor to assimilate vv 10–14 to vv 1–9, suffered further reworking.[7]

Interpretation

■ **19:1** The lament (קינה) to which the prophet is summoned in the introduction did not have its origin primarily in the subjective "compassion" of men, as Jahnow has demonstrated with full references. It was at first a "ceremony," a "custom," which grew primarily on animistic or pre-animistic bases, but which could then be filled out with personal feelings of compassion. In view of Ezekiel's harshness, even if we do not speak directly of "grim Ezekiel," it is advisable to keep this character of the קינה in mind.[8]

■ **19:2** It begins with the form of an interrogative exclamation. The fuller איכה (Lam 1:2; 2:1; 4:1) or איך (26:17; Is 14:4, 12) with a following verbal clause, which is typical of laments, is replaced by the more restrained מה with a following nominal clause.[9] The description of the "death" (איך נפלת Is 14:12; cf. Amos 5:2 נפלה), which follows immediately as a rule, is here preceded by the history prior to the death. The reference to the original nobility of the mother, preserved in the mournful מה אמך לביא, which is to be understood mournfully as the following events show, brings out the

contrast of then and now, which is a particular feature of the lament.[10]

But who is the mother, who reappears again in the addition in v 10? The first question is not to be separated from the second of who are meant by the two lion cubs. With the first, of whom v 4 mentions his deportation to Egypt, scarcely anyone but Jehoahaz can be intended, who, as Josiah's son, was deported to Egypt by Pharaoh Neco according to 2 Kings 23:33ff. In the second (vv 5–9) Klamroth would find Jehoahaz's successor Jehoiakim, of whom then a deportation to Babylon would be attested here in line with 2 Chr 36:6.[11] This view is today refuted by the evidence of the Wiseman Chronicle. In another way Noth has renewed the interpretation in respect of Jehoiakim. He finds in the "being shut up in a cage" ("ils le mirent dans une cage") and in the "imprisonment" (v 9b is to be read מְצָרוֹת "bonds" or מַצֶּרֶת following Akkadian maṣṣartu "custody") a reference to the encirclement of Jerusalem by soldiers and the death of the king in Jerusalem under siege which followed. He believes he can find the deportation of Jehoiachin first mentioned only in the third strophe vv 10–14. Against this view we must object that it ignores the sharp break after v 9 and destroys the clear parallelism of (ו)יבאהו in vv 9 and 4, which in both cases implies a real deportation. Above all, however, it falls down on the understanding of סוגר (see below to v 9), which is not to be understood in line with Sennacherib's words about the siege of Jerusalem: "he himself [Hezekiah] I shut up like a bird in a cage (kīma iṣṣūr quppi) in Jerusalem, his residence" as a metaphor of siege, but as the deportation of a prisoner.[12] Thus the majority of commentators, undoubtedly with more justification from the text, seek to find a deported king also in the second lion cub. Ewald, Bertholet, Heinisch, Hölscher, *Hesekiel*, and others think of Jehoiachin, the son of Jehoiakim who was taken to Babylon (2 Kings 24:15).

Or should the other king deported to Babylon, Zede-

---

7 However, this must be left to the detailed exposition, and the question of its chronological placing dealt with after that.

8 Jahnow, *Leichenlied*, 202.

9 Jahnow, *Leichenlied*, 136.

10 Jahnow, *Leichenlied*, 99.

11 Klamroth, *Exulanten*, 10f.

12 *AOT* 353.

kiah, be found here? From 2 Kings 23:31 and 24:18 it becomes clear that Jehoahaz and Zedekiah were sons of the same mother (Hamutal, the daughter of Jeremiah from Libnah). Accordingly Oort, Kraetzschmar, von Orelli, Herrmann, Fohrer and others relate the reference to the "mother" in Ezek 19 to the queen mother, who received in Judah the privileged position of גבירה.[13] The deportation of the "mother of the king (Jehoiachin)" is expressly mentioned in 2 Kings 24:15.

This reference to Hamutal, and the interpretation of the lion cubs in reference to Jehoahaz and Zedekiah, is at first attractive, but becomes on closer examination very improbable. Would Ezekiel, where he sets together the kings who suffered deportation (the short political life of Jehoahaz had otherwise no particular importance for Ezekiel), have left out of reckoning the king with whom he himself had shared this fate and according to whose years he, as an exile, dated his prophetic messages?[14] That "the influential and ambitious Hamutal" had "had her hand in" the accession to the throne of her two sons and had therefore played a very prominent political role (Kraetzschmar) is an unsubstantiated postulate.

Thus the mother, who is first referred to in the metaphor of the lioness, must be seen as Judah, or more precisely the Davidic royal house which ruled in Judah and from which the particular kings emerged. Already Gen 49:9 uses in a prominent way the metaphor of the royal lion for the royal tribe of Judah.[15] Also the use of the metaphor of the royal growth of the vine in vv 10ff can very well be understood in this direction.[16]

However why is Jehoiakim, who compared with Jehoahaz and Jehoiachin was undoubtedly the more important king and with whom the features of violence are readily connected, not mentioned in the series?

The difficulty of his not being mentioned loses weight when we abandon the false view, created by the present unity of vv 1–14, that a series of three kings is referred to here. In the original structure of the oracle two kings are mentioned in parallel (for the parallelism of deportation to West and East cf. Hos 9:3, further 7:11; 11:11; 12:2), who only gain prominence from their common fate of deportation and who were in no way important politically. Their fate is mourned in the form of a lament. We cannot then avoid the question whether Ezekiel has been aroused to his קינה by the two lament oracles in Jer 22:10 (Jehoahaz: 22:11f is a secondary prose comment) and 22:28 (Jehoiachin: a slightly glossed saying, originally composed metrically and with specific Jeremianic features; cf. the triple question מדוע—אם—ה). The extensive oracle about Jehoiakim in Jer 22 contains understandably no particular lament features.

What was said in Jer 22 in separate sayings about two different kings has been strengthened in Ezekiel into a comprehensive lament about the fate of the royal house. As a lioness-mother, who could dwell among other lions, i.e., any royal powers, this royal house has provided its particular kings.[17]

■ 19:3 When it is said in a strikingly impersonal way of the young lion which represents Jehoahaz that he is "exalted" (העלה parallel to שים v 5) to become a young lion by the lioness, i.e., the "maternal" royal house, thereby stressing the features of carnivorous bloodlust, this can scarcely be understood as something blameworthy in the sense of a decline from an originally peaceful way of life (Kliefoth, Breuer).[18] Rather it describes, within the scope of the chosen metaphor, the normal growth and development of the king. The particular historical position of Jehoahaz, who can

---

13 Georg Molin, "Die Stellung der Gᵉbira im Staate Juda," *ThZ* 10 (1954): 161–175.

14 See above pp. 114f.

15 See also above p. 126.

16 See above p. 319.

17 For the parallelism of the nouns לביא (note a) and ארי, which derive from the Asiatic and African regions respectively, but which in Hebrew were no longer properly differentiated, see Ludwig Koehler, "Lexikologisch-Geographisches," *ZDPV* 62 (1939): 121–124. According to Theodor Nöldeke, *Beiträge zur semitischen Sprachwissenschaft* (Strassburg: Trüb-

ner, 1904), page 70 note 10, כפיר denotes on the other hand a "half-grown lion cub;" according to Koehler, 121, it means more precisely "a young lion who seeks its own food." From 19:3, 5f, it is clear that כפיר in this particular metaphor is the individual regent standing in his own authority.

18 Kliefoth; Joseph Breuer, *Das Buch Jecheskel übersetzt und erläutert* (Frankfurt: Sänger & Friedberg, 1921).

19 Meissner, *Babylonien* 1, 74, 73.

20 Erman-Ranke, 275.

21 See the "taming" of prisoners with a ring through

scarcely have had scope for much exercise of power between the death of Josiah and his summons to Riblah in his three month rule, is not considered further.

■ **19:4** Thus the description of the enemy's intervention, which is again quite vaguely described, dispenses with any moral or religious emphasis on a "righteous retribution." In the picture of the lion net, by means of which the lion in a pit was robbed of his freedom, we have described metaphorically how Jehoahaz lost his freedom. The hunter in the Gilgamesh epic who laments Enkidu's misfortunes already speaks of hunting with pits (I, 109, 136). In the deportation to Egypt the historical reference enters into the picture with harsh reality. Is this also the case in the reference to being carried away, "with hooks"? It is narrated of Ashurbanipal that he captured lions alive and had them imprisoned in cages in order to let them free again on the occasion of another hunt, just as before him Tiglath Pileser speaks of the capture of elephants.[19] A picture of hunting from the old Egyptian kingdom also shows lions and lionesses, which were led before their captors in great wooden cages.[20] A text such as Ezek 29:4 leads us to think that animals were caught with hooks. However, Ezek 38:4; 2 Chr 33:11; Is 37:29 (= 2 Kings 19:28) make it clear that prisoners, when being finally deported, were treated in a similar way.[21] The use of this metaphor of the lion must certainly not be taken to imply that Jehoahaz (in 608 B.C.) was transported to Egypt from Riblah in this humiliating fashion, which was used for the deportation of prisoners at the end of a war. 2 Kings 23:33 ויאסרהו, if the ויסירהו of 2 Chr 36:3 is not preferred, appears to mention only his being put in chains.

■ **19:5** Vv 5–9 tell of the parallel removal of Jehoachin. Once again the lioness, after her disappointment with the first young king, had brought up a cub to be a "young lion." In view of the thematically conditioned omission of Jehoiakim we must not search here for references to concrete events at the accession of the new king in besieged Jerusalem.

■ **19:6, 7** The proud walking about among the lions, the lust for prey, and the destruction of cities and lands should not be interpreted historically and concretely of Jehoiachin's actions, but simply serve to elaborate pictorially his awesome royal majesty. In the scale of the description in vv 6f, which has been enlarged in comparison with the brevity of v 3b in the first strophe, we can scarcely avoid noting Ezekiel's closeness to Jehoiachin, who was "his king" in a particularly fateful way.

■ **19:8** With the second lion episode also the reaction of the surrounding world should be understood solely as a part of the literary image, and not moralistically as a reference to the punishment of a particularly oppressive rule of Jehoiachin. Here also, in a strangely impersonal way, the summoning of "troops" is mentioned. In the indefiniteness of the גוים (also v 4) the mystery of the authoritative Lord is hinted at, who rules as sovereign over peoples and provinces. The description of the captured lion is more fully elaborated, corresponding to the generally broader scope of vv 5–9. Vv 5–9 are not to be shortened, with Noth, in the interests of strophic similarity with the length of vv 2–4. Beside the pit-trap, a net (cf. 12:13; 17:20) is also mentioned. Thus Marduk in the Primeval Contest (*Enuma elish* IV: 41, 95) goes out to meet Tiamat equipped with a net. Pictures of Assyrian royal hunts show how the servants go out with hunting dogs, spears, and nets.[22] The Eagle stele of Eannadu of Lagash shows a victorious king (or god?), who holds captive his human enemies in a net.[23]

■ **19:9** The hapax legomenon סוּגַר, which cannot be isolated from the Akkadian *šigāru*, is like this latter word usually translated "cage." This interpretation was established by M. Streck in connection with the translation of Annals VIII, 11 (29 IX 111).[24] However, already in 1934, B. Landsberger pointed out that Annals VIII, 11, can only be translated as a statement by the Assyrian king about a rebellious Arab prince: "I put a neckband upon him (*šigaru* [sic] *aškunšuma*), bound him with bears and dogs and made him guard

---

their lip *ANEP* 524, and the comments of Parrot, *Babylon*, 91. Cf. on v 9.

22 Meissner, *Babylonien* 1, 74.

23 *ANEP* 298, cf. 307.

24 M. Streck, *Assurbanipal II*, VAB 7, 2 (Leipzig, 1916), page 67 note 8. Cf. Baer-Delitzsch, xv.

the city gate."[25] Since, however, *šigāru*, according to its determinative, must have been made of wood, E. I. Gordon has examined this further and has shown that it must have been a wooden neck-stock, made up of four pieces (Vogt: *coagmentum quoddam ligneum, in quod collum captivi immittitur = collare ligneum*), in which prisoners as well as wild animals were held captive.[26] A newly found stele from the period of the dynasty of Akkad, described and illlustrated by F. Basmachi, has now added an illustration to our literary knowledge.[27] In a leading scene six prisoners in a line are shown held in *šigāru*. To this may be added that a tablet from Nippur, on its reverse side, gives a stele inscription of Sargon of Akkad: "he captured Lugalzaggesi, king of Uruk, in battle, and brought him in a *gišši-gar* to Enlil's gate."[28] Should we regard the neck-shafts in which prisoners are pictured on the palace gate of Balawat as a further development of the neck-stock?[29] Since סוגר, which was evidently still correctly understood by 𝔗 קולרין, was used both for animals and for human prisoners, its mention in 19:9 does not need to go beyond the scope of the literary image.

As in v 4b the mention of the place of deportation brings the historical reality fully into the image. In the reference "they brought him to the king of Babylon," which is more precise than in v 4b, an exact knowledge of the place of Jehoiachin's custody in the royal palace of Nebuchadnezzar is to be seen.[30] In the two textual additions in v 9a, the first (note a) seeks to carry over the element of deportation with hooks or rings from v 4. The second (note b) seeks to clarify the fact of Jehoiachin's imprisonment in Babylon.

Unlike vv 2–4, vv 5–9 are concluded by a purpose clause (v 9bβ) which shows the end of the original unit at this point. Since the silence of the lion's voice over the mountains of Israel, which is expressed there, is anticipated by v 7b (קול שאגתו), the removal of this clause as suggested by Noth is not to be followed. Rather by its reference to the "mountains of Israel,"

this relates the whole lament to the rest of Ezekiel's preaching.[31] What took place with Jehoiachin's deportation was a judgement upon Israel, the people of Yahweh. What is said in Ezek 6 in a thematic oracle against the "mountains of Israel" is here made concrete in reference to the fate of the two young kings.

Setting

The oracle in vv 2–9 appears not yet to have in mind the complete destruction of Judah and so must have arisen before 587. Nevertheless in the misfortunes of the two kings, deported respectively to the West and East, the great catastrophe which was to overtake the land had begun to dawn.

Furthermore the lament betrays the particular proximity of the mourner to Jehoiachin and his involvement in the latter's fate. Authorship by the prophet Ezekiel, who shared in the same exile, is thus also made probable by the subject matter.

Aim

A lament was the "ceremonial" (see above on v 1) reference to the fact of death. In uttering a lament for the kings who were deported in opposite directions, Ezekiel sets before his compatriots the reality of death which had entered the Davidic royal house. By this act the Commander of the nations (cf. to vv 4, 8) summons the mountains of Israel, the special people of God, v 9bβ, to judgement.

The declaration of the certain fact of death which had overtaken "Israel," must first of all not be overlooked. It is quite conceivable that this plain lament, affirmed by its composition as from God himself, gave a complete and final "affirmation," directed against the circles of those who wanted to regard the judgement upon Jehoiachin as only provisional and who hoped for a rescinding of it (Jer 28f; analogous expectations by the elders in Ezekiel 8:1; 14:1; 20:1). In connecting the deportation of Jehoiachin with that of Jehoahaz in

---

25 Benno Landsberger, *Die Fauna des alten Mesopotamien nach der 14. Tafel der Serie ḤAR-ra = ḫubullu*, ASAW phil.-hist. Kl. 42, 6, 81.

26 E. I. Gordon, "Of Princes and Foxes: The Neckstock in the newly-discovered Agade Period Stele," *Sumer* 12 (1956): 80–84.

27 F. Basmachi, *Sumer* 10 (1954): 116–119.

28 Gordon, "Princes," 80.

29 Meissner, *Babylonien* 1, plate 69.

30 See above pp. 114f.

31 See above pp. 185f.

32 For the traditio-historical meaning of the vine we may compare what was said on p. 319.

a single lament, Ezekiel proclaims about Jehoiachin what Jer 22:10 says earlier about Jehoahaz: "He will return no more." This rejects any way of avoiding God's judgement, even pious avoidance which took refuge in the promise regarding the Davidic dynasty (2 Sam 7) and from it thought it could infer that God could not give up the young lion from Judah, the son of the royal lioness (Gen 49:9f). God speaks to his people in judgement, and this also concerns its messianic representative. There is no way out from the impending "death" of the son of David.

The "ceremonial" origin of the lament must not, however, be allowed to hide the fact that in it something of the hidden "compassion" of God with the downfall of such a strong and youthful king is expressed—does God have any pleasure in the death of anyone (18:32)? By the particular character of Ezekiel's message, it must further be said that God suffers the dishonoring of his name in the downfall of the young lion from Judah, when it is said among the nations: "These are Yahweh's princes who have had to go away from his land" (cf. 36:20). The judgement upon God's people is God's own suffering in that by it his own name enters into the twilight of dishonor.

■ **19:10–14** In vv 10–14 the oracle about the young king has undergone a further expansion. Its composition with metaphors and phrases from Ezek 17 raises the question whether this third strophe in Ezek 19 has not been formulated with the express intention of subsequently adding as a conclusion the lament of ch. 19 to ch. 17, the basic text and additions of which are no doubt older than 19:1–9. That the threatening oracle concerning Zedekiah's treason should be rounded off in vv 10ff with a lament which mourns the total downfall of the royal house may be felt as wholly appropriate.

Setting

Vv 10–14 presuppose the complete downfall of the royal house and must therefore have been composed after 587 B.C. In their basic text they contain a statement about this total downfall and are appended here as a kind of comprehensive summary of vv 1–9. A secondary addition has then attempted to blend in a particular saying about king Zedekiah. To this later addition we owe the ambiguity of the present text as a whole. If we can then derive the basic text of vv 10–14,

which belongs to the time after the year 587, from the prophet's own hand, then the later elaboration, which obscures the clarity of the text, must be ascribed to the later work of the school.

Interpretation

■ **19:10** The addition is similarly couched in the firm קינה meter. However, it lacks the introductory call to lament. This makes a formal distinction between the new image of the vine and the introduction of the image of the lioness (v 2).[32] In a slight variation from the similar use of the metaphor in 17:6ff the vine here is not a symbol of an individual king, but represents the "mother," i.e., the entire Davidic royal house, following vv 2ff. The mention here also of roots in a well watered place (17:5, 8) is then, unlike 17:5, not grounded in the installation of Zedekiah by his Babylonian master, but is a symbol of the grace assured to the Davidic royal house by God. The promise of fruitfulness and increase, which was given to the people of God as a whole in the promise to the patriarchs (J, Gen 12:1ff and other passages; P, Gen 17:2, 4, 6), is rooted in the promise of Nathan, 2 Sam 7, so far as the Davidic house is concerned.

■ **19:11aα** Here there is also promised what is described historically in v 11aα: the gift of a succession of kings, who are represented in the metaphor of the shoot, or branches, of the vine. The representation of a person by a branch is also found in the priestly narrative of Aaron's rod (Nu 17:16ff). By the explicit designation as rulers' scepters (שבטי משלים), the reference to rulers is emphatically given. In the further description of the staffs as מטות עז their power is further stressed. The contrast with the despising of the vine in Ezek 15 does not then come to mind. Throughout a certain artificiality of the metaphor is not to be denied.

■ **19:12** Since the violent actions of the young lion in vv 1–9, within the framework of the parable, had fully motivated the reactions of the surrounding world, the destructive intervention of hostile powers here comes quite unexpectedly. What in the parable of the vine in 17:9f had its proper purpose in the treasonable conduct of the vassal towards his suzerain, which is described immediately beforehand, becomes here the unexplained intervention of a foreign power, which is only manifest in its anger (בחמה). The mysterious failure to name the agent of the judgement recalls the concealment of those who are summoned in vv 4, 8. However, beyond what is said there, we find that here there is left out even any mention of the agent of the judgement who is summoned. The identity of the hands which tear the vine out of its ground and throw it away is left obscure (cf. Dan 2:34). The scorching east wind which then follows (17:10) is a normal feature of the summer weather of Palestine. Nothing at all is said about where the fire, which finally consumes the vine shoots and recalls 15:4ff, comes from.

■ **19:13** Even in the final verses, couched in double-fives (vv 13, 14aβ), the final result of the catastrophe is simply stated without any attempt at a narrative assimilation to what precedes: the transplanting of the vine into dry desert soil, which no longer allows the growth of royal shoots, i.e., the end of the story of the Davidic house in the deportation of its whole tribe.

■ **19:14aβ** The plain statement of its concluding clause v 14aβ recalls rather remotely the concluding statement of the original two-strophe poem in v 9b. Over against the silencing of the king's voice on the mountains of Israel, which is stated there, there stands here the loss of a royal branch on the royal vine. The blessing of fertility and propagation is lost with the removal of the blessing of the (promised) land. Has the ancient promise of God to the house of David come to nothing?

■ **19:11aβb** A later hand has sought to introduce still more clearly into this event of the fall of the Davidic house the guilt and punishment of the last king Zedekiah. Thus in v 11aβb, in a grammatically incorrect appendix to the preceding, the proud conceit of Zedekiah, who is now represented by a particular individual shoot (rod), is shown up, with a verbal borrowing from 31:3, 10. He is compared to the world tree, described in Ezek 31, with its top in the clouds. With this addition an element of critical accusation enters into the lament.

■ **19:12bα** The brief insertion in v 12bα (note c) merely seeks to add the interpretation that the royal branches mentioned in v 11a also perished.

■ **19:14aα** An element of reproach, and of inner motivation of the judgement, is again found in the addition of v 14aα, which affirms in regard to Zedekiah, in a late interpretative remark to v 12b, that the fire which consumes the shoot of the vine has arisen from the royal branch itself and has burnt up the remaining branches (בדים were not previously mentioned). In the burning of the royal vine there blazes the fire kindled by Zedekiah's own treason (Ezek 17). The kingship is destroyed by its own sin.

■ **19:14b** The concluding remark קינה היא, which reappears in 32:16 and which is reminiscent of the Priestly Document's style,[33] is carried further in a different way from 32:16 by a reference to the "death" that has meanwhile occurred ותהי לקינה. In the briefest possible way the prophet (or his disciple) thereby bows to the Lord of history: God's word, in calling him to a lament, has proved right.

Aim

The additional strophe carries further, into a new phase of history, the message which is already to be found in the lament of vv 2–9. At the same time it expands it. What was aimed in vv 2–9 against false hopes, which could be related to Jehoiachin, is here finally expressed about the royal house as a whole. The blessed soil, on which alone the royal house could flourish, is taken from it. No life remains from which new hope could be expected. To men's eyes, a future for the Davidic dynasty, which was scorched and burnt in the desert, has become impossible. Nothing is said here of the divine possibility which alone, according to 17:22–24, could offer hope.

In adding vv 10–14 the prophet upholds this harsh judgement, without any attempt to reduce the lament over this tragic end. The school, with their further interpretation, has added to it, in a way which recalls the great general confession of the Deuteronomistic History, a reference to the guilt (of pride) by which the last king had himself kindled the fire which destroyed him and his house.

A hope for the future is only possible for faith, where it upholds a lament for death under the divine judgement, without detracting from it. Cf. further 37:1–14.

33   See above p. 123 to 1:28.

The Sinful History of the People of Israel. The Judgement and Salvation of the Second Exodus

Bibliography

M. Friedmann

הציון הוא ביאור לנבואת יחזקאל

(Vienna, 1888).

D. H. Müller

Biblische Studien IV: *Strophenbau und Responsion in Ezechiel und den Psalmen*, (Wien: Hölder, 1908), 1–27.

E. Rohland

Die Bedeutung der Erwählungstraditionen Israels für die Eschatologie der alttestamentlichen Propheten, Unpub. Diss. (Heidelberg, 1956).

W. Wiebe

Die Wüstenzeit als Typus der messianischen Heilszeit, Unpub. Diss. (Göttingen, 1939).

20

1 And it happened in the seventh year, in the fifth month, on the tenth (day) of the month,[a] that some of the elders of Israel[b] came in order to inquire from Yahweh, and they sat down before me. 2/ Then the word of Yahweh came to me: 3/ Son of man, speak with[a] the elders of Israel[b] and say to them: Thus has [the Lord][c] Yahweh said: Have you come to question me? As I live, I will not allow myself to be questioned by you![d] says [the Lord][e] Yahweh. 4/ Will you (not rather) judge them—judge,[a] son of man! Make known[b] to them the abominations of their fathers 5/ and say to them: Thus has [the Lord][a] Yahweh said:

On the day when I chose Israel,[b] then I raised my hand to the descendants of the house of Jacob (in an oath)[c] and revealed myself to them in the land of Egypt and raised my hand to them (in an oath),[c] in which I declared: I am

20:1 1a The lack of any reference to the month in 𝔊[B] and the following reference to the day of the month τῇ πεντηκαιδεκάτῃ τοῦ μηνός rests on a misunderstanding of 𝔐 בחמשי בעשור לחדש. The text of 𝔏[S], which in *quinta mensae* (= *mense*) *quinta decima mensis* rests on this mistake, has arisen by a subsequent addition of the name of the month (following 𝔐 or 𝔊).

b 𝔊, including 𝔊[O] (𝔏[S]) read (τοῦ) οἴκου Ισραηλ. But cf. 14:1.

3 3a 𝔐 את. 32 MSS אל, but cf. the parallel 14:4. דבר את again 2:1; 3:22, 24, 27; 44:5. דבר אל in 2:2, 7f; 3:1, 4, 10f; 11:25; 12:23; 20:27; 24:18; 32:21; 33:2; 37:19, 21; 40:4, 45; 41:22; 43:6.

b 𝔊 (but not 𝔊[B]) + οἴκου, 𝔖 בני.

c אדני is lacking in 2 MSS[Ken] 𝔊 𝔏[S] 𝔆, see Excursus 1.

d 𝔊 (𝔏[S]) renders more freely εἰ (Σ οὐκ) ἀποκριθήσομαι ὑμῖν. Cf. note d to 14:4.

e אדני is lacking in 𝔊 𝔏[S] 𝔆[Sa], see Excursus 1.

4 4a Related to Yahweh by 𝔊 (𝔏[S]) εἰ ἐκδικήσω αὐτοὺς ἐκδικήσει.

b הודיעם. 𝔊 διαμάρτυραι, 𝔏[S] *testificare*, cf. note a to 16:2.

5 5a אדני is lacking in 𝔊 𝔏[S]. 𝔆[Bo] *deus israel*, see Excursus 1.

b 𝔐 בישראל. 𝔊 (𝔏[S]) τὸν οἶκον Ισραηλ, cf. note c to 12:23 and *VT* 8 (1958): page 79 note 11.

c 𝔊 translates 𝔐 ואשא ידי by ἐγνωρίσθην, anticipating the following ואודע. It has, as the translation of the usage in vv 5b, 6 by ἀντελαβόμην τῇ χειρί μου (differently in vv 15, 23, 28, 42) shows, failed to understand the sharp accentuation of the declaration of an oath, which, theologically, is conveyed by the entire description of the chapter. Thus it weakens the "swearing" an oath here to "revealing himself" and in vv 5b and 6 to "promising help."

Yahweh, your God. 6/ On that day I raised my hand to them (by which I promised them on oath),[a] that I would bring them out of the land of Egypt into a land which I had investigated[b] for them, which flows with milk and honey and which is a jewel[c] among all lands. 7/ And I said to them: Let each one throw away the loathsome things on which his eyes are fixed, and do not render yourselves unclean with the idols of Egypt. I am Yahweh, your God.

8 But they were rebellious against me and would not listen to me. Not one[a] threw away the loathsome things on which his eyes were fixed, and they did not let go the idols of Egypt. Then I thought to pour out my anger upon them in order to exhaust my anger upon them in the midst of the land of Egypt. 9/ But I acted (mercifully)[a] for my name's sake, that it might not be profaned[b] before the eyes of the nations, in whose midst they were, (and) before whose eyes I had revealed myself to them (with the promise) to lead them out of Egypt. 10/ And I led them out of the land of Egypt[a] and brought them into the desert.

11 And I gave them my statutes and made known to them my laws, through which men may live,[a] if they do them. 12/ And I also gave them my sabbaths, that they might be a (covenant-) sign between me and them, so that they might know that I—I, Yahweh[a]—sanctify them.

13 But the house of Israel rebelled against me in the desert. They did not walk in my statutes[a] and despised my laws, through which men may live if they do them, and they completely desecrated my sabbaths. Then I thought to pour out my anger upon them in the desert, in order to destroy them utterly. 14/ But I acted (mercifully)[a] for my name's sake, that I might not be profaned[b] before the eyes of the nations, in the sight of which I had brought them out. 15/ But I lifted my hand to them in the desert (in making an oath to them) that I would not bring them into the land, which I had given 'them' (?),[a] which flows with milk and honey and which is

6

6a Cf. note c to v 5.

b 𝔊 ἡτοίμασα αὐτοῖς (𝔊^A ὤμοσα then 𝔏^S iuravi illis) has failed to understand the תרתי of 𝔐, but certainly does not simply presuppose the נתתי used by 𝔐 in v 15 and by 𝔗 𝔊 (יהבת) which harks back to v 6 and is correctly translated by 𝔊 in v 15 by ἔδωκα. Against Cornill, Ehrlich, *Randglossen*, Herrmann, Toy, who would read נתתי, we must keep the unusual reading of 𝔐, since it fits better in the present context, which speaks of the preparatory action of Yahweh. But cf. note a to v 15.

c 𝔐 צבי. Strikingly 𝔊 has here and in v 15 κηρίον ἐστί "it is a honeycomb." Cooke thinks of an interchange with צוף. 𝔊^Bmg δυνατή Θ δύναμις, Clem ἐπαινουμένη, Σ θρησκεία, Ἁ first edition reads στάσις, second edition (cf. Jerome) *inclytum*.

8 8a 𝔊 𝔖 𝔏^S 𝔆 𝔈 𝔄 show no equivalent for the איש of 𝔐. This (attested by 𝔗) could possibly have come into the text in dependence on v 7, so Cornill, Bertholet, Cooke, Fohrer.

9 9a עשׂה, used absolutely, is not impossible with Ezekiel (cf. 8:18; 36:22, 32; cf. also the formula דברתי ועשׂיתי 17:24; 24:14; 36:36; 37:14) and therefore (against Cornill) is not to be changed in accordance with the interpretative rendering of 𝔊 ואחוס in.

b 𝔐 הֵחֵל. A change to הָחֵל (Toy, Bertholet) is not necessary, since the nip'al of חלל is also not unknown in Ezekiel (7:24; 22:16, 26; 25:3), and already 𝔊 shows this tradition of interpretation.

10 10a V 10a has fallen out in 𝔊^B, 967 and others 𝔆^Sa 𝔆 (𝔏^S) by homoioteleuton with v 9, Ziegler, *Ezechiel*.

11 11a 𝔗 thinks of eternal life וייחי בהון בחיי עלמא.

12 12a Cf. 14:4 (7).

13 13a 𝔊 (= 𝔊^B) misunderstands the introductory וימרו לבית ישראל בי בית ישראל as ואמר לבית ישראל and consequently recasts what follows into an address by the insertion of an imperative: ἐν τοῖς προστάγμασί μου πορεύεσθε. In the strangely disconnected לא הלכו (καὶ οὐκ ἐπορεύθησαν) which then remains, the connection with 𝔐 is then resumed. 𝔊^A carries through this recasting in direct speech and positive admonition right up to the conclusion of v 13aα, only to begin once again then with the correct translation of 𝔐 13aα and to carry it through fully. So also 𝔏^S. The whole structure of Ezek 20 points to 𝔐 as the original text.

14 14a Cf. note a to v 9. Instead of ואעשׂ (v 9) here ואעשׂה; cf. 18:14, 28.

b Cf. note b to v 9.

15 15a 4 MSS (𝔊 𝔏^S 𝔖 𝔙) add להם, which is accepted by Cornill, Herrmann, Bertholet. נתן used absolutely without a dative would be unusual. נתתי is well attested. However, in view of the otherwise demonstrably stereotyped repetition of previously used formulations, we may question whether the more colorful תרתי of v 6 had stood here instead of the weaker נתתי. An original omission of להם could more easily be understood beside תרתי

a jewel[b] among all lands. 16/ For they had rejected my laws, and had not walked in my statutes, and had desecrated my sabbaths[a]—for their hearts remained set on their idols.[b] 17/ But my eye spared them,[a] so that I did not destroy them and I did not finish them[b] off in the desert.

18 And I said to their sons in the desert: Do not walk in the statutes[a] of your fathers and do not follow their laws, and do not make yourselves unclean[b] with their idols! 19/ I am Yahweh, your God. Walk in *my* statutes and follow *my* laws and do them! 20/ And keep my sabbaths holy, so that it may be a (covenant-) sign between me and you, that you may know that I—I Yahweh[a]— am your God.

21 But the sons (too)[a] rebelled against me. They did not walk in my statutes and did not keep my laws, so that they should follow them, through which the man who does so may live. 'And'[b] they desecrated my sabbaths. Then I thought to pour out my anger upon them, in order to exhaust my anger upon them in the desert. 22/ [But I withdrew my hand.][a] But I acted (mercifully)[b] for my name's sake, that it might not be profaned[c] before the eyes of the nations, in the sight of which I had brought them out. 23/ Nevertheless[a] I lifted my hand to them in the desert (in an oath) that I would scatter them among the nations and disperse them throughout the lands 24/ because they had not kept my laws and had rejected my statutes, and had desecrated my sabbaths, and their eyes had remained fixed on the idols of their fathers. 25/ I also gave to them bad statutes[a] and laws, through which they could not live,[b] 26/ and I made[a] them unclean through their offerings, when they offered all the firstborn (by fire)—that I might fill them with horror [, that they might know that I am Yahweh].[b]

27 Therefore speak to the house of Israel, son of man, and say to them: Thus has [the Lord][a] Yahweh said: Yet further thereby[b] have your fathers insulted me,

(in v 6 it stands beside תרתי) than beside נתתי.

b 𝕲 κηρίον, 'A στάσις, Σ θρησκεία, Θ δυναμις, cf. Note c to v 6.

16 16a For the construction cf. Blau, "Gebrauch," page 9 note 3.

b 𝕲 translates loosely καὶ ὀπίσω τῶν ἐνθυμημάτων τῶν καρδιῶν (𝕲ᴮ 𝕷ˢ 𝕮ᴮᵒ καρδίας) αὐτῶν ἐπορεύοντο.

17 17a 𝕿 וחס מימרי עליהון.

b אתם – אותם cf. note a to 2:1.

18 18a The masculine plural חקים is found in Ezekiel further 11:12; 20:25; 36:27. 𝕲 νόμιμα 𝕿 גזירת.

b 𝔐 אל תטמאו is given a double translation by 𝕲 (𝕷ᶜˢ): μὴ συναναμίσγεσθε καὶ μὴ μιαίνεσθε.

20 20a Cf. note a to v 12.

21 21a The καί added by 𝕲 (𝕷ᶜˢ) is a loose translation and does not indicate the loss of a גם in 𝔐 (against Cornill, Bertholet).

b Varᴾ 𝕲 𝕷ᶜˢ 𝕾 𝖁 and the parallel v 13 support the addition of the copula.

22 22a 𝔐 והשבתי את ידי is not attested by 𝕲 𝕷ᶜˢ 𝕾. The use of the perfect consecutive in the narrative context of vv 21f, the phrase השיב יד which is otherwise never used of Yahweh in Ezekiel (but of men in 18:8, 17; 38:12), and the omission of the passage in the parallel descriptions in vv 9, 14 appear to demonstrate that the statement is not original.

b Cf. note a to v 9.

c Cf. note b to v 9.

23 23a 𝔐 גם. Following the analogy of vv 15, 25, we should expect וגם, so MSS Edd. 𝕲 (𝕷ᶜˢ), which translates the וגם אני in vv 15, 25 by καὶ ἐγώ, gives here simply καί; cf. 𝖁 𝕿 = 𝔐. Torrey's interpretation (*Pseudo-Ezekiel*, 89f) of the section vv 23–26 as a series of three rhetorical questions, which all expect a negative answer and which may therefore be regarded as an Aramaism, is not to be followed. Cf. the exposition.

25 25a For 𝔐 חֻקִּים cf. note a to v 18.

b 𝕿 offers a significant paraphrase of v 25: "But I rejected them because they were rebellious against my word and would not receive my prophets. I expelled them to a place far away and handed them over to the ones who hated them. And they followed their own foolish impulses and made for themselves bad statutes and laws, through which they could not have life."

26 26a Understood by 𝕲 as a future. So Σ (according to Jerome), already from v 25.

b 𝔐 למען אשר ידעו אשר אני יהוה is not attested by 𝕲 𝕷ᶜˢ 𝕮ˢᵃ Just Jeromeᵗᵉˢᵗ, and it is also shown to be a later insertion by its linguistic usage (the introduction of the recognition formula by למען אשר, the use of the imperfect for this, and the introduction of what is to be known by אשר).

27 27a אדני is lacking in 𝕲 𝕷ˢ 𝕮, see Excursus 1.

b The adverbial accusative עוד זאת is found again 36:37, translated by 𝕾 in both places by תוב בהדא, and misunderstood by 𝕲 ἕως τούτου as עד זאת (36:37 correctly as ἔτι τοῦτο).

in breaking faith with me. 28/ When I brought them into the land which I had sworn, with my hand upraised, to give to them—where they (then) saw any high hill or any leafy tree, there they slaughtered their sacrifices[a] [and there they brought their gifts which provoked me to anger],[b] and there they set out their sweet-smelling offerings and poured out their drink offerings. 29/ And I said to them: what is the high place about, to which you go up?[a] Thus its name has become "high place" to the present day.

30 Therefore speak to the house of Israel: Thus has [the Lord][a] Yahweh said: You are making yourselves unclean with the behavior[b] of your fathers. In following their abominations you are committing their immorality. 31/ And in offering[a] your gifts [, in making your sons pass through the fire][b] you are making yourselves unclean for all your idols right up to the 'present'[c] day. Should I then let myself be questioned by you, house of Israel? As I live, says [the Lord][d] Yahweh, I will not let myself be questioned by you.

32 [a]It will never happen, what has arisen (as a thought) in your spirit, that you say: "We shall become like the nations, like the families of the (heathen) lands and worship wood and stone." 33/ [a]As I live, says [the Lord][b] Yahweh, with a strong hand and an outstretched arm and with outpoured wrath I will be king over you. 34/ And I will bring you out of the nations and gather you from the (heathen) lands to which you have been scattered, with a strong hand and an outstretched arm and outpoured wrath. 35/ And I will bring you into the desert of the nations and enter into judgement with you there face to face.

28 28a In 𝕲 καὶ ἔθυσαν ἐκεῖ τοῖς θεοῖς αὐτῶν (𝕷[CS] *et sacrificaverunt illic sacrificia diis suis* shows, however, a text expanded in accordance with 𝔐) the τοῖς θεοῖς αὐτῶν is either an inner Greek scribal error for τὰς θυσίας αὐτῶν (Cooke), or a theological reinterpretation in the direction of wholesale worship of foreign gods, but not (against Bertholet) a witness for an original לאלהיהם (instead of את זבחיהם).

b 𝔐 ויתנו שם כעס קרבנם is lacking in 𝕲 and may represent a theologically motivated addition (cf. 𝕲 note a), since the noun כעס is never otherwise found in Ezekiel (for the verb cf. 8:17; 16:26, 42; 32:9). The original text contained an objective listing of the individual kinds of sacrifice.

29 29a The unusual, but not impossible, use of the definite article with the predicate הבאים (cf. further 1 Sam 4:16; Is 66:9; Zech 7:6 Cooke) is intended to strengthen the wordplay הבאים – הבמה. Driver, "Linguistic Problems," 67, reads באים שמה, cf. Dtn 4:5.

30 30a אדני is lacking in 𝕲 𝕷[CS] 𝕮[Sa], see Excursus 1.

b 𝔐 הבדרך אבותיכם is interpreted by 𝕲 (𝕷[CS]): ἐν ταῖς ἀνομίαις τῶν πατέρων ὑμῶν.

31 31a 𝔐 בשאת מתנותיכם is supported by Ps 96:8 (Ju 3:18; 2 Sam 8:6; 1 Chr 18:2, 6) as a possible reading. Cf. משאותיכם v 40. 𝕲 ἐν ταῖς ἀπαρχαῖς τῶν δομάτων ὑμῶν would point to מתנותיכם. If, however, we regard v 31a, with its resumption of the אתם נטמאים from v 30, as a later interpretative addition, then we should give preference to the smoother connection of 𝔐 by ובשאת than to the more clumsy בראשית (𝕲), which has been influenced from v 40 and which would introduce a new notion. Cf. note b.

b For 𝕲 ἐν τοῖς ἀφορισμοῖς we must compare v 40 τὰς ἀπαρχὰς τῶν ἀφορισμῶν ὑμῶν as a translation of ראשית משאותיכם (also 48:8), where 𝕲 ἡ ἀπαρχὴ τοῦ ἀφορισμοῦ corresponds to 𝔐 התרומה אשר תרימו. In the במשא[ו]ת of the Hebrew original which we thus presuppose, we must see an original בשאת of 𝔐 (note a) with a slight scribal error. In any case 𝕲 appears not to have had before it the בהעביר בניכם באש with which we must compare the related v 26, and its translation in 𝕲 is to be compared (the note in BH³, which claims that 𝕲 only lacked בניכם באש, is false). This clause is thus a part of a second stage of interpretative editing which was still not present to 𝕲.

c With Eb 22 6 MSS[Ken] 𝕲 𝕷[CS] 𝔗 we must add הזה.

d אדני is lacking in 𝕲 𝕷[CS] 𝕮 𝕰 𝔄, see Excursus 1.

32 32a 𝕲 𝕷[CS] connect v 32aα with v 31.

33 33a 𝕲 (𝕷[CS]) add an introductory διὰ τοῦτο and then regard v 33 as a concluding sentence to v 32.

b אדני is lacking in 𝕲 𝕷[CS] 𝕮, see Excursus 1.

35 35a The nipʿal of שפט is found in 17:20; 38:22. It brings out particularly strongly the taking of a stand in a lawsuit. Cf. further 1 Sam 12:7; Is 43:26; Jer 25:31. Cf. the analogy of the nipʿal of ענה Ezek

36/ As I entered into judgement with your fathers in the desert of the land of Egypt, so will I enter into judgement with you, says [the Lord]ª Yahweh. 37/ I will cause you to pass under the rod,ª and 'I will number you exactly' '.ᵇ 38/ And I will cut off the rebels and those who are disloyal to meª from among you. From the land of their exile I will lead them, but theyᵇ shall not come into the land of Israel. And you shall know that I am Yahweh.ᶜ

39 But you, house of Israel, thus has [the Lord]ª Yahweh said: 'throw away'ᵇ each of you his idols [serve (?), and afterwards, if you will not obey me]ᵇ and profane my holy name no more with your gifts and your idols. 40/ For on my holy mountain, the high mountain of Israel, says [the Lord]ª Yahweh, there will the whole house of Israel serve me altogetherᵇ [in the land].ᶜ There I will receive them with favor, and there I will demand your gifts and your offerings of firstlings,ᵈ alleᵉ your holy gifts. 41/ I will receive you favorably, with sweet-smelling offerings, when I bring you out from the nations, and gather you from the (heathen) lands into which you have been scattered, and I will prove myself to you as the Holy One in the eyes of the nations. 42/ And you will know that I am Yahweh, when I bring you into the land of Israel, into the land which I have sworn (to give) to your fathers, with upraised hand. 43/ And there you will remember your ways and [all]ª your deeds, with which you have made yourselves unclean, and you will utterly loathe yourselves on account of all your evil deeds [, which you have

14:4, 7.

36   36a אדני is lacking in 𝕲 𝔏ᶜˢ 𝕮, see Excursus 1.

37   37a כל אשר יעבר תחת השבט is used in Lev 27:32 for a herd that has been counted.

b 𝔐 והבאתי אתכם במסרת הברית has given trouble to the early translators. Ἀ καὶ εἰσάξω ὑμᾶς ἐν δεσμοῖς τῆς διαθήκης, Σ καὶ καθαρῶ ὑμᾶς διὰ κλοιοῦ (iron collar) τῆς συνθήκης, correspondingly 𝔅 in vinculis foederis; hence Kraetzschmar: "in the bond (מסרת = מאסרת) of the covenant." Θ καὶ διάξω ὑμᾶς ἐν παραδόσει τῆς διαθήκης, cf. 𝔗 במסרת קיימא. 𝕾 ואעלכון במרדותא דדיתיקי. Cornill, accordingly, regards it as justified to emend במסרת to במוסר: "And bring you in chastisement." Without changing the consonantal text, Driver, "Studies. 8," 297, conjectures מֹסֶרֶת "chastisement" derived from יסר; Hitzig would read במסרת הַבְּרִית "in the crucible of purifying." However against all these attempts 𝕲 (𝔏ᶜˢ) καὶ εἰσάξω ὑμᾶς ἐν ἀριθμῷ must point to the original reading. הברית is therefore a scribal error, being a dittography of the וברותי which follows in v 38. So already Ewald, Smend. The expression הביא במספר is to be understood as "to count in," following 1 Chr 9:28. It continues the metaphor of the parallel first half of the verse.

38   38a 𝕲 (𝔏ᶜˢ) διότι misunderstood 𝔐 בי as כי.

b 𝔐 יבוא. With Eb 22 MSS (versions) we must read יבאו. Cf. note a to 10:3.

c Surprisingly 𝕲ᴮ reads here κύριος κύριος, see Excursus 1.

39   39a אדני is lacking in 𝔏ᶜˢ. 𝕲ᴮ κύριος κύριος, see Excursus 1.

b V 39a is clearly disturbed in its second half. 𝕲 appears to have had before it roughly the same text. Hitzig believed that he could discern underneath ἐξάρατε, which it reads in place of 𝔐 לכו עבדו, a העברו (so also Cornill, who compares Zech 13:2 "clear away") or better still בערו (so also Bertholet). However, a glance at the related statement in v 7 איש שקוצי עיניו השליכו rather suggests that we should see in the לכו a remnant of an original [הש]לכו. The summons that then follows here איש גלוליו השליכו is continued in v 39b in a text that is free from objection. What comes in between appears to be a fragmentary clause (corrupted at the beginning?), which has entered here in error from quite another place. Cf. 3:7; 20:8.

40   40a אדני is lacking in 𝕲 𝔏ᶜˢ. 𝕲ᴮ κύριος κύριος, see Excursus 1.

b For כל בית ישראל כלה cf. note a to 11:15.

c 𝔐 בארץ is not attested by 𝕲 𝔏ᶜˢ 𝕾 and is undoubtedly a (meaningful) gloss seeking to make the text clear.

d For 𝔐 משאותיכם cf. note a to v 31. 𝔗 אצוותכון misunderstood it as משארותיכם "kneading-troughs" (or their content), cf. Dtn 28:5, 17. 𝔅 decimarum vestrarum, i.e. מעשרותיכם.

e ב-essentiae, cf. Gesenius-Kautzsch § 119 i.

43   43a 𝔐 כל, not attested by Eb 22 𝕲 𝔏ᶜˢ, is to be

403

done].[b] **44/ And you will know that I am Yahweh, when I deal with you for my name's sake—not in accordance with your evil ways and your corrupt deeds, [house of Israel,][a] says [the Lord][b] Yahweh.**

deleted since it disturbs the balance of the two parallel clauses (את עלילותיכם – את דרכיכם).

b 𝔐 אשר עשׂיתם was not in the original text according to 𝔊 𝔏[cs].

44 44a 𝔐 בית ישׂראל is lacking in 𝔊 𝔏[cs].

b אדני is lacking in 𝔊 𝔏[cs], see Excursus 1.

Form

Both Cooke, who derives the chapter from the prophet himself, and Hölscher, who denies it to the prophet in its entirety, regard Ezek 20 as a self-contained unit. The thematic correspondence of the two halves of the chapter (exodus, judgement in the desert, demand for the putting away of idols) and the evenness of the prosaic style of speech immediately seem to support this view.

However, there are not lacking considerations against it which make it more probable that the declaration of judgement in the first half has been supplemented by the promise of salvation in the second. There is at first an analogy between the starting position in chs. 8–11; 14:1–11; and ch. 20. Both in the basic text of chs. 8–11 and in 14:1–11 the request of the elders of Israel for a decision from God is met with refusal and a threat of judgement. Should we expect this to be any different in the original structure of Ezek 20? More important, however, is the fact that Yahweh's explicit command to the prophet to speak in 20:4 orders him to "judge" and to "make known the abominations of their fathers." The parallel texts (for "judging" 22:2, cf. 23:36; for the "making known abominations" 16:2; 22:2) show that in each case the prophet's words keep to the theme commanded by Yahweh. Is it only in Ezek 20 that it is to be expanded by a promise of salvation? To this must be added that the correspondence of the two halves of the chapter in style and details of expression is not so close, on further examination, as would appear at first glance from the identity of the theme. The rough sequence of two oaths in vv 31 and 33 (the parallelism in the parallel formulations in 14:16, 18, 20 and 17:16, 19 do not form a genuine analogy) offers a particular stylistic clumsiness. This leads on to the further question of the exact limits between the original text and its expansion.

Bertholet and Fohrer make a division after v 32 and use the quotation in v 32 (as others have done before them) as an important feature for the understanding of the situation of the question in vv 1ff. The expansion then begins directly with the oath in v 33. However,

there are serious reasons for doubting this. The conclusion of vv 1–32 with a quotation is unusual. The quotation comes awkwardly. Thus Herntrich would see v 32 as an isolated (but genuine) single verse. However, the beginning in v 33 is not satisfying. The oath formula חי אני, which is found sixteen times in the book of Ezekiel, never introduces a prophecy.[1] In 16:48 it gives an element of emphasis into reproach that has already been set out. More frequently it marks the transition from reproach to declaration of judgement (cf. in the double declaration of judgement in 17:16, 19, which answers the accusing account of Zedekiah's sin in 17:12–15; further 14:16, 18, 20; 34:8; in 5:11; 35:6, 11 it is introduced directly with לכן). In the remaining passages it introduces the divine antithesis to an assumption (20:3, 31), or a saying of the people being addressed set out in the form of a quotation, so 18:3 after 18:2; 33:11 after 33:10; 33:27 slightly removed from 33:24. Yet this last named manner of use of the oath formula appears in the oath of 20:33, which answers the quotation in 20:32. The section vv 32f cannot therefore be isolated in accordance with the clearly recognizable style of Ezekiel. Rather, with Herrmann and others, we must see the beginning of the expansion of Ezek 20 in v 32. This means, however, that the quotation in v 32 cannot be used to illuminate the situation of vv 1–31, as has often been done.

Noteworthy in the section vv 1–31 is the repeated declaration of a conclusion in vv 27 and 30, introduced with לכן, and a subsequent command to speak. Examination of the contents shows that a conclusion which is called for by the content of what precedes, i.e., the repeated refusal to give a divine answer, is first pronounced in vv 30f, whilst vv 27–29 contain a clumsily introduced appendix to the narrative account of vv 5–26. Since vv 27–29 are separated from what precedes also by the fact that they fall outside the stereotyped pattern of vv 5–26, they must be regarded as an element of later editorial expansion and separated off from the original text.

The basic prophecy which is then left in vv 2–26, 30f (for v 31aα cf. the exposition) contains a rebuff to the request by the elders, as the framework in vv 3 and 31aβb brings out clearly. Whereas in the parallel in 14:1–11 the rebuff was motivated by a direct unmasking of the inquirers as idolaters, in 20:4–26 the prophet is commanded to proclaim reproach along the lines of a theological survey of history, which first turns directly to the immediate situation of those addressed with the question of v 30. Thus, unlike in 22:2ff, where the "judging" of the city of blood is accomplished in the form of a confrontation with the divine law in the form of a listing of individual offenses, the "accusing" of the people is wrapped up in a narrative of Israel's history, as in 16:2ff and 23:1ff.[2] Unlike chs. 16 and 23, however, any allegorical dress is completely omitted. The divine word says nothing here of marriage to a specially chosen bride (16, 23), nor of the vine (15, 19:10–14), or the lioness (19:1ff), but speaks quite simply of "Israel" (v 5) and its history with God. In the lament form of the "general confession," in which the community or the individual renders honor to God by public confession of the sinful history of Israel, this proclamation by the prophet later found an echo in the prayers of the worshipping community.[3]

Ezek 20, however, is still not completely understood, if we simply find in it a free recounting of favorite stories of early Israel. G. von Rad has shown that Israel, at a very early period, formulated certain credo-like summaries of its account of its original encounter with Yahweh, which could not easily be expanded by its subsequent historical experience.[4] Ezek 20 can only be understood, in its traditio-historical background, when we see how the prophet takes up here the sacred core of the credo formulation which he had received and retells Israel's history on the basis of it. This is exactly similar in the figurative addresses with the sacred images of Israel as the bride of Yahweh and as a vine.

The accusing prophetic historical account must therefore be oriented antithetically to the narratives which told, at Israel's festivals (Passover, Ex 13:8) and on other occasions of Israel's worship, the main outline of the credo-formulations of Yahweh's saving actions at the time of the exodus. (Cf. Ps 105, the counterpart to the "general confession" of Ps 106.) What is there celebrated as Yahweh's saving action appears in Ezekiel recast into a history of Israel's disobedience, deserving of judgement. The stress on the feature of Israel's disobedience at the time of the exodus could certainly link up with older features of the tradition: the murmuring of the people in the wilderness,[5] the sin over the golden calf (Ex 32), and the sin over the sending out of the spies (Nu 13f; 1:19–46). However, in the radical representation of the period of the exodus from this viewpoint, which, as will be shown in the detailed exposition, goes far beyond the material furnished by the tradition in certain passages, we can doubtless see the specific emphasis of Ezekiel himself. The acceptance that 20:1–31 derives from Ezekiel undoubtedly receives strong support from this closeness which it shows to the theological position of Ezek 15, 16, and 23.

In his prophetic historical account Ezekiel takes up only elements from the "short historical credo" (von Rad). Since the history of the patriarchs had already been stamped earlier with the idea of Yahweh's free and gracious promise, mention of it is lacking in this account which is oriented towards a proclamation of judgement, although 33:24 shows a knowledge of the story of Abraham. A pale reference to it may be seen at most in the reference to the "seed of the house of Jacob" (v 5) (cf. on the text). It is also understandable from the major theological character of the chapter that any description of the settlement in the land, which is promised in v 6 and which would be expected from the "short historical credo," is completely absent, since it represented a feature of the gracious character of the history. The subsequent addition in vv 27–29 shows that afterwards the absence of this was felt, and an attempt made to fill the gap.

---

1 See above p. 176.
2 See above p. 335.
3 See Gunkel-Begrich, *Einleitung*, 132; von Rad, *OT Theology* 1. Cf. especially Ps 106, which reflects Ezek 20 in its wording, and also Dan 9, Ezra 9, Baruch 1:15ff, and *4 Ezra* 3:4ff, which also includes the primeval history.
4 Gerhard von Rad, "The Form-critical Problem of

the Hexateuch" in *The Problem of the Hexateuch and Other Essays*, tr. E. W. Trueman Dicken (New York: McGraw-Hill, 1966), 1–78; von Rad, *OT Theology* 1.
5 Noth, *Pentateuchal Traditions*, § 8h: "The Murmuring of the People."

We can see a distinctive feature of Ezekiel's composition in the parallel casuistic outlining of three phases of history within the exodus events. This recalls the casuistic series of three generations in Ezek 18 and the casuistic structure of 3:17ff; 14:12ff; 33:1ff. We may perhaps find a prophetic prototype for such a stylizing of history in the scheme of the series of plagues given in Amos 4:6ff (Is 5:25; 9:7–20; 10:1–4), which, however, lacks the specific legal casuistic form of Ezekiel, as well as any connection with the credo history.

In spite of the balanced stylizing of the three phases of the exodus period, we cannot find here a scheme of metrical strophes, as Müller and Fohrer, each in different ways, believe they can demonstrate.[6]

Setting

The date in 20:1 places the prophecy in the year 591. The same verse also shows the prophet's location in exile. For the apparent difficulty that the inquirers in v 31 are addressed in regard to their child sacrifices, as still being continued, see note b to v 31 and the exposition.[7]

Interpretation

■ **20:1** We do not know how the historical circumstances of the exiles and of the citizens of Jerusalem had changed in the period of at least eleven months since the proclamation of the great vision of judgement upon Jerusalem (8:1) up to the tenth day of the fifth month of the seventh year of Jehoiachin's exile, a point of time in the summer of 591 (according to Parker-Dubberstein August 14th, 591). Nor do we know why on that day the elders of Israel came and sat before the prophet.[8] It is expressly noted that they wanted to inquire of Yahweh. Scholars have sought to answer the question why they came to the prophet from v 32. Thus A. Menes, J. A. Bewer, and others believe, following Friedmann, that they can find in the request of the

elders the desire to establish a sacrificial cult of their own in Babylon.[9] Fohrer thinks of the desire to set up an image of Yahweh "of wood and stone." The conclusion drawn above that with v 32 a secondary expansion of Ezek 20 begins, however, prohibits using v 32 for an elucidation of v 1. It is also substantially improbable that the exiles would have come with such a request to the prophet if it concerned an image, which would have directly opposed the ancient command of Yahweh (Ex 20:4). Rather, as we have conjectured for 8:1 and 14:1, by their request the elders would have been seeking a word from the prophet which announced the ending of the deportation of Jehoiachin and his fellow exiles. Ezek 36:37 may offer an example, although clearly for a later period: where Yahweh "lets himself be questioned" (אִדָּרֵשׁ) he proclaims afresh the old patriarchal promise of the increase of the people (ארבה אתם).

■ **20:2** The divine word, which is introduced with the usual formula for the receipt of a message, proclaims a totally different oracle, just as in 8:1ff and 14:1ff[10].

■ **20:3, 4** After a refusal, couched in the emphatic oath form (cf. 14:3), there follows a command to the prophet, at first formulated as a question and then passing over into the imperative, to pronounce judgement on the inquirers by accusing them of the sins of their fathers. As in 16:1ff and 2:3 the solidarity of those who belong to the people of God with their history becomes plain. At the same time the conclusion of the speech of accusation in v 30 makes clear that those addressed have still not broken free altogether from the ways of their fathers. Thus, behind the historical survey which follows, which does not establish a fixed and unalterable fate, there is hidden implicitly the call of the "freedom to repent" (Ezek 18).

■ **20:5–26** The fearful thing in the "accusing" and "making known of abomination" which the prophet is called to perform consists in the fact that this does not mean the history of sins which occurred alongside the

---

6 The close connection in which the recasting of the credo-narrative of Ezek 20 stands to H and P in its description of the divine revelation and lawgiving is best demonstrated in connection with the detailed exposition.

7 For the form, location, and date of vv 32ff see below pp. 413f.

8 See above p. 236 to 8:1; p. 306 to 14:1.

9 A. Menes, "Tempel und Synagoge," *ZAW* 50 (1932): 272f; Julius A. Bewer, "Beiträge zur Exegese des Buches Ezechiel," *ZAW* 63 (1951): 195–197.

10 See above pp. 144f.

great history of Israel's salvation, is set in the shadows on the sidelines, but that he has to declare the great events of this very history as stations in the way of the frightful sins committed by Israel. Ch. 23 seeks to make clear in another way how the words of Israel's "credo" become great accusations against it.

In three phases, formulated in schematic parallelism, the "saving history" of the credo which accuses Israel is unfolded in a casuistic legal style, which was familiar to the prophet from his priestly background. Each of the three phases shows how Israel received the instruction of its God in an area of life which was intended by God to bring salvation (vv 5–7, 10–12, 17–20). Each time Israel behaved rebelliously against this instruction (vv 8a, 13a, 21a) so that Yahweh's holy anger blazed up and threatened the destruction of Israel (vv 8b, 13b, 21b). Then Yahweh repeatedly restrained himself "for his name's sake" (vv 9, 14, and 17, 22). In an evident heightening this restraint is increasingly elaborated with stronger threats of judgement (lacking in the first phase; in the second phase vv 15–16; in the third phase vv 23–26). Thus the three phases do not stand simply alongside each other as cases to be considered individually (which distinguishes them from the legal casuistic of Ezek 18), but possess an inner historical movement towards judgement, which then stands as a concrete threat over the third phase. For the immediate present of the exiles being addressed it was a reality which had already taken place.

The introductory description of the salvation to which Yahweh had called Israel at the beginning of its history begins impressively.[11] For the first and only time in the book of Ezekiel the verb בחר is used, which plays an important role in the contemporary Deuteronomic terminology.[12] Its pre-Deuteronomic setting K. Koch believes he can find in the credo-hymns of the Psalter on the basis of an examination of a semantic study.[13] The ideas of Deuteronomy may further be recalled when the following history of Yahweh with

Israel is emphatically set under the pronouncement of a divine oath.[14] The linguistic consideration that Deuteronomy uses the verb שבע for an oath (Dtn 1:8; 4:31; 6:10; 7:12f; 8:1; 11:9, 21 and other passages), whilst throughout Ezek 20 uses the phrase נשׂא יד (vv 5, 6, 15, 23, 28, 42, cf. 36:7; 44:12; 47:14; שבע in Ezekiel only in 16:8; 21:28; in 32:4 it is a text error) and even more the fact that in the references mentioned in Deuteronomy the oath is always given to the patriarchs (Abraham, Isaac and Jacob), whilst here it is given to the people coming out of Egypt, opposes placing Ezek 20 too close to Deuteronomy. The linguistic contacts much more strongly (in spite of K. Koch) place Ezek 20 close to the language of the Priestly Document (in particular Ex 6).[15] Admittedly the verb בחר is lacking there, but an important role is played by God's self-disclosure in his name (Ex 6:2, 6, 8; in v 7 in the recognition formula), the promise of the land (נשׂאתי את ידי Ex 6:8), the recognition of God and his giving of himself to be recognized (ידע Ex 6:3; v 7 in the recognition formula), exactly as in Ezek 20. K. Koch may be right in his comment that an element of the range of meaning of בחר in the Psalms, to which the mention of the patriarchs belongs, may have entered by the בית יעקב.[16] This need not undermine the consideration that Ezek 20, unlike Ex 6, clearly avoids any explicit reference back to the patriarchs and sees Israel's origins solely in the exodus from Egypt, as in ch. 23.[17]

Ezek 20 recounts the history of Israel's election not simply as a sacred story. Rather, in a thoroughgoing theological reflection the divine call that is evident in it is made plain.[18] The similarity of the formulations to those of Ex 6 suggests that Ezekiel was following a priestly theology in this. Yahweh's election encounter with Israel means both his self-revelation and his entering into a binding relationship with the people. The noetic and the voluntative elements of the divine revelation are swallowed up in a distinctive way in the formulation of Ezek 20. Yahweh's action towards Israel

---

11   For ביום with a following infinitive (A. Fischer, "Zur Siloahinschrift," *ZDMG* 56 [1902]: 804) and its use in the description of events which begin an era, see above pp. 338f to 16:4.

12   Vriezen, *Erwählung*.

13   Klaus Koch, "Zur Geschichte der Erwählungsvorstellung in Israel," *ZAW* 67 (1955 [1956]): 205–226.

14   Horst, "Eid," especially 371–373.

15   Koch, "Geschichte," page 218 note 30. This was already seen by Müller, *Strophenbau*, 20.

16   Koch, "Geschichte," page 218 note 31.

17   For the parallelism of the two election traditions see Kurt Galling, *Die Erwählungstraditionen Israels*, BZAW 48 (Giessen: Töpelmann, 1928).

18   See Walther Zimmerli, *Das Alte Testament als Anrede*,

is an oath (וָאֶשָּׂא יָדִי ל"), a freely undertaken obligation which fundamentally involves a third party as a witness and guarantor between the two parties to the covenant, which Yahweh will never henceforth go back on. Thereby it is at the same time a handing over and a disclosure of the mystery of his own person (וָאִוָּדַע לָהֶם). In the self-disclosure sworn to the covenant partner: "I am Yahweh, your God," both are contained as in a fundamental covenant declaration (also Ex 20:2aα). In the handing over of his name in the self-disclosure of the theophany address, Yahweh reveals the mystery of his being, allows himself to be invoked by his people, and, at the same time, leaves himself vulnerable in the zone of his accessibility to men in that he can no longer be assured that his name will not be misused.[19] (It is inculcated in Israel's sacral law [Ex 20:7] that such dishonoring is not allowed to take place in the community.) In the covenant declaration which is contained in the revelation of the divine name: "I am (Yahweh) your God," for which K. Elliger, "Ich bin," suggests the title "favor formula" (German *Huldformel*), he binds himself to the people whom he has called in his name which he has made known. From now on his name is pledged to this people, into whose history it has entered. Through it, it may be honored, but through it also it may come to dishonor, without his being able to guard against such an eventuality on account of his faithfulness and the promise he has made. In his act of election God takes the risk of such a possibility endangering his honor.

■ **20:6** However, election is not merely a general activity. It belongs to the people Israel in its concrete history and in its actual obedience. Thus vv 6f unfold the basic declaration of Yahweh's act of election. It is no accident that here, as in Ex 6 and in the prologue of the Decalogue, the reference to the free gracious action of Yahweh stands at the beginning. The prior action of Yahweh remains the basis of all his relationship to his people (the word "covenant," which naturally comes to

mind here, is lacking).[20] Yahweh promises that he will bring up his chosen people from Egypt. Nothing is said here of the oppression by the Egyptians, unlike in Ex 6 (and Ezek 23). Reference to the "crying out" of the oppressed (זעק in different connections in 9:8; 11:13; 21:17; 27:30) or to the "redemption" (גאל and פדה are lacking in the vocabulary of Ezekiel) play no role in Ezekiel, unlike Deuteronomy (and Dtr) and Deutero-Isaiah. However, the promise of the land, which plays a central role in Ezekiel's preaching, is very much more fully adduced.[21] In a threefold statement, which is almost liturgical in its solemnity (Nu 6:24–26; Is 6:3; Jer 7:4; 22:29), it is laid down: 1) Yahweh himself has searched it out. Nu 10:33, with the use of the verb תור, says that the ark, and in Dtn 1:33 Yahweh himself in the pillar of cloud and fire, has searched out the camp site (Nu 10:33 the resting-place מנוחה) for his people in the desert. Does the present assertion represent a spiritualizing and heightening of the spy narrative of Nu 13f?[22] 2) The reference to the land flowing with milk and honey, which possibly has as its background the mythology of Paradise, which is already found in the older Pentateuchal sources (Ex 3:8, 17; 33:3; Nu 16:13f), and in Deuteronomy (6:3; 11:9; 26:9, 15), H (Lev 20:24) and P (Nu 14:8, so Noth), reappears, where Ezekiel is citing the tradition which he had received.[23] 3) The description of the land as "splendor" (צבי) appears to have arisen in the time immediately before Ezekiel. It is first demonstrably used in Jer 3:19 in what is undeniably still a quite free usage (ארץ חמדה נחלת צבי צבאות גוים).[24] Later it becomes in the book of Daniel (Dan 8:9; 11:16, 41, 45) an apocalyptic code word for the "promised land."

■ **20:7** However, Yahweh's election does not only mean a blessed destiny. It is a summons which calls for responsibility. With a significant fresh introduction Yahweh's demand in terms of law, which had been proclaimed from of old in Israel's covenant cult, is formulated in v 7.[25] In this we must not overlook the formal

BEvTh 24 (München: Kaiser, 1956).

19 Zimmerli, "Jahwe," 193–195 (= *Gottes Offenbarung*, 24–27).

20 See above p. 352.

21 See above pp. 185f, 203f.

22 For the spiritualizing of the story of the manna in Dtn 8:3 see von Rad, *OT Theology* 1.

23 Gressmann, *Messias*, 155–158; H. Usener, "Milch

und Honig," *Rheinisches Museum für Philologie* NF 57 (1902): 177–195.

24 Miller, *Verhältnis*, 107.

25 Alt, "Origins of Law."

dependence on earlier legal language. The introductory אִישׁ, which relates the law to the individual (such individual application is not lacking in the Decalogue), is to be found in אִישׁ אִמּוֹ וְאָבִיו תִּירָאוּ Lev 19:3 (cf. the אִישׁ אִישׁ formulations of H which have a counterpart in Ezek 14:3, 7).[26] We find the elevated legal language in the repetition of legal pronouncements (cf. the pairs of laws in Lev 19:3, 4 and other passages). Above all we find rich parallel material in H emphasizing the legal demand by the motive clause of Yahweh's self-proclamation, a form which represents a further development of the proclamation of law which we find in the Decalogue with the prefatory divine self-introduction.[27] In contrast then, in the formulation of the basic demand laid upon Israel, we can discern the language of the prophet himself; idols and "abominations," which render Israel unclean, are repeatedly the great enemies of Yahweh throughout the entire preaching of Ezekiel.[28] Corresponding to the situation of the exodus from Egypt we have here the "idols of Egypt."[29]

In comparison with the Pentateuchal narrative it is striking how decisively Ezekiel summarizes the process of revelation into a single event. What is there broken up into at least three acts: Yahweh's revelation of his name in connection with the call of Moses (Ex 3, 6); the giving of the promise of the exodus and the settlement in the land by Moses to the people (Ex 4:30f; 6:6 in P simply commands this, and the carrying out is not explicitly narrated); the giving of the laws on the mount of God in the wilderness (Ex 19ff), is here concentrated at the beginning in the act of revelation to Israel whilst it is still in Egypt. Also the promise of the land, which according to the Pentateuch had already been given to the patriarchs, is here included without any reference back to earlier events. We must be careful here not to draw conclusions about a different view of the history which Ezekiel may have received and seek to find a tradition of a giving of the law to Israel whilst it was already in Egypt. The arbitrary summarizing is Ezekiel's own work and is to serve to strengthen his message.

■ **20:8** This is also true, however, of the assertion of Israel's disobedience, which is expressed by means of vocabulary known in Ezekiel from his call-narrative.[30] We can as little obtain from this a reliable historical account of the "condition of religious apostasy from which Moses summoned the tribes" as from the harsh description of the unchastity of the two women in Egypt of Ezekiel 23.[31] Later Jewish tradition first began to tell of this (actually on the basis of Ezek 20:8).[32] Rather we are concerned here, as in Ezek 15, 16, with an overall radical judgement upon Israel which allows it, even in its earliest period, no place for any bright period of obedience.[33] We can best find an occasion for such a negative judgement upon Israel in Egypt in remarks such as Ex 5:21 about the complaints of the Israelite representatives in the face of the making of their forced labor more severe. In this nothing is said about religious disloyalty.

Thus Yahweh's anger blazes up against the unwillingness of Israel to listen. Israel is threatened with destruction whilst it is still in the land of Egypt.

■ **20:9** However, the force of the reality of Israel's election then manifests itself. In this election Yahweh had revealed his name, without any special protection, to the eyes of the nations in that he had bound it to Israel. The destruction of Israel, to whom Yahweh had promised deliverance from Egypt in conjunction with the revelation of this name, would mean a profanation of this name over which all the world would then surely begin to mock.[34] The reference to such an endangering of the name of Yahweh, whose honor in the world was at stake, is already to be found in the older intercessory prayers of Moses after Israel's sin over the golden calf (Ex 32:12) and over the spies (Nu 14:13ff). It goes back to the early period in Egypt.

■ **20:10** Already the gracious act of the exodus from

26 See above pp. 302f.

27 See B. Gemser, "The Importance of the Motive Clause in Old Testament Law," *VT Suppl* 1 (1953): 50–66; Zimmerli, "Jahwe," 181–186 (= *Gottes Offenbarung*, 12–17).

28 See above pp. 186f.

29 For the formulation שִׁקּוּצֵי עֵינָיו cf. 18:6.

30 For בֵּית מְרִי see above p. 134; for מרה p. 175; for

31 Martin Buber, *The Prophetic Faith*, tr. Carlyle Witton-Davies (New York: Macmillan, 1949), 43.

32 George Foot Moore, *Judaism in the first centuries of the Christian era, the age of the Tannaim* 2 (New York: Schocken, 1971).

33 See above pp. 336f.

34 Cf. Ezek 36:20; see Sheldon H. Blank, "Isaiah 52:5

לֹא יָאבוּ לִשְׁמֹעַ אֵלַי of 3:7. cf. the לֹא אָבוּ לִשְׁמֹעַ אֵלָי

Egypt, which in the older credo is the primary datum of Yahweh's freely given love for his people, becomes here an act of God's inner faithfulness and his upholding of the honor of his name over against his sinful people. More radically than this we cannot trace the unmerited freedom of the action of divine grace.

■ **20:11** However, the fact of sin was repeated in a fearful way among the people when they had been brought out into the freedom of the desert. Once again Yahweh proclaims his law to his people. When mention is no longer made here simply of putting away the idols of Egypt, but quite generally in great breadth of the revelation of the "laws and statutes," we must find in this (against Jahn) a recollection of the comprehensive lawgiving at Sinai, admittedly in a quite loose formulation.[35] To this is added a reference to the character of the commandments which make life possible and which is found with the same words in Lev 18:5. This must certainly derive from the laws of admission to the sanctuary.[36] The mention of the sabbath law also points in the direction of the Sinai lawgiving. In view of the fact that it is taken up again in vv 13, 16, 20, 21, 24, we should certainly not deny it to the original text of Ezek 20 (Jahn, Hölscher, *Hesekiel*; cf. Cooke).[37] It was undoubtedly an ancient Israelite institution of inactivity at intervals of seven days (Ex 20:8–11; 23:12; 34:21; Lev 19:3, 30; 23:3; 26:2; Dtn 5:12–15). It appears with the meaning of a confessional sign of the Yahweh covenant (Ex 31:12–17; 35:2f), together with circumcision, to go back to the exilic age.[38] In the book of Ezekiel sabbaths are mentioned again in the plural in 22:8, 26; 23:38; 44:24; 45:17; 46:3, and in the singular in 46:1, 4, 12. Also here they are referred to as special gifts, which like a piece of legal proof, mark out Israel from the nations of the world as Yahweh's own and therefore a "consecrated" (Ex 19:4–6; Dtn 14:2) people (cf. the variations of formulation in ch. 20).[39] When Elliger wants to translate the אני יהוה מקדשם, which is found similarly in Lev 20:8; 21:8;

22:32 (cf. further Ex 31:13; Lev 21:15, 23; 22:9, 16; Ezek 37:28): "I, Yahweh, am one who wills them (you) to be holy," then the imperative formulation, which is directly in line with H, threatens to obscure the fundamental indicative, which is certainly brought out by the variations in ch. 20 (but cf. Lev 20:7 besides 20:6).[40] The close connection of the sabbath motivation of 20:12 with Ex 31:13 must not be explained by a literary-critical reduction of the text in various ways, but by a reference to Ezekiel's origin in the priestly legal tradition with its fixed language.

■ **20:13, 14** Once again, however, Israel rebels and despises not only the commandments and the life promised in them, but disgraces its own honor in that it despises the sign of the sabbath, so that it is once again threatened with the danger of destruction under the divine anger. Once again it is only Yahweh's regard for his own honor or his name pledged to Israel which saves it. However, when the wilderness generation, who have been brought out from Egypt, are threatened that they will not see the promised land, we cannot fail to see in this a recollection of the concrete tradition of the episode with the spies and the consequent condemnation to a forty year long wandering in the wilderness (Nu 13f; Dtn 1:19–46).

■ **20:17** Israel may survive, even though the achievement of the promised salvation is delayed for a generation.

■ **20:18** To the second generation in the wilderness also the divine law is given again. It is first formulated negatively as a warning against the "statutes of the ancestors"; we may question whether the masculine בחקי is used in conscious distinction from the חקות of Yahweh (v 11), cf. v 25. In 11:12; 36:27 it is used freely for the laws of Yahweh.

■ **20:19f** There then follows, parallel to vv 11f, but in a slightly varied formulation, a positive exhortation. It remains unclear whether the connecting אני יהוה אלהיכם (v 19aα) is to be understood as a reinforcing

---

and the Profanation of the Name," *HUCA* 25 (1954): 1–8.

35 See above p. 175 to 5:6; Jahn, *Buch*, xv.

36 See above pp. 376f; see also the חקות החיים of 33:15.

37 For the sabbath see Ernst Jenni, *Die theologische Begruendung des Sabbatgebotes im Alten Testament*, ThSt 46 (Zollikon-Zürich: Evangelischer Verlag, 1956); in

Judaism Moore, *Judaism* 2; and see the Mishnah tractate *Šabbat*.

38 Martin Noth, "The Laws in the Pentateuch: Their Assumptions and Meaning" in *The Laws in the Pentateuch and Other Studies*, tr. D. R. Ap-Thomas (Philadelphia: Fortress, 1967), 1–107.

39 Zimmerli, *Erkenntnis*, 49–57.

40 Elliger, "Ich bin," 17.

motive clause for v 18 (see above to v 7) or in line with the classical Decalogue (also Lev 18:2f) as a preamble to the commandments of vv 19f—so the verse division of 𝔐. Similarly we cannot decide with certainty whether, with this third inculcation of the law, Ezekiel has in reply adhered to the stylistic requirements of the scheme, or whether he had in mind a tradition of a giving of the law to the generation born in the desert at the end of its stay there, as we have it in the "Deutero-Nomium" and particularly in the idea of the covenant in Moab Dtn 28:69.

■ **20:21, 22** With rigid uniformity, however, for the third time the disobedience of Israel and the unleashing of the divine anger is asserted. Here also, however, we are again left with the faithfulness of Yahweh, in the binding of his name to Israel. The historical result of this loyalty, the giving of the beloved land to the second generation of those in the wilderness, is remarkably left unexpressed. Everyone knew that Israel had entered into the land. Therefore it was unmistakably clear that Yahweh's entrusting of his name to Israel did not simply mean the unlimited possibility of treating his honor with contempt. In a clear heightening when compared with the threat against the first desert generations (vv 15f), we are shown, in a double threat, the seriousness of the divine anger, which is made known in both spheres of the divine revelation, in the future historical guidance vv 23f, as in the revelation of the divine law vv 25f.

■ **20:23f** The divine threat in history possesses immediate actuality for its own time—and at the same time for Ezekiel's compatriots. The scattering among the nations (twice expressed as in 12:15; 22:15; 29:12; 30:23, 26; 36:19) had become a reality in his day for Jehoiachin and those deported with him. We have raised the conjecture that the elders who sat before the prophet were awaiting a divine oracle which would promise the revoking of the partial judgement upon Jerusalem in 597. Instead of this the prophetic word sets before them a divine message which asserts already for the beginnings of the desert period the final judgement of exile upon all Israel. It is possible that this striking motivation of the exile had its origin in an older

and more concrete tradition. According to Ex 32:34 Yahweh sent away the people who had sinned over the golden calf with the threat: "On the day when I will punish them, I will visit their sins upon them." A comparison with Dtn 4:25–28 raises the possibility that in Ex 32:34 the fate of the idolatrous Northern Kingdom (2 Kings 17) is hinted at. Ez 20:23f applies the threat radically against the whole of Israel, even that part of it which was in Judah and Jerusalem. For all Israel Yahweh's forbearance with those who journeyed through the wilderness and the achievement of the settlement in the land was bound up with the declaration of the subsequent withdrawal of the pledge of the divine honor, in which the announcement of Israel's election had been given a historically concrete form (v 6). Does all this not then mean (in spite of v 22) the destruction (לכלותם v 13) of Israel and the venting of wrath (לכלות אפי ב[ה]ם vv 8, 21) upon it?

■ **20:25f** No less strange is the second factor: the turning of the law as a way of life (vv 11, 13, 21) into a way of death by the divine ordaining of "bad statutes." Should we, as in v 18, here take the use of the masculine חקים as a simple terminological distinguishing of the harmful from the saving will of God and regard the expression לא טובים, instead of the more direct רעים, as a softening of such a harsh statement? Even so the statement that Yahweh makes his law, which is otherwise celebrated as light (Ps 119:105) and a way of life (see above to v 11), the occasion of punishment is quite unique in the Old Testament. V 26a has directly in mind the demand of the firstborn by Yahweh which is earlier to be found in Ex 22:28. Whilst more peaceful times silently presuppose the possibility of the redemption of human firstborn by an animal sacrifice (Ex 13:13, 15), there came into currency in the time of Ahaz and Manasseh, undoubtedly under various foreign influences, a literal interpretation of the command.[41] Ezekiel could not simply dismiss this rigorous interpretation with a gentle wave of the hand. Undoubtedly it is the language of an age which was deeply affected by mystery and by the real possibility of the collapse of its own righteousness which dared to consider the mystery of a divine punishment, itself contained in the law, without dismissing

41   See above p. 344 to 16:20.

411

such an idea.[42] The Pauline recognition of the nature of the law (Rom 5:20; 7:13; Gal 3:19) is here hinted at a distance in a specially limited formulation (in a different way Jer 31:31–34). Kittel rightly opposes Hölscher, who ascribes the "only original idea in the whole chapter" to a redactor: "what redactor or editor would have dared to express a saying of such surprising boldness?"[43] J. A. Bewer's reconstruction of the text into a completely ordinary understanding, achieved by conjectural transpositions, recalls the tortuous re-interpretation of 𝔗 (note b to v 25).[44] Only the recognition formula, added in v 26bβ (note b), derives from the hand of a disciple and affirms that in the mystery of such strange actions, Yahweh can be recognized in the mystery of his being, which here means the incomprehensibility of the holy Judge.

Thus Ezekiel, in vv 5–26, retells the "saving history" memorized in the credo to the elders of Israel who were expecting a gracious word from God. This history was one in which Israel had responded to the electing action of its God with incredible disobedience so that Yahweh, in spite of his forbearance for the sake of his name, must declare the accomplishment of a radical judgement, which he had set mysteriously within his law, as long ago as the end of the central era of salvation (cf. the presentation in Hos and Jer!). The great history of Israel under David and the monarchy is never once mentioned in all this.

■ **20:30** But if much already applied to that earliest generation, how then could the representatives of the people—in this way the address in vv 30f turns to its conclusion—who have not really turned back in the depth of the manner of their ancestors, expect a promise of deliverance? As in 14:1ff, there is set before the people, in the persons of its representatives, the fact of the abomination of its idolatry.[45]

■ **20:31** In v 31aα, with its resumption of the אתם נטמאים from v 30, we cannot altogether suppress the suspicion that we are faced with a piece of later exaggerated elaboration, which at the same time makes a bridge across to v 39. The offering of gifts to idols by those who had been deported is otherwise nowhere so plainly spoken of. 14:1ff speaks more reservedly. A still later hand has then very clumsily (note b) felt it necessary to refer here again to the practice of child sacrifice, which, so far as we can see, was connected with a place of sacrifice in the valley of Hinnom near Jerusalem (cf. Jer 19).

■ **20:27-29** A further piece of later exegetical elaboration is found in vv 27–29. The glossator, who recalls in his language the glossator of 6:13 aβ–14,[46] has overlooked the close connection of the original oracle to the outline of the credo and has attempted to add briefly a reference to Israel's history in the land, which is missing in the credo and which is also a history of sin. In the עוד זאת (again in 36:37) the later character of the verse becomes clear. In a Deuteronomistic manner the worship of the high places is mentioned as the particular sin of Israel in the land (cf. to Ezek 6). It is described by the verb גדף (5:15 the noun גְּדוּפָה), which is never otherwise used by Ezekiel for "insulting" Yahweh, in which clearly the חלל of the original text is paraphrased. Thus Israel pays back Yahweh for its entry into the land in which he had fulfilled his original promise, v 6. Willfully it chose the places provided by nature and offered at them meal offerings, incense (?), and libations.[47] A later hand has emphasized still further (note b) the affront to God represented by such gifts. In v 29, where in a wordplay the expression במה is explained by the element of מה and בוא (according to van den Born with sexual overtones), we should likely see a gloss that has been added later. Bewer's attempt to reconstruct v 29 more radically by textual changes and transpositions is not convincing.[48]

Aim

The prophet answers men who came to him in need and confusion of heart. The world of their pious assurances

---

42 Cf. further above pp. 145f to 3:20 and p. 308 to 14:9.

43 Rudolf Kittel, *Geschichte des Volkes Israel* 3 (Stuttgart: Kohlhammer, 1927–1929), 169; Hölscher, *Hesekiel, der Dichter*, 110. See also Spiegel, "Ezekiel," 276f, against Torrey's interpretation.

44 Julius A. Bewer, "Textual and Exegetical Notes on the Book of Ezekiel," *JBL* 72 (1953): 159–161.

45 For "acting immorally" (זנה) cf. above p. 342 to 16:15.

46 See above pp. 191f.

47 von Rad, *OT Theology* 1.

48 Bewer, "Exegese," 195–197; Bewer, "Textual Notes," 159–161.

and divine promises had been broken. Both land and temple had been lost. They looked for a word from God which would bring afresh to them God's "yes" and assure them of a return to the old life in the land.

On what basis could they still hope for this? They had bound themselves to their confession of faith. God, so they believed, was still the God who had chosen his people and who had made this election manifest historically in the exodus from Egypt. However much was broken, in the central statement: "thy God, who brought you up from the land of Egypt, the house of slavery" (Ex 20:2) there lay the most inward, final, and unshakeable fact, in which faith could always find shelter and upon which it could dare to look for the word of God.

The frightening element in the prophet's oracle is that it penetrates into this inner resort and shows that there is in it no place where God's people can find protection and secure themselves in a last, unassailable fortress and know themselves to be safe. Even where faith made confession of this central history of God with his people and spoke of the primal act of God's saving election, it encountered an accusation against its own, and the whole community's sinful humanity. He meets the message which convicts him of his sin and which makes the judgement which is to come upon him into an inescapable necessity which upholds God's law.

With a stern ruthlessness the prophet attacks the central statement of the confession of faith—that great initial sacred history in which God, in an unheard of way, had committed himself to man in his name. Phase after phase he narrates it and shows how in the people whom God had called, brought up, and repeatedly endowed with gifts, there was nothing to be found but disobedience, rebellion, and a ripeness for punishment. Repeatedly there was present the leaning to other powers, the idols and abominations, instead of a leaning to the One who had called the people. Repeatedly there was present the despising of every sign of sabbath rest, which God had given to his people, so that they might celebrate thereby their sacred relationship to God. But they had repeatedly transgressed this with their everyday work and its godless cares.

The history of God's mighty acts, in which he had entrusted his name to the community, is therefore at the same time a history of a threat to man in judgement. There is no place at which the community can settle down comfortably in the certainty of its election because it has been excused from judgement. On the contrary, precisely where God does his greatest works will his inescapable judgement (vv 23f) and the mystery of his wrath within the law (vv 25f) be revealed.

The prophet addresses men who were exploring the possibility of a change in their history which would still make finally possible for them a deliverance back into their old way. They wanted to keep a continuity with what was old—is not the very meaning of the divine saving history the preservation of this certainty? They wanted to remain the sons of their natural fathers (v 30). Wherever men of God's chosen people seek out a way of escape for themselves, they can only be confronted by the negative divine question: "Should I allow myself to be inquired of by you?" even when they offer to God the words of his own great history, written as a confession of faith. God's judgement sweeps away all man's own righteousness, even for one who belongs to God's people, and comes to him out of the very center of God's revelatory history. There is no way by which the community can bypass this judgement.

Form

The basic text of vv 1–31 has later undergone an expansion.[49] Vv 32ff start from a saying which is set in the mouths of those addressed by the prophet (v 32). God counters this with his own word (vv 33ff) with the impassioned emphasis of an oath. This is the form of the disputation oracle which is already familiar from 18:2ff.[50] Here, however, the divine rejoinder, otherwise than in ch. 18, does not expand casuistically the fate of a pious or wicked individual, but contains a great declaration about Israel's history, which is given in the form of a proof-oracle with the recognition formula in v 38 as a first conclusion. The section vv 39–42 is certainly disturbed at its beginning (note b to v 39), starting off in the imperative, but then in the motivation in vv 40–42 again taking up the form of a

---

49 For the process of expansion and the inner development of the message cf. the comments on pp. 333f to Ezek 16.

50 See above pp. 374f; also p. 280 to 12:21ff.

proof-oracle (expanded by the compensatory v 42αβb ״בהביאי״). In its content we must certainly not separate this continuation from vv 32–38, since here there first comes the positive elaboration of the negative answer to what is said in the quotation in v 32. Vv 43–44 are also then formulated as a proof-oracle (expanded by the compensatory v 44αβb ״בעשותי״), which carries further the details in regard to the inner attitude of those who have been delivered and in its content forms an altogether suitable conclusion.

Thus the whole section vv 32–44, which is probably, but not certainly, to be regarded as having been formulated in stages (van den Born), is to be designated a disputation saying, which is set out, in its divine rebuttal, as a threefold proof-oracle, with an imperative introduction (admonition) of the middle element.

Setting

The oracle looks out from the situation of exile to a coming salvation. The quotation in v 32 enables us to see into the resignation of the exiles after the complete collapse of all their hopes of a restoration after the burning of Jerusalem in 587. On the other hand in vv 40ff we can see a stage on the way to the concrete expectation of a new temple, as in chs. 40–48. Thus it must be set before 40:1, i.e., in the period between 587 and 573/72, perhaps closer to the second date. If we find in chs. 40–48 a genuine kernel of Ezekiel material, then we shall see no compelling ground for denying to the prophet Ezekiel this well-defined, and in part quite unique, oracle, from which lines of thought lead to Deutero-Isaiah.

Interpretation

■ **20:32** Through his prophet Yahweh answers an idea which has arisen among the exiles (for העלה על רוחכם cf. 11:5, also 14:4, 7; 38:10) and which appears to have gained some force among them. The נהיה כגוים, which is as a rule interpreted as a cohortative, has usually been understood as the expression of a definite idolatrous decision, and the content of the questioning of God in v 1 has usually been found in the words of the people, as already mentioned. A glance at the related text 1 Sam 8:5, 20 (van den Born) would support this understanding. Against it, however, it is more correct to find in v 32, in accordance with 33:10; 37:11, the

expression of a deep despair. V 32 takes up, in continuation of vv 1–31, an idea which is only conceivable as a reaction of the exiles to the preaching of vv 1–31. If the judgement of being scattered among the nations by Yahweh is already an accomplished fact (v 23), a judgement, the finality of which was unmistakably confirmed by the year 587 with its ending of all hopes of a return to an intact Jerusalem, is any hope left of any other future than dispersion among the nations with all its bitter religious consequences? In the formulation of the oracle, with its parallelism of גוים and ארצות, we can discern Ezekiel's language (cf. 11:16; 12:15; 20:23; 22:15; 29:12; 30:23, 26; 36:19, also the ארצות—עמים 11:17). The reference to worship of "wood and stone" can, following Jer 2:27, be derived from the polemic against Canaanite nature worship (cf. Volz, Rudolph on the text). Texts such as Dtn 4:28; 28:36; 29:16; 2 Kings 19:18 and the parallel Is 37:19, as also the present text, show that it had gained a much extended meaning, and here also the worship of Babylonian images made of precious metal (Is 44:9–20) may be included.

■ **20:33** Yahweh's word opposes such voices which resign themselves to the necessity of assimilation to the heathen lands where they have gone and which thereby appear to have affirmed for themselves the logic of the inescapable message of vv 1–31 (does not Jeremiah's warning to the exiles Jer 29:5–7 also point in this direction?). It promises a new exodus out of the slavery of the world of the nations. The announcement of a second exodus in the desert is foretold in Hos 2:16f. There it comes threateningly to the people who are still in the land, as the possibility of judgement upon (North) Israel which had become satisfied in Canaan. At the same time, in a double sense, which recalls some of Isaiah's formulations, it also contains the promise of a new positive relationship to Yahweh, from which it can then move again to a gift of the land and its vineyards. [51] In Ezek 20 it takes on a unique change of emphasis. The "bringing up" will be a mighty act of deliverance for the people of God scattered among the nations. However, the idea is directly bound up with this that in the desert a great act of judgement will take place which will separate the sinners from the obedient, before a new entry into the promised land takes place. The full unfolding of this is found in the message of the new exodus and the return to Zion in Deutero-Isaiah, the prophet of the later exilic period, in whom the aspects of woe and judgement have been completely swallowed up by the overwhelming jubilation at the imminent salvation. Ezek 20 represents a middle position between Hos 2 and Deutero-Isaiah (as also in the connection of the assertion with a reference to Yahweh's kingship), which again confirms his position in the early exilic age.

Yahweh's promise of the new exodus is given in v 33 a majestic interpretative preface. That Yahweh acts "with a strong hand and outstretched arm and wrath poured out," which is repeated in v 34, takes up, in the first two clauses of its hymnic three parts, the stereotyped statements of the credo account of the exodus.[52] Not by accident the reference to the "arm of Yahweh" also plays a considerable part in Deutero-Isaiah's great message of deliverance (40:11; 51:5, 9; 52:10; 53:1). The phrase added in third position "with wrath poured out" is a formulation deriving from Ezekiel's own usage (שפך חמה in 7:8; 9:8; 14:19; 20:8, 13, 21; 22:22; 30:15; 36:18, besides שפך זעם 21:36; 22:31), which leaves it ambiguous whether here, as with "hand" and "arm" which are used against the Egyptians, the wrath is also to be thought of as turned against the hostile powers who hold Israel prisoner, or whether, as the allusion to 20:8, 13, 21 makes possible and what follows makes explicitly clear, it refers to God's wrath against sinners in the house of Israel itself (so also in the related formulation in Jer 21:5). The most surprising feature, however, is that there appears in this exodus terminology the predication of Yahweh as king, which is only found in Ezekiel of Yahweh here (the verb מלך again 17:16 in a secular usage, the noun מלך often of human kings). We cannot find in this a subtle polemic against the מלך worship, which is referred to in the child sacrifice of vv 26, 31 without mention of the מלך name (so Kraetzschmar, Herrmann). Rather we should consider, with van den Born, whether the mention of

the kingship of Yahweh has been occasioned by an association of the kind found in 1 Sam 8, where, in connection with the desire of Israel "to be like the nations," the kingship of Yahweh is announced (admittedly with a quite different result there and also in connection with the different problem of the calling of a human king). In Ezek 20 the concern is not with the proclamation of Yahweh's kingship, but with the manifestation of God's kingship through his acts in history.[53] This also distinguishes Ezek 20, in its formulation, from Deutero-Isaiah, with whom the proclamation of Yahweh's kingship is celebrated as a world wide act of enthronement and as a climactic event at the end of the miraculous return of the people through the desert in the style of the יהוה מלך hymns (Is 52:7–10).[54] ■ 20:34 Yahweh's great assertion of his kingship over Israel is then made historically concrete in the continuation in v 34.[55] As the first exodus concerned the deliverance of the people, groaning under forced labor in the one land of Egypt, so the second exodus will go further, when it will bring about the gathering of the people who are scattered in many lands. In addition to the Babylonian exiles this may also have in mind the places of exile of the North Israelites 2 Kings 17:6 and the groups which had fled to Egypt Jer 43f. The same assertion is also found in v 41 (34:13). As the first exodus led "into the desert of the land of Egypt" (v 36a), so will the second exodus correspondingly lead out from the world of the nations into "the desert of the peoples." The expression, which reappears in the War Scroll from Qumran (1:3) as a fixed religious term, must be a very schematic new coining of Ezekiel's, like several other construct formulations with the name Israel, and not an expression current in normal geographical terminology.[56] Its more precise geographical meaning need not be looked for (Cooke: desert between Babylonia and Palestine, similarly van den Ploeg and others) since, even if we think of the gathering of the Egyptian diaspora, it cannot be geographically local-

---

51 See Wolff, *Hosea*, on the text.

52 See above p. 408 to v 6; see above p. 294 to 13:9, also Dtn 26:8 and other passages.

53 Cf. Diethelm Michel, "Studien zu den sogenannten Thronbesteigungspsalmen," *VT* 6 (1956): 55: "the exercise of lordship."

54 See Kraus, *Königsherrschaft*, 102–109, where the late dating of the יהוה מלך hymns is certainly refuted

by Is 6:5. Michel, "Studien," 68, differently. For Yahweh's kingship see further Sigmund Mowinckel, *Psalmenstudien. II. Das Thronbesteigungsfest Jahwäs und der Ursprung der Eschatologie* (Kristiania: Dybwad, 1922); Alt, "Gedanken," 345–357.

55 But which does not, against Kuhl, "'Wiederaufnahme,'" 3, necessitate the excision of v 34.

56 For Qumran: E. L. Sukenik, *The Dead Sea Scrolls of*

ized to a single region.[57] The desert is important here simply as the typological counterpart to the first "desert of Egypt." That Yahweh here confronts his people "face to face" is clearly intended to recall, as an antitype, that first desert encounter at the mountain of God (Dtn 5:4, similar encounters are described with the same expression in Gen 32:31 Jacob; Ex 33:11; Dtn 34:10 Moses; Ju 6:22 Gideon), from which the frightened people tried to escape (Dtn 5:5, 23–27; Ex 20: 18f). Ezekiel here knows of no escape from such a dangerous encounter with God. Yahweh's judgement will then be accomplished upon the people.

■ **20:36** When Ezekiel also sees this judgement as a typological counterpart to the earlier judgement in the desert, we may ask whether he here has in mind the judgement upon the first generation of Israel in the desert which is described in vv 15f and which fell upon the entire nation. Alternatively he may have in mind the Exodus traditions of judgements upon individuals in which sinners were destroyed from the midst of the people by a divine punishment, cf. Nu 16:31ff.

■ **20:37f** Furthermore Yahweh's act of judgement (nip‘al of שפט again in 17:20; 38:22) is also described as an event involving decision.[58] Yahweh ,who is not only accuser, but also judge, separates those who have rebelled against him (cf. 2:3) like a shepherd who makes his flock pass under his staff (again Jer 33:13; Lev 27:32) in order to count them (for הביא במספר cf. the מנה of Jer 33:13, also Is 40:26) and to separate them (Mt 25:31ff).[59] The immediate fate of the rebellious, which is to take place in the desert, is not described. It is sufficient to say that they do not experience the redemption.[60] Once again it is clear that the individual's life in Israel is entirely dependent on the life of the community.[61] The concept of ארץ מגורים, which here denotes the land of exile, becomes in P, where alone it is again found in the Old Testament, a designation of the land promised to the patriarchs, but which they did not actually receive (Gen 17:8;

28:4; 36:7; 37:1; Ex 6:4).

■ **20:39** With his announcement of the coming action of Yahweh, the prophet at the same time calls his fellow exiles, in their present despair, to "know" (=acknowledge).[62] However, the decision has not yet been made who is to be accepted and who rejected. Yahweh does not will the end of those who were apparently sentenced to death, but desires rather that they should repent (18:32). The imperative which arises from this, and which is significantly introduced with a new summons to the house of Israel, must be intentionally formulated in dependence on the law given at the beginning of Israel's history (v 7). The summons to "throw away" idols is illuminated in the parallel clause (for the text cf. note b) by the warning not to dishonor Yahweh's name by offerings to idols. It has rightly been noted that חלל is used here, unlike in vv 9, 14, 22, of an active dishonoring of the divine name (שם קדשי again in 36:20–22; 39:25; 43:7f; cf. Lev 20:3; 22:2, 32, Amos 2:7) (Blank, "Profanation"). A true honoring of the divine name with a pure offering will only be possible when Yahweh will have once again opened up the way to the place of his presence.

■ **20:40** Thus in v 40 the oracle once again turns to the great divine promise. The casting away of idols does not occur in a vacuum, but in the joy of a great hope. It may be a certain difficulty in v 40 that the promise of Yahweh is first expressed in the third person to the house of Israel (40abα), only to fall back again in vv 40bβ, 41ff into the direct speech of the preceding verses. Since textual surgery is not recommended by the closely interwoven nature of the statements we must conjecture that 40abα, as a fundamental divine word to the "house of Israel," is given a certain emphasis; 40bβ–42 then bring the concrete explanation and a further emphasis, which should be closely bracketed with vv 32ff. In a double reference to place, emphasized by the formula for a divine oracle (which should not, with Fohrer, be reduced by textual surgery) and by the

the Hebrew University (Jerusalem: Hebrew University Press, 1955), plate 16; see Hans Bardtke, "Der gegenwärtige Stand der Erforschung der in Palästina neu gefundenen hebräischen Handschriften. 29. Die Kriegsrolle von Qumrān übersetzt," ThLZ 80 (1955): 401; J. van der Ploeg, "La Règle de la Guerre, traduction et notes," VT 5 (1955):375 and 394. VT 8 (1958):77–79.

57   Van der Ploeg, "Règle de la Guerre," 394.

58   The process of trial is very clearly described in Is 43:26. See Gemser, "rîb," especially p. 131; Begrich, Studien, 19–42.

59   For the identity of witness and judge see Begrich, Studien, 36f.

60   Cf. 13:9; see above pp. 294f.

61   See above pp. 381f.

שׁם, which is repeated three times for emphasis and which is related to this place reference, v 40 seeks to give expression to the enduring faithfulness of Yahweh to his election history, which will not give up even the chosen place of his dwelling against all tendencies to assimilation.[63] In the taking up of the exodus tradition in a new exodus, there is interwoven a taking up of the Zion tradition (without the name Zion) in the reference to a new temple.[64] Only here in the book of Ezekiel do we find in the mouth of Yahweh the expression הר קדשׁי, which is particularly evident in the book of Isaiah (11:9; 56:7; 57:13; 65:11, 25; 66:20), but which is also found in Ps 2:6; Joel 2:1; 4:17; Ob 16; Zeph 3:11. Peculiar to Ezekiel, however, is the הר מרום ישׂראל (17:23, plural 34:14), which points to the temple mount in the light of the mythical mount of God.[65] Israel's worship remained bound to this central shrine. Here it can expect the divine declaration of pleasure at the sacrifices offered to him.[66] When the priestly technical term רצה is elaborated in v 40 by דרשׁ, which belongs to the prophetic terminology of hearing, the intention must lie in setting against the negative use of the word in the basic text (1, 3, 31), its transformation into an oracle of hope. The expression תרומה, which pictures the "lifting up, taking away" of the offering that is to be consecrated, is found (besides a similarly general usage in 44:30) in chs. 45 and 48 in a quite special limitation of the "contribution" from the land. ראשׁית "firstfruits" occurs again in 44:30; 48:14. Also in the non-specialized term משׂאת "present" (2 Sam 11:8 of a secular gift from the king), which is only found here in Ezekiel, the "lifting up" of the gift comes to expression. קדשׁ designates quite generally the taboo character of the gift.

■ 20:41f It is not wholly clear how exactly בריח ניחח is to be understood. Is it a ב-essentiae, which compares the offerer metaphorically to the smell that is pleasing to God? Or does it denote, with ב-pretii, the sacrificial act on account of which the worshipper is accepted by

God? Or should we, with BH³, change the text to a כ?

In the concluding statement of v 41, which recapitulates what precedes and which points on to the recognition formula of v 42, what stands out as new is solely the ונקדשׁתי בכם. The gracious fulfillment of Yahweh's history, which points his people to the mystery of his own being, is at the same time the way of his revelation to the nations, which will once and for all put an end to the desecration of his name. The Godhead and praiseworthiness of the God who had pledged his name to Israel will become plain throughout the world through his free loyalty to the people who had fallen under his holy judgement.

■ 20:43f Then also the final event will be able to take place: the humble and shamefaced recognition of his faithfulness by those who have found deliverance through it. The process of remembering, self-loathing, and recognition, which is described in three phases and which is said in the addition 6:8–10 of those who escape from the "bankrupting" of Jerusalem, will then finally take place among the exiles who will have returned to their land.[67] The evil past will not be suppressed and forgotten in a harmful way, but will be kept in mind. However, in loathing this past there will take place a true repentance, which will consciously achieve its true end and which will find its true goal in an acknowledged return to Yahweh. The mystery of Yahweh's being, however, will then clearly be the mystery of one who is not compelled to follow the law of human activity, in its scheme of retribution, but of one whose inner loyalty maintains what it has promised and thereby demonstrates his holiness.

Aim

The oracle in vv 32–44 speaks to men who, in their great despair, can no longer believe that God's people, upon whom judgement has rightly fallen, still have a future and who, in this despair, would become like men who do not know the living God. To these men there is

62 Zimmerli, *Erkenntnis*, 39–47 (= *Gottes Offenbarung*, 78–88).
63 See above pp. 174f to 5:5.
64 See Rohland, *Erwählungstraditionen*, 194–199.
65 Cf. further to 40:2; also the remarks on הרי ישׂראל above pp. 185f.
66 For this significance of רצה, which is further illustrated by its polemical use in prophetic oracles

(Amos 5:22; Hos 8:13; Jer 14:12; Mal 1:10), see Ernst Würthwein, "Amos 5, 21–27," *ThLZ* 72 (1947): 147f. In Ezekiel it is found again in 43:27.
67 See above pp. 188–190.

proclaimed the great joy that God remains at work, even through the darkest night of his people. Indeed, with those who have suffered the direst judgement he begins afresh.

In this God's action is not like that of a man, who, after he has failed with his first piece of work, then tries again elsewhere with the fullest possible denial of the "past." Rather God's history continues, even where it achieves something new and allows the old to be forgotten (2 Cor 5:17), in a remarkable faithfulness to that which it had begun at the start. The promise of the beginning is not withdrawn.

God's fulfillment of his history, however, has nothing to do with the slick recognition of a happy ending, in which, as in folktales, everything comes out all right in the end, so that men can only rub their eyes in surprise as though waking out of sleep. Nor has it to do with the sinner, who feels safe in his old age and wants to sleep off God's judgement, as Jonah sleeps through the storm from God in the hold of the ship (Jonah 1:5), and who yet afterwards appears to be justified.[68] Even the fulfillment of God's history remains a summons, which calls for responsible action and in no way bypasses God's judgement. Thus the law given at the beginning is not annulled, but continues to stand over God's people.

The community was called upon, even when all its supports had been knocked away and its own weakness and self-righteousness set under judgement, to reject all other gods and to know no other than the one who had called it long ago. It was called upon, even in its spiritual poverty, not to seek any new place or any new, arbitrary, form of prayer, but to let itself be guided to the place and manner of prayer by the original divine instruction, which God would not allow to fall away. It is to know that, when it walks according to his word and prays with all its resources, it will be accepted before God (רצה).

The message commands the people not to forget that it deserved judgement, even when God had led it out of the night of that judgement into a new life, but to remain mindful of its guilt. It was to turn to a recognition of God, who is faithful even in his judgement, out of a genuine sense of honor and a sincere rejection of its disobedience.

The people who thus give up any false assurance on the basis of their past and who entrust themselves to the future promised by God will both live and worship God in truth.

---

68   See above p. 413.

The formula for the coming of a message, which is repeated four times (vv 1, 6, 13, 23), appears to divide up Ezek 21 into four separate units. However, a glance at the content shows that vv 1–4 and 6–12 are joined together by v 5, analogously to 17:1–10, 11–21, into an overall unity of allegory and interpretation. The interpretation follows the catchphrase "sword," which dominates the song of vv 13–22 and also determines the sign-action of vv 23ff, according to 𝔐 (but cf. note a to v 24), which shows how "the sword of the king of Babylon" comes.

Closer examination shows further that the section vv 23–37 concludes, in the appended vv 33–37, in a "sword" oracle against the Ammonites, in which among other things statements from the song of the sword in vv 13–22 reappear. (Cf. the analogy of 23:36–49 in the overall structure of ch. 23.) This forbids our treating vv 13–22 and 23–37 simply as separate units. They are at least joined together redactionally by vv 33–37.

We may also see an element of loose formal dovetailing together in the instruction to the prophet to raise a lament at the message of the sword, which is found in vv 11f within the section vv 1–12, and in v 17 in the section vv 13–22. The repetition in the concluding section (v 36, for v 37 cf. note a) of the metaphor of fire, which dominates the introductory section in vv 1–4, may point to the intention of the framework of the chapter.

All these factors suggest that we should see in Ezek 21 a redactionally planned composition which is held together not only by its common theme (this factor is also found in the parallelism 12:22–25 and 12:26–28), but also by elements of content which are interconnected. The three separate units, which in the history of their formation were at one time quite separate, are to be considered together in their later interrelatedness.

21

A. The Sword of Yahweh

1 And the word of Yahweh came to me: 2/ Son of man, turn your face southwards[a] and prophesy[b] towards the south[c] and prophesy against[d] the forest (of the fields) 'in the south'[e] 3/ and say to the forest in the south: Hear the word of Yahweh: Thus has [The Lord][a] Yahweh spoken: Behold, I am kindling a fire within you. It will consume in you every green tree and every dry tree. The burning flame[b] will not be extinguished, and every face will be scorched by it, from the south to the north, 4/ and all flesh will see[a] that I, Yahweh, have kindled it. It will not be extinguished.

5 Then I said: Ah, [Lord] [a]Yahweh, they[b] say of me: Does he not speak (only) in riddles?

21: 2a 𝔐 תימן, by 𝔊 Θαιμαν (𝔏ᶜ *thaeman*, 𝔏ˢ *theman*) misunderstood, following 25:13, as a proper name, denoting the "right," i.e., in the normal orientation facing the east (see above p. 166 to 4:6), the south. Cf. further 47:19; 48:28.

b 𝔐 הטף literally "drip." It is used of prophetic speech again in v 7 and Amos 7:16; Mic 2:6, 11. 𝔊 ἐπίβλεψον, 𝔏ᶜˢ *aspice*, 𝔖 חור appear to presuppose here and in v 7 a misreading of הבט, which is never found in Ezekiel.

c 𝔐 דרום, interpreted by Montgomery, "Hebraica," 130f, as "bow" (of the ecliptic) and in Ezek 40–42 the normal designation of the south, was again understood by 𝔊 Δαρωμ (𝔏ᶜˢ *dagon*) as a proper name. From the designation of Southern Palestine at a later time as Δαρωμα, Eissfeldt, *Baal Zaphon*, page 17 note 1, suggests that דרום is a secondary development as a direction from an original name of a region (cf. Burrows, "Daroma"). Cf. Tallquist, *Himmelsgegenden*, 116.

d על—אל cf. note a to 1:17.

e The syntactically impossible יער השדה נגב of 𝔐 is taken up again in v 3 in abbreviated form as יער הנגב. 𝔊 ἐπὶ δρυμὸν ἡγούμενον Ναγεβ (𝔏ᶜˢ *in silvam summam nageb*), which also takes the נגב of 𝔐 as a regional designation, appears to have had before it the same text, except for the misreading of השדה as השרה. The reading with ר could be original if 𝔊 יער אשר בנגב עבא דבתימנא points to an original. However, since the simple יער הנגב of v 3 too is thus reproduced in 𝔊, it is very uncertain. Thus it still remains the most probable conjecture that שדה is a secondary interpretative gloss, and the original text ran, as in v 3, יער הנגב (Jahn, *Buch*, Hölscher, *Hesekiel*, Fohrer). Reider, "Etymological Studies," 119f, with reference to arabic *sdw* and *sdj* "stretch forth," conjectures a translation of 𝔐 as "(woodland), which extends towards the south." Driver, "Linguistic Problems," 67, changes to שדה הנגב and points to the parallel terms שדה מואב and שדה אדם.

3 3a אדני is lacking in 𝔊 𝔏ᶜˢ 𝔊ˢᵃ, see Excursus 1.

b 𝔐 להבת שלהבת. 𝔊 ἡ φλὸξ ἡ ἐξαφθεῖσα, 𝔏ˢ *flamma accensa*, 𝔙 *flamma suscensionis*, 𝔗 paraphrases more freely. שלהבת again Job 15:30; Sir 51:4, and in later Hebrew. Cf. שלהבתיה Song 8:6. להבה is the older Hebrew word, cf. Is 5:24; Hos 7:6. The doubling serves for emphasis.

4 4a 𝔐 וראו. 𝔊 (𝔏ˢ) καὶ ἐπιγνώσονται shows that ראה here is used more loosely instead of the usual ידע of the recognition formula (so then in v 10). Cf. further 39:21 and see Zimmerli, *Erkenntnis*, 7f.

5 5a אדני is lacking in 𝔏ˢ 𝔊 Tyc, whilst 𝔊 here reads κύριε κύριε, see Excursus 1.

b 𝔗 האינון 𝔊 הא הנון do not justify the addition of הנה in 𝔐.

5　　Then the word of Yahweh came to me:
7/ ᵃSon of man, set your face against
Jerusalem and prophesyᵇ againstᶜ 'its
sanctuary'ᵈ and prophesy againstᶜ the
land of Israel 8/ and say to the land of
Israel: Thus has Yahweh spoken:ᵃ
Behold, I am against you,ᵇ and
I will draw my sword from its sheath
and cut off from you both righteousᶜ
and wicked. 9/ Because I will cut off
from you both righteous and wicked,ᵃ
therefore my sword will be drawn from
its sheath againstᵇ all flesh from the
south to the north,ᶜ 10/ and all flesh
will know, that I, Yahweh, have drawn
my sword from its sheath. It will not
(again) be sheathed.

11　　But you, son of man, groan! With
breaking loins and bitter pain groan
before their eyes. 12/ And when they
say to you: Why are you groaning?
then say: Becauseᵃ something I have
heard is coming. Every heart will be in
despair, and every hand will fall limply
down, every spiritᵇ will become faint,
and all knees will run with water.
Behold it is coming and will happen,
says [the Lord]ᶜ Yahweh.

7　7a 𝕲 (𝔏ˢ) adds here διὰ τοῦτο προφήτευσον, in
order to connect vv 6ff more clearly with vv 1–5.
　b Cf. note b to v 2.
　c על—אל cf. note a to 1:17.
　d the impossible מקדשׁים of 𝔐 is to be changed
with 3 MSSᴷᵉⁿ MSᵈᵉ ᴿᵒˢˢˡ ⁴⁴⁰ 𝕲 𝔏ˢ 𝕾 to מקדשׁם,
or is this still an error for מקדשׁה?

8　8a 𝔏ˢ 𝔄 Tyc agree with 𝔐, whilst the messenger
formula is completely lacking in 𝕲ᴮ, ¹⁰⁶, undoubtedly in error. The later tradition then shows
as usual the double designation of God (𝕲ᴮᵐᵍ κύριος
κύριος, 𝕲ᴸ αδωναι κύριος, cf. 𝕾 𝔗 𝔙, also MSS Edd).
　b See above p. 175 to 5:8.
　c 𝕲 ἄδικον καὶ ἄνομον, a classical example of a
correction for dogmatic reasons. 𝔗 finds an elegant
middle way of interpretation: "and I will lead your
righteous men into exile, in order to destroy the
wicked among you (i.e., those who remain in the
city)." The same translation in v 9.

9　9a Has fallen out, undoubtedly by homoioteleuton, in a considerable part of the 𝕲 tradition
(𝕲ᴬ, ¹⁰⁶ ᵃⁿᵈ ᵒᵗʰᵉʳˢ, cf. 𝔏ˢ 𝕲ˢᵃ Tyc Jerome). The לכן-
clause of v 9b requires the יען-clause of v 9a as its
presupposition. Cf. further the exposition.
　b על—אל cf. note a to 1:17.
　c 𝔐 צפון After v 3 we should expect צפונה, so
Origen.

12　12a על—אל cf. note a to 1:17.
　b 𝕲 καὶ ἐκψύξει πᾶσα σὰρξ καὶ πᾶν πνεῦμα (𝔏ˢ et
exturpebit omnis caro et omnis spes) expands the statement.
　c אדני is lacking in 𝕲 𝔏ˢ, see Excursus 1.

Form

The section 21:1–12 connects a divine declaration of
judgement (vv 1–10) with a description of the prophetic suffering and groaning at the vision of the coming
judgement (vv 11–12). We feel at once directly reminded of Jeremiah, in whose preaching the prophetic
suffering at the visions and auditions of the coming
judgement is particularly strongly expressed.[1]

If we then look more closely at the form in which this
series of sayings is set out, we find ourselves once again
in the sphere of Ezekiel's own language. Indeed we
may consider that the stereotyped school language,
which characterizes the book of Ezekiel as a whole so
unmistakably, appears in 21:1–12 in a particularly
marked way. This led Hölscher, Hesekiel, to deny this

oracle to Ezekiel especially emphatically.

Whereas with Jeremiah the expression of his own
suffering appears quite directly in his own words, in
Ezekiel, in the manner that is customary to him, everything is once again swallowed up in the word of God.
Yahweh commands the prophet to groan. A question
from those around him, which has its counterpart in
12:9; 24:19; 37:18; cf. 21:5, makes it necessary for the
prophet to give a public explanation for his expression
of grief. In this reformulation the act of groaning is set
in line with the prophet's sign-actions.[2] The closest
parallel of content (not form) in Ezekiel is to be found
in 12:17–20. Out of the prophet's human and direct
expression of suffering (as in Jeremiah) the divine
instruction to adopt a "significant" attitude has arisen.

1　　Hans Joachim Stoebe, "Seelsorge und Mitleiden
　　bei Jeremia," WuD NF 4 (1955): 116–134.
2　　See above pp. 156f.

The "demonstration" (לעיניהם v 11) makes possible the subsequent full formulation of the divine threat of judgement, which in v 12bβ receives its full weight of emphasis through the binding divine affirmation הנה באה ונהיתה (again in 39:8).

However, the announcement of judgement in vv 1–10 too is completely clothed in the garment of the language of the Ezekiel school. Already in the introductory summary to Ezek 21 it is laid down that the repeated introduction of an allegory and its interpretation through the formula for the coming of an oracle have their parallels in the allegory of 17:10 and its interpretation in vv 11ff. Even more sharply than by the question of meaning in 17:12a the allegory is here characterized in its obscurity by the rebuke of the people, which the prophet cites in his cry to God.[3] The strongly preserved parallelism of allegory and interpretation goes beyond the situation of ch. 17 and is also formally preserved in the form of a proof-oracle.[4] However, the parallelism reaches further into the introductory formulas of vv 2f and 7f. The משל and its interpretation are emphasized by the prophet, at God's command, by an expressive action.[5] Here as there this is very strongly reinforced by a threefold parallelism (cf. again 25:3) in God's commands.

Setting

The place at which the oracle was formulated can certainly not be Jerusalem itself (against Herntrich). The prophet is commanded to face south. In the interpretation this is explained in regard to Jerusalem and the land of Israel. An interpretation in regard to the geographical region of the Negeb is prohibited, not only by the normal linguistic usage of the book of Ezekiel, but also expressly by the interpretation in vv 5–10 (cf. further to v 2). Herntrich's isolation of vv 1–4 from vv 6–10 separates sections that are clearly related to one another by the strong parallelism of vv 1–4 and 6–10. The oracle was delivered to the exiles.

The threat against Jerusalem and the Temple presupposes that both entities still exist. Nothing is to be found that indicates that the siege of the city is already in progress. Thus, on the basis of its content, the oracle can best be placed before 589 B.C. On the other hand, certain formal considerations (the close connection between allegory and interpretation, as well as the free deviations in the use of the recognition formula, see below to ראה v 4, כל בשר vv 4, 10, and the הנה באה ונהיתה which only reappears in 39:8), do not completely settle the question whether the oracle, with its strongly stylized character, has not first come to its present form somewhat later, in the school of Ezekiel. Then it would have been placed by the redactor at the beginning of the series of sayings about the sword (the sword of Yahweh, the sword, the sword of the King of Babylon) as the oracle which is most clearly defined theologically. However, v 10b certainly does not presuppose the continuation in v 35a (see below to vv 33–37).

Interpretation

■ **21:1, 2** Within the framework of the coming of a message the prophet (Son of man) receives the commission to turn his face to the south and to direct his prophetic word there.[6] Uniquely in the book of Ezekiel the expression הטיף is used here beside the usual נבא (here and in v 7). In the qal this verb denotes "dripping down" (Ju 5:4 of rain from the clouds; Job 29:22; Prv 5:3; Song 4:11 metaphorically of words from the lips). In the hip'il it is used again in Mic 2:6, 11 and Amos 7:16 of the preaching of prophets. In Mic 2:6, 11 the word undeniably has a derogatory sense.[7] This is not so clear in Amos 7:16. In Ezek 21:2, 7 there is no derogatory note. Whether the expression originally denoted an ecstatic "slavering" of the prophet (A. Jepsen), or, as the first mentioned text more probably supports, it was originally regarded as a metaphorical comparison (G. Hölscher), in Ezekiel 21 it is a freely

3   See what is said on p. 360 about the inner relationship of משל and חידה.
4   For the variation from ידע of the recognition formula to the related ראה cf. note a to v 4.
5   See above p. 182.
6   See above pp. 144f; pp. 131f; for such expressive actions see above pp. 182f.
7   See Quell, *Propheten*, 135f.

used synonym for the verb נבא, which is usually used in Ezekiel.[8]

The three parallel expressions for the direction of looking and preaching, to which the prophet is directed, are all understood by 𝕲 as place names (cf. the notes). In fact in 25:13 תימן denotes a place in Edom. However, quite apart from the express clarification by the name Jerusalem in v 7, its mention here would be wholly mysterious. Thus here, as in 47:19; 48:28, תימן must be understood as a geographical direction. The same is true of דרום, which is used only as a geographical direction in all its Old Testament occurrences (Dtn 33:23; Job 37:17; Eccl 1:6; 11:3; Ezek 40:24, 27f, 44f; 41:11; 42:12f, 18) (cf. also note c). נגב, on the contrary, in the Old Testament first denotes "land that is dried out," i.e., the region south of the Judean mountain range with its poor rainfall, the hollow of Beersheba and the desert region which extends south of it. From this the expression has become in the Old Testament a straightforward geographical direction. Thus from this in Daniel 11:25, 19 Egypt can be described as הנגב, and its king as מלך הנגב (Dan 11:5f and other passages). With reference to Is 21:1f Herntrich, followed by Bertholet, seeks to understand vv 1–4 as a threat against the steppe region in the south of Palestine.[9] However, there are great difficulties with this. We cannot reckon, even in antiquity, with a description of the Negeb as a forest region because the rainfall conditions can have been little different from what they are today (Prof. Evenari, Jerusalem, orally). If, however, we adduce support from Is 21:13, where apparently the arid desert shrubs can be described as יער (although Ezek 21:3 speaks of עץ לח and עץ יבש), there also stands against this interpretation that historically, after 597, when the Negeb was possibly separated from Judah (Jer 13:19),[10] a threat directed against the Negeb is scarcely probable. To this must be added the fact that throughout all of Ezekiel's proclamation of judgement, events concerning separate regions play no role at any point. Only Jerusalem as the center and representative of the land of Israel is important.[11] In this Ezekiel's distance from the land comes to expression. What then would be the point of a special oracle here against the Negeb? Finally the linguistic factor must be considered that in the book of Ezekiel נגב is otherwise only found as a designation for the geographical direction (besides 21:2f, 9, also 40:2; 46:9; 47:1, 19; 48:10, 16f, 28, 33). Thus the word in 21:2f, 9 must be understood in parallel to the other two terms as a geographical direction.

W. F. Albright has conjectured that "the forest of the south" means the Lebanon, which, from the perspective of Ugarit, would be seen as a counterpart to the forests on Casius and Amanus, the *spn* of North Canaanite mythology.[12] Ezekiel would then have veiled Jerusalem under the title of Lebanon (cf. 17:3). However, this view of adducing a terminology never actually found in Ugarit runs into considerable difficulty. Thus the question remains to be answered on what grounds Jerusalem and the land of Israel could be described as "the forest in the south."

Two literary images appear to be relevant in this nomenclature. That judgement is referred to under the metaphor of fire is often to be found in Ezekiel (5:4; 10:2, 6f; 15:4–7; 16:41; 19:12, 14; 21:37; 23:25, 47; 24:10, 12 and other passages; cf. the reference to "the fire of wrath" 21:36; 22:21, 31; 38:19). From the reference to the fire which consumes the vine (15:4–7) or the noble ruler's scepter (19:12, 14) the way is not very far to the metaphor of the forest fire. This is already to be found in the prophetic preaching of Isaiah (9:17; 10:17ff, also Zech 11:1f). More directly Jer 21:14, where the palaces of Jerusalem appear to be compared to a forest (יער) and there is mention of a fire which Yahweh kindles in them, may have influenced Ezekiel.

Thus the reference to "the forest in the south" may quite simply have in mind Judah, lying in the south of

---

Alfred Jepsen, *Nabi; soziologische Studien zur alttestamentlichen Literatur und Religionsgeschichte* (München: Beck, 1934), 11; Hölscher, *Profeten*, 32.

9 Herntrich, *Ezekielprobleme*, 104f.

10 Albrecht Alt, "Judas Gaue unter Josia," *PJ* 21 (1925): 108; differently Noth, "Einnahme," 155f.

11 *VT* 8 (1958): 84f.

12 W. F. Albright, "Recent Progress in North-Canaanite Research," *BASOR* 70 (1938): 23.

Syria. More probably, however, with the strongly stylized language of the oracle, we should accept the view that here a counterpart to the saying about the foe from the north, which is developed fully in Jeremiah and which is also discernible in Ezek 38f (38:6, 15; 39:2), is intended.[13] Woe comes from the north upon the "forest of the south." The prophet looks and preaches in the direction of the woe that is about to come upon Jerusalem. Thus the identification of the foe from the north with the Babylonians, which is already evident in Jeremiah for the days of Jehoiakim (Jer 36:29), is tacitly presupposed. It is quite plainly set out in 21:23ff.

■ **21:3, 4** The prophet first of all addresses the forest with a summons to pay attention and then with the full divine message of judgement. Fire will rage through the forest without pity, consuming both fresh and dried up wood (the doubling with לח and יבש is also found in 17:24). Nothing will escape its flames, and every face will be marked with burning scars. In Lev 13:23, 28 a noun צָרֶבֶת "scorching, scar" is derived from the hapax legomenon צרב. All this will not be a blind catastrophe of nature, but an event proving Yahweh's inexorable judgement. Unusual in the recognition formula is not only the variation of the customary ידע to ראה (note a), but also the widening of the subject of the recognition (which reappears in v 10). All flesh, i.e., all the world will know that Yahweh is at work here.[14] The expression is only used here in Ezekiel for the widening of the recognition formula. (Cf. further the reference to גוים in 36:23, 36; 37:28; 39:7, 23, also the additions in 17:24; 29:6; 39:22.) The burning of the forest thereby takes on the significance of a sign which will be seen by the whole world.

■ **21:5** This parable, which veils what is referred to in a deep mystery, is answered by the complaint of the hearers that the prophet is speaking in (unintelligible) proverbs (ממשל משלים). This retort is greeted by the prophet with a groan of lamentation (אההּ cf. 4:14; 9:8; 11:13) to God.

■ **21:6–8** Thus the further coming of a message is at the same time a granting of the prophet's request. The interpretation which is given in it joins smoothly on to the figurative address. The verbs of vv 2f reappear word for word in the command to speak (vv 7f). However, in place of the mysterious instruction to face a particular direction there now appears clearly the name of the addressees: Jerusalem, its sanctuary, the land of Israel. In place of the forest fire the sword appears, which Yahweh draws from its sheath, admittedly another metaphor (Hölscher), but a metaphor of a weapon of war which is very much closer to the reality than the metaphor of the forest fire. It becomes a mythical declaration when Yahweh speaks of the "sword," the meaning of which is to be dealt with more fully in vv 13ff as *his* sword (חרבי).[15] By this personal entrance of Yahweh in mythical language, the harshest reality of judgement is mentioned, about which vv 23ff then show clearly that it will be accomplished historically by the king of Babylon. Yahweh himself strikes unmercifully in a judgement which overtakes righteous and wicked alike (thus interpreting the עץ לח and עץ יבש of v 3). The formulation appears to be in flat contradiction to the statements of Ezek 18 and also to know nothing of the preservation of a remnant, as Ezek 9 leads us to expect. The versions (note c), as also the Talmudic interpretation in *b. 'Abodah Zarah* 4a which interprets the righteous as "only incompletely pious," show how much difficulty the formulation occasioned. The double expression can only be understood when we see in it a form of speech which does not intend to differentiate the righteous and the wicked individually in a casuistic manner, but which sets out an undivided whole by summarizing two opposites.[16] We must further note that here, unlike Ezek 18, the address is not to those who have already been smitten and abandoned to the death of exile and who are summoned to return, but to those who still think that they

---

13   Cf. above pp. 119f to 1:4.

14   For כל בשׂר, which is frequent in P (Gen 6:12f, 17, 19 and other passages), Deutero-Isaiah and Trito-Isaiah (Is 40:5f; 66:16, 23f; 49:26, similarly in the recognition formula of a proof-oracle), see A. R. Hulst, "*Kol baśar* in der priesterlichen Fluterzählung" in *Studies on the Book of Genesis*, OTS 12 (Leiden: Brill, 1958), 28–68, especially 43f.

15   Pp. 432f.

16   For such two-part descriptions of totalities see above p. 191 and see A. M. Honeyman, "*Merismus* in Biblical Hebrew," *JBL* 71 (1952): 11–18.

can escape the judgement.

■ **21:9** V 9 then offers a particular difficulty. For one thing the logic of the לכן־יען-clause is not easy to see. Secondly, as Hulst points out, the כל בשׂר, which refers in v 10 as in v 4 to the witnesses of the divine judgement, is differently used here for those who are themselves punished in this judgement.[17] This judgement is thereby extended to "all the world." Finally v 9 is also striking for its broad repetitions of sayings from v 8. The suspicion arises that we have here an addition which has been introduced into its context by means of a "resumption."[18] Its intention must be to bring out in the מנגב צפון an additional element from v 3b into the interpretation. Further it seeks to extend the declaration of judgement to cover the whole world, and it does this by the taking over of כל בשׂר from v 10. Therewith it brings an element of obscurity into what is otherwise a very clear declaration of judgement which originally added the recognition formula on to v 8, formulated analogously to v 4, but with the use of ידע of the strict style of the formula. In the sword which Yahweh draws against his chosen place and which no man can force back into its sheath, he reveals himself in his action before the whole world.

■ **21:11** That this judgement is not simply an appointed fate, but an act of suffering, is made clear in the concluding sign-action, once again in a very harshly objective way. Yahweh commands the prophet to groan (אנח). The verb אנח, which according to the evidence of 9:4 is parallel to אנק, expresses, according to 24:17, an overwhelming experience of pain which precludes any outward expression. Such pain the prophet is commanded to show "before their eyes" with "breaking loins" and in "bitter pain." The loins, on which men fasten a sword for battle or a sackcloth for lamentation, are the center of physical strength (Job 40:16; Nah 2:2). When they are "broken" (מחץ Dtn 33:11), seized with trembling (חלחלה Nah 2:11; Is 21:3), brought to tottering (29:7), then this strength has gone.[19]

■ **21:12** To the people's question why this should be seen in the prophet, he must answer with the message of doom which had sounded in his ears (cf. the related

formulation in Jer 10:22). It takes up words from the great description of the day of Yahweh. 7:26 speaks of the overwhelming reports of disaster; 7:17 of the utter despair of everyone at these events which shows itself in the loss of strength in men's hands and the uncontrollable wetting of their knees. The statement is expanded here by a reference to the weakness of their hearts and the failing of their spirits. The grimness of that "day" (cf. יום in vv 30, 34) is outlined by the groaning and despair of the prophet. In the harsh concluding sentence which states the inevitability of the coming disaster there echoes the הנה באה of 7:5, 6, 10 (cf. 30:9; 33:33).

Aim

Where fire and sword hold sway man's courage fails him, and all pretensions are finished with. In the twofold declaration of metaphor and interpretation the prophet's word announces these same two powers of evil.

The most dangerous threat of the prophet's preaching, however, lies in the message that in the fire and the sword it will not be simply anyone who is wielding them, but God himself who will kindle the fire and unsheathe the sword. This too will not be against any people at a distance, who may or may not have deserved such a fate, but against his own people with its land, its city and its sanctuary. In the prophet's groaning we hear that, in what is to happen, a truly catastrophic event, even in God's estimate, will be accomplished upon his own people.

All this seeks to establish that where God encounters his people their fate is hopeless, and they have not simply to fear a benevolent grandfatherly rebuke, but death itself. There can be no easy taking hold of "life," still existing in some untouched corner for the darling child of election. "Life" is only conceivable where God's people despair of their own lives and give in to God's judgement, in fear of the sword which they cannot put back into its sheath. When they receive the message with which God himself returns the sword to its sheath (see below v 35) it is because he wills to speak out of his own free faithfulness about his peace.

---

17 Hulst, "*Kol baśar*," 43f.
18 Kuhl, "'Wiederaufnahme'."
19 For מרירות "bitterness, pain" cf. the מר of 3:14.

B. The Sword

Bibliography

F. Delitzsch
"Assyriologische Notizem zun Alten Testament.
IV. Das Schwertlied Ezech. 21, 13–22," *ZK* 2
(1885): 385–398.

21

13 And the word of Yahweh came to me:
    14/ Son of man, prophesy and say:
    Thus has 'Yahweh'ᵃ said:
    [say:]ᵇ
    A sword, a sword is sharpened
    and burnished.ᶜ

15 It is sharpened to bring about a slaughter,
    to flash brightly,ᵃ is it burnished.ᵇ [. . . .]ᶜ

21:    14a 𝔐 (BH³) כה אמר אדני is quite without anal-
14   ogy in the book of Ezekiel. 𝔅 (BH²) read here כה
       אמר יהוה, which appears a further three times (11:5;
       21:8; 30:6). 𝔊 (𝔏ˢ ℭ) κύριος is no help. The entire
       later tradition, as also 𝔊 𝔅 𝔗, point to the customary
       כה אמר אדני יהוה. But cf. 21:8. So we must reckon
       either with a secondary change of an original יהוה
       to אדני (cf. to 18:25, 29) or with the abbreviation of
       a כה אמר אדני יהוה. See Excursus 1. But cf. also
       note b.

       b 𝔐 אֱמֹר is out of place after the messenger form-
       ula (see above p. 133) and the preceding ואמרת and
       is to be deleted with 𝔊ᴸ· ¹³⁰ 𝔏ˢ ℭᴮᵒ. Or has it been
       subsequently construed out of a miswritten יהוה
       (cf. note a)?

       c In the parallel to the perfect הוחדה the passive
       participle מְרוּטָה of 𝔐 is striking. The explanation
       in vv 15a, 16b, which takes up the הוחדה literally,
       then presupposes in the parallel also a perfect puʻal
       (or passive qal, Bauer-Leander § 38n') מֹרָטָה (dag-
       hesh forte affectuosum Gesenius-Kautzsch § 20 i, cf.
       נָתַגּוּ 27:19). This is how we should also read v 20.
       𝔐 מרוטה has been influenced here from v 33. 𝔊 (𝔏ˢ)
       ὀξύνου καὶ θυμώθητι (instead of ἑτοιμάζου? Cf. Katz,
       "Septuaginta," 280) understood the verbs here and
       in the following as imperatives. 𝔗 finds threatened
       in the doubled חרב the sword of the king of Babylon
       and the sword of the Ammonites. Cf. the analogous
       individualizing interpretation of 𝔗 in note b to 16:6.

15   15a The analogy of the parallel first clause leads
       us to expect an infinitive construct after the second
       למען also. Bauer-Leander § 57 t" believe they can
       interpret הֲיֵה as an infinitive form, similar to the
       imperative, after the analogy of קְטֹל. Bertholet reads
       הֱיֹת. Further 𝔊 ὅπως γένῃ εἰς στίλβωσιν appears to
       point to a reading למען היה (הית) לברק, which is
       also supported by the עשויה לברק (v 20). More
       radical textual emendations, such as to בָּרֹק בָּרָק
       (Herrmann, Fohrer), הָהֵל ברק (Cornill, Toy), or to
       היה לה הרג (Ehrlich, *Randglossen*) then become un-
       necessary. For the usage היה ל "to become some-
       thing" cf. 1 Kings 2:2. 𝔅 *ut splendeat*, 𝔊 דתברק sum
       up the expression more briefly, whilst 𝔗 paraphrases
       freely.

       b For מרטה cf. note c to v 14.

       c 𝔐 או נשיש שבט בני מאסת כל עץ, in spite of all

the effort expended on it, so far eludes any satisfactory interpretation. The versions offer no help
for an understanding of it. 𝔊, which connects the
concluding מרטה of v 15a with 𝔐 או נשיש, translates this section: ἑτοίμη (Katz, "Septuaginta," 280,
adds ἧς, which is adopted by Ziegler) εἰς παράλυσιν.
𝔏ˢ *paratus in dissolutionem*. Forms of מרט which were
not understood are twice translated by ἕτοιμος in
v 16, differently in 21:14, 33; 29:18; cf. 21:20. The
equivalent of εἰς παράλυσιν remains obscure (in spite
of Cornill). The further translation σφάζε ἐξουδένει
ἀποθοῦ πᾶν ξύλον may point to a Hebrew original
טבחי בזי מאסי כל עץ, behind which we may find
simply the wrongly written (or misunderstood) text
of 𝔐. 𝔖 corresponds to the first half of 𝔊 in division
and translation. The second half adheres closely to
𝔐. 𝔗 paraphrases 𝔐 freely: "Because the tribe of
the house of Judah and Benjamin rejoiced when the
house of Israel was carried away as prisoners, because they had served idols and had again committed idolatry with images made of wood(,16 so
he recompensed them, in delivering them into the
hand of the king of Babylon. . . .)." In regard to this
questionable section we can simply outline some
considerations: 1) in its interpretation v 15b cannot
be separated from v 18. The catchphrase שבט מאסת
is found in both places and must be understood
similarly in both. 2) V 16 joins on directly to v 15a
over v 15b. Thus v 15b gives the impression of being
a later addition. The same is true of v 18 which is
already striking for its concluding formula for a
divine saying, which occurs here in an address to
the prophet. The only formal analogies in the book
of Ezekiel in 14:13–20; 43:19, 27 are no real counterparts on closer examination. Thus v 18 also must
be understood as an independent addition, introduced as a gloss in connection with v 15b. 3) It then
remains quite uncertain whether the additions in
vv 15b and 18 really should be interpreted from the
context, or whether they contain quite independent
remarks introduced from outside. The vocabulary
of both additions, which does not show any closer
contacts with Ezek 21, would support this. Should
we interpret v 15b from the Wisdom vocabulary:
". . . my son you have refused (מָאַסְתָּ) the rod and
every counsel (עֵצָה)"? Cf. Bewer, "Exegese," 197f,
and "Textual Notes," 161f, who in the rest connects
בני with או נשיש and wants to read איך אשיבנו "How
shall I turn it back" (so "Exegese"), or אין ישיבנו
"none shall turn it back" ("Textual Notes"). A-
gainst the direct connection of the participle מֹאֶסֶת
with שבט, as 𝔐 suggests, there stands especially the
fact that שבט is otherwise always construed as a
masculine. Delitzsch's ("Schwertlied") view that
שבט is of common gender is a pure *petitio principii*.
Cf. also Albrecht, "Geschlecht," 92. This difficulty
also weighs against the conjecture of van den Born,
which is otherwise very attractive, of understanding
vv 15b and 18 as allusions to the Judah saying of

16 And one[a] gave it to him, who scoured it,[b]
to grasp it (firmly) in the hand.
It is sharpened, [a sword][c] burnished[d]
is it,
so that it is given into the hand of the
destroyer.

17 Cry out and howl, son of man, for it has
come to my people; it has come
among the princes of Israel. They are
'delivered'[a] to the sword together
with my people. Therefore beat your
thighs.[b]

[18/ For it is tested . . ., says (the Lord)[a]
Yahweh.][b]

Gen 49:8–12 (שבט v 10, בני v 9, cf. further to Ezek
21:32b): "The scepter of my son despises all wood
(i.e., all scepters of other powers)." Cf. further 19:
11, 14.

16 16a 𝕭 *et dedi* may point to a ואתן (so Bertholet,
Fohrer). However, its reading is probably to be understood as a smoothing of the harsh impersonal
reading of 𝔐 "one gave," which is also attested by
𝕲 𝕾 𝕿.

b 𝔐 לְמָרְטָה may be understood as a lengthened
infinitive (Gesenius-Kautzsch § 45d) parallel to the
following לתפש. The harsh asyndesis which then
arises and the difference in form of the two parallel
infinitives, however, make it appear more probable
that the form is to be understood as לְמֹרְטָה (Ehrlich, *Randglossen*), a suffixed participle. In this case
more radical emendations to למרצח (Hölscher,
Hesekiel, Cooke, Bertholet—the verb רצח is otherwise never found in Ezekiel) or לטובה (Toy) become superfluous.

c If we do not accept with Cornill (following
MS[Ken 96]), Herrmann and Fohrer that חרב, which
is already clearly attested by 𝕲 𝔏[S], is a gloss, then
we can with Cooke understand the preceding היא
as the introduction to an explanatory remark: "that
is to say." However, the parallelism with the second
היא which follows, as well as the analogous repetition of היא in the adjoined v 17 (see below), rather
supports the first interpretation.

d For the form מרטה cf. note c to v 14.

17 17a 𝔐 מְגוּרֵי was already found by 𝕲, which seeks
to find in it the root גור (παροικήσουσιν, 𝔏[S] *habita-
bunt*). A root מגר is attested in Ps 89:45 in the pi'el
with the meaning "to throw down" (biblical Aramaic Ezra 6:12), and the "ground form" in Syriac
with the meaning "to fall." Since the formation of a
passive participle qal from an intransitive ground
stem is difficult and in Ezek 35:5, in a section which
is related in its thought, the usage וַתַּגֵּר עַל יְדֵי חֶרֶב
(hip'il of נגר with a similar meaning in Jer 18:21;
Ps 63:11) occurs, it is more probable that we should
make the slight change to מֻגָּרֵי (Herrmann, Bertholet, Bewer). Cf. the analogous miswriting of מרטה
note c to v 14. For the connection of the construct
state with the following prepositional expression cf.
Gesenius-Kautzsch § 130a.

b 𝕲 (𝔏[S]) κρότησον ἐπὶ τὴν χεῖρά σου presupposes
ידך and interprets following the ויספק את כפיו of
Nu 24:10; Job 27:23; Lam 2:15 (but cf. Ezek
21:19). Jer 31:19, on the other hand, gives good
reason for keeping to 𝔐 ספק אל ירך. For על—אל cf.
note a to 1:17.

18 18a אדני is lacking in 𝕲 𝔏[S] 𝕮, see Excursus 1.

b 𝔐 כי בחן ומה אם גם שבט מאסת לא יהיה is fully
confirmed by 𝕲 (𝔏[S]) ὅτι δεδικαίωται καὶ τί, εἰ καὶ
φυλὴ ἀπώσθη; οὐκ ἔσται. 𝕾, which connects the end
of v 17 with v 18, deviates slightly from 𝕲: "clap
your hands because this [i.e., Israel] has been justified (מטל דאזדקת הדא), and if the tribe (שרבתא)

428

19 But you, son of man, prophesy and clap
  your hands together!ᵃ
   Twice,ᵇ 'three times'ᶜ the sword shall
   rage.
   It is a sword of death, 'a mighty sword
   of death,
   which whirls round them (?).'ᵈ
20 That hearts failᵃ

is rejected shall it (he?) not be (לא תהוא)?" 𝕭 *quia
probatus est et hoc cum sceptrum subverterit et non erit.* 𝕿
paraphrases and interprets here also: "For the prophets have prophesied against them, but they have
not returned. What will now happen at their end?
Say: surely the tribe of the house of Judah [Rashi
adds: and Benjamin] will be carried off and will not
be established on account of their evil deeds." Cf.
for the whole note c to v 15. So far a really convincing interpretation of the verse has not been found.
Cf. Bewer, "Exegese," 198f: "For a testing is made.
And why, if you despise (מָאַסְתָּ) the root, should it
not happen?" Ziegler, *Ezechiel*, interprets the שבט
in another direction: "The testing is coming and the
rejected scepter will be no more." Van den Born
understands the second half of v 18a, in which he
would simply delete the negation, as an (elliptical)
oath in which Yahweh affirms that Zedekiah is not
the scepter, who must despise all other trees on account of his election (cf. to v 15b): "For he is tested.
And what? No, (I swear it) he shall not be the scepter which despises.."

19 19a על—אל cf. note a to 1:17.

 b 𝔐 וְתִכָּפֵל, understood by 𝕲 καὶ διπλασίασον,
𝕷ˢ *et itera* as a qal and read as the continuation of the
command to the prophet. According to 𝕲 𝕭 𝕿 the
impersonal nip'al is to be read.

 c 𝔐 שְׁלִישָׁתָה ("his [?] third") is certainly attested
by 𝕲 ἡ τρίτη (ῥομφαία), 𝕷ˢ *tertius* (*gladius*), 𝕿
תליתיתא. However, we may be inclined here to follow 𝕭 *ac triplicetur* (also 𝕲, which relates the following חרב to what precedes and translates וסיפא
דתלתא, apparently without attesting any ordinal
number and having a copula before this clause) and
to read וְשָׁלְשָׁה, Cf. 1 Kings 18:34. Does 𝔐, in line
with Zech 13:8, intend to speak of the destruction
of two thirds by the sword?

 d 𝔐 חרב חלל הגדול החדרת להם has arisen by a
false division of the words at two points. From an
original חרב חללים גדולה the plural ending of
חלל(י)ם, which is to be expected in the resumption
after what has gone before, has been erroneously
related to the following word and wrongly written
as the definite article. The feminine ending of
גדולה, which cannot be dispensed with, has then
consequentially been related as a definite article to
the following parallel attribute. 𝕲 καὶ ἐκστήσει
αὐτούς and 𝕭 *qui obstupescere eos facit* point to an
הַחֶרְדַּת in the Hebrew original (if 𝕲 originally read
ἐκστήσεις, following 𝕲ᴮ, ⁹⁶⁷ ᵃⁿᵈ ᵒᵗʰᵉʳˢ—against Ziegler—then הֶחֱרַדְתָּ is presupposed). Instead of a derivation from חדר "to go round," Bewer, "Exegese," 198, conjectures a derivation from חָדַר with
the meaning "to penetrate," following Ehrlich,
Randglossen, Authorized Version, American Revised
Version.

20 20a The introduction of an infinitive with ל after
למען is striking. If we do not accept that it is a consciously unusual expression to obtain a threefold

429

and 'the collapsing'[b] are many
  in all their gates,
'they are given over'[c] to the 'killing' of
  the sword, ' '[d]
It is made to flash,
  'burnished'[e] for slaughter.
21 'Prove your sharpness'[a] to the right ' '[b]
    (and) to the left,[c]

---

alliteration with ל (cf. further Ewald, *Lehrbuch* §
315c), we may conjecture that 𝔐 has misread an
original הָמוּג (so BH³, Herrmann, Fohrer and
others). The ὅπως μὴ θραυσθῇ of 𝔊ᴮ (𝔊⁹⁶⁷ without
μή) certainly appears to point to the presence of ל
at an early stage.

b 𝔐 הַמִּכְשֹׁלִים "the stumbling blocks." 𝔊 οἱ ἀσ-
θενοῦντες, 𝔏ˢ *infirmi*, 𝔖 כריהא point to הַמְּכֻשָּׁלִים.
Cf. Jer 18:23.

c In 𝔐 אבחת, which Baer-Delitzsch, X, believe
they can understand as a synonym to טבחת, is unintelligible. 𝔊 (𝔏ˢ) παραδέδονται εἰς σφάγια ῥομφαίας
points to a reading נתנו לטבח (ה)חרב, as the translation of 𝔐 טבח in 𝔊 of vv 15, 20b and 33 with
σφάζειν, or σφάγια and σφαγή shows. Since in the
section comprising vv 19–22 the address of Yahweh
in the first person otherwise first appears in the conclusion, we must follow 𝔊 𝔏ˢ also in the reading of
the verb. 𝔖 𝔗 𝔙 attest נתתי.

d 𝔐 אח is understood by 𝔊 εὖγε (cf. Katz, "Septuaginta," 280), which is repeated in the parallel
statement, as a cry of lamentation similar to הֶאָח in
26:2; 36:2 (= 𝔊 εὖγε). The introduction of ὀξεῖα in
Σ′Α 𝔊ᴸ Thdrt appears to support a Hebrew original
חדה, which is followed by Cornill. Ehrlich, *Randglossen*, seeks to understand it as an abbreviation of
אבחת חרב and to delete it. Toy, Bertholet emend
to אַךְ (which is found in Ezekiel only in 46:17 as a
participle of restriction), BH³ regards אַתְּ as probable, which carries forward the direct address to
the sword from v 21 already on to v 20.

e 𝔐 מְעֻטָּה "covered (?)," 𝔙 *amicti*. After the parallel in v 15 should we expect a derivation from מרט:
מְרוּטָה (מ)מֹרָטָה or (v 33)? Driver, "Linguistic Problems," 68, and Reider, "Contributions," 90, would
leave 𝔐 מעטה and understand it from the Arabic
m'ṭ "to draw (the sword)."

21 21a 𝔐 התאחדי gives no satisfactory sense understood from אֶחָד (Abulwalid points to the Arabic
'ḥd X "to isolate oneself," thence Smend: "to direct
his entire power, attention to [ב] something"). 𝔊
(𝔏ˢ) διαπορεύου ὀξύνου, 𝔙 *exacuere* point to a derivation from חדד, which is also supported from vv 14–
16. Cornill thinks of a Syriac type *Ettaphal* formation, and Driver, "Linguistic Problems," 68, to an
Aramaic by-form אחד from חדד. Just as much,
however, a simple scribal error from התחדי is possible. The hitpa'el, which 𝔊 seeks to translate with
the preceding διαπορεύου, introduces the idea of
proving himself.

b 𝔐 השימי "put (?)" (for the hip'il of שים cf. note
a to 14:8) is not attested by 𝔊 𝔏ˢ 𝔙 MSᴷᵉⁿ¹²⁶ and
is to be deleted as a mutilated dittography of הַשְׂמִילִי,
so Hölscher, *Hesekiel*, and others. Driver, "Linguistic Problems," 68, conjectures הָשֵׂמִּי, and in "Ezekiel," 154, הוּשְׂמִי and understands this from the
Arabic *sāma* "to draw out of a sheath."

c הַשְׂמִילִי instead of הַשְׂמָאִילִי, cf. Bauer-Leander §
50v.

22 for which your edge[d] is ordered.[e]
And I also will clap[a] my hands together
and vent my anger. I, Yahweh, have
spoken.

d 𝔐 פָּנֶיךָ is emended by some (Bertholet, Bewer, "Exegese," 198, following Ju 3:16; Prv 5:4) to פִּיּוֹתֶיךָ. Eccl 10:10, however, shows that the text of 𝔐, which is unanimously supported by the versions, is quite unobjectionable. Cf. further note e.

e 𝔐 מֻעָדוֹת from יעד hop'al "to be asked to come, to be ordered." פָּנִים is otherwise construed in the Old Testament as a masculine and in the Mishnah as a feminine, but cf. ZAW 25 (1905): 336. According to Driver, "Ezekiel," 154f, we should read מוּעֶדֶת, since a collective expression can be treated as a feminine singular, cf. Jer 36:23; Mic 2:9.

22 22a אל—על cf. note a to 1:17.

Form

An answer to the question about the form of the saying in 21:13–22 is very closely related to the answer to the question about the originality of the present text and whether it has been subsequently worked over. Study of the text has shown that vv 15b and 18 probably must be cut out as subsequent additions. Furthermore Hölscher, *Hesekiel*, following considerations seen by Rothstein, has pointed out that in vv 14b, 15a, 16 we cannot deny that explanatory glosses have been made to an original text. Two sentences about the sword, which are preserved in a five-beat meter and which fit together without difficulty (vv 14b, 16a), have been commented on by a sentence which falls outside the five-beat meter. On the basis of this consideration Hölscher analyses the whole section of vv 13–22. He removes all elements in which the prophet himself is addressed, i.e., besides the introduction in vv 13, 14a, also vv 17, 19a and the concluding v 22 which corresponds to v 19a. He also removes from what remains in vv 19b–21 some elements (in v 19b besides the first חרב the section חרב חללים up to הגדול, in v 20 למען למוג לב, the נתתי אבחת and אח). There is then left a short clear address to the sword. Cooke follows Hölscher.

Against this analysis, which is at first attractive, there must be set some further formal considerations which suggest a modification of Hölscher's view. The present text as a whole is joined together by the repeated command to prophesy (vv 14, 19). The introductions to the two strophes into which the song then divides cannot be so easily removed from the text as

would appear in Hölscher's view. This is especially true of v 19, which is closely related to what follows. The introductory formula of the messenger saying, which follows הנבא in v 14, is left out in v 19 with good reason, since the action which appears in place of it is already a part of the message. The copula before the תכפל must certainly not then be removed and possibly replaced by a colon to introduce direct speech. To this must be added the consideration that the catchword כף holds together the two parts as a key word.[20] If we then question whether a conscious connection is intended between the "hand" which grasps the sword (v 16) and the "hand" which claps into the second "hand" and thereby doubles the effectiveness of the sword (v 19), it is scarcely difficult not to feel that in the form וְתִכָּפֵל the כף of v 19 (16) is echoed in a wordplay. The "doubling" of the sword and the "clapping into the hands" thereby are brought into a close relationship, even in sound. With the concluding statement, according to which Yahweh himself claps his hands together (v 22), there can be no doubt that it should be understood as an intense heightening of v 19. Then the suggestion that כף in v 16 should already be regarded as a catchword cannot be altogether wrong. Hölscher's breaking up of the verses which contain the catchword therefore becomes questionable. In the context of considerations of form we must further assert against Hölscher that the addition in v 15a is certainly not a prosaic explanatory gloss. It is preserved in two four-beat clauses, built up regularly in parallel. The same rhythm must also be intended in the addition in v 16b.

---

20 See Martin Buber, "Leitwortstil in der Erzählung des Pentateuchs" in Martin Buber and Franz Rosenzweig, *Die Schrift und ihre Verdeutschung* (Berlin: Schocken, 1936), 211–238.

These varied considerations lead to the following conclusions: the song of the sword in 21:13–22 is constructed as a unit in two strophes. The first strophe, which deals with the manufacture and delivery of the sword, contains two clauses formulated in a five-beat meter (vv 14b, 15a, 16), to each of which has been added a comment couched in double fours. The call to the prophet to raise a lament which then follows (v 17), which is reminiscent of the element vv 11f in the section vv 1–12, represents an intentional echo of the description of the sword. However, since it comes too soon in the overall structure of the sword song (cf. the conclusion in vv 11f) and in its content also we could rather remove it from the sword song (see below), it must be a later addition. In the second strophe the presence of any additional commenting is less easy to discern. Yet we cannot with complete certainty rule it out. For the rest the beginning and end are clearly dovetailed so that Hölscher's radical reduction is not to be supported.

The analysis given raises three possibilities in regard to the question of authorship: 1) Ezekiel was the author only of the original basis. The additional comments come from a later hand. The close connection between the additions in vv 15a and 20, which takes up the statements of v 15a and which even according to Hölscher belongs firmly to the basic section of vv 19–21, makes this view improbable. 2) Ezekiel himself added comments to a sword song which he took up, and then developed it independently first of all in the second strophe. This explanation cannot be completely excluded. We could then point to the analogy of Ezek 7 where the independent elaboration and development of an older prophetic announcement of judgement (בא הקץ) is clearly demonstrable. Besides this we must seriously keep open the possibility that Ezekiel 3) developed more fully in a second phase a brief sword saying of his own, the earlier form of which can only be fragmentarily recovered. For this process of the elaboration in a stronger and more concrete form of a saying of his own there are not lacking analogies in the book of Ezekiel.

Setting
We cannot adduce from the text information which would make possible a closer determination of the place where the prophecy was uttered. The reference to hearts made fearful by the sword certainly does not serve as proof against a derivation from the Babylonian exiles.[21] Chronologically the threat of the sword and its being aroused to a murderous slaughter (v 21) would point to a time before the fall of Jerusalem. Against this the summons to lamentation (v 17) appears to presuppose the battle against people and princes (plural) as something that has already happened (היתה). Accordingly v 17 must have been added after the fall of Jerusalem.

Interpretation
■ **21:13, 14** There begins in v 13, introduced by a fresh formula for the coming of a message, a divine saying which commands the "son of man" to proclaim a fearful song of the sword, with the full weight of a divine utterance.[22] Vv 13–21 are distinguished from the saying about the sword of Yahweh (חרבי vv 8–10) in the preceding verses (vv 1–12) in that the sword, as an instrument of judgement, appears here to take on an independant personal existence. In v 21 the prophet's word becomes a direct address to the sword. Such hypostasizing of the sword is found in mythical language in Gen 3:24, where reference is made to a fiery sword which bars the approach to paradise like a flickering flame. The late prophetic saying in Is 27:1, in which the sword is clearly put into the hand of Yahweh, shows that this also had a place in the mythology of the battle with the dragon of chaos. Yahweh punishes the dragon בחרבו הקשה והגדולה והחזקה. In the Ugaritic parallel to this reference to the battle with the dragon explicit mention of the sword is lacking.[23]

Reference to the sword (of Yahweh) had already gained a place in the language of earlier prophecy. Besides the early Israelite conception of Yahweh as a warrior,[24] which was encouraged by the ideas of the holy war, there was influence from particular images of the mythical power of the sword in the surrounding world. Thus in Amos, besides the direct statements that Yahweh executes judgement with the sword (4:10; 7:9; 9:1), we find the other conception according to which Yahweh commands the sword for judgement (צוה Amos 9:4, cf. Jer 47:7; שלח Jer 9:15; 49:37). In the sayings of the prophets it can further be said that Yahweh summons the sword (קרא Jer 25:29; Ezek

38:21), that this consumes (אכל Is 1:20; Jer 12:12; 46:10; Na 2:14, and also Dtn 32:42, and in narrative 2 Sam 2:26; 11:25; 18:8), and that it gets drunk (רוה Is 34:5; Jer 46:10). Indeed Jer 15:3 introduces it alongside dogs, birds, and wild animals as the first of the four families (משפחות) of judgement. (Cf. the use of חרב היונה Jer 46:16; 50:16; also 25:38 [with emended text].) Thus there arises in the prophetic preaching the form of a sword song, thematically controlled, in which the sword's raging is described (Jer 50:35–38) or is adjured directly in personal address (Jer 47:6f; Zech 13:7f).

Thus Ezekiel with his sword song stands in line with a prophetic tradition of speech which he was not the first to coin, but which he has developed in his own way.

The basis of the first strophe of the song is formed in two lines which describe the manufacture and delivery of the mysterious and fatal sword. The repetition of the חרב for emphasis has its parallels in Ezekiel in the אחיך אחיך of 11:15 (a more distant example of the stylistic device of repetition may be found in the book of Ezekiel in יען ביען 13:10, יען וביען 36:3—again in Lev 26:43, see below to v 19). Unlike the vigorous address in Gen 22:11; 1 Sam 3:10; Ps 22:2, in neither text are we concerned with direct address (against van den Born). With all the fateful power that is given to it the sword is seen throughout with full sobriety as a weapon which first comes from the hand of a maker (cf. Is 54:16f). Thus its blade is sharpened (חדד, the adjective חד is used of the sword in 5:1; Is 49:2; Ps 57:5; Prv 5:4) and burnished (מרט 29:18 of the baldness or wounds inflicted by carrying baggage; it is used of polished metal again in 1 Kings 7:45).

■ **21:15a** The additional comment, in a statement which is sharply formulated in parallel and which connects up with the two acts of preparation, adds a reference to the purpose of the sword in which its threatening use as a weapon of judgement is announced. It is appointed to "slaughter and to flash." The verb טבח, which is not again used in Ezekiel (the noun טֶבַח, besides v 15, is found again in vv 20, 33), first of all denotes the slaughtering of animals in order to prepare them for a meal (Gen 43:16; Ex 21:37; Dtn 28:31; 1 Sam 25:11, hence טַבָּח the "cook" 1 Sam 9:23f, feminine 1 Sam 8:13). Jer 25:34; 51:40 show how the picture of the slaughtering of (sacrificial) animals can then become a picture of judgement upon the nations and their shepherds. Thus, in Is 34:2, without any reference to the slaughter of animals, it is used of the judgement of the sword (Is 34:5) of Yahweh on the day of wrath (cf. Lam 2:21 or Ps 37:14 for the killing of the poor by the sword of the wicked). For the "flashing" of the sword, which here takes on a threatening note as a parallel to "slaughter," we must compare Dtn 32:41 which, in different words, connects the sharpness and the "flashing" of the sword (אם שנולי ברק חרבי). Na 3:3 (alongside להב חרב) and Hab 3:11 speak of the "flashing" of the spear, i.e., of its metal tip.

■ **21:16** The text of the older original basis of the song then spoke of the delivery of the sword into the hand of the one who was to wield it. The subject of the handing over, whom we can only regard as Yahweh from the overall content of the song, is left in a mysterious anonymity in the text of the song itself. If we keep to the text of 𝔐 then also the hand into which the sword is put is also left in the dark. If we emend the text with Ehrlich (note b), then the smith who burnishes the sword is also appointed to wield it by the power that lies mysteriously in the background. In any case the addition in v 16b then discloses menacingly: the person who wields the sword will be one who is ready to kill (the participle הֹרֵג also in 28:9; cf. further 2 Kings 9:31). For Ezekiel's day this points undeniably to Nebuchadnezzar, the leader of the Babylonian army. In the context of the oracles against the nations, 30:24f then says plainly that the sword of Yahweh has been given by him into the hand of the king of Babylon.

■ **21:19** The original song of the sword then followed

21 Herntrich, *Ezekielprobleme*, 106.

22 See above pp. 144f; pp. 131f.

23 Otto Eissfeldt, *Baal Zaphon, Zeus Kasios und der Durchzug der Israeliten durchs Meer*, BRA 1 (Halle: Nie-meyer, 1932), 24; Gressmann, *Ursprung*, § 10: "Jah-we als Kriegsgott," 71–85.

24 See Henning Fredriksson, *Jahwe als Krieger* (Lund: Gleerups, 1945), for his being equipped with a sword, see especially pp. 95–97.

directly on v 16 with a second strophe. The fresh divine address to the prophet, which calls him again to carry out the expressive gesture of 6:11, arises out of the first half of the song of the sword by an inner relationship.[25] In v 16a its original text had pointed in veiled language to the threatening hand (כַּף) which wielded the sword. In the addition in v 16b the menacing character of this hand (יָד) is more fully brought out. Now, in an emphatic gesture, the prophet is to strike "hand" in "hand" (van den Born goes so far as to speak of a sword dance) in order to effect by this very gesture the coming event.[26] Since the gesture which he is summoned to make is the triumphant gesture of the victor over the vanquished, by this action the victory of the menacing hand is anticipated.[27] This is further emphasized by the formulation of v 19b with its use of the verb כפל, which is otherwise only found in the technical vocabulary of P (Ex 26:9; 28:16; 39:9). In the double cutting with the sword (וְתִכָּפֵל) the ear catches in the Hebrew text a further allusion to the hand which wields it (v 16) and which exults over its victory (v 19). In 𝔐 the idea may be expressed that the sword receives authority to rage (Zech 13:7f) over the third portion which is measured out to it (5:2, 12). In the original text, restored with aid of 𝔅 (note c), by a simple increase of numbers the ever more severe raging of the sword is mentioned. O. Eissfeldt, "Schwerterschlagene," has shown that the expression חַלְלֵי חֶרֶב, as also the simple חָלָל, denotes not simply those who have fallen in battle, but in a narrower sense those who have been "murdered" or "executed."[28] If the sword in Ezekiel's song of the sword is indeed "a sword of judgement and not a sword of battle" and is described further in a twofold statement as חרב חללים גדולה (note d, for the doubling cf. above to v 14), this recalls the "harsh, great, and mighty sword" of Is 27:1.[29] Then, as Eissfeldt lays down quite generally for the the sword sayings of Ezek 21, this expression, in dependence on the formulation in Isaiah, states that the terrible sword is a "sword of judgement and not of battle" which pierces, or encompasses (חדר), those who have come under judgement.[30] Thus it then controls the power of the divinely aroused panic which brings despair to the hearts of men, as is to be seen in the holy war of Yahweh (Ex 23:27f; Josh 2:9 and other passages).[31] At the same time it also controls the power to bring death in the streets "in all their gates." Once again any closer definition of those referred to in the suffix is left obscure in prophetic mystery, although it was immediately clear to the prophet's hearers.

The menacing independent existence of the sword then becomes quite clear where it is summoned, in a further heightening of the message, to perform its insatiable work fully, as in Jer 47:6 and Zech 13:7 in imperative address.

■ **21:21** We cannot make out with complete certainty whether the description of the sword in v 20b, which repeats with slight variation the statements of v 15a, belongs to the description which precedes or to the imperative of v 21 as a summons to those being addressed. In it, with great severity, the sword is now commanded to prove its sharpness and, like a raging attacker, to let its strokes fall to right and left, wherever the mysterious will which is at work in it determines, and according to the turning of its "face," which is mentioned here like that of a man.

■ **21:22** First in v 22 the one who ordered the preparation of the sword, gave it into the hand, struck fear before it, and incited it to its wild raging, appears out of his mysterious hiddenness. Now we can perceive the "I" (וגם אני אכה) of the God who appears in the final sentence as the one who controls history by his word. He appears himself with the expressive gesture, which he had commanded his messenger to perform in v 19. Now we can discern the hand of the ruler of history himself behind the hand which wields the instrument of judgement, behind that in which the sword is placed (v 16), and behind the handclapping of the prophetic messenger which both anticipates the triumph over the sword's enemies (v 19a) and at the same time effects the doubling of its fury (19b). With the clapping of his own hands he arouses the fury of the sword to the uttermost, declaring his triumphant victory and finally exhausting his anger. The formula is found again in 5:13, 16:42; 24:13.

■ **21:17** The year 587 began the historical fulfillment of

---

25 See above p. 184.
26 See above p. 156.
27 See above p. 184.

28 See above pp. 186f.
29 Eissfeldt, "Schwerterschlagene," 77.
30 Eissfeldt, "Schwerterschlagene," 77.

the harsh threat which is expressed here in the veiled language of prophecy. In the call to lament, which has been introduced in v 17 after 587, the historical contours become clearer. The call to make loud lamentation (זעק and הילל are also found together in Hos 7:14; Is 65:14; Jer 47:2, and in the reverse order in Is 14:31; 15:3f; Jer 25:34; 48:20, 31; 49:3 צעק), together with the designation of the people as עמי in the mouth of Yahweh (13:9f, 19, 21, 23; 14:8f; 25:14; 33:31; 34:30; 36:12; 37:12f; 38:14, 16; 39:7; 44:23; 45:8f; 46:18), contains a note of softness in the lament which is not often found in Ezekiel. We can perceive here a deep pain in God himself that the sword must come against his people along with the "princes of Israel" (again 19:1; 22:6). Plainly there is in mind here not only the fall of 587 but the whole history of suffering of the last princes of Judah, such as is dealt with in part in Ezek 19. In this the note of accusation is in the background and only the lament is in the forefront (as in ch. 19). The "beating of the thighs," which appears in Jer 31:19 as a gesture of remorse, must also be understood here as a gesture of lamentation. Similarly in *Odyssey* 13, 198, Odysseus laments in this way (cf. Achilles *Iliad* 16, 125).

■ **21:15b, 18** Still later the additions in vv 15b and 18 have been added. If van den Born's interpretation is in the right direction, then here the mystery of the messianic promise and judgement is raised.

Aim

History has a terrifying aspect for men, even when they belong to the people of God, because of its conjunction of forces. It moves in its own way, in opposition to men, and threatening them. It contains fearful, supernatural forces which can injure, terrify, and destroy because man is alone in facing them.

The threatening feature of Ezekiel's sword song lies in the fact that the prophet does not minimize this reality of history with an illuminating pious word, but accords it validity in his message from God. There is as reality the sword. Indeed, God himself has appointed it, brightly burnished, flashing and ready, to execute a grim slaughter. Then also the hand which grasps the sword and gives it movement, intelligence to look out for weak spots, and the power to strike, is real and of God. The prophet's word in no way denies to all these threatening realities their power. Quite the contrary! The prophet is commanded, by the clapping of his hands together, to redouble the power of the forces that threaten Israel, to heighten the fear of them to panic proportions, and finally to incite them to absolute fury by an unheard-of summons so that they may strike out in all directions and in their raging execute a fearful destruction. In conclusion the prophet is empowered to name the name of God himself as the center of power at work in the sword and to point to God as the one whose signals authorize the forces of death.

Thus the prophet speaks of the "wrath of God" which is revealed against the unrighteous nature of his people (Rom 1:18). This does not take place simply in a hidden background in which God and the soul are alone, and alongside of which in another room history and all that gives it meaning take place, quite apart from that hidden dialogue. God deals with his sinful people even through the forces which wield the sword that he has drawn.

If this is so, then there can be no stoic withdrawal into another world, withdrawn from the actual events, in which man shields himself from this attack in the calmness of his spirit or soul. It is then true that God himself will be encountered in this battle (cf. Gen 32:25ff). Here the wrath of God casts man into the depths of fear and grief so that he can only cry out in his abandonment: "My God, my God, why hast thou forsaken me?" (Ps 22:2).

At the same time, however, this harsh message affirms that there is no "sword" in the world in which God himself, by his word, does not remain the real power, and that every power can only rage and terrify so long as it is aroused by God's wrath. Thus all help consists solely in the fact that God himself makes known his saving righteousness in a world which stands under the revelation of his wrath. This he does by his speaking again (v 22), which means life out of death (37:1–14).

---

31   See von Rad, *Krieg*, 10f.

C. The Sword of the King of Babylon

P. R. Ackroyd
"The Teraphim," *ET* 62 (1950/51): 378–380.

W. L. Moran
"Gen. 49:10 and its Use in Ez. 21:32," *Biblica* 39 (1958): 405–425.

F. Oefele
"Die Leberschau Ezek. 21:26," *ZAW* 20 (1900): 311–314.

21

23 And the word of Yahweh came to me: **24/** And you, son of man, make two ways [, upon which the sword of the king of Babylon comes].[a] They must both start from one[b] land. And you shall set a signpost ' '[c] at the beginning of each way[d] **25/** [, so that the sword can come]:[a] "Rabbah[b] of the Ammonites" and "Judah,[b] which has

21: 24 24a P. Rost, "Miscellen," 393, has offered the conjecture that 𝔐 לבוא חרב מלך בבל, which clumsily anticipates what is to come and reappears again in v 25, has entered from the margin, as an attempt at improving v 25. However, more probably the words mentioned must be regarded as an interpretative note (correct in its content, but coming too soon in the context), exactly as in the לבוא חרב of v 25. Cf. also note a to 4:1.

b The אחד of 𝔐, which is striking alongside the feminine ארץ and which Driver, "Ezekiel," 145, would regard as a "colloquialism," with reference to 𝔐 דמות אחד of 1:16, is possibly to be emended with 2 MSS^Ken to אחת. Aalders seeks to support the possibility of a masculine construction of ארץ from Gen 13:6; Is 9:18. More radical emendations, such as the change of מארץ to ממקום (Hitzig) or מדרך (Oort, "Ezechiël," 513f), are certainly not to be accepted.

c 𝔐 בָּרֵא (23:47 "to cut to pieces") is not attested by 𝔊 and is a misplaced dittography of the nearby בראש. For this miswriting cf. also note d.

d For the second בָּרֵא of 𝔐 we have as a counterpart in 𝔊 ἐν ἀρχῇ. Thus we must read here also בראש (cf. note c) and connect this with the beginning of v 25a. The repeated בראש דרך then offers a certain difficulty. Herrmann would delete בראש דרך עיר in v 24 as a gloss. However, since something must be said about the two ways, it is better to accept a distributive understanding of the double statement. Thus in v 25 Cornill and Toy add עיר after דרך. More probably, however, the עיר in v 24 has arisen out of the miswriting of an original יד (Oort, "Ezechiël," Bertholet, Fohrer, cf. Ehrlich, *Randglossen*). 𝔊 supports 𝔐.

25 25a Cf. note a to v 24, also note b to v 25.

b The repeated את, which is mostly emended following 𝔊 ἐπί, 𝔖 על to אל (Ehrlich, *Randglossen*, Bertholet) or to על (Cooke), can scarcely be a simple scribal error. Rather the two expressions introduced with את are syntactically dependent on שים as fuller definitions of the repeated יד (note d to v 24). The relationship is now confused by the insertion of לבוא חרב, to which 𝔊 𝔖 have then related the two place references as descriptions of the destinations, by a simple interchange.

26 its stronghold in Jerusalem."ᶜ

For the king of Babylon has arrived atᵃ the forking of the roads, the starting-point of the two ways. He has cast the arrows to receive an oracle; he has enquired of the teraphim; he has observed the liver. 27/ Into his right (hand) the lot marked "Jerusalem." has fallen [, so that he sets up battering rams],ᵃ so that he opens his mouth 'with shouting,'ᵇ raises his voice in a battle cry, sets battering rams against the gates,ᶜ heaps up a siege ramp, builds siege works. 28/ However, in their eyes it appears to them [, who have sworn solemn oaths (?),]ᵃ as a

c 𝕸 יהודה בירושלם בצורה at first glance arouses little confidence. Since 𝕲 𝕷ˢ 𝕾 read the copula before "Jerusalem" and 𝕲 (𝕷ˢ) translates as καὶ ἐπὶ τὴν Ἰουδαίαν καὶ ἐπὶ Ἱερουσαλημ ἐν μέσῳ αὐτῆς, many have concluded that the original reading was יהודה וירושלם בתוכה (Cornill, Ehrlich, *Randglossen*, Herrmann, Toy, Cooke and others). It is then remarkable how such a clear text could have been corrupted into such an obscure one. Thus 𝕸 is worth serious consideration. It has in its favor the formal consideration that the mention of the destinations that has been incorporated, "Rabbah of the Ammonites," sums up the names of city and people in a single grammatical expression. It has beside it a similar summarizing expression for the second destination, whilst 𝕲 breaks this up into two references and so destroys the formal parallelism of the saying. If we seek to restore a formation "Jerusalem of the Judeans," exactly parallel to "Rabbah of the Ammonites," then it immediately becomes clear that Ezekiel cannot have selected such a phrase because 1) this is for Ezekiel a theologically impossible formulation (see below) and 2) the רבת or רבה which still carries the emphasis "the great" would have no real counterpart appropriate to Jerusalem. This results in the chiastic formulation יהודה בירושלם בצורה "Judah, which is inaccessible in Jerusalem," alongside the רבת בני עמון which similarly has three accents. So also 𝕭 *Judam in Jerusalem munitissimam*. The prepositional phrase בירושלם would then have the force of defining more precisely בצורה (analogous to a general statement in the construct state), so that the article which would otherwise be expected with בצורה can be omitted. Cf. further the exposition. That 𝕲 translates בצורה with ἐν μέσῳ αὐτῆς Blau, "Hebräisch," 97, believes he can understand from the Mishnaic מְבָצָּר "standing in the midst." 𝕿 paraphrases in its own way ועל דבית יהודה דנפקו מירושלם למתב בקירוין כריכן.

26 26a אל – על cf. note a to 1:17. We can better find the caesura of the verse after הדרכים.

27 27a 𝕸 לשׂום כרים is already attested by 𝕲, but must nevertheless be regarded as an addition which anticipates the similar statement of v 27b. The saying is also better in place after the two parallel three beat clauses, which speak of the initial war cries. So Oort, "Ezechiël," 513f, Herrmann, Bertholet, Fohrer.

b 𝕸 ברצח "in murder," only again in Ps 42:11 in an uncertain text. The ἐν βοῇ of 𝕲 (𝕷ˢ *in clamorem*) fits very much better with the parallel בתרועה and points to a reading בְּצֶרַח. Cf. Is 42:13 (also Jer 4:31 with emended text?).

c 𝕸 על שׁערים. 𝕲 (𝕷ˢ 𝕾) render more precisely ἐπὶ τὰς πύλας αὐτῆς.

28 28a 𝕸 שׁבעי שׁבעות להם has no counterpart in 𝕲 𝕷ˢ 𝕾 and must be cut out as a subsequent addition. Its meaning is already contested in the ver-

'lying oracle,'ᵇ where it shows guilt whereby they are then afflicted.

29 Therefore thus has [the Lord]ᵃ Yahweh said: Because men denounce you in your guilt,ᵇ in that your offenses are revealed, so that your sins are evident in all your deeds—because you have been denounced,ᵇ therefore you shall be apprehended with a (strong) hand.ᶜ

30 And you, 'wicked offender,'ᵃ prince of Israel, whose day has come in a time of final punishment, 31/ thus has [the Lord]ᵃ Yahweh said: 'Take off' ᵇyour diadem, 'throw away'ᵇ your crown!

sions. Ἀ ἑπτὰ ἑβδομάδες αὐτοῖς; Θ ἑβδομάζοντες ἑβδομάδας αὐτοῖς; 𝕭 et sabbatorum otium imitans; 𝕿 paraphrases v 28aαβ: "And they did not know that he lay in wait forty-nine times and sat down because of the matter, until I gave him the hour in which you should be given into his hands." Since in what follows in vv 30–32 the king Zedekiah is especially attacked because of his guilt, Ezek 17 supports that we should think of the oath (there אלה beside ברית) which he broke. Should we then look behind שבעי for an abstract formulation שבעים (Gesenius-Kautzsch § 124d)? Or should we think of a superlative formulation (Gesenius-Kautzsch § 133 i), in which for variety a masculine plural form of שבעה is used (which is never otherwise found) (cf., however, the use of תהלות and תהלים)? Tsevat, "Vassal Oaths," 202, points to parallels in the Rabbinic sphere for such elative formations. We should also consider Fohrer's conjecture of נשבעי. Cf. BH³.

b 𝕸 כקסום שוא. Instead of the infinitive form (𝕲 ὡς μαντευόμενος presupposes כְקֹסֵם), which is read as written plene by Kethib and defectively by Qere, we must read with 𝕲 (and 𝕸 vv 26, 27) the noun קֶסֶם.

29 29a אדני is lacking in 𝕲 𝓛ˢ, see Excursus 1.

b Whilst in 29a 𝕸 is vocalized as a hip'il הַזְכַּרְכֶם (for the form cf. Gesenius-Kautzsch § 53 1; Bauer-Leander § 480''), in 29b the nip'al הִזָּכְרְכֶם is used. 𝕲 levels this off in translating both as active: ἀνθ' ὧν ἀνεμνήσατε (𝕲²⁶ in 29b ἀνεμνήσθητε); 𝓛ˢ recordati estis ... ammonuistis; 𝕭 twice recordati estis; 𝕿 the other way round both times חלף דאידכרתון. V 29a shows the active full formulation of the legal usage. The repetition in b, which offhand is passed over in 𝕲 with an abbreviation (אתדכרתון 29a), but which may be original as an emphatic resumption from v 28b (differently Oort, "Ezechiël," 513f, Cornill, Herrmann, Hölscher, Hesekiel, Bertholet, Fohrer), points to a negligent elliptical formulation, which is related in the passive form directly to the guilt of the accused person. We cannot be sure in the active הַזְכַּרְכֶם of 29a whether the suffix should be understood as subject ("because you have denounced . . .") or as object in a neutral formulation ("because one has denounced you"). The formulation of v 28 (subject "the lot") and v 29αβb (passive) supports the second interpretation.

c 𝕸 בכף, interpreted by 𝕿 ביד מלכא דבבל, but misunderstood by 𝕲 ἐν τούτοις, 𝓛ˢ in istis as בהם. 𝕾 supports 𝕸. An emendation to באף (Ehrlich, Randglossen) or בהם (Cornill, Herrmann, Bertholet, Fohrer) is not necessary.

30 30a 𝕸 חָלָל רָשָׁע. The חַלְלֵי רְשָׁעִים of v 34 raises the question whether we should not vocalize more correctly חֲלַל רָשָׁע, i.e., as a construct formation. Cf. also note a to 3:19. For the nomen rectum as the designation of a genus cf. Gesenius-Kautzsch § 128 l.

31 31a אדני is lacking in 𝕲 𝓛ˢ ℭᴮᵒ, see Excursus 1.

b 𝕸 הַשָׁפִּיל; הָרִים; הָסִיר. With 3, 5 and 11

Everything is finished !ᶜ Raise the 'low,'ᵈ
'bring down'ᵇ the 'high' !ᵈ 32/ Ruins,
ruins, ruins will I make it.ᵃ 'Finish with
it'ᵇ by the time whenᶜ he comes to
whom judgement belongs and I give it
(to him).ᵈ

33 But you, son of man, prophesy and say:
Thus has [the Lord]ᵃ Yahweh spoken
againstᵇ the Ammonites and againstᵇ
those who mock you, and say (?):ᶜ
Sword, sword, drawn to slaughter,
burnished to destroy,ᵈ 'to flash like

MSSᴷᵉⁿ respectively we should read the infinitive
absolute הָרֵם; הַשְׁפֵּל. ⑤ ἄφελοῦ; ἀπόθου. In
what follows it translates with finite verb forms.

c 𝕸 זאת לא זאת, ⑤ αὕτη οὐ τοιαύτη ἔσται, literally: "This is not this." Ehrlich, *Randglossen*, points to
2 Kings 9:37.

d In 𝕸 הַשְּׁפָלָה "the punctuators intend to recommend the masculine form as the more correct,"
Bauer-Leander § 62 y. The parallel וְהַגְּבֹהַּ would
support the masculine interpretation, for which we
could then better read in the text הַשָּׁפֵל (Cooke).
So 𝕭 *humilem – sublimen*. However, the neutral interpretation is also possible, in which we should
vocalize הַשְּׁפָלָה and then read 𝕸 וְהַגְּבֹהָה (והגבה
has arisen by haplography, cf. the ה which follows
subsequently). So Herrmann, Bertholet, Fohrer.

32 32a Bertholet and others relate the feminine suffix of אֲשִׂימֶנָּה to the city of Jerusalem, the mention
of which in v 27 admittedly lies at some distance.
More probably we should leave open its connection
in a neutral generality. The threefold עַוָּה may have
influenced the form.

b 𝕸 גם זאת לא היה, ⑤ οὐδ' αὕτη τοιαύτη ἔσται
support our seeking an interpretation of the sentence in the direction of the זאת לא זאת of v 31.
Only היה may be abbreviated out of an original
תהיה (the reading הָיָה conjectured by Driver, "Linguistic Problems," 68, is less probable). So Moran,
"Gen 49:10." A more radical emendation of the
text to גם אות לא יהיה (Hitzig, Ehrlich, *Randglossen*,
Bewer, "Textual Notes," 162) or to אוי לה כזאת
תהיה (Cornill) is not necessary. ⑤ passes over the
passage here as already in v 31.

c עד is not to be understood here as pointing to a
goal. Brockelmann § 163b: "עד, like the Latin *dum*,
may not only denote the goal, but also the period of
time until then."

d 𝕸 ונתתיו. The text seems to be mutilated. If the
suffix is related to המשפט, we should then expect a
לו. So Cooke, following ⑤ καὶ παραδώσω αὐτῷ.
However, in the vocative style of the whole of vv 31f
the originality of such an abrupt sentence is in no
way impossible. 𝕿 relates v 32 to Gedaliah in a free
interpretation.

33 33a אדני is lacking in ⑤ 𝔏ˢ 𝕮ᴮᵒ, see Excursus 1.
b אל – על cf. note a to 1:17.
c The repeated ואמרת is out of place after the
prophetic introductory formula; however, unlike
the אמר of v 14, it is well attested in the tradition.
d 𝕸 להכיל may formally be derived from כול
"to encompass" as well as from אכל (Gesenius-
Kautzsch § 68 i) "to let consume." Neither yields
a completely satisfying sense. ⑤ εἰς συντέλειαν, 𝕭 *ut
interficias* may point to a connection with כלה. If we
do not emend immediately to לְכָלָה (Bertholet), we
shall have to accept a by-form לְהָכֵל (כלל or כול
would then wrongly be written plene) for כלה. We
may reject a further emendation to לההל (Cornill,
Toy).

lightning,'ᵉ 34/ to bring you (at the
time), when men saw visions of lies
about you and gave oracles of lies
concerning you, down onᵃ the necks of
the shameless wicked men,ᵇ whose day
has come in a time of final punishment. 35/ 'Put it back'ᵃ in its sheath!ᵇ
At the place in which you were
fashioned, in the land of your origin,
I will judge you, 36/ and I will pour
out my wrath upon you. The fire of my
anger I will kindle against you and I will
give you into the hand of barbarians,ᵃ
men who forge destruction. 37/ [You
will be given as fuel for the fire.]ᵃ Your
blood will be in the midst of the land.
You shall no more be remembered, for
I, Yahweh, have spoken.

34

35

36

37

e 𝔐 בָּרָק is to be revocalized after למען as בְּרֹק.
Cf. Ps 144:6. 𝔊 introduces a ἐγείρου (in clumsy imitation of v 15) probably in order to separate the two
purpose clauses which strike harshly together (in
dependence on the ἐξεγέρθητι of Zech 13:7?). 𝔊
translates the whole of v 33bβ simply by ומברק.

34a 𝔐 אל – על cf. note a to 1:17.

b For 𝔐 חללי רשעים, which is not to be emended,
cf. note a to v 30.

35a Instead of 𝔐 הָשֵׁב imperative "with the a
preserved in pause in the context," Bauer-Leander
§ 56 u'', we must read the infinitive absolute הָשֵׁב.

b 𝔐 אֶל־תַּעְרָהּ is misunderstood by 𝔊 μὴ κατα-
λύσῃς as אַל תַּעֲבֹר, cf. Jer 51:43 (in 𝔊 Jer 28:43).
𝔙 revertere ad vaginam tuam.

36a 𝔐 אנשים בערים. 𝔊 ἀνδρῶν βαρβάρων has possibly deliberately been selected as a play on בער.
The double emphasis of disorder and wildness,
which is present in the saying here, is well captured
in this translation.

37a 𝔐 לאש תהיה לאכלה betrays itself as a subsequent insertion by its bad grammatical assimilation (second masculine in a section which otherwise
uses the feminine). Cf. 15:4, 6.

Form

The repetition of the address ואתה בן אדם in vv 24 and
33 divides the unit vv 23–37 into two parts. The second
(vv 33–37) is a divine saying against the Ammonites
(but see below). It is made up in vv 33f of borrowings
from the preceding sections, and represents a later
addition to the prophecy of vv 23–32. It does not derive
from Ezekiel himself as will be demonstrated in detail
in the exposition.

In vv 23–32 Yahweh first of all commands the
prophet to perform a sign-action. This makes evident a
"situation at a road junction," which concerns the
alternative of a road to Rabbat Ammon or one to
Jerusalem. In a further passage (vv 26f), joined on with
כי expressing a reason, the prophet is informed of the
meaning of the action which he has been commanded
to perform, and of its significance for Jerusalem (v 28).
This opens the way for the divine saying, set out in
direct address, which is given to the prophet (vv 29–32).
Again this is divided up into separate sections. An
address to the people (second person plural), which
arises quite directly from what precedes, has added to
it in vv 30–32 a saying to the "prince of Israel" (second
person singular). This first addresses him in reproach
(v 30) and then with the divine message (vv 31f) in
which there is a repetition of the introductory messenger

formula.

Fohrer seeks to separate the address to the prince
from the rest of the section and to regard it as an independent unit. In its content, however, the concrete
application of the declaration of judgement, which is
left hidden in v 29 in the two brief words בכף תתפשׂי,
against the prince who is responsible (see below to
v 34b) may be regarded as a meaningful development.
Also it moves wholly within the framework of the events
and message of vv 24–29, so that no compelling necessity exists for separating off vv 30–32.

The connection of 21:24ff with the "narratives of
sign-actions" is evident, and we must compare what
has been said more fundamentally about them above.[32]
At the same time, however, we must assert that the
present text has its own distinctive character within
these narratives. Certainly here also, in the manner
that is significant of Ezekiel, everything is completely
swallowed up in the divine word, and the performance
of the action is not further described. However, as a
distinctive feature, it is striking that the sign-action
which the prophet is commanded to perform is not
fully unfolded. The prophet is to make a representation
of the two roads with their signposts. However, after
this, it is not then said that he is also, in the sign, to
portray the obtaining of an oracular decision and the

choice of the route in his action, which we should expect following the analogies in chs. 4f and 12, also 24:15–24 and 37:15–28. In accounting for this it is inappropriate to speak of a "disordered presentation" (Hölscher, *Hesekiel*). The impression that already in vv 24f we have before us a "bad mixture of image and reality" (Hölscher) has arisen especially from the additions introduced by a redactor in vv 24a (note a) and 25 (note a), who wanted to bring out the catchword "sword" here also. The original text points to a structure which was clear throughout, even though the sign-action which the prophet was commanded to perform has been forced into the background even more sharply than usual on account of the message proclaimed in the divine word. Thus vv 24–32 are skillfully constructed in a threefold pattern: 1) the action which the prophet is commanded to perform as a sign, and which is left in a fragmentary condition in regard to the event which is "signified," is followed by 2) the address of Yahweh to the prophet which reveals to him the action of the king of Babylon and interprets it in all its seriousness. From this arises 3) the plain command to preach to Jerusalem and its king.

The text is preserved in an elevated and clearly rhythmic prose. In it we encounter again the short cola, which are to be read with two or three accents and which we find particularly clearly in Ezek 7 and 16.[33] These formal peculiarities, which recall the other preaching of Ezekiel, forbid that we should deny to him this unit, even with all its formal distinctiveness of structure. This is supported by the distinctive and concrete historical message of the prophecy.

Setting

Herntrich and Bertholet affirm particularly strongly of this oracle that it shows the immediacy of having been delivered in Jerusalem itself. "If this unit had been uttered in Babylon it would have been a fiction. But it carries no traces of being fictional."[34] Admittedly the

declarations of judgement upon the people (v 29) and prince (vv 30–32) are spoken with a peculiar directness. Yet on closer examination undoubted features of a real verbal dialogue, such as for example we find in the prophecies of Amos or Jeremiah, are missing. The words of accusation are, in the end, couched in a general formulation. Above all the references to the king and the land show a considered distance. "Judah, which has its stronghold in Jerusalem" is already some distance away from the terminology current in the land "the cities of Judah and Jerusalem." Also the term "prince of Israel" for Zedekiah, the King of Judah, is the result of theological reflection.[35] The prophecy was spoken in the geographical distance of exile, as also the breadth of Yahweh's address to the prophet itself supports (vv 24–28). At Nebuchadnezzar's departure those in exile could very well have had information about the king's varied war aims.

In date the oracle belongs to the year 589 B.C., in which Nebuchadnezzar, after the defection of Zedekiah (and Ammon), marched westwards. O. Eissfeldt has offered the conjecture that the threat directed against the Ṣafā region in Jer 49:28–33 may also have this campaign as its background.[36] The decision of the Babylonian king about the choice of the first target of his campaign had still not been made by the time of Ezek 21:23ff. The unrest of the exiles, whose hearts were fearful with uncertainty, is echoed in the prophecy, as also the passionate anger of the prophet at Zedekiah's irresponsible action (cf. to Ezek 17).

Interpretation

■ **21:23, 24** In a fresh encounter the command is given to the "son of man" to mark out two roads.[37] The verb שִׂים, which is frequently (forty-one times) used in the book of Ezekiel (4:2; 21:27 the placing of battering rams; 4:4 imposition of guilt; 6:2; 13:17 and other passages, the turning of the face; 17:5 placing a tree; 19:5 a young lion and others), allows no completely

32 See above pp. 156f.
33 See above p. 201; p. 334. Cf. vv 26b, 27, 31.
34 Herntrich, *Ezekielprobleme*, 107.
35 *VT* 8 (1958): 84f; 79.
36 Otto Eissfeldt, "Das Alte Testament im Lichte der safatenischen Inschriften," *ZDMG* NF 29/104 (1954): 97.
37 For the formula for the coming of a message see

above pp. 144f; see above pp. 131f.

clear definition of the action demanded of the prophet. As in 4:1 is he to draw a plan on a tile? Or is he to draw it with his finger in the sand (John 8:8 ἔγραφεν εἰς τὴν γῆν), or is he to mark it with a sharp tool, and to make a right-angled fork with an ordinary stick? Only two more precise instructions are given: 1) The roads are to start out from *one* land. In the mention of the "land," as in the עיר of 4:1, an element of interpretation enters into the description of the sign. However, the mention of the sword of the king of Babylon, for whom the road is to be made ready and which comes rather early, must derive from the redactor of Ezek 21 (cf. notes a to vv 24 and 25). The picture which arises of the parting of the two roads, implicit in the mention of the common starting-point, is a development of the picture of a situation requiring a decision (cf. Heracles at the parting of the ways; Mt 7:13f; *Barnabas* 18–20; *Didache* 1ff). Here also we are concerned with a decision of a historical kind.

2) At the beginning of each of the two roads Ezekiel is to set up (again שׂים) a marked signpost. The noun יד used here designates in 1 Sam 15:12 the memorial sign which Saul set up (מציב) for his victory over Amalek. We must think of an inscribed memorial stone in the manner of the Mesha inscription. The memorial stone (יד) of Absalom is designated in 2 Sam 18:18 a מצבת. Since it was to preserve the memory of a name (בעבור הזכיר שׁמי), we should not exclude here also that it was inscribed, as we may conjecture also for יד ושׁם, which Is 56:5 promises in the temple (court) to eunuchs.[38] Signposts, such as marked roads in Mesopotamia,[39] are otherwise referred to in the Old Testament by the word נס (Is 5:26; 11:12; 13:2 and other passages). יד then seems to be clearly distinguished from נס, as the simple designation for a signpost (27:7 then "mast"), by its inscription.

■ **21:25** The two inscriptions of the signposts in Ezekiel's sign-action are notably formed with three words (cf. note c). In each the name of a capital city is connected with the relevant name of the land. The capital city of the Ammonites (present day *'ammān*) is, as a rule, abbreviated as "the great" (רבה). Cf. 2 Sam 11:1; 12:27, 29 and other passages. So then also Ezek 25:5.

Besides this, however, we find, in order to distinguish it from Rabbah in Judah (Josh 15:60), the fuller name רבת בני עמון (Dtn 3:11; 2 Sam 12:26; 17:27; Jer 49:2). It must be used in the present text with the force of a name of honor with an obvious meaning. This becomes clear from the parallel designation of the capital city of Judah, the name of which does not at first carry any correspondingly obvious rank of honor, and the defended character of which must therefore be expressed in another way. According to the older tribal geography, Jerusalem lay in the territory of the tribe of Benjamin (Josh 18:15ff). As a Jebusite city it was conquered by David and incorporated by him into the region of Judah of which he had already been chosen as king (2 Sam 2:4). Legally it remained his personal property as "the city of David."[40] The political dualism of Judah-Jerusalem, which continued after the separation of the two kingdoms, is still freely presupposed in Jeremiah's terminology.[41] Accordingly Jerusalem could not simply be defined as "Jerusalem of the Judeans," parallel to "Rabbah of the Ammonites." Thus, as already mentioned, some note of emphasis, corresponding to רבה, which would bring out the prestige and importance of the city, was necessary. It came therefore to the distinctive formulation: "Judah, which has its stronghold in Jerusalem." The faith in the special foundation of the city of God and its ultimate inviolability, which is expressed in the Zion psalms (46, 48, and others) and in Isaiah (28:16) and which is also presupposed in Ezek 38f, shines ambiguously through this nomenclature. In view of the real threat of judgement this title for Jerusalem could only be regarded as very questionable in its immediate situation. It reflects the dangerous sense of security of those still in Jerusalem, against which the judgement threatened by the prophet had to be proclaimed. The fall of the בצורה is also mentioned in Is 25:2; 27:10, cf. 36:1.

■ **21:26–28** This indeed is the revelation which Yahweh is giving to his prophet in the explication of the symbolic action (vv 26–28): the fortress of Jerusalem is threatened quite directly by the army of the Babylonian king. The catchword "sword," which in the redactional

---

38   See also Kurt Galling, "Erwägungen zum Stelen-
      heiligtum von Hazor," *ZDPV* 75 (1959): 9f.
39   Meissner, *Babylonien* 1, 341.

40   See Alt, "Jerusalems Aufstieg."
41   *VT* 8 (1958): 84f.

additions to vv 24f seeks to determine the theme, is not repeated. Instead, we have clearly described how the King of Babylon faced the decision about his campaign route, which would become a decision of judgement upon Jerusalem. From 2 Kings 25:6 we learn that Nebuchadnezzar, in his campaign of the years 589–587, had his center of operations in Riblah, a place the name of which, according to the evidence of 6:14, had a somber memory for Israel.[42] Commentators have constantly put forward conjectures where the forking of the ways was located, at which Nebuchadnezzar had to decide to take the road to Rabbah or to Jerusalem. A Babylonian army could reach a decision for the route to Jerusalem as early as Riblah and march south along the coast road past the Phoenician cities. However, it could also march along the east side of Antilebanon to Damascus and then decide there whether it would strike directly south on the east Jordanian plateau against Rabbah or west into the Jordan valley. It could then cross either by the sources of the Jordan south of Hermon or at the mouth of the Yarmuk valley south of the sea of Gennesaret and march against Jerusalem. For the present text, however, it is significant that any reference to the location of this decision is lacking. Since the prophet simply receives the commission to draw two roads "which go out from a land," he could also have in mind a decision which takes place directly at the borders of Mesopotamia. The prophet draws a fictional scene in which all the importance of a strategic decision is summed up, which would mean for Jerusalem a speedy judgement.

■ **21:26** War plans were not decided without the instruction of the deity. David took his decisions with the aid of a prophetic oracle (1 Sam 22:5) or that of the priestly ephod (1 Sam 23:9–12; 30:7f); cf. further 1 Sam 23:2, 4; 2 Sam 5:19, 23. Saul was in an uncontrollable anxiety because Yahweh no longer answered him before battle "neither by dreams, nor by lot (Urim), nor by the prophets" (1 Sam 28:6). So also

Thutmosis IV, at the news of a rebellion in Nubia, went up to the temple in order to receive council from Amun, who then spoke with him like "a father to a son."[43] Also in Assyria, before a campaign in the field, the gods were inquired of by means of sacrifice, and in the actual battle "the soothsaying priest went before the troops." By observation of livers and oil, through the interpretation of the dreams of the king or his own visions, he was able to declare what was to happen and so to assist the making of the right decision.[44]

In the threefold inquiry of deity which, according to Ezek 21:26, the Babylonian king conducted at the forking of the ways, features of Israelite oracle seeking are mixed with others of a specifically Babylonian coloring. The arrow oracle is otherwise nowhere else specially mentioned in the Old Testament. The reference to shaking out (קלקל) the arrows comes close phenomenologically to the procedure for the use of lots, which is otherwise well known in the Old Testament. This is especially so for the casting of lots with אורים and תמים. The lot which was cast (ירה Josh 18:6; השליך Josh 18:18; הפיל Is 34:17; Prv 1:14; ידד Joel 4:3; Ob 11; Na 3:10), so that one of the two differently marked stones was thrown out (יצא Nu 33:54; Josh 16:1; עלה Lev 16:9f; נפל Ezek 24:6), could also be said to be "cast in the lap" (הוטל Prv 16:33). Thus in the present text, where we are clearly concerned with deciding between two alternatives, we should think of casting arrows (from a quiver?), in which one arrow is thrown out. From v 27, where admittedly nothing further is said directly about arrows, the variant practice is also conceivable that the inquirer, after shaking up the arrows, puts his right hand into the quiver and finds the divine decision in the arrow which his hand seizes upon.[45] The scenes of shooting arrows in 1 Sam 20:20–22 and 2 Kings 13:14–19 are better left out of any explanation of Ezek 21:26. In the Babylonian sphere the arrow oracle has not so far been attested. However, there is evidence of it in the Bedouin-Arabian sphere.[46]

42 See above pp. 191f.
43 H. Bonnet, *Reallexikon der ägyptischen Religionsgeschichte* (Berlin, 1952), 562.
44 Meissner, *Babylonien* 1, 101.
45 So F. Küchler in *W. W. von Baudissin Festschrift*, BZAW 33 (Berlin, 1918), 290.
46 For example, the story, which was later wrongly ascribed to the *imra' alḳais*, of the man who abused

and cursed the oracular arrow of the stone idol of *ḍulḫalaṣa* in *tabāla*, when this told him to seek blood revenge for his father. Julius Wellhausen, *Reste arabischen Heidentums gesammelt und erläutert* (Berlin: Reimer, ²1897), 46f; R. Klinke-Rosenberger, *Das Götzenbuch kitāb al-'aṣnām des ibn al-kalbi*, Sammlung orientalistischer Arbeiten 8 (Winterthur: Winterthur, 1941), 48. Mohammed expressly forbids the

The inquiry of the teraphim, which is also mentioned in second place, appears to denote a common secular practice in Israel. We can certainly not reach a single clear understanding of its nature and meaning from the Old Testament references to it, so that Ackroyd has to conjecture that we have in the תרפים a collective name for various cult objects. When Rachel, according to Gen 31:19, 34f, takes with her the teraphim of her father and hides them underneath her, under a camel saddle, we may deduce a not too large representation of a family god (deriving from the Arameans?). The strange comedy in 1 Sam 19:13, 16, in which Michal deceives her husband's pursuers by teraphim put in David's bed, with a skin of goat's hair serving as an imitation of his head, leads us to think of a mask (for oracles?). The story of the Danite image mentions teraphim beside an ephod as the property of a sanctuary (Ju 17:5; 18:14, 17f, 20, similarly Hos 3:4). That the teraphim, which were strongly disapproved of later by the stricter Yahweh faith (1 Sam 15:23; 2 Kings 23:24), were a means of inquiry of God is also shown by Zech 10:2.[47]

Finally in "observing the liver," which is otherwise never mentioned in the Old Testament, but which is known from Babylonian accounts as a practice, already well-known at an early period and well refined in its details, we appear to come at last to a typically Babylonian feature.[48] A clay model from the period of the first Dynasty of Babylon shows the division of a liver into more than fifty segments, on which important marks are drawn for interpretation.[49] To this must be added text books of liver observation and collections of omen texts. In the palace of Mari no less than thirty-two models of livers were found.[50] That the observation of livers, however, was also not unknown in Canaanite

Palestine is shown by the find of a (markedly more primitive) model of a liver in Megiddo VII (1350–1150) and in Canaanite Hazor (Temple II, area H, of the excavations of 1958).[51]

The threefold action of the Babylonian king is summarized in the formulation קָסַם קֶסֶם. In distinction from 13:9, 23; 22:28 (the noun קֶסֶם only in 13:6, מִקְסָם in 12:24; 13:7), where a prophetic oracle is denoted by this expression, here the entire activity of procuring oracular decisions at the forking of the roads is in mind. Its designation as "the mother of the road" (אֵם הַדֶּרֶךְ)[52] shows how this "junction of two roads" (following v 24, not to be deleted as a gloss with Herrmann, Cooke, Fohrer) had routes going from it in two directions.

■ 21:27 When the oracular arrow "Jerusalem" (thought of as inscribed, following Nu 17:17, cf. Ezek 37:16?) falls into his right hand, the decision is taken. In an almost unbearable concentration of expression there is quite directly bound up with this a reference to the evil which will then come upon Jerusalem. Fierce shouting will be heard. צֶרַח is connected in Zeph 1:14 with the "Day of Yahweh," and in Is 42:13 the shouting of a warrior is ascribed to Yahweh himself. The noun is found in Jer 4:31 of the desperate cries of the dying. The war cry (תְּרוּעָה), which was originally at home in the sphere of the holy war, will be heard, and battering rams will be set up against the gates of the city.[53] Then siege walls will be built and siege works erected.[54]

■ 21:28 The coming danger is in no way lessened by the fact that in Jerusalem the Babylonian king's use of oracles could be ridiculed and ignored like the lying oracle of a false prophet (13:6, 9, 23). We should not ask the question: "How then could Jerusalem hear of that particular scene at the road junction in the far distance?" Only Jerusalem's unpreparedness for judge-

---

use of the arrow oracle for the division of portions of meat in *Sura* 5:4.

47 See also Georg Hoffmann and Hugo Gressmann, "Teraphim, Masken und Winkorakel in Ägypten und Vorderasien," *ZAW* 40 (1922): 75–137.

48 Meissner, *Babylonien* 2, 267–275.

49 *ANEP* 594.

50 Parrot, *Babylon*, page 144 note 1.

51 For Megiddo, *ANEP* 595 beside 594; for Hazor, *IEJ* 9 (1959): page 84 and plate 12c. For other evidence of the observation of livers see *RGG*³, s.v.

52 Scarcely satisfactorily interpreted by Joseph Reider,

"Contributions to the Scriptural Text," *HUCA* 24 (1952/3): 90f, by reference to Arabic *'umm eṭ-ṭarīk* as "the main part of the road," i.e., top part.

53 Paul Humbert, *La 'terou'a'; analyse d'un rite biblique*, Université de Neuchâtel; recueil de travaux publié par la Faculté des lettres 23 (Neuchâtel: Secrétariat de l'université, 1946); von Rad, *Krieg*, 11.

54 See above p. 162 to 4:2. See also Yigael Yadin, "Hyksos Fortifications and the Battering-Ram," *BASOR* 137 (1955): 23–32, who dates the invention of the battering ram back to the beginning of the second millenium B.C.

ment is concerned in the statement, since the city always regarded itself as secure in the face of the military plans of a foreign ruler, who took his campaign decisions with a technique of oracle-giving which was despised in Israel. With all sharpness the prophet formulates the surprising claim that in that "heathen" oracle the judgement of God is present, which reveals guilt, and upon it also the ministering of punishment will occur. A later addition, which is not attested by 𝕲 𝕷 𝕾 (note a), points to Zedekiah's crime of treason, which was fully described in Ezek 17.[55]

The expression מזכיר עון, like תפש, stems from the vocabulary of legal practice. Thus in the directions for the trial by ordeal of a woman suspected of adultery in Nu 5:13 תפש denotes being caught in the act. The meaning "to arrest" is found in 1 Kings 13:4; 18:40; 20:18; 2 Kings 10:14; Jer 26:8; 37:13f.[56] The sacrifice that is then necessary for the proof of guilt is then called in Nu 5:15 a מנחת זכרון מזכרת עון (in v 18 מנחת הזכרון). According to 1 Kings 17:18 the widow of Zarephath, whose son is threatened with death, despisingly reproaches the prophet, who has his lodging in her house, באת אלי להזכיר את עוני.[57] According to Nu 5, the divine oracle is called for when a question of guilt cannot be determined by men. Ezek 21:28 (29) must be regarded in the light of this background, where the prophet affirms with all sharpness that the oracular decisions, which the Babylonian king receives at the junction of the roads and which those in well-defended Jerusalem believe they can despise, carry within themselves the full weight of a divine decision, in spite of the Israelite contempt for such an oracle technique. Through it guilt will be revealed, brought to proof, and from there the "affliction," which continues the accusation, will be legally possible.[58] If Reventlow, "Mazkir," is correct

in his understanding of the title of the office of מזכיר (2 Sam 8:16; 20:24; 1 Kings 4:3) as the public prosecutor in law, then the Babylonian king is introduced directly into a specific official function in Israel. Unlike the משיח-office of Cyrus in Is 45:1, it is here a threatening office of one who sets in motion the processes of divine judgement.

■ 21:29 What stands in v 28, still in connection with the address to the prophet, appears again in v 29 in a command to preach publicly to the people. This is set out as a motivated declaration of judgement, in which the element of motivation has undergone a development which disrupts the balance of the saying. Its introductory יען הזכרכם is repeated again, with slight variations (note b), after the broad elaboration in two infinitive formulations in bα. There then follows in two short words the declaration of judgement (bβ). Motivation and declaration of judgement elaborate the assertions of v 28b. Thus it is now said here that Jerusalem's acts of rebellion and its sinful deeds will be revealed by the king of Babylon.[59] In הזכרכם, which is vocalized in two different ways (note b), there is expressed ambiguously that, beside the foreign accuser from Babylon, Jerusalem is itself its own accuser by its deeds. This public "denunciation" of Jerusalem will now be followed by its being dealt with by the stern hand (of the king of Babylon).

■ 21:30–32 The declaration of judgement reaches its climax then in an oracle addressed to the responsible prince of Israel, by which only Zedekiah can be meant. In the king's fate it will become plain how the "punishment," expressed in v 29 figuratively with a general legal term, will be accomplished historically upon Jerusalem-Judah. V 30 begins with an impassioned address.[60] The designation of the king of Judah as a

---

55 See now further Matitiahu Tsevat, "The Neo-Assyrian and Neo-Babylonian Vassal Oaths and the Prophet Ezekiel," *JBL* 78 (1959): 199–204.

56 Cf. above p. 307 to 14:5.

57 Cf. further Ezek 29:16.

58 For the forensic stamp of זכר and הזכיר see further Begrich, *Studien*, page 26 note 2; Hans-Joachim Kraus, *Psalmen*, 2 volumes, BK 15 (Neukirchen-Vluyn: Neukirchener, 1960), on Ps 109:14; Henning Graf Reventlow, "Das Amt des Mazkir. Zur Rechtsstruktur des öffentlichen Lebens in Israel," *ThZ* 15 (1959): 161–175.

59 For פשע see above pp. 308f to 14:11; for the noun עלילה, which, apart from this reference, is always in parallel with דרך, see above p. 316 to 14:22f.

60 For the title נשיא see above pp. 209, 273, 364 and below to 37:22–24.

prince of Israel (plural 19:1; 21:17; 22:6) again shows an elevated theological language at a distance from the direct political reality, see Excursus 2. The gloss in v 28 (note a) recalls, in dependence on Ezek 17, Zedekiah's broken vassal oath. The summons in v 30 makes no mention of any specific guilt of the king, but gives a summary accusation in the reproachful description חָלָל רָשָׁע. חָלָל does not here mean "the slain" ("You, as a guilty fallen warrior" Ewald, Smend), nor should we vocalize with Koehler-Baumgartner רֻשַׁע ("slain by wrongdoing"). Rather חלל is to be understood here with Gesenius-Buhl, from חָלַל "to desecrate," as "dishonored, impious" (*b Berakot* 18b combines both possibilities: "wrongdoer, who even during your lifetime will be called 'dead'"), which is clearly distinct from the innocent חֹל "profane" (cf. 22:26). This must certainly also here reflect indirectly the sacrilege of breaking the covenant, which places Zedekiah in the sphere of the sacriligious. Again we can see in this a priestly way of reckoning. It motivates the harsh threat, which is also built in to the summons to the prince: his "day" has come in a time of עֲוֹן קֵץ. Once again we encounter in this a strongly formulated assertion, with a very sharply defined vocabulary. The reference to the "day" recalls the harsh language of the day of Yahweh, as does the perfect בא which is connected with it.[61] Admittedly here this is altered by being related personally to the king as an individual, to whom then the suffix of יֹום is related. (Cf. 1 Sam 26:10; Ps 37:13.) In Ezek 7 also the reference to the "day" (of Yahweh) is connected with a further reference to the "end" (קֵץ). It is introduced here in the pregnant formulation עֲוֹן קֵץ, which recurs again in v 34 and 35:5. In view of the variety of meanings of עֲוֹן it denotes ambiguously both "guilt," which involves its own consequences, and "punishment," which is inflicted as a consequence.[62] The presence of the first meaning is certainly to be affirmed, against C. A. Ben-Mordecai, who wants to find only the second here

("ultimate calamity, final crash").[63] The reference to the end is then not to be understood here in connection with a philosophical doctrine of the end of time. As in Ezek 7 the end of all the old security of Israel in the face of the advent of the wrath of Yahweh, which will burst forth on account of the fullness of guilt (cf. Gen 15:16), is brought to expression.[64]

■ **21:31** The declaration of judgement (vv 31f) introduced by the messenger formula follows the impassioned and direct command. It is no longer preserved in the form of an address, but contains expressions, set out in the style of abrupt cries, which work like individual hammer blows and which finally have the effect, almost like an oath, of summoning the disaster.

First of all it is a call for the setting aside by the prince of his tokens of honor, with the violent removal of the insignia of his office. The turban (מִצְנֶפֶת) otherwise appears in the Old Testament (Ex 28:4, 37, 39; 29:6; 39:28, 31; Lev 8:9; 16:4) and in Sir (45:12) as a designation of the high priest's headband. However, it has entered into the high priests' adornment as an element of the older royal apparel.[65] On the other hand, the "coronet" (עֲטָרָה), about which, according to Barrois, nothing can be concluded with certainty from the Old Testament narratives, is still clearly mentioned as a sign of kingship, in Ps 21:4; 2 Sam 12:30 (also in the original text of Zech 6:11, 14).[66] It was sometimes a work of beaten gold, but it could also be of a linen material, set with a precious stone, with a diadem, or with decorative bands (cf. the Assyrian tiara). The removal of the insignia means the removal of royal authority.

In a series of further commands, which are in part no longer fully clear in their exclamatory brevity, an act of disaster becomes clear, which appears to extend beyond the fate of the person of the prince.[67] The cry appears to express the end of previous honor. The experience of humiliation (הַשָּׁפֵל) is also found in Jer 13:18, in an accusation against the king and queen and linked with

---

61   Cf. 7:12 and see above pp. 201f.
62   See also above pp. 164f, 167.
63   C. A. Ben-Mordecai, "The Iniquity of the Sanctuary: A Study of the Hebrew Term עָוֹן," *JBL* 60 (1941): 311–314.
64   See above pp. 203f.
65   Martin Noth, "Office and Vocation in the Old Testament" in *The Laws in the Pentateuch and Other Studies*,

     tr. D. R. Ap-Thomas (Philadelphia: Fortress, 1967), 235–236.
66   Barrois, *Manuel* 2, 55f.
67   For זאת לא זאת cf. note c.

removal of the crown. Has Ezekiel been influenced by this saying of Jeremiah's? Alongside the humiliation he immediately sets an exaltation, as in 17:24 (although in the reverse order). However, even if the adjectives are to be understood here as masculine (but cf. note d), the clause does not announce the exaltation of the humiliated Jehoiachin by the humbling of the now exalted Zedekiah (Smend, Ziegler *Ezechiel*). 21:31 is distinct from 17:24, where such an idea is rendered probable by the theme of the newly planted cedar branch, in that here the immediate context speaks only of judgement. In spite of the overthrow of all the old order, it is best not to speak of a "complete chaos" (Moran) because Old Testament faith, as may be adduced for 17:24, sees behind the humbling and exalting by Yahweh the act of a sovereign upholding of justice.[68]

■ **21:32** In the threefold עוה Herrmann has been able to argue, on the basis of parallels from Babylonian magical texts, that it carries something of the echo of a coercive magical saying.[69] In עַוָּה, which is only found here in the Old Testament, Moran, by reference to עוה "to twist," would hear a strong emphasis on "distortion." In any case we should not overlook that in the threatening formulation of v 32a the "I" of Yahweh begins to appear quite openly.

How then should we understand the conclusion of the royal saying in v 32b? It has long been noted that there is a striking similarity in bβ to Gen 49:10, the Shiloh text which was already understood messianically by 𝔗. Accordingly it is believed that we must see in Ezek 21:32 a reference to a future after the judgement. The אשר לו המשפט of 𝔐 is translated in this context (corresponding to the interpretation of שׁילה in Gen 49:10 as שֶׁלוֹ) with 𝔊 ᾧ καθήκει as "for whom it is fitting" (Smend), "who has a claim (to it)" (Kraetzschmar, Ziegler, *Ezechiel*), "who has a right to it" (Fohrer), "who is right" (Herrmann), "to whom the right be-belongs" (Cooke), "die er recht op heeft" (van den

Born), "die het recht heeft" (Aalders), "cui est jus (debitum)" (Knabenbauer). Bertholet affirms "a fleeting glance into a brighter future," whilst Herrmann says firmly: "v 32b can hardly be understood otherwise than in the narrower messianic sense." Fohrer does not believe he can go so far, but accepts the proposition that Ezekiel has interpreted in his own way "that obscure saying (i.e., Gen 49:10) and applied it to Jehoiachin." S. Mowinckel again conjectures that the saying is a conscious interpretation of an old messianic promise by the school of Ezekiel, which, in the early post-exilic age, set the hope of a genuine shoot of David against the governors and princes sponsored by the Persian overlords.[70] The great difficulty of all these interpretations consists in the fact that they all start from an understanding of the word משפט which is never so found in Ezekiel. An examination of the linguistic usage of משפט in the book of Ezekiel, to which Moran correctly points, indicates 23:24b as the closest parallel for the interpretation of 21:34. Here the phrase ונתתי . . . משפט, admittedly clarified still further by the added לפניהם, is found with the interpretation "to allot judgement." From this the understanding of the whole verse as a threat, which was already proposed by Auvray, becomes very probable.[71] Certainly the עד must not be regarded as indicating the terminus, if we wish to avoid an impossible reckoning of periods of time (against Auvray, Moran, note c). The word indicates that all that which has been threatened in the preceding impassioned words will come upon Jerusalem and its king by the man to whom Yahweh himself (as in 23:24) has committed the task of judgement. From this the saying takes on a clear relationship to the introductory symbolic action which shows how Nebuchadnezzar was sent out against Jerusalem by the oracular decision given at the junction of the roads. As the idea lies behind v 28 that he was commissioned as accuser in this mysterious and unusual way, so in v 32 it is affirmed further that Yahweh himself has also ordained him to

---

68 Moran, "Gen 49:10," 418; for exaltation-humiliation as a prerogative of royal power see also Donald John Wiseman, *The Vassal-treaties of Esarhaddon* (London: British School of Archaeology in Iraq, 1958), page 44 lines 191f.

69 Johannes Herrmann, "Zu Jer 22:29; 7:4," *ZAW* 62 (1949/50): 322.

70 Sigmund Mowinckel, *He That Cometh*, tr. G. W.

Anderson (Nashville: Abingdon, 1956), 174f.

71 P. Auvray in the *Bible de Jérusalem* (1949).

accomplish the judgement. If we affirm a relationship of the saying to Gen 49:10, which also would be supported by the use of the figurative images of the Judah oracle (Gen 49:8–12) in Ezek 19 (Moran), we can establish that Ezekiel has surprisingly made the ancient promise the vehicle of a message of total judgement.

■ **21:33–37** 21:23–32 have shown how the king of Babylon, in his campaign against the west, was guided by the decisions of an oracle to take the road to Jerusalem. What then happens to Rabbat Ammon, the name of which stood second on the signpost at the road junction? The lack of an answer to this question, which originally lay outside the field of view of the message of vv 23–32, was subsequently felt. In vv 33–37 a later addition has sought to answer this question in close dependence on the statements of the two preceding sections vv 15–22 and 23–32. We may raise the question whether it was the redactor of the whole chapter who also placed vv 33–37 under the catchword of "sword." Certainly it was not Ezekiel himself, to whom we cannot ascribe the citing of his own declarations, which is on the one side slavish, and on the other both inexact and replete with rearrangements of statements (cf. also 23:36ff). Vv 33–37 presuppose in any case the connection of the two sections in ch. 21 under the catchword "sword." The relationship to vv 1–13 is less clear.

In their details vv 33–37 raise considerable difficulties for their interpretation. After the introduction (v 33) the whole is to be understood as an oracle against the Ammonites, a conclusion which is also dictated by the oracle's position after vv 23–32 and its material connections with what precedes which in no way can be eliminated. Since it turns against the "gloating" of the Ammonites, the end of Jerusalem is presupposed, which according to the information of the foreign nation oracle in 25:1–5, 6–7 (cf. also Zeph 2:8) was greeted by the Ammonites with shameful delight.

After an introductory call to the prophet (v 33a) the oracle begins in v 33b with a summons to the sword. Since v 34 continues the saying in the second singular feminine, it must be understood as a vocative address. Vv 33f concern the destructive activity of the sword. In vv 35–37 then, after v 35a has spoken of the sheathing of the sword (note a) in a clause which is treated with unnecessary suspicion by Hölscher, *Hesekiel*, and Fohrer, a judgement upon the object addressed is expressed, in the form of an address in the second singular feminine. It is not at all clear, as most commentaries do not fail to observe, what entity could be meant other than the sword previously addressed. Even for those who change the address to the sword in v 34b (Cornhill, Ehrlich, Toy, Bertholet, Fohrer read אוֹתָה), the evidence remains lacking how the second feminine singular in vv 35b–37 can be understood otherwise than in relation to the sword—even though in the concluding statement a people appears as the entity addressed in the sword.

But this means that two possibilities can be considered for the interpretation: 1) Here the Ammonites are meant by the sword, unlike in what precedes. This has, as a consequence, the view that the Ammonites have attacked Jerusalem with the sword—a view which is in no way historically attested for the year 587 (for the historical position see below to 25:1–7). Indeed by the remark made in v 33a that we are concerned with the punishment of the "gloating" of the Ammonites this is expressly excluded.[72] Thus this interpretation proposed by Cooke is inapplicable. 2) The sword, as already in what precedes, represents the Babylonians and their king. Then the threat against the Ammonites, which we expect after the introduction in v 33a, is to be found in vv 33b, 34. The Ammonites are threatened with judgement in the same words as the city of Jerusalem previously. Beyond it vv 35–37 then speak of an end of judgement in an act of judgement upon the very instrument that executes it—a surprising assertion for the book of Ezekiel. It is otherwise not found in Ezekiel's own words, but can be supported by the preaching of Isaiah (10:5ff). The third possibility of interpretation, which is often found in commentaries, according to which vv 34f speak of the sword as the Babylonians, but then go on to speak in vv 35–37 of judgement upon the Ammonites (cf. Bertholet, Fohrer), is excluded by 𝔐, however much we should prefer this interpretation from the content elsewhere of Ezekiel's preaching.

If we recognize that throughout the sword is inter-

---

72 For the view of a second destruction of Jerusalem in the fifth century B.C. (Julian Morgenstern, "Jerusalem—485 B.C.," *HUCA* 27 [1956]: 101–179, especially 109–114) see below to 25:1–7.

preted as the "sword of the king of Babylon" (cf. v 24), as Bewer argues for 𝔐, and van den Born, at least for an original text underlying 𝔐 here, then the call for the sheathing of the sword (v 35) appears as a complete contrast to the statement about the drawing (הוציא) of the sword in vv 8–10.[73] Also in this case the remark that the judgement will take place in the land of the origin of the sword becomes more meaningful than in the application to the Ammonites, in which case it would merely state the obvious. (Cf. the parallel statements regarding Egypt in 29:14.)

■ 21:33 The beginning of the section is entirely borrowed from v 14—even to the superfluous repetition of the introductory אֱמֹר here in the form ואמרת (cf. note b to v 14). Here, however, the address and motivation of the command to speak have already entered into the introduction.[74] In the saying itself, first of all the beginning of the sword song from v 14 is cited. To this is added directly a statement of purpose from the addition in v 15. This shows some transposing of the statements. That in place of the "sharpened" sword the "drawn" (literally "opened," cf. Ps 37:14) sword appears perhaps already anticipates v 35, the command to sheathe it. The following passive participle qal מרוטה is similar to פתוחה.[75] If להכיל is rightly understood (note d), then this emphasizes the threatening side of the sword still more strongly. Its destructive wrath is now directed according to v 33a against Ammon.

■ 21:34 The statements of v 34 are cited from the section vv 23–32. The sword rages against Ammon because in Ammon lying oracles have been given in its favor (thus the לך must be understood differently from the להם of v 28). The formal correspondence of v 34aα, which has been expanded by a parallel statement in the formal language which is otherwise normal in Ezekiel (cf. vv 13:6f, 9, 23; 22:38), with v 28aα must not prevent us from recognizing that the statement must here be interpreted differently. What is referred to in v 28 as the mistaken judgement of the people of Jerusalem

regarding the historically effective oracle of the Babylonian king at the junction of the roads has become here, in line with Ezek 13, a false instruction from the native seers of Ammon which in reality points the road to their judgement. Thus here the impious men, who are described by the expression which in v 30 qualifies the "prince of Israel," are affected by the judgement which in v 28 is proclaimed against the prince. By way of elaboration there is added the comment that the sword will come upon their necks. The figure of speech, which Jahn surprisingly wanted to interpret as a bond of friendship between Ammon and Judah, is not otherwise found in the Old Testament.

■ 21:35 This entire proclamation of judgement upon Ammon preserved in the form of a citation is followed in vv 35–37 by a continuation which leaves behind altogether the parallel Ammon-Israel (Judah) and strikes out into a new area of proclamation. This certainly does not justify (against Bewer) the separation of vv 35–37 as a unit on its own.[76] Rather the continuation arises quite consciously out of the citation, which belongs to what precedes. The summons to the sword to stop, which basically is interested less in the end of the judgement upon Ammon than in that upon Israel, appears to have arisen quite formally. It commands a halt to the action of vv 8–10, in order thereby to prepare at the same time the coming judgement upon the instrument of judgement itself. The cry "sheathe it again" is obviously made with reference to the removal of the people bringing judgement from Palestine, where they have raged against Jerusalem and Ammon, to the place of their origin.[77] In an important parallel it is further designated as the "the place where you were created."[78] In Ezekiel the verb ברא in the nip'al is found again 28:13, 15 (pi'el 23:47 in a different sense). The striking emphasis on the createdness of those addressed again fits better with the arrogant superpower than with the small kingdom of Ammon. Yahweh will bring judgement upon the instrument of judgement,

---

73 Bewer, "Textual Notes," 162f.
74 For a reference to the shameful delight of the Ammonites cf. to 25:3.
75 Cf. notes c to v 14, b to v 15, e to v 20.
76 Bewer, "Textual Notes," 162f.
77 For מכרותיך see above p. 322 note b to 16:3; cf. 29:14.
78 For the verb ברא, which originally stemmed from

cultic language, see F. Böhl, "ברא, bārā, als Terminus der Weltschöpfung im at.lichen Sprachgebrauch" in At.liche Studien Rudolf Kittel zum 60. Geburtstag, BWAT 13 (Stuttgart, 1913), 42–60; Paul Humbert, "Emploi et portée du verbe bârâ (créer) dans l'Ancien Testament," ThZ 3 (1947): 401–422.

which has fulfilled its usefulness, in its own homeland. Is 37:29, 34 similarly refers to such a return of the Assyrian king and then in 37:38 to the judgement upon Sennacherib in his own city of Nineveh.

■ **21:36** In a further description of the judgement, echoes of Ezekiel's language are mixed with quite distinctive independent formulations. The "outpouring of wrath" is elsewhere expressed by Ezekiel with the use of the word חמה (7:8; 9:8; 14:19; 20:8, 13, 21 and other passages—with זעם again 22:31). The "breathing out blazing wrath" (אש עברתי again 22:21, 31; 38:19) could be influenced by 22:21 where, in connection with the allegory of the furnace, breathing out (נפח instead of הפיח 21:36) is appropriately mentioned. We may further question whether in v 37aα, which has certainly been added later (cf. note a), it is only by chance that the image of fire reappears, which was earlier dominant in the first sword prophecy (vv 1–12). The "giving into the hand" has its counterpart in 16:39; 23:9, 28. The reference to "barbarians" (note a to v 36), who are to bring judgement upon Babylon, is peculiar. Should we see in this a remote allusion to the Persians, who came from the previously little known Iranian highlands? The חרשי משחית, in both words, strikingly recalls Is 54:16. Also the statement that blood will be in its land at once recalls Ezekiel's summary formulations, according to which blood comes upon a person (18:13), or his head (33:4), or in the midst of a city (22:13; 24:7), but however it presents, in combination with בתוך הארץ, an entirely distinctive formulation. In this we shall scarcely, following 24:7f, have to think of blood which is covered with earth and is therefore hidden and silenced by it, although soon afterwards the extinguishing of any memory (again 25:10) is mentioned (so Smend, von Orelli). It must refer to the blood of judgement, which the strange judge will himself exact in the land (Herrmann).

The אני יהוה דברתי, which for the first time is joined by כי (cf. further 26:14, also 23:34; 26:5), concludes the oracle.[79]

Aim

The forceful prophetic oracle vv 23–32, which is tense and which is shot through with intense excitement, was given at a time of far-reaching decision. The Babylonian army, which was to punish Zedekiah's treason, had started out from Babylon. Among the circles of the exiles something of the war aims of Nebuchadnezzar may have been heard. The questions arose compulsively: where would the blow fall? Would it begin with Ammon or Egypt, so that further room for maneuver would be left to Jerusalem? Or would it be Jerusalem?

Behind the obvious considerations there lay the basic questions: it was not a matter of a particular nation, but of the remnant of the people of God which had its last line of defense in the fortress of Jerusalem. How would its destiny be decided? As the heathen army approached it, there was "the oracle-priest at the head of the troops," who thought that by the superstitious practices of his techniques of oracle-giving he could determine the outcome.[80] Jerusalem stood, highly exalted (Ps 48), defended by God himself (Ps 46), the city at the center of the earth,[81] of which Isaiah had preached that the enemy who thought they could destroy the place of God's costly foundation stone (Is 28:16) would be trampled upon on God's mountain (Is 14:25, cf. Ezek 38f). This was the city in which men knew God's prophetic word rather than superstitious oracle practices (Dtn 18:9–22). In it lived the Davidic ruler on whom the ancient divine promise rested (2 Sam 7) and of whom the community knew that God would stand up for his anointed one against the raging of the heathen (Ps 2). The entire sacred tradition of the historically founded community was at risk in this hour when the angry king of Babylon marched out to deliver the blow of destruction. Must not God himself at this hour, when everything was at stake, stand by his history, his tradition, for the religious benefit of his people—against the heathen, idolatrous pressure which had set out to destroy the city of God?

The prophet answered this question by his sign-action, out of which his message was preached. His answer was an uncompromising "No!" God is not with the revered sacred city and he does not act through the decisions of the legitimate office-bearers of the people of God. He is with the heathen ruler and lets his decision

79 See above p. 176 to 5:15.
80 See above p. 443.
81 See above pp. 174f to 5:5.

be given by the strange work of the heathen practice of an oracle-priest—not in the temple in Jerusalem, but at the crossroads beyond the borders of the land of Israel. Therein the sovereignty of God is preached who can even make the most distant person—a king who knows nothing of him and a heathen mantic priest who appears blatantly to dishonor his name—into an agent of his judgement. To the people of God, however, it is proclaimed that they must consent to such, even when he stands outside of their pious forms and confessions, but yet has been made by God into a discloser and accuser of their guilt.

Remorselessly God here hunts his people down out of the defenses of their seeming piety in their own self-sufficient lives. The task of being judge is handed over to the heathen ruler before whom the disloyalty of the chosen bearer of highest honor in the community becomes clear and his sacred insignia are rolled in the dust. In all this God is at work. There can be no hiding in a place of piety, no defense behind consecrated offices and traditions. God can deal with his people from out of the midst of the heathen world and call it to give account by heathen men. God is entirely free in his judgement, which stands as a threat directly over his own people. When, according to *b 'Abodah Zarah* 4a, Raba says: "The Holy One, blessed be he, said to Israel: When I judge the Israelites then I will not judge

it as the nations of the world, of which it is said: Ruins, ruins, ruins will I make it (Ezek 21:32), rather will I punish it as with the pecking (פיד) of a hen (i.e., bit by bit)" then the sacred power of the divine judgement, which Ezekiel proclaimed, is completely denied.

The late postscript in vv 33–37 makes two necessary additions to this. If—so runs the first—a fugitive from the judgement should consider he has the right to treat with contempt the judgement which has come from God, then he will know that God's sword will also at last turn against him. God's judgement will also bring those who have been spared to fear and remorse (Rom 11:19f).

The other runs: If the instrument of God's judgement should itself choose to have an unlimited office, then it will know that that judgement, in its holy righteousness, will also confront the instrument of its own activity. In all this the people are to learn that God's ultimate purpose is not that the sword should be unsheathed, but that it should come to be put back in its sheath.

22

The City of Blood

1 Then the word of Yahweh came to me:
2/ And you, son of man, will you (not)
judge—judge[a] the city of blood! And
make known to her all her abominations
3/ and say: Thus has [the Lord][a]
Yahweh spoken: 'You city,'[b] which
sheds blood in its midst, so that its
time (of judgement) comes, and which
makes for itself[c] idols, so that it
becomes unclean—4/ through your
blood,[a] which you have shed, you have
burdened yourself with guilt, and
through your idols, which you have
made, you have become unclean and
have brought near your days[b] (of
judgement) and 'brought on the time'[c]
(=the end) of your years. Therefore I

22: 2a The second התשפט of 𝔐 is not attested by 4
2 MSS 𝔊 (𝔊⁹⁶⁷ agrees with 𝔐) 𝔖. The doubling of
התשפט, however, is shown by 20:4, where 𝔊 also
agrees, to be an idom of Ezekiel's. 23:36, which is
undoubtedly secondary, shows a subsequent simplifying of the expression. In 𝔊 the diversity in the
translations of the formula here and in 23:36 (εἰ or
οὐ κρινεῖς) on the one hand and in 20:4 (note a to
20:4) on the other is striking.

3 3a אדני is lacking in 𝔊 (attested by 𝔊ᴮ) 𝔏ˢ 𝔙, see
Excursus 1.

b 𝔊 'Ὦ πόλις, 𝔏ˢ o civitas. Cornill, Bertholet, Fohrer would also add here an אוי and refer to 24:6,
where 𝔊 𝔏ˢ translate a (הדמים) עיר אוי with the
same words. Graphically it is more probable that
the article of עיר has fallen out after יהוה by haplography, and originally העיר was intended as an
address form (cf. v 5 and Gesenius-Kautzsch § 126e).

c 𝔐 עליה literally "with her," parallel to the
בתוכה of a. So 𝔗 𝔖 בגוה. Ehrlich, Randglossen: "over
and above." 𝔊 κατ' αὐτῆς, 𝔏ˢ adversus se, 𝔙 contra
semetipsam understand על as adversative.

4 4a 𝔐 דמך "thy blood," anticipating what follows,
means "the blood poured out in you." The reading
of 𝔊 (𝔏ˢ) ἐν τοῖς αἵμασιν (plural αἵματα as in v 2)
αὐτῶν, to which we must add "the men in the city"
as a word of relation, seeks to avoid this duplication
of the expression. 𝔖 בדמא, 𝔗 בחובת דם זכיי smooth
the text by giving up the suffix of 𝔐 דמך.

b 𝔐 ימיך, since Cornill's categorical judgement
on the text, is usually changed to יומך, cf. Jer 50:31.
However, appeal to 𝔗 does not amount to proof,
since its יום תבריך is not a translation, but represents an explanatory paraphrase. 𝔊 𝔖 𝔙 support 𝔐.
The plural usage of "the approach of the days (of
judgement)" is found in 12:23. It is further supported by the parallel plural שנות.

c 𝔐 ותבוא עד שנותיך "And you have come to
your years," which may be understood from the
usage בוא בימים found in Gen 18:11; 24:1; Josh
13:1 for age and the approach of death, raises difficulties on account of its masculine form. However,
ותבוא could have arisen from וַתָּבֵא by a scribal
error with the transposition of א and ו which is often
found (cf. note a to 14:1). Besides the causative-
accusatory ותקריבי of the parallel expression the
purely indicative form of expression of 𝔐 is also
striking in its content. Since 𝔊 καὶ ἤγαγες καιρὸν
ἐτῶν σου, 𝔙 et adduxisti tempus annorum tuorum also
support the expected causative formulation here,
we should prefer the reading וַתָּבֵאִי and conjecture
behind עד an error for עת. The latter is also supported by 𝔖 עידן בישתך and 𝔗 זבנא דשניכי. Or was
there an עד roughly synonymous with עת (note c
to 16:7)? Cf. also Driver, "Linguistic Problems,"

have made you a disgrace among[d] the nations and an object of scorn in all lands. 5/ Those near (to you)[a] and those far from you rejoice over you, who are famous for your uncleanness[b] and great on account of your (evil) tumult![c]

6 See, the princes of Israel[a] in you have each one thrust in his (powerful) arm[b] to shed blood. 7/ Men despise their father and mother in you; the alien[a] they have ill-treated[b] in your midst; they oppress orphans and widows in you. 8/ You treat my sanctuaries with utter contempt[a] and desecrate my sabbaths.[a] 9/ Slanderers[a] are in you, who work to shed blood. And on[b] the mountains men in you have feasts. They commit lewdness in your midst. 10/ In you 'a man has' intercourse with the wife of his father;[a] men in you violate women in their monthly uncleanness. 11/ Each one commits outrage with the wife of his neighbor, and each lewdly defiles his daughter-in-law, and each abuses his sister in you, the daughter of his father.[a] 12/ In you men have accepted bribes in order to shed blood; you[a] take usury and interest and violently wrest unjust gain from your neighbor, and have forgotten

68.

d 𝔐 לגוים, MSS Edd בגוים.

5 5a 𝔊 πρὸς σέ, 𝔖 לכי (the sequence near-far is thereby reversed, cf. 6:12) explicitly add the word of relation lacking in the first member of 𝔐.

b Literally: unclean in name (title).

c 𝔐 רבת המהומה. 𝔊 πολλὴ ἐν ταῖς ἀνομίαις, 𝔖 סגיאת בעוליה, 𝔙 grandis interitu must be regarded as interpretations and not as evidence of a different underlying text (BH³).

6 6a 𝔊 οἴκου Ἰσραηλ.

b 𝔐 לְזְרֹעוֹ is understood by 𝔊 πρὸς τοὺς συγγενεῖς αὐτοῦ, 𝔖 לשרבתה as לְזַרְעוֹ and apparently interpreted of the favoritism towards relatives of the rulers of Jerusalem. So also would Honeyman, "Euphemism," 222, and van den Born understand it.

7 7a 𝔊 adds the copula, cf. note a to 1:4. For the rest 𝔊 𝔖, in their translations of לַגֵּר by πρὸς τὸν προσήλυτον and לאינא דמתפנא לותי (similarly 14:7; 22:29; 47:22f), already think of the proselytes of a later time who had turned to the Yahweh faith (לותי).

b For the form of expression עשה בעשק we must compare, beside the עשה בחמה of 22:12, עשה בלא משפט 8:18; 23:25, עשה בשנאה 23:29 22:29 with emended text). In 23:25, 29 (22:29 with emended text), however, the object is introduced with את and not with ל. Cf. 22:14. Since in 18:18; 22:29 the formulation is found with a cognate object עשק עשׁק we must consider whether in the present text also the עשו בעשק could have arisen from a scribal error for עשקו עשק. 𝔗 אנסו אונסא could support this.

8 8a 𝔊, which at the beginning adds the copula (note a to 1:4) and at the conclusion adds ἐν σοί, assimilates the verbs to the 3rd plural of v 7.

9 9a 𝔐 אנשי רכיל is understood by 𝔊 as ἄνδρες λῃσταί "robbers," and by 𝔖 as גברא תגרא "traders." 𝔊 again introduces ἐν σοί.

b על – אל cf. note a to 1:17. For the rest the textual tradition is clear. There are no grounds for a change to על הדם following 33:25 (against Herrmann, Toy, Bertholet).

10 10a literally: "men in you uncover the shame of their father." The versions clearly attest גלו, instead of 𝔐 גלה, which is to be expected following the parallel ענו. Geiger, Urschrift, 394f, argues for taking גלה as a deliberate weakening of the shocking expression.

11 11a 𝔖 takes all, and 𝔊 the first and third verbs as third person plural.

12 12a 𝔊 𝔖 add respectively ἐν σοί and בכי and read here (𝔖 also with the following verbs) the third person plural. However, the second person singular of 𝔐 must be original, since 𝔐 seeks to avoid the monotony of a repeated לקחו, and the conclusion of the speech in v 12 undoubtedly emphasizes a personal address.

13 me, says [the Lord][b] Yahweh.

13 See, I clap "with my hands"[a] at your
unjust gain which you have made, and
at your 'bloodguilt,'[b] which has
occurred in your midst. 14/ Will your
courage last; will your hands remain
firm in the days[a] when I deal with
you? I, Yahweh, have spoken and I will
act. 15/ And I will scatter you among
the nations and disperse you among the
lands and destroy your uncleanness in
you.[a] 16/ I will let myself be profaned[a]
by you in the eyes of 'the nations,'[b]
and you will[c] know that I am Yahweh.

b אדני is lacking in 𝕲 𝕮, see Excursus 1.

13 13a 𝔐 והנה הכיתי כפי אל בצעך. 𝕲 ἐὰν δὲ ἐπάξω
χεῖρά μου πρὸς χεῖρά μου ἐφ' οἷς συντετέλεσαι (so
𝕲⁹⁶⁷, in 𝕲ᴮᵛ πρὸς χεῖρά μου is lacking). If we do not
regard ἐπάξω as an inner Greek corruption from
πατάξω which is found in the later witnesses (cf.
Wevers, "Septuaginta-Forschungen," 127), then
this points to a reading והנה הבאתי כפי אל כפי.
Here we should regard הבאתי, or הביתי as a corruption of an original הכיתי; although in 𝔐 we
must further conjecture the omission of a (עַל =)
אל כפי after כפי אל by haplography. Cf. 𝕾. For the
idiom הכה כף אל כף cf. 21:19, 22, besides the
shorter הכה בכף 6:11.
  b 𝔐 דמך. The following היו demands the reading
דמיך, attested by 𝕲.

14 14a The change from 𝔐 לימים to ליום, which
Ehrlich, *Randglossen*, BH³, Bertholet conjecture by
reference to v 4, is unsupported in the tradition and
is not demanded by v 4; cf. note b to v 4.

15 15a V b is lacking in 𝕾.

16 16a 𝔐 ונחלת בך, 𝕲 καὶ κατακληρονομήσω ἐν σοί,
𝕾 וארתכי, 𝖁 *et possidebo te* derive ונחלת from נחל
"to inherit" and introduce the Deuteronomistic
idea, not found in Ezekiel, of Israel (Jerusalem) as
the inheritance of Yahweh, cf. von Rad, "Promised
Land"; Wildberger, "Israel." However, 𝕲 𝕾 𝖁 𝕿
(ואיתקדש בך), 'Α καὶ κατακληροδοτήσω ἐν σοί, καὶ
κατα(σ)τρώσω σέ must be followed in reading the
first person singular, and ונחלתי be restored, and
this be derived from חלל, Gesenius-Kautzsch § 67 u.
Cf. the exposition. Breuer translates 𝔐 "Thus you
will recover yourself again in the eyes of the nations;" Driver, "Three Notes," page 357 note 2,
would take נחל as "to sift (pass through a sieve)."
נחל in Ezekiel in 46:18; 47:13f.
  b 𝔐 גוים, better הגוים with MSSᴷᵉⁿ 𝕲 𝕾 𝕿.
  c 𝕲 𝕿 second person plural, 𝕾 second person singular feminine.

Form

First of all the formula for a divine saying in v 12 serves
at once as external evidence for the question about the
structure and unity of 22:1–16. Van den Born has made
the conjecture that the following verses 13–16 then
represent a subsequent expansion of the unit. The
formula would then be regarded as a concluding formula of the original section.

In order to answer this question we must consider the
structural purpose which underlies the whole section.
This is clearly expressed in the introduction in vv 1f.
The prophet is summoned, as in 20:4 (cf. the echo in
23:36), to "judge" and "to declare abominations."
This matter of "accusation" has already been found in

chs. 16 and 20.[1] After this introduction we should then
specifically expect in the saying that follows a revelation of sin as a part of a process of judgement. This is
what we find in 20:5ff where the "abominations of the
fathers" are revealed in a review oriented towards the
historical order of Israel, and from this the threat of
judgement which stands over contemporary Israel is
made known.

The "accusation" in 22:1ff characteristically differs
in two points from the formulation of the accusation in
20:1ff. Whereas in Ezek 20 the history of the fathers is
told in the third person to the men who came to inquire
of the prophet, and this is thoroughly adhered to, in
22:1ff the oracle changes almost immediately into

direct address to the Jerusalem of the present. The bloody city of Jerusalem is thereby very fully apostrophized. The resumption of the initial address (v 3aβb) in v 5b shows that the whole complex 3aβ–5 must be understood form-critically as an elaborate vocative summons. The corpus of the accusation proper first begins with vv 6ff. This elaborate mode of address, for which we may find a formal counterpart in the comforting statements about the people addressed in Deutero-Isaiah's oracles of salvation (such as 41:8f in the section 41:8–13), hides within itself a certain anticipation of what follows. Thus vv 3aβ–4a(5b) contain a reproachful description of those addressed. In vv 4b–5a there then follows, introduced with על כן, already a divine threat of punishment.

To this we may add a further consideration: whilst the accusation of sin in Ezek 20 is unfolded with the materials of Israel's historical traditions, in 22:1ff this unfolding takes place quite simply according to the divine law set out without any mention of the dimension of historical depth. This is presupposed in the form of a series of apodictic laws, which in content stand particularly close to H. This brings Ezek 22:1ff very close to the formulations of ch. 18 and 33:10ff, where the righteous and the unrighteous are described by reference to such a series of laws.[2] Whereas in ch. 18, however, something of the context of such a series of laws in worship in the temple can be seen, at which "life" was promised, in ch. 22 all this is dropped, and we can now only see the naked series of laws, by which norm the unrighteousness of the city of blood is revealed. Instead of it the series of laws here therefore is now very firmly embedded in the theme of ch. 22. Through a threefold "in order to shed blood" (is the number three a pure chance, in view of its liturgical importance in Is 6:3; Jer 7:4?) it is clearly linked in vv 6, 9, 12 with the oracle against "the city which sheds blood." Through the בך "in you," which is repeated no less than nine times, and the emphatic בתוכך "in your midst," which appears twice, it is finally joined to the vocative of the introduction 3aβ–5. These considerations oppose our seeing in vv 6ff an addition as Fohrer does. We should thereby rob the accusatory speech of its particular

force.

However, the question raised by van den Born is still not answered, whether vv 13–16 belong to the accusation as an original element. The fact that in the summons in 3aβ–5 reference is already made to the divine judgement shows that it is not impossible that after the accusation in vv 6–12 a declaration of judgement has been set out. Van den Born has rightly pointed out the striking introduction of this legal pronouncement by והנה, instead of the expected על כן or לכן as in v 4. והנה is only used in 16:27 in a section which has probably been added later to introduce a legal pronouncement (there in respect of a review of the past) directly after reproach. We can further point out that the conclusion of the legal pronouncement of vv 13–16 at first begins somewhat abstrusely with the catchword בצע which has just been used (v 12), before going on secondly to use the particular catchword דם, which we expect here. Beyond it the formulation of the threat as a proof-saying, which brings a new accent into the accusation (cf. the analogous subsequent addition in 20:26), makes it more probable that an original accusation, which ended with a concluding formula in v 12, has subsequently been expanded by an explicit threat of judgement in the form of a proof-saying.

Regarding the formal structure of 22:1ff we can further establish that the *parallelismus membrorum* (very marked in the address vv 3aβ–5) gives to the oracle the character of an elevated style without our being able to mark a fixed meter. It is the style of smooth, metrically stylized prose, which is repeatedly found in Ezekiel.

Setting

The concreteness of the accusations against Jerusalem is for Hölscher an argument for not regarding the saying as genuine: "In the mouth of Ezekiel, living at a remote distance, the detailed descriptions of conditions in Jerusalem stand out strangely."[3] With the same argument, however, Herntrich and Bertholet believe they can show that Ezekiel must himself have spoken in Jerusalem: "Either the section was spoken in Jerusalem, or it is a purely literary construction."[4]

Once we recognize, however, that the prophet has

1   See above p. 335; p. 405.
2   See above pp. 374–377.
3   Hölscher, *Hesekiel, der Dichter*, 117.
4   Herntrich, *Ezekielprobleme*, 107.

not put together here separate perceptions of misdeeds in Jerusalem, but, as in the description of the wicked in 18:10–13, measures this against existing collections of laws and then (as in a different way also in chs. 16, 20, 23) utters a total judgement, then the heaping together of the most concrete declarations shows again a certain distance from actual events in Jerusalem. What we find in Hos 4:1f or Jer 7:9f further supports this. A certain trait of doctrinaire speech, which derives from an overall view, and which simply makes affirmations, without enumerating individual facts, is not to be denied here (as also in another way in ch. 20). Ezek 22:1ff also introduces into the process the spiritual understanding of judgement upon Jerusalem by those already sitting in the darkness of judgement. For those in Jerusalem Ezek 22 could only be an immense exaggeration.

Had the catastrophe of 587 already taken place? In view of the material parallels in 20:1ff and its dating, we can certainly not exclude that 22:1–16 also is concerned with a reckoning with the sins of Jerusalem before the ultimate fall of the city.

Interpretation

■ **22:1, 2** The address, which comes to the "son of man" as a divine event, commands him to take up the task of "making accusation" against the bloody city.[5] As already in 20:4 the forensic "judging" (שפט) is explained in the parallel by a formulation of priestly-legal language. For הודיע תועבות we should compare the הודיע of v 26 and 44:23. Over against the office of the priest who gave instruction in ritual ordinances there appears here the office of the priest-prophet making accusation against ritual offenses (תועבות). His "judging" in this introductory speech is already set firmly under the viewpoint of sacral law. In the reproach "bloody city" (עיר הדמים) alone that need not be so. When Nahum, who spoke a generation before Ezekiel, attacked Nineveh as the "bloody city" (3:1), this had in mind the political brutality of Assyrian domination and the "plundering" (2:14) of the lion (2:12f). Isaiah's polemic against the bloodstained hands of the people of Jerusalem (1:15) also had in mind the social

oppression of the poor, as the continuation shows. However, the fundamental position of P's "Blood Law" in Gen 9:4f shows how closely in priestly thinking crimes of blood, the sins of social oppression, and ritual disorder come together, which the modern mind holds apart. Thus in H an offense against the correct method of sacrifice can be designated as bloodguilt: "It shall be reckoned as blood (guilt) against this man; he has shed blood" (Lev 17:4).[6] Blood is a "quite peculiar liquid."[7] In crimes involving blood not only is man's physical life power touched, but also a fundamental taboo, which is also encountered in ritual offenses.[8] Thus "bloodguilt," in the priestly understanding, becomes a comprehensive category of guilt.

■ **22:3** Thus we can understand that the reproach "bloody city," which reappears in 24:6, 9, but has already been prepared for in 7:23; 9:9; 11:6, can be interpreted in the summons vv 3aβ–5 by a double accusation of shedding blood (regarded as a legal offense also in 16:38; 23:45) and of making idols. Both belong fundamentally together. Where a proper fear before the One, who alone is holy, is lost and men impiously prepare their unclean idolatry,[9] there reverence for life and the life of one's neighbor disappears.

■ **22:4** Just as man by his idolatry dangerously involves himself with uncleanness, so by shedding blood he enters into "guilt." The Hebrew verb אשם (in Ezek again 25:12; 35:6 with emended text) must therefore clearly not be interpreted onesidedly morally or forensically. It contains at one and the same time the assertion that the "guilty" person has entered into a sphere of corruption and harm. The root אשם can hardly be separated etymologically from the root שמם. Thus in Ps 34:22 "to be condemned" (so ZB) is parallel to "to be killed"; in Is 24:6 it is parallel to "to be consumed by the curse." 2 Chr 19:10 sees as a consequence of becoming guilty the intervention of the divine wrath (קצף). Similarly Ezek 22 also is aware that uncleanness and "guilt," like a harmful infection of the human body, bring on the day of destruction. According to v 3 the bloody city is threatened with "its time" (for עת as the καιρός of judgement cf. 7:7, 12; 21:30, 34; 35:5). According to v 4 it itself brings near the days (of judge-

---

5   See above pp. 131f; pp. 144f.

6   See Gerardus van der Leeuw, *Religion in Essence and Manifestation*, tr. J. E. Turner (New York: Harper

& Row, ²1963).

8   Johnson, *Vitality*, 71–74.

9   See above pp. 186f for גלולים.

ment), and it brings on its "years" (see note c).[10] Thereby in the "years" the long period in which the judgement has been due is touched upon (cf. 4:4–8).

To the vague references to the judgement which is to follow the critical time of the "moment of destiny"[11] there is immediately added the personal declaration according to which it is Yahweh himself who hands over Jerusalem to the scorn of the surrounding peoples, of which Ps 79:4 complains.

■ **22:5** In sharp dissonance with the conclusion of the speech vv 3aβ–5 the city's claim to high honor and its humiliating fall are set side by side. Because the "name," i.e., the reputation of the city has made known its uncleanness to everyone, and because its greatness (for רַבָּה as the title of a city cf. 21:25) has become great disorder, and that means here social injustice, and because of the bloodshed in it (cf. Am 3:9; Ezek 7:7 remains obscure), Yahweh prepares to make it a laughingstock and an object of scorn by its neighbors. (Thereto 16:57, also 25:3, 6).

■ **22:6–12** The strictures which are brought against Jerusalem, bloodshed and idolatry, are in no way given historical definition here. We have already heard them earlier in Ezekiel. We also look in vain for a historical definition in the great corpus of accusation, which in vv 6–12 follows the summons vv 3aβ–5. We can at best find such a definition in the first part of the list of sins in which in particular the "princes of Israel" are accused of violence (and therefore bloodshed).[12] The history of Israel's monarchy is thereby summarized in a single overall judgement, which combines all the concrete allegations of earlier prophets (Nathan, David 2 Sam 12; Jer 22 and other passages) and does away with all the brighter statements which can be put together from 1 and 2 Kings. In the fullness of the judgement which is to come upon Jerusalem Ezekiel declares the total disobedience of the city before the law of Yahweh, beginning with its kings. Of this disobedience he had to speak with all severity·and plainness.

If we look for an element of structure in the loose mass of accusations in vv 6–12, in the sequel to which the princes fall into the background and Jerusalem alone is addressed directly, then we can best see such in the clauses ending with the expression לְמַעַן שְׁפָךְ דָּם, which for their part connect the series of accusations with the general theme "city which sheds blood" (v 3). Thus the three sections vv 6–8, 9–11 and 12 can be separated out. We cannot, however, speak of a concise structure. The further fact that the units, which are nine times characterized by בָּךְ "in you" and twice by בְּתוֹכֵךְ "in your midst," come close to a number of ten units raises the question whether a conscious decalogue series was intended. It is scarcely right, however, to attempt to restore this clear series, by excisions or additions. For this the formal structure of the individual clauses is much too unclear. A "decalogue" could at most stand in the background as a quite general, and certainly not firmly kept, pattern. In any case this consideration is not important for an understanding of the whole.

■ **22:6** The three verses 6, 9 and 12, which are characterized by the thematic final clause already mentioned, all have to do with crimes of a social nature, which in fact could also point throughout to a quite graphic meaning for bloodshed. This is at once very clearly to be seen in the strictures on the princes and their violence, who forget that the "strong arm" of dominion belongs to God alone, in whose power also is the law of mercy (Is 51:9f; 52:10; Ps 89:14; Dtn 5:15; 26:8 and other passages), and who breaks the arm of the wicked (Ps 10:15).[13] The formulation appears without any visible dependence on an older formulated law code.[14]

■ **22:7** The oldest Israelite law codes deal with those who curse father or mother. Ex 21:17; Lev 20:9 use the pi'el קלל; Dtn 27:16, the hip'il of קלה "to treat contemptuously." In a positive way the honoring (כבד) of parents is commanded in the Decalogue Ex 20:12; Dtn 5:16. In Lev 19:3 reverence (ירא) is commanded.

---

10   See note b for קרב of the approach of judgement; cf. 9:1; 12:23, also 7:7f; 30:3.

11   See above p. 204.

12   For the title נשׂיא ישׂראל 21:30, see above pp. 445f, plural 19:1; 21:17.

13   Cf. above p. 165 to 4:7 and below to 30:24f.

14   For the form of speech cf. Jer 17:5.

Also concern for aliens is an ancient Israelite commandment (Ex 22:20; 23:9, 12).[15] Widows and orphans are also directly mentioned (Dtn 14:29; 16:11, 14; 24:19–21; 26:12f, cf. Jer 7:6; 22:3, the latter only in Ex 22:21; in H they are not mentioned).[16]

■ **22:8** With v 8, however, which has a clear counterpart in Lev 19:30 את שבתתי תשמרו ומקדשי תיראו, it abruptly changes in the conclusion of the first group of clauses into ritual commands. Against the מקדשי תיראו of Lev 19:30, which especially commands reverence for the sanctuary and must have formed the legal basis for the death sentence threatened by the priests against Jeremiah in Jer 26, the reference to the קדשי in Ezekiel is limited to a general command to reverence for holy things (sanctuary, sacrifice, temple vessels, cf. the laws of chs. 40–48). All this is treated with contempt in Jerusalem.[17] The formal transition to a direct reference of the verbs (חללת—בזית) to the city being addressed, which makes the characteristic בך (בתוכך) superfluous, and the transition to sacred law raise the question whether v 8 is a subsequent addition (so Cornill, Hölscher, *Ezechiel*, Fohrer). The fact of an analogous material transition from v 9a to v 9b and the corresponding formal change to a direct declaration against Jerusalem in v 12 do not make this conclusion appear probable. The above connection with H also is no argument against v 8 being authentic.

■ **22:9** This reappears clearly in the second group of statements. The prohibition against going about as a slanderer is only found in the Old Testament in Lev 19:16 (cf. Prv 11:13; 20:19). When there the further ruling follows: לא תעמד על דם רעך, then it becomes clear how readily a lying slander incurred bloodguilt (analogously Mt 5:21f). The contemporary lament of Jeremiah (6:28; 9:3) shows that Ezekiel actually mentions here other well-known diseased aspects of contemporary Jerusalem life. The further stricture against "eating on the mountains" concerns especially, as we have already noted in connection with 18:6, the

pre-Josianic period.[18] Here also Jerusalem's sinful history, analogous to ch. 16 (and ch. 20, 23 for Israel) is seen and condemned as a whole.

■ **22:10** The accusation of זמה, which then follows and is formulated in general terms, acts as a heading to the offenses which follow and which are violations of sexual taboos as they are especially clearly laid down in Lev 18 and 20.[19] So incest with a father's wife (or concubine), of which Lev 18:8 expressly states that her nakedness is the nakedness of the father (cf. Lev 20:11). Sexual relationships in marriage with a woman during the time of her period have already been mentioned in 18:6.[20]

■ **22:11** In three clauses, with similar formal structure, and where the introductory איש reflects legal formulations with an introductory איש (cf. 20:7), the following are brought in: the abomination (תועבה) of intercourse with a neighbor's wife (Lev 18:20; 20:10, also Ezek 18:6), the offense (זמה) of becoming unclean with the wife or bride of one's son (Lev 18:15; 20:12), and uncleanness (טמא) with a half sister (Lev 18:9; 20:17).[21] The whole threefold group, which holds clearly together both in form and content, is clearly characterized by the connecting בך at the end as a connected element. Thus in the second series of statements, beside the reference to those who go about as malicious slanderers in Jerusalem, there especially stand references to disorders of sexual life. We can find a confirmation of the latter in Jeremiah's laments about adultery among his people (5:7; 7:9; 9:1; 23:10, also 29:23). Perhaps we should look beyond this to the stricture of Amos (2:7) and also Hosea against Israel (4:2, 13f, 7:4) as a background to Ezekiel's polemic. In the formulation of his strictures Ezekiel, in his close connection with H, clearly goes his own way over against them.

■ **22:12** The third group of statements points, in a more firmly bound thematic, to disorders in the sphere of property and money. The prohibition against accepting

---

15 Cf. above p. 303 to 14:7.
16 For הונה cf. p. 380 to 18:7; for עשה בעשק cf. the בצע בעשק in 23:25, עשה בשנאה 23:29, עשה בחמה 22:12. This is Ezekiel's language.
17 Cf. the concrete accusations of Ezek 8. For the sabbath command see above p. 410 to 20:12.
18 Cf. p. 380 to 18:6.
19 See above p. 345 to 16:27.

20 See above p. 380.
21 See above pp. 408f; see above p. 383 to 18:12f; see above p. 380.

a bribe, which brings about miscarriage of justice and blood guilt, was again already current in the older laws of Israel (Ex 23:8; Dtn 10:17; 16:19; 27:25). Mention of it is lacking in H. Laments about bribery in Jerusalem are found in prophecy in Is (1:23; 5:23), and Ezekiel has already spoken in 18:8 of getting rich by usury and interest.[22] With the catchword of violence, by which unjust gain is extorted, there is a reference back to v 7. Since the form of speech in this third group of statements, as already in v 8, is changed into a direct address to the city by the verbal construction, there is really no more room for the repetition of the characteristic בך. The particular climax in the change of style from a description to a personal confrontation is reached in the short concluding remark of the accusation: "You have forgotten me." In this there appears, out of the objective reality of broken laws, a personal offense to God throughout it all. Over against the "you" of the city there appears the "I" of God. "Forgetting" Yahweh is frequently spoken of in Hosea (2:15; 8:14; 13:6, also 4:6), in Dtn (6:12; 8:11, 14 etc.) and in Jeremiah (3:21; 13:25 etc.). In the book of Ezekiel the usage is only to be found again in 23:35. It recalls the similarly unique use of בחר in 20:5 or of מלך in relation to Yahweh in 20:33, when this speech usage, which is otherwise rare in Ezekiel, is used once.[23] This makes it possible that the summing up in a quite personal formulation of disobedience against Yahweh's commands, which is not otherwise common in Ezekiel, is here plainly in place. Similarly also the counterpart of remembering (זכר) Yahweh is only once to be found in Ezekiel in 6:9.

Thus it now becomes quite clear that we are dealing in the whole full listing of laws that have been broken, not with several things, but ultimately with one thing: the turning away from the Lord, who gives to everything in life its order. Ezekiel loves to express this elsewhere more sharply with the word מרה "to be rebellious," (cf. 20:8, 13, 21) and also the phrase בית מרי.[24] In essence he stands exactly where Hosea stood in his list of offenses in Hos 4:2, or Jeremiah with his list in 7:9. In both prophets more is meant than the summing up of individual offenses. They both, together now with

Ezekiel as a third, want to accuse the people of disobedience against an overall will, which is in the form of the classical decalogue, and in Ezekiel in the form of a (decalogue-like?) series of laws formulated in the manner of H. They "forget" God and thereby dishonor him, who looks for obedience, not in any hidden "spirituality," but in the multiplicity of concrete situations in life. In the heightened accusation of sin, which goes far beyond Hos 4:2 and Jer 7:9, we can see the radical sharpening of the "accusation" which Ezekiel makes.

■ **22:13–16** The conclusion, vv 13–16, must have been added either by Ezekiel himself or his school somewhat later. In content it emphasizes once again what has already been said in the address vv 4b–5a: Yahweh will punish disobedience. The emotional sign-action of handclapping, over unjust gain (בצע from v 12) and over bloodshed (דם בתוכך from v 3), introduces his declaration of judgement and reveals his wrath.[25] In the form of a question the city is shown its weakness in the face of the "days" on which Yahweh will deal with it (referring back to the ימיך of v 4). Yahweh's speech, however, hides within itself an event.[26] This event means the scattering of the people (as 12:15; 20:23, cf. 29:12; 30:23, 26), through which it perishes in its uncleanness (תמם again 24:10f; 47:12), and the terrible act occurs that Yahweh himself, who has committed his name to his people, is set in the forum of the nations as one who is dishonored, as 36:20 fully illustrates. The forensic character of לעיני הגוים has been rightly stressed by H. Graf Reventlow, "Die Völker." In such an event Yahweh will show who he is. In the removal of uncleanness we must think, according to the context, not of a reassuring statement in line with 36:25, but of the harsh destruction of those who are unclean in a remorseless judgement to annihilation. Thus in 24:1–14 the metaphor is used of rusted metal thrown into the fire.

Aim

The prophet is called by God to be the accuser of the city of God in which his people spend their lives. In his first words, where he names it as the "bloody city" with

---

22 See above pp. 380f.
23 P. 407; p. 415.
24 See above p. 134 to 2:5.

25 P. 184 to 6:1; p. 434 to 21:22.
26 For the formula v 14b cf. 12:25, 28; 17:24; 24:14; 36:36; 37:14.

threatening names, he accuses it of bloodguilt and idolatry. Where it should show forth God's purity, it is famous for its uncleanness. Where it should live with its neighbors in the quiet of a God-given space, it is entirely dominated by the unrest that is within it.

In all this the prophet is not simply a moral or religious critic on his own account. The oracle 22: 1–16 makes clear, especially in its main part vv 6–12, something quite different. God's people had a law, containing the divine will that was preached to it, in which God's gracious attitude to this people rested. In his law God had placed his hand upon his people so that in all the areas of its life it might belong to him and remember him, where a man was concerned with father or mother, or with alien, orphan or widow, and also where he was concerned with the Holy One and with the rhythm of time and its weeks. God had taken hold of man's most physical side, the intercourse between husband and wife, just as he had with dealings in money or property. In the law which God had given to his people, he had, in grace, set his sign upon all these things, so that thereby, in obedience to the law, they might thankfully confess him as God and not forget him in any sphere of their lives.

However, the terrifying thing had happened that this very law, which constituted the wisdom and honor of God's people (Dtn 4: 6–8) and by which light was shed upon its path (Ps 119: 105), had become the terrible accuser of the city of God and had as witnesses the prophets who accused the people of sin. In careless playing with power by the rulers, in lack of justice for the aliens and foreigners, in contempt for parents, in sexual disorder, and in selfish use of time, as though it were a possession which simply belonged to man each day—on every side the law of God proclaimed: "you have forgotten God" (v 12)! So also in selfish use of, and dealings with, money, and in the careless greed for possessions, in contempt for those parts of the world which were holy and in the profanation of what was sacred.

The prophet had to show that God would not let his holy will be mocked. The heat of his anger had to blaze where he was forgotten by his people in the various parts of life as the Lord and master. God's will does not simply come to terms with the uncleanness of his people, which disregards his laws. It blazes angrily until all selfishness is destroyed, and so long as any uncleanness remains. It burns so fiercely that God himself, in the eyes of the world, is put in question, since he has given over his own people to judgement, to become an object of scorn among the people. Yet the prophet had to preach that God revealed himself in the mystery of his name even where such death prevailed, under the accusation of the holy law which he had revealed to his people. God himself, in his holy wrath against his own people, becomes to the world an object of scandal and folly (1 Cor 1: 22–24).

Israel in the Smelting Oven

Bibliography

L. Köhler
  "Alttestamentliche Wortforschung. B*e*dīl und *b*e*dīlīm"; *ThZ* 3 (1947): 155–156.

22

17 Then the word of Yahweh came to me: **18/** Son of man, the people of the house of Israel[a] have become for me 'dross.'[b] They are all copper and tin[c] and iron and lead inside a (smelting) oven. They have become dross [silver].[d]

19 Therefore 'speak (?)':[a] Thus has [the Lord][b] Yahweh spoken: Because you have all become dross, see, therefore I will gather you together in the midst of Jerusalem. **20/** 'As'[a] men gather together silver and copper and iron and lead and tin in a (smelting) oven and kindle fire under[b] it, in order to smelt it,[c] so will I gather (you) together in

---

22:
18 18a Literally: the house Israel.

b K לסוג, Q לסיג. Since not only where it is repeated in vv 18b and 19a, but also in all the other texts in the Old Testament (Is 1:22, 25; Ps 119:119; Prv 25:4; 26:23) the plural form is used, and also 𝕲 𝕾 appear to point to a plural original, we must read לסגים. For the translation of the word cf. the exposition.

c The Hebrew בדיל is to be understood according to Koehler, "B*e*dīl," as a loanword from the Sanskrit *pātīra*.

d 𝕲 translates the concluding בתוך כור סגים כסף היו with ἐν μέσῳ ἀργυρίου ἀναμεμειγμένος ἐστί, omits any counterpart to 𝔐 כור, and changes the sequence סגים כסף. 𝕾 בגו כורא דחליטין בסאמא passes over the היו of 𝔐 and subordinates סגים כסף as a relative clause of the list of impure metals: "which are mixed with the silver." The excision of כור (BH³, Cornill, Fohrer) does not come in question, since the usage בתוך כור is anchored much too firmly in the following interpretation (v 22, cf. אל תוך כור v 20, interpreted in אל תוך ירושלם v 19). The כסף occasions a certain awkwardness, which is often avoided by putting it as in v 20 before נחשת at the head of the list of metals (BH³, Cooke, Herrmann, Bertholet). 𝕾 𝕿 (לפסולת כספא) 𝖁 (*scoria argenti*) understand כסף as a closer definition (as permutative?) of סגים, which could be considered if we could regard כסף as originally belonging to 𝔐. Driver, "Linguistic Problems," 69, would read סיג מכסף "dross without silver."

19 19a 𝕲 introduces additionally here (διὰ τοῦτο) εἶπον, which smooths the following transition to direct speech.

b אדני is lacking in 𝕲 𝕮ᴮᵒ, see Excursus 1.

20 20a That in 𝔐 קבצת כסף כן אקבץ ... is an intentional comparison, is beyond doubt. 𝕲 καθὼς εἰσδέχεται, 𝕾 איך דמתכנש, 𝕿 כמיכנש make it probable that we should add the comparative particle, analogous to the כהתוך ... כן of v 22, and read the first word כקבצת.

b Literally: against it.

c 𝔐 להנתיך. According to Bauer-Leander § 15 l the retention of נ without assimilation is to be found particularly in pausal forms. Certainly 𝕲 τοῦ χωνευθῆναι and 𝕾 דנתפשרון arouse the suspicion that here

461

my anger [and my wrath]ᵈ [and gather]ᵉ and smelt you. 21/ [And I will gather you together.]ᵃ And I will kindle against you the fire of my wrath, and you shall be smelted in it. 22/ As silver is smelted in a (smelting) oven,ᵃ so shall you be smelted in it (i.e., in the fire of my anger), and you shall know that I—I Yahweh—have poured out my wrath upon you.

an original nipʻal form לְהִנָּתֵךְ may subsequently have been changed into a hipʻil through plene-writing.

d 𝔐 ובחמתי is not attested by 𝔊. 𝔖, by passing over the והנחתי (note e), connects it with the following והתכתי אתכם, which is impossible on account of its form as a perfect consecutive. ובחמתי must have been added subsequently in dependence on v 22.

e 𝔐 והנחתי "and set it" or "leave" (𝔙 *et requiescam*) is scarcely right. 𝔗 ואסיף "and I will destroy," with its interpretation, appears to be dependent on the following והתכתי, which 𝔗 translates with ואישצי. The καὶ συνάξω of 𝔊, however, appears to point to a וכנסתי, in which the וכנסתי אתכם of v 21, which is lacking in 𝔊, is anticipated. Since 𝔊 omits a translation of the form both in vv 20 and 21, כנס in Ezekiel is otherwise found again only in the uncertain reading of 39:28, the suspicion is great that the וכנסתי in the original text behind 𝔊 in v 20, and additionally in 𝔐 in v 21 (with אתכם), has first been added subsequently. The textual tradition offers no support for an emendation to ונפחתי (BH³, Bertholet, Fohrer, van den Born).

21   21a 𝔐 וכנסתי אתכם is lacking in 𝔊 𝔖, cf. note e to v 20.

22   22a The nominal form התוך of 𝔐 is a קְטוּל-formation, derived from the hipʻil, according to Bauer-Leander § 61 γγ. Bertholet, Fohrer want to find in it a mixed form from הַנָּתֵךְ and הָתַּךְ.

Form

The short oracle breaks up into an address by Yahweh to the prophet (v 18), in which the nature of Israel is shown to him in a simile, and a message to the people (vv 19–22 second person plural). The transition to the latter takes place directly in 𝔐, without being separated by an express command to speak. We can easily add this from 𝔊 (note a to v 19). The message itself is given as a three-part proof-saying, in which a brief motive clause (v 19aβ יען) is followed by a broadly constructed declaration of judgement with two explicit comparisons (כן . . . כ in vv 20 and 22) and a final, verbally expanded, recognition formula.

Further the distinctiveness of this oracle consists in that its argument proceeds with a simile which is given no detailed justification, but is simply presupposed as a given fact. It is justified, as other qualifying similes in Ezekiel (Israel as a vine ch. 15; the unfaithful wife ch. 16; the two unfaithful women ch. 23 and others), in the older prophetic tradition. Certainly there is a close connection, even in the formulation, with Is 1:22, 25 as a direct basis. Whilst on the one hand the argu-

ments proceed wholly on the basis of given material, on the other hand we can also see clearly how the whole is recast in Ezekiel's distinctive manner of expression. This is true not only for the new content and the actualizing of the old simile (cf. the exposition), but also for the form and language. Beside the formulation as a proof-saying, the replacing of the verb צרף, which is apparently almost unavoidable in reference to dross and smelting (Is 1:25; Jer 6:29; Prv 25:4; 27:21), by the root נתך, which is used no less than five times in vv 20–22, is characteristic of the oracle. The root צרף is not found at all in the book of Ezekiel. The linguistic distinctiveness of Ezekiel again becomes very clear in this.

Setting

The address to the "house of Israel," which is concentrated in Jerusalem, and the lack of any reflection of the political dualism Jerusalem-Judah which is so clearly marked in Jeremiah (as Jer 7:2; 26:2, see Excursus 2) points, against Herntrich, to a location far from Jerusalem as the place of origin of this oracle.

"Israel" is an entity seen from a distance, not the people in Judah and Jerusalem, standing before the eyes of the citizens of Jerusalem.

Chronologically the oracle belongs in the period close to the siege of Jerusalem, which is soon to begin, therefore somewhere about 589 B.C. The oracle proclaims this siege as a harsh catastrophe and at the same time justifies its inner necessity.

Interpretation

■ **22:17** The account of the fresh coming of a message tells first of the coming of a word of Yahweh to the prophet (son of man).[1] In this he is told in a simile what the people of Israel is like: "The people of the house of Israel have become dross for me." The היה ל of this expression, which expresses, according to C. H. Ratschow, an "evidence of an inner reality," clearly points in this to the earlier text of Is 1:21ff as the source from which this judgement stems.[2] In continuation of the introductory איכה היתה לזונה קריה נאמנה (this picture has been unfolded in Ezek 16) the further metaphor is used there in parallelism כספך היה לסיגים. V 25 then describes the refining process of the סיגים. Jeremiah's later use of this metaphor (Jer 6:28–30, cf. further Is 48:10; Zech 13:9; Mal 3:2f) moves further in a different direction from the original text and is certainly not the direct background of Ezek 22:18.[3]

The noun סיג, which is connected with the root סוג "to deviate, to separate off," denotes the separating off of worthless material in the process of smelting. More precisely Cooke and Köhler, "B^e dīl," have described how the process of refining silver takes place in two phases. In a first phase, by the addition of other minerals to the lead-silver ore from which the silver is obtained, the sulfur elements are removed. These combine with the other metals present to form the corresponding sulfides, materials which are subsequently removed as dross. In a second process, the so-called refining, the mixture of silver and lead that remains has the lead removed by the addition of a flux through oxydation to PbO (lead oxide). According to Köhler Is 1:22, 25 is concerned with this second process, which can easily go wrong and leave a silver-like

dross. Against Köhler, however, the question must be raised whether סיג in any case can denote only the dross, the unfortunate produce of the second process, and not, in a broader sense, the final useless product of both processes. Ezek 22:17–22 could support this, where not only lead and iron, but also a number of other metals are mentioned.

It is clear in any case that the present oracle, based on Is 1:21ff, simply repeats the one statement which is expressed there against the inhabitants of Jerusalem and relates it to the "house of Israel." This, in Yahweh's judgement (היו לי), is dross, useless material and unacceptable. The process which goes wrong, which possibly underlies Is 1:21, and the process of successful refining, which is first clearly attested in Is 1:25, must be kept away from Ezekiel's message. V 18bα "they are all copper, tin, iron and lead in the furnace" clarifies the statement cited from Is 1, which is further emphasized in the concluding סגים היו (bβ), in a direction which differs from Is 1. Exactly as in Ezek 15, in the allegory of the vine, it is here laid down in the metaphor of dross that, in the eyes of Yahweh, Israel is something useless and worthless. Rightly therefore in v 18 the silver, which is what is acceptable and is to become, after further refining, the pure material of the smelting process, is left out.

■ **22:19** On the basis of this assertion which Yahweh makes to the prophet, there then emerges the message to the house of Israel, which the prophet is called to give, introduced by the messenger formula.[4] Where here a motivation is first given (v 19aβ), which is to justify the following declaration of judgement, this is not a real argument which engages in dialogue with the accused, "you have all become dross," which would allow accusation and defense in speeches for and against. Rather it refers back to a judgement which God has already previously given, which was proclaimed in the earlier prophecy of Isaiah and for which a reason was given there. In Is 1:21, 23 it was unfolded how the once honorable city has been dishonored by its leaders and has despised Yahweh's law. In the redactional placing of Ezek 22:1–16 before vv 17–22 (and in the ordering of vv 23–31 after vv 17–22?) something

---

1   See above pp. 144f; pp. 131f.
2   Ratschow, *Werden*, 10.
3   See also Miller, *Verhältnis*, page 2 note 2 and page

113.

4   See above p. 133.

of this motivation may be carried over. In vv 19–22, however, only the divine judgement is stated and the punishment arising from it adduced.

The "logic" of the divine judgement is reminiscent of the logic of Ezek 15. Thus as the useless vine, of which Ezek 15 speaks, can only be used in the fire, so is it clear from the inner logic of the situation that dross and fire belong together. The true message is found in v 19 in the historical actualization: "See, therefore I will gather you in Jerusalem."

■ **20:20–22** What this really means is fully elaborated in the two following similes. As the metals, in the process of refining silver, are all together in the furnace (the silver is rightly included here because we are no longer concerned with the comparison with the house of Israel, but with a description of the smelting process), so now the furnace is made ready and the fire lit (vv 20f). As silver is put in the heat of the fire, so will Israel go in the fire (without itself being the silver).

A slight logical inconsistency is not to be denied in this whole address. The traditional metaphor, which is used in Is 1:25 positively of Jerusalem and which shows the aim of a successful refining process (cf. the statement about Abraham *Cairo Damascus Document* B 20:3 הוא האיש הנתך בתוך כור), is here simply used in regard to judgement. Israel is not identified with the genuine silver, although v 22, in the course of the metaphor, speaks of the process which the silver also undergoes. The argument here is simply based on its nature as dross, and only the process of judgement in fire is stressed. It is said of such burning that Yahweh undertakes it and stirs it up like a smelter. It belongs with this that the chronological sequence of events also is awkwardly misconceived. Dross is an end product of a smelting process. It is thrown away after the completion of this process. In Ezekiel's argument, however, the nature of Israel as dross is already affirmed at the beginning of the statement. Under this dross fire appears to be kindled afresh. This is in place in Is 1:25 where refinement is to take place out of the further heating. Thus the second process of refining is in mind there, which is here in the distance, because only a burning of destruction is to be proclaimed.

Whilst therefore the logic of the smelting process in this secondary development of an early metaphor, which was quite clear in Is 1:21ff, is far from being free from objection, yet, just as in Ezek 15, where similarly a secondary development strangely breaks up an earlier image (the vine), it is unmistakable. Yahweh himself is at work, when now the house of Israel (in its Judean remnant) is shut up within the walls of Jerusalem, and the fire begins to burn hot. He himself has brought them all together and in his anger has lit the fire, fanned it with bellows with which the smelting furnace was made hot (Jer 6:29) until even the toughest metal begins to melt.[5] Here he shows himself to be at work in the mystery of his being.

Aim

Israel had been able to speak of the miracle of its election as those who had been brought out of the iron-(smelting)-furnace of Egypt (Dtn 4:20; 1 Kings 8:51; Jer 11:4). In such a deliverance it had become accepted. The message of the prophet Ezekiel is cutting in its harshness. Because of its sins, Israel in his days had become useless dross, for which the fire of the furnace was once again the proper place. Over its history there stood God's "No!"

This "No" did not take place at some fringe point. In Jerusalem, the chosen city, God had gathered his people together in order to light the fire of judgement under it there. The prophet could not speak of a miscarriage of God's history. God willed that this also should be taken as a part of the historical events in which he made himself truly known to the world.

The loss of his own reputation in which God could now find in his people only dross and no silver becomes quite unmistakable (as in Ezek 15). God's face here becomes terrifying when he reveals himself as the God who is holy in his judgement.

---

5   See the illustration in *BA* 1 (1938): 5.

Survey of the Corruption of All Classes in the Land

Bibliography

D. H. Müller

"Der Prophet Ezechiel entlehnt eine Stelle des Propheten Zephanja und glossiert sie," *WZKM* 19 (1905): 263–270.

22

23   Then the word of Yahweh came to me: 24/ Son of man, say to it:[a] You are a land which has not been 'rained upon,'[b] upon which no shower has fallen[c] in the days of wrath.[d] 25/ 'Her princes'[a] in her midst were like the growling lion, who tears his prey. They have eaten men, have seized[b] their possessions[c]

22:
24   24a 𝔐 לה has no clear word of relation in what precedes. It cannot be עיר (v 3) because in what follows it is the land that is clearly referred to (ארץ v 24a, also עם הארץ v 29). בית ישראל in v 18 is masculine. Thus, like 𝔗 (את ארעא דישראל), we must accept an ארץ or אדמת ישראל as the unexpressed word of relation.

b 𝔐 ארץ לא מטהרה (so 𝔗 ארע לא מדכיא היא) is striking, less on account of its being the real puʿal of טהר than on account of the circumstantial paraphrase of a simple ארץ טמאה. Thus 𝔊, with its reading γῆ ἡ οὐ βρεχομένη, points to an underlying ארץ לא מטרה (= ממטרה Gesenius-Kautzsch § 52 s), which is supported by the parallel גשמה (note c), for the original text.

c 𝔐 לא גשמה points to a noun גֶּשֶׁם (Bauer-Leander § 72 i), which is otherwise not found in the Old Testament, instead of the usual גֶּשֶׁם. The connection must be understood therefore as a nominal clause: "its rain (does) not (fall)." The vocalizing as puʿal (גֻּשְׁמָה) could smooth the text. 𝔊 smooths the text still further: οὐδὲ ὑετὸς ἐγένετο ἐπὶ σέ. 𝔖 combines in v 24 the readings of 𝔐 and 𝔊: אנתי ארעא לא הויתי דכיא ולא אצטבעתי ולא נחת עליכי מטרא.

d 𝔐 זעם is supported by the concluding repetition in v 31 and is not to be emended with Ehrlich, *Randglossen*, Herrmann to זרם. Driver, "Linguistic Problems," 69, would understand זעם here as "bad weather."

25   25a 𝔐 קשר נביאיה "the band of its prophets" (so also 𝔙; 𝔖 מרדו נבייה) presupposes קשרו) yields impossible sense because a mention of prophets in this speech first follows in v 28, with specific mention of the offenses of the prophets there, whilst here offenses of the political rulers are mentioned. Thus 𝔗 avoids the difficulty by the translation ספרהא. The correct reading is preserved by 𝔊 ἧς οἱ ἀφηγούμενοι ἐν μέσῳ αὐτῆς. We must therefore emend to אשר נשׂיאיה.

b 𝔐 יקחו. The reading לקחו (Herrmann, Bertholet, BH³) offers throughout a smooth series of perfect statements and graphically presents no difficulties, cf. Delitzsch, *Schreibfehler* § 119 a. However, a glance at the related descriptions in 18:5–9, 10–13, and their striking change of tense calls for caution in the acceptance of such an emendation.

and treasures; they have made many into widows in her midst. 26/ Her priests have done violence to my law and profaned my holy offerings. They did not make a distinction between what is holy and what is profane, and they do not teach the distinction between unclean[a] and clean, and they shut their eyes before my sabbaths so that I was profaned in their midst. 27/ Her officials in her midst were like wolves, who tear their prey, to shed blood [, and to destroy (men's) lives],[a] to acquire unjust gain.[b] 28/ Her prophets then painted them with whitewash; they saw false visions and prophesied lies to them[a] in saying: Thus has [the Lord][b] Yahweh said, when Yahweh has not spoken. 29/ The people of the land practiced violence and committed[a] robbery. ' '[b] They oppressed the unfortunate and the poor, and they 'acted[c] unjustly' towards the alien. 30/ I looked for a man among them[a] who would build a wall and go before me into the breaches to defend the land,[b] so that I might not destroy it, but I found none. 31/ So I poured out my wrath upon them, and I utterly destroyed them in the heat of my anger. I requited their actions upon their own head, says [the Lord][a] Yahweh.

Reference to the versions, therefore, is not compelling because in ch. 18 these similarly smooth out the change of tense.

c חסן, according to the accentuation, is to be linked with the following and not to what precedes, as 𝕲 ἐν δυναστείᾳ and 𝕾 בעשינותהון.

26 26a The article in הטמא is striking and is lacking in the parallel reference 44:23. 𝕲 translates loosely καὶ ἀνὰ μέσον ἀκαθάρτου καὶ τοῦ (lacking in 𝕲⁹⁶⁷) καθαροῦ. Read טמא.

27 27a 𝔐 לאבד נפשות is lacking in 𝕲. It represents, beside the characteristic לשפך דם (vv 6, 9, 12 למען שפך דם), a weaker addition, which disturbs the intentional variation between ל and למען.

b בדיל לקבלא ממון דשקר 𝖝 and 𝖂 et avare ad sectanda lucra clarify each in their own way.

28 28a 𝕲 passes over להם, whilst 𝕾 also joins להון to the preceding clause.

b אדני is lacking in 𝕲, see Excursus 1.

29 29a 𝔐 וגזלו גזל will not be subordinated to עשקו עשק as in 18:18. Thus here we must reckon with the weakening of the Hebrew perfect consecutive under Aramaic influence. Gesenius-Kautzsch § 112 pp.

b The copula is lacking in 8 MSS^Ken, 𝕲 𝕾 𝖂. Read ענו.

c The repetition of עשקו in the same verse is striking, the doubling of the assertion of unrighteousness (lawlessly doing violence) is unusual, and is not to be compared with the usage with an inner object in 18:18; 22:29a. 𝕲 ἀναστρεφόμενοι presupposes עשו as in v 7, which, with Cornill and others, is to be restored. For the construction עשה את cf. note c to 7:27.

30 30a Literally: out of them.

b 𝕲 has not properly understood the text. For the variants of the 𝕲 tradition see Ziegler, *Ezechiel*, 80f.

31 31a אדני is lacking in 𝕲 𝕮^Bo, see Excursus 1.

Form

The oracles of the great writing prophets concern themselves repeatedly with the whole life of the people of God. Thus, besides oracles to the king or to individual groups, among whom sins are particularly concentrated (priests, Hos 4:4ff; women of Samaria, Amos 4:1ff, and of Jerusalem, Is 3:16ff; prophets, Mic 3:5ff; Jer 23:9ff and others), we find quite early the speech forms of a general sermon in which a number of groups, each with its own particular offenses, are listed. In Mic 3:11 princes, priests, and prophets are mentioned together; and in Jer 5:31 prophets and priests. Ezekiel 22:23–31, in its central section vv 25–30, represents a particularly broadly worked out pattern of such preaching to all authorities. The corruption which pervades all sections is here set out in an individualizing way in order to make clear the radical nature of wickedness in the land.

In such an address to particular sections of society, which had become a current form of prophetic polemic, a certain typifying has unavoidably arisen. The particular problem of the present text, however, is occasioned by the close connection with the address of Zeph 3:3f, which lists princes, judges, prophets, and priests and which exceeds the usual typifying. Müller, "*Zephanja*," who has pointed with particular emphasis to this context, is certainly right when he thinks of a direct familiarity of the author of Ezek 22:23–31 with

Zephaniah's oracle. Since the familiarity extends beyond the section Zeph 3:1–4 (5) to cover also the unit 3:6–8, in that the threat of Zeph 3:8 is also echoed in the concluding section of the unit Ezek 22:23–31, the author of Ezek 22:23–31 must also have had before him a collection of the words of Zephaniah. V 31, however, has, for its part, a close counterpart in the second from last verse of the section 21:33–37, which is regarded as secondary.

Under these circumstances can the oracle have derived from Ezekiel? A quotation from Zephaniah is already to be found in 7:19. Its absence in the older tradition (note b to 7:19) and its formal distinctions from the context easily shows there its secondary nature. In 22:23–31, however, the whole oracle has arisen as a free development out of the basis of the Zephaniah oracle. Such a process of free elaboration of early elements of prophetic preaching is not at all unusual in Ezekiel. We can think of the full acceptance and development of the theme of the unfaithful wife (ch. 16), of the two faithless women (ch. 23), the bad shepherds (ch. 34) from Hosea and Jeremiah. We can further also point to the taking up of stereotyped sayings, such as the speech of Amos concerning the end (cf. in Ezekiel 7) or the oracle of the dross from Isaiah (cf. to Ezek 22:17–22), whereby again material taken over is commented upon and further elaborated by Ezekiel. 22:23–31 shows this process in still further measure. The process itself, however, is quite usual in Ezekiel. Thus we cannot from this determine with certainty whether vv 23–31 come from Ezekiel himself or rather from the circle of his disciples. A late date is opposed by 44:6–15, a section which is certainly not presupposed by 22:26.

With its description as a sermon against institutional groups, however, the section 22:23–31 is still not fully defined as to its form. If the reconstruction of the text of v 24 following 𝕲 is right (cf. note b), then this begins by a direct address to the land threatening it with judgement, which is described metaphorically as the withholding of rain. A judgement which has already happened, however, is spoken of by the conclusion in v 31, in the third person plural. If in v 24 we follow 𝔐, then the metaphor, by which the saying in v 24 begins with

reproach, is displaced. (Cf. the exposition.) In any case 22:23–31, unlike Zeph 3:1–4, is not reproach ,which gives the reason for the catastrophe before it happens, but an appeal to those upon whom judgement has already fallen. The saying has the function of making clear to people who have undergone judgement its rightness, and bringing it to recognize this. The sermon has become an element of prophetic "reminiscence."[1]

Setting

Conclusions about the location and date of the oracle are clear enough in all this.

22:23–31 stems from the time after 587. The final judgement upon the remnant of Israel, which has hitherto been spared, has taken place.

Those addressed are not a group of those remaining in the land, but first of all the land itself, which has been made desolate (cf. 33:29). In that the oracle then passes over to a description in the third person, it is clear that no actual situation exists in which people are being addressed. The עם הארץ mentioned in v 29 is (against Herntrich) no proof for the "Jerusalem situation" of those addressed. Rather we must think of an oracle to the circle of the exiles, who are to be brought to a real submission under a righteous judgement by the sermon reviewing the past.[2]

Interpretation

■ **22:23** With the formula for the coming of a message, an address to the prophet is described (son of man), in which he receives from God a command to speak.[3] The land, which must be presupposed as the object addressed by God's word (note a), is told of the day of wrath. The catchword זעם, which reappears in v 31 in the conclusion (otherwise in Ezekiel only 21:36), must here have been determined by Zephaniah 3:8. In the preaching of the prophets it was already, Is 10:5 (25); Jer 15:17; Na 1:6; Hab 3:12, an expression for Yahweh's intervention in judgement, and it receives in Dan 8:19; 11:36 the emphasis of a technical term. The event on the יום זעם, which can be compared with the עת עון קץ of 21:30, 34, is described by the metaphor of drought. This reference to a continuing state of affairs

---

1   See below p. 469 for זכר.
2   Cf. further 6:8–10, see above pp. 188–190.
3   See above pp. 144f; pp. 131f.

of a time (יום) of woe may not be felt to be particularly happy. Its real content is certainly easily understood: drought is a divine judgement (1 Kings 17:1; Jer 14:1ff) and death for a land. "Rain is blessing 34:26; Lev 26:4; Dtn 11:14, and not to be rained upon is not to be blessed, Zech 14:17" (Herrmann).

The inner force of this metaphorical description of a day of judgement, which is without any analogy in Ezekiel, inevitably raises the question whether 𝔐, with its reading, can still be right. It begins with reproach, which then in vv 25–30 is clarified by a sermon: "you are not a purified land." Since 24:13 repeats the accusation of Jerusalem's lack of purity in connection with another metaphor, and the coming purification in the promises of salvation 36:25, 33; 37:23 is strongly emphasized, this accusation would not be without its contact with the rest of Ezekiel's preaching. All that is then striking is that the ritual component, which is otherwise present in statements about purity, is wholly in the background in the unfolding of the sermon. The declaration which follows in v 24b must then, if we relate the היא to b and see in it the introduction of an interpretive explanation ("this means . . .") or take the following words by themselves, following the accentuation of 𝔐, contain a more detailed explanation of a. Since, according to 36:25, the purification of men takes place by their being sprinkled with clean water, this process could have been interpreted with reference to the land being rained upon. However, for this, any clear parallel is lacking in Ezekiel. Cf. the discussion of the question whether, according to Ezek 22:24, the great flood has come upon the land of Israel or not, *b Zebaḥim* 113a.

■ **22:25** With v 25 the text begins a sermon against the authorities. In comparison with Zeph 3:3f it is expanded with a fifth element. The condemnatory description is also considerably expanded against the four corresponding members in Zephaniah. There is further a change in the order. The priests are moved from last (fourth) place in the series into second place. There is also a change within the groups addressed, which must be connected with the different linguistic usage of Ezekiel. In place of the שרים of Zephaniah there appear

in Ezekiel the נשיאים (note a to v 25), and in place of the שפטים the שרים.

In Zeph 3:3f the lack of mention of the king in the accusation is striking—is it reverence for the law of Ex 22:27? In Zeph 1:8 the king's sons are certainly mentioned—but beside them appear the שרים. These bearers of highest honor after the king form in Zeph 3:3 the first group of officials. In Ezek 22 this is altered. Ezek 17 has shown how the guilt of the last days of Jerusalem was the direct responsibility of the ruler. Whilst the description of judgement in 7:27, in its נשיא, had in mind the particular king at the time of judgement,[4] the reproach here reviews, in the plural, the whole succession of kings (as already in v 6). The metaphor of the lion, which is now turned against them, no longer portrays the royal honor, as in Ezek 19, but the fierce greed and violence of the kings.[5] They murder the living (cf. 19:3, 6) in order to enrich themselves. They make many women in the land into widows.[6] In substance we are reminded of the crimes of the king in 2 Sam 11 and 1 Kings 21, as well as of Jer 22:17.

■ **22:26** The priests, who in the priestly-prophetic book of Ezekiel appear not by accident in the place directly after the kings, are first, as in Zeph 3:4b, although in different order, accused of violence against the *torah* of Yahweh and the profaning of Yahweh's sanctuaries (cf. v 8). The phrase חמס תורה, which occurs in the Old Testament only in these two places, affirms that the priests, in the sphere of their own special activity, take the divine instruction, apparently defenselessly (cf. the analogy of the חמס גר Jer 22:3) given into their hands, and use it arbitrarily for their own benefit.[7] Behind this there stands the knowledge that *torah* can only be received as a gift and communicated by obedience, i.e., by listening.[8] However, in such misuse that which is holy is profaned. The clear distinction between the spheres holy-profane, clean-unclean, which no man can manipulate, becomes ignored. The great program of Ezek 40–48 then shows how in the coming age of salvation these distinctions will be set up afresh and guaranteed. In this connection 44:23 also sets out the new obligation of the priesthood to give true *torah* (Hag 2:10ff) and to teach "knowledge" (דעת).[9] A par-

---

4   See above p. 209.
5   See above p. 394.
6   הרבה, as in 11:6, otherwise cf. Jer 15:8, Ps 109:9.
7   See Begrich, "Tora."
8   See above pp. 212f. to 7:26b.
9   For הבדיל and הודיע see above p. 336 to 16:2.

ticularly important case of disregard for the distinction between holy and profane according to the laws of the age is found in the disregard for the law of the sabbath.[10] Abayyeh in *b Šabbat* 119b, by citing the present text, explains the destruction of Jerusalem by breach of the law of the sabbath. In all this the ultimate end is not the breaking of laws, but that Yahweh himself is driven into the sphere of the profane and robbed of his holiness. Among the older prophets it is above all Hosea who condemns the priests of his day for misuse of their obligation to give true instruction (Hos 4:6).

■ **22:27** Next in third place there then appears in Ezekiel the שרים, who are mentioned in Zeph 3:3 in first place. They appear in place of the שפטים, who are not mentioned in Ezekiel.[11] Among other things the character of the statement as a quotation becomes clear in that the "in their (or your) midst" becomes, when Ezekiel formulates it, בתוכה, as in 22:3, 7, 9. The present text, however, in dependence on Zeph 3:3, has קרב. בקרבה. קרב is found in the book of Ezekiel otherwise only in 11:19; 36:26f in the pregnant meaning of "inside." Since the metaphor of the lion in v 25 has already been used for the princes, there remains here for the officers only the lesser metaphor of the wolf, which is associated in Zeph 3:3 with the judges and which also, in its allusion to a less noble species of animal, conveys a similarly violent attitude. The description of the wolf in Zephaniah, which is hardly clear, is here given in the normal vocabulary of Ezekiel.[12] In substance the officers are accused of the same offenses as the princes. In earlier prophecy cf. Is 1:23; 3:14; Hos 9:15.

The accusations against the prophets also differ from Zephaniah's formulations. They are found in Ezek 13. Instead of honoring truth in a genuine attack against sin, the prophets whitewash the truth (13:10f; 14f), see lying visions, give lying oracles (13:6–9), and claim to have God's word when Yahweh has not spoken (13:6).

In fifth position are mentioned the "people of the land," the landowning nobility (of Judah), who already appeared in 7:27 beside the princes.[13] In the description of them the vocabulary reappears which in Ezek 18

describes the wicked: extortion (18:18), robbery (18:12, 18), oppression of the poor (18:12). Jer 7:6 speaks of injustice against the alien (בלא משפט Jer 22:13). These are offenses against which prophecy since Amos had raised its voice in the name of the old covenant law of Israel.

■ **22:30** The concluding remark in v 30 recalls Jeremiah's despairing attempt to find in the streets of Jerusalem one man who does right (Jer 5:1ff). According to this Yahweh himself has made the attempt without success (cf. Eccl 7:27f).[14] What has been said in Ezek 13 of the prophets, that they have not built up the walls (13:5 גדר גדר) or gone into the breaches (13:5 עלה בפרץ; in Ps 106:23 עמד בפרץ) in order to prevent the destruction (20:17; 30:11), is here affirmed in a final review of all strata among the people.

■ **22:31** Thus Yahweh must pour out his wrath (21:36; Zeph 3:8, cf. 22:22), and destroy with the heat of his anger (21:36; 22:21; 38:19), and bring the action of the people back onto their own heads (9:10, 11:21).

Aim

The prophetic voice speaks to man upon whom God's wrath has fallen. The scorching heat which torments the drought-stricken land does not need first to be announced. It has already come to men.

There cannot have been lacking voices who, in this position, wanted to do away with all historical reflections. The present was enough to think about. Since Ezekiel also, surprisingly, had proclaimed to the exiles (as in 11:14ff; cf. ch. 18) that in the present the hope of a better dawn had not wholly disappeared, there were clearly also voices who were inclined to forget everything about the past and to refer only to the message of this better hope more vitally than ever. Against them the book of Ezekiel repeatedly insists on the necessity of remembering (זכר 6:9; 16:61; 20:43; 36:31), in which the nation's history took on a contemporary meaning. The oracle 22:23–31 achieves something of this "remembering," which takes place not only in the message of judgement, but is also present in that of the possibility of the new life which faces the people.

10　See above p. 410 to 20:12, also 22:8.
11　For the juridical function of the שָׂרִים cf. Jer 26:10ff.
12　For טרף טרף cf. v 25, also 19:3, 6; for שפך דם

22:3f, 6, 9, 12; for בצע 12f; 33:31.
13　See above p. 209.
14　See Miller, *Verhältnis*, 112.

In this "remembering" the earlier history of the people of God is summarized in such a way that in it any human boasting is done away with. The history is not here set out in its chronological dimension, as in chs. 16, 20, 23. This history is examined with regard to those leading officials who had taken part in it. It is not the nameless and historically unimportant people who are examined, but those who exercised leadership in name, reputation, and authority in the nation (Jer 5:1ff).

We could undoubtedly also put together a much brighter history. It can easily be constructed from the historical narratives of the Bible. The impulse to a history of despairing disobedience of every high official does not arise from a seeking after gloomy pictures, but from the yardstick of divine holiness, in which God's commands are given to his people. Under this yardstick everything appears in the dark light of disobedience; the story of the princes, the officers and of the landed nobility is a history of violence and contempt for the weak. The story of the priests, who know and should teach the difference between the divine and human realms, is a history of selfish presumption. The story of the prophets, who receive God's word most directly, is a history of vague outpourings: where God speaks threateningly they give harmless lies, and again they offer comforting assurances when God has declared no such thing.

The people of God (the worshipping community, not the "world" which has no knowledge of God) are examined whether they will listen to this prophetic "remembering" of their history or whether they will try to find salvation in an apparently pious forgetting and suppression of it.

Oholah and Oholibah

Bibliography

Cf. to 16:1–63.

F. Delitzsch
Wo lag das Paradies? (1881), 233–241 (I. Die Länder und Völker *Kû* und *Sû*. II. Aramäerstämme in und bei Babylonien).

E. Klauber
Assyrisches Beamtentum nach Briefen aus der Sargoniden-zeit, LSS V 3 (1910).

D. H. Müller
"Strophenbau und Responsion in Ezechiel und den Psalmen," *Biblische Studien IV* (Wien: Holder, 1908), 28–36 (Ezekiel Kap. 23).

A. Salonen
Hippologica Accadica, AAF Ser. B Tom.100 (1956).

H. Winckler
Altorientalische Forschungen, 2. Reihe, Band II, Heft 1 (1899): 253–259 (Ko'a und Sho'a).

23

1 Then the word of Yahweh came to me: 2/ Son of man, (there were) two women, daughters of the same mother. 3/ They played the whore in Egypt, (already) in their youth they played the whore.[a] There[b] their breasts were pressed and there their virgin bosoms were handled.[c] 4/ The elder was named Oholah and her sister Oholibah. And they became mine and bore sons and daughters. [And regarding their names:[a] Oholah is Samaria and Oholibah is Jerusalem.][b]

5 But Oholah was unfaithful to me[a] and was filled with desire for her lovers,

23: 3a The זנו of 𝔐 is certainly not attested by 𝔊 𝔖 𝔄 Arm. ℭ. The versions, however, must here have smoothed over the terse narrative clauses (already found in v 2) for stylistic reasons.

b שמה (𝔊 ἐκεῖ, 𝔖 𝔗 תמן) is also used in 32:29f; 48:35 in a purely local sense, with no emphasis on direction. Besides the use of the variation beside the parallel שׁם, a euphonic regard for avoiding the harsh coming together of two מ will certainly have determined the choice of the fuller שׁמה.

c 𝔊 ἐκεῖ διεπαρθενεύθησαν (then also 𝔊 אתבתלי, cf. v 8), scarcely points to a Hebrew original without דדי (Cornill, Hölscher, *Hesekiel*), but must be understood as a free paraphrase of the original. However, the revocalizing of 𝔐 עשׂו to עֻשּׂוּ (corresponding to the puʿal of the parallel מעכו) is to be considered seriously. דדים is only found again vv 8, 21 Prv 5:19; the particular emphasis of the piʿel and puʿal of עשׂה (again vv 8, 21) is without parallel in the Old Testament. Herrmann conjectures a connection with עסס "to crush" (Mal 3:21), Mishnaic Hebrew עסה "to press." See also Driver, "Difficult," 54.

4 4a 𝔐 is the only Old Testament occurrence of the contracted form -ān of the third plural feminine suffix to a feminine plural in ־וֹת, see Diehl, *Pronomen*, 43. Cf. note a to 16:54.

b Following αβγ we do not expect a further statement about the name, which more correctly belongs to αα. This lateness of b shows the half verse to be an interpretative gloss in the manner of the glosses of Is 7:17, 20; 8:7.

5 5a 𝔐 תחתי (chose whoredom) in my place. 𝔊 (ἐξεπόρνευσεν . . .) ἀπ' ἐμοῦ, 𝔖 מני. Cf. note b to 16:32.

b A glance at vv 7, 12, and 𝔗 בני אתור (cf. also

[for Assyria],[b] warriors,[c] 6/ clothed in blue purple, ambassadors and governors. They were all handsome young men, cavalrymen, riding on horses.[a] 7/ And she turned her lust[a] towards them. The best of the Assyrians were they all. And she made herself unclean with the idols of all those for whom she was filled with desire.[b] 8/ Yet she never gave up her immorality[a] with the Egyptians,[b] for in her youth they had lain with[c] her and handled her virgin bosom,[d] and poured out their immorality upon her.[e] 9/ So I abandoned her to her lovers, the Assyrians, for whom she had been filled with desire. 10/ They stripped her bare, took away her sons and daughters, and killed her with the sword, so that she became a byword[a] among women and (so) judgement[b]

𝕲 𝕾 𝖁) supports the view that בני has fallen out. So Ehrlich, *Randglossen*, Herrmann, Fohrer. More probably, however, the אל אשר, which is linguistically different from vv 7, 12, and which anticipates v 7aβ, shows the hand of a glossator. על – אל cf. note a to 1:17.

c 𝔐 קרובים cannot here be translated "those who are approaching" or "neighbors" in spite of 𝕲 τοὺς ἐγγίζοντας αὐτῇ, 𝕾 דקריבין לה, 𝖁 *appropinquantes*. In the latter case, we should at least expect the article. But what then does it mean? The Assyrians are not the "neighbors" of Israel. In the first case, which from the side of its content alone would then be possible, besides missing the article, we also miss an אליה (cf. 43:19; Dtn 4:7; Josh 9:16 and other passages) which indicates the movement of those who are approaching. קר[ו]בים without the article is found again in a parallel connection in v 12 (v 23 with emended text). It is inserted there between the attribution of power and authority to the Assyrians, which here first follows in v 6. Accordingly the קרובים in v 5 is also to be expected as the first element of a list, which then follows in v 6. Ehrlich, *Randglossen*, understands it as "lords" who have access to the king. Accordingly Herrmann: close confidants of the king, van den Born: *hovelingen*. We may adduce for this the parallel of the Akkadian *qur(ru)būti* "body guards, guardsmen" (Salonen, *Hippologica*, 229f; Klauber, *Beamtentum*, 105–111, read erroneously as *mutir-pūti*). More correctly, however, Ewald points to the closeness with the word קְרָב "war," which points to a meaning "ready for war" (considered by Koehler-Baumgartner). A change to קרואים "highly regarded" (Cornill, cf. note c to v 23), or רבים (Toy), or קרדים following Akkadian *qurādu* "warlike" (Haupt in Toy; Šanda, *ZKTh* 26 [1902]: 205) is not necessary.

6   6a Galling, "Ehrenname," pages 133f note 2, would think here rather, as in 38:4, of a chariot driver.

7   7a For 𝔐 תזנותיה cf. note a to 16:15.

b 𝔐 ובכל אשר עגבה בכל גלוליהם. The second formulation defines the first more precisely. An emendation of the text is not necessary. 𝕲 ἐν πᾶσι τοῖς ἐνθυμήμασιν αὐτῆς is a loose translation.

8   8a For תזנותיה cf. note a to 16:15.

b 𝔐 literally: from Egypt. In the ממצרים there also lies a temporal emphasis: the whoredom familiar from the time of Egypt.

c For אתה – אותה cf. note a to 2:1.

d Cf. note c to v 3.

e For the expression cf. 16:15.

10   10a 𝔐 שם. 𝕲 λάλημα, 𝕾 translates שם twice: תמן ממלאא. The use of שם is certainly unusual, but not unintelligible. Cf. on the subject 36:3, also Jer 29:22. Thus a change to שמה (Ehrlich, *Randglossen*, Herrmann, Koehler-Baumgartner) or שנינה (BH³, Bertholet, Fohrer) is not necessary.

b 𝔐 שְׁפוטִים. Otherwise in Ezekiel only שפטים is

was passed on her.ᶜ

But her sister Oholibah saw it, and she
gave herself up to lust even worse than
her sister, and in her immorityᵃ was
worse than the immorality ᵇ of her sister.
12/ She was filled with desire forᵃ the
Assyrians, ambassadors and governors,
warriors,ᵇ splendidlyᶜ dressed, cavalrymen who rode on horses,ᵈ very
handsome young men. 13/ And I saw
that she had made herself unclean. Both
had acted in the same way. 14/ But she
carried her immoralityᵃ still further.
When she saw men in figured reliefᵇ
on the wall, figures of Chaldeans,ᶜ
drawn with vermilion, 15/ with a belt
fastened round their waists,ᵃ turbans
with loose ends on their heads, they all
looked like high officers,ᵇ a copy of the
Babylonians,ᶜ whose homeland is
Chaldea.ᵈ 16/ she was filled with desireᵃ
for them, when she saw them with her
eyes and sent messengers to them to
Chaldea.ᵇ 17/ Then the Babylonians
came to her as lovers and made her
unclean with their immorality. And
when she had become unclean through
them, her desire for them departed.ᵃ

found (5:10, 15; 16:41 and other passages). Should
we read this here? שָׁפוֹט is otherwise only found
2 Chr 20:9.

c 𝕲 expands: εἰς τὰς θυγατέρας (𝕲ᴬᵠ + αὐτῆς) in
dependence on 16:41.

11   11a For 𝔐 תזנותיה Cf. note a to 16:15.

b The expression זנונים, which has here been
chosen in order to secure a variation from the adjoining תזנות, is only found again in v 29. It is especially frequent in Hosea (1:2; 2:4, 6; 4:12; 5:4);
otherwise in Gen 38:24; 2 Kings 9:22; Na 3:4
(twice).

12   12a על – אל cf. note a to 1:17.

b 𝕲 τοὺς ἐγγὺς αὐτῆς cf. note c to v 5.

c מכלול again in 38:4 in an analogous description of military dress. Cf. מכללים 27:24; מכלל Ps
50:2. That 𝕲 mentions here תכלתא, assimilating to
v 6, certainly does not necessitate an emendation of
the text (against Herrmann, Bertholet, Fohrer).
𝕿, with its גמר, also testifies indirectly in v 6 to a
process of assimilation in exactly the reverse direction. 𝕲 εὐπάρυφα "with a beautiful hem."

d Cf. note a to v 6.

14   14a For 𝔐 תזנותיה cf. note a to 16:15.

b For 𝔐 אנשי מחקה cf. note b to 8:10. An emendation of the text to אנשים מחקים (Cornill, Toy,
Bertholet) or אנשים חקקים (Koehler-Baumgartner,
Cooke) is also not necessary, in spite of 𝕲 ἄνδρας
ἐζωγραφημένους and 𝕭 viros depictos, cf. also 𝕿 𝕲.

c Instead of K כשדיים (again 2 Chr 36:17) we
should read Q כשדים with vv 15f, 23.

15   15a The verbal adjective חָגוֹר is only found here
in the Old Testament.

b שליש literally "the third man" (in a chariot).
According to Alt (orally), we should accept from
2 Kings 7:17 השליש אשר נשען על ידו that the adju-
tant of the chariot force, who stood as "third man"
beside the driver in the chariot, had the task of supporting the fighting soldier when the chariot was
turning, and so ensuring that he was able to shoot.
Cf. the Akkadian šalšu, šalšu rakbu, tašlišu (tašlišu),
Salonen, Hippologica, 213–218, also Klauber, Beamtentum, 111–115.

c 𝔐 בבל is not attested by 𝕲 (but 𝕲 𝕭 𝕿 differ),
but cannot be omitted in the text since otherwise
this becomes syntactically obscure. Can we also
adduce the three-beat rhythm of the three preceding groups of expressions?

d For כשדים as a territorial name cf. note b to
16:29.

16   16a Q demands, in agreement with v 20, the form
ותעגבה, following Bauer-Leander § 40 t,z; 49v "af-
fect-Aorist." Gesenius-Kautzsch § 48 d.

b 𝔐 כשדימה. 𝕲 (𝕲 𝕿), as already in 11:24 more
fully εἰς γῆν Χαλδαίων. Cf. note b to 16:29.

17   17a יקע perhaps an onomatopoeic formation "to
cradle," used in Gen 32:26 of the hips. In Ezek
23:17f; Jer 6:8 it is used with נפש as subject. Further
in 23:18, 22, 28 the נקע by-form.

18/ She had made her immorality[a] public and made herself naked. Then I turned away from her,[b] as I had turned away from her sister.[b] 19/ She[a] played the whore still more.[b] She remembered[c] her youth, when she had played the whore in Egypt, 20/ and was filled with desire[a] for her lovers (?),[b] whose flesh is like the flesh of the donkey, and whose seed[c] is like the seed[c] of horses. [21/ And you longed for the immorality of your youth, when men in Egypt[a] handled[b] your breasts, to press[c] your virgin bosom.][d]

22 Therefore, Oholibah, thus has [the Lord][a] Yahweh said: Behold, I will rouse your lovers against you, from whom your desire has turned away, and bring them against you from all sides, 23/ the Babylonians and all the Chaldeans, Pekod and Shoa and Koa [all Assyrians][a]

18   18a For 𝔐 תזנותיה cf. note a to 16:15.
      b Cf. note a to v 17.

19   19a 𝔊 already in v 19 changes to direct address, which is first in place in v 22. However, cf. also v 21 𝔐, and see note d.
      b For 𝔐 תזנותיה cf. note a to 16:15.
      c 𝔐 לזכר literally: in order to remember.

20   20a For 𝔐 ותעגבה cf. note a to v 16.
      b 𝔊 פלגש, in Hebrew certainly a foreign loanword (cf. Greek παλλακίς, παλλακή), is otherwise in the Old Testament a designation for a concubine (Gen 22:24; 35:22 and other passages). According to Morgenstern, "Additional Notes," 56f, the word would originally have denoted a woman who stayed in her father's house, in accordance with the custom of the "*beena* marriage" (matriarchate). Neufeld, *Marriage Laws*, 123, on the other hand, finds in it originally a designation for an ordinary prostitute. A masculine use of the term is not otherwise found. So Jahn, *Buch*, and Koehler-Baumgartner read instead פלשתים, for which 16:27 may be adduced in support, but where the Philistines are certainly regarded as Yahweh's weapon of punishment. However, the context in 23:20 points to the Egyptians. 𝔊 ἐπὶ τοὺς Χαλδαίους is simply guessing; also 𝔖 ואתנקפת לעבדיהון "and she clung to her deeds," 𝔗 ואיתרעיאת למיהוי שמשא "and she longed to be his servant" (thus better שמוטא "his prostitute," Cooke, *Dalman WB*, and others), 𝔙 *et insanivit libidine super concubitum eorum* offer a free paraphrase. The translation given in the text remains uncertain.
      c 𝔐 זרמה is connected as a rule (Gesenius-Buhl, Zorell) with זרם "heavy rain." So 𝔙 *fluxus*, as also 𝔗 צחנתא "something abominable." However, a metathesis of ר and מ and a connection with זמורה "shoot, twig" would also be possible. So Koehler-Baumgartner: the male sex organ. 𝔊 αἰδοῖα and 𝔖 חנא appear to have understood it in this way. Cf. note c to 8:17, also above pp. 244f.

21   21a 𝔐 ממצרים "out of Egypt." Does 𝔊 ἐν Αἰγύπτῳ presuppose a במצרים (so MS[Ken 30]) or a simple מצרים (so MSS[Ken 28], de Rossi 737)? The latter could be taken as an accusative of place, or with an active reading of בעשות (cf. note b), as subject. Eissfeldt, "Zeilenfüllung," 89, suggests that the first מ of 𝔐 ממצרים could be regarded as taken over from an מ which once stood at the end of the line as *custos*.
      b 𝔐 בַּעְשׂוֹת. Following vv 3, 8 we should read בְּעְשׂוֹת, or (note c to v 3) בְּעָשׂוֹת.
      c 𝔐 למען. The analogy of vv 3, 8 suggests the reading of לְמַעֵךְ or לִמְעֹךְ.
      d The change to direct speech, which comes too soon and which is first in place from v 22 on, and the (inaccurate) citation of earlier statements in v 21, the content of which does not carry further, betrays it as a subsequent addition.

22   22a אדני is lacking in 𝔊 𝔆, see Excursus 1.

23   23a The asyndetic introduction of כל בני אשור, which is smoothed out in 𝔊 𝔏 (Sabatier) 𝔖 by the

with them,[b] handsome young men,
ambassadors and governors, high
officers and highly respected men,[c] all
of them men[d] who ride on horses.[e]
24/ And they will come against you
from the North (?)[a] 'with' chariots[b]
and wheels, and with a host from
among the nations. Bucklers, shields
and helmets[c] they will set against you
on all sides. I will give them authority
to execute judgement, and they will
judge you according to their laws.
25/ And I will turn my zeal against you,
and they will deal with you[a] in anger.
They will cut off your nose and your
ears, and your posterity[b] will fall by
the sword. [They will take your sons
and your daughters, and what is left of

addition of the copula, makes the expression appear either as an apposition to the three preceding national names or as a subsequent addition, which does not then fully fit in. Since, however, the Assyrian nation is never presented as a unity of those three past nations, the mention of the Assyrians in this connection appears historically very questionable, so that the second view is the more probable.

b אתם – אותם cf. note a to 2:1.

c Since the enumeration otherwise works with the predicates mentioned in vv 5f and 12, and since קר[ו]א[י]ם, where it is used absolutely in the Old Testament, either refers to invited guests (1 Sam 9:13, 22; 2 Sam 15:11; 1 Kings 1:41, 49; Zeph 1:7; Prv 9:18) or those who have been called by the community (קרואי העדה Nu 1:16; 26:9), we may first conjecture a scribal error in 𝔐 קרואים from קרובים (cf. note c to v 5). However, 𝔐 is also attested by 𝔊 ὀνομαστούς, 𝔙 nominatos (also 𝔏 זמינין?). Thus we must reckon with a free variation and understand the absolute קרואים as "called, highly esteemed."

d 𝔐 כלם is wrongly attached to the following verse by 𝔊 πάντες ἥξουσιν.

e Cf. note a to v 6.

24 24a 𝔐 הֹצֶן is so far uninterpreted. 𝔊 𝔗 Kimchi and 10 MSS[Ken] read חֹצֶן, which is found in Ps 129:7; Is 49:22; Neh 5:13 with the meaning "bosom," but this does not clarify the verse here. Baer-Delitzsch, xi, following Akkadian analogies, accept a meaning "heap." Cornill adopts this, and Bertholet considers a reading מִצָּפוֹן, following 𝔊 ἀπὸ βορρᾶ. Graphically closer is the reading המון (Smend, Cooke). For the reading of 𝔊 the description of the campaign of Nebuchadnezzar against Tyre in 26:7ff, with its echoes in 23:24 and its מצפון, can be adduced. Reider, "Contributions," 91, chooses with Ben Yehuda the reading הֹצֶן which, is interpreted following Arabic ḥiṣān as "stallion." In any case the interpretation remains uncertain.

b 𝔐 רכב. 26:7 and the following ובקהל (cf. Wernberg-Møller, "'Pleonastic'," 323) would support here the reading ברכב (Bertholet, BH³). However, the uncertainty in the interpretation of the preceding הצן permits no certain decision.

c קובע is found again 1 Sam 17:38. Much more frequently we have the form כובע, Ezek 27:10; 38:5. "It is hard to say which form is the original. There can as well have been an influence from the ʿayin to make כ to ק, as an influence from the beth to change ק to כ," LidzEph 2, 135. 𝔊 did not understand the saying.

25 25a For אתך – אותך cf. note a to 2:1, also note b to 22:7.

b With אחרית "that which is after" the question arises whether "in the sequence of generations" means posteriores, future descendants (cf. Jer 31:17, with its parallel בנים, or Ps 109:13 parallel דור אחר) or looks to the coming judgement on those who

475

you^c will be burnt with fire.]^c 26/ And
they will strip off your clothes and take
away your finery. 27/ And I will put an
end to your immorality and your
whoredom^a from the land of Egypt,
and you will no (more) raise your eyes
to them,^b and remember Egypt no more.

28 Thus has [the Lord]^a Yahweh said:
Behold, I will give you^b into the land of
those whom you hate—into the hand of
those from whom your desire has
turned away. 29/ And they will deal
with you^a in their hatred, and take all
you have earned, and leave^b you naked
and exposed, and your whorish^c
nakedness will be uncovered.^d 'Your'^e
immorality and your whoredom^f
30/ 'have'^a brought this on you because^b

are still there *reliqui*, the surviving remnant (so Amos
9:1). In the context of the metaphor of an individual person (and his children) the first interpretation
is preferable. However cf. note c.

c Beside אחרית, בניך ובנותיך cannot here mean
"descendants," but must, as in Amos 9:1, point to
the "survivors, the remnant." b interprets the metaphor of a (Oholibah) in terms of the reality represented by her (the political entity Jerusalem or Judah). Since v 26 returns again to the metaphor and
the double understanding of אחרית in v 25a and 25b
appears somewhat harsh, we must see in v 25b a
piece of subsequent interpretation. For the play on
variants in the concluding words of 𝕲, which are
taken actively, see Ziegler, *Ezechiel*, 80f.

27 27a 𝔐 ואת זנותך. The formation זנות is only again
found in Ezekiel in 43:7, 9. A glance at the connection of זמה and תזנות in 29:35 suggests that here
a ת has fallen out through haplography, and the
original text is to be read as תזנותך, which corresponds with the linguistic usage in ch. 16 and 23.

b As the word of relation for 𝔐 אליהם we must
think of the "lovers." In the usage נשׂא עינים אל
there is otherwise found in Ezekiel as object only
גלולים (18:6, 12, 15; 33:25, cf. 6:9; 20:24). For
the usage here cf. Gen 39:7. Should we see the work
of a "commentator" here, who had in mind as object not the "lovers" but the "idols of Egypt"
(20:7)? Cf. v 30.

28 28a אדני is lacking in 𝕲 𝔏^s 𝕮, see Excursus 1.
b The suffixed form נְתַנֵךְ occurs again in 25:4, Is
22:1, cf. Gesenius-Kautzsch § 91 e, Bauer-Leander
§ 48 s''.

29 29a אתך – אותך cf. note a to 2:1.
b 𝔐 ועזבוך is not attested by 𝕲 𝔏^s. Thus the יגיעך
of 𝔐 corresponds in 𝕲 to τοὺς πόνους σου καὶ τοὺς
μόχθους σου. We may question whether we are faced
here with a simple double translation, as in 16:14
(note a), or whether 𝕲 misunderstood ועזבוך as
ועזבוניך (27:12, 14 "merchandise").
c For זנוניך cf. note b to v 12.
d 𝔐 נגלה has to be understood as a participle:
"is revealed." However, perhaps we should restore
perfect consecutive ונגלתה (Herrmann, Bertholet).
The acceptance of a third person masculine perfect
(Aalders) is very difficult, in spite of Joüon 150 k.
e 𝔐 וזמתך ותזנותיך connects the two words with
the preceding, 𝕲 only the first. The *scelus tuum et
fornicationes tuae* of 𝔅, which is added asyndetically,
may here have preserved a recollection of the original point of division of vv 29/30. With 𝔅 we should
read זמתך and begin the new sentence v 30a with
this word.
fFor תזנותיך cf. note a to 16:15.

30 30a Instead of עשׂה we should read עשׂו, cf. 𝔗.
The infinitive absolute of 𝔐 is a vocalization of embarrassment made necessary in consequence of the
false verse division. For the form of expression cf.
Jer 4:18.

you have gone whoring after the nations,ᶜ because you have made yourself unclean with their idols.

31 You have followed in the way of your sister,ᵃ and I will put her cup into your hand.ᵇ 32/ Thus has [the Lord]ᵃ Yahweh said: You shall drink the cup of your sister, which is deep and wide, [she will become an object of mockery and scorn]ᵇ and which holds much.ᶜ 33/ You will become full of grievous drunkenness.ᵃ A cup [of horror and]ᵇ devastation is the cup of your sister [Samaria].ᶜ 34/ And you shall drink it and empty (it completely) and 'taste its dregs' (?)ᵃ [and tear out your breasts],ᵇ for I have spoken, says [the Lord]ᶜ Yahweh.

35 Therefore thus has [the Lord]ᵃ Yahweh said: Because you have forgotten me and have cast me behind your back, you will bear (now) your immorality and your whoredom.ᵇ

36 And Yahweh said to me: Son of man, will you (not) judge Oholah and Oholibah!ᵃ And make known to them their abominations!ᵇ 37/ For they have

b 𝔐 בְּזְנוּתֵךְ. The ב, like the following עַל אֲשֶׁר, defines the cause of the punishment, which is therefore not repeated in 𝔊 𝔏ˢ 𝔗.

c גוים without the article is also found 7:24; 19:4, 8; 22:16.

31 31a For הלך בדרך cf. note a to 18:11.

b 𝔐 בידך. MSS 𝔊 𝔖 𝔗 plural.

32 32a אדני is lacking in 𝔊 𝔏ˢ 𝔗 𝔄, see Excursus 1.

b The passage, in which Oholibah is presupposed as subject (or is it intended as an address in the second masculine singular, wholly out of the context? So Aalders), is not attested by 𝔊 𝔏ˢ 𝔗 𝔄 and is shown to be an addition by the way in which it breaks up the context.

c 𝔐 מְרֻבָּה. If we do not accept this as a noun which is otherwise not found, we have to presuppose a vocalization מַרְבָּה with 𝔊 𝛴 𝔖ʰ, cf. Ex 36:5.

33 33a שכרון of 𝔐 is not to be emended in accordance with 21:11 to שברון (so MSSᴷᵉⁿ ⁸⁹, ¹¹², Cornill, Ehrlich, *Randglossen*, Cooke, Bertholet), but rather שכרון ויגון form a zeugma: "drunkenness which leads to sorrow."

b 𝔐 שׁמה ושׁממה. 𝔊 𝔏ˢ attest only one of the two synonymous expressions (𝔊⁹⁶⁷ corresponds to 𝔐). Thus שׁמה, which is completely lacking in Ezekiel apart from the present text, but which is frequent in Jeremiah, represents an addition—Ezekiel uses the expression שׁממה twenty-one times, משׁמה five times, four of them in the double expression שׁממה ומשׁממה, cf. further to 35:7. In the original text, accordingly, we should see a two-beat expression.

c In the original text of 𝔊ᴮ שמרון is not attested (although it is in 𝔊⁶⁹⁷ 𝔏ˢ, accepted for 𝔊 by Ziegler). Since שמרון, instead of the expected אהליבה, is striking also in its content, it is possibly an old interpretative addition as in v 4b.

34 34a 𝔐 ואת חרשׂיה תגרמי "and you shall gnaw its potsherds" (so 𝔙, also Driver, "Ezekiel," 155) appears roughly to have been found by 𝔊, although the remaining versions translate very differently, but is not seriously convincing. ויח פרעונותה תקבלין 𝔗 avoids the difficulty by interpreting the simile. 𝔖 וסערכי תגזין "and you shall cut your hair" is a free rendering from the general context of mourning. In the translation Cornill's conjecture ואת שמריה תגמאי (similarly Ehrlich, *Randglossen*, ואת שמריה תגמרי) is accepted as helpful. The interpretation remains questionable.

b 𝔐 ושדיך תנתקי. The stichos is lacking in 𝔊 𝔏ˢ. Its insertion, which harks back to the mention of שדים in vv 3, 21, must already presuppose the reading חרשׂיה of 𝔐 in the preceding stichos.

c אדני is lacking in 𝔊 𝔄 (𝔏ˢ *deus*), see Excursus 1.

35 35a אדני is lacking in 𝔊 𝔏ˢ 𝔄, see Excursus 1.

b For 𝔐 תזנותיך cf. note a to 16:15.

36 36a 𝔐 התשׁפוט, 𝔊 οὐ κρινεῖς in the sense of an imperative, cf. 20:4; 22:2.

b 𝔐 וְהַגֵּד, according to Rubinstein, "Finite Verb," 363, could also be understood as an infinitive

committed adultery, and blood is on their hands, and they have committed adultery with their idols, and the very children which they have borne to me they have offered to them[a] for food.[b] 38/ This too they have done to me: they have defiled my sanctuary [on that day][a] and desecrated my sabbaths. 39/ And when they had sacrificed their sons to their idols, they came into my sanctuary [on that day][a] to desecrate it. And behold, they did this within my house. 40/ They[a] also sent to men, who were to come from afar, to whom a messenger was sent,[b] and they came— for these[c] you washed yourself, you painted your eyes and put on finery,[d] 41/ and you sat yourself[a] upon a bed that had been made ready,[b] and before which a table was spread, and you laid my incense and my oil upon it.[c] 42/ With loud voices 'they sang' (?)[a] . . .[b] and

absolute in the context of a verb-infinitive absolute construction.

37 37a 𝔐 להם. We expect להן. So MSS Edd. Up till now the correct feminine suffix forms have been used in vv 36f. In what follows the masculine forms are used.

b 𝔊 διήγαγον αὐτοῖς δι᾽ ἐμπύρων (𝔏ˢ *per ignem*, 𝔖 בנורא) is a free elaboration, which does not necessitate a change of 𝔐.

38 38a 𝔐 ביום ההוא is lacking in 𝔊 𝔏ˢ and is to be deleted. Clearly the addition here and in v 39 seeks to emphasize that the defiling idolatry and the entering into Yahweh's sanctuary occur on one and the same day. This would be more correctly expressed by בעצם היום ההוא.

39 39a 𝔐 ביום ההוא is lacking in 𝔊 𝔏ˢ, as in v 38.

40 40a 𝔐 תשלחנה (assimilated by 𝔗 to the following second person singular and changed to the perfect שלחת) is not attested by 𝔊 𝔏ˢ. However, it can hardly be left out. For the preceding כי as "a connective between the adverb (אף) and the rest of the clause" see Blau, "Adverbia," 134f. In the final use of the participle (באים) Driver, "Ezekiel," 155, with reference to 1 Chr 15:16, sees an Aramaism.

b 𝔐 שלוח. 𝔊 (𝔏ˢ 𝔖) ἐξαπέστελλον possibly read שלחו.

c By לאשר which 𝔊, in order to smooth over the disturbance of the sentence construction found in what precedes (note a) translates with εὐθύς, an addition comprising vv 40bβ–41 and formulated in the second singular feminine is added on.

d 𝔐 ועדית, as the וישבת in v 41, appears to betray a late linguistic usage which has lost a feeling for consecutive form under Aramaic influence. However cf. note a to 22:29.

41 41a Cf. note d to v 40.

b 𝔐 כבודה is either to be taken as a noun (Ju 18:21, "valuable possessions," Ps 45:14 "splendor") or as the feminine of an adjective כבוד which is otherwise not found. More probably, however, following 𝔊 (ἐπὶ κλίνης) ἐστρωμένης, 𝔏ˢ (*super lectum*) *stratum*, it is a scribal error for רבודה (cf. Prv 7:16).

c 𝔐 שמת עליה. 𝔊 (𝔏ˢ) εὐφραίνοντο ἐπ᾽ αὐτοῖς appears to have had before it a form שמחו, which may then point to an original שמתי. The עליה of 𝔐 is either to be taken neutrally ("thereto") or to be emended to עליו. The section present in the second singular feminine appears to end here.

42 42a 𝔐 וקול המון שלו בה "And the sound of a careless multitude is in it." For the lack of dagesh in ב after ו cf. Gesenius-Kautzsch § 21c. 𝔊 καὶ φωνὴν ἁρμονίας ἀνεκρούοντο "with voices in unison they sing" appears to presuppose a verb in place of שלו and not to have known בה, which has no clear word of relation. Cornill שרו, Toy שרים would point in the direction of 𝔊.

b 𝔐 ואל אנשים מרב אדם מובאים סובאים ממדבר "and to men out of the multitude of men who were brought drunken out of the desert." 𝔊 καὶ πρὸς

they^c put bracelets on^d their hands and a beautiful crown on their head. 43/ . . .^a 44/ And 'they came'^a to her.^b As a man comes to a prostitute, so they came to Oholah and Oholibah, the immoral women.^c 45/ Righteous men will pass judgement upon them,^a as a man passes judgement upon an adulteress and such who shed blood,^b for they are adulteresses, and blood is on their hands. 46/ [For]^a Thus has [the Lord]^b Yahweh said: One might summon^c a host against them^d and give them over to terror^e and plunder. 47/ And with stones they^a [the assembly which is

ἄνδρας ἐκ πλήθους ἀνθρώπων ἥκοντας ἐκ τῆς ἐρήμου shows that מובאים סובאים is to be regarded as a dittography, but does not help further in understanding the text. Is the mention here of the coming of men from new directions? 𝔊, which translates the text with great freedom, thinks of people from Arabia: "men who came from Sheba and from the desert"; similarly 𝔗, which speaks of "men round about from the desert."

c Following the masculine ויתנו of 𝔐 there must be meant here the men who put ornaments on the women. It is certainly not to be excluded that ויתנו appears here for the third person feminine plural of נתן, which is never found in the Old Testament. There could then be mention here of the preparations of the women themselves, as in v 41.

d אל – על cf. note a to 1:17.

43 43a 𝔐 ואמר לבלה נאופים עת יזנה תזנותה והיא remains obscure. 𝔊 καὶ εἶπα Οὐκ ἐν τούτοις μοιχεύουσι; καὶ ἔργα πόρνης καὶ αὐτὴ ἐξεπόρνευσε. Driver, "Ezekiel," 155, understands ל as a particle of exclamation before a verbal adjective derived from בלה "to wither" (cf. Josh 9:5) and reckons at the conclusion with an aposiopesis: "Oh! The women jaded with adulteries! Now they will commit whoredom with her and she . . .!" We must add something like: (she)'ll enjoy it! However, we must reckon on with a more radical corruption of the text.

44 44a 𝔐 ויבוא; the versions support ויבאו, cf. note a to 14:1.

b The singular אליה presupposes that here only one woman was spoken of. The same also appears to be the case in v 43. Thus vv 43–44aα fall out from the context as a separate element.

c 𝔐 אשת הזמה shows an unusual plural formation from אשה which, however, is intelligible, following Baer-Delitzsch, xi, and Driver, "Linguistic Problems," 175, as influenced from the Akkadian aššati. Following 𝔊 τοῦ ποιῆσαι ἀνομίαν Cornill, Ehrlich, Randglossen, Herrmann, Toy, Bertholet, Cooke would emend to לעשות [ה]זמה.

45 45a 𝔐 אותהם only here. Cf. Gesenius-Kautzsch § 103b. It could be a scribal error arising from the directly following מ, from an original אותהן. So some MSS and cf. note d to v 46.

b 𝔐 ומשפט שפכות דם. 𝔊 (𝔏ˢ) καὶ ἐκδικήσει αἵματος may be a free abbreviation. In 16:38 𝔐 has ושפכת דם, which has no counterpart in 𝔊.

46 46a 𝔐 כי is lacking in MS^{Ken 224} 𝔊 𝔏ˢ and is to be deleted as a scribal error and dittography of כה.

b אדני is lacking in 𝔊 𝔏ˢ 𝔆, see Excursus 1.

c 𝔐 הַעֲלֵה, which could be an imperative according to its form, is better understood as infinitive absolute with the following נָתֹן.

d 𝔐 עליהם, in line with אותהם in v 45 (note a), may be a scribal error for עליהן?

e זעוה by-form for זועה Koehler-Baumgartner; only here in Ezekiel, more frequent in Jeremiah.

47 47a 𝔐 ורגמו. 𝔊 (𝔏ˢ) καὶ λιθοβόλησον must have

summoned]^b shall stone them, and with their swords they shall hack them^c in pieces.^{d} They shall kill their^e sons and their^e daughters, and they shall burn their houses with fire. 48/ And I will put an end to immorality in the land and all the women will be warned^a not to be immoral as you,^{b} 49/ and 'men'^{a} will bring your immorality upon you, and you must bear the guilt (which you have committed) with your idols,^{b} and you shall know^c that I am [the Lord]^d Yahweh.

had before it the infinitive absolute רגום (and misunderstood it as imperative). This reading is supported by the preceding נָתַן and the following ברא. For an explanation as verb-infinitive absolute construction see Rubinstein, "Finite Verb," 363f, also 366f note 3.

b Ehrlich, *Randglossen*, would translate 𝔐 אבן קהל by "stones thrown by the people." Also 𝔊 λίθοις ὄχλων, 𝔏^s *lapidibus turbarum* take קהל as genitive with אבן and thereby show the difficulty in the interpretation of קהל without the article. This is certainly to be regarded as the subject, clumsily inserted after v 46, and to be cut out as foreign to the original text (Cornill, Herrmann, Toy, Bertholet, Cooke).

c 𝔐 אותהן only here, cf. Gesenius-Kautzsch § 103b, also note a to v 45.

d בָּרָא pi'el only again Josh 17:15, 18 with the meaning "to cut down." Ezek 21:24 text error. An emendation to כרת (Rothstein) or בתך (Bertholet, Cooke) is not necessary. Driver, "Linguistic Problems," 175, would emend to ואבדו, following the Eastern Syriac translation in Mt 26:52.

e 𝔐 בניהם ובנותיהם again shows confused suffix forms—under the influence of the directly preceding בחרבותם, correctly written with masculine suffix relating to קהל?

48   48a 𝔐 וְנִוַּסְּרוּ reflexive-passive nitpa'el, again וְנִכַּפֵּר Dtn 21:8, frequent in late Hebrew. Cf. Bauer-Leander § 38s.

b 𝔐 כזמתכנה, 𝔊 (𝔏^s) κατὰ τὰς ἀσεβείας αὐτῶν.

49   49a 𝔐 ונתנו could be joined with the plural subject in v 47, over v 48, but is better to be understood neutrally; cf. the passive translation of 𝔊 (𝔏^s) καὶ δοθήσεται. 𝔗 understood וְנִתְּנוּ; the first person in 𝔊, which connects best with v 48 and also corresponds with the use of נתן על to denote intervention for punishment (7:3, 8f), is probably a smoothing over.

b For the form תִשֶּׂאינָה cf. Gesenius-Kautzsch § 76b.

c The masculine וידעתם of 𝔐 again has in mind the community being addressed.

d אדני is lacking in 𝔊 𝔏^s, see Excursus 1.

Form

The redactional section 23:1–49 shows itself to be a formulation closely related to ch. 16, not only in its theme, but also in its formal structure. Here also a number of expansive additions, which depend upon the main element, have been added to the basic element of a figurative address drawn in harsh colors. In the sphere of the kernel section itself a basic text must have been expanded with subsequent additions. The mutual influence of ch. 16 and 23 is to be seen here, though

naturally now in the reverse direction.[1]

In the analysis, first of all, vv 36–49, which are introduced by ויאמר יהוה אלי which is unusual in Ezekiel (cf. note a to 4:13, note a to 9:4, and below to 44:2, 5), are separate from what precedes. Both content and linguistic usage show vv 36–49 to be a secondary section, strongly affected by quotations. We can also recognize in vv 32–34 a relatively independent song of the cup of reeling, on the grounds of its theme and introductory messenger formula and the concluding oracle formula.

It is joined to the theme of the preceding by the transitional v 31. In v 35 a threat with a motive clause (יען) has been added with a separate introductory formula. Also the section vv 28–30, introduced with its own messenger formula, appears as a weak summary of what has already been said, couched in more general terms.

Thus we are left to begin with the section vv 1–27. However, in this kernel section also we must still reckon with additions. The extent of the subsequent elaboration may be disputed. After the removal of additions in vv 4b, 7b, 8, 9b, 10b, 12–14a, 18, 21, 23aβb, 25b, 26, the exclusion of which will be justified in the following exposition, the basic text runs as follows:

> Then the word of Yahweh came to me: / Son of man, there were two women, / daughters of the same mother. / They played the whore in Egypt, / already in their youth they played the whore. / There their breasts were pressed / and there their virgin bosoms were handled. / The elder was named Oholah / and her sister Oholibah. / And they became mine / and bore sons and daughters. /
>
> But Oholah was unfaithful to me / and was filled with desire for her lovers, / warriors clothed in blue purple, / ambassadors and governors. / They were all handsome young men, / cavalrymen riding on horses. / And she turned her lust towards them. / The best of the Assyrians were they all. /
>
> So I abandoned her to her lovers. / They stripped her bare, / took away her sons and daughters, / and killed her with the sword. /
>
> But her sister Oholibah saw it, / and she gave herself up to lust even worse than her sister, / and in her immorality was worse than the immorality of her sister. / When she saw men in figured relief on the wall, / figures of Chaldeans drawn with vermilion, / with a belt fastened round their waist, / turbans with loose ends on their heads, / they all looked like high officers, / a copy of the Babylonians, / whose homeland is Chaldea, / she was filled with desire for them, when she saw them with her eyes / and sent messengers to them to Chaldea. / Then the Babylonians came to her as lovers / and made her unclean with their immorality. / And when she had become unclean through them, / her desire for them departed. /
>
> She played the whore still more. / She remembered her youth, / when she had played the whore in Egypt, / and was filled with desire for her lovers (?), / whose flesh is like the flesh of the donkey, / and whose seed is like the seed of horses. /

> Therefore, Oholibah, thus has the Lord Yahweh said: / Behold, I will rouse your lovers against you, / from whom your desire has turned away, / and bring them against you from all sides, / the Babylonians and all the Chaldeans, / Pekod and Shoa and Koa. / And they will come against you from the North (?) / with chariots and wheels / and with a host from among the nations. / Bucklers, shields and helmets / they will set against you on all sides. / I will give them authority to execute judgement, / and they will judge you according to their laws. / And I will turn my zeal against you, / and they will deal with you in anger. / They will cut off your nose and your ears, / and your posterity will fall by the sword. / And I will put an end to your immorality / and your whoredom from the land of Egypt, / and you will no more raise your eyes to them / and remember Egypt no more.

For the metric features of the saying we must refer back to what was previously said.[2] Since the *parallelismus membrorum* can be very clearly seen in certain verses (cf. vv 2–3a), Hölscher, *Hesekiel*, believes here also that he can reconstruct a complete poem (seven strophes [Müller gives a different strophic division]). However, a uniform meter cannot really be worked out. The length of line varies especially between two and three beat units, and also four beat units are not lacking (e.g., v 14b—double fours). On the other side, however, the parallelism of expression in some parts, which is not to be overlooked, forbids Fohrer's solution of the short-verse strophes. Thus we must reckon here with an exalted narrative style, which sometimes approximates closely a firm metric rhythm, but then slips back again into a freer movement (cf. the 3 lines of vv 10a or 11).

Unlike the saying about the whorish Jerusalem in ch. 16, the story of the two whorish women, Oholah and Oholibah, is first told by Yahweh to the prophet (vv 1–21). First in the change to the declaration of judgement upon Obolibah in v 22 does the saying turn formally to address directly the younger sister. Any explicit command to the prophet to speak is lacking. The actual address to Judah-Jerusalem, which alone in Ezekiel's day represented God's covenant people, thereby comes to expression very sharply.[3]

A glance at the history of tradition of the imagery

---

1   For the process of growth which is recognizable behind the redactional section 23:1–49 we must compare what was said above on pp. 333f in respect to

ch. 16.

2   Pp. 333f.

3   For the address to the people as a "corporate per-

used here of Yahweh and his two wives has already raised the question whether ultimately a mythological background lies behind it. Hempel affirms: "Anat-Bethel . . . and Ašam-Bethel, the popular consorts of Yahweh, are made by the prophet himself, for whom sexual excesses are an abomination (18:6), in the most extravagant sexual fantasy, into symbols of the people, as Oholah and Oholibah, to whom God has become married."[4] He would thereby illuminate Ezek 23 quite directly from the syncretistic popular faith that is evident at Elephantine.[5] Against this Fohrer points more cautiously to Jer 3:6–11, behind which direct old Canaanite conceptions must stand, such as are to be seen in Ugarit in the narratives of El, who seduces and impregnates two goddesses.[6] With the reference to Jer 3:6ff Fohrer points in the right direction, beside which Kuhl's reconstruction of a secular love song, which is supposed to lie behind Ezek 23 and which Fohrer similarly would adduce, is superfluous.[7] A glance at the Old Testament traditions, which present themselves very clearly at this point, is entirely sufficient to explain the choice of imagery in Ezek 23. The reference to Israel as the unfaithful wife of Yahweh appears in prophetic preaching for the first time in Hosea and is markedly historicized.[8] It is then freely applied by Jeremiah in 3:6ff, after Josiah's movement towards a greater Israel, to which Jer 31f also belongs, to the two divided kingdoms, each of which is embodied in the figure of a woman. In this the women are given fixed names, which are self-descriptive. Beside the מְשֻׁבָה יִשְׂרָאֵל (3:6, 8, 11, 12) appears בָּגוֹדָה יהודה (or בֹּגֵדָה) (3:7f, 10f). Every feature of divine marriage relating to fertility and procreation is here completely suppressed in the presentation of the complete humanity of the two women, who are spoken to in regard to their guilt, and called to repentance in the sphere of their responsibility as being created. Ezekiel stands on the shoulders of Jeremiah, in taking up this imagery and elaborating it in detail in accordance with its own thoroughness

(analogous to Ezek 16, 34). Yet there are no longer in mind here, as in Hos 2, Jer 3 and Ezek 16, the immoral practices with the local Canaanite Baals, but the political relations of the two kingdoms with foreign powers. Thus here it is no longer the Baals who become Yahweh's rivals, but the political and historical figures of the smartly dressed Assyrian and Babylonian warriors. Admittedly in the whole unit Yahweh, who is the real husband, is standing rather in the background as the rival lover before the great theme of the rivalry of the historical lovers in the south (Israel's youthful love) and in the east (later love). The זנה has undeniably already become a very fixed concept. The increasing harshness of the imagery from Jer 3:6ff to Ezek 23 (the divorcing of the משׁבה ישׂראל [Jer 3:8] becomes the killing of Oholah, and this same punishment, which is left unexpressed in Jer 3 for the בגודה יהודה, is now fully affirmed for Oholibah) corresponds with the whole character of Ezekiel's preaching.

With the allegory of the two women Ezekiel combines in a surprising way, going beyond Jer 3, Israel's credal proclamation of its origin out of Egypt. The very names Oholah and Oholibah, which have here completely displaced the national names Israel and Judah (cf. further the exposition, especially to v 4b), recall in an archaizing manner the period of tent-dwelling in the wilderness (cf. Hos 12:10 and see below). It is then again certainly the specific feature of Ezekiel's transformation of the history into a condemnation of sin that this recollection of Egypt is not chosen in order to show the bright early history of God's deliverance, but that, as in Ezek 20, it has become entirely a vehicle for an accusation against Israel's shameless resorting to Egypt, which had become actual in Ezekiel's day.

Setting

From this some conclusion about the date of the basic oracle of vv 1–27 is possible. It reflects very clearly the time of strong dependence of Judah upon Egypt. Since

---

4   Hempel, *Literatur*, 168.
5   See Albert Vincent, *La religion des Judéo-Araméens d'Éléphantine* (Paris: Geuthner, 1937).
6   See Gordon, *Ugaritic Textbook*, text 52, translated in Gordon, *Ugaritic Literature*, 57–62. See also Walter Baumgartner, "Ugaritische Probleme und ihre Tragweite für das Alte Testament," *ThZ* 3 (1947):

sonality" cf. above pp. 334f.

96f.
7   *Hesekielprobleme*—unprinted manuscript, no date, p. 78.
8   See Wolff, *Hosea*, on Hos 1:2, also above p. 335.

Yahweh threatens in it that this attachment to Egypt shall be brought to an end, we can point to a time after Zedekiah's defection from Babylon (ch. 17), but before the time of the capture of Jerusalem in 587.

As to the place where the saying was spoken no definite indications are to be found.[9] For a location among the exiles nothing stands in the way.[10]

Interpretation

■ **23:1** The narrative of the two unfaithful women, which is first told to the prophet (son of man) as a personal communication from Yahweh, without any command to preach, begins as in ch. 16 with a prologue, which tells their previous history.[11] In terse sentences this hurries on to the mention of the marriage between Yahweh and the women (ותהיינה לי 23:4 corresponds to ותהי לי 16:8) and registers the birth of sons and daughters by which the marriage receives its confirmatory seal. Whereas 16:9–14 describes in some detail the honor that it means to belong to Yahweh, to which the mention of the beginnings in Egypt might have given rise (cf. Hos 11:1; 13:4), any such description of Yahweh's gracious gift is completely lacking here.

■ **23:3** After the brief mention of the common origin of the two women, behind which lies an affirmation of the unity of Israel, there comes a mention of the place of the youthful days of the women connected quite harshly with a reference to their sins. Whereas 16:3 lets us see the sinful burden of Jerusalem in its inheritance from its ancestors, here it is carried back explicitly to the youthful years of the two women with the sins of their youth. The intact virginity of the girls, who should have kept themselves pure to the one alone to whom they belonged, has already been denied by the prophet in ch. 16. We may question whether, as in 20:7, Israel's proximity to the idols of Egypt is in mind. Since, however, in ch. 23 immorality denotes more broadly political dependence, this association lies further away. It is superfluous to set out here a more immediate history which points from the early immorality of Israel to its connection with Yahweh. In its exposition the text seeks to affirm simply the basic fact, twice repeated in another way in ch. 16 and 20, that Israel in its history derives from an initial call by Yahweh to whom it owes its existence as a people (sons and daughters), and that it, on the other hand, from its very origins stands under a grim shadow, with reference to its human character and conduct.

■ **23:4** Jer 3 had described the two women with the qualifying names of משבה and בגודה (בגדה), but at the same time added to these quite freely the names Israel and Judah which were in current use in the political sphere. Since "Israel" in Ezekiel is the emphatic name for the whole people of God, the antithesis Israel-Judah is impossible for him.[12] The subsidiary name has here become a full proper name. Just how far, and in what direction, this has a qualifying force is contested. The traditional interpretation (Jerome, Knabenbauer, Ewald, Herrmann, Aalders) overhears in the names a different valuation of the two women: Oholah, who has "her (own) tent in her," is the sinful Northern Kingdom with its own distinctive worship at the high places. Oholibah "my tent in her" points to the Southern Kingdom with its legitimate Yahweh temple.[13] However, this interpretation is not without difficulty. It points, more precisely, to the name forms אָהֳלָה and אָהֳלִיבָה. The interpretation of the feminine endings of the two names in 𝔐 as weakened suffixes is extremely bold and is not supported by the oft-quoted analogy of the name חֶפְצִי־בָהּ of 2 Kings 21:1 (Is 62:4), since here the consonantal ה is clearly preserved. Also the references to the Jerusalem sanctuary as אהל is not supported in Ezekiel (41:1 is a textual error); we must then refer only to the אהל מועד of P. Thus others (Smend, Cooke, Fohrer), under the weight of the second objection, leave aside the idea of seeing a different evaluation in the two names, which would in any

---

9   So also Herntrich, *Ezekielprobleme*, 108.
10 Cf. the remarks below p. 487.
11 For the introductory formula for the coming of a
    message see above pp. 144f; for son of man see above
    pp. 131f.
12 See Excursus 2 and *VT* 8 (1958): 75–90.
13 So also Arnulf Kuschke, "Die Lagervorstellung der
    priesterschriftlichen Erzählung. Eine überlieferungs-
    geschichtliche Studie," *ZAW* 63 (1951): 90.

case be surprising in the context of the other statements in Ezek 23, and take the י in אהליבה as י-*compaginis*. They then think, in regard to the אהל in both cases, of the tents of the high places and translate both names as rebukes: "who has a tent" and "tent in her." Steinmann in particular thinks, with reference to 2 Sam 16:22, of the marriage tent (*tente nuptiale*). Here also, however, there are grammatical difficulties against this understanding of the name Oholibah. With this belongs the question whether 16:16, where במות טלאות, but not אהל, is mentioned, can really support the negative emphasis, which is generally tacitly accepted, of "tent of a high place."[14] אהל is otherwise not found in Ezekiel (for 41:1 see above) and also does not appear elsewhere in the Old Testament with this negative emphasis. Names formed with the element אהל otherwise appear frequently: Oholiab from the tribe of Dan Ex 31:6 and other passages; Ohel, the grandson of Zerubbabel 1 Chr 3:20; Oholibamah, the wife of Esau Gen 36:2, 5 and other passages, the name of an Edomite tribe Gen 36:41; 1 Chr 1:52, and references from Phoenicia and the Arabian region.[15] So in the interpretation of the names of Ezek 23 we must keep carefully to the normal interpretation of אהל. The names of the two women must simply, in Ezekiel, echo and set forth the slightly archaizing sound of Bedouin names, indicating that the two girls with the similar sounding names (Ewald points here to the sons of Ali, Hasan and Husein) did not belong in Egypt and were not born there. They belonged to a people who came from the desert and who dwelt in tents, pasturing flocks there (Gen 4:20). Just as in the reference to the Cananite-Amorite-Hittite origin of Jerusalem, we come up against a feature of good historical tradition here.[16] This need not altogether exclude that, for an Israelite ear, there was an element of word play (Seeligmann), with a double meaning in אָהֳלִי בָה, which would take on significance from the אהל מועד.

A later hand has sought to interpret the obscure names of the women of the allegory more explicitly in terms of the political entities which underlie them, and somewhat late, by taking up the שמותן of the beginning of the verse, added the interpretation of Samaria and

Jerusalem.[17] In avoiding the direct opposition of Israel and Judah we can thus undeniably see the aftereffect of Ezekiel's use of the name Israel (see above).

With striking brevity in the basic text, after the introduction of the names of the women, there is mention of their marriage to Yahweh and their children. This marriage forms the legal basis for the intervention of the husband which comes later, who is more than simply the human partner in a marriage. In the description of their sins, however, for both women, unfaithfulness against their true husband is stressed less strongly than careless moving from one lover to another. This is to be understood from the contemporary situation of the oracle, which is directed sharply against Zedekiah's pro-Egyptian policy.

■ **23:5–10** Verses 5–10 then narrate the history of the older sister, without mentioning, as should properly be expected, the changed location of the two women which has taken place meanwhile, in that they have now moved out of Egypt and into the land of Canaan. Also, by passing over the long intervening period of history in the land of Canaan (the period of the judges, the age of David and the early monarchy), allusion is made directly to the Assyrian age with its removal of Northern Israel into exile, threatened by the earlier prophecy (Hosea). This represents the counterpart of the exiling of Judah which is later very directly threatened.

■ **23:5** Oholah is burnt up with immoral desire. Beside the word זנה, which is found in Hosea and Jeremiah, we have the expression עגב, which is found again only in 16:37 (with emended text) and Jer 4:30, besides the six occurrences in ch. 23. (vv 5, 7, 9, 12, 16, 20). The noun is found in עגבה 23:11, עגבים in 33:31f. The woman's conduct is not made clear as to its inner motives, but is simply to be understood from the original character of the woman, which she has already shown in the sins of her youth. Unlike 16:15, where the woman's beauty, as a cause of wanton immorality, is mentioned, in ch. 23 all emphasis is placed on the description of the lovers and their desirable features. These are described as finely clad warriors (for קרוב cf. note c). Bluish (תכלת, and reddish ארגמן) purple from Elishah elsewhere adorns the beautiful ships of Tyre

---

14 See above p. 343.

15 Bernhard Moritz, "Edomitische Genealogien. I," *ZAW* 44 (1926): 87f. For its interpretation, which is

certainly not to be restricted to the אהל מועד nor to "the tent of the high place," see also Noth, *israelitischen Personennamen*, 158f.

(27:7). 27:24 mentions it as one of the goods with which Tyre carries on its trade. Further it plays in Ex 25ff and Nu 4 (cf. 2 Chr 2:6, 13; 3:14) an important role among the fabric parts of the sacred tent, the priestly clothing, the covering of the sacred utensils when moving camp (cf. Nu 15:38); Jer 10:9 the clothing of idols; and in Est 1:6 in the furnishing of the royal festival chamber. The stress on the warlike character of the Assyrians is certainly in place. The two foreign loanwords פֶּחָה (abbreviated from Akkadian *bēl pīḫati*) "ambassador" and סָגָן (Akkadian *šaknu*) "representative, ambassador" are found together again in Jer 51:23, 57 (Aramaic Dan 3:2f; 27 in the reverse order in a long series of official titles).[18] The Assyrian provincial system becomes evident in this. The youthfulness of these men, who are singled out as the élite of the Assyrians, emphasizes their military skill as well as their beauty which is attractive to women. Whether they are finally designated as "cavalry" or "charioteers" (note a) cannot be decided with certainty. According to J. Wiesner, there exist illustrations of Assyrian cavalry. "But the chariot units were the kernel of the Assyrian army; soldiers fought from them with bows and thus continued the assault tactics of the second millenium."[19]

■ **23:7** A later hand has added, in the clumsy and long prose line v 7b, the idea that the real cause of Oholah's uncleanness took place in intercourse with the idols of the Assyrians. The picture is demonstrably disturbed by this addition, which has a certain historical justification (2 Kings 21:5; 23:4f, 11f).

■ **23:8** Verse 8 must also belong to a late (different) hand (Hölscher, *Hesekiel*, van den Born), who ascribes to Oholah already the offense of further adultery with Egypt. This offense is introduced in v 17b clearly as an unexpected surprise (cf. the harsh introductory יקע "to cradle" note a to v 17) and as a heightening of the sin of Oholibah. In contrast, the לא עזבה of v 8, which is (partially) a repetition of the vocabulary of v 3 and

which then also reappears in the secondary v 21, and the dependence of v 8b on the language of 16:15 looks rather opaque, and destroys the heightening effect of v 17, which is already anticipated by v 11 (cf. Jer 3:11). The expansion in v 8 has then also made necessary the gloss in v 9b. In content the addition in v 8 recalls that the Northern Kingdom had already embroiled itself with Egypt against Assyria, as the polemic of Hosea (7:11; 8:9; 12:2) attests as well as 2 Kings 17:4. When this treaty-politics (German *Bündnispolitik*) is described as a perpetuation of the youthful immorality with Egypt, then the bypassing of the intervening period can be particularly strongly seen. Israel's treaty-politics with Egypt cannot historically be called a perpetuation of the old love of the exodus period. However, the glossator was not seeking a "historical" illumination of events, but to set in an accusing light a continuing feature of Israel's sinful nature.

■ **23:9f** Oholah's immorality is answered by Yahweh's judgement. Since it was a judgement that had already happened, it could be mentioned in a historical survey. As in 16:37, 39, it consisted of an abandonment to her lovers, who, after the shameful custom of the victors of those times, carried off in triumph the captured women, stripped them bare (cf. Is 47:2f), took away their children to sell into slavery, and killed the women themselves. This has in mind the events of 2 Kings 17. This is then further clarified by additions. By taking up the ביד of v 9a, v 9b adds that the lovers who have been summoned for judgement are none other than the Assyrians, who were the object of such unclean desire. This clarification has become necessary by the too early introduction in v 8 of the old-new Egyptian lovers. It makes clear that only the Assyrian lovers have been commissioned to deliver judgement. V 10b then takes over from 16:41 the statement that this judgement makes Oholah a subject of women's gossip. The clumys sequence of the clauses 10bα and 10bβ, which appear in 16:41 in the materially proper sequence, already

---

16 See also pp. 337f to 16:3.
17 Kuhl, "'Wiederaufnahme'."
18 On *bēl pāḫati* or *pīḫati* see Klauber, *Beamtentum*, 99–104; Benno Landsberger, *Materialien zum sumerischen Lexikon. Vokabulare und Formularbuecher* (Rome: Pontifical Biblical Institute, 1937), 125–135. For the quantity of the first vowel see Albrecht Goetze, "Short or Long *a*?" *Or* 16 (1947): 245f. According
19 to Klauber, *Beamtentum*, 100, *šaknu* was occasionally used in a simple exchange with *bēl pīḫati* (*pāḫati*). Wiesner, *Fahren*, 70. For the terminology see especially Salonen, *Hippologica*, 208–218, "Besatzung des 2-rädrigen Streitwagens"; 218–226, "Reiter (Kavallerie), Kuriere, Eilboten."

shows formally the character of 23:10b as an addition. In content also the witness of the women in the trial scene of 16:39–41 is better in place than in the Oholah scene, especially when in the fully worked-out Oholibah scene it lacks any counterpart.[20]

■ **23:11–27** As in Jer 3:6ff this Oholibah scene, which constitutes the main aim of Ezek 23, is now set out systematically. The contact with the ותראה בגודה אחותה יהודה of Jer 3:7 extends to the text of v 11. The younger sister has before her the warning example of the elder. However, she refuses to see with her eyes and to take warning. As Jer 3:6ff, with a truly Jeremianic passion, is shot through with grief at the hardness of Judah, from whom Yahweh had expected something different, so Ezek 23, on the other hand, shows again a much harsher form of speech. V 11 states briefly the even more serious unclean desire of Oholibah, to go on to set it out in more detail.

■ **23:12–14a** In this it is striking that v 12 repeats first the sin of Oholibah in almost the same words in which v 5b had described the offenses of Oholah with the Assyrians. To this in v 13 is added Yahweh's affirmation about the likeness of the two sisters, to go on in v 14a, in different words, to take up again the statement of v 11 about the greater number of Oholibah's sins. This "recapitulation" strongly arouses the suspicion that vv 12–14a are an elaborative addition.[21] Their origin is again to be understood from the desire for a greater historical completeness. Also Judah had had, as is to be seen from Hosea and Isaiah, its phase of alliance with Assyria. Should this be completely passed over in the allegorical description? Thus with a slight change of sequence in the description of the Assyrians (the sequence 1, 2, 3, 4 in vv 5f becomes 2, 1, 4, 3 in v 12) and with the variation of תכלת of v 6 to מכלול in v 12, the description is repeated from vv 5f. Yahweh's affirmation in v 13 then emphasizes somewhat pedantically that the action of Oholibah is the same as that of Oholah. V 14a then takes up the assertion, expected since v 11, that the sins of Oholibah are more than those of her sister.

■ **23:14b–17a** This increase of sin first of all consists of the unusual way in which Oholibah has attached her-self to the Chaldeans. Unfortunately in this description for the present-day reader the details are not fully intelligible. It is here said of Oholibah that she, her desire aroused by wall carvings, sent messengers to Babylon in order to allure the Chaldeans. Clearly the prophet must have had in mind here a special mission which made the first contact with the Babylonians. We can scarcely think here of the contacts which Hezekiah made with the Chaldean Marduk-apal-iddin (Merodachbaladan), the great enemy of Sargon II (721–705) and Sennacherib (705–681), according to 2 Kings 20:12ff (= Is 39), more than a hundred years before Ezekiel's days (against van den Born).[22] Rather it must concern the first contacts which took place in Josiah's time with the initial breakup of the Assyrian kingdom with Nabopolassar. Are the final stand which Josiah made against Neco, as the latter hastened to assist the crumbling Assyrian kingdom against the Babylonians and Medes (2 Kings 23:29; 2 Chr 35:20, cf. the Wiseman Chronicle), and the subsequent enthronement of Jehoahaz, which was clearly anti-Egyptian in intent, to be understood against a background of arrangements with the Neo-Babylonians? We know nothing further about this and can only raise the question.

■ **23:14b** The accusation that the first contacts with the Babylonians were occasioned by familiarity with images drawn on walls with vermilion, which represented Babylonian officials, remains thoroughly obscure. If Jer 22:14 attests the practice mentioned here of using vermilion for the decorative elaboration of contemporary buildings by Jehoiakim in Jerusalem, then we may think in the present connection rather of paintings outside Jerusalem which drew the attention of the Judeans to the Babylonians. According to A. Parrot, the technique presupposed here of sketching an outline with reddish paint (חקקים בששר, Jer 22:14 משוח בששר appears to have in mind painting on a flat surface) is found in *tell aḥmar* (*til barsib* on the upper Euphrates) and in the Cassite paintings from Dur-Kurigalzu.[23] Ezekiel's horror of all pictorial representations, which also strengthens here the emphasis on the unprecedented nature of Oholibah's actions,

---

20 See above pp. 346f.
21 Kuhl, "'Wiederaufnahme'."
22 See Bruno Meissner, *Könige Babyloniens und Assyriens*

(Leipzig: Quelle Meyer, 1926), 168, 175, 184f, 193f, 198; Wolfram von Soden, *Herrscher im alten Orient*, Verständliche Wissenschaft 54 (Berlin: Springer,

can already clearly be seen in ch. 8.

■ **23:15** The אנשי מחקה על הקיר of 23:14 has its counterpart in the שקץ וכל גלולי בית ישראל מחקה על הקיר of 8:10.[24] Oholibah, however, allows herself to be befooled by the splendid appearance of the officers (for שליש cf. note b to v 15), their belts (Is 5:27), and flowing turbans—or should we think of the סרוחי טבולים as "long hair and a band round the head," following Herodotus I 195? It is said additionally in v 15, of the Chaldeans whose pictures Oholibah sees, that "Chaldea is their land of origin" (cf. 16:3). If "land of the Chaldeans" in 1:3 and 12:13 denotes quite generally the Babylonian land of exile, then the city of Babylon appears here to be distinct from "Chaldea" (כשדים) as a territorial name vv 15f; 11:24; 16:29). In v 23 the Babylonians (בני בבל) are distinct from the Chaldeans (כשדים). This could show a knowledge of the foreign origin of the Aramean Chaldeans, whose ruler Marduk-apal-iddin, one hundred years earlier, had his seat in the Southern Babylonian "Sea-land" on the Persian Gulf.[25] We can better trust such a distinction drawn by a prophet dwelling among Babylonian exiles than one speaking in Jerusalem.

■ **23:16–17a** Therein lies the first extra in Oholibah's sin, that she was roused to such desire by the colored pictures of men that she summoned the subjects of the pictures by messengers in order to share her bed with them and to commit adultery with them and become unclean.

■ **23:17b–21** To this is added the second feature, that, after she had become unclean with the Chaldeans, she was filled with revulsion at this immoral affair, so that she turned faithlessly against her lovers to a renewed love affair with the Egyptians. In the account of this turning away there is reflected in proverbial simplicity the story of the ages of Jehoiakim and Zedekiah.

■ **23:17b** In place of Jehoahaz, who continued Josiah's policy, Judah was forced to accept Jehoiakim as king by Pharaoh Neco (2 Kings 23:33f). After the battle of

Carchemish (605), which brought the whole of Syria-Palestine into Nebuchadnezzar's power, for three years he paid tribute to the Babylonian king. After the defeat of Nebuchadnezzar in the battle against Egypt (601–Wiseman Chronicle) he withdrew his loyalty (2 Kings 24:1). The intervention of the Babylonians in the year 598/97 was not able to ensure a permanent loyalty to Babylon. Ch. 17 describes a further defection by Zedekiah. In all this secret negotiations with Egypt played an important role.

■ **23:19f** In vv 19f allusion is made to this as a rediscovery of the old love. By a strong sharpening of the description of the immorality with Egypt there is expressed how repugnant the action of Oholibah was. With forceful sharpening of the diction the lasciviousness of the Egyptians is described. Admittedly the exact interpretation of פלגש, which must contain a defamatory heightening of מאהבים (vv 5, 9, 22), can no longer be made out (cf. note b to v 20). Yet all the clearer is the comparison with the "flesh," i.e., the sexual member of the ass and the seed, or eventually also the sexual member (cf. note c), of the horse.[26] What here denotes the coarse sensuality of the Egyptians is expanded in b Berakot 25b and 58a to all non-Jews, whilst b 'Arakin 19b uses verse 20 for a peculiar process of reckoning in affirming a vow. In all this we can raise the question how far here, aside from the exaggerated language which sets out in drastic metaphors the power of Egyptian political conspiracy, we are to find any actual evaluation of national character. (Cf. Gen 12:11f; 39:7ff and the quotation in Ezek 16:26.)

■ **23:18** The original text here again has undergone additions. In v 18 a remark has been added, quite obviously suggested by the catchword יקע, about Yahweh's turning away (נקע) from Oholibah as he had turned away from Oholah. It breaks up the connection of vv 17b and 19 in a clumsy way. After the mention of the sobering turning away of Oholibah from her Babylonian lovers we expect nothing less than new

1954), 96, 106f.
23 Parrot, *Babylon*, page 145 note 1. For painted reliefs in Assyria see Meissner, *Babylonien* 1, 325f.
24 See above pp. 240f.
25 See above p. 111.
26 See *TWNT* 5, page 283 note 3, s.v. ὄνος, for classical references and illustrations of the lust of the ass. For the horse cf. Jer 5:8 (13:27).

information about the woman's shameless uncovering of herself such as follows in v 18a and motivates Yahweh's turning away. The new turning to immorality is first stated in v 19. Thus v 18 falls out of its context and anticipates prematurely the reaction of Yahweh, which can be seen fully in v 22.

■ **23:21** In verse 21, however, the too early direct address in the second person singular shows up the addition (cf. note d). This verse passes over v 20 and connects up again with v 19 (נעוריה), elaborating the youthful sins once again with the harsh details of v 3.

■ **23:22** In v 22 the saying changes to direct address to Oholibah. The direct declaration of judgement begins (parallel to the direct address to the זונה in 16:35ff). The handing over to the lovers from the East, who have previously been summoned by messengers, must now fearfully also happen to Oholibah. From all sides the hostile armies which have been "aroused" by Yahweh himself will advance.[27]

■ **23:23** Among them the Babylonians, i.e., the oldest settled inhabitants of the capital city, are distinguished from the Aramean Chaldeans.[28] Three further groups of people, the names of which with their thick 'O' sounds are undoubtedly deliberately quoted for their sound, are then listed in order. פְּקוֹד, mentioned again in Jer 50:21 in connection with an oracle against Babylon, denotes an important Aramean tribe *puqudu* in east Babylonia. It is not only mentioned by Tiglath-pileser III, but also in the inscription of Sargon II in a list of those conquered by Marduk-apal-iddin.[29] שׁוֹעַ, mentioned again in Is 22:5, has mostly been connected with the Sutaeans, who are known from Mari, from the Amarna letters, and from Assyrian royal inscriptions.[30] They were a nomadic group of the Syro-Arabian desert, which was later to be found east of *diyāla*. However, this identification remains very uncertain. This is even more true of the identification of the קוֹע, which stands alongside שׁוֹעַ to rhyme with it, with the *qutū* (so Delitzsch, otherwise Zimmern), which would be located

in the same east-*diyāla* territory.

The mention of the Assyrians which then follows in 𝔐 must already, in the consideration of note a to v 23, be claimed as an interpretative addition. We may question whether the fact that the *sutū* and *qutū* (?) were neighbors has provoked the mention of the Assyrians. However, it has more probably been introduced as a result of the addition of v 12. Thus the description of the Assyrians has been called forth, with attributes stemming from vv 5f, which differs again from the sequence in v 12. Not only is the כלם ordered differently and the פרשים suppressed, but also the קרובים לבשי תכלת of vv 5f (12) is replaced by שלשים וקרואים. שלשים stems from v 15.

■ **23:24** The advance of the Babylonian army against Oholibah-Jerusalem will take place with great expenditure: levy of war weapons (chariots and wheels is a hendiadys, for the subject see above to v 6) and levy of men. 16:40 had spoken of the קהל which the lovers there had called up to carry out the legal sentence of stoning against the adulteress. In the oracle against Oholibah, which is oriented politically and militarily, the קהל עמים advances as an army in order to hem in Jerusalem with its weapons, which no defense can withstand. צנה means the large shield, arched and flat at the bottom, whilst the מגן must mean the simpler round shield, covered with leather and sometimes made with a humped center.[31] If the text originally spoke of the enemy coming from the North (note a), then in this we can find an echo of the older prophetic threat of the "foe from the north" (Jer 4:6f and other passages).[32] The whole description is repeated more elaborately in the Gog-episode in Ezek 38f.

Oholibah will be handed over in judgement by her legitimate husband Yahweh to this host and their barbaric methods of war.

■ **23:25** In their wrath Yahweh's jealousy (קנאה 5:13; 16:38, 42) will be let loose upon Oholibah. The laws for the conduct of war in Dtn 20 show that Israel, in its

---

27 See Hans Bardtke, "Der Erweckungsgedanke in der exilisch-nachexilischen Literatur des Alten Testaments" in *Von Ugarit nach Qumran*, BZAW 77 (Berlin, 1958), 9–24.

28 See above p. 487 to v 15.

29 See Sina Schiffer, *Die Aramäer; historisch-geographische Untersuchungen* (Leipzig: Hinrichs, 1911), page 4 especially note 4, pp. 126ff; A. Dupont-Sommer,

Les Araméens, L'Orient Ancien Illustré 2 (Paris: Maisonneuve, 1949), 74.

30 J. R. Kupper, "Les nomades en Mésopotamie au temps des rois de Mari," *BFPLUL* 142 (1957): 83–145.

31 For צנה see the illustration *BRL*, 457; for מגן see the illustration *BRL*, 458; for the helmet see *BRL*, 279f.

wars, was conscious of being under the authority of its
God, and thereby a certain law of humanity. Thus
there is almost completely lacking in Israel's law any
punishment involving mutilation. But things were
different in the surrounding nations. The Assyrian
illustrations of war show quite freely flaying, impaling,
blinding, and physical mutilation which was the order
of the day for prisoners.[33] Oholibah will be delivered
up to this grim practice of Babylonian victory for
mutilation and the killing of her children (note b). The
punishment of cutting off the nose and ears is attested
in Egypt in connection with the punishment of a plot
against Rameses III (Turin Papyrus), and among
the Hittites as a punishment for a negligent temple
servant.[34]

The obscurity of אחרית in v 25aγ has called forth in
v 25b an explanatory addition which speaks explicitly
of the fate of the sons and daughters who are carried off.
אחרית is distinguished from this and related to what is
left of the property in the land which will be burnt by
the enemy with fire.

■ **23:26** In v 26, however, we find an assimilation to
16:39, where the mention of the loss of clothes and
finery is completely in place in the whole picture which
had told of the giving of these things to the bride
(16:10–13). This feature has been taken over into v 26
with almost literal repetition. The original text concluded with the threat of Yahweh that he would put
a complete end to Oholibah's dependence on Egypt.
In this the end goes back to the beginning at v 3 and
sharply brings out again the anti-Egyptian direction of
the oracle.

Aim

The allegory of the two sisters, which is directed
particularly to Oholibah (Judah-Jerusalem), once
again has the intention of striking at the heart of an
inbuilt election faith of the chosen people. Remorselessly all its pride, its consciousness of being God's
people "from Egypt" (Hos 13:4), is destroyed. Whereas
Ezek 16 had given some space to a description of the
exaltation of God's people by him and his rich gifts to
them, here this is completely suppressed. From the first

recognizable impulses of love onwards, the girls Oholah
and Oholibah became corrupted. There is no noble,
innocent love, not even at the beginning of the history
of God's people. Beyond this Oholibah, the remnant of
the people which was spared in the first judgement, had
not taken the least warning from the exemplary fate
of her sister, but had gone still further along her paths.

We can again hear in this a message in which the
prophet had to alarm the community which had become complacent in its holy election-tradition. In the
confession of faith of the Old Testament people of God,
the name "Egypt" plays an important role. It awakened
in Israel recollections of its great encounter with God
and his call made in his own presence. This very word,
noble in its basis, but leading to pious complacency, is
taken up in the prophetic preaching in all its sharpness
and made relevant for the present and the decisions
which were currently facing the remnant of Judah.
What is Egypt today? For the Jerusalem of the prophet's
time it was no longer the place to which men had said
goodbye in obedience to God's guidance, but had
become a great temptation, the place of the most impious immorality and sin of God's people with powers
other than God's own sovereign power. Isaiah had
spoken of trust in the military aid of Egypt and of
treaties with it as something done behind Yahweh's
back (Is 30:1–5; 31:1–3). In the later prophecy of
Ezekiel, which presupposed this earlier prophetic
preaching, all of this is taken up in the condemnatory
metaphor of "immorality" (זנה) and "immoral desire"
(עגב). The community is remorselessly faced with its
crime in which it has, from the very beginning, repeatedly given its love to what has a reputation on
earth because it is resplendent with weapons and appears to be youthful and vital.

By such denial of true love for the One to whom the
community really belongs (v 4 ותהיינה לי), which then
leads to the fickle oscillating from one to another and
to becoming ensnared in the vagaries of world history,
the community of God comes to grief. In judgement the
whole horror of the one to whom they have sold themselves will come upon them. God needs no angel from
heaven; he judges men through that which they have

---

32   Cf. above pp. 119f to 1:4.
33   Cf. above p. 272; also Meissner, *Babylonien* 1, 111–
      113; *AOBAT* 129, 132, 141; *ANEP* 368, 373.
34   *ANET* 215, 207.

chosen for themselves in their own godless love.

■ **23:28–30** The addition in vv 28–30 carries forward the ideas of the declaration of judgement in vv 22–27, beginning with a new messenger formula and with slight variations of expression and detail. The נקע—יקע, which in vv 17, 22 expressed the revulsions against the Babylonian lovers, is interpreted in v 28 by שׂנא (so also in the addition 16:37). The second ביד clause (v 28b) gives the impression of being a subsequent reference back to vv 17, 22. V 29aα[1] varies v 25 by replacing the בחמה by בשׂנאה; v 29aα[2] varies v 26b, whilst the following stichos v 29aβ takes over the "naked and bare" from 16:7 (vv 22, 39). The stripping of the women naked stems from v 10 (cf. 16:36f, also 23:18). Becoming unclean with idols was also introduced in the addition v 7 in connection with the narrative about Oholah. From all these considerations vv 28–30 are to be regarded as a formulation by the school of Ezekiel which, directly under the impact of the downfall of Jerusalem (v 29), summarizes again the punishment in close dependence on 23:1–27 (and Ezekiel 16). In an appended motive clause (v 30) it points to the immorality and becoming unclean among the nations and their idols as the cause of the judgement.

■ **23:31–34** The second addition, vv 31–34, describes the judgement under the image of a cup of woe. This again is a clear reference back to the history of the two sisters.

■ **23:31** From this v 31 forms the transition to the section vv 32–34, which connects with vv 28–30 and is introduced independently by the messenger formula. It is firmly emphasized by כי אני דברתי and is rounded off by the formula for a divine message.

The image of the cup filled with strong drink so that whoever drinks from it sways and falls is to be found before Ezekiel in Jeremiah and Habakkuk.[35] Jer 25:15, 17, 28 shows the metaphor in a prophecy from the time of Jehoiakim in elaborating the divine judgement on the nations. According to Hab 2:16 the כוס ימין יהוה will be given to the mysterious tyrant who has made "his neighbors" drunk. Neither of the two texts can be the first occurrence of the metaphor, which has already been quite specifically changed in both. Jer 51:7 then describes Babylon as כוס זהב ביד יהוה, which presupposes a previous prophecy of doom in which Babylon is the instrument of the divine judgement. Similarly Is 51:17, 22, in reference to the destruction of Jerusalem by the Babylonians, speaks of the כוס חמתו (i.e., of Yahweh) and of the כוס התרעלה. (Cf. Ob 16; Jer 49:12; Lam 4:21; Ps 60:5; 75:9; Mt 20:22; 26:39; Rev 14:10.)

Ezek 23:32–34 paints a picture of the cup and of the effects of drinking what it contains, in a prophecy behind which we can trace the seeking after a metric form. However, in the face of the undeniable glosses and scribal errors which it has undergone, its original form can no longer be recovered with certainty. Is the קינה rhythm intended?[36] Or are three-beat units continually connected with two-beat units, so that we come to a three-strophe structure each of three three-line strophes? Some rhyme elements are also not to be overlooked, (v 32 הרחבה / העמקה; v 33 שׂכרון / יגון; v 34 ומצית / ושׂתית). Note also the threefold repetition of כוס at the beginning of the lines. The division of 𝔐 may point to a three-part structure.

■ **23:32** The first strophe (v 32, 3:2:2) then first describes the great size of the cup—we can see in this the greatness of the judgement. A later additional remark (note b), formulated in the third person feminine singular, adds that the woman (who is addressed directly in the original prophecy) will become an object of scorn and mockery as a consequence of the judgement (36:4, cf. 16:57).

■ **23:33** The second strophe (v 33, originally also 3:2:2?) mentions the ruin and desolation which are a result of drinking the cup of judgement. In the additions in 𝔐, which point to a form 3:3:3, we find not only שׁמה, which is not Ezekiel's usage (note b), but also שׁמרון, which makes clear that it is: "thy sister Samaria." This recalls the gloss of v 4b and derives from the allegory of Oholah.

■ **23:34** The third strophe (v 34, originally 3:2:2?) finally describes, if Cornill's restoration of the text is right (note a), the finality of the act of judgement, in which the cup is emptied to the dregs—and this at the express command of Yahweh. The addition ושׂדיך תנתקי

35   See Gressmann, *Ursprung*, 129–136; Hugo Gressmann, "Der Festbecher" in *Sellin-Festschrift* (1927), 55–62; W. Lotz, "Das Sinnbild des Bechers," *NKZ*

28 (1917): 396–407.

36   See above pp. 391f to ch. 19.

(note b), which is not attested in 𝕲 𝔏ˢ, points back to v 3 (v 21) and shows how the judgement falls on the breasts of the adultress which were once shamelessly offered to the Egyptians.

Linguistically and stylistically no compelling grounds can be adduced against the derivation of the original text of vv 32–34 from Ezekiel himself. The taking up of earlier prophetic motifs and images is repeatedly to be found in Ezekiel—the original text of 23:1–27 also offers an example of this process. As a close formal parallel we may also adduce the original text of the song of the sword in 21:23–32. A certain difficulty for the view of an origin from Ezekiel chiefly arises from the redactional ordering in the whole of ch. 23. The prophecy of the cup of judgement in its formulation cannot be thought of without the history of the two sisters. However, it is not directly connected with the original text of vv 1–27, but only with verses 28–30 which are undoubtedly secondary. Does it then stem from the hand of a disciple of Ezekiel, as a section first added after vv 28–30? We cannot thus decide with certainty the question of the original derivation from Ezekiel.

■ **23:35** The prophecy of doom which then follows in v 35 and which is of the יען—לכן type, making it an independently introduced motive clause (in which, as in 16:43, the לכן is shortened to a simple וגם), does not add anything materially new. The offense of adultery, as in Dtn, is described as "forgetting" Yahweh,[37] and in stronger imagery as "throwing Yahweh behind one's back" (only again 1 Kings 14:9; Neh 9:26; cf. Is 38:17). The judgement is described in the terminology used in 16:52 as a "bearing (of the punishment) of wantonness and immorality."[38] This was the language of Ezekiel's school in Ezek 16 also.

■ **23:36–49** Whereas the three additions in vv 28–35, in language and content, stand quite close to the prophet and his preaching, this cannot be said of vv 36–49. Here a new level of independence from the original text is evident both in the language and the extent of the dependence on Ezek 16 (and 23).

The section, which is introduced with an introductory formula which is otherwise alien to Ezekiel,[39] contains in its first half (vv 36–44) an account of the sins of the two women, and then in vv 45–49 a description of the punishment. In detail the style has strikingly run wild. In vv 37–40bα Yahweh describes in narrative the actions of the two women. In v 40bβ it changes to address in the second person singular form (to Oholibah alone?), but then returns in v 42, without any reason, into the descriptive third person feminine plural style. In v 45 Yahweh again describes the nature of the judgement, only in v 46 to go back again into direct speech with an introductory messenger formula, directed not at the sinning women, but at a circle of people who assist in the judgement, who are not clearly defined. Then again in vv 48f it changes into second person feminine plural. The text cannot be from one hand but is broken up by additions, which Hölscher may have correctly noted.[40]

■ **23:36** The reproach begins in v 36 with the summons to the prophet, known from (16:2) 20:4; 22:2, to declare (הודע is here replaced by הגד) the sins, without, as in other references, continuing with a command to speak and going on with the divine message introduced directly with the messenger formula. The form is therefore only imperfectly imitated.

■ **23:37** A causal כי leads in to a description of the sins: adultery and bloodguilt (following 16:38, cf. further 23:45). What is perhaps a subsequent addition v 37aβb (or is the ו really intended to add a further sin?) makes this clearer; adultery with idols and bloodguilt through offering child sacrifices (16:20f, העביר as 16:21).

■ **23:39** The original continuation of v 37aα may be found in v 39 (Hölscher) (dl ו), where is mentioned the slaughtering (שחט 16:21) of children and the entering of the sanctuary which follows this and by which this latter is defiled.

■ **23:38** In v 38, in which Hölscher would see a gloss to v 39, there enters the idea of the defiling of the sanctuary by the profaning of the sabbath (20:13, 16, 21; 22:8). The women's sin, in marked deviation from the original text of Ezek 16:23, is thereby made into an offense against holiness. The orientation towards the twofold law of Lev 19:30 (=26:2), analogous to Ezek

---

37   But cf. above pp. 458f to 22:12.
38   See above pp. 350f.
39   See above p. 480.

40   Hölscher, *Hesekiel, der Dichter*, page 124 note 1.

22:8, is not to be overlooked.

■ **23:40** After these sins, which are mostly taken over from Ezek 16, there is then added the section vv 40–44, which has been subsequently glossed and which is strongly disturbed in parts of the text. It describes the coming of foreigners to commit adultery with the women, woven together from reminiscences from chs. 16 and 23. 23:16 had mentioned the sending abroad of messengers in connection with the adultery with the Chaldeans. Beyond the insertion vv 40bβ–41, which is formulated as an address in the singular and loosely connected by לאשׁר, vv 42–44 continue the original narrative text.

■ **23:42** Whereas in 42aα mention is made of noise at a festival (note a), 42b tells how the foreign men (or the women themselves? note c) adorn the two women with bracelets and headbands. From 16:11f the adorning of the foundling child by Yahweh is repeated here in a similar, but distorted, formulation.

■ **23:43, 44** V 43 is unintelligible (cf. note a), but appears, as v 44a, to speak only of one woman, who is resorted to like a prostitute. The subheading v 44b then summarizes the conduct of the two women together.

■ **23:40bβ–41** The insertion in the singular in 40bβ–41 describes the scene of adultery still with reference to the conduct of the woman, who washes and paints her eyes for her visitors, puts on finery (16:11, 13), prepares the bed for adultery, sets a table in front of it, and puts on it the sweet-smelling cosmetics given by the husband.[41] The description recalls Prv 7:14ff.

Thus the whole description of the offenses in vv 36–44 shows a clearly recognizable mixture and in part a highly novel development of features from the (already expanded) content of Ezek 16 and 23.

■ **23:45–49** This is true also of the declaration of judgement in vv 45–49. The adulterers, whom Yahweh summons in 16:37f in order to execute judgement according to the laws of adultery and murder, have here become "righteous men." Their work as judges, however, is the same as there. To this is added also here a command to the assembly (קהל 16:40, cf. 23:24), which executes by stoning and hacking to pieces (16:40). The killing of children and the burning of houses recalls what is said

in 23:25f and 16:41; similarly the conclusion in v 48a recalls the conclusions in 16:41 and 23:27. The reference to the warning example, which is then added and which sees in this judgement upon the two adulterers a warning to other women, is new. Out of the function of the women as witnesses in 16:41 (and 23:10) there has entered here a didactic and warning purpose in a somewhat schoolmasterly way. Then follows the guilt formula, well-known from other concluding sections (16:52, 54, 58; 23:35), however in a fresh and varied form.[42] In place of the נשׂא זמה of v 35 and 16:58, we have here the active usage ונתנו זמתכנה עליכן which is taken up in the parallel by נשׂא חטא, which is also found in Lev 19:17; 20:20; Is 53:12 and other passages. The masculine חטא is otherwise not found in the book of Ezekiel. Once again this is defined by reference to the "sin with the idols." Finally the recognition formula is added, which again interprets Yahweh's judgement as a sign, by which Yahweh proves himself in his own personal sovereignty. Only here and in 13:9; 24:24; 28:24; 29:16 is אדני also found in the recognition formula. (Cf. note d.)

Aim

The entire section vv 36–49 contains a surprising rationalizing of the history of Oholah and Oholibah. The normal prophetic attitude in proclaiming judgement upon the people of God for its sinful ways is very much in the background. The narratives Chs. 16 and 23 are made into didactic example-stories of a righteous divine judgement upon sinful, adulterous, and murderous women, who are to serve as a warning example so that other women in the future may not do likewise. No longer is it the house of Israel which is given a warning, but individual women in their moral and social conduct. The depth of the prophetic preaching is far from being reached in this by a long way. It witnesses to the truly human way which the prophetic tradition also has taken up, so that occasionally this is also not lacking in the editorial additions to the prophetic books. The prophetic word of judgement, in a great narrowing down, is made into a moral admonition which applies to everyday life.

---

41 *BRL*, 435–437.
42 See above pp. 350f to 16:52.

The Cauldron on the Fire.

Bibliography

J. L. Kelso
"Ezekiel's Parable of the Corroded Copper Cauldron," *JBL* 64 (1945): 391–393.

24

1 And the word of Yahweh came to me in the ninth year, in the tenth month, on the tenth (day) of the month: 2/ Son of man, write[a] down the date[b] of this day [this very day].[c] The king of Babylon has this very day invested[d] Jerusalem. 3/ Declare a parable to the house of rebelliousness and say to them: Thus has [the Lord][a] Yahweh said:

Set a cauldron on (the fire), set (it) up,[b] and pour in water.[c] 4/ Put in 'pieces of meat,'[a] plenty of good pieces, fill it[b] with leg and shoulder, the best of the bones.[c] 5/ Take[a] the best[b] of the flock, and pack round[c] 'the pieces of wood'[d]

24: 2a K כתוב beside Q כְּתָב־ can not only point to an imperative כְּתוֹב, but also to an original infinitive absolute. However, in what follows the imperative is always written defectively (אסף – יצק – שפת). Against this the infinitive absolute appears לקוח (v 5).

b Literally: the name.

c 𝕲 γράψον σεαυτῷ εἰς ἡμέραν ἀπὸ τῆς ἡμέρας ταύτης has before it an incorrect reading of a, in which the repeated היום is already to be found. Against this 𝕲 𝔙 do not show that the words את עצם היום, which we can readily regard in b as an explanatory addition, did stand in the text they had before them. Certainly the possibility of subsequent smoothing in 𝕲 𝔙 is not to be ruled out altogether.

d סמך properly: to lean upon, to support. סמך על is used of hostile attack also in Ps 88:8. It contains a reference to a hard-pressed attack. For על – אל cf. note a to 1:17.

3 3a אדני is lacking in 𝕲 𝓛ˢ 𝕮, see Excursus 1.

b The second שפת is lacking in 𝕲 𝕾 𝕮 𝕲 𝔄. However, this could be a smoothing over. Ezekiel loves doubled repetitions, cf. הנבא 20:4; 22:2, התשפט 37:9, also חרב 21:14.

c 𝔐 בו. Since סיר is treated in what follows as a feminine, we should expect בה, so Bertholet, Fohrer.

4 4a 𝔐 נתחיה is certainly determined here by the אליה which is next to it. 𝕲 τὰ διχοτομήματα, 𝕾 נכסא support the reading נתחים. The verb and noun נתח repeatedly occur in the language of sacrifice (Ex 29:17; Lev 1:6, 8, 12; 8:20; 9:13; 1 Kings 18:23, 33, again Sir 50:12). But cf. also the ritual of the amphictyonic levy 1 Sam 11:7; Ju 19:29; 20:6.

b 𝔐 מלא is not attested by 𝕲 𝓛ˢʷ 𝕾; perhaps a secondary addition.

c 𝕲 ἐκσεσαρκισμένα, 𝓛ʷ *carnata* (𝓛ˢ *separata*) *ab ossibus*, 𝕾 דשמיט גרמה are interpretations: off the bone, the best pieces.

5 5a The infinitive absolute, which is striking here standing alone between imperatives, raises the question whether originally here further members of the series of verbs שפת – יצק – אסף – (מלא?) – (לקוח – דור – רתח – בשל were intended as infinitive absolutes. Cf. also note a to v 10.

b 𝔐 מבחר. 𝕲 ἐξ ἐπιλέκτων κτηνῶν, 𝓛ˢʷ *de electis pecoribus*, 𝕾 מן גביא דענא support an original ממבחר.

c For דור cf. Koehler-Baumgartner, also Σ σύνθες . . . κυκλοτέρως; 𝕲 ὑπόκαιε, 𝓛ˢʷ *combure*, 𝕾 שגור (kindle).

d 𝔐 העצמים "the pieces of bones," already found

6 under it. Seethe 'its pieces of meat'ᵉ and 'cook'ᶠ its bones in it.

6 Therefore thus has [the Lord]ᵃ Yahweh said: Woe to the city of blood! to the pot on which is 'rust,'ᵇ and the rust of which cannot be removed from it. [Piece by piece have men removed it—no lot is cast for it.]ᶜ 7/ For the blood (shed by it) is in it. On the bare rock has sheᵃ done it, she has not poured it outᵃ on the earth to cover it with dust. 8/ To make anger flare up, to call down vengeance, I have setᵃ the blood (shed by it) on the bare rock, so that it may not be covered.

9 Therefore thus has [the Lord]ᵃ Yahweh said: Woe to the city of blood!ᵇ Therefore I will make the woodpileᶜ great, 10/ pile upᵃ the logs, kindleᵃ the fire, cookᵃ the meat and 'pour away the

in 𝕲, but in meaning scarcely possible. The conjecture of Böttcher, who reads העצים (cf. v 10), expanded by the conjecture of Driver, "Linguistic Problems," 175, of reading the following תחתיה of 𝔐 as מתחתיה, would solve the riddle. When 𝕭 translates the beginning of v 10: *congere ossa*, it supports beautifully the possibility of an interchange of עצים and עצמים.

e 𝔐 רתחיה. With 2 MSSᴷᵉⁿ we should read נתחיה and restore the parallelism also found in v 4: נתחים – עצמים. "Its pieces of meat" = "the pieces of meat found in it."

f Since the verbs in the parable (*mašal*) vv 3b–5 are preserved throughout in the imperative or infinitive absolute (cf. note a), we must also read בַּשֵּׁל here instead of 𝔐 בשלו (the qal is only found again in Joel 4:13 with the meaning "become ripe").

6 6a אדני is lacking in 𝕲 𝕾ᵂ 𝕮ˢᵃ, see Excursus 1.

b With reference to 16:44 𝔐 חֶלְאָתָה could be understood as a suffix form with softening of the ה before the following ב Gesenius-Kautzsch § 91 e. However, since the suffix is effectively superfluous beside the following statement, it is more probable that we have a scribal error for a simple חֶלְאָה. According to Dalman, *Arbeit* 5, 183: verdigris. Ehrlich, *Randglossen*: "dirt" (as 𝕿 זיהומתיה). 𝕲 ἰός is related to חלה "to be ill."

c V 6b offers considerable difficulties of intelligibility. 𝕲 attests simply bα; b is fully attested by 𝕾 𝕾ˢ 𝕿, whilst 𝕾ᵂ only translates bβ. For the form הוֹצִיאָהּ we may consider whether it should be understood as a perfect hip'il with suffix or whether with the vocalization הוֹצִיאָה it should be understood in relation to סיר as third person feminine singular perfect hip'il without suffix or as an emphatic imperative. Since v 7 joins smoothly on to v 6a, v 6b arouses the suspicion of being an addition. Cf. the exposition.

7 7a 𝔐 שפכתהו . . . שמתהו, taken by 𝕲 (𝕾ˢᵂ) in dependence on v 8 as first person: τέταχα αὐτό . . . ἐκκέχυκα αὐτό.

8 8a 𝔐 נתתי. The change of person from v 7 is striking, although the clear support for the first person forbids an emendation to נתנה (Ehrlich, *Randglossen*, Fohrer). Cf. note a to v 7.

9 9a אדני is lacking in 𝕲 𝕾ˢᵂ 𝕮, see Excursus 1.

b 𝔐 אוי עיר הדמים is lacking in 𝕲 𝕾ˢᵂ. It stands in v 6 at the beginning of the reproach at a more appropriate place, as here at the beginning of an announcement of judgement. Thus it is questionable in its originality (Cornill, Bertholet, Fohrer). Cf. 16:23 note b.

c 𝔐 המדורה clearly refers back to the דור of v 5. The noun is found again Is 30:33. 𝕲 τὸν δαλόν, 𝕾ᵂ *tritionem* (firebrand), 𝕾ˢ *populum* according to 𝕲ᴮ τὸν λαόν (a scribal error for ΔΑΛΟΝ?), 𝕾 מעמרא (dwelling).

10 10a The translation seeks to preserve the ambiguity of 𝔐. The verbs התם . . . הדלק . . . הרבה הדלק . . . הרקח could be understood both as infinitive ab-

broth,'ᵇ [that the bones may be burnt,]ᶜ
11/ and 'set' (it)ᵃ [empty]ᵇ on itsᶜ coals,
that it may become hot and its bronze
may glow and its uncleanness in it
melted away, its rust consumed.ᵈ
12/ ' 'ᵃ But its much rust will not come
off in the fire, that its corrosion should

solutes and also imperatives. In the first case the
continuation of the statement in v 9b would lie in
the setting out of naked verbal concepts, according
to which Yahweh is the subject of the action. So 𝔊
𝔏ˢʷ 𝔖. Also 𝔗, where the interpreted parable points
in this direction. Accordingly Bertholet, Ziegler,
Ezechiel, Fohrer. The continuation of 𝔐 in v 11
והעמידה, however, appears compellingly to point
to an understanding as imperative. So most commentaries. But cf. note a to v 11. The inner movement of the text, from its introduction in v 9b on,
points to a relating of the statement to Yahweh.
What was stylized in vv 3b–5, in a mysterious parable, as a summons to an unknown third person, is
here set out as the action of Yahweh (גם אני).

b 𝔐 והרקח המרקחה "and anoint the anointing
pot (anointing mixture?)" is unintelligible. 𝔊 καὶ
ἐλαττωθῇ ὁ ζωμός, 𝔏ˢ *et minuatur ius* (cf. 𝔏ʷ) "and
the broth becomes little" must point to וְהָרֵק הַמָּרָק
as the original reading. So Ehrlich, *Randglossen*, cf.
Kraetzschmar, Bertholet. Also הרחק(Hölscher,
Hesekiel) is graphically close. The catchword רקה
is taken up again in v 11. Driver, "Linguistic Problems," 175f, reads וְהָרְתַּח הַמֶּרְתָּחָה "and stew the
stew" and refers to רתח Job 41:23.

c 𝔐 והעצמות יחרו is lacking in 𝔊 and shows itself to be an addition, not only by the transition to
the imperfect, but also by the use of the feminine
plural עצמות, with which elsewhere in Ezekiel only
"dead bones" are designated (6:5; 32:27; 37:1,
3–5, 7, 11), whilst the "pieces of bone" in 24:4f are
called עצמים. There also appears a new emphasis
here which breaks up the image: the destruction of
human bones by burning them (cf. 2 Kings 23:16
and other passages).
The חרה stems from v 11, where it is related to the
pot.

11a 𝔐 והעמידה can only be understood as imperative. However, 𝔊 καὶ στῇ (𝔏ˢʷ *et stet*) points to
a free translation of והעמד, which would then be
understood in the sequence of infinitive absolute
forms of v 10 (note a). 𝔖 ואקימיוהי also points to
this understanding, which also stands behind the
interpretation in 𝔗. Also the reading ואעמידה is to
be considered. Bertholet, Fohrer read והעמדתיה.

b 𝔐 רקה is lacking in 𝔊 𝔏ˢʷ. It could have become necessary as a clarification (of the right meaning), when v 10bα was wrongly copied (note b to
v 10). The two-beat structure of the surrounding
lines speaks for the text of 𝔊.

c 𝔐 גחליה "its coals" (i.e., those that were underneath it in the first action [vv 9f]). The feminine
suffix relates back to the סיר, mentioned in vv 3–5,
which is the subject in what follows, without its
being expressly mentioned. Vv 6–10 are passed over.

d For the Aramaizing form of 𝔐 תתם cf. Gesenius-Kautzsch § 67 g.q.

12a 𝔐 תאנים הלאת "with pain it (the cauldron?
the rust?) has made weary (?)" is lacking in 𝔊 𝔏ˢʷ

melt (?).[b] 13/ On account of your abominable uncleanness,[a] because I cleansed you, but you would not be clean from your uncleanness, you will never again be clean, until I have satisfied my anger upon you. 14/ I, Yahweh, have spoken [, it is coming,][a] and I will do (it). I will not leave it unnoticed,[b] nor will I spare [nor will I let myself relent].[c] According to your conduct and your deeds 'I will judge you,'[d] says [the Lord][e] Yahweh.[f]

and is to be deleted as a miswritten scribal dittography of the preceding תתם חלאתה. Otherwise Driver, "Linguistic Problems," 176.

b 𝔐 באש חלאתה was not understood by 𝔊 (𝔏ˢʷ) καὶ καταισχυνθήσεται (בוש – באש) ὁ ἰὸς αὐτῆς. The understanding of the expression which is conjectured by the translation is found also in the paraphrase of בנורא תתוקד מסניאות חובהא צ. The lack of the last חלאתה in 𝔙 et non exivit de nimia robigo eius neque per ignem suggests that we should perhaps also delete this concluding saying (Herrmann, Toy, Bertholet).

13:   13a For the construction בטמאתך זמה cf. note c to 16:27, where Gesenius-Kautzsch § 131 r is to be followed. 𝔊 ἀνθ' ὧν ἐμιαίνου σύ, καὶ τί . . . presupposes בטמאתך ומה. Further 𝔐 בטמאתך . . . יען is not attested by 𝔊 𝔏ˢʷ. It could be a subsequent clarification.

14   14a 𝔐 באה in content is a variant of ועשיתי, which, however, breaks up the sequence of the stereotyped formula דברתי ועשיתי also found in 17:24; 22:14; 36:36; 37:14. Although 𝔊 already attests it, it must be of secondary origin. For באה cf. formulae such as הנה באה ונהיתה 21:12; 39:8, cf. 33:33.

b פרע in Ezekiel only here.

c 𝔐 ולא אנחם is lacking in 𝔊 𝔏ˢʷ and is certainly an addition, since it adds a third statement to the two preceding parallel expressions.

d 𝔐 שפטוך "they judge you" = "men judge you." The versions offer here the first person, which is to be expected after the strong introductory אני יהוה. Read with MSS שפטתיך; cf. 7:3, 8; 16:38; 36:19, also 11:10f; 18:30 and other passages.

e אדני is lacking in 𝔊 𝔏ˢʷ ℭ, see Excursus 1.

f The addition in 𝔊 (cf. 𝔏ˢʷ) διὰ τοῦτο ἐγὼ κρινῶ σε κατὰ τὰ αἵματά σου καὶ κατὰ τὰ ἐνθυμήματά σου κρινῶ σε, ἡ ἀκάθαρτος ἡ ὀνομαστὴ καὶ πολλὴ τοῦ παραπικραίνειν (cf. 22:5), which Ewald, Hitzig, Smend took as original, is to be regarded as an addition which was possibly already found in the Hebrew original of 𝔊.

Form

The section 24:1–14, through the emphatic dating in vv 1f, points immediately to the short saying in vv 3b–5, which the prophet is to proclaim to the people as a parable.[1] It is a prophecy of vital appeal, given in direct singular address, in which one imperative affirms the others. We immediately feel drawn back to sayings such as 4:1ff; 5:1ff—sayings in which Yahweh commands the prophet to perform a sign-action. The introductory imperative is there continued by perfect consecutive. So then Kraetzschmar and others find here also a command to the prophet to perform a sign-action. Schmidt and Cooke vary this view to one in which the prophet was preparing himself a meal, and the introductory

word from God made this everyday activity meaningful as a sign-action. It is a consequence of this view when Fohrer goes a step further and removes from its position the introduction in v 3a, which commands that vv 3b–5 should be delivered to the people as a משל, and makes this the introduction of the following interpretation in vv 6a, 7, 8a. Can, however, an interpretation be described as a משל? How also can the subsequent inappropriate repositioning of v 3a be explained?

Thus van den Born must be on the right lines when he points to the analogy of a "work song" for vv 3b–5.[2] By the song, in which those addressed are deliberately left obscure, the listeners are called to a quiet everyday occupation, which is described in all the details of the work involved, until finally everyone can picture the steaming cooking pot. This everyday action, as a מָשָׁל, is full of a hidden, threatening significance.

With the picture of the steaming cauldron, which is already to be found in 11:1ff with a somewhat different emphasis, Ezekiel takes up afresh a feature of the prophetic tradition which he had before him, in order to relate it to the events of his days. The story of the "death in the pot" from the Elisha tradition (2 Kings 4:38–41), which is recalled here by the introductory שְׁפֹת הַסִּיר (also the יָצַק v 40f), which also occurs there, cannot be more closely adduced. We have seen in an earlier connection that there are other lines of tradition between the book of Ezekiel and the Elisha stories.[3] However, we must point to Jer 1:13. Against the usual understanding of the סִיר נָפוּחַ, we must think not so much of the woe coming from the North as the city of Jerusalem cast into the fire of judgement by the foe from the North. In this case the parallels are quite clear. As Ezek 22:18 takes up the picture of Is 1:22 (25), so we have in the apparently everyday work song of 24:3b–5 the threat of the סִיר נָפוּחַ known from the early preaching of Jeremiah, given prophetic actualization in the days of Ezekiel.

Ezekiel 17:2 and 21:5 make clear that a prophetic מָשָׁל demands an interpretation. 24:6–14 satisfies this demand. However, these verses are not a single unit. They are divided by the twofold לָכֵן כֹּה אָמַר יהוה in vv 6 and 9 into two sections vv 6–8 and 9–14. This gives rise to the confusing fact that vv 6–8 not only lack any interpretation of vv 3b–5 as an act of judgement, which is clearly intended, but enlarge the parable of vv 3b–5 by the idea of rust on the cauldron added to it, which has not so far been mentioned. At the same time this further elaboration of the parable (along the lines of reproach) seeks to provide a motive for the threat expressed in vv 3b–5. An explanation of the content of the allegory is then found in vv 9f, a section which again runs in brief three- and two-beat half lines. Here the "I" of God who is behind the event becomes evident. In vv 11ff then it is no longer only the features of the מָשָׁל of vv 3b–5 which are taken up. Here also a development of the imagery of vv 6–8 comes into play. A gram-

matical feature strengthens the suspicion that in vv 11f we have a new note, which is not related to vv 3b–5, but to vv 6–8. V 9b begins its interpretation with the emphatic assertion that Yahweh himself is acting. In view of this we must understand the verbal forms of v 10 quite obviously as infinitive absolutes (cf. note a to v 10) and see in them the further elaboration of Yahweh's action. However in v 11 this is no longer possible, since וְהַעֲמִידָהּ can only be understood as imperative, parallel to the imperatives of vv 3b–5. In content v 10b connects up with v 11, in which the features added subsequently in vv 6–8 to the parable are interpreted. Thus we must also reckon v 10b to the later development. Thus the original interpretation of the מָשָׁל of vv 3b–5 is to be found in vv 9b and 10a, whilst vv 10b, 11ff contain the development of the interpretation in regard to vv 6–8.[4]

Thus the analysis shows that in 24:1–14 we again have before us a prophetic saying which has been subsequently expanded. A מָשָׁל in vv 3b–5, originating from Jer 1:13, has been given an introduction in vv 1–3a and is interpreted in vv 9–10a. This has then been expanded by a later interpretative addition (cf. the analogy of 12:1ff). This interpretative addition is couched in the scheme: reproach-threat. The threat in vv 9–10a, with the use of the introductory formula in v 9, is prefaced in vv 6–8 by reproach, stylized as a woe-oracle. This seeks to justify the threat of judgement by a development of the content of the allegorical material of the מָשָׁל. The original threat of vv 9–10a has correspondingly been expanded in vv 10b, 11ff. Still later further small additions have been made, which in part are not found in 𝕲 (cf. the notes and the exposition).

Setting

According to the reference of 24:1f the original text derives from the period of the beginning of the siege of Jerusalem. From the content of the prophecy this reference is altogether probable.

However, the later interpretation must already have had in mind the event of the fall and burning of the city. It is intended to make intelligible, within the content of this original parable, the surprisingly harsh fate of

---

1   For מָשָׁל see above p. 360.

2   See Hempel, *Literatur*, 19; Eissfeldt, *OT Introduction*, 88f.

3   See above p. 159 to 3:24, p. 236 to 8:1.

4   How far the section vv 10b–14 can be regarded as a consistent unit can best be examined in the context

Jerusalem. We cannot therefore be far off the time of the year 587, since we find in it nothing of the new hope, such as is later fully unfolded in chs. 40ff. The derivation of the addition from Ezekiel himself cannot altogether be excluded, although the circle of the school, who have preserved the oracles, may also possibly be the authors.

Herntrich accepts that the משל was spoken in Jerusalem itself, as the army of Nebuchadnezzar advanced. Bertholet leaves the possibility open that Ezekiel may have been "in a neighboring city" and from there have affirmed the beginning of the siege. We cannot separate the saying about the boiling cauldron in 24:1ff from the related prophecy in 11:1ff, which was localized among the exiles.[5] The localizing of the saying (24:1ff) among the exiles, as also its later interpretation, has nothing against it from the content.

Interpretation

■ **24:1f** The coming of the message, which the prophet experiences (son of man), is dated to the tenth day of the tenth month of the ninth year of the reign of Jehoiachin.[6] According to Parker-Dubberstein this is January 15, 588 B.C. The date is impressed on the prophet explicitly and commanded to be noted. It is the date of the beginning of the pressing of (for סמך אל cf. note d to v 2) the siege of Jerusalem by the king of Babylon.[7] This is known also from 2 Kings 25:1 (Jer 52:4, cf. 39:1), where it is reckoned according to the reign of Zedekiah, which coincides with that of Jehoiachin. The fasting of the tenth month, which was held in the period of exile and which is explained in Zech 8:19 as ended, but which was adopted again in Judaism after the destruction of Jerusalem by Titus, is understood as a recollection of this day of the beginning of the siege, which thereafter remained an especially significant day.[8] This is opposed by the view of R. Simon, who saw in it (b Roš Haššanah 18b) a recollection of the event of Ezek 33:21 on the fifth day of the tenth month.

The exact noting of this day, which is surprisingly well confirmed by coincidence on the one hand of the date in 2 Kings 25, which was apparently quite independently preserved, and on the other by Ezek 24, has repeatedly given trouble to commentators. Are we to reckon with a power of farsightedness in Ezekiel which made it possible for him to affirm precisely a date which historically related to somewhere else?[9] More detailed consideration points to the conjecture that the similarity of the dates does not rest on a pure chance. The formulation of the date in Ezek 24:1 differs in two ways from the other date formulations in Ezekiel. Where elsewhere in Ezekiel the date is connected with the formula for receiving a message, the date always stands directly after the ויהי, which is afterwards taken up by a היה. So 26:1; 29:17; 30:20; 31:1; 32:1, 17 (in 29:1 the introductory ויהי has completely fallen out). Also in texts formulated somewhat differently 1:1; 8:1; 20:1; 33:21 (also 3:16) the date follows immediately after the introductory ויהי. 40:1 begins with a note of the date. Thus 24:1 demonstrably differs from what is otherwise usual in Ezekiel by its striking tardiness in giving the date. To this we may add the deviation in the manner of numbering the month, which, where it is not altogether missing, is always, apart from 32:1, expressed by the simple ordinal number and the preceding ב. In 32:1 it is lacking because it could not be formed from the number twelve. In order to avoid a misunderstanding, it is therefore formulated here בשני עשר חדש. In 24:1, however, in spite of the existing ordinal number, it is formulated בחדש העשירי with the preceding בחדש. This formulation reappears exactly similarly in 2 Kings 25 (Jer 52:4, also 39:1). Thus the suspicion arises that the date of 24:1 has been added following 2 Kings 25:1. A dependence in the reverse direction is quite improbable (against Fohrer), in view of the peculiarity described above of the formulation in Ezek 24:1 over against the other formulations in the book of Ezekiel. This means then that the date of Ezek 24:1 has been subsequently assimilated to the date of

---

5   See above pp. 259f. For the "farsightedness" of the prophet cf. the detailed exposition to vv 1f.
6   See above pp. 144f; pp. 131f; p. 115.
7   מלך בבל 17:12; 19:9 and other passages, with the name Nebuchadnezzar 26:7; 29:18f; 30:10.
8   Moore, *Judaism* 2.
9   Cf. above pp. 259f, p. 284.

of the detailed exposition.

the historical account. This means for the account of Ezek 24 that originally here either no date was given, or another date was replaced by that of 2 Kings 25:1.

With this, however, all conclusions on the basis of the precision of the prophet's preaching are removed. That the circles of the exiles would have followed the advance of Nebuchadnezzar's army with extreme anxiety is to be accepted, even without the date of Ezek 24:1. That one day the prophet delivered a prophecy in this anxiety, charged with his prophetic authority, which made plain the beginning of the siege, need cause us no surprise in view of the excitement which is evident in Ezekiel's words which accompanied the events of this final act of judgement (cf. Ezek 4f, 12, 17, 21, also 23). Even the explicit written attestation of this saying appears in no way unusual from Is 8:1ff; Hab 2:2f.[10] An inaccuracy in the note of the date, in earlier prophecy, had in no way the force of negating the truth of a message.[11] The decisive feature is the "so" of the beginning of the siege, not the exact reckoning of "when." That a later age, which saw the prophet more strongly in the guise of a calculating apocalypticist, set great store on a precise note of the date, which as a fast day had already become important, is only too intelligible. In Ezek 24:1f we find simply this process of subsequent assimilation.

■ **24:3** At the time of the beginning of the siege Ezekiel receives the commission to preach to the "house of rebellion" a prophetic parable (מָשָׁל).[12] As according to Nu 21:17f the high task of digging for spring water was accompanied by a song, so here the מָשָׁל accompanies the domestic task of preparing a splendid meal. The oracle addresses the unknown person who was entrusted with the task and encourages him to set the iron, or copper, cauldron[13] on the hearth, to pour in water in order to cook the pieces of meat in it (1 Sam 2:13f). The best pieces of meat, the upper leg (יָרֵךְ) and the shoulder (כָּתֵף), and pieces of bone, which give strength and flavor to the broth, with all from the best of the cattle are to fill the cauldron (meat and bones in a cauldron also in Mic 3:3). Wood was then to be set under the cauldron, and all its contents were to be heated and cooked with the meat. It is noteworthy that

in this regard the lighting of the fire is not mentioned.

The work song stands first, without any interpretation, and even in its formulation it contains no hidden background features. It appears to be the joyous call to a cheerful task in making ready for a feast. In a transition, which recalls the harsh surprise in Isaiah's song of the vineyard (Is 5:1–7), there then follows in vv 9–10a a great change, which reveals the reality of judgement lying hidden in the harmless song.

■ **24:9** Whereas Isaiah's song of the vineyard offers a complete interpretation in regard to the human, as well as the divine, partner of the event, vv 9–10a are content, if the deletion of v 9aβ with 𝕲 (note a) is right, with revealing who is really acting in the procedure of cooking. In the emphatic גַּם אֲנִי Yahweh himself steps out from the harmless occupation and transforms it into an allegory of the threatened judgement.

■ **24:10a** Yahweh himself will make the pile of wood so high that the fire cannot very quickly be put out. He takes a great deal of wood, lights the fire, cooks the meat until it is ready (in the הָתֵם there is a threatening note of "bringing to an end"). Now the lighting of the fire is mentioned: Yahweh himself is the dangerous fire-lighter. If v 9aβ is an original part of the text, then in the introductory woe cry those who are threatened by this fire, the inhabitants of Jerusalem, are clearly mentioned. In the undiscerning and arrogant statement of 11:3 the people of Jerusalem have brought this judgement upon their own heads.

Aim

The original saying of 24:1–5, 9–10a has in mind the judgement upon those left behind in Jerusalem by the first deportation of 597 B.C. In the catastrophe of that year, they looked upon themselves with vain pride as the *élite* who had been spared. They claimed for themselves the right to the possession of the inherited gift of God (Jerusalem, the land) and looked down upon those who had gone into exile at that time (11:15). With thoughtless temerity they had once again thought of themselves hidden safely in Jerusalem and said: "It is the pot, and we are the meat" (11:3).

Into such complacency God's word enters. Its threat-

---

10   Cf. above pp. 112f.
11   Cf. what was said above on pp. 259f to 11:13.
12   For "house of rebellion" see above p. 134; for מָשָׁל

see above p. 360.
13   Barrois, *Manuel* 1, 387f; *BRL* mentions סִיר under "pottery."

ening interpreters are the Babylonian armies, which, at the time when the prophecy was proclaimed among the exiles, were encamped in siege around the walls of Jerusalem. The place of protection became the place of danger. Under the protecting pot God himself had kindled a fire, well-supplied with logs of wood to make a fire that could not quickly be put out and which now does its work on the valuable food set in the pot utterly and completely up to the bitter end (התם).

Thus God answers those who had been blinded by being spared the judgement, regarding it as a promise of greatness and thinking to be able to lull themselves in the security of being among the elect. In that this prophecy, however, was proclaimed among the exiles, it destroyed all the comforting hopes which believed that they would soon go back to a Jerusalem which had been spared the judgement.

Interpretation

■ **24:6–8, 10b–14** The judgement took place in 587—even more harshly than the original משל had anticipated. It not only overtook the inhabitants of Jerusalem and brought upon them a fate like that which in 597 had come to the first exiles. The city itself, with its temple, was reduced to ashes one month after its capture at the express command of Nebuchadnezzar (2 Kings 25:8f). In the later interpretation which the original משל has undergone, the shock of this heightening of judgement can still be felt. At the same time this later interpretation seeks to give expression more clearly than was the case in the original משל to Jerusalem's guilt.

This took place by the introduction of reproach before the announcement of doom in vv 9f. This ignores the fact that already vv 3b–5 contain an announcement of doom, and that fundamentally the reproach should have been put before vv 3b–5. From v 9 the introduction is repeated. If v 9aβ, in spite of its omission in 𝔊, belongs to the original text, then the call to Jerusalem as the city of blood was taken over with it. For the rest, however, there is a difference from 22:1ff in that no offenses are listed which made Jerusalem the city of blood, but this element is brought in by the expansion of the image of vv 3b–5. No longer is there mention of the pieces of meat in the cauldron, but of the cauldron itself and of the uncleanness which clings to it. Re-

garding this we cannot make out with certainty whether an iron cauldron is in mind, which has begun to rust, or whether, as Kelso conjectured, a copper cauldron is thought of, in which the metal quickly decays because it has been bent, dented, and scratched, or because it has been cast when too hot, and air bubbles have formed in the metal. In any case a serious "sickness" (חלה—חלאה note b) of the metal is thought of which cannot be removed by exterior cleaning.

■ **24:7** Passing over the later addition in v 6b (cf. below), v 7 gives reasons for the uncleanness which v 6a expresses figuratively, but drops the figurative dress. The uncleanness of the city consists in the shedding of innocent blood. This develops the image of the city of blood in line with 22:1ff. Beyond ch. 22, however, it establishes that the city of blood, because no atonement has been made, cries out to heaven. Ancient belief, with its dynamistic-animistic conceptions which are frequently evident in the Old Testament, affirmed that the (power of) the soul lay in the blood.[14] Thus in ritual laws the avoidance of eating blood is strongly insisted upon (Gen 9:4; Lev 17:10–14; Dtn 12:16, 23f, also Ezek 33:25). Blood that has not been covered, i.e., not correctly covered with earth and buried, retains something of its power and, in the case of murder (Gen 4:10), cries out to the heavenly avenger. Job requests the earth not to cover his blood (Job 16:18) because he does not wish the outcry over his unjustified misfortunes to come to an end. In the statement of Ezek 24:7 that the blood (unjustly shed) in Jerusalem has been poured out on bare rock (again 26:4, 14, of rocks washed clean by the sea) expression is given to this idea of the dangerous vitality of the blood of the city, the assertions of which cannot be silenced. In Jerusalem no one took the trouble to atone according to law for the murder.

■ **24:8** Verse 8 gives the statement a surprising twist with reference to God—he himself has therefore seen to it that the blood was not covered over and thereby the call for his avenging action silenced. He himself was concerned that he should be provoked by the blood so that his anger should flare up and seek vengeance—a striking counterpart to the divine remembrance of his own mercy in the rainbow in Gen 9:12–17. The threatening application of this idea, according to which in the guilt mirrored by man's uncovered blood Yahweh himself is already at work in punishment (kindling his anger), recalls 3:20 and 14:9.[15] It is certainly not to be deleted (Herrmann). With v 8 we reach the addition to the threat of the original text in vv 9, 10a, in which Yahweh himself appears.

■ **24:10b** This divine threat is now set out in the elaborated image in vv 10b–14. The infinitive absolutes in v 10a, which declare Yahweh's kindling of fire under the cauldron filled with meat, are still veiled in v 10b and then changed back in v 11 quite clearly into the imperative style of vv 3b–5. A further action is added to the cooking of the pot, which expresses in a new way the harsh judgement which is to befall the inhabitants of the city itself.

■ **24:11** The cauldron, after its contents have been cooked, is to be emptied of its contents (מרק) (a later hand has added the burning of the bones, cf. note c) and then again placed empty on the fire. In this way it will begin to glow red-hot. Its iron (copper?) will be set on the white-hot coals, and its uncleanness will be burned out (in the melting of the pot?), and so an end made of its rust (תתם).

■ **24:12** Verse 12, once again going back behind the concluding remark of v 11, states that without this destruction its uncleanness could not be removed from it.

■ **24:13** What is said in v 12 in the metaphor of rust is again interpreted in v 13: the rust means its uncleanness, which is wickedness.[16]

Vv 13b–14, however, summarize by a new declaration of the action. The lack of readiness to be cleansed of uncleanness leads to the fact that Yahweh's anger, in all its destructive severity, must vent itself.[17]

■ **24:14** He will follow his words with action (note a to v 14) and will not spare (חוס otherwise always connected with עין, 5:11; 7:4, 9 and other passages), but will judge Jerusalem according to its deeds (cf. 36:19). The new catchword טהר, which appears no less than three times in vv 13b–14, arouses the suspicion, as the new formal beginning in v 13b, that here, in a late phase of the text composition, we have a further summary.

■ **24:6b** We must also recognize an addendum in v 6b. It goes back directly from the mention of rust (v 6a),

which is explained in v 7 by the bloodguilt of Jerusalem, to the mention of pieces of meat in vv 4f. At best we must see in the sentence an allegorical appendix, which seeks to supplement one feature of the process of judgement. The cauldron (which must be understood as the subject) pours out its contents piece by piece without any lot being cast for them. This must point to the forcible removal of all the remaining population of the city. Over against what happened in 597 are we to think of no casting of lots to choose those who are to be deported?

Aim

The expansion of the original משל has taken place out of a deep sense of shock. The judgement of the year 587 exceeded that which was expected from the analogy of the events of 597. In view of the scale of judgement there emerged afresh an insight into the depth of Israel's underlying guilt. Out of the fire of judgement which raged over Jerusalem and its temple, faith is perceptible for those who are willing to hear: *nondum considerasti quanti sit ponderis peccatum.*

Thus the prophetic message carries the confession of sin into yet greater depth. Not only are individual inhabitants of Jerusalem guilty of it, but the whole city of God is consumed with uncleanness—so radically that all attempts at cleansing it no longer have any purpose.

So God's judgement must also increase to its full severity; it must destroy so completely (התם) that nothing is left from the past. This is the prophetic (only Old Testament prophetic?) knowledge of God's judgement, which leaves no island of escape on which the old can be preserved, but reaches to the utmost limit of death. Hope for the people can only arise where it submits to the fact of such judgement which takes away all human pride.

---

14 Cf. above p. 456 to 22:2.
15 See above pp. 145f; p. 308.
16 For זמה see above p. 345.

17 For הניח חמה ב cf. 5:13; 16:42 (21:22).

The Prophet's Grief over the Death of His Wife, a Sign of Grief over the Fall of Jerusalem.

Bibliography

Cf. to 3:22–5:17.

J. B. Bauer
"Hes. 24:17," *VT* 7 (1957): 91–92.

J. Hempel
"Eine Vermutung zu Hes. 24:15ff," *ZAW* 51 (1933): 312–313.

24

15 Then the word of Yahweh came to me: 16/ Son of man, behold, I am taking from you the delight of your eyes by sudden death. You shall neither lament nor weep [, nor shall your tears run].[a] 17/ Groan in deathly stiffness,[a] make no lamentation, bind your turban about you, and put[b] your shoes on your feet. Do not cover your upper lip and do not eat the 'bread of lamentation'.[c]

24:
16

16a 𝔐 ולוא תבוא דמעתך is lacking in 𝔊 𝔏 𝔆. It is superfluous beside the ולא תספד ולא תבכה, which is formally concise and in which, as in the following clause, the prophet is subject. It makes a transition in the context from the sphere of ritual lamentation to that of personal feeling. The stichos is also noteworthy on account of its plene writing of ולוא. Standing alone לא is never written plene in the book of Ezekiel, and ולוא only in 16:56. In the last mentioned reference it fulfills the function of a הלא, which alone otherwise is often written הלוא (13:7, 12; 17:9; 24:25; 34:2; 37:18; 38:14). Cf. note a to 16:56 (where ולוא is to be read instead of ולא).

17

17a 𝔐 האנק דם מתים is usually emended: Cornill, Bertholet to התאפק דם משתומם (restrain yourself, be silent); Ehrlich, *Randglossen*, to האנק דומם גם. Fohrer deletes האנק דם and, with Toy, changes to אבל מתים. Bewer, "Exegese," 200, reads הָאָפֵק דְּמָעֹתֶיךָ and sees a variant of this in v 16bβ, which is lacking in 𝔊, which confirms the reconstruction of v 17aα. Driver, "Ezekiel," 155f, emends to דֹּם הֵאָנֵק "Do not groan aloud." Bauer, "Hes. xxiv 17," considers a reading האנק דם מת ימ[ן י]אבל לא־תעשה "Groan, lament in silence for the dead, (but) days of lamentation do not make!" 𝔊 (𝔏ˢʷ) στεναγμὸς αἵματος ὀσφύος, however, had doubtless already the consonantal text of 𝔐 before it. The only exception is the change of מתים to מתנים. 𝔖 and 𝔙 tried in their own way to deal with this consonantal text of 𝔐. 𝔗 שתוק על מיתך smooths the דם מתים by the introduction of a suffix. For the interpretation of the passage, where the text is certainly intact, it is important to notice that דמם does not mean "keeping silent," but "ceasing to move." Thus it can be interpreted by עמד (Josh 10:12f of the sun's standing still, 1 Sam 14:9 of soldiers creeping forwards). In Job 31:34 it means staying at home in fear, rather than going out; in Ex 15:16 lying still as a stone. Thus דם מתים can be understood as the motionlessness of the dead or as a fixed immobility in the face of coming death (Lev 10:3). דם here in the three-beat v 17aα¹ is the counterpart to עשה (אבל) of v 17aα².

b Cohen, "Studies," 181f, conjectures here a second meaning for שׂים of "bind."

c The reference given by Ehrlich, *Randglossen*, to

18   [And I spoke to the people in the
morning.]ᵃ And my wife died in the
evening, but I did on the next morning
as I had been commanded. 19/ Then the
people spoke to me: Will you not tell
us, what this that you are doing means
[for us]?ᵃ

20   Then I spoke to them: The word of
Yahweh came to me: 21/ Say to the
house of Israel: Thus has [the Lord]ᵃ
Yahweh spoken: Behold, I will
desecrate my sanctuary, your proud
treasure, which your eyes delight in
and your desire 'looks for'.ᵇ And your
sons and your daughters whom you
have left behind will fall by the sword.
22/ And you will do as I have done: you
shall not cover your upper lip, nor will
you eat the 'bread of lamentation'.ᵃ
23/ Your turbansᵃ you will (bind) on
your heads and your shoes on your feet.
You shall not wail nor weep, but you
will pine away in your wickedness and
groanᵇ one to another. 24/ And Ezekiel
will be a sign to you. Just as he has
done you will do. When it happens,ᵃ
you will know that I am [the Lord]ᵇ
Yahweh.

25   And you, son of man, surelyᵃ on the day
when I take away from them their
treasure, the eminent joy which their
eyes delighted in and their desire
looked for, their sons and their
daughters—26/ on that day a survivor
will come to you, so that your ears may
hear it.ᵃ 27/ On that day your mouth
will be opened [towards the survivor],ᵃ
and you will speak and be no more
dumb, and you will be a sign to them,
and they will know that I am Yahweh.

the funeral meal prepared by neighbors, which
would therefore be designated with an obsolete use
of אנשים as "food of others," is not satisfactory. We
must read with 𝔗 (לחם אבילין) 𝔙 (cibos lugentium)
and following Hos 9:4 (cf. Dtn 26:14) לחם אונים.

18   18a aα is hardly in order, since in it the prophet's
speech is anticipated, which is, however, first provoked by the question of the people. 𝔊 (𝔏ˢᵂ 𝔆), in
which aβ is lacking, clearly had before it an erroneous text. For its explanation see Cornill. The remaining versions go along with 𝔐. So we must either
accept with BH³, Herrmann, Rothstein a scribal
error of ואדבר from ותדבר or ודברת and see in aα
the conclusion of the command of vv 16f, or better
delete aα as a clumsy addition. Bertholet's transposition to vv 16–18a, 21aβ, 24–27, 18b–20, 21aαb,
22–23 (thus taking vv 27, 19–23 without 21aβ as
secondary) arouses little confidence. Neither is the
pluperfect translation of ותמת and ואעש (Ehrlich,
Randglossen) satisfactory.

19   19a 𝔐 לנו is not attested by 𝔊 𝔏ᵂ 𝔆 𝔗 and is to
be deleted as an erroneous repetition of the preceding.

21   21a אדני is lacking in 𝔊 𝔏ˢᵂ 𝔆ᴮᵒ, see Excursus 1.
b The מחמל, which is only found here in the Old
Testament, has as its counterpart in the parallel in
v 25 משא. Already 𝔊 (𝔏ᵂ) ὑπὲρ ὧν φείδονται (αἱ
ψυχαὶ ὑμῶν) had before it מחמל, without being able
to understand it. 𝔙 super quo pavet anima vestra. The
variation of the expressions (עינים) מחמד and
(נפשם) משא in v 25 forbids that we should, with 4
MSS 2 Edd, simply emend the מחמל in v 21 to a
second מחמד. The root חמל is attested in the Old
Testament only with the meaning "to feel compassion" (and derivatives). The Talmudic חמילה
"wrapper, coating" shows, however, that at least in
later Hebrew the meaning "to bear, carry," cf.
Arabic ḥml, was also known. Therefore מחמל is
simply a synonym for משא: "The thing to which
men lift their eyes, i.e., their desire." So also Kopf,
"Etymologien," 172.

22   22a Cf. note c to v 17.

23   23a 𝔐 ופארכם, better with Varᴳ ופאריכם.
b 𝔐 ונהמתם understood by 𝔊 παρακαλέσετε, Σ
παρακληθήσεσθε, 𝔆 ותביאון as ונחמתם. נהם denotes
in Is 5:29; Prv 28:15 the growling of lions, Is 5:30
the roaring of the sea. It is here a variant repetition
of the אנק of v 17.

24   24a Or: thereby, that it comes. The expression is
lacking in 𝔊.
b אדני is lacking in 𝔊 𝔏ˢ, see Excursus 1.

25   25a 𝔐 הלוא passed over by 𝔆.

26   26a 𝔐 להשמעות אזנים appears to be a pure Aramaism. Ehrlich, Randglossen, would understand the
form as a scribal error for an original להשמיע את
אזניך.

27   27a 𝔐 את הפליט. 𝔊 (𝔏ᶜˢ) πρὸς τὸν ἀνασῳζόμενον,
𝔙 cum eo qui fugit. 𝔆 ונפתח פומך מתפצינא makes
הפליט the subject, whilst 𝔗 במיתי משיזבא para-

phrases into a general statement. The suspicion that
את הפליט (Bertholet, Fohrer), and possibly also the
ותדבר joined with the copula ו, is a subsequent insertion cannot be wholly ruled out.

Form

The section 24:15–27, beginning with the formula for
the coming of a message in v 15, is marked off clearly
into two units vv 16–24 and 25–27, not only by the
double address to the prophet in vv 16 and 25, but also
by the corresponding double recognition formula in
vv 24 and 27. The repetition of statements from vv
16–24 in the section vv 25–27 (removal of the delight of
the eyes v 16, cf. vv 21 and 25; designation of the
prophet as a מופת in vv 24 and 27; recognition formula
in vv 24 and 27) shows that the second part cannot be
understood in isolation from the first, but has arisen in
dependence on vv 16–24.

Vv 16–24 tell first of all of Yahweh's announcement
that the prophet's wife will die. In connection with this
a specific line of conduct is prescribed for Ezekiel (vv
16f). The occurrence of what has been announced and
Ezekiel's conduct (v 18) call forth a question from the
people (v 19), which provides the occasion for a particularly important divine word to the questioners, in
which Yahweh sets forth the prophet, by his action, as
a "sign" for the people (vv 21–24). In view of this
speech, to which the whole prophecy builds up from
the beginning, Ezekiel's speech to the people in v 18aα,
which is quite open in its content, appears much too
soon. The suspicion is great that v 18aα has either been
moved from its original position before v 20 (as a
marginal note?) to this false position or is simply an
addition. We can see further that in the important
divine speech in vv 21–24 the prophet speaks in vv 22f
unmistakably in the first person and points to the
example of his action. V 24 returns to a speech from
God. Thus vv 22f are to be regarded as a clumsy subsequent elaboration, which repeats the statements of
vv 16f. They do not belong to the original text. This is
to be found in vv 21, 24 and is constructed formally as
a proof-saying in two parts. When Irwin puts 24:24 with
1:3 because in both passages Ezekiel is spoken of in the
third person and calls 24:24 "a passage that cries out

to high heaven its spurious origin," he completely
overlooks that in 24:24, unlike in 1:3, we are dealing
with a passage in a section of divine speech.[1]

The section vv 16–24, in its original form, shows
itself to be a combination of a sign-action with a proof-
saying.[2] The element of declaration of judgement in the
proof-saying is therefore not preserved as a pure divine
word, but by the prophet's suffering and action it
becomes a direct sign-event before the eyes of the people.
Similarly, seen from the other side, the symbolic action,
by its development into a proof-saying, becomes an
element of God's self-revelation to his people. The sign-
action is thus, unlike as in 4:1ff, not completely swallowed up in the divine word, but is set out in the manner
of 12:1ff as a narrative, in which the divine word
nevertheless has already entered into the exposition.
It differs from 12:1ff and 4:1ff in that it not only knows
of an action which the prophet performs, but also of an
experience of suffering which comes to him directly
from God. In connection with this suffering the prophet
must then adopt a specific line of conduct commanded
by God. This gives the whole event a striking ambiguity: the prophetic suffering becomes a vehicle for a
message to be practiced by the prophet. (Cf. further the
exposition.)

Setting

The question about the location and date of the symbolic event and the message which it contains can be
answered with satisfactory precision. When Herntrich
in his exposition restricts the term מחמד עינים to Jerusalem and its temple and concludes from this that
Ezekiel himself must have been in Jerusalem (the city is
only "the delight of their eyes" for the people living in
Jerusalem), this is a counsel of despair.[3] It leaves completely out of consideration that the prophet is to
become a sign to those around him by his shattering
grief. A population living in Jerusalem, which was
threatened by troops frustrated by a long siege, would

---

1   Irwin, *Problem*, 272.
2   See above pp. 156f.
3   Herntrich, *Ezekielprobleme*, 110.

have been menaced in quite another way than by this intangible grief. This clearly speaks in favor of a group of people involved in the great disaster at a distance. To this may be added the clear reference to "your sons and your daughters whom you have left behind" (v 21), which we, together with its (shortened) echo in v 25, can scarcely cut out on critical grounds.[4]

As the date of the event of vv 15ff we can scarcely adopt that mentioned in 24:1 (see also above to vv 1f). However, the redaction of the book must be so far correct when it sets the event close to the fall of Jerusalem. The siege of the city appears already, beyond what is said in vv 3b–5, to be reaching its climax. The bitter end is imminent.

Interpretation

■ **24:15** The prophet receives the harsh announcement of the immediately imminent death of his wife, which at first concerns him quite personally (son of man).[5]

■ **24:16** This understanding of the saying in v 16a, which stands beyond question for 𝔐 by the following ותמת אשתי (v 18), is now admittedly not beyond doubt. Hölscher, *Hesekiel*, sees a subsequent addition, not only in the במגפה, but he also defends the thesis of Jahn that only the divine words in vv 16–17 derive from the prophet Ezekiel himself. In their original meaning these verses speak, according to Hölscher, not of the prophet's wife, but of Jerusalem. Thus the meaning of the verses 16f is quite simply this: "Jerusalem will fall, with no one lamenting it."[6] See also van den Born, Matthews.

The scholars mentioned can rightly adduce that the designation מחמד עינים, which is interpreted in Lam 2:4 of the youthful Jerusalem destroyed by conquest (cf. מחמדי בטנם Hos 9:16), can denote "any favorite possession, silver and gold, wife and children" (Hölscher), as in 1 Kings 20:6. However, we must question whether the . . . הנני לקח ממך can really be used so simply of the event of the destruction of the city and temple and describe this event as a "taking away." According to

its usage elsewhere, לקח always appears to contain a note of spatial removal. Thus plunder is removed (30:4; 38:13; 46:18), jewelry is stolen (16:39; 23:26, 29), sons and daughters are taken away (as slaves) (23:10, 25). It can also be said of ecstatic transportation that the spirit (3:14)[7] or the hand of God (8:3) snatches away, and the personified sword can be said to "snatch away" as an instrument of punishment (33:4, 6). In the context of the last-named passages we also have to see 24:16, where the "taking away" means the removal of Ezekiel's wife by death. The added במגפה is quite without suspicion in this connection, in that by this word not only can the "blow" of a disastrous battle (1 Sam 4:17; 2 Sam 18:7) be expressed or the blow of the divine anger in a long lasting plague (2 Sam 24:21, 25), but also, especially in the priestly language, the fatal blow of divine judgement (Nu 14:37, cf. 17:13–15; 25:8f, 18f; 31:16, also Ps 106:29f).[8] Thus Yahweh removes Ezekiel's wife by her sudden death, which completely overwhelms the prophet.

We find here once again one of the rare passages in Ezekiel in which his personal experience is caught up in his prophetic message. It is therefore relevant to recall once again the limitations about what we can learn from this of the prophet's biography.[9] The expression מחמד עיניך must certainly not lead us to sentimental considerations (Schumpp: "It implies a happy marriage"). Lam 2:4 and Hos 9:16 show that phrases of this kind for a close relative were in general use. Besides this we have in the background here the particular message which was intended. In its reference to the temple, which is then more fully elaborated in v 21, this expression from Ezekiel, the priest, is quite properly in place with regard to the prophet's message. R. Johanan is so far right in regard to the sequence of statements of 24:16 when he says: "When a man's first wife dies, it is as though the temple had been destroyed in his days" (*b Sanhedrin* 22a).

The passage in any case affirms that Ezekiel was

---

4   Cf. the exposition, also Spiegel, "Ezekiel," 307.

5   For the formula for the coming of a message see above pp. 144f; for son of man see above pp. 131f.

6   Hölscher, *Hesekiel, der Dichter*, 130.

7   See above p. 139.

8   See also Johannes Hempel, *Heilung als Symbol und Wirklichkeit im biblischen Schrifttum* (Göttingen: Vandenhoeck & Ruprecht, ²1965), 243.

9   Expressed on pp. 156f.

married, and that probably also means (Jer 29:6 can scarcely be opposed to this) that he was not alone in 597, but was deported with his wife.[10] His wife died suddenly and unexpectedly, not "old and full of days" (Gen 25:8), roughly ten years after the deportation and shortly before the fall of Jerusalem at the time of the renewed siege. Any other circumstances, which would be of great interest for a biographer, are left obscure. Ezekiel can only therefore speak about this event because it anticipated symbolically the great disaster which was to overtake Jerusalem. In this Ezekiel appears again in the context of a type of prophetic preaching which he had already used earlier. The figures of the wife and children of Hosea (Hos 1–3) and also the wife and children of Isaiah (Is 7:3 [14?]; 8:1–4, 18) appear similarly in the light of the message of Hosea and Isaiah. We can also point to Jeremiah, who conversely, by not marrying, became a sign of the coming judgement (16:1–4) and who thereby comes close to Ezekiel, who became a witness of the same message by his grief at losing his wife.[11]

The prohibiting of any mourning, which is found in Jeremiah in direct reference to the passage mentioned (אל תלך לספוד ואל תנד להם 16:5), is explained in Ezekiel in a way which is characteristically different from Jeremiah. Whereas with Jeremiah the painful imposition not to marry or to mourn, which sets him apart as an individual (cf. the מפני ידך בדד of the confession of 15:17) by making impossible all "normal" relationships, shows the removal of God's salvation (כי אספתי את שלומי 16:5), with Ezekiel it is the grim harshness of suffering, which symbolically shows the immense suffering of Israel that is coming. (Cf. already the paralysis [3:15], the dumbness [3:26], and the pathological immobility [3:25; 4:4–8].) Everything was prohibited to him which was customarily shown when a person died, in the way of conduct on the part of the persons left, and also in the way of ritual precautions and ceremonial lamentation.

■ 24:17 To this ceremonial, which could be described as a whole by ספד or עשה אבל, there belonged loud wailing, which could find its spoken expression in the lament.[12] The mourner unties his turban in order to let his hair hang loose and to cover it with earth (or ashes), and at the same time he takes off his sandals. Just as with the covering of the upper lip, which is mentioned, i.e., of the entire head down to the upper lip, we are faced with a very ancient custom by which at one time the person left sought to make himself unrecognizable to the dead person who returned as a ghost (revenant). The customs were even maintained after their animistic basis had fallen away. The custom of giving bread to the mourners in order to call them back again to the world and the joy of living by this gesture of human friendship points in another direction. If, as note c conjectures, the reading לחם אונים is correct, we can consider with H. Cazelles and T. Worden whether this preserves a custom which had its origin in Canaanite fertility cults, in which lamentation was made for the dead god by ritual meals.[13] Ugaritic parallels support this.

All these activities were prohibited to Ezekiel by divine command. With unnatural hardness he must give expression to his grief only in deep, silent desolation.

■ 24:18 The broad divine announcement and the command that went with it are followed in v 18 by a brief note about the actual death and Ezekiel's behavior in accordance with God's command, which is stated with the same stereotyped phrases as in 12:7; 37:7. The stylizing into the sequence evening-morning is already found in 12:7f. It corresponds to the Priestly Document's description of a day in Gen 1 (cf. further Ezek 33:22).

The event has repeatedly given expositors on all sides difficulty, as something completely strange. Thus Hölscher could quote Hengstenberg's words: it would be "strange if God so far humbled his servant that he took away his wife from him on no other ground than in order to give a mimic representation of the future circumstances of the people." This feeling of strangeness overlooks the subordination of the entire narrative under the sole point of view of the message, which has already been clearly established. The questions which are so interesting biographically and psychologically of the chronological sequence of God's word in vv 16f and the death of Ezekiel's wife—the question whether in the

---

10   See Janssen, *Juda*, 35.
11   Miller, *Verhältnis*, 94.
12   See Jahnow, *Leichenlied*, and also above pp. 391f.

13   H. Cazelles, *RB* 55 (1948): 54–71; T. Worden, "The Literary Influence of the Ugaritic Fertility Myth on the Old Testament," *VT* 3 (1953): 290f; see above

preceding divine speech the whole imposition regarding Ezekiel's behavior is already expressed does not interest the prophetic narrative. The entire painful experience of the prophet together with his behavior at God's command, which serves the people of the house of Israel as a message, is made clearly evident. The commentator who inquires from the quite different viewpoint of modern biographical concern may well ask the question whether, in accordance with the psychological experience at the beginning, there stood the unexplained foreboding about his wife's sudden death. We may ask further whether the prophet, severely shocked by the occurrence of the tragedy, was incapable of any normal human reaction, including proper mourning (עשׂה אבל), and this would fit with other aspects of the prophet's immobility to make a well-defined picture of his psychological peculiarity. First we see the "natural" human reaction of the prophet, which he could then only interpret, exactly like the sudden blow of his wife's death, as part of the message God had commanded him to preach. The modern commentator may question whether it was only in a subsequent concentration, in the face of the people's question, that everything was worked together into a clear message and symbolic action in which everything from the start took place at the divine command. The prophet himself does not answer these questions, but only allows us to hear the compelling message given to him, which is evident in and through his experience.

■ **24:19** That this was provoked by the people's question completely corresponds with the stereotyped form of the narrative, which is also to be found in 12:9; 37:18 (cf. 17:12; 21:5, 12).

■ **24:20** Thus Ezekiel proclaims the message which Yahweh is declaring through his suffering and the action of the people. It is a unique phenomenon in the book of Ezekiel that the prophet, in his answer to the people, should refer back to the event of the coming of the message, which made him a messenger.[14] We must

therefore be warned by this fact against ascribing all the formulae for the receipt of a message to a redactor as, for example, Hölscher does. The formula here has its place in the speech of the prophet himself.

■ **24:21** In the divine message there is now unfolded what the death of the prophet's wife foretold: God is removing from the house of Israel that which it loves. In this it is no longer the verb לקח (see above to v 16) that is used, but it is said concretely that the temple will be desecrated, and the relatives of the exiles will be killed.[15] The meaning of God's temple for the house of Israel is described with a threefold predication. The מחמד עיניכם, which connects with v 16, is preceded by the title גאון עזכם, in which both Israel's trust, which here has in mind its impenetrable fortress, as well as its pride in this place are brought to expression. The following מחמל נפשׁכם (note b) contains a roughly synonymous description to מחמד עיניכם, in which the נפשׁ replaces the eyes as the seat of human favorable desire.

Beside the holy place, on which Israel's faith hangs, mention is made of those to whom the natural affection of the exiles was closely bound: "your sons and your daughters whom you have left behind." This need not be understood with pedantic literalness, that it was simply the older generation which was deported. Jer 29:1ff speaks expressly against this. In fact it is clear from this that it was not simply whole families which were deported, but that a selection was made (in part by lot?), among which the older generation must have been more strongly represented.[16] The lack of any mention of a deportation in the Wiseman Chronicle similarly points to the conclusion that in the view of the Babylonians there was no deportation in the technical sense but a (provisional?) removal of hostages.[17] Such would especially have been taken from the older, politically significant, generation. Thus then younger relatives of the exiles remained behind.[18] That just young people would be killed in the impending catastrophe is attested by the severity of this disaster.

---

pp. 242f to 8:14f.

14 See above pp. 144f.

15 For the desecration of the sanctuary, in which Yahweh deals a direct blow at his own holy order (Lev 19:30 and above to 22:8), cf. 7:24; 25:3; Dan 11:31.

16 See above p. 501 to 24:6b.

17 See above pp. 364f.

18 Cf. the designation אנשׁי גאלתך 11:15, see above p. 261.

■ **24:24** In this blow it will become clear that Ezekiel, by his mysterious behavior, is a "sign" for the people.[19] By the time this happens and by the fact that it does, Yahweh will reveal the personal mystery of his being.[20] As the "sign" in a lawsuit has the power of an attestation, so will the fulfillment of what is declared in Ezekiel's action prove the truth of Yahweh's being.

■ **24:22f** The general reference to the fact that in Ezekiel's strange inaction the total paralysis of the exiles at the terrible news awaiting them is prefigured was not enough for a later scribe. Without keeping to the style of the divine speech, he has in vv 22f listed once again in detail the features of the behavior commanded in vv 16f, with a connecting ועשיתם כאשר עשיתי, which anticipates the ככל אשר עשה תעשו.[21] These are now all related to the people. The series of three groups of two-beat units containing negative statements is thereby reordered: not covering the upper lip and not eating the bread of lamentation stand first, covering the head and feet come second, and not weeping is in third place. The positive description of Ezekiel's conduct (corresponding to v 17aα) appears appropriately at the end. The groaning of the prophet has as its counterpart here the groaning one to another (נהם), in which the "pining away" (nipʿal of מקק also in 4:17; 33:10, cf. Lev 26:39) in one's own sins is expressed. To the description of the judgement there then is added an element of motivation and confession of guilt.

■ **24:25–27** What then follows in vv 25–27 is clearly formally connected with vv 15–24, although its content points in another direction. The point of connection for this narrative is the time of the city's fall, which is described with the phraseology of vv 16a, 21, slightly changed and expanded. In dependence on v 24 the event of 33:21f is introduced under the viewpoint of a sign-action of the prophet. The whole passage, which begins in a strangely slow way with a question, appears to presuppose the event as known, and its originality in the present position is very suspicious.

Further it is not in itself unified. It is striking that the ביום קחתי מהם in v 25 corresponds to a twofold ביום ההוא in vv 26 and 27. This is stylistically hardly acceptable and has certainly first been introduced by a secondary insertion.

■ **24:25** The appendix in vv 25ff must originally have comprised only vv 25 and 27. With a renewed address

to the prophet (cf. v 16) attention is then drawn to the day of the city's fall. With a new metaphor which uses the לקח of v 16, this is described as a day on which their strength (מעוז in the book of Ezekiel only again in 30:15, more frequently in Is, Ps, Dan 11) and their great joy (משוש only here in Ezekiel) will be taken away from them (i.e., the house of Israel v 21). In this twofold statement the מקדשי גאון עזכם of v 21 is consciously varied. The following מחמד עיניהם corresponds exactly to the expression in vv 16, 21, whilst the מחמל נפשכם of v 21 appears slightly altered in משא נפשם (cf. note b to v 21). The removal of the sons and daughters is quoted in abbreviated form from v 21.

■ **24:27** On this day of disaster, so runs v 27, Ezekiel will again be able to speak and so will become a sign to them (i.e., to the house of Israel), in which Yahweh will demonstrate the personal mystery of his being (corresponding to v 24).

In these statements the event of 33:21f is clearly quoted somewhat carelessly, in that there the loosing of the prophet's tongue is set at the moment at which the announcement of the city's fall reaches him. The inexactness is a consequence of the introduction of this "sign-action" into the event of the death of Ezekiel's wife. Since this is directed towards the day of the city's fall, that other event must also be set at this terminus because for the glossator the connection with the statements of vv 16, 21 is important.

■ **24:26** The appendix in v 26, with its clumsy disturbance of the correspondence between ביום in verses 25 and 27, is to be explained from the fact that a later hand noted the disagreement in 24:25, 27 as against 33:21f and has attempted to render the statement more precisely. The loosing of the prophet's tongue occurs at the moment of the arrival of the messenger. In a clumsy way the detail of 33:21f is anticipated. Also the introduction of את הפליט in v 27 (note a) must go back to the same hand. However, the text is not really clarified by this insertion. Now v 25 mentions the moment of the city's fall, and v 26 gives the impression that the messenger on the very day of the fall came to Ezekiel. Herntrich considers, in regard to this, whether at the end Ezekiel was seated in a house in besieged Jerusalem and had received there an announcement of the fall of the city by a messenger (hardly a conceivable situation on the day of the overthrow of the city which had been

Ezekiel 24:15–27

starved out). Or perhaps (so afterwards especially Bertholet) he had lived in a country town near to Jerusalem, in which the news could still arrive on the same day. Yet all these are misleading questions, out of place because of the actual nature of the text. Vv 25–27 are to be regarded as a redactional appendix, which is intended to form a bridge over the collection of oracles against foreign nations in Ezek 25–32 and to link up with Ezek 33. The material questions, which are found in the statements of vv 25–27, must be considered together with 33:21f.

Aim

The oracle 24:15–24 (25–27) first of all makes clear once again the office of prophet. Because God's word is not simply information and a doctrinal idea, but the intervention of the divine judgement, the messenger of God can therefore be called unreservedly into the service of the divine message, with all his private experience. In the grievous suffering of the prophet, in which there is no longer any room for ordered rites of mourning, Israel's encounter with God's judgement is already present in advance. Thus the messenger (as

already in 4:4–8) becomes a full witness ($\mu\acute{\alpha}\rho\tau\upsilon\varsigma$), who suffers with his people in judgement.

This shows how remorselessly God's judgement must destroy and cannot even be held back before the holy ones, to whom rightly the most costly aspects of the love of the people of God belong (v 21). Because God acts in this way, he sets his own honor at stake in the judgement, and himself becomes an object of scorn and contempt in the eyes of the world. Into what depth of foolishness does God's judgement lead, where men regard it with their own cleverness! In his judgement does God not put himself to death in the eyes of the world?

Yet even so the prophet holds unswervingly that in such an event God reveals himself to his world in the truth of his own being.

---

19 See above p. 271 to 12:6, 11, and see Keller, *OTH*, 96.
20 For the double meaning of ב see Zimmerli, *Erkenntnis*, 14–16.
21 Kuhl's principle of "resumption" ("'Wiederaufnahme'") must be expanded by the phenomenon of "anticipation" for the insertion of additions.

509